D0215592

Introduction to Clinical Psychology

Science, Practice, and Ethics

Jeffrey E. Hecker

University of Maine

Geoffrey L. Thorpe

University of Maine

Boston • New York • San Francisco
Mexico City • Montreal • Toronto • London • Madrid • Paris
Hong Kong • Tokyo • Cape Town • Sydney

J.E.H.: To Lee and Olivia
G.L.T.: To Beth and Tim

Series Editor: *Kelly May*
Series Editorial Assistant: *Adam Whitehurst*
Marketing Manager: *Taryn Wahlquist*
Senior Production Editor: *Annette Pagliaro*
Editorial Production: *Walsh & Associates, Inc.*
Composition Buyer: *Linda Cox*
Manufacturing Buyer: *JoAnne Sweeney*
Cover Administrator: *Linda Knowles*
Text Design and Composition: *Publishers' Design and Production Services, Inc.*

For related titles and support materials, visit our online catalog at www.ablongman.com.

Copyright © 2005 Pearson Education, Inc.

All rights reserved. No part of the material protected by this copyright notice may be reproduced or utilized in any form or by any means, electronic or mechanical, including photocopying, recording, or by any information storage and retrieval system, without written permission from the copyright owner.

To obtain permission(s) to use material from his work, please submit a written request to Allyn and Bacon, Permissions Department, 75 Arlington Street, Boston, MA 02116 or fax your request to 617-848-7320.

Between the time Website information is gathered and then published, it is not unusual for some sites to have closed. Also, the transcription of URLs can result in unintended typographical errors. The publisher would appreciate notification where these errors occur so that they may be corrected in subsequent editions.

Library of Congress Cataloging-in-Publication Data

Hecker, Jeffrey E., 1959–
    Introduction to clinical psychology : science, practice, and ethics / Jeffrey E. Hecker, Geoffrey L. Thorpe
        p. cm.
    Includes bibliographical references and index.
    ISBN 0-205-27774-8
    1. Clinical psychology.   I. Thorpe, Geoffrey L.   II. Title.

  RC467.H388   2004
  616.89–dc22

                                                                    2003063232

Printed in the United States of America

10 9 8 7 6 5 4 3 2   RRD 08 07 06 05

C O N T E N T S

PREFACE

Welcome to *Introduction to Clinical Psychology: Science, Practice, and Ethics*. We are excited to share our passion for clinical psychology with you. We had several goals in writing this textbook. First, we wanted to provide a broad overview of the field of clinical psychology. Our discipline is diverse and expanding, and we wanted to develop in students an appreciation of the breadth of the field. Second, we wanted to write a user-friendly textbook. The writing style was designed to be more conversational than academic. The intended audience for this book is advanced undergraduate and beginning-level graduate students in psychology. We strove to write in a style that was readily accessible to students at this level of training. Third, we wanted to cover some topics in greater depth than is typical of many books of this type on the market. For example, we discuss research methods in psychotherapy in some depth (Chapter 10), since we feel that understanding how evidence is gathered about whether a psychotherapy works is important to contemporary clinical psychologists. Similarly, we devote an entire chapter to biological models (Chapter 4) because of the importance attributed to the biological bases of problematic behavior in today's world and because these models are having an increasing impact on the science and practice of clinical psychology. Finally, we sought to integrate discussion of the science and practice throughout the text since our view is that the two should go hand in hand.

The reader will soon discover several characteristics of the text. There is an *emphasis upon science* throughout the book. We are unapologetic advocates of the scientist-practitioner model of training and practice (see Chapters 1 and 2). We believe that one of the strengths of the discipline, and a characteristic that sets it apart from other mental health disciplines, is an emphasis upon science. Therefore, we critique research and practice in clinical psychology from a scientific perspective. What are the limitations of our research methods? How strong is the scientific basis for the assessment and intervention strategies used by practitioners? We discuss these and related questions with the hopes that students will develop an appreciation for their complexity.

There is also an *emphasis upon controversies*. The field of clinical psychology was shaped by controversies. Significant advances in psychological assessment and psychotherapy were triggered by vehement criticisms of the state of the art and equally fervent defenses of time-honored practices. Conflict over the way clinical psychologists should be trained was present at the birth of the discipline and continues today. Conflict and controversy will continue to shape the discipline. Rather than shy away from controversies or soft-peddle differences, we sought to immerse students in the conflicts. Our hope is to raise more questions than we answer.

We believe that it is important to understand where a discipline came from in order to understand where it is today. Therefore, we cover the development of the field in some detail in Chapter 2 and provide additional historical information in other chapters as needed. However, the reader will find a strong *emphasis upon contemporary clinical psychology* throughout the text. We want students to understand what clinical psychology is all about at the beginning of the twenty-first century.

Finally, as the subtitle of our text indicates, there is an *emphasis upon ethics* through-out the book. We discuss ethical dilemmas faced by clinical psychologists in every chap-ter. In the Focus on Ethics boxes, the reader is introduced to ethical challenges and provided some information about how psychologists manage these challenges. Students will become familiar with the ethical standards psychologists use as guides to negotiate their way through ethical dilemmas. Our decision to discuss specific ethical issues within certain chapters was arbitrary. For example, we discuss ethical issues associated with advertising in the Focus on Ethics box in the chapter on Clinical Neuropsychology (Chapter 14). This is no way meant to imply that neuropsychologists are more likely to deal with ethical issues in advertising than are other psychologists. We recognize that only a minority of students who read this book will pursue careers in clinical psychology. Nonetheless, we believe that it is important for everyone to grapple with questions about what is right and what is wrong and why. It is our hope that exploration of how clinical psychologists as individuals and how psychology as a discipline have struggled with these issues can help readers develop their own personal ethics.

Acknowledgments

Producing the first edition of a textbook is a task that involves many people beyond the authors. We are grateful to many colleagues and students who helped in a variety of ways. Several friends provided valuable comments and critiques of draft chapters, including Sue Righthand, Bruce Kerr, Larry Smith, Sandy Sigmon, and Anne Hess. We appreciate their thoughtful comments. We would also like to thank the external reviewers who were appro-priately critical, but also supportive, in their feedback: Clint Bowers, University of Central Florida; Michele M. Carter, American University; Cynthia M. Hartung, Oklahoma State Uni-versity; Lynne Kellner, Fitchburg State College; Roxann Roberson-Nay, University of Mary-land; David A. Smith, Ohio State University; Richard Wenzlaff, University of Texas-San Antonio; and Eric Zillmer, Drexel University. Several students participated in gathering and organizing information, most notably Elizabeth Ranslow, Jamie Scoular, Jared Bruce, Becky Garnett, and Margaret Smith. We are grateful to Mary P. for her kind permission to quote the excerpt from "Black Raspberry Tales" in Chapter 12, and to Sheryl L. Olson, Ph.D., of the University of Michigan, who permitted us to draw outline material from the Behavioral Assessment chapter in the second edition of *Behavior Therapy: Concepts, Procedures, and Applications* by Geoffrey L. Thorpe and Sheryl L. Olson (Boston: Allyn and Bacon, 1997).The support and encouragement of Carol Thorpe are greatly appreciated, as are her many hours of work in compiling the references. Secretarial support was graciously provided by Sandy Page and Kathy McAuliffe. We also wish to thank the editorial staff at Allyn and Bacon for their encouragement, support, and guidance. Finally, we are indebted to the stu-dents at the University of Maine, whose passion for learning motivated us to write this book.

PART ONE

Introduction and Foundations

CHAPTER

1

Definition and Training

Stop for a moment before reading any further. Take a minute to think about what you know, or think you know, about clinical psychology. On a piece of scrap paper (a 3×5 card or self-stick note will do), complete this sentence: "Clinical psychology is . . ."

Over the past several years the first author has used this exercise to begin his introduction to clinical psychology class. The responses he has gotten have been extremely interesting, ranging from the bluntly honest ("Clinical psychology is . . . I have absolutely no clue") to the dramatic ("Clinical psychology is searching for clues, analyzing backgrounds, tying together leads, hopefully concluding with somewhat of an answer to the problem—a detective of the mind, if you will"). Organizing students' responses to this incomplete sentence exercise into various categories has illuminated a picture of how clinical psychology is perceived by this sample of undergraduates. Far and away, most students associate clinical psychology with some type of therapeutic activity. Fully 79 percent of the responses identify clinical psychology as a field that is involved in psychological treatment. The most common type of response (44 percent), in fact, is to define clinical psychology in terms of therapy. The second most common type of response (35 percent) also emphasizes therapy but includes one or more other endeavors (e.g., research, assessment, diagnosis). A minority of students define clinical psychology as a research or scholarly discipline (10 percent).

Although the sample is neither randomly selected nor representative of undergraduate psychology majors throughout the country, my suspicion is that the identification of clinical psychology with psychotherapy is fairly common. As we will see later, in this chapter, this view of the field, while not inaccurate, does not capture the richness of the subject. There is so much more to clinical psychology.

Definition

Division 12, the Society of Clinical Psychology of the American Psychological Association, offers the following definition of clinical psychology. "The field of Clinical Psychology integrates science, theory, and practice to understand, predict, and alleviate maladjustment, disability, and discomfort as well as to promote human adaptation, adjustment, and personal development. Clinical Psychology focuses on the intellectual, emotional, biological, psychological, social, and behavioral aspects of human functioning across the life span, in varying cultures, and at all socioeconomic levels" (Society of Clinical Psychology, 2002). If your response to the incomplete sentence task approximated this definition, then maybe you don't need this book. If it didn't, read on.

We will not try to one-up the Society of Clinical Psychology by offering our own definition of the field. Rather, we will attempt to give you a sense of what clinical psychology is all about in four ways. First, we will describe some of the general characteristics of the discipline. Second, we will describe the professional activities and work settings of clinical psychologists. Third, we will seek to define clinical psychology by distinguishing it from related disciplines. Finally, in the second half of this chapter we will examine in some detail the training of clinical psychologists.

Characteristics of Clinical Psychology

Emphasis on Science

Clinical psychology is a subdiscipline of psychology. Many in the general public probably equate psychology with clinical psychology. It is the largest subdiscipline of psychology. The majority of doctoral degrees in psychology are awarded in clinical psychology (American Psychological Association, 1997, 1999) and clinical psychology is listed as the specialty area of the majority of the members of the American Psychological Association (American Psychological Association, 1997) and the majority of psychologists in the United States (Stapp, Tucker, & VandenBos, 1985)

We might be congratulated, sarcastically, for our keen grasp of the obvious when we point out clinical psychology's relationship to the larger discipline of psychology. But we do so because recognition of clinical psychology as a specialty within psychology is important to have if one is to understand the discipline. Psychology is the branch of science that is devoted to studying and understanding behavior. As a subdiscipline of psychology, clinical psychology is imbued with the values and assumptions of science. A couple of the assumptions of science that are particularly important for understanding clinical psychology are *determinism* and *empiricism*. Determinism is the assumption that all events have causes and that these causes are potentially knowable. Science assumes that the causes of events are not random but follow some order or set of rules. These rules are also potentially discoverable. Events can be understood if we can identify all of the relevant rules. For psychology then, the causes of behavior are potentially knowable and are assumed to follow a set of rules that are also identifiable.

Empiricism is the assumption that science concerns itself with events that are observable and measurable. This is common sense. How can one study a phenomenon if the phenomenon cannot be observed? Historically, the argument that psychology should concern itself only with observable events is associated with *behaviorism* (see Chapter 3). John Watson launched behaviorism with a 1913 paper in which he argued that the only acceptable form of psychological data is observable behavior, thus excluding mental processes from psychology altogether. A strict empirical approach to science, however, is not tenable. Scientists have long recognized the need for nonobservables in science. Gravity is a phenomenon that cannot be directly observed but is extremely useful in understanding the action of objects of different mass.

Hypothetical constructs are not directly observable but are known by their relationship to observable events. Gravity is an example of a hypothetical construct. While we cannot observe gravity directly, the validity of statements about gravity can be tested through observation. Examples of hypothetical constructs in clinical psychology include anxiety, depression, self-efficacy, and intelligence. None of these constructs can be observed directly but predictions about observable behaviors (e.g., trembling, crying, approaching a feared situation, and performance on a test) can be made based upon these hypothetical constructs and these predictions are open to empirical test. Accepting that hypothetical constructs have a place in science does not mean the death of empiricism. The validity of a hypothetical construct can be tested by examining relationships among observable events.

In addition to the scientific assumptions that pervade clinical psychology, clinical psychology is a discipline that employs and values scientific methods. As such, there is a strong emphasis upon research in clinical psychology. Many but not all clinical psychologists do research. However, even those who do not are taught to value research and to apply knowledge gained through research to address practical problems.

Emphasis on Maladjustment

There are, of course, many subdisciplines of psychology besides clinical psychology. There are, for example, 52 other divisions of the American Psychological Association besides Division 12. Clinical psychology is a specialty within psychology that concerns itself with abnormal behavior and emotional suffering. For the most part, clinical psychology concerns itself with problems with which human beings struggle. As researchers, clinical psychologists apply scientific methods to understand how problems such as phobias, self-induced vomiting, compulsive gambling, and many others develop and are maintained. As clinicians, psychologists seek to understand the problems their clients experience and apply that understanding to help them gain relief. The focus upon "maladjustment, disability, and discomfort" is one of the characteristics that sets clinical psychology apart from other subdisciplines of psychology.

Emphasis on the Individual

Another characteristic that helps distinguish clinical psychology is its emphasis upon the individual. Psychology, as a science, seeks to understand the general relationships among variables that govern behavior. That is, psychology is interested in understanding behavior at a *nomothetic* level. Clinical psychology is interested in this level of understanding. However, the emphasis in clinical psychology is upon how general principles can be applied to understand the individual. This *idiographic* level of understanding is central to the practice of clinical psychology. An example may help illustrate the nomothetic-idiographic distinction. Research studies find that between 7 percent and 15 percent of women experience a period of significant depression after the giving birth and that acute life stressors are a risk factor for postpartum depression (Swendsen & Mazure, 2000). Clinical researchers have also found that the degree of social support and the range of coping strategies that a new mother has influence whether she becomes depressed and the severity of depression. This nomothetic information is used by the clinical psychologist to develop an idiographic understanding of the client referred for postpartum depression. What are the significant stressors faced by this woman? How does she cope? Who supports her? With the answers to these and other questions, the clinician develops an understanding of this particular woman's experience of postpartum depression. Treatment is based upon this idiographic understanding.

Emphasis on Helping

A fourth characteristic of clinical psychology is that it is a helping profession. Clinical psychologists work to help people who are in psychological distress. If the findings or our informal study using the sentence completion task ("Clinical psychology is . . .") are at all valid, you probably already associate clinical psychology with treatment. This association of clinical psychology with psychotherapy is interesting, given that psychotherapy was not really a significant function for clinical psychologists throughout the first half of the profession's history (see Chapter 2).

None of the four characteristics of clinical psychology discussed—scientific assumptions and values, concern with psychological distress, emphasis on the individual, and helping profession—are unique to clinical psychology. Many disciplines within psychology apply a scientific approach to understand human behavior (e.g., personality, social, cognitive psychology). Other disciplines, most notably psychiatry, are concerned with human maladjustment. And there are, of course, many other helping professions (e.g., medicine, nursing, social work). It is the integration of these characteristics within a single discipline that distinguishes clinical psychology. Clinical psychology applies the assumptions and methods of psychological science to problems of human behavioral, emotional, and mental functioning to better understand and treat these problems.

Activities and Work Settings of Clinical Psychologists

Another way of learning about what clinical psychology is involves looking at what clinical psychologists do. Clinical psychologists meet privately with people who are in psychological distress to help them overcome their problems. But clinical psychologists do so much more. They are involved in research, writing, teaching, assessment, consultation, administration, and other professional activities.

Research

Most clinical psychologists are products of graduate programs that include extensive training in research design, methods, and statistics. Clinical psychologists who train in traditional scientist-practitioner programs (see section on training) must conduct at least one piece of original research in order to obtain their degree. In fact, training in research is one of the characteristics that distinguishes clinical psychology from most other helping professions.

Although many clinical psychologists are involved in research in one form or another, a minority consider "researcher" to be their primary professional identity (Norcross, Karg, & Prochaska, 1997b). It is more typical for researcher to be one of the professional hats worn by a clinical psychologist. In fact, even clinical psychologists who are university professors report that, on average, they spend about a quarter of their professional time engaged in research (Norcross et al., 1997b).

The types of research clinical psychologists conduct is extremely varied. A quick perusal of the table of contents of a recent volume of the *Journal of Consulting and Clinical Psychology* received at the time of this writing show studies on adolescent physical aggression (Andrews, Foster, Capaldi, & Hops, 2000), work adjustment of bipolar patients (Hammen, Gitlin, & Altshuler, 2000), treatment of spit tobacco users (Hatsukami, Grillo, Boyle, Allen, Jensen, Bliss, & Brown, 2000), posttraumatic stress disorder (Schnurr, Ford, Friedman, Green, Dain, & Sengupta, 2000), prevention of delinquent and violent behavior (Stoolmiller, Eddy, & Reid, 2000), couples therapy (Jacobson, Christensen, Prince, Cordova, & Eldridge, 2000), and telephone-administered treatment of depressive symptoms in people with multiple sclerosis (Mohr, Likosky, Bertagnolli, Goodkin, Van Der Wende, Dwyer, & Dick, 2000).

Survey studies of clinical psychologists tend to find that a minority of psychologists publish the lion's share of research. In fact, over twenty years' worth of survey studies have repeatedly found that the modal number of publications for clinical psychologists is 0 (Garfield, & Kurtz, 1974; Norcross & Prochaska, 1982; Norcross et al., 1997b). But this number is misleading. These same survey studies tend to find that most psychologists do publish at least one article (81 percent in the most recent survey; Norcross et al., 1997b). About three-quarters of clinical psychologists report having presented at least one paper at a conference and about one-quarter have published at least one book (Norcross et al., 1997b).

Teaching

Clinical psychologists are engaged in a variety of forms of teaching. About 50 percent of clinical psychologists report that they spend some portion of their professional time teaching (Norcross et al., 1997b). Between 15 and 20 percent are employed as professors at colleges, universities, and other academic institutions (American Psychological Association, 1999; Norcross, Karg, & Prochaska, 1997a). Clinical psychology professors typically teach courses that are within the domain of clinical psychology. At the undergraduate level, courses might include abnormal psychology, tests and measurement, introduction to clinical psychology, and systems of psychotherapy. Graduate courses taught by clinical psychologists include psychological assessment, theories of psychopathology, psychotherapy, clinical research methods, professional ethics, and any number of focused advanced seminars such as forensic psychology, child psychopathology, child assessment, neuropsychology, health psychology, or geropsychology.

In addition to traditional classroom-based courses, clinical psychologists engage in a variety of other forms of teaching. Perhaps one of the most challenging but also most gratifying forms of teaching is clinical supervision. Here the clinical psychologist works with graduate students to help them develop clinical skills in assessment, psychotherapy, or other applied activities (e.g., consultation). Many graduate programs in clinical psychology have affiliated training clinics where students work with real people presenting with real problems under the supervision of a licensed psychologist. Clinical supervision includes didactic instruction in the theoretical and empirical basis for clinical activities but also draws from the clinical supervisor's own experience. Clinical supervision might take the form of modeling interviewing, testing or therapy skills, observing the trainee, listening to audiotape recordings of therapy sessions, or critiquing videotaped sessions along with the supervisee. Clinical supervisors often need to help supervisees manage their own anxiety about clinical work or to work through feelings aroused by the client. Box 1.1 explores some of the ethical issues that can arise in clinical supervision.

BOX **1.1**

Focus on Ethics: Ethical Issues in Clinical Supervision

The Psychological Services Center is the training clinic affiliated with the doctoral training program in clinical psychology at the University of Maine. The clinic provides outpatient psychological services, including psychological assessment and psychotherapy, to people from the surrounding community. When a potential client contacts the clinic, the case is assigned to a graduate student clinician and a clinical supervisor. The supervisors are licensed psychologists, most of whom are also faculty members in the Department of Psychology. The clinician-supervisor team takes responsibility for the case. Typically, the graduate student has most of the face-to-face contact with the client. The supervisor may observe the clinician directly through a one-way mirror as he or she works with the client. Alternatively, the supervisor may listen to audiotapes of therapy sessions or watch videotapes. The supervisor and clinician meet regularly to discuss the case, to develop plans for future sessions, and for the supervisor to give the clinician feedback and help him or her work through problems that arise. These procedures, which are representative of those used in most training clinics, create a host of opportunities for ethical dilemmas to arise.

One basic ethical challenge faced by clinical supervisors every time they agree to supervise a case is the multiple levels of ethical responsibility inherent in clinical supervision. Supervisors have responsibility to assure that the clients are provided the best possible services. At the same time, they have a responsibility to their supervisees to assure that the student clinicians have the best possible learning experience. Fortunately, in most instances, working toward one goal facilitates movement toward the other. The better the learning experience for the clinicians, the more the clinicians improve, and the more the clinicians grow and develop, the better the service to the clients. Ideally, the more conscientious supervisors are about observing therapy sessions, about providing timely and constructive feedback, about providing the supervisee with complementary resources (e.g., books or tapes), about modeling therapeutic techniques, and about creating a supervisory relationship in which students feel comfortable bringing up issues and concerns, the more the students will learn and the better served clients will be.

In reality, however, there are times when working toward the goal of helping supervisees develop as clinicians and the goal of providing clients with the best possible service may conflict. It is a cliché to say that we learn from our mistakes, but it is often true. For developing clinicians, some of the most powerful learning experiences may be those times during which they struggle, falter, or screw up. Students need to have the opportunity to try new things. Supervisors must balance the sometimes conflicting ethical responsibilities to clients and to supervisees. They must assure that clients receive adequate and appropriate services as supervisees learn to implement clinical techniques and procedures.

BOX **1.1** **Continued**

A second area of clinical supervision that creates ethical challenges is evaluating supervisees' performance in clinical practice. In most courses, the instructor can specify at the outset exactly what the expectations are for that course and how students will be evaluated. Students know when the exams will be given, generally what topics the exams will cover, and what kinds of test items will be included (e.g., essay, short answer, multiple choice). They know whether the course includes a research paper and what percentage of the grade the paper is worth. On the other hand, when students begin a semester of practicum training in psychotherapy, for example, the instructor can only provide an outline of what is expected (e.g., how many clients the student will see, how often they will meet for supervision, etc.). Each student who takes the psychotherapy practicum will have a different experience. Neither the supervisor nor the student can know at the outset exactly what kinds of clients the student will see, what issues those clients will present, what crises might arise, and what emotional reactions the student may experience as he or she works with a client. For one student, a semester of practicum training may include helping a client through an acute suicidal crisis. For another student, the experience may involve coping with feelings of romantic attraction to a client. For a third, practicum may include helping a highly motivated client work through a structured treatment protocol for learning to manage anxiety. All three students are evaluated on a variety of criteria, which might include their ability to deal effectively with their own feelings in therapy, their ability to convey warmth and empathy to the client, their willingness to raise issues in supervision, and their openness to corrective feedback. Surely, for these hypothetical students, their performance in each of these criterion areas is dependent not only upon their skills and professional development but also upon the clients with whom they are working. For the supervising psychologist, the ethical challenge is to evaluate each practicum student in a fair and equitable manner given the variability in experiences across students.

A third way in which the clinical supervisor to supervisee relationship can present ethical challenges is the fact that it creates opportunities for exploitation. Several commentators have noted the parallels between the therapist-client relationship and the clinical supervisor-supervisee relationship (e.g., Koocher & Keith-Spiegel, 1998; Sherry, 1991). Just as in the therapist-client relationship, there are inequities in the clinical supervisor-supervisee relationship. Supervisees are expected to disclose personal information about their thoughts and feelings, whereas supervisors are not. The supervisor and supervisee frequently meet alone. Supervision sessions can be emotionally charged. Just as therapists do, clinical supervisors try to help supervisees develop self-awareness and exploration. At the same time, the supervisor is evaluating the student clinician. In addition, the supervisor may have other relationships with the student that are also characterized by an inequity of power (e.g., research supervisor, classroom teacher). The inequity of the relationship creates opportunities for abuse. It is upsetting to note that survey studies have found that sexual contact between clinical supervisors and their supervisees occurs fairly often (Glaser & Thorpe, 1986; Levenson & Shover, 1979, cited in Koocher & Keith-Spiegel, 1998). The Ethics Code (American Psychological Association, 2002) expressly prohibits sexual relationships between psychologists and their supervisees since such relationships impair the supervisor's ability to be objective and because there is such a potential for supervisor-supervisee sexual relationships to be exploitative.

There are, of course, many other ways, besides sexual, in which clinical supervisors can exploit their supervisees. Some are obvious (e.g., requiring supervisees to do extra work for which the supervisor receives financial compensation). Others are more subtle (e.g., using supervision time to discuss the supervisor's own clinical experiences without adequately discussing the supervisee's case). In order to minimize the opportunities for abuse, alternatives to one-on-one supervision are sometimes used. Some supervisors meet with multiple supervisees at one time. Group supervision

(continued)

B O X **1.1**   **Continued**

allows students to learn from others' experiences and diffuses the intimacy created in individual supervision. Another alternative is to have multiple supervisors. A third approach is sometimes called "vertical supervision" in which a team of students at different levels of training work under the direction of the psychologist supervisor. The more senior student clinicians supervise the less seasoned supervisees, with the psychologist overseeing the whole team. In this model the more advanced students receive training not only in clinical skills but also in clinical supervision.

No approach to clinical supervision completely avoids ethical challenges. As we will illustrate throughout the book, ethical issues arise in every area of clinical psychologists' professional lives. The goal for training in professional ethics is not to learn how to avoid ethical dilemmas. Instead, the goal is to learn how to manage ethical issues as they arise.

Clinical psychologists who do not hold academic positions are also frequently involved in teaching. Psychologists are often called upon to do in-service training for other helping professionals or paraprofessionals. For example, a clinical psychologist might provide telephone hotline volunteers training in crisis intervention. Psychologists may train medical students in basic interviewing skills or teach a group of lawyers about the limitations of psychological tests. Clinical psychologists also often share their knowledge with psychologists and other professionals through continuing education workshops or grand rounds presentations.

Before leaving the topic, we think it is important to point out that while many clinical psychologists teach as part of their professional work, very few receive formal training in teaching while completing their graduate education. More typically, psychologists learn teaching by doing. The absence of teaching training from graduate curricula is unfortunate given the prominent role teaching plays in the lives of many clinical psychologists.

Psychotherapy

Psychotherapy involves helping people to understand and resolve problems. The term *psychotherapy* encompasses a broad array of psychological interventions including behavior modification, individual counseling, family therapy, parent training, and others. The prototype for psychotherapy is a one-on-one meeting between the therapist and client to discuss the client's problems. This form of therapy, referred to as individual psychotherapy, is the most common form of therapy engaged in by clinical psychologists (Norcross et al., 1997b), but it is not the only form of psychotherapy. Therapy can include meetings in groups, with couples, or with extended families. The variety of presenting problems that psychotherapy can be used to address is practically endless. Anxiety, depression, eating disorders, psychoses, alcohol abuse, drug addiction, relationship difficulties, compliance with medical procedures, sexual functioning, traumatic memories, phobias, shyness, and a host of other issues might prompt someone to seek help from a psychotherapist.

Psychotherapy has become the predominant activity of clinical psychologists. It is their most frequently engaged in activity. Eighty-four percent of clinical psychologists in a recent survey reported that they engaged in psychotherapy (Norcross et al., 1997b). The percentage of time spent in psychotherapy varied according to the work setting of the psychologists. University professors spent about 10 percent of their time, clinical psychologists in hospital settings spent about 40 percent of their time, and private practitioners about 60 percent of their time in psychotherapy (Norcross et al., 1997b).

Psychotherapy has clearly been the growth area for psychologists over the past forty years. But there is strong evidence that this growth cannot continue and that, in fact, psychotherapy may play a less central role in the professional lives of psychologists in years to come. Changes in health-care delivery systems in the United States and increased competition from other professional groups interested in providing psychotherapy services has resulted in a shrinking market for psychologist-psychotherapists. The opportunities for psychologists as psychotherapy providers will likely shrink in the future (Cummings, 1995; Norcross et al., 1997b). One of the challenges facing clinical psychology today is to develop alternative career opportunities for its professionals.

Assessment

After psychotherapy, psychological assessment is the most frequently engaged in activity by clinical psychologists (Norcross et al., 1997b). Psychological assessment involves collecting information about people's behavior, interests, emotions, thoughts, intelligence, interpersonal styles, and so on and integrating this information to develop a greater understanding of the person. Clinical psychologists use interviews, psychological tests, and observations to collect the data upon which they base their assessments.

The procedures used in any given psychological assessment will vary depending upon the goal of the assessment. Some of the general goals of psychological assessment are to diagnose, to formulate treatment plans, to make predictions about future behavior, and to evaluate the outcome of a psychological intervention. The complexity of psychological assessment can best be appreciated by looking at the types of questions clinical psychologists evaluate. Consider for a moment the following assessment questions:

A child is failing the fourth grade. Why and what can be done to help?

A 24-year-old suffers a head injury in a car accident. What impact has this had upon his intellectual functioning?

A 33-year-old woman seeks a therapist and complains that she has lost her zest for life. What can be done to help her?

A 39-year-old women becomes violently ill on the way to her outpatient chemotherapy treatments. Why and what can be done to help her?

A 46-year-old man has been convicted of sexually abusing his 8-year-old stepdaughter. What level of risk does he pose to the community? Can he benefit from psychological treatment?

A 52-year-old business executive is referred to a psychotherapist by the company's employee assistance program because he has begun losing his temper with his employees frequently. What is going on?

A 76-year-old woman spends most of her days in bed, rarely talks to her children when they visit, and is not keeping up her personal hygiene. She suffered a minor stroke eight years ago. Her husband died three years ago. Is she depressed, or is her behavior due to deterioration in brain functioning?

Consultation

When functioning in the role of consultant, a clinical psychologists may utilize skills in teaching, research, assessment, or even psychotherapy. Clinical psychologists are often hired by organizations to provide advice and share their expertise. A school might hire a clinical psychologist to evaluate students who present significant behavior problems. The psychologist evaluates students and then works with the staff to design learning environments that best suit to the students' needs. A clinical psychologist might consult with a pediatric oncology center to develop strategies to help patients comply with unpleasant medical procedures. In a business setting, a clinical psychologist might be hired to help employees learn to manage stress. A correctional facility might hire a clinical psychologist to provide staff training in suicide prevention. Clinical psychologists have been hired by law enforcement agencies to assist in hostage negotiations (Hatcher, Mohandie, Turner, & Gelles, 1999). A clinical psychologist might be hired by a mental health agency to help develop methods of evaluating the efficacy of clinical intervention services provided by the agency.

The first author has provided consultation services to a federally funded job training program for the past fifteen years. The program provides job training and basic education to disadvantaged adolescents and young adults. The author's experience illustrates how several of the skills of a clinical psychologist are used in the role of consultant. The typical ten-hour consulting day begins with a review of the students who have been referred for evaluation. The referrals are prioritized and the morning is spent conducting brief evaluations of from four to eight students. These evaluations consist of clinical interviews, telephone interviews with relevant staff members, and reviews of medical and/or disciplinary records. The afternoon is devoted to meetings with various groups of staff members. The consultant meets with the on-site counseling staff to review the students evaluated that day and to develop case management plans. Typically, a portion of this meeting is devoted to staff development activities such as training in referral writing. A meeting with the residential life staff focuses upon a discussion of the management of students who present behavioral problems in the dormitories. A formal staff training meeting occurs in the later afternoon. The consultant meets with about one-quarter of the staff at a time to provide more formal training in areas such as conflict resolution, talking to students about sexual issues, anger management, or managing job-related stress. After that training, the consultant might meet with individual staff members to help them with specific problems or concerns. Recent examples include helping the health education instructor develop a curriculum on anxiety and depression and meeting with the substance abuse specialist to develop a set of semi-structured group therapy exercises. The consultant also meets with the center's director to discuss staff problems and identify training needs.

Some clinical psychologists find consultation work to be personally and financial rewarding enough that they make it their primary professional activity. It is more typical, however, for clinical psychologists to spend only a portion of their professional time consulting. More than half of clinical psychologists report doing some consultations but typically they spend less than 10 percent of their time in this activity (Norcross et al., 1997b). In addition to paid consultation work, psychologists also frequently provide informal consultation to professional colleagues without charging a fee. Informal consultation with one's colleagues is considered an important component of professional development by many clinicians (Cohen, Sargent, & Sechrest, 1986).

Administration

Although not the most glamorous of professional activities, many clinical psychologists find themselves holding administrative responsibilities as their careers develop. At universities, clinical psychologists are department chairs, deans, vice presidents, and presidents. Psychologists also frequently occupy administrative positions in hospitals, clinics, and mental health agencies. On average, clinical psychologists report spending about 10 percent of their time with administrative duties (Norcross et al., 1997b).

Why do so many clinical psychologists end up in administrative positions? We know of no research that might shed some light upon this question. And we acknowledge that one could propose a variety of reasons, some of which may not paint a very flattering picture. Nonetheless, we prefer to speculate that clinical psychologists have some skills and characteristics that make them suited for administrative work. First, through their training in research, clinical psychologists develop strong organizational skills. Second, through their clinical training, clinical psychologists develop strong interpersonal skills. It may be this combination of a highly organized individual who is skillful at interacting with people in a variety of emotional states that lends itself to successful administrative work.

Research, teaching, assessment, therapy, consultation, and administration are six general categories of work engaged in by clinical psychologists. One of the interesting things about clinical psychology as a career choice is that it opens doors to a variety of professional opportunities. But a clinical psychologist need not walk through only one door. In fact, it is unusual for a clinical psychologist to spend all of his or her time in one type of professional activity. Variety is the norm. Table 1.1 summarizes the findings from a survey of clinical psychologists conducted in 1995. The table suggests that it is rare for clinical psychologists to limit their professional life to only one type of activity. Not surprisingly, psychologists in private practice spend most of their time in assessment and psychotherapy and university professors spend theirs doing research and teaching. The distribution of times spent in different activities varies by work settings, but clinical psychologists tend to spend some portion of their professional time in a variety of different activities. Box 1.2 provides some examples of the variety of activities clinical psychologists engage in a typical week.

The variety of activities engaged in by clinical psychologists is matched by the variety of work settings. Clinical psychologists are employed at four-year colleges, universities, medical schools, dental schools, solo private practices, group practices, mental health clinics, businesses, all branches of the military, general and psychiatric hospitals, and Veterans Administration medical centers. Table 1.2 provides information on the primary employment sites for clinical psychologists reported in survey studies over a twenty-two-year period. The one area of clear growth has been private practice. While 23 percent of psychologists reported that they worked in private practice in 1973, that percentage jumped to 40 percent

TABLE 1.1   **Activity Profiles of Three Groups of Clinical Psychologists**

	Private Practitioners		University Professors		Hospital Psychologists	
	% involved	Mean % of time	% involved	Mean % of time	% involved	Mean % of time
Psychotherapy	95	61	68	11	91	41
Diagnosis/ assessment	78	17	44	3	86	22
Research/ writing	22	2	92	27	46	5
Teaching	25	2	97	34	48	6
Clinical supervision	46	4	69	8	68	8
Consultation	53	7	53	5	55	5
Administration	28	3	55	10	57	10

Source: Adapted from Norcross, Karg, & Prochaska (1997b).

B O X **1.2**

A Week in the Life of Two Clinical Psychologists

Clinical psychologists' professional time is filled with a variety of activities. We asked two psychologists who have different primary work settings to describe typical weeks in their professional lives.

Work Site: Mental Health Department, Community Hospital.

Responsibilities: Psychotherapy and psychological assessment services to outpatients; consultation to inpatient psychiatric unit and other medical units; supervision of master's-level clinicians; administrative and committee meetings; on-call crisis intervention coverage.

Monday
    8:00 - check messages, e-mail, return calls
    9:00 - psychotherapy client
    10:00 - psychotherapy client
    11:00 - case conference -review new cases
    12:00 - continuing education luncheon
    1:00 - intake new psychotherapy client
    2:00 - consult with psychiatrist re: inpatients
    3:00 - intake new psychotherapy client
    4:00 - supervision of masters-level clinicians
    5:00 - paperwork

Tuesday
    8:00
    9:00 - check messages, return calls, prepare
    10:00 - score/interpret psychological testing
    11:00 - report writing
    12:00 - lunch
    1:00 - psychotherapy client
    2:00 - psychological evaluation
    3:00 - psychological evaluation continued
    4:00 - psychotherapy client
    5:00 - paperwork

BOX **1.2**   **Continued**

Wednesday
8:00
9:00 - check phone and e-mail, return messages
10:00 - multidisciplinary team meeting
11:00 - staff meeting
12:00 - lunch, paperwork, phone calls
1:00 - psychotherapy client
2:00 - psychological evaluation
3:00 - evaluation continued
4:00 - psychotherapy client
5:00 - paperwork

Thursday
8:00 - check phone and e-mail, return
    messages
9:00 - psychological evaluation
10:00 - evaluation continued
11:00 - evaluation continued
12:00 - lunch, return calls
1:00 to 5:00 - on call for clinical emer-
    gencies and crisis intervention
3:00 - score/analyze psychological testing
4:00 - write reports as time allows
5:00 - catch up

Friday
8:00 - check phone and e-mail, return messages
9:00 - report writing
10:00 - psychotherapy client
11:00 - Policy Committee
12:00 - Wellness Committee
1:00 - psychotherapy client
2:00 - consultation with inpatient psychiatry
3:00 - consultation continued
4:00 - consultation continued
5:00 - return messages

Work Sites: Department of Psychology, public university; part-time private practice.

Responsibilities: Teach undergraduate and graduate courses; supervise doctoral students' research; clinical supervision; administrative and committee meetings; research; scholarly publishing. Private practice responsibilities include psychotherapy and psychological assessment.

Monday
8:30 - check phone and e-mail, return messages
9:00 - course preparation
10:00 - teach undergraduate abnormal psychology
11:00 - meeting with research lab
12:00 - lunch
1:00 - case conference
2:00 - clinical faculty meeting (every other week)
3:00 - faculty meeting (once a month)
4:00 - return calls, paperwork, etc.
5:00 - go home

evening - prepare for next day's assessment

Tuesday
8:30 - review cases for day
9:00 - psychological evaluation
10:00 - evaluation continued
11:00 - evaluation continued
12:00 - score tests, begin report
1:00 - report writing
2:00 - psychotherapy client
3:00 - psychotherapy client
4:00 - psychotherapy client
5:00 - psychotherapy client
6:00 - psychotherapy client

evening - catch up on therapy contact notes

(continued)

B O X **1.2**   **Continued**

Wednesday

8:30 - check phone and e-mail, return messages
9:00 - course preparation
10:00 - teach undergraduate abnormal psychology
11:00 - swim or work out
12:30 - group clinical supervision
1:00 - group supervision continued
2:00 - individual supervision
3:00 - office hours/return messages
4:00 - office hours continued
5:00 -

evening - read to prepare for Friday seminar

Thursday

8:30 - check phone and e-mail, return
       messages
9:00 - scholarly writing
10:00 - research activities (data analysis)
11:00 - continued
12:00 - basketball
1:00 - scholarly writing and
2:00   research activities (data analysis)
3:00 - continued
4:00 - continued
5:00 - psychotherapy client
6:00 - psychotherapy client

evening - read to prepare for Friday seminar

Friday

8:30 - check phone and e-mail, return messages
9:00 - Human Subjects Committee (HSC, once per month)
10:00 - HSC or seminar preparation
11:00 - seminar preparation
12:00 - lunch or swim/work out
1:00 - teach graduate seminar
2:00 - seminar continued
3:00 - seminar continued
4:00 - return messages

by 1995. What is not included in Table 1.2 is information about part-time private practice. Fully 60 percent of clinical psychologists who did not indicate private practice as their primary employment reported that they engaged in part-time private practice. Combining the full-timers and part-timers, a full 76 percent of the clinical psychologists surveyed were engaged in some private practice. The ability to set one's own hours and to be one's own boss are attractive features of solo private practice. In the 1970s and 1980s it represented a relatively lucrative option for full- or part-time employment. The changes in health-care delivery that took place in the United States in the 1990s and that continue today have cut the profits and increased the hassles associated with private practice. Some commentators have suggested that the days of the independent practitioner are numbered (e.g., Cummings, 1995).

Distinguishing Clinical Psychology from Related Professions

A third approach to understanding clinical psychology is to look at what it is not. Clinical psychology is one of several helping professions that concerns itself with human psychological distress. There is considerable overlap in the activities of clinical psychologists and those of

TABLE 1.2 Primary Employment Sites for Clinical Psychologists

Employment Site	1973 %	1981 %	1986 %	1995 %
Psychiatric Hospital	8	8	9	5
General Hospital	6	8	5	4
Outpatient Clinic	5	5	4	4
Community Mental Health Center	8	6	5	4
Medical School	8	7	7	9
Private Practice	23	31	35	40
University, Psychology	22	17	17	15
University, Other	7	5	4	4
VA Medical Center	—	—	—	3
None	1	1	4	1
Other	1	12	10	11

Source: Adapted from Norcross, Karg, & Prochaska (1997a).

related professions. Clinicians with graduate level degrees in medicine, psychology, social work, nursing, or education might, for example, provide psychotherapy. Legitimate questions for someone interested in the mental health field and considering post-undergraduate education to ask are: Why clinical psychology? and What sets this field apart from the others? We will endeavor to highlight the characteristics of clinical psychology that distinguish it from related professions. Our intention here is to answer the second question but not the first. Everyone must choose his or her own educational path. Clinical psychology is the right road for some. But for others, it would be the wrong avenue to travel.

Psychiatry

Probably the most commonly asked question of any clinical psychologist is some variations of "What's the difference between a psychologist and a psychiatrist?" The short—somewhat flip—answer has been to say, "Psychiatrists prescribe medication, psychologists don't." This answer never did justice to the many differences between the two professions and may not be true for very long. There is a concerted effort underway for psychologists to obtain the legal privilege to prescribe medications (Deleon & Wiggins, 1996). In 2002, New Mexico became the first state to pass legislature allowing licensed psychologists with appropriate training to prescribe medications. We will distinguish the two disciplines by describing differences in training, theoretical models, and professional activities.

Psychiatry is a medical specialty. The undergraduate education of most psychiatrists had a heavy emphasis upon course work that prepared them for medical school (e.g., biology, chemistry). Psychiatrists complete four years of post-baccalaureate training in a medical school and obtain a medical degree (M.D.). Medical school training for psychiatrists is the same as that of physicians who specialize in other areas. After medical school, psychiatrists complete a one-year internship in general medicine. Typically, the internship consists of a series of rotations lasting one month or so, during which new M.D.s work with resident and attending physicians in different specialty areas. Focused training in psychiatry does not begin until the residency. Psychiatrists complete a three-year psychiatric residency, after which they take examinations to become board certified in psychiatry.

The training of clinical psychologists is quite different. At the undergraduate level, training typically is in psychology or a related social science. Students take course work in the psychological approaches to understanding normal and abnormal behavior (e.g., learning, personality, cognition). Graduate school is typically designed to last five years, although it may take longer. The first four years of training occur at the home institution and involve course work in psychology, practicum training in the clinical areas (e.g., assessment, psychotherapy), and training in research. The fifth year of training is the pre-doctoral internship, which is usually spent at another institution and involves twelve months of full-time clinical work. The degree in clinical psychology (Ph.D. or Psy.D.; see below) is awarded after the student defends his or her doctoral dissertation.

Besides the differences in training content and training methods that distinguish psychiatry from clinical psychology, the difference in training philosophy may be the most important distinction of all. In medical school, students learn facts about biochemistry, anatomy, and physiology. In graduate school, psychology students learn about theories and how to critically evaluate research. The last thing that medical students do before they are awarded the M.D. is take the Hippocratic oath. The last thing that graduate students in psychology must do is defend their dissertation research. Sandford Goldstone, a mentor to the first author and colleague of the second, captured well the important distinction in training philosophies between the two disciplines. To paraphrase Dr. Goldstone, "When they are through with their training they take an oath. When we are through we get into an argument." As Dr. Goldstone's comment suggests, the final steps in medical and psychological training may tell us a lot about the way the two professions approach their work. Physicians learn facts and use this knowledge to understand and treat patients. Psychologists learn to think as researchers, to evaluate probabilistic findings, and to defend their views by citing the data.

Differences in training content highlight the differences in models for understanding human behavior that distinguish the two professions. Psychiatry is strongly dominated by the biological model of human behavior. Historically, American psychiatry allied itself with psychoanalysis in the first half of the twentieth century. The past fifty years, however, have witnessed the ascendancy of biological psychiatry. In clinical psychology, there has been far less agreement regarding the most appropriate model for understanding behavior (see Chapters 3 and 4). The biological basis of human behavior and psychological distress is only one of several ways of understanding for a clinical psychologist.

Clearly, there is overlap in the professional activities of psychologists and psychiatrists. Both types of clinicians make diagnoses, for example. Psychologists may use psychological tests to assist in the diagnostic process, whereas psychiatrists, who do not receive training in psychometric testing, typically do not. Both disciplines consider psychotherapy to be within their professional purview. As we have seen, this has become the dominant activity of clinical psychologists. Training in psychotherapy begins early in graduate school and is a significant component of most internships. The ascendance of biological psychiatry has been accompanied by a decrease in the importance of psychotherapy in the professional training and practice of psychiatry (Fleck, 1995).

Counseling Psychology

Counseling psychology is the specialty of psychology that is most similar to clinical psychology. Like clinical psychologists, counseling psychologists complete five years of graduate training that includes a one-year full-time internship. They receive training in research and must complete a dissertation. In most states, clinical and counseling psychologists are licensed under the same law. The clinical work of counseling psychologists involves psychological assessment, therapy, and consultation.

Traditionally, the distinction between clinical and counseling psychology has been in the areas emphasized in training and practice. Counseling psychologists have tended to deal with problems of adjustment in healthy individuals or more minor forms of maladjustment. Typical activities that defined counseling psychology included career and educational counseling. There was less of an emphasis upon testing in counseling psychology, and when it was used, testing tended to involve vocational interest inventories, aptitude testing, and personality. The prototypical work setting for a counseling psychologists was the college or university counseling center. Student counseling centers typically emphasize outreach programs (e.g., eating disorders awareness presentations), prevention (e.g., workshops for married students), and short-term counseling.

The practice of counseling psychology has changed over the past few decades. Counseling psychologists have expanded their areas of practice beyond career and short-term counseling to include more general psychotherapy. They have expanded their work settings to include private practice (Vredenburgh, Carlozzi & Stein, 1999; Zook & Walton, 1989), health care (Ruth-Roemer, Kurpin, & Carmin, 1998), and psychiatric institutions. The validity of the distinction between clinical and counseling psychology may be fading and some commentators have suggested that it is no longer justified (e.g., Beutler & Fisher, 1994).

School Psychology

School psychology is another specialty area that has some characteristics in common with clinical psychology. School psychologists work with educators to help them meet the intellectual, social and emotional needs of school-age children. A significant component of the work of school psychologists involves psychological testing. They typically rely heavily upon tests of intelligence, academic achievement, and behavior functioning. School psychologists are called upon to make diagnoses about learning disability, attention deficit hyperactive disorder, or mental retardation. They consult with schools to help them create learning environments that promote children's academic and personal development. They may help teachers to develop and refine their classroom management skills. School psychologists sometimes may provide brief therapy for students.

Some school psychologists receive a doctorate degree. In 1997, for example, 95 doctoral degrees in school psychology were awarded (American Psychological Association,

2000). Most school psychologists, however, have only masters-level training. The National Association of School Psychologists recognizes the masters as the degree necessary for entering the profession. In contrast, clinical psychology has always viewed the doctorate as the entry-level degree.

Social Work

Social work is a profession whose roots are in social service. Traditionally, social workers have worked with the poor and disenfranchised segments of the population (Richie, 1992). In mental health settings, the social work role historically had been to take the social history, hook patients up with social resources (e.g., disability benefits, welfare), and arrange for residential or vocational placements. The traditional roles of different professions working as a multidisciplinary team in a psychiatric hospital or community mental health center would be as follows. At intake, the social worker would take a social history, the psychiatrist would conduct a diagnostic interview, and the psychologist would administer psychological tests. The team, usually with the psychiatrist as its head, would meet to develop a treatment plan. In treatment, the psychiatrist would prescribe and monitor medications, the psychologist would conduct psychotherapy, and the social worker would provide support services for the family and mobilize community resources as needed (e.g., halfway house, food stamps, job training, etc.).

These traditional roles have disintegrated over time. As the profession has aged, social workers are less likely to be satisfied with their traditional roles. Contemporary clinical social workers make diagnoses and conduct psychotherapy. They are also likely to occupy important administrative positions in hospitals, clinics, or other social services agencies.

Given its history, it is not surprising that theories of clinical social work tend to emphasize the role of social factors such as poverty, racism, and sex-role stereotyping in psychological distress. Social work intervention is often directed toward empowering the disenfranchised.

The training of clinical social workers is markedly different from that of a clinical psychologist. The Masters in Social Work (M.S.W.) is the degree required for clinical practice. M.S.W. programs typically do not provide training in research. There is usually no masters thesis requirement. Clinical training takes place in the field under the supervision of a licensed social worker. To become a Licensed Clinical Social Worker (L.C.S.W.), most states require the M.S.W. and one to two years of supervised clinical work. The L.C.S.W. may practice psychotherapy as well as other clinical activities. Clinical social workers are employed by public and private agencies such as child protective services, community mental health centers, and psychiatric hospitals. A growing number of social worker are employed in private practice (Strom, 1993).

Other Related Professions

The mental health field is not limited to individuals with training in psychology, psychiatry, or social work. A growing number of states are recognizing other groups of professionals. In California, one can become licensed in Marriage, Family, and Child Counseling (M.F.C.C.). Typically, an M.F.C.C. has a masters degree in psychology, education, counseling, or a related profession. Two years of supervised experience is required for licensure. M.F.C.C.s can practice independently. Several states have similar types of licenses. In Maine, for example, one can become a Licensed Clinical Professional Counselor, while in Massachusetts, with similar credentials one can be a Licensed Mental Health Counselor. It is difficult to comment upon these disciplines since education, clinical experience, and supervision of these professionals varies so greatly.

As the preceding discussion indicates, it is not easy to distinguish clinical psychology from other mental health professions by focusing upon clinical activities. Several professions engage in diagnosis, assessment, and psychotherapy. In the next section of this chapter we turn our attention to the training of clinical psychologists. The models and methods of training clinical psychologists may be the feature that most clearly distinguishes the discipline from others.

Training in Clinical Psychology

The hallmark of training in clinical psychology is the integration of science and practice. The *scientist-practitioner model* has been the preeminent approach to training in clinical psychology over the past fifty years (Norcross et al., 1997a; Stricker, 2000). One of the basic assumptions of scientist-practitioner model is that science and practice must continually inform each other. What better way for this to occur than for clinical psychologists to be trained as scientists and practitioners? But this training must not be separate. Clinical psychologists are not scientists on Mondays, Wednesdays, and Fridays and practitioners on Tuesdays and Thursdays. Scientist-practitioner training is not training in science plus training in practice (Belar, 2000). Integration of science and practice defines the model. "Scientist-practitioner psychologists embody a research orientation in their practice and a practice relevance in their research" (Belar & Perry, 1991, p. 7).

Graduate training programs that adhere to the scientist-practitioner model prepare students in three broad areas: research, assessment, and intervention. Students are trained to conduct psychological research but also to apply knowledge drawn from psychological research in their practice. "The graduate of this training model is capable of functioning as an investigator and as a practitioner, and may function as either or both, consistent with the highest standards in psychology" (Belar & Perry, 1991, p. 8). In order to prepare scientist-practitioners, graduate programs provide didactic instruction in core content areas in psychology (e.g., biological bases of behavior, learning and cognition, social influences upon behavior, individual differences). Didactic instruction is coupled with experiential learning through clinical practica to prepare students to deliver psychological services. Students learn to critically evaluate the scientific status of assessment and intervention techniques at the same time they are learning to apply these techniques. Research training usually includes research mentoring, in which the graduate student works closely with a research advisor, along with instruction in research design, methods, and statistics. Students design and carry out an independent research project, the doctoral dissertation, at the culmination of their research training.

The scientist-practitioner model of training is often referred to as the *Boulder model,* named for Boulder, Colorado, the city where a committee of psychologists met in 1949 and formally adopted this model of training for clinical psychology (see Chapter 2). The Boulder model has been alternatively hailed and denigrated over the years. While opinions vary, we feel it is important for the reader to know that we fall strongly in the camp of supporters of scientist-practitioner training. Boulder model thinking pervades this book. When Boulder model training succeeds, the product is a unique type of health professional. We can do no better that to quote the authors of a policy statement that emanated from a national conference on scientist-practitioner training in capturing the ideal graduate of a Boulder model training program. "The scientist-practitioner model produces a psychologist who is uniquely educated and trained to generate and integrate scientific and professional knowledge, attitudes, and skills so as to further psychological science, the professional practice of psychology, and human welfare" (Belar & Perry, 1991, pp. 7–8).

But the scientist-practitioner model is not the only approach to training clinical psychologists. And while most clinical psychologists describe their training as Boulder model (Norcross et al. 1997b), the percentage of newly graduated doctorates in clinical psychology from Boulder model training programs has been shrinking for several years (Rice, 1997). The most common alternative to the Boulder model is the *Vail model,* also named for a city in Colorado that hosted a major training conference (see Chapter 2). The Vail model, which is sometimes called the *scholar-practitioner model,* deemphasizes the need for research experience in training and emphasizes training in the delivery of psychological services. The Vail model training program prepares its graduates for careers in clinical practice.

Vail model training may occur within a psychology department at an accredited university, which is the home for most scientist-practitioner training programs. But practice-oriented training also takes place within so-called "free-standing" schools of professional psychology. These schools are private, for-profit, and not affiliated with a university. One of the largest free-standing schools is the California School of Professional Psychology, which currently has four campuses. These schools represent a controversial development in the history of clinical psychology and are a marked departure from the model graduate training program envisioned by the attendees at the Boulder conference (Raimy, 1950). Box 1.3 outlines some of the differences between training in a free-standing professional school and a university-based graduate program in clinical psychology.

Students who receive graduate training in clinical psychology that emphasizes psychological practice sometimes receive a Psy.D. (Doctorate of Psychology) as opposed to a Ph.D. in psychology. The first Psy.D. training program was developed at the University of Illinois and commenced in 1968 (Peterson, 1968). While this program was eventually eliminated, many other Psy.D. programs have sprung up over the years. In 1999, 39 of the 199 doctoral training programs in clinical psychology accredited by the American Psychological Association offered the Psy.D. (American Psychological Association, 1999)

The relationship between the Psy.D. degree and professional training schools is not one to one. That is, not all professional schools offer the Psy.D. and not all Psy.D. degrees are awarded by professional schools. In 1993, for example, more professional school graduates earned the Ph.D. than the Psy.D. (American Psychological Association, 1993, cited in Rice, 1997). Many of the accredited doctoral training programs that offer the Psy.D. are affiliated with universities.

BOX **1.3**

Training in a Free-Standing Professional School versus a University-Based Doctoral Program

The traditional homes for doctoral training programs in clinical psychology have been departments of psychology within regionally accredited universities. The late 1960s and early 1970s, however, witnessed the birth of new homes for training clinical psychologists. Professional schools of psychology, sometimes referred to as free-standing because they are not affiliated with accredited universities, sprang up first in California and then throughout the United States. In this box we will discuss some of the differences in the experiences of students who receive their training in a professional school as compared to a university.

One of the first differences students will note—and for some students the most important—is in the cost. With few exceptions, it is more expensive to receive training in a professional school. There are two main reasons for the cost difference. First, free-standing schools are much more dependent upon tuition for financial stability. In contrast, universities rely upon a wider variety of sources of financial support, including indirect support from research grants, public moneys, and endowments. Second, it is far more common for students in university-based doctoral programs to receive financial support. Students commonly work as research or teaching assistants during their graduate years at a university. In contrast, students in professional schools rarely receive financial support from the institution (Norcross, Sayette, & Mayne, 1998).

A second difference is class size. Professional schools tend to accept much larger classes of students than do university-based programs. Given the reliance upon tuition dollars to pay the bills, the motivation to accept large classes is obvious. It is not uncommon for the entering class of a professional school to be on the order of thirty to sixty students, whereas university-based programs tend to accept classes of about five to ten students. To illustrate the difference we will use our own graduate program as an example, compared to the Massachusetts School of Professional Psychology (MSPP; geographically, the closest professional school). Nine students were offered a place in our entering class for fall 1999 (12 percent acceptance rate). Five students entered our program that fall. According to their website, MSPP routinely has entering classes of approximately thirty-five students. Forty-two percent of the applicants were offered admission in fall 1999.

A third difference between professional schools and universities is the makeup of their respective faculties. The faculties at professional schools tend to be primarily clinical in their orientations and experience. Typically, they do not do research. A relatively large percent of the faculty of professional schools hold part-time positions. These part-time faculty typically have clinical jobs as their primary form of employment. Advocates for professional school training argue that these clinician faculty are strong professional role models for their students, who, by and large, are interested in clinical positions upon graduation. At a traditional university, the graduate students are trained by full-time faculty members who are researchers as well as teachers and clinicians. A typical clinical faculty member is a tenure-track or tenured professor who devotes 25 percent, 50 percent, or more of his or her time to research. Student contact with clinically oriented professional psychologists is often limited to practicum supervision.

The fourth difference between training in the two types of schools is related to the third. Training at a university has a much stronger research orientation than does training at a professional

(continued)

BOX **1.3** **Continued**

school. Graduate students are involved in research throughout their training. Typically, they work closely with a research advisor, assisting on the advisor's studies as they develop their own line of research. Students complete an independent research project, the doctoral dissertation, at the conclusion of their training. In professional schools there is very little emphasis upon research. Students may do a dissertation project but this does not necessarily involve collecting original research data. These schools emphasize clinical functions. Students are trained to consume research as it relates to clinical practice, whereas students in university programs are trained to be producers of research.

What are the differences between Psy.D. and Ph.D. training? The main difference, of course, is the relative emphasis placed upon research and practice. Ph.D. programs, particularly those that endorse the scientist-practitioner training model, place a heavy emphasis upon research training and production. In Psy.D. programs students do receive some research training but usually are not required to carry out an empirical study. Professional training schools allow for a wider definition of what might be considered acceptable dissertation research, including theoretical analyses, surveys, analyses of archival data, qualitative investigations, case studies, and public policy investigations (Peterson, Peterson, Abrams, & Stricker, 1997).

Within programs that offer a Ph.D. in clinical psychology there is great variability in the training experiences students receive. There are marked differences between traditional research-oriented training programs and professional-applied programs in clinical psychology. Research-oriented programs tend to have smaller faculty to student ratios, higher quality faculty (in terms of publications), more full-time and fewer part-time faculty, smaller class sizes, and they admit students with higher GRE scores than professional-oriented Ph.D. programs (Maher, 1999). A trend that is of concern for many research-minded clinical psychologists is that the percentage of Ph.D.s in clinical psychology being offered by lower-quality programs is increasing (Maher, 1999). Graduates of schools with an applied orientation tend to score lower on a standardized test used for licensure than graduates of research-oriented programs (Yu, Rinaldi, Templer, Colbert, Siscoe, & VanPatten, 1997).

While Psy.D. and Vail model training programs do not provide the same level of research training as Boulder model programs, that should not be construed to mean that the scientific foundations of psychology are ignored. On the contrary, training in science should be part of any graduate program in clinical psychology. The importance of training in the scientific foundations of clinical psychology have been affirmed at every major conference on training since the meeting at Boulder (Ellis, 1992). The educational model promoted by the National Council of Schools and Programs of Professional Psychology (an organization of professional schools) views professional practice as a form of science (Peterson et al., 1997). "The properly trained professional psychologist is a scientist in the sense that the skilled physician is a local clinical, biological scientist and the skilled engineer is a local physical scientist" (Peterson et al., p. 376). It is this training in critical, scientific thinking that sets clinical psychologists apart from other professionals.

A third variation on graduate training in clinical psychology has emerged in recent years. The *clinical-scientist* model of training, as the name implies, strongly emphasizes scientific research. The goal of clinical scientist training programs is to produce psychologists who will further our applied knowledge through research. It is not that clinical scientist programs do not train students in psychological assessment and intervention. Rather, they limit the scope of the training to practices that have sufficient scientific support. The product of a clinical-scientist program is individuals who will "think and function as a scientist in every respect and setting in their professional lives" (McFall, 1991, p. 85).

Graduate training programs that adhere to the clinical-scientist model have recently formed the Academy of Psychological Clinical Science. The academy provides these programs with the opportunity to share information and resources to work toward the organization's goals, which include fostering "the training of students for careers in clinical science research, who skillfully will produce and apply scientific knowledge" (Academy of Psychological Clinical Science, 2003).

Graduate training programs in clinical psychology vary with respect to how strongly they adhere to any one model of training over another. Some programs are strongly practice oriented, whereas others, such as those that belong to the Academy of Psychological Clinical Science, place significantly more emphasis upon research training. But it would be inaccurate to imply that every graduate training program can be neatly pegged into one of these three categories. Within the same scientist-practitioner model programs some students may gear their training experiences toward careers in clinical practice, while others will aspire to careers in clinical science and gear their training accordingly. When planning for graduate training in clinical psychology, it is important to know the training philosophy espoused by the program; however, it is also important to look within the program to understand the possibilities it offers.

In the next section of this chapter we will take the reader through the educational life of a clinical psychologist from undergraduate preparation through post-graduate continuing education.

Undergraduate Preparation

Training in clinical psychology occurs at the graduate level. But in order to participate in graduate-level training, one must first, of course, complete a course of bachelor's-level education. A strong undergraduate education in psychology is the best preparation for specialized training in clinical psychology. Course work in the basic areas in psychology such as biological bases of behavior, learning, social, cognition, perception, and developmental psychology lay the groundwork for specialized training. Courses in clinically relevant areas of psychology are important as well (e.g., abnormal psychology, tests and measurement, and personality theory). Most psychology majors will complete a sequence of courses in research design and statistics. These are critically important courses for students interested in scientist-practitioner training.

At most universities, the psychology department is housed within a college of liberal arts and sciences. Students therefore are typically required to take a breadth of courses to fulfill the requirements for a liberal arts degree. A broad-based education makes sense for the student interested in a career in clinical psychology. Graduate training programs are interested in well-educated students. Undergraduate course work in other sciences, such as biology or chemistry, is usually looked upon favorably. Mathematics and computer science are also valuable. Finally, course work in other social sciences (sociology or anthropology in particular), introduces students to nonpsychological perspectives on understanding human behavior.

However, having a well-rounded liberal arts education with an emphasis in psychology usually will not be enough to garner acceptance into most graduate programs in clinical psychology. Students can obtain five basic things to improve their chances of acceptance into graduate school in psychology:

1. High grade-point average
2. Good scores on the Graduate Record Examination
3. Research/scholarly experience
4. Clinically relevant experience
5. Strong letters of recommendation

The acceptance standards for graduate training in clinical psychology are competitive. One of the factors considered by training directors is grade point average obtained in undergraduate courses. While there is no hard and fast cutoff for acceptable grade point average, and different programs give different weights to this criterion, the higher the GPA the better. For example, it would not be uncommon for a doctoral program in clinical psychology to set 3.5 (on a 4-point system) as the *minimum* required GPA for consideration (Fiore, 1991). Some of the more prestigious graduate programs might set the minimum GPA even higher. One limitation of the GPA is that it is not standardized, making it difficult to compare GPAs across different institutions. It is unlikely that GPA is ever considered alone. A candidate with somewhat lower grades might be accepted if he or she has significant research accomplishments, for example. In addition, different training programs may emphasize different parts of the GPA. Some look at the GPA obtained over the entire undergraduate education, while others are more interested in the GPA for the last two years of college.

The Graduate Record Examination (GRE) is a standardized test used by most graduate schools to assist in evaluating applicants. The GRE is to acceptance into graduate school what the SAT (Scholastic Aptitude Test) is to acceptance into college. The general GRE test yields two scores: Verbal and Quantitative. A third general score, Analytic, was dropped from the test in 2002. In addition to these scores, many graduate programs are interested in students' scores on the GRE subject test in psychology. Applicants' scores on these provide information that allows application committees to make comparisons of student from different undergraduate institutions. As with the undergraduate GPA, students accepted into graduate programs in clinical psychology tend to have high GRE scores (e.g., 600 or higher in most areas).

The third basic thing to do to prepare for graduate school in clinical psychology is to obtain research experience. Probably the most common way an undergraduate gains research experience is by working as a research assistant for a psychology professor at his or her undergraduate institution. Many psychology departments offer a limited number of course credits for students who work as research assistants. Conducting independent research as part of a research methods course or as an honors thesis is also a good way to get one's feet wet as a researcher. Presenting research at a conference, or better yet being a co-author on a published paper, shows strong interest in research and is looked upon very favorably by directors of clinical psychology training programs (Piotrowski & Keller, 1996). Active participation in research is important for a variety of reasons. Students learn about doing research, which can help them to determine whether a career that involves research is a good match for them. Second, it is a great way for students to get to know faculty members and for faculty members to know them. This is extremely important when it comes time for letters of recommendation. Third, research involvement is valued highly by directors of clinical psychology training programs (Piotrowski & Keller, 1996), particularly directors of scientist-practitioner and clinical-scientist programs. Interestingly, however, directors of Psy.D. programs also give considerable weight to applicants' research work when evaluating applications (Piotrowski & Keller, 1996).

Reflecting the science-practice nature of clinical psychology, in addition to research experience, clinical experience can help an applicant create a successful application. Work as a hotline counselor, a volunteer at a psychiatric facility, a psychology technician, or other clinically relevant experiences help round out an application. While it is true that most application committees value research experience over clinical work (Piotrowski & Keller, 1996), the latter can help support an application. Directors of Psy.D. programs, in fact, tend to weigh clinical and research experience equally (Piotrowski & Keller, 1996). In addition to the functional value of helping to build a strong application, clinical experience helps students learn about the applied aspects of clinical psychology. As with research experience, exposure to this type of work can help students make decisions about the type of graduate program that best matches their career goals.

The fifth basic component of a graduate school application is letters of recommendation. All graduate programs require them; most require at least three. It is best if these letters are from individuals who are familiar with different aspects of the student's education and training. At least two of the letters should come from psychology faculty (Fiore, 1991). These might be faculty with whom the student has had more than one class or for whom the student worked as a research assistant. Psychologists, or professionals from related disciplines, who supervised the student's clinical work also frequently provide letters of recommendations.

In addition to the basic five described above, an additional consideration in preparing oneself for graduate training in clinical psychology is what area within the broad field is of greatest interest. Clinical psychology is an expanding discipline. As it grows, there is a move toward increased specialization. Students who can focus their interests are more likely to be able to identify programs and faculty members with similar interests. The match between the applicant and potential faculty mentors is extremely important. This is particularly true for research-oriented graduate programs within which graduate students work closely with a research mentor. A close match between an applicants' research experience and interests and those of a potential research mentor can override less than stellar GPA or GRE scores when faculty choose who to accept.

Graduate Training

As our earlier discussion indicated, the graduate school experiences of clinical psychologists vary based upon the training philosophy of the training program and a myriad of other factors. Keeping this variability in mind, in the following section we endeavor to give you a sense of the basic components of graduate training in clinical psychology.

Most graduate programs require advanced course work in the basic areas of psychological science. Scientist-practitioner programs, for example, typically include training in the following content areas: biological bases of behavior, cognitive-affective bases of behavior, social bases of behavior, and individual behavior (Belar & Perry, 1991). How these basic content areas are covered varies depending upon the competencies and interests of the training faculty. Biological bases of behavior may be covered through courses in neuropsychology, neuroanatomy and physiology, circadian rhythm, or endocrinological influences on behavior. Similarly, courses in psychopathology, personality theory, or child development would all be relevant to developing a knowledge base about individual differences in behavior.

Course work and experience in clinical psychology are, of course, central to any training program. Graduate seminars in psychological assessment, pscyhotherapy, and psychopathology typically make up the core clinical courses. Many programs require that students receive training in professional ethics and legal issues germane to clinical psychology. Specialized courses in areas such as neuropsychology, psychopharmacology, health psychology, family systems therapy, or consultation in medical settings might round out the clinically oriented course work.

Doctoral training programs typically require that students complete a doctoral qualifying examination before they are officially considered to be doctoral candidates. These examinations often take place over several days and rigorously evaluate not only students' knowledge but their ability to present their ideas in written and oral formats. The doctoral qualifying examinations, sometimes referred to as comprehensive exams, usually fall somewhere around the midpoint of students' graduate careers and mark a transition from graduate student to doctoral candidate. Some more research-oriented programs require students to write a grant proposal or a review paper in lieu of the qualifying exam.

Much of the clinical training of graduate students takes place outside of the classroom. Usually by no later than their second year in training, students participate in practical training. They work with real clients under the supervision of licensed psychologists. Practicum training may occur in a training clinic affiliated with the graduate program, or it may take place in the field. Students often obtain 1,000 or more hours of practicum training prior to internship (Hecker, Fink, LeVasseur, & Parker, 1995). These clinical hours include a variety of professional activities including assessment and psychotherapy, supervision, writing case notes and reports, case conferences or clinical rounds, and consulting with other professional on clinical issues.

Training in the more applied aspects of clinical psychology continues after students leave their graduate programs and before they complete the doctoral degree. The American Psychological Association requires that training include a one-year pre-doctoral internship in order for graduate programs to be accredited by the professional organization The internship year is a full twelve months of applied clinical experience. Graduate students compete for slots in accredited internship programs. Typically, the internship year is completed at an institution not affiliated with the graduate training program. Internships, in fact, may be great geographical distances from training programs. Students from our training program here in Maine, for example, have done their internships in several New England states but also in

Florida, Mississippi, California, Texas, Hawaii, Oklahoma, and British Columbia, to name a few.

Research training is another significant aspect of graduate work in clinical psychology. Training programs typically require courses in research design and advanced statistical analysis. But research training, like clinical training, involves a great deal of experiential, hands-on learning. Particularly in traditional scientist-practitioner and clinical-scientist programs, students work closely with mentors, learning about research and developing expertise in a particular area experientially. Graduate students often present research papers at conferences and many co-author, or sometimes solely author, published empirical studies, review papers, book chapters, or other scholarly works.

The relationship between the graduate student and his or her research advisor can be one of the most important associations in the professional development of a clinical psychologist, particularly for those interested in careers that emphasize research (Blount, Frank, & Smith, 1993). The relationship can be an intense one since the research mentor must play a variety of roles including critic, professional role model, supporter, and confidant over five years or more of training. When it works well, the relationship between research mentor and graduate student changes over time so that by the time the Ph.D. is awarded, their interactions are more akin to colleagues than teacher and student. Long after receiving their Ph.D.s many psychologists still identify themselves with their research mentors. (For example, in a recent e-mail with a psychologist whom I had never met, she oriented me to her professional views by writing, "What would you expect from one of Borkovec's students?" Thomas Borkovec was her research advisor.)

Involvement with research in one form or another is a hallmark of scientist-practitioner training. In addition to collaborating with their research advisors, graduate students will need to produce independent research. Many, but not all, doctoral programs require the completion of a master's thesis. All Ph.D. programs require a doctoral dissertation. The dissertation represents the culmination of the student's research training. It requires mastery of an area of scholarly literature, creativity in designing a research study that will contribute to the literature, perseverance in carrying out the project, collecting and analyzing the data, and writing the final dissertation. The dissertation must meet the approval of a committee of faculty members. Often the last thing that a clinical psychology graduate student has to do before the doctorate is conferred is orally defend the dissertation in front of the dissertation committee and others. In this "argument," students must demonstrate not only that they have a grasp on a large amount of factual information, but that they can present and defend their own interpretation of the information and their opinions.

Table 1.3 contains a sample program of study from a scientist-practitioner model graduate training program.

Post-Doctoral Training

It has long been recognized that there is a need for training in clinical psychology to continue beyond the awarding of the doctoral degree. Post-doctoral training in psychology has been discussed at every major training conference on clinical psychology including the original Boulder Conference (Belar, Beiliauskas, Klepac, Larsen, Stigall, & Zimet, 1993; Raimy,

TABLE 1.3   Sample Program of Study for a Scientist-Practitioner Model Graduate Program

Year One

Fall	Spring	Summer

Psychological Assessment I
Adult Psychopathology
History and Systems of
   Psychology
Directed Research
	Psychological Assessment II
	Seminar in Psychotherapy
	Research Methods
	Directed Research
		Seminar in Ethics and
		   Professional Issues
		Practicum
		Directed Research

Year Two

Fall	Spring	Summer

Seminar in Cognitive
   Behavior Therapy
Advanced Psychological
   Statistics
Cognitive Psychology
Practicum
Directed Research
	Child Psychopathology/
	   Therapy
	Multivariate Statistics
	Practicum
	Social Psychology
	Directed Research
		Practicum
		Directed Research
		Doctoral Qualifying
		   Exam

Year Three

Fall	Spring	Summer

Topics in Clinical
   Psychology
   (Forensic Psychology)
Child Psychopathology
Practicum
Directed Research
	Topics in Clinical
	   Psychology
	   (Women's Health
	   Psychology)
	Theories of Learning
	Practicum
	Directed Research
		Practicum
		Directed Research
		Dissertation Proposal
		   Due

Year Four

Fall	Spring	Summer

Seminar in Physiological
   Psychology
Dissertation
Practicum
	Topics in Clinical
	   Psychology
	   (Clinical Supervision)
	Dissertation
	Practicum
		Practicum
		Dissertation Defense

Year Five

Fall	Spring	Summer
Internship	Internship	Internship

1950). Specialty areas within clinical psychology were the first to develop criteria for post-doctoral training (e.g., health psychology, Stone, 1983; clinical child psychology, Tuma, 1985; and clinical neuropsychology, INS-Division 40 Task Force Report, 1987). Most states have codified the need for post-doctoral training in their licensing laws. One year of post-doctoral training is the typical prerequisite for licensure (Stewart & Stewart, 1998). There is general agreement in the field that a period of supervised post-doctoral experience should be required for licensure (Frances & Wolfe, 2000).

Psychologists who plan to practice under state licenses are not, however, the only group for whom post-doctoral training is helpful. Psychologists pursuing careers in academia and research also frequently complete one or more years of organized post-doctoral training. Research post-doctoral training fellowships are typically supported by grants. The post-doctoral training period is a time to develop a research speciality and to establish the track records of scholarly publications one needs to secure an academic position.

Post-doctoral training is far less regulated than graduate training in clinical psychology (Frances & Wolfe, 2000). State licensing laws require a year of *supervised* practice, not a year of organized post-doctoral study. Oversight of what constitutes supervision is minimal in most states. There has been an effort in recent years to better organize and regulate post-doctoral training in psychology. The Association of Psychology Postdoctoral and Internship Centers lists post-doctoral training programs that meet some basic criteria. In 1997, the American Psychological Association established guidelines for post-doctoral training in psychology and began accrediting post-doctoral training programs. APA accreditation is voluntary and so far does not carry much weight with licensing boards or organizations representing specialties within psychology. As of this writing, there are only six APA-accredited post-doctoral training programs in psychology.

In 1992, a National Conference on Post-Doctoral Training in Professional Psychology was held in Ann Arbor, Michigan. In the policy statement that emanated from the conference, the attendees identified three groups of psychologists for whom a post-doctoral residency would be appropriate (Belar et al., 1993, p. 1286):

1. Professional psychologists who plan to practice or supervise practice in a specialty or general practice setting
2. Professional psychologists who wish to teach professional courses at the graduate level, supervise in, or direct a professional psychology program
3. Professional psychologists who are preparing for a career involving research on clinical problems

Continuing Professional Education in Psychology

In a 1972 article in the American Psychologist, Samuel Dubin estimated that the half-life of a doctoral degree in psychology is about ten to twelve years. In other words, about ten years after completing a doctoral training program, the graduate can expect that about half of the knowledge acquired is obsolete. Given the rapid growth of the discipline over the past thirty years, we would argue that ten to twelve years is probably a high estimate. The past three decades have witnessed dramatic technological advances impacting clinical practice, an explosion of practice-relevant empirical research, and an increasing trend toward specialization. The need for clinical psychologists to educate themselves throughout their professional lives is obvious.

The American Psychological Association has recognized the need for psychologists to acquire professionally relevant knowledge throughout their professional careers. APA defines continuing professional education as follows:

> Continuing Professional Education (CPE) in psychology is an ongoing process consisting of formal learning activities that (1) are relevant to psychological practice, education and science, (2) enable psychologists to keep pace with emerging issues and technologies, and (3) allow psychologists to maintain, develop, and increase competencies in order to improve service to the public and enhance contributions to the profession. (APA website)

Most state licensing boards have also recognized the need for ongoing education for psychologists. In forty states psychologists must participate in formal continuing education activities in order to maintain their licenses to practice psychology. Typically, this means that psychologists must provide the licensing board with documentation of continuing education activities. Probably the most common way for psychologists to obtain continuing education credit is to attend workshops or scientific meetings that have formal learning objectives. Other ways for psychologists to obtain credit for continuing education activities are to read books or participate in structured web-based learning programs. To get credit for these types of activities, psychologists must complete an assessment of their learning. Just like in your undergraduate psychology courses, it's not enough to read the book—psychologists have to show they know what it said.

In addition to maintaining competence and staying abreast of new developments in the field, psychologists use continuing education activities to expand their areas of competence. For example, a psychologist whose practice has involved a combination of psychotherapy and consultation to schools might wish to extend his or her practice to include some forensic work (e.g., custody evaluations). Extending one's areas of proficiency is not something that clinical psychologists should take on lightly. Practicing beyond their areas of competence is one way that psychologists get into legal and ethical hot water. Responsible expansion of competence usually involves some combination of the following steps:

1. Psychologists should choose areas of expansion that are related to their current competencies. A psychologist who specialized in behavioral treatment of attention deficit hyperactivity is probably on solid ground if he or she seeks to expand practice to include working with children who are noncompliant with medical treatments. This same psychologist would be on much shakier footing if he or she sought to move into psychoanalytic treatment of adult personality disorders.
2. Psychologists should develop a plan of study to prepare themselves for the new area of practice. This plan of study would ideally include an organized plan for reading in the area as well as participation in formal continuing education programs such as weekend workshops.
3. Psychologists should arrange for supervision by more experienced colleagues as they begin to do work in a new area.

Psychologists who obtain a significant amount of advanced training and continuing education in a given specialty area will sometimes choose to obtain voluntary credentials demonstrating their advanced proficiency. There are a variety of types of voluntary credentials psychologists can obtain if they so choose. Some of these advanced "certifications" require minimal documentation by way of proof of the psychologists' competency. Quite frankly, the main function of some of the more questionable credentials seems to be to placate the psychologists' vanity. Unscrupulous professional psychologists can probably obtain a veritable alphabet soup of letters to place after their names. The following example was taken from a book on professional ethics in psychology: Roger A. Droit, Ph.D. (c), MAT, C.Ht. When asked to explain the abbreviations, Mr. Droit indicated that Ph.D. (c) meant that he was a Ph.D. candidate (in other words, he had not yet finished his degree), the MAT stood for Master of Arts in Teaching, and the C.Ht. stood for Clinical Hypnotist (a credential he had obtained via a correspondence course) (Koocher & Keith-Spiegel, 1998). Another favorite example of bogus credentials is the organization that periodically sends solicitations to the authors in which they are informed that they may already qualify for an advanced credential in forensic psychology. The solicitation explains that the applicant should award himself or herself a certain number of points for having a doctorate degree, a certain number for each psychological evaluation completed for forensic purposes, as well as points for relevant books read or workshops attended. If one's point total is greater than 100, the applicant has already qualified for the credential (provided he or she sends in a check for the application and membership fee).

Lest the reader get the wrong impression, we want to be clear that not all voluntary credentialing is bogus and obtained for questionable reasons. The most well-recognized and well-respected voluntary credential for professional psychologists is the ABPP, the American Board of Professional Psychology. The board was established in 1947 with the goal of serving the public by certifying psychologists competent to deliver high-quality services in specialty areas. The primary purpose of board certification is to communicate to the public that the psychologist has demonstrated expertise in a specialty area within psychology. Board-certified psychologists may list ABPP after their doctorate degree (for example, Geoffrey L. Thorpe, Ph.D., ABPP).

When the board was originally formed, and throughout much of its history, ABPP certification was awarded in one of four areas: clinical psychology, counseling psychology, school psychology, and industrial psychology. In recent years, however, reflecting the diversity and increasing specialization of professional psychology, ABPPs are now awarded in twelve different speciality areas. Currently, the American Board of Professional Psychology is the governing body for twelve distinct member boards. These are listed in Table 1.4.

The requirements for the ABPP are quite rigorous. A doctoral degree, licensure, and at least five years of experiences are minimum. The candidate must also demonstrate specialized training, evidence of substantial experience, and continuing education in the specialty area. A committee of board-certified psychologists reviews samples of the psychologist's work (e.g., reports of psychological evaluations, transcripts of therapy sessions) and conducts an oral examination that usually takes four to five hours to complete. The examination usually includes the candidate's doing some type of live clinical activity (e.g., evaluation, interacting with a real client, conducting clinical supervision).

TABLE 1.4   **American Board of Professional Psychology and Member Boards**

American Board of Professional Psychology

American Board of Behavioral Psychology	American Board of Group Psychology
American Board of Clinical and Health Psychology	American Board of Industrial/Organizational Psychology
American Board of Clinical Neuropsychology	American Board of Psychoanalysis in Psychology
American Board of Clinical Psychology	
American Board of Counseling Psychology	American Board of Rehabilitation Psychology
American Board of Family Psychology	
American Board of Forensic Psychology	American Board of School Psychology

The ABPP diploma is generally considered a prestigious credential. While licensure is a credential that is required to practice psychology, the ABPP is a voluntary credential that carries no legal weight. While licensure signals to the public that the psychologist has the minimal competencies needed to practice psychology, the ABPP signals advanced proficiency.

Ethics and the Development of a Clinical Psychologist

Ethics is the branch of philosophy that deals with moral judgments. Ethics provide guidance for making moral decisions, for deciding what is "right" versus "wrong," "good" versus "bad," or "appropriate" versus "inappropriate." For example, one approach to ethical decision making is *teleology,* which argues that actions should be judged by their consequences. An action is morally right if it results in more positive than negative outcomes. For example, if a lifeboat with ten people on it can only operate safely with eight, is it okay to force two off to save the rest? An alternative approach to justifying ethical decisions is referred to as *deontology*. In contrast to teleological justification, in the deontological approach a small set of moral principles are used to judge the morality of an action. For example, one might use the principle that being honest is ethically correct. Difficulties with the deontological approach arise when more than one ethical principle is involved. For example, is it okay to lie (violate the principle *be honest*) in order to save someone's life (adhere to the principle *preserve life*)? The classic example of this dilemma is a physician in Nazi-occupied Europe who is asked if there are any Jewish patients in the hospital (Haas & Malouf, 1995). Should the physician accurately report that there are Jewish patients (be honest)? Or should he or she lie in order to protect the Jewish patients (preserve life)?

Professions generate ethics codes to guide their members in making decisions on ethical matters and so that they have a basis to judge the appropriateness of their members' actions. The Hippocratic oath was the first profession-generated ethics code (Koocher & Keith-Spiegel, 1998). The development of a set of professional ethics is an important milestone in the development of any profession. Psychology published its first set of ethical principles in 1952 (see Chapter 2, Box 2.2, for history of the APA ethics code). The most recent version of the ethics code, *Ethical Principles of Psychologists and Code of Conduct,* was approved by the governance of the American Psychological Association in August 2002 and published later that year. The Ethics Code, as it is referred to, is reprinted in Appendix A.

The Ethical Principles of Psychologists and Code of Conduct (APA, 2002), referred to as the Ethics Code, consists of four parts: Introduction, Preamble, General Principles (of which there are 5), and Ethical Standards (of which there are 89). The Introduction discusses intent and scope of the Ethics Code. The Preamble and General Principles are aspirational in nature. They express goals toward which psychologists should aspire. The five General Principles are Beneficence and Non-Maleficence, Fidelity and Responsibility, Integrity, Justice, and Respect for the People's Rights and Dignity. The principles are written in aspirational language (e.g., Principle B: "Psychologists establish relationships of trust with those with whom they work."). As such they are essentially unenforceable. Instead, the intent of the General Principles is to "inspire psychologists toward the highest ethical ideals of the profession." The Ethical Standards, in contrast, are written in concrete enough language so that they can be used to more easily determine whether a psychologist's behavior is inconsistent with the standard and hence sanctionable (e.g., "Psychologists do not engage in sexual intimacies with current therapy clients/patients."). If a psychologist's actions violate one of the ethical standards, it can form the basis for imposing sanctions against the psychologist by the American Psychological Association, a state licensing board, or others.

Having a professional code of ethics does not assure that psychologists' behavior will always adhere to the ethical standards. Gerald Koocher and Patricia Keith-Spiegal (1998) identify several characteristics of psychologists who behave in ethically questionable or unprofessional ways: (1) Some are ignorant of, or misinformed about, the ethical standards (e.g., "I didn't know I couldn't have sex with my psychotherapy clients; I never charged them for those sessions."). (2) Some psychologists practice outside their areas of competence (e.g., "I've been doing psychotherapy with adults for years. I don't see why I can't see kids as well. After all, they're just like adults, only shorter."). (3) Some are insensitive to the feelings and needs of the people with whom they work (e.g., the psychologist who responds to a client's questions about the theory underlying a projective test by saying, "It's quite complicated. I don't think you'd understand."). (4) Some psychologists are clearly exploitative (e.g., the psychology professor who makes herself first author on a paper based upon her doctoral student's dissertation). (5) Some behave irresponsibly (e.g., A psychologist drops a psychotherapy client from his practice after the client comes to a therapy session in an acute suicidal crisis. He provides the client with names of other therapists but takes no steps to assure that the client actually gets in to see someone else. The psychologist explains, "I have a part-time practice. I'm not set up to deal with suicidal clients."). (6) Some psychologists unethical behavior appears to be motivated by vengeance (e.g., a psychologist lets loose a barrage of derogatory statements toward his client after the client complains that she is not getting any better).

Ethical dilemmas may be an unavoidable part of the professional life of a psychologist. No matter what professional activity clinical psychologists engage in, ethical issues are likely to arise. In order to be prepared to deal with these, psychologists must first recognize that there is an ethical problem (or at least the potential for a problem), identify some relevant standards to help guide their actions, and know what resources to turn to for help (Bersoff, 1995; Haas & Malouf, 1995; Koocher & Keith-Spiegel, 1998).

We believe that training in ethics and ethical decision making should begin at the very start of one's education in clinical psychology. But we do not view training in ethics as something that should take place separate from training in the content areas of clinical psychology. Ideally, consideration of ethical issues should be interwoven throughout one's education as well as one's professional life. In this book, we practice what we believe. One of our goals is to introduce students to the kinds of ethical issues clinical psychologists face and to provide some direction as to how to deal with them. Our method of accomplishing this goal is to present and discuss ethical issues throughout the text. In the Focus on Ethics sections of each chapter, we discuss an ethical issue that is related to the focal topic of the chapter. We hope to raise your awareness of the complexity of professional ethics and to spur on the process of ethical development that will continue throughout your life.

2 History and Recent Developments

When seeing a new clients, whether for assessment, therapy, or consultation, one of the first things clinical psychologists do is take a history. Clients are asked about the history of their presenting problem as well as their general psychological and social development (see Chapter 6). In order to develop a thorough understanding of their clients, psychologists need to know how the clients got to where they are today. What interpersonal relationships, social pressures, educational experiences, upheavals, traumas, successes, and failures influenced their clients? In much the same way, we believe that for students to understand contemporary clinical psychology, they must understand its history. Just as clinical psychologists understand their clients by examining the development, growth, and maturation of their lives, students can understand the discipline by exploring its development, growth, and maturation.

No discipline develops in a vacuum. The inception of clinical psychology was the product of a variety of social, political, scientific, and philosophical factors, and these factors continued to influence the field as it developed. The German word *Zeitgeist* means the ideological outlook or climate of the times. Just as clinical psychology's birth was a function of the Zeitgeist of the late nineteenth century, what clinical psychology is today is a function of the Zeitgeist of the early twenty-first century.

The following sketch of the history and development of clinical psychology is necessarily incomplete. For the reader interested in a more in-depth discussion of the history of the field we recommend *A History of Clinical Psychology* (Reisman, 1991), *Clinical Psychology since 1917: Science, Practice and Organization* (Routh, 1994), or "Hippocrates meets Democritus: A History of Psychiatry and Clinical Psychology" by Donald Routh (1998), which is Chapter 1 of *Comprehensive Clinical Psychology* (Bellack & Hersen, 1998). Much of the following account of the history of clinical psychology is based upon these sources.

Ancient Roots

Lightner Witmer founded the first psychological clinic at the University of Pennsylvania in 1896, and that is the year most scholars recognize as the birth of clinical psychology. But one can identify predecessors to the field dating back many centuries. Unlike the roots of a tree, it is difficult to trace an unbroken connection from the ancient roots of clinical psychology to its budding new developments. Nonetheless, the striking similarity between the ideas of some ancient scholars and contemporary psychological thought deserves mention. Similarly, one can recognize functions of clinical psychologists in the methods of ancient practitioners.

First, as clinical psychology is a discipline involved in studying and treating mental disorder, it is worth noting that awareness of mental illness, as distinct from physical illness, can be dated as far back as 2100 B.C. to the ancient Babylonians (Brems, Thevenin, & Routh, 1991). In fact, most ancient cultures, including those in South and Central America as well as the ancient Hebrews, recognized and attempted to treat mental disorders. Typically, mental illness was viewed from a religious perspective, and treatments such as prayer, wearing of amulets, or religious rituals were used. It interesting to note, however, that despite the religious lens through which psychological disorders were viewed, some ancient writings suggest recognition of psychological factors and treatment. For example, foreshadowing Freud, ancient Hebrew scholars viewed dreams as expressions of unacceptable wishes and recommended unrestrained communication about one's worries and troubles (Brems et al., 1991).

Western cultures traditionally trace the roots of medicine and philosophy to the ancient Greeks. A predecessor of contemporary thought about the biological bases of mental illness (see Chapter 4) can be found in the writings of Hippocrates (c. 446–377 B.C.), who hypothesized that psychopathology resulted from imbalances in one or more of the four bodily humors: blood, black bile, yellow bile, and phlegm. An excess of black bile, for example, was considered to be the source of melancholy (depression). The term *melancholy* means "black bile" in Greek (Routh, 1998). Hippocrates also organized mental conditions into types, some of which are still in use today. *Phrenitis* was use to describe the condition in which a person had a high fever and talked nonsense. The condition cleared when the fever subsided. *Mania* described the person who was acutely agitated in the absence of fever. *Hysteria* was used to describe women who presented with vague or difficult-to-understand bodily complaints. *Paranoia* described the person whose thinking was bizarre in the absence of fever.

The writings of the Greek philosophers also foreshadowed ideas that would reappear centuries later in psychiatry and clinical psychology. Socrates (c. 470–399 B.C.) believed that the answers to all questions lay inside the individual and wrote about the healing powers of speaking and self-expression (Brems et al., 1991). Plato's (c. 428–347 B.C.) writings about the soul are strikingly similar to Freud's ideas about personality. Plato believed the soul had three levels, the *logistikon* (residing in the head and responsible for logic and reason), the *thumos* (residing in the chest and responsible for courage and aspirations), and the *alogistikon* (residing in the stomach and responsible for instincts and appetites) (Brems et al., 1991). Finally, Aristotle (c. 384–323 B.C.) believed in the healing power of words spoken by patients with mental disorders. All three of these well-known Greek philosophers advocated for humane treatment of the mentally ill.

The Greek philosophers were, of course, not the only ancient scholars to study and theorize about mental illness. Mental disorders, like all forms of illness, result from an imbalance of the powers of "yin" and "yang," according to the *Yellow Emperor's Book of Internal Medicine,* which was published in China in the second century B.C. (Routh, 1998). This book includes description of traditional Chinese medical treatments including some, such as acupuncture, that are still in use today.

In addition to writing and thinking about psychopathology, the ancient Chinese also preceded modern clinical psychology by using mental tests for assessing and categorizing individuals. Examinations, which included tests of mental abilities, were used to recruit and select civil servants for over 1,000 years prior to the development of psychological tests in Europe and the United States (Routh, 1998).

While the writings of the ancient Greeks, as well as the writings and practices of the ancient Chinese, foreshadowed important ideas that what we would now associate with clinical psychology, it is difficult to discern a direct link between these ancient writings and the modern discipline. In Europe, the link was clearly broken during the Dark Ages. Medieval Europe saw a deterioration of science and philosophy and the ascendance of religion. Mental illness, like most everything, was viewed through a religious lens. Psychopathology was understood as the product of demonic possession or other supernatural forces. Following from this point of view, religious rituals were the treatment of choice. Illustrative of the medieval Zeitgeist was the publication *Malleus Malificarum* ("The Witches' Hammer"), which was a manual for the identification, torture, and trial of witches. The book was endorsed by the pope and went through nineteen editions over a 300-year period (Routh, 1998). Perhaps reflective of women's powerlessness during that period of time, convicted witches (females) outnumbered sorcerers (males) 50 to 1 and were the victims of about 150,000 religious executions in the Dark Ages (Brems et al., 1991).

Although religious thinking about the causes and treatment of abnormal behavior did not recede quickly, the Renaissance saw the reemergence of a scientific and more humanistic approach to people with mental disorders. Important figures during this period of time included Paracelsus (1493–1541) and Johann Weyer (1515–1588). Both men were physicians who rejected spiritual causes of psychological and emotional difficulties. Paracelsus introduced a completely biological approach to mental illness. He argued that human behavior could be understood as a function of biological processes. He practiced a form of medicine that was similar to what we might call homeopathy today (Brems et al., 1991). Weyer made a careful study of individuals identified as sorcerers and witches and was successful at discerning physical causes for their unusual behaviors. Through his observations, Weyer developed a sophisticated descriptive classification system that included toxic psychoses, senile psychosis, hysteria, delusions, paranoia, depression, and epilepsy. Weyer became an outspoken critic of witch hunts and the brutality of faith-based treatment of the mentally ill. In 1583, he published *De Praestigiis Daemonum* ("The Slight of Hand of Demons"), which disputed the *Malleus Malificarum*. Weyer's book was placed on the pope's list of forbidden readings (Routh, 1998).

Eighteenth and Nineteenth Centuries: Laying the Groundwork for Clinical Psychology

In the eighteenth and particularly the nineteenth centuries important social and scientific developments set the stage for the birth of clinical psychology. Four areas that laid the foundation for clinical psychology were improved *understanding of mental disorders,* scientific approaches to the *measurement of individual differences,* the *emergence of scientific psychiatry,* and the concept of *hysteria and the ascendance of psychological determinism.*

Understanding of Mental Disorders

The gradual shift away from a religious and toward a medical model of mental illness took a few hundred years to complete. By the eighteenth century, mental illness, or "madness," was generally accepted as falling under the purview of the medical profession. With the acceptance of the medical model came the development of psychiatry as a speciality branch of medicine. The early pioneers of psychiatry included Benjamin Rush (1745–1813) in the United States, Philipe Pinel (1745–1826) in France, Vincenzo Chiarugi (1759–1820) in Italy, and Francis Willis (1718–1807) in England.

Unfortunately for the mentally ill, the advent of psychiatry resulted in treatment that was, at best, only slightly less horrific than what they endured under the witches' hammer. The mentally ill were housed in asylums, where they were often chained or otherwise restrained. In most asylums beatings were common, and patients were ridiculed and mistreated by their guardians. They were fed the coarsest of slops. Visits by physicians were infrequent and "treatment" usually consisted of some method of adjusting bodily fluids including purges, blood letting by leeches or other means, and vomits. Benjamin Rush, for example, was given to bleeding his patients frequently and likely hastened the death of many through his treatments. While these methods may seem barbaric by current standards, they were perfectly logical in light of eighteenth-century psychiatry's understanding of mental illness. The generally accepted view was that most forms of mental illness were caused by an inflammation of the brain due, presumably, to an excess of blood in that area (Dain, 1964). Bleeding, therefore, made sense. Depression or melancholy, unlike other forms of psychopathology, was thought to result from a lack of blood to the brain. Instead of bleeding his depressed patients, Benjamin Rush strapped them to a device he created that spun them around, forcing blood to their brains (McKown, 1961). The starvation diets many psychiatric patients were kept on also had a scientific rationale. Deprived of calories, the patients' bodies could not produce excess blood, phlegm, or excrement, which was thought to be causing their loss of reason.

In the late eighteenth century, significant efforts were made to reform the way in which the mentally ill were treated. This shift in treatment philosophy has come to be known as the *moral treatment movement*. This movement was initiated, nearly simultaneously, by Phillipe Pinel in France and William Tuke (1732–1822) in England.

Phillipe Pinel was named doctor in charge of the insane at the Bicetre Hospital in Paris on August 25, 1793. When he took control of the facility, he was sickened by what he observed. Patients were housed in filthy narrow cells that were sweltering in the summer and freezing in the winter. They sometimes slept four or more together on a dirty sack. Food was a ration of bread doled out in the morning, sometimes supplemented by thin gruel. Scurvy and dysentery were common. Pinel could not accept a medical or philosophical rationale for what he observed. He wrote, "Forgetting the empty honours of my titular distinction as a physician, I viewed the scene that was opened to me with the eyes of common sense and unprejudiced observations" (Pinel, 1806/1962). Pinel set about changing the conditions at the Bicetre. He removed the chains from most patients, insisted that cells be kept clean, doubled bread rations and distributed them three times a day rather than one, added other foods to the patients' diets, prescribed work therapy, and prohibited brutality by his staff.

In his book *A Treatise on Insanity,* Pinel described "the moral treatment of the insane," which included good food, comfortable lodgings, work therapy, considerate treatment, entertainment, and mild exercise.

William Tuke was a wealthy tea merchant and devout Quaker who in 1791 began to investigate the state of English asylums for the mentally ill when he learned that a fellow Quaker died while a patient of the York Asylum for the Insane (McKown, 1961). When Tuke investigated the York Asylum, like Pinel, he was appalled by what he saw. In 1796, Tuke and his son Henry founded the York Retreat in order to house Quakers who had become mentally ill. The Retreat was a large brick farmhouse set on several acres of land. No walls separated the farm from the road. Patients were allowed to stroll the grounds on gravel walks lined with flowers and shrubs. The Retreat was partially self-sufficient with fruit orchards, vegetable gardens, dairy cows, poultry, and rabbits. Although not prescribed work therapy, as Pinel's patients had been, patients at the Retreat were expected to do what they could to help around the farm. The York Retreat initially was overseen by William Tuke and subsequently by a line of Tuke men, including Henry, Samuel, and Dr. Daniel Hack Tuke. These men presided over the Retreat as a traditional father would over his family, dealing with patients in a firm yet compassionate manner. The Tukes, especially Samuel Tuke, who published *A Description of the Retreat* in 1813, were instrumental in spreading moral treatment to the United States.

The moral treatment movement was relatively short-lived and may have been a victim of its own success. The first institution in the United States based upon the premises of moral treatment was the Friends Asylum in Pennsylvania, which accepted its first patient in 1817. Three other institutions—the McLean Asylum, the Blooomingdale Asylum, and the Hartford Retreat—were founded by 1824. These institutions reported striking rates of success. Bolstered by these claims, reformers—most notably Dorothea Dix (1802–1887)—agitated for reform and for government support for institutions to treat the mentally ill. Ms. Dix campaigned tirelessly for public support for treatment facilities for the mentally ill. New Jersey was the first to respond and erected an institution in 1848. In the following years, the construction of over thirty other state institutions for the mentally ill were a direct result of Ms. Dix's efforts.

By the mid nineteenth century, numerous institutions in the United States were employing moral treatment. However, within twenty years, most institutions had abandoned the tenets of moral treatment and had evolved into custodial institutions for housing the chronically mentally ill. A variety of factors have been implicated in the downfall of moral treatment, including the influx of chronic and severely disturbed as well as poorly educated immigrant patients, the enormous size of the institutions, and the lack of zeal and conviction in the institutions' superintendents and psychiatrists compared to the moral treatment reformers (Bockoven, 1963; Dain, 1964; Levine, 1981).

Although it predated clinical psychology, the moral treatment movement is significant for the field because it anticipated a shift from a purely medical to psychological treatment. In addition, it facilitated the development of institutions devoted to the treatment of the mentally ill. Finally, the moral treatment movement was instrumental in shifting societal views of the mentally ill from useless individuals who needed to be ostracized from society to a more humanistic view of the mentally ill as human beings deserving of compassion despite their irrationality (Brems et al., 1991).

Measurement of Individual Differences

One of the important figures in the early history of psychological testing was Sir Francis Galton (1822–1911). Although the types of tests that Galton developed bear little resemblance to modern psychological tests, he was one of the first to advocate for, and practice, a scientific approach to the measurement of *individual differences* (i.e., the dispersion of characteristics in the population). Galton was a fascinating man with an insatiable curiosity. He was the prototypical aristocrat-scholar who devoted himself to intensive study of various topics simply because they piqued his interest. Before he developed an interest in the measurement of individual differences, Galton had already made a name for himself in the scientific community. He had gone to medical school but never completed his medical training because he was distracted by other interests. Galton explored areas of Africa that were previously uncharted by Europeans. For this work he was given a fellowship in the Royal Geographical Society. He later published a book on meteorology.

Galton was in his forties when he read *The Origin of Species,* which was written by his cousin Charles Darwin and published in 1859. Galton was strongly influenced by Darwin's theory of evolution and saw practical implications of the theory for human evolution. He saw in the theory of evolution an opportunity to improve the British race. Galton began collecting an assortment of data on men from varying social classes, including aristocrats, businessmen, and university personnel. He analyzed these data using the principles of statistical probability and the normal curve distribution. The result of this work was the publication in 1869 of *Hereditary Genius,* which, as the title implies, argued that intelligence is inherited. Galton was an unapologetic advocate of eugenics. Since his studies suggested that brighter parents had brighter children, he argued that a better race of humans could be created if more intelligent and successful people were encouraged to mate.

Based upon the premises put forth in *Hereditary Genius,* Galton believed it was critically important that objective methods of measuring and identifying gifted people be developed. Galton's choice of tasks to use in the measurement of individual differences followed from the assumption that all knowledge is acquired through the senses. Galton reasoned that intellectually gifted people would have more sensitive sensorily systems and that intellectually limited people would be relatively sensory insensitive. Galton's tasks, therefore, included tests of color sensitivity, hearing acuity, ability to discriminate between varying weights, and reaction times.

Galton established a laboratory at the South Kensington museum in 1885 and for the next six years measured various characteristics of over 9,000 people. Unfortunately, not much was learned about human intelligence as a result of all this testing. However, Galton did improve upon statistical methods used for analyzing data on individual differences and inspired others to continue with this pursuit.

With respect to the history of clinical psychology, one of the most important people inspired by Galton was James McKeen Cattell (1860–1944). Cattell, an American, had received his doctorate in 1886 in the laboratory of Wilhelm Wundt in Germany, where his dissertation focused upon individual differences in reaction times. After finishing his doctoral degree, Cattell spent a year at Cambridge University, where he met Galton and was highly impressed. Upon his return to the United States, he established a psychology laboratory at the University of Pennsylvania, where he studied tasks similar to those being used by Galton.

In an article published in 1890, Cattell was the first to use the term "mental test." In this article, Cattell laid down some of the important principles of psychological testing. He argued, for example, for the importance of the adoption of a standard battery of tests that would be administered in exactly the same fashion by different researchers, allowing for comparison of results across investigators. Cattell suggested that the following tests make up a standard battery: the strength of hand squeeze, the time it takes to move one's arm a set distance, the ability to discriminate two points of pressure, the ability to discriminate between two weights, reaction time to sound, reaction time to naming colors, accuracy of bisecting the middle of a 50 cm line, judgment of 10 seconds time, and the number or letters remembered after one presentation. Although these tests did not prove to be measures of important individual differences, Cattell's work foreshadowed the methods for developing standardized tests of intelligence.

Emergence of Scientific Psychiatry

During the nineteenth century there was a growing faith in science and the scientific method. It was in this context that scientific psychiatry emerged as a legitimate discipline. The first order of business for a scientific approach to psychiatry was the development of a system for classifying psychiatric disorders. The nineteenth century saw the initial identification, naming, and detailed description of several major psychiatric conditions. For example, J. Langdon Down described a syndrome involving mental retardation that continues to bear his name. General paresis was identified as a syndrome caused by syphilis. Ewald Hecker published a monograph on *hebephrenia,* describing its symptoms and deteriorating course.

Probably the most significant nineteenth-century contributor to the development of modern psychiatry was Emil Kraepelin (1855–1926), who published the first edition of his textbook on psychiatry in 1883. In the textbook, which would eventually go through eight editions, Kraepelin provided a rich and detailed description of *dementia praecox,* a syndrome marked by hallucinations, delusions, progressive deterioration in intellectual functioning, and incongruent emotional expression. In later editions, he described subtypes of the condition including paranoid, hebephrenic, and catatonic. Dementia praecox is what we would now call schizophrenia. Kraepelin differentiated dementia praecox from manic-depressive illness. The former condition was believed to have *endogenous* causes (i.e., due to inherent, constitutional factors), while the latter was an example of a condition he thought was due to *exogenous* factors (i.e., caused by external conditions). Kraepelin argued that all mental disorders could be divided into those with endogenous and exogenous causes. Kraepelin believed endogenous diseases were incurable but that patients with exogenous disorders had a more favorable prognosis.

The emergence of scientific psychiatry helped set the stage of clinical psychology in a variety of ways. First, improved classification created a need for improved methods of making differential diagnoses. Assessment, as we will see, is one of the cornerstone activities of clinical psychology. Diagnostic assessment was one of the first practical problems psychological tests were developed to address. Second, the differentiation of mental retardation from other psychiatric conditions created a need for valid instruments for assessing intellectual functioning. Third, psychiatric classification systems, most notably Kraepelin's, identified some psychiatric conditions that may have nonbiological causes. The most important psychiatric syndrome for which nonbiological causes were considered was *hysteria*.

Hysteria and the Ascendance of Psychological Determinism

Hysteria referred to a condition in which patients presented with vague or unusual medical complaints, many of which appeared to be neurological, for which no physical basis could be identified. Patients with hysteria, usually adolescent or young-adult females, had such problems as anxiety, fatigue, memory loss, anesthesia (loss of feeling, including sensory impairments), and paralyses, none of which could be traced to recognizable biological abnormalities or physical malfunctions. The typical patient was an intelligent and well-educated yet politically powerless young woman whose allotted role in society was a rigidly predetermined ritual of marriage, child-bearing, domestic duties, and household management. Modern commentators point out that some of the symptoms of hysteria—those involving passivity, dependency, and emotionality—largely matched the contemporary expectations for women's behavior (Bernheimer, 1990; Kahane, 1990). Most European physicians dismissed hysterics as devious fakers seeking sympathetic attention.

Unlike his contemporaries, the brilliant French neurologist Jean Martin Charcot (1825–1893), was fascinated by the phenomena of hysteria. Charcot believed that hypnotism, a newly discovered procedure that was garnering a great deal of attention in European intellectual circles, was a condition that could only be induced in hysterics. Charcot believed that one could not study hysteria without hypnosis since the two phenomena were so closely related. By conducting objective neurological examinations of people under hypnosis, Charcot believed that he had demonstrated that the hysteric's symptoms could not be produced by conscious deception (Zilboorg & Henry, 1941).

One of Charcot's pupils, Piere Janet (1859–1947), dismissed Charcot's idea that a hypnotic trance could only be induced in patients with hysteria. After carefully examining the histories of his hysteric patients (taken while they were under hypnosis), Janet discovered that many of them had experienced a significant emotional shock prior to the onset of the hysterical symptoms. The patients reported no conscious memories of these traumas when not under hypnosis. Janet speculated that the emotionally shocking events had been pushed into some unconscious part of the patients' minds. Janet's thinking was that this forgetting was a maladaptive feature of the hysteric's personality.

A contemporary of Janet, who also studied briefly with Charcot, was a young Viennese physician named Sigmund Freud (1856–1939). Although we will delay the telling of Freud's story until Chapter 3 when we discuss the development of psychoanalysis, suffice it to say that Freud's writings about the psychological causes of hysteria and other conditions had a dramatic impact on psychiatry in Europe and the United States. For our current purposes, it is important to note that the work of Charcot, Janet, and others—notably Joseph Breuer (1841–1925) and Hippolyte Bernheim (1837–1919)—had a significant impact on Freud's thinking about psychopathology.

Although Freud was a trained as a physician and developed the related discipline of psychoanalysis, his impact upon the field of clinical psychology was significant. Freud opened the door to nonbiological (and nonspiritual) thinking about mental disorders. His psychoanalytic treatment, and the varied psychodynamic therapies it spawned, were the dominant approaches to psychotherapy for most of the twentieth century. Furthermore, Freud's ideas about the unconscious influenced the development of psychological testing, most notably the development of projective techniques (see Chapter 8). Finally, Freud, perhaps more than any other figure, firmly ensconced the importance of psychological factors in understanding human behavior.

The Birth of a Discipline: 1890–1910

In the 1890s psychology was a young but rapidly growing science. The first psychology laboratories had been established in 1879 by Wilhelm Wundt (1832–1920) at the University of Leipzig in Germany and William James (1842–1910) at Harvard University in the United States. G. Stanley Hall (1844–1924) established the second U.S. laboratory in 1883 and James McKeen Cattell opened the third in 1888. By 1900, however, there were over forty psychology laboratories in the United States (Benjamin, 1996). Psychology was defining itself as a scientific discipline devoted to understanding the human mind and behavior. However, very early on there were those who saw the applicability of the young science to alleviating human problems. Lightner Witmer (1867–1956) and Alfred Binet (1857–1911) were two of those pioneers.

Witmer received his bachelor's degree from the University of Pennsylvania in 1888. He became an assistant to Cattell at Pennsylvania but later transferred to the University of Leipzig to complete his Ph.D. under Wundt. After completing his degree, Witmer returned to the University of Pennsylvania, where he continued his research. There are various stories about how Witmer got interested in applied psychology (Reisman, 1991). In one version, he was challenged by a public school teacher to demonstrate the practical use of the new science of psychology by helping a child overcome a chronic problem with poor spelling. Witmer identified that the child had a visual problem and had some success at improving the boy's spelling. Encouraged by his success, Witmer began to work with other children with learning difficulties.

In 1896, Witmer established the world's first psychological clinic. The clinic worked primarily with children who were having difficulties in school. Today these children would likely be labeled mentally retarded, learning disabled, or autistic. The type of work done in the clinic was a predecessor to the field of school psychology (Fagan, 1996).

Witmer attended a meeting of the American Psychological Association in 1896 and described his new psychological clinic for his colleagues. Witmer proposed that psychologists should continue to function as scientists but also apply what they learned to address practical problems. He shared his vision of the psychological clinic as a place where public service, research, and instruction of students could be carried out at the same time. To say that his audience was not enthusiastic about what Witmer proposed would be kind. His talked "stimulated the elevation of some of his colleagues' eyebrows but little else" (Reisman, 1991, p. 39). Fortunately, Witmer was hard-headed and continued with his work, expanding the operations of his clinic, training students, and publishing case studies and original research.

While some historians of psychology have deemed Witmer worthy of little more than a footnote, his contributions to clinical psychology were substantial (McReynolds, 1996). In addition to establishing the first clinic, Witmer was the first to formally propose a new helping profession, distinct from medicine and education, to be called clinical psychology. He established the field's first journal, the *Psychological Clinic,* and was its first editor. The journal operated until 1935 and is considered to be the forerunner of the *Journal of Consulting Psychology*. Finally, Witmer established the first training program in clinical psychology and provided a framework for what clinical training should look like (e.g., doctoral-level education that included supervised clinical experience). By the 1920s, many of Witmer's graduates were making significant contributions of their own, mostly in the area of school psychology. Another interesting outgrowth of Witmer's training clinic was that it attracted and welcomed a relatively large number of women. Consequently, women were well represented in the field of school psychology throughout the twentieth century (Fagan, 1996).

Alfred Binet was another important figure in the birth of clinical psychology. Like Witmer, Binet's main contribution was triggered by an interest in applying psychology to helping children in the educational setting. Like many of the key figures in the early days of clinical psychology, Binet pursued a variety of interests before making his lasting mark upon clinical psychology with his studies of intelligence. Binet obtained a law degree in 1878 but never practiced. His scientific curiosity drew him to study, but not practice, medicine. Binet was influenced by Charcot and in the 1880s turned his attention to psychological research. He did some early experiments and published books and papers on hypnosis, hysteria, and fetishism, among other topics. In 1889 he co-founded the first psychological laboratory in France as well as the first French journal of psychology. Binet received a doctorate of sciences degree in 1894 and in 1895 became director of the psychology laboratory he had co-founded.

In 1904, the Minister of Public Instruction in Paris appointed a commission to study how to best serve the needs of impaired children in the educational system. The plan was to develop special classes to assist these children. The problem faced by the commission was how to identify the children who could not benefit from instruction in the regular classroom. Binet, along with Theodore Simon (1873–1961), the chief medical doctor of an asylum in Paris, offered to assist with the problem. The product of their collaboration was the 1905 Binet-Simon scale, composed of 30 items arranged in order of difficulty. Binet and Simon continued to work with and define their scale and produced a more sophisticated version in 1908. The new edition included more items, which were grouped by age levels from 3 to 13. They selected items for the scale by systematically testing them with normal children. The rule was that if more than 60 percent but less than 90 percent of the children at a given age got an item right, it was considered appropriate for that age and was included in the test (Watson, 1978). Table 2.1 includes items from both ends of the 1908 Binet-Simon scale. In the 1908 edition, Binet and Simon introduced *mental age* as the score for their scale. If a child got all the items right at the age 8 level of the test, he or she was considered to have a mental age of 8. Binet and Simon developed a classification system for children based upon their performance on the scale. An *idiot* had a mental age of 2 years or lower; an *imbecile's* mental age was from 3 to 7 years; and a *moron* had a mental age above 7 years. A third version of the scale was published in 1911 that extended the scale from age 3 to adult.

TABLE 2.1   Items from the 1908 Binet-Simon Scale

Age 3 Years
1. Points to nose, eyes, mouth.
2. Repeats sentences of six syllables.
3. Repeats two digits.
4. Enumerates objects in a picture.
5. Gives family name.

Age 4 Years
1. Knows sex.
2. Names certain familiar objects: *key, pocketknife,* and *penny.*
3. Repeats three digits.
4. Indicates which is longer of two lines 5 or 6 cm in length.

Age 12 Years
1. Repeats seven digits.
2. Finds in one minute three meanings for a given word: *obedience.*
3. Repeats a sentence of 26 syllables.
4. Answers problem questions (common-sense test).
5. Gives interpretations of pictures.

Age 13 Years
1. Draws the design that would be made by cutting a triangular piece from a once-folded edge of quatro-folded paper.
2. Rearranges in imagination the relationship of two triangles and draws the results as they would appear.
3. Gives differences between pairs of abstract terms, as *pride* and *pretension.*

Source: Watson, 1978, pp. 360–361.

Binet's scale was revolutionary in several ways. First, by choosing items based upon how normal children responded, Binet had created the first, albeit crude, norm-referenced test of intelligence. This reflected Binet's idea that the best way for psychologists to study individual differences was first to understand the norm and than look at how the individual differed from the norm. Second, the items Binet chose for his scale reflected his thinking about intelligence. Remember, "mental tests" had already been introduced by Cattell. Unfortunately, Cattell's tests proved not to be particularly valid measures of anything, especially intelligence. Unlike Cattell's tests, which focused upon sensory and motor functioning, Binet's tasks measured complex intellectual processes such as judgment, problem solving, abstract reasoning, and memory. These types of tasks proved to be useful in measuring individual differences among children.

Although not without its critics, the Binet-Simon scale was quickly adopted by researchers and clinicians interested in intelligence and the classification of defective children. For example, in 1909, the city of Rochester, New York, appointed an examiner to use the Binet-Simon scale to identify students for special classes that had been developed for subnormal children. Henry Goddard (1886–1957), who was the director of the research laboratory at the Institute for Backward Children at Vineland, New Jersey, learned about the Binet-Simon scale in 1908 and set about revising it for general use in the United States. Goddard, who is given credit for coining the term "moron" to identify the higher functioning among the intellectually impaired, published an English version of the Binet scale in 1911. Interest in Binet's work was not limited to France and the United States; his scale was quickly adopted for use in Belgium, Germany, Italy, and England as well (Reisman, 1991).

Alfred Binet died suddenly in 1911 at the age of 54. His contributions to the fledgling field of clinical psychology were enormous. First, Binet's scale was the forerunner of modern tests of intelligence. His recognition that assessing what is commonly meant by intelligence requires complex tasks was a breakthrough for mental testing. Second, his development of the mental age concept foreshadowed the creation of the intellectual quotient (see Box 7.2 for discussion of measuring IQ). Third, Binet was an early example of what would later come to be called a scientist-practitioner. He demonstrated how the young science of psychology could be utilized to address practical human problems. Finally, the success of Binet's scale was a key factor in initiating a boom in psychological testing.

Witmer and Binet were certainly important figures in the birth of clinical psychology but we do not want to give the reader the impression that they were that were the only important pioneers of this era. For example, in the 1890s other early psychologists made preliminary efforts to study psychopathology from a psychological perspective. For example, in 1896, James Sully organized a psychological laboratory for the study of "difficult children." And in 1897 William Krohn (1868–1927), who was a founding member of the American Psychological Association, established a laboratory for studying people with mental illness at the Eastern Hospital for the Insane in Kankakee, Illinois (Reisman, 1991). In addition, psychological clinics were established at the University of Iowa and at Clark University in 1909. Other evidence that clinical psychology was gaining acceptance in academia can be taken from the fact that both the University of Minnesota and the University of Washington added courses on clinical psychology in the first decade of the new century and both schools later established psychological clinics (Reisman, 1991).

Another important development in this time period was the creation of the first professional organization for psychologists in the United States. The American Psychological Association was founded in 1892 by G. Stanley Hall and six other "rugged pioneers." In its first year the organization boasted 31 members. By 1910, the APA had grown to 222 members. At this period of its development, clinical psychology did not feature at all prominently in the workings and discussions of the APA. Nonetheless, the organization was to play an important role in defining and regulating the field in its later development.

Childhood: World War I through World War II

If clinical psychology was born in the 1890s, the period starting with World War I and ending with World War II could be considered its early and middle childhood. The field was developing but was still struggling to create its own identity. Nonetheless, the advancements that took place in the thirty years between 1915 and 1945 were crucial to the later blossoming of clinical psychology. We have organized the discussion of this epoch in the field around three areas: *assessment, theory,* and *professional development.*

Assessment

In 1914, relatively minor skirmishes in the Balkans region of Europe erupted into full-scale warfare. By 1916, the first "world war" was in full swing, and by 1917 the United States declared war on Germany and threw itself into the "war to end all wars." This was a period of fervent patriotism for many Americans. Men and women from all walks of life, including academia, were expected to do their part, and many psychologists responded to the call. The practical problem of selecting people, mostly men, for their suitability for enlistment spurred the rapid development of tests of mental abilities.

When the United States entered WWI, APA president Robert Yerkes (1876–1956) formed a committee to work with the Army to develop methods of classifying recruits according to their abilities. Among the more important products of the group's work was the development of two group administered test of intelligence called the Army Alpha and the Army Beta. The Alpha test was a verbal scale for use with English-speaking recruits. The Beta was a nonverbal test of intelligence that was developed to assess men whose primary language was not English.

During the war over 1,700,000 men were tested in groups and another 80,000 plus were examined individually. This was the first time that normative data on psychological tests were gathered on such a large scale. In some ways, the picture of the young-adult American male that emerged from this massive testing was not particularly flattering. Over 500,000 were found to be illiterate, about 8,000 were discharged due to low intellectual ability, and another 20,000 were assigned to units where their work would not be intellectually challenging. The average mental age of the U.S. soldier was estimated to be 13.5 years. Findings of these type were made public and spawned an interest in intellectual testing.

The period between the two world wars saw a huge amount of work in the area of intellectual testing. In the tradition of the Army Alpha and Army Beta, several group-administered tests of intelligence and mental abilities were developed in the 1920s, including the Otis Classification Test (1923), the Institute of Educational Research Intelligence Scale (1925), Miller Analogies Test (1926), and others. Individually administered tests of mental abilities were also developed. Lewis Terman revised the Binet scale, collected normative data from a sample of children and adults in the United States, and published the Stanford-Binet Scale in 1916. The Stanford-Binet scale was the most popular individually administered test of intelligence in the 1920s and 1930s. However, other individually administered tests designed for measuring intelligence were also developed and gained popularity during that period of time. For example, the Goodenough Draw-A-Man Test (1926) measured a child's intelligence by scoring a drawing the child produced in response to the instructions "draw a man."

A major revision of the Stanford-Binet Scale was published by Lewis Terman and Maud Merrill in 1937. The test included age levels ranging from 2 years to a "Superior Adult III" category. The test had two equivalent forms, L and M, to minimize practice effects when the same individual was tested on separate occasions and was normed on a sample of over 3,000 individuals chosen to represent a cross-section of the United States population.

The 1937 edition of the Stanford-Binet was the preferred measure for assessing children's intelligence for the next two decades.

Along with the 1937 revision of the Stanford-Binet, the publication of the Wechsler-Bellvue scale in 1939 was the most significant development in the area of intellectual testing during that era. David Wechsler was chief psychologist at the Bellvue Psychiatric Hospital in New York City when he developed his test of intelligence (see Box 2.1 for a brief biography of Wechsler). He was dissatisfied with the available methods of measuring intelligence in adults because they tended to be upward extensions of measures originally designed for children. He wanted to create a scale that had clinical utility in evaluating adults who had suffered deterioration in their mental abilities. The Wechsler-Bellvue was one of the first individually administered intelligence tests developed for use with adults. The inclusion of verbal and nonverbal items was innovative and contributed to the rapid acceptance of the test (Matarazzo, 1972). The Wechsler-Bellvue was the first in a series of tests of intelligence that bear Wechsler's name and that became the most popular IQ tests used in the United States.

Advances in psychological testing were not limited to the arena of intellectual assessment in the period between the world wars. Psychologists were also devoting their attention to developing tests for measuring personality and diagnosing mental disorders. Once again, the practical issues facing the military in WWI prompted important developments in psychological testing. In 1917 Robert Woodworth (1869–1962) created the first test for detecting mental disturbances. Called the Psychoneurotic Inventory but labeled the Personal Data Sheet so that the soldiers completing it would not be alarmed, the test served well as a screening instrument for identifying recruits suffering with various mental conditions (Reisman, 1991).

In 1921 Herman Rorschach (1884–1922) published *Psychodiagnostik,* in which he described a method of diagnosing patients, and characterizing features of their personalities, based upon their responses to a set of ten ink blots. Rorschach showed, for example, that his inkblot method was useful in identifying individuals with schizophrenia. Unfortunately, Rorschach died shortly after the publication of his monograph and it was left to others to develop and popularize the test.

Next to the Rorschach, the Thematic Apperception Test (TAT) is probably the best-known projective test of personality. And, like the Rorschach, it was first published and popularized in the period between the world wars. Henry Murray (1893–1988) developed the test at the Harvard Psychological Clinic and published it in 1938.

The other major test to appear on the scene in this time period was the Minnesota Multiphasic Personality Inventory (MMPI). Developed in the late 1930s by a psychologist and a neurologist at the University of Minnesota Hospitals, the MMPI was an empirically derived test designed for the purpose of making differential diagnoses among psychiatric disorders. The MMPI, originally published in 1943, became the most widely used clinical assessment instrument of all time.

World War II triggered another growth spurt in psychological testing. Once again, psychologists were asked to develop and improve upon tests that could be used for the evaluation and classification of military personnel. In addition to general tests of intellectual ability and academic achievement, psychologists helped develop tests for the selection of naval officers, pilots, submarine personnel, and spies. It has been estimated that in 1944 alone, over 60 million standardized tests were administered to 20 million people (Reisman,

BOX **2.1**

David Wechsler, an Early Scientist-Practitioner

David Wechsler emigrated to the United States from Romania at age 6. He received his bachelor's degree from the College of the City of New York in 1916 at age 20 and his master's degree a year later from Columbia. As fate would have it, the United States entered into World War I in 1917, significantly impacting Wechsler's intellectual development and interests. While waiting to be inducted, he worked under the supervision of the eminent psychologist E. G. Boring, scoring and interpreting the performance of thousands of newly recruited troops on the Army Alpha. Once in the Army, his first assignment once again involved intellectual measurement. He assessed recruits using the Stanford-Binet and other scales. Later, while still in the Army, he had the opportunity to work with Charles Spearman whose theorizing about a "g" factor in intelligence (see Chapter 7) impressed Wechsler. After his discharge from the armed services, Wechsler won a scholarship to study in France, where he met Theodore Simon.

Wechsler earned his Ph.D. from Columbia in 1925. After holding a variety of positions, he accepted the post of Chief Psychologist at Bellevue Psychiatric Hospital in 1932. It was there that Wechsler turned his intellectual and creative talents toward the problem of measuring adult intelligence. Wechsler (1939) pointed out several problems with the available instruments for measuring intelligence in adults. He noted that most were developed for assessing intelligence in children and adapted for adult use by adding more difficult items. In addition, he pointed out the fact that the mental age method of measuring intelligence was not applicable to adults. As an alternative Wechsler offered the deviation IQ, which related the individual's IQ score to the average score for similarly aged people (see Chapter 7, Box 7.2, for discussion of methods of measuring IQ). The deviation IQ is one of Wechsler's many significant contributions to the area of intellectual assessment (Matarazzo, 1972).

Although Wechsler developed the Wechsler-Bellvue scale before there ever was a Boulder conference, he is a good example of a scientist-practitioner. Wechsler was trained first as a psychological scientist. He used his knowledge of the principles and methods of his science to help better understand the clinical problems he faced at Bellvue Hospital. His work with clinical populations informed his scientific work, the results of which improved his, and countless others', clinical practice.

1991). In addition to the use of testing for classification, the use of tests as part of an individualized diagnostic evaluation also grew during the war. The physical and psychological trauma suffered by soldiers produced a need for idiographic clinical assessment. The recently developed MMPI, Wechsler-Bellvue, and Rorschach were used extensively during the war and the identification of clinical psychology with these tests grew stronger.

Theory

The dominant theory in psychiatry and clinical psychology at this point in history was clearly psychoanalysis. Freud was hardworking and productive throughout his life, and the period between the world wars was no exception. Although many view his earlier work, notably *Interpretation of Dreams* (1900), as his most important, his later writings contributed significantly to the dispersion of his ideas and his legacy. Freud published *Beyond the Pleasure Principle* in 1920, *The Question of Lay Analysis* in 1926, *The Ego and the Id* in 1927, *Inhibitions, Symptoms, and Anxiety* in 1936, and *Moses and Monotheism* in 1939. His ideas were further promulgated by his many students and followers, most notably his daughter Anna Freud (*The Ego and Mechanisms of Defense,* 1937).

In the 1920s and 1930s, psychoanalysis had its most direct impact upon the developing field of clinical psychology through its influence upon psychological testing. Although neither Rorschach nor Murray were Freudian, the influence of psychoanalytic thinking can be seen in how others interpreted their tests. Psychoanalytic symbolism appeared in interpretation of psychological, particularly projective, testing. For example, Card IV of the Rorschach inkblots was referred to as the "father card" in many circles because the inkblot is commonly seen as a monster figure. Another example of the influence of Freudian thinking upon the interpretation of projective material is in human drawings in which the nose is commonly seen as a phallic symbol (Handler, 1996).

Outside of psychoanalysis, other important theory development was occurring around this time. In Russia, Ivan Pavlov (1849–1936), a physiologist, was doing his landmark work on classical conditioning. Pavlov had already had a successful career as a physiologist before beginning his work on reflex learning. In 1904 he won a Nobel Prize for his work on digestion. Pavlov was, in fact, studying the functioning of saliva in digestion when he became interested in conditioning. Pavlov had noticed that the dogs he studied began to salivate when they saw the meat—before it was given to them. Pavlov reasoned that the normal salivation to food on the tongue had become conditioned to the sight of the food. Pavlov devoted his keen intellect and strong work ethic to working out the parameters of this form of learning. In his elegant demonstrations of *classical conditioning* in dogs, Pavlov showed that stimuli that previously did not call forth a reflex response (e.g., salivation) would come to do so following a particular experimental procedure. Initially, healthy dogs routinely produced saliva in response to the presentation of food. But Pavlov showed that, under special conditions, dogs could also learn to salivate in response to a bell being rung, or a whistle being blown, or even the presentation of a diagram of a circle on a piece of white card. The experimental procedure that produced such results involved repeatedly presenting the new stimulus (e.g., the bell being rung) a fraction of a second before, the reflex-eliciting stimulus (e.g., the food). The *pairing* of the two stimuli was made repeatedly until the response normally produced in the reflex began to be produced by the new stimulus. In Pavlov's terminology, the original connection between the food and the salivation is an *unconditioned reflex* (unconditioned, because no new learning is required). Specifically, the food is an *unconditioned stimulus* (UCS) and the salivation is an *unconditioned response* (UCR). After several pairings of the bell and the food, such that the previously neutral sound of the bell could elicit salivation in the dogs, the bell has become a *conditioned stimulus* (CS). This conditioned stimulus had now taken on the power to trigger salivation itself. Salivation in response to the conditioned stimulus, the bell, is referred to as the conditioned response (CR).

Although not initially aware of Pavlov's work, John B. Watson (1878–1958) initiated a new branch of psychology, *behaviorism,* with an article entitled "Psychology as a Behaviorist Views It" in 1913. The article was a bold statement in which Watson sought to redefine psychology from a science of consciousness to a science of behavior. Watson is considered the founder of U.S. behaviorism. He is well known for his provocative statements about the importance of the environment and learning in shaping human behavior. One of his more famous quotes captures the essence of Watson's view: "Give me a dozen healthy infants, well-formed, and my own specified world to bring them up in and I'll guarantee to take any one at random and train him to become any type of specialist I might select" (Watson, 1928, p. 10).

While Watson sought to create a new psychology, his most famous experiment had to do with a clinical phenomenon—phobia. His demonstration of fear conditioning in *Little Albert* paved the way for conditioning models of anxiety disorders. In this study, Watson and his collaborator Rosalie Rayner demonstrated that a healthy 11-month-old child, who showed no fear of a white rat, developed an intense fear of the rat and related stimuli after several learning trials in which the rat was paired with the sudden sound of a steel bar being struck (Watson & Raynor, 1920).

Watson's academic career was cut short in 1920 when divorce proceedings were initiated against him, and sensational publicity resulted. He was asked to resign his professorship at Johns Hopkins University. Later that year, he married Rosalie Raynor. Watson went on to have a successful career in advertising.

In a sequel to Watson and Raynor's (1920) famous study, Mary Cover Jones (1924) used conditioning principles to eliminate an irrational fear in a young child. A 2-year, 10-month old boy named Peter had an extreme fear of rabbits. Jones treated Peter's fear in the following manner. The boy was placed in a relaxing playroom, with nonfearful children, and given something enjoyable to eat. The rabbit was introduced to the room and gradually brought closer and closer to Peter. Eventually, he was able to touch the animal without showing signs of distress.

The demonstrations by Watson and Raynor (1920) and Mary Cover Jones (1924) were interesting and pioneering. However, they did not have an impact on psychotherapeutic practices at the time, which were dominated by psychoanalysis and derivative psychodynamic therapies. Nonetheless, they laid the groundwork for the behavior therapy movement that would have a significant impact upon clinical psychology in the 1950s and later.

Professional Developments

Over the first fifty years of the existence of the field, the professional activity associated with clinical psychology was testing. Paralleling the growth in development of psychological tests occurring in the period between world wars, there was growth in the number of psychologists working outside of academia. Psychologists were employed in child guidance clinics, psychiatric clinics, hospitals, psychoeducational clinics, juvenile detention facilities, and industry. Although professional psychologists expanded their clinical activities in the 1930s, they functioned largely as psychological examiners prior to WWII.

Psychologists' identification with the relatively new field of applied psychological testing created opportunities for business and professional development. In 1921, for example, James McKeen Cattell founded the Psychological Corporation and convinced some 200 other psychologists to buy shares of stock in the venture. Originally set up as an organization that would sell psychological tests, consult to companies on psychological matters, and carry out studies for clients, it blossomed as a developer and marketer of psychological tests. The Psychological Corporation set standards for the tests it marketed and in so doing had a moderating influence on the extravagant claims being made about some psychological tests. The Psychological Corporation became a successful company that is still a major player in the multimillion-dollar psychological testing business.

As more psychologists found employment outside of universities, the American Psychological Association struggled with how to deal with these nontraditional psychologists. On the one hand, APA wanted to be the one organization to represent all of psychology. On the other hand, it was formed as an organization devoted to the promotion of the science of psychology. Qualification for membership reflected the organization's scientific emphasis. In the 1921, for example, membership in APA required a Ph.D. in psychology and published post-doctoral research. By 1926, APA created an associate member status. While full membership still required publications, one could be an associate member without ever having published a paper. By the early 1930s, associates outnumbered members of the organization.

There were several efforts by clinical psychologists to form their own professional organizations in the early years of the discipline. As early as 1917, a group of 49 psychologists formed the American Association of Clinical Psychologists (AACP). Two years later, this organization was incorporated into APA becoming the Section of Clinical Psychology (Brems et al., 1991). In 1921 a disgruntled group of clinical psychologists formed the New York State Association for Consulting Psychology. In 1930, this organization expanded to create the Association of Consulting Psychologists. In 1937, the American Association of Applied Psychology (AAAP) was formed. In 1938, AAAP took over the publication of the *Journal of Consulting Psychology,* which was created the year before by the Association of Consulting Psychology. By the close of the 1930s, there were over 2,000 members and associates of APA, of which about 40 percent did not hold academic positions and about 12 percent defined themselves as clinical psychologists (Reisman, 1991). The clinical psychologists in APA were frustrated. They had disbanded the Clinical Section of APA in 1937 and many sought an organizational home in AAAP.

By the late 1930s many clinical psychologists were also frustrated with the limited roles of psychological examiners and diagnosticians. These psychologists were interested in treatment and some were beginning to conduct psychotherapy, albeit on a limited basis. The expansion of psychologists into psychotherapy was not greeted positively by their colleagues in psychiatry. In fact, the medical profession as a whole fought against clinical psychologists' moving beyond psychological testing. In the 1920s, psychiatry fought against clinical psychologists functioning as diagnosticians. They were okay with psychologists doing the testing to establish IQ, for example, but the diagnosis of mental retardation was viewed as the purview of the psychiatrist (Reisman, 1991). By the 1930s, diagnosing was an accepted professional activity of clinical psychology, but psychotherapy was seen by psychiatry as a service that could only be provided by a medical professional. Efforts by organized psychiatry to limit the scope of psychological practice continued throughout the twentieth century and to the present time (e.g., psychiatry is vigorously fighting psychologists' efforts to obtain prescription privileges today).

Professional psychology was changing rapidly as the 1930s gave way to the 1940s, and the APA recognized the need to change if it was to remain vital as the premier organization representing psychology. In 1939, there were 618 members of APA and 1,909 associates. The associates were restless and it was widely recognized that the impediment to membership was the post-doctoral research requirement. Meanwhile, the AAAP was growing, reaching

615 members in 1941. By 1942 work was underway to reorganize APA to maintain the growing number of clinical members and to entice those who had defected to return to the organization. A joint committee of APA and AAAP developed a constitution that redefined the objective of APA to be "to advance psychology as a science and means of promoting human welfare." The change in stated objective, as well as the internal organization of the APA, marked a shift toward greater attention to the concerns of professional (i.e., nonacademic) psychologists. The other major change included in the new constitution was that the publication requirement for membership was dropped. In 1944, the constitution was accepted and AAAP voted itself out of existence and transferred its membership to APA.

At this point of the world's history, of course, the changes in a relatively small professional organization were inconsequential compared to the massive reorganization of governments and world powers that was taking place as a result of WWII. But our focus is on clinical psychology, and for our discipline the changes that coincided with, and followed, WWII were as dramatic as those that were happening on the larger world stage. As with the WWI, WWII called for the processing and classification of millions of men for military service. Many individuals were rejected from military service because of psychological difficulties. In fact, "mental disease" ranked second to visual defects as the most common reason for rejection (Rowntree, 1943). In addition, the large number of psychological, neurological, and physical casualties of the war created a huge demand for diagnosticians and therapists. Psychologists, many of whom were already stretching their professional activities to include psychotherapy, were ready and willing to fill the need for psychotherapists. Early in WWII, psychologists tended to be used for selection and classification of military personnel. But as the war progressed and the casualties mounted, more and more psychologists were called upon to provide clinical services. Over half of the psychologists who served in the armed forces during WWI provided some counseling or psychotherapy services. Perhaps the most important way in which WWII impacted the development of clinical psychology was that it triggered a chain of events that pushed the field to define itself and create a model for training.

Adolescence: Post WWII and the Development of an Identity

Not to drag out the analogy to a child's development too far, in many ways the years immediately following WWII represent the adolescence of clinical psychology. Developmental psychologists recognize that the most important psychological challenges for adolescents are to develop a sense of identity and the capacity to function independently. The first task the field had to take on was defining itself and the next was to struggle for independence.

Prior to WWII, very few graduate programs offered training in clinical psychology. Some graduate programs offered a few clinical courses and a few had clinical practicum experiences available. But for most psychologists, clinical training took place after graduate school and most of it was "on the job." The APA was ambivalent about getting involved with the training of clinical psychologists. By 1935, however, pressure had grown in the organization to make a statement about what clinical psychology is and how clinical psychologists should be trained. The APA Committee on Standards of Training was formed and

defined clinical psychology as "that art and technology which deals with the adjustment problems of human beings" (Report of Committee, 1935). The committee recommended that
psychologists wishing to identify themselves as clinical should have a Ph.D. and a year of
supervised experience. Indicative of APA's ambivalence at the time, the committee published its report and promptly disbanded.

By the end of the WWII the APA's interest in clinical training had changed dramatically. The organization responded to the demand for clinicians that followed the war. For
example, there were 16 million U.S. veterans of the war and an additional 4 million pre-WWII
veterans; 44,000 of these veterans were in Veterans Administration hospitals. The VA
announced that it needed 4,700 clinical psychologists. In addition to the need for trained
clinical psychologists, the APA was also responding to the huge amount of money that was
being invested into training of clinical psychologists through the VA and the United States
Public Health Service. The VA and the USPHS asked the APA to help them identify graduate training programs in clinical psychology that provided appropriate and high-quality
training. The APA responded to this request by appointing a committee, chaired by David
Shakow, to develop a model for training clinical psychologists.

Shakow's committee issued its report, which has come to be known as the Shakow
report, in 1947 (American Psychological Association, 1947). The report recommended that
clinical psychologists be trained at the doctoral level. Training was envisioned as lasting four
years, the first two of which were at the university and were devoted to training in the science of psychology, research methods, and statistics, as well as diagnostic and therapeutic
methods. The third year of training was to be spent on internship and devoted to full-time
clinical work. In the final year of training, the doctoral student would return to the university to carry out his or her dissertation research. The committee recommended that course
work cover general psychology, psychodynamics of behavior, diagnostic methods, research
methods, therapy, and related disciplines. The committee's report emphasized the importance of training in research and the continuity between clinical psychology and the field
of psychology in general:

> A clinical psychologist must first and foremost be a psychologist in the sense that he can be
> expected to have a point of view and a core of knowledge and training which is common to
> all psychologists. This would involve an acquaintance with the primary body of psycholog-
> ical theory, research, and methods on which further training and interdisciplinary relationships
> can be built. Preparation should be broad; it should be directed to research and professional
> goals. Participants should receive training in three functions: diagnosis, research and therapy,
> with the special contribution of the psychologist as a research worker emphasized through-
> out. (American Psychological Association, 1947)

Beginning in 1948, the APA started to accredit doctoral training programs in clinical
psychology. Shakow's committee had specified that accredited programs were to be site-vis-
ited every five years by two or more psychologists who would evaluate the training program.

In 1949, the National Institute of Mental Health funded a conference on graduate
training in Boulder, Colorado. The APA was represented at the conference, which was also
attended by representatives from the university doctoral training programs in clinical psychology, internship training sites, and some practicum agencies. After two weeks, the Boul-

der conference attendees essentially reaffirmed the recommendations described in the Shakow report. Probably of greatest importance to the field was the endorsement the clinical psychologist as both a *scientist* and a *practitioner*. The following training principles were included in the conference report: (1) Clinical psychologists were to be trained at university psychology departments; (2) they were to be trained as scientists first and clinicians second; (3) they should be required to complete a one-year internship of full-time clinical work; (4) they should be trained in diagnosis, research, and therapy; and (5) they should be required to complete original research making a contribution to the field and culminating in the Ph.D.

The scientist-practitioner model of training was recognized as a unique experiment by the Boulder conference participants. In most disciplines, graduate training is geared toward practice or research, but not both. In medicine, for example, students learn facts about anatomy, physiology, biochemistry, and the like, and how to diagnose and treat illnesses. They do not learn how to—nor are they expected to—carry out research to contribute to the knowledge base in these areas. In Boulder model training, on the other hand, participants develop the skills to apply psychological knowledge (e.g., diagnose and treat) but also to contribute to that knowledge base.

The years immediately preceding and following the Boulder conference were years of incredible growth for training in clinical psychology. Grant money was available from the USPHS graduate training programs and hundreds of funded internships at VA facilities were created. The GI bill was amended to include graduate education, so that psychology programs were inundated with applications from veterans who brought with them their own funding (Baker & Benjamin, 2000). Consequently, the number of graduate training programs in clinical psychology grew. In 1947, there were twenty-two universities offering doctoral training in clinical psychology in the United States. Two years later, in 1949, that number had grown to forty-two (Reisman, 1991). Still, these programs continued to receive far more applicants then they could possibly train. Training directors were in a position to be able to choose the best and brightest from their large pools of applicants.

Growth in clinical training grew through the 1950s and 1960s. Starting in the late 1940s, the National Institute of Mental Health began making training grants available to university psychology programs. These grants provided support for teaching costs and graduate assistantships. The goals of the program were to support the creation of new graduate programs and to improve the quality of existing programs. By 1962, there were 60 APA-accredited graduate training programs in clinical psychology, 55 of which were supported by NIMH training grants (Brems et al., 1991).

Looking back in time, the years immediately following World War II can be seen as a period of striking optimism about clinical psychology. There was abundant support for training of clinical psychologists and for clinical research. The rapid growth of clinical psychology was by and large a U.S. phenomenon. Some numbers illustrate the point. By 1968, there were approximately 12,000 psychologists in the United States who identified themselves as clinicians (Cates, 1970, cited in Reisman, 1991). By comparison, around the same period of time, it was estimated that there were 2 in Bulgaria, 76 in Finland, 134 in Denmark, 14 in Ireland, 183 in Norway (Bard, 1966, cited in Reisman, 1991), 94 in Rumania, 253 in Sweden, 345 in Great Britain, 60 in Yugoslavia, and about 30 in Greece (Vassiliou & Vassiliou, 1966, cited in Reisman, 1991).

In the United States, the field had captured the public's interest and there were unprecedented numbers of applicants to training programs. By 1950 clinical psychology had established itself as a scientific and professional discipline.

Adulthood: Milestones and Growing Pains

The fifty-plus years since the Boulder conference have witnessed continued growth and change for clinical psychology. In the following pages we highlight some of the important controversies and developments in the field. Taking the year 1950 as a rough jumping-off point, we trace developments up to the present in the following areas: *training, psychotherapy, psychological testing, professional practice, specialization,* and *growth.*

Training

The conference in Boulder, Colorado, was not the last time a group of interested psychologists gathered to discuss the training of clinical psychologists. These conferences (like Boulder, named for their locations) provided proponents and detractors of the scientist practitioner model forums to air their views. The first conference in which an alternative to the Boulder model was formally proposed was held in Miami Beach in 1958. Although the participants in the Miami Beach meeting continued to support Boulder model training, they encouraged exploration of alternatives, including masters-level training and professional training that would culminate in a Doctorate of Psychology (Psy.D.).

Perhaps reflective of the rebellious times, in the 1960s there was growing discontent with scientist-practitioner training among a vocal group of clinical psychologists. While university faculty tended to support the Boulder model, students and practitioners were more critical. They complained that too much time and effort was spent developing research skills that most graduates never used after receiving their Ph.D.s and that too little time and effort was devoted to clinical training. In addition, many practitioners did not like the skeptical atmosphere in which clinical methods were taught. Student felt pulled in different directions when they reviewed scholarly material critical of the very assessment and intervention strategies they were learning to apply in clinical practica. In addition, students were frustrated by the length of typical Ph.D. training programs. It was not unusual for students to take seven or more years to complete the Ph.D., often due to delays in completing the doctoral dissertation. There was a cry for alternative approaches to training.

In 1968 the University of Illinois, which already had a respected Ph.D. program in clinical psychology, initiated a Psy.D. program that deemphasized research and required more training in clinical assessment and treatment methods relative to the Ph.D. program. Another alternative was the start of the professional schools of psychology. The first professional school, the California School of Professional Psychology, was founded in 1969.

In 1974, another training conference was held, this time in Vail, Colorado. The Vail conference produced a series of recommendations for loosening the regulations that govern the training of clinical psychologists. The Vail attendees endorsed the Psy.D. as a legitimate alternative to traditional Ph.D. training. Second, whether training culminated in a Ph.D. or Psy.D., the scholar-practitioner model (see Chapter 1) was also endorsed as an alternative to the scientist-practitioner model. Finally, in the anti-intellectual spirit that was popular toward the end of the 1960s and in the early 1970s, the Vail conferees proposed that masters-level training should qualify individuals to use the title *psychologist*.

Clearly, the emphasis of the Vail conference was toward a liberalizing of training. Some of what came out of the Vail conference was eventually accepted by the APA and influenced the criteria for program accreditation (e.g., scholar-practitioner training and the Psy.D.) but most of the other recommendations fell flat. Most notably, the APA continued to promote the idea that doctoral-level training was a prerequisite for use of the title psychologist and, in fact, recommended the abolition of terminal masters programs in clinical psychology.

The next major conference on training clinical psychologists took place in Salt Lake City, Utah, in 1987. While the proceedings of the Utah conference included an acknowledgment of the legitimacy of the Psy.D., they also emphasized the importance of training in research for every clinical psychologist (Bickman, 1987). The Utah conferees called for greater diversity in clinical psychology training with respect to gender, age, race, and sexual preference. Finally, the most controversial recommendation was that by 1995, all professional schools should be affiliated with a regionally accredited university. The latter recommendation was not accepted by the APA's office of accreditation.

As mentioned in Chapter 1, a more recent development has been the self-identification of so-called clinical scientist training programs (McFall, 1991). Clinical scientist training puts the emphasis back upon research. Students in a clinical-scientist program are taught to apply scientific standards to evaluate clinical methods and to apply only those methods for which there is significant scientific support. More importantly, clinical scientist training teaches students to evaluate their own clinical work scientifically and to contribute to the clinical science literature.

Psychotherapy

In the early adulthood of clinical psychology, psychoanalysis and psychoanalytically oriented therapies were dominant. In psychoanalytic circles, "controversial" modifications to traditional psychoanalytic techniques, such as having the patient sit in a chair rather than lie on a couch and seeing patients less often than daily, were hotly debated. But outside of psychoanalytic circles, major paradigm shifts in the way that psychotherapy was conceptualized and carried out were occurring. Theories of personality and psychotherapy that did not rely upon the unconscious were developed and promoted by mavericks such as Carl Rogers, Joseph Wolpe, Albert Ellis, Aaron Beck, and others.

In his 1951 book, *Client-Centered Therapy,* Carl Rogers (1902–1987) eschewed the need for interpretation of unconscious drives and motives in psychotherapy. In fact, he argued against the need for interpretation altogether. Rogers saw the role of the psychotherapist to be understanding the world as the client experienced it and communicating that understanding to the client. Rogers believed that all human beings have the capacity to grow and move toward *self-actualization,* "the inherent tendency of the organism to develop all its capacities in ways which serve to maintain or enhance the organism" (Rogers, 1959, p. 196). In client-centered psychotherapy, the therapist creates circumstances that allow the client to shed *conditions of worth* (internalized beliefs about standards one must achieve to be loved and valued) and release his or her capacity for personal growth. Rogers was a pioneer, not only in his thinking about psychotherapy, but also in being one of the first to test his ideas through empirical investigation. Rogers made recordings of his therapy sessions so that they could be studied, a practice unheard of at the time and shocking to traditional psychoanalysts. Rogers proposed his ideas about the psychotherapy conditions that are necessary for change as hypotheses to be tested and set about testing them. Consequently, Rogers initiated a new era of psychotherapy research.

Around the same time that Rogers was developing and testing his ideas about psychotherapy, the first generation of modern behavior therapists were developing a whole different approach to understanding and treating emotional and behavioral disorders. Behavior therapy involved the application of principles of classical and operant conditioning to clinical disorders. Joseph Wolpe was a behavior therapy trailblazer. Trained in psychoanalysis, Wolpe was frustrated with the disappointing results he achieved applying psychoanalytic procedures with traumatized veterans of World War II. He searched for an alternative and found it in the literature on *experimental neurosis,* a condition marked by anxious behavior in laboratory animals exposed to certain learning procedures. Drawing upon this literature, Wolpe conducted his own laboratory experiments in which he demonstrated that anxiety in cats, conditioned for experimental neurosis, could be overcome by eliciting a response incompatible with anxiety while presenting them with anxiety-provoking stimuli. In his 1958 book, Wolpe proposed the concept of *reciprocal inhibition* as a principle of behavior change that relied upon countering anxiety by a competing feeling state (Thorpe & Olson, 1997). Wolpe developed the psychotherapy technique *systematic desensitization* based upon the principle of reciprocal inhibition (see Chapter 13).

In addition to Wolpe, other pioneers of the behavior therapy movement included Hans Eysenck (1916–1997) in England and B. F. Skinner (1904–1990) in the United States. Eysenck and his colleague Monte Shapiro developed the first graduate program in clinical psychology in Great Britain. Eysenck was discouraged by the wide gulf between psychology and what students were being taught in clinical training programs (primarily psychoanalytic approaches to assessment and therapy) in U.S. training programs he visited. He and Shapiro created their program to train students in a scientifically oriented clinical psychology (Thorpe & Olson, 1997). Although it had not yet been named, much of the early work done by Eysenck and his students came to be known as behavior therapy. B. F. Skinner demonstrated that the behavior of laboratory animals could be modified by controlling the consequences of specific responses. In an elegant series of studies using standardized learning environments, Skinner articulated the principles of *operant conditioning.* Applying these principles to chronic psychiatric patients on a hospital ward, Skinner demonstrated that these patients showed the expected learning patterns when the consequences of their behavior were controlled (Thorpe & Olson, 1997). Following from Skinner's lead, other clinical researchers developed therapy techniques, including the token economy (Ayllon & Azrin, 1968) and various child behavior management strategies (e.g., Bijou & Baer, 1966), by applying operant conditioning principles.

While it was derided by some of its critics as being too symptom-focused, thus ignoring the supposed root causes of clients' problems, behavior therapy continued to expand and grow throughout the 1960s and 1970s. The development of behavior therapy was spurred by a commitment to empirically evaluating behavioral interventions. Consequently, an immense empirical literature examining specific behavior therapy techniques grew. By the end of the 1970s, systematic desensitization, for example, represented the most intensely researched psychological intervention ever developed (Wilson & O'Leary, 1980). Behavior therapy researchers, such as Gordon Paul and Isaac Marks, have continually set the standard for psychotherapy outcome research.

Behavior therapy has expanded dramatically since the early pioneers applied learning principles to alleviate human suffering. This growth has included an expansion beyond the application of classical and operant conditioning to include cognitive learning. *Cognitive-behavior therapy* is the term now favored by many to describe this approach to psychotherapy. The two most influential early developers of cognitive behavior therapy were Albert Ellis (b. 1912) and Aaron Beck (b. 1921). Ellis was a clinical psychologist and prolific writer, researcher, and clinician (see Ellis, 1991, for a humble autobiography of his life in clinical psychology) who first described his ideas about cognitive behavior therapy in the 1950s. Through his clinical work, Ellis noticed that his clients tended to hold beliefs and think in ways that contributed to their emotional distress. Ellis developed an approach to therapy (rational emotive behavior therapy) in which he very directly educated his clients about how their beliefs contributed to their problems. Like Ellis, Aaron Beck began developing his cognitive therapy for depression in the 1950s. Although developed independently, Beck's cognitive therapy shares some features with rational emotive behavior therapy. Like Ellis, Beck advocated rationally challenging clients' irrational beliefs. But he also suggested that therapists and clients work together to develop experiments to test out the clients' beliefs. Beck's cognitive therapy uses empathic questioning to challenge clients' beliefs.

Cognitive behavior therapy has steadily grown in popularity since it was first described almost 50 years ago. Currently, about half of the licensed psychologists who are members of APA define their orientation as cognitive-behavioral or behavioral (Resnick, 1997). Cognitive behavioral approaches have been tested empirically and have been shown to be helpful for a variety of clinical problems (see Chapter 13). Using the number of related articles published in the major journals (e.g., *Journal of Consulting and Clinical Psychology, Clinical Psychology: Science and Practice*) as the measure of an approach's standing in the field, cognitive-behavior therapy appears to be the dominant approach to psychotherapy in clinical psychology at the present time.

Psychodynamic therapies, client-centered and other so-called humanistic therapies, behavior therapy, and cognitive-behavior therapy represent major approaches to psychotherapy, but clearly not all therapies can be fit neatly into one of these four areas. Starting in the 1960s, the number and types of psychotherapies has proliferated. In 1979, Larry Beutler published a survey of the field in which he concluded that there were over 130 types of psychotherapy. By the mid-1980s estimates of the number of therapies had grown to over 400 (Karuso, 1985, cited in Kazdin, 1994). The growth in the types of psychotherapy practiced was matched by a growth in the number of clinical psychologists choosing psychotherapy practice as their primary form of employment (see Chapter 1, Table 1.2).

For its first fifty years, clinical psychology was identified with psychological testing. Over its second fifty years, the field has redefined itself as one most strongly associated with psychotherapy. As we saw in Chapter 1, no matter what their work setting, most contemporary clinical psychologists spend some portion of their time conducting psychotherapy.

Psychological Testing

Psychological tests developed in the 1920s and 1930s have proven to be remarkably enduring in terms of their popularity among clinical psychologists. In the 1950s, the Rorschach,
Stanford-Binet, Wechsler-Bellevue, TAT, and the MMPI were the instruments most often
used by clinicians and most frequently studied by clinical researchers. By 1951, there were
1,219 publications dealing with the Rorschach, 493 regarding the Stanford-Binet, and 371
on the Wechsler-Bellevue (Sunberg, 1954, 1961, cited in Reisman, 1991). In retrospect, the
1940s and 1950s can be seen as the heyday of psychological testing. Clinical psychologists
were applying psychological tests in a variety of settings and for a wide variety of purposes.
Tests were used to make diagnostic, treatment, placement, and educational decisions.
Although not without critics, as a discipline, clinical psychology had faith in the value of
psychological testing.

The 1960s, however, was a period during which questioning "authority" and rebellion
against "the establishment" was the norm. It is perhaps not surprising then that the 1960s
witnessed the beginning of a strong backlash against psychological testing. A 1965 special
issue of *American Psychologist* was devoted to criticism of psychological testing and papers
in its defense. Criticism of testing came from a variety of perspectives. Many pointed out the
poor reliability and validity of many psychological tests, particularly projective tests (e.g.,
Rabin & Hurley, 1964). Behavior therapists had little use for instruments designed to measure unconscious conflicts, defense mechanisms, or personality traits. They advocated for
direct observation of behaviors of interest and *functional analysis* (see Chapter 9). Humanists such as Rogers did not see the need for constructs such as psychiatric diagnoses, the
unconscious mind, or stable personality traits. Testing, therefore, was of minimal importance
to the client-centered therapist.

Projective personality tests such as the Rorschach and TAT have been the victims of
particularly scathing attacks. By the late 1950s, in fact, several reviews of the literature had
appeared that were highly critical of projective tests. For example, Jensen (1959) wrote, "No
general conclusion concerning reliability is possible even with respect to any particular
techniques. The reported reliabilities are usually lower than is considered acceptable in the
case of objective tests" (p. 133). And Eysenck (1958) weighed in as well: "There is no satisfactory evidence for any of the numerous claims made for these devices" (p. 120). In 1978,
Peterson reviewed the literature on the Rorschach and concluded that the data did not justify its use in clinical practice. In a 1965 review of the TAT, Zubin, Eron, and Shumer (1965)
concluded, "It is not possible to regard the TAT as a valid instrument of personality assessment, as such" (p. 462). A similarly negative conclusion about the TAT was reached by
Swartz (1978) thirteen years later. In 2000, the authors of a comprehensive review of projective techniques concluded that while there was some support for the validity of a few of
the indexes derived from the TAT and Rorschach, the instruments are routinely used for purposes for which they are invalid or for which there is little research support (Lilienfeld,
Wood, & Garb, 2000).

Intellectual testing has also been virulently attacked from a variety of quarters. Once
again, these attacks first appeared in the 1960s, at which time it was discovered that certain
minority groups scored, on average, about one standard deviation lower on IQ tests than white
children and adults. This finding led to intense scrutiny of IQ tests and a variety of criticisms.

It was discovered that many tests did not include minority groups in their standardization samples and that test items often reflected white, middle-class values and sampled a narrow range of abilities. In addition, some critics thought that the tests were being used to segregate minority children from whites in educational settings and to discriminate against minorities in the employment arena. The APA responded to the mounting criticism of intelligence testing in a special report issued to its members (Cleary, Humphreys, Kendrick, & Wesman, 1975). The authors of the report summarized the evidence, which showed that black children, on average, scored about 15 points below white children on IQ tests across school years. However, the report argued that this did not justify segregation of children along racial lines, nor should it be taken as evidence or genetic differences between the races. Despite the committee's efforts to strike a conciliatory tone, the report was met with criticism by some minority groups. Speaking for minority psychologists, one black psychologist wrote, "Psychological testing historically has been a quasi-scientific tool in the perpetuation of racism . . . it has provided a cesspool of . . . fallacious data which inflates the egos of whites by demeaning Black people and threatens to potentiate Black genocide" (Jackson, 1975, quoted in Reisman, 1991, p. 342).

Despite the criticisms psychological tests have faced over the past forty-plus years, the number of published tests continues to grow. What then has been the consequence of all the scrutiny of, and commentary about, psychological testing? It appears that the testing enterprise has improved in a variety of ways: (1) The standards for normative data have increased substantially. Contemporary psychological tests need to show that they include adequate representation of the subgroups that make up the population to which findings are to be generalized. A test of general intelligence, for example, must have normative data on a sample of people who approximate the distribution of races in the United States. (2) In addition to representativeness in norm sampling, most contemporary psychological tests strive to be inclusive in item content as well. For example, pictures used in test items include images of non-white people. (3) Perhaps one of the most significant consequences of the critical attention paid to tests of intelligence and personality has been the proliferation of specific tests designed to measure specific attributes. Thousands of tests designed to measure specific emotions (e.g., anxiety, depression, anger), personal characteristics (e.g., assertiveness, parenting confidence), cognitive skills (e.g., short-term memory, nonverbal problem solving), academic achievement (e.g., reading comprehension, mathematical computations), and many other attributes have been developed. (4) Popular tests are periodically revised and the new editions attempt to address the problems identified in the earlier versions. Notably, in the 1970s John Exner undertook to develop a uniform system for administering, scoring, and interpreting the Rorschach that could be used reliably (see Chapter 8). The Wechsler scales of intelligence have also been periodically updated, as have major tests of academic achievement. A major revision of the MMPI was finally published in 1989. (5) Finally, test developers have taken some steps to minimize the misuse of psychological test data. For example, the 1986 revision of the Stanford-Binet scale dropped the use of the term "IQ" in favor of a standard age score that, hopefully, more accurately reflects what the score is (i.e., an appraisal of how someone is functioning relative to age-matched peers, not a measure of innate intellectual ability).

Ironically, the strong backlash against psychological testing that began in the late 1950s and continued though the 1980s has not been accompanied by a decrease in the popularity of psychological testing. While this period of time did witness a decline in the amount of time clinical psychologists spent in psychological testing (in 1959 it was estimated that clinical psychologists spent 44 percent of their time on diagnosis and assessment, but by 1976 that estimate had dropped to 24 percent; Reisman, 1991), the decline was more likely due to psychologists' increasing involvement in psychotherapy. The continued popularity of some psychological tests, particularly projective tests, has baffled many observers. In 1982, Anne Anastasi summarized the apparent paradox succinctly: "Projective techniques present a curious discrepancy between research and practice. When evaluated as psychometric instruments, the large majority make a poor showing. Yet their popularity in clinical use continues unabated" (p. 564). As we commented at the beginning of this section, succeeding generations of clinical psychologists have shown a striking loyalty to some of the earliest tests developed. A survey conducted in the mid-1980s found that the top ten most frequently used tests by psychologists included the MMPI, WAIS, Rorschach, TAT, and projective drawing techniques (Lubin, Larsen, Matarazzo, & Seever, 1985). Ten years later, Watkins, Campbell, Nieberding, and Hallmark (1995) found the list to be essentially unchanged.

Professional Practice

Over clinical psychology's first fifty years, there was a small but slowly growing number of psychologists who offered their services for a fee. After World War II, the number of psychologists interested in professional practice expanded rapidly. Clinical psychology's adulthood has witnessed a continued expansion of professional practice. Through the years, professional psychologists have had to fight for recognition of their services and to expand their position in the professional marketplace.

A significant milestone in the development of any profession is the legal recognition that the profession, in fact, exists. For psychology, the battle for legal recognition was fought over a thirty-five-year period. To understand psychology's struggle for legal recognition, it is important to understand a bit about the way *licensing* and *certification* laws work. A licensing law restricts the performance of certain functions to individuals who are recognized members of that profession (e.g., only people holding certain professional licenses can legally write orders for prescription medications). A certification law, on the other hand, controls only the use of a title. For certification an individual must meet certain standards specified by statute. Only those individuals who have demonstrated that they meet those requirements can use the title protected by certification (e.g., psychologist). Another important thing to know about licensing is that professional licenses are issued by states. There is no federal license to practice psychology. Each state sets its own standard for licensure or certification.

The first certification law for psychologists went into effect in Connecticut in 1945. The law required that those wishing to use the title *psychologist* have a Ph.D. and one year of professional experience. Many other states sought to follow Connecticut's example in the late 1940s and 1950s. But certification and licensing legislation ran into tough resistance from the medical community in some states. The American Medical Association actively opposed licensing laws, conceding that certification may be acceptable, because physicians wished to prevent psychologists from practicing psychotherapy (Gerty, Holloway, & MacKay, 1952). Psychiatry acknowledged that some psychologists might be able to perform therapy under supervision in a medical setting, but warned that the public would be harmed if psychologists were allowed to provide psychotherapy in private practice.

Despite resistance from organized medicine, psychologists won a series of battles in state legislatures to obtain certification and licensing laws in the 1950s. During that decade Kentucky, Minnesota, New York, Maine, Washington, California, Florida, New Hampshire, and Maryland all passed certification laws, and Georgia and Tennessee passed licensure laws. In the subsequent two decades all states eventually passed either certification or licensing laws and many states were able to change the language of their laws from certification to licensure. In 1980, Missouri became the last state to license psychologists.

The passage of licensing laws was an important stepping stone for professional psychology, paving the way for other legal victories. Perhaps one of the most important was psychologists' fight to obtain payment for their services from medical insurers. In the 1970s, psychologists won important legal suits against insurance companies (e.g., *Blueshield of Virgina v. McCready* and *Wyatt v. Strickney*). In these cases, the courts held that patients should have the freedom to choose among mental health professionals who provided the same services (e.g., psychotherapy). Therefore, other mental health professionals, in addition to psychiatrists, should be eligible for third-party payment for their services. The fight for access to third-party payors continued through the 1980s. However, by the close of that decade clinical psychologists could receive reimbursement for their services from all the major insurance providers, including the federal programs (e.g., Medicaid, Medicare).

Another area in which psychologists have fought for and won expanded practice opportunities has been gaining so-called *hospital privileges*. This means that psychologists in many states can admit a patient to a hospital and provide treatment to the patient while he or she is hospitalized without arranging for supervision from a physician. Once again, it was organized medicine, most strongly psychiatry, that fought against hospital privileges for psychologists. In 1990 an important legal case was settled in California *(CAPP v. Rank)* that upheld psychologists' rights to hospital privileges. Currently, about fifteen states have passed legislation allowing psychologists hospital privileges.

The battles won in the 1970s and 1980s created unprecedented opportunities for psychologists in private practice. These opportunities, along with the unbridled expansion of training programs (see Robiner, 1991), resulted in spectacular growth in private-practice psychologists. In 1974 there were 20,000 psychologists licensed to practice. By 1990, that number had increased to 63,000—a 300 percent increase over fifteen years (Shapiro & Wiggins, 1994). Since the early 1990s, however, the unprecedented growth in opportunities for private practice psychologists has slowed due to changes in the way health care is delivered and paid for in the United States.

The health-care system in the United States was traditionally set up as a fee-for-service system. That is, a service (e.g., setting a broken bone) cost a certain amount (determined by the provider) and the patient receiving the service paid for it. People bought health insurance, or the insurance was provided by an employer or the government, to cover all or some portion of the services provided. The insurer would pay the actual cost of the service. Psychologists providing psychotherapy services, for example, charged their clients for the service (e.g., $90 for one hour of psychotherapy). Insured clients either paid the psychologist directly and then submitted their receipts to the insurance company for reimbursement, or paid the psychologists a portion of the fee and the psychologists billed the insurance company directly for the rest. Under this system, the health-care providers set their fees and determined what treatments were needed. Under this system, psychologists had maximum autonomy.

The fee-for-service system was good for health-care providers and good for most patients. Unfortunately, it was also extremely expensive and the rate of increase in health-care costs far outstripped the rate of inflation. For example, in 1954 health-care expenditure in the United States was about $12.7 billion, or about 4.4 percent of the gross national product (GNP). By 1994, expenditure on health care had reached $1 trillion, or about 13 percent of the GNP (McGrew, Glueckauf, Bond, & Frank, 1996). Concern about this growth led to calls for reform of the health-care system. While the government was not successful in reforming the way health care is delivered in the United States, the health-care insurance industry has reformed the way health care is reimbursed. The changes brought by the insurance industry have dramatically changed the way psychologists practice. In 1985, 80 percent of health-care plans were traditional fee-for-service; by 1995 only 20 percent followed the traditional model (Resnick, 1997).

Most private-practice psychologists now work within some form of *managed care*. Managed care refers to a variety of systems within which health-care providers provide services that are overseen (or managed) by the third-party payer or a company hired by the insurance company (for a more thorough discussion of the definition of managed health care see Bobbit, Marques, & Trout, 1998). In a prototypical managed-care system, psychologists must have their credentials reviewed by the managed-care company in order to be designated as a provider. The psychologist contracts with the managed-care company to provide services to people whose insurance benefits are managed by that company. The fee for specific services is set by the managed-care company, as is the number of sessions for which the psychologist will be reimbursed. Psychologists seeing clients for psychotherapy must have their treatment plans approved by the managed-care company. The number of psychotherapy session for which the client has approval is set. If the psychologist believes that additional sessions are necessary, he or she must petition the managed-care company for approval.

As you might have guessed, clinical psychologists bristle under managed-care systems and for most private practice psychologists, managed care is a four-letter word. Several surveys have found that most practicing psychologists feel that managed care has had a negative impact upon their work (Phelps, 1996; Tucker & Lubin, 1994). Psychologists' complaints are many (see, for example, Austad, Hunter, & Morgan, 1998). Concerns about the continuity of care have been expressed by many psychologists, including the ethical dilemma they face when the managed-care company refuses to approve services deemed necessary by the clinician. Others have voiced concern about the intrusion of the managed-care company into the psychotherapy relationship (Fox, 1995). Therapists must share personal information about their clients in order to obtain approval for services. Managed care clearly favors short-term psychotherapy over traditional long-term insight-oriented psychotherapy, which upsets proponents of the latter (Pipal, 1995). Within managed health care, practice guidelines are used to evaluate the appropriateness of clinicians' treatment plans. Some critics of practice guidelines have argued that these limit the autonomy and stifle the creativity of clinicians. Others have argued that practice guidelines are often determined by political forces rather than scientific evidence (Jacobson & Hollon, 1996). Finally, many psychologists complain of being swamped by paperwork created by the managed-care system. There are lengthy applications to be designated as a provider, treatment plans for each new client, and forms for requesting additional sessions.

In the short term, the impact that the managed-care revolution has had on psychological practice has been profound. Many psychologists are leaving private practice and seeking other avenues of employment. Others are shifting the focus of their practices to areas such as forensic psychology, neuropsychology, or business consultation in order to escape the burden managed care has placed upon psychotherapy practice. Still others are limiting their psychotherapy practices only to those clients who can afford to pay for therapy themselves.

By and large, professional psychology has taken an adversarial stance against managed care (e.g., Fox, 1995). Some psychologists have brought suit against managed-care companies, as have some clients who believe they were denied services unfairly. If successful, these types of suits may limit the intrusiveness of some managed-care practices but are not likely to make the beast go away. Several commentators have warned that psychologists need to learn to play ball within the managed-care environment or get out of the game. They argue for the acceptance of managed care as a reality (Kiesler & Morton, 1988; Hayes, 1996). However, rather than forecast the consequent destruction of professional psychology, some see in managed care exciting opportunities for scientifically minded psychologists (e.g., Hayes, 1996; Strosahl, 1994). Managed care forces practitioners to justify their treatment plans and to demonstrate that what they do is effective. Managed care has spurred the identification and use of treatments that have empirical support (Barlow, 1996; Rehm, 1997). The long-term impact managed care will have upon professional psychology has yet to be determined.

Specialization

The first generations of clinical psychologists were considered to be trained in the specialty area of clinical psychology after completing their doctoral degrees (Wiens, 1993). As specialists, one might expect that clinical psychologists would have mastery of the knowledge in their discipline. It is self-evident, however, that with the rapid growth of the discipline no one person can truly master all of the knowledge in clinical psychology. By the close of the 1980s, APA's Division of Clinical Psychology and the Council of University Directors of Clinical Psychology proposed that clinical psychology is a field rather than a discipline (Resnick, 1991). While this change in definition might seem a trivial semantic exercise, it acknowledged the growing need for specialization for professional practice as well as scholarly research. With the new definition, training in clinical psychology is viewed as laying the foundation upon which mastery of specialty knowledge is built.

Evidence for the specialization of clinical psychology can be seen in the professional organizations representing the field. The growing number of divisions within APA attests to the increasing specialization of the field. There are currently 53 divisions, fully 20 of which are clearly related to clinical psychology (e.g., 22, Rehabilitation Psychology; 29, Psychotherapy; 40, Clinical Neuropsychology; 53, Clinical Child Psychology). Division 12 (Division of Clinical) was formed to give clinical psychologists a professional home within APA. The increased diversity of clinical psychology is evident in the current organization of Division 12. Renamed the Society of Clinical Psychology in 1999, the division currently has six sections for clinical psychologists who share various interests (see Table 2.2). The

TABLE 2.2   Sections of the Society for Clinical Psychology

Section II	Clinical Geropsychology
Section III	The Society for a Science of Clinical Psychology
Section IV	Clinical Psychology of Women
Section VI	Clinical Psychology of Ethnic Minorities
Section VII	Emergencies and Crises
Section VIII	Association of Medical School Psychologists

Note: Sections I (Clinical Child Psychology) and V (Society of Pediatric Psychology) left Division 12 to form their own Divisions (53, Clinical Child Psychology, and 54, Society of Pediatric Psychology).

twelve different ABPP certifications available to clinical psychologists further reflects the field diversification (see Table 1.4).

The trend toward increased specialization within clinical psychology is likely to continue and will place strain upon the discipline. Some graduate programs already offer doctoral-level training with emphasis upon one or more areas of specialization such as health psychology, clinical neuropsychology, or forensic psychology. Some observers of the field see specialization as more appropriately conducted after the doctorate has been earned through designated post-doctoral training programs (Wiens, 1993). This model is more akin to traditional training of physicians who obtain their medical degrees over four years of general training and only specialize after receiving their M.D. In addition to implications for training, there are several other issues that increasing specialization is presenting to the field: (1) As the number of clinical psychologists aligning themselves with specific specialty areas increases, the connections between the specialty and the broader field are likely to fray. (2) Practice issues will need to be worked out as well. For example, will only those clinical psychologists who seek certification in clinical neuropsychology be allowed to conduct neuropsychological evaluations, or will clinical psychologists with adequate training in neuropsychological assessment still be able to do this type of work without certification in neuropsychology? (3) Will the standard of care for psychologists who specialize be higher than that of generally trained psychologists? Regardless of whether psychologists seek certification in specialty areas, in contemporary clinical practice all psychologists must define their areas of competence. It is no longer acceptable to view oneself as a general clinical psychologist who is competent to work with any problem that comes through the door.

Growth

In the first decade of the twenty-first century, most Americans probably equate *psychology* with *clinical psychology*. Many college students taking their first introduction to psychology course are surprised to hear the field defined as a scientific discipline and disappointed that the course includes minimal coverage of counseling or psychotherapy. This association of the broader field with clinical psychology is not surprising, given that for many people their only exposure to psychology is through the mass media. But the association of psychology with clinical psychology cannot be blamed entirely on the media. The reality is that in the United States, clinical psychology has grown to become the largest discipline within psychology and one of the largest providers of mental health services.

One indicator of the growth of clinical psychology is the increase in number of training opportunities available for students interested in the field. In 1969 there were 70 APA-approved doctoral training programs. By 1979 there were over 100. In 1989 the number had grown to 157 and by 1999 there were over 200 (including programs offering combined training in clinical/counseling or clinical/school). The number of non-APA-accredited programs is harder to estimate, but there are substantial numbers of these as well. For example in 1989, there were 45 professional programs in clinical psychology, of which only 22 were APA accredited (Reisman, 1991). Many of these nonaccredited programs produce large graduating classes annually. While prior to 1940 over 70 percent of Ph.D.s in psychology were in the experimental area, by the mid-1980s over 50 percent of the doctoral degrees in psychology were awarded in clinical and that percentage has continued to grow (Reisman, 1991).

The ascendance of clinical psychology can also be seen in the makeup and governance of the APA. In 1999, over 50 percent of APA members identified themselves as clinical psychologists. The APA, which at the turn of the twentieth century was a small organization of academic psychologists that required proof of scholarly work for membership, had, by the turn of the twenty-first century, become a professional guild that devotes a large portion of its resources to supporting the practice of psychology. Although APA continues to support scientific psychology (e.g., its journals are among the best in any area of psychology), during the second half of the organization's life it has been increasingly dominated by clinical interests. Clearly reflective of this shift toward clinical psychology is the background of the APA presidents. In the 1980s five of the ten APA presidents were clinical psychologists. Of the ten people who served as president in the 1990s, nine were clinical psychologists and the tenth, Frank Farley, had published in a variety of areas, including clinical. Perhaps even more indicative of the change in the organization was the election of the first non-Ph.D. psychologist to the presidency of APA. Dorothy Cantor, Psy.D., served as the organization's president in 1996.

Understandably, the shift in APA priorities toward practice left many academic and research psychologists feeling alienated. Numerous psychologists who viewed themselves as "pure" scientists felt alienated in APA. In 1988, a plan to reorganize APA was put to a vote. The plan called for a restructuring into separate assemblies of academic and nonacademic psychologists. It was hoped that by separating the organization into two bodies with different dues, it would address the concerns of academic psychologists who resented having their dues used to promote practice issues. The reorganization plan was rejected by the membership and immediately thereafter a group of psychologists interested in an organization devoted exclusively to scientific psychology formed the American Psychological Society (APS). The founding members of APS consisted of 22 former APA presidents and about 400 other distinguished scientific psychologists. Formed in August 1988, within six months APS had 5,000 members. By 2001, membership had reached about 15,000.

APS does not limit membership to psychologists holding academic positions, nor does it exclude APA members. The society's mission is "To promote, protect, and advance the interests of scientifically oriented psychology in research, application, and improvement of

BOX 2.2

Focus on Ethics: The APA Ethics Code

The explication of a code of ethics is a milestone in the development of any profession. A code of ethical standards is an implied social contract between the profession and the public (Koocher & Keith-Spiegal, 1998). The stated objectives of the ethics codes of most professions share similar themes: to promote welfare and avoid exploitation of consumers, to maintain competence and act responsibly, and to uphold the integrity of the profession. In practice, ethics codes function to protect the public and to protect the profession. The former is usually explicitly stated but the latter is often the primary motivator behind the development of ethical guidelines. Fortunately, in most cases, ethical standards usually serve both functions simultaneously. By protecting the public against unscrupulous behavior by its members, a profession also protects its credibility. The following history of the American Psychological Association's ethics code is adapted from Canter, Bennett, Jones, and Nagy (1994).

Although the American Psychological Association did not create its first ethics code until 1952, it created its first committee for dealing with ethical issues in 1938. The Committee on Scientific and Professional Ethics (CSPE) was formed that year and one of its recommendations was that the association create a continuing committee (the CSPE was a temporary entity) to "investigate complaints of unethical conduct . . . and to formulate from time to time rules or principles of ethics for adoption by the Association" (Olson, 1940, p.721, cited in Canter et al., 1994). For over ten years the committee advised members and dealt with ethical complaints without any authoritative set of principles to guide it.

The first Committee on the Ethical Standards for Psychologists was formed in 1947 and was chaired by the eminent learning theorist Edward C. Tolman. True to psychology's principles as an empirical science, the committee gathered data from the APA membership (there were about 7,500 members at that time) on ethical situations and dilemmas. They collected over 1,000 responses to their request for members "to describe a situation they knew of first-hand, in which a psychologist made a decision having ethical implications, and to indicate . . . the ethical issues involved" (APA, 1953, p. vi, cited in Canter et al., 1994). Using this "critical-incident" method, the committee derived a set of ethical principles that was adopted by the organization in 1952 and published in 1953. The original document was 171 pages and included 162 "principles" and 148 "subprincipless," each of which was accompanied by an example ethical situation from the membership survey. Fortunately, a 19-page summary version was also published, *Ethical Standards of Psychologists: A Summary of Ethical Principles* (APA, 1953).

The APA ethical principles have gone through numerous revisions since the 1953 version. Revisions were adopted in 1958, 1962, 1965, 1972, 1977, 1979, 1981, 1989, 1992, and 2002. Some of these have been substantial modifications to their predecessors, while others represented relatively minor modifications. Why so many revisions? Many factors have created pressure to revise the ethics code: (1) The profession continues to grow and change and the code needs to change to accommodate new developments; (2) as committees apply the ethics code, they discover its flaws and weaknesses; and (3) legal challenges to the code have forced the profession to make certain modifications.

The most severe sanction that the APA can deliver against one of its members for violating the ethics code is expulsion from the organization. But membership in the American Psychological Association is voluntary and not required for the practice of psychology. Violation of the ethics code, however, can result in penalties much more severe than expulsion from APA. State licensing boards, state psychological associations, and other organizations have adopted the code. And violation of the ethics code can be used against psychologists in malpractice cases.

BOX **2.2** **Continued**

When the ethics code is used in legal proceedings, it is often scrutinized with particular care. In one legal case brought against a state licensing board *(White v. the North Carolina State Board of Examiners of Practicing Psychologists),* for example, the court ruled that the language in parts of APA's ethics code was too vague to be used to determine that a specific violation had occurred.

Each successive version of the Ethics Code was intended to avoid, or at least minimize, some of the problems encountered implementing its predecessor. For example, the 1992 version was the first to break the principles down into two major sections: General Principles and Code of Conduct. This clearly delineated aspirational parts of the document from the enforceable standards. The current version of the code followed this tradition and includes five General Principles and 89 specific standards, organized under ten headings. The latter are intended to be specific enough so that it is clear when a psychologist has run afoul of one or more. In reality, some standards are very specific (e.g., "Psychologists do not engage in sexual intimacies with students or supervisees who are in their department, agency or training center or over whom psychologists have or are likely to have evaluative authority."), while others include qualifiers (e.g., "A psychologist refrains from entering in a multiple relationship if the multiple relationship *could reasonably be expected* to impair the psychologist's objectivity, competence, or effectiveness . . ." [italics added]). The 2002 version of the *Ethical Principles and Code of Conduct* is reprinted in Appendix A.

The ethical standards is not the only document published by the APA concerned with ethical issues. The organization has produced guidelines in a variety areas that have relevance for ethical decision making and behavior. These include the *Guidelines for Providers of Psychological Services to Ethnic, Linguistic, and Culturally Diverse Populations* (APA, 1990), *Guidelines for Computer Based Tests and Interpretations* (APA, 1987b), *General Standards for Providers of Psychological Services* (APA, 1987a), *Standards for Educational and Psychological Testing* (1985), *Ethical Principles in the Conduct of Research with Human Participants* (1982), *Guidelines for Ethical Conduct in the Care and Use of Animals* (1986), *Guidelines for Child Custody Evaluations in Divorce* (APA, 1994), *Guidelines for Psychological Evaluations in Child Protective Matters* (APA, 1998) and *Guidelines for Psychotherapy with Lesbian, Gay, and Bisexual Clients* (APA, 2001).

human welfare." About 13 percent of APS membership consists of psychologists with clinical or other applied orientations.

Concluding Remarks

As clinical psychology has grown, it has diversified tremendously. The diversity of clinical psychologists' theoretical orientations, professional activities, and ideas about the definition and future of their field might be seen as a threat the unity of the discipline. Is there really a clinical psychology? Or are there multiple clinical psychologies? As this brief history of clinical psychology illustrates, unity has never been the field's strong suit. Rather, clinical psychology as we know it today is the product of many varied and often, clashing viewpoints. Consequently, the discipline is not a comfortable home for someone looking for structure and certitude. The issues the field is struggling with today (e.g., how to adapt to managed care, whether psychologists should pursue prescription privileges, what the relationship is between clinical psychology and the larger science of psychology) will shape what happens to the field in the years to come. But undoubtedly as those issues are resolved, new ones will develop. And the beat goes on.

3 Psychological Models in Clinical Psychology

The Role of Theoretical Models

We usually think of a *model* as an ideal pattern for some project, such as an architect's scaled-down mock-up of the design of a new shopping mall, or an attractive person's display of the latest fashion in cosmetics or clothing. A model can demonstrate how things work, such as a small-scale working replica of a steam engine, or how something is done, such as a therapist showing an anxious client how to deal safely and calmly with a phobic situation. Similarly, a *theoretical model* is a simplified pattern that shows how something might look or how a process might work. For example, in the early 1900s physicists described a theory of atomic structure—a positively charged nucleus surrounded by a system of electrons—that served as a model of the atom.

How Models Help

Like any other topic of study, psychology is a complex subject that would be difficult to grasp "all at once" without some guiding ideas or principles. Models can help by suggesting possible patterns for human experience and behavior, patterns that can be explored and studied until they outlive their usefulness or are replaced by other models. For example, in some cultures mental illness is thought to be caused by demonic possession. Accepting that model of abnormality can quickly suggest possible treatments, such as luring the offending spirit away from the person or driving it out through prayers or tortures. Another model that has been popular in clinical psychology is that of the "black box"—the view that instead of trying to find out what goes on inside someone, psychologically or biologically, we can make progress by looking for meaningful connections between stimulus "inputs" and response "outputs." Models like these can simplify the subject matter and suggest specific hypotheses for study, allowing us to focus our attention on the essentials.

Dangers of Models

One problem with adopting a theoretical model is that in the end it might prove unworkable, unhelpful, or just plain wrong. That might not be too bad—at least we would have advanced our understanding of what not to pursue—provided that we did not invest too much time and effort in testing the model. Staying with an unworkable model diverts our attention from more worthwhile alternatives. For example, in the mid-1800s physicians and scientists were trying to understand the causes of syphilis, a chronic disorder leading eventually to a progressive deterioration in physical and cognitive functioning. But researchers made little progress until they arrived at the biological model of an infectious disease caused by a microorganism. The original model—tracing the paralysis and dementia associated with syphilis to environmental causes—produced some ludicrously inaccurate hypotheses, such as the idea that the disease was caused by soldiers' disappointment at military defeats in the Napoleonic Wars.

Studying genetics and pharmacology has advanced knowledge tremendously and has been responsible for major breakthroughs in mental health treatment in the last half century. But focusing exclusively on a biological model for mental disorders can be just as misleading as looking solely for environmental influences and psychological factors. Biological and behavioral (or psychological) processes not only co-exist; they operate in interaction to produce and maintain most mental disorders, requiring us to adopt a multidimensional approach (Barlow & Durand, 2002; Durand & Barlow, 2003; Kleinman, 1988).

Mental disorders have multiple causes and can be remedied by a variety of treatments, both biological and psychological. Finding significant genetic factors in a disorder does not necessarily mean that psychological treatment will not work, and finding psychological causes does not invalidate medical treatment, such as the use of medication (Gottesman, 1991). Statements like "Obsessive-compulsive disorder has been found to be a biologically based condition" provide convenient sound bites for the mass media, but make little sense to mental health professionals (Barlow & Durand, 2002).

Despite the enormous popularity in the news media of biological models of mental disorder, research data often show that psychological models have stronger scientific support. For example, Seligman (1998) reviewed a broad range of studies on biochemical and cognitive causes of depression, examining heritable mechanisms, laboratory analogues, longitudinal measurement, experimental manipulations, specific treatment ingredients, and global treatment effectiveness. He was surprised to find about twice as much scientific support for cognitive, rather than biochemical, causation. An exclusive focus on a single model could lead to inaccurate conclusions and distract attention from successful treatment modalities.

With these cautions about the dangers of one-dimensional models in mind, we will trace the theoretical foundations of clinical psychology by presenting the traditional approaches to psychopathology and mental health treatment in this chapter and the next. Because psychologists do not all agree upon one particular theoretical model, comprehensive coverage requires that we review several: psychoanalysis, interpersonal models, humanism, behaviorism, cognitive models (this chapter), and the biological bases of human behavior (Chapter 4).

Psychoanalysis

In the Western world, psychoanalysis was the traditional or "default" model of personality, psychopathology, and psychotherapy for at least the first half of the twentieth century. Practically every other technique and theory of mental health has a connection with psychoanalysis. In some cases, such as projective tests for personality assessment or interpersonal therapy to treat depression, the link is straightforward because very similar theoretical assumptions are made. In other cases, such as cognitive and behavioral treatment interventions, the link is indirect because behavior therapy was initially established as an alternative to psychoanalytic concepts and methods. Either way, psychoanalysis provided the impetus for the whole range of newer developments, and its significance for clinical psychology is undeniable.

Development

Sigmund Freud (1856–1939) developed psychoanalysis as (1) a theory of psychological development, personality, and neurosis; (2) a method for studying symbolic cognitive processes and the unconscious; and (3) a technique of psychotherapy. The story of Freud's own professional development as a physician specializing in neurology parallels the story of the original development of psychoanalysis.

Neuroses and Hysteria.   In the late 1800s European physicians were becoming very familiar with the *neuroses,* a group of disorders thought to have psychological origins. The best known of these was *hysteria,* a pattern of symptoms that appeared to be neurological but that made little sense medically. (The term *hysteria* is no longer used as a diagnosis since it derives from the ancient theory that attributed its cause to a wandering uterus!) Treating hysteria successfully eventually involved dealing with such subtle matters as buried emotions; mixed feelings; hidden wishes; suppressed anger; and thoughts, dreams, and images that turned out to be symbolic of patients' real issues. The study of hysteria in the late 1800s led directly to the development of psychoanalysis.

Mesmerism and Hypnotism.   Many years before Freud, the Austrian physician Franz Anton Mesmer (1734–1815) was devising treatments for hysteria using electricity and magnetism. He moved to Paris in 1778 and practiced what became known as *mesmerism* in luxurious surroundings with a wealthy, fashionable clientele. In his salon clients formed a circle around a copper bath and dipped iron rods into magnetized water, making a vital connection with the stars and planets. Mesmer would touch the clients one by one with a magnetized wand, gazing steadily into their eyes to establish *rapport,* a special, trusting relationship. Gradually becoming restless, then agitated, then convulsive, each client would experience a *grand crisis* of the nervous system, a finale that guaranteed cure (Bromberg, 1975; Zilboorg & Henry, 1941).

Mesmer was eventually discredited as a fraud, but some practitioners, continuing to use a form of his technique, put their patients into trances for therapeutic purposes. One successful application was in producing anesthesia during surgical operations. The technique became known as *hypnotism,* eventually thought to work not by magnetism, electricity, or the alignment of the planets, but by mobilizing patients' expectations, beliefs, or suggestibility. Hypnotism also produced an extraordinary revival of long-forgotten memories (Bromberg, 1975).

The Parisian neurologist Jean Martin Charcot (1825–1893) began to study hypnotism scientifically in 1875. He believed that the only people who could be hypnotized were patients with hysteria, so studying one meant studying the other. At the time most physicians dismissed patients with hysteria as deliberate fakers and malingerers, but Charcot took it seriously and attributed the disorder to psychological trauma. By conducting objective neurological examinations of people under hypnosis, Charcot showed that subjects' reactions could not be the result of conscious deception (Zilboorg & Henry, 1941).

Impressed by Charcot's pioneering research, Sigmund Freud obtained a traveling fellowship and studied with him in Paris (Ryckman, 2000). Influenced by his observations of Charcot and by the work of Josef Breuer in Vienna, Freud experimented with hypnosis as a therapeutic technique after his return to Austria. Breuer had used hypnosis successfully to treat a young woman with a complex case of hysteria. This famous case of Anna O. (see Box 3.1) inspired Freud to begin his investigations into what ultimately became known as psychoanalysis.

Freud tried a series of techniques, and explored several theories about the therapeutic change process, before his approach crystallized into psychoanalysis. (These techniques and theories are described in detail in Chapter 11.) Rather than refining specific treatment strategies, Freud eventually focused on understanding the strong pressures that keep patients unaware of their real issues and safeguard neurotic symptoms from practically all efforts to remove them. His discovery of these forces of *repression* and *resistance* was vital to his new approach. Abandoning hypnosis, Freud recognized that the intense personal relationship between doctor and patient was far more important than the use of any particular technique. He recognized this "new situation" by calling his method *psychoanalysis* (Freud, 1925/1989).

BOX 3.1

The Case of Anna O.

"Anna O." was really Bertha Pappenheim, an intelligent and well-educated young woman who became the first German social worker and an influential feminist. While caring for her ailing father, she developed classic symptoms of hysteria, including paralysis, memory loss, deafness, and states of mental confusion. Her physician, Josef Breuer, found by chance that Anna's clouded states of consciousness cleared up when she expressed key emotions in words (Freud, 1925/1989). He followed up by hypnotizing her and asking her to tell him what was troubling her at that moment, a technique that successfully resolved her confusion and other symptoms.

For example, Anna had a strong aversion to drinking water. She had no idea where this came from, but the problem was intense enough to prevent her from drinking even when extremely thirsty. This was later traced to an incident in which she had seen a little dog drink from a glass. This had disgusted her so much at the time that she had somehow suppressed her memory of the incident. But when, during hypnosis, Anna recalled not only the incident but also the emotional reaction she had had at the time, her symptom was immediately relieved and she could drink water freely again. Jokingly, Anna called the new treatment "chimney-sweeping"; in serious conversation, she referred to it as "the talking cure" (Breuer, 1895/1989, p. 68; Breuer & Freud, 1895/1974).

Key Assumptions

The elements of Freudian theory form three intertwined strands. One of these is a *structural theory* of personality and the topography of the mind, a theory that postulates different mental structures to deal with different emotional and behavioral tasks. Another is a theory of human development stating that, early in life, individuals progress through a series of standard *psychosexual stages,* each marked by a sensual preoccupation with a particular part of the body coupled with the need to confront a certain challenging conflict. Finally, there is the all-pervading concept of the *unconscious,* the label for the hidden workings of dynamic mental processes, operating beyond our awareness, that cause most of our emotionally significant behavior. We'll present the structural and stage theories one at a time, then weave the strands together in a discussion of symptom formation and psychoanalytic case material.

Structure of the Personality

The Pleasure Principle.   Freud believed that the mind is energized by two basic instincts: a positive, life-giving force and a destructive, aggressive force. The life-giving force, Eros, has two components: self- preservation and sexuality. The energy of the sexual part is known as *libido*. The minds of newborn children have practically no structure initially, so infants tend to go directly into action to satisfy the demands of the instincts; the guiding principle is the *pleasure principle*. Simply stated, the motto is "If it feels good, do it!"

Primary Process.   Infants' thinking patterns are dominated by hallucinatory images, the type we are familiar with when we are daydreaming or dreaming. This form of cognition is known as *primary process,* a form of wishful thinking that coincides with the infant's difficulty in separating fantasy from reality. But even very young children soon realize the need to deal with the frustrations of reality. The pleasure principle is unrealistic because infants cannot always gratify their needs immediately. The child may feel extremely hungry, yet the parent still seems to take forever to take care of the feeding. Or the child may reach for an attractive object, but the parent communicates displeasure and rapidly places it out of reach. The child's own wants can even come into conflict, so that satisfying one impulse frustrates another. For example, a very young child cannot urinate and be dry at the same time (Karon & Widener, 1995). Children learn that, while the pleasure principle is fine when you can get away with it, it is unworkable as a general approach to life.

The Reality Principle and Secondary Process.   When children learn to make allowance for practical realities, they begin to operate according to the *reality principle*. Learning to deal with the world more realistically actually influences the development of the mind, which becomes differentiated into two structures, the *id* and the *ego*. The id is the original pleasure-seeking mind, driven by instincts, and the ego is the newer, realistic one, driven by the need to compromise with the demands, pressures, and frustrations imposed by the outside world. When some form of threat arises, the mind produces anxiety, which serves as a signal to the ego to deal effectively and practically with the problem (Farrell, 1981).

Consistent with the reality principle is the development of a more mature thinking style, *secondary process* thinking, that realistic, pragmatic, goal-oriented, rational cognitive activity that we associate with waking life in adulthood.

The Id, the Ego, and the Superego.   Freud wrote about different types of behavior (plea-sure-seeking versus realistic, for example) as if they are the product of different parts of the mind, a style that helps some readers and confuses others. He eventually called the original pleasure-seeking, instinct-driven part the "it," the realistic part the "me," and a third, the conscientious and value-driven part, the "over-me," using the everyday German words. It was the English translator who used the Greek and Latin forms *id, ego,* and *superego,* cre-ating further confusion for many students (Karon & Widener, 1995). In Freud's model, the *id* is a collection of unknown and uncontrollable unconscious mental forces. The *ego* is "a coherent organization of mental processes" associated with consciousness (Freud, 1923/1989, p. 630), but the ego is not the same thing as the conscious part of the mind. Part of the ego itself is unconscious—the part that operates the various defensive strategies that resist ther-apeutic progress and allow us to deceive ourselves about the real reasons for our behavior. The *superego* is an ideal ego that, as the conscience, exercises moral censorship on behavior. The superego contains the commands and prohibitions that we learn from parents, teachers, and others in authority during our childhood years. It both arises from, and allows resolu-tion of, the Oedipus complex that all humans have to negotiate at about the age of five (Far-rell, 1981; Freud, 1923/1989; Lapsley, 1994).

Stages of Psychosexual Development.   To Freud, an essential theme in the young child's psychological development is the growth of the sexual instinct, which is focused upon a particular part of the body, an *erotogenic zone,* from which the child derives pleasure and satisfaction. Which part of the body this is depends on the child's stage of psychosexual development. Like other stage theories, Freud's assumes that people progress through the same stages in the same order and at approximately the same pace.

The Oral Stage.   The first erotogenic zone is the mouth, and the first stage of psychosexual development is the *oral stage.* According to Freud, we pass through this stage during approx-imately the first 18 months of life. The newborn infant is already equipped with a sucking reflex that allows him or her to feed from the mother's breast or from the bottle, but the breast or the bottle are not always available. The resulting frustration is the first significant psychological challenge faced by the infant. Unusual difficulties in learning to deal with this form of frustration at this time of life could lead to an oral *fixation,* a form of "hangup" about feeding, causing difficulties later in life in any activity related to food, drink, or the mouth. Fixations could stem from encountering either too much or too little frustration in the oral stage. The child who is always fed as soon as the need arises is just as vulnerable to fixation as the child who experiences severe feeding deprivation; neither is able to learn to deal with an appropriate level of frustration. Unconsciously, the oral stage brings the hid-den threat of the loss of the parent who brings food.

The Anal Stage.   The second erotogenic zone in Freud's theory is the anus, and the second stage the *anal* (or anal-sadistic) *stage.* The challenge presented at this stage derives from adults' desire for the child to be toilet trained. We pass through this stage approximately between the ages of 18 months and 4 years. For the child, the conflicting tendencies are between being tidy, clean, dutiful, and cooperative versus being messy, rebellious, and unco-operative. Ideally, the adults caring for the young child will approach toilet training sensitively, presenting neither too great nor too small a challenge at each point. If fixation does occur at the anal stage, the child is vulnerable to developing certain extremes of personality that may be symbolically related to toileting behavior: uncooperative, mean, stingy, and emotionally constricted at one extreme; and generous, giving, careless, wasteful, and emotionally expressive at the other.

The Phallic Stage.   The third erotogenic zone is the genital area, but the third stage is not the genital but the *phallic* stage (Farrell, 1981). Freud believed that we pass through the phallic stage approximately between the ages of 4 and 6. At about the time that the ego separates from the id, infants direct their libido toward themselves, a time of *primary narcissism*. But the ego then begins to invest libidinal energy into other people and things, or rather into mental representations of them ("objects")—usually the mother's breast at first, then the mother (the word *object* refers to the internal image of the mother, not to the mother herself). The child's sexual interest in the mother becomes prominent in the phallic stage, and from this point the course of psychosexual development diverges for males and females (Farrell, 1981).

Take the example of Maria, a girl of about 5 years of age. According to the theory, on entering the phallic stage she develops an unconscious wish to give her mother a child, just as a boy of the same age would. But Maria comes to realize at some level that she has no penis, and holds her mother responsible for this. Rather than accepting this as a biological difference between females and males, the 5-year-old girl assumes that she once had a large penis but lost it through castration. The parallel situation in the male is fear that he will be castrated: "The girl accepts castration as an accomplished fact, whereas the boy fears the possibility of its occurrence" (Freud, 1924/1989, p. 665). The close relationship Maria had with her mother breaks down, and she turns to her father instead, wishing for a child from him—a child to take the place of a penis. According to Freud, Maria has developed "penis envy." Her mother is now a rival for the father, and Maria's Oedipus complex has begun. This is not easily resolved, and it can only be handled by a perpetual Oedipal attachment to her father (Farrell, 1981; Freud, 1923/1989).

As in the other stages, failure to negotiate the phallic stage successfully can lead to fixation. In this case, incomplete resolution of the frustrations involved can lead females and males to have difficulties with rivalry or competitiveness in adult life, and, more important, problems in the development of the superego. Freud believed that males develop stronger superegos than females because of the different challenges posed to them by the Oedipus complex (Farrell, 1981). The case of Little Hans (see Box 3.2) illustrates Freud's exploration of the Oedipus complex of a 5-year-old boy with a phobia of horses.

The Latency Stage and the Genital Stage.   After progressing through the minefields of the first three stages of psychosexual development, children enter a period of relative psychosexual calm, the *latency stage,* in which the chief challenges faced are those presented by the changes of puberty and the need to adapt socially in the school years. After puberty comes the *genital stage* in the teenage years, in which young adults learn to focus their sexual interests upon another person.

The Defensive Strategies of the Ego.   The focus of psychoanalytic theory is upon the work of the ego in confronting the demands of the id, the superego, and external reality. In

BOX **3.2**

The Case of Little Hans

Hans, whose mother had been one of Freud's patients, suddenly developed an extreme fear of horses at the age of 5. Believing that only the father could persuade Hans to talk openly about his problems, Freud delivered his treatment through correspondence with the father, meeting Hans himself only once (Freud, 1909/1955).

Theoretically, Hans was progressing through the phallic, or Oedipal, stage of psychosexual development, unconsciously harboring sexual desires for his mother and wishing to possess her and displace his father, now a jealous rival. But great anxiety would have been aroused by the unconscious fear of castration by his father, so Hans would have found it necessary to abandon his sexual interest in his mother. The standard way to resolve this is through *repression,* but Hans's ego would not be strong enough yet. He could only obtain sufficient power by *identifying* with his father, thus incorporating some of his strength. Resolving the Oedipus complex in this way has a dramatic effect on mental development, even changing the structure of the mind itself so that the *superego,* containing many characteristics of the father, emerges from the ego (Lapsley, 1994).

In Freud's analysis, Hans's unconscious fear of his father had been displaced onto horses, so that a horse is a symbol for the father. Freud drew evidence from Hans's spontaneous comments, his reports of fleeting thoughts and fantasies, and his behavior.

Concerning Hans's feelings toward his mother: He asked her to touch his penis after a bath; he had a fantasy of seeing her naked; and he touched his genitals as he watched her. He said he and his mother had some imaginary children. He said he wanted to marry her and enjoyed accompanying her to the bathroom. He admitted to being jealous of his father (Conway, 1978; Freud, 1909/1955).

Concerning Hans's feelings toward his father: When playing (at horses!) in his room, Hans ran up to his father and bit him. Hans told his father he wanted him to "knock up against a stone and bleed, and then I'll be able to be alone with [Mommy] for a little bit" (Freud, 1909/1955, p. 82).

Concerning castration fears: Hans described a daydream: *"The plumber came; and first he took away my behind with a pair of pincers, and then gave me another, and then the same with my widdler* [penis]" (Freud, 1909/1955, p. 98, original emphasis).

Concerning the connection between the father and a horse: Hans compared his father's moustache with a black muzzle of the kind horses wear. Once, when the father was leaving the breakfast table, Hans said: "Daddy, don't trot away from me;" his father was struck by Hans's use of the word "trot" (Conway, 1978, p. 285).

Freud argued that the phobia served a purpose in addition to symbolizing an unconscious conflict. By avoiding horses, Hans had to avoid going outside at all (in 1908 most of the traffic in Vienna was horse-drawn), and this kept him at home close to his mother.

Freud's theorizing about the Little Hans case was strongly criticized by behavior therapists years later on the grounds that it was speculative and unscientific (Wolpe & Rachman, 1960). Nonetheless, psychoanalysts treasure this case history as a classic example of psychoanalytic interpretation that illustrates some of the principal themes in the Freudian approach to understanding neurotic disorders (Cheshire, 1979; Conway, 1978).

performing this often delicate balancing act, the ego has to make many compromises. Constant instinctual demands for food and sex must be attended to, but so must the dictates of practical reality and pressure from the conscience. The ego can deal with some of these conflicting demands only by resorting to certain defensive strategies that unconsciously either conceal the person's real wants or distort external reality (Cramer, 1994). Accordingly, psychoanalysts place great emphasis upon *psychic determinism,* the view that unconscious processes underlie all mental life and behavior, none of which—dreams, slips of the tongue, lapses of memory, mistakes—are accidental or insignificant (Farrell, 1981).

Defense Mechanisms.   The ego uses several strategies to protect the individual from excessive mental excitation. These strategies are the *defense mechanisms.* Anna Freud, Sigmund Freud's daughter, proposed that the defense mechanisms deflect potentially disturbing emotions arising either from the unconscious instincts of the id, or from external reality (Cramer, 1994). The best known defense mechanism is *repression,* the capacity for which develops very early in life during the oral stage. Take Farrell's (1981) example of a baby boy, Joe, whose mother has problems in breastfeeding him and handles the situation rather ineptly. Joe reacts badly to this frustration and becomes anxious about feeding. To protect Joe from being overwhelmed by this anxiety, the ego exerts energy to oppose the impulse responsible for the anxiety, the impulse to feed. The feeding impulse undergoes *primal repression,* and Joe appears to lose interest in feeding. Primal repression deals with the anxiety produced by the challenges in all the childhood stages of psychosexual development. But in older children and adults, repression is thought to work differently. When Joe as a young adult becomes interested in fondling and sucking the breasts of his sexual partner, anxiety may arise because the wish threatens to reactivate the feeding trauma of childhood. In response to the anxiety, the ego represses the wish, making it unconscious for Joe. Together with the wish to suck breasts, related wishes—to suck candy, chew gum, and the like—also get repressed, because they also have dangerous links to the feeding trauma and the ego therefore withdraws energy from them. Now, Joe has no idea that he really wishes to suck even candy, let alone someone's breasts. This is *repression* proper (Farrell, 1981).

In *regression,* a defense mechanism that plays an important role in psychoanalytic treatment, the individual falls back upon earlier routines when faced by a challenge. For example, regression occurs when the elementary school student, encountering a threat of some kind, starts thumb-sucking and playing the role of a preschooler; or when an older child reverts to wetting the bed when a baby brother or sister is born.

The other defense mechanisms include denial and projection (Cramer, 1994). *Denial* means disavowing the emotional significance of a potentially troubling event (not disavowing the event itself). For example, an office worker looks out of the window and sees that the adjacent building is on fire, then says to a co-worker, "Don't those flames look pretty against the sky!" In using denial, this person is not obscuring the existence of the fire, but its emotional significance—the possibility of injury or death to the occupants, or of distress to the onlookers. In *projection,* "the owner of an unacceptable thought or feeling projects the thought outward and attributes it to some other individual: The unacceptable thought 'I hate Tom' becomes 'Tom hates me'" (Cramer, 1994, p. 93). Projection is also used in unconsciously handling one's guilt over misbehavior by blaming another person for being the instigator.

Psychoanalysts believe that defense mechanisms are only partly successful. They hold dangerous impulses in check, but only at the expense of a great deal of mental energy. Excessive use of defenses in a rigid fashion is sometimes associated with psychopathology (repression may be correlated with hysteria, and projection with paranoia), but defenses can also be adaptive and promote healthy adjustment (Cramer, 1994; Farrell, 1981).

Psychoanalytic Theory of Symptom Formation.   The symptoms of a neurotic disorder are themselves a form of unconscious mental defense, and their pattern reflects possible psychosexual fixations as well as symbolizing the underlying conflict. For example, the development of a phobia (an unrealistic fear of a specific item or situation) would reflect the operation of subtle unconscious processes, requiring the interpretation of symptoms in terms of their symbolic meanings. Take the example of a young woman whose promising career in advertising is threatened by her newly acquired fear of heights. Given appropriate indications from the client's personal history, a psychoanalyst might hypothesize that the woman never satisfactorily resolved her Oedipal issues, and that any competitive successes in life would arouse unconscious fears of rivaling her mother. The client develops a fear of heights (as opposed to fears of snakes, darkness, or the number 13) because of a symbolic relationship to fears of going up in the world and also because the fear serves a purpose in preventing her from continuing the threatening rivalry: Someone with a fear of heights can hardly compete in a business world demanding daily exposure to air travel, express elevators, and high-rise buildings. To the psychoanalyst it would be irrelevant to try to help the client by giving her tranquilizers, or by helping her cope with elevators; the real issue is the unconscious Oedipal material on the theme of rivalry with a parent.

Influences on Clinical Psychology

Psychoanalysis has had a profound influence upon clinical psychology because it was the first systematized school of psychotherapy. Every form of psychotherapy today has *some* link with psychoanalysis, because even those that developed from contrasting theoretical assumptions were described by their authors as alternative approaches—and that meant spelling out how they differed from the Freudian approach. Psychoanalysis itself spawned several related methods that fall into the broad category of *psychodynamic* therapies. Carl Jung and Alfred Adler, both early associates of Freud, went on to develop their own distinctive models of psychopathology and psychotherapy, and these in turn inspired others to make further innovations. *Ego psychology, self psychology,* and *object relations theory* are examples of psychodynamic therapies that emerged in the 1930s and 1940s in Europe and the United States.

Psychoanalysis has influenced psychological assessment by alerting clinicians to the idea that much of human experience and behavior has hidden origins. Clinicians who use projective testing methods are influenced by psychoanalysis to probe for clients' unconscious defensive styles and cognitive content. Psychoanalysis has also inspired empirical research into psychological processes, although this is certainly not the area with which it is most closely identified. Laboratory experiments on animals in the 1940s and 1950s were often designed to test psychoanalytic hypotheses, such as the links between frustration and fixation (Yates, 1962) and between conflict and anxiety (Masserman, 1943).

Clinical psychologists who are drawn to the psychoanalytic model view what they do as similar to detective work. When clients consult psychologists for evaluation or psychotherapy things are not necessarily what they seem to be, and it can be intellectually exciting to discover hidden links that explain otherwise incomprehensible symptoms. For example, one of our colleagues mentioned a secretary who was having trouble typing certain letters on her keyboard. Drawing from his familiarity with keyboards and typing, he astounded the secretary by correctly surmising that she was having concerns about her marriage. The letters she could not type were on the keys normally struck by her ring finger. And a fellow student from college who went on to train at the Tavistock Clinic, a major psychoanalytic center in London, described working there with a young boy with fears of aggression. In therapy he drew detailed pictures in crayon of military vehicles, guns, and tanks, but they were only outlines—nothing was filled in. When the psychologist told the boy it was okay to feel and express his anger, he immediately started filling in the gun barrels with solid color.

By maintaining a careful, disciplined alertness to the details and nuances of clients' reported problems and manner of self-presentation, psychoanalytic psychologists can help their clients in a thoroughgoing and genuine way by developing hypotheses about their defensive styles, "blind spots" in their self-appraisals, or the "real" motives behind symptoms. When such clinical impressions converge to form a consistent picture, the psychoanalytic model allows psychologists to attain fundamental insights into the meanings underlying clinical phenomena, insights that proponents argue would be unattainable with other models.

Current Status

The psychoanalytic model remains popular with mental health professionals and has continued to capture the interest of philosophers, authors, and screen writers. Literary criticism was strongly influenced by psychoanalysis in the 1900s, and this now goes both ways—psychoanalytic theorists have also learned much from contemporary thought in the humanities (Messer & Wolitzky, 1997). As a result, students interested in psychoanalytic thought today can learn from experts in many academic departments on the typical college campus. It sounds like a joke, but sometimes when a student calls the psychology department for information on contemporary psychoanalysis, he or she is advised to check with the departments of philosophy, English, modern languages, or anthropology for more expert coverage.

Although the current classification manual for mental disorders in the United States (American Psychiatric Association, 1994) largely omits Freudian terms, psychoanalysis strongly influenced the categorization of many of the disorders recognized today. Many professionals believe it next to impossible to study personality and psychopathology without a solid understanding of the psychoanalytic model. Psychoanalytic concepts also underlie many approaches to psychological assessment, ranging from projective methods to questionnaire evaluations.

The most formal application of psychoanalytic theory, the system of psychotherapy known as *classical psychoanalysis,* is practiced with only a tiny minority of mental health clients because of its great demands on their time and their money (Barlow & Durand, 2002). But various less intensive forms of psychoanalytically oriented psychotherapy are widely practiced today (Auld & Hyman, 1991; Karon & Widener, 1995). Examples are *supportive-expressive psychotherapy* (Luborsky, 1984, 1997), *time-limited dynamic psychotherapy* (Binder, Strupp, & Henry, 1995; Levenson & Strupp, 1997), and *interpersonal therapy* (Klerman, Weissman, Rounsaville, & Chevron, 1984; Markowitz, 1998; Markowitz & Swartz, 1997).

Interpersonal Models

Interpersonal theory stems from the work of the American psychiatrist Harry Stack Sullivan, who emphasized the idea that "we come to treat ourselves as we have been treated by our parents" (Henry, 1997, p. 224). Early relationships and encounters with other people, *interpersonal transactions,* shape our view of ourselves and create behavioral tendencies that persist over the life span. Mental health problems such as depression, anxiety, somatoform disorders, and substance abuse can be seen as rooted in the patterns of early interpersonal relationships. At the same time, specific life events and current interpersonal issues are strongly linked to clients' present mood states. Learning to alter the interpersonal environment can help clients alleviate their symptoms and reduce excessive negative emotions (Markowitz & Swartz, 1997).

Development

The interpersonal models originated in the ideas of significant individuals who had begun their careers as psychoanalysts, but later rejected important aspects of Freudian theory in favor of a focus on clients' interpersonal functioning. Carl Jung and Alfred Adler are the best known of the early innovators who departed from Freud's views (their systems of psychotherapy are described in Chapter 11). Of these two, Adler is especially relevant to the interpersonal perspective.

Alfred Adler.   Alfred Adler (1870–1937) accepted Freud's psychodynamic theory and agreed with several specific hypotheses—that symptoms are purposeful, dreams are meaningful, and early childhood experiences are highly significant in personality development. But Adler rejected the stages of psychosexual development and the Oedipus complex, and stressed instead each individual's search for a positive role within the family, the prototype for all other social interactions. In the process we form conclusions that contain errors and partial truths together with accurate judgments. Everyone creates a *cognitive map* or lifestyle, an implicit set of convictions that serve as guides for dealing with other people. These convictions include the *self-concept* (the sense of who one is); the *self-ideal* (the sense of who one should be); the *world-concept* (the sense of what the natural and social world demands); and the *ethical convictions* (the sense of what is right and wrong). Discrepancies between self-concept and self-ideal may result in inferiority feelings that could expand into the pathological *inferiority complex* (Mosak, 1995; Ryckman, 2000). Therefore, rather than viewing repressed sexuality as fundamental, Adler stressed a social view of neuroses. Being preoccupied with feelings of inferiority to others is debilitating, but constructive engagement in interpersonal relationships is the key to a creative and fulfilling life (Bloch, 1982; Mosak, 1995).

U.S. versions of psychoanalysis developed after Freud's lectures at Clark University in Worcester, Massachusetts, in 1909. In the following decades many prominent psychoanalysts left continental Europe for the United Kingdom and the United States to escape the threat of Nazi persecution, and some of them made revisions to the psychoanalytic theory of personality to accommodate the experiences of immigrants adjusting to life in a new country. Others followed Adler by rejecting the theory of infantile sexuality and emphasizing social interaction. Yet others focused on the ultimate significance of early, pre-Oedipal parent-child interactions. The terms used to describe these new approaches include ego psychology, object relations, and the *cultural school* of psychoanalysis; *neo-Freudians* was the label both for the innovators in general and for the specific subgroup who gave prominence to interpersonal relationships in personality, psychopathology, and psychotherapy (Arlow, 1995; Auld & Hyman, 1991). Erich Fromm, Karen Horney, and Harry Stack Sullivan represent the Adler-like neo-Freudians who rejected the libido theory and stressed the importance of interpersonal issues (Bloch, 1982; Ehrenwald, 1976; Farrell, 1981; Walker, 1959).

Erich Fromm.   Erich Fromm (1900–1980) was born in Germany and earned a doctorate in sociology in Heidelberg in 1922. He trained with prominent Freudians such as Karl Abraham, who had made important contributions to the psychoanalytic theory of depression. Fromm later disagreed with traditional psychoanalytic views on sexuality and aggression. Freud believed that in return for the advantages of living in a civilized society we have to restrict our personal freedom, making it necessary to repress our instinctive urges. Fromm was more optimistic, viewing aggression as caused by the frustrations of living in human society, not by an automatic, innate drive. Similarly, he explained the sense of inferiority experienced by many women in terms of how they were treated in contemporary society. Fromm emigrated to the United States in the early 1930s at a time when a significant number of Americans were immigrants or the children of immigrants. Observing that so many people were successfully facing the tasks and challenges of adapting to a new culture, Fromm and other neo-Freudians turned away from inborn instincts as primary explanations of human behavior and toward socialization and acculturation processes (Ryckman, 2000; Walker, 1959).

Karen Horney.   Karen Horney (1885–1952), a German physician who had been analyzed by Karl Abraham, emigrated to the United States in the 1930s. Recognizing that what is "normal" in one culture may be seen as abnormal in another, she emphasized cultural rather than biological factors in human development, especially concerning gender differences. She believed that children begin life with basic anxiety, but it can be overcome with appropriate nurturing from parents or other caregivers. Children who have been deprived of this vital parental love develop low self-esteem and patterns of impairment in social relationships. We can try to deal with our basic anxiety by our orientation with regard to other people; we can move *toward, against,* or *away from* others. People with neuroses tend to have inflexible attitudes and behavior, and fail to develop their potential because of inner conflict (Bloch, 1982; Ryckman, 2000).

Harry Stack Sullivan.   Harry Stack Sullivan (1892–1949) was born in the United States and became known as the founder of the *Washington school* of psychiatry, in addition to having been a prominent figure in the cultural school (Ehrenwald, 1976). Like Fromm and Horney, Sullivan focused on clients' interpersonal functioning and saw the psychotherapist as a participant observer of human communication, interaction, and relationships. He viewed personality as the enduring pattern of social interactions. The self consists of the *reflected appraisals* of parent figures and other significant adults. If parents are excessively critical of their children, the children grow up to criticize themselves and thereby live with anxiety. If parents are loving toward their children, children grow up capable of "love, fellowship and good social adjustment in general" (Ehrenwald, 1976, p. 304). Sullivan was optimistic about the treatment of inpatients with schizophrenia and other psychoses, and he made positive contributions in that area.

Interpersonal Psychotherapy.   The most recent development from the interpersonal perspective has been *interpersonal psychotherapy,* an intervention devised in the 1970s specifically for the treatment of depression (Klerman, Weissman, Rounsaville, & Chevron, 1984; Weissman & Paykel, 1974). Interpersonal psychotherapy began as a research intervention and has become an accepted time-limited treatment protocol (Weissman & Markowitz, 1998), detailed further in Chapter 11.

Key Assumptions

In the 1940s, the assumptions of the interpersonal model were that assessment and psychotherapy make more sense when they focus on clients' past and current social relationships than when they aim at gaining insight into psychosexual stages, repressed instincts, and the Oedipus complex. By the 1960s, the introduction of the major tranquilizers had made community treatment a possibility for many people with chronic mental illness. That in turn increased professionals' awareness that mental disorders occur within a social system, and that family life, friendships, and work influence clients' well-being and need to be taken into account in treatment. This also implied going beyond the traditional approach of diagnosing specific symptoms, and adding the important dimension of assessing clients' *social adjustment* (Weissman & Paykel, 1974).

The interpersonal model also focuses on the social roles taken by the individual in close relationships. Key social roles are those of parent, child, sibling, and spouse, and also important are the roles of friend, neighbor, and co-worker. The link with mental disorders goes both ways: Problems in social roles can contribute to psychopathology, and the presence of a disorder can impair social functioning (Klerman et al., 1984).

Clinicians using the model of interpersonal psychotherapy draw concepts from Sullivan and others from the interpersonal school, but do not commit themselves to any particular assumptions about the etiology of disorders. Interpersonal problems occurring at the time of onset of a depressive disorder are viewed as a pragmatic treatment focus. Rather than dealing with the client's lasting personality characteristics, interpersonal psychotherapists deal with current social functioning and direct treatment toward dysfunctional relationships associated with the present depressive episode (Weissman & Markowitz, 1998).

Influences on Clinical Psychology

The interpersonal model has been influential in bringing clinical psychologists into contact with social psychiatry. By focusing on interpersonal relationships, Harry Stack Sullivan, Gerald Klerman, and other psychiatrists have established an image of psychiatry different from the traditional *medical model* of symptoms and diseases. By rejecting the Freudian theory of instinctual drives, mental health professionals following the interpersonal model show that one may adopt a psychodynamic orientation without accepting traditional psychoanalysis. By playing a central role in well-controlled research on interpersonal psychotherapy for depression, Myrna Weissman, Ellen Frank, and other psychologists have helped establish an empirically supported intervention drawn from psychodynamic theories and traditions.

Current Status

Interpersonal psychotherapy is the most obvious achievement of contemporary interpersonal models. Typically, psychodynamic clinicians have been less interested in quantitative research than psychologists in more experimental areas, but interpersonal therapy has been evaluated in controlled studies in recent years and the findings have been positive (Spanier & Frank, 1998). Interpersonal psychotherapy is accepted as an empirically supported intervention of proven efficacy for depression (DeRubeis & Crits-Christoff, 1998), and studies in the 1980s and 1990s have also demonstrated its value in the treatment of bulimia nervosa (Fairburn, 1998).

Humanism

The humanistic model is strongly tied to psychotherapy approaches that emphasize people's inborn potential for positive and healthy development. This form of humanism, a model of personality, psychopathology, and psychotherapy, has its scholarly origins in existential philosophy. Existentialists reject the idea that we are largely controlled by biological, intrapsychic, and social forces, stressing instead our innate freedom to choose and act. To existentialists, freedom is inseparable from responsibility—the idea that we can and should accept the consequences of our free choices, whether they work out well or poorly. Above all, existentialists and humanists value living in, and being intensely aware of, the present moment, as opposed to worrying about the future or ruminating about past mistakes. This present-centered focus—tuning in to our here-and-now experience of living—automatically confronts us with the unavoidable matter of our eventual death. Coming to terms with our mortality, and thus healthily confronting angst or existential anxiety, is the key to healthy development and a fulfilling life.

Development

Humanistic versions of psychotherapy began to arise as rivals to psychoanalysis in the United States and Europe in the 1940s. Humanism is usually discussed in connection with experiential therapies that emphasize the process, rather than the content, of psychotherapy sessions. Humanistic therapists do not structure their interventions around techniques or control the content of therapy sessions, because central to the model is the ideal of making our own choices, as opposed to slavishly following someone else's ideas about what we should do.

The development of the humanistic model in mental health work began with a group of European existential analysts who broke away from Freudian psychoanalysis in the 1940s and 1950s. They included psychiatrists who had been trained in psychoanalysis, yet resisted its central assumption that human experience and behavior are governed and determined by internal forces foreign to our conscious experience. Instead, they embraced existentialism and stressed the importance of our direct, conscious experience of the world at the present moment.

One of the best-known existential analysts was Ludwig Binswanger (1881–1966). He earned his medical degree from the University of Zurich and studied psychiatry with Eugen Bleuler and Carl Jung, themselves early psychoanalysts who later parted company with Freud. Binswanger came to believe that to understand an individual fully it is essential to explore three separate *modes of existence:* the *world around us,* the world of things and events; the *world with us,* the world of interactions with other people; and our *own world,* the world of one's private, inner, subjective experience (Hergenhahn, 1992).

Existential Analysis.   The modes of existence described by Binswanger form the all-important *worldview,* the general perspective by means of which we live our lives as individuals. Existential analysts believe that neuroses or mental disorders result from negative or narrowly conceived worldviews or *designs.* For example, one patient's design centered on the vital importance of continuity:

> Any disruption of continuity—a gap, tearing, or separating—produced great anxiety. One time she fainted when the heel of her shoe fell off. Separation from the mother also evoked anxiety. . . . Holding onto mother meant holding onto the world; losing her meant falling into the dreadful abyss of nothingness. (Hergenhahn, 1992, p. 505)

Client-Centered Therapy.   The most significant development in the United States for the humanistic model was the introduction of *client-centered therapy* in 1940 by Carl Ransom Rogers (1902–1987). His central hypothesis about psychotherapy was that "a self-directed growth process would follow the provision and reception of a particular kind of relationship characterized by genuineness, non-judgmental caring, and empathy" (Raskin & Rogers, 1989, p. 155). Rogers's approach, also known later as *person-centered therapy,* stemmed from humanistic psychology, which was influenced by Alfred Adler but developed most directly from the work of Abraham Maslow (see Box 3.3).

Carl Rogers was born in a Chicago suburb to parents who were religious fundamentalists. He was socially isolated in childhood. When he was 12 the family moved to a farm west of Chicago, where his father aimed to extend his civil engineering expertise to scientific farming. Rogers took a great interest in the work of the farm and became an agriculture major at the University of Wisconsin, where he was active in Christian associations and considered training for the ministry. He changed majors to history and graduated in 1924,

BOX **3.3**

Abraham Maslow (1908–1970)

Maslow initially endorsed behaviorism and had trained with the pioneer experimental psychologists Edward Titchener, Harry Harlow, and Edward Thorndike, but he came to reject scientific psychology for reducing people entirely to their habits and cognitive structures while ignoring their poetic, romantic, and spiritual aspects.

> Maslow's point was not that psychology should stop attempting to be scientific or stop studying and attempting to help those with psychological problems but that such endeavors tell only part of the story. Beyond this, psychology needs to attempt to understand humans who are in the process of reaching their full potential. (Hergenhahn, 1992, p. 511)

Maslow proposed that there is a hierarchy of human needs, the lowest of which—food, shelter, and sex, for example—are shared with other animals, and the highest of which are uniquely human: the *esteem needs,* such as the need to contribute to human well-being. Having reached the level of esteem, one is in a position to progress to *self-actualization,* reaching one's full creative potential.

then moved to New York to attend Union Theological Seminary, where he took several psychology courses. After two years, he switched to Teachers' College at Columbia University, where he studied testing, measurement, diagnostic interviewing, and interpretive treatment. He completed an internship at The Institute for Child Guidance, a psychoanalytically oriented agency, where he learned projective testing and detailed history-taking. Rogers then worked for twelve years at a Rochester, New York, child-guidance center as an administrator and psychologist (Hergenhahn, 1992; Raskin & Rogers, 1989).

After taking an academic position at Ohio State University, Rogers introduced *client-centered therapy* on December 11, 1940, in a paper titled "Some Newer Concepts in Psychotherapy." In this presentation to the Psi Chi chapter at the University of Minnesota he argued that clients move toward independence and insight when the counselor avoids advice and interpretation and, instead, consistently recognizes and accepts clients' feelings. The book *Counseling and Psychotherapy,* an expansion of his talk, contained a lengthy transcript of a series of therapy sessions. Arguably, the field of psychotherapy research began in 1943 with a dissertation investigating Rogers's method (Cain, 2002; Raskin & Rogers, 1989).

For twelve years Rogers was professor and head of the counseling center at the University of Chicago. In 1957 he published a classic paper in which he argued that genuineness, unconditional positive regard, and empathy are the three essential therapist-offered conditions for psychotherapeutic change. He moved to the University of Wisconsin in 1957, where he conducted an ambitious study of schizophrenia, and to La Jolla, California, in 1964.

Key Assumptions

Humanists and existentialists focus upon:

- Our direct, conscious experience of the world as it seems to us as individuals.
- The need for each individual to confront the inevitability of death and thus to live more fully in the present.
- The fact that making choices and taking responsibility for them are inescapable.
- The ultimate importance of personal freedom and our search, as individuals, for meaning in life.

The central idea is to accept the unique viewpoint of the individual, fully understanding this *phenomenological world* as it seems to him or her:

> *The human world is the structure of meaningful relationships in which a person exists and in the design of which, generally without realizing it, he or she participates.* That is, the same past or present circumstances can mean very different things to different people. . . . For to be aware of one's world means at the same time to be designing it, *constituting* one's world. (May & Yalom, 1989, p. 366; original emphasis)

Assumptions of Existential Analysts.   Consistent with Binswanger's view that mental disorders may be caused by distorted worldviews, existential analysts feel that stressful life events that force us to confront our inaccurate or unworkable assumptions can lead to panic, depression, or spiritual crises. For example:

> Mabel defines herself as superior in the academic realm, but on graduating from a small high school and entering a large university, she encounters many persons with similar gifts. She panics, misinterpreting her changed grade level as evidence that her mind is failing. (Bugental & McBeath, 1995, pp. 113–114)

Bugental and McBeath (1995) cite similar examples: a wealthy woman whose life had been idyllic until the sudden death of her child confronted her with her vulnerability to tragedy and an idealistic young man who pleased his parents by entering the ministry, but found his faith challenged when brought up against the difficult lives of his parishioners, and then felt trapped and guilty for fear of failing his family.

Existential analysis has some elements in common with psychoanalysis, but the differences are important. The emphasis in existential analysis is on understanding the person's life history in terms of his or her world design, rather than explaining it in terms of general theories of development. If there are "areas of incompleteness" in the personality, the therapist helps the person to experience this, rather than trying to tell the person what is wrong. Therapist and client are seen as equals, and the focus is on their shared "plane of common existence" (Binswanger, 1956/1976, p. 377). When clients describe their dreams, they are taken seriously as an important aspect of life and a specific way of existing, not as a trivial byproduct of "real" existence (Binswanger, 1956/1976).

Assumptions of Client-Centered Therapists.   Carl Rogers also stressed the importance of the phenomenological world in his client-centered therapy, arguing that as individuals we can safely rely upon our own inner sense of what feels right for us in guiding us toward optimal development.

The Actualizing Tendency.   Rogers noted that many physical processes show a formative tendency, a trend to developing order out of chaos. In people, this formative process includes an *actualizing tendency,* an automatic, constructive progression toward realizing one's full creative potential. The actualizing tendency is in-built, just as the tendency of a healthy plant to grow, given adequate sunlight, soil, and water, is inherent in the plant itself.

The Organismic Valuing Process.   Personality, our sense of self, develops as we interact with others, and interactions involving evaluation are especially important. Healthy development involves symbolizing, perceiving, and organizing our experiences in relation to the self, but maladjustment occurs when significant experiences are ignored, denied, or distorted. When we use the actualizing tendency as a guiding principle in life, trusting our innate sense of what feels right, we live according to our *organismic valuing process* and are likely to live fulfilling, productive, self-actualizing lives. In other words, living according to one's true inner feelings is healthier than using the standards and judgments of other people as the guide (Hergenhahn, 1992; Raskin & Rogers, 1989).

Conditions of Worth.   Unfortunately, problems can arise because of our need for *positive regard* from others. When others value us and show positive regard (love, warmth, sympathy, acceptance) with no strings attached, we tend to develop in a healthy manner and can live according to the organismic valuing process. But when others give positive regard only when we behave, think, and feel in certain specified ways, then *conditions of worth* get established: the notion that we are only worthy or worthwhile when we operate according to the rules of others. The values of others can replace the organismic valuing process as a guide to living, and the distortions that arise are responsible for mental disorders and incomplete personality development (Hergenhahn, 1992).

Therapeutic Principles.   Carl Rogers's central idea was that "people have vast inner resources for self-understanding and self-directed solutions if they feel heard and understood in a facilitative relationship of warmth and acceptance" (Shlien, 1992, p. 1083). Consistent with the theory that conditions of worth are responsible for mental health problems, Rogers's therapeutic approach involves counteracting those damaging conditions by providing an atmosphere of complete acceptance, empathy, and nonjudgmental valuing. Therapy is therefore *nondirective*. A client-centered therapist does not seek to give advice or tell a client what to do, because the client's in-built organismic valuing process and self-actualizing tendency are the keys to guiding the client in a healthy direction. The therapist's task is to help the client tune in to his or her own inner resources.

While client-centered therapists do not judge or evaluate their clients' decisions, feelings, or behavior, it is consistent with the model to direct the process of therapy (though not the *content*). For example, "the therapist can suggest in a nonimposing way that the client try engaging in particular in-session exercises" (Bugental & McBeath, 1995, p.129).

Initially, the focus was entirely upon the client, but later the importance of the therapist as a person in the relationship was recognized. When therapists are fully themselves and their awareness of current experience is operating at full intensity, they are to be trusted and their behavior is constructive. Essential qualities the client-centered therapist provides are:

- *Genuineness,* or congruence and consistency on the part of the therapist.
- *Unconditional positive regard,* in that the therapist accepts the client regardless of his or her choices about what to talk about and how to talk about it.
- *Empathy,* or an attitude of profound interest in the client's world of meanings and feelings.

Basic concepts on the client side of the process include *self-concept,* especially self-regard; *locus of evaluation* (when clients gain in self-esteem they tend to shift the basis for their standards and values from other people to themselves); and *experiencing,* which becomes more flexible, open, and creative when the therapeutic process helps clients abandon their rigidity.

Influences on Clinical Psychology

The humanistic model inspired the development of existential analysis, client-centered therapy, and related schools of counseling and psychotherapy. Since most clinical psychologists describe themselves as eclectic in their choice of therapeutic methods, the humanistic model influences many practicing clinicians. Even therapists whose primary allegiance is to psychodynamic or cognitive-behavioral models will occasionally draw from the humanistic model when the occasion demands. For example, not every client presents focused problems or has a diagnosable mental disorder. In such cases, a structured treatment of choice drawn from the professional research literature may not be available. It may be more to the point to help the client explore certain problems, issues, or preoccupations in a less structured way. A very similar idea has recently been formulated by Steven Hayes and his colleagues as *Acceptance and Commitment Therapy,* in which radical behaviorist and humanistic models come together to create an experiential approach to behavior change (Hayes, Strosahl, & Wilson, 1999).

As the following case example illustrates, it could be misleading to treat every psychotherapy referral as a case demanding a specific form of focused therapeutic intervention.

Case Illustration.   May and Yalom (1989) presented the following case illustration. "David" was a 50-year-old scientist who had decided to separate from his wife after twenty-seven years of marriage. He sought therapy because he was anxious about telling his wife. Describing his wife as boring, David told his therapist that he had left her several times in the past but only for brief periods. Now that their children had grown up, David saw very little to hold the marriage together, and, besides, he was interested in a younger woman.

The therapist helped David explore several existential themes, including *responsibility*—his sense of moral duty toward his wife and the marriage, and his own possible contribution to his wife's limited existence by restricting her role to that of homemaker. Another important question was whether David's apparent dissatisfaction with his wife might really have represented dissatisfaction with his life in general, or with some other aspect of it. In that connection, David described a dream in which a friend who was dying of cancer was sinking into the soggy ground near David's swimming pool:

> I used a giant power auger to drill down into the quicksand. I expected to find some kind of void under the ground but instead I found a concrete slab five to six feet down. . . . I found a receipt . . . for $501. I was very anxious in the dream about that receipt since it was greater than it should have been." (May & Yalom, 1989, p. 397)

The dream was explored as involving themes of death and aging; for example, the idea of someone nearly being six feet under, and the concrete slab suggesting a tombstone. The numbers "five to six feet" and $501 were poignant because David had had the dream on his 51st birthday! The therapist reasoned that if David was truly more troubled about his age than he realized, then leaving his wife might be an attempt to solve the wrong problem. The existential analysis proceeded to deal with David's concerns about aging and death. In the end David did leave his wife, but he based his decision on a fuller recognition of his existential situation. When new anxieties arose during the transition from the marriage to a new relationship, the therapist offered support but did not try to alleviate the anxiety: The need to confront, rather than to avoid or try to minimize, existential anxiety is a central theme in this theoretical approach (May & Yalom, 1989).

Current Status

Treatment approaches informed by the humanistic model enjoy support from many clinicians as the "third force" (after psychodynamic and behavioral approaches) in psychotherapy. Because the humanistic model emphasizes phenomenology, here-and-now experiencing, and clients' perception of the world rather than objective external reality, most of its adherents traditionally avoided scientific psychology and objected to quantifying human experience and behavior in numerical terms. As a result, humanistic psychotherapists have not made a priority of conducting controlled research on specific therapeutic techniques.

However, contemporary humanistic psychologists have shown considerable interest in systematic research on the *process* of therapy, and a formidable amount of work in this tradition has been reviewed recently (Cain & Seeman, 2002; Hill, 2001; Hill & O'Brien, 1999). Carl Rogers favored research on the therapeutic process, and he conducted some difficult and challenging quantitative studies. These included the *Wisconsin project* in the 1960s, a massive report on the treatment of sixteen clients with schizophrenia. Although the results of this ambitious study were disappointing in respect of therapeutic outcome (perhaps not surprisingly, with such a challenging disorder as schizophrenia as the target), Rogers and his colleagues made progress in solving some of the methodological problems in research of this kind (Rachman & Wilson, 1980). Nonetheless, many psychologists now accept humanistic approaches less for their demonstrated scientific standing than for their intuitive appeal as suitable interventions for clients with generalized distress or unfocused malaise.

Process-experiential therapy is a contemporary example of treatment along humanistic lines that illustrates current practice in this field. Process-experiential psychotherapy draws from the humanistic model and from current research on emotion and cognition. It cites the importance of innate self-actualization, the here-and-now, and the nurturing of "more adaptive functioning by continuously focusing the client on his or her experiencing" (Goldman & Greenberg, 1997, p. 402). Clients create new meaning by identifying and symbolizing internal experience. Therapy facilitates "conscious choice and reasoned action [through] increased access to and awareness of inner experience and feeling" (pp. 402–403). The therapist accepts and enters the client's frame of reference, tunes in to the client's experience, and guides the client's attention to what the therapist senses as most pertinent for the client at a particular moment. Therapists formulate "process diagnoses," which identify the ways in which people interfere with their own experience. Maladaptive "emotion schemes" underlie psychopathology. Determinants of emotional disturbances are (1) problems in symbolizing feelings, (2) activating emotion schemes that produce negative feelings, and (3) inability to integrate certain emotion schemes. Therapists therefore go beyond what is apparent on the surface and restructure core maladaptive emotion schemes. Therapeutic tasks include *empty-chair techniques,* in which the client talks to a troublesome part of the personality—for example, one's pride—by imagining that it is seated in an adjacent empty chair. The client then moves over and sits in the empty chair to take the role of his or her pride, for example, and continues the dialogue. In this way, the client has an opportunity to focus on an aspect of his or her personality that has not yet been fully recognized or understood. Such techniques help clients to create a more unified and harmonious sense of self.

Process-experiential therapy and other humanistic psychotherapies are reviewed in greater depth in Chapter 11.

The Behavioral Model

Behavior therapy, behavior modification, and applied behavior analysis are overlapping approaches to mental health work that together draw from the behavioral model. We'll use the phrase *behavior therapy* as the generic term for these approaches.

The behavioral model was gradually established as an alternative to psychoanalysis between the 1930s and 1950s. Psychoanalysts had compared mental health problems such as neuroses, or anxiety-based disorders, with medical problems such as infectious diseases. If Little Hans fears horses, they argued, it must be the result of some deeper, more fundamental cause, such as unresolved Oedipal issues. The medical analogy is that the phobia is merely a symptom of the underlying disease, just as fever and chills can be symptomatic of a systemic infection. Medical professionals can try to bring fevers down directly by giving the patient a cold bath, but such symptomatic treatment does not get to the root cause of the problem and would not work as a fundamental cure. To do that, the infection must be dealt with. By analogy, it did not make sense to psychoanalysts to remove Hans's phobia by means of some practical procedure. The underlying disease had to be confronted.

The simplest generalization about behavior therapy is that it began by questioning this medical analogy. It's an interesting hypothesis that a phobia could be an offshoot of a deeper problem, but how do we know that for sure, and how could we test it definitively? What would have happened if Freud had helped Little Hans to deal with his fear and avoidance of horses in some systematic and structured way? Would it necessarily have missed the point to have dealt directly with the problem as presented by the client? Behavior therapists questioned the image of wise, omniscient doctors who could determine unfailingly what was really going on, at the same time viewing their clients' ideas about their problems with suspicion as the products of irrational, unconscious forces. Dissatisfaction with the disease model of psychopathology was redoubled by the fact that the concepts used by psychoanalysts to explain the origins of mental disorders were subjective, mentalistic, and very hard indeed to pin down to anything clearly and unambiguously observable. Early behaviorists like John B. Watson rejected mentalistic concepts like mind, the unconscious, and repression because of the great difficulty of building a science of psychology upon such slippery foundations—the chief difficulty with such subjective material being that different observers could give widely varying interpretations of the same clinical phenomena. As an alternative, Watson proposed focusing on the objectively observable behavior of the individual, and making that the target of investigation and therapy. Hans Eysenck, one of the originators of behavior therapy, summarized this view in a famous statement to the effect that getting rid of the "symptom" is the same thing as getting rid of the neurosis.

As an alternative to the medical disease model, behavior therapists drew their hypotheses from known behavioral processes like classical conditioning and based their therapeutic interventions upon the results of laboratory experiments. Behaviorism and empiricism were the essential philosophical concepts, and experimental psychology was the chief source of therapeutic techniques and theoretical processes.

Development

Established as an alternative to psychoanalysis and humanistic methods, behavior therapy draws from experimental psychology and is strongly influenced philosophically by empiricism and behaviorism. Rejecting psychoanalysis on theoretical and empirical grounds, the pioneers of behavior therapy in South Africa, the United Kingdom, and the United States used the principles of conditioning and learning to develop innovative treatment procedures. Examples of behavior therapy techniques can be found throughout recorded history, but the systematic use of behavioral approaches in mental health work began in the 1950s. Behavior therapy has since been broadened by the contributions of creative clinicians and by new theoretical developments. Practicing behavior therapists share many of the characteristics of traditional therapists in seeking to form close, collaborative therapist-client partnerships. Yet behavior therapy differs from the other approaches in its use of specific techniques addressed to specific problems, and in its adherence to experimental research in validating principles and procedures.

Joseph Wolpe. In the early 1940s Joseph Wolpe was working as a physician at a South African military hospital. The patients were combat veterans who were suffering from post-traumatic anxiety disorders. Initially employing psychoanalytic methods, Wolpe obtained disappointing results and looked for alternative ideas on the treatment of anxiety. He read the literature on *experimental neurosis* (laboratory-induced anxiety) and discovered that conditioned fear in cats could be overcome by eliciting feeding responses that compete with anxiety. Conclusions from these experiments led Wolpe to develop the concept of *reciprocal inhibition,* a general principle of behavior change that relied upon countering anxiety by a competing feeling-state (Wolpe, 1958, 1982). Wolpe's work was original because of its foundation in laboratory experiments, its basis in clearly stated theoretical principles, and its stimulation of practical, goal-oriented treatment techniques.

Hans Eysenck and Monte Shapiro.   In the 1950s Hans Eysenck established the first British graduate program in clinical psychology at the University of London's Institute of Psychiatry. Critical of psychoanalytic approaches because of their lack of experimental support, Eysenck insisted that they would have no place in his program. Instead, he proposed "the development of a theory of neurosis and treatment based on modern learning theory, particularly Pavlovian conditioning and extinction" (Eysenck, 1984, p. 3). Eysenck was supported in this project by his colleague Monte Shapiro, who viewed each client as similar in some ways to a participant in an individually tailored experiment (Shapiro, 1966), an approach that continues to be a strong tradition in behavior therapy.

Eysenck and Shapiro were disappointed to find that traditional clinical training programs had little connection with mainstream psychology (Yates, 1970). Students interested in clinical psychology had usually graduated from college with a psychology major, with a background in scientifically oriented courses in learning, motivation, perception, social behavior, developmental psychology, research and statistics, and so forth. But in graduate school the same students were required to forget about mainstream psychology and study the works of Freud, interpret projective tests, describe character defenses, and delve for unconscious meanings underlying clients' behavior. Why not make clinical psychology more like psychology? The efforts made by Shapiro, Eysenck, and their colleagues in London to devise a scientifically oriented clinical psychology were essential to the development of behavior therapy, not only in Britain but worldwide.

Eysenck viewed common clinical problems like anxiety and hysteria as resulting from the interplay of personality factors and learning events. This inspired his associates to begin to use learning-based treatment methods, such as the Mowrers' (1938) bell and pad treatment for nocturnal enuresis (bed wetting) in children. Like Wolpe, Eysenck and his colleagues drew their treatment interventions from the theories of Pavlov (1927) and Hull (1952), but initially their work continued independent of Wolpe's (Franks, 1969).

John B. Watson and B. F. Skinner.   John B. Watson is closely identified with *behaviorism,* one of the theoretical mainsprings of behavior therapy. His demonstration of fear conditioning in *Little Albert,* an infant who developed fears of a white rat and related stimuli after learning trials in which the rat was paired with the sudden sound of a steel bar being struck, paved the way for conditioning interpretations of anxiety disorders (Watson & Rayner, 1920).

The work of B. F. Skinner (1904–1990) and other operant learning theorists led directly to practical therapeutic techniques. In a series of studies in standardized learning environments, Skinner showed that animal behavior is modifiable by controlling the consequences of specified responses. In a typical experiment, a pellet of food was delivered to a food-deprived pigeon if, and only if, it made a designated response, such as pecking at an illuminated disk on the wall of the experimental chamber. If the pigeon's response rate increased as a result of this procedure, the delivery of food was said to *reinforce* the pecking behavior. This work was extended, with suitable modifications, to human volunteers, and the same general learning patterns were seen. Skinner (1953) argued that operant learning principles provide a basis for understanding the whole spectrum of human behavior, normal and abnormal.

Extending his work on operant learning from the laboratory to the hospital ward, Skinner (1961) showed that chronic psychiatric inpatients also displayed the typical learning patterns displayed by rats, pigeons, and students. In an unpublished progress report in 1954, Lindsley and Skinner were, in fact, the first to use the term *behavior therapy* (Yates, 1970).

Although this research did not involve treatment, it provided a foundation for therapy based on operant learning. Teodoro Ayllon (1963) demonstrated that operant learning methods could be used to increase adaptive behavior in chronic psychiatric inpatients, and he developed ward-wide behavior management programs known as the *token economy* from the same principles (Ayllon & Azrin, 1965, 1968).

Behavior Therapy Techniques. Behavior therapists have developed specific treatment techniques for each broad class of disorders. For example, behavioral treatment plans for anxiety disorders, schizophrenia, and depression would differ notably from one another. The first targets of behavior therapists in the late 1950s included the anxiety-related disorders. The original treatments were stimulated by principles of classical conditioning and by experimental neurosis phenomena (Eysenck & Rachman, 1965; Wolpe, 1958, 1990; Wolpe & Lazarus, 1966).

Key Assumptions

Classical Conditioning. Wolpe (1958) drew from the work of Pavlov (1927) and Masserman (1943) in designing his original studies of fear acquisition and removal in cats. In his famous demonstrations of *classical conditioning* in dogs, Pavlov had shown that stimuli that previously did not call forth a reflex response like salivation may come to do so following a particular experimental procedure. Initially, healthy dogs routinely produce saliva in response to the presentation of food. But Pavlov showed that, under special conditions, dogs could also learn to salivate in response to a bell being rung, or a whistle being blown, or even the presentation of a diagram of a circle on a piece of white card. The experimental procedure that produced such results involves repeatedly presenting the new stimulus (for example, a bell being rung) a fraction of a second before the food, the reflex-eliciting stimulus. This *pairing* of the two stimuli was made repeatedly until the response normally produced in the reflex began to be produced by the new stimulus. In Pavlov's terminology, the original connection between the food and the salivation is an *unconditioned reflex* (unconditioned, because no new learning is required). Specifically, the food is an *unconditioned stimulus* (UCS) and the salivation is an *unconditioned response* (UCR). After several pairings of the bell and the food, such that the previously neutral sound of the bell could itself elicit salivation in the dogs, the bell has become a *conditioned stimulus* (CS). This conditioned stimulus had now taken on the power to trigger salivation itself. Salivation in response to the conditioned stimulus, the bell, is referred to as the *conditioned response* (CR). The effects of classical conditioning can be undone gradually in a process of *extinction*. The procedure involves systematically presenting the CS without the UCS—presenting the bell without the food—on several occasions. Gradually, the dog stops producing saliva in response to the bell.

Behavior therapists like Wolpe speculated that anxiety disorders in humans could arise through classical conditioning mechanisms. The type of conditioning involved would have to be aversive, as in the case of elementary school students who become fearful of public speaking after their classmates ridicule them while they are making presentations in front of the class. If classical conditioning is at work, the unwanted anxiety is a conditioned response, and the needed treatment involves an extinction procedure of some kind. (With the fearful public speakers, that could mean encouraging the students to make classroom presentations without being ridiculed by classmates.)

But Wolpe's research convinced him that simply presenting the CS without the UCS, the usual method for obtaining extinction, does not readily work with anxiety responses. He proposed that anxiety has to be countered by a competing feeling state before it can be reduced. Accordingly, in his studies of cats with experimental neuroses he found it necessary to feed them as part of the extinction procedure. Feeding competes with and inhibits anxiety, and anxiety competes with and inhibits feeding. Because the competing process goes both ways, he called the process *reciprocal inhibition,* stating the general principle as follows:

> If a response antagonistic to anxiety can be made to occur in the presence of anxiety-evoking stimuli so that it is accompanied by a complete or partial suppression of the anxiety responses, the bond between these stimuli and the anxiety responses will be weakened. (Wolpe, 1958, p. 71)

Wolpe used a combination of techniques—reciprocal inhibition at each step in a graded progression of feared stimuli—in designing behavioral treatment for people with various anxiety disorders. Observing that muscle relaxation techniques can be used to inhibit anxiety, and that humans can respond just as readily to imagined scenes as to real situations, Wolpe developed the technique of *systematic desensitization* to treat people with phobias and other specific, situational fears.

Systematic Desensitization.   There are three key elements to the systematic desensitization procedure: relaxation training, assembling an anxiety hierarchy, and presenting hierarchy items for the client to imagine while deeply relaxed. Several versions of relaxation training have been described, but research has not clearly shown that any particular method is preferable (Hecker & Thorpe, 1992). One that involves teaching clients systematically to tense, then relax, various muscle groups is in common use today (Bernstein & Borkovec, 1973). The *anxiety hierarchy* is a carefully prepared list of items, ordered along a dimension of gradually increasing anxiety-eliciting potential, representing a cross-section of the client's feared situations. Someone with a phobia of heights might compile a hierarchy literally consisting of a series of steps. The first, a situation causing least anxiety, might be "standing on the bottom rung of a step-ladder in your kitchen," the second might be "standing on the second rung," and so forth. The last, most anxiety-evoking item in a list of 20 or so, might be "climbing to the top of a commercial radio antenna in a high wind." After the preliminary relaxation training and construction of the anxiety hierarchy, the therapist carefully describes the first scene from the hierarchy, ensuring that the client can imagine it without anxiety. If the client signals anxiety, the therapist discontinues the presentation of items and helps reinstate deep relaxation and calm before proceeding. After several presentations of the scene without anxiety, the therapist proceeds to the next, and ultimately the entire hierarchy is covered in this fashion.

Since 1958 research findings and theoretical developments have improved the practice of behavior therapy and modified its techniques. Today systematic desensitization has been supplanted by such methods as graduated practice in real-life situations.

Operant Learning.   *Operant learning* phenomena are essential to behavior therapy. Humans are always operating in the context of environments that may reinforce, extinguish, or punish certain behaviors we may produce (Skinner, 1953). Because such behavioral contingencies are always present, they exert their influence on both normal and abnormal behavior in any situation in which behavior occurs. Behavior therapists believe that abnormal behavior becomes understandable when the contingencies operating are known. Changing the contingencies can change the behavior.

Schaefer and Martin (1969) provide an example from an inpatient setting. The staff of a hospital for patients with mental retardation were alarmed at the number of "head bangers" in the institution. Many patients had adopted a pattern of deliberately banging their heads against the wall. This behavior was obviously harmful, because the patients' heads were often bleeding after such episodes. No fault could be found with the treatment staff. In fact, they were unusually sympathetic and caring people. Whenever a patient started head banging, a nurse would hasten to offer comfort and would even give the patient candy or chocolate. However, this treatment did not seem very helpful. The patients tended to start banging their heads whenever they saw a nurse arriving with a supply of candy (Schaefer & Martin, 1969, pp. 47–48).

Behavior therapists would certainly not discourage the nurses from being sympathetic and would not want them to stop giving candy to patients. But Schaefer and Martin did not hesitate to recommend some changes in the ways the ward staff *scheduled* their offerings of candy and sympathy. Bringing candy and words of comfort only when patients bang their heads on the wall creates a behavioral contingency of *positive reinforcement* in which we might expect the head banging to continue. The logical remedy would be to advise the staff to offer reinforcement at any time *other* than when the patients are banging their heads, thus placing the head banging under *extinction* and positively reinforcing incompatible behavior. Behavior therapists would make careful observations of the effects of this change in procedure in order to ascertain whether, indeed, the predicted results will ensue.

Influences on Clinical Psychology

In addition to the specific treatment techniques associated with behavior therapy, its distinctively scientific approach to clinical assessment and the validation of treatment interventions set it apart from other models and continue to influence the field.

Research Methods and Behavioral Assessment.   One of the characteristic features of behavior therapy is its commitment to experimental hypothesis-testing. Research designs for evaluating the effects of behavior therapy include case histories, clinical series, single-case experiments and multiple baseline designs, crossover studies, and group designs. In evaluating behavior change processes that underlie treatment effectiveness, researchers often wish to rule out the effects of nonspecific factors that arise in any investigation, such as participants' guesses as to what is expected of them—the *demand characteristics* of the experimental situation.

Behavioral assessment is a vital component of behavior therapy. Early approaches to behavioral assessment focused on identifying the types of controlling variables that were related to discrete problem behaviors occurring in particular situations. Over time, the field has broadened to encompass standardized measures and multiple measures of problem behavior that may include cognitive or affective responses. In contrast with other approaches to assessment, the chief function of behavioral assessment is to facilitate behavior therapy. Behavioral assessment is used to:

- Develop clear and specific descriptions of presenting problems.
- Identify variables related to the onset and maintenance of these problems.
- Evaluate the severity of the client's problems.
- Identify effective treatment options.
- Provide a means of evaluating treatment implementation, progress, and outcome.

Behavioral assessment techniques cover a wide range of specific methods and situational contexts, including behavioral interviews, rating scales, self-report questionnaires, analog techniques, self-monitoring techniques, direct observation, and measures of psychophysiological responses.

Current Status

If we cite the publication of Wolpe's (1958) *Psychotherapy by Reciprocal Inhibition* as marking the beginning of behavior therapy as a systematic clinical enterprise, then it has been in progress for over forty-five years. Those years have witnessed rapid development in the concepts, procedures, and applications of behavior therapy. At first, conditioning and learning principles inspired the design of treatments for specific problem behaviors and clinical disorders. This work was marked not only by conditioning applications but also by scientific validation of procedures. Behavior therapists soon demonstrated that there was no empirical basis for the concerns of psychoanalysts that clients or patients would develop new symptoms after successful behavior-focused treatment. Behavioral treatment was indeed successful, and in a wide range of applications, more demonstrably so than any prior approach to psychotherapy.

As empirical data and clinical experience accumulated, behavior therapists had to rethink some of their theories. New techniques, like *flooding* (confrontive exposure of anxious clients to feared situations), were effective when the prevailing theories predicted they would fail. Theorists gradually began to question the adequacy of classical conditioning in explaining unnecessary anxiety in specific situations, and it also became clear that more diffuse disorders like depression and generalized anxiety deserved greater attention. Studies of operant learning showed that people respond less to the objective contingencies than to the contingencies as perceived by the individual (Bandura, 1969; Meichenbaum, 1995). Such developments aroused the interest of many behavior therapists in the *cognitive model,* to be reviewed next.

Keeping pace with therapeutic progress, advances in *behavioral assessment* allowed clinicians to monitor clients' self-reports, behavioral performances, and physiological responding in structured, objective, psychometrically respectable ways (Barrios, 1988; Farrell, 1993; Nelson, 1983).

In recent years behavior therapy has been extended to such problems as distress in intimate relationships, nightmares and obsessional thoughts, and severe medical disorders in children and adults. Consistent with its standing as a leading approach, behavior therapy is covered prominently in textbooks on contemporary psychotherapies (e.g., Bongar & Beutler, 1995; Corsini & Wedding, 1995; Gurman & Messer, 1995; Prochaska & Norcross, 2003), in addition to having its own immense professional literature. Behavior therapy's continuing appeal derives partly from its scientific grounding and the empirical validation of its procedures, and partly from its humane application of psychological principles to a wide diversity of clients and patients.

The Cognitive Model

The most behavioristic versions of behavior therapy have traditionally shunned mentalistic concepts like dreams, images, thoughts, and expectations because of significant practical problems in achieving acceptable *reliability*—interobserver agreement—in detecting and measuring such phenomena for scientific purposes. But clinicians often find it difficult to maintain such methodological purity when working with real-world clients who are distressed by troublesome feelings and plagued by uncomfortable ideas. In such contexts, focusing entirely on behavior, while not impossible, poses a considerable challenge. The cognitive model became attractive to the large proportion of behavior therapists who accept more pragmatic forms of behaviorism than those of Watson and Skinner and who wish to add the cognitive elements of clients' functioning—especially their attributions, their self-statements, and their assumptions about themselves and the world—to clinical case formulations and therapeutic interventions. Today, some clinicians who draw from the cognitive model to inform their professional work have little if any allegiance to traditional behavior therapy.

The cognitive model focuses on clients' symbolic representations of their experience and behavior, attending to the thoughts and images that intervene between external environmental events and the individual's behavior. Advocates of the cognitive model agree, of course, that the environment influences our behavior, but not in a directly controlling sense as in early accounts of conditioning as an automatic process. Instead, our thoughts about, and appraisals of, incoming stimuli are viewed as a vital part of the equation, an active mediating process. Such thoughts and appraisals can themselves be essential targets of therapeutic modification.

Clinical psychologists using the cognitive model in basic research might investigate psychopathology by assessing clients' recognition thresholds to briefly displayed words touching on clinically relevant themes, thereby studying attentional and cognitive processing biases that can help explain the development and maintenance of certain disorders. In the therapeutic arena, psychologists might use any of a variety of cognitive restructuring therapies to treat aspects of depression, anxiety disorders, and even schizophrenia. These therapies include the *cognitive-behavior modification* of Donald Meichenbaum, the *cognitive therapy* of Aaron Beck, and the *rational emotive behavior therapy* of Albert Ellis (Thorpe & Olson, 1997).

Development

There were three chief strands in the development of the cognitive model during the 1970s. First, behavior therapists recognized that many of their established techniques were not entirely behavioristic, and inescapably required that clients attend directly to their cognitions. Wolpe's systematic desensitization, for example, demands that clients mobilize specific images and make subjective judgments of distress levels (Locke, 1971). Arnold Lazarus (1971, 1976) recognized this explicitly by incorporating the cognitive domain as one of seven key modalities of his *multimodal* approach to psychotherapy.

Second, the whole of psychology "went cognitive" in the 1970s and 1980s, probably as a result of both conceptual and methodological advances. For example, Albert Bandura showed that, although we indeed respond to behavioral contingencies along the lines spelled out by behavioristic learning theorists, people are influenced more by their view of what those contingencies are than by the experimental arrangements as objectively specified (Bandura, 1969). Studies showing that even classical conditioning is not an automatic process that "happens to" a passive subject converged with this cognitive trend, leading to an acceptance of people's *expectations* as an essential component both of learning in general and of therapeutic behavior change in particular (Rescorla, 1988).

Third, the cognitive restructuring therapies that had been developed independently since the 1950s by Beck and Ellis were brought into the mainstream of experimentally oriented clinical psychology by Meichenbaum and others. For example, in research on public speaking anxiety in students, schizophrenia in psychiatric inpatients, and hyperactivity in children, Meichenbaum and his colleagues enhanced therapeutic effectiveness by asking clients to rehearse specific self-statements in order to focus their attention on, and guide their behavior toward, more constructive routines (Meichenbaum, 1977). In the 1970s, a variety of procedures aimed at cognitive modification were greeted enthusiastically by many behaviorally oriented clinicians, researchers, and students.

Key Assumptions

The central idea that people can be influenced more by their thoughts about events than by the events themselves dates from Stoic philosophy. Freeman and Reinecke (1995) quote the Roman philosopher Epictetus as follows:

> What upsets people is not things themselves but their judgements about the things. . . . So when we are thwarted or upset or distressed, let us never blame someone else but rather ourselves, that is, our own judgements. (p. 183)

If people are upset more by their thoughts than by actual events, it follows that appropriate treatment interventions could be aimed at helping people think in more benign and less disturbing ways.

Social learning theorists view learning as an active process, reflecting learners' attempts to organize and reorganize their patterns of experience and behavior (Freeman & Reinecke, 1995; Meichenbaum, 1995; Persons, 1994). Following his encyclopedic review of behavior change research, Bandura (1969) concluded that the active development of *expectancies* is the essential element in the processes underlying classical and operant conditioning (see also Reiss, 1980; Rescorla, 1988; Rescorla & Solomon, 1967).

Bandura's social learning theory focuses attention on behavior, the person, and the environment as the key reciprocally interacting variables in psychological functioning. In this model, the focus of interest in the person is on his or her internal symbolic activity and cognitive processes. Behavior change processes operate largely by altering cognitive factors like *self-efficacy* (Bandura, 1977). Self-efficacy refers to the person's expectations about his or her ability to produce behavior that successfully meets the demands of challenging situations. Perhaps ironically, treatments involving behavioral enactments, as opposed to deliberate attempts at cognitive restructuring, are the most effective methods for promoting cognitive change in Bandura's model (Wilson, 1982). Observational learning processes are at the root of effective therapy methods like *participant modeling* (Bandura, 1971a), in which clients learn to handle real-life feared situations under the guidance of the therapist, who demonstrates successful coping behavior.

Influences on Clinical Psychology

Cognitive-Behavioral Interventions. Cognitive modification procedures like *rational emotive behavior therapy* (Ellis, 1962, 1995) and *cognitive therapy* (Beck, 1976, 1995) are very much in the mainstream of clinical psychology today, to such an extent that practically the entire spectrum of behavior therapy procedures have been regrouped and relabeled under the heading *cognitive-behavioral* interventions. Verbal persuasion, rational disputation, modeling of positive self-statements, and suggesting more benign attributions are now the preferred techniques of a generation of empirically oriented psychotherapists. Although part of the success of the cognitive model may be attributable to faddishness, the foundation of its enduring appeal to scientific clinical psychologists is its consistent empirical backing by the positive results of carefully controlled therapeutic outcome studies. Beck's cognitive therapy alone has been applied successfully to depression, panic disorder, personality disorders, marital dysfunction, and bulimia (Barlow & Durand, 1999, 2002; Durand & Barlow, 2003), and cognitive procedures have also been shown effective in the treatment of the acute and chronic symptoms of schizophrenia (Thorpe & Olson, 1997).

Cognitive Psychology and Cognitive Neuroscience. The experimental techniques of cognitive psychology have enhanced the study of psychopathology by providing an objective basis for the study of attentional biases and cognitive processing errors. The impetus for this work largely derived from contemporary clinicians' general interest in the role of cognitive phenomena in the assessment, etiology, and treatment of psychopathology.

Recent methodological advances allow assessment of fundamental cognitive processing biases that, unlike attitudes and beliefs, are not immediately accessible to self-report. These cognitive biases involve the selective processing of emotionally relevant information, and are therefore highly pertinent to emotional disorders such as depression, generalized anxiety, and phobias (Mineka, 1992). In the context of emotional disorders, interpretive, attentional, memory, judgmental, associative, and interpretive biases have all been investigated (McNally, 1994, 1995; Mineka & Sutton, 1992).

For example, *attentional bias,* an apparently automatic process in which individuals attend disproportionately to environmental threats, has been viewed as an important factor in arousing and perpetuating anxiety disorders (McNally, 1995). Anxious individuals show an attentional bias toward environmental threats representing their specific concerns (Williams, Mathews, & MacLeod, 1996). For example, people with panic disorder focus attentively on fear-relevant bodily sensations such as a racing pulse, thus enhancing anxiety. Because of this attentional bias, potentially threatening stimuli are processed more frequently and intensely, creating a vicious circle in which increased anxiety makes threat-relevant stimuli more salient. Recording reaction times to, or recognition thresholds for, threat-relevant material tests objectively the degree to which individuals have allocated processing resources to such stimuli (Williams, Mathews, & MacLeod, 1996; Williams, Watts, MacLeod, & Mathews, 1988, 1997), providing compelling information on anxiety mechanisms.

In a study measuring recognition thresholds, panic disorder clients and nonanxious individuals were presented with sentence stems such as *"When Jane's heart was pounding, she was _____."* Next, words representing alternative sentence endings were presented sequentially for very brief, sub-threshold durations, which were gradually increased to the point at which the participant could recognize the word. In this example, the words were *reading, running,* and *dying.* Nonanxious participants quickly recognized the word *running,* while panic disorder clients—consistent with their suspected preoccupation with bodily sensations associated with medical catastrophes—rapidly selected *dying* (Clark, 1986; Clark & Beck, 1988).

Research dealing with attentional bias have also used a methodological tool called the emotional *Stroop* task, which presents a series of words printed in different colors. Participants are asked to name the colors in which the words are printed, ignoring the semantic content of the words themselves. Words that individuals find threatening or disturbing attract the attention powerfully, distracting participants from the task of naming the ink color. Delays and errors in naming the colors of key words form an objective index of these words' threat value (MacLeod, 1991).

Current Status

The cognitive model pervades both clinical practice, in the form of cognitively derived therapeutic interventions, and research on psychopathology, in that it informs controlled studies of various forms of processing biases held to underlie many disorders. Yet the appeal of the cognitive model to many practitioners probably draws more from the energetic and innovative therapies of such charismatic leaders as Albert Ellis (1962, 1995) and Arnold Lazarus (1976, 1995) than from the careful conceptual and empirical work of scientists like Peter Lang (1979, 1985) on *bioinformational theory,* Edna Foa (Foa & Kozak, 1986) on *emotional processing,* and Albert Bandura (1977, 1986, 1994, 1995) on social learning theory and self-efficacy.

BOX **3.4**

Focus on Ethics: Boundaries of Competence

As we have seen, clinical psychologists can choose different theoretical models to guide their professional activities in assessment and treatment. Each of these models has its advantages and disadvantages, and although individual practitioners may be strong adherents of one or another model, one cannot ethically fault a colleague for preferring a different model to one's own.

However, there are some important ethical considerations in one's choice of theoretical model, one of which is *competence*. This important topic is covered in the Ethics Code (American Psychological Association, 2002) under Standard 2, Competence, which states, in part, "Psychologists provide services, teach, and conduct research with populations and in areas only within the boundaries of their competence, based on their education, training, supervised experience, consultation, study, or professional experience" (2.01, Boundaries of Competence). Ethical psychologists actively pursue continuing professional education and development throughout their careers (Nagy, 2000; Pope & Vasquez, 1998).

According to this important ethical standard, one would only practice in an unfamiliar area after seeking, and gaining, appropriate professional training and reaching an acceptable level of competence. What would clearly be impermissible, for example, would be for a qualified behavior therapist to decide, out of the blue, to "branch out" and have a shot at being a psychoanalyst, having heard a few presentations on the subject and deciding that he or she has a fairly good idea of what it's all about. The same would go, of course, for the competent psychoanalytically oriented psychologist who, suddenly deciding that behavior therapists' *in vivo* exposure adventures with phobic clients sound like a lot more fun that sitting in a dreary office all day, impetuously embarks on a behavior modification project with a client without the appropriate training or background.

4 Biological Models in Clinical Psychology

The biological model of mental disorders and their treatment encompasses the fields of genetics, anatomy, and physiology and includes the entire range of medical interventions, from neurosurgery to pharmacotherapy. At its simplest, accepting the biological model means attributing mental disorders to underlying physical disease. Chromosomal abnormalities, biochemical imbalances, brain injury, malnutrition, and the whole spectrum of medical diseases can all play significant roles in psychopathology, and today few scientists or clinicians would find that view controversial. The most common disagreements in this area today focus on how wide is the range of mental disorders with significant biological underpinnings and to what degree a holistic, interdisciplinary approach—including the contributions of medical, psychological, and sociological professionals—makes the best sense in providing adequately comprehensive treatment.

The medical model is associated with a variety of professional interventions. These include genetic counseling, to advise parents on possible risks to their natural children when familial patterns of psychopathology have been identified. It is associated with neurology and neurosurgery and with the technical advances in medical imaging that give unprecedented nonintrusive access to anatomical structures and physiological processes. And it is associated above all in the public mind with prescribing and dispensing medication—pharmaceutical products designed to treat practically any recognized mental disorder. In appraising the biological model fairly and accurately, psychologists face the challenge of deciding where in the spectrum of possible viewpoints—from an exclusive biological determinism to a single-minded emphasis on psychological and environmental causation—lies the most defensible position. This is made the more difficult because of some common logical errors that can be too uncritically accepted by the unwary.

One of these is the notion that if a disorder is most strongly associated with biological abnormalities, then a medical intervention must be the logical remedy. Another is that if the use of a medication successfully alleviates the signs and symptoms of a mental disorder, then only biological, not psychological, processes can be operating. Such statements ignore the familiar clinical observation that even a severely mentally retarded individual whose disorder is clearly linked to irreversible brain damage can sometimes gain the most benefit from a program of educational and psychological interventions. And even the most potent medication with specific efficacy for a given disorder may owe much of its value to psychological factors such as placebo and expectancy effects.

The converse is equally true. Even if it were possible to establish that a client's anxiety disorder is unequivocally linked to adverse conditioning events and environmental circumstances, that still would not prove that medication would be useless as treatment.

It is true that certain chemicals trigger panic attacks much more often in panic disorder clients than in nonanxious individuals and that medications used to treat panic can block this chemical provocation of panic. It is also true that behavior therapy techniques, without medication, can do exactly the same thing (Barlow, 1988). Furthermore, it is true that *positron emission tomography* scanning (the PET scan), a brain imaging technique, can show dramatic changes in protein metabolism in the central nervous system following successful pharmacological treatment of obsessive-compulsive disorder. It is also true that PET scans show the same dramatic pre-post changes in clients treated solely by psychological, not pharmacological, interventions (Barlow & Durand, 2002). Both biological and psychological processes influence psychopathology and its treatment, calling for a multidimensional view of mental disorders and mental health. It will be helpful to keep these observations in mind as we review the essentials of the biological model.

Development

The development of the biological model coincides with practically the entire history of human thought and civilization. When ancient people first looked for biological causes of human behavior (what actually makes us move, speak, or experience emotions), the brain was just about the last part of the body they even considered. They started with breath, a quality that was obviously essential to life. In Hebrew, Greek, and Latin the words for breath came to mean "soul" or "spirit." The heart, as in expressions like "stout-hearted" and "heavy-hearted," has always been connected with emotions. As a significant organ in human psychological functioning, the brain was ignored for centuries. Aristotle thought it was probably just a refrigeration unit, a device for cooling the blood (Asimov, 1994).

Electricity and the Nervous System

The nerves of the brain (at least, the nerves of a dead brain) look gray, but the nerve fibers connecting the brain with the rest of the human body look like white strings. The word *nerve* derives from the Latin word for a string or cord. In ancient and medieval times, the nerves were thought to be hollow tubes carrying fluids known as "animal spirits." Luigi Galvani, the Italian anatomist, made the connection between electricity and the nervous system in the 1780s by studying the twitching of a dead frog's leg when an electric current was passed through it. By the late 1800s electricity was understood quite well, and this helped advance understanding of the nervous system. Just as breaking an electrical circuit can switch off a light, severing a certain nerve in the human body could produce deafness or paralysis, for example (Asimov, 1994).

Phrenology

The European mystic Emanuel Swedenborg (1688–1772) brought mind and brain together in the 1740s. He identified the brain's cerebral cortex as the seat of consciousness, perception, sensation, and thought, while the spinal cord and the structures of the brain stem control automatic and habitual movement (Bromberg, 1975). But the structure of the brain itself was still unknown by the end of the 1700s. The Viennese physician Franz Joseph Gall believed that the parts of the brain were highly specialized, so that the dozens of human personality characteristics and abilities were each controlled by a particular brain region. Gall had begun by noticing that his patients with prominent eyes also had superior memory functioning. He was highly skilled at dissection and, theorizing that differences in mental ability were in direct proportion to the quantity of gray matter in the brain, demonstrated that at least some people with severe mental retardation had relatively little cerebral cortex. Unfortunately, Gall's potentially helpful scientific study of craniology was taken to ridiculous extremes by his followers, who thought that individuals with especially well-developed talents would show bumps on their skulls to indicate the correspondingly well-developed brain regions. The pseudoscience of *phrenology* involved feeling for bumps on patients' skulls in order to gauge their personality attributes (Asimov, 1994; Bromberg, 1975).

The Case of Phineas Gage

Phineas Gage was a 25-year-old railroad work crew foreman who suffered a dramatic injury on September 13, 1848, when blasting rock out of a gorge in Cavendish, Vermont. A hole had been drilled in the rock, and Gage had charged the hole with gunpowder. An assistant had been told to pour sand in, so that when the three-and-a-half-foot-long tamping iron was pounded down, sparks would not set off the gunpowder. Startled by an extraneous sound, Gage and the assistant looked away at the crucial moment; then Gage turned back and pounded in the tamping iron, unaware that the assistant had not yet poured in the sand. The explosion launched the tamping iron right through Gage's head, entering below the left eye and exiting through the top of the skull. He was thrown through the air and immediately had convulsions.

Miraculously, Gage recovered. He was even able to speak to his workmates shortly after the accident, and he joked with the doctors who treated him. He made steady progress in the following weeks, and several months after the accident he was shopping in Cavendish and planning a trip out of town. But his personality had undergone a profound change. John Harlow, one of the treating physicians, later described this as follows:

> The equilibrium, or balance, between his intellectual faculties and animal propensities seems to have been destroyed. He is fitful, irreverent, indulging at times in the grossest profanity. . . . A child in his intellectual capacity and manifestations, he has the animal passions of a strong man . . . his friends and acquaintances said he was 'no longer Gage.' (Restak, 1984, pp. 149–150)

This case, and others like it, taught neurologists a great deal about the functions of the regions of the brain that were injured.

Tremendous advances were made in medicine and neuroscience in the 1900s. Among the most significant in the past fifty years were the pharmaceutical revolution, which dramatically improved the outlook for the most severe and persistent mental illnesses, and the rapid development of computer-assisted medical imaging, allowing not only for more precise diagnostic studies but also for real-time investigations of physiological processes.

Key Assumptions

The Brain and the Nervous System

All of the workings of the human body are relevant in one way or another to clinical psychology and mental health work, but for understandable reasons the brain receives the most attention. The human brain obviously has a great deal to do with higher mental functions like intelligence, memory, and learning. It is also essential in regulating breathing, the rhythm of the heart, body temperature, and blood chemistry; allowing us to walk, move, and stay upright; processing input from the sense organs so that we can see, hear, taste, feel, and touch; and organizing the myriad facets of our experience and behavior so that we may live, learn, feel emotions, communicate with others, avoid pain, and seek pleasure. Because the brain is ultimately essential to all human experience and behavior, it is highly relevant to our understanding of abnormal behavior patterns resulting from physical malfunctions in the brain's "machinery."

The brain's anatomical structures serve a variety of specific functions. Its workings have a great deal to do with the rapid building up and breaking down of complex protein molecules. It has miles of neural "wiring" that works according to elaborate electrochemical principles. Nerve impulses travel along the nerve cells in waves of electrical activity, and they get from one nerve cell to another by sending tiny packets of materials across minute gaps. Other chemicals are busily demolishing these materials almost as soon as they are constructed. And all the anatomical structures, molecules, nerves, electrochemical principles, gaps between nerve cells, and packets of materials have long names of many syllables that derive from ancient Greek and Latin terms.

Hormone Action versus Nerve Impulses. The two types of coordination in the human body are hormone action and nerve impulses. Hormone action involves the buildup of chemicals that are released into the bloodstream, circulate throughout the body, and have their effect when they reach particular organs. This is a relatively slow process. The other type of coordination involves the nervous system. Nerve impulses travel along specialized nerve cells, *neurons,* by means of an electrochemical process. Neurons provide special high-speed pathways for the relay of transmitted information, which travels to and from specific organs (Asimov, 1994).

The Human Brain. The central nervous system in humans consists of the brain and spinal cord, each encased within bone (the skull and the backbone). The brain is composed of neurons and *glial* cells (support cells). When fully developed, the brain weighs 1450 to 1480 grams (about three pounds), and specialists estimate that it contains over ten billion neurons and one hundred times as many glial cells. Only two or three million of the neurons extend out of the brain to control muscle movements, so an astronomical number of brain cells are left to serve other functions (Kolb, Whishaw, & Cioe, 1994; Restak, 1984).

Neurons.   Neurons vary in shape, size, and function, but they all create bioelectrical impulses that may be transmitted to other neurons. The vast majority of neurons in the brain connect only with other neurons, but in the peripheral nervous system (the part outside the central nervous system) some neurons receive stimulation from sense organs and others transmit impulses to muscles and glands.

The simplest way to understand the structure and function of neurons is to look at a stylized drawing, as in Figure 4.1. Each neuron has a *cell body,* a roughly spherical structure that contains the cell nucleus. Within the cell body, metabolic processes maintain the cell and synthesize necessary materials for proper cell function. Neurons also have extensions that allow interaction with other neurons (or with sense organs, muscles, or glands). These extensions are the branchlike *dendrites* (named from the Greek word for tree) that receive incoming signals, and the stringlike *axon* that extends away from the cell body and trans-

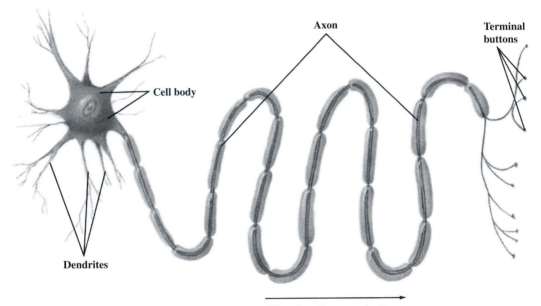

FIGURE 4.1   The basic structure of a neuron, showing the cell body, the axon with its end buttons, and several dendrites.

From Baron, Robert A. *Psychology: The Essential Science* © 1989. Published by Allyn and Bacon, Boston, MA. Copyright © 1989 by Pearson Education. Reprinted by permission of the publisher.

mits information to other cells. Neurons are interconnected by their axons and dendrites. A neuron may have as many as 15,000 connections with other neurons (Kolb, Whishaw, & Cioe, 1994).

Many of the neurons outside the brain have axons that are covered by a sheath formed from glial cells. This is the *myelin sheath,* which speeds the transmission of the nerve impulse and gives the neuron a white color. (The "gray matter" of the brain is so called because the gray-colored cell bodies predominate there.) The end of an axon branches into tiny swellings called *end buttons* that make contact with other neurons or with muscles or glands (Brown & Morris, 1994; Chiras, 1991).

The Nerve Impulse.   Neurons operate in binary, "on-off" fashion; they are either activated, responding at full strength, or resting, not responding at all. Neurons vary in the threshold of stimulation needed to activate them. Some dendrites make activation less likely when they are stimulated, and others make activation more likely. It is possible for a neuron to remain at rest even when several other neurons are stimulating it, provided that there is an even balance of excitatory and inhibitory influences (Restak, 1984). When a neuron is triggered to respond, a bioelectric impulse travels from a dendrite to the cell body and from the cell body along the axon. There is a tiny difference in electrical potential or voltage between the inside and outside of a resting neuron, measurable in thousandths of a volt. The outer membrane of the resting neuron keeps a high concentration of charged particles, usually sodium ions, outside. When the neuron is activated, part of the cell membrane suddenly becomes more permeable to sodium ions, which rush into the neuron and change its electrical polarization at that site from negative to positive. This is known as *depolarization.* Immediately afterward, there is a process of *repolarization* in which that part of the cell returns to its polarized state; sodium ions stop flowing in and potassium ions flow out. The nerve impulse is a wave of depolarization that travels rapidly along the axon toward the end buttons at a rate of about one and a half feet per second. In the case of myelinated axons, those with a myelin sheath, the depolarization jumps from one section to another at a rate of 600 feet per second (Chiras, 1991).

The Synapse.   One neuron connects with another at a tiny gap one millionth of an inch wide known as the *synaptic cleft.* The junction itself, the combination of the end button from the sending neuron, the synaptic cleft, and the dendrite of the receiving neuron, is the *synapse.* The neuron that transmits the impulse is the *pre-synaptic* neuron; the receiving neuron is the *post-synaptic* neuron (Chiras, 1991; Restak, 1984). Figure 4.2 is a schematic diagram of the major components of a synapse.

End buttons contain vesicles that store chemicals known as *neurotransmitters.* When the nerve impulse reaches an end button, calcium ions rush in, causing the release of neurotransmitters into the synaptic cleft. They cross the gap and attach to special receptors in the post-synaptic neuron. This process in turn leads to depolarization of the receiving neuron at that point, and if the stimulus is above the threshold and received by an excitatory dendrite, the nerve impulse travels along the receiving neuron (Chiras, 1991; Restak, 1984).

Neurotransmitters are extremely short-lived in the synaptic cleft. There are three principal mechanisms for removing them once they have served their function: (1) removal by enzymes that break them down into their chemical components; (2) reabsorption into or

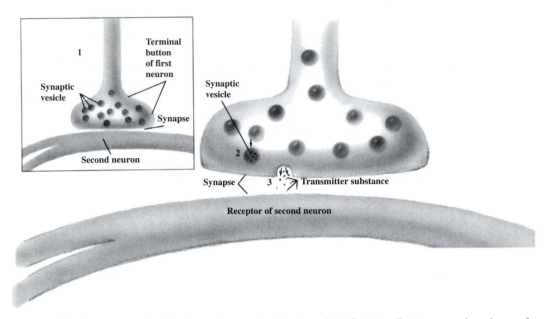

FIGURE 4.2   A synapse, showing the end or terminal button of the first (sending) neuron, the release of neurotransmitters, and the receptor of the second (receiving) neuron.

From Baron, Robert A. *Psychology: The Essential Science* © 1989. Published by Allyn and Bacon, Boston, MA. Copyright © 1989 by Pearson Education. Reprinted by permission of the publisher.

reuptake by the sending end button; and (3) diffusion into the immediate environment (Chiras, 1991).

Of the many neurotransmitters, *acetylcholine* (abbreviated ACh) is especially well understood. ACh is released by nerves that stimulate muscle contraction and is usually secreted by densely myelinated neurons that supply a fast signal. The removal of ACh after synaptic transmission is accomplished by an enzyme, *cholinesterase* (ChE), which is located in the synaptic space and breaks ACh down into choline. This in turn is taken up by the sending neuron, so the mechanism for removing ACh involves two of the three processes noted above, enzyme action and reuptake (Azmitia, 1994).

Brain Structure and Function

The functioning of the central nervous system is organized in a hierarchy so that the same behavior is controlled, with increasing degrees of subtlety, by successive anatomical levels. The spinal cord, the lowest anatomical level, controls the basic units of behavior, such as the reflexes that cause muscles to respond to sensory stimuli. Each higher level of the nervous system brings more sophisticated control over these basic behaviors. The cerebral cortex, the highest level, not only adds considerable flexibility to the limited movement sequences controlled by lower centers, but also integrates our behavior in space and time, allowing us to plan ahead and to deal with abstract concepts (Kolb, Whishaw, & Cioe, 1994). Ultimately, the cortex allows us to adjust our behavior to the highest values and standards of conduct that we choose.

The entire brain is wrapped in three layers of protective coverings, the *meninges*.

The Meninges.   These three membranes lie between the human skull and the brain. The outermost is the *dura mater* (literally, the "hard mother"); under that is the *arachnoid* ("cobweb"); and under that, tightly wrapping the brain, is the *pia mater* ("soft mother"). The *cerebrospinal fluid* (CSF) circulates between the pia mater and the arachnoid, floating the brain in a volume of fluid barely enough to fill a teacup (Restak, 1984). The CSF also fills the tiny central canal in the middle of the spinal cord and the four hollows or *ventricles* within the brain itself. Medical practitioners can extract samples of the CSF by means of a *lumbar puncture*, in which a needle is inserted between the fourth and fifth lumbar vertebrae in the small of the back to withdraw the fluid (though painful, the procedure is safe because the spinal cord itself does not extend that far down the backbone). The pressure and composition of the CSF can help detect abnormalities such as brain tumors or meningitis, an infection and inflammation of the brain's coverings (Asimov, 1994; Restak, 1984).

Descriptions of the human brain divide it for convenience into three principal areas: the hindbrain, the midbrain, and the forebrain.

The Hindbrain.   The top of the spinal cord passes through a hole in the base of the skull and broadens into the *brain stem*. The lowest part of the brain, the part nearest to the spinal cord, is the *hindbrain*, a region at the brain stem that includes the medulla oblongata, the pons, and the cerebellum. The first structure encountered on the way up is the *medulla oblongata* ("a longish marrow," or soft organ), appearing as a slight swelling of the brain stem. Next comes a more pronounced bump, the *pons* ("bridge"), which connects the hindbrain with the midbrain. The *cerebellum* ("little brain") is attached to the brain stem and lies behind and above it. The cerebellum is divided into two hemispheres with gray, wrinkled surfaces (Asimov, 1994; Kolb, Whishaw, & Cioe, 1994). (The basic structure of the human brain is shown in Figure 4.3.)

The structures of the hindbrain have a great deal to do with the more automatic aspects of the activity of our muscles, such as breathing and standing still. Much of the brain's sensorimotor coordination is performed by the cerebellum, which operates to control that continuous correction of muscle movements involved in such activities as picking up a pencil or remaining upright on ice skates (Asimov, 1994). The medulla and pons also contribute to the control of major movements, balance, and equilibrium, and are involved in salivation, swallowing, and the gag reflex.

The Midbrain.   The midbrain consists of structures that regulate whole-body movements in response to visual and auditory stimuli. One important region of the midbrain is the *reticular formation* (from the Latin for "little net"), an area with a mixture of gray and white matter that gives it a netlike appearance (Asimov, 1994; Kolb, Whishaw, & Cioe, 1994). The reticular formation is part of the reticular activating system that filters sensory information and is involved in the arousal mechanisms controlling sleep and wakefulness (Asimov, 1994).

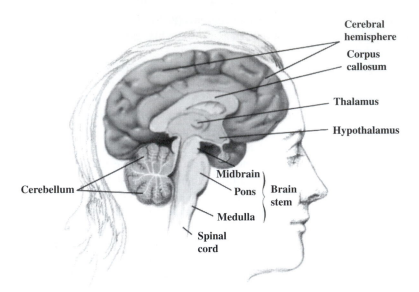

Cerebral
hemisphere

Corpus
callosum

Thalamus

Hypothalamus

Midbrain
Pons   Brain
stem

Medulla

Spinal
cord

Cerebellum

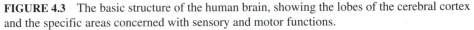

FIGURE 4.3   The basic structure of the human brain, showing the lobes of the cerebral cortex and the specific areas concerned with sensory and motor functions.

From Baron, Robert A. *Psychology: The Essential Science* © 1989. Published by Allyn and Bacon, Boston, MA. Copyright © 1989 by Pearson Education. Reprinted by permission of the publisher.

The Forebrain.   Anatomically, the forebrain is divided into five areas: the basal ganglia, the limbic system, the thalamus, the olfactory (related to the sense of smell) bulbs and tract, and—largest and most prominent, taking up 80 percent of the forebrain volume—the cerebral cortex.

The *basal ganglia* are a collection of *nuclei* (aggregations of neurons) beneath the cortex that connect it with the midbrain. The basal ganglia chiefly have a motor function; damage to their structures can affect posture and may be associated with abnormal muscle movements (Kolb, Whishaw, & Cioe, 1994).

The *limbic system* is a collection of structures that are usually described together because they share a role in regulating emotional expression, but it is not really a system and its structures have different functions. The structures of the limbic system, including the *hypothalamus,* are essential to the mediation and expression of emotional, motivational, sexual, and social behavior. The limbic system is involved in controlling hormone secretion, regulating internal homeostasis, and monitoring hunger and thirst; it is also involved in memory storage and emotional expression. The hypothalamus is concerned in all aspects of hormonal and autonomic functions and controls eating and drinking; it is "the central core from which all emotions derive their motive force" (Joseph, 1994, p. 68). Direct electrical stimulation of part of the hypothalamus causes feelings of intense pleasure in humans, and rats will tirelessly press a lever to produce electrical stimulation of that area, apparently preferring this to food or sex. Accordingly, the hypothalamus is the site of the "pleasure center." Parts of the hypothalamus and other limbic structures have neurons that produce and respond to *enkephalins,* opiate-like substances. When humans ingest narcotics, it is these limbic structures that are activated. People with tumors infiltrating the hypothalamus sometimes laugh uncontrollably, whistle, sing, and tell obscene jokes. Some people with such tumors have "died laughing," but their laughter has not reflected their feelings and has been labeled "sham mirth" (Joseph, 1994, p. 70). The similar phenomenon of "sham rage" can occur in people whose aggressive outbursts are the result of tumors in the nerve fibers leading down from the hypothalamus (Restak, 1984).

The *thalamus* is the channel for information from the limbic system and brainstem to be relayed to the cortex (Chiras, 1991). All sensory input except for smell is received by the thalamus and transmitted to the cortex; the olfactory bulbs and tract deal with smell directly (Kolb, Whishaw, & Cioe, 1994).

The cerebral hemispheres form the largest part of the forebrain and the most noticeable brain structure, overlaying most of the rest of the brain. The outer layer of the hemispheres is the *cerebral cortex* (literally, "bark" or "outer rind"), which, because the unmyelinated nerve cell bodies lie on top, appears gray. The cortex is wrinkled into folds, giving the appearance of a walnut; the many convolutions triple the surface area of the gray matter of the cortex. The folds are called *gyri* (plural of gyrus; pronounced with a soft "g" and meaning "rolls"); the valleys are called *sulci* (plural of sulcus; pronounced with a soft "c" and meaning "valleys"). Especially deep sulci are called *fissures.*

The main topographical features of the cerebral hemispheres—the most obvious gyri, sulci, and fissures—are essentially the same from brain to brain, allowing them to be mapped and charted as in Figure 4.3. For example, the *frontal lobe* is the part of each hemisphere lying in front of the central sulcus and above the *lateral fissure* (Asimov, 1994; Chiras, 1991). The other lobes are the *temporal,* the *parietal,* and the *occipital,* each named for the cranial bone lying above it.

The cortex can be divided into sensory, motor, and association areas. *Sensory areas* receive neural messages from the sense receptors; *motor areas* send the messages that control movement; and the *association areas* do not have particular sensory or motor functions. At a finer level of detail, particular areas of the brain are known to be intimately connected with very specific functions. For example, brain damage at one particular location may leave a person unable to "see," yet able to detect the color and location of a visual stimulus. Damage at another may allow someone to hear, but prevent identification of the particular sound (Kolb, Whishaw, & Cioe, 1994).

The frontal lobe contains the *precentral gyrus,* immediately in front of the central sulcus, controlling movement in the opposite part of the body. Damage to this area causes paralysis (Restak, 1984). Some brain regions that are closely identified with specific functions have been named after the scientists who first explored them successfully. The third left frontal gyrus is known as *Broca's area* because, in 1861, the French surgeon Pierre Paul Broca showed by postmortem examinations that patients with *aphasia* (inability to speak or to understand speech) had suffered damage to that region (Asimov, 1994). Damage to the very front of the brain, the *prefrontal fibers,* may lead the individual to act without inhibition; the prefrontal cortex is responsible for allowing appropriate inhibitory control of our actions. It was the damage to Phineas Gage's prefrontal area that led to his personality change, his loss of inhibition, and his inability to plan ahead (Restak, 1984).

Behavioral Genetics

It is important to find out about the possible heritability of mental disorders for several reasons. People with severe mental illnesses might choose not to start families if it were known that their disorder was always passed on to children. Establishing clear patterns of heritability might help identify people at risk for a disorder, or might eventually reveal the actual biological and behavioral mechanisms affected by particular genes, thus leading to new ideas about treatment. Or it might be found that people inherit just a vulnerability to a disorder, actually developing it only when other factors also come into play, such as an impoverished environment, certain child-raising practices, or significant life events. Knowing this could allow preventive measures to be taken.

Gregor Mendel.   The founder of modern genetics was Gregor Mendel (1822–1884), an Austrian monk who studied the patterns of inheritance determining the characteristics of garden pea plants, particularly the color of their flowers. Mendel established that the color of a given flower—red or white—was determined by the transmission of "factors" (*genes*) contributed by the parent plants. The gene responsible for red flowers was *dominant,* because mating red with white always produced red in the next generation. The gene for white was *recessive,* because mating a second-generation red with a pure red produced white one time in four. Mendel's observations of the transmission of other characteristics, such as pea color (green or yellow), length of plant stem, and whether peas were wrinkled or smooth led to the same conclusions (Nagoshi, 1994). The notion of dominant and recessive heredity attracted the interest of medical researchers in the early 1900s, and applying Mendelian concepts rapidly paid off when it was found that certain human variations like *albinism* accorded perfectly with the model (Gottesman, 1991).

It soon became clear, however, that even the most obvious and severe mental disorders do not conform to a simple Mendelian model. Careful research by Ernst Rudin in 1916 showed immediately that *schizophrenia,* the classic major mental disorder, could not be controlled by a dominant gene. He studied a number of people with schizophrenia and observed that none of their parents had the disorder. A recessive gene could not be responsible either, because only about 4.5 percent of the siblings also had the disorder, rather than the 25 percent predicted by a recessive model. Rudin did notice that a further 4 percent of the siblings had mental disorders other than schizophrenia. Speculating that the disorder might involve genes at two different locations, Rudin calculated that, if that were true, 6.25 percent of siblings would have schizophrenia. The observed value was different enough that he abandoned this hypothesis (Gottesman, 1991).

Human Genetics.   Every human being develops from the union of two *gametes,* specialized reproductive cells: an egg from the mother and a sperm from the father. The fertilized egg or *zygote* contains all of the hereditary material that is transmitted from one generation to the next. The zygote divides to form two cells in a process of *mitosis;* these divide in turn; and by the time a few billion cells have been produced a recognizable human embryo is forming. Although cells differentiate and become specialized (as nerve, muscle, or bone cells, for example), each cell nucleus contains *chromosomes,* rodlike units that carry the specific hereditary factors, *genes.* As cells divide, the chromosomes are duplicated also, and as a result the hereditary material in the original zygote is represented in every cell. At the point of cell division the nucleus of a cell contains 46 chromosomes. Half of each chromosome—with a full complement of all of its genes—reaches each new cell. Usually, then, every cell has a complete and equivalent set of genes, and these are duplicates of those in the original zygote. Genes operate and influence bodily processes by providing chemically coded information that guides the production of enzymes and other proteins (Carson, 1975; Monsanto Company, 1990; Nagoshi, 1994).

The 46 chromosomes of a normal cell can be grouped as 23 pairs, as each type of chromosome appears twice. One chromosome from each pair, or one set of 23 chromosomes, derives originally from the mother, and the other from the father. (The gametes are unusual in that each has only one set of 23 chromosomes. The process involved in making just one set available also recombines the genes—not creating new ones but placing them in new combinations.) The two members of each pair of chromosomes usually look similar to each other, but in males the pair known as the sex chromosomes look different; one chromosome, known as Y, is shorter, and the other, X, is longer. Females have two X chromosomes in this pair. Accordingly, normal males have the chromosome formula XY, and normal females have the chromosome formula XX. Mothers always contribute an X chromosome to this pair, but fathers contribute either an X or a Y, determining the sex of the child (Carson, 1975; Nagoshi, 1994).

The sex chromosomes contain several genes that are not related to sexual traits or characteristics. Such genes are referred to as "sex-linked" in their inheritance, and as a result they have properties that differ from those of genes carried on the other chromosomes. For example, a recessive gene carried on the X chromosome causes a form of color blindness. If we call the recessive color-blindness gene c, and the normal equivalent C, females (who have two X chromosomes) can have the patterns CC, Cc, cC, or cc. As the c gene is recessive, only the cc pattern is associated with color blindness. The Y chromosome does not contain the genes for color vision, so males (who have an X and a Y chromosome) will be color blind whenever the mother passes on a c gene. For example, if the father carries the color-normal C gene on his X chromosome, and the mother has the cc color blind pattern, all the daughters will be normal (the X from the father carries the dominant C gene), but all the sons will be color blind (the Y from the father has no gene for color vision, and the X from the mother has the c gene). The counterpart to sex-linked inheritance is *autosomal* inheritance, in which the inherited genes are carried by any of the other pairs of chromosomes (Carson, 1975).

Monozygotic and Dizygotic Twins.   In the rare case when two unfertilized eggs are simultaneously released by a woman's ovaries, it is possible for both to be fertilized by different sperm cells and form embryos, eventually being born as twins. When twins are formed in this way, developing from two separate zygotes, they are known as *fraternal* or *dizygotic* twins. Genetically, such twins are no more alike than any brothers or sisters from the same parents. Dizygotic twins may or may not be of the same sex.

In the case of *identical* or *monozygotic* twins, only one egg is fertilized, but when the zygote first divides to form two cells they become separated, implant separately in the wall of the uterus, and form two distinct embryos. Monozygotic (from one zygote) twins share identical genetic information (and are, therefore, always of the same sex). There are several possible ways in which monozygotic twins could become biologically different from each other, such as through subtle differences in the intrauterine chemical or physical environment; but because they share the same genes, identical twins are especially interesting targets of study by behavioral geneticists.

Family Trees and Human Pedigrees.   Clinical psychologists are interested in abnormal behavioral tendencies, such as displaying bizarre behavior or reporting hallucinations. Such observable characteristics or traits can be referred to as *phenotypes,* and one area of interest is the degree to which they run in families or have a genetic basis. The specific genetic characteristics of individuals, or the patterns of genes in their cells, are referred to as *genotypes,* and these can be assessed indirectly from the degree of similarity between different pairs of relatives (Carson, 1975; Gottesman, 1991).

The research methodology involved in assessing genotypes begins with a form of family tree, which in turn starts with a designated individual who has the trait or disorder of interest. For example, Ernst Rudin began by identifying individuals with schizophrenia, and then went on to study their relatives. In a study like this the person with schizophrenia is known as a *proband,* or an "index" case. Beginning with a proband with schizophrenia, and then studying various people among his or her relatives with different theoretical levels of shared inheritance, allows assessment of possible genetic factors in schizophrenia.

A significant problem here is that members of the same family, particularly siblings growing up in the same household with their biological parents, share a common physical and social environment in addition to sharing a certain percentage of their genes. Genetic and environmental factors could cause any similarities observed in the behavior of family members.

Family, Twin, and Adoption Studies

Because of the continual interaction of biological and environmental factors in human behavior, it is extremely difficult to hold one factor constant while studying the other, raising significant methodological problems. We would like to answer questions like these: Is the person depressed because she inherited depressive genes from her parents or because she grew up in a family of hopeless pessimists? Would she still have developed depression if she had been adopted at birth and raised in an energetic, cheerful, fun-loving family? The family, twin, and adoption studies were designed to help answer such questions.

Family Studies.   To return to the example of schizophrenia, the lifetime prevalence rate—the percentage of people who will develop the disorder sometime in their life—is about 1 percent (American Psychiatric Association, 1994). If it turned out that the close relatives of people with schizophrenia show the same prevalence of schizophrenia as people in general, that would clearly count against the hypothesis that there is a significant genetic basis for this disorder. But what if the relatives showed a 10 percent prevalence of schizophrenia, 10 times the normal rate? That still would not prove the existence of a genetic factor, because social factors like poverty or poor parenting might also run in the family and cause abnormal behavior, quite apart from possible genetic factors. Nonetheless, family studies can show whether closer relatives are at greater risk for a disorder than more distant relatives, and findings like that could be interpretable along genetic lines.

Twin Studies.   When twins grow up together in the same household, their general environment, if not their specific individual experience, seems identical. How similar the twins are to each other *genetically* depends on whether they are identical (monozygotic, MZ), or fraternal (dizygotic, DZ), pairs. MZ twins have 100 percent genes in common, while DZ twins share only 50 percent of their genes. If one member of a twin pair develops schizophrenia in adulthood, the other twin could be examined for signs of the disorder. If both have the disorder, they would be *concordant* for schizophrenia (twins could also be concordant in *not* having the disorder). If MZ twins showed greater concordance than DZ twins for depression, this could support a genetic basis for the disorder (Gottesman, 1991; Neale & Oltmanns, 1980).

Adoption Studies.   Adoption studies can be extremely useful in disentangling genetic from environmental influences. The procedure is to find children who were adopted into mentally healthy families, yet whose natural parents had a serious disorder. Because the adoptees have been separated from their natural parents, they have also been separated from any adverse environmental factors associated with growing up with a mentally disordered parent. Yet the adoptees will always carry within themselves any genetically transmitted factors that might cause the disorder (Nagoshi, 1994).

A related approach is to begin with adoptees who have developed a disorder, and then to examine the mental health of the adoptive and natural parents. Yet another approach is to examine cases of *cross-fostering*—cases in which the children of apparently normal biological parents are adopted by parents who develop a disorder.

The Example of Schizophrenia.   The results of family, twin, and adoption studies have shown that "genes are responsible for making some individuals vulnerable to schizophrenia" (Barlow & Durand, 2002, p. 435). However, no single "schizophrenia gene" has been identified. An individual's vulnerability to developing schizophrenia appears to be the result of a combination of different genes. To illustrate this, if there were a single gene for schizophrenia, identical twins would be highly concordant for the disorder, even if environmental factors were also involved. But even with the highest possible genetic vulnerability, the chances of an individual developing schizophrenia are similar to the results of a coin toss. If Jane has an identical twin, Joan, who has schizophrenia, the likelihood that Jane will have schizophrenia is a little short of 50 percent. The same goes for an individual whose mother and father both have schizophrenia (Barlow & Durand, 2002; Gottesman, 1991).

We noted earlier that the prevalence of schizophrenia in the general population is about 1 percent. Research clearly shows that having close relatives with the disorder increases one's risk of having schizophrenia; the closer the blood relative, the higher the risk. If one has a brother or sister with the disorder, the chances of having the disorder oneself is five or ten times the general prevalence. Even so, the odds are clearly against it (Gottesman, 1991).

Influences on Clinical Psychology

Studying the structure and function of the nervous system has led to significant advances in our understanding of many abnormal behavior patterns and has made it possible to design effective pharmacological and, sometimes, surgical treatments. For example, biomedical treatments for depression and schizophrenia are based on knowledge of how neurotransmitters work. Some of the medications used with depression inhibit the reuptake of certain neurotransmitters, making more of these chemical messengers available to pass on neural impulses. Others used with schizophrenia do the opposite, blocking receptors in the receiving neurons so that lesser amounts of the neurotransmitter are able to cross the synapse. Yet other medications may alter the general excitability of neurons by influencing the delicate balance of ions on either side of nerve cell membranes, affecting the transmission of nerve impulses along axons. Finally, knowing that damage to prefrontal brain areas can remove behavioral inhibitions has, in the past, justified surgical interventions to treat otherwise incurable obsessional states.

Studying genetic factors in mental disorders may allow the development of preventive measures. For example, one form of mental retardation is related to *phenylketonuria* (PKU), a condition marked by the absence of an enzyme that normally breaks down the amino acid *phenylalanine*. PKU is caused by a recessive autosomal gene that fails to code for the enzyme. Phenylalanine builds up in the child with the disorder and depresses the levels of other essential amino acids, interfering with normal nervous system development (Nagoshi, 1994). Fortunately, detecting the disorder early allows the child to be placed on a diet low in phenylalanine, much reducing the adverse effects of the metabolic problem.

Another genetic defect responsible for mental retardation is *Down syndrome* (American Association on Mental Retardation, 1992; Chiras, 1991), caused by an error in cell division when the female gamete is formed, producing an extra chromosome 21. Down syndrome occurs once in 700 births and is far more common in children born to mothers over the age of 35. The extra chromosome disrupts normal growth and development. Fluid from the *amnion,* the sac surrounding the developing fetus, contains fetal cells; this fluid can be withdrawn in a procedure known as *amniocentesis,* allowing medical professionals to test for the presence of various genetic defects (Chiras, 1991). Unfortunately, such testing can only reveal the presence of a defect. There is no viable way to prevent the consequences of the genetic error.

Family, twin, and adoption studies have been widely used by researchers investigating the heritability of schizophrenia and other disorders. One helpful role that clinical psychologists can take in this area is to educate and inform clients and their relatives about patterns of heritability, referring them to other professionals as necessary.

One of the most significant implications of the biological model in clinical psychology is the use of contemporary medical imaging techniques in basic research on psychopathology. Psychologists working in medical settings are usually in the best position to take advantage of this technology.

Medical Imaging Techniques

Positron emission tomography (PET) is a brain imaging technique in which radioactively tagged chemicals can reveal the chemical activity of the brain, highlighting the parts of the brain involved in performing an experimental task. Glucose, normally the brain's "fuel," is commonly used as the tracer (National Institute of Mental Health, 1997).

Magnetic resonance imaging (MRI) employs a scanner consisting of an extremely powerful magnet. Radio wave signals, creating a varying magnetic field much weaker than the steady field of the main magnet, are sent to the part of the patient's body under study. The returning signals are converted into images by a computer attached to the scanner. Pictures of almost any part of the body can be obtained at almost any angle. MRI scanners are especially helpful in viewing the body's soft tissues, such as the brain, spinal cord, and nerves (Ballinger, 1996).

Computed tomography (CT) is a radiographic method that supplies detail of the internal structure of materials in three dimensions. The technique uses computer processing of X-ray data (ARACOR, 1998).

Current Status

At the time of writing, few clinical psychologists are directly involved in prescribing medication and employing traditional medical procedures, but this is a fast-moving area in which the next few years will be likely to see significant changes in the scope of psychological practice. As an example of these trends, specially trained clinical psychologists in New Mexico are now licensed to prescribe specific psychotropic medications. Meanwhile, only the most insular of clinical psychologists would completely ignore the biological model in working professionally with clients. Unless the client's presented problems are entirely in the realm of counseling, in which he or she is seeking a forum for general self-improvement or personal discovery rather than a problem-oriented treatment plan to address a distinct disorder, the psychologist would practically always seek to consult with treating psychiatrists or other physicians to ensure coordination of treatment. In many cases, treating psychologists see the client more often than the medical professionals and are therefore in a good position to monitor medication side effects and changes in the client's mental status. With the client's formal authorization, the psychologist can rapidly communicate such information to other professionals when necessary.

Integrating Biological and Psychological Models

To reiterate our introductory comments, discussion of the role of neurons, brain structure, and genetics in mental disorders can misleadingly suggest that the causes of disorders must be *either* biological *or* environmental. There is a related myth to the effect that biological causation would require biological treatment and that psychological causation would require psychological treatment. But biological processes and environmental influences are both legitimate subjects of study. Biological and environmental phenomena operate whenever we study human behavior, and events in biological and environmental domains of necessity co-occur to produce human behavior. Mendel's garden peas would have failed to produce colored flowers at all if they had been raised in total darkness without water or nutriment, regardless of their genetic composition. World-renowned scientists like Albert Einstein or Marie Curie presumably had genetically controlled biological mechanisms underlying their highly developed cognitive skills, but if they had been raised as feral children without human contact it is unlikely that their genes would have found expression in superior works of science and scholarship. And in the potentially tragic example of PKU, discovery of its genetic cause led to a simple environmental modification—restriction of the diet in the first few years of life—that successfully prevents the otherwise catastrophic effects of the disorder. Identifying a clear genetic basis for this disorder made environmental modification more, not less, relevant to its treatment (Neale & Oltmanns, 1980).

Biological and Behavioral Processes

Similar arguments apply to the distinction between biological and behavioral (or psychological) processes: They co-exist (Kleinman, 1988). Finding significant genetic factors in a disorder would not logically invalidate either pharmacological or psychological treatment for it (Gottesman, 1991). Despite the well-known interaction of biological and behavioral processes in the mental health arena, the news media often present simplistic, one-dimensional accounts of the causation of disorders in purely biological terms. For example:

> Yesterday's newspaper was interesting and fairly typical. On page 8 I was told that the inner ears of lesbians differ slightly from heterosexual women and that this shows that sexual orientation is biologically determined. On the front page I learned that a particular sequence of nucleotides tends to be different in people who smoke versus those who do not, and that addiction is biologically determined. On page 4 I was informed that the brains of those with dyslexia are subtly different than those without dyslexia, and that dyslexia is biologically determined. (Hayes, 1998, p. 95)

One problem with observations like these is that they are based on correlational data. Which comes first, the biological variant or the behavioral characteristic? Presumably, years of smoking could possibly affect nucleotides, just as nucleotides may influence smoking. In any event, such extreme biological reductionism seems similar to explaining a Mozart performance by examining the inner workings of the piano and observing the operation of the mechanical linkage between the keys and the hammers striking the strings. Of interest, certainly, but arguably not the definitive statement of what Mozart's music is all about.

Finally, research data often show that psychological models of mental disorders have stronger scientific support than biological models. Seligman (1998) reviewed a broad range of studies on biochemical and cognitive causes of depression, examining heritable mechanisms, laboratory analogues, longitudinal measurement, experimental manipulations, specific treatment ingredients, and global treatment effectiveness. He concluded that there was approximately twice as much scientific support for cognitive, rather than biochemical, causation. An exclusive focus on biological models could lead to inaccurate conclusions and distract attention from successful treatment modalities.

BOX **4.1**

Focus on Ethics: Consultations and Referrals

In Box 3.3 we noted that psychologists are ethically obliged to practice only within the bounds of their established competence. At least as important ethically is the need for psychologists to make appropriate referrals to other professionals when necessary. In the Ethics Code (American Psychological Association, 2002), Principle B, Fidelity and Responsibility, reads in part: "Psychologists consult with, refer to, or cooperate with other professionals and institutions to the extent needed to serve the best interests of those with whom they work." Standard 3.09, Cooperation with Other Professionals, states: "When indicated and professionally appropriate, psychologists cooperate with other professionals in order to serve their clients/patients effectively and appropriately."

Consider the following scenarios:

> A woman telephones a male psychologist to ask for an appointment, saying that she has just managed to extricate herself from an abusive relationship with a man against whom she has recently obtained a protection order. She would like to have several sessions with a psychologist to process her feelings about this disastrous relationship and to gain some insight into why she is having persistent nightmares and problems in being around men at her workplace. The psychologist has two highly competent female colleagues who specialize in the consequences of domestic violence at a local women's health center. Does the male psychologist take on the case?

Arguably, the appropriate response to this scenario is not obvious. If the psychologist himself is competent in dealing with the sequelae of domestic violence, he would not necessarily refer the client to a female colleague, though he could ask the client if she might prefer to work with a female therapist. If he does not have that competence, he would be best advised to refer the client to a colleague who is competent in that area, or to seek supervision from the colleague while treating this client.

> A client attends an intake session with a psychologist, having asked for treatment for depression. During the interview, the client mentions that he has been experiencing severe headaches and back pain for some weeks, though one of his relatives who works in a human services agency has convinced him that it's "all in his head" and that he's simply somaticizing his depressive issues.

What the psychologist should do in this case is straightforward. A medical consultation is necessary. It's possible that the client's physical complaints are not grounded in actual medical problems or biological abnormalities, of course, but they might be, and the psychologist is not competent to assess that. Far better for the client to consult a physician and be sent back to the psychologist with a clean bill of health than for him to be diagnosed months later with an inoperable brain tumor that could have been treated if detected earlier (Koocher & Keith-Spiegel, 1998).

When in doubt, psychologists should always refer a client for a consultation if there is a chance that another professional has the expertise and skill to contribute successfully to the management of the case (Nagy, 2000).

PART TWO

Psychological Assessment

5 General Issues in Psychological Assessment

The development of psychological tests was a significant milestone in the development of clinical psychology. Psychological assessment was the defining activity of clinical psychology in the first half of the twentieth century, and some continue to see assessment as the one activity that most clearly distinguishes clinical psychology from related disciplines.

Our plan for this chapter is to introduce the reader to some of the important issues in psychological assessment. The process of psychological assessment can be broken down into four stages: planning, data collection, data processing, and communicating findings. In the planning stage, psychologists determine what questions are to be addressed in the assessment and how to go about collecting information. The data collection stage involves gathering information via observations, interviews, testing, and record reviews. As the data are collected, psychologists are entering the processing stage. Its at this stage that the information is organized and interpreted. Finally, clinical psychologists communicate the assessment results. In practice, of course, each stage of the assessment overlaps with the others. The assessment plan (stage I) is modified as more information is collected (stage II) and interpreted (stage III). Nonetheless, we have organized our discussion of general issues in psychological assessment around the four stages.

Stage I: Planning the Assessment

Psychological assessment starts with a referral question. Someone wants to know something about an individual and believes that a psychologist can find it out. Sometimes the person asking the referral question is the client. A person who feels compelled to wash his or her hands 100 or more times a day might pose a straightforward question to a psychologist: "What's wrong with me?" Psychologists assess psychotherapy clients before initiating treatment. The questions in this type of assessment might be "Is this person likely to be helped by psychotherapy?" "What are the treatment goals?" and "What are the psychological and situational factors underlying the problem?"

Psychological assessments are also initiated by people other than the patient or client. A primary-care physician, a school system, the court, or a parent might refer someone to a psychologist for assessment. Sometimes people referring someone to a psychologist are not sure what it is they want to learn from the evaluation. Its the psychologist's job to try to help them formulate their concerns into a question that a psychological evaluation can address.

In some cases, referral sources want to know something that the psychologist cannot possibly tell them. For example, a psychologist might be asked, "Will Mr. Townsend (a patient on a psychiatric ward) harm anyone if he is released into the community?" As we will see in Chapter 16, while a psychologist may be able to provide information on the level of risk Mr. Townsend presents and the circumstances that would increase or decrease the risk of violence, the psychologist cannot answer the question as presented (i.e., "yes he will" or "no he won't") with much accuracy. In cases such as these psychologists need to educate referral sources about what can be learned from a psychological assessment.

Historically, the psychologist's role in some institutions and agencies has been administrator and interpreter of psychological tests. Our colleagues in psychiatry have been accused of viewing psychologists this way. They might refer a patient to the psychologists for "a psychological" or "a Rorschach and MMPI." Contemporary clinical psychologists would be reluctant to accept the referral under these circumstances. Instead, they would likely question, with varying degrees of tact, what it is the psychiatrist is interested in knowing.

Coming to some agreement with the client, or the people who referred the client, about what can and cannot be determined with a psychological assessment is the first thing a psychologist should do when accepting a new referral. The goal of any psychological evaluation follows from the referral question. Goals pursued in psychological evaluations can be grouped into three types: classification, description, and prediction.

Classification

One of the traditional goals of psychological assessment is to classify individuals. Although there are many ways in which people can be classified, the use of diagnostic labels is the predominant one in clinical psychology today. Although criticized by many (e.g., Albee, 1970; Carson, 1994, 1996; Follette & Houts, 1996; Szasz, 1961), the use of diagnostic labels for both clinical and research purposes has become the norm for clinical psychology. The classification system most often used by psychologists is the *Diagnostic and Statistical Manual of Mental Disorders* currently in its fourth edition (DSM-IV, American Psychiatric Association, 1994).

The first edition of the DSM was published in 1952 (DSM-I, American Psychiatric Association) and consisted of a glossary of descriptions of the diagnostic categories. DSM-II appeared in 1968 (American Psychiatric Association), and though it expanded the number of diagnostic categories from 60 to 145, it was very similar to DSM-I in that the descriptions were heavily influenced by psychoanalytic theory and were couched in psychiatric jargon. Diagnosis required a high degree of inference about internal states. For example, according to DSM-II, "Phobias are generally attributed to fears displaced to the phobic object or situation from some other object of which the patient is unaware" (American Psychiatric Association, 1968, p. 40).

Work began on the third edition of the DSM in 1974 and the manual was published in 1980 (DSM-III, American Psychiatric Association). DSM-III introduced several important changes in the way mental health problems were diagnosed. First, unlike its predecessors, the manual strove to be atheoretical so that it would be acceptable to clinicians and researchers from any theoretical camp. Second, DSM-III presented explicit diagnostic criteria for each disorder with specific rules about the number of criteria that had to be met for each diagnosis. The criteria were set so that diagnoses could be made with the lowest level of inference. Guidelines for making differential diagnoses were also provided. The third innovation was the multiaxial system. Giving a full DSM-III diagnosis involved describing the individual on five axes:

I. Clinical syndromes (e.g., schizophrenia, major depression)

II. Personality disorders and developmental disorders (e.g., borderline personality disorder, developmental reading disorder)

III. Physical conditions (e.g., diabetes)

IV. Severity of psychosocial stressors (e.g., recent divorce, loss of job, death of a loved one)

V. Highest level of adaptive functioning in the past year (a number rating rating from 1, "Superior," to 7, "Grossly Impaired")

The goal of the multiaxial system was to broaden clinician's and researcher's views of patients beyond the primary diagnosis to consider physical and situational factors and to recognize the heterogeneity of impairment among individuals with the same disorder.

Although DSM-III had its faults, it marked a significant improvement in the classification of mental disorders. One product of this improvement was the huge growth in both the quantity and quality of research into mental disorders that followed its publication. As the knowledge base grew, the flaws in DSM-III became clearer. One weakness, for example, was the use of hierarchical rules for diagnoses. In the DSM-III system, certain disorders superseded others so that if a person met criteria for more than one disorder only the diagnosis higher in the hierarchy was given. This system was artificial and suppressed information on comorbity (i.e., a single person meeting criteria for more than one disorder). For example, if a person met criteria for agoraphobia with panic attacks and generalized anxiety disorder in DSM-III, they were only given the former diagnosis. An interim revision of DSM-III was published in 1987 (DSM-III-R, American Psychiatric Association, 1987), which kept many of the positive features of DSM-III but eliminated some of the problems such as the hierarchical organization.

DSM-IV was published in 1994. This revision of the manual benefitted from improved quality and substantial quantity of research on mental disorders produced since the publication of DSM-III. Three sources of empirical data were used in revising DSM for the fourth edition (American Psychiatric Association, 1994). First, work groups of experts in the different classes of disorders were formed and assigned the task of systematically and comprehensively reviewing the published literature in their areas. The literature reviews were directed toward specific issues such as the clinical utility of each disorder (i.e., how does knowing the disorder help the clinician) or the appropriateness of specific diagnostic criteria. Second, existing data sets were reanalyzed in order to gather more information on issues for which there was insufficient published data or in cases where published findings painted a confusing picture. Researchers shared data sets with the work groups, which allowed them to explore how changing one or more diagnostic criteria would influence findings. The third source of data was a series of twelve field trials carried out to explore the impact of suggested changes to the diagnostic system.

The DSM-IV contains over 300 diagnoses and describes decision rules for arriving at each. The DSM-IV retained the multiaxial system introduced in DSM-III with the following modifications: Personality disorders and other significant maladaptive personality characteristics, along with mental retardation, are included in Axis II. Other developmental disorders, such as Expressive Language Disorder, are now included in Axis I. For Axis IV, rather than rating the severity of stressors, a checklist of nine descriptive categories of psychosocial and environmental problems is used. And Axis V is a rating of Global Assessment of Functioning, which is the clinician's rating of the individual's overall level of psychological health ranging from 90, indicating good functioning, to 1 indicating markedly impaired functioning. Table 5.1 includes examples of DSM-IV multiaxial diagnostic formulations.

In 2000, the American Psychiatric Association published the Diagnostic and Statistical Manual of Mental Disorders—Fourth Edition—Text Revision (DSM-IV-TR; American Psychiatric Association, 2000). There are no substantive changes from the DSM-IV in the diagnostic criteria for any disorder. There are no new disorders and no new subtypes of disorders. The changes from to DSM-IV have been to the text that accompanies the descriptions of some disorders. Recognizing that the DSM-IV is used not only as a diagnostic manual but also as an educational tool, a decision was made to revise the text to assure that it included the research findings published subsequent to 1992. (Although the DSM-IV was published in 1994, text was based upon literature available up to 1992.) Since the diagnostic manual is

TABLE 5.1   Examples of DSM-IV Multiaxial Diagnoses

Example 1

Axis I	309.81	Posttraumatic Stress Disorder, Chronic
	305.00	Alcohol Abuse
Axis II	301.6	Dependent Personality Disorder
Axis III		None
Axis IV		Threat of job loss
Axis V	GAF = 35	(current)

Example 2

Axis I	300.4	Dysthymic Disorder
	315.1	Mathematics Disorder
Axis II	V71.09	No diagnosis
Axis III	382.9	Otitis Media
Axis IV		Victim of child neglect
Axis V	GAF = 55	(current)

Example 3

Axis I	V61.1	Partner Relational Problem
Axis II	V71.09	No diagnosis
Axis III		None
Axis IV		Unemployment
Axis V	GAF = 83	(highest level past year)

Source: Adapted from American Psychiatric Association (1994).

used as an educational tool, the publishers felt that it was important that the text accompanying the diagnostic criteria reflect state-of-the-art knowledge.

The DSM-IV-TR represents the latest iteration of the popular system for categorizing mental disorders. The developers of the DSM recognize that the classification system is imperfect and that it will continue to be revised as new scientific evidence is collected. Critics of the diagnostic manual are skeptical about whether the changes seen in each new version are really the product of sober consideration of scientific findings. In any event, the accumulation of scientific knowledge is not the only rational basis for change in a classification system. Conceptual developments—advances in the way we view, value, or judge human behavior, leading to newer and more appropriate definitions of pathology—can be equally important.

A famous example of the impact of changes in social mores on psychiatric nomenclature is its handling of homosexuality. Gay men and lesbians were classified as having a mental disorder in DSM-I and DSM-II (American Psychiatric Association, 1952, 1968). With the publication of DSM-III (American Psychiatric Association, 1980), homosexuality was no longer a disorder unless it was "ego dystonic" (i.e., "There is a sustained pattern of homosexual arousal that the individual explicitly states has been unwanted and a persistent source of distress," p. 282). In DSM-III-R, homosexuality cannot be found in the list of mental disorders. However, the term does appear in the index, where the reader is directed to see Sexual Disorder Not Otherwise Classified, under which one finds "persistent and marked distress about one's sexual orientation" (p. 296). With DSM-IV, the word "homosexuality" does not even appear in the index, although "persistent and marked distress about sexual orientation" (p. 538) is still offered as an example of a Sexual Disorder Not Otherwise Classified.

Another controversial example can be seen in the proposed category "premenstrual dysphoric disorder." Several groups, including the Committee on Women of the American Psychological Association (1985) protested when this disorder was first suggested. They were offended by the pathologizing of a common and normal fluctuation in women's mood. Others welcomed the proposal because it would have given legitimacy to a pattern that causes genuine distress and temporary impairment in a minority of women. But there is the concern that approving the new category could buttress negative stereotypes about women and give ammunition to those who would restrict women's vocational opportunities. Thus far, premenstrual dysphoric disorder has not made it into the official nomenclature but diagnostic criteria for the disorder are included under Criteria Sets and Axes Provided for Further Study in DSM-IV-TR.

Criticisms of Diagnoses.   While some critics decry the influence of political and social factors on a nosological system that is supposedly based in science, others condemn the whole idea of diagnosing mental disorders. Several common criticisms of the diagnostic process have been noted. First, the use of a diagnostic label to describe a human being's behavior or emotional problems implies an understanding of the problem that is often not there. For example, a man seeks help from a mental health professional because he is distressed by an inability to have or maintain an erection. His medical doctors have found no physiological cause for his problem. His problem would be labeled male erectile disorder. While the label may assist the man in getting reimbursement from his insurance company, it really has no other function. By giving the problem a label, the clinician has not furthered his or her understanding of this man's condition. To explain the man's difficulty having an erection as being due to male erectile dysfunction involves circular reasoning (Man: "Doctor, why can't I get an erection?" Doctor: "Because you have male erectile dysfunction." Man: "How do you know I have this disorder?" Doctor: "Because you can't get an erection.").

A second commonly cited concern about diagnostic labels is their association with the medical model. The client's behavior is assumed to be the product of some disease state, according to this model. Clinical psychologists, particularly those trained in behavioral and humanistic traditions, tend to be uncomfortable with this way of understanding of understanding human behavior.

A third commonly voiced criticism of psychiatric diagnoses is their poor reliability. In this context, reliability refers to the agreement between two diagnosticians about the presence of specific diagnoses is a given individual. The diagnostic reliability of mental health disorders has tended to be quite poor historically. Psychiatric diagnoses using the first two editions of the DSM were notoriously unreliable. Improving the diagnostic reliability of mental disorders was one of the main goals of the major revision of the DSM that resulted in the creation of the third edition. Field trials using the DSM-III tended to find acceptable diagnostic reliability for the major mental disorders. But concerns about the reliability of psychiatric diagnoses remain (Sarbin, 1997). For example, reliability trials for the DSM-IV were not initiated until after the manual's publication and only a small number of diagnoses are being investigated (Kutchins & Kirk, 2000).

Finally, critics note psychiatric labels carry with them a negative social stigma. Individuals with psychiatric diagnoses in their medical histories may be discriminated against in job opportunities, housing, or social relationships (see Goffman, 1963). The mentally ill are viewed with suspicion by others and their behavior, which might seem perfectly normal in another person, can be misinterpreted as pathological. A well-known experiment conducted by Temerlin (1968) illustrated this point very effectively. Temerlin made an audiotape of an interview with an actor who was instructed to act slightly anxious but otherwise to respond to questions normally. The interview was then presented to a group of clinicians, one-third of whom were told that the person on the tape was being interviewed for a job. Another third of the clinicians were told that interview was with an interesting psychiatric patient who "looks neurotic but actually is quite psychotic." The final third of the clinicians were also told that the person on the tape was a psychiatric patient but the neurotic-psychotic suggestion was reversed. Temerlin found that what the clinicians were told strongly influenced the way in which they interpreted the responses of the person on the tape. Those who were told that the man was psychotic rated him as much more pathological than the clinicians in the other conditions. How the subject was labeled also impacted the diagnoses given by the clinicians: 15 of 25 psychiatrists and 7 of 22 clinical psychologists assigned a psychotic diagnosis to the man who had been labeled psychotic. None of the clinicians in the other two conditions diagnosed a psychotic disorder.

The criticisms of the use of diagnostic labels to describe individuals experiencing problems in living clearly have merit. However, these criticisms need to be balanced against the benefits of a system for classifying individuals into groups with similar characteristics. First, categorization of people in psychological distress helps researchers study the causes and treatments of their problems. The publication of DSM-III ushered in the modern era of research into mental disorders. Much of this research was made possible by improvement in diagnostic reliability of the diagnostic system. Second, accurate labeling can facilitate treatment. Knowing that other individuals who share important characteristics with the client respond favorably to certain treatments and not others can save the client from unnecessary distress and speed improvement. The treatment utility of diagnostic labels (i.e., whether knowing the diagnosis helps the clinician choose the best treatment) varies considerably. However, the association between diagnosis and treatment is much better with some other disorders. For example, the diagnoses panic disorder, bipolar disorder, and major depression have strong treatment utility. We know something about what is helpful for these disorders. Third, reliable and valid labels aid communication between professionals. By using appropriate labels, professionals can efficiently communicate a great deal of information.

Description

While psychiatric diagnoses can facilitate research, treatment planning, and communication, they fall short as descriptors of complex human beings. It should come as no surprise that a system that is made up of discrete categories cannot adequately capture all the intricacies and complexities of a human life. A second goal, therefore, of psychological assessment is often to provide a comprehensive *description* of the individual. The need to go beyond simple classification to providing rich descriptions of persons and the environments within which they live was recognized by clinical psychologists as long ago as the 1930s and 1940s (Murray, 1938; Rapaport, Gill, & Schafer, 1945, 1946). Traditionally, a detailed descriptive assessment would include a battery of psychological tests and interviews as well as observations of the individual in question. Behavior therapists have also been interested in detailed descriptive assessment of their clients, although they tend to use tools such as structured observation, interview, checklists, and behavioral diaries (Ciminero, Calhoun, & Adams, 1986; see also Chapter 9).

Psychological assessment geared toward providing a thorough description of the client tends to rely more heavily upon *dimensional,* as opposed to categorical, descriptors (Eysenck, 1970; Millon, 1991). Eysenck, for example, has empirically derived two dimensions of personality, neuroticism and extraversion. An individual's personality style can be plotted on these two dimensions. Other approaches involve rating people on several dimensions of personality (e.g., Widiger, Trull, Hurt, Clarkin, & Frances, 1987). In addition to personality traits or dimensions, environmental factors impacting upon the individual and the *person by situation* interaction are also explored in a comprehensive psychological assessment.

Descriptive psychological assessments can serve several functions. They are a rich source of research hypotheses and the data from a descriptive assessment can be used in research. For example, in studies of behavioral treatment of obsessive-compulsive disorder, pretreatment levels of depression have been shown to be negatively associated with treatment outcome (Foa, Grayson, & Steketee, 1982). Descriptive assessment can also help with treatment planning. Hypotheses about the variables that control the individual's problem behavior can be developed. These would provide the targets for intervention. For example, a detailed assessment of a depressed client can help to identify which aspects of the problem to target for treatment (e.g., sleep disturbance, suicidal ideation, and so on). Personality assessment can sometimes help clinicians plan psychotherapy strategies (see Butcher,

1990; Retzlaff, 1996, for examples). Finally, the data from descriptive assessments can be used to evaluate treatment outcome.

One criticism that has been leveled against comprehensive psychological assessment is that the findings often lack treatment utility. Recall that this is the same point has been made about psychiatric diagnoses. The weak relationship between assessment findings and treatment is a frequently cited criticism of traditional assessment batteries (Ciminero, 1986). A comprehensive psychological assessment, including tests of intellectual and personality functioning, interviews, and observation, provides a great deal of information, but much of this information has little if any impact upon what the clinician actually does with a client. In the current health-care delivery environment, there is an emphasis upon brief assessment and treatment. Thorough descriptive assessments that do not directly impact diagnosis or treatment planning may not long be practical for most practitioners.

Prediction

A third goal of psychological assessment is to make some prediction about a person's future behavior. "Will my psychotherapy client attempt to kill herself before our next session?" "Is Mr. Wyman likely to harm someone if he is released from the hospital?" "Can Charlie be mainstreamed into regular elementary school?" "Will Mr. Wood benefit from a specialized sex offender treatment program?" Questions such as these require a psychologist to predict a client's behavior in the future.

When a psychologist predicts that a certain behavior will occur and it does, it is referred to as a *true positive* prediction. If the prediction is that the behavior will occur and it does not, that is a *false positive*. Take the case where a psychologist is asked to predict whether alcoholic clients will remain sober for six months after leaving a treatment program. A true positive prediction would be when the psychologist says a person will stay sober and that person does; it would be a false positive prediction if the psychologist says a person will stay sober but that person falls off the wagon. The term *true negative* is used to describe the prediction that, in this case, the person will relapse into alcohol abuse and the person does. *False negative* describes the prediction that the person will relapse but the person stays sober. The *sensitivity* of a psychological assessment is the probability that when a behavior is predicted to occur it actually does and *specificity* refers to the probability that when a behavior is predicted not to occur it does not. In other words, sensitivity is the probability of a true positive and specificity is the probability of a true negative. In our example, the sensitivity of the psychologist's predictions is the percentage of the people who remain sober who were predicted to remain sober. If 20 people stayed sober and the psychologist accurately predicted 16 of them, sensitivity is 80 percent. Specificity would be the percentage of the people who relapse and were predicted to relapse. If 80 people relapsed and the psychologist accurately predicted 60 of them, specificity is 75 percent. (The terms sensitivity and specificity are also used to describe the accuracy of diagnostic procedure. A diagnostic test that is both sensitive and specific will pick up most of the cases of the disorder and falsely diagnose people without the disorder infrequently.) If you think about it for a moment, you will see that sensitivity and specificity are related. If the psychologist predicted that every patient discharged from the alcohol treatment program would stay sober, his assessment is highly sensitive (he correctly predicted all the people who stay sober) but not specific at all (he incorrectly predicted sobriety for all of those who started drinking again).

Psychologists are not fortune tellers. Education and training does not endow them with a special ability to see into the future. Instead, psychologists integrate information from a variety of sources and try to make informed guesses about how people are likely to behave in the future. This is an extremely difficult task. Psychologists' ability to accurately predict a person's behavior is affected by the *base rate* of the behavior of interest. Common phenomena are easy to predict. For example, a psychologist who predicts that a 14-year-old client will become sexually active sometime over the next eight years is on pretty solid ground. Rarer behaviors (e.g., murder, suicide) are much harder to predict. We will use suicide prediction to illustrate the base rate problem.

The Base Rate Problem. Even the most experienced clinician is bound to be wrong more often than not when he or she predicts that someone will commit suicide. The reason is that suicide is an infrequent, or rare, event. The base rate for suicide in the general population is about 1.2 per 10,000 people (Fremouw et al., 1990). That means that less than .0002 percent of the population will die by suicide. Even when people present with some of the risk factors described in Box 5.1, the true probability that they will kill themselves is actually quite low. For example, the chances that someone who has made a suicide attempt will complete suicide within the next year is about 2 percent. That means that while the risk for suicide among people who have recently attempted is about 10,000 times higher than for the general population (2/.0002), 98 percent of them will not kill themselves within a year of the attempt (100 percent–2 percent). No matter how sensitive the assessment methods, when one predicts a low base rate phenomenon, the chances of a false positive prediction are quite high.

The following example may help to clarify the issue of predicting low base rate phenomena. Let's say that the base rate of suicide among people diagnosed with major depression is 5 per 1,000 per year (actual estimates vary from about 2.3 to 5.7 per 1,000 for people diagnosed with depression; see Fremouw et al., 1990). Now let's say a psychologist has an assessment method that has .80 specificity and sensitivity. That is, the method will correctly identify 80 percent of people who will commit suicide within the next year and 80 percent of those who will not commit suicide. If the psychologist applies the method to 1,000 people with major depression, four of the five (80 percent) clients who would kill themselves would be correctly identified (true positives). And 796 of the 995 (80 percent) who would not commit suicide would be correctly identified (true negatives). One of the clients who would commit suicide, therefore, would be incorrectly identified as nonsuicidal (false negative). Finally, 199 of the nonsuicidal clients would be incorrectly identified as suicidal (false positives). Therefore, of the 203 (199 + 4) clients who were predicted to be suicidal, only about 2 percent (4/199) would actually have killed themselves. If the method was used to determine which patients should be hospitalized for their own protection, 98 percent (199/203) of those hospitalized would, in fact, not have required hospitalization to protect them from killing themselves (see Table 5.2)

The problem of overprediction (i.e., lots of false positives) will occur whenever one is dealing with low base rate events. When predicting a phenomenon that occurs infrequently,

TABLE 5.2   Suicide Prediction: A Hypothetical Example

Psychologist's Prediction	True Outcome		Totals
	Suicide	*No Suicide*	**Totals**
Suicide	4 (True Positive)	199 (False Positive)	203
No Suicide	1 (False Negative)	796 (True Negative)	797
Totals:	5	995	1,000

one would be correct most of the time if one simply never predicted that the phenomenon would occur. To use the above example, if the clinician predicted that none of the clients would kill themselves, he or she would have been right 99.5 percent of the time (995/1,000). However, five people would have committed suicide. By applying the test, the clinician actually would be correct less often overall (80 percent correct: [4 + 796]/1,000), but four people would have been prevented from killing themselves.

In addition to the base rate problem, another factor that limits psychologists' ability to predict future behavior accurately is psychologists' limited knowledge of the wide variety of situational influences that will impact the client. For example, a psychologist who does not know that the patient he has recommended for release from the hospital will discover his wife in bed with another man when he gets home cannot weigh this information in the assessment of the patient's suicide risk. See Box 5.1 for discussion of suicide risk factors.

In clinical settings, psychologists asked to make prediction about the future behavior of clients must weigh the costs of accurate and inaccurate predictions. Consider the psychologist treating a paranoid client who is particularly agitated during a session and makes some general threats about "getting even with the bastards." The client has a history of violence and the psychologist is faced with the decision of whether it is appropriate to have the client hospitalized. The psychologist in this situation is faced with the task of predicting whether the client will harm someone. In making the decision, the psychologist must weigh the costs of each possibility: psychologist does not hospitalize and the client does not harm anyone (true negative; minimal costs); psychologist does not hospitalize and the client harms someone (false negative; high costs to the person who is harmed; to the client, who now has legal problems; and to the psychologist, who may be sued by the client and/or the victim); psychologist hospitalizes and the client would not have been dangerous (false positive; high cost to the client, whose freedom is unnecessarily restricted and who may be required to pay for the hospital stay); psychologist hospitalizes and the client would have harmed someone (true positive; cost to the client weighed against protection of the victim and the psychologist).

Clinical versus Statistical Prediction.   Psychologists are often asked to make predictions about how an individual will behave at some point in the future. Data are gathered from

BOX **5.1**

Suicide Risk Assessment

Clinical psychologists must grapple with the ethical and legal issues presented by individuals who are at risk of committing suicide in any clinical setting they work. Whether the individual is an acutely despondent psychotherapy client being seen in a private practice, a troubled teenager being evaluated by a psychologist consulting to a group home, or a person who has been brought to the hospital to be considered for involuntary hospitalization, the clinical psychologist must make a judgment about suicide risk and take appropriate action. In researcher settings as well, psychologists may not be immune from the responsibility of considering the risk of suicide presented by their research participants (Sigmon, 1995). Psychologists have an ethical obligation to manage the problem of suicide competently (Bongar, 1992) and may face malpractice suits if they fail to do so.

The possibility that someone with whom a psychologist has a professional relationship will commit suicide is considerable. Chemtob, Hamada, Bauer, Torigoe, and Kinney (1988) found that 22 percent of the clinical psychologists they surveyed had experienced a client's death by suicide. Not surprisingly, when clients kill themselves, it has a significant impact, both professionally and personally, upon mental health professionals (Chemtob, Bauer, Hamada, Pelowski, & Muraoka, 1989). Psychologists rank work with suicidal clients as the most stressful professional activity (Deutsch, 1984).

Assessing suicide risk is a challenging endeavor. To do so competently requires an understanding of research on suicide risk factors and how to apply it (Fremouw, Perczel, & Ellis, 1990). Risk factors for suicide can be organized into three types: demographic, clinical, and psychological. What follows is a brief summary of some of the better-known risk factors (see Fremouw et al., 1990, for a more detailed presentation and discussion).

Demographic Risk Factors

Sex: Men commit suicide about three times more often than women, although women will make suicide attempts about three times more frequently than men.

Age: Suicide risk tends to increase with age. This is most true for white males. The period of greatest risk for white females is between 33 and 64 years of age, with their risk decreasing at age 65 and beyond. Nonwhite men and women are most likely to kill themselves between the ages of 25 and 34.

Race: White males are the group at greatest risk for suicide. About 70 percent of all completed suicides are white male. Other races kill themselves at about half the rate of whites. The only exception to this is certain Native American tribes (e.g., Apache and Southwest Pueblo), who have suicide rates even higher than white males.

Marital status: Unmarried people are more likely to kill themselves than are married people. This is true whether one is separated, widowed, divorced, or never married. The risk of suicide in unmarried people in increasing order is single, widowed, divorced, separated.

Living arrangements: People who live alone are at greater risk for suicide.

Living environment: Suicide rates are higher for urban compared with suburban and rural populations.

Employment: The unemployed kill themselves at a higher rate than do the employed.

Clinical Risk Factors

Daily functioning: People who maintain a household, hold a job, and socialize are at low risk for suicide. People who struggle in these areas are more likely to kill themselves.

(continued)

B O X   **5.1**   **Continued**

Lifestyle A person whose life is marked by frequent changes in jobs, friendships, and living arrangements presents a greater risk for suicide.

Psychiatric history: A person who has a history of significant psychiatric problems is at higher risk. A history of schizophrenia, depression, alcohol dependence, or personality disorder, in particular, suggests an increased risk for suicide.

Medical history: People with chronic or terminal illnesses are more likely to kill themselves.

Family history of suicide: When a family member or significant other has killed himself or herself, it increases the probability of suicide in the client.

Previous suicide attempts: For a person who has attempted suicide, the chances that he or she will eventually commit suicide are about 10 percent to 15 percent. One to 2 percent of people who attempt to kill themselves will complete a suicide within the next year.

Psychological Risk Factors

Depression-anxiety: Perhaps not surprisingly, people who kill themselves tend to be experiencing high levels of subjective distress. They may be anxious and depressed. Many people believe that suicide is often motivated by a desire to escape psychological pain.

Hostility: People who have a history of anger and hostility expressed toward themselves and others are at greater risk for suicide compared to those without such a history.

Hopelessness: People who commit suicide tend to be hopeless about the future. They believe that the future is bleak and that they cannot do anything about it.

Disorientation/disorganization: Individuals who have poor reality contact and difficulty thinking rationally are at risk for suicide. Some psychotic individuals kill themselves in response to command hallucinations (i.e., they hear voices telling them to take some action). Higher rates of suicide are seen in individuals with schizophrenia or organic brain impairment.

Suicide plan: In general, the more specific and well-worked out an individual's plan for committing suicide, the greater the risk. Risk is particularly high for people whose specific plan is highly lethal and easily accessible (e.g., "I am going to take the gun from my desk drawer and shoot myself in the head").

Final arrangements: Giving away of one's possessions, writing a suicide note, or making plans for the care of pets or loved ones suggests the person is at significant risk for committing suicide.

There are no formulas for combining these risk factors to determine the probability of a successful suicide. In general, the greater the number of risk factors, the higher the risk. However, the presence of one or two significant risk factors in the absence of any others requires action. For example, a suicide note that details a lethal suicide plan indicates high risk even when no other demographic, clinical, or psychological risk factors are present.

interviews, psychological testing, background records, and observations. The psychologist then combines the data and comes to some conclusion about how the individual in question is likely to behave. There are generally two methods of combining information for the purposes of making predictions. Using the *clinical method,* a psychologist constructs a model to explain the person's psychological functioning and uses this model to predict how the individual will behave in the future (Wierzbicki, 1993). The psychologist gathers a great deal of data about a person and integrates this information to paint a picture of the person as a unique individual distinct from all others. The model offers an explanation of why the person will behave or feel in certain ways in the future (Dawes, 1994). In contrast, the *statistical method* (sometimes called the *actuarial method*) involves classifying the person based upon characteristics he or she shares with others. The person is then predicted to behave the way similar people have behaved in the past. Insurance companies, for example, determine premiums based upon an actuarial prediction about how likely it is that an individual will get into an accident based upon the accident rates of people of the same age, marital status, gender, and with similar driving records. The statistical method does not attempt to explain why the person will behave the way he or she will.

Professional psychologists tend to rely upon the clinical method in their practice work. They use their training in theories of human behavior, their understanding of relevant research findings, and their experience to draw conclusions about how people are likely to behave. Based upon this training, knowledge, and experience, psychologists may claim expertise, thus implying that their ability to make certain predictions is greater than that of the average person. And as Robyn Dawes (1994), a strong critic of professional psychology, notes, this expertise is used to justify the high fees psychologists sometimes charge for their expert opinions. But it is reasonable to ask, "How well do these mental health experts do in comparison to actuarial predictions?" (Dawes, p. 82). In his book *House of Cards: Psychology and Psychotherapy Built on Myth,* Dawes concludes that the answer is not very well.

Dawes's book appeared forty years after another text strongly critical of the clinical method. In 1954, Paul Meehl published *Clinical versus Statistical Prediction: A Theoretical Analysis and Review of the Literature,* in which he examined the findings from about twenty published studies that compared the clinical and statistical methods. The studies were quite varied in the behaviors that were predicted (e.g., academic success, criminal recidivism). Meehl concluded that of the studies he reviewed, "in all but one . . . the predictions made actuarially were either approximately equal or superior to those made by the clinician" (p. 119). In a later paper, Meehl (1965) noted that the one study favoring clinical prediction employed a questionable statistical analysis. The following example gives a flavor of the type of studies reviewed by Meehl (1954). A statistical combination of three variables (marital status, length of psychotic episode, and patient "insight" into his or her condition) was superior to the hospital's medical and psychological staff members at predicting response to electroshock therapy (described in Dawes, 1994).

In his review, Meehl focused upon studies that compared methods of integrating information for the purposes of making predictions. The studies he examined primarily compared clinicians to statistical formulas when both predictions were based upon the same data. In another important literature review, Jack Sawyer (1966) expanded upon Meehl's review by examining 45 studies including many in which clinicians had more information than that included in the statistical model. His review also included studies in which the experts had access to the statistical model's predictions prior to their own data collection (i.e., the clinician would know what the formula predicted before interviewing the person). The latter type of study allowed for an examination of whether clinicians could improve upon the statistical method. Sawyer's review also examined the role clinical judgments might play in predictions. Sawyer came to the same conclusion as Meehl regarding the relative accuracy of predictions based upon clinical and statistical methods of integrating data: The statistical approach was clearly superior. This was true even when clinicians had access to information not used in the statistical formulas. Furthermore, Sawyer concluded that clinicians could not improve upon the accuracy of statistical prediction. In fact, when clinicians knew the actuarial predictions and were instructed to improve upon them, they tended to do worse than the statistical predictions alone. Sawyer did, however, conclude that there was a role for clinicians in the prediction process. The most accurate predictions were made by statistical formulas that included both clinically derived and mechanically derived data. "This suggests that the clinician may be able to contribute most not by direct prediction, but rather by providing, in objective form, judgements to be combined mechanically" (p. 193).

As one might expect, the conclusions drawn by Meehl and Sawyer were not received enthusiastically by professional psychology. Meehl's 1954 book sparked an intense debate that continued over the next three decades (Holt, 1986; Meehl, 1986; Sarbin, 1986). Several counterarguments have been offered with some frequency (Dawes, 1994; Wierzbicki, 1993). First, methodological weakness of the individual studies included in the reviews have been pointed out (Holt, 1970). Flaws can, in fact, be found in many of the studies, particularly those included in the earlier reviews. Nonetheless, even accepting that some of the research is weak, the sheer volume of studies showing a consistent superiority for actuarial predictions make it difficult to ignore the conclusion. For example, Meehl (1986) writes:

> There is no controversy in social science which shows such a large body of qualitatively diverse studies coming out so uniformly in the same direction as this one. When you are pushing 90 investigations, predicting everything from the outcomes of football games to the diagnosis of liver disease and when you can hardly come up with a half dozen studies showing even a weak tendency in favor of the clinician, it is time to draw a practical conclusion.

A second common defense of the clinical method is to argue that the research studies comparing clinical to actuarial methods did not use experts to make clinical predictions. Holt (1970), for example, pointed out that in 23 of the 45 studies reviewed by Sawyer (1966), the people making clinical predictions were not trained psychologists or psychiatrists. Several studies used psychology graduate students as judges and one even used sports writers. The fact that many studies did not use true experts is used to argue that the overall findings cannot be generalized to real clinical situations. Dawes (1994), however, points out that, while many studies did not use experts, many did. And the latter did not find experts to be superior. In fact, many found that experts performed no better than nonexpert judges such as graduate students. In one study, in fact, psychologists were no more accurate than their secretaries at distinguishing the responses of schizophrenic from brain-injured patients on a neuropsychological test (Goldberg, 1959, cited in Dawes, 1994).

A third criticism of the research is that many of the studies did not *cross-validate* their findings (Holt, 1970). In this type of research, to cross-validate means to create a statistical formula to predict a criterion using one data set and then applying the formula to a new set of data. Statistical formulas are usually created by using regression procedures. These procedures create the optimal prediction equation for a specific set of data. When the formula is used to make predictions with a new set of data (cross-validation), it is never as successful as with the original sample (Wierzbicki, 1993). When a statistical formula created with a specific data set is compared to a clinician's prediction with the same data set, the statistical formula will have a clear advantage. To be fair to Meehl, it should be noted that he pointed out this problem with the original data set he reviewed in his 1954 book. Holt noted that fully one-third of the studies cited by Sawyer (1966) did not use cross-validation. This is an important criticism. However, two-thirds of the studies reviewed by Sawyer did use some form of cross-validation and the statistical method was superior in these investigations.

The fourth frequently offered argument against the superiority of the statistical method is that the studies demonstrating this effect lack "ecological validity" (Dawes, 1994; McArthur, 1956). In other words, the tasks presented to clinicians were not representative of the tasks they face in actual practice. For example, in some studies neuropsychologists were asked to make judgments about patients based solely on the patients' responses to psychological tests. Critics point out that this is something a neuropsychologist would never do in practice. Dawes counters this argument by pointing out that the tasks clinicians were typically asked to do would be components of real-world evaluations. For example, while neuropsychologists would not blindly interpret test findings, interpretation of test scores would be part of the overall evaluations. If clinicians do not do well on the components of an evaluation, why should one suspect that they would do better on the entire task? Dawes offers the following analogy. If he claims to be able to play a complicated piano concerto brilliantly, but shows that he cannot play scales very easily, we are unlikely to believe his claim about the concerto—and with good reason.

The types of arguments offered in defense of the clinical method assume that if methodological inadequacies were corrected or different tasks or judges were used, the clinical method would emerge as superior. This is, of course, only an assumption. Thus far, the data are not there to support it. Subsequent to his 1954 book, Meehl periodically updated his review of the literature and continued to draw the same conclusion (Meehl, 1957, 1965, 1986). More recently, Dawes, Faust, and Meehl (1989) published an article in the prestigious journal *Science* in which they reviewed close to 100 studies comparing clinical and statistical methods in the social sciences. They concluded that in almost every study actuarial predictions equaled or surpassed those based upon clinical judgment.

It may provide some solace to clinical psychologists to know that they are not alone in falling short when compared to the statistician. Studies in medicine are finding that computer programs can outperform physicians in some diagnostic and prognostic tasks (see Dawes, 1994, for examples). Statistical formulas, for example, have been found to be better at predicting future heart attacks than physicians (Lee et al., 1986, cited in Dawes, 1994).

The debate about the relative merits of statistical and clinical prediction is essentially over and the result is humbling for those schooled in the clinical method. "The consensus of opinion is that statistical prediction is more accurate than clinical prediction" (Milner & Campbell, 1995, p. 21). "People's behavior and feelings are best predicted by viewing them as members of an aggregate and by determining what variables *generally* predict for that aggregate and how" (Dawes, 1994, p. 101; italics in original). While some clinicians may be disheartened, true scientist-practitioner psychologists need not be. The variety of contexts within which psychologists are asked to make predictions about others is considerable. There are no published tables of statistical formulas to which clinicians can turn in most clinical situations. However, as scientists, clinical psychologists should have the skills to approach the problem systematically: review the literature to identify likely predictor variables, collect the necessary data, and develop, test, and modify prediction equations.

Stage II: Data Collection

Jerome Sattler (1988) describes interviews, norm-referenced tests, observations, and informal assessment methods as the four "pillars" of psychological assessment. To these we would add a fifth: examination of life records. This set of five strategies are the basic methods of data-collection in psychological assessment. A detailed discussion of interviewing, norm-referenced testing, and observational methods will be presented in the following chapters. At this point we provide an overview of the methods of psychological assessment.

The clinical interview is undoubtedly the most common method for gathering information in psychological assessment. It is part of almost any evaluation and is often the only method psychologists use to collect information about their clients. No matter what one's theoretical orientation, the interview provides a straightforward means of gathering information. The popularity of the clinical interview is probably related to its convenience and flexibility. Interviews can be carried out almost anywhere and require no special equipment. They can be organized around specific goals and adapted for a variety of purposes. They can vary in level of formality depending upon the objective. Interviews provide "self-report" data: the individual's report about his or her thoughts, feelings, and behaviors and those of others. Clinicians need to be mindful, of course, that this information is prone to distortion based upon the circumstances of the assessment, the individual's mood, the impression he or she hopes to create upon the clinician, and other factors.

Perhaps the greatest advantage of psychological testing is that it allows the clinician to compare the performance of one individual with that of hundreds, or in some cases thousands, of others who have taken the same test. Instructions for test administration are *standardized*—that is, everyone is administered the test in the same manner—and the testing situation, while not exactly the same for every individual, is generally consistent for each examinee. The psychological test then is a systematic way of collecting a sample of an individual's behavior under precisely specified conditions so that it can be compared to the behavior of similar individuals under the same conditions.

Norm-referenced tests are systematic means of collecting samples of behavior under relatively standardized conditions. They are designed to help us understand some aspects of people's knowledge, skills, and personality (Green, 1981). "Norm-referenced tests are standardized on a clearly defined group, termed the norm group, and scaled so that each individual score reflects a rank within the norm group" (Sattler, 1988, p. 3). Tests have been developed for assessing every conceivable area of human functioning. The quality of psychological tests varies considerably. The responsibility for evaluating tests and choosing those that are appropriate given the individual being evaluated and the goals of the assessment falls to the psychologist. When we discuss types of psychological tests in Chapters 7 and 8, we will discuss some of the factors psychologists consider when choosing tests. Some of the statistical and psychometric concepts that are important to test selection are reviewed in Appendix B for the interested reader.

Observation provides valuable assessment information. It can be used to assess directly areas of interest. For example, an assessment of parenting skills might include an observation of the parent with his or her children. Observations are also used to collect information that helps clinicians develop hypotheses about the data collected through interviews and psychological testing. Observing an otherwise relaxed and eloquent parent fidget and stammer when asked about discipline strategies would likely color the way in which the clinician interprets the parent's response. Evidence of anxiety, depression, or distractibility may lead a psychologist to hypothesize that the score on an intelligence test underestimates a child's true intellectual abilities. Observational methods vary in degree of formality and similarity to the natural environment.

A wide variety of strategies can be grouped under the rubric of informal assessment techniques. The term refers to strategies psychologists use to gather important information about a specific individual for which there is no norm-referenced assessment method available. An example might be asking a child, after the completion of a standardized test, to try again to answer some items he or she missed on a timed subtest, only the second time there is no time limit. In this manner, the psychologist is attempting to gather information about why the child failed the items during the formal administration of the task. While informal assessment strategies can provide useful information, they must be used with caution since the technical qualities of the methods (e.g., normative responses, reliability, validity; see below) are unknown (Sattler, 1988).

As all of us proceed through life, a partial record of our accomplishments, failures, and problems accrues. Academic, employment, arrest, and hospital records provide valuable information about important life experiences. Accessing these records in a psychological assessment can serve a variety of purposes. Records can direct the psychologist toward areas of inquiry that might have been overlooked otherwise (e.g., "Tell me about this assault conviction"). They can also provide a reference against which the client's self-report is gauged. Gaining access to an individual's arrest record can help the clinician interpret the client's response to the question "Have you ever been arrested?" Checking collateral sources of information is particularly important when the client is heavily invested in the outcome of the evaluation. For example, child protective services records would be an important source of information when evaluating a parent in a child abuse case.

Stage III: Processing Assessment Data

How psychologists go about conducting psychological assessments is guided by their theoretical orientation. Psychologists' theoretical models direct the goals of the assessment, the methods used, and, most importantly, the way in which findings are interpreted. Psychologists view assessment findings through theoretical glasses. Theory guides how one makes sense of clients' behavior. The same piece of information means different things to different psychologists. For example, a male college student reports that he becomes extremely anxious whenever he initiates conversation with a female peer. The psychoanalyst might see the client's anxiety as a sign that he has poor control over id-driven sexual impulses. A trait-oriented psychologist might take the client's report as evidence of neuroticism. A cognitive therapist would hypothesize that the client holds negative beliefs about his ability to cope with the interaction and irrational ideas about the consequences of behaving less than perfectly. A behavior therapist might view the client's report as evidence of a conditioned emotional reaction learned from prior negative experiences interacting with females. Finally, a psychologist who adheres to a medical model might view the young man's report as evidence of social phobia.

Most clinical psychologists do not rigidly adhere to one theoretical viewpoint. A cognitive-behavioral clinician might also see the client as meeting diagnostic criteria for social phobia. The clinician can use the diagnosis to facilitate treatment planning or communication with referral sources without necessarily conceptualizing the problem as being the product of an underlying disease state. Surveys of psychologists reveal that the most frequently identified theoretical orientation is "eclectic" (Zook & Walton, 1989). Nonetheless, the fact that psychologists tend not to adhere slavishly to one theoretical perspective does not mean that they do not have a working model of behavior that guides, either implicitly or explicitly, their interpretation of assessment findings.

One broad distinction that is often made between ways of viewing psychological assessment data is the *sign* versus *sample* interpretation of human behavior (Wiggins, 1973). In the sign approach, human behavior is viewed as a sign of some underlying characteristic. For example, psychodynamic psychologists view responses to psychological tests as signs of underlying personality dynamics. Trait theorists view assessment findings as signs of underlying personality traits. And in the medical model, assessment data is examined for evidence of underlying disease states or mental illness. The alternative interpretation is to view assessment behavior as a sample of clients' behavior. This view is associated with the behavioral perspective. No underlying causes are inferred. Rather, clients' responses to psychological tests, or observed behavior, or what clients report about their behavior, are viewed simply as samples of the ways in which the client behaves in various contexts. When a client's behavior is viewed as a sign of some underlying characteristic, it involves a considerable level of inference on the clinician's part. On the other hand, viewing assessment findings as samples requires very little inference.

A third way of viewing assessment findings is not tied to any particular theoretical perspective. Assessment data can be viewed as *correlates* (Wiggins, 1973). Viewing data as correlates involves a midlevel of inference between signs (high inference) and samples (low inference). Inferences made about the individual are based upon the known correlates of the observed behavior. For example, if a psychologist is told that person A took an overdose of Tylenol and was rushed to the emergency room for treatment, the psychologist might infer that the individual is a women in her 20s who is moderately depressed and has felt little emotional support from significant others. These inferences are based upon what is known about individuals who attempt suicide by overdose (Fremouw et al., 1990). The psychologist might also infer that the woman has a borderline personality disorder since suicide attempts are very common in people described as borderline (Linehan & Kehrer, 1993), although this inference is riskier since most people who make a suicide attempt are not borderline. In drawing inferences based upon known relationships, the psychologists could be wrong, of course. Person A could be a 60-year-old male with Alzheimer's disease. But the psychologist's inferences are the best guesses based upon the characteristics most strongly correlated with unsuccessful suicide by overdose. Another illustration might bring home the point about viewing assessment findings as correlates more clearly. What can you tell about a person if the only thing you know about him is that he plays in the National Basketball Association? Think about it for a minute. If you conclude that he is over six feet tall, African American (in 1997 about 80 percent of NBA players were African American), attended college, is wealthy, and has exceptional athletic ability, in all likelihood you are right on target.

Clinical Judgment

When clinical psychologists combine psychological assessment findings, some degree of subjectivity enters into the process, for better or worse. *Clinical judgment* is the term used to describe the subjective component of clinicians' decision making about their clients. Conventional wisdom holds that clinical judgment is something that develops with training and experience. As the professional gains more experience, it is assumed that the validity of his or her clinical judgment improves. Often the processes involved in clinical judgment cannot be explained other than by reference to the clinician's experience. Clinical judgment has been described as "intuitive" (Wiggins, 1973) and therefore not open to scientific scrutiny. A strong faith in the validity of clinical judgment was modeled by Freud, who did not see value in experimental tests of psychoanalytic interpretations (Shakow & Rapaport, 1964).

As a field, clinical psychology was generally accepting of the validity of clinical judgments throughout the first half of the twentieth century (Wierzbicki, 1993). In the 1950s, however, Paul Meehl (1954) and others raised serious concerns about clinical judgment and called for experimental study of its accuracy. Meehl wrote, "We of all people, ought to be highly suspicious of ourselves . . . [and] have no right to assume that entering the clinic has resulted in some miraculous mutations and made us singularly free from the ordinary human errors which characterized our psychological ancestors" (pp. 27–28).

Since Meehl's call to action, scores of studies of clinical judgment have been published. By and large these studies have shown that clinicians' judgments are highly suspect. More importantly, these studies have identified some of the factors that affect clinical judgment. Some of the most well-established factors are discussed below. The interested reader should see Wierzbicki (1993) for a more detailed discussion.

Preconceived Notions. Clinicians' judgments about their clients are influenced by what they expect to find (Arkes, 1981). We all have "implicit personality theories" (Bruner & Tagiuri, 1954) that lead us to expect that certain characteristics go together. For example, when subjects were told that a boy is "aggressive," they expected him to be cold and self-centered and not friendly or charitable (Shweder, 1977, cited in Arkes, 1981). Similarly, clinicians hold assumptions about what client characteristics go together. The strength of these preconceived notions can overpower findings that are inconsistent with the expectations biasing the clinician's judgment.

Simply identifying an individual as a mental health client or patient can influence the way that person's behavior is perceived. As we saw earlier, an interviewee whom clinicians believed to be a psychiatric patient was judged more negatively than if the clinicians thought he was a job applicant (Temerlin, 1968). In another famous—or some might say infamous (Spitzer, 1975)—study, Rosenhan (1973) documented how the behavior of twelve healthy people who gained access to a mental facility by falsely claiming they heard voices was interpreted as pathological by hospital staff.

Clinicians' beliefs about people based upon their gender, race, or socioeconomic background can influence their clinical judgments. Gender, race, or class biases, however, are not as pervasive as some have suggested (e.g., Sleek, 1996). Older literature reviews failed to find consistent evidence that clinical judgment is negatively influenced by clients' race

(Abramowitz & Dokecki, 1977; Abramowitz & Murray, 1983) or gender (Abramowitz & Dokecki, 1977; Whitley, 1979; Davidson & Abramowitz, 1980), although some evidence of social class biases was identified (Lopez, 1989). In a more recent review of the literature, Garb (1997) has identified some evidence of biases consistently found by researchers. Garb is careful to define bias as the situations "when the accuracy of judgments varies as a function of client race, social class or gender" (p. 99). Notice that the definition refers to the *accuracy* of judgment. Diagnoses, clinician's ratings, or intelligence estimates, for example, may vary as a function of race, gender, or socioeconomic status for reasons other than the biases of the clinicians. For example, the fact that epidemiological studies find a higher prevalence of depression in women than in men is generally believed to be a reflection of the true difference between the sexes and not a product of biased diagnosticians. Evidence of gender bias would be variability in the accuracy of clinical judgment associated with the gender of the client. For example, McNeil and Binder (1995; cited in Garb, 1997) found that more false positive predictions were made about the likelihood that a male patient would be violent and more false negative predictions were made about female patients' potential for violence. When clinicians were wrong, they were more likely to predict that a male would be violent and he was not; and that a female would not be violent and she was. This type of evidence indicates gender bias.

Some of the consistent biases found by Garb (1997) include the following. African American and Hispanic patients are more likely to be given a diagnosis of schizophrenia than are white patients, who are more likely to be diagnosed with psychotic affective disorder. Women are more likely to be diagnosed with histrionic personality disorder and men with antisocial personality disorder even when clinicians are presented with the exact same background information about the clients. And clinicians are more likely to recommend psychotherapy for middle-class clients than for poor clients. Middle-class clients are also expected to do better than lower-class clients.

Although Garb (1997) has found evidence for race, class, and gender influences upon clinical judgment, it important to note that his review summarizes many areas in which biases based upon these factors could not be found. For example, race (African American versus white) did not effect clinicians' predictions about children's academic, vocational, or social functioning (Huebner & Cummings, 1986, cited in Garb, 1997). Gender bias in the diagnosis of a variety of psychiatric disorders such as schizophrenia, posttraumatic stress disorder, alcohol abuse, delusional disorder, and others could not be found. Nor could gender bias be found in clinician's treatment decisions about children and adolescents. The interested reader should see Garb (1997) for a comprehensive review of the research on gender, social class, and racial influences upon clinical judgment.

Confirmation Bias.   While clinicians' perceptions of their clients' behavior may be influenced by their preconceived notions about the clients, these notions also may affect the way clinicians go about gathering additional information. Psychologists form hypotheses about their clients based upon the information they receive with the referral, their preconceived notions, and the information they gather early in the assessment. Psychologists tend to form initial opinions about their clients quite quickly (Meehl, 1960). These early hypotheses are then tested as the clinician gathers more information. Unfortunately, psychologists, like most people, are prone to look for information that is consistent with their hypotheses and fail to elicit information that is inconsistent. This tendency is known as the confirmation bias.

The kinds of questions clinicians ask and the way they word questions are influenced by their hypotheses about their clients. For example, if a psychologist forms the hypothesis that a client is introverted, he is likely to ask a question like "What factors make it hard for you to really open up to people?" But if the psychologist thinks the person is an extrovert, the question is more likely to be "In what situations are you most talkative?" (Snyder, 1981, cited in Arkes, 1981). These questions are likely to yield information that is consistent with the clinician's original hypothesis. Clinicians tend not to pursue information that will disconfirm their hypotheses. The tendency to pursue confirmatory information is very strong and not limited to mental health professionals. Even people trained in the scientific method tend to use confirmatory as opposed to disconfirmatory strategies to test hypotheses. Mahoney (1976; cited in Wierzbicki, 1993) presented a hypothesis-testing task to 15 psychologists, 15 physical scientists, and 15 Protestant ministers. None of the three groups used disconfirming strategies to any great degree. In fact, 85 percent of the experiments used to test hypotheses were confirmatory.

Hindsight Bias.　　When clinical psychologist learn several facts about a client, including the client's diagnosis, they are likely to believe that would have arrived at that diagnosis themselves if given the other information. The hindsight bias refers to "the tendency to believe, once the outcome of an event is known, that the outcome could have been predicted more easily than is actually the case" (Wedding & Faust, 1989, p. 237). Professionals and nonprofessionals are prone to the hindsight bias.

Arkes, Wortman, Saville, and Harkness (1981) provided one group of physicians with a case history and four possible diagnoses. Four other groups of physicians were given the same case history and possible diagnoses. Each of these four groups was told that one of the four choices was the true diagnosis, but each group was told a different diagnosis was correct. Arkes and colleagues found that each group of physicians rated as most likely the diagnosis they were told was correct. Arkes, Faust, Guilmette, and Hart (1988) replicated this finding with a group of neuropsychologists.

Overconfidence.　　The hindsight bias tends to build clinicians' confidence in their judgments. Several other factors also conspire to inflate clinicians' confidence without improving the validity of their clinical judgments. Training and experience are often touted as the means by which one develops clinical judgment. But empirical studies suggest that experience is not always such a good teacher. Several reviews of the literature on the relationship between experience and clinical judgment have drawn the same conclusion (Dawes, 1994; Faust & Ziskin, 1988; Garb, 1989). "Virtually every available study shows that amount of clinical training and experience are unrelated to judgmental accuracy" (Faust & Ziskin, 1988, p. 32). Even a strong defender of clinical judgment reached the same conclusion, "results on experience and validity were disappointing" (Garb, 1989, p. 391).

Why isn't there a relationship between clinical experience and validity of clinical judgment? Dawes (1994) argues that clinicians are prone to certain biases that create "the illusion of learning" (p. 122) from experience. The first bias is the tendency to vividly recall instances in which one's judgments were accurate and to overestimate their frequency. Clinicians are bound to be right at least some of the time, even if only by chance. The neuropsychologist, for example, is likely to recall easily the time she suspected that a patient had a tumor in his left temporal lobe and this suspicion was confirmed by neurological examination. The more commonplace examples when the clinician's suspicions were not confirmed did not make such a strong impression and are more difficult to recall.

The second bias is the tendency for clinicians to draw conclusions about the characteristics of a particular type of person by examining only those people. A psychologist may note that a high percentage of individuals with schizophrenia report that they had intense arguments with their parents when they were teenagers. The psychologist may falsely conclude that parent-child discord in adolescence is an early marker for schizophrenia. This line of reasoning is faulty since the psychologist has not examined the frequency with which nonschizophrenic people recall heated arguments with their parents during adolescence. Arkes (1981) and others have also noted this bias in clinical judgment. A more ridiculous example may make the point clearer. If you discover that over 90 percent of alcoholic clients drank milk as children, would you conclude that milk drinking in childhood is a risk factor of alcohol abuse?

The third bias that bolsters the illusion that one learns from experience occurs when the consequence of the clinician's judgment creates an outcome that makes it difficult for the clinician to be wrong. For example, psychologists may develop confidence in their ability to predict which clients are truly suicidal and which are not based upon experience working on the admissions unit at a local psychiatric hospital. Each time the clinician believes that a person is a true suicide risk, hospitalization is recommended. In the rare instances when the clinician judges the person not to be a risk, discharge is recommended. In the former case, predictions are never tested because the person is protected from committing suicide while in the hospital. And the predictions are unlikely to be wrong in the latter case given the low base rate for suicide. Once again, a more extreme example may make the point. A waiter who "knows" from his experience that well-dressed people are better tippers makes a special effort to provide them excellent service. At the same time, he provides poorly dressed customers with the minimum service. Surely the waiter's experience will confirm his hypothesis. (Example is taken from Einhorn & Hogarth, 1978, cited in Dawes, 1994).

Reducing Impact of Biases.   Arkes (1981) offered the following suggestions for reducing the impact of biases upon the validity of clinical judgments. First, *search for alternative explanations.* As we have seen, clinicians tend to be swayed by their original hypotheses about clients. By explicitly forcing themselves to consider alternatives, the clinicians may improve the accuracy of their judgments. Second, *understand the impact of base rates.* Arkes actual suggestion is to "think Bayesian" (p. 327), referring to statistical models based upon Bayes theorem (see Arkes, 1981, for discussion). In short, understanding the impact of the base rate of a phenomenon upon our ability to predict it can help prevent overconfidence in our judgments. Arkes's third suggestion is to *decrease reliance on memory.* Our recall of what characteristics a client presented is affected by our hypotheses about the client. If we believe that the client is depressed, we are more likely to recall information consistent with that hypothesis (e.g., difficulty sleeping) and less likely to recall inconsistent information (e.g., optimistic about the future).

Computer-Assisted Assessment

For better or worse, computers are an integral part of our lives. From running our cars and checking out our groceries to managing our money, computers are ubiquitous. It is not surprising, therefore, that computer-assisted psychological assessment is one of the fastest growing areas in professional psychology. There is, in fact, a long relationship between psychological assessment and computer technology. As early as the late 1950s, computers were used to score personality tests, develop profiles, and even offer rudimentary interpretations (Fowler, 1985). Today, with PCs or Macs on nearly every psychologist's desk and easy access to the Internet, there is a sizable market for computer assessment software that developers have been eager to tap. There are now software packages available to assess personality, intelligence, vocational interests, neuropsychological functioning, academic achievement, and a variety of other areas (Cohen et al., 1992). Computers can be of assistance in every phase of psychological assessment from data collection through data integration and interpretation.

Several potential advantages of computer-assisted psychological assessment have been identified (see Butcher, 1987; Jackson, 1986). These include the following:

1. *Professional time savings.* The psychologist does not have to be with the examinee as he or she takes a test or provides background information. Assessment data can be collected by trained assistants. Scoring procedures that are laborious when done by hand can be completed in seconds by the computer.

2. *Test-administration consistency.* Recall that one of the biggest advantages of psychological tests is that they allow us to compare an individual's behavior to the behavior of a normative sample who responded to the same instructions and test stimuli as the individual. Consistency in test administration, therefore, is very important. For some tests, the examiner is required to present test materials, record verbatim responses, and monitor response times simultaneously. The examiner can sometimes feel as if he or she needs a third hand and an extra pair of eyes. Computers administer the test the same way to every test taker and can simultaneously record response times to the microsecond if need be.

3. *Rapid turnaround time between test administration and scoring/interpretation.* With scoring and interpretation software for personal computers, the psychologist can get results and interpretation almost immediately after assessment data have been collected. Even when test data are sent to a service for scoring and interpretation, turnaround can be very rapid with the use of scanners, e-mail, and fax machines.

4. *Scoring accuracy.* One of the great strengths of computers is their ability to do mundane, repetitive tasks accurately and rapidly. The computer does not get bored. Its attention does not wane. Thus, for psychological testing, scoring errors can be virtually eliminated.

5. *Data analysis.* Computers can combine data and carry out complex mathematical and statistical analysis quickly and accurately. Such analysis would not be possible if it had to be done by hand.

6. *Assessment of special populations.* Psychological assessment data can be collected on individuals with spinal cord injuries, speech impairments, cerebral palsy, or other

disabilities with the assistance of specialized computer software (see Wilson, Thompson, & Wylie, 1982, for an example). Using traditional assessment strategies with special populations is sometimes impossible.

While there are clearly many advantages to computer-assisted assessment, there are also limitations and potential dangers when using computers. Despite their ubiquity, some people are intimidated by computer technology. Responding to prompts appearing on a computer monitor can be anxiety provoking for some and negatively impact the validity of the assessment. Cohen and colleagues (1992) note that computer-administered tests can rob some people of their preferred test-taking strategies. For example, some people like to review previous responses before responding to new ones while other like to skip around and answer questions they are sure they know before going to more difficult items. While these strategies may be available when taking the test in a traditional paper-and-pencil format, they may not be an option when the test is computer administered. Consistency in test administration, therefore, can be a two-edged sword.

For the psychologist, the time saved by rapid scoring and interpretation of assessment data can be offset by the time it takes to master the computer software. Particularly for the psychologists for whom psychological assessment makes up only a small part of their professional activities, the financial and temporal investment in computer-assisted software may not be worthwhile.

When computers are used to collect assessment data, the psychologist may miss an important opportunity to observe the individual's behavior. People taking psychological tests do much more than just respond to test items. Some doodle, others talk to themselves, and others fidget nervously. Sometimes test takers arrive at correct responses but then "overthink" and contaminate their answers. Qualitative data such as these may be missed when the computer gives the test rather than the psychologist. In addition, if the psychologist is not observing the assessment, he or she may be unaware of important test-taking factors that have affected the results. Interruptions, distracting noises, or sleepiness may all impact the test taker during the assessment. Finally, the psychologist loses out on the opportunity to build rapport with the examinee when the computer administers the assessment.

The most controversial area of computer involvement in psychological assessment is computer-generated interpretation. Paul Meehl (1973) noted that the computer provides the ideal means of combining and interpreting actuarial data. Clinical judgment is eliminated, something Meehl strongly applauds. Others, however, have raised the alarm about computer-generated interpretive reports. The ease with which computers produce interpretive reports may lead some psychologists to overlook serious validity problems. In 1986, Joseph Matarazzo, a former APA president, was highly critical of the burgeoning computer-generated interpretation industry. In no uncertain terms, Matarazzo characterized the majority of programs available at that time as unvalidated. He described the behavior of people in the business of selling interpretive software as "undisguised hucksterism of the crassest kind" (1986, p. 15). We explore the debate over computer-generated interpretation of personality assessment data in some detail in Chapter 8. For now, we simply note that the availability of interpretive software and computer-generated interpretive services does not relieve the individual psychologist of the burden of determining the validity of the interpretive report for his or her client. Just as a psychological test is not either valid or not valid (it may be valid for certain purposes with certain clients but not others), the validity of interpretive software depends upon the clientele with whom it will be used and the purposes of the assessment.

Stage IV: Communicating Assessment Findings

Psychological assessment can be a challenging and time-consuming task. An enormous amount of data is collected about a single individual. There may be interviews with the client and collateral sources, informal and formal observations, and psychological testing, as well as medical, mental health, or other life records. The report is where the psychologist brings all this information together. What impact a psychological assessment will have depends not only on the substance of the findings and recommendations, but also on how effectively the psychologist can communicate them. Given the importance of psychological assessment in the history of clinical psychology and in contemporary practice, and considering the emphasis clinical psychologists place upon the connection between research and practice, there is surprisingly little research on psychological reports (see Ownby, 1992, for a review of relevant research). What follows is a distillation of observations and recommendations from experts in this area.

Goals

As we saw at the outset of this chapter, the primary goal of a psychological assessment is to address the referral questions. It follows then that the first goal of a psychological report should be to respond to the question or questions asked by the person who referred the client for assessment. How well the referral question is answered depends upon how clearly the referral source and the psychologist communicated about the assessment at the outset. Having come to some agreement about the questions (e.g., diagnosis, treatment recommendations, dangerousness, and so on), the psychologist then addresses these in the report.

In addition to addressing the specific referral questions, a good psychological report will serve other purposes as well (Ownby, 1992; Sattler, 1988). First, the report should provide data that helps the recipient to understand the client. Ideally, anyone reading the report will learn some things about a client that he or she did not know beforehand. Second, the report should impact the recipient so that he or she interacts with the client differently as a result of knowledge gained through the report: A teacher alters the way materials are presented to a pupil; a judge decides for or against probation for a particular criminal; the multidisciplinary treatment team at a psychiatric hospital modifies its treatment plan. A third purpose of a psychological report is to provide a written record of historical information, interview, test, and observation findings, as well as treatment recommendations at a specific point in time. An accurate record of this kind may be used for a variety of purposes, including research, program evaluation, assessing the efficacy of interventions for the specific individual, or as background information against which future assessment findings might be interpreted. A fourth purpose of a psychological report, pointed out by Sattler, is that it may serve as a legal document in a variety of types of proceedings.

Writing Style

For psychological assessment findings to have an impact, they must be presented clearly and in a manner that is useful to the recipient. Thus, the style in which a report is written is very important. How well does the following personality description fit you?

> You are a person with a variety of interests. There have been times in your life when you weren't sure you had made the right choices. With close friends you tend to feel relaxed and at ease. You can be yourself. But there are still parts of you that you don't share with anyone. You feel frustrated at times, particularly when things don't go your way. When you think about the future, you tend to feel anxious, particularly when thinking about what you want to do with the rest of your life. You recognize that you have faults. You're not perfect. But you try to be the best person you can be.

If you can relate to the brief description provided above, congratulations—you are probably a lot like most people your age. The description is so general and vague (e.g., "You feel frustrated at times") that it could apply to just about anyone. Don't feel bad if you were thinking that the description really matched you. The tendency for people to accept general descriptions as accurate for themselves is so common that it has been given a name: the "Barnum effect," named for the circus promoter P. T. Barnum, who said, "there's a sucker born every minute." Horoscope writers, palm readers, and fortune tellers rely on people's tendency to interpret general statements as personally meaningful to ply their trade. Unfortunately, Barnum statements, such as "You enjoy a certain amount of change and variety in life" and "You find that study is not always easy" (Dickson & Kelly, 1985), sometimes appear in psychological reports. Statements such as these are either so general that they apply to everyone or so vague that they carry no meaning.

Clarity is the number one priority in writing a psychological report. Jerome Sattler (1988, pp. 733–745) offered the following recommendations, among others, to improve clarity in reports.

Include in the report relevant material and delete potentially damaging material. Reports should include information that is relevant to the referral question, important to know about the client, and useful to the recipient. Just because a piece of information may be factual and highly interesting (e.g., "Mr. Moon's father once worked as a roadie for the Rolling Stones") does not mean that it belongs in the report. The psychologist needs to consider whether the information will contribute in any way to the understanding of the client. The reader needs information that helps him or her understand the client's uniqueness, relates to the referral question, and demonstrates the client's attitudes, feelings, or behavior.

Avoid undue generalizations. Conclusions and generalizations about a client should be supported by the assessment findings. Statements describing general characteristics of the client should follow from data contained in the body of the report and the basis of the conclusions should be made clear (e.g., "Keith suffers reading disorder. While his intellectual skills are in the average range, his reading achievement is significantly below that of his age-matched peers").

Use behavioral referents to enhance the report's readability. Providing examples that illustrate the points the psychologist is making about the client can make the report more interesting to read. For example, the statement "Mr. Daltry has poor impulse control" is made clearer if the psychologist adds, "as indicated by his history of physical assaults, poorly planned robberies, and anger outbursts."

Communicate clearly and eliminate unnecessary technical material. Ideally, the statements made in a psychological report leave no room for misinterpretation. Ideas should be presented in a logical and orderly fashion. Ambiguous phrases such as "quite a few," "very often," and "seldom" should be avoided. Jargon or highly technical terms should not be used when ideas can be expressed in everyday language. In describing testing results, specific subscales should not be referred to by name unless it is absolutely necessary, and then they should be accompanied by a brief explanation.

Eliminate biased terms from reports. Language that implies that the psychologist is biased toward one group or another should not appear in a psychological report (American Psychological Association, 1994a). Word choices can reflect subtle biases. For example, referring to *man* and *wife* in the same sentence can imply inequality between men and women since the terms are nonparallel (e.g., *man* and *woman* or *husband* and *wife* are parallel). Biases can also be more blatant (e.g., "The child had the disheveled look characteristic of children raised on welfare"). The child may have appeared disheveled and he or she may be raised on welfare but it reflects the psychologists' biases to draw a connection between the two.

In writing a psychological report, it is helpful to know who is the intended audience. A report would be written one way if it was to be sent to another psychologist and quite another if the audience is an elderly individual's home health aide. As we have seen, how one carries out a psychological assessment and interprets the findings is greatly influenced by one's theoretical orientation. Acknowledging this, the psychologist cannot assume that the reader of the report shares his or her orientation. Terms peculiar to one's orientation should be replaced by phrases that capture the ideas behind the terms. Ownby (1992) provided the following example of a report that accurately reflects the writer's psychodynamic formulation without using the term "reaction formation."

> Mr. Strongarm is conflicted about several dynamically important issues, including dependency needs and sexual identity. He has dealt with these conflicts by developing an exaggerated masculine identity in which he demands absurdly high levels of performance from himself at work and even in sports activities in which he engages ostensibly so that he can "relax." (p. 125)

Organization of the Report

There is no universally agreed upon format for psychological reports. Some may be written as letters to the referral source and others are formatted as more formal documents. Typically, the report will have headings like *Identifying Information, Reason for Referral, Background Information, Behavioral Observations, Assessment Results and Interpretation,* and *Summary and Recommendations.*

The Identifying Information section usually includes the name, age, sex, and race or ethnic background of the client as well as any other relevant identifying information. An example of the first sentences in this section of a report might be "Brian Jones is a 52-year-old white male who is originally from Great Britain but has resided in the United States for over 25 years. Mr. Jones is currently a patient on the drug-rehabilitation unit at St. Christopher's hospital." Additional information included here might be the grade in school if the client is a child, or the type of employment for an adult. The assessment procedures used in the evaluation are also often included in this section.

The next section of the report usually describes the reason for the referral. This section includes the name of the referral source, the specific questions the referral source would like addressed, and a summary of specific behaviors or symptoms that led to the referral: "Mr. Jones was referred by the multidisciplinary substance abuse treatment team for diagnostic assessment and treatment recommendations. Specifically, the treatment team has asked for assistance in making a differential diagnosis between cocaine-induced paranoia and paranoid personality disorder. Mr. Jones holds the apparently delusional belief that he was formerly a member of a famous rock and roll band, the name of which he will not reveal, and that his former bandmates are plotting to kill him. He claims that he has been hiding out in the United States for over 25 years."

In the Background Information section of a psychological report, relevant history is described. What is considered relevant, of course, depends upon the purpose of the assessment. Areas that might be covered in the background section include family of origin, education, employment, sexual, marital, medical, legal, mental health, and substance abuse. Some of these areas would be skipped altogether and others given greater emphasis in different evaluations. With children, for example, the psychologist will usually describe the child's development, family background, and school performance in some detail. The following is an example provided by Sattler (1988, p. 727).

> Mick, a 12-year, 9-month-old adolescent, is the youngest of five children. He lives with his mother, who has been married three times. He last saw his father when he was 5 months old and just beginning to crawl. He first walked alone at 15 months and achieved bowel control at 2 years of age. However, bladder control was never achieved, and he remains enuretic at the present time.
>
> He attended a Head Start Program at the age of 4 years, but was referred to a child guidance clinic because of behavioral problems. He received a diagnosis of hyperactivity at this time. When Mick was 5 years old, his maternal grandmother died of a stroke, and Mick became extremely depressed. His mother noted that shortly afterwards Mick told her that he knew in advance that his grandmother was going to die; he claimed that he had psychic abilities.
>
> At 6 years of age, Mick attempted suicide by throwing himself in front of a car after his mother had been hospitalized for hypertension; however, he was not seriously injured. Mick told her he believed she was going to die and he wanted to die too. This attempted suicide resulted in Mick's referral to County Mental Health where he was treated for the suicide attempt and also for hyperactivity and enuresis.
>
> When Mick was 9 years old, his youngest sister attempted suicide by drug overdose. Mick was upset for several months. At the age of 10 years, he was expelled from school for alleged sexually inappropriate behavior, including touching other children's genitalia. He was subsequently transferred to another school, where he currently attends special education classes. Academically, he has always performed poorly.
>
> According to Mick's mother, their relationship has always been close, although recently he has become "difficult to get along with." She described Mick as a social isolate—having

no friends and preferring to spend his time alone or with her only. He has had no serious medical problems.

In the Behavioral Observations section, the psychologist paints a picture of the client in the evaluation. The goal is to describe the person in the context of the evaluation so that the reader has a sense of what it was like to be with the client during the assessment. The following might be included in the behavioral observations section of a report:

- Physical appearance including dress and distinguishing features (e.g., scars, tattoos, facial hair)
- Attitude toward the evaluation (e.g., "friendly and cooperative," "distant and reserved")
- Speech pattern (e.g., rapid, deliberate, mumbles)
- Activity level (e.g., fidgety, relaxed)
- Unusual mannerisms or odd behaviors (e.g., "Periodically throughout the evaluation, Mr. Entwistle would abruptly drop to the floor and do a set of 10 pushups.")
- Use of colloquialisms (e.g., "I was wicked mad.")
- Responses to testing materials (e.g., reactions to successes and failures)

The Assessment Results and Interpretation section of the report is where the major findings are described. This section might be organized in several ways. Ownby (1992) describes three models for reporting findings. In the *hypothesis-oriented* model, the psychologist describes the assessment findings relevant to each referral question. In the fictitious Mr. Jones example presented above, the psychologist might first describe the findings consistent and inconsistent with cocaine-induced paranoia and then do the same with paranoid personality disorder. This model of organizing findings makes it easy for the referral source to locate the responses to his or her questions. In the *domain-oriented* model, the psychologist organizes findings around different domains of functioning, such as intellectual, academic achievement, personality, and psychopathology. This approach has the advantage of being comprehensive and providing information on both the strengths and weaknesses of the client. The third approach is the *test-oriented* model. Here findings are organized around the tests administered. While this approach makes it clear where the findings come from, it does not have many other advantages.

In the final section of the report, the psychologist summarizes and integrates the findings. No new material should be included here. Rather, the most important conclusions are spelled out succinctly. This section may be the only part of the report some will read, so it is important to make every word count. Recommendations based upon the assessment findings are usually saved until the end of the report.

Concluding Comment: Testing versus Assessment

What's in a name? The title of this chapter refers to psychological assessment, not psychological testing. Our word choice was deliberate. Psychological assessment is not the same as psychological testing (Matarazzo, 1990), although the former often includes the latter.

Testing involves gathering scores on psychological tests and interpreting these scores nomothetically by comparing them to normative data. Psychological assessment is a much more complicated endeavor that involves the idiographic interpretation of test findings as well as personal history data, observations, information from collateral sources, and the referral question. Nomothetic information is used in psychological assessment but it is interpreted within the context of all that is known about an individual.

An example may illuminate the distinction between testing and assessment. Mr. Hopkins, a 42-year-old man, is encouraged to see Dr. McLaughlin, a psychologist, by his wife, who is concerned about how he is dealing with the recent death of his mother. As part of the intake evaluation, Dr. McLaughlin interviews Mr. Hopkins and his wife and administers tests measuring anxiety and depression as well as a personality inventory. Mr. Hopkins reports that he was saddened by his mother's death, although his facial expression reveals little emotion as he discusses his feelings about the loss. Ms. Hopkins describes her husband as a responsible person who has been a good provider for her and their children. She notes that he also took care of most of his mother's living expenses over the last several years of her life. Over the course of their marriage he has always been the one to remain calm as they faced life's challenges, while she was always more emotional. She states, "He has been my rock," but reports that since his mother's death he has been "distracted" and "irritable." She also notes that he has lost interest in sexual relations. Mr. Hopkins does not disagree with his wife's report but attributes his irritability and lack of interest in sex to vague "pressures" at work. On psychological testing, Mr. Hopkins's scores on the measures of anxiety and depression are mildly elevated but in the normal range. There were no clinically elevated scales on the personality test; however, the pattern of scores suggests that Mr. Hopkins is a rigid man who functions best in structured situations in which behavioral expectations are clear. He is emotionally constricted and holds stereotypical beliefs about appropriate sex-role behavior.

In this example, psychological testings suggests the absence of pathology. Mr. Hopkins's scores do not indicate clinically significant depression or anxiety, nor do they suggest a personality disorder. Psychological assessment paints a different picture of Mr. Hopkins. An integration of the data suggests that he is emotionally distraught but has been unable to express his feelings. His personality style makes it difficult for Mr. Hopkins to grieve the loss of his mother. While the psychological testing does not indicate significant pathology in this example, the findings play an important part in the hypothetical model Dr. McLaughlin develops to explain Mr. Hopkins's presenting problems. This fictitious example illustrates what some researchers believe is a common tendency for standard mental health scales to fail to distinguish true mental health from the "illusion of mental health" (Shedler, Mayman, & Manis, 1993, p. 1117).

In Chapters 7 and 8 we will discuss psychological tests in greater detail, including their strengths and weaknesses. However, the reader should keep in mind that most of the research on psychological tests has studied testing, not psychological assessment as defined above. There is surprisingly little research on the reliability and validity of idiographic interpretation of data from multiple tests and other sources of information.

Tests are tools. Like any tools, their utility cannot be separated from the persons who use them. A hammer and chisel can turn a stone into a beautiful piece of art when employed by a skilled sculptor. In the hands of the untrained, however, these same tools can be dangerous, defacing rather than enhancing the stone. In a similar manner, in the hands of a well-trained psychologist—one with knowledge of psychometrics, psychopathology, theories of human behavior, and relevant empirical findings—psychological tests are powerful tools for understanding and helping individuals. But, as with the hammer and chisel, these tools have the potential to do harm if applied in an uninformed or simplistic manner.

BOX 5.2

Focus on Ethics: Releasing Assessment Data

Normally, if clients want to see their test data (e.g., test scores), psychologists provide them with this information. With clients' permission, psychologists also provide test data to specific people designated by the client. However, there are circumstances under which psychologists may refuse to release test data. Ethical Standard 9.04 includes the sentence "Psychologists may refrain from releasing test data to protect a client/patient or others from substantial harm" (American Psychological Association, 2002).

But how can someone be harmed by releasing test data? Two examples illustrate the potential for harm. A psychologist releases raw assessment data to another mental health professional who does not have appropriate training to interpret the data (e.g., a social worker or a psychiatric nurse) and the other professional draws erroneous conclusions from the data, which could impact his or her work with the client, inadvertently causing the client harm. Psychologists should be cautious, therefore, when deciding whether to release raw test data to another professional. D. L. Shapiro (1991), for example, cites a case in which the courts ruled that a psychologist did not have to release raw psychological data to a psychiatrist because the latter was not a "qualified person."

As a second example, consider the case in which a neuropsychologist is compelled to release raw test data to the attorney for the defendant in a lawsuit in which the plaintiff has claimed of loss of memory functioning secondary to brain impairment caused by the defendant (Tranel, 1994). The attorney might draw the jury's attention to difficult test items that were missed ("If failing this item means you suffer from memory loss, then I guess we all must be brain damaged") or correct responses to items tapping areas of memory functioning that were unimpaired by the injury ("Pretty good memory for someone who is supposedly so impaired"). The jury may be persuaded by this biased interpretation of test items taken out of context.

Tranel (1994) interprets the APA ethical standard to mean that psychologists should only release test data to other qualified professionals. In most cases, this means another psychologist. He recommends that when a psychologist receives a request to release raw psychological data to someone who is not necessarily qualified (e.g., an attorney), the psychologist should offer to provide an interpretation of the data or recommend that the recipient engage the services of another psychologist to whom the data could safely be released.

In addition to harm that may be caused by release of individuals' test data, psychologists also need to be cautious about releasing test materials (e.g., test manuals, protocols, or test stimuli). Prior access to test materials can invalidate conclusions drawn from clients' responses to test items. Imagine the situation in which questions from a commonly used test of intelligence became widely available on the World Wide Web. Clients could study test materials before taking the test. Given that the normative sample did not have the same prior exposure to test materials, it would be inappropriate to interpret clients' scores based on how they compare to the norm group. Clients'

(continued)

B O X **5.2**   **Continued**

scores would likely overestimate their true intellectual abilities. Ethical standard 9.11 reads, "Psychologists make reasonable efforts to maintain the integrity and security of tests and other assessment techniques consistent with law."

There are circumstances, however, in which psychologists can be compelled to release psychological test data by way of a subpoena or court order. Judges and attorneys are not necessarily qualified to use these data appropriately. What is a psychologist to do when the law and the ethical code conflict? Ethical standard 1.02 (Relationship of Ethics and Law, American Psychological Association, 1992) provides the following guidance:

> If psychologists' ethical responsibilities conflict with law, psychologists make known their commitment to the Ethics Code and take steps to resolve the conflict in a responsible manner.

In the case of a subpoena to release psychological data, this means that the psychologist should explain to the judge the ethical conflict created by the request and suggest an alternative course of action (Tranel, 1994) such as releasing the data to another psychologist who would act as consultant to the court. Not all judges are open to such arrangements but many will respect the psychologist's dilemma.

CHAPTER

6 Clinical Interviewing

The clinical interview is the most widely employed assessment tool in clinical psychology (Watkins, Campbell, Nieberding, & Hallmark, 1995). Often, an interview is the only method a psychologist uses when evaluating a client. But even when an assessment also includes testing, observation, or other data collection methods, the interview almost always plays a central role. Defined simply, an interview is a conversation. Taken out of context, it can be difficult to distinguish an interview between a psychologist and client from a social conversation.

> JULIA: How have you been?
>
> BETH: Fine.
>
> JULIA: Really?
>
> BETH: I don't know. I guess not. It seems like all that Jim and I do lately is fight. He wants do things with his buddies, and I understand that; it's just that we both work long hours all week and there doesn't ever seem to be time for the two of us on the weekends.
>
> JULIA: I thought you and Jim had planned to go away together this past weekend?
>
> BETH: So did I. But it never happened.
>
> JULIA: What went wrong?

Julia and Beth could be friends catching up with one another over a cup of coffee or Julia could be a psychotherapist and Beth a therapy client following up on last session's homework assignment and setting the agenda for the day's session. It is impossible to tell from this brief snippet of conversation taken out of context.

There are several characteristics that distinguish a clinical interview from a social conversation. The first is the different social roles of the two participants. The psychologist is in the role of professional. Depending upon the circumstances of the interview, adopting the professional role may bring with it the expectation that the psychologist has some knowledge or expertise not available to everyone and will help the client. The interviewee may adopt the role of "patient," adapting his or her behavior to that role. A second distinction between a clinical interview and a social conversation is the settings in which they occur. Clinical interviews usually take place in a professional setting such as a hospital, clinic, school, or professional office. A third characteristic that sets the clinical interview apart from a social conversation is that the former is one-sided. The flow of information is, for the most part, from the client to the psychologist. The skilled clinician is able to maintain a natural flow to the conversation while eliciting information about the client's beliefs, attitudes, feelings, and personal history. The clinician's opinions, beliefs, and background generally are not shared. Let's take the conversation between Julia and Beth a bit further.

> **BETH:**   I told him I wanted to go to the coast. At first he said yes but then he "remembered" a softball tournament he had agreed to play in.
>
> **JULIA:**   Let's review the situation from the start. When did you first bring up the idea of a weekend getaway?

It seems clearer now that Julia is a therapist. She does not share her opinion about Jim's behavior, nor does she share personal experiences as a friend might. Instead, Julia tries to elicit additional information so that she can get a clearer understanding of the problem. If Julia were to respond by saying, "Grant tries to pull the same kind of stuff with me. I just tell him, fine, if you like softball so much go ahead, just don't expect to find me waiting around for you when you get home." While this type of response may be common enough between friends, it is hard to imagine a clinical situation in which it would be appropriate.

The fourth defining characteristic of a clinical interview is that it has an objective or purpose. In fact, a clinical interview has been called a conversation with a purpose or goal (Mattarazzo, 1965). The questions asked by the clinician are chosen for a reason. The information gathered will help the psychologist achieve the objective of the interview. The purpose of the interview depends upon the circumstances of the assessment. There are, however, several common types of clinical interviews.

Types of Clinical Interviews

While categorizing interviews for teaching purposes is helpful, it may also distort reality. Oftentimes, more than on type of interview is carried out in a single meeting between psychologist and client. Common types of interviews are described below.

Intake

The first meeting between a psychologist and client is usually to conduct an intake interview. The primary purpose of the interview is to determine the nature of the client's problem. Why is this individual looking for help? The second purpose of the interview, which follows from the first, is to determine whether the psychologist, or the agency where he or she works, has the resources and competencies to help the individual.

For the client seeking help for personal problems, the intake interview is particularly important. He or she is meeting with the psychologist for the first time and may not know exactly what to expect. As the interview proceeds, the client may find the psychologist, a total stranger, asking about painful and very private experiences. Most of us would find such an experience anxiety-provoking. Given the stress of the situation, perhaps it is not surprising that as many as half of all clients who come for an intake interview never return for treatment

(Baekeland & Lundwall, 1975). In the initial interview, the psychologist must balance the need to gather information with the need to help the client feel at ease and build rapport.

When a client seeks psychotherapy, the main goals of the first interview are to define the problems to be worked on in therapy and establish the goals of treatment. The kinds of questions the therapists asks might include "What is the main problem for which the client is seeking help?" "Why is the client seeking help right now?" "What are the client's expectations?" "How would the client expect things to be different if therapy is 100 percent successful?" "What are the important aspects of the problem?" At the conclusion of the successful pre-therapy interview, the psychologist should have a thorough understanding of the presenting problem and have identified potential strategies for intervention (Wilson, Spence, & Kavanagh, 1989).

The way in which therapists help clients articulate their problems can have a significant impact upon the success of therapy. Writing from a cognitive-behavioral perspective, Kanfer and Scheft (1988) suggest six "think rules" to guide clinicians helping clients to define their problems:

1. *Think Behavior:* To set the stage for change, the clinician and client define the problem, and possible solutions, in terms of action. What actions define the problem? What actions would alleviate the difficulty? For example, if a client describes his problem by saying, "When my boss criticizes me, I feel that I will blow up," the therapist asks "When that happens, what do you think about? "What do you do?" and "What physical sensations do you experience?" (Kanfer & Scheft, 1988, p. 109).

2. *Think Solution:* Both therapists and clients tend to focus upon problems. Many people seeking help may see the role of psychotherapy client as consisting of little more than describing problems. Therapists are also socialized to identify problems. But asking clients to think about how problem situations might be handled differently provides valuable information about the appropriate targets for treatment and possible therapeutic strategies. It also helps to socialize the person to the role of client as collaborator with the therapist (Beck, 1994).

3. *Think Positive:* What are the client's strengths? What resources does he or she have to help overcome the problem? Has the client successfully coped with similar problems in the past?

4. *Think Small Steps:* When establishing goals for therapy, the therapist should help the client think in increments. For example, a severely agoraphobic client may have the goal of feeling comfortable doing her Christmas shopping at a crowded shopping mall. The therapist helps the client think of the incremental steps toward this outcome. Overcoming her fear of leaving the home is a necessary first step toward conquering the crowded shopping mall.

5. *Think Flexible:* In discussing potential treatment strategies, therapists and clients think of several possible approaches to change. Therapy can be viewed as a series of trial-and-error experiments in which the therapist and client experiment with potential solutions.

6. *Think Future:* Clients often come to therapy with the expectation that they will uncover the roots of their problems. Although an understanding of how a problem developed can be helpful, this understanding by itself is unlikely to change the problem in the

future. In defining the goals and strategies of therapy, the therapist helps the client keep an eye to the future.

It is important for psychotherapy clients to know what they are getting into before beginning psychotherapy. The Ethics Code (American Psychological Association, 2002) emphasizes the importance of obtaining a client's *informed consent* before commencing psychotherapy. In Box 6.1, we discuss some of the ethical and professional issues presented by the need for informed consent for psychotherapy.

Case History

Traditionally, in many mental health centers it was the role of the social worker to do an intake interview and obtain a detailed psychosocial history of the client. The psychologist's role was to conduct psychological testing, and the psychiatrist would do a mental status exam and diagnostic interview. The professionals would meet to share information and arrive at a treatment plan. These professional role boundaries have eroded over time. In many settings the psychologist does the intake, history taking, testing, and diagnostic assessment.

The case history, sometimes called the psychosocial history, is a detailed description of a client's background. The history provides information that may be necessary to formulate a complete diagnosis. However, knowing a person's history also helps the clinician to understand how the presenting problems fit in the broader context of the person's life.

Case-history interviews tend to be broadly focused. Typical information gathered in a case history interview might include:

a. *Birth and Development:* Were there complications in pregnancy or during birth? Did the client reach developmental milestones (e.g., walking, talking, toileting) at the normal ages?

b. *Family of Origin:* Who raised the client? Did the family remain intact? What was the client's relationships like with parents, siblings, extended family? Have any family members experienced mental health, substance abuse, significant medical or legal problems?

c. *Education:* How far did the client go in school? Did he or she repeat any grade or receive special education services? Were there significant behavioral problems in school (e.g., suspensions or expulsions)?

d. *Employment:* What types of job has the client held? Has the client ever been fired? If so, why? Has the client changed jobs often? Why?

e. *Recreation/Leisure:* How does the client spend his or her free time? What are his or her hobbies or interests?

f. *Sexual History:* How did the client learn about sex? What were the circumstances of the client's first sexual experience (e.g., coercive, in the context of a romantic relationship, one-night stand)? What is the nature of client's current sexual functioning?

g. *Dating and Marital:* When did the client start dating? Significant romantic relationships? How many times has the client been married?

h. *Alcohol and Drugs:* What is the nature and the pattern of client's alcohol and drug use? Has the client experienced legal, employment, or social problems secondary to alcohol or drug use?

BOX 6.1

Focus on Ethics: Informed Consent

Standard 3.10, *Informed Consent,* of the Ethics Code reads as follows:

> When psychologists conduct research or provide assessment, therapy, counseling, or consulting services in person or via electronic transmission or other forms of communication, they obtain the informed consent of the individual or individuals using language that is reasonably understandable to that person or persons except when conducting such activities without consent is mandated by law or governmental regulations as otherwise provided in this Ethics Code.

There is little controversy about the general idea of obtaining individuals' informed consent before involving them in research, psychological assessment, or therapy. The process of obtaining informed consent can be viewed as a means of empowering people by providing information and encouraging personal responsibility. For clients, informed consent offers some level of protection from unscrupulous or incompetent professionals. For psychotherapists, assuring that clients are fully informed about treatment can improve the quality of services delivered in several ways. It encourages consideration and discussion of realistic expectations about outcome. It opens the door for communication about misinterpretations or dissatisfactions on clients' part that may have resulted in premature termination (Hare-Mustin, Marecek, Kaplan, & Liss-Levenson, 1979). In addition, assuring that clients have understood the goals, methods, and likely outcomes of psychotherapy ahead of time can protect psychologists from malpractice suits (Roston & Sherrer, 1973).

While the concept of informed consent is easy to accept in the abstract, challenging issues arise when one considers the specifics of obtaining consent. There are three components to informed consent: *knowledge* (does the person have the information he or she needs to make a rational choice?), *freedom to choose* (has the person been coerced so that he or she does not really have the option of refusing?), and *capacity* (does the person have the ability to understand the information and make a free choice?) (Stromberg et al., 1988). Our discussion of the issues associated with informed consent is organized around these three components.

What information is necessary for clients to possess in order to provide truly informed consent? For psychological assessment, clients need to know the purpose of the assessment, the procedures to be used, who will have access to the results, the fees, and the limits of confidentiality. For psychotherapy clients, information about the goals of treatment and the procedures to be used is the bare minimum. For example, socially anxious clients should know ahead of time if treatment involves group therapy sessions during which they will be asked to participate in role playing of challenging social encounters (Hope & Heimberg, 1993). Psychotherapy clients should be informed about the psychologist's business practices: fees, cancellation policy, office hours, emergency coverage, and the like.

But what should potential psychotherapy clients be told about prognosis? A therapist wants to be positive about the potential benefits of psychotherapy in order to motivate clients for treatment. However, it would be unethical to paint an unrealistically rosy picture. Should therapy clients be told what percentage of people with similar problems get better with the proposed form of treatment? But exactly what does "better" mean (e.g., free of symptoms or just better able to cope?)? Reliable information about expected outcomes is not available for many of the problems clients bring to psychotherapy (see Chapter 10 for discussion). Even for problems for which there is considerable research evidence that psychological treatment works, reasonable questions can be raised about how these research findings generalize to practice outside of the research setting (Feinstein & Raw, 1997). Clients' need for accurate information needs to be balanced against the potential negative impact the information may have upon their motivation for treatment and expectations for a positive outcome.

(continued)

B O X **6.1**   **Continued**

In addition to information about prognosis, it is generally agreed that psychologists should provide clients with information about alternative approaches to treatment. In describing alternatives, therapists must be careful to characterize the alternative approach fairly. Saying, "Of course, if you just want to escape your problems, I could always refer you to a psychiatrist for medication," is not a reasonable way of describing pharmacotherapy as an alternative to psychotherapy for depression. Of course, providing clients with information about alternatives does not mean that therapists must catalogue every possible approach. Psychologists should be aware of the resources in their community and be knowledgeable about the most common alternative approaches to treatment.

Finally, the theoretical orientation of the professional can impact what information is deemed appropriate to share with clients. Writing from a psychoanalytic perspective, Lebensohn (1978) bemoaned the deleterious effects of informed consent. After describing how informed consent for psychoanalysis would involve explaining the psychoanalytic technique, the likelihood that the patient will develop a strong emotional attachment to, and perhaps become dependent upon, the analyst, the possibility that treatment will fail or that the client will get worse, the limits of confidentiality, and the possibility of divorce or suicide, Lebensohn writes, "having properly executed the above form, you may now enter the private consulting room and feel free to tell the psychiatrist anything and everything that comes to mind" (Lebensohn, 1978, p. 36).

The second component of informed consent, freedom of choice, is most frequently threatened when psychological services are mandated by others. Clients may be legally coerced, for example, when assessment or therapy is mandated as a condition of probation or when parole decisions are influenced by prisoners' willingness to undergo evaluation or treatment. Is it unethical for psychologists to provide professional services under circumstances such as these? Probably not, but psychologists must take care not to participate in the coercion. It is one thing for a therapist to provide court-ordered treatment to a convicted sex offender, for example. It is quite a different thing for the therapist to use the threat of incarceration to coerce a client into accepting forms of treatment the client finds objectionable. The latter clearly would be unethical. Just because therapy is court-ordered does not mean anything goes. The therapist has the responsibility to inform the client about treatment procedures, likely outcomes, and potential side effects. The client has the right to refuse the recommended treatment or parts of it. It is then up to the therapist to decide whether there are viable alternatives approaches.

Clients' capacity is a critical issue in determining whether informed consent has truly been given. Taking an extreme view, one could argue that individuals with mental disorders do not have the capacity to give informed consent (Moore, 1978). From this perspective, providing clients with information about risks, benefits, and treatment alternatives is pointless. "All the knowledge in the world will not help a depressed patient make a non-depressed choice. . . . How can the patient make a reasonable choice regarding behavior control when their choosing mechanism is so often the very object of the procedure?" (Neville, 1972, pp. 7–8, cited in Widiger & Rorer, 1984). Consistent with this point of view are research findings that show that many clients voluntarily admitted to a psychiatric hospital could not say what they had consented to or what the consent procedure had involved (Appelbaum, Mirkin, & Batemen, 1981). Impairment in clients' capacity to provide truly informed consent due to their mental disorder presents a serious ethical dilemma. Most professionals would be uncomfortable denying much-needed treatment. There are no simple answers. When it is has been determined that the client is legally incapable of giving consent, psychologists should seek consent from individuals authorized to act on the client's behalf. When there has been no legal determination of incompetence yet questions about capacity are present (e.g., severely depressed client), the psychologist needs to proceed cautiously, frequently revisiting the issue of informed consent.

    i. *Physical Health:* Has the client had significant medical problems (e.g., head injuries, chronic illnesses)?

    In addition to gathering the factual information described above, the clinician is also interested in learning about the client's attitudes and emotional responses to these historical events. The case history interview also provides the clinician with the opportunity to make observations about the client's speech pattern, thought processes, emotion regulation, memory, and other processes (see Mental Status Exam section).

    Most competent adults are able to provide the kind of historical information needed to complete a psychosocial history. With children and more severely disabled adults, however, it is often necessary to rely upon other sources to gather this information. Parents or other relatives are valuable sources of information. Depending upon the circumstances of the assessment, it can be extremely enlightening to gather information from employers, spouses, previous mental health providers, or friends of the interviewee. In a forensic assessment (see Chapter 16), comparing information provided by the client with that obtained from collateral sources can be extremely enlightening. For clients seeking psychotherapy services, even when the client provides consent for the clinician to contact other sources, some clinicians are reluctant to do so for fear of the impact this may have upon the developing therapy relationship. However, there is often no substitute for the kind of information that can be obtained from significant others in the client's life.

Diagnostic

The purpose of the diagnostic interview is to elicit the information necessary to arrive at a diagnostic formulation. The model for a diagnostic interview is, of course, a medical one. The diagnostician asks a series of questions about the presence or absence of "symptoms" and based upon the information gathered determines a diagnosis. One's view of the value of the diagnostic interview is inexorably tied to one's opinion about the value of psychiatric diagnoses. As we discussed in Chapter 5, the use of diagnostic labels to describe consumers of mental health services is a controversial enterprise. We will discuss diagnostic interviewing in some detail in the second half of this chapter.

Mental Status Exam

The mental status examination comes from the psychiatric tradition. It is considered to be analogous to the physical examine in general medicine (Siassi, 1984). Although usually described as a type of interview, the mental status exam is really a protocol for organizing one's observations of the client. The exam actually takes place throughout the interview, but the clinician may need to ask specific kinds of questions in order to gather information about certain phenomena. Siassi recommends that mental status exam observations be made throughout the clinical interview and that the clinician switch to direct questioning at the end of the interview in order to elicit the information needed for the mental status exam. The following topic areas are typically covered in the mental status exam section of a report.

    a. *General Appearance and Behavior:* In this section, the clinician may comment upon the gait, posture, dress, gestures, personal hygiene, and level of activity of the client.

b. *Speech and Thought:* Is the client's speech coherent? Does it follow a normal progression? Is it slow or fast? Are there long silences? Does the client's speech appear
pressured (i.e., Does it seem that the client is having a difficult time speaking fast
enough to express his or her thoughts?)? Does the client use unusual words? Is there
evidence of delusional thinking? Is the client evasive and defensive or frank and
open?

c. *Consciousness:* Is the client alert and attentive? Is there a clouding of consciousness?

d. *Perception:* Is there evidence of hallucinations either during the interview or in the
past?

e. *Obsessions and Compulsions:* Does the client engage in compulsive activity (e.g.,
repeatedly checking his or her own pulse)? Does the client report intrusive and
repetitive thoughts? Does he or she recognize the irrationality of the obsessions and
compulsions?

f. *Orientation:* Does the client understand where he or she is; what time of day, week,
or year it is; and who he or she is? For example, the client who adamantly insists that
he is Jesus Christ and that the psychologist is Pontius Pilot is probably not fully oriented to person, place, or time.

g. *Memory:* Can the client accurately account events from the distant past (e.g., where
he or she was born, the names of parents, and so on)? Recent memory is assessed by
inquiring about the client's knowledge of current events. Short-term memory can be
assessed by asking the client to remember the names of three items or a set of numbers and then checking his or her recall a few minutes later.

h. *Attention and Concentration:* Is the client easily distracted or is he or she able to sustain attention? Having the client count backward from 100 by 7s is one technique
some clinicians use to assess level of concentration. This strategy is called serial 7s.

i. *General Information:* Can the client name the president and his immediate predecessors? Can he or she provide the approximate dates of important historical events
(e.g., World War II)?

j. *Intelligence:* Mental status observations usually include a gross estimate of the
client's level of intellectual functioning based upon his or her educational history,
vocabulary, general fund of information, and reasoning abilities.

k. *Insight and Judgment:* Can the client provide a reasonable account of his or her problems? Does the client demonstrate an understanding of the probable outcomes of certain actions?

l. *Higher Cognitive Functioning:* Can the client think abstractly? A commonly used strategy for assessing abstract thinking is to ask the client to interpret a proverb. For example, a client might be asked, "What does the saying 'Don't count your chickens before
they are hatched' mean?" An answer that suggests the ability to think abstractly might
be something like "It means don't jump the gun. It's not a good idea to assume that
everything is going to work out in your favor." The client who responds, "Well, chickens come from eggs and you shouldn't count eggs because you might break them" may
tend to think more concretely.

The mental status examination usually appears in the report of a psychological or psychiatric evaluation. In a hospital setting, the mental health professions may record mental status observations in a clients chart. Box 6.2 contains an example mental status examination.

BOX **6.2**

Mental Status Exam

The patient is a slightly disheveled 29-year-old white alert female who is initially hostile but cooperates later. She appears to be oriented to person, place, and date. She is concentrated throughout the interview, showing good comprehension. Her answers are goal-directed. Her affect is labile and irritable with restricted range of affective expression. Mood is generally depressed. She acknowledges sleep and appetite disturbance, vague suicidal thoughts (but no plan), and appears hopeless. The client acknowledges auditory and visual hallucinations of brief duration. She has some insight into their morbid nature. Some obsessive worries and fears may still be present, but client refuses to elaborate on them. She denies suicidal thoughts. Immediate, recent, and remote memory are intact. Her concentration is slightly impaired on serial 7 backward; she makes two calculation errors. She can multiply 2×192, which suggests at least average intelligence. The client shows some insight but does not recognize the impact of her job upon her depression. Judgment appears to be adequate at the present time (adapted from Othmer & Othmer, 1994, pp. 310–311).

Unstructured mental status exams, while common in practice, can be criticized on at least two grounds. First is questionable reliability. There are likely to be differences between clinicians in how the various mental status areas are assessed and the exact interpretation of clients' responses. A second criticism is the lack of normative data against which to interpret a client's responses to mental status questions. How fast does it usually take people to do serial 7s? Does this change with age and is speed of serial 7s correlated with IQ?

A number of structured mental status examinations have been developed in response to these criticisms. One of the earliest and still most widely used is the Mini Mental Status Examination (Folstein, Folstein, & McHugh, 1975). This is a 30-item test that evaluates orientation, recall, short-term memory, attention/concentration, and language comprehension. As the name implies, it is brief—about 10 minutes to complete. The developers of the Mini Mental Status Examination have collected normative data and provide cut-off scores that allow for comparison with normal, demented, and psychiatric populations. The examination relies heavily upon written and verbal responses and therefore is inappropriate for use with some populations, such as individuals for whom English is a second language (Matthews, 1997).

Crisis

There are times in which psychologists must interact with people who are in crisis. For example, psychologists who work on the admission units of psychiatric hospitals or who provide emergency consultation at general hospitals often deal with clients in crisis. Some agencies, such as suicide prevention hotlines or walk-in mental health centers, are created to help people who are in crisis. However, clinicians often find themselves dealing with unexpected crises. The least-impaired psychotherapy client can suddenly appear in crisis when unexpected life stressors occur.

In most crisis situations, the psychologist does not have access to many of the assessment tools he or she typically relies upon. The individual in crisis cannot be asked to complete a lengthy battery of psychological tests or to provide written consent and wait while the clinician obtains copies of prior mental health records. The problem has to be dealt with at the moment. When interviewing a client in crisis, the clinician tries to provide reassurance, assess the problem, and explore potential resources, all the while projecting a calm and confident manner. The goal of the crisis interview is to resolve the problem immediately at hand so that a catastrophic outcome (e.g., suicide) is avoided. For some individuals, one or two interviews with a skilled clinician will resolve the crisis and they are able to resume their lives without further need of mental health service. For others, the crisis interview is the first step toward developing permanent solutions to long-standing problems. Finally, there are those clients for whom crises are the norm. These clients are often very taxing to work with and require a great deal of skill and patience from their therapists (see Linehan & Kehrer, 1993, for discussion of a model for dealing with chronically suicidal clients).

The Importance of Rapport

Rapport has been defined as "the sense of mutual trust and harmony that characterizes a good relationship" (Giordano, 1997). It is generally accepted that rapport is a necessary condition for successful clinical work. It may be impossible for a clinician to obtain important information about a client's behavior, feelings, and attitudes if the client does not trust the clinician or if the interaction is acrimonious. The client who perceives the clinician as caring, interested, competent, and trustworthy will respond to the directive "Tell me about your sex life" very differently from the client who perceives the clinician as bored, incompetent, or manipulative.

There are innumerable techniques for building rapport. Greeting the client in a warm and friendly manner, shaking hands, and offering a cup of coffee can all be seen as strategies for building rapport. Much has been written about techniques for building rapport (see for example Brenner, 1982; Cormier & Cormier, 1991; Giordano, 1997). Carl Rogers (1957) probably captured the essence of the successful clinician's attitude when he described empathy, genuineness, and unconditional positive regard (see Chapter 12). While there is disagreement over whether these conditions are sufficient for therapeutic change, there is general agreement that they are important, and perhaps necessary, for effective clinical work regardless of the clinician's orientation (see, for example Beck, Rush, Shaw, & Emery, 1979; Teyber, 1988; Wilson & Evans, 1977).

Establishing rapport can be particularly challenging when the clinician and client come from different cultural or socioeconomic backgrounds. Our cultural experiences shape our view of ourselves, others, and the world. Clinicians' and clients' perceptions of each other are strongly influenced by their cultural upbringing. Consequently, it may take longer to establish rapport with a culturally different client. In their book *Culture-Centered Counseling and Interviewing Skills,* Paul Pedersen and Allen Ivey (1993) emphasize the importance of clinicians' recognizing their own cultural biases. To presume that one is free of bias is naive and dangerous. The process of building rapport with a culturally different client involves educating oneself about the communication patterns used in the client's culture. The client presents a pool of words, behaviors, and concepts and defines these for the clinician as they interact. The challenge for the clinician is to understand the client's words, behaviors, and concepts so that these can be used to communicate effectively. Pedersen and Ivey emphasize the need for patience on the clinician's part. Establishing rapport with a culturally different client usually takes longer than it does when working within one's own culture.

Communication Strategies

Verbal Strategies

Consider the following questions:

> CLINICIAN A: "How would you describe your relationship with your parents?"
>
> CLINICIAN B: "Did you have a good relationship with your parents?"

Both clinicians are interested in learning the same information about their clients. Clinician A words the question so that the client can provide a full range of answers. This is a good example of an *open-ended question.* Open-ended questions don't limit a client's responses. Open-ended questions tend to start with words such as *what, how, when, where,* and *who* (Cormier & Cormier, 1991). Other ways of asking for the same information in an open-ended fashion might be "Tell me about your relationship with your parents," or "What is your relationship with your parents like?" Clinician B's wording of the question limits the client's choice of responses. It can be answered with a simple "yes" or "no" and provides much less information.

Open-ended questions are used frequently in an initial interview or when initiating discussion of a new topic area. As the interview progresses, however, the clinician is interested in gathering more specific information. Three examples of appropriate closed questions might be "Of all the problems we discussed, which bothers you the most?" "Is there a history of depression in your family?" "Are you planning to look for a job in the next few months?" (Cormier & Cormier, 1991, p. 114). Closed questions help to narrow the topic area of discussion and are useful in gathering specific information. While asking direct questions such as these is a straightforward means of gathering information, there are several mistakes that beginning clinicians make with some frequency. One of these is to both ask and answer a question. For example, in assessing alcohol use a clinician was heard to ask, "How much beer do you typically drink on a week night . . . a six pack?" There are probably two reasons clinicians fall into this style of questioning. First is to fill in the silence. Learning to be comfortable with silence is an important clinical skill (Cormier & Cormier, 1991; Giordano, 1997). Second, by offering a possible answer, the clinician may feel as if he or she is helping the client by letting him or her know the type of answer the clinician expects. The problem with answering one's own question, of course, is that it may influence the client's response. The second problem is a bit more subtle but equally problematic. In this case the clinician's choice, or wording, of questions is influenced by what the clinician expects to hear. Consider the following interchange.

> CLIENT: "My wife just rags on me all the time. She is constantly putting me down."
>
> CLINICIAN: "Have you always felt humiliated by your wife or has this developed recently?"

The client in this case never said that he felt humiliated. Instead, the clinician assumed that the client would have felt this way when he was put down by his wife. It is just as likely that the client's emotional reaction would have been anger or sadness.

A skilled interviewer uses a combination of open and closed questions. A metaphor for conceptualizing the flow from open to more direct questions is to think of questioning as a funnel. Initially, open-ended questions are used and a broad range of responses is possible. As the discussion of a particular topic area progresses, the questioning becomes more focused and the degree of freedom in responding narrows, just as the space in a funnel gets narrower and narrower. Questioning about a marital relationship might progress something like this:

> "How would you describe your marriage?"
> "What are these arguments like?"
> "What do you enjoy about the relationship?
> "Have you and your husband ever separated?"
> "How long have you been married?"

It is important to communicate in a manner that clients can understand. While this statement may seem obvious, sticking with this simple dictum can be difficult. A gross assessment of the client's level of intelligence and verbal abilities can be made based upon background information such as age, education level, and occupational status. However, this assessment needs to continue as the clinician gathers additional information about the client through their interactions.

Nonverbal Strategies

Much of what gets communicated in an interview occurs nonverbally. It has been estimated, for example, that 65 percent of the meaning of a message is gleaned from nonverbal behavior (Birdswhistell, 1970, cited in Cormier & Cormier, 1991). Skilled clinicians read a client's nonverbal behavior for clues about the client's emotions, attitudes, and behavior. The client who never makes eye contact with the clinician may be anxious or depressed. Fidgeting might suggest anxiety or agitation. Slouching in the chair with arms folded can signal boredom, or the client may be communicating resentment toward the interview process. Clinicians need to take into consideration the client's cultural background when developing hypotheses based upon the client's nonverbal behavior. In some cultures, for example, averting one's eyes is a sign of respect.

Just as the client's nonverbal behavior conveys a great deal of information to the clinician, the clinician's facial expressions and body posture say a lot to the client. It is important for clinicians to be attentive to the nonverbal messages they send to clients. Being attentive and conveying interest facilitates communication. Clients are often asked about highly personal issues. They are more likely to share this information with a clinician they perceive to be interested in what they say and to care about them as a person. Egan (1986) describes several "microskills" for communicating interest to clients. He uses the acronym SOLER as a mnemonic device for recalling these skills. The S stands for *squarely* facing the client (i.e., having one's shoulders squared to the client and facing him or her directly). O reminds the clinician to adopt an *open* posture. Crossing one's arms or legs can signal defensiveness, but an open posture says that the clinician is open to what the client has to say. L is for *lean* toward the client. In North American cultures leaning toward someone conveys the message that the listener is interested in what is being said. E is for *eye contact.* Frequent eye contact shows interest. Finally, R stands for *relax.* Beginning clinicians often find the latter the most difficult microskill to master. However, it may be the most important. In most clinical contexts some degree of anxiety on the part of the client is common. A relaxed clinician helps the client to relax and open up in the interview.

When there is inconsistency between verbal and nonverbal messages, the latter tend to be given greater credence (Cormier & Cormier, 1991). *Congruence* is sometimes used to describe harmony or consistency between verbal and nonverbal information (Cormier & Cormier, 1991). It is perhaps not surprising to note that researchers find congruence between a clinician's verbal and nonverbal messages to be positively associated with how facilitative clinicians are rated by their clients. The question "How would you describe your relationship with your wife?" will likely lead to one type of response if asked by a clinician who is staring out the window and tapping a pencil and quite another from a clinician who makes eye contact with and leans toward the client.

Listening Skills

Being a good clinical interviewer involves much more than simply knowing what questions to ask. Effective interviewing requires effective listening. Listening might seem like a passive process. The listener receives information. And, in fact, listening in some contexts is more passive than in others. Listening to one's psychology professor lecture about the relationship between schedules of reinforcement and rates of extinction might require very little action on the part of the student. However, even in this situation, some action on the part of the listener can facilitate communication. The student who asks questions when things are not clear and summarizes what the instructor says in his or her notes is likely to get more out of the lecture than the student who simply sits and listens. When listening is an active process, the listener gains more information.

The term *active listening* has been used to describe the strategies used by clinicians to facilitate communication with clients (Egan, 1986). Cormier and Cormier (1991) describe four basic listening responses: clarification, paraphrase, reflection, and summarization. *Clarification* refers to questioning that helps the clinician understand an ambiguous message. Typical clarifying responses start with phrases such as "Are you saying that . . ." "Could you describe for me . . ." "Say what you mean by . . ." and end with repetition of the client's own words. In addition to clarifying the message, clarification responses confirm the accuracy of the clinician's perception and highlight for the client exactly what he or she has communicated.

Paraphrasing involves taking what the client has said, rephrasing it, and saying it back. The clinician tells the client, in the clinician's own words, what he or she understood the client to say. Paraphrasing communicates to the client that he or she has been understood. In addition, it also provides the client with an opportunity to clarify the message if the clinician has misunderstood. A third function of clarification is to encourage the client to say more about an important topic. Finally, paraphrasing can be used as a strategy to gently redirect the client back to the topic at hand. Consider the following interaction:

CLIENT: "School has always been really difficult for me. I really have to work hard to do well. My grades have always been good but it hasn't been easy. Not like my sister. Megan has always just waltzed right through school. She just reads a chapter once and its all there for her when test time comes."

THERAPIST: "So while you've done well in school, you've had to work very hard."

Reflection is similar to paraphrasing but rather than the clinician rephrasing the content of what the client has said, reflecting involves describing the emotional component of the client's message. Cormier and Cormier (p. 95) provide the following example to illustrate the distinction between paraphrasing and reflection:

CLIENT: "Everything is humdrum. There's nothing new going on, nothing exciting. All my friends are away. I wish I had money to do something different."

COUNSELOR PARAPHRASE: "With your friends gone and no money around, there is nothing for you to do right now."

COUNSELOR REFLECTION: "You feel bored with the way things are for you right now."

Summarizing, the fourth listening response described by Cormier and Cormier (1991), is an extension of paraphrasing and reflecting. It involves tying together two or more distinct parts of what the client has said. Summarizing is sometimes used to identify and check out a common theme that reappears across different contexts. Summarizing, like paraphrasing and reflection, provide the client with an opportunity to clarify what he or she has communicated. It also demonstrates for the client that the clinician is listening and cares about what the client has to say. Table 6.1 summarizes the basic listening responses.

Clinical interviewing is a deceptively challenging task. Clinicians in training, and even seasoned professionals, often struggle to build rapport with clients while simultaneously gathering necessary information. In Box 6.3 we discuss some common pitfalls encountered in clinical interviews.

Diagnostic Interviewing

The goal of a diagnostic interview is classification of the client and his or her problems. The assumption underlying diagnostic interviewing is that psychiatric disorders make themselves apparent through sets of signs or symptoms. In addition, disorders are believed to have predictable courses, rates of occurrence among family members, and treatment responses. The cause of a disorder does not need to be known for classification purposes and identifying possible etiological factors is not the primary goal of a diagnostic interview. Rather, the goal is to classify the client's complaints or dysfunctions according to a diagnostic system.

TABLE 6.1 **Definition and Intended Purposes of Listening Responses**

Response	Definition	Intended Purpose
Clarification	A question beginning with, for example, "Do you mean that" or " Are you saying that," plus a rephrasing of the client's message.	1. To encourage client elaboration. 2. To check out the accuracy of what you heard the client say. 3. To clear up vague messages.
Paraphrase (responding to content)	A rephrasing of the content of the client's message.	1. To help the client focus on the content of his or her message. 2. To highlight content when attention to feelings is premature or self-defeating.
Reflection (responding to feelings)	A rephrasing of the affective part of the client's message.	1. To encourage the client to express more of his or her feelings. 2. To have the client experience feelings more intensely. 3. To help the client become more aware of the feelings that dominate him or her. 4. To help the client discriminate accurately among feelings.
Summarization	Two or more paraphrases or reflections that condense the client's message or the session.	1. To tie together multiple elements of the client message. 2. To identify a common theme or pattern. 3. To interrupt excessive talking. 4. To review progress.

Source: Adapted from Cormier and Cormier (1991).

In the United States at this time that system is usually the DSM-IV (American Psychiatric Association, 1994).

In the diagnostic interview, the clinician observes the client's behavior, inquires about his or her symptoms in detail, and gathers relevant personal and family history. Recall that the DSM-IV utilizes a multiaxial system. Therefore, in addition to inquiring about the criteria for specific mental disorders, the interviewer also gathers information about stable personality characteristics (Axis II), general medical conditions (Axis III), life stressors (Axis IV), and general ability to function (Axis IV). The same psychiatric disorder may manifest itself very differently in different clients. Some clients experience more than one disorder at the same time (this is referred to as comobidity). Different clients have different coping mechanisms, different levels of psychosocial support, and face different types of life challenges. They may or may not have accompanying medical conditions. By using the multiaxial diagnostic system, the clinician attempts to put some order onto the myriad of information obtained in the assessment.

There are many methods for conducting diagnostic interviews. These vary in their goals and degree of structure. (See Hersen & Turner, 1985; Othmer & Othmer, 1994; Shea,

BOX **6.3**

Common Interviewing Pitfalls

The journey from undergraduate psychology student to professional psychologist is challenging, exciting, and sometimes painful. Not only is there a great deal of psychological theory and research to master, but the developing professional must also learn about such nonacademic topics as health-care policies, record keeping, licensure, ethical standards, professional appearance, supervisor expectations, and malpractice insurance, to name a few. An important transition on the journey is the step from student to clinical psychology trainee. An interesting book titled *Basic Skills and Professional Issues in Clinical Psychology,* edited by Janet Matthews and Eugene Walker (1997), was written to help prepare students for their first professional experiences in psychology. In a chapter on interviewing skills, Peter Giordano (1997) describes some of the common pitfalls beginning clinicians fall into during their first clinical interviews.

The authenticity pitfall: Hearing the advice "be yourself" may seem comical to the psychology trainee who is struggling to make sure to maintain eye contact, express empathy, observe the client's nonverbal behavior, ask open-ended questions, and record what the client is saying. But the advice is sound nonetheless. Too often beginning clinicians adopt a persona when they enter the clinical setting. They try to be their supervisor or a master clinician whose work they admire. Certainly there is some value in learning from professional models. However, the attention one must devote to maintaining the persona diverts one from the client.

The jargon pitfall: This pitfall is related to the first. In order to sound professional, beginning clinicians often use professional jargon where simpler language would be more effective. Asking "Are you anhedonic?" will likely elicit a blank stare from most clients, but "Do you feel like you don't enjoy things the way you used to?" is a question most people can understand.

The slave-to-the-intake-form-pitfall: Many agencies provide a suggested outline of topics to be covered during an initial interview. Some even use an intake form to be completed by the clinician. Probably out of a sense of insecurity, many beginning clinicians feel overwhelming pressure to make sure that all possible topics are covered during the intake interview. By focusing on the form, the beginning clinician will likely miss what is important to the client.

The diagnostic label pitfall: Prior knowledge of diagnostic labels can influence the topic areas the clinician chooses to cover in the intake interview. One of us had the experience of interviewing a client for a study on the treatment of panic disorder. The client was referred by another clinician in the community who described her as "agoraphobic." After 45 minutes or so of interviewing, during which both the clinician and the client struggled through a long series of questions about panic attacks and agoraphobic avoidance, the clinician noticed that the client's hands were red and chapped. This led to inquiries about hand washing, which revealed that the client suffered with a rather severe case of obsessive-compulsive disorder. The expectation that the client's problem was panic disorder with agoraphobia impeded the assessment process.

The apology pitfall: It is quite natural for a new clinician to feel insecure about his or her competence when beginning professional work. There are times when clients will directly challenge the new clinician's competence by questioning his or her age or life experiences. A veteran with PTSD may want to know whether the psychologist has ever served in the military or seen combat. A harried mother may inquire whether the clinician has children. A grieving widower may want to know whether the psychologist has ever lost a loved one. In such circumstances, clinicians may feel the need to apologize for their lack of experience.

Instead of apologizing, its better to answer the question in a straightforward, nondefensive manner, while at the same time conveying confidence in one's ability to help. A clinician whose competence is challenged because he or she does not have children might respond:

BOX **6.3** **Continued**

You are right. I don't have children of my own. . . . However, because you are a parent and I am not, you may help me understand how a parent feels in certain circumstances. With your input and my understanding of principles that psychologists have learned from research and practice over many years, I am in a better position to be of help to you. (Giordano, 1997, pp. 76–77)

The reassurance pitfall: Interviewing people about their personal lives and problems can sometimes leave a clinician feeling overwhelmed. The objective life stressors faced by some people are striking. Clinicians drawn to the field by a desire to help others want to do something. It is a natural tendency to want to offer reassurance to the client. But reassurance needs to be communicated carefully while acknowledging the reality of the client's situation.

Hearing clients' sometimes tragic stories can produce a strong urge to do something to make the client feel better. However, it may trivialize the client's problems if the clinician were to close out the interview by saying something like "Don't worry. I'm sure everything is going to work out fine." Instead, it would be more appropriate to acknowledge the strength it took to come in for help and to praise the client's willingness to discuss the difficult topics. "I really appreciate your willingness to share with me some of the painful experiences you've had. I know that it's not easy to discuss these kinds of things. It takes a lot of strength to recognize that it's time to ask for help to deal with all that you are facing."

1988; and Morrison, 1993, for examples.) Unstructured clinical interviews are probably the most popular method of arriving at a diagnosis.

In an unstructured clinical interview, the clinician develops hypotheses about the client and his or her symptoms over the course of the assessment. In a high-quality interview, hypotheses are tested by looking for information that is consistent, but also information that is inconsistent, with the hypotheses. As we saw in Chapter 5, clinicians tend to search for confirming information and ignore information inconsistent with their original hypothesis.

Othmer and Othmer (1994) propose five steps in diagnostic interviewing. In the first step, the clinician looks for *diagnostic clues* in the client's chief complaint, behavior, history, and presentation. Based upon these clues, the clinician will create lists of possible psychiatric disorders, excluded disorders, and unexplored disorders. In this step of the interview, the clinician tends to ask open-ended questions such as "What kind of problems brought you here?" or "Tell me what's troubling you." In order to be comprehensive, questioning tends to expand the areas of discovery (e.g., "Are there other problem areas we haven't discussed?"). In the second step, the clinician inquires about specific *diagnostic criteria.* Specific questions relating to specific criteria are asked. Example questions might include "Have you ever heard voices or seen things that no one else could hear or see?" "Did you ever have a problem with binge eating, when you would eat so much food so fast that it made you feel sick?" or "Have you ever been bothered by embarrassing, scary, or ridiculous thoughts that come into your mind over and over even though you tried to ignore or stop them?" The specific questions depend upon the clues the clinician picked up on in the first step. With further questioning the lists of unexplored and possible disorders shrinks and the list of excluded disorders grows. The third step of the interview is to get a *psychiatric history.* In this step a history of the disorder is gathered. Has the client received mental health services in the past? For what problems? What were the outcomes? In addition, the clinician gathers information about premorbid functioning (i.e., how the person was doing before developing the disorder) and family history (i.e., whether others in the client's family have suffered with mental disorders). The fourth step is to arrive at a *diagnosis.* Here is where the clinician condenses the various data into a handful of diagnostic labels and ratings. Othmer and Othmer suggest the fifth step in the diagnostic process is to arrive at a *prognosis* for the patient. Based upon the five diagnostic axes, as well as ancillary information gathered during the interview, the clinician estimates the likely future course of the disorder and the client.

Unstructured interviewing is probably the method used by most practicing clinicians to develop diagnostic formulations of their clients. Unfortunately, most reviewers have pointed out problems with the reliability of this approach (e.g., Wiens & Matarazzo, 1983). Structured clinical interviews are an alternative method for gathering the information upon which to base a psychiatric diagnosis.

Structured Interviews

In an unstructured clinical interview, the clinician uses his or her judgment to decide what questions to ask, what areas of inquiry can be skipped, and what issues require additional probing. A whole host of factors can influence the clinician's decisions. Theoretical orientation, personal biases, clinical experience, time available, and mood of the clinician might all affect what questions the clinician chooses to ask and what he or she chooses to ignore. In addition, a variety of client factors including age, gender, ethnicity, socioeconomic status, and physical appearance can influence the clinician's choices. Variability among clinicians with respect to what questions are asked, which observations are judged to be important, and how the interview information is organized contributes to poor interjudge diagnostic reliability (Ward, Beck, Mendelson, Mock, & Erbaugh, 1962).

Structured interviews improve diagnostic reliability by standardizing the interview process. In a structured diagnostic interview, questions are predetermined. The clinician is provided with a set of rules that guide decisions about which areas to probe, the sequencing of inquiries, and the system for rating client responses (Rogers, 1995). In structured interviews even the exact wording of questions is standardized.

There are several well-developed structured diagnostic interviews. These interviews vary in comprehensiveness. The Structured Clinical Interview for Axis I DSM-IV Disorders (SCID-I; First, Spitzer, Gibbon, & Williams, 1995), for example, covers nearly all diagnoses, while the Anxiety Disorders Interview Schedule—Fourth Edition (ADIS-IV; Brown, DiNardo, & Barlow, 1994) gathers in-depth information about the anxiety disorders and related conditions but only minimal data about other disorders. The Comprehensive Drinker Profile (CDP; Miller & Marlatt, 1984) was developed to assess alcohol abuse and dependence as well as clients' potential to benefit from alcohol treatment. An overview of the more well-developed diagnostic and structured interviews is presented by Rogers (1995).

Structured diagnostic interviews offer several advantages over unstructured interviews (Rogers, 1995). First, diagnostic reliability is improved by the use of structured interviews. Second, structured interviews tend to be more comprehensive. Clinicians tend to focus upon the presenting problem and associated symptoms. Harkness (1992) found that, after establishing the presence of a single mental disorder, most clinicians tend to stop the diagnostic investigation. Studies of clinic and community samples indicated that the rates of comorbidity (i.e., the presence of two or more mental disorders in the same person) are considerable (Clark, Watson, & Reynolds, 1995; Lilienfeld, Waldman, & Israel, 1994). Third, by following a structured interview, clinicians are more likely to apply the diagnostic criteria correctly. The structured interview increases the clinicians' awareness of diagnostic decision rules such as minimum number of required diagnostic criteria and exclusion guidelines. Fourth, structured interviews provide guidelines for, and improve the reliability of, ratings of psychopathology. The DSM-IV is a categorical system. That is, diagnostic rules are set to determine whether clients meet criteria for mental disorders. It is a yes/no decision. The client meets criteria or does not. Diagnostic interviews often include guidelines for rating the severity of client's problems.

While structured interviews clearly have their advantages, some clinicians have reservations about their use. Some are concerned that following a standardized interview may negatively affect rapport building. In addition, clients may be put off if the interviewing process seems unnatural or mechanized. Finally, in paying strict attention to the wording and decision rules in the diagnostic interview, the clinician may miss important observations. With these potential limitations in mind, it is important to note that research studies suggest that rapport is not strongly affected by structured interviewing.

Research on Diagnostic Interviewing

Reliability. The most common method of determining diagnostic reliability is to look at the level of agreement between two diagnosticians. If in most instances in which one clinician determines that a client has a specific mental disorder the other clinician also forms the same diagnostic impression, and if the clinicians also tend to agree on the clients who do not have the disorder, then there is good reliability. Historically, diagnosing of mental disorders was a strikingly unreliable enterprise (Matarazzo, 1983; Ward et al., 1962).

In a seminal paper on the subject, Ward and colleagues (1962) described the factors underlying the poor reliability of psychiatric diagnoses. They argued that when clinicians disagree on diagnoses, there are three possible causes: diagnostician variability (i.e., the clinicians ask different questions or make different observations), criterion variability (i.e., the diagnostic criteria are not clearly defined), and client variability (i.e., the clients are inconsistent in their clinical presentations). In 1962, Ward and colleagues estimated that most of the cases of diagnostic disagreement were due to the ambiguities of the diagnostic system. However, they also pointed out that a substantial proportion of the cases of diagnostic disagreement could be attributed to variability in the behavior of the clinicians. The introduction of objective diagnostic criteria with the DSM-III (American Psychiatric Association, 1980) was aimed at the first source of variability. Structured diagnostic interviews were designed to reduce the number of diagnostic disagreements that could be attributed to differences among interviewers.

The assessment of diagnostic reliability is a deceptively tricky enterprise. The most straightforward approach to the problem would be to examine the number of times two clinicians agree that a diagnosis is present or not compared to the total number of cases. Let's take a simple example (see Figure 6.1). Two clinicians interview the same 100 patients. Dr.

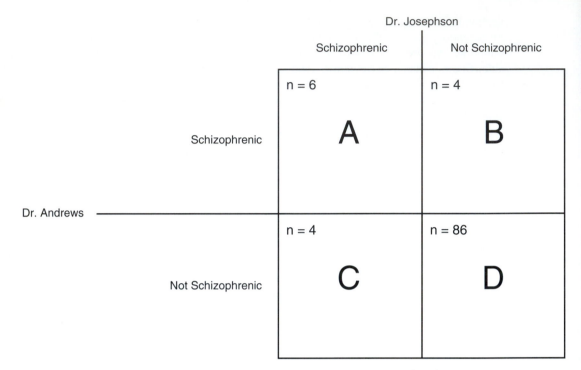

FIGURE 6.1   Diagnostic agreement/disagreement between Drs. Josephson and Andrews.

Andrews diagnoses schizophrenia in ten clients. Dr. Josephson also diagnoses schizophrenia in 10 clients—6 of the clients diagnosed schizophrenic by Andrews plus 4 that Andrews did not think were schizophrenic. Figure 6.1 shows that in 6 cases, Drs. Andrews and Josephson agreed on the diagnosis of schizophrenia (cell A); in 4 cases Dr. Andrews thought the client schizophrenic but Dr. Josephson did not (cell B); in 4 cases it was Josephson who said schizophrenia and Andrews said no (cell C); and in 86 cases both diagnosticians agreed the clients did not have schizophrenia (cell D). Overall Drs. Josephson and Andrews agreed 92 percent of the time (A + D/N or 6 + 86/100). This suggests very good reliability. However, close inspection of Figure 6.1 reveals that most of the diagnostic agreement was due to the large number of case in which both clinicians agreed that the disorder was not present (cell D—86 cases). The *overall percent agreement* is generally considered to be a poor measure of reliability particularly when diagnosing rare disorders. The base rate of a disorder (i.e., how often it occurs in the general population) influences diagnostic reliability. Two clinicians will agree most of the time if they both always diagnose the absence of a rare disorder.

An alternative procedure for determining diagnostic reliability that takes into account the likelihood of chance agreements is the *kappa coefficient*. One formula for calculating kappa is:

$$\frac{AD - BC}{AD - BC + N(B+C)/2}$$

Applying this to the data in Figure 6.1, we arrive at a kappa coefficient of .56. This is a more sober, and accurate, estimate of the diagnostic agreement between Drs. Andrews and Josephson. Kappa is the statistic most often reported by researchers investigating diagnostic reliability. The kappa coefficient can be used not only to estimate reliability between different clinicians but also to estimate test-retest reliability. In the case of diagnostic reliability, test-retest would be the agreement between diagnostic formulations obtained at two different points in time. A kappa coefficient above .75 indicates excellent reliability (Cicchetti, 1994).

Reliability for Structured Diagnostic Interviews. How reliable are diagnostic interviews? One way to answer this question is to say that there is greater diagnostic agreement between clinicians when structured interviews are used when compared with unstructured interviews (Matarazzo, 1983). Beyond that, however, it is important to point out that the reliability of a structured interview cannot be determined separate from a number of factors. As Ward and colleagues (1962) pointed out, diagnostic reliability is determined by the reliability of the interviewers' behavior, but also by the diagnostic criteria used and the consistency of the patients' behavior. Other factors also influence reliability including characteristics of the interviewers (e.g., training, motivation), the study methods used (e.g., two diagnosticians observing the same interview; two independent interviews; test-retest; live or videotaped interviews), and characteristics of the study sample (e.g., hospitalized sample; clinic sample; gender distribution). Recall that reliability is influenced by the base rate of the problem (Williams et al., 1992).

With the above caveats in mind, one can examine the kappa coefficients reported by various researchers. In a large test-retest reliability study of 592 patients from six different sites, Williams and colleagues (Williams, Spitzer, & Gibbon, 1992) found an average kappa of .68 for lifetime diagnoses (i.e., has the person ever met diagnostic criteria for the disorder) using the Structured Clinical Interview for DSM-III-R. Williams and colleagues summarized findings from several studies using different diagnostic interviews and different study methodologies that reported similar or higher kappa coefficients. It appears, therefore, that structured diagnostic interviews are an acceptably reliable method of collecting information upon which to base a diagnosis.

Validity. "The validity of diagnostic interviewing is inextricably tied to the validity of diagnosis itself" (Rogers, 1995, p. 4). Answering a question such as "Is the SCID a valid instrument for diagnosing schizophrenia?" assumes schizophrenia to be a valid construct. There is no "gold standard" for psychiatric diagnoses. If a diagnostic instrument indicates the presence of a mental disorder, there is no absolute standard against which one can compare the accuracy of the diagnosis. For many medical disorders such gold standards do exist. For example, a physician may diagnose mononucleosis based upon a patient's complaints of high temperature and sore throat as well as evidence of swollen lymph nodes upon physical exam. The physician, however, has available a blood test (the heterophil antibodies test) to confirm the diagnosis. For mental disorders there is no independent test of the presence of the disorder that is universally accepted as the standard in the field.

One approach used to validate structured diagnostic interviews is to examine content validity. Do the questions on the interview accurately reflect the diagnostic criteria? This question is usually easily answered. For example, on the SCID interview there is a one-to-one correspondence with the diagnostic criteria of the DSM (Rogers, 1995). It is important to be clear that this approach validates the diagnostic interview as a measure of the disorder as defined by the diagnostic system. It would be tautological to argue that the correspondence between the interview and the diagnostic criteria is evidence of the validity of the disorder.

A second approach to validating structured diagnostic interviews is to look at the convergent validity between the instrument and another method of arriving at the diagnosis. For example, one study investigated the validity of the SCID interview by comparing diagnoses made by an experienced psychiatrist who was provided with an audiotape of the SCID interview to the diagnoses made by another experienced psychiatrist who reviewed the patients' clinical records. These researchers found good agreement between the two diagnosticians (Maziade, Roy, Fournier, & Cliché, 1992). In a study of the ADIS (DiNardo et al., 1985), clinicians' diagnoses of agoraphobia matched up well with clients' ratings of the fears on a questionnaire measure (Barlow, DiNardo, Vermilyea, Vermilyea, & Blanchard, 1986).

How well an interview identifies a client as having one disorder and not another is a measure of its discriminant validity. One could imagine a single question diagnostic interview that would probably do a pretty good job of identifying people with major depression (e.g., "Are you depressed?"). This measure would likely have good *sensitivity* for major depression (i.e., it correctly classifies people with the disorder). However, the measure would have poor *specificity* (i.e., it would inaccurately classify a large number of people without major depression as having the disorder). The single-question interview could be said to have poor discriminant validity. The issue of discriminant validity, or specificity, is a problematic one for diagnostic interviews. It is not uncommon for clients to meet criteria for two or more psychiatric diagnoses. For example, Sanderson and colleagues (Sanderson, DiNardo, Rapee, & Barlow, 1990) found that approximately 70 percent of clients interviewed with the ADIS-R (DiNardo et al., 1985) qualified for more than one anxiety disorder and about one-third met criteria for a mood disorder. There are at least three possible explanations for such findings: (1) There is a great deal of comorbidity among the anxiety disorders and between anxiety disorders and depression. (2) The structured interview has poor discriminant validity. (3) The validity of specific diagnoses within the DSM system is poor. Regarding the third possibility, the validity of the general diagnosis of anxiety disorder may be valid, but the validity of specific anxiety disorders poor.

Reasonable questions about the construct validity of the DSM system can be raised (see for example Carson, 1996; Follette & Houts, 1986). Box 6.4 summarizes some of the criticisms of the DSM and describes some proposals for alternative approaches.

Interviewing with Children

When a child is referred to a clinical psychologist for assessment or treatment, it is usually the parents or other adults who the psychologist will interview about the presenting problem. The assessment might include behavioral checklists completed by adults who know the child, observations of the child, and perhaps psychometric testing. In fact, it is generally

BOX **6.4**

Alternatives to DSM

Classification plays an important role in science. The history of medicine is replete with illustrations of how diagnostic classification was the first step in discovering the causes of various diseases. For example, classifying groups of people together based upon their symptom presentation was a necessary first step in identifying the causes of tuberculosis, leprosy, and cholera in the nineteenth century (see Spring, Weinstein, Lemon, & Haskell, 1991). A more contemporary example is the relatively rapid identification of the Human Immunodeficiency Virus (HIV) as the cause of Acquired Immune Deficiency Syndrome (AIDS). Classification has played an important role in the development of our understanding of some mental disorders as well. Emil Kraepelin's (1856–1926) pioneering work on the disorder he called dementia praecox laid the foundation for the study and treatment of schizophrenia, as the condition is now called.

To accept that classification is a necessary step in a scientific approach to understanding abnormal behavior does not mean one must accept the DSM system, however. One can agree that nosological systems are valuable because they can facilitate communication among researchers and help organize research efforts without accepting that the current diagnostic system is the best, or even an effective, means of achieving these goals. Similarly, to acknowledge that classification can help clinicians choose among treatment alternatives, communicate among themselves, and make predictions about future course and associated problems does not mean that one must endorse the DSM. In other words, there could be alternatives to the DSM that would do a better job of achieving the goals of a classification system.

The reality is that at this point in time no well-developed rival to the psychiatric diagnostic system exists. However, alternatives to the DSM system have been suggested by a variety of scholars (e.g., Leary, 1957). In an interesting special series of the *Journal of Consulting and Clinical Psychology* (Volume 64), several possible alternatives to categorical psychiatric classification were offered by behaviorally oriented scholars. One of the central ideas of behavioral assessment is that understanding the *function* of behavior is more important than its descriptive qualities (sometimes referred to as its *topography*). Two behaviors that look the same may serve very different functions. For example, two individuals may frequently consume alcohol to the point of severe intoxication, but drinking serves a different function for each individual. In a traditional diagnostic system, the focus is on the topography of the behavior (i.e., both people drink too much). From a behavioral perspective, the drinking behavior of these two individuals may serve very different functions (Wulfert, Greenway, & Dougher, 1996). One of them may drink to get "high." Drinking serves to increase the enjoyment of social situations. For the second individual it helps him or her to escape negative feelings—it serves a different function.

Traditionally, proponents of behavioral assessment have eschewed classification system. However, examples of behavioral alternatives to, and modifications of, psychiatric diagnostic systems have recently been described. Hayes, Wilson, Gifford, Follette, and Stroshal (1996) argue that a classification system based upon functional analysis of behavior is feasible. In the example described above, we saw that the same behavior, drinking alcohol, can serve different functions in different individuals. Hayes and colleagues point out that the converse is also true—behaviors that are topographically different (i.e., they look different) may serve the same function. *Experiential avoidance* is suggested as one dimension for classification of overtly different behaviors. In this classification system, a wide variety of forms of psychopathology could be viewed as maladaptive means of avoiding unpleasant private experiences, such as negative emotions or unpleasant memories.

(continued)

B O X   **6.4**   **Continued**

Hayes and colleagues (1996) note that the concept of experiential avoidance appears under different guises in most psychological theories of therapy. The goal of psychoanalysis is to help the client to face memories that were so painful they had to be repressed. Rogers advocated "openness to experience" as a key goal of client-centered therapy. Perhaps most obviously, behavioral approaches to anxiety disorders all involve some form of *exposure* to previously avoided situations, images, or feelings. Additional evidence for the significance of experiential avoidance comes from studies of traditionally classified psychopathology. In panic disorder, for example, clients avoid experiencing a variety of normal human emotions (Hecker & Thorpe, 1992). Individuals with obsessive-compulsive disorder seek to escape or avoid aversive thoughts and unpleasant emotions. The function of hand washing is to escape the anxiety associated with the thought of contamination and to avoid the thought of contaminating others (Steketee, 1993). Finally, studies of victims of assault have shown that those who avoid reminders of the trauma in the period of time immediately following the traumatic event are more likely to develop posttraumatic stress disorder (Foa & Riggs, 1995). Given the significance of avoidance in various forms of psychopathology and the central role exposure to avoided experiences plays in a variety of forms of psychotherapy, Hayes and colleagues argue that experiential avoidance is a more meaningful category around which one could categorize psychopathology than the current diagnostic dimensions (e.g., mood disorders, anxiety disorders, and so on), which by and large emphasize topography.

The behavioral approach to classifying abnormal behavior is, of course, not the only alternative to the psychiatric system. Follette and Houts (1996) call for development of multiple systems for classifying psychopathology. The different systems can then compete based upon how well they succeed at helping us to understand etiology, predict course, and treat individuals who experience various problems of living. Citing philosophers of science (e.g., Feyerband, 1982), they suggest that competing systems are more likely to lead to scientific progress than is adherence to a single nosology.

Criticisms of psychiatric classification systems are as old as the classification systems themselves (see, for example, Greisinger, 1867), as are calls for alternative systems. Despite these protests, the psychiatric diagnostic system is more dominant in the mental health field today than at any time in the past. Granting agencies organize funding sources around the DSM, scientific journals reflect psychiatric categories (e.g., *Journal of Anxiety Disorders; Schizophrenia Bulletin*) and insurance companies require that clients be given diagnostic labels before they will pay for mental health services. Despite its weaknesses, therefore, it appears as though the DSM is here for the foreseeable future.

---

accepted that adult informants and direct observations can provide a more accurate picture of a child's behavioral deficits and strengths than can the child's own description (Bierman, 1983). Having said this, it is important not to lose sight of the unique and important role child interviews play in assessment. Only children themselves can tell us about their direct experiences, their perceptions of problems, their hopes, and their fears. Developing a valid understanding of the cognitive and emotional factors mediating children's behavioral problems often requires interviews with the children (Bierman, 1983).

Interviewing children presents its own unique set of challenges. Reliance upon the strategies used with adults can yield incomplete, distorted, or in some cases no information from a child. Open-ended questions are the cornerstone of the adult clinical interview. "Tell me about your family" is an appropriate means of initiating a new topic area with an adult client. The same statement may yield only a blank stare, or a difficult-to-interpret response (e.g., "My daddy is tall") from a preschooler. Clinicians need to develop a new set of verbal strategies if they are to succeed at interviewing child clients. Similarly, the context within which interviews are conducted is very different with children and adults. An adult usually understands the social role of patient or client. Adults will usually comply with expectation that they sit in a chair, make eye contact, and engage in a dialogue with the psychologist. Typically, children do not appreciate such expectations. Interviewers must show flexibility. A successful child interview may occur while sitting on the floor drawing pictures, over the course of a game of checkers, or while playing with dolls. Finally, clinicians must be resourceful. It takes energy, enthusiasm, and creativity to keep a child interested in the clinical interview.

Developmental Considerations

Children's verbal skills, memory, conceptual skills, and organizational skills are not fully developed. Understanding children's level of cognitive development can help clinical psychologists structure clinical interviews and interpret children's responses. Karen Bierman (1983) has described the importance of children's cognitive development in the clinical interview. Her description of cognitive abilities at various stages of child's development are summarized below.

Preschool-age children think in simple and concrete terms. The world is interpreted in terms of black-and-white categories: good and bad, nice and mean, beautiful and ugly. Children live in the present and only interpret events in terms of what impact they have on them (egocentrism). Preschool-age children's conception of social roles tend to be quite rigid. One study found that children at this age describe a mother as someone who takes care of children. If a mother fixes a car, she is no longer a mother (Moore, Cooper, & Brickhard, 1977, cited in Bierman, 1983). Similarly, another study found that some preschoolers believed that if a "father studied and became a doctor," he could no longer be a father (Kooistra, 1964, cited in Bierman, 1983).

As children get older, their abilities to think and express themselves develop. By their early grade-school years, for example, children can recognize that a woman becomes a mother when she has a child and that she continues to be a mother regardless of what other activities she engages in (Moore et al., 1977, cited in Bierman, 1983). Children in these middle childhood years begin to use more complex constructs in understanding the world. "After age 7, children begin to make an increasing number of psychological inferences about other people, pertaining to their thoughts, feelings, personality, attributes, and general behavioral dispositions" (Bierman, 1983, p. 224).

By adolescence, young people begin to form a complex understanding of the world similar to that seen in adults. There is a recognition that behavior is influenced by multiple factors and that individuals can have a mixture of positive and negative attributes. There is an increased understanding of social roles and the world is seen as more predictable and understandable. There is, of course, considerable variability in the cognitive and verbal skills of adolescents. Many are still unable to articulate their feelings and describe their experiences with accuracy (Sattler, 1988).

Interview Techniques

A variety of strategies have been developed to facilitate child interviews. One way to categorize these strategies is to break them into two sets—those providing alternative stimuli to which the child can respond and those providing alternative means for a child to respond (Bierman, 1983).

In the adult interview, the stimuli presented to the interviewee are verbal questions, usually worded in an open-ended format. As can be seen from the previous discussion, younger children do not have the cognitive capacity to respond to this broad style of questioning. Questions can be modified so that they provide the child with a more concrete set of responses to choose from. For example, the open-ended questions "Describe your mom" becomes "What do you like best about your mom?" "What do you like least about your mom?" (Sattler, 1988). A second means of providing the child with an alternative to straight verbal questioning is to provide the child with visual stimuli to which he or she can respond. A common strategy is to have a child draw a picture of himself or herself or of the family and to then have the child talk about the drawing. This strategy can relieve some pressure the child may experience when he or she has to talk directly about himself or herself. It is usually easier to talk about a picture than it is to talk about oneself. Bierman (1983, p. 234) describes an example in which the interviewer might elicit information from a child of recently divorced parents. The clinician shows the child a picture and says, "Here are a mom and dad and a little girl about your age. The mom and dad are divorced." The clinician might then ask questions such as "What do you think happened?" "What does the little girl feel?" "What will happen next?"

A second set of strategies for conducting interviews with children involves providing them with alternatives to verbally answering the clinicians' inquiries. Children may lack the vocabulary or the cognitive sophistication to describe their thoughts and feelings. They can be provided with a variety of means for expressing themselves. For example, the clinician might provide the child with simple pictures of faces expressing various emotions and encourage them to choose among the faces in response to the clinician's questions. In the following example, the therapist (T) has provided the boy (B) with pictures of sad, happy, and mad faces (from Bierman, 1983, p. 236).

T: "How would you feel if you got to stay in the place where you live now?"

B: (*He points to sad.*)

T: "How would you feel if you could live with your mom?"

B: (*He points to happy, and then circles happy with a felt pen*)

T: "How did you feel when you had to leave your mom's?"

B: (*He points to sad.*)

T: "How come you had to leave?"

B: "Cause they were fighting."

T: "How did you feel when your mom and dad were fighting?"

B: (*Points to mad.*) "Real mad."

T: "What happened?"

B: "Nothing . . . I don't know . . . I ran away."

T: "It must have been scary."

B: "It was."

Several additional techniques have been suggested by to facilitate the process of interviewing children. The following list is adapted from Kanfer, Eyberg, and Krahn (1983) and Sattler (1988).

Use descriptive comments. Simple descriptive comments are a way of showing the child that the clinician is paying attention and of encouraging the child to continue appropriate behavior. Statements such as "You are working hard on your drawing," or "It looks like you're getting ready for a tea party" are examples of descriptive comments.

Give praise frequently. Praise rewards the child for talking about areas that the interviewer considers to be important. Examples might include "Sometimes it's hard to talk to a grown-up about these things, but you are doing a great job," or "I sure am learning a lot about your family. You are a great teacher." As a general rule, the younger the child is, the more praise is needed.

Use simple questions. Open-ended questions are usually not appropriate for younger children. They require a level of abstraction that is beyond their developmental level. Similarly, if-then or other forms of two-part questions can be confusing to children. For example, if a psychologist conducting a custody evaluation was to ask a 5-year-old, "If you lived with Mommy and Jack but got to see Daddy every other weekend, would you be happy or sad?" is not likely to get an interpretable response. Whatever the child's response, he or she would most likely be answering only one part of the question (i.e., would you be happy or sad if you lived with Mommy and Jack, or would you be happy or sad if you got to see Daddy every other weekend).

Be tactful. While this advice probably applies to most adult interviews as well, it is particularly important to avoid sounding critical or judgmental when interviewing a child. Sattler (1988, p. 422) offers the example of a child who complains about a teacher. It would be tactless for the interviewer was to respond, "Do you always have trouble with teachers?" A more appropriate response might be "Have you found other teachers to be as upsetting as this one has been for you?" Another example might be asking an adolescent, "What was the last grade you completed?" as opposed to saying, "When did you quit school?"

Use special care when asking about culturally unacceptable behavior. Starting at about age 5, children develop an increasing awareness of what behaviors are generally considered socially acceptable and those that are unacceptable. In a clinical setting, the psychologist is often interested in behaviors that might be viewed as culturally unacceptable. For example, children may not want to talk about domestic violence that occurs between their parents. There are a variety of strategies that can be useful when inquiring about such behaviors. One method is to first ask about positive, socially acceptable behaviors. In the case of domestic violence, the interviewer might say something like "Most moms and dads get along real well sometimes and not so well at other times. What is it like at your house when your Mom and Dad are really getting along well together? . . . What kinds of fun things do they like to do together?" After the child has had a chance to talk about positive interactions, the interviewer can then inquire about problems: "What is it like when they just aren't getting along . . . when they are mad at each other?" Another strategy to use when inquiring about sensitive areas is to let the child know that the interviewer is already aware of the negative behavior, so that the child is not in a position of having to admit or deny it. If the interviewer initiates questioning about domestic violence by asking, "Do your Mom and Dad hit each other when they argue?" the child is faced with having to admit to this socially unacceptable behavior. Instead, if the interviewer words the question in such a way as to show the child that the interviewer assumes the unacceptable behavior occurs (e.g., "What sorts of things do your mother and father fight about?"), it may help the child avoid feeling as if he or she is the one who let the cat out of the bag. In using this approach, the interviewer must be sure that the unacceptable behavior has occurred, otherwise there is the risk of leading the child into describing things that never happened. (See Chapter 16, Box 16.2, for examples of leading interview questioning.)

Try to understand silence. Assessment interviews primarily rely on verbal communication to gather information. When a child is silent, the interviewer is gathering no verbal information. For the inexperienced interviewer, particularly the student-clinician, silence can be very anxiety-producing. It is important for the interviewer to try to understand the child's silence before attempting to prompt the child to speak. Children are silent for a variety of reasons. They may resent having to meet with the interviewer. They may be characteristically shy. They may be frightened. Or they may be willing to talk but not know what to say. The interviewer looks to the child's nonverbal behavior, the circumstances of the interview, prior experiences with the child, and information from collateral sources to develop an understanding of the child's silence. Choosing an appropriate method for breaking through a child's silence requires an understanding of the silence. For the reticent child, engaging in parallel play may ease the pressure on the child and create opportunities to initiate the interview in a non-threatening fashion. For the child who is angry about having to meet with the psychologist, it might be more helpful to encourage the child to talk about the reasons he or she doesn't want to be there. This allows the interviewer the opportunity to build rapport through empathic listening and also to clarify misconceptions about the purpose of the interview.

Handle anxiety through support and reassurance. It is not at all unusual for children to be anxious about meeting with a psychologist, particularly for an initial assessment interview. There are no sure-fire techniques for avoiding or eliminating children's anxieties about clinical interviews. Some general strategies to keep in mind, however, can be helpful. The interviewer wants to avoid questioning that will generate guilty feelings. "Matter of fact acceptance by the interviewer of everything the child says is the most effective means of avoiding the development of anxiety" (Yarrow, 1960, p. 582). When difficult areas are being discussed, it is important to reassure the child and to acknowledge the sensitivity of the topic area. Sometimes at the end of an interview it is helpful to remind children about confidentiality, if that is appropriate, to praise the children for their efforts, and to thank them for their participation.

Issues of Cultural Diversity in Clinical Interviewing

"Multiculturalism is a social-intellectual movement that promotes the value of diversity as a core principle and insists that all cultural groups be treated with respect and as equals" (Fowers & Richardson, 1996, p. 609). Some critics of psychology view it as an oppressive, anti-multicultural institution devoted to perpetuation of the status quo, one that views middle-class American norms as universally applicable (see Jahoda, 1988; Sue & Sue, 1990, for discussion of this view). This portrayal of organized psychology, however, is probably not altogether fair. There is considerable evidence to suggest that organized psychology has embraced the values of multiculturalism. For example, attention to cultural differences is one of the criteria by which training programs in professional psychology are evaluated for accreditation purposes (American Psychological Association, 1986). Furthermore, in 1988 the American Psychological Association established a Task Force on the Delivery of Services to Ethnic Minority Populations. The task force published guidelines for practitioners who provide services to ethnic, linguistic, and culturally diverse populations in 1990 (American Psychological Association, 1990). While perhaps not as quickly as its critics would have liked, professional psychology appears to have endorsed multiculturalism.

While any professional activity engaged in by clinical psychologists can be influenced by cultural factors, the clinical interview seems particularly vulnerable to cultural influences (Pedersen & Ivey, 1993; Sue & Sue, 1990). Different cultures have different styles of communication. When the clinician and client are from different cultures, the opportunities for miscommunication are abundant. Derald Sue and David Sue (1990) have described some of the variations in communication styles among different cultures in American society. Native Americans, for example, tend to speak slowly and softly. They are comfortable with long silences and tend to be more indirect and low-key in their communication styles. In contrast, African Americans tend to speak with more affect, use prolonged eye contact when speaking, and are quicker to interrupt when conversing with peers. Asian Americans and Hispanics have some similarities in communication style. They tend to speak softly and avoid eye contact when interacting with persons perceived as having higher status. European Americans are characterized by speaking loudly and relatively rapidly. They tend to make more eye contact when listening and use head nods a great deal. European Americans, particularly males, tend to be direct and task-oriented in their communication. A quick scan of these communication style variations shows how easily communication patterns can be misinterpreted. As a simple example, a European American male psychologist might misinterpret avoidance of eye contact in a Japanese American child as evidence that the child is anxious, whereas the child would view additional eye contact as a sign of disrespect.

The task of understanding the impact cultural differences may be having upon the clinical interview and minimizing the risk of miscommunication and misunderstanding is a challenging one. Several writers have suggested guidelines for culturally sensitive interviewing. The following recommendations are drawn from the American Psychological Associations Guidelines (American Psychological Association, 1990), Sue and Sue (1990), and Pedersen and Ivey (1993).

1. Psychologists need to be aware of their own cultural background and experiences, values, and biases and how these may influence their behavior and interpretations in the clinical interview. Psychologists might ask themselves if they would have handled an interview differently if the client had shared the psychologists' cultural or ethnic background.
2. Psychologists need to educate themselves about the communication styles of ethnic groups and cultures with whom they work. The broad generalizations about the communication styles characteristics of broad ethnic groups described above only provides a gross outline for interpreting clients' behavior. Clearly, there are significant variations within Native American and African American groups in our society. Understanding the local communication norms is important.
3. Clinicians should be willing to modify their characteristic communication styles in order to facilitate communication. Understanding is not enough. Psychologists may need to model clients' communication patterns if they are to succeed at eliciting information from culturally different clients (Pedersen & Ivey, 1993).

BOX **6.5**

Interviewing as Intervention: Motivational Interviewing

Throughout this chapter clinical interviewing has been discussed as an assessment strategy. As we have seen, the clinical interview is the most frequently used assessment strategy by clinical psychologists (Watkins et al., 1995). Interviewing, however, also plays an important role in psychological intervention. In fact, most forms of psychotherapy consist of a series of clinical interviews.

How clients are interviewed about their problems can have a significant impact upon their motivation to change problematic behavior (Kanfer & Schefft, 1988; Miller & Rollnick, 1991). William Miller (1983) has developed an approach to interviewing that is designed to help people recognize personal problems and to develop in them the motivation to do something about them. Motivational interviewing is a set of techniques designed to help people recognize how their behavior creates problems for them and others and to motivate them to do something about it.

The strategies used in motivational interviewing are not confrontative, argumentative, or coercive. Instead, clinicians join with clients in developing an understanding of the problem behavior and how it does and does not work for them. The responsibility for changing problem behavior lies squarely with the client. "The strategies of motivational interviewing are more persuasive than coercive, more supportive than argumentative. The counselor seeks to create a positive atmosphere that is conducive to change. The overall goal is to increase the client's intrinsic motivation, so that change arises from within rather than being imposed from without" (Miller & Rollnick, 1991, p. 52).

BOX **6.5**   **Continued**

There are five general principles to motivational interviewing:

1. **Express empathy.** Empathy involves understanding the way the client perceives the world, being able to see things the way the client does. Communicating that understanding to the client is the heart of expressing empathy. Expressing empathy, however, should not be confused with agreeing with or approving of a client's behavior or worldview. Rather, expressing empathy means being nonjudgmental. It is uncritical acceptance of the client. Part of understanding clients is understanding and accepting the ambivalence they feel about the problem behavior.

   CLIENT: "I worry sometimes that I may be drinking too much for my own good."

   THERAPIST: "You've been drinking quite a bit."

   C: "I don't really *feel* like it's that much. I can drink a lot and not feel it."

   T: "More than most people."

   C: "Yes. I can drink most people under the table."

   T: "And that's what worries you."

   C: "Well, that and how I feel. The next morning I'm usually in bad shape. I feel jittery and I can't think straight through most of the morning."

   T: "And that doesn't seem right to you."

   C: "No, I guess not. I haven't thought about it that much, but I don't think it's good to be hung over all the time. And sometimes I have trouble remembering things."

   T: "Things that happen while you're drinking."

   C: "That, too. Sometimes I just have a blank for a few hours."

   T: "But that isn't what you meant when you said you have trouble remembering things."

   C: "No. Even when I'm not drinking, it seems like I'm forgetting things more often, and I'm not thinking clearly."

   T: "And you wonder if it has something to do with your drinking."

   C: "I don't know what else it would be."

   T: "You haven't always been like that."

   C: "No! It's only the last few years. Maybe I'm just getting older."

   T: "It might just be what happens to everybody when they reach 45."

   C: "No, it's probably my drinking. I don't sleep very well, either."

   T: "So maybe you're damaging your health and your sleep and your brain by drinking as much as you do" (Miller & Rollnick, 1991, pp. 75–76).

2. **Develop discrepancy.** Motivation to change is fostered when clients perceive a discrepancy between their personal goals and their behavior (Miller, 1985). In motivational interviewing it is generally assumed that people experience a stronger motivation to change when they are the ones who describe the negative consequences of their behavior rather than being

(continued)

B O X   **6.5**   **Continued**

confronted with the negative consequences by someone else. In the following example, the doctor (D) has been interviewing a patient (P) about her smoking, focusing upon what she likes about smoking and how cigarettes fit into her day. As the interview progresses, notice how the doctor elicits from the patient the problems associated with smoking. It is the patient who points out the negative consequences of smoking.

D: "It sounds like these cigarettes do different things for you. After some of them, like the first one of the day and those after meals, you notice the biggest effect, and this can be relaxing. Others, like those in between, have less of an effect, and you even said it was like just keeping the habit going."

P: "Yes, that's exactly right."

D: "Where does the coughing come in?"

P: "Well, that's my smoker's cough. I've had it for years."

D: "Do you know what it means about your lungs?"

P: "Yes, I know it's not good for me. It's like my lungs are telling me, 'Stop it!' "

D: "What about some of the other effects of smoking on your body?"

P: "Well, they say it's not good for your heart and it can cause cancer and that sort of thing. I feel guilty about my smoking; the kids are always going on at me."

D: "You've told me quite a bit about your smoking this morning. It's relaxing sometimes, but it also makes you feel guilty."

P: "Yes, I know it's bad for me. It costs so much each day, and the kids are always moaning about it."

D: "Can I ask you, what really concerns you about your smoking?"

P: "I suppose I can put up with the coughing. Even the money is not too serious. It's really that I just feel hooked on the damned things, like I don't know where it's going to end."

D: "You feel hooked on them."

P: "Yes, as I told you earlier, I enjoy some of them, but most of them do nothing for me."

D: "It's like you don't really know why you smoke some of them."

P: "That's right (Rollnick & Bell, 1991, pp. 211–212)."

3. **Avoid argumentation.** Most people become defensive when they are directly confronted with negative aspects of themselves or their behavior. People often dig in their heels when they are directed to change their behavior. In motivational interviewing a "gently persuasive style" rather than an overt confrontational style is used.

C: "I don't like not remembering things."

T: "That doesn't seem normal to you."

C: "No. But I don't think I'm an alcoholic. I've known some alcoholics, and I'm not like that."

T: "Your situation doesn't seem that bad to you."

C: "No, it doesn't. I've quit drinking for weeks at a time with no problem. And I can have a couple of drinks and leave it alone. I have a good job and family. How could I be an alcoholic?"

T: "That must be confusing to you, as you think about it. On the one hand you can see some warning signs that you are drinking too much, and you worry about that. On the other hand, you don't seem to fit how you picture an alcoholic."

C: "Right. I mean I've got some problems, but I'm not a drunk."

T: "And so thus far it hasn't seemed like you needed to do anything about it. But you're here. Why now?" (Miller & Rollnick, 1991, p. 143).

4. **Roll with resistance.** If not argue, then what does a therapist do with a client's resistance to change? In motivational interviewing, the therapist goes with the client's resistance, perhaps even exaggerating the argument against change. In the following brief example, a businessman who abuses cocaine resists the idea of cutting back on his cocaine use. The therapist does not challenge the resistance head on; instead, he or she elicits more information from the client.

C: "I couldn't decrease my cocaine use. If I did, the company would go bust. I need it to keep me going; I really need to work 80 hours a week."

T: "You seem to be a very generous person, in a way. You are willing to risk damage to your health to save the company. Could you tell me a bit more about these pressures that are resting on your shoulders?"

5. **Support self-efficacy.** Self-efficacy is a person's belief that he or she can carry out or succeed at a specific task (Bandura, 1977). People tend not engage in a task if they feel they can't cope with the demands it places upon them. Helping people to change then involves not only showing them that there is a need to change but also supporting their belief that they can do what it takes to create change.

C: "What's the use? I've tried to quit, and I think I'm hopeless. I'm tired. I'm worn out. I don't want to try any more."

T: "It may seem a trite saying, that 'It's always darkest before the dawn,' but it's also true. When people are at their lowest point, at the bottom of the valley, it's hardest to see the light. I think that all of the efforts you've put into trying shows how very much you *want* to recover. I admire you for that. So don't give it up now. You remember that wheel of change we talked about? Every time you go around it, you're one turn closer to getting off. You've discovered a lot of things that *don't* work for you. Now let's use that strong desire of yours, and move on to find what *will* work for you" (Miller & Rollnick, 1991, p. 109).

7

Intellectual and Educational Assessment

Some might argue that the birth of clinical psychology was marked by the development of the Binet-Simon scale of intelligence. Others might say that it was the establishment of the first psychology clinic by Lightner Witmer. Whichever side you take, there is agreement that the development of tests of intelligence was instrumental in the creation of the field. As we saw in Chapter 2, the success of tests of intelligence spawned the development of other types of psychological tests and marked the first steps toward professionalization of the field.

In this chapter, we provide an overview of the general area of intellectual assessment. Starting with definitions and theories of intelligence we will introduce the reader to the more commonly used tests of intelligence. In the third section of this chapter we grapple with some of the more contentious questions in the area of intelligence testing: What do these tests actually measure? Is intelligence inherited? Are there racial differences in intelligence? The chapter concludes with a discussion of other types of tests that are used, usually in conjunction with intelligence tests, in the educational arena. But we start with intelligence.

Intelligence

Definition

Defining exactly what intelligence is has proven to be a surprisingly difficult task. In 1921, a symposium involving thirteen psychologists expert in the area of intellectual assessment considered the definition. The symposium proceedings, reported in a special issue of the *Journal of Educational Psychology,* revealed that the experts had thirteen different views on the nature of intelligence. Observing this diversity of definitions led one commentator at the time to suggest, somewhat cynically, that intelligence is what intelligence tests measure (Boring, 1923). And the situation has not changed much in the intervening years. In 1986, Sternberg and Detterman found that twenty-four prominent scholars had twenty-four different definitions of intelligence. Such disagreement should not be a source of dismay, however. Science advances through disagreement. New knowledge is often engendered by rigorous debate. In addition, a closer look at the various definitions of intelligence reveals that, while distinct, they had many features in common. In the 1921 survey, the elements that appeared most often in the various definitions were "(a) higher level abilities (such as abstract reasoning, mental representation, problem solving, and decision making), (b) ability to learn, and (c) adaptation to meet the demands of the environment. In the 1986 survey, the most common elements were (a) higher level abilities, (b) that which is valued by culture, and (c) executive process" (Sternberg, 1997, p. 1030). In fact, a survey of over 1,000 experts from a variety of fields—including psychology, sociology, education, and genetics—indicated a significant degree of consensus on the important elements of intelligence (Snyderman & Rothman, 1987). Of the thirteen descriptions rated by the respondents, there was nearly unanimous agreement that *abstract reasoning, the capacity to acquire knowledge, and problem solving ability* were important elements of intelligence. Table 7.1 lists the behavioral descriptions rated in the survey and the percent of agreement among the experts.

Take a look at the example definitions of intelligence listed below. What common elements can you discern? (Note: The middle four definitions appear in Sattler (1988, p. 45).

. . . intelligence, that is to say, reasoning, judgment, memory, the power of abstraction. (Binet, 1890, quoted in Matarazzo, 1972, p. 65)

. . . *adjustment or adaptation of the individual to his total environment,* or limited aspects thereof . . . the capacity to reorganize one's behavior patterns so as to act more effectively and more appropriately in novel situations . . . the *ability to learn* . . . the extent to which (a person) is educable . . . the *ability to carry on abstract thinking* . . . the effective use of concepts and symbols in dealing with . . . a problem to be solved. (Freeman, 1955, pp. 60–61)

Intelligence, as a hypothetical construct, is the aggregate or global capacity of the individual to act purposefully, to think rationally and to deal effectively with his environment. (Wechsler, 1958, p. 27)

. . . the resultant of the processes of acquiring, storing in memory, retrieving, combining, comparing, and using in new contexts information and conceptual skills; it is an abstraction. (Humphreys, 1979, p. 115)

TABLE 7.1   Important Elements of Intelligence

Descriptor	% of Respondents Checking as Important
Abstract thinking or reasoning	99.3
Problem-solving ability	97.7
Capacity to acquire knowledge	96
Memory	80.5
Adaptation to one's environment	77.2
Mental speed	71.7
Linguistic competence	71
Mathematical competence	67.9
General knowledge	88.3
Creativity	59.6
Sensory acuity	24.4
Goal directedness	24
Achievement motivation	18.9

Source: Adapted from Snyderman & Rothman (1987).

> . . . a human intellectual competence must entail a set of skills of problem solving—enabling the individual *to resolve genuine problems or difficulties* that he or she encounters, and, when appropriate, to create an effective product—and must also entail the potential for *finding or creating problems*—thereby laying the groundwork for the acquisition of new knowledge. (Gardner, 1983, pp. 60–61)
>
> Intelligence comprises the mental abilities necessary for adaption to, as well as shaping and selection of, any environmental context. (Sternberg, 1997, p. 1030)

One element of several of these definitions is adaptation, the ability to modify one's behavior to meet the demands of the situation. The ability to think abstractly, using symbols or mental representations, is a second. The ability to acquire new information or to learn through experience is a third. While we would like to offer the reader a definition of intelligence that integrates the central elements of the most important definitions offered to date, we are not so foolish as to think that we could provide a definition that would satisfy everyone. The quest for a satisfactory definition of intelligence has been called "an unending search" (Matarazzo, 1972).

Theories of Intelligence

Perhaps not surprising, given the lack of consensus on the definition of intelligence, a myriad of different theoretical models of intelligence have been offered. A sampling of theoretical models is presented below. For a more thorough treatment of theories of intelligence, the interested reader might see Sattler (1988), Anastasi and Urbina (1997), and Matarazzo (1972).

Spearman's Two-Factor Theory.   One of the earliest theoretical models of intelligence was proposed by Charles Spearman (1927). Spearman was a British psychologist who made significant contributions to the development of statistical methods used in psychological research. It is not surprising, therefore, that Spearman's theory was built upon observations about the correlations among various tests of intelligence. Spearman posited that performance on intellectual tasks is determined by a general factor (g) and one or more specific factors (s). The g factor was thought of as a kind of mental energy. All intellectual tasks require some amount of g. The more highly two functions were correlated, the more highly saturated they were with g, according to Spearman. Tests that are thought to have high g loadings involve abstract reasoning, comprehension, and problem solving. The s factors are more heavily involved in tasks that are less complex. Tests that involve recognition memory, visual-motor coordination, motor speed, and attention are poor measures of g since they have lower intercorrelations and are presumed to be more strongly influenced by s factors.

Spearman's theory is frequently referred to as a two-factor theory but this may be a misnomer (Anastasi & Urbina, 1997). Although two factors, g and $s,$ are specified, g is the only factor that accounts for the correlation among different intellectual functions. As such, Anastasi and Urbina suggest that it might be more accurately described as a single-factor theory.

Supporters of the g construct point to factor analytic studies of various intelligence measures that show considerable intercorrelation among measures. The appropriate interpretation of these factor analyses, however, has been controversial. Critics of the concept of $g,$

or general intelligence, argue that it does not make sense to base a theory of intelligence upon the observed relationships among test scores (e.g., Gardner, 1983; Gould, 1981). In a very real way, this view of intelligence is a more complex version of Boring's (1923) cynical definition of intelligence as whatever the tests measure.

Thurstone's Primary Mental Abilities.   A sharp contrast to Spearman's theory is the multiple factor view offered by Thurstone (1938). Thurstone's theory was based upon three assumptions regarding mental abilities: "(1) several fundamental abilities working together influence performance on a mental test, (2) the number of tasks in a mental battery will exceed the number of fundamental abilities tapped in the battery, and (3) performance on any specific task in a battery does not depend upon the operation of all of the fundamental abilities" (Kaufman & Harrison, 1991, p. 99). Based upon these assumptions and his observations about the correlations among different mental tests, Thurstone identified the following primary mental abilities: *verbal, perceptual speed, inductive reasoning, number, rote memory, deductive reasoning, word fluency, and space or visualization.* Thurstone developed the Primary Mental Abilities Tests to measure these factors.

Cattell and Horn's Fluid and Crystalized Intelligence.   Robert B. Cattell and John Horn developed an of innovative theory that posited two types of intelligence: *fluid* and *crystallized* (Horn & Cattell, 1966). Fluid intelligence is one's native abilities believed to be largely determined by genetics and biological factors. Fluid intelligence develops throughout childhood and into adolescence but plateaus in late adolescence or early adulthood. Crystallized intelligence is one's acquired skills and knowledge and, therefore, is strongly influenced by one's environment and culture. Crystalized intelligence can continue to develop throughout the life span. Cattell (1963) suggested the analogy of a coral reef to explain the differences and relationships between fluid and crystallized intelligence. Fluid intelligence is like the living coral organism, whereas crystalized intelligence is coral structure that forms about the organism.

Different mental tasks are believed to be more or less strongly influenced by the two forms of intelligence. Tasks that require new learning (e.g., paired associates), novel problem solving (e.g., classification of figures), or more concentration are thought to be purer measures of fluid intelligence. Crystallized intelligence is assessed by measures of vocabulary, general information, and abstract word analogies. These tests involve retrieval or application of acquired information. Crystallized intelligence is strongly influenced by formal and informal education. One criticism of many of the standard measures of intelligence is that they are overrepresented by tasks that assess crystallized intelligence, while fluid intelligence has a significantly smaller influence on the test performance (Kaufman & Harrison, 1991).

One of the interesting applications of Cattell and Horn's theory is understanding the impact of brain injury. In general, fluid intelligence is thought to be more sensitive to the effects of a brain injury; whereas crystallized intelligence is thought be more resistant to impairment. Some individuals with dementia, for example, may not be able to recall a list of paired words (e.g., dog-kettle, fish-sand, apple-carrot) learned 20 minutes earlier (impaired fluid intelligence) but easily remember nursery rhymes they learned in early childhood (crystallized intelligence). Cattell and Horn's theory has had a strong influence on the development of the latest version of the Stanford-Binet intelligence scale, which we will discuss below.

Developmental Models.   A very real intellectual lineage runs through the theories of intelligence discussed thus far. Cattell carried out research with both Spearman and Thurstone. Horn was Cattell's student. All of these theoreticians relied heavily upon factor analysis in their work. Jean Piaget's background and methods stand in stark contrast to these men. Piaget received his doctorate in biology in 1918. By 1920, however, he was working with Theodore Simon in Binet's laboratory in Paris. While administering psychological tests to children, Piaget became much more interested in the incorrect responses children gave rather than the correct ones. In chatting with the children about their performance, Piaget gained insight into their reasoning. In addition, he began to note that children of the same age often gave the same wrong answers. These observations, along with careful study of his own three children, provided the foundation upon which Piaget developed his theory of intellectual development.

Piaget's developmental model proposes that cognitive processes develop through an interaction between the developing brain and the child's life experiences. The child's cognitive structures must repeatedly reorganize as the child adapts to his or her changing biology and environment. Two natural tendencies govern the child's interactions with the environment: *organization* and *adaption*. Organization is the tendency to combine two or more distinct schemes into one more complex and integrated scheme. A *scheme* is a kind of framework for making sense of one's experiences. Adaptation includes two complementary processes: *assimilation* and *accommodation*. In assimilation, the child takes in new information and fits it into existing schemes. Accommodation is the process of modifying existing structures to take into account new information and experience.

Piaget proposed a hierarchical model of intellectual development that is divided into four periods: *sensorimotor, preoperational, concrete operations,* and *formal operations.* Each period includes several substages. The model is hierarchical in the sense that each period builds upon, or evolves from, the previous. Therefore, no stage can be skipped in intellectual development. Children make sense of the world using the cognitive structures available to them at the time. As they develop, however, the structures become increasingly inadequate as inconsistencies between the cognitive rules and the children's experiences become more frequent. Children need to develop new structures in order to handle these inconsistencies. The new structures by necessity involve a higher order of thinking.

To say that Piaget's writings have had a significant impact upon developmental psychology is like saying the Beatles influenced popular music. In the applied arena, Piaget's theories of intellectual development have had a significant influence upon educational practices. Surprisingly, however, Piaget's theory has had a relatively small impact upon psychometric assessment of children's intelligence. Although considerable effort has been put into development of a Piagetian battery of assessment instruments, the product of these efforts have fallen short in one way or another (Kaufman & Harrison, 1991). Although there are similarities between Piagetian and psychometric approaches, there are also marked differences. For example, by focusing upon how an individual performs relative to a normal sample, the psychometric approach emphasizes differences between that individual and the sample. In contrast, a Piagetian approach is more interested in changes within a single individual over the course of development (Elkind, 1974).

Multiple Intelligences.   Two more contemporary theories of intelligence, or more accurately intelligences, deserve attention before leaving the issues of theory. In his 1983 book, *Frames of Mind,* Harvard psychologist Howard Gardner proposed a dramatically different approach to understanding intelligence. Gardner rejects the idea of a singular intelligence. Instead, he posits the existence of multiple intelligences.

Gardner developed his theory of multiple intelligences by reviewing evidence from a wide variety of sources including "studies of childhood prodigies, gifted individuals, brain-damaged patients, *idiot savants,* normal children, normal adults, experts in different lines of work, and individuals from diverse cultures" (Gardner, 1983, p. 9). Gardner's criteria for an intelligence is that it must function to enable an individual to "*resolve genuine problems or difficulties*" (Gardner, p. 60) but also have the potential for "*finding and creating problems*" (Gardner, p. 61). To qualify as an intelligence, a faculty must be useful and valuable within the culture in which the individual lives. In his book, Gardner describes several intelligences: *linguisitic, musical, logical-mathematical, spatial, bodily-kinesthetic,* and *personal intelligences.*

Another contemporary theorist who has posed the existence of multiple intelligences is Robert Sternberg (1985). Sternberg's triarchic theory of human intelligence posits the existence of three forms of intelligence: *analytic, practical,* and *creative.* Analytic intelligence is an academically oriented intelligence. It is this type of intelligence that is measured by most conventional tests. This form of intelligence is useful for remembering information, evaluating it, and determining its value. Practical intelligence comes into play in solving practical problems. Practical intelligence refers to adaptive thinking outside of an academic setting. It is probably best to think of creative intelligence as a "candidate intelligence" (Sternberg, 1997). That is, it requires further study to determine whether the construct has acceptable validity.

Sternberg and his colleagues have developed the Triachic Abilities Test (Sternberg, 1993a) to measure analytic, creative, and practical intelligence. Thus far, the instrument has been used only in research settings. In one study, for example, Sternberg and company tested 199 high school students with the instrument. Based upon their scores, students were categorized as high-analytic, high-creative, high-practical, high in all three abilities, or low in all three abilities. The students were then placed into one of four sections of an experimental introduction to psychology course. The different sections were designed to emphasize either memory-based learning, analytical thinking, creative thinking, or practical thinking. The researchers found that students who received instruction that matched their strongest intelligence performed substantially better than those who were taught in a section that did not match their highest intelligence (Sternberg, 1997).

Sternberg's and Gardner's theories mark a radical shift in thinking about intelligence. Like Piaget's model of intellectual development, however, Gardner's and Sternberg's ideas have had a stronger impact in the field of education than in clinical psychology. To date, no widely used assessment instruments have assessed intelligence as it is understood by these theories.

B O X   **7.1**

Focus on Ethics: Who Is Qualified to Use IQ Tests?

Marge N. O'Vera, Psy.D., retested a child who had been given the Wechsler Intelligence Scale for Children—Third Edition (WISC-III) by another examiner a few months earlier. The youngster, who was mildly mentally retarded, earned IQ scores 3 to 5 points higher when O'Vera tested him, and O'Vera told the child's parents, "This is a sign that he could be making some real intellectual progress." (Koocher & Keith-Spiegel, 1998, p. 148)

The appropriate use of tests of intelligence involves much more than simply knowing how to administer and score a standardized test. Even if we assume that Dr. O'Vera gave the test in an appropriate manner and followed the scoring procedures faithfully, her comments to the parents were grossly inappropriate and raise serious questions about her competence to use IQ tests.

Identifying minimum standards for users of psychological tests is a difficult endeavor. The question "Who is qualified to use psychological tests?" is best answered, "It depends." Competence for use of psychological tests is dependent upon the test in question, the population to be tested, and the purpose for which the test results will be used. For intelligence testing, we have identified some of the more important areas of competence.

Administration and Scoring: While standardized administration and scoring of a test of intelligence does not guarantee competent test use, it is clearly a prerequisite. One of the great strengths of standardized tests is that a person's performance can be compared to hundreds or even thousands of other people who have been given the same task under similar, if not identical, conditions. The test scores are useless if the conditions under which they are obtained differ in some important way from the conditions under which the standardization sample was tested. The psychological examiner needs to build rapport with the client so that he or she is sufficiently motivated and comfortable when taking the test. The examiner needs to create a setting for test administration that is appropriate for the tasks involved. The score of the Block Design subtest of the WAIS-III (the subtest requires that the examinee reproduce a pattern by organizing a set of red and white blocks), for example, will not be interpretable if the examinee has to balance the blocks on a clipboard on his or her lap or if there is an interruption during this timed task. Being able to administer and score intelligence tests in a standardized fashion, and to evaluate factors that may have affected testing circumstances, are minimal competencies for using these tests.

Knowledge of Psychometrics: A thorough understanding of psychometric concepts and theory is also crucial for appropriate test use. The psychological examiner must be familiar with the terms *standard deviation, mean, percentile rank, standard error of measurement, reliability,* and others. The degree of change in the scores upon which Dr. O'Vera based her optimistic statements about the child's "intellectual progress" are well within the range expected given the imperfect reliability of the test. In other words, the higher scores are likely due to chance or trivial factors and should not be seen as evidence of improved intellectual functioning. Dr. O'Vera either does not understand psychometric theory, is ignorant of the psychometric properties of the WAIS-III, or has purposely chosen to give misinformation. The first two possibilities would mean she is not competent to have used the test. The latter suggests she is either cruel or misguided.

Theories of Intellectual Functioning: Scores produced by an intelligence test need to be interpreted within some theoretical framework. The clinician must have a conceptual context for making sense of the overall IQ and other scores produced by the test.

BOX **7.1** **Continued**

Knowledge of Special Populations: IQ tests are often used as part of a larger battery of assessment strategies for the purposes of diagnosis, treatment planning, or making prognostic statements about a client. Sophisticated use of test findings requires that the examiner have an understanding of the specific population from which the client was drawn. A set of test scores obtained by a elderly patient with dementia would mean one thing but the same pattern of scores produced by an adolescent would suggest something very different. The concurrent and predictive validity of test scores are different for different populations. An understanding of the clinical syndrome a client suffers with, or the common sequella following a certain type of brain injury, provide the necessary context within which test scores are interpreted. Once again, Dr. O'Vera's statements provide an example that suggest incompetence in this area. Her statement to the parents suggest striking ignorance about mental retardation.

Knowledge of the Specific Test: As we have seen, there are several tests of intelligence. These tests differ with respect to the theoretical model used in their development, the quality and representativeness of normative samples, and their psychometric properties. To use the tests appropriately, the examiner must understand the specific features of that test. The test manual is the starting point for learning about a test. However, for most tests research articles and critical reviews continue to appear for some time after test publication. The competent examiner keeps abreast of new developments about the test.

Measurement

Stanford-Binet Scales. The current edition of the Stanford-Binet Intelligence Scale is the intellectual heir to the original Binet-Simon Scale. Binet's test was a milestone in the development of clinical psychology. The success of the test had a significant impact on the development of the fledgling field of clinical psychology (see Chapter 2).

The Binet-Simon scale was translated and adapted for use by several scholars in Europe and the United States (Kaplan & Saccuzzo, 1993). The link, however, between the original scale and the current Stanford-Binet was forged by Lewis Terman and his associates at Stanford University. The Stanford-Binet Intelligence Scales, as the test came to be called, became extremely popular and for the first half of the twentieth century was the premier test of intelligence in the world. Terman published the first edition of the Stanford-Binet in 1916 (Terman, 1916). His research team added many items to the 1911 Binet-Simon and eliminated or revised many others. The new test was standardized on an American sample of approximately 1,000 children and 400 adults. This first edition of the Stanford-Binet set the standard for modern individually administered tests of intelligence. The 1916 Stanford-Binet was the first to include detailed instructions for administering and scoring and the first to use the IQ (Anastasi & Urbina, 1997).

The Stanford-Binet has gone through many revisions. The first major revision appeared in 1937 (Terman & Merrill, 1937).The authors developed two parallel forms of the test: L and M to allow for retesting of the same individual with minimal practice effects. The 1937 Stanford-Binet was completely restandardized on a sample of over 3,000 individuals chosen to represent a cross-section of the United States populations. By current criteria the effort to represent the U.S. population was woefully inadequate. The sample overrepresented individuals from higher socioeconomic levels and urban populations. In addition, the "representative sample" was made up entirely of white Americans born in this country (Anastasi & Urbina, 1997). The third edition of the Stanford-Binet was published in 1960 (Terman & Merrill, 1960). The 1960 edition, or Form L-M, combined the best items from the two 1937 forms. Interestingly, Terman and Merrill did not restandardize the 1960 version, so that IQ was calculated using 1937 norms. In 1972, Form L-M was restandardized using a more representative sample of over 2,100 people (Terman & Merrill, 1973). Prior to the publication of the fourth edition in 1986, Form L-M was used with reference to the 1972 norms.

The Stanford-Binet Intelligence Scale: Fourth Edition represented a major revision of the scale. The test was designed to assess intelligence in a manner more consistent with contemporary theoretical models of intelligence. The test is based upon a three-level hierarchical model of intelligence. At the top of the hierarchy is *g* or general intelligence. At the next level is *crystallized abilities, fluid abilities (abstract/visual reasoning;* Horn & Cattell, 1966), and *short-term memory.* The third level in the hierarchy falls under crystallized abilities, which are divided into *verbal* and *quantitative reasoning.* Figure 7.1 illustrates the three-level hierarchical model underlying the contemporary Stanford-Binet.

Organization of the Stanford-Binet, 4th Edition.   The fifteen subtests of the Stanford-Binet are organized into four categories, which represent the four major content areas: *Verbal Reasoning, Abstract/Visual Reasoning, Quantitative Reasoning,* and *Short-Term Memory.* The subtests included in each content area are described in Table 7.2.

Raw scores on the subtests are converted into *standard age scores,* which have a mean of 50 and a standard deviation of eight. Content scores are calculated for each of the four content areas. These scores have a mean of 100 and a standard deviation of 16. The Composite Score (comparable to overall IQ) also has the mean set at 100 and the standard deviation at 16.

Evaluation.   The Stanford-Binet appears to be as good a measure of general intelligence as any other individually administered instrument (Laurent, Swerdlik, & Ryburn, 1992). It

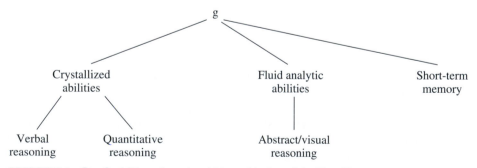

FIGURE 7.1   Stanford-Binet three-level hierarchical model of intelligence.

TABLE 7.2   Content Areas and Subtests of the Stanford-Binet

Verbal Reasoning	Abstract/Visual Reasoning	Quantitative Reasoning	Short-Term Memory
Vocabulary	Pattern analysis	Quantitative	Bead memory
Comprehension	Coping	Number series	Memory for sentences
Absurdities	Matrices	Equation-building	Memory for digits
Verbal relations	Paper-folding and -cutting		Memory for objects

was normed on an adequate standardization sample. Administration and scoring instructions are clear and there is considerable information available to assist interpretation (see, for example, Sattler, 1988). The test appears to discriminate well between normal, gifted, and neurologically impaired populations. The Stanford-Binet may be the instrument of choice for assessing the intelligence of gifted children because the wide age range of the test eliminates ceiling effects (Laurent et al., 1992).

There are some weaknesses to the Stanford-Binet. First and foremost, disagreement about the factor structure of the instrument raises questions about appropriate interpretation. It appears that the factor structures changes from a two-factor to a four-factor organization as the sample gets older. A second weakness applies to work with the younger end of the age range. It can be difficult to establish a basal level with younger intellectually impaired children (Laurent, Swerdlik, & Ryburn, 1992). Finally, administration of the Stanford-Binet is somewhat more difficult than other tests since the examiner must score each item as the test is administered.

A fifth edition of the Stanford-Binet Intelligence Scale was introduced in 2003. The new scale was carefully normed and all items were reviewed for gender, ethnic, cultural, regional, and socioeconomic biases. The fifth edition is organized in a slightly different manner from the fourth. It produces a Full Scale IQ, Verbal and Nonverbal IQ, and five Composite Indices. Another change for the fifth edition is that the standard deviation for the various scores have been set at 15 (as opposed to 16, which had been the tradition with earlier versions of the Stanford-Binet). The fifth edition is too new to have been evaluated by researchers and clinicians in the field but shows great promise.

Wechsler Scales.   The most popular individualized tests of intelligence are those derived from a battery of tests developed by David Wechsler and first published in 1939 (Harrison, Kaufman, Hickman, & Kaufman, 1988). There are three basic Wechsler scales: one designed and standardized for adults, one for children and adolescents, and one for preschool-age children. The three scales share many features. In addition to measuring general intelligence, the Wechsler scales are thought by many to be useful in diagnosing organic brain damage, learning disabilities, psychoses, and emotional difficulties impacting intellectual functioning.

The Wechsler-Bellevue (Wechsler, 1939) provided the foundation for the later instruments bearing Wechsler's name. The story behind the Wechsler-Bellevue is worth summarizing since it can help one understand the strengths and weaknesses of the current Wechsler Scales.

BOX **7.2**

Measuring IQ

Although the Binet-Simon scale can be considered the forefather of most modern measures of IQ, the term *intelligence quotient* (IQ) was not coined until after Binet's death. Binet, however, did set the stage for the development of the concept of IQ. Binet was interested in the ratio of a child's *mental age* (MA) to the child's *chronological age* (CA). Mental age was defined by the number of items the child correctly completed on the Binet-Simon scale. If a child completed all the items expected of a 7-year-old, for example, he or she was assigned a mental age of 7. Each item beyond those expected of 7-year-olds that the child correctly completed was worth so many months of credit. Children whose mental age exceeded their chronological age were considered to have advanced levels of intelligence. Children who scored below their chronological age were thought to have delayed intellectual development. For Binet then, an index of intelligence could be represented by the formula:

$$\frac{MA}{CA}$$

In 1912 German psychologist William Stern noted a problem with Binet's ratio that had to do with the fact that intelligence does not increase in the same increments from year to year. He suggested an alternative approach for indexing the relationship between mental and chronological age. It was Stern who coined the term *Intelligence Quotient* and offered the following formula to calculate IQ:

$$IQ = \frac{MA \times 100}{CA}$$

Stern's formula helps to account for the decreasing rate of intellectual development as children grow older. An example will help illustrate. Using Binet's simple formula, a 4-year-old child who obtains a mental age of 3 would seem to be as delayed as a 10-year-old who obtains a mental age of 9. Both children would appear to be one year behind. But the amount of intellectual growth children experience between ages 3 and 4 is much larger than the typical change from age 9 to age 10. The 4-year-old is likely more delayed intellectually than the 10-year-old in this example. Applying Stern's formula, the children would obtain IQ scores that more accurately represent the degree of intellectual delay. The 4-year-old would have an IQ of 75 (3/4 × 100) and the 10-year-old would have an IQ of 90 (9/10 × 100). Stern's formula was adopted by Lewis Terman when he developed the Stanford-Binet scale.

While the mental age to chronological age ratio approach made sense for assessing intelligence in children, the logic did not apply for adults. Adult intellectual development appears to level off some time in late adolescence or early adulthood. It was David Wechsler (1939) who introduced the concept of the *deviation IQ* as an alternative to the mental age approach. Wechsler's approach to defining IQ assumed that intelligence is normally distributed in the population. IQ was measured by how far the person's score deviated from the mean score for similarly aged people. In developing an IQ scale, Wechsler needed to administer his measure to a fairly large group of similarly aged people, then calculate the mean and standard deviation of the distribution of scores. For the sake of convenience, the mean is transformed to equal 100 and the standard deviation

BOX **7.2**   **Continued**

converted to 15. One of the advantages of the deviation IQ is that it allows for the easy conversion of IQ score into percentile rank. For example, someone with a deviation IQ of 100 is known to score higher than 50 percent of the normative sample. With an IQ of 115 (i.e., one standard deviation above the mean), we know that the person scored above about 84 percent of the normative sample.

The deviation IQ has several advantages over the mental age to chronological age quotient (Matarazzo, 1972). The interpretation of IQ is much clearer. IQ represents, in clearly defined units, how a person scored relative to the normative sample. Second, it is not handicapped by any assumptions about the relationship between mental and chronological age. Stern's approach to IQ assumes a precise relationship between the rate of growth of mental and chronological age that is simply not there. Finally, the deviation IQ provides an index of adult intelligence that remains stable as the individual ages.

The advantages of the deviation IQ have been recognized by most test developers. In the 1960 version of the Stanford-Binet, a deviation approach was adopted. The deviation method is now the standard approach to defining IQ.

Wechsler did not develop new tasks to measure adult intelligence. Rather, he selected tasks from the measures available at the time. His rationale for choosing the tasks that would become the Wechsler-Bellevue was sometimes clinical, sometimes empirical, and sometimes theoretical (Kaufman, 1990). For example, he included an arithmetic subtest because performance on math tasks tended to correlate well with other measures of intelligence, the items were easily created and standardized, and because the task seemed "worthy of a grownup" (Wechsler, 1958, cited in Kaufman, p. 67). Wechsler finally settled upon eleven subtests for the Wechsler-Bellevue. Six of the subtests were combined to yield a Verbal IQ score, the other five were used for calculation of a Performance IQ. Scores on all eleven subtests were combined to yield a Full Scale IQ. Wechsler standardized his test on a sample of adults who matched the United States population at the time on several important variables such as age, sex, education, and occupation level.

The 1939 Wechsler-Bellevue scale was modified, restandardized, and renamed the Wechsler Adult Intelligence Scale (WAIS) in 1955. In 1981, the Wechsler Adult Intelligence Scale—Revised (WAIS-R) was published. This edition was a slightly modified version of the WAIS ("a cosmetized WAIS," Kaufman, 1990, p. 64) with completely new standardization samples. The most recent version of the WAIS, the Wechsler Adult Intelligence Scale—Third Edition (WAIS-III) was published in 1997.

Given Wechsler's original goal of developing a measure of adult intelligence that was more than a simple upward extension of the available children's tests, it seems ironic that the WAIS spawned measures of children's intelligence that were downward extensions of the adult test (Anastasi & Urbina, 1997). The Wechsler Intelligence Scale for Children (WISC), designed for use with 6- to 16-year-olds, was first published in 1949. Adding to the irony, the test was criticized for being insufficiently child-oriented. The WISC was reincarnated as the WISC-R (Wechsler Intelligence Scale for Children—Revised) in 1974. In addition to a completely new standardization sample, many of the test items were rewritten to be more child-friendly. For example, an Arithmetic subtest word problem that asked the child about "cigars" was changed to "candy bars." The third edition of the child scale (the WISC-III) was published in 1991 (Wechsler, 1991). The Wechsler scales were extended to even younger ages with the development of the Wechsler Preschool and Primary Scale of Intelligence (WPPSI) first published in 1967 and revised in 1989 (WPPSI-R). This test is normed for use with children from 3 years to 7 years and 3 months.

Organization of the Wechsler Scales. All three of the Wechsler scales are organized in the same way. Each test has from five to seven Verbal subtests and five to seven Performance subtests. Separate Verbal and Performance deviation IQs are calculated as well as a Full Scale or overall IQ. The IQ scores have a mean of 100 and a standard deviation of 15. Scaled scores for each of the subtests have a mean of ten and a standard deviation of three. Presentation of all subtest scores in the same units allows for comparison of relative strengths and weaknesses across subtests. While the WAIS-III and the WPPSI-R each has one or more unique subtest, most of the subtests are the same across all three measures. Table 7.3 lists the Wechsler subtests, which scales they appear in, and the intellectual functions they purport to assess.

TABLE 7.3 Wechsler Subtests

Subtest	V[1]	P[2]	WAIS-III	WISC-III	WPPSI-R	Functions Assessed
Vocabulary	X		X	X	X	vocabulary knowledge
Similarities	X		X	X	X	abstract reasoning
Arithmetic	X		X	X	X	concentration/basic math skills
Digit Span	X		X			immediate memory/ concentration
Information	X		X	X	X	range of knowledge
Comprehension	X		X	X	X	judgment/social reasoning
Picture Completion		X	X	X	X	alertness to detail
Digit Symbol-Coding		X	X	X		visual-motor functioning
Block Design		X	X	X	X	nonverbal reasoning
Matrix Reasoning		X	X			nonverbal fluid reasoning
Picture Arrangement		X	X	X		planning ability/social reasoning
Letter-Number Sequencing	X		X			working memory
Symbol Search		X	X	X		processing speed
Object Assembly		X	X	X	X	analysis of part-whole relations
Mazes		X		X	X	nonverbal problem solving
Animal Pegs		X			X	visual motor speed
Geometric Design		X			X	perceptual recognition and motor
Sentences		X			X	short-term auditory memory

[1]Verbal, [2]Performance

The organization of the Wechsler tests into Full Scale, Verbal, and Performance IQs reflects Wechsler's thinking about intelligence. Over fifty years of research on the Wechsler scales, however, has rather consistently found that more than two factors are assessed by these tests. The latest version of these scales have taken this research into consideration and show clinicians how to organize test findings with respect to the underlying factors. For example, the data collected in the development of the WISC-III was subjected to several exploratory and confirmatory factor analyses. A four-factor model seems to best accommodate the data. The four factors are *Verbal Comprehension, Perceptual Organization, Freedom from Distractibility,* and *Processing Speed.* A similar factor structure is evident in the WAIS-III with a factor labeled *Working Memory* replacing Freedom from Distractibility. The WISC-III and WAIS-III allow for calculation of Index Scores for each factor. Like IQ scores, the Index scores have a mean of 100 and a standard deviation of 15.

Evaluation.   The Wechsler scales have many positive features to recommend them. They have been extensively normed taking care to standardize the tests on samples that are representative of the U.S. population. While administration of the Wechsler scales requires specialized training, the tests are organized so as to ease administrations. Test materials provide scoring guidelines that are easy to use and extensive statistical information is easily accessed in the test manuals. Test reliability is high with IQ and Index Scores having very good reliability and subtests acceptable reliability. Given the popularity of the Wechsler scales, there is a substantial research base that is constantly expanding. The popularity of the tests has also resulted in a plethora of supportive materials such as computer-assisted interpretation programs, interpretive guides, and training manuals.

Despite their many strengths, the Wechsler scales have their limitations. Critics point out the weak theoretical foundation of the Wechsler scales. Interpretation of scores is based upon empirical findings, not a comprehensive theory of intellectual functioning. In addition, some critics, notably Sternberg (1993b), have pointed out the limited treatment utility of Wechsler tests. The connection between test findings and educational strategies, for example, is not always clear (Shaw, Swerdlik, & Laurent, 1993).

Kaufman Scales.   The newest individually administered comprehensive tests of intelligence on the scene are those developed by Alan and Nadeen Kaufman. Alan Kaufman worked for the Psychological Corporation for several years in the late 1960s and early 1970s. During this time, he worked very closely with David Wechsler on revising the WISC. Kaufman supervised the standardization of the WISC-R before assuming an academic position. Subsequent to his work on the WISC-R, Alan Kaufman, along with his wife, set out to develop their own individually administered instrument designed for the same purposes as the Wechsler scales and the Stanford-Binet. Unlike these older instruments, which were not developed out of a theoretical model of intellectual functioning, the Kaufman scales have a strong foundation in theory. In addition, the Kaufmans took advantage of newer developments in test construction (Kaufman & Kaufman, 1983a, 1983b, 1993).

The Kaufman Assessment Battery for Children (K-ABC; Kaufman & Kaufman, 1983a, 1983b) is an individually administered test of intellectual functioning designed for use with children between the ages of 2½ and 12½. The test is appropriate for use with all children, including those with many forms of physical handicap and learning disabilities, as well as children from cultural minorities and those for whom English is a second language.

The theoretical basis for the K-ABC is drawn partially from the work of Luria (1966) and others (e.g., Das, Kirby, & Jarman, 1975). These theoreticians identified two types of information processing: sequential and simultaneous. Sequential processing involves arranging information in temporal or spatial order. Tasks such as memorizing lists of spelling words or following a set of rules or directions require sequential processing. Simultaneous processing involves synthesizing many pieces of information at the same time. Understanding the overall meaning of a story or comprehending broad scientific principles require simultaneous processing (Kaufman, Kaufman, & Goldsmith, 1984). The K-ABC is designed to assess these styles of information processing. Understanding how a child processes information should help the diagnostician to identify the basis of learning problems and suggest methods for remediation.

Organization of the K-ABC.   There are four scales in the K-ABC: Sequential Processing Scale, Simultaneous Processing Scale, Mental Processing Composite (a combination of the Sequential and Simultaneous scales), and Achievement Scale. The Sequential Processing Scale has three subscales; the Simultaneous has seven; and the Achievement has six. The number of subtests administered depends upon the child's age, ranging from seven at age 2 years, 6 months to thirteen at ages 7 and older. A global score is obtained for each of the four scales. The mean of each is 100 and the standard deviation is 15.

Kaufman Adolescent and Adult Intelligence Test.   The Kaufmans have more recently designed a measure of adolescent and adult intellectual functioning—the Kaufman Adolescent and Adult Intelligence Test (KAIT; Kaufman & Kaufman, 1993). Once again, the Kaufmans set out to develop a theoretically sound test. Like the Stanford-Binet: Fourth Edition, the KAIT was influenced by Cattell and Horn's theory of crystallized and fluid intelligence (Horn & Cattell, 1966). In addition, Luria's (1980) and Piaget's (1980) ideas about adult intellectual function influenced the test development.

The KAIT is designed for use with individuals between the ages of 11 and 85. The test is composed of two scales: Crystallized Scale and Fluid Scale. The former assesses concepts likely to have been acquired through school and other experiences. The latter assess the person's ability to solve new problems. The Core battery is made up of three subscales of each scale. An Expanded battery is recommended for assessment of individual with known or expected neuropsychological dysfunction. The manual provides information supportive of reliability and validity.

Evaluation of Kaufman Scales.   The Kaufman scales have many features to recommend them. They were both carefully standardized. For example, the K-ABC was standardized on 2,000 children who were chosen to represent the 1980 U.S. census findings. Both measures are relatively easy to administer and score. They both include special instructions for bilingual and hearing-, speech-, or language-impaired examinees. The strong theoretical bases of these tests represents an important shift from the first generation of individually administered intelligence tests. Finally, both scales, but particularly the K-ABC, were designed so that educators could easily use the results to design interventions. These scales are relatively young and therefore have not undergone the degree of scrutiny applied to the Stanford-Binet and Wechsler scales. Time will tell whether they live up to their considerable promise.

Interpretation of Individually Administered Tests of Intelligence

When used by a skilled examiner, the Stanford-Binet, Wechsler, and Kaufman scales yield a great deal of information about an individual. An overall estimate of the client's general level of intellectual functioning is only one piece of information drawn from the tests. Assessment of complex problems such as mental retardation, learning disabilities, giftedness, brain impairment due to head injury or stroke, and behavioral disorders require sophisticated analysis of test scores and synthesis of other information. Many schemes have been proposed for analysis of the major intellectual assessment instruments (see for example Sattler, 1988; Kaufman, 1990). One approach is to examine test scores in a sequential pattern from the most general to the most specific. At each level of analysis, the psychologist develops hypotheses about the possible meaning of individual test scores and the variability among scores. These hypotheses are tested against other data drawn from the test and other sources.

The most reliable and valid single score derived from tests of intelligence is the overall IQ (Composite Score on the Stanford-Binet; Full Scale IQ on the Wechsler Scales; Mental Processing Composite on the Kaufman Scales). This score provides the best estimate of the individual's general level of intellectual functioning compared to other similarly aged people in the United States. The score is a global index of the person's cognitive abilities. While the overall IQ is the most reliable score the tests yield, it is not perfectly reliable. Therefore, psychologists routinely calculate a *confidence interval* around the obtained IQ score. The confidence interval provides a range of scores within which the psychologist can be fairly sure the client's true IQ score actually falls. Table 7.4 lists some generally accepted qualitative phrases used to describe clients' general level of intellectual functioning based upon their overall IQ scores.

TABLE 7.4   Qualitative Descriptions of WAIS-III Full-Scale IQ Scores

IQ Score	Classification
130 and above	Very Superior
120–129	Superior
110–119	High Average
90–109	Average
80–89	Low Average
70–79	Borderline
69 and below	Extremely Low

Source: Adapted from Wechsler (1997).

In the second level of analysis, the factor scores, as well as the differences among factor scores, are examined. For the Wechsler scales the psychologist traditionally looks at the Verbal and Performance IQs and the discrepancy between the two scores. There have been hundreds of studies of the so-called V-P discrepancy and volumes have been written about its interpretation. In general, the Verbal scales assess verbal comprehension skills while the Performance scales assess perceptual organization skills. A significant verbal-performance difference can be caused by a variety of factors. For example, a Verbal score significantly lower than the Performance might be due to language difficulties, cultural factors, or educational deprivation. A significant Verbal-Performance difference favoring the Verbal score is sometimes seen in brain-damaged individuals. Interpretation of Verbal-Performance differences needs to be made with caution. The skilled psychologist considers not only the magnitude of the difference but also the base rate of such differences in the specific type of person being assessed (e.g., how often is V-P difference of this magnitude observed in a normal population; Matarazzo, 1972; Grossman, Herman, & Matarazzo, 1985). In addition to Verbal-Performance differences, the examiner is interested in the differences among the various factors identified through factor analyses of the tests. For example, consistently lower scores on subtests that make up the Freedom from Distractibility factor on the WAIS-III can suggests attentional difficulties.

At the third level of analysis, the variability among specific subtests is examined. On what subtests did this person obtain the highest scores? Which ones yielded the lowest? What do these tests have in common? What hypotheses are suggested by the pattern of subtest scores? For example, certain configurations among WAIS-R subtests have been identified and strategies for interpreting these have been suggested (see for example, Kaufman, 1990). Once again, the clinician should proceed cautiously when interpreting subtest scatter. Subtests scores tend to be less reliable than general IQ and factor scores. Therefore, a certain degree of variability is expected by chance. There are general rules (e.g., "When comparing a person's performance on two groupings of subtests, compute his or her mean age-corrected scaled score for each grouping. Differences of 1 standard deviation [3 points] may be considered significant" Kaufman, p. 481), as well as fairly complicated statistical approaches, for interpreting subtests scatter.

The final phase of test interpretation is qualitative. Here the examiner considers the client's behavior outside of responses to test items. Does the child fidget a great deal? Does he or she make eye contact with examiner? Are there any unusual movements or expressions? Slow, hesitant responses may suggest depression, for example. In addition to these qualitative extra-test behaviors, the psychologist looks at specific test items for clues about the clients' performance. For example, test items within each subtest are arranged according to difficulty, with easier items first and more difficult items later. A child who answers the first four test items correctly and then misses the rest is different than a child who gets an item right, misses three or four, gets another one right, then misses a few, and so on. Each child may receive the same score on the subtest but for very different reasons. The psychologist might suspect that anxiety or difficulties with attention contributed to the second child's poor performance.

It is the integration of the information obtained from each level of analysis with life history and findings from other tests that is the "art" of psychological assessment (Matarazzo, 1972). Individually administered tests of intelligence are tools that, when used by well-trained and skilled clinicians, can help develop a thorough understanding of clients' psychological functioning.

Screening Measures

Psychologists interested in knowing something about a client's intellectual ability often do not want to put the time into administering and scoring a full-length individually adminis-tered intelligence test. Sometimes their reasoning is good (e.g., they only have access to a client for a limited period of time). At other times it is not (e.g., they are only interested in a global IQ score and erroneously believe that is all one gets from the full test anyway). What-ever the reason, abbreviated forms of the individually administered intelligence tests have been developed and are quite popular.

Short-forms of the Stanford-Binet and the Wechsler scales have been around almost as long as the scales themselves. Terman and Merrill (1937), for example, identified four tasks at each level that could be given as a shortened form of the Stanford-Binet. Several short-forms of the WAIS have been proposed over the years (see Kaufman, 1990, Chapter 5 for discussion). For example, one popular method of obtaining an IQ estimate with the WAIS-R was to administer only the Vocabulary and Block Design subtests or these two plus one other from the Verbal and Performance scales (Silverstein, 1985).

What is lost in exchange for the time savings is the ability to do finer-grain analyses of the specific subtest and factor scores. The reliability of these tend to be more severely com-promised, limiting the inferences one can draw based upon them. The use of short-form intel-ligence tests can be justified for screening purposes. However, these scores should not be used for classification or for drawing inferences about neuropsychological functioning or intellectual strengths and weaknesses.

Instead of abbreviating longer tests, psychologists interested in saving time often turn to brief measures of intelligence. These tests usually take 20 minutes or so to complete. Two screening tests that have been popular for some time are the Slosson Intelligence Test (Jensen & Armstrong, 1985; Slosson, 1982) and the Shipley Institute of Living Scale (Shipley, 1940). Despite their popularity, both tests have significant problems and psychometric limitations. For example, the standardization sample of the original Slosson is unrepresentative of the population at large (Oakland, 1985; Reynolds, 1985). A revised edition of the test was pub-lished in 1991 and addressed some but not all of the original tests weakness. Weaknesses include an underrepresentation of minorities and children with disabilities in the standardiza-tion sample and norm tables for adults that combine data for all subjects 18 years and older. The Shipley scale has never been updated since it was originally published in 1940. It also has a poor standardization sample and shows marginal test-retest reliability. Despite its limita-tions, the Shipley was one of the five most commonly used tests in the 1980s (see Kaufman, 1990).

The Wechsler Abbreviated Scale of Intelligence was published in 1999. The WASI is made up of Vocabulary, Block Design, Similarities, and Matrix Reasoning subtests. The test yields Verbal, Performance, and Full Scale IQ scores familiar to Wechsler scale users. The WASI is more than an abbreviated version of the WAIS. While it includes subtests from the WAIS, it has some unique items and was standardized independently. In developing the

WASI, the test publishers avoided most of the problems associated with short forms. While shorter than the full WAIS-III , the WASI takes somewhat longer to administer than other commonly used brief intelligence tests.

Another relative newcomer is the General Ability Measure for Adults (GAMA; Naglieri & Bardos, 1997). This test is self-administered and there is a 25-minute time limit. The GAMA norms were based upon a sample of 2,360 adults who ranged in age from 18 to 95. The sample matched the 1990 U.S. census data with respect to gender, race/ethnicity, education level, and region of the country. The sample was broken down into eleven normative age groups so that IQ scores are based upon age-matched peers. The GAMA yields an overall IQ score and four subtest scores: *Matching, Analogies, Sequences,* and *Construction.* The test instructions require a third- to fourth-grade reading level; however, the test items are completely nonverbal. Support for the validity of the GAMA comes from studies conducted by the tests publisher (National Computing Service) showing a correlation with the WAIS-R Full Scale IQ of .75 and with the Kaufman battery of .70. At this point, the GAMA shows considerable promise. It remains to be seen whether it will stand the scrutiny of independent researchers.

Issues and Controversies

Debates about what IQ tests actually measure have been around since the first Binet-Simon scale. Misconceptions about IQ underlie many of the controversies surrounding the use of IQ tests. For the general public, the terms *IQ* and *intelligence* are synonymous. In professional use, however, the term *IQ* should never be used apart from the test from which it was derived (Anastasi & Urbina, 1997). As we have seen, tests of intelligence differ in content, normative structure, and theoretical underpinnings

Two points about the use IQ are worth making before we begin to discuss some of the more contentious issues in this area of science and practice. First, the term is appropriately used as a *descriptive* and not *explanatory* concept (Anastasi & Urbina, 1997). An IQ score provides a summary description of an individual's behavior at a specific point in time. Scores on IQ tests describe a person's performance. They do not explain what caused a person to perform that way. It would be tautological to say that a person's mental retardation is due to a low IQ. Poor performance on IQ test is part of the definition of mental retardation (American Psychiatric Association, 1994).

The second point that deserves emphasis when considering the meaning of IQ scores, and the appropriate use of IQ tests, is that the scores, or tests, should be used to develop a better understanding of individuals, not to label them (Anastasi & Urbina, 1997; National Commission, 1990). Careful consideration of individuals' performance on tests of intelligence, along with other information, should be the starting point for developing means for helping them achieve their maximum potential. Anastasi and Urbina (1997, pp. 295–296) make the point with the following example: "If a reading test indicates that a child is retarded in reading, we do not label the child as a nonreader and stop; nor do we administer a nonverbal test to conceal the handicap. Instead, we concentrate on teaching the child to read."

Correlates of IQ

The concurrent and predictive validity of intelligence tests have been examined in a variety of ways. One of the most common methods of exploring validity has been to look at the relationship between IQ scores and academic performance. Most reviewers have drawn the conclusion that the correlation between performance on tests of intelligence and performance in school is about .50 (Brody, 1985; Kaufman, 1990; Matarazzo, 1972; Neisser et al., 1996). To put it another way, about 25 percent of the variance in school performance (usually measured as grades) can be accounted for by IQ scores. Conversely, 75 percent of the variance in school performance can be attributed to factors not measured by tests of intelligence. The relationship between IQ and academic performance has generally been found to be stronger in elementary years and weaker for college students (Brody, 1985).

In addition to grades, IQ is also correlated with how long people continue in school. The correlation between IQ and total years of education is about .55 (Neisser et al., 1996). The average IQ for a college graduate is about 115, for a high school graduate it is about 100, and for someone who finished only the eighth grade it is approximately 90 (Kaufman, 1990).

Given the relationship between IQ and academic achievement, it is not surprising to find that IQ is also positively correlated with occupational success. That is, individuals who work in jobs that are generally considered high status in our culture (e.g., physician, executive, engineer) tend to have higher IQs than people who work in lower-status jobs (e.g., construction, food service, factory worker). People who work in professional and technical jobs have an average IQ around 112, skilled laborers' average IQ is about 100, and unskilled workers have a mean IQ of about 87 (Kaufman, 1990). In addition to occupational success, IQ has also been found to correlate positively with job performance (Hunter, 1983).

The causal connection between intelligence (as measured by IQ tests), academic success, and occupational success is unknown. It might be tempting to argue that greater intelligence causes some people to do better in school and achieve more professionally. However, it is just as logical to argue that greater academic success leads to both better scores on IQ tests and a better job. In addition, the possibility of another variable (e.g., motivation) underlying the relationships among IQ test scores, school performance, and occupational success seems just as feasible.

Most intelligence tests measure verbal abilities, numerical abilities, and ability to use abstract symbols. These abilities are very useful for school learning. "Most intelligence tests can therefore be regarded as measures of scholastic aptitude and academic intelligence. The IQ is both a reflection of prior educational achievement and a predictor of subsequent educational performance" (Anastasi & Urbina, 1997, p. 296). Given the increasing importance of information taught in our educational system for success in our modern and increasingly technical society, it is not surprising that IQ tests are also predictive of occupational success.

Heritability of IQ

Few questions have intrigued scientists and lay persons alike as much as the question of how much of who we are is determined by our genetic makeup and how much is the result of environmental influences. The nature-nurture debate has been the most contentious when the issue in question is intelligence. In the heat of this debate, scientific findings are sometimes lost, and at other times distorted for political purposes. There is substantial evidence that genetic factors play a significant role in determining performance on intellectual tests. We will review this evidence here. We discuss one of the more sensitive implications of this finding in Box 7.3 where we examine the issue of race and IQ.

There are a variety of types of evidence pointing to the strong influence of genetic factors on IQ. Most of this evidence comes from studies that have examined the correlations among IQ scores for various family members. Nature has provided scientists with naturally occurring experiments that allow for the exploration of genetic and environmental factors affecting IQ. Monozygotic (MZ) or identical twins share 100 percent of their genetic makeup. Dizygotic (DZ) or fraternal twins have the same amount of shared genetics as nontwin siblings. MZ twins raised together have all their genes in common and are raised in the same environment. DZ twins raised together share an environment but have only half of their genes in common. Examining the correlations between IQ scores for MZ and DZ twins sheds some light on the relative contribution of genetic and environmental factors. Across various studies, the correlation between IQ scores for pairs of MZ twins raised together is about .86, whereas it is only about .60 for DZ twins. Stronger evidence of genetic influence come from studies of MZ twins who were raised in different homes. Correlations ranging from .68 to .78 have been found across various studies (Neisser et al., 1996). The IQ scores for nontwin siblings reared apart is about .24 (Kaufman, 1990).

B O X   **7.3**

Race and IQ

Few areas of study have been as charged with debate as the subject of racial and ethnic differences in IQ. Do some racial/ethnic groups score higher than others on tests of intellectual functioning? If so, what are the group differences due to? Are there social policy implications to these findings? What do the findings about group differences mean for the specific individuals who make up the groups? In this box we will look at the findings on racial and ethnic differences in performance on standardized tests of intelligence and try to make sense out of what is a complicated area of inquiry.

To start off, numerous investigations have demonstrated that the average IQ scores for various racial and ethnic groups in the United States differ. White Americans of European descent as a group score about 15 points, or one standard deviation, higher on individually administered tests of intelligence than African Americans (Herrnstein & Murray, 1994; Jensen, 1985; Neisser et al., 1996; Suzuki & Valencia, 1997). Hispanic Americans score somewhere between African Americans and European Americans, while Asian Americans score slightly above European Americans (Lynn, 1993; Suzuki & Valencia, 1997). While there is general agreement about differences among whites, blacks, and Hispanics, there is less consensus about Asian Americans. Flynn (1991), for example, estimated the average IQ of Chinese and Japanese American children to be no different than whites. The average IQ for Native Americans is about 90 (Vraniak, 1994). The group difference that has drawn the most attention is that between black and white Americans, and this is the difference we will discuss in the most detail here. While the most controversial, this is also the difference that has been demonstrated most consistently. Some evidence suggests that the gap between the mean IQs for blacks and whites in the United States has decreased over the past twenty-five years (e.g., Thorndike, Hagan, & Sattler, 1986; Vincent, 1991; Williams & Ceci, 1997), with more recent studies finding the difference to be in the neighborhood of 10 IQ points (Neisser et al., 1996).

BOX **7.3** **Continued**

Before we explore factors that may account for this difference, it is important that we clarify exactly what we mean, and do not mean, when we talk about racial differences in IQ. The group differences we will be discussing refer to the average differences in performance between individuals who are grouped, usually by self-selection, according to race or ethnicity. We are not describing the difference in intelligence between any single member of one group and a member of another group. In addition, it should be kept in mind that we are talking about the differences in means between two distributions that have considerable overlap. Much more of the variability in IQ scores within the population of the United States can be accounted for by differences within racial and ethnic groups than between them (Loehlin, Lindzey, & Spuhler, 1975; Suzuki & Valencia, 1997)

A wide variety of explanations for black–white differences in IQ have been offered. One approach has been to attack the validity of the tests themselves. For example, it has been suggested that the way the tests are constructed and administered favors white over black Americans. Blacks may be less familiar with the vocabulary used in the tests. The tests may be administered more often by white than black examiners. Blacks may be less motivated to try on tests that reflect the dominant white culture's values. These explanations hold an intuitive appeal, particularly for those of us who are uncomfortable with the notion of systematic black–white differences. Nonetheless, while plausible, these factors have not been shown to account for the observed mean IQ difference when they have been examined in controlled studies (Neisser et al., 1996; Reynolds & Brown, 1984). A problem with the argument that it is something in the tests, per se, that is systematically biased against blacks is that the predictive validity of the tests is as good for blacks as it is for whites (Jensen, 1980; Reynolds & Brown, 1984). The performance of African Americans on IQ tests is as strongly correlated with the relevant criterion variables (e.g., school performance) as the scores for whites. If one views IQ as a measure of academic aptitude and achievement as many experts do (e.g., Anastasi & Urbina, 1997), IQ tests appear to be as good a measure of these attributes for blacks as they are for whites.

If not the characteristics of the tests themselves, then what else might account for racial differences in average IQ? Several plausible environmental factors have been explored. Many of these factors are associated with economics. As a group, African Americans have lower incomes that Americans of European descent. A higher proportion of black Americans live in poverty compared to whites. Factors associated with poverty may account for black–white differences in IQ. For example, poorer nutrition, inadequate prenatal care, worse schools, and less intellectually stimulating home environments are all associated with poverty. It may be these factors rather than race per se that is negatively impacting African American intellectual functioning. Support for this viewpoint come from studies that show a positive correlation between socioeconomic status and IQ (White, 1982, cited in Neisser et al. 1996). But average economic differences between blacks and whites alone can not account for differences in performance on IQ tests. Black–white differences on IQ tests are not eliminated when groups are matched for socioeconomic status (Loehlin et al., 1975).

Much of what is important about the experience of being black in America is not necessarily related to economic status. To be part of a minority group that has been systematically discriminated against politically, economically, and socially impacts one's self-image in important ways. It has been argued that children who are members of persecuted minority groups may develop the belief that hard work and perseverance on their part will not be rewarded (Ogbu, 1978). Such attitudes, the argument goes, would negatively affect one's performance on IQ tests as well as the variables that

(continued)

B O X **7.3**   **Continued**

IQ predicts (e.g., school and occupational performance). Along similar lines, it has been argued that important aspects of the African American culture conflict with what is valued in the culture of U.S. school systems. Individualism (i.e., that one is completely responsible for one's successes and failures) and maintaining control of one's emotional expression are strongly valued in U.S. schools as they operate today. In contrast, African American culture values community responsibility and affective expression (Boykin, 1994). From this point of view, psychometric assessment of IQ fits nicely with the values of U.S. schools, but is inconsistent with African American culture.

In contrast to arguments that stress economic and cultural influences upon IQ test performance, some have argued that race differences in IQ can best be accounted for by genetics (Herrnstein & Murray, 1994; Jensen, 1969, 1985; Rushton, 1995). This argument is clearly the most controversial and clearly the one that has engendered the most acrimony. The types of findings that are usually used to support arguments for a genetic basis for race differences in IQ include the following: the evidence pointing to the influence of hereditary factors in intelligence; the racial differences in IQ seen in the United States appear in other countries as well; the mean IQ for mixed race offspring tends to be in the middle between the mean of the two parental groups; African children born and raised in African countries score lower than matched groups of white children in some studies (Rushton, 1995, 1997). It is beyond the scope of this brief review to examine this evidence in detail. Suffice it to say that the evidence cited above is open to multiple interpretations and not all reviewers have drawn the same conclusions (e.g., Neisser et al., 1996).

One strategy for parceling out the relative contributions of environmental and genetic factors is to look at children from one race who have been raised in the cultural environment of another. The Minnesota Transracial Adoption Study (Scarr & Weinberg, 1976, 1978a, 1978b; Weinberg, Scarr, & Waldman, 1992) employed this strategy. This study involved biological and adoptive children of 101 middle-class families with two white parents. One hundred seventy-six adopted black children (i.e., one or two biological parents were black) and 145 biological white children were tested in this study. The white parents of these children had above-average intelligence (about 119) and education. The biological parents of the black children were estimated to have average intelligence and education based upon adoption records. The first set of reports to emanate from this study suggested that environmental factors had a significant impact upon the intellectual development of the black children. Their average IQ (110) was considerably higher than would have been predicted had these children been raised by their natural parents. Nonetheless, other findings from the same study suggest genetic influences. The average IQ of the adopted black children was still lower than the IQ of their adoptive parents and the biological children of these parents. Furthermore, when these children were retested at age 17, the black children were found to have lost some of the advantages they had shown when they were younger. In the retest, their average IQ was only about 97 (Weinberg, Scarr, & Waldman, 1992).

While studies like the Minnesota Transracial Adoption Study provide valuable information about the nature and nurture of racial differences in IQ, they do not provide the final word. Clearly the adoptive children in these families differed from the biological offspring in more than just their genetic makeup. For example, the children with two black birth parents were not adopted until they were, on average, about 32 months of age (Neisser et al., 1996). In addition, although raised in white families, the adopted children still had the experience of growing up black in America.

Studies of MZ twins reared together and reared apart provide the data upon which estimates of the heritability of IQ are based. Heritability refers to the percentage of the variance in the population that is due to heredity (Vandenberg & Vogler, 1985). The heritability estimate for IQ is about .50. In other words, about 50 percent of the variability in IQ scores in the *population* can be attributed to genetic differences among individuals (Kaufman, 1990; Neisser et al., 1996). General cognitive ability, as measured by IQ tests, is one of the most highly heritable complex behavioral traits (Plomin, 1997).

The estimates of the heritability of IQ change with the age of the sample studied. When heritability estimates are based upon younger samples of children, they hover around .45. However, as the sample gets older, heritability estimates increase. By late adolescence, heritability is estimated to be about .75 (Neisser et al., 1996). This change across the life span of the sample studied appears to reflect a true change in heritability. For adult samples, 75 percent of the variance in intelligence appears to be due to genetic factors. This change in the degree to which individual differences in intelligence reflect genetic differences from childhood to adulthood seems quite puzzling. A panel of experts on intelligence offered the following explanation: "One possibility is that as individuals grow older their transactions with their environments are increasingly influenced by the characteristics that they bring to those environments themselves, decreasingly by the conditions imposed by family life and social origin. Older persons are in a better position to select their own effective environments, a form of genotype-environment correlation" (Neisser et al., 1996, p. 86).

Given the evidence for genetic influences on IQ, one might wonder if there is an IQ gene. Behavioral geneticists don't think so. The complex factors that contribute to IQ scores are most likely influenced by multiple genes. However, some progress has been made toward identifying the groups of genes that may work together to influence IQ (Chorney et al., 1998).

Heritability estimates are easily misinterpreted. The fact that heritability refers to the proportion of the variance in the distribution of intelligence in the *population,* not in the individual, deserves repeating. A heritability estimate of .75 does *not* mean that 75 percent of an individual's intelligence is determined by genetics.

A second common misinterpretation of the heritability findings is the conclusion that if a trait is strongly influenced by genetic factors it is immutable. This is simply not true (Angoff, 1988; Neisser et al., 1996). An illustration of the complicated relationship between genetics and environment demonstrates the changeability of heritable traits. There is strong evidence that height is determined to a large extent by genetic factors. The heritability of height is estimated to be .80 (Kaufman, 1990). Nonetheless, there is strong evidence that average heights continue to increase over generations (Olivier, 1980). For example, in Japan, the average height of young men increased approximately 4 inches from the 1940s to the 1980s (Angoff, 1988).

Malleability of IQ

Given the facts that heritability estimates for IQ fall well below 1.00 and that traits that are highly heritable are influenced by environmental factors, the question of what environmental experiences can significantly impact IQ is particularly intriguing. Biological, cultural, educational, social, and family influences have all been examined. Given the interaction between genetics and life experiences (as suggested by the change in heritability of IQ with age discussed above suggests), distilling the cause-and-effect relationship between environmental factors and IQ can be difficult. Nonetheless, there is substantial evidence that IQ is effected by environmental factors.

The quantity and quality of one's educational experience seems to be a likely variable that would influence mental abilities and hence IQ. As we have seen, IQ correlates well with school performance. While the causal direction of that relationship is unclear, there are multiple sources of data showing that performance on IQ tests is influenced by one's education (Ceci, 1991). For example, some children start school a year earlier than their peers who are very close in age because of the cut-off date for admission used by their school system (e.g., two children who are within a few days of each other in chronological age may be in different grades because one child's birthday is before, and the other after, the cut-off). When these children are studied, the ones who have been in school longer tend to have higher scores. Another illustration of the influence of education on IQ is the fact that test scores tend to decrease over the summer vacation. A dramatic example of the effects of education on IQ was provided by a naturally occurring experiment in the 1960s when one Virginia county closed its schools for a number of years to avoid forced integration. Most of the African American children in the county had no formal education during that time period. On average, these children scored 6 IQ points lower per missed year in school compared to a matched comparison group (Green, Hoffman, Morse, Hayes, & Morgan, 1964, cited in Neisser et al., 1996).

Occupational and cultural factors have also been shown to influence intelligence. For example, some evidence suggests that "intellectual flexibility" is influenced by the complexity of one's job (Kohn & Schooler, 1973, 1983). The influence of cultural factors upon intellectual functioning are suggested by examples such as the following: "Rice farmers in Liberia are good at estimating quantities of rice (Gay & Cole, 1967); children in Botswana, accustomed to story-telling, have excellent memories for stories" (Dube, 1982) (Neisser et al., 1996, pp. 86–87). Finally, biological events such as malnutrition, lead poisoning, and prenatal alcohol use have all been shown to have negative effects upon intellectual functioning.

Perhaps one of the most intriguing findings pointing to the malleability of IQ is that test scores, much like height, have steadily risen since the tests were developed at the outset of the twentieth century (Flynn, 1984, 1987). The "Flynn effect," named for James Flynn, who was the first one to systematically describe this trend, is very well documented in the United States and other technologically advanced countries. IQ tests are restandardized periodically to correct for this trend and to preserve 100 as the average IQ. Flynn has estimated the rise in average IQ to be about 3 points per decade. So someone who scores 100 on a recently standardized IQ test would have scored 106 if the test used twenty-year-old norms. There are a variety of possible explanations for the Flynn effect. Most, however, focus upon broad societal changes. The population of the United States has become increasingly urban and television and computers provide people with access to more information and a wider variety of viewpoints then they might otherwise have been exposed to (Neisser et al., 1996). Additionally, nutritional factors that might account for the increase in average height may also account for improved intellectual functioning (Lynn, 1990). Whatever the reason, the

Flynn effect points to culture-wide environmental influences upon IQ. Natural selection simply could not account for such rapid increases in test scores.

Intelligence over the Life Span

Is IQ a stable trait? What happens over the life span? Children clearly become more intelligent as they get older, but what about adults? Does intelligence rise across the life span, or do we start to lose our intellectual abilities as we get older? Exploration of questions such as these can help us to understand the construct of intelligence and also shed light on what exactly is being measured by tests of intelligence. Researchers have used a variety of methods to address these questions and the conclusions drawn depend to a large extent upon the methods used. Let us begin to explore the issue of intelligence test performance by looking at the evidence for the stability and instability of IQ scores through childhood and adolescence.

Longitudinal studies involve following the same set (or cohort) of people over time. Longitudinal methods have been used to study the stability of children's intelligence through childhood and into their adults years. A common strategy is to test a group of children at one point in time, say 5 years old, and then test the same group of children again at some later point, say age 10. The correlation between the two sets of IQ scores provides some information about the stability of IQ. A considerable number of research studies have employed this methodology and found that IQ scores tend to be quite stable from middle childhood through adolescence and into the adult years (see Anastasi & Urbina, 1997, for review). Depending upon the ages at which the children were originally tested and the interval between assessments, the correlations run between .45 and .85. The older the children were at the time of the original assessment and the shorter the time from the first and second testings, the greater the correlations tend to be. For example, one study found that the correlation between scores for children tested at age 3 and again at age 4 was .83, whereas the scores at age 3 correlated .46 with scores obtained from the children at age 12 (Sontag, Baker, & Nelson, 1958). In another study, the correlations between a group tested at age 14 and again at age 25 was .85 (Bradway, Thompson, & Cravens, 1958, cited in Anastasi & Urbina, 1997).

The correlational research described above provides useful information about how groups of children tend to perform. When the focus of the research is shifted, however, from the group to the individual, a very different picture emerges. Longitudinal studies that have looked at what happens to individual children's test scores over time reveal that IQ scores tend to rise and fall, sometimes dramatically, and that these rises and falls appear to be related to environmental events. The California Guidance Study (Honzik, Macfarlane, & Allen, 1948, cited in Anastasi & Urbina, 1997) was the first to document the changes that occur in individual IQ scores with repeated assessment. Fully 59 percent of the children showed IQ changes of 15 or more points from one testing period to another. IQ changes were not random but appeared to be related to the emotional climate in the child's home and to the degree to which the parents were concerned about their children's educational accomplishments. In this study, while the overall correlations between sets of test scores at different points in time were generally high, individual children sometimes showed striking changes in test performance.

Similar to the findings regarding changes in children's intelligence through the years, what one concludes about intellectual functioning through the adult years depends to a great extent upon the research methods employed. Longitudinal studies are extremely time-consuming and costly since one has to keep track of the original cohort of subjects over several years. *Cross-sectional* studies employ an alternative methodology. Instead of studying the same group of people over time, in cross-sectional research different groups of varying ages are studied at the same time. To examine changes in intellectual functioning over the adult years, for example, groups of adults at different ages are studied at the same time (e.g., groups of subjects ages 25–34, 35–44, 45–54, and so on). Inferences about changes in intellectual functioning are made by examining the mean scores of each group of subjects. Data of this sort tend to suggest that intellectual functioning peaks in the mid-20s and declines at a steady rate over successive decade of life (see, for example, Anastasi & Urbina, 1997, Figure 12.1, p. 331).

Cross-sectional studies typically suggest a steady decline in intellectual functioning starting at about age 30. However, if one takes into consideration the Flynn effect, it is obvious that these findings are due to cohort differences rather than deterioration in intellect associated with age. If, as Flynn and others have shown, the average IQ is increasing, it seems reasonable to attribute the decline in average scores starting at about age 30 to differences in the samples tested.

Longitudinal studies of intellectual functioning in adulthood clearly show that the deterioration suggested by cross-sectional findings is grossly misleading. The Seattle Longitudinal Study is a particularly high-quality example of longitudinal research (Schaie, 1994). The study was initiated in 1956 and the sample was most recently retested in 1991. Figure 7.2 summarizes some of the findings from the Seattle study. As you can see, declines in intellectual abilities do not appear to begin in earnest until about age 60 and the rate of performance decline varies across cognitive tasks.

Educational Assessment

Testing is pervasive in educational settings. Most forms of psychological tests are employed in the school setting. IQ tests are frequently used to classify children into subgroups. Assessment instruments developed for specific educational reasons are also commonly used in U.S. schools. Some tests are used to assess the amount of knowledge the student has obtained to date. Others are used to assist in making prognostic decisions about the child's likelihood of benefitting from certain types of educational experiences. Still other tests, often used in combination, have the goal of diagnosing specific types of learning difficulties. In this section we will provide a brief overview of various types of educational tests and describe some of their typical uses.

Tests of Aptitude and Tests of Achievement

Tests used in academic settings are often classified under the heading of *aptitude* or *achievement* tests. But as we will see, a dichotomy cannot be drawn between achievement and aptitude tests. The two types of tests are probably better understood as falling along different

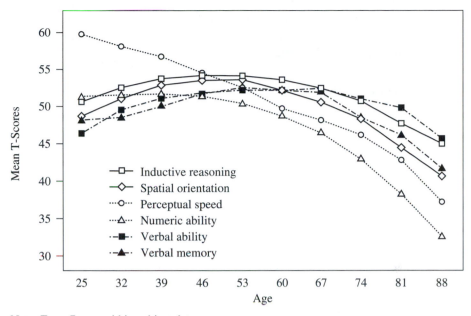

Note: From 7-year within-subject data

FIGURE 7.2 Average changes in various areas of intellectual functioning in a longitudinal sample through the adult years.

Source: Schaie, K. W. (1994). The course of adult intellectual development. *American Psychologist, 49,* 304–313. Figure 6, p. 308. Copyright © 1994 by The American Psychological Association. Reprinted with permission.

points on a continuum. One way that aptitude and achievement tests are distinguished is in their respective goals. Aptitude tests are thought to tell us about future performance. Achievement tests, on the other hand, evaluate what a person has learned as a result of a specified educational experience. A second distinction has to do with the specificity of the experiences that are thought to effect performance on achievement and aptitude tests. Achievement tests measure one's performance after a relatively standardized set of experiences (e.g., college algebra), whereas aptitude tests measure learning from essentially unknown, and certainly uncontrolled, learning experiences.

The distinctions between achievement and aptitude tests often do not hold true when the tests themselves are scrutinized. For example, performance on the Graduate Record Exams (GREs) is clearly influenced by what has been learned through formal education prior to graduate school. However, the test also predicts, to a certain degree, performance in graduate school.

Aptitude and achievement tests might be more productively thought of as falling along a continuum of "Tests of Developed Abilities" (Anastasi & Urbina, 1997). At one end of this continuum might be tests that assess performance in a specific subject area (e.g., French vocabulary) where the information is acquired through a specific course or courses. Further along on the continuum would be tests that are more broadly oriented to assess skills such as mathematical reasoning or reading comprehension. At the opposite end of the scale would be tests designed for use cross-culturally that do not depend upon specific language skills or educational experiences.

Tests of Aptitude

Having exposed the fallacy of dichotomizing tests of aptitude from tests of achievement, it may seem odd to have headings: Tests of Aptitude and Tests of Achievement. Nonetheless, we use this organizational strategy as a convenience and to maintain continuity with traditions in the field.

Aptitude tests are most often used to determine an individual's readiness to for some future learning experience. In fact, for younger school children, aptitude tests are often referred to as "readiness" tests. The Metropolitan Readiness Test, for example, is designed to assess the degree to which kindergarten and first-grade children have the prerequisite skills to benefit from formal education in reading and mathematics. For some reason, when tests are developed for adults, the term *aptitude* usually replaces *readiness.* An aptitude test that is familiar to most college students in the Scholastic Aptitude Test (SAT), which is used to assess one's readiness to do college-level work. The Graduate Record Exam (GRE) is another aptitude test that many readers of this book may soon become familiar with if they haven't already. These tests could be called the "College Readiness Test" and the "Graduate School Readiness Test" since they essentially measure students' readiness for different levels of advanced education (Cohen et al., 1992).

The Metropolitan Readiness Test, SAT, and GRE are all group-administered aptitude tests that are used primarily for placement purposes. Other tests of aptitude, in contrast, are used for individual assessment and are designed to yield information that can assist educators in developing an educational plan to meet the needs of a specific child. The Detroit Tests of Learning Aptitude (currently in fourth edition, DTLA-4; Hammill, 1998) is an example of such a test. The DTLA-4 is designed for use with children and adolescents from age 6 years to 17 years, and 11 months. It consists of ten subtests that can be combined to produce sixteen composite scores. The DTLA-4 attempts to measure academic skills that are acquired through general experience and not specific courses. As such, the test evaluates students' ability to reason, concentrate, recall information, and use vocabulary. Subtests of the DTLA-4 include *Word Opposites,* which assesses knowledge of vocabulary and antonyms; *Design Reproduction,* which assesses short-term memory, spatial relations, and attention to detail; and *Symbolic Relations,* which assesses ability to think abstractly and see theoretical and practical relationships. The DTLA-4 is used in combination with other tests and collateral information to diagnose learning difficulties and to assist in the development of plans for remediation (see Box 7.4 on page 223).

Tests of Achievement

Tests of achievement are designed to measure some area of accomplishment. What has this person achieved? For second graders a test of achievement should cover addition and subtraction as well as basic vocabulary. In other words, the test should assess information and skills the child would have been expected to master in the first and second grades. At the college level, tests of achievement in psychology might include questions about classical and operant conditioning, theories of personality, and basic psychometric concepts. Information a psychology major should presumably have mastered in the course of his or her education. The exams you take in this class are achievement tests.

There are group-administered tests of achievement such as the Metropolitan Achievement Test. But clinical psychologists are more likely to use individually administered tests of achievement. An example of a widely used individually administered measure is the Wide Range Achievement Test (currently in its third edition, WRAT-III; Wilkinson, 1993). The test measures reading, spelling, and arithmetic with three subtests by those names. The test is normed on samples ranging in age from 5 years to 74 years, 11 months so that it can be used with students ranging from kindergarten through adulthood. The test yields Standard Scores and Grade Scores for Reading, Spelling, and Arithmetic so that the examiner can determine where the person is relative to age-matched peers but also has some general indication of the instructional level for that person (e.g., reading level comparable to a child who has completed the fifth grade).

The WRAT-III Reading subtest is purposely designed to eliminate, as much as possible, the effects of comprehension. That is, to perform on the Reading subtest, test-takers need only to pronounce the words on a list; they do not need to demonstrate knowledge of the words' meanings. The authors argue that this attribute of the test makes it particularly valuable in diagnosing reading difficulties and developing intervention strategies (Wilkinson, 1993). A child who shows good vocabulary comprehension on a test such as the WISC-III but performs below age level on the Reading subtest of the WRAT-III is having difficulty coding written words. It would be inappropriate to develop a remedial program that emphasizes comprehension for such a child.

A strength and weakness of the WRAT-III is its brevity. With only three subtests, the test can be administered quickly and serves some purposes well. For example, the Reading subtest can be administered as a screening measure to determine whether an individual has the required reading ability to complete a paper-and-pencil questionnaire. With only three tests, however, the examiner can draw only a limited amount of information from the test.

The Peabody Individual Achievement Test—Revised (PIAT-R) is another individually administered test of achievement that has somewhat broader coverage than the WRAT-III. The PIAT-R has six subtests: *Mathematics, Reading Recognition, Reading Comprehension, Spelling, Written Expression,* and *General Information.*

Achievement tests are often administered along with intelligence tests in order to gather information about both the child's intellectual ability and the level of achievement that child has obtained. Significant differences between ability and achievement can suggest the presence of specific learning disabilities, which is the topic we turn to next.

Learning Disabilities

Learning disability is a term that has been used loosely to refer to any type of difficulty in learning. Sattler (1988) distinguishes between the broad use of the term, in which it applies to difficulties in learning that might be attributed to any type of factor including mental retardation, brain injury, or emotional disturbance, and the more narrow use of the term. The latter is a more circumscribed use and is more consistent with laws governing educational mandates for children with learning disabilities. Sattler (1988, p. 598) defines the more narrow sense of the term as follows: "(Learning disability) refers to the failure, on the part of a child who has adequate intelligence, maturational level, cultural background, and educational experience, to learn a scholastic skill."

The federal government provided a definition of *specific learning disability* in Public Law 94-142:

> . . . a disorder in one or more of the basic psychological processes involved in understanding or in using language, spoken or written, which may manifest itself in an imperfect ability to listen, think, speak, read, write, spell or do mathematical calculations. The term includes such conditions as perceptual handicaps, brain injury, minimal brain dysfunction, dyslexia, and developmental aphasia. The term does not include children who have learning problems which are primarily the result of visual, hearing, or motor handicaps, of mental retardation, of emotional disturbance, or of environmental, cultural, or economic disadvantage. (*Federal Register,* 1977, p. 65083)

Public Law 94-142, originally titled the Education for All Handicapped Children Act (1977) and later renamed the Individuals with Disabilities Education Act (1990), mandates that all children with mental or physical disabilities be identified; guarantees these children a publicly financed education; and requires that individually tailored education plans be developed for each child.

Psychological testing plays an important role in the process created by PL 94-142. First, the identification of children to be placed in programs funded by 94-142 involves testing. Children may be identified as having a *specific learning disability,* for example, if their level of academic achievement in a specific area (e.g., reading, writing) is significantly less than what would be expected given their age, ability, and educational opportunities. IQ scores are often used as one factor in determining a child's ability and standardized achievement tests are used to measure academic achievement. Second, assessment of children's cognitive strengths and weaknesses is a necessary prerequisite to developing individualized education plans.

Public Law 94-142 created a need for psychologists trained to evaluate and provide educational recommendations for school-age children. In addition, tests have been developed to facilitate the diagnosis of specific learning disabilities. Sometimes referred to as psycho-educational test batteries, these test kits generally contain two types of tests: tests that measure general intellectual abilities and aptitude for academic success and tests that measure achievement in specific areas such as reading, mathematics, and written language. The Woodcock-Johnson Psycho-Educational Battery—Revised (Woodcock & Johnson, 1989) is an example. The battery is divided into two major sections: Tests of Cognitive Ability and Tests of Achievement. The Woodcock Johnson Battery is comprehensive. There are 21 tests (7 standard and 14 supplemental) in the Cognitive Ability battery and 18 (9 standard and 9 supplemental) in the Achievement battery. By examining the relationships among scores on the various tests and composite scores, the examiner attempts to determine whether there is a discrepancy between the examinee's ability and his or her achievement, and what the test-takers' strengths and weaknesses are with respect to both ability and achievement.

Since the passage of 94-142, educators have increased their awareness of the high frequency of children, college students, and adults who are handicapped by learning disabilities (see, for example, Gregg, Hoy, & Gay, 1996). Box 7.4 contains an example report on a learning disability assessment.

BOX 7.4

Learning Disability Assessment

PSYCHOEDUCATIONAL EVALUATION

NAME: Peter Zayler   SCHOOL: Alfred Newman Elementary
DOB: 05/17/93   GRADE: Kindergarten; AGE: 5 yr, 10 mo
DOE: 03/06/99   EXAMINER: William Zeman, Ph.D.

REASON FOR REFERRAL: Peter Zayler is a 5-year, 10-month-old boy who was referred by his Special Services Director, Terri McGilligan, for an evaluation to develop an understanding of the difficulties he is experiencing in the classroom and to determine whether he qualifies for special education services. The results of this evaluation will be used in conjunction with teacher observations, performance records, and complementary evaluations conducted by school personnel to help determine Peter's educational needs.

BACKGROUND INFORMATION: Peter has been experiencing difficulties following his teacher's instructions and staying on task in the classroom. His behavior is often disruptive to the class. His teacher is concerned that he is not progressing at the same rate as his classmates. She noted that he needs considerable individual attention in comparison to his peers. Peter's mother is concerned about the difficulties he is experiencing in school. She has observed similar problems (e.g., staying on task) at home.

EVALUATION PROCEDURES
        Review of school records
        Stanford-Binet Intelligence Scale—Fourth Edition (SB:FE)
        Peabody Picture Vocabulary Test—Revised (PPVY-R)
        Beer Developmental Test of Visual-Motor Integration (VMI)
        Classroom Observation

TESTING BEHAVIOR: Peter presented as a friendly young boy. He warmed up to the examiner quickly and was cooperative with testing procedures. As time progressed, however, it became very difficult to keep Peter focused on the tasks at hand. He would move about the testing room despite being instructed to remain in one place and often had to be redirected to attend to the testing procedures and materials. Peter often responded impulsively. For example, he would play with the testing materials and answer before all the directions were given. This types of behavior was particularly disruptive during two subtests of the SB:FE: Bead Memory and Quantitative. The scores from these subtests are of questionable validity. Given the referral information, it seems likely that Peter's behavior during the evaluation was representative of his behavior in other learning/educational settings. Therefore, the results of this evaluation are considered to be an accurate representation of his current abilities.

(continued)

B O X   **7.4**   **Continued**

ANALYSIS OF TEST RESULTS

Intellectual: On the Stanford-Binet: Fourth Edition, Peter obtained an overall Composite Standard Score (SAS) of 83. The chances that his true score on this measure falls in the range between 78 and 88 is 95 out of 100. This score suggests overall intellectual functioning in the Low Average range. Peter's Verbal Reason SAS was 97 (Average range), his Abstract/Visual Reasoning SAS was 84 (Low Average range), his Quantitative Reasoning SAS was 78 (Slow Learner range) and his Short-Term Memory SAS was 84 (Low Average range).

Peter's scores in each area of ability are summarized below. Individual subtests have mean score of 50 and a standard deviation of 8.

Verbal Reasoning		*Abstract/Visual Reasoning*	
Vocabulary	49	Pattern Analysis	43
Comprehension	44	Copying	43
Absurdities	53		

Quantitative Reasoning		*Short-Term Memory*	
Quantitative	39	Bead Memory	36
		Memory for Sentences	46
		Memory for Digits	49

Inspection of inter-subtest variability reveals a reasonably stable pattern of performance within the Average range with the exception of the Quantitative and Bead Memory subtests, which were areas of weakness in the Low Average range. Disruptive test-taking behaviors were likely a contributing factor to Peter's lower scores on these subtests. As indicated earlier, Peter's performance on these subtests were affected by his impulsivity. If the SAS for Short-Term Memory is recalculated without the Bead Memory score, it is 94 (Average range). Similarly, if Quantitative Reasoning is deleted from the calculation of the Composite SAS, the revised SAS is 91 (Average range).

Receptive Vocabulary: The results of the Peabody Picture Vocabulary Test—Revised, a test of nonverbal receptive vocabulary knowledge, yielded a Standard Score of 92, which is in the Average range. This score indicates that Peter performed better than 30 percent of the children in the normative sample and translates to an age equivalent of 5 years, 3 months. This score is consistent with the Verbal Reasoning area score on the SB:FE.

Visual-Motor: On the Beery Developmental Test of Visual-Motor Integration, Peter obtained a Standard Score of 89, which is in the Average range. This scores indicates that Peter performed better than 23 percent of the children in the normative sample and translates to an age equivalent of 5 years, 2 months.

CLASSROOM BEHAVIOR

Observation: Peter was observed in his classroom prior to the testing. Peter was observed to be off-task frequently and required a great deal of the teacher's individual attention. He frequently walked back and forth from his assigned work area and the areas where other children were working. Peter often disrupted the other children and his intrusions appeared to be unwelcome by most of the children. Peter was easily distracted by materials in and around his work area. For example, on one occasion Peter returned to his seat after being directed to do so by his instructor. He was in the seat less than five seconds before a stack of story books caught his attention. He got out of the seat, picked up the books, and began to flip through them. The books were taken away by the instructor, who then directed Peter back to his seat. Peter frequently made unsolicited comments about the difficulty of the work assignment (e.g., "I'm having a hard time," "Too many words"). Peter

---

frequently engaged in biting or chewing behavior during the observation period, for example, chewing on crayon wrappers, his shirt cuff, and an eraser.

SUMMARY

Peter's overall intellectual functioning appears to be in the Average range. His vocabulary knowledge and ability to reason with words, while average for a child his age, are relative strengths for Peter. Peter's short-term memory skills and his ability to reason quantitatively are relative weaknesses. Peter's visual-motor development is on par with his intellectual functioning.

Peter appears to be on the high end of the distractibility continuum for children his age. Similarly, he appears to have difficulty controlling his impulses and is highly active. In the classroom setting, he requires considerable one-on-one attention from an adult. He is easily distracted by stimuli in the classroom environment. He requires frequent redirection in order to accomplish school tasks.

RECOMMENDATIONS

1. The level of inattention, distractibility, and impulse control problems observed in this evaluation suggests the possibility of attention deficit-hyperactivity disorder (ADHD). A definitive diagnosis of ADHD would require additional assessment. Referral for further assessment of the possibility of ADHD is recommended.

2. Peter's performance on the tests of cognitive functioning, while mostly in the average range, were consistently at the lower end of this range. These findings are consistent with Peter's teacher's concern that, while Peter started off the academic year performing at a level on par with his classmates, he has not progressed at a similar rate. Peter may be showing signs of stable learning difficulties. If this is the case, the discrepancies between his scores and the scores of age-matched normative sample will become larger as he progresses. Therefore, reassessment of Peter in 18 months is recommended.

3. Given the behavioral difficulties Peter is presenting, it is recommended that a behavioral management plan be developed. In general, the plan should outline strategies for reinforcing appropriate classroom behavior with the teacher's attention and small rewards, while at the same time implementing a set of negative consequences for disruptive behavior. For example, Peter could earn stickers or checks in a notebook for maintaining attention on assigned tasks for specified periods of time. Brief time-out can be used to reduce the frequency of disruptive behavior. The examiner is available to Peter's teacher to assist in the development of an appropriate behavior management plan.

4. Peter's performance on tasks of visual motor perception and coordination suggest a mild delay in this area. Increasing the opportunities for Peter to utilize these skills may remedy this deficit. Peter should be encouraged to engage in activities that utilize these skills both at home and at school. Some recommended activities include coloring in coloring books, playing with constructive toys such as Lincoln Logs or Legos, and drawing (particularly coping geometric shapes).

5. Peter's development of quantitative reasoning skills may be enhanced if he is encouraged to practice numerical skills. He should be encouraged to practice basic computational skills such as counting coins or game pieces. Another activity of this type is adding the dots on a die by counting the dots on two and later three sides.

William Zeman, Ph.D.   Date
Licensed Psychologist

CHAPTER

8

Personality Assessment

We began Chapter 7 by describing various ways of defining intelligence. We saw that *intelligence* was surprisingly difficult to define. Well, if you thought intelligence was difficult, try taking a stab at *personality*. Once again, the term is one with which we are all familiar, but when used in a scientific or professional context, proves challenging to delineate.

In everyday parlance, personality is usually used in one of two ways (Hall & Lindzey, 1978). The first is evaluative. "He's got a lot of personality" usually means the person is interesting, fun to be with, and has good social skills. "She has no personality" means the opposite. When used this way, the quantity of personality a person is thought to have refers to his or her level of social adroitness and likableness. In a similar fashion when we say, "Tom has a great personality" we are evaluating Tom's social skills (as opposed to his physical appearance) positively. The second way the term frequently is used by the general public is to describe a dominant or outstanding feature of another. We might say a person has a "fearful personality" or a "bubbly personality" or a "passive-aggressive personality." In this use, a salient characteristic that is highly typical of the person is chosen to provide an overall description.

In 1937, the well-known psychologist Gordon Allport reviewed the extant literature and distilled over fifty different definitions of the term *personality.* In 1970, Calvin Hall and Gardner Lindzey published an authoritative textbook on personality. Rather than offer a definition of personality, these authors concluded, "it is our conviction that *no substantive definition of personality can be applied with any generality . . . personality is defined by the particular empirical concepts which are a part of the theory of personality employed by the observer* (emphasis in original; Hall & Lindzey, 1970, p. 9).

How one understands personality is inextricably tied to one's theoretical orientation. For the psychoanalyst, personality refers to the dynamic struggle between drives to satisfy unconscious, usually sexual, desires and the needs to function in the real world. For psychologists who subscribe to a humanist-existentialist viewpoint, one's personality is one's phenomenal experience of the world at the moment including the knowledge of one's mortality. Behaviorally oriented psychologists have traditionally eschewed the term *personality* in favor of the view that individual differences in behavior are better understood in terms of reinforcement history and skill variability. Considering personality from these different viewpoints illustrates the futility of a single definition.

For clinical psychologists the approach one takes to assessment of personality is also closely tied to one's theoretical perspective. Psychologists who believe that unconscious conflicts are important determinants of clients' emotional and behavioral difficulties will choose assessment instruments they believe assess these unconscious processes. On the other hand, clinical psychologists who are more empirically minded will choose assessment instruments where the behavioral and emotional correlates of the scores derived from the measures are well established.

One system for organizing different approaches to personality assessment has been to distinguish *projective* from *objective* methods. Projective methods tend to be less structured and involve a greater degree of judgment in scoring and interpretation. Clients have a fairly large degree of latitude in choosing how to respond. Objective methods, on the other hand, are more highly structured, scoring is objective, and interpretation involves relatively less subjective judgment. Clients have a limited number of choices in how they respond to the test items.

In this chapter we will provide an overview of the methods of personality assessment most frequently used by clinical psychologists. Both projective and objective methods will be discussed and evaluated. We will conclude by discussing the role of personality assessment in contemporary clinical psychology.

Projective Methods

Three children are lying on the ground in an open field looking up at puffy white clouds in the sky. The first child says that she can see the image of a ballerina pirouetting through the air. The second child looks at the same sky and sees the face of an old man scowling down at him. The third child sees two rams butting heads. What do their different perceptions of the clouds tell us about these children? Does what each child see in the clouds provide us with clues about their self-esteem, relationships, impulse control, moral development, mood state, or need for achievement? Or is it more likely that what each child chose to say about the clouds has more to do with what they had seen on television recently, whether they had played this game before, or what they thought might sound "cool" to their friends.

The idea that what people perceive when they respond to some ambiguous stimulus provides important information about their personality is the basic assumption underlying projective methods of psychological assessment. Consequently, psychologists have developed a variety of methods for systematically assessing the ways in which people respond to a variety of ambiguous stimuli by using inkblots, pictures, sentence stems, drawings, and verbal instructions. These varied projective methods have the following characteristic in common:

1. All projective methods share the assumption that when people try to make sense of some vague or ambiguous stimulus, their understanding of that stimulus is determined by their feelings, experiences, needs, and thought processes. This assumption has been called the *projective hypothesis.* Put simply, the projective hypothesis assumes that a person will project something important about him or herself onto an ambiguous stimulus. Lawrence Frank (1939) is usually credited as the first to use the term "projective methods." Frank compared the projective methods to an X-ray. In both technologies a stimulus is "passed through" an individual yielding a picture of the internal structure that can only be interpreted by a trained professional.

2. Projective methods are relatively *unstructured*. The tasks allow for an almost inexhaustible variety of possible responses. In order to avoid contaminating a person's responses, instructions for projective methods are often general and can be vague themselves (e.g., "Tell me what you see." "There are no right or wrong answers.").

3. The purpose and procedures used in projective tests are usually *disguised* to some degree. The client does not know the way in which their responses will be analyzed and interpreted.

4. Projective methods are usually used as a *global approach* to assess the individual's entire personality. This is particularly true in a clinical setting where these instruments have been used most often. Typically, the psychologist puts together a comprehensive description of the client's psychological functioning, rather than identify a particular trait, based upon the information gathered through the projective assessment.

5. Proponents of projective methods argue that these techniques are particularly effective, and may be the only means available, for evaluating unconscious elements of the personality. The assumption is that the information gathered with the projective test could not be gotten otherwise. Quoting Frank (1939, p. 395), "the most important things about an individual are what he cannot or will not say."

6. Interpretation of projective tests is usually based upon, or has been strongly influenced by, psychoanalytic thinking. The relationship between projective methods and the Freudian concept of *projection* is not straightforward. Projective methods are not procedures for assessing projection. Freud used the term *projection* to describe a defense mechanism whereby an individual attributes his unacceptable, unconscious thoughts and feelings onto others. Responses to projective stimuli are not necessarily defensive nor unconscious (Zubin, Eron, & Shumer, 1965, cited in Wierzbicki, 1993). Clearly, however, the development of projective techniques in the first half of the twentieth century was strongly influenced by the popularity of psychoanalysis. The acceptance of *psychic determinism* and the importance placed upon unconscious processes paved the way for projective testing.

7. In the clinical settings, projective methods are used in an *idiographic* manner. While normative data are available for some projective tests, these instruments are used to develop a model of the personality functioning of the individual.

Projective methods were developed in clinical settings, and it is in these settings that they have predominantly been used. As we will see, when these methods have been evaluated as psychometric instruments, often they have been found wanting. Nonetheless, through the decades they have maintained their popularity in clinical settings (Bellack, 1993; Lubin, Larson, & Matarazzo, 1984; Piotrowski, Sherry, & Kelly, 1985; Watkins, 1991) and these instruments continue to be taught in many APA-accredited doctoral training programs in clinical psychology (Piotrowski et al., 1985). We will discuss the continued popularity of projective methods later in this chapter. At this point, we turn our attention to the most popular of all the projective methods, the Rorschach.

Rorschach

History.   Hermann Rorschach was a Swiss psychiatrist who had a strong interest in art and drawing. His father had been an art teacher and Rorschach published papers on the analysis of psychiatric patients' artwork early in his career. Three significant influences upon Rorschach's thinking and professional work can be identified. First, Rorschach worked under the supervision of Eugen Bleuler, who published his work on dementia praecox, coining the term *schizophrenia,* in 1911 while Rorschach was doing his psychiatric residency. Second, like most European psychiatrists of his day, Rorschach was influenced by psychoanalytic thinking and employed psychoanalytic techniques in his work with some patients. Third, Rorschach was influenced by the writings of Carl Jung, particularly Jung's writings about the use of word-association tasks as a means of exploring unconscious material. In 1921, Rorschach published *Psychodiagnostik,* in which he described a method of diagnosing patients, and describing characteristics of their personality, based upon their responses to a set of ten inkblots (see Box 8.1 for a brief history of the Rorschach cards). The book contained Rorschach's observations about the responses of hundreds of patients and nonpatients to his inkblots. Among his many observations, Rorschach noted that the schizophrenic group responded much differently than the other groups. Thus the seeds of the Rorschach technique

---

B O X **8.1**

The Story of Rorschach's Ten Inkblots

The ten inkblots that appeared in Rorschach's book are the same ten blots that have been used over the eighty-plus years since its publication. While systems for administering, scoring, and interpreting the Rorschach have varied, the blots themselves have not been altered through the ages. The story of how the famous ten inkblots came into existence make an interesting historical footnote (Exner, 1986).

Rorschach originally used about forty inkblots in his research. When he first organized his materials for publication, he based the manuscript on the fifteen blots he used most often. Rorschach's manuscript was rejected by several publishers. His one offer for publication came with the proviso that he limit the number of inkblots to six in order to reduce the cost of publication. Rorschach refused. He did revise the manuscript, however, and tried with another round of publishers. Rorschach's friend Walter Morganthaler championed Rorschach's book and was able to obtain a contract with a small publisher, the House of Bircher, in Bern. Once again, the cost of reproducing the inkblots was an issue for the publisher. Rorschach had to revise his manuscript again, this time describing and including replications of only the ten inkblots he used most frequently. Little did the publishers know what a significant impact their refusal to publish fifteen inkblots would have upon the future of psychological assessment.

In addition to reducing the number of Rorschach inkblots, the House of Bircher changed the test in ways they could never have foreseen in 1921. Reproduction of the inkblots altered the stimuli in three ways. The reproduced inkblots were smaller than the original, and some of the colors were slightly different. The most important alteration to the test stimuli, however, was the introduction of shading in the reproduced figures. Rorschach's original inkblots were all solid colors; there were no variations in shading. When the blots were reproduced for publication, there were marked differences in the degree to which the ink saturated the plates. As a consequence, the figures that appeared in *Psychodiagnostik* were very different than the blots studied by Rorschach. As we describe elsewhere in this chapter, how examinees use the variations in shading to form percepts is believed to reveal important information about their personality. The House of Bircher's failure to accurately reproduce the Rorschach figures resulted in a whole new dimension of test interpretation.

as a diagnostic instrument were sewn. Unfortunately, Rorschach died of complications of appendicitis in 1922, one year after the publication of his famous book. He was 37 years old.

There was not a strong response to Rorschach's book during the short period of time between its publication and his untimely death. Very few copies of the manuscript sold and the original publisher declared bankruptcy not long after Rorschach's death (although Rorschach's book was not to blame). His work might have had little impact upon psychiatry or clinical psychology had it not been for three of Rorschach's close friends: Walter Morganthaler, Emil Oberholzer, and Georgi Roemer (Erdberg & Exner, 1984). These three men continued to teach Rorschach's method and to keep the Rorschach alive.

Born in Europe, the Rorschach grew to prominence in the field of psychological assessment in the United States. Five psychologists with very distinct background became interested in the Rorschach and promoted its development in the United States: Samuel Beck, Bruno Klopfer, Zygmut Piotrowski, Marguerite Hertz, and David Rapaport (Erdberg & Exner, 1984). Although beyond the scope of this chapter, the story of how each of these psychologists got involved with the Rorschach and their influences upon the test's development make for fascinating reading. The interested reader should see Chapter 1 of *The Rorschach: A Comprehensive System* by John Exner (1986) for a full account.

Although Beck, Klopfer, Piotrowski, Hertz, and Rapaport shared ideas about the Rorschach, it would inaccurate to say that they worked together to popularize the test. The fact was that each had his or her own ideas about the test and their disagreements about the instrument were frequently aired in professional journals—often times in hostile exchanges. One consequence of this rancor was that five different systems for administering, scoring, and interpreting the Rorschach were popularized in the United States. While these approaches shared common features (e.g., each used the same ten inkblots; administration always included a free-association phase followed by inquiry about the aspects of the blot used in the response), they were clearly five distinct Rorschach systems (Erdberg & Exner, 1984; Exner, 1986). The two most popular systems were those developed by Beck and Klopfer. Beck, whose training was in experimental psychology, insisted upon the development of extensive normative data and rigorous validation of each interpretive element. Klopfer, on the other hand, who was influenced by phenomenological thinking, encouraged examiners to use their own experience and judgment in coding and interpreting material (Erdberg & Exner, 1984).

The various approaches to the Rorschach can be organized into two types (Weiner, 1977). First, the test can be viewed as a perceptual-cognitive task. Here the basic task is to organize an ambiguous stimulus into something that is meaningful. How a person goes about this task is thought to represent how he or she would behave in situations that share some of the same elements with the testing situation. For example, the person who focuses upon minute details of the test stimuli and is not able to organize these details into a meaningful integrated percept would be expected to deal with real-life situations in a similar manner. One might say that such a person has a difficult time seeing the forest because all the trees demand his or her attention. In this approach to Rorschach interpretation it is not the content of the responses so much as the structure that is important. Emphasis is placed upon how color, form, and location determine the choice of responses.

The second type of approach to interpretation sees the central value of the Rorschach method as being a "stimulus to fantasy" (Erdberg & Exner, 1984). This type of interpretive strategy places greater emphasis upon the content of responses. The person's responses are viewed as symbolic representations of internal personality dynamics. An example may help to illustrate this approach to interpretation. Very early in one of the authors' graduate training he administered the Rorschach to a 17-year-old client. In response to the first card, the young man stated, "It looks like a bat." This is a common response to Card 1 of the Rorschach. When the examiner asked if the subject saw anything else in the inkblot, there was a long delay before the young man responded, "A hollow log." Approaching the task as a stimulus to fantasy, the author's supervisor saw great significance in the second response. By responding "A hollow log," the examinee was communicating something important about his self-perception. The supervisor saw the response as the youth's way of saying, "I don't know who I am. Behind my exterior facade there is nothing there. I am hollow."

Although very popular among clinicians, early evaluation of the Rorschach from a psychometric perspective found the instrument wanting (e.g., Cronbach, 1949; Eysenck, 1952; Holzberg, 1960; Jensen, 1959; Windle, 1952; Zubin, 1954). One of the difficulties in evaluating the Rorschach lay in the variability across systems. There really was no Rorschach test, per se. Rather, there were many Rorschach methods. There were many other difficulties with the test as a psychometric instrument as well. The following problems have proven particularly strong impediments to establishing the reliability and validity of the instrument: variability in the total number of responses, the influence of examiner effects, the individual significance attributed to specific blots, and the interdependence of scores. In a 1952 review of the literature on the reliability of the Rorschach, Hans Eysenck drew the following conclusion: "The literature here is in such a confused state that it is almost impossible to derive any agreed conclusions" (p. 164).

Defenders of the Rorschach have sometimes argued that in the hands of an expert, the instrument has great validity. They emphasize the need to evaluate the examiner and the instrument together. Holzberg (1960, p. 374), for example, argued, "the Rorschach method cannot be isolated from the interpreter, the Rorschach and the psychologist being one integral methodology." Arguments such as these cannot be defended from a scientific perspective because to do so would allow one to dismiss evidence contradictory to one's view. Negative findings about the validity of the Rorschach are assumed to be due poor examiners; examiners who produce positive findings are assumed to be expert.

By the 1960s the Rorschach had a poor reputation as a psychometric instrument. Among the many problems with the Rorschach, those most frequently cited included: "(a) lack of standardized rules for administration and scoring, (b) poor interrater reliability, (c) lack of adequate norms, (d) unknown or weak validity, and (d) susceptibility to situational influences" (Wood, Nezworski, & Stejskal, 1996, p. 3). In contrast, the instrument continued to be extremely popular among clinicians, the majority of whom simply ignored formal scoring systems or developed their own idiosyncratic methods of interpreting their findings that borrowed from one or more interpretive systems (Exner & Exner, 1972). Survey studies found that less than 20 percent of clinicians faithfully adhered to a single scoring/interpretive system (Exner, 1986). For a discipline that emphasized the relationship between science and practice, the situation was an embarrassment.

Contemporary Rorschach Use. Despite its many detractors, the Rorschach has not gone away. It was has been called "a test that has repeatedly outlived its obituaries" (Peterson, 1994, p. 396). Contemporary efforts to understand and use the Rorschach in a scientifically defensible manner were spearheaded by John Exner. Exner established the Rorschach Research Foundation in 1968, whose original goal was to study the strengths and weaknesses of each of the five major Rorschach systems. By the early 1970s the thrust of the foundation's efforts had shifted to the development of a new system that integrated those features of the existing systems that had empirical support and to establish an empirical foundation for aspects of the Rorschach that appear to have the greatest clinical utility. For the past thirty-plus years, Exner's foundation (known by most people as *Rorschach Workshops*) has worked to develop a psychometrically sound Rorschach system (Exner, 1991, 1993; Exner & Weiner, 1994).

Exner's "Comprehensive System" for the Rorschach combined those elements of the earlier Rorschach systems that had the most empirical support. Those components of the other systems with the best reliability and validity data were included. Exner standardized administration, scoring, and interpretation, basing his system on empirical comparisons among the various practices. Exner's system is essentially atheoretical. It is not based upon a particular theory of personality or psychopathology. Rather, the system is based upon what works. For example, if a certain combination of scores has been shown to reliably distinguish people with schizophrenia from those without the disorder, then this set of scores was included in the Comprehensive System.

The Exner system places greater emphasis upon the structure of responses rather than their content. Each response is coded on several scoring categories (see below). The "structural summary" is a compilation of score totals, ratios, among various scoring categories, and percentages. In all over 50 percentages, ratios, and scores are included in the structural summary. Interpretation is based upon this summary record. Some inferences are based upon a single scoring category, others are based upon a combination of two or more findings. More complex inferences are based upon complex groupings of various score summaries. For example, the *Egocentricity Index* is derived by adding the number of "pair" responses (e.g., two teddy bears, two rocket ships) to the number of reflection responses (e.g., a dog looking in a mirror, a mountain reflected in a lake) times three and divided by the total number of responses. The Exner system produces scores on several indices such as this (e.g., *Schizophrenia Index, Depression Index,* and *Suicide Constellation*) and recommends cut-off scores for each, which allows for inferences about the likelihood that certain conditions or disorders are present.

Exner's Comprehensive System has continued to evolve over the past twenty-five-plus years since the publication of the first edition of *The Rorschach: A Comprehensive System* (Exner, 1974). Exner and his colleagues have collected a great deal of normative data on normal children, adolescents, and adults as well as people suffering with a variety of mental health conditions. They have generated a great deal of data supporting the inter-rater reliability of the scoring method and the validity of various inferences drawn from test scores. Exner Workshops regularly sponsors workshops and seminars in which clinicians and researchers are trained to administer and score the Rorschach according to Exner's well-worked-out system. Adequately trained testers have been shown to have high rates of interscorer reliability. The Exner system has increased in popularity to the point at which now it is considered by most to be the standard approach to Rorschach assessment. This has resulted in improved quality and quantity of Rorschach research (e.g., Masling, 1997; Shontz & Green, 1992; Weiner, 1996, 1997).

Exner's Comprehensive System clearly marks an advance above the first generation of Rorschach methods. However, the system is not escaped criticism. Some take issue with the atheoretical approach (e.g., Lerner, 1991). Others continue to warn that even Exner's approach to the Rorschach falls short on psychometric grounds and question the data that appear to support Exner's approach to the Rorschach (e.g., Garb, Florio, & Grove, 1998; Wood et al., 1996a, 1996b). Commonly cited criticisms of the Exner system include the following: (1) Interscorer reliability estimates reported by Exner are inflated since they are based upon statistical procedures that take advantage of chance agreements (see Wood et al., 1996a); (2) Exner's books (e.g., Exner, 1991, 1993; Exner & Weiner, 1994) selectively review literature on the validity of the various scores, ratios, and percentages included in the structural summary, ignoring studies published by other researchers that yield contradictory findings; (3) the data supporting the reliability of the Exner scoring system are based upon carefully trained raters who work for Rorschach Workshops; field trials that examine the reliability of clinicians in the field are few and far between; (4) administration, scoring, and interpretation of the Rorschach using the Comprehensive System is extremely time-consuming raising questions about cost-benefit analysis and incremental validity. For example, there are much easier ways of assessing whether a client is depressed compared to the client and professional time needed to derive a score on Exner's Depression Index; (5) interpretations of the meaning of various Rorschach scores often have not been subject to cross-validation; (6) most of the research supporting the Comprehensive System has been produced by Exner and his colleagues at the Rorschach Workshops. Many of the studies cited by Exner are unpublished. A significant portion of the research supporting the Exner system, therefore, has not been reviewed by other scientists. In the science of psychology, research is typically reviewed by other experts in the field before publication in what are sometimes referred to as "peer-reviewed" journals. Independent scholars have not had the opportunity to scrutinize much of the research basis for the Comprehensive system.

While Exner is the best-known contemporary approach to the Rorschach, it is not the only game in town. Aronow and his colleagues (1994, 1995) have developed an approach in which the Rorschach is used as standardized clinical interview. Interpretation focuses upon the content of the responses rather than perceptual or structural determinants. The authors do not recommend their approach for research purposes but suggest this use of the Rorschach in clinical settings in which clinicians are interested in developing an idiographic understanding of their client. Lerner (1991) has developed an approach to the Rorschach that is explicitly tied to psychoanalytic theory. As might be expected from a psychoanalytic approach, Lerner views the fundamental value of the Rorschach as an instrument for accessing the unconscious working of clients' minds.

Administration, Scoring, and Interpretation.   The following overview of Rorschach administration and scoring is based upon the Exner method. For a discussion of alternative methods, the interested reader might see Aronow, Reznikoff, and Moreland (1994) or Lerner (1991).

There are two phases to the administration of the Rorschach: the Response (or Association) phase and the Inquiry Phase. The Response phase starts when the subject is presented with the first inkblot and the question *"What might this be?"* The examiner writes down the subject's responses verbatim. Questions from the subject about the acceptable responses or procedures are responded to nondirectively (e.g., Subject: "Can I turn it?" Examiner: "It's up to you." S: "Do you want me to show you where I see it?" E: "If you like."). The Response phase proceeds through all ten inkblots in the same manner—the examiner hands each card to the subject and records everything that he or she says. Subjects are not limited to the number of responses they give to each blot. Exner recommends taking the card from the subjects after six responses to the first card and after five response to any of the next nine cards.

The Inquiry phase begins after the subject has had a chance to respond to all ten Rorschach cards. The purpose of the Inquiry phase is for the examiner to gather enough information so that all responses can be scored adequately. In the Inquiry phase, the examiner tries to find out what it was about each card that led the subject to give the response. The instructions for the Inquiry phase include the following: "*I want you to help me see what you saw. I'm going to read what you said, and then I want you to show me where on the blot you saw it and what there is there that makes it look like that, so that I can see it too. I'd like to see it just like you did, so help me now.*"

In scoring a Rorschach protocol, the examiner must identify the location on the blot used in creating the response. For example, if the subject uses the entire blot it is scored W (Whole); areas commonly used to form percepts are scored D (Common Detail); and unusual sections of the blot are scored Dd (Unusual Detail). If the subject uses the white space it is scored S (White Space Details). In addition to location, responses are scored for the "determinants" used to form the response. Scoring the determinants is extremely important since the totals, percentages, and ratios of various determinants is what appears on the structural summary, which is the basis for Rorschach interpretation. Some of the basic categories of determinants are *Form* (e.g., Response: "A bat." Inquiry: "You can see the wings here, the head here and the feet here."), *Movement* (e.g., R: "It looks like two women dancing." I: "Just the way it looks like they are swirling around" [a human movement response]; R: "The space shuttle blasting off." I: "This looks like fire coming out of the bottom and it looks like it is shooting up in the air" [an inanimate movement response], *Color* (e.g., R: "Blood." I: "The red looks like splattered blood."), *Texture* (e.g., R: "A bearskin rug." I: "This part looks furry."), and *Shading* (e.g., R: "Smoke." I: "Just the way the shade varies from gray to black.").

Interpretation of the Rorschach protocol is based upon an analysis of the frequency with which different determinants are used by the subject to forms responses, the ratio of one type of determinant to another, and the percentage of the total number of responses that used certain determinants. What follows is brief sampling of the kinds of interpretations that are associated with different types of determinants. The inclusion of some human movement responses in a Rorschach protocol is generally viewed positively. The absence of any such response suggests interpersonal deficits. The quality of the human movement responses is important. Human movement that is frequently aggressive (e.g, "Two warriors trying to stab each other") is associated with aggressive verbal and nonverbal behavior. How subjects use color in creating their responses is thought to indicate something important about their emotional life. Well-formed responses that integrate color into the percept suggest that the subject can manage his or her emotional responses effectively (e.g., R: "A crab." I: "These look like legs and claws and the red reminded me of a crab."). On the other hand, complete denial of the color in the blots (i.e., color is never used as a determinant) suggests that the subject tends to stifle emotional expression. Finally, poorly formed responses that are based upon only the color of the blot suggests that the subject may be impulsive and has poor control over emotional expression (e.g., R: "A party." I: "It's just all the color, man."). Texture responses are thought to suggest dependency needs. A woman who sees a furry stuffed animal in every inkblot would be thought to be highly dependent and to have a strong need for nurturance.

The above examples are only a small representation of the many factors considered when interpreting a Rorschach protocol. Remember, the Exner system produces over 50 totals, ratios, and percentages to be interpreted. The plethora of information one might get from a Rorschach protocol is seen by some as the instruments strength and by others as its curse. Clinicians who use the instrument view it as a rich source of information from which they can develop hypotheses about their clients. For the more empirically minded psychologist, the sheer volume of information gleaned from a protocol presents a nightmare for interpretation. For this psychologist, the Exner system can't be accepted as a whole. The validity of each interpretation needs to be demonstrated. He or she needs to know who was in the sample upon which this interpretation was validated and whether the findings were ever checked on an independent sample. What were the percentages of false-positive and false-negative findings? Because these types of data are often difficult to identify, many psychologists remain skeptical about the Rorschach method.

Thematic Apperception Test

The Thematic Apperception Test (TAT) was first described in 1935 in an article by Christina Morgan and Henry Murray. Murray and his colleagues developed the test at the Harvard Psychological Clinic and he described the method more fully in his 1938 book, *Explorations in Personality.* In the TAT the examinee is shown a series of ambiguous sketches and asked to create a story about what he or she thinks is going on in each picture. Murray argued that the test was a valuable method of getting at aspects of the client's personality that are unconscious or which the client does not wish to reveal. The TAT, Murray (1943, p. 1) writes, is:

> [a] method of revealing to the trained interpreter some of the dominant drives, emotions, sentiments, complexes, and conflicts of personality. Special value resides in its power to expose underlying inhibited tendencies which the subject is not willing to admit, or cannot admit because he is unconscious of them.

In its original form, the TAT was intimately tied to Murray's theory of personality. Murray's personality theory emphasized the importance of each individual's psychological *needs.* Primary (or *viscerogenic*) needs derive from the necessity to satisfy certain physiological cravings. The needs for water, food, sex, and shelter from the elements are examples of primary needs. Secondary (or *psychogenic*) needs are more psychological in nature. They originally derive from primary needs but do not have strong connection to biological processes. Examples would include needs for achievement, affiliation, autonomy, and recognition. Murray (1938) lists twenty-six different needs. While listing needs simplifies matters, Murray recognized that needs do not function in isolation. They may conflict, in which case the satisfaction of one need interferes with the satisfaction of another (e.g., the need for dominance and the need for affiliation), or there can be a *fusion* of needs in which different needs produce the same behavior (e.g., the need for power and the need for achievement).

For Murray, understanding of personality cannot be accomplished by understanding only the individuals needs, but must also include an understanding of "press." Press refers to the determinants of behavior that lie in the environment. "The press of an object is what it can do to the subject or for the subject—the power that it has to affect the well-being of the subject in one way or another" (Murray, 1938, p. 121). Press is made up, not only of objective aspects of the environment, but also the person's subjective interpretation of the world. By understanding not only a person's motives but also the ways in which he or she views the environment, we are more likely to be successful at understanding and predicting behavior. *Thema* is the interaction between needs and press. The emphasis in Murray's theory of personality is on idiographic understanding of the individual personality. What are the strongest needs for the individual, how do the needs interact, and what aspects of the environment are important in determining behavior?

The TAT was developed by Murray to study his theory of personality. Thus, the original interpretive strategies were designed to yield information relevant to his theory. Murray's test, more than his theory, has had a strong impact upon clinical psychology.

Administration and Scoring.   There are thirty-one TAT cards, each with a black-and-white sketch or picture. Some of the pictures are recommended for adult men, others for adult women, some for both men and women and others for boys and girls between ages 7 and 14. Each picture depicts some kind of ambiguous event. Murray (1943) recommended a standard set of twenty cards be used for men and women in a specific order. In clinical practice, psychologists tend to pick a set of cards based upon the themes that the cards are believed to pull for and the psychologist's preferences. Researchers often choose a standard subset of the cards.

Typically, the examinee is asked to tell a story about the picture, explaining what each character is doing, what each one is thinking and feeling, what led up to the situation, and how it turns out. The examiner records the subject's response verbatim. Audio recording is often used to assure that the story is gotten word for word. If the subject leaves out part of the story, the examiner is allowed to ask for more information (e.g., "What led up to this?" "How does it turn out?").

The first task for the test interpreter is to identify the "hero" or "heroine" of the story. This is the central character. The assumption is that the hero or heroine represents the subject. The second task is to identify the motivations and feelings of the hero or heroine. These provide clues about the subject's needs. Third, the situational forces impacting upon the hero and heroine are identified. What interferes with the hero's efforts to achieve his goal? What environmental resources does the heroine draw upon? The goal here is to develop hypotheses about press. The fourth level of analysis is to identify the themes, or the interactions between the hero or heroine and his or her environment. Certain TAT cards are designed to pull for information about certain common themes such as parent-child interactions and heterosexual situations (Groth-Marnat, 1990).

Evaluation.   Perhaps the biggest challenge in evaluating the TAT is that the methods employed under this label are quite diverse. Three factors contribute to this diversity. First, while Murray recommended a certain set of cards for adult men and another set for women, others who have worked with the TAT have chosen different subsets of the thirty-one pictures. The result is that one study of the TAT may employ a totally different set of projective stimuli than another. The second factor is the variety of administration and scoring methods that have been employed. In the 1970s a half-dozen or more approaches to the TAT were taught in graduate-level assessment courses (Vane, 1981). Finally, there is the distinction between what takes place in a research setting and what actually happens in the offices of clinicians who employ the TAT in practice. Clinicians choose the cards they prefer and very few use objective scoring systems when interpreting TAT responses (Klopfer & Taulbee, 1976). Box 8.2 contains example TAT stories along with interpretive comments.

BOX 8.2

Example TAT Stories and Commentary

The following are example TAT stories produced by two individuals, John and Amy, followed by commentary about the stories. The stories and commentary are copied verbatim from Newmark (1996, pp. 173, 181–182).

Card 4: A woman is clutching the shoulders of a man whose face and body are averted as if he were trying to pull away from her.

> **JOHN:** This reminds me of a 1940s movie of some sort with swashbuckling hero—Rhett Butler character—Dietrich or somebody saying, "Don't go! Don't go!" "But I have to." Sort of like High Noon or something. So he'll go take care of the bad guys coming in on the train and he and she will go off in the sunset together and live happily ever after.

Commentary: This story provides distance from the client and a tongue-in-cheek vision of stereotyped roles for men and women. An honest, sincere, self-searching young man should not deal with this critical card in such casual terms. The matters portrayed here appear to be of central importance and it is possible to wonder whether he feels that relationships and romantic love are beyond his grasp.

> **AMY:** This woman wants this man's attention and, well, she wants it in a physical way—not sure if necessarily sexual—might be because of eyes half-closed, veiling. He's looking away, not looking at anything in picture—fact of picture on wall behind head, he's thinking of another woman. . . . I can't even think of a situation that could lead up to this. He's not being very responsive to her, not doing it intentionally to get her to act that way. Doesn't care either way—what she does. She obviously cares more about him than he does about her from the picture—but you can't tell. Or think I've decided that she wants some kind of sexual contact with this man. That's why he's turned his head away—thinking of someone else, or doesn't know how to tell her that he doesn't feel the same way.

Commentary: A single theme is repeated here. Sexual focus with physical cues again—"eyes . . . veiling." Man rejects woman because of "thinking" about another woman with resultant lack of responsiveness. Her caring is unrequited. The use of "I" indicates a loss of distance, signaling the intensely personal nature of this story.

(continued)

B O X   **8.2**   **Continued**

Card 13MF: A young man is standing with downcast head buried in his arm. Behind him is the figure of a woman lying in a bed.

> **JOHN:**   ... OK. I see this being 6 A.M.—sun's just coming up and the fellow is wiping brow—whew! What a night! And the woman in the bed is still asleep. I think they are probably college students—hardly any furniture in there—bed looks like made by putting your mattress on the floor. This is a fairly strapping young man—can see muscles—pecs—through shirt. These two people have some affection for each other but I don't think their relationship is going to last any length of time.

Commentary: The departure from conventional storytelling here is the physical description of the young man. The "Whew! What a night!" and the emphasis on physique may constitute a protest that the storyteller is really a lusty, robust male—even macho in the sense of proving or demonstrating male sexual prowess. The other side of the coin, however, is recognition that satisfying a woman sexually (and otherwise as well) is not an easy task. The fragility of the relationship in this story and the potential independence of affection from sexuality suggest that in his own perceptions, at least, the necessary conditions for an enduring relationship are not present.

> **AMY:**   Well, this looks like she's nude. She's in a one-person, single bed. Man looks like he's turned away—sort of anxiety. He's fully dressed. Might be he walked in and saw her undressed. Maybe she wants to have sex with him. Maybe he doesn't want to with her. He's being very dramatic, looks away, putting hands over his eyes. He's in a dilemma. I can't figure out why the bed is so close to the ground. Looks like it's a single bed. Looks like she might be touching his leg with her hand. Might be he's telling her something that he's ashamed of—can't understand why she would be laying there nude if they were having such a serious conversation about something else.

Commentary: The response is immediate here: a nude woman who wants sex and an anxious man who rejects her. There is a physical description of the card and a misinterpretation of "touching his leg" that suggests loss of distance and personalization. The client appears critical, bewildered, and confused about the picture and her interpretation.

With the diversity of approaches that fall under the heading of TAT in mind, one must be careful about drawing overall conclusions about the reliability and validity of the test. Several sets of specific scoring methods have been developed and many of these have been shown to have adequate interscorer reliability (Groth-Marnat, 1990). Typically, these systems show that reliable scores can be obtained on scales that are designed to assess a rather narrow range of personality characteristics such as need for affiliation or achievement. It has been much more difficult to show that two clinicians agree when using the test to develop an overall picture of a clients personality functioning. Internal consistency of the instrument is impossible to evaluate since the various cards are not comparable (Entwisle, 1972). Test-retest reliability coefficients tend to be low (Groth-Marnat, 1990; Dana, 1996).

As one might expect, given the limited support for reliability, the validity of the TAT has been very difficult to establish. The data that most strongly support validity come from studies that have examined the constructs of achievement, affiliation, and power (Lundy, 1988). For example, a positive correlation between need for achievement and grade point average have been found; subjects who score high in need for achievement are seen as more socially attractive and prefer tasks that require greater internal, as opposed to external direction (studies reviewed by Groth-Marnat, 1990).

The validity of the TAT, as it is used by most clinicians in practice, has not been established. Some early studies found that when experienced clinicians produced descriptions of TAT subjects, these descriptions tended to match independent descriptions that were based upon histories (Arnold, 1949; Harrison, 1940; cited in Groth-Marnat, 1990). However, these findings have not been replicated. Laboratory studies raise serious questions about validity. For example, variations in instructions have been shown to have a strong impact upon the types of stories produced by research subjects (Lundy, 1988). Use of marijuana prior to testing influenced the types of stories produced (West, Martindale, Hines, & Rother, 1983).

The TAT seems to be particularly vulnerable to the influence of examiner effects. Interpretation of TAT stories is a subjective process. Questions can be raised about how much of the interpretation reflects important aspects of the client's personality and how much it tells us about the examiner. The contamination of interpretation of projective test findings by clinician-relevant material has been called *eisegesis* (Dana, 1966). In a way, the task of interpreting a TAT story could be viewed as a projective test itself—the examiner responds to an ambiguous stimuli (the TAT stories) and says what he or she thinks it means. The problem of examiner effects is particularly important when the examiner and the test subject are from different cultural backgrounds (Dana, 1993).

Once one of the most frequently used tests by clinical psychologists (Wade, Baker, Morton, & Baker, 1978), the TAT has decreased in popularity in recent years. Survey studies have shown that by the end of the 1980s its frequency of use had dropped off dramatically (Piotrowski & Keller, 1989; Pitrowski & Lubin, 1990). The TAT, however, has spawned some interesting offspring. The Tell-Me-A-Story (TEMAS) is a picture-story-telling task that is designed for use with cultural minorities (Constantino, Malgady, & Rogler, 1988). This test uses pictures of Hispanic and African American characters in situations suggesting interpersonal conflict. The Senior Apperception Test is designed for elderly clients (Bellack, 1993). The pictures pull for themes that would be relevant to older clients (e.g., loneliness, family conflict). A TAT-type of test has been developed for children who have been maltreated. Some of the images suggest abuse, others neglect, and others contain courtroom themes (Caruso, 1988). The test is designed to gather information about a child's experiences as well as attitudes and feelings about these experiences.

Projective Drawings

What does an artist's work tell us about the artist? Does the evolution of Picasso's work over his lifetime tell us important things about changes in his personality? Emmanual Hammer (1958) thought it did: "when an artist paints a portrait, he paints two, himself and the sitter " (p. 8). If an artist's creations provide us clues about the artist as a person, what about the doodles and sketches the rest of us produce? Can we tell something important about a person based on marks made on a scratch pad while talking on the phone? It is intuitively appealing to think that the answer is yes. Surely the person whose doodles include lightning bolts and arrows is different from the one who draws bunny rabbits and kittens. But can we agree on what the doodles mean about each person, and if we agree, do our speculations match up with what we know about the person from other sources? That is, as scientist-practitioners, psychologists should not be satisfied with the intuitive appeal of drawing analysis. Questions of reliability and validity arise when we begin to think about drawings as psychological tests.

The first effort to develop a formal psychological test based upon drawings was made by Florence Goodenough. Her *Draw-A-Man Test* (Goodenough, 1926) was actually proposed as a method of assessing children's intellectual development. The test was updated by Harris (1963). The Goodenough-Harris version of the test has standardized administration and scoring procedures and reasonable norms. Interestingly, although it was the first test developed based upon the interpretation of drawings, the Goodenough-Harris test may be the most psychometrically sound projective drawing test in contemporary use (Groth-Marnat, 1990).

Perhaps it is not surprising, given the history of our field, that in the 1940s and 1950s there developed a strong interest in the use of drawings as a projective test of personality. Machover (1949) gave us the *Draw-A-Person* test and Buck (1948) gave us the *House-Tree-Person.* As the name suggests, in the latter test, the subject is asked to draw a house, a tree and a person. In later variations of the House-Tree-Person, the subject is first asked to draw the items in pencil and a second time in crayon (Jolles, 1952, 1971). In addition, the *Draw-A-Family* (Hulse, 1971) and *Kinetic Family Drawing* (Burns, 1970) were developed to assess not only personality but also family dynamics. The popularity of the latter test grew with the development and popularization of family therapy.

Specific instructions and detailed scoring criteria have been developed for all of these drawing tests (see, for example, Koppitz, 1968, 1984). It is fair to say, however, that in clinical settings these scoring/interpretive procedure generally are ignored. Instead, intuition and clinical lore guide interpretation. Box 8.3 contains some examples of common interpretations.

Psychometrically, it has been difficult to establish the reliability and validity of projective drawing tests. Early reviews of the literature were quite negative (e.g., Harris, 1972; Suinn & Oskamp, 1969; Swensen, 1957, 1968). When global ratings of subjects based upon their projective drawings are made, some studies have found reasonable reliability and validity (Groth-Marnat, 1990; Kahill, 1984). The poorest showing, psychometrically speaking, has been for interpretations based upon specific aspects of the drawings (e.g., pencil pressure, head size, eyes).

One of the more intriguing findings in the research on projective drawings has less to do with what they can tell us about clients and more to do with what they tell us about clinicians. Even when they are fully aware of the problems with reliability and validity, clinicians tend to put stock into their interpretations of projective drawings. The term *illusory correlation* was coined by Chapman (1967) to describe the tendency of people to see relationships between things that they think should go together—even when faced with evidence that there is no real connection. In one study, for example, undergraduate subjects were presented with a series of human figure drawings and a list of symptoms of psychiatric patients who had produced the drawings. The students perceived an association between aspects of the drawings and patient characteristics. The interesting thing about these associations is that

BOX **8.3**

Interpretations of Human Figure Drawings

The following interpretations are taken from a chapter by Leonard Handler (1996) titled *The Clinical Use of Drawings: Draw-A-Person, House-Tree-Person, and Kinetic Family Drawings.*

Head. The head is considered to be very significant when interpreting human figure drawings since the head is thought to be the seat of fantasy and intellectual life. A very large head might be interpreted to mean that a client has a strong fantasy life. Alternatively, it might signal that a client has an inflated self-image, overvalues intellectual skills, or perhaps aggressiveness. When the head is unusually small, it might be interpreted as a sign of feelings of inadequacy, sexual impotence, intellectual inadequacy, or low self-esteem. If there is a great deal of hair on the head it may indicate sexual preoccupation or possibly compensation for feelings of sexual incompetence. The absence of hair might be interpreted as feelings of sexual weakness, castration fears, or low physical energy.

Nose. From a psychoanalytic perspective, the nose is seen as a phallic symbol. A pronounced nose might be viewed as a sign of sexual striving. From a less analytic perspective, the nose is viewed as an indicator of male clients' need for power. Failure to include a nose at all in the drawing may indicate shyness, social or sexual withdrawal, or feelings of inadequacy

Ears. Large ears are suggestive of paranoid tendencies and may give clues of auditory hallucinations. It is not unusual for the ears to be omitted altogether in drawings produced by normal subjects.

Beards/Mustaches. The inclusion of facial hair is often interpreted as an effort by male subjects to enhance masculinity and sexual status. It can suggest a need to compensate for feelings of inadequacy.

Breasts. When unusually large breasts are produced by a male subjects it is thought to indicate emotional immaturity, maternal overdependence, psychosexual immaturity, and strong dependency needs. For women, large breasts suggest identification with a dominant mother, exhibitionism, and possibly narcissistic tendencies.

Hands. The use of hands in a drawings is believed to be indicative of interpersonal relations and desire for affection. The person who produces a drawing in which the hands are behind the back might be viewed as evasive. It might be hypothesized that this individual harbors guilt feelings about masturbation. Clenched fists suggest anger and aggressive tendencies. Outstretched hands may be seen as a plea for help or an invitation for interpersonal contact. Failure to produce fingers might be taken as a sign of a lack of confidence in interpersonal relationships.

Profile View. When the face is drawn in profile it suggests a tendency to be evasive and a reluctance to face, or openly communicate, with others. Social withdrawal or at least a reserved interpersonal style is expected. A profile drawing might also suggest oppositional tendencies.

they were very similar to the interpretations that are frequently made by individuals with expertise in projective testing (e.g., large head means strong fantasy life). In another study, subjects were told that interpretive statements about a set of human figure drawings were "correct." They were then given a list of personality descriptors and asked to describe what aspects of the drawings were associated with the descriptors. Subjects tended to ignore the "correct" associations they had been taught. Instead they listed intuitively derived associations (e.g., big eyes mean paranoia; Chapman & Chapman, 1967). Research with psychology graduate students and professional psychologists as subjects have shown that they are as susceptible to illusory correlations as are undergraduates (Chapman & Chapman, 1967, 1969; Starr & Katkin, 1969).

Interest in projective drawings peaked in the 1950s and 1960s. At one point, projective drawings were second to the Rorschach as the most popular tests used in mental health facilities (Sundberg, 1961). The publication of several negative reviews of the validity of these tests dented their popularity. Nonetheless, these tests have continued to be used frequently. Survey studies have found them to be among the more frequently used tests (Lubin et al., 1984, 1985; Piotrowski & Zalewski, 1993; Prout, 1983). For the scientifically minded psychologist it is difficult to explain the longevity of projective drawing tests. Perhaps one method of reconciling the dismal psychometric findings with the high frequency of use is not to think of these methods as tests at all. At the conclusion of a review of the literature on adult human figure drawings, Kahill (1984) offered the following suggestion:

> . . . rather than making futile attempts to turn itself into a scientific instrument, figure drawing should more properly take its place as a rich and potentially valuable clinical tool that can provide working hypotheses and a springboard for discussion with the patient. (p. 288)

Objective Methods

It is traditional to distinguish objective from projective personality scales. Objective personality tests are probably more accurately described as *self-report inventories* since these instruments ask respondents to report on their behavior, attitudes, emotions and so on. There are a variety of characteristics that distinguish objective from projective personality tests. For self-report inventories, respondents are forced to choose among a set of possible responses (e.g., true or false). Scoring of these measures involves much less judgment than projective tests and the purpose of the test items is more obvious. For example, most people might guess that the test item "I cry easily" is getting at depression; but what a false response to the item "I sometimes tease animals" means about the person is less clear. (Both items are taken from the MMPI and are included in scale 2—Depression.)

Like projective tests, self-report inventories are not used exclusively for the purposes of identifying personality characteristics. While they are commonly referred as "personality tests," they are used to assess such things as mood states, attitudes, interpersonal style, and psychopathology.

Typically, objective personality tests consist of a series of statements, most of which are self-referent (e.g., "I have never been in trouble with the law"), and respondents are asked to decide whether the statement is true or false for them. Scores on various scales of attitudes, mood, personality characteristics, interpersonal style, and so on are determined by combining respondents' scores on the items that make up the scales. So, for example, a test may have a scale for assessing depression. The scale is made up of a subset of the items from the whole test. A different subset of items is combined to form a scale for anxiety and a third might be combined to assess hostility. While this may seem straightforward enough, two questions need to answered. How are test items chosen? How is it determined which items belong together to form a scale? As it turns out, there are a variety of methods for developing a self-report inventory. In the next section of this chapter, we will describe four well-known inventories, each of which was developed using a different approach to answering these two questions.

MMPI/MMPI-2/MMPI-A

The best-known of the self-report inventories is the *Minnesota Multiphasic Personality Inventory*. The test was originally developed as a diagnostic aid but its applications have expanded far beyond psychiatric diagnosis. The MMPI has been used in counseling, medical, business, military, employment, forensic, and other settings. The literature that has grown around the MMPI since its original publication in 1943 is extensive; by the 1980s over 8,000 research references could by cited (Graham & Lilly, 1984; Lubin et al., 1985).

The MMPI is the best example of a test developed using the *empirical criterion keying method* of test construction (Anastasi & Urbina, 1997). In this approach test items are chosen based upon their ability to discriminate one group of people from another. For example, if 70 percent of people who are depressed respond "true" to the statement "I wish I could be as happy as other people seem to be" and only 15 percent of nondepressed people respond to this same item with "true," it would be chosen to appear on a scale measuring depression. The item is chosen for its ability to distinguish two groups of people, not for its content. To use another example from the MMPI to illustrate, "People generally demand more respect for their own rights than they are willing to allow for others" is an item from scale 1 Hypochondriasis. The item was chosen because individuals identified as hypochondriacal tended to respond "false" and nonhypochondriacal people tended to respond "true." The fact that there is no obvious reason why people who tend to worry about their health and have somatic complaints should be more likely to think this statement false than those without health concerns is not important.

Paul Meehl (1945) captured the rationale behind the empirical criterion keying method well when he wrote:

> . . . the verbal type of personality inventory is *not* most fruitfully seen as a "self-rating" or self-description whose value requires the assumption of accuracy on the part of the testee in his observations of self. Rather is the response to a test item taken as an intrinsically interesting segment of verbal behavior, knowledge regarding which may be of more value than any knowledge of the "factual" material about which the item superficially purports to inquire. Thus if a hypochondriac says he had "many headaches" the fact of interest is that he *says* this. (p. 9)

From this perspective, a self-report test can be viewed as a standardized set of stimuli to which the examinee responds. What is of interest is how people who share certain characteristics tend to respond to the stimuli. The item is of interest if it correlates with a certain set of behaviors.

The MMPI.   The MMPI was developed in the late 1930s by Starke Hathaway, Ph.D., a psychologist, and J. Charnley McKinley, M.D., a neurologist. Starke Hathaway's training was as a physiological psychologist. He worked at the University of Minnesota Hospitals as a research psychologist in the Department of Neurology. J. Charnley McKinley was the head of that department and the person to whom Hathaway reported. Hathaway and McKinley were interested in developing a reliable, valid, and cost-efficient method of diagnosing patients for research purposes. The questionnaire measures available at the time were insufficient for a variety of reasons. Most had been rationally derived based upon their authors' preferred theories. They tended to be narrow in focus (e.g., assessing only neuroticism) and, although face valid, had poor psychometrics when evaluated empirically.

Hathaway and McKinley set out to develop a scale that was empirically derived and would assess a variety of problem areas and was reliable, valid, and efficient to use. They were influenced by the methods K. B. Strong had used in developing a measure of vocational interests. To develop their test, Hathaway and McKinley collected over 1,000 potential items. These were derived from existing personality tests, psychiatric textbooks, case records, interviews with clinicians, and their own clinical experience. Many of the original 1,000 statements were eliminated due to redundancy, lack of clarity, insignificance, or irrelevance. The final pool consisted of 504 items that were considered to be clear, readable, and balanced between positive and negative wording. The items were written as first-person declarative statements so that subjects could respond either true or false.

The next task in the development of the MMPI was to identify a group of patients who were considered to be relatively pure examples of the various diagnostic groups of interest. The diagnostic system utilized at the time of the MMPI's development reflected a view of psychopathology organized around three types of conditions: neuroses, psychoses, and characterological disturbance. Eight specific diagnostic groups were formed for the purposes of test development: Hypochondriasis, Depression, Hysteria, Psychopathic Deviate, Paranoia, Psychasthenia, Schizophrenia, and Hypomania. These groups represented the major categories of psychiatric patients being treated at the University of Minnesota Hospitals at the time. As you may have guessed by the names, the diagnostic grouping reflected thinking at that time about classification of psychopathology. The approximately 50 patients in each subgroup were chosen to represent relatively pure examples of the various conditions. For example, the patients in the Psychopathic Deviate category were chosen because they appeared to be good examples of this problem and did not appear to meet criteria for any of the other conditions.

Using the empirical criterion keying method required a comparison group of "normal" people—that is, a group of people who did not seem to suffer with any of these conditions. Normals were family members and friends of patients who were being treated at the hospital. The primary criteria for inclusion in the normal group was willingness to complete the test and the absence of any medical or psychiatric condition for which the person was receiving treatment. The sample of 724 normals were closely representative of the population of individuals living in Minnesota in the 1930s.

Once data were collected from the normals and the psychiatric patients, their responses could be compared. Any item that correctly differentiated the two groups would be included on that scale. This was determined by examining the proportion of true versus false responses given by the patient sample compared to the proportions of each response given by the normals. Inferential statistics were used to determine whether the proportions or true and false responses were different in the two samples. For example, the item "Much of the time my head seems to hurt all over," was answered true by 4 percent of the normal sample and 12 percent of the hypochondriasis sample. Since this was a statistically significant difference, the item was included in the Hypochondriasis scale (Groth-Marnat, 1990).

In order to remain on the scale, an item had to survive cross-validation. In this procedure, the ability of a test item to distinguish between patients and normals was tested with a new sample of normal subjects. Alternative normal samples used to cross-validate the original MMPI items included recent high school graduates, general medical patients, and Work Projects Act (WPA) workers. The items that survived cross-validation were selected for the eight scales. Normative data, including the means and standard deviations, were calculated for each scale using data from the original normative sample.

Two scales were subsequently added to the original eight MMPI scales: the Masculinity-Femininity scale and the Social Introversion scale. The original intention of the Masculinity-Femininity scale was to identify individuals with a homosexual orientation. Fifty-five items designed to evaluate sexual orientation and sex-role interest patterns were added to the original item pool. A group of identified homosexuals and a group of, presumably, heterosexual male soldiers were administered these items. While very few of these items were found to discriminate between the homosexual and heterosexual samples, they were included anyway because they were somewhat more successful at discriminating men from women in the original normative sample. Items for the Social Introversion scale were chosen if they discriminated between subjects who scored high and those who scored low on another test of social introversion-extroversion.

With the addition of the 55 items for the Masculinity-Femininity scale to the original 504, the total number of MMPI items reached 559. Interestingly, the original MMPI contained 550 unique items. Apparently, the fate of the nine missing items remains a mystery (Groth-Marnat, 1990).

The developers of the MMPI were concerned that the information yielded by their new instrument might not be valid for some respondents because of their test-taking attitude. Test takers might alter the impressions they give by purposely responding to test items inaccurately. In order to assess test-taking attitude, Hathaway and McKinley created four *validity* scales: the Cannot Say (?), the Lie (L), the Infrequency (F), and the Correction (K). The ? scale is a simple count of questions not answered and questions for which the person responded both true and false. The MMPI was considered invalid if too many (i.e., more than 30 items) were left blank. The Lie scale includes items that assess obvious or unsophisticated efforts to present oneself in a favorable light. For example, a false response to the item "I gossip a little at times" suggests that the person is not willing to admit to common foibles. The F scale is composed of items that were endorsed less than 10 percent of the time by the normal sample. A high score on the F scale indicates that the examinee endorsed a high number of unusually deviant items. This can indicate a purposeful intention to appear worse off psychologically than one really is. An exaggeration of symptoms can be seen in people who are malingering (e.g., someone who is faking mental distress or illness in order to avoid some responsibility such as armed service) or in those who are desperate for help. High F scores can also be produced by people who are mentally confused, poor readers, or grossly psychotic.

The final validity scale is the K scale. This is designed to be a more sophisticated measure of psychological defensiveness than the L scale. K scale items comparing psychiatric patients who produced normal MMPI profiles (the defensive sample) from true "normal" subjects who also produced normal MMPI profiles. Later in the MMPI's development, the idea was developed that K scores could be used as a correction to modify the raw score produced by some of the other scales. Some portion of respondents' raw scores on the K scale are added to clinical scales 1, 4, 7, 8, and 9 to correct for the their defensiveness.

Evaluating the examinee's test-taking attitude is usually the first step when interpreting the MMPI. This is accomplished by examining the pattern of scores among the three basic validity scales (L, F, and K). A high score on the L and K scale, accompanied by a low score on F, suggests a "fake good" response style. Here the test taker likely denied problems in an effort to present himself or herself in the best possible light. The opposite pattern of scores (high F with low L and K) suggests the opposite. Here the examinee appeared to have exaggerated psychological distress possibly as a cry for help or to avoid some responsibilities.

The basic MMPI then consisted of the four validity and ten clinical scales listed in Table 8.1. Examination of the pattern of scores among these 14 scales formed the basis for MMPI interpretation. However, these scales were not the only ones developed using the basic MMPI items. Scores of other clinical and research scales were developed over the years. These measures, often referred to as supplemental scales, were usually developed using the same logic as was used for the original scales. Items were selected based upon their ability to discriminate one group of respondents from another. Other MMPI scales were derived through rational inspection of the scale items. Harris and Lingoes (1955, cited in Butcher et al., 1992) developed a popular set of subscales of several of the basic MMPI clinical scales based upon their analysis of the content of the scale items. For example, they developed five subscales of scale 2: D1—Subjective Depression, D2—Psychomotor retardation, D3—Physical Malfunctioning, D4—Mental Dullness, and D5—Brooding. Clinicians use these scales to interpret elevations on scale 2.

The basic MMPI remained unchanged for nearly fifty years. The test is the most widely used clinical testing instrument in history. But the MMPI has not escaped criticism. Perhaps the most damaging criticism of the test is the makeup of the original standardization sample. The "normal" sample was all white, mostly from rural Minnesota, almost all Protestant, largely of Scandinavian descent, who worked as farmers or in blue-collar positions and had an average education level of eighth grade (Graham, 1990). Clearly this group was not representative of the United States. Other commonly identified problems with the MMPI include low to moderate levels of reliability, high item overlap across scales, and high correlations between different scales. In addition, there were widely recognized problems with the content of many test items. Some were poorly worded. For others, the terms used were obsolete or frankly offensive, especially for those items related to sex and religion.

TABLE 8.1 MMPI Validity and Clinical Scales

Scale #	Original Scale Name	Abbreviation	Meaning of High Score
Validity			
	Cannot Say	?	Left many items blank and/or answered both T and F.
	Lie	L	Unsophisticated lying to present self in positive light.
	Frequency	F	Endorsed many unusual items. Fake-bad or very disturbed.
	Correction	K	More sophisticated attempt to present oneself positively.
Clinical			
1	Hypochondriasis	Hs	High degree of concern about health and body functioning.
2	Depression	D	Depressed mood. General dissatisfaction with life.
3	Hysteria	Hy	Somatic complaints and denial of psychological problems.
4	Psychopathic Deviate	Pd	Antisocial attitudes and behavior. Aggressive.
5	Masculinity-Femininity	Mf	Nonstereotypical sex-role interests.
6	Paranoia	Pa	Suspicious. Morally self-righteous. Hypersensitive.
7	Psychasthenia	Pt	Chronic anxiety, indecisiveness agitation, obsessive features.
8	Schizophrenia	Sc	Bizarre though processes. Feels peculiar or different.
9	Hyopmania	Ma	High energy. Elevated mood. Increased activity level.
10	Social Introversion	Si	Shy, introverted, socially inept. Lacks self-confidence.

MMPI-2. After years of discussion and debate, an effort was undertaken in 1982 to revise and restandardize the MMPI. Revision of the MMPI involved several stages (see Butcher, Dahlstrom, Graham, Tellegen, & Kaemmer, 1989). First, a team of recognized MMPI experts was assembled by the test publisher. This team rewrote items that were awkwardly worded or that used obsolete language. In the end, 14 percent of the original MMPI items were rewritten. One hundred and fifty-four new items were also written to cover topic areas that relate to contemporary problems. A version of the MMPI with 704 items was administered to a standardization sample.

The second edition of the MMPI (the MMPI-2) was standardized on a sample of people solicited from several regions of the United States. The normative sample consisted of 2,600 subjects chosen to represent the population according to 1980 U.S. census data on age, gender, minority status, social class, and education. The 704-item version of the MMPI was eventually culled down to 567 items.

A great effort was made to maintain as many characteristics of the original MMPI as possible in the new scale. Consequently, the MMPI-2 kept most of the original scales intact so that fifty-plus years of research findings would be applicable to the new scale. The original validity and clinical scales reappear in the MMPI-2. In addition, however, some new scales have been added.

There are three new validity scales in the MMPI-2. The F(B), or Back Side F scale, was developed to detect a deviant response style to items that appear later in the test. Some subjects become bored and careless and others may change their response style as they work their way through the test. Since all the items of the F scale appear in the first 370 items, they do not detect test-taking attitude for the end of the test. The addition of the F(B) scale was deemed necessary because the items that make up the Content Scales (scales new to the MMPI-2 see below) appear at the end of the test.

Two additional validity scales added to the MMPI-2 were designed to assess psychologically inconsistent responses to similar items. The True Response Inconsistency Scale, TRIN, consists of twenty pairs of items for which it would be logically inconsistent to respond with both true or both false statements (e.g., "Most of the time I feel blue" and "I am happy most of the time"). The TRIN scale is scored so that a high score indicates a tendency to respond true to most items ("yea-saying") and a very low score indicates a tendency to respond with false ("nay-saying"). The Variable Response Inconsistency Scale, or VRIN, is similar. A high score on VRIN indicates that a large number of test items were scored in a logically inconsistent manner. The VRIN score can help one interpret the meaning of a high F scale. If VRIN is also high then the elevated F scale may be due to random responding. Whereas a low VRIN with a high F suggests purposeful exaggeration of psychological distress.

The other new scales for the MMPI-2 are the Content Scales. These scales were not developed using the empirical criterion keying method. Rather, as the name implies, these scales were formed by gathering together items that have similar content. For the MMPI-2 items, three different raters read each item carefully and placed it into a content category. An item was only included in the category if all three raters thought it belonged there. In addition, each item had to correlate .50 or higher with the total score for that content scale in order to be included in the scale. The MMPI-2 content scales are listed in Table 8.2 along with a brief description of each.

MMPI-A.   The MMPI was originally developed for use with an adult population between the ages of 16 and 65 (Hathaway & McKinley, 1940). However, almost from the very beginning the instrument was used with younger adolescents. A considerable research and clinical literature developed about the use of the MMPI with adolescents in psychiatric, substance abuse treatment, correctional, and medical settings (see Butcher et al., 1992, for overview). Despite this literature, normative data for adolescents were not published until the 1970s (Dahlstrom, Welch & Dahlstrom, 1972; Marks et al., 1974) and these norms were based upon data collected decades earlier. Although some have argued for the use of adult normative data for interpreting the MMPI protocols of adolescents (e.g., Hathaway & Monachesi, 1963), there is a considerable amount of research data showing that when adolescents' scores are plotted against adult norms, the results tend to overpathologize the adolescents (Butcher et al., 1992).

TABLE 8.2   MMPI-2 Content Scales

Scale Name	Characteristic of High Scorers
ANX (Anxiety)	Many symptoms of general anxiety, tension, somatic complaints, sleep difficulties, worries, and difficulty concentrating.
FRS (Fears)	Many specific fears including blood, animals, high places, leaving home, dirt, water, and natural disasters.
OBS (Obsessiveness)	Ruminate about problems, difficulty making decisions, excessive worries, may engage in compulsive behaviors such as checking or washing.
DEP (Depression)	Depressed mood, uncertain about the future, unhappy, cry easily, feel hopeless and empty. Suicidal thought may be present.
HEA (Health Concerns)	Many physical symptoms across different body systems including neurological, gastrointestinal, respiratory, and other.
BIZ (Bizarre Mentation)	Report auditory visual or olfactory hallucinations. Paranoid ideation. Strange or peculiar thoughts.
ANG (Anger)	Irritable, grouchy, impatient, easily annoyed, stubborn.
CYN (Cynicism)	Expect hidden or negative motives behind others' actions. Do not trust others.
ASP (Antisocial Practices)	Report problems behaviors during school years, legal difficulties, and beliefs that it is okay to break the law.
TPA (Type A)	Hard-driving, fast moving, work-oriented. Impatient. Tend to become annoyed easily.
LSE (Low Self-Esteem)	Low opinion of themselves. Negative attitudes about their appearance and value. Low self-confidence.
SOD (Social Discomfort)	Uneasy around others. Prefer to be by themselves. Shy.
FAM (Family Problems)	Considerable family discord. Childhood and/or marriage is viewed negatively.
WRK (Work Interference)	Report behavior or attitudes that contribute to poor work performance.
TRT (Negative Treatment Indicators)	Report negative attitudes about doctors and mental health treatment. Believe that no one can understand them.

In 1989, work began on the development of a version of the MMPI designed explicitly for use with adolescents. The MMPI-A, published in 1992, was the result of that work. As was the case with the MMPI-2, the MMPI-A was designed to preserve many features of the original MMPI. In addition, many of the positive features of the MMPI-2 were incorporated into the adolescent version. However, an effort was made to change some of the negative characteristics of the MMPI such as the length, the awkward wording, and the objectionable content. The final instrument was shorter (478 items) and more user-friendly for adolescents. The MMPI-A was standardized on a representative sample of about 1,600 male and female adolescents between the ages of 14 and 18. In addition, a clinical sample of over 700 adolescents recruited from a variety of treatment facilities in the Minneapolis area were used to develop and validate the scale.

The MMPI-A includes the same four validity scales and ten clinical from the original MMPI as well as the additional validity scales included in the MMPI-2. The MMPI-A includes fifteen content scales that were developed using the same methods as the MMPI-2 content scales.

The MMPI-A marks a significant advance over the earlier practice of using of the MMPI with adolescents. Specific strengths of the instrument include normative data from a nationally representative sample, adolescence-relevant content areas, and expanded methods for assessing profile validity. Despite these improvements, the MMPI-A has some noteworthy problems. While 478 items is significantly shorter than 566, it still represents a lot of material for an adolescent to wade through. Successful completion requires considerable sustained attention. Another issue is the reading level required for the test. A seventh-grade reading level is recommended. Many youth seen in clinical settings cannot read at this level. Perhaps the greatest concern is the sensitivity of the test. It has been suggested by some that the MMPI-A has an unacceptably high false negative rate. That is, normal profiles are often produced by adolescents with known psychopathology (Archer & Krishnamurthy, 1996).

Evaluation.   The MMPIs certainly have a lot of positive attributes. They are relatively easy to administer. There is an abundance of books and articles on the instruments to aid clinicians with interpretation. Computer programs exist for administering, scoring, and interpreting the test. As mentioned earlier, it is the most popular clinical instrument of all time, so most mental health professionals are familiar with it, which aids communication. Some of the problems with the original MMPI were addressed with the creation of the MMPI-2 and MMPI-A, but the creation of these new scales has also presented problems. The developers of the new scales tried to correct weaknesses of the old scale without altering it so greatly that research findings and clinical lore that developed around it could not be applied to the new versions. There is considerable debate about whether this goal was achieved. For example, the MMPI-2 manual contains information that allows the examiner to compare scores generated by the MMPI-2 with scores that presumably would have been produced by the same person had he or she completed the MMPI. While some have endorsed this approach as a defensible means of taking advantage of MMPI interpretive data while using the more user-friendly MMPI-2 (Humphrey & Dahlstrom, 1995), others doubt the wisdom of this strategy (Ben-Porath & Tellegen, 1995).

Another commonly cited difficulty with the MMPIs is the use of outdated and misleading labels for the clinical scales. For example, scale 8 (Sc) is the Schizophrenia scale. While the original hope was that this scale could be used to identify individuals who suffer with this disorder, it was quickly demonstrated that that was not the case. While people with schizophrenia tend to score high on this scale, so do people with other severe mental disorders as well as normal people who are experiencing a great deal of stress. The MMPI-2 user will know that a person who scores high on scale 8 may feel alienated and/or apathetic, may have poor family relationships, and tends to hold unusual beliefs. But a high scorer does not necessarily have all of these attributes. Retention of the label invites misinterpretation.

The strengths of the MMPI (e.g., ease of administration, familiarity) may also be viewed as weaknesses since they create the opportunity for misinterpretation. While many mental health professionals are familiar with the behavioral correlates of elevation on the basic validity and clinical scales, they may be less cognizant of the influence of demographic and cultural variables on scale scores. The same pattern of scale scores can have very different meanings based upon the age, ethnicity, education level, and socioeconomic status of the respondent. We know, for example, that elevations on scales 1, 2, and 3 are common in older samples and in people with serious medical conditions (Hecker, Norvell, & Hills, 1989). Scores on Scale 9 tend to decrease with age (Groth-Marnat, 1990). In addition to age, differences have been found between different ethnic groups (Greene, 1987). Research studies with the MMPI frequently reported that African Americans tend to score higher on scales F, 8, and 9 (Green & Kelly, 1988; Smith & Graham, 1981). Hispanics, Asian Americans, and Native Americans all seem to produce patterns of scale scores that are unique to their subgroup (Greene, 1987). Finally, we know that education level influences scale scores. Highly educated respondents tend to produce lower L and F scores and higher scores on scale 5. Valid interpretation of a particular subject's MMPI clinical scale scores requires awareness of these subgroup variations in normative responding.

The MMPI never achieved its original goal of being an efficient method of arriving at a diagnosis. Nonetheless, the instrument can produce valuable clinical information. The MMPIs are best used as methods of developing clinical hypotheses about clients. These hypotheses need to be tested against other information one gathers about the individual.

The Millon Scales

Personality theory did not play a role in the development of the MMPI. Rather, items were selected and scales formulated based upon their ability to discriminate between groups of people. In contrast to this purely empirical approach, some tests have been developed with an explicit theory of personality in mind. The TAT is a good example of a personality test whose development was guided by a particular theory of personality.

The self-report inventories developed by Theodore Millon are probably the best examples of contemporary measures developed in within the framework of a personality theory. The Millon Clinical Multiaxial Inventory (MCMI; Millon, 1983) was derived from Millon's biopsychosocial theory of personality and psychopathology (Millon, 1969, 1981). In the original model, personality types were derived based upon two dimensions: primary sources of reinforcement and pattern of coping behavior. The MCMI is currently in its third edition (MCMI-III; Millon, Davis, & Millon, 1997). The test has evolved to incorporate new empirical findings as well as developments in Millon's thinking about personality.

The theoretical model upon which the MCMI-III is based is grounded in evolutionary theory. According to this view humans are predisposed to behave in certain ways because these behaviors have survival significance. Typically, behaviors are naturally selected because they increase the probability of survival and/or reproduction. Here Millon's thinking is influenced by sociobiologists who examine the interaction between biology and social functioning (e.g., Wilson, 1975, 1978).

Millon's theory holds that there are four basic domains in which evolutionary principles are exhibited: *existence, adaptation, replication,* and *abstraction* (Millon et al., 1997). These domains are viewed as polarities with contrasting survival strategies at each end of the pole. Most "normal" individuals have the capacity to operate at one pole or the other. "Despite the presence of relatively enduring and characteristic styles, adaptive flexibility typifies most normal individuals; that is, they are able to shift from one position on a polar continuum to another as the circumstances of life change" (Millon, 1996, p. 89). *Existence* refers to the tendency to engage in life-enhancing or life-preserving behaviors. At the life-enhancing end, behavior is oriented toward improving the quality of life, while the life-preserving pole is marked by avoiding things that may jeopardize existence. The domain of *adaptation* is viewed as a polarity between passive and active strategies for coping with one's circumstances. In the *Replication* domain, the goal is to produce and protect offspring. The two ends of this polarity are marked by strategies to promote oneself at one end and strategies to protect and nurture others at the other end. The classification system proposed by Millon is embedded in the polarities derived from these first three domains. The basic polarities are pleasure-pain (*existence*), passive-active (*adaptation*), and other-self (*replication*).

The personalities of most healthy people achieve some degree of balance in these polarity pairs. There is flexibility and capacity to adapt to situational demands. In the personality disorders, however, there are either deficiencies, imbalances, or conflicts within each domain. For example, the Avoidant personality is strongly oriented toward avoiding pain and rarely acts in life-enhancing ways. The Avoidant takes an active approach to pain avoidance. The reproductive strategies of the Dependent personality are oriented toward nurturing others and they take a passive approach to their environment.

Millon's personality theory is heady stuff and not easy to grasp with a cursory reading. The central idea is that the personality disorders can be understood as dysfunction in one or more of these evolutionarily driven domains. The implications of theory for the development of the Millon inventories is significant. In stark contrast to the purely empirical (atheoretical) manner in which the MMPI was constructed, the MCMI development was theory driven.

The MCMI was developed and validated in three stages. The first stage of validation Millon calls "theoretical-substantive." In this stage, the items are generated to represent Millon's theoretical framework. The items for each scale were developed on the basis of theoretically derived definition of each syndrome. In the second stage of validation ("internal-structural"), the degree to which the items making up a scale hang together empirically is examined. The internal consistency of the scales is important here. In addition, the degree to which the scales correlate is explored. According to the theory, certain scales should be correlated with one another and others should not. In the third phase of the validation ("external-criterion"), the empirical relationship between the scales and a variety of other measures of the syndromes are examined. Three generations of research were used to examine the external-criterion validity of the MCMI-III. The validation process actually began with the MCMI-I. The relationship between the clinical syndrome scores of the MCMI was compared with various two-point code-types of the MMPI. The second generation of studies looked at the relationship between scale scores and the ratings of diagnostic judges who were experienced clinicians and familiar with Millon's theory. The third generation of validation studies looked at the correlations between the MCMI-III scale scores and several other well-known tests of personality and psychopathology (Millon et al., 1997).

MCMI-III. The MCMI-III is the latest version of Millon's scale for assessing adult personality disorders and psychopathology. The scale was normed on a clinical population. Consequently, the scale scores derived from the subjects' responses to the test items are transformed into base-rate (BR) rather than T-scores or some other scale that assumes a normal distribution. Personality disorders and clinical syndromes are not normally distributed in the clinical population. The point of BR scores is not to define where a person falls on a continuum; rather it is to indicate whether he or she belongs to a particular diagnostic category. The transformation of raw scores to BR scores is based upon estimates of the prevalence of the various personality disorders and clinical syndromes in the population. For example, "if 5 percent of the clinical population is deemed to possess a schizoid pattern as its primary personality style, and another 2 percent the schizoid pattern as a secondary feature, then the raw scores have been transformed so that the normative sample reflects these *prevalence* or *base* rates" (Millon & Davis, 1996, p. 126).

Base rate conversion scores were created by setting BR equal to 0 for a raw score of 0 on the scale. The BR was set to 115 for the maximum raw score and 60 was set as the median raw score for the normative clinical sample. The BR score of 75 was set so that the percentage of subjects in the normative sample who were rated as having the personality or disorder *present* was equal to the estimated base rate of the disorder. The BR of 85 or higher captured the percentage of subjects in the normative sample who were rated as having the disorder *prominent* (McCann & Dyer, 1996).

The MCMI-III has 175 items, which are written at about an eighth-grade reading level. Most clients can complete the scale in 30 minutes or less. There are a total of 28 scales, which are organized into five groups. The instrument is best known as a measure of personality disorder. There are eleven *Clinical Personality Patterns* that closely coincide with the Axis II personality disorders in the DSM-IV (American Psychiatric Association, 1994). Three additional personality scales are organized under the heading of *Severe Personality Pathology.* Under the heading *Clinical Syndromes* are seven scales that assess Axis I disorders commonly seen in outpatient settings. There are also three scales, organized under the heading *Severe Syndromes,* that assess more severe psychopathology such as different forms of psychosis. Table 8.3 lists the MCMI-III scales.

Like the MMPI, the MCMI has scales for measuring test-taking attitude and response bias (scales X, Y, and Z). These scales were created empirically for the MCMI-II by having student subjects respond to the test under specific instructional sets. For example, Scale Y (Desirability) was created by asking subjects to respond in such a manner as to appear as psychologically healthy as possible. Scale Z (Debasement) assesses subjects tendency to overreport or exaggerate problems. Scale X (Disclosure) is not composed of a set of specific test items; rather it is made up of weighted raw scores of the clinical personality pattern scales. Low scores suggest a tendency to be secretive and defensive. High scores suggest that the respondent may be seeking attention or sympathy by overreporting concerns. There is a fourth scale that assesses respondents' approach to the test, the V or Validity scale. This scale consists of three items that have such unusual content that endorsement suggests the

TABLE 8.3   MCMI-III Scales

Scale	Scale Name
Modifying Indices	
X	Disclosure
Y	Desirability
Z	Debasement
V	Validity
Clinical Personality Patterns	
1	Schizoid
2A	Avoidant
2B	Depressive
3	Dependent
4	Histrionic
5	Narcissistic
6A	Antisocial
6B	Aggressive (Sadistic)
7	Compulsive
8A	Passive-Aggressive (Negativistic)
8B	Self-Defeating
Severe Personality Pathology	
S	Schizotypal
C	Borderline
P	Paranoid
Clinical Syndromes	
A	Anxiety
H	Somatoform
N	Bipolar: Manic
D	Dysthymia
B	Alcohol Dependence
T	Drug Dependence
R	Post-Traumatic Stress Disorder
Severe Syndromes	
SS	Thought Disorder
CC	Major Depression
PP	Delusional Disorder

respondent was either not paying attention, responded randomly, or was being purposely oppositional. One of the items, for example, reads, "I flew across the Atlantic thirty times last year." With the exception of a subset of pilots and flight attendants, few people would be honest if they responded true to this item. If a person endorses two or more of these items, the test is assumed to be invalid.

The primary purpose of the MCMI-III is to assist mental health professionals in making diagnostic and treatment decisions for individuals who present with emotional and/or interpersonal difficulties (Millon et al., 1997). The instrument is designed for use with clinical, not normal populations. Remember, the test was developed and normed on a clinical population. It is not appropriate to use the instrument as a general measure of personality functioning for normal subjects. The test developers suggest that outpatient mental health clinics, college counseling centers, general and psychiatric hospitals, and independent or group practices are all appropriate professional settings for using the MCMI-III. The test has also been used criminal and civil forensic settings (McCann & Dyer, 1996).

The MCMI-III can be hand-scored but this is a time-consuming and cumbersome process. The test publisher, National Computer Systems, Inc., offers two scoring options. For a small fee, it will computer-score all 28 scales and provide a profile that includes scale cut-off lines indicating the BR score of 75 and 85. For a larger fee, it will provide not only the profile but a detailed computer-generated analysis of the personality and symptom picture with suggestions for psychotherapy. The test provides information that clinicians can use to form hypotheses about clients. These hypotheses are then tested against information gathered through interviewing, personal history, and other data sources (Millon & Davis, 1996).

Clinicians find many attributes of the MCMI-III appealing. It is considerably shorter and takes much less time to complete than the MMPI. The measure uses diagnostic terms and an organizational structure that is consistent with the contemporary psychiatric classification system. The MCMI has been updated relatively frequently in order to maintain its coordination with new editions of the *Diagnostic and Statistical Manual.* Dr. Millon served on the Personality Disorder Work Group for the DSM-IV and his influence can be seen in the diagnostic criteria. In addition, the MCMI-III manual facilitates comparison between the Clinical Personality Patterns and the DSM-IV personality disorders. The frequent revisions not only keep the test tied with changes in nosology but also help assure that the normative sample is representative of clients seeking professional help. The instrument seems to be a valuable tool to assist clinicians in making diagnostic decisions particularly when there is a question of personality disorder. The measure can also be used for outcome assessment when the treatment target is personality dysfunction (Goncalves, Woodward, & Millon, 1994; Retzlaff, 1996).

There are some noteworthy shortcomings and limitations to the MCMI. First, there is fair amount of item overlap across the various scales that impairs the instruments ability to make differential diagnoses. Second, patients who are experiencing anxiety and depression frequently produce elevations on scales that purport to measure stable personality characteristics (Millon & Davis, 1996). The interaction between "traits" (i.e., personality) and "states" (i.e., clinical syndromes) is inevitable, according to Millon, and is consistent with his view of psychopathology (Millon & Davis, 1996). Other limitations of the instrument include the difficulty of hand-scoring, the relatively high required reading level, and the fact that the instrument is not appropriate for use with normal populations.

Other Millon Scales. The Millon Adolescent Clinical Inventory (MACI; Millon, Millon, & Davis, 1993) is a 160-item true-false inventory designed for use with adolescents between the ages of 13 and 19. The test requires a sixth-grade reading level. The MACI is similar in development and organization to the MCMI. It is designed for use with adolescents in clinical settings. The Millon Behavioral Health Inventory is for use with adults in medical or physical rehabilitation settings (MBHI; Millon, Green, & Meagher, 1982). This instrument is in the process of being updated (Millon et al., 1997). Finally, there is the Millon Index of Personality Styles (MIPS; Millon, Weiss, Millon, & Davis, 1994), which is designed to assess personality functioning in "normal" adults. The MIPS is appropriate for use in counseling settings in which individuals are seeking help with work, family, or social problems. This instrument was standardized on normal adult and college samples. Like the other Millon inventories, the development of the MIPS was guided by Millon's theory about personality functioning.

NEO-Personality Inventory

Factor analysis is a statistical method that examines the interrelationships among a large set of variables. In test construction, the relationships that are examined are among test items. Factor analysis has been used to develop tests of personality. The technique is usually associated with trait theory. In constructing a test of personality, a researcher would administer a set of test items to a large number of people. The intercorrelations among the test items is then calculated and examined. Items that are highly correlated presumably measure the same thing. If items are not strongly related, then they probably are measuring different constructs. In factor analysis, the items that belong together (i.e., are correlated) are organized into factors. Using advanced statistical techniques, factor analysis can determine the number of factors that best describes a set of test items. The content of the items that make up a factor is examined, the researcher names the factor, and then develops hypotheses about what he or she has measured. The reliability and validity of the factor can then be examined using the usual psychometric procedures.

One of the pioneers in the use of factor analysis to develop a measure of personality was R. B. Cattell (1946, 1950, 1957). Cattell collected as many personality trait names as he could find from the dictionary as well as psychological and psychiatric literatures. Combining items that were obviously synonyms, Cattell put together a shorter list of personality trait descriptors. He then had associates rate a large and heterogenous group of adults on these traits. Cattell subjected these trait ratings, along with self-report questionnaire findings, to factor analysis. In this way, he developed a list of the traits that describe human personality. Using factor analytic procedures, Cattell developed the Sixteen Personality Factor Questionnaire (Cattell, Saunders, & Stice, 1950). The 16 PF as the test is called is currently in its fifth edition (Cattell, Cattell, & Cattell, 1993).

A more contemporary model of personality that is based upon factor analytic work is the "Five-Factor Model" (Costa & Widiger, 1994; McCrae & John, 1992; Wiggins & Pincus, 1992). Interestingly, several personality researchers have arrived at the conclusion that five factors can account for the relationships found among a wide range of personality variables. In fact, there is a surprising level of consensus among investigators of trait models of personality (Anastasi & Urbina, 1997). Where there is controversy is in agreeing upon what it is that these five factors measure and what they should be labeled.

Costa and McCrae (1992) have developed a test to assess personality according to their perspective on the Five-Factor Model. The NEO Personality Inventory—Revised (NEO-

PI-R), the latest version of their test, is designed to assess normal personality but is appropriate for use in some clinical settings. The NEO-PI-R provides scores on five major "domains" of personality: Neuroticism (N), Extraversion (E), Openness to Experience (O), Agreeableness (A), and Conscientiousness (C). The name NEO derives from the initials of the first three factors. "NEO" is the proper name of the test, however, not an abbreviation (Costa & McCrae, 1992). In addition to the five domains, the test yields scores on 30 "facets" that represent subfactors of each domain. The NEO-PI-R domains and facets are listed in Table 8.4.

One of the more interesting features of the NEO-PI-R is that it is available in parallel forms. Form S is a self-report version and Form R can be completed by an observer who knows the person well, such as a friend or spouse. Both versions have the same test items, but one is written in the first person (Form S) and the other in the third person (Form R). Both versions yield scores on the five domains and 30 facets.

The five basic traits assessed by the NEO-PI-R are conceptualized as continuous dimensions. These traits are believed to be approximately normal in their distribution in the population. The normative data for each scale, therefore, are approximately normally distributed. The profile form upon which the raw scores are graphed are broken down into five levels: *very low* (T score < 35, 7 percent of normal sample), *low* (T = 35 to 44, 24 percent of sample), *average* (T = 45 to 55, 38 percent of sample), *high* (T = 56 to 65, 24 percent of sample), and *very high* (T > 65, top 7 percent of sample). Given the conceptualization of these traits as dimensional, as opposed to categorical, it is not surprising that the developers of the NEO-PI-R do not offer cut-off scores for the identification of personality types such as "neurotics" or "extraverts." Each domain or facet score of the NEO-PI-R should be compared to the normative sample when interpreting and not compared to the person's other domain or facet scores. A person who scores at the 75th percentile on Depression (N3) and the 25th on Positive Emotions (E6) is more likely to feel depressed and less likely to feel

TABLE 8.4   Revised NEO-Personality Inventory: Domains and Facets

Neuroticism (N)	*Extraversion (E)*	*Openness to Experience (O)*
Anxiety (N1)	Warmth (E1)	Fantasy (O1)
Angry Hostility (N2)	Gregariousness (E2)	Aesthnetics (O2)
Depression (N3)	Assertiveness (E3)	Feelings (O3)
Self-Consciousness (N4)	Activity (E4)	Actions (O4)
Impulsiveness (N5)	Excitement-Seeking (E5)	Ideas (O5)
Vulnerability (N6)	Positive Emotions (E6)	Values (O6)

Agreeableness (A)	*Conscientiousness (C)*
Trust (A1)	Competence (C1)
Straightforwardness (A2)	Order (C2)
Altruism (A3)	Dutifulness (C3)
Compliance (A4)	Achievement (C4)
Modesty (A5)	Self-Discipline (C5)
Tender-Mindedness (A6)	Deliberation (C6)

happy than most people. But since positive emotions are more commonly experienced than negative ones, the person is still likely to feel happy more often than depressed (Costa & McCrae, 1992).

The NEO is available in a briefer version (i.e., 60 items as opposed to 240 for the NEO-PI-R) called the NEO Five-Factor Inventory (NEO-FFI). The briefer tests yields scores on the five domains only and not the 30 facets. The authors suggest that the NEO-FFI is appropriate for use in some types of research, when there is limited time available for testing, or where only global information about personality is needed.

The original version of the NEO-PI was published in mid-1980s (Costa & McCrae, 1985). In the subsequent years an impressive amount of research has been done on the instrument and the five-factor model (see, for example, Costa & McCrae, 1994). It is the measure of choice for assessing personality traits. The clinician employing the NEO-PI-R needs to be aware of the measures limitations. The inventory assumes that respondents will be honest and forthcoming when responding to test items. There are no scales of test-taking attitude or validity. Form R represents an important development since it provides a standardized means of assessing a third-person's view of the test subject. Defensiveness would be one hypothesis to explore when there are significant discrepancies between Form S and Form R results.

In evaluating the NEO-PI-R one needs to be mindful of exactly what factor analysis is: "a technique for grouping items into relatively homogeneous and independent clusters" (Anastasi & Urbina, 1997, p. 367). The procedure does not identify "truth." The relationships it discovers are limited by the types of questions asked and the reliability and validity of the individual test items. Because a factor has been identified through factor analysis, and given a certain label by the researcher, one cannot conclude that the factor is a valid measure of the construct implied by the label. Creating a factor that is homogeneous and statistically pure (i.e., not contaminated by other factors) is an important first step; however, establishing the construct validity of the factor (see Appendix B) requires further empirical investigation.

The Place of Personality Assessment in Contemporary Clinical Psychology

In Chapter 5 we described three common goals of psychological assessment to be classification, description, and prediction. Personality assessment measures are used to help clinical psychologists achieve these goals. How central a role these tests should play in each type of assessment, however, is open to question.

In clinical settings, psychologists commonly use tests of personality and psychological functioning such as the ones described in this chapter to assist in formulating a diagnosis. Critics of psychological tests point out that the tests themselves are not particularly reliable or valid diagnostic instruments (e.g., Dawes, 1994). And while there are scores of studies that have examined how people with different diagnoses tend to score on common psychological tests, the clinical implications of these findings are questionable. While the mean score for a clinical sample may be statistically different than the mean score for a control group, overlap in the two distributions of scores is often considerable. Defenders of tests of personality and psychopathology argue that these instruments are rarely used by themselves. Typically, clinicians integrate psychological test findings with information gathered via interview and from other sources (e.g., arrest records, interview with spouse, and so on) to arrive at a diagnosis. The test data provide the clinician with clinically relevant information against which clinical hypotheses can be tested. Alternatively, possible diagnoses may be suggested by the tests. The diagnostician can then look for collateral information to either support or disprove each diagnostic possibility.

Personality test data are used frequently to help clinicians develop more detailed understanding of their clients that go beyond simple diagnostic formulations. People who suffer with depression are more different than they are similar. Depressed clients who have a dependent personality style are different than depressed clients who are narcissistic. The former may cling to significant others and constantly seek reassurance from their therapists, while the latter may tend to feel anger and hostility toward loved ones who are not fulfilling their needs. They may believe that they should be the most important clients on their therapists' caseload and may become enraged over a canceled appointments or therapists' vacations. Personality testing provides a time-efficient means of developing a broader understanding of one's client.

Clinicians use personality test findings to help them make predictions about their clients' behavior. One of the common predictive questions faced by clinical psychologists is whether this client will benefit from psychotherapy, or what type of therapy will be most effective for this particular client. A great deal has been written about the therapeutic implications of different personality test scores and patterns (e.g., Butcher, 1990; Retzlaff, 1996). However, much of this literature is based upon rational arguments and clinical lore. Research on psychological testing and research on psychotherapy tend to have progressed along two relatively independent tracks (Sechrest, Stickle, & Stewart, 1998). In fact, critics of traditional personality testing have pointed out the tenuous relationship between assessment findings and intervention. Other types of predictive questions psychologists might use personality test data to address include risk for suicide, risk for violence, likelihood for success in a residential treatment program, and others. Once again, testing data should not be used alone to answer these complicated questions. We know very little about the hit-and-miss rates for tests used to address these clinically meaningful questions. Test data is just one source of information clinical psychologists might consider. For most clinicians in applied settings faced with difficult predictive decisions, how test findings and other sources of information should be integrated to arrive at a decision is more of an artistic than a scientific endeavor.

Personality testing is used by many clinical psychologists engaged in basic and applied research. For the researcher, the tests may be the only reliable means of assessing the construct of interest. In intervention studies, personality tests and tests of psychological functioning may be used to assess therapeutic change or as predictors of therapeutic response. In basic research, test data might be used to test hypotheses about the fundamental nature of personality.

BOX **8.4**

Focus on Ethics: Computer-Generated Narrative Interpretation

The publishers of the most popular self-report inventories provide test-users with the option of purchasing computer-generated interpretive reports. Users of the MMPI-2 and MCMI-III, for example, can send completed questionnaires to the testing service and receive back not only scores on all the various subscales of each measure, but also a narrative report or series of interpretive statements about the examinee's test-taking attitude, diagnosis, personality, and prognosis for psychotherapy. The following is an example paragraph taken from an automated interpretive report of a Millon Adolescent Clinical Inventory (Millon, Millon, & Davis, 1993) completed by a 16-year-old youth seen by one of the authors.

> The MACI profile of this adolescent suggests that he exhibits a veneer of friendliness and sociability. Although he often is able to make a good impression on casual acquaintances, his characteristic unreliability, impulsiveness, deep resentment, impatience, and moodiness are seen frequently by peers and family members. He is excitable, persistently seeks stimulation, and engages often in immature, defiant, and self-dramatizing behavior. Relationships with peers and family may be shallow and tenuous, frequently characterized by caustic comments, lies, and hostile outbursts. He tends to act on impulse without deliberation and with poor judgment, often getting into imbroglios, if not fights. Seen often as irresponsible and undependable by others, he may be truant, disposed to run away, or become involved with drugs. His short-lived enthusiasms may be followed by legal and family difficulties, personal disillusionment, and resentment toward authorities.

The option of having a computer generate interpretive statements about a client is an appealing one for many psychologists. The interpretive report offers significant time savings. Rather than spending time figuring out what a set of test scores mean and translating the interpretation into a comprehensible narrative form, psychologists can let the computer do the work for them. In addition to the time savings, computer-generated interpretation of the test findings offer other advantages. A high-quality automated interpretation program utilizes an extensive data base of information about the correlates of various test scores and test patterns. The computer program uses more information than the average psychologist can access when generating an interpretive report. When confronted with an unusual pattern of test results, clinicians may resort to speculation about their meaning. A computer program, on the other hand, may be able to derive an interpretation based upon a pool of similar cases (McCann & Dyer, 1996). Computers are good at storing and retrieving large quantities of information. The interpretive rules and algorithms upon which automated interpretations are based can be updated as new information about test correlates appears (Jackson, 1985). In many ways the computer is the perfect tool for the actuarial approach to assessment. In addition, the higher-quality interpretive services hire test experts as consultants when developing their interpretive software. By using the testing service, average psychologists take advantage of a broader base of information and a higher level of expert knowledge than they themselves possess.

In addition to its capacity for information storage and integration, the computer has the advantage of its objectivity. The computer does not know, like, or dislike the client. It does not have to deal with the client's insurance provider. It is unaware whether the client is tall, short, handsome or homely. Therefore, the interpretation of test results is based upon what is known about the correlates of the test indicators and only that information. Whereas psychologists may be influenced by feeling about, or prejudices toward, their clients, the computer program is not. Computer-generated interpretive reports can provide a valuable "outside opinion" about one's clients (Butcher, 1990).

BOX **8.4** **Continued**

The time savings offered by computer scoring and interpretation services is very tempting for busy psychologists. But, like most things that tempt us, there is the risk of harm if one does not proceed with caution. In the name of time-saving, psychologists may risk misuse or misinterpretation of test findings. Two potential dangers are: (1) misuse resulting from lack of knowledge about the testing service and (2) misinterpretation resulting from overreliance on the interpretive program.

What should psychologists know about a computer test interpretation service before deciding to use it? The short answer to this question is: usually a lot more than they can tell by reading the advertisements. Psychological testing is big business for test publishers and a significant portion of that business is in test scoring and interpretation services. In the late 1980s the annual revenues for the larger testing companies was in the hundreds of millions of dollars (Haney, Madaus, & Lyons, 1993). Test publishers want psychologists to use their tests and their testing services. Psychologists in practice routinely receive advertisements hawking the "cost efficiency," "improved patient care," and "increased therapy time" that will result from using one testing service or another. It is the psychologists' responsibility to look beyond this surface to really know about the test and testing service. At a minimum, a psychologist should know about a test's reliability; concurrent, predictive, and construct validity; and the makeup and features of the normative data base (see Chapter 5). In addition, however, a whole new series of questions about the automated interpretation system should be answered by psychologists before they use the system. "How were the interpretive statements derived from the scores? What is the theoretical rationale and the research base of the system? Were the statements derived from quantitative analyses or from expert clinical judgment? If the latter, some information regarding the qualifications of the particular experts should be given" (Anastasi & Urbina, 1997, p. 76).

The APA Ethical Principles and Code of Conduct make clear that it is the psychologist's responsibility to be knowledgeable about the automated services they use. Ethical Standard 9.09 (b) reads:

> Psychologists select scoring and interpretation services (including automated services) on the basis of evidence of the validity of the program and procedures as well as on other appropriate considerations.

The ease with which computerized testing services can be used is one of their strengths but also one of their dangers. Computer-generated test interpretations are not meant to stand alone. When used properly they provide the competent practitioner with an independent source of information that is used to supplement the other data gathered by the clinician (Bersoff & Hofer, 1995). Findings from self-report inventories need to be interpreted in the context of what else is known about the client. The example MACI interpretive information reproduced above was only one source of information used by the author in his evaluation of the adolescent. This information was integrated with data from interviews with the young man and his parents, reports from other mental health professionals, police records, and other psychological test data.

The bottom line is that while automated testing services may alleviate clinicians of some of the work involved when using psychological tests, they do not alleviate them of the responsibility for the end product.

CHAPTER

9

Behavioral Assessment

Like other clinical psychologists, those who employ cognitive-behavioral treatment interventions conduct assessments for such purposes as describing and understanding clients' problems and monitoring therapeutic change (Cone, 1998). In doing so, these psychologists draw from a range of concepts and specific assessment methods known collectively as *behavioral assessment.* Historically, this distinct group of methods was necessary because pioneer behavior therapists such as Joseph Wolpe, Teodoro Ayllon, and Nathan Azrin were making what were then considered to be highly nontraditional assumptions about etiology, assessment, and treatment. For example, in the 1950s, when behavior therapy began to emerge as a systematic clinical enterprise, psychoanalytically oriented therapists looked for unconscious causes underlying mental disorders, and examined their clients for signs of across-the-board personality traits and enduring defensive styles. By contrast, behaviorally oriented therapists looked for behavioral contingencies and reinforcers influencing particular client behaviors, and assessed their clients' specific responses to particular situations.

Today, behavioral assessment typically includes focused interviewing about the elements of a client's problems in the context of their interpersonal and physical environment. Parents, teachers, institutional direct-care staff, and others are interviewed if the client is a very young child or a nonverbal adult. Behavioral assessment traditionally includes the direct observation of a client's behavior in structured, problem-relevant situations. Questionnaires and rating scales are used when these target specific behaviors, thoughts, images, bodily sensations, and emotions. Behavioral assessment can even extend to monitoring physiological reactions that indicate emotional activation in specific contexts, as in the example of a combat veteran with posttraumatic stress disorder whose heart rate is measured while the soundtrack of a war movie is played (Blanchard, Kolb, Gerardi, Ryan, & Pallmeyer, 1986).

However, behavioral assessment is not a fixed set of tests or procedures but an approach or a paradigm, a set of principles to be used flexibly (Ramsay, Reynolds, & Kamphaus, 2002).

Conceptual Basis

Cognitive-behavioral therapists do not necessarily reject all traditional forms of mental health assessment. Many use the MMPI-2 and other validated inventories in broadly evaluating a client's personality and psychopathology, and a sizable proportion even use projective tests like the Rorschach. But in assessing the client, the problem, and the interaction of the two for the purpose of designing a specific, behaviorally oriented treatment plan, behavioral assessment comes into its own as a unique strategy in the mental health field. The therapist carefully assesses the nature, context, and development of each client's emotional, cognitive, and behavioral difficulties. A detailed behavioral assessment guides selection of specific intervention techniques and establishes the basis for evaluating therapy progress and outcome. In this highly individualized form, behavioral assessment is inevitably an essential component of behavior therapy.

Behavioral assessment chiefly emphasizes empirically based methods that focus on designated observable behaviors, as far as possible avoiding any need for inference (Haynes, 1998). Behavioral assessment has been characterized as follows: "The objective description of specific human responses that are considered to be controlled by contemporaneous environmental events and whose consistency and/or variability are directly related to the consistency and/or variability of the environment" (Cone, 1987, p. 2).

Consistent with the principal assumptions of behavior therapy, in this quotation the main influences on human behavior are viewed as environmental, justifying the need to assess each individual's interaction with key external stimuli. Behavioral assessment typically focuses on conditioning and learning phenomena, such as the behavioral contingencies, reinforcers, and stimulus pairings operating in a client's natural environment, and his or her responsiveness to such events. Because the most distinctive behavioral assessment methods are idiographic (specific to the individual client) rather than nomothetic (based upon group normative data), behavioral assessment has sometimes been faulted for lack of appropriate psychometric standardization of the kind that prevails in trait-based personality evaluations (Ramsay et al., 2002).

Ironically, behavioral assessment has been criticized not only for failing to establish group norms for all methods. The detailed attention to specifics that is characteristic of behavioral assessment can also limit therapists' ability to make generalizations about individual clients' behavior in different settings (Nelson, 1983).

The behavioral assessment of *personality* is based initially upon the straightforward idea that people tend to repeat the behavior that was reinforced when they last encountered a situation. The behavior may or may not be produced in a different situation, depending upon the learning contingencies that applied there (Mischel, 1968). Consequently, there is little interest in personality traits or dispositions assumed to reside within the individual. Instead, behavior therapists assess the client's actions, thoughts, and feelings in particular situations, avoiding assumptions about the cross-situational consistency of behavior. Current assessment practices in behavior therapy reflect recent cognitive and social learning formulations in which the interaction of environment, behavior, and symbolic processes within the individual is stressed (Wilson, 1995).

Typical Procedures

Behavioral assessment usually begins with a detailed examination of specific environmental influences on the client's behavior. In the typical outpatient setting, the behaviorally oriented clinical interview is usually the starting point. Guided by learning concepts such as conditioning and reinforcement, the therapist inquires about the situations in which the problem behavior occurs, about possible pairings of stimuli within those situations, and about the possible reinforcing or punishing consequences of the problem behavior. Questions like "how," "when," "where," and "what" are typical features of assessment interviews in behavior therapy, consistent with the focus on the specifics of behavior in situations. The question "why" is rarely asked because it is less useful (Wilson, 1995). Behavior therapists often make direct observations of behavior in the natural environment in order to gather data and test hypotheses about potential conditioning and learning events. Whether information is gathered via an interview or through direct observation, assessment often leads directly to treatment. To take a simple example, when a behavior therapist observes that a parent appears to be reinforcing a child's temper tantrums unintentionally by giving attention as a consequence, an appropriate treatment plan based on this assessment information would be to ask the parent to reschedule the attention-giving, breaking the contingency between the problem behavior and the potentially reinforcing consequence.

Treatment goals are discussed carefully with the client, who is the chief decision maker, with the therapist serving as a resource. (Exceptions may occur in the case of very young children or severely disturbed adults for whom other responsible people have to make decisions on treatment.) Issues presented by the client are taken seriously and assigned primary importance, although the therapist may become aware of issues that the client does not initially regard as important (Swan & MacDonald, 1978; Wilson, 1984).

Traditional Approaches to Assessment

Behavioral assessment grew both from the need to establish a system for classifying problems and processes behaviorally, and from dissatisfaction with psychodynamic formulations and traditional diagnostic classification. Assessment of psychological disorders has had a long and varied history. Currently, there are many different approaches to the evaluation of psychological symptoms. We can place behavioral assessment in context by reviewing other approaches briefly here.

Syndrome-Based Diagnosis

Syndrome-based diagnosis is the oldest and most influential approach. It owes a great deal to Emil Kraepelin (1856–1926), a German psychiatrist who pioneered modern approaches to classification. The central assumption is that certain signs or symptoms tend to cluster together in clinically meaningful ways to define psychological disorders or *syndromes* (from the Greek words for "running together"). For example, the symptoms of depression often include dysphoric mood, reduced energy and activity level, nonrestorative sleep, poor appetite, self-criticism, feelings of guilt, and perceptions of hopelessness. Collectively, these symptoms define the syndrome of depression. Initially, the criterion for identifying a syndromal grouping was expert judgment: the consensual opinions of experienced clinicians, based on careful observations of case material.

The *DSM-IV* (*Diagnostic and Statistical Manual of Mental Disorders,* Fourth Edition; American Psychiatric Association, 1994) presents the classification system most widely used in the United States today. The *DSM-IV* is the prime example of diagnostic classification based on the syndromal approach.

There are many advantages to syndrome-based diagnosis. First, clients' problems often fall into meaningful clusters. When this is the case, the cluster of problems is a suitable treatment target. Indeed, outcomes can be better when the cluster is seen as a distinct disorder than when it is seen as a collection of isolated issues. Second, a single diagnostic term summarizes a great deal of information, facilitating communication between professionals with disparate backgrounds. Third, grouping clinical symptoms into syndromes facilitates research into the causes, correlates, and treatment of various disorders (Klein & Riso, 1995).

One major disadvantage of syndromal diagnosis is the tendency for syndromal groupings to become *reified,* or treated as though they are entities in themselves and represent actual diseases (First, Francis, Widiger, Pincus, & Davis, 1992). To cognitive-behavioral therapists and many other clinical psychologists, most diagnostic categories in mental health are viewed as, at best, *metaphors* for medical diseases. Furthermore, categorical systems lose many of their advantages if different syndromal groupings have high degrees of *comorbidity* or diagnostic overlap, and that is clearly the case with the *DSM-IV* (Klein & Riso, 1995).

Some of the criticisms of *DSM-IV* (and of psychiatric diagnosis as a whole) have even wider implications. One criticism focuses on the drawback that some diagnostic labels seem aimed at the problems of particular groups of people and not others and may therefore be used to discredit broad categories of individuals (such as political dissidents, ethnic minorities, and women). Benjamin Rush (1745–1813), pioneer of American psychiatry and signatory of the Declaration of Independence, introduced the diagnosis *anarchia,* a "form of insanity" in which people were unhappy with the new political structure of the United States (Brown, 1990). Similarly, the disease *drapetomania,* identified by Samuel Cartwright in 1843, was seen only in African slaves and its symptoms involved a "compulsion to run away." African Americans were also supposedly vulnerable to *dyaesthesia Aethiopica,* a disorder in which the psychopathology involved "paying no attention to property" (Brown, 1990). More recently, critics of the *DSM-III* (American Psychiatric Association, 1980) chided its authors for gender bias because it retains several diagnoses that reflect negative stereotypes of women (Kaplan, 1983), although the proponents of categorical classification point out that there are also many diagnoses reflecting negative stereotypes of men (Williams & Spitzer, 1983/1995). We could note that the essential problem here is the negative stereotyping itself, not just a perceived lack of evenhandedness.

Another broad criticism of diagnosis is that, in their attempt to collect clusters of symptoms into categories, the classifiers sometimes make decisions that are quite arbitrary. This criticism has been expressed as follows:

> Grouping patients according to selected properties rather than in terms of their total phenomenology is analogous to classifying a car by observing any four of the following eight properties: wheels, motors, headlights, radio, seats, body, windshield wipers, and exhaust systems. While an object with four of these properties might well be a car, it might also be an airplane, a helicopter, a derrick, or a tunnel driller. (Chang & Bidder, 1985, p. 202, cited in Brown, 1990)

These critics would rather deal holistically with the human being involved, not focus upon a set of problems. Yet this is ironic, because another disadvantage of diagnosis is that it can be mistakenly applied to *people,* not to problems. Agoraphobia, for example, is a disorder encompassing anxiety about traveling far from home, fear of crowded, public places, and panic attacks, and the diagnostic label is properly applied to the set of problems, not to the person. When a *person* is described as "an agoraphobic," then he or she is being defined and labeled in terms of a disorder, surely a dehumanizing practice.

Perhaps of greatest concern to cognitive-behavioral psychologists is the practice of using *DSM-IV* diagnostic categories to select participants for psychotherapy research, implying that the diagnostic label is all-important in describing and defining the individual's psychological status. Acierno, Hersen, and Van Hasselt (1998) selected the following apt quotation criticizing "an uncritical and simplistic reliance on diagnostic labels . . . based on the erroneous assumption that once persons have been assigned [one], they are sufficiently similar to be randomly assigned to different-treatment conditions" (Eifert, Evans, & McKendrick, 1990, p. 164, cited in Acierno et al., 1998, p. 47).

Empirically Based (Dimensional) Classification

Rather than relying on the opinions of expert clinicians, dimensional approaches to classification involve the use of statistical techniques to identify groupings of interrelated symptoms. Data are derived from symptom rating scales or questionnaires completed by large numbers of individuals. Multivariate statistical techniques such as factor analysis and cluster analysis are used to reveal relevant dimensions or clusters. *Factor analysis* simplifies a large number of variates in a collection of data by reducing them to a smaller number of hypothetical variates. Using dimensions identified by factor analysis, clinicians can locate the severity of symptoms, or the degree to which one shows evidence of a trait, at some point on a scale. Using *cluster analysis,* clinicians can identify groupings of discrete problem behaviors that tend to be highly intercorrelated. Behavior therapists have tended to favor dimensional over syndromal approaches to classification, because rating a client's behavior along a continuum rather than placing it in one or another category allows recognition of nuances (Quay, 1986).

Eysenck (1966a) was a leading defender of dimensional classification. His empirically derived personality dimensions of neuroticism and extraversion led to predictions about the suitability of behavior therapy for particular clients. He argued that it was a mistake to ignore individual differences in personality:

> No physicist would dream of assessing the electrical conductivity, or the magnetic properties, or the heat-resisting qualities of random samples of matter, or "stuff in general;" [he or she] would insist on being given carefully purified samples of specified elements . . . much energy was spent on the construction of [the] table of the elements, precisely because one element does not behave like another. Some conduct electricity, others do not, or do so only poorly; we do not throw all these differences into some gigantic error term, and deal only with the average of all substances. (Eysenck, 1966a, p. 2)

Eysenck used this argument to justify classifying people's personality characteristics. For example, clients who score high on a scale of introversion are more conditionable than others. According to Eysenck, people with high conditionability are especially prone to develop anxiety disorders, hence assessing clients' conditionability is potentially important in research on behavior therapy for anxiety.

However, there are disadvantages to classifying personality and psychopathology on dimensional scales. Methods like factor analysis encourage the view that people's behavior can be described entirely in terms of stable dispositions, such as personality traits. This can be misleading, and in fact contradicts the usual assumptions made by behavior therapists, who have always stressed the importance of the immediate environment of conditioned, discriminative, and reinforcing stimuli in understanding human behavior. Because of the workings of behavioral contingencies and reinforcement processes, behavior tends to be *situation-specific* rather than reflecting enduring traits within the person.

Traditional Psychodynamic Approaches

In traditional psychodynamic approaches to assessment, personality is defined by inferred, underlying constructs such as unconscious intrapsychic dynamics. These underlying features are seen as stable aspects of individuals which produce consistency in a person's behavior across different situational settings and across time. The purpose of assessment is to identify these unconscious dynamics and to provide a diagnostic label if they are "pathological," or viewed as causing mental disorders. A person's response to an assessment instrument is rarely of interest in its own right. Rather, it is viewed as an indirect manifestation of personality traits or dynamics that cannot be directly observed. For example, a person's responses to ambiguous test stimuli such as pictures or inkblots may indicate the presence of unconscious motivational conflicts underlying the client's presenting problem. Assessment of personality traits or unconscious motives may lead to a diagnosis, with general implications for treatment. Nonetheless, there is little direct relationship between traditional psychodynamic assessment and treatment (Goldfried & Kent, 1972).

Defining Features of Behavioral Assessment

In its purest form, behavioral assessment emphasizes the empirically based measurement of precisely specified observable behavior, using a variety of methods, modalities of client functioning, and settings in which the problem behaviors can arise. Assessing the specific environmental stimuli than can control behavior is of fundamental importance (Cone, 1998; Haynes, 1998). The paradigm "emphasizes the use of minimally inferential assessment methods. Consequently, direct measurement of a client's behavior is preferred to retrospective reports" (Haynes, 1998, p. 9).

Behavioral therapists carefully examine the nature of their clients' problems and the critical factors that influence them. In concert with factors that exist "within" a person, such as patterns of psychophysiological, cognitive, or affective responding, contextual factors in the environment are seen as major determinants of behavior. Thus, in contrast with more traditional views of personality and psychopathology, individual behavior is not viewed as inherently stable across different life situations. Furthermore, a client's overt responses to assessment instruments are of interest in their own right, and must be sampled as extensively and accurately as possible. In contrast with traditional approaches, a primary function of behavioral assessment includes selection of appropriate treatment techniques and evaluation of treatment progress and outcome. Assessment itself can be viewed as the first stage of behavior therapy.

However, behavioral assessment is hardly a static or even well-defined enterprise (Cone, 1998). From the time of its initial development, behavioral assessment has broadened significantly in scope. Many of these changes remain controversial. Thus, we will begin with a brief overview of the development of behavioral assessment, then consider current conceptualizations and controversies.

Development of Behavioral Assessment

Behavioral assessment emerged during the 1960s, partly as a reaction to weaknesses inherent in traditional models of assessment (Kanfer & Saslow, 1969). Syndromal diagnosis and psychodynamic procedures (such as projective tests) were criticized because of their limited scientific validation and questionable utility in suggesting treatment approaches. Early approaches to behavioral assessment were *idiographic,* tailored to the unique features of each client. Consistent with the emphasis upon conditioning and learning principles, assessment focused on specific behavior in specific surroundings.

During this early period, researchers developed such behaviorally focused assessment devices as *behavioral avoidance tests,* such as those used by Lang and Lazovik (1963) to assess fear of snakes. In a behavioral avoidance test for a client with a specific phobia of snakes, a live snake is placed in a glass container at the far end of a room or corridor. The client approaches the snake, stopping only when increasing subjective anxiety has reached a level at which he or she is unwilling to proceed further. Measuring the distance from the snake at the point that the client stops provides an index of behavioral avoidance.

Other observational measures of problem behavior in specific environmental contexts were developed, such as Paul's (1966) use of structured ratings of twenty key behaviors while speech-anxious participants delivered actual talks.

Behavioral assessment continued to expand during the 1970s. This decade has been called the "honeymoon" period in the development of behavioral assessment, because it was marked by great optimism and conceptual confidence (Nelson, 1983). Approaches to the behavioral assessment of specific psychological disorders proliferated. Inaugural issues of two journals, *Behavioral Assessment* and *Journal of Behavioral Assessment,* were published. However, during the late 1970s behavioral assessment entered a self-critical phase that Nelson (1983) referred to as the "period of disillusionment." The idiographic emphasis of the early behavioral assessment techniques represented a potential strength, but was taken too far. If assessments are truly unique to each case, then generalizations across clients with similar features are impossible. Leading behavior therapists argued that behavioral assessment must meet traditional psychometric standards such as reliability, validity, and standardization (e.g., Goldfried & Linehan, 1977). Lack of standardization of materials and procedures makes cross-study comparisons impossible, while normative data, or *norms,* provide useful standards for decisions about who needs therapy and can help therapists set treatment goals. Normative standards also provide objective indices for the evaluation of outcome.

Similar concerns were expressed about concepts of situational specificity. It is advantageous to start with the idea that behavior may be situation-specific. But if behavior is *always* specific to particular situations, then how can therapists make convincing generalizations about their clients' problems? Gradually, the idiographic, situationally focused approach of earlier approaches to behavioral assessment has given way to a broader, transactional view of psychological disorders. Assessment techniques have broadened accordingly, much to the approval of many behavior therapists and the chagrin of others.

Psychometric principles, familiar to all clinical psychologists in the context of intelligence, aptitude, and objective personality testing, can be applied to any form of assessment, including behavioral assessment (Haynes, 1998). The chief focus is upon the *construct validity* of an assessment procedure—the degree to which conclusions drawn from the results of the assessment are indeed true to the targeted construct. For example, Paul's (1966) *timed behavioral checklist* of performance anxiety, used to assess public speaking anxiety, shows acceptable construct validity if participants who score as anxious on this behavioral test are indeed anxious about public speaking as gauged by other accepted criteria. Of course, it could be of interest to researchers, clinicians, and clients to assess behavior in a public speaking situation in its own right, whether or not it correlates with anything else. As Haynes (1998) points out, such information could be highly accurate, in that the public speaking performance was assessed with great fidelity, yet still invalid, if it was intended as a measure of anxiety across situations and assessment methods yet showed no correlation with any other criterion.

Current Views

How has the field of behavioral assessment broadened in response to earlier criticisms? Psychologists now show much greater appreciation for the complexity of factors that converge to potentiate and maintain behavior disorders (Haynes & O'Brien, 1990). For example, cognitive and affective-physiological responses account for much of the variance in the onset, maintenance, and cessation of behavior disorders (Parks & Hollon, 1988). Incorporating affective and cognitive variables into behavioral research and treatment has required significant broadening of assessment options. Similarly, dynamic, multivariate models of setting and response interrelationships have greater explanatory power than static, univariate models (Haynes, 1991; Mash & Hunsley, 1990). In explaining why a particular person develops a behavior disorder at a particular time, it is common to find multidirectional interrelationships among responses, persons, and settings (Haynes and O'Brien, 1990).

Yet many of the core assumptions underlying behavioral assessment remain unchanged. For example, there is widespread agreement that functional analyses of problem behavior should be conducted using minimally inferential assessment tools (Cone, 1998). Furthermore, it is widely assumed that modifying setting and response variables associated with the problem behavior will lead to improved functioning (O'Brien & Haynes, 1993).

A related issue concerns the changing role of "traditional" diagnostic categorization in behavioral assessment. During the initial development of behavioral assessment, traditional diagnostic labels were rejected outright as useless or even harmful. The *DSM-II* (American Psychiatric Association, 1968), the reigning diagnostic system at that time, was vaguely formulated, had been shown empirically to be unreliable, and unashamedly anchored many key concepts to psychodynamic theory. However, the manual was completely revised in 1980, and in the *DSM-III* the diagnostic criteria were specified in more concrete terms. The current *DSM-IV* drew from empirical studies in the published literature to develop and refine diagnostic categorizations (First et al., 1992). Thus, many behavior therapists now incorporate syndromally based diagnosis into their assessment practices.

There are a number of ways in which syndromal diagnosis can be useful to behaviorally oriented clinicians. Syndromal diagnosis may provide an initial step in identifying diagnostic classes that can be further differentiated in functional analysis. As First and colleagues (1992) stated, "they act as a modular unit—[DSM diagnosis] providing the frame and behavior analysis a more finer grained and more specific picture of the particular problem confronting the patient" (p. 304). Furthermore, the *DSM-IV* and its predecessors have facilitated communication with other professionals who do not share the behavioral viewpoint (Nelson & Barlow, 1981).

Krasner (1992) offered a dissenting opinion. He argued that efforts to integrate syndromal classification and functional analysis represent a weakening of behavioral assessment. As a result, behavioral assessment is in danger of losing its "root identity," particularly the strong emphasis on assessing social contextual factors related to the onset and maintenance of disordered behavior. This issue remains controversial.

Concerning current practices in behavioral assessment, Haynes (1998) has surveyed both treatment outcome research studies and the reports of practicing behaviorally oriented clinicians. Researchers used trait-based self-report measures in more than 75 percent of the articles published in *Journal of Consulting and Clinical Psychology* between the early 1960s and the mid-1990s. Drawing from that same sample of research reports, Haynes showed that structured behavioral observation and self-monitoring, two prominent behavioral assessment techniques, were used far more often than projective techniques and personality inventories. However, the use of those hallmarked behavioral assessment methods peaked in the mid-1980s. In surveys conducted in 1989 and 1990, practicing behavior therapists reported that they used the clinical interview most often; personality questionnaires and self-report inventories over half the time; self-monitoring about half the time; and structured behavioral observation less than a quarter of the time (Haynes, 1998). Direct behavioral observation to identify controlling variables prior to treatment declined in the mid-1980s even among behavioral clinicians working with autism and other developmental disabilities (Groden & Lantz, 2001).

Functional Analysis

The overarching goal of behavioral assessment as an essential component of behavior therapy is to integrate assessment information into a clinical formulation to guide treatment interventions (Haynes, 1998). The clinical formulation that results from a behavioral assessment is most often referred to as the *functional analysis,* a phrase that signals behavior therapists' interest in identifying the potentially controllable discriminative stimuli, behavioral contingencies, and reinforcers influencing the client's problem behavior. "The overriding question is, 'What factors are contributing to or responsible for the target behavior?'" (Kazdin, 2001, p. 102).

Identifying the antecedent conditions and consequences of a particular behavior could show that it occurs more frequently at some times of day, when particular people are present, or when certain consequences occur. For example, Kazdin (2001) cited the example of an 8-year-old child, Kathy, who often fought physically with her younger sister. The mother was asked to chart occurrences of unacceptable behavior (fighting) and acceptable behavior (playing cooperatively). The charts revealed, among other things, that when Kathy fought with her sister, her mother would take Kathy to her room and remain with her until she calmed down, sometimes reading to her. When Kathy played appropriately, the parents would "leave well enough alone" (Kazdin, 2001, p. 108). One of the hypotheses that emerged from this assessment was that Kathy's fighting was reinforced by having private time with her mother. Appropriate interventions based on that hypothesis included making private time with her mother contingent upon Kathy's playing cooperatively, not fighting.

Repp and Horner (1999) illustrated the use of functional analysis with clients who put their hands in their mouths, sometimes biting their hands. Typical behavioral interventions to address problem behavior of this kind include overcorrection and differential reinforcement of other behavior. In *overcorrection,* the client is asked to remedy the damage done by the behavior, actually going beyond what would be minimally required, contingent upon the occurrence of the inappropriate behavior. In this example, overcorrection could mean requiring the clients to clean their teeth with antiseptic toothpaste and to have their hands treated with antibacterial medication. *Differential reinforcement of other behavior* (DRO) involves delivering positive reinforcement contingent upon a client's having spent at least a certain minimal interval of time *not* engaging in hand-biting. Without a functional analysis of the problem behavior, overcorrection and DRO could have been implemented as potentially suitable behavioral interventions. However, a functional analysis might reveal that another, quite different approach is more fitting.

For example, the functional analysis might show that the clients put their hands in their mouths when they could not predict what was required from them in a pending task. Assessment of the consequences might reveal that the problem behavior served as an escape response, effectively taking the client out of the difficult situation. If that were the case, making the task more predictable, or giving pertinent information to the clients, would be more appropriate treatment interventions (Repp & Horner, 1999).

In general terms, how does a functional analysis actually facilitate the conduct of behavior therapy? There are five main functions:

1. Description of the problem
2. Identification of controlling variables
3. Evaluation of adaptive significance
4. Selection of treatment
5. Evaluation of outcome

Problem Description

Problem description is necessary before important comparisons can be made, such as comparing the behavior before and after treatment and across situations, and comparing the client with other individuals (Cone, 1998). The most obvious first step in behavioral assessment is to obtain a clear description of specific problems that the client would like to change. Often, when clients seek psychotherapy they present vague descriptions of their problems such as, "I just don't get much pleasure out of life any more," "I feel tense and wound up a lot," or "I just can't seem to get along with my spouse (or child or parents)." The therapist's task is to encourage the client to "translate" these complaints into specific problems amenable to change. For example, the person who complains of relationship problems may be referring to verbal arguments that tend to recur and are organized around specific conflict issues. The characteristic frequency, duration, and intensity of the problem are then delineated in order to determine the severity of the problem. One client may describe mild arguments with a spouse that last for a few minutes and occur once or twice a month; another may describe daily fights involving shouting and physical violence.

Identifying Controlling Variables

Once a specific problem (or set of problems) is identified, the next step is to examine the types of antecedent and consequent stimuli that could be maintaining it. This is the essence of functional analysis—identifying important relationships between the environment and the behavior that are potentially controllable (Tryon, 1998). It would be difficult to exaggerate the importance of functional analysis: "The well-documented large effect sizes associated with reinforcement contingencies [indicate] that they must be evaluated as part of any comprehensive behavioral assessment and that they must be considered as part of any comprehensive behavioral intervention" (Tryon, 1998, p. 96).

Kanfer and Saslow (1969) proposed a conceptual model, the *S-O-R-C-K* model, which helps guide clinicians through the stages of behavioral assessment. *S* refers to *stimuli*, antecedent events or discriminative stimuli that function to cue the problem behavior. *O* refers to the *organism,* or characteristics of the individual that cannot be directly observed but may play a role in perpetuation of the problem (for example, a biological predisposition to behave impulsively or to entertain dysfunctional thoughts that precipitate depressive feelings). *R* refers to *responses* or behaviors identified by the client as problematic. *C* refers to the immediate *consequences* of the behavior, and *K* to *contingencies* or current schedules of reinforcement. Thus, a comprehensive analysis of controlling variables must include analysis of precipitating events (which may be characteristics of specific situational contexts), individual predispositions that the client brings to the situation, current environmental variables, and the types of positive and negative consequences which help maintain the problem.

Adaptive Significance of the Problem Behavior

How does the problem behavior affect the person's ability to function effectively in different life contexts? In order to evaluate this important issue, the clinician might use criteria such as comparison of the problem with some "normal" standard; danger to self or others; and impairment of social, occupational, or personal functioning (Kazdin, 1985).

Selection of Treatment

Controlled studies of comparative treatment efficacy have sometimes indicated specific interventions for particular subgroups of clients; for example, people with alcoholism who are internalizers versus externalizers, people with claustrophobia who respond with increased heart rate versus behavioral avoidance, and people with public speaking anxiety whose fears are specific versus generalized (Acierno et al., 1998). These interesting findings notwithstanding, there is no *general* behavioral model for selecting an appropriate treatment strategy. If a client identifies more than one problem, it is necessary to decide which specific problem behaviors should be changed first, and available research has not yet provided all the answers. For example, a woman who was housebound as a result of severe agoraphobia became vulnerable to being asked to look after the children of several neighbors in the daytime. The neighbors' rationale was that, since she seldom left her house anyway, why could she not provide free daycare services for her community? The first decision confronting the client and the therapist was whether to work first on the client's agoraphobic avoidance or on her assertiveness problem, her difficulty with saying "no" to unreasonable requests (Hecker & Thorpe, 1992).

Although there are no absolute rules for selecting among alternative treatment goals, useful guidelines have been offered by several clinicians. For example, Nelson and Hayes (1979) have suggested the following criteria for selecting among various treatment targets:

- Dangerousness to self or others
- Behaviors that are highly irritating to others
- Behaviors that are easiest to change (in order to increase the client's feelings of hopefulness and sense of personal efficacy)
- Behaviors at the beginning of a chain of linked behaviors

Once priorities have been assigned for alternative problems, assessment data can be used to develop an intervention with a high probability of success. In guiding the choice of treatment, primary considerations are the nature of the client's problem and the nature of the controlling variables.

Evaluation of Treatment Progress and Outcome

The final assessment function involves evaluation of treatment progress and outcome. According to Barlow, Hayes, and Nelson (1984), evaluation of treatment effects can be addressed by three different questions:

1. Is the treatment being implemented successfully?
2. Is the treatment effective in alleviating the client's presenting problems?
3. What are the implications of the treatment effects for clinical science?

Reflecting the idiographic emphasis, early behavioral approaches to treatment evaluation involved single subject designs that were focused on discrete target behaviors. In line with the broadening conceptual paradigms in behavior therapy, current approaches have emphasized the need to treat multiple target behaviors and assess outcome from many different perspectives (Farrell, 1993). Finally, it is essential to show that treatment effects generalize across different situations, and across time (McGlynn & Rose, 1998).

Behavioral Assessment Methods

Behavior therapists tend to use multiple assessment techniques and methods, the exact nature and number being determined by the unique features of each case.

Behavioral Interviews

Among behavior therapists, the behavioral interview is almost universally employed to gather information concerning problem behavior (Guevremont & Spiegler, 1990). The therapist's general goals are to establish a warm, supportive, and trusting relationship with the client, and to achieve detailed information about the nature, development, and current context of the client's stated problems. The first of these goals has priority, because even the most perfectly executed information-gathering interview will be pointless if the client fails to return for a second meeting due to poor rapport with the clinician (Sarwer & Sayers, 1998). Detailed information from interviewing allows the clinician to develop a preliminary model of controlling factors related to target behavior, and to select settings and methods for assessment and variables for treatment evaluation and design (Haynes, 1991).

Guidelines for the characteristics of helpful behavioral interviewing can be suggested, but controlled research is lacking (Sarwer & Sayers, 1998).

Establishing a good relationship. Although behavior therapy is generally time-limited and problem-focused, this does not preclude the necessity of establishing good rapport with clients. General characteristics of successful therapists have been detailed elsewhere (e.g., Egan, 1982). Good relationship-building skills involve the ability to show respect and caring to the client, the ability to listen carefully and to be empathically responsive to the client's distress, and the ability to present oneself as genuine. These therapist skills are probably necessary to the success of all forms of psychotherapy. In addition, successful behavior therapists must possess good structuring skills and strike a balance between allowing clients to ventilate painful feelings and obtaining essential information about the problem behavior. All of these qualities require excellent judgment and interpersonal skill, typically achieved through advanced training.

Achieving adequate information. The information-gathering procedure has been likened to a funnel (Hawkins, 1979) in that, initially, a wide range of life events are discussed, narrowing to more specific information as the interview progresses. The therapist attempts to obtain a picture of the entire person in his or her social milieu. The following areas are usually assessed:

- Psychosocial adjustment, reflecting the number, type, and severity of emotional or behavioral problems, at the present time and in the past, and the quality of the client's social relationships. Past history is usually explored, although not in the detail achieved by psychodynamic practitioners. Information about the client's overall history of social adjustment is obtained, subdivided into areas such as relationships with family, friends, intimate partners, teachers/employers, and co-workers.

- Academic and vocational adjustment. General information about the client's history of academic and vocational achievement is also obtained, including present level of vocational success and satisfaction and relevant information about school achievement.
- Medical history and status. Pertinent medical information is obtained, such as the client's history of serious illnesses and past inpatient or outpatient treatments. Frequently, clinicians also inquire whether close relatives have had histories of severe psychological and physical disorders.
- Assets. The client's personal strengths or assets are carefully assessed. These might include quality of the client's social support system and special areas of competence, such as high intelligence or good social skills.
- Motivation. Clinicians ask how the client has tried to handle the problem in the past, and how well these efforts have succeeded. It is important to ascertain the strength of the client's motivation to change and whether the client has positive expectancies that change can occur, since these cognitive factors affect how hard people will try (Bandura, 1986). For example, a therapist might ask, "How would your life be different if your problem were no longer a problem for you?"

Through skilled questioning and possibly the use of other assessment techniques, the therapist and client narrow the focus to one or more well-defined problems. The therapist probes to achieve clear descriptions and examples. Once specific problems have been identified as appropriate for treatment, the therapist moves to an explanation of potential controlling variables.

Behavioral interviews provide a wealth of information that is used in treatment planning, implementation, and evaluation. However, despite the widespread use of this assessment tool, there is a dearth of information about the reliability and validity of behavioral interviews (O'Brien & Haynes, 1993; Sarwer & Sayers, 1998).

Structured Interviews

Structured interviews and rating scales were originally designed to provide differential diagnoses of clients' presenting problems, and to assess the severity of symptoms associated with diagnostic categories (Morrison, 1988). Contemporary structured interview protocols are specific to particular problem areas and go beyond straightforward diagnostic classification; they also provide additional data relevant to research and treatment. Questions refer to the duration, content, course, and severity of specific symptoms. Examples of better known instruments include the *Schedule for Affective Disorders and Schizophrenia* (SADS; Endicott & Spitzer, 1978); *Diagnostic Interview Schedule* (DIS; Robins, Heltzer, Croughan, & Ratcliff, 1981); and the *Structured Clinical Interview for the DSM* (SCID; Spitzer & Williams, 1985).

For anxiety disorders, the *Anxiety Disorders Interview Schedule—IV* (ADIS-IV; Brown, DiNardo, & Barlow, 1994) is routinely used by cognitive-behavioral researchers and clinicians, and because of its impressive interrater reliabilities and construct validity it is regarded as the state-of-the-art behavioral assessment tool for these disorders (McGlynn & Rose, 1998). In addition to obtaining information pertinent to arriving at a diagnosis, the ADIS-IV elicits material on the history of the client's problems and the situational and cognitive factors influencing anxiety.

Structured interviews have several advantages. They are reliable, inexpensive, fairly easy to administer, and they allow modest flexibility in interview content. However, they have important disadvantages as well, particularly for behaviorally oriented clinicians. Structured interviews require lengthy administration times (e.g., the SADS takes between 1.5 and 2 hours to administer). Moreover, some instruments do not provide information about contextual factors related to problem behavior: Diagnosis alone is insufficient for treatment formulation (Persons, 1991). Finally, the validity of many structured interview formats has not been adequately established. Use of structured interviews is typically confined to clinical situations where a precise diagnostic label is required, such as treatment studies of individuals who suffer from the same type of disorder.

Questionnaires

Frequently, self-report checklists and questionnaires are used during the initial stages of therapy to identify the range and intensity of the client's presenting problems. Behavioral self-report questionnaires have focused on observable phenomena such as the frequency and type of undesirable behaviors. Unlike self-report questionnaires employed in traditional assessment, behavioral questionnaires are highly problem-focused. For example, the Wolpe and Lang (1969) *Fear Survey Schedule* consists of 72 items on which clients rate the degree of fear corresponding to different situations or objects. More recently, in line with the "cognitive revolution" in behavioral therapy, questionnaires have been designed to assess the type and frequency of maladaptive thoughts (Parks & Hollon, 1988; Smith, 1989). For example, on the widely used *Beck Depression Inventory-II,* clients assess the frequency of self-critical and suicidal thoughts.

Self-report questionnaires are advantageous because they cover a wide range of clinical disorders, and are easily administered, quick, and inexpensive. Because of these practical virtues, they are frequently used in screening, and in evaluations of treatment progress and outcome. An example of a specific self-report questionnaire to assess a focused problem area is the *Revised Children's Manifest Anxiety Scale* (see Ramsay et al., 2002). Potential limitations of self-report questionnaires have included the possibility of distortion, bias, or misinterpretation in the client's responses; lack of attention to situational specificity; and in many cases, questionable validity (O'Brien & Haynes, 1993). For these reasons, data derived from self-report questionnaires should always be supplemented with other sources of information about the client's problem.

Behavior Rating Scales

Typical behavior rating scales are multifaceted, assessing a wide range of behaviors on several different dimensions. The most widely used rating scales for children's behavior are the *Child Behavior Checklist* (CBCL) and *Conners' Rating Scales-Revised* (see Ramsay et al.,

2002). Ratings are usually made by teachers and parents, conferring the advantages of assessing behavior across situations with independent informants. However, these ratings tend to be impressionistic, global ratings that may be subject to various forms of bias.

Analogue Techniques

Analogue techniques involve asking the client to respond to contrived situations in the clinic or laboratory that are similar to real-life problem situations. A range of media and techniques have been used, including paper-and-pencil responses to written scripts, asking the client to attend to audiotaped or videotaped situations, asking the client to enact problematic social interactions in the consulting room, or asking the client to assume various roles of persons involved in troubling social exchanges. For example, Goldsmith and McFall (1975) assessed interpersonal skills of adults by asking them to respond to a contrived script, and Lang and Lazovik (1963) have assessed avoidance behavior in phobias by devising behavioral avoidance tests. Analogue techniques may be very useful in generating hypotheses about the nature of the client's problems. However, since analogue situations are simulated and of necessity different from the context in which the target behavior typically occurs, the degree of correspondence between contrived stimuli and real-life problems they represent may not be great and has rarely been tested by clinicians (Haynes, 1998; Nay, 1977). For this reason, analogue methods should be used cautiously and supplemented with other sources of information about the problem at hand.

Self-Monitoring

Self-monitoring involves recording aspects of one's own behavior for use in treatment. Self-monitoring is especially helpful in the case of low frequency events, which would be difficult to observe independently. If the presenting problem involves some sort of "private event," such as cravings or dysfunctional thoughts, self-monitoring is one of the only means available for assessment.

Traditionally, clients have been asked to compute frequency counts of discrete behaviors that are short in duration (such as number of drinks taken or cigarettes smoked). A variety of assessment tools have been used, including written diaries, mechanical counters, timing devices, and computers. If a given response occurs very frequently, the client might be asked to record behavior only during certain time periods each day. In the case of behaviors that are not discrete, such as studying, exercising, practicing, or writing, the client may be asked to record the time spent on the activity each day. Finally, clients may be asked to keep daily records of negative thoughts that are keyed to certain life situations. For example, recording immediate cognitive reactions to upsetting situations can help one assess dysfunctional thought patterns relevant to anxiety or depression.

If self-monitoring is to be successful, the target behavior must be carefully defined and the client must be adequately trained. The advantages of self-monitoring are many:

- It can be can be carried out anywhere.
- It permits sampling of low-frequency private events, such as illicit drug use or sexual behavior.

■ It promotes insight into how one's own behavior is related to situational and other factors.

■ It can be reactive, in that self-monitoring may in itself promote positive change (although this is a disadvantage of the technique as well).

Potential drawbacks of self-monitoring include noncompliance, reactivity, and inaccuracy. In trying to circumvent noncompliance, it is important that the therapist selects a recording method appropriate to client's problem, trains the client in self-monitoring techniques, then follows up with phone or mail contacts.

The reactivity problem is more difficult to deal with. When individuals self-record their own behavior, it tends to change in frequency. Generally, positive target behaviors tend to increase in frequency under self-monitoring, whereas negative target behaviors tend to decrease. Finally, when independent checks of self-monitored data have been conducted, many investigators have reported poor accuracy. Thus, the assessment function of self-monitoring is hampered by problems of reactivity and inaccuracy, particularly in situations where pretreatment baseline data must be obtained. For these reasons, self-monitoring should be used with caution and supplemented with other forms of assessment data.

Direct Observation

Direct observation of problem behaviors in natural settings (such as homes, schools, or residential treatment facilities) played an important role in the initial development of behavioral assessment and continues to be one of its hallmarks (Tryon, 1998). The greatest advantage of *in vivo* observation is that problem behavior can be observed in its customary situational context, leading directly to hypotheses about possible controlling variables. For example, direct observation of bizarre, inappropriate behavior, in its context, on the part of someone hospitalized with schizophrenia may reveal that the patient gains a lot of attention from the staff for this behavior. This hypothesis can be directly tested, using behavioral treatment methods.

However, the many potential limitations of *in vivo* observation preclude its widespread use in clinical practice. The following drawbacks are most salient:

1. Reactivity. Perhaps the greatest drawback of observational methods is reactivity to the presence of the observer (Foster, Bell-Dolan, & Burge, 1988). People tend to behave differently when they know that they are being observed by others. Research suggests that reactivity effects are greater under some conditions than others. For example, studies of individuals in residential treatment facilities have revealed little evidence for reactivity to observation, whereas studies of normal families and the families of boys referred for behavior problems have revealed strong reactivity effects (Romanczyk, Kent, Diament, & O'Leary, 1973). Reactivity problems can be minimized by decreasing the intrusiveness of the observers, and by scheduling an adaptation period that allows the individual(s) to habituate to the presence of the observer.

2. Reliability of observations. Achieving acceptable interrater reliability requires intensive training. Diverse factors have been found to affect reliability, including the complexity of social behaviors and interactions under observation, observers' awareness that a reliability assessment is being conducted, observer fatigue, and the tendency for observers to "drift" from the original coding criteria over time (Taplin & Reid, 1973). Scheduling unannounced reliability checks and allowing sufficient rest periods may help attenuate these problems.

3. Validity of observations. Validity is influenced by many factors, including the comprehensiveness of the coding system, the number of observations conducted, the nature of the validation criterion (what the results of direct observation are to be correlated with), and the extent to which different situations relevant to the problem behavior are adequately sampled (Foster et al., 1988; Tryon, 1998). The problem of the validity of sampling runs parallel to the problem of generalizability: "Trait theorists assume generalizability across assessment contexts. Behavioral clinicians have too often assumed rather than demonstrated generalizability" (Tryon, 1998, p. 83).

4. Cost-efficiency. Direct observation is expensive and time-consuming. This impracticality has been a critical obstacle to frequent use of observational methods in general clinical practice.

Psychophysiological Recording Methods

Psychophysiological recording methods are used to assess patterns of physiological responding relevant to behavior disorders or health problems. Common assessment targets have included cardiovascular responses, respiratory activity, gastrointestinal activity, electrodermal activity, cortical activity, and muscular activity (Sturgis & Gramling, 1988, 1998). Psychophysiological measures have proven useful in assessments of diverse clinical problems, particularly fear and anxiety, problems of sexual arousal, and health-related disorders. However, interpretation is complex, because psychophysiological data are influenced by many different types of individual, setting, and procedural variables. For example, like observational measures, these measures can be reactive to situational variables that are irrelevant to the problem behavior (Farrell, 1993). Moreover, the reliability and validity of many psychophysiological measures have not been well established. Finally, these measures require specialized equipment and expertise, which limits their practicality.

Assessment of Dysfunctional Cognitions

Rational emotive behavior therapy (Ellis, 1962, 1995), cognitive therapy (Beck, 1976, 1995), and other interventions aimed at cognitive restructuring call for specific assessment techniques to evaluate dysfunctional or maladaptive cognitions. Most commonly, these take the form of structured questionnaires to assess clients' self-statements, automatic thoughts, cognitive schemas, and irrational beliefs.

Self-Statements

The assessment of self-statements in specific situations originated in the work of Meichenbaum and his colleagues. For example, Meichenbaum, Gilmore, and Fedoravicius (1971) asked speech-anxious volunteers to record what they had "said to themselves" covertly when participating in an *in vivo* behavioral test of public-speaking anxiety at the start of the experiment, and those self-statements became the focus of analogue treatment. Unhelpful self-statements such as "I'm not sure I can do this. What if I faint or make a fool of myself?" would ideally be replaced by potentially helpful, coping self-statements such as "I may not be the world's greatest speaker, but I'll simply go ahead and do as well as I can. What's the worst that can happen, anyway?"

Because self-statements of this kind are assumed to be highly situation-specific, it would be practically impossible to design a validated questionnaire containing the whole range of maladaptive self-statements found in clients in general across all problem issues and diagnostic categories. One approach used by researchers has been to present people with vignettes or hypothetical scenarios describing frustrating events and then ask the participants to rate the likelihood that they would entertain each of a list of particular, designated self-statements if that situation actually arose in real life. The *Situational Self-Statement and Affective State Inventory* (SSSASI), designed by LaPointe and Harrell (1978) and further studied by Harrell, Chambless, and Calhoun (1981), presents a series of five vignettes describing irritating events and disappointing outcomes, such as not receiving an expected raise at work, having an argument with a dating partner, or having one's application to join a community committee rejected. After reading each vignette, respondents indicate to what degree they would experience certain emotional reactions as well as specific self-statements. Examples of the thoughts are: "I've really done a lousy job. I've let everybody down. My work just hasn't been any good. I don't think I can do any better," and "That liar! I know she's been seeing someone else for weeks. Somehow I'll find out who it is." Examples of the feelings are *dejected, depressed, helpless,* and *suspicious, distrustful, wronged.* Although the self-statements were phrased so as to avoid direct references to emotion, the thoughts and the feelings mapped onto the five affective categories of depression, anxiety, anger, suspicion, and rational concern. The SSSASI possesses satisfactory psychometric properties of discriminant validity, test-retest reliability, and internal consistency (Thorpe, Parker, & Barnes, 1992; Thorpe, Walter, Kingery, & Nay, 2001).

The original research on the SSSASI showed that particular thoughts correlate with specific feeling states, supporting the central cognitive therapy hypothesis that particular unhelpful self-statements are linked to emotional distress. These findings with nonclinical participants have been replicated with psychiatric inpatients and outpatients, with the additional result that the clinical respondents endorse the negative thoughts and feelings significantly more strongly than nonclinical participants (Thorpe, Barnes, Hunter, & Hines, 1983).

Automatic Thoughts and Cognitive Schemas

Treatment focused on altering clients' unhelpful self-statements has been shown effective as an intervention for depression (Rush, Beck, Kovacs, & Hollon, 1977). It is also possible to approach this correlational link between thoughts and feelings the other way around, by gauging the effects of different levels of depression on self-statements. This was accomplished in a quasi-experimental study by Dobson and Shaw (1986), who assessed two types of cognitions relevant to depression.

Cognitive therapists hypothesize that some self-statements, schema-based cognitions or *schemas,* are always present in people who are prone to depression, whereas other self-statements, *automatic thoughts,* are present only during an actual episode of depression. Schemas are fundamental, pervasive, and enduring, and it is relatively difficult to gain access to them. An example of a depressive schema could be *Whenever things start to go well, there's bound to be a huge disappointment coming.* By contrast, automatic thoughts are fleeting, situation-specific, and fairly readily accessible, such as "Oh, no! The boss wants to see me in the office! I'm going to lose my job!"

Dobson and Shaw assessed different groups of depressed inpatients and waited two weeks while they received state-of-the-art treatment. Depressed patients who improved with treatment showed significant changes in their automatic thoughts, whereas their schemas were unaffected, consistent with prediction. The *Automatic Thoughts Questionnaire* used in this study is commonly used in the cognitive-behavioral assessment of depression.

Irrational Beliefs

Surveys of *irrational beliefs* are important in research and clinical settings for assessing constructs relevant to rational emotive behavior therapy (REBT) (Smith, 1989).

The *Common Beliefs Survey—III* (CBS-III; Bessai, 1976, 1977), a 54-item inventory of irrational beliefs, is an example of the earlier questionnaires used in REBT research. Rather than comprising a disjointed list of specific, arbitrarily chosen ideas, the 54 items of the CBS-III form six empirically derived factors that make up two scales. The *evaluation* scale consists of the three factors: Blame Proneness, Self-Downing, and Perfectionism. The *locus of control* scale consists of the three factors: Importance of the Past, Importance of Approval, and Control of Emotions. This original factor structure was confirmed and replicated in a study of 264 medical patients by Tosi, Forman, Rudy, and Murphy (1986).

Recent research has shown that the CBS-III has satisfactory psychometric properties. Three of its factors—Self-Downing, Perfectionism, and Importance of the Past—correlate significantly with scores on the self-statements in the SSSASI, mentioned earlier, attesting to the construct validity of those subscales. Two factors—Self-Downing and Perfectionism—significantly discriminate patients from nonpatients (Thorpe, Parker, & Barnes, 1992).

Reflecting recent developments in REBT theory (Ellis, 1995), contemporary surveys focus on three or four general beliefs in preference to earlier lists of eleven or twelve specific ideas. Irrational thought *processes,* such as "demandingness," are assessed in addition to areas of thought *content,* such as "need for achievement" (Bernard, 1998). Factor analysis provided the empirical basis for distilling higher order, more general beliefs from the earlier more specific ones.

The *General Attitude and Belief Scale* (GABS; Bernard, 1998) is a contemporary irrational beliefs scale that includes such subscales as Self-Downing, Need for Achievement, and Rationality. Sample items from the GABS include: "I believe I would be a worthless person if I achieved poorly at tasks that are important to me" (Self-Downing subscale), and "I must do well at important things and I will not accept it if I do not do well" (Need for Achievement subscale).

Inventories of irrational beliefs are especially amenable to traditional psychometric standardization because the constructs assessed appear very similar to personality traits (Walter, Thorpe, & Kingery, 2001). This stands in marked contrast to the more traditional forms of behavioral assessment considered earlier in this chapter because of the idiographic, situation-specific focus of typical behavioral assessment strategies.

BOX **9.1**

Focus on Ethics: Using Unstandardized Assessment Methods

Consider the following scenario:

> A psychologist complains to a state licensing board that a colleague has been using unstandardized assessments routinely in her clinical practice and, on the basis of these evaluations, has frequently made confident treatment recommendations with direct implications for the health and well-being of young children with severe psychological impairments. The licensing board takes the matter seriously and asks the licensee to explain why her conduct should not be seen as representing clear violations of Ethical Standards 2.04 and 9.02(b).

Ethical Standard 2.04, Bases for Scientific and Professional Judgments, states: "Psychologists' work is based upon established scientific and professional knowledge of the discipline." Ethical Standard 9.02, Use of Assessments, reads in part: "(b) Psychologists use assessment instruments whose validity and reliability have been established for use with members of the population tested. When such validity or reliability has not been established, psychologists describe the strengths and limitations of test results and interpretation." In this context, how could a psychologist justify using unstandardized assessment methods with no normative data with which to compare a client's responses?

Nagy (2000) provides a vignette to illustrate the problem with assessment measures that have not been adequately researched. He describes a young therapist who develops an inventory of marital distress, drawing items from her clinical experience with many couples. This psychologist fails to establish that the inventory meets even minimal psychometric standards of reliability and validity, but goes ahead and uses it anyway to make clinical decisions about new couples entering treatment with her. Not mentioning to clients that the test is experimental, the psychologist sometimes makes recommendations on the basis of a couple's test scores that they consider a trial separation, thus risking potentially significant harm.

But is using an unstandardized method always unacceptable? To return to our own scenario, suppose that the psychologist replies to her licensing board as follows:

> Yes, it is true that I use assessment methods with no normative data that allow me to compare a client's scores with anyone else's, and it is true that, in a traditional sense, the psychometric properties of my assessment technique are unknown. But let me explain that the assessment method I use involves direct behavioral observation of the self-injurious behavior of children with autism. I assess each child individually over many hours within his or her residential treatment program. I tally the precise frequency with which a child attempts self-injury and carefully observe what stimuli are presented or withdrawn in temporal contiguity with the problem behavior. This allows me to assess for antecedent and consequent events that may exert powerful influences on the behavior and permits me to raise hypotheses about which stimuli to alter in order to gain therapeutic control over the self-injurious behavior.

BOX **9.1** **Continued**

As this example shows, it seems ironic that behavior therapy, arguably the most research-oriented and empirically based of the psychotherapies, could be faulted because its assessment methods are often idiopathic and do not allow for group comparisons or for the compilation of normative data. If the purpose of assessment is to measure general intellectual functioning or to place a client's personality characteristics along a series of trait-based continua, then the psychologist would be remiss if he or she used methods without standardization or group norms. If, as in this example, an idiographic approach makes sense because the aim is therapeutic, not to compare the particular client with others, then there is no ethical violation and the method used is appropriate to the professional task being undertaken.

We cannot resist ending this section on the ethics of assessment with an ironic quotation from Tryon (1998):

It is notable that the American Psychological Association has published test-user guidelines that prohibit the use of unvalidated tests but remains silent regarding the use of unvalidated clinical procedures [treatment interventions]. (p. 96)

PART THREE

Intervention

10 Psychotherapy: Research Issues and Efficacy

The astute reader will likely detect a pattern in this book. Chapters often begin with a discussion of the difficulties encountered when attempting to define some important terms used by clinical psychologists. It started in Chapter 1 when we struggled to define exactly what is clinical psychology. The theme repeated itself in Chapters 7 and 8 when we described the challenges of defining the terms *intelligence* and *personality* respectively. The dilemma presents itself again here. This time the problem word is *psychotherapy*.

What Is Psychotherapy?

This is a good question, but one that it very difficult to answer. It has been suggested, with only mild sarcasm, that it may be easier to do psychotherapy than it is to define it (London, 1986). In preparing this chapter we reviewed many suggested definitions of psychotherapy. And although we found many suitable candidates, the definition with which we felt most comfortable was one offered by John Norcross (1990, p. 218):

> Psychotherapy is the informed and intentional application of clinical methods and interpersonal stances derived from established psychological principles for the purpose of assisting people to modify their behaviors, cognitions, emotions, and/or other personal characteristics in directions that the participants deem desirable.

One might quibble with Norcross's definition by, for example, challenging the meaning of some of the key terms and phrases. What exactly is meant by "interpersonal stances," and who decides which "psychological principles" are "established" and which are not? But such an enterprise is not worth the time of the authors or the reader. The scope of "psychotherapy" is so broad that no single definition is likely to satisfy everyone. One count has the number of different psychotherapy techniques for adults at over 400 (Karuso, 1985, cited in Kazdin, 1994b). And psychotherapies for children and adolescents number over 200 (Kazdin, 1988). It is not only the number of psychotherapies that make the task of defining psychotherapy so challenging but also the diversity of approaches. Psychotherapy has been used to describe everything from primal screams (Janov, 1970) to biofeedback (Blanchard & Epstein, 1978). In light of the volume and heterogeneity of psychotherapies, it is not surprising that most definitions can be found lacking.

A better way to understand what psychotherapy is might be to look at the characteristics of the participant and their relationship. We will endeavor to give the reader a sense of psychotherapy by describing the clients, the therapists, and their relationship.

The Psychotherapy Client

Psychotherapy clients presumably seek help because they are distressed, demoralized, or in some way dissatisfied with themselves or their lives (Frank, 1961). Carl Rogers (1957) described psychotherapy clients as those "in a state of incongruence" (p. 96), meaning that there is a discrepancy between their true self and their experience of themselves. The picture one forms from these descriptions is of someone in acute psychological distress reaching out for help. For many psychotherapy clients this is probably an accurate depiction, but not for all. The reality is that the types of individuals who might be considered appropriate candidates for psychotherapeutic intervention vary quite markedly. Many seek therapy voluntarily, while others are directly or indirectly coerced into treatment. Psychotherapy clients vary in age, income, academic background, ethnicity, gender, cultural identity, intellectual ability, personality style, and presenting problems, among other factors.

If there is such variability in the types of individual participate in psychotherapy, perhaps another approach to understanding who psychotherapy clients are would be to look at who benefits from psychological treatment. One means of addressing this question is to examine the types of problems that improve with psychological intervention. We know, for example, that people with depression (Craighead, Craighead, & Ilardi, 1998), panic disorder (Barlow, Esler, & Vitali, 1998), obsessive-compulsive disorder (Franklin & Foa, 1998), and bulimia nervosa (Wilson & Fairburn, 1998) tend to benefit from specific types of psychotherapy (see Table 10.4 for a list of mental health problems that improve with psychotherapy), while those with other problems—for example, anorexia nervosa (Wilson & Fairburn, 1998) and schizophrenia (Kopelwicz & Liberman, 1998)—often do not improve with psychological intervention by itself. There are two difficulties with defining who are appropriate psychotherapy clients by looking at their presenting problems. First, not all problems for which people seek psychotherapy fall neatly into one diagnostic category or another. Second, a careful look at the research supporting psychotherapy for specific problems reveals that not all clients improve to the same degree. While many people improve with psychological treatment, some don't and a few get worse.

Another approach to defining the psychotherapy client would be to look at who seeks psychotherapy and who stays involved with psychological treatment after it has been initiated. Studies tend to find that a disproportionate percentage of people who seek psychotherapy are white, middle or upper-middle class, and better educated (e.g., Kadushin, 1969). Similarly, several studies have found that clients from lower socioeconomic classes tend to drop out of treatment earlier (e.g., Pilkonis, Imber, & Rubinsky, 1984). Ethnicity has also been studied as it relates to psychotherapy use, completion, and success. In a large-scale study of over 13,000 Asian American, African American, Mexican American, and European American consumers of community mental health services in Los Angeles County, Sue, Fujino, Ju, Takeuchi, and Zane (1991; described in Garfield, 1994) found that Asian and Mexican American's were underrepresented among psychotherapy users, whereas African Americans were overrepresented. African Americans tended to have less positive outcomes. Perhaps not surprising, an ethnic match between therapists and clients was associated with longer involvement in psychotherapy and better outcome.

Conventional wisdom has it that as people get older, they are more set in their ways, rigid, and resistant to change. Following from this assumption, elderly clients were assumed to make poorer psychotherapy subjects. Earlier studies tended, in fact, to find a weak negative relationship between age and prognosis in psychotherapy studies (Luborsky, Chandler, Auerbach, Cohen, & Bachrach, 1971). Studies supporting the view that elderly clients make poorer psychotherapy clients tended to involve long-term analytically oriented psychotherapy (Garfield, 1994). More recent studies of shorter-term, cognitive-behavioral and brief dynamic psychotherapies have found that these interventions yield positive results, comparable to those found with younger clients, when delivered to elderly depressed patients (Thompson, Gallagher, & Breckenridge, 1987). In general, it appears that the elderly are as responsive to briefer, problem-oriented psychotherapy as are other adult clients.

A host of client variables that relate to treatment outcome have been studied (see Garfield, 1994, for review). For many of these variables, there exists a study or two demonstrating a correlation with outcome. But inconsistent findings and failures to replicate are common and it is difficult to draw general conclusions about many of these variables. One exception is the relationship between the degree of disturbance and treatment outcome. A fairly consistent finding is that the severity of the clients' pathology at pretreatment is negatively correlated with treatment outcome. For example, while people who are more severely depressed at the outset of treatment tend to improve with psychotherapy, they are often still depressed at posttreatment (e.g., Burns & Nolen-Hoeksema, 1991; Hoberman, Lewisohn, & Tilson, 1988). Similar findings have been reported for people with panic disorder (Keijsers, Hoogduin, & Schaap, 1994).

The Psychotherapist

Besides the client, the other main participant in the psychotherapy relationship is the therapist. Who are psychotherapists? Many psychotherapists are doctoral-level clinical psychologists, but a doctorate in clinical psychology is not a requirement. People from a wide variety of other disciplines function as psychotherapists, including social work, psychiatry, nursing, counseling psychology, educational psychology, and others. Studies of therapists from different professional disciplines have not found that psychotherapy clients consistently prefer one discipline over another, nor that professionals from one discipline are always more effective therapists than those from a different professional background (Beutler, Machado, & Neufeldt, 1994).

In fact, even people without graduate-level training sometimes function as therapists. These "nonprofessional" therapists can be quite effective. Empirical studies comparing professional and nonprofessional therapists have have not been too encouraging for those of us involved in higher-level training of mental health providers. Literature reviews tend to find no systematic advantage for professionally trained therapists over nonprofessional therapists (Berman & Norton, 1985; Weisz, Weiss, Alicke, & Klotz, 1987). Similarly, therapists' level of experience has not consistently emerged as a significant predictor of treatment outcome (Beutler et al., 1994).

If not professional training, than what other characteristics define a psychotherapist? Writers describing the preferred characteristics of therapists from a variety of different theoretical orientation tend to highlight similar therapist attributes (e.g., Beck, Rush, Shaw, & Emery, 1979; Pipes & Davenport, 1999; Rogers, 1957; Teyber, 2000). Psychotherapists take a *nonjudgmental* stance with their clients. They express empathy, warmth, and caring. They place clients' interests, needs, and problems above their own during the therapy hour. Psychotherapists are *genuine*—that is, honest with themselves and their clients.

A final attribute shared by psychotherapists, regardless of their theoretical orientation or professional training, is that they are recognized as socially sanctioned healers (Frank, 1961). When people consult psychotherapists, there is an unspoken recognition by both parties that the therapist will play the role of helper.

Characteristics of psychotherapists have been studied extensively (see Beutler et al., 1994, for review) and this literature is extremely complex. For many therapist attributes, the relationship to treatment outcome is moderated by client characteristics and type of therapy. A few factors, however, have emerged as fairly robust predictors of treatment outcome. Therapists' well-being, their expectations about client progress, and their competence tend to be associated with treatment outcome. The positive finding for therapist competence is reassuring for those of us involved with training clinicians. At first glance, this finding might seem inconsistent with the research we had alluded to earlier that has found no relationship between therapists' level of experience, or their level of training, and outcome. But competence is different from amount of experience or level of professional training. Anyone who has been involved in training psychotherapists knows that some students take to the role of psychotherapist quite naturally, whereas others, regardless of amount of experience or training, never quite master the role.

The Psychotherapy Relationship

The relationship between the psychotherapy client and therapist is unique. As you will see in the following chapters, some schools of therapy see the relationship as the primary mechanism of change. Other approaches view the relationship as facilitative of, but not necessary for, change. Rather than discuss the therapy relationship through the lens of a particular theoretical orientation at this point, we will discuss some of the features of the psychotherapy relationship that cut across theoretical orientation and that distinguish the relationship from most others.

One characteristic that helps to define the therapy relationship is the setting within which it takes place. Psychotherapy occurs in a socially sanctioned place of healing (Frank, 1961). Clients are typically seen in a professional office. The frequency and length of meetings is planned and subject to strict limitations. Typically, psychotherapy clients are seen for weekly 50- to 60-minute appointments. Contact between therapists and their clients outside of the therapy hour is governed by specific rules. In fact, it is generally considered professionally unwise, and ethically risky, for psychotherapists and clients to have any type of relationship outside of their professional one.

Unlike most other relationships, the psychotherapy liaison has a specified purpose—to help the client achieve his or her goals. This should be the sole reason why the relationship has formed. Therefore, when the goals have been achieved the relationship should end. Therapists and clients join together to help the clients overcome their problems. This aspect of the therapy relationship is sometimes called the "therapeutic alliance" (Gaston, 1990). This subjective sense, shared by the therapist and client, that they are working together plays an important role in therapy.

The information that psychotherapy clients share with their therapist is confidential. While there are limits to confidentiality, the trust that the therapist will not disclose what the client says to anyone makes the therapy relationship unlike most other. The freedom to share one's greatest fears, one's most personal memories, one's doubts, and one's hopes with someone who accepts this information without passing judgment occurs rarely in human relationships. As such, the relationship is often a very intimate one. Yet the professional nature of the relationship, the fact that personal information is shared by one participant and not the other, and its time limits distinguish the relationship between therapist and client from other close connections.

Integrating what we have said so far about client, therapist, and relationship, a picture of what psychotherapy is begins to emerge. Psychotherapy involves the coming together of one or more persons in distress with a socially sanctioned helper for the purpose of overcoming the client's problem. A relationship develops in which the information shared with the therapist is kept in confidence; the client's, as opposed to the therapist's, issues are the focus; there are strict limitations on the place and time of contact; and there is an understanding that the relationship is time-limited.

Research Issues

"In the absence of science, opinion prevails" (Nathan & Gorman, 1998b, p. ix). This quote is taken from the preface of the book *A Guide to Treatments That Work,* which summarizes the scientific evidence for psychological and pharmacological treatments of psychiatric disorders. The quote captures one of the arguments for a scientific approach to clinical psychology—the best way to advance knowledge is through the application of scientific methods. But are all phenomena understandable via the scientific method? What about psychotherapy? Scientific research attempts to isolate specific variables so that they can be scrutinized carefully. The process of isolating a single variable or small set of variables tends to simplify complex phenomena. Does this simplification change the phenomena? For example, in the case of psychotherapy, does the process of administering a therapy in a uniform manner to several different clients somehow change the therapy so that it loses some important characteristic (e.g., flexible responsiveness to clients' needs)? These are the types of questions that psychotherapy researchers must grapple with on a daily basis. Such questions have led many clinicians to adopt a cynical view of the relevance of scientific studies of psychotherapy to their day-to-day work with patients (Edelson, 1994; Havens, 1994). We explore the relationship between psychotherapy research and psychotherapy practice in Box 10.1.

B O X   **10.1**

The Scientist-Practitioner-Psychotherapist

Think for a moment about the Boulder model of training clinical psychologists. Clinical psychologists are trained as scientist and practitioners. The goal of Boulder model training is not to produce professionals who function as scientists on Monday, Wednesday, and Friday and practitioners on Tuesdays and Thursday. Rather the goal is integration of science and practice. Clinical psychologists carry with them the values, methods, and knowledge of science into the clinical arena. If this is the ideal, then how would a clinical psychologist go about practicing psychotherapy. In other words, what would a scientist-practitioner-psychotherapist look like?

At a minimum level, scientist-practitioner-psychologists would be consumers of the psychotherapy research literature and would base clinical decisions upon empirical findings. In the absence of relevant empirical research, clinicians would base their decisions upon appropriately validated theory. Does this happen? Unfortunately, most of the available evidence suggests that it does not, or at least not as often as the developers of the scientist-practitioner model might have hoped. A survey by Morrow-Bradley and Elliot (1986) of psychologist-psychotherapists found that only about 30 percent of the respondents reported that they used psychotherapy research frequently to inform their psychotherapy practices. Psychotherapists cited many problems with the psychotherapy research literature that limited its utility. Many pointed out that the research questions, or the populations studied, were of little relevance to their practices. Others criticized the emphasis upon group statistics and statistical significance between groups. Knowing that one group of subjects outperformed another group provides little guidance for dealing with individual clients. Finally, some therapists acknowledged that they simply did not have the time to sift through research articles.

There are reasons to believe that the gap between psychotherapy research and psychotherapy practice may be closing. Three recent developments may facilitate the consumption and use of psychotherapy research by psychotherapists. First, information about which forms of psychotherapy have been shown in clinical trials to be helpful for specific types of clinical problems is now more readily available. Division 12 of the American Psychological Association, for example, began to publish and update a list of treatments that enjoy empirical support in 1995 (see Table 10.4). The publication of these lists and other efforts to identify empirically supported treatment alleviate the practitioner of the time-consuming task of poring over research journals to identify the treatments supported by research. Second, training in the specific types of psychotherapy is becoming easier to obtain. Several publishing companies have begun publishing practitioner-guide books that describe the treatments in enough detail that a generally well-trained clinician could apply them. In addition, clinicians have access to workshops, videotaped presentations, and web-based instruction in the empirically supported treatments. The third factor that may facilitate the closing of the scientist-practitioner gap is the increased pressure upon psychotherapists to defend their clinical practices applied by insurance carriers and managed care corporations. Although "managed-care" is a four-letter word to most practitioners, the increased accountability associated with this form of health-care delivery may force them to change their practices to include therapies that have some measure of scientific support.

Goals of Psychotherapy Research

Psychotherapy research, like any research endeavor, begins with a question. Does interpersonal psychotherapy help people with bulimia nervosa? What is the best treatment for depression? What are the characteristics of people with panic disorder who improve significantly with treatment? How does cognitive therapy help people with depression? Are therapist characteristics associated with positive outcome in client-centered therapy? What components of cognitive behavior therapy for social anxiety are responsible for therapeutic change? The goal of any given study is to answer the researcher's question.

The short list of research questions in the preceding paragraph give a flavor of the variety of psychotherapy research goals. In general, the goals of psychotherapy research can be organized under three headings: (1) to understand the efficacy of various forms of treatment for various problems (research designed to address this goal is frequently called *outcome* research); (2) to understand the mechanisms by which treatments work (this type of research is often called *process* research); and (3) and to understand the factors that influence the efficacy of specific treatments. When one considers the variety of types of problems for which psychotherapy has been, or could potentially be, applied (e.g., there are over 300 diagnostic categories in the DSM-IV) and the number of types of psychotherapy, it quickly becomes apparent that the quantity of possible research questions is, for all intents and purposes, infinite.

How then do psychotherapy researchers decide upon the research questions they want to explore? In contemporary clinical psychology it is often the case that new research questions are generated by previous research. The research enterprise is one that expands as it develops. For every question a study answers it may generate several new ones. Let us illustrate with a real example. In the mid-1960s Meyer reported on a series of patients with obsessive-compulsive disorder whom he treated by exposing them to obsessional cues (e.g., having compulsive hand washers purposely soil their hands) and then strictly preventing them from engaging in the compulsive behavior (e.g., not allowing hand washing). Meyer originally reported on the successful treatment of two patients (Meyer, 1966) and later on a larger sample (Meyer & Levy, 1973; Meyer, Levy, & Schurer, 1974). These uncontrolled investigations led to a series of controlled studies in which the treatment, exposure with response prevention, was compared to a variety of control conditions and found to be consistently effective with about 70 percent of patients studied (see Foa, Steketee, & Azarow, 1985, for review). The success of exposure with response prevention led to questions about the contributions of the two main components of treatment. In a series of studies comparing the relative effects of exposure and response-prevention, Foa and her colleagues discovered that the combination of the two techniques was superior to either intervention alone (Foa, Steketee, Grayson, Turner, & Latimer, 1984; Foa, Steketee, & Milby, 1980; Steketee, Foa, & Grayson, 1982). This line of research fueled theoretical thinking about mechanisms of action underlying exposure with response prevention and other exposure-based treatments (see, for example, Foa & Kozak, 1986; Hecker & Thorpe, 1987). A variety of other research questions developed out of the studies showing exposure and response prevention to be helpful for most people with obsessive-compulsive disorder, including: Can the effects of exposure with response prevention be enhanced by the addition of a pharmacological treatment (e.g., Marks et al., 1980)? How effective is exposure with response prevention compared to pharmacological treatment (Foa, Kozak, Steketee, & McCarthy, 1992)? Does inclusion of spouses in the treatment of people with obsessive-compulsive disorder enhance the efficacy of exposure with response prevention (Emmelkamp, van der Helm, van Zanten, & Ploch, 1990)? Can people with OCD successfully apply exposure with response prevention therapy on their own (Fritzler, Hecker, & Losee, 1997)? Will modified versions of exposure with response prevention therapy be helpful for other mental health problems such as bulimia (Leitenberg, Rosen, Gross, Nudelman, & Vara, 1988)?

Not all lines of psychotherapy research can be traced to a single case or series of cases. But the *case study* is a valuable strategy for developing research hypotheses. The case study is an in-depth investigation of a single person or situation. In psychotherapy, it usually involves a thorough exploration of an individual, including personal history and detailed exploration of the therapeutic strategies that seem to be responsible for therapeutic change. The case study method was the only technique used by Freud (for example, the case of Anna O.; see Chapter 3). The case study is a good method for generating research hypotheses; it cannot, however, be used to answer research questions.

The research strategies used by a psychotherapy researcher are determined by a variety of factors, the most important of which is the research question. Questions about the relative efficacy of two psychotherapies lead to certain types of research designs and methods, whereas questions about how a treatment works would require a different design and method to answer.

Psychotherapy Research Strategies

Psychotherapy research studies usually fall into one of three major types: *true experiments, quasi-experiments,* and *passive-observational* (sometimes call naturalistic) designs (Kazdin, 1994). In true experiments, the researchers exert the greatest degree of control over the independent variable or variables of interest. A psychotherapy study that would be classified as a true experiment would have the following characteristics: (1) Participants are carefully selected and are relatively homogeneous for the problem of interest (e.g., all meet DSM-IV criteria for panic disorder and no other psychiatric condition, are not receiving pharmacological treatment, and are of similar age and educational experience); (2) participants are randomly assigned to treatment conditions (e.g., cognitive-behavior therapy, interpersonal psychotherapy, or wait-list control); and (3) treatments are delivered by competent therapists who faithfully follow the treatment protocol. From a research standpoint, true experiments allow us to make the strongest inferences about the relationship between the independent variable (e.g., the treatment) and the dependent variable (e.g. the disorder).

There are times, however, when researchers cannot control all the characteristics of a study. That is, some independent variables are influenced by the experimenter but not fully controlled. When the conditions of a true experiment are not quite met, but are only approximated, the research is referred to as quasi-experimental (Cook & Campbell, 1979). Often what distinguishes a quasi-experiment from a true experiment is whether subjects are randomly assigned to conditions. For example, if a researcher wanted to compare the relative effects of cognitive-behavior therapy (CBT) and interpersonal psychotherapy (IPT) for the treatment of panic disorder, he or she might train the therapists in clinic A in CBT for panic disorder and the therapists who work in clinic B in IPT. The researcher then compares the success rates for clinics A and B. This is a quasi-experiment because participants are not randomly assigned to treatment conditions. In a quasi-experiment it is usually impossible to confidently conclude that differences observed in the dependent variable are due to differences in the independent variable. In our example, if the researcher found that people with panic disorder seen at clinic A did better than those seen at clinic B, he or she could not be sure that the difference was due to CBT being a better treatment than IPT. It is possible that characteristics of the clients seen at the two clinics (e.g., different education levels) might be responsible for the different outcomes. Other differences between the two clinics (e.g., physical qualities of the buildings, support staff, access to parking) may have affected participants' motivation for and success in treatment. With a quasi-experimental design, one can't be sure.

In both true experiments and quasi-experiments, independent variables are manipulated by the experimenters. In passive-observational designs the experimenter does not attempt to control the variables of interest but rather allows them to vary as they will. The experimenter observes and looks for relationships among different variables. Naturalistic studies often involve relatively large numbers of subjects so that there is opportunity for variables of interest to vary enough so that relationships among them can be discovered. An interesting example of this type of research was published by Burns and Nolen-Hoeksema (1992). They were interested in the relationship between therapeutic empathy and clinical improvement in depressed patients treated with cognitive behavior therapy. Over the course of the study 185 depressed patients were treated with cognitive-behavior therapy. Although the researchers were interested in empathy, they did not systematically manipulate the level of empathy exhibited by the therapists. Rather, they simply asked the patients to rate how warm, caring, and empathic their therapists were. Using sophisticated statistical procedures, they showed that there was a direct relationship between the amount of empathy experienced by patients and their degree of improvement over the course of therapy.

Psychotherapy Research Designs

The specific research design used by psychotherapy researchers is primarily determined by the research questions but is also influenced by such factors as the number and types of participants the researcher has access to, the researcher's financial resources, the research setting, and others. In the following section we will describe some more frequently used psychotherapy research designs.

Single-Subject and Small N Designs.   While the bulk of psychotherapy research reported in the clinical literature involves a large number of subjects who have been randomly assigned to different treatment conditions, it is possible to conduct valid research using only one subject. This approach to research is called *single-subject experimental design* (Barlow & Hersen, 1984; Hayes, 1981; Kazdin, 1982). Although these designs are most closely associated with behavioral approaches to therapy, there is no reason why they could not be used to test therapies drawn from other theoretical orientations (e.g., Kolko & Milan, 1983).

In single-case experimental and small N design studies, the researcher/clinician repeatedly measures the behavior of interest (the dependent variable) and looks for changes in the behavior that coincide with introduction of the treatment (the independent variable). The logic underlying single subject and small N experimental designs is based upon the assumption that the changes observed in the dependent variables that coincide with the introduction and/or cessation of the independent variable are unlikely to occur by chance when they appear repeatedly.

There are several essential requirements for a single-case experimental design study. First, the client's behaviors, thoughts, or feelings, which are the target of the intervention, need to be specified in such a manner that they can be repeatedly measured. Repeated measurement might involve tracking the frequency of a specified type of thought (e.g., client pushes a golf counter every time she thinks about binge eating), counting how often a certain behavior is engaged in (e.g., how many cigarettes smoked), or rating the intensity of an emotional experience (e.g., daily rating of depressed mood). Repeated assessment is essential because the therapist/researcher needs to know the pattern and stability of the behavior before intervening. Repeatedly assessing the behavior over a period of time establishes the *baseline* level of the behavior. The second requirement of single-case experimentation is that the intervention must be clearly specified. It must be clear when the intervention has been implemented and when implementation has ceased. The third essential component is *replication*. The logic of single-case experimental design dictates that the influence of the independent variable upon the dependent variable must be repeatedly demonstrated.

Single-case experimental designs are traditionally described using a series of uppercase letters. Each letter represents a different phase of the study. The baseline phase is usually indicated by letter A. The introduction of the first intervention is denoted by the letter B and subsequent interventions are symbolized using successive letters (i.e., C, D, E, and so on). A common example would be an A/B/A/B design. In this design, treatment B is introduced after an appropriate baseline period; it is withdrawn and then reintroduced. The following example illustrates the A/B/A/B design. Johnston, Kelley, Harris, and Wolf (1966) intervened with a preschool-age boy (Don) who was excessively shy and passive. Typically, Don stood quietly in the playground as the other children played. The researcher noted that the more the teachers encouraged Don to play, the more he withdrew. They hypothesized that, although well intended, the teachers might be reinforcing passive behavior by their attention. The therapists/researchers decided to test their hypothesis. Treatment consisted of having the teachers ignore Don when he stood alone but attend to Don when he played appropriately. They targeted times spent using a popular climbing apparatus as the first place to apply the treatment. Figure 10.1 illustrates their findings. During five days of baseline observation (A), Don played on the climber during less than 10 percent of his free time. During the intervention period (B) the teachers attended to any approximation of the desired behavior. The teachers then withdrew their attention for climbing (second A) and finally reintroduced attention contingent upon climbing behavior (second B). As the bar graphs illustrate, Don climbed on the apparatus when the teachers attended to this behavior but not when their attention was withdrawn. The fact that the relationship between attention for climbing and climbing was repeatedly shown supports the hypothesis that Don's behavior was strongly influenced by teacher attention.

Single-case experimental designs can be used to address a variety of important questions. The A/B/A/B design examines whether treatment B leads to changes in the targeted behavior or not. More complex questions can be addressed as well. For example, single-case experimentation can be used to examine the relative benefits of two forms of treatment

Percentage of outdoor play spent climbing

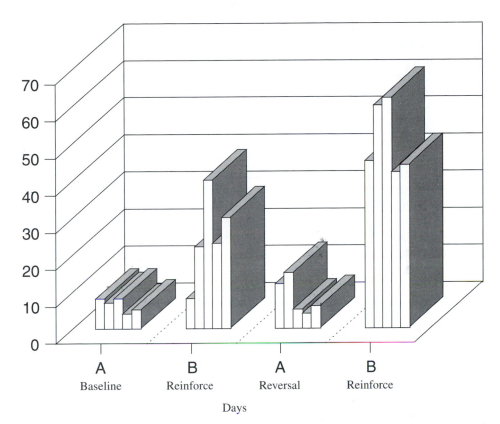

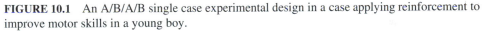

FIGURE 10.1   An A/B/A/B single case experimental design in a case applying reinforcement to improve motor skills in a young boy.

Adapted from Johnston, Kelley, Harris, & Wolf (1966). An application of reinforcement principles to development of motor skills of a young child. *Child Development, 37,* 379–387.

(A/B/A/C) or whether adding new components to an intervention leads to additional improvement (A/B/B+C/B).

The basic A/B/A/B design is appropriate for some types of psychotherapy but not others. The approach has been a particularly productive one for behavior therapists approaching problems from an operant perspective. Changing the contingencies of reinforcement changes the frequency of behaviors. The design lends itself to operant approaches because reinforcers can be introduced and withdrawn. The A/B/A/B design can be used to test the effects of medications as well. For example, the frequency of disruptive behavior of a child with attention-deficit hyperactivity disorder can be observed before psychostimulants are administered, while the child is on the medication, when it is withdrawn and then reintroduced. The effects of the medications are reversible. Designs that require that the therapeutic effects of an intervention disappear when the treatment is withdrawn are not appropriate for interventions that are designed to have a lasting effect (e.g., we don't expect a broken arm to return to its fractured state once the cast is removed).

When interventions are expected to have lasting effects, alternative research designs need to be employed. *Multiple baseline* designs can be useful for these types of intervention. In a multiple baseline single-subject experiment, the therapist/researcher intervenes with different behaviors after varying lengths of baseline observation. If each behavior improves coincident with the introduction of treatment, it is logical to assume that the treatment caused the observed change in the target behavior.

The logic of the multiple baseline can be applied with a small group of participants presenting the same or similar problems. In a study with a multiple baseline across individuals, at least one behavior is recorded across several individuals. The treatment is introduced to each individual after a different length of baseline assessment. For example, a researchers interested in the impact of medication X on children with attention problems might employ a multiple baseline design across three children to test the drug's effects. The percentage of time spent on task for each child is measured every day by a classroom observer. The medication is given to each child after a different number of days of baseline assessment (e.g., 5, 8, and 11). Let's say that during baseline assessment, the percentage of time spent on task for child 1 varies from 10 percent to 16 percent over five days of baseline. For child 2 it varies from 8 percent to 14 percent over 8 days, and for child 3 it varies from 12 percent to 21 percent over 11 days of baseline assessment. If each child's percentage of time on task jumps to over 80 percent coincident with the introduction of medication X (i.e., for child 1, day 6; for child 2, day 9; and child 3, day 12), it would provide strong evidence that taking the medication caused the improvement in on-task time.

Between-Group Designs.   The majority of psychotherapy studies that appear in the professional journals utilize *between-group* designs. The basic elements of a between-group design psychotherapy study include one group of individuals who receive a specific treatment (the *experimental group*) and another group who receive no treatment (the *control group*). The two groups of subjects are assessed before and after a course of psychotherapy. If the experimental group improves more from pre- to posttreatment, the researcher can conclude that psychotherapy is more helpful than the passage of time. This basic building block of between-group design research is sometimes called pretest-posttest control group design (Kazdin, 1994b).

The logic of between-group design research goes something like this. If the researcher can hold everything constant between pretreatment and posttreatment for two groups of subjects, with the exception that one group receives psychotherapy and the other does not, then it is safe to conclude that it is the psychotherapy that caused any differences observed between the two groups. In reality, of course, researchers cannot keep everything constant between psychotherapy and control groups over the course of treatment. One or more clients may lose a job, have a car accident, get a promotion, get divorced, get the flu, or run a marathon during the interval between pre- and posttreatment. It is impossible for the researcher to control for all of these *nuisance* variables. Instead, researchers rely upon *random assignment* to treatment and control conditions to balance out these factors. The assumption of random assignment is that the presence of these nuisance variables will be evenly distributed between the treatment and control group if participants are assigned randomly to each condition. While this assumptions is a fair one for studies in which a fairly large number of participants are included, it is not necessarily accurate when there is a small N, as is common in many studies of psychotherapy (Hsu, 1989).

Many psychotherapy researchers do not use a "no treatment" condition as the control group. There are ethical and methodological problems with simply assessing but not treating groups of people who are in psychological distress. It is not ethically defensible to recruit people for a study of psychotherapy and then not provide them with treatment. Methodologically, the no-treatment control group presents problems as well. Individuals who are not receiving treatment may feel discouraged and search elsewhere for help. Instead of receiving no treatment, they may receive another form of help (e.g., medication, another psychotherapy) between pre- and posttreatment. As an alternative to no treatment, psychotherapy researchers often use a *wait-list* control. Participants in a wait-list control group are told that they will receive treatment at the end of a set waiting period. This way participants are less likely to lose hope and seek treatment elsewhere.

Wait-list control conditions are appropriate for determining whether a psychotherapy is more effective than the simple passage of time. However, the inferences one can draw from a treatment versus no treatment design are limited. While it may be appropriate to conclude that the treatment produced more change than no treatment using such a design, it would be inappropriate to conclude that the treatment worked for the reasons the researcher thinks it worked. The main limitation of the active-treatment versus no-treatment design is that there are a variety of plausible explanations for why participants in the active treatment condition improved and the no-treatment participants did not.

The problem of identifying the active ingredient in treatment is one that medical researchers have grappled with for a long time. In drug treatment studies, the researchers want to be sure that it is the pharmacological agents that caused the change. In these studies the pharmacological agent of interest is compared to a pharmacologically inert substance, called a *placebo*. If the real medication outperforms the placebo, then the researcher can attribute the improvement to the pharmacological agent and not the psychological effects of undergoing treatment or taking "medicine."

Following from the drug-study approach, psychotherapy researchers may want to use a placebo psychological intervention as the comparison group in a between-groups design study. Borrowing the placebo design from medicine is more complicated, however, than it might first seem. Remember, in pharmacotherapy studies, the placebo condition controls for psychological effects. Do we really want to control for psychological effects when studying psychological interventions? Defining placebo this way would, of course, be ludicrous for psychotherapy researchers.

There are at least two approaches one might take to create a placebo psychotherapy. One would be to create a treatment that is credible (i.e., believable to the clients) but should not work according to the theory upon which the active treatment is based (Parloff, 1986). The problem with a definition of placebo that includes the "theoretically inert" notion is that there are a multitude of theories of psychotherapy. "(V)irtually every currently established psychotherapy would be considered inert, and therefore a placebo, from the viewpoint of other established theories of cure" (Critellie & Neumann, 1984, p. 33).

An alternative way of defining a placebo psychotherapy is to say that the placebo treatment is one that includes only "common factors" that are present across different psychotherapies. Empathy, therapeutic alliance, positive expectations, and confronting problems are examples of factors that are present in a variety of psychotherapies (Weinberger, 1995). Common factors are components of psychotherapy that are not specific to any one approach to treatment. Placebo psychotherapy would be an intervention that includes these components but not other components that are assumed to be important for therapeutic change. When an intervention is shown to be superior to a common-factors placebo it can be concluded that the specific intervention adds to the effect of the common factors alone.

This approach has some merit. However, it is not clear that labeling a common-factors intervention as a placebo really adds to our knowledge in any way. Several commentators have suggested abandoning the placebo concept for psychotherapy research because of the conceptual and practical problems it creates (e.g., Horvath, 1988; Senger, 1987; Wilkins, 1986). The placebo construct carries with it negative connotations that do not help further our understanding of psychotherapy, nor does it facilitate our efforts to develop the most efficacious therapeutic interventions.

From the basic pretest-posttest control group design building block, more and more complicated research designs can be constructed. We will describe some of the more common designs below.

The most basic research question a researcher might ask is whether a particular treatment is helpful for a particular clinical problem. Psychotherapies are typically made up of a variety of components that are delivered together as a package. The most basic question then is "Does the treatment package alleviate the problem?" Edna Foa and her colleagues used such a design to study the efficacy of a brief cognitive-behavioral treatment package for preventing long-term problems in women who had recently been raped (Foa, Hearst-Ikeda, & Perry, 1995). Twenty women who had recently been raped were studied. Ten of the women were treated with a brief prevention program based upon a cognitive behavioral intervention that had been shown to be helpful for rape victims with PTSD (Foa, Rothbaum, Riggs, & Murdock; 1991). The brief prevention program consisted of four meetings with a therapist and included education about the common reactions to sexual assault, breathing and relaxation training, imaginal reliving of the assault, confronting feared but objectively safe situations, and cognitive restructuring (i.e., helping the women to think objectively about themselves and challenging irrational beliefs related to the trauma). The other ten women received no treatment but were assessed five times over a 12-week period (assessment-only control). The women who received the brief prevention intervention showed greater decreases in depression and PTSD symptoms than the control subjects over the course of the treatment period and two months after the program had ended. Immediately following the brief intervention program, 10 percent of the women who had received the treatment met criteria for PTSD. By contrast, 70 percent of the women in the control group met criteria for PTSD.

After a treatment package has been shown to lead to therapeutic change, researchers often turn their attention to identifying the components of treatment that lead to change. *Dismantling designs* are used to address the questions: What components are necessary for change? What components are sufficient? And what components facilitate therapeutic change (Kazdin, 1998). In a dismantling design, different components of the treatment are isolated. In a typical study of this type, one group of subjects receives the entire treatment package and other groups receive various components.

Neil Jacobson and several colleagues used a dismantling design to experimentally test the theory of change proposed to explain how cognitive behavior therapy helps people who are depressed (Jacobson et al., 1996). It had already been established that cognitive behavior therapy is an effective treatment for depression (Dobson, 1989). The treatment, as described by Aaron Beck and colleagues (Beck, Rush, Shaw, & Emery, 1979), consists of several components. Early in treatment, depressed clients are encouraged to become more active and put themselves into contact with people and situations that are reinforcing. For example, clients are instructed to plan enjoyable activities to be engaged in between therapy sessions. As therapy progresses, clients are taught to identify negative thoughts that are associated with downward shifts in mood. Therapists then help clients to see the irrational nature of these thoughts and to change them so that they are more logical and positive. Finally, late in therapy clients' core beliefs about themselves and assumptions about the world are identified and alternative beliefs and assumptions are developed. Jacobson and colleagues (1996) treated 150 depressed individuals with one of three forms of cognitive behavior therapy: (1) behavioral activation only (this intervention focused exclusively upon helping clients to become more active); (2) activation and modification of dysfunctional thoughts (this intervention included activation but also modification of maladaptive automatic thoughts); and (3) the full cognitive behavioral treatment including exploration and modification of core beliefs and assumptions. Following from the theoretical formulation proposed by Beck and colleagues (1979), Jacobson and colleagues (1996) predicted that the full cognitive behavioral treatment would be more effective than the behavioral activation component alone or in combination with challenging of automatic thoughts. Contrary to their predictions, however, they found no evidence that the full treatment was any more effective than its components. The findings of Jacobson and colleagues raise serious questions about what theory of change best accounts for the success of cognitive behavior therapy of depression and what are the necessary and sufficient conditions for change. The study is an excellent example of how a dismantling design can be used to test a theory about the mechanism of change for a specific psychotherapy.

A research strategy that can seem quite similar to the dismantling design is the *constructive research strategy*. The research questions addressed with the constructive design are, however, quite different from those addressed with the dismantling strategy. Constructive designs are used to examine how to improve upon an established treatment. A treatment package may be developed by starting with the core component and adding components to see whether they lead to enhanced benefits. *In vivo* exposure therapy is the treatment of choice for people suffering with severe agoraphobic avoidance. With the therapists support, agoraphobic clients go into situations that they typically avoid (e.g., a crowded shopping mall) and stay there until their anxiety subsides (Hecker & Thorpe, 1992). Using a constructive research strategy, Arnow, Taylor, Agras, and Telch (1985) found that a group of agoraphobic clients who received couples communication training after a course of in vivo exposure therapy were doing much better eight months following treatment compared to a group of agoraphobics who had exposure therapy but not couples communication training.

Between-group designs are not only used to examine the impact of a single treatment or treatment package. They can be used to compare the efficacy of two or more treatments. In the most basic comparison design, treatment A is provided to one group of participants and treatment B to a second. For example, O'Leary, Heyman, and Neidig (1999) compared two forms of group therapy for wife abuse. Married couples were accepted into the study if there had been repeated instances of husband-to-wife physical aggression. Half of the couples received Gender Specific treatment. In this condition, men were seen in groups of six to eight for therapy that emphasized that the male is solely responsible for past abuse and for stopping abusive behavior. The wives of these men were also seen for group therapy that focused upon identifying characteristics of abusive relationships, understanding the effects of violence, and evaluating the advantages and disadvantages of staying in their marriage. The other half of the subjects received Physical Aggression Couples Treatment (Heyman & Neidig, 1997). In this treatment, groups of six to eight couples met together for fourteen sessions. The focus of this treatment was on the couples' working together to accept responsibility for the escalation of angry interchanges and to eliminate physical and psychological aggression in their homes. Both treatments resulted in significant reductions in psychological and physical aggression, but the conjoint couples' intervention led to significantly greater improvement in the husbands' marital adjustment. Unfortunately, neither treatment consistently led to an elimination of physical aggression in the treated couples. Over a one year follow-up period 75 percent of the husbands committed acts of physical aggression.

From the basic comparison of two alternative treatments, comparison designs can increase in complexity. One of the largest-scale and best-known studies of psychotherapy used a more complex design to examine the efficacy of two forms of treatment for depression: Interpersonal Psychotherapy and Cognitive Behavior Therapy. The National Institute of Mental Health Treatment of Depression Collaborative Research Program (NIMH-TDCRP) compared the two psychotherapies to each other but also to an established treatment (Imipramine) and a stringent control condition (placebo drug plus clinical management) (Elkin, 1994). The design of the NIMH-TDCRP study allowed the researchers to examine several research questions: Is each treatment effective (CBT versus placebo; IPT versus placebo)? Is one treatment more effective than another (CBT versus IPT)? How does each psychotherapy compare with an established drug treatment (Imipramine versus CBT; Imipramine versus IPT)?

Factorial design studies are another form of between-group design that allows researchers to look at more complex research questions. In factorial designs, the impact of two or more factors are examined alone or in combination. The simplest factorial design includes two variables, each of which has two levels or conditions. For example, psychotherapy might be considered one variable with two levels: therapy A and therapy B. The other factor of interest might be therapist gender which would, of course, have two levels also male and female. Combining each level of each variable results in a 2×2 design.

The main reason for using a factorial design is to examine the combination of two or more variables. Factorial designs are used to test whether there is an *interaction* between two or more variables. An interaction means that the effect of one variable (e.g., type of treatment) is dependent upon another variable (e.g., gender of the therapist). In our hypothetical study, an interaction would be found if participants who receive treatment B improve to a significantly greater degree if treatment is provided by a female therapist.

Factorial designs can be used to study the effects of two or more types of treatment. Four findings are possible when treatments are combined: an additive effect (i.e., the effects of each treatment combines to equal the sum of the two treatment effects); inhibitory effects (i.e., the effects of the combined treatment is less than the more powerful treatment alone); interaction effects (i.e., the effects of the two treatments is greater than either alone) or reciprocal effects (i.e., the combined treatment is as effective as the more powerful treatment alone).

There is a growing interest in the combined effects of psychological and pharmacological treatments for people suffering with mental disorders. There is considerable evidence supportive of each of these approaches to treatment delivered by themselves for a variety of conditions including anxiety, depression, and more severe mental disorders. If psychological treatments and pharmacological treatments are helpful, might combining the treatments lead to even greater benefits? Isaac Marks and colleagues looked at this question in a study of the treatment of panic disorder with agoraphobia (Marks et al., 1993). They looked at two factors: drug treatment (alprazolam versus placebo) and psychological treatment (exposure versus relaxation). Relaxation exercises are considered a credible treatment but has not been shown to be helpful for people with agoraphobia. Thus, by some definitions relaxation would be considered a placebo psychological treatment for panic disorder with agoraphobia. Marks and colleagues found that both exposure and alprazolam were effective treatments and that there were some advantages to the combined treatment over the course of therapy. However, after treatment was discontinued the participants who received alprazolam deteriorated, while those who received exposure therapy maintained their gains. The combination of alprazolam and exposure therapy actually did worse than exposure alone over the long run.

Factorial designs are also helpful when examining the interaction of client characteristics with type of therapy. As such, factorial designs allow us to look at what kind of people improve with what kind of treatment. In the NIMH-TDCRP study described above, although not a true factorial design, post-hoc (i.e., after the fact) hypotheses about interactions between depression severity and type of treatment were explored. It appears that with less severely depressed patients, all the treatments were equally effective, but for the severely depressed patients there was an advantage for drug treatment (Elkin et al., 1995; see Jacobson & Hollon, 1996, for alternative interpretation of the NIMH-TDCRP severity by treatment interactions).

It has been suggested that the ultimate question for psychotherapy researchers is "What treatment, by whom, is most effective for this individual with that specific problem, under which set of circumstances?" (Paul, 1967b, p. 111). Although it is probably impossible for any single research study to answer this question, factorial designs are valuable tools for gathering relevant information. Taking a step back and thinking about this ultimate psychotherapy research question, however, also illustrates the practical limitations of factorial designs. With each new factor, or new levels of a given factor, introduced into the design, the number of subject cells grows rapidly. For example, in a simple 2 by 2 design there are four cells. Introduce a third factor with two levels and there are now eight cells. If the new factor has three levels the number of cells jumps to 12. Even a simplistic research design that looks at only two levels of each of the factors suggested by the ultimate psychotherapy question results in a large number of treatment cells. A study that looks at two types of treatment (e.g., psychodynamic versus behavioral) delivered by two types of therapists (e.g., male versus female), for two different client samples (e.g., African American versus European American); under two treatment circumstances (e.g., rural versus urban setting) results in a factorial design with 16 cells. Following a general rule of 25 participants per treatment cell (Kazdin & Bass, 1989), this study would require 400 subjects.

Analogue Research

Not all psychotherapy research is carried out in a clinical setting with clients seeking help for mental disorders or life problems. There are a variety of reasons why clinical researchers may need to carry out their research in the controlled environment of a research laboratory. Psychotherapy research is often carried out in circumstances that approximate the clinical setting. When the difference between the clinical situation and the research conditions differ markedly, the term *analogue research* is used to describe these types of studies. In analogue psychotherapy studies, treatment is conducted under conditions that are analogous to but not exactly the same as the actual clinical situation.

Analogue client samples have frequently been used in psychotherapy studies. College students who are moderately fearful of public speaking might be used in an analogue study of social phobia, for example. Analogue samples can be useful to researchers in several ways. First, it is often easier to obtain a relatively large analogue sample than it is to recruit a clinical sample. College students are the most frequently studied analogue population. They are a captured subject pool who are responsive to inexpensive inducements to participate in research (e.g., extra credit). Second, when studying clinical samples seeking help the researchers must be carefully to balance the clients' needs against the requirements of the research design. For example, a depressed research client may present with acute suicidal ideation that needs to be addressed despite the fact that the research protocol prescribes a different set of interventions for that session. Analogue samples tend to be less complex. Finally, it is ethically defensible to offer analogue samples more circumscribed treatment that may isolate only one component of a problem, whereas working with clinical samples brings with it the ethical responsibility of providing acceptable care.

Analogue samples frequently have been used in studies of anxiety reduction methods. In fact, one often-cited criticism of the early research literature on systematic desensitization is that most of the studies had been conducted with moderately fearful college students (Thorpe & Olson, 1997). Nonetheless, this type of research played an important role in developing our understanding of anxiety reduction and has complemented the research carried out with clinical population. As an example, we can point to one of our own studies of anxiety reduction in which we used an analogue sample (Hecker, 1990). An issue in the anxiety treatment literature had to do with the relative merits of exposure therapies carried out in imagination (i.e., clients imagine themselves in anxiety-producing situations) as compared to those carried out in real life (e.g., clients actually place themselves in situations that are associated with increased anxiety). We had argued in an earlier paper that the method of exposure treatment was less important than whether the clients experienced an initial increase in anxiety followed by habituation of the anxiety response during treatment (Hecker & Thorpe, 1987). To test this hypothesis we treated 36 female college students who reported a significant fear of snakes and who could not bring themselves to touch a snake during a pretreatment behavioral test. Half of the participants participated in two sessions of imaginal exposure therapy that involved ten trials of vividly imagining frightening encounters with snakes over two sessions. The other half received in vivo exposure therapy in which the participants were presented with a live snake housed in an aquarium ten times over two sessions. Heart rate was recorded over a baseline period and across all exposure trials. The results showed that both treatments resulted in significant improvement on the measures of snake fear. The in vivo condition showed greater improvement on one measure. More importantly, we found that there was a similar pattern of heart rate activity across the two treatment conditions. Both treatments results in activation of a fear response (as indicated by heart rate increase) and habituation of that response across trials.

Our study illustrates some of the advantages of using analogue samples. We were able to recruit a large number of participants who were moderately fearful of snakes. These participants could be treated in a highly controlled setting that allowed us to measure their heart rate and deliver treatment in a highly structured fashion (e.g., ten 3-minute trials of exposure) over two sessions. Our findings helped to elucidate the physiological correlates of anxiety reduction and complemented the findings of clinical research trials (Hecker & Thorpe, 1987).

It is probably inappropriate to draw a sharp distinction between analogue and clinical research (Kazdin, 1998). In a sense all clinical research is analogue. There are a variety of ways in which any psychotherapy research trial may differ from treatment as actually practiced in the field. Whether it is subject selection (i.e., psychotherapy studies often have rather strict inclusion criteria (e.g., no comorbid medical or mental health condition), manner of recruitment (i.e., advertising for research participants), assessment procedures (i.e., psychotherapy studies usually involve more extensive assessment than typically used in practice), treatment delivery (i.e., treatment is delivered in a more structured fashion with limits set on number of sessions), or a host of other ways, psychotherapy studies differ from psychotherapy practice. It is probably more accurate to think of psychotherapy research falling on a continuum of approximation to clinical treatment. At one end of the continuum would be laboratory-based studies of analogue client samples. At the other end would be clinical trials carried out in working clinics with clients who have sought treatment without inducement.

Validity of Psychotherapy Research

As we have seen psychotherapy studies can be designed to address a variety of different research questions. Whatever the goals of a particular study, researchers want to be confident that the conclusions they draw from their research are well founded and accurate. In other words, researchers want to be able to draw *valid* conclusions. Four types of experimental validity have been identified: *internal validity, external validity, construct validity,* and *statistical conclusion validity* (Kazdin, 1994b).

In experimental research, the term *internal validity* refers to the confidence with which a researcher can conclude that changes observed in the dependent variable were caused by the independent variable. In psychotherapy research, the independent variable is usually the type of psychotherapy the participants receive. The dependent variable is the change in their symptoms (e.g., depression). The internal validity question, then, is to what extent can the changes observed in the participants be attributable to the intervention as opposed to some other factor. Questions about internal validity are frequently raised when quasi-experimental designs are used. Since random assignment was not used one cannot be sure to what extent the differences observed between the experimental and control treatments are due to the treatments and not some other difference between the two groups. Differences in the expertise, or enthusiasm, of the therapists delivering one intervention from those delivering another can compromise the internal validity of a psychotherapy study. If the therapists are highly motivated and well trained in one intervention but are not enthusiastic about or particularly adept at delivering the comparison treatment, this poses a serious threat to the internal validity of study. Differences observed between the two groups are as likely due to the therapists' skill and enthusiasm as they are to differences in the treatments themselves.

External validity refers to the confidence with which one can conclude that the results of the psychotherapy study can be generalized beyond the research setting. If psychotherapy A was found to be more effective than psychotherapy B in a controlled research trial, how likely is it that this difference will be observed in another clinical setting with different clients and different therapists? Psychotherapy outcome studies have frequently been criticized for having poor external validity. Research clients are often carefully selected (e.g., they have the problem the researcher is interested in treating (e.g., bulimia) but no other conditions (e.g., major depression). They may receive treatment free of charge. Treatment is delivered in a relatively structured format following a treatment manual. Therapists have been carefully trained and are closely supervised. Clients are seen for a fixed number of therapy sessions. The type of treatment clients receive is usually determined randomly rather than by matching treatment to clients' specific needs. There are sound arguments for each of these research strategies and each is important and helps assure the internal validity of the study. However, following each of these strategies limits the degree to which the findings of the study can be generalized to the "real world."

There are several challenges to generalizing controlled psychotherapy outcome studies to the real world. One challenge is assessing the importance or meaningfulness of the change clients experience in therapy. In Box 10.2 we discuss various methods of assessing the "clinical significance" of treatment outcome.

BOX **10.2**

Clinical Significance of Psychotherapy Outcome

Traditionally, psychological research relies upon statistical analyses to draw inferences about the impact one variable has upon another. Researchers look for "statistically significant" differences between groups of people who are in the experimental and control groups. To be statistically significant, the difference between the mean scores of the two groups must be greater than would be expected by chance. In the social sciences, it is traditional to accept that the difference between groups is not due to chance if the probability of the observed difference, or a larger one, is less than 5 percent. This is sometimes referred to as the .05 level of significance. A more conservative cut-off point is .01 (i.e., the probability that the observed difference or a larger one occurring by chance is 1 out of 100). The significance level is referred to as the alpha level and is set by the experimenter.

BOX **10.2** **Continued**

In psychotherapy outcome studies, the logic of statistical analysis is applied as follows. Researchers look at how much a group of treated clients change from before treatment to after treatment. If the probability that the group mean would change as much as it did is less than 5 percent, than the researcher concludes that the improvement is significant. When there is a control group, certain statistical analyses can tell us whether the difference in rates of change between the experimental and control groups is greater than would be expected by chance.

But what does this all mean for people receiving psychotherapy? Would a person seeking help ask a prospective therapist, "Does the mean score for a group of people who have a problem like mine improve more than would be expected by chance when they receive the treatment you offer?" Of course they would not. They are more likely to ask, "Am I going to get better?" or "Can I overcome my problem?" Statistical analyses that compare the mean scores for different groups of clients are of limited value when answering these types of questions.

Psychotherapy researchers have started to look beyond statistical significance of psychotherapy outcome data to consider the *clinical significance* of the findings (Kendall, 1999). Actually, the importance of looking beyond the question of whether mean scores improve more than chance has been recognized for some time (Jacobson, Follette, & Revenstorf, 1984; Kazdin, 1977), but there is little consensus about the best way to assess the clinical significance of treatment (Kazdin, 1999; Ogles, Lunnen, & Bonesteel, 2001). We'll summarize five approaches to measuring clinical significance.

One way of framing the question of clinical significance is to ask, Is the client like most "normal" people after treatment? Let's say that we are interested in treating depression. We could choose a measure of depression and then administer it to a large group of normal (i.e., nondepressed) people. We could then calculate the mean and standard deviation of the distribution of scores of nondepressed people. A client would be considered to be clinically significantly improved if, after treatment, his or her score on the measure of depression is within the range of the normal distribution (e.g., within two standard deviations of the mean of the nondepressed group). This approach to measuring clinical significance is logical and defines outcome in a way that is relatively easy to understand—is the client like most people after treatment? There are some limitations to this approach, however. First, a researcher must have information on the distribution of scores for normal people on the outcome measure of interest—information that is not always available. Second, for some outcomes there may, in fact, be no normal distribution. For example, self-induced vomiting is rare. It is likely that for a sample of 100 people who do not suffer with an eating disorder, the average number of times they induce themselves to vomit in a week's time is zero, and there may be no variance around this mean. Third, it is possible that clinically meaningful improvement may occur but the client is still outside of the normal range. To take the self-induced vomiting example further, if a client with bulimia induces vomiting twice every day during a two-week pretreatment period and only three times over the entire two weeks of posttreatment assessment, this would appear to be clinically significant change. Nonetheless, the client is still outside the normal range.

An approach to defining clinically significant outcome that complements the within-normal-distribution approach described above is to say that clients have clinically significant outcome if their score on a measure at posttreatment is not likely to be taken from the distribution of scores for people with that problem. For example, let's say the mean score on our measure of depression for a group of depressed clients is 40 and the distribution of scores has a standard deviation of 10. A client who scores 20 or below (i.e., at least two standard deviations below the mean) at posttreatment

(continued)

BOX **10.2**   **Continued**

would be considered to have reached a clinically significant level of improvement. The probability that a score below 20 came from the depressed population is less than 5 percent. These first two approaches to measuring the clinical significance of outcome have been worked out in some detail by Neil Jacobson and his colleagues (see Jacobson & Truax, 1991; Jacobson, Roberts, Berns, & McGlinchey, 1999).

A third approach to defining clinical significance of outcome is to use the subjective evaluation of significant individuals who have contact with the client (Foster & Mash, 1999; Kazdin, 1994b; Wolf, 1978). These subjective evaluations typically involve global ratings of how the client is doing before and after treatment. Global ratings might be made by expert judges (e.g., mental health professionals) based upon samples of the client's behavior (e.g., face-to-face interviews or videotape recordings). Alternatively, ratings can be made by significant others in the client's life such as parents or spouses. Advantages of this approach to clinical significance include its simplicity and its ecological validity. There are, however, several factors that should be considered when using subjective evaluations to measure outcome. First, subjective evaluations may not correspond to actual behavior. For example, a mother's ratings of her child's behavior may be as much as function of the mother's level of depression as it is of the child's behavior. Second, the subjective evaluation of a third party may be a poor measure of a client's mental health. A husband may be threatened by his wife's newfound assertiveness and rate her mental health adjustment as worse after therapy compared to before when she was less likely to speak her mind.

The fourth approach to measuring clinical significance is to expand the scope of the assessment to include broad measures of functioning. It is possible for a psychotherapeutic intervention to have a significant impact on some highly circumscribed target behavior (e.g., skin picking) but little impact on the client's overall quality of life. The inclusion of a quality-of-life measure with a battery of more specific measures of treatment outcome can provide useful information about the overall impact of treatment (Gladis, Gosch, Dishuk, & Crits-Christoph, 1999).

One final approach to the assessment of clinically meaningful treatment outcome deserves mention. Information relevant to treatment outcome is produced in everyday life. Some of this information is recorded for reasons that have nothing to do with the researcher's hypotheses. Nonetheless, these measures may be critically important to the research questions. We are referring here to so-called *social impact* measures (Kazdin, 1994b). Arrests, hospitalizations, number of days truant, death, divorce, and missed work days are all examples of social impact measures. These measurements get at the bottom line—is the impact of the treatment meaningful to the society at large? Are sexual offenders who undergo treatment less likely to be arrested for future offenses compared to those who do not receive treatment? Do fewer couples who participate in one approach to marital therapy end up divorced compared to another approach? Do social skills training programs help people with schizophrenia function without hospitalization?

It has become increasingly common for psychotherapy researchers to report on the clinical significance of treatment outcome along with traditional statistical significance. Unfortunately, measures of clinical significance usually suggest more humble conclusions about treatment efficacy than those suggested by traditional between-group statistical analyses. (e.g., Jacobson & Truax, 1991; Jacobson, Wilson, & Tupper, 1988; Robinson, Berman, & Neimeyer, 1990).

Construct validity has to do with the mechanisms of change. Given that change has been observed, what is responsible for the change? Psychotherapies may work for reasons that have nothing to do with the mechanisms of change proposed by the therapies' developers. Joseph Wolpe (1958, see Chapter 13) proposed that *reciprocal inhibition* was responsible for the decreases in anxiety observed when fearful clients go through systematic desensitization. While it is fairly well established that systematic desensitization is helpful for some types of anxiety-based problems, reciprocal inhibition has been discredited as a credible theoretical mechanism underlying the observed changes (see Thorpe & Olson, 1997, for discussion).

A fourth type of validity that is important for psychotherapy researchers to consider is statistical conclusion validity. Statistical analyses are applied in most types of psychological research to determine the probability that changes observed in the dependent variable were due to chance. In a psychotherapy study, for example, repeated measures analysis of variance may be used to determine whether the degree of change observed from pre- to posttreatment was greater for one treatment than for another. Several factors can influence whether the observed differences between the two treatment conditions are found to be statistically significant (i.e., not likely due to chance). These factors include the strength of the effect (i.e., how truly different the two treatments are in terms of efficacy), the reliability of the instruments used to measure the effect, the appropriateness of the statistical tests used, and the number of participants studied. Threats to statistical conclusion validity include anything that could affect the interpretation of statistical findings. For example, it is not uncommon for studies comparing two types of psychotherapy to find the interventions to be equally effective (see below). Some people have used this failure to find statistically significant differences between interventions as evidence that all psychotherapies are equally effective. In an influential review paper, Kazdin and Bass (1989) pointed out that most psychotherapy studies have used small numbers of subjects and therefore have low statistical power. In other words, it may be that differences did exist between the treatments but the statistical procedures used were inadequate to detect these differences. In other word, the conclusion that the two psychotherapies are equivalent may lack statistical conclusion validity.

Does Psychotherapy Work?

Eysenck's Challenge and Meta-Analysis

The second half of the twentieth century saw a boom in the practice of psychotherapy. One might take the sheer popularity of psychotherapy as evidence of the power and efficacy of the procedures. If so many people want psychotherapy, it must be a highly effective method for relieving human suffering. Right? As scientist, of course, clinical psychologists do not accept popularity as evidence of efficacy. Soft drinks, alcohol, and cigarettes are popular but most of us would not conclude that these substances must, therefore, be good for consumers.

One of the first people to ask the question Does psychotherapy work? was the eminent psychologist, Hans Eysenck. In 1952 he published a paper in which he reviewed all of the studies of psychotherapy treatment outcome available at the time. Although published a half century ago, Eysenck's review is a good starting point for examining the efficacy of psychotherapy because the review, and the response to it, illustrate the complexities and challenges hidden behind the simple question Does psychotherapy work?

Eysenck identified 24 published studies that reported on psychotherapeutic treatment of "neurotic" patients. None of the studies reviewed by Eysenck included control groups. Therefore, in order to evaluate the effectiveness of the treatment, he had to estimate the rate at which the patients would have improved without treatment. Eysenck used two studies to estimate the "spontaneous recovery" rates for neurotic patients. One study reported that 72 percent of "neurotics" seen in state hospitals recovered (Landis, 1938). The other reported on 500 neurotics seen by their general medical practitioners (Denker, 1946). Eysenck concluded that about 72 percent of these patients recovered with this nonspecialized care. Based upon these two studies, Eysenck concluded that the spontaneous recovery rate for neurosis was 72 percent.

Eysenck then turned his attention to the 24 studies of psychotherapy. Since these studies did not report results in any uniform manner, Eysenck developed his own classification system to summarize treatment outcome. Patients were determined to be either: (1) cured or much improved, (2) improved, (3) slightly improved, or (4) not improved, died, or discontinued treatment. Based upon this system of "forcing" results into these categories Eysenck concluded that the percent of psychotherapy clients who improved (defined as being in category 1 or 2 above) was no higher than the spontaneous recovery rate. Comparing these recovery rates to his estimate of the rate of spontaneous recovery, Eysenck concluded that from the available evidence the answer to the question Does psychotherapy work? seemed to be no. Eysenck was well aware of the limitations of the data he had reviewed. He was careful to make clear it would be inappropriate to conclude that his review disproved the possibility that psychotherapy was effective. Rather, the most appropriate conclusion was that the available data did not support that it was effective. In subsequent reviews of the literature, Eysenck continued to be critical of the quality of psychotherapy studies and stood by his conclusion that the evidence did not support the effectiveness of psychotherapy (Eysenck, 1960, 1966b).

The responses to Eysenck's papers were spirited. Several clinicians and scholars came to the defense of psychotherapy and were critical of Eysenck's conclusion (e.g., Bergin, 1971; Luborsky, 1954; Sanford, 1953; Strupp, 1963a, 1963b). Arguments put forth in defense of psychotherapy included the following: (1) Eysenck was very conservative in his judgments about outcome when he forced the data into his four categories. A different subjective assessment would have lead to much different conclusions. (2) The studies upon which the 72 percent spontaneous recovery rate were based likely employed lower criteria for improvement than the psychotherapy studies, thus the 72 percent is an overestimate of the true rate of recovery without psychotherapy. (3) The idea that the neurotics in the control studies improved "spontaneously" is inappropriate. These patients received some treatment through the state hospitals and their family doctors. In addition, they may have sought counsel from friends, family members, clergy, or others that helped to ease their distress. (4) Eysenck's review essentially used a quasi-experimental approach (i.e., the patients were not randomly assigned to treatment or control conditions), and there are good reasons to believe that the two samples were different in several ways other than the fact that one received psychotherapy and the other did not. (See Wierzbicki, 1993, for discussion of these and other criticisms of Eysenck's review.)

Perhaps the most salient response to Eysenck's review was to question the value of the entire endeavor. Given the range of therapies included under the heading of "psychotherapy," the range of therapists employed in the various studies (e.g., different levels of experience, training backgrounds, and so on), and the range of problems included under the heading "neuroses" any general conclusion drawn from an effort to aggregate the outcomes from these studies is doomed to be meaningless. Responding to Eysenck's review, one commentator wrote, "From the point of view of science, the question 'Does psychotherapy do any good? has little interest because it is virtually meaningless. . . . The question is, which people, in what circumstances, responding to what therapeutic stimuli?" (Sanford, 1953, pp. 335–336).

Despite recognition by many that any effort to aggregate all of the psychotherapy literature together to draw a single conclusion about the effectiveness of psychological treatment was bound to lead to meaningless conclusions, there were those who persisted nonetheless. After Eysenck's papers, the psychotherapy outcome literature review published by Smith and Glass (1977; and later Smith, Glass, & Miller, 1980) probably had the biggest impact upon the psychotherapy research field. Like Eysenck, Smith and Glass attempted to review all of the psychotherapy outcome literature. And, like Eysenck, the publication of their review was followed by a vigorous response from psychotherapy scholars and clinicians (e.g., Rachman & Wilson, 1980) Unlike Eysenck, however, Smith and Glass drew a very positive conclusion about the effectiveness of psychotherapy.

Perhaps the most significant thing about the Smith and Glass (1977) review is that it introduced the use of a statistical technique for reviewing psychotherapy outcome literature. Meta-analysis is a set of statistical procedures for aggregating the results from different studies on a single topic. To conduct a meta-analysis the reviewer derives a measure from each study that is comparable across different studies. The measure drawn from each study is called the "effect size." Statistically, the effect size is defined as "the mean difference between the treated and control subjects divided by the standard deviation of the control group" (Smith & Glass, p. 753). The formula for determining an effect size is $ES = (\bar{X}_t - \bar{X}_c)/SD_c$, where ES refers to the effect size, $\bar{X}_t$ is the mean of the treated group, $\bar{X}_c$ is the mean of the control group, and SD_c is the standard deviation of the control group. What does this mean? Well, statistically the effect size is in a unit of measurement that can be interpreted with respect to the distribution of the control group scores. We'll use some numbers to illustrate. Let's say that a psychotherapy study looked at the efficacy of a treatment designed to improve self-esteem. The participants in the treatment group received the psychotherapy and the control subjects did not. At the conclusion of treatment, the mean score on a measure of self-esteem for the treated group was 72, while the mean control group score was 60. Now, let's say the standard deviation of the distribution of scores for the control group is 12. The effect size for this study would be 1 ($(72 - 60)/12 = 1$). With an effect size 1, we know that the treated group scored, on average, one standard deviation higher than the control group. Assuming that the scores for the control group are approximately normally distributed, we can conclude that the mean score of the treated group is at about the 84th percentile of control. So the "average person" treated with psychotherapy is expected to improve to the level of the 84th percentile of the control group at the end of treatment. If an effect size for a study is 0, than the treatment and control groups are not different. In other words, the treatment had no effect.

In a meta-analysis, one or more effect sizes is calculated for each study reviewed. The reviewer then calculates the mean effect size for all the studies. For a meta-analysis of psychotherapy outcome research, the mean effect size can be interpreted as an indicator of how well the "average person" receiving the psychotherapy is doing compared to the people who were in the control the condition.

In conducting their meta-analysis of the psychotherapy outcome literature, Smith and Glass (1977) tried to identify every available study of psychotherapy. They identified 375 experimental studies of psychotherapy. They calculated an effect size for any outcome measure reported by the original investigators so that they ended up with 833 effect sizes. Averaging all of these effect sizes together, Smith and Glass determined that the mean effect size for patients who received psychotherapy was .68. Smith and Glass interpreted this to mean that "the average client receiving therapy was better off than 75% of the untreated clients" (p. 754). They hailed this as strong support for the beneficial effects of psychotherapy.

In an extension of their original meta-analysis, Smith, Glass, and Miller (1980) examined an even larger set of psychotherapy studies (n = 475 studies producing 1,766 effect sizes), which they reported on in book form. Their reanalysis essentially replicated their original findings. In the Smith and colleagues' meta-analysis the average effect size for all psychotherapies was .85.

The response to the Smith and Glass (1977) meta-analysis was as least as large, and as lively, as that which followed the publication of Eysenck's (1952) review. A large number of scholars were critical of meta-analysis as it was used by Smith and Glass (see, for example, Eysenck, 1978, who referred to it as "An exercise in mega-silliness," as well as Eysenck, 1983, Kazdin and Wilson, 1978, Rachman and Wilson, 1980, and Searles, 1985). Some of the more striking criticisms include the following: (1) Smith and Glass ignored the quality of the research design of studies they included. (2) The control groups against which psychotherapies were compared were different in different studies. In some studies, the psychotherapy was compared to a no-treatment control group. In others, clients in the control condition received placebo treatment or another intervention. The effect sizes derived from these studies, therefore, are not truly comparable. (3) Although Smith and Glass (1977) argued that they included all psychotherapy studies available at the time, it was pointed out that many studies of behavior therapy were excluded (Rachman & Wilson, 1980). (4) The heterogeneity of the studies aggregated together via meta-analysis raised serious questions about how meaningful is the average effect size. For example, in the Smith and Glass meta-analysis, effect sizes derived from a wide variety of outcome measures are averaged together. What does it mean to average together an effect size derived from a measure of depression with another derived from a measure of grade point average? (5) Similarly, the heterogeneity of psychotherapies studied (e.g., gestalt, cognitive therapy, transactional analysis) raised questions about the meaning of a statistic based upon the average of these diverse interventions. (6) Finally, although strong advocates for meta-analysis, Smith and Glass appear to have violated some of the mathematical assumptions underlying the technique, such as including multiple, highly correlated effect sizes drawn from the same study (see Landman & Dawes, 1982, for discussion).

Although not a particularly good example of the use of meta-analysis to evaluate the psychotherapy outcome literature, the publication of the Smith and Glass (1977) meta-analysis had a significant impact upon the field. Through the process of critically evaluating the Smith and Glass meta-analysis, the parameters for how the method could be appropriately used to review this literature emerged. Some of the parameters of high quality meta-analysis include the following. First, a specific type, or relatively homogeneous set, of interventions are reviewed. For example, Dobson (1989) conducted a meta-analysis of cognitive therapy for depression. To be included in the meta-analysis, a study had to have employed a specific approach to psychotherapy for depression (i.e., Beck's cognitive therapy of depression, Beck et al., 1979) and used a specific measure of depression (Beck Depression Inventory; Beck, Ward, Mendelson, Mock, & Erbaugh, 1961). Thus Dobson's meta-analysis avoided three of the problems present in Smith and Glass (1977): heterogeneity of interventions, heterogeneity of outcome measures, and multiple effects sizes taken from single study.

Meta-analysis is now a generally well-accepted tool for evaluating psychotherapy outcome literature. Contemporary meta-analytic reviews usually focus upon one form of psychotherapy and/or one problem or disorder. The results of these meta-analytic reviews tend to support the efficacy of psychotherapy. Table 10.1 contains a sample of meta-analytic reviews that have been published in recent years.

Empirically Supported Treatments

In the 1990s, psychotherapists and psychotherapy researchers experienced tremendous pressure to get the word out about effective psychotherapies. This pressure came from a variety of sources. First, sparked by the 1992 presidential campaign, various political and

TABLE 10.1   A Sample of Meta-Analytic Reviews of Psychotherapy Outcome

Researchers	Patient Diagnosis/Treatment	Number of Studies	Effect Size
Allen, Hunter, & Donohue (1989)	Public Speaking Anxiety	97	.51
Christensen, Hadzi-Pavlovic, Andrews, & Mattick (1987)	Obsessive compulsive disorder/ Exposure treatment	5	1.37
Mattick, Andrews, Hadzi-Pavlovic, & Christensen (1990)	Agoraphobia	51	1.62
Trull, Nietzel, & Mann (1988)	Agoraphobia	19	2.10
Dobson (1989)	Depression/Cognitive therapy	10	2.15
Robinson, Berman, & Neimeyer (1990)	Depression	29	.84
Gaffan, Tsaousis, & Kemp-Wheeler (1995)	Depression/Cognitive therapy	11	.93
Giblin, Sprenkle, & Sheehan (1985)	Family therapy	85	.44
Laessle, Zoettle, & Pike (1987)	Bulimia	9	1.14
Lyons & Woods (1991)	Rational emotive therapy	70	.98
Benton & Schroeder (1990)	Schizophrenia	23	.76

Source: Adapted from Lambert & Bergin (1994).

social constituencies were engaged in a debate about the future of health-care policy in the United States. It seemed quite possible that psychotherapy might be excluded from coverage under whatever policy emerged. Second, the health insurance industry was undergoing a substantial change. "Managed care" was emerging as a new model for health-care delivery. In a traditional fee-for-service model, the health-care provider decided what procedures would be used and the insurance company paid for it. Under managed care, assessment and treatment decisions have to be approved by the insurance provider or someone designated by the insurance company to oversee clinical decisions. For psychotherapists, this meant increased pressure to justify the procedures they used based upon efficacy and cost-effectiveness. Third, guidelines for treating mental disorders were being developed by other professions. For example, the American Psychiatric Association (1993) issued clinical practice guidelines for major depressive disorder, which emphasized pharmacological treatment and minimized the role of psychotherapy in the treatment of depressed individuals. Psychotherapists were rightly worried about the promulgation of such guidelines, and psychotherapy researchers were incensed because the guidelines did not reflect what was known about effective psychological treatments for depression. Finally, pressure came from pharmaceutical companies. Pharmacological treatments were being developed for a variety of conditions that can also be treated with psychotherapy (e.g., depression, panic disorder, obsessive-compulsive disorder). Pharmaceutical companies have enormous promotional budgets that they employ to disseminate information about their medicines to practitioners as well as consumers. There is no comparable mechanism for psychotherapy researchers to disseminate information about effective psychological treatments. As a consequence, research studies showing that psychological treatments are very helpful for some psychological conditions (e.g., exposure with response prevention for obsessive compulsive disorder) are often not generally known beyond a relatively small circle of clinical researchers and clinicians. In contrast, word of research demonstrating the efficacy of a new medication spreads very quickly to health care providers and consumers with the help of pharmaceutical sales representatives and direct advertisement.

It was in this context that David Barlow, the president of Division 12 of the American Psychological Association created the *Task Force on Promotion and Dissemination of Psychological Procedures.* Barlow believed very strongly that clinical research into psychotherapy had produced enough evidence to show that there are effective psychological interventions for a variety of psychological problems. Given the social and political forces described above, Barlow knew that psychology had to be proactive in getting the word out to insurance companies, consumers, and psychologists about these effective treatments. The task force released its initial report in 1995 (Task Force on Promotion and Dissemination of Psychological Procedures). The task force chose the term "Empirically Validated Treatments" to refer to those interventions for which there was a reasonable amount of empirical support. There were, in fact, two levels of Empirically Validated Treatments: "Well-Established Treatments" and "Probably Efficacious Treatments." The criteria for each are listed in Tables 10.2 and 10.3.

In its original report as well as two subsequent updates (Chambless et al., 1996, 1998), the Task Force provided lists of treatments for various disorders or life problems that met their criteria for either well-established or probably efficacious treatments. The 1998 updated list is reproduced in Table 10.4. Note that the Task Force members labeled the list as "Exam-

TABLE 10.2   Criteria for Empirically Validated Treatments: Well-Established Treatments

I. At least two good group design studies, conducted by different investigators, demonstrating efficacy in one or more of the following ways:
  A. Superior to pill or psychological placebo or to another treatment.
  B. Equivalent to an already established treatment in studies with adequate statistical power (about 30 per group; cf. Kazdin & Bass, 1989).
  OR
II. A large series of single-case design studies demonstrating efficacy. These studies must have:
  A. Used good experimental designs and
  B. Compared the intervention to another treatment as in I.A.

FURTHER CRITERIA FOR BOTH I AND II:
III. Studies must be conducted with treatment manuals.
IV. Characteristics of the client samples must be clearly specified.

Source: From Task Force on Promotion and Dissemination of Psychological Procedures (1995). Training in and dissemination of empirically-validated psychological treatments: Report and recommendations. *Clinical Psychologist, 48,* 3–23.

ples of Empirically Validated Treatment." The inclusion of the word "Examples" is not trivial. There is recognition that the lists are not complete and never will be. Our knowledge of effective treatments is always changing. The psychotherapy outcome literature is continually growing and it is expected that the list of effective psychological treatments will continue to grow as well.

TABLE 10.3   Criteria for Empirically Validated Treatments: Probably Efficacious Treatments

I. Two studies showing the treatment is more effective that a waiting-list control group.
  OR
II. Two studies otherwise meeting the well-established treatment criteria I, III, and IV, but both are conducted by the same investigator.
  Or one good study demonstrating effectiveness by these same criteria.
  OR
III. At least two good studies demonstrating effectiveness but flawed by heterogeneity of the client samples.
  OR
IV. A small series of single case design studies otherwise meeting the well-established treatment criteria II, III, and IV.

Source: From Task Force on Promotion and Dissemination of Psychological Procedures (1995). Training in and dissemination of empirically-validated psychological treatments: Report and recommendations. *Clinical Psychologist, 48,* 3–23.

TABLE 10.4 Examples of Empirically Validated Treatments

Well-Established Treatments	Citation for Efficacy Evidence
ANXIETY AND STRESS:	
Cognitive behavior therapy for panic disorder with and without agoraphobia	Barlow et al. (1989) Clark et al. (1994)
Cognitive behavior therapy for generalized anxiety disorder	Butler et al. (1991) Borkovec et al. (1987)
Exposure treatment for agoraphobia	Trull et al. (1988)
Exposure/guided mastery for specific phobia	Bandura et al. (1969) Ost et al. (1991)
Exposure and response prevention for obsessive-compulsive disorder	van Balkom et al. (1994)
Stress Innoculation Training for coping with stressors	Saunders et al. (1996)
DEPRESSION	
Behavior therapy for depression	Jacobson et al. (1996) McLean & Hakstian (1979)
Cognitive therapy for depression	Dobson (1989)
Interpersonal therapy for depression	DiMascio et al. (1979) Elkin et al. (1989)
HEALTH PROBLEMS	
Behavior therapy for headache	Blanchard et al. (1980) Holroyd & Penzien (1990)
Cognitive-behavior therapy for bulimia	Agras et al. (1989) Thackwray et al. (1993)
Multicomponent cognitive-behavior therapy for pain associated with rheumatic disease	Keefe et al. (1990a,b) Parker et al. (1988)
Multicomponent cognitive-behavior therapy with relapse prevention for smoking cessation	Hill et al. (1993) Stevens & Hollis (1989)
PROBLEMS OF CHILDHOOD	
Behavior modification for enuresis	Houts et al. (1994)
Parent training programs for children with oppositional behavior	Walter & Gilmore (1973) Wells & Egan (1988)
MARITAL DISCORD:	
Behavioral marital therapy	Azrin et al. (1980a) Jacobson & Follette (1985)

Source: Adapted from Chambless, Baker, et al. (1998).

David Barlow and the Division 12 Task Force were not the only ones to recognize a need to pull together the psychotherapy outcome literatures toward the goal of promoting the use of psychotherapies that enjoy some level of empirical support. Some efforts were aimed at mental health consumers. For example, in a book titled *What You Can Change and What You Can't,* Martin Seligman (1994) presented a guide to help consumers of mental health services understand mental health disorders and psychotherapies and drugs that have been shown to be helpful for these problems. Other efforts were directed at mental health practitioners. In the volume mentioned earlier in this chapter, *A Guide to Treatments that Work* (Nathan & Gorman, 1998), distinguished clinical scientists "present the most rigorous, scientifically based evidence for the efficacy of treatments" (p. x) for DSM-IV disorders. That volume includes chapters reviewing both psychological and pharmacological treatments. Other efforts were aimed at psychotherapists and psychotherapy researchers. For example, a special volume of the *Journal of Consulting and Clinical Psychology* was devoted to a discussion and commentary on "empirically supported psychological therapies" (Kendall, 1998) and included reviews of psychological treatments for adult mental disorders (Baucom, Shohan, Mueser, Daiuto, & Stickle, 1998; DeRubeis & Crits-Chrisoph, 1998), marital distress (Baucom et al., 1998), problems seen in children and adolescents (Kazdin & Weisz, 1998), and various health problems (Compas, Haaga, Keefe, Leitenberg, & Williams, 1998).

If controversy is a sign of the strength of a discipline, clinical psychology is one strong discipline. The reaction to the efforts to produce a list of empirically supported psychotherapies rivals the response to Meehl's review and Smith and Glass's meta-analyses. One criticism is directed toward the name itself. The word "validated" implies a stamp of approval that is absolute and might even imply a legal stamp of approval (Garfield, 1996). In fact, there is some agreement that empirically supported is a preferred term and reflects status of the research more accurately (i.e., the treatment has empirical support). In another salient criticism, Garfield (1996) pointed out that the lists of empirically validated treatments tend to be organized by DSM diagnostic categories. Garfield and others are skeptical of the reliability and validity of the psychiatric diagnoses and bemoan the implicit verification of the medical model this organizational scheme promotes (Goldfried & Wolfe, 1998). The focus upon psychiatric diagnostic categories ignores important individual differences among clients. Individuals who meet diagnostic criteria for the same diagnosis are not identical and the treatment literature shows that they have variable responses to treatment. Just as the empirically supported treatments ignore client variables, therapist variables are not included in the lists either. The reality is that not all therapists are created equal. By focusing upon certain type of psychotherapy outcome studies, the empirically supported psychotherapy lists ignore another body of empirical literature that has demonstrated the influence of therapist characteristics upon treatment outcome. For example, Luborsky and colleagues (1988) reanalyzed data from four published studies and found that therapist characteristics accounted for more of the variance in outcome measures than did therapy techniques. Another salient criticism of the efforts to identify empirically supported treatments is that the list highlights the differences between therapies and ignores their commonalities (Garfield, 1996). Common factors shared by different therapies may account for the treatment effects (e.g., Weinberger, 1995; see below for discussion of common factors). Finally, several critics have questioned the external validity of randomized controlled trials of psychotherapy

(Borkovec & Castonguay, 1998; Drodz & Goldfried, 1996; Garfield, 1998; Persons & Silberschatz, 1998).

Despite the concerns raised by critics of the efforts to disseminate information about psychological treatments that have research support, the benefits of these efforts seem to outweigh the concerns. Five benefits of identifying empirically supported treatments can be identified: (1) Providing consumers of mental health services with information about treatment efficacy empowers these consumers. (2) Condensing information about research findings into an easily digestible form makes it easier for practitioners to keep abreast of developments in the field. Knowing what treatments have empirical support can help psychologists plan their continuing education. (3) It would be inappropriate to conclude that psychotherapies that do not appear on the list are ineffective. In many cases, the interventions simply have not been carefully tested. Productions and disseminations of the empirically supported treatments may promote research into under-studied forms of therapy. (4) The publication of the Division 12 Task Force's findings instigated a great deal of discussion in the field about psychotherapy research and practice. Several of the top journals devoted special sections to the topic including the *American Psychologist, Clinical Psychology: Science and Practice, Journal of Consulting and Clinical Psychology,* and *Psychotherapy Research, and Practice.* The type of critical analysis triggered by the Task Force is vital to the health of the field. (5) The reality is, decisions are being made about what treatments should be reimbursed by third-party payers and what treatments should not. Most of the concerns about the external validity of psychotherapy outcome studies to clinical practice are true for studies of pharmacological treatment as well. Yet these treatments are being vigorously promoted. If organized psychology does not promote effective psychotherapies than who will.

Efficacy versus Effectiveness Research

Far and away the most common research strategy employed to test whether a psychotherapy is helpful is a randomized control trial in which the psychotherapy of interest is compared against no-treatment or an alternative therapy. Hundreds of psychotherapy outcome studies of this type have been published. These studies are of variable quality. The better ones include all or some of the following methodological features (Seligman, 1995):

1. Clients are randomly assigned to the treatment and comparison conditions.
2. Factors such as the credibility of the treatment conditions, the training level of the therapists, expectancy about potential gain, and amount of therapist-client contact are carefully controlled so that plausible alternative explanations for treatment-control differences can be ruled out.
3. Treatment delivery is guided by a well-worked-out manual and compliance to the treatment manual is closely monitored.
4. Clients are seen for a fixed number of therapy sessions.
5. Treatment outcomes are clearly specified and operationalized.
6. Raters blind to the type of treatment clients have received are used to assess outcome.
7. Clients are carefully selected so that they meet diagnostic criteria for one disorder and not others.

8. Clients are seen for follow-up assessment as fixed periods of time after treatment (e.g., 6 and 12 months).

The more tightly controlled the study (i.e., the more of the above features are present), the more confident the researchers can be that any differences observed between the treatment and control conditions are due to the experimental treatment. Psychotherapy studies of this type are referred to as *efficacy studies* (Seligman, 1995). They examine the efficacy of a specified treatment for a certain disorder. Efficacy studies have been used to determine whether or not a treatment is considered empirically supported.

Efficacy studies are not the only research paradigm that can be used to assess questions about whether psychotherapy works. Martin Seligman (1995, 1996) has argued that *effectiveness studies* are another viable paradigm. An effectiveness study examines the effects of a psychotherapy as it is actually delivered in the field. In contrast to efficacy research, in an effectiveness study, treatment manuals are not used, duration of treatment is determined by the client's progress or other real-world factors (e.g., insurance limits, client or therapist moves), clients may have multiple problems, and they choose their therapists and therapy modality based upon availability, therapists' reputations, and the clients' belief that they will be helped by the therapist/therapy. In effectiveness research, psychotherapy clients might be surveyed about the response to the treatment they received. Alternatively, naturally occurring information may be gathered about clients who received treatment. For example, divorce rates for clients seen for marital therapy, rearrest records for treated sexual offenders, or rehospitalization rates of severely mentally ill patients may be gathered to examine the impact of psychological interventions delivered in the field.

Efficacy and effectiveness research can be seen as two complementary approaches to addressing questions about whether psychotherapy is helpful. The main purpose of an efficacy study is to establish that the treatment has an effect. For the effectiveness study, the goal is to demonstrate the generalizability, feasibility, and cost effectiveness of the treatment (Jacobson & Christensen, 1996). Effectiveness research is carried out after a treatment has been shown to be helpful under controlled conditions. Unfortunately, there are very few examples of effectiveness research in the psychotherapy field at this point in time. A notable, and controversial, example is the *Consumer Reports* study discussed in Box 10.3.

Are All Psychotherapies the Same?

In *Alice in Wonderland* the dodo bird, having judged a race, proclaims the happy verdict that "everyone has won and all must have prizes." In a well-known and often-cited paper that reviewed comparative studies of psychotherapy, Luborsky, Singer, and Lubosky (1975) concluded that the so-called "dodo-bird conclusion" applied: All psychotherapies appear to be helpful and there is no strong evidence that any one approach is more helpful than any other. Smith, Glass, and Miller (1980) drew essentially the same conclusion based upon their meta-analysis of psychotherapy outcome. More contemporary literature reviews (e.g., Lambert & Bergin, 1994) often have drawn similar conclusions.

But not everyone is willing to endorse the dodo-bird conclusion. Advocates of behavior therapy have pointed out that when differences are found, they tend to favor behavioral approaches (e.g., Giles 1983a, 1983b; Rachman & Wilson, 1980). In addition, even a casual

BOX **10.3**

The *Consumer Reports* Study

When making a major purchase such as a car, computer, or stereo people frequently use information about customer satisfaction when deciding what product to buy. If 9 out of 10 customers are satisfied with a product, that's usually taken as a strong endorsement. If this information is helpful or car buyers, what about consumers of mental health services? Is "customer satisfaction" information useful in evaluating psychotherapy? The publishers of the consumer information magazine *Consumer Reports* think it is. They employed the same methods they used to learn about customer satisfaction with cars, toasters, and microwave ovens to find out about people's satisfaction with mental health treatment.

Consumer Reports conducts an annual survey of its readers that includes questions about their experiences with appliances, automobiles, and services. In the 1994 survey of its readership, *Consumer Reports* included questions about mental health professionals as well as others to whom readers may have turned to for help with emotional problems (e.g., physicians, medications, self-help groups). *Consumer Reports* sent out 180,000 questionnaires to its readership and 22,000 were returned. Of these, 7,000 respondents indicated that they had sought help for an emotional problem; however, about 3,000 sought help only from a friend of loved one. Approximately 4,100 went to a mental health professional (2,900), their family doctor, or a support group. Twenty-six questions were asked about mental health professionals and parallel questions were asked about physicians, medications, and self-help groups. The data with respect to the question of whether psychotherapy was helpful was organized into three composite scales: Specific Improvement (was there improvement in the problem for which the client sought treatment), Satisfaction (how generally satisfied with treatment was the person), and Global Improvement (how the person is doing overall after treatment). Some of the more important findings included the following:

1. Psychotherapy helped. People who had worked with mental health professionals reported that they improved. Approximately 90 percent of the respondents who described themselves as feeling *very poor* or *fairly poor* when they started therapy reported that they were doing *very good, good,* or at least *so-so* when they completed the survey.

2. Respondents who participated in psychotherapy for a longer period of time tended to improve more than those who received briefer treatment.

3. Psychotherapy alone was as helpful as psychotherapy plus medication.

4. Psychologists, psychiatrists, and social workers were all rated as helpful and there was no difference in overall improvement for the respondent who worked with one of these three types of professionals. Respondents who worked with psychologists, psychiatrists, or social workers reported greater improvement than those who worked with marriage counselors.

5. Family doctors did just as well as mental health professionals in the short run but worse over the long term.

6. Those respondents who chose to seek therapy on their own and were active consumers of treatment (e.g., checked out their therapists ahead of time, followed through with homework, did not miss appointments) improved more than those who took a more passive approach to therapy.

7. No approach to psychotherapy did any better than another other approach.

BOX **10.3** **Continued**

From a traditional research perspective, the *Consumer Reports* study is seriously flawed. While the subject sample is large, there is no reason to believe that it is representative of the population of people who seek mental health services. Outcome data are retrospective and limited to self-report only. Without a control group it is impossible to say whether the degree of improvement reported by the respondents is more than would have been expected with the passage of time. Despite these flaws, the *Consumer Reports* study stands as one of the few examples of an effort to gather information about the outcome of psychotherapy as it is practiced in the field.

perusal of the list of empirically validated treatments (see Table 10.4) reveals a predominance of cognitive-behavioral approaches. Still, when behavioral or cognitive-behavioral treatments are directly compared to another well-developed treatment within a single carefully controlled study, differences in treatment efficacy have been difficult to find. Two well-known examples will suffice to illustrate this point.

Sloane, Staples, Cristol, Yorkston, and Whipple (1975) conducted a comparison study of behavior therapy and short-term analytically oriented psychotherapy that set a new standard for psychotherapy research at the time it was published. Ninety-four clients who sought treatment for anxiety or personality-related problems at an outpatient clinic were randomly assigned to one of the two comparison treatments or a minimal-treatment wait-list group. The therapists were recognized experts and proponents of their respective approaches to therapy. An independent evaluator, blind to treatment conditions, evaluated each participant at pretreatment and four months after treatment commenced. There were no differences between the behavior therapy and the analytically oriented psychotherapy on any of the target symptoms. There was a slight advantage for behavior therapy on measures of global improvement and social functioning. At eight-month follow-up there were no differences between the treatment conditions.

Another landmark study comparing two well-developed psychotherapies was the National Institute of Mental Health-Treatment of Depression Collaborative Research Project (NIMH-TDCRP, Elkin et al., 1989; Imber et al., 1990). The two psychotherapies in this study, cognitive behavior therapy (CBT) and interpersonal psychotherapy (IPT), were compared to each other as well as antidepressant medication (imipramine) along with careful clinical management and a placebo medication plus clinical management. Both psychotherapies were specifically developed for treatment of depression (Beck et al., 1979; Klerman, Weissman, et al., 1984). Over 250 carefully diagnosed depressed clients were seen in this study, which was carried out at four different locations in the United States. The therapists were well trained and carefully supervised. The NIMH-TDCRP findings are quite complex and have been reported and debated in several publications (e.g., Elkin, 1994; Jacobson & Hollon, 1996). Overall, however, the basic outcome finding was that depressed clients in all treatment conditions (including the placebo plus clinical management) tended to improve. Direct comparisons between CBT and IPT revealed no significant differences on any of the major outcome measures. In post-hoc analyses, when clients were divided into two groups based upon severity, severely depressed participants who received interpersonal psychotherapy did better on some measures than those who received the placebo treatment. The difference between the cognitive behavior therapy and placebo conditions was not statistically significant for either the severely or mildly depressed patients.

Why has it been difficult to find differences in treatment efficacy between psychotherapies that are so clearly different in theoretical underpinnings and treatment techniques? At least three possible explanations can be offered (Lambert & Bergin, 1994; Stiles, Shapiro, & Elliott, 1986). First, treatments may achieve similar outcomes but via difference processes. In other words, treatments may be equally effective for different reasons. This is a plausible hypothesis but will require more sophisticated research methodologies than have been used thus far to be fully tested. Second, the failure to find treatment differences may be due to limitations of the research methods used in comparison studies. As discussed above, the finding that two psychotherapies are equivalent may lack statical conclusion validity. The third explanation for the equivalence of outcome among psychotherapies is that, while therapeutic strategies differ, there are *common factors* shared by different therapies that account for therapeutic change.

Common factors refer to characteristics of psychotherapy that cut across different treatment modalities. The common factors argument is that the shared qualities of different therapies are more important than the characteristics unique to each treatment. The term *nonspecific factors* has also been used to describe shared characteristics of different therapies. But common factors is preferred since the term nonspecific does not apply once a factor has been specified.

Although not the first to call attention to factors that are characteristic of all psychotherapies (see, for example, Rosenzweig, 1936), Jerome Frank (1961) is perhaps the best-known promoter of the view that the therapeutic change is primarily a function of factors shared by most therapeutic approaches. He argued that four elements common to most psychotherapies include: (1) an emotionally charged, confidential relationship between therapist and client; (2) a setting that is recognized as a place of healing (e.g., a doctor's office); (3) a conceptual framework for understanding how the problem developed; and (4) some forms of therapy rituals that follow from the theory.

Frank (1961) further identified the common mechanisms by which different psychotherapies produce therapeutic change. Psychotherapy, regardless of its specific form, provides clients with opportunities for new learning. It raises the client's expectancy that change is possible. Psychotherapists help clients to have success experiences and to develop a sense of mastery over their problems. Through the therapy relationship, clients overcome feelings of alienation from other people. Finally, in psychotherapy clients become emotionally aroused.

Following from Frank, there have been several attempts to summarize what the most important common factors in psychotherapy might be (see Arkowitz, 1992; Goldfried, 1992; Kleinke, 1994; Weinberger, 1993). Weinberger (1995), for example, highlighted five common factors that have been shown to have some empirical relationship to outcome: (1) the therapeutic relationship, (2) expectations of therapeutic success, (3) confronting or facing the problem, (4) providing an experience of mastery over the problem, and (5) attributing therapeutic success to personal or internal factors. He argued that different approaches to psychotherapy vary in the degree to which they capitalize upon these change factors.

Of the different common factors identified, therapeutic empathy is one that has received a great deal of theoretical and empirical attention. Carl Rogers (1957; see Chapter 13) argued that the therapists' empathic understanding of their clients and their ability to communicate that empathy were central to therapeutic change. Rogers assertion has been empirically evaluated in numerous studies (Orlinsky & Howard, 1986). Although correlations are often modest, there is a considerable body of evidence showing a relationship between clients' experience of therapeutic empathy and treatment outcome.

Another therapy relationship factor that has been examined empirically is *therapeutic alliance*. Therapeutic alliance refers to the collaborative bond between the therapist and client that develops as they work together to help the client overcome his or her problem. The term has its origins in psychoanalytic psychotherapy and has been emphasized by psychodynamic writers and researchers (Horvath & Luborsky, 1993). Therapists and clients work together toward the clients' goals in all forms of psychotherapy. Whether those goals are to explore possible childhood origins of adult problems or to conquer a hierarchy of feared situations when therapy is working well, the therapist and client experience an important bond. Therapeutic alliance, then, is a good example of a common factor. Empirically, therapeutic alliance appears to be related to outcome across a variety of different therapies for a variety of different problems. For example, in the NIMH-TDCRP study, alliance was related to outcome for patients in all four treatment conditions (CBT, IPT, imipramine and clinical management, and placebo and clinical management; Krupnick et al., 1996). In a study of alcohol abuse treatment, therapeutic alliance predicted drinking behavior during treatment and twelve months after treatment (Connors, Carroll, DiClemente, Longabaugh, & Donavan, 1997). Some studies have found that clients experience higher levels of therapeutic alliance when participating in cognitive-behavior therapy compared to other treatments (Carroll, Nich, & Rounsaville, 1997; Raue, Goldfried, & Barkham, 1997).

Concluding Comments

Psychotherapy has been called an art by some (Bugental, 1987) and a science by others (Karasu, 1980). It has also been described as a means of social control (Hurvitz, 1973) and a mechanism for purchasing friendship (Schofield, 1964). Just as in the story of the blind men and the elephant, the conclusions one draws about psychotherapy probably depend upon which aspects of the phenomenon one chooses to focus. One does not have to subscribe to the view that psychotherapy is a science to appreciate that a great deal can be learned about the phenomenon through the application of scientific methods of inquiry. As clinical psychologists and proponents of the scientist-practitioner model, we believe that the scientific study of psychotherapy is the best way to advance our knowledge and to protect the consumer. In the following chapters, we will describe the major approaches to psychotherapy and evaluate the empirical status of each.

BOX 10.4

Focus on Ethics: Information for New Clients

Psychotherapy is a professional service. Psychotherapy clients are consumers and as such they have the right to know about the service they are buying. And yet, what does the general public know about psychotherapy? What should clients expect when they seek psychotherapy services? Several factors conspire to make it challenging for consumers to know what to expect when they seek help from a psychotherapist. First, for many psychotherapy clients, the only information they have about this service is what they have gleaned from the mass media. Unfortunately, the depiction of psychotherapy and psychotherapists in movies, books, and television frequently bears little resemblance to reality. Second, psychotherapy refers to an extremely heterogenous set of activities. The experience of one client is likely to be very different from that of another depending upon their presenting problem, the theoretical orientation of the therapist, and other factors. Finally, the fact that many people are in a psychologically vulnerable state when they pursue psychotherapy may interfere with their ability to be wise consumers.

It is the responsibility of professional psychologists to educate their clients about the services the clients are buying and the parameters within which those services will be delivered. Psychologists have an ethical responsibility to discuss with their clients issues such as the type of therapy they provide, the anticipated course of treatment, their fee and how it will be handled, confidentiality issues, and reasonably expected risks and benefits (see Ethical Standard 10.01, American Psychological Association, 2002). Some psychologists use written informed consent agreements (Handelsman & Galvin, 1988). At the very least, therapists should discuss the following issues with their clients: *treatment goals* (What problems will be addressed? What are expected outcomes?), *the process of therapy* (How will the therapist and client work together? What are the responsibilities of each? What risks are associated with the treatment?), and *parameters of the therapist's practice* (What are the fees and what methods of payment are accepted? What are the limits of confidentiality? When is the therapist available? What should the client do in case of emergency?) (Koocher & Keith-Spiegel, 1998).

The following two examples are taken from the book *Ethics in Plain English: An Illustrative Casebook for Psychologists* (Nagy, 2000). In the first, the therapist provides useful information very early on in his professional contact with the client. In the second, the therapist misrepresents treatment and neglects to provide information the client needs to make an informed decision about whether to pursue therapy.

Rosemary, a depressed 46-year-old woman with chronic pain in her lower back from a two-year-old work injury, contacted Dr. Tellem for psychotherapy and nonmedical interventions for her pain. She was expecting that one hypnotic session could relieve her suffering and hoped that antidepressant medication could alleviate her depression. Dr. Tellem explained over the phone that treatment would be longer, consisting of history taking, relaxation training, biofeedback or self-hypnotic training, psychotherapy, and possibly other interventions. He explained that his theoretical orientation was cognitive-behavioral, discussed coordinating treatment with her physician, and explained the necessity of signing a consent form. He told her the cost of therapy and indicated that because he was not listed as a provider on her managed health care plan, he would be considered an "out-of-system provider," thus it was possible that partial payments could be made by the insurer. The patient, however, would be expected to make a copayment, the exact amount of which could be determined with a telephone call to the managed health care case manager.

BOX **10.4** **Continued**

Dr. Tellem handled the inquiry from Rosemary in an ethically responsible manner. He provided her with the information she needed in order to make an informed choice about whether to begin therapy with him. Further along in this vignette, Rosemary expresses surprise at both the projected length of therapy and the cost. She had contacted another potential therapist, who assured her of relief in two to three sessions. Rosemary is impressed with Dr. Tellem's openness and the fact that he encouraged her to ask questions. She decides to consult him for treatment.

During a telephone conversation, Dr. Sunnyview informed Janet, her new patient who was depressed and anorectic, that individual psychotherapy would rapidly provide relief for her symptoms and help her to be more productive at work. She virtually promised that treatment would be effective in nine sessions or less. This time frame was consistent with the number of sessions that had been allotted by the patient's managed care carrier, and Dr. Sunnyview wanted her patient to know that she could make a great amount of progress within that limited number of sessions. She said nothing about the possibility that depression sometimes was exacerbated during the course of therapy or the possibility that treatment might well last longer. She never discussed the need for or the logistics of seeking any required additional sessions from the managed care carrier.

Dr. Sunnyview used sophisticated psychological terms, which Janet did not understand, in describing her theoretical orientation. She said nothing about confidentiality, the possible need for hospitalization, fees, or the frequency of sessions. In fact, she expected the patient to come three times each week and pay in advance for each week's therapy, and she offered no possibility of a sliding fee or deferred payments.

When the patient appeared for her first session and learned of these expectations, she was quite disappointed because she could not afford to come as often or pay the high fee of $175 for each 45-minute session. Disappointed, she promptly dropped out of treatment and avoided contacting another therapist for several months. She felt shameful and betrayed by her meeting with Dr. Sunnyview, as though she was expected to understand in advance the financial obligation and other details of the treatment.

Dr. Sunnyview falls far short of her ethical obligation to provide Janet with relevant information about her treatment and her business practices. Perhaps most egregious is the unrealistically positive characterization of the outcome the client could expect and the time frame within which the dramatic progress could be made. The distorted information Dr. Sunnyview provides Janet is the most flagrant problem in this vignette. However, Dr. Sunnyview's failure to discuss the fee, her expectations about payment, the limits of confidentiality, and the possible need to coordinate treatment with other providers is equally indefensible.

11 Psychodynamic Psychotherapy

Every form of psychotherapy is based on certain assumptions, such as the obvious one that people can be helped to overcome personal problems and change for the better. What assumptions underlie the various psychodynamic psychotherapies? Psychodynamic theorists propose that much of mental life and activity is unconscious, and neurotic symptoms are the result of the ego's defensive efforts against repressed conflicts. Healthy development involves making constructive use of such conflicts; unhealthy development reflects a failure to deal with them adequately and may produce a mental disorder. Freud's emphasis on social development and early childhood experiences supports an environmental or psychological view of personality and psychopathology. If mental disorders are caused by environmental factors, then treatment involves helping clients to adjust to them or avoid them (Bell, 1980). If the ego adapts to continually changing internal and external environments, biological, psychological, and social, then the mind is *dynamic,* or active and changeable. The rationale for psychodynamic therapy is that, because the mind is dynamic and adaptive, mental symptoms are treatable (Bromberg, 1975).

Psychoanalysis

Background and Basic Principles

Freud's Early Clinical Work.   Returning to Vienna in 1886 after his four-month visit to Charcot's clinic in Paris, Freud started a private practice as a specialist in nervous diseases (Freud, 1925/1989). Few therapeutic techniques were available at that time. Physicians could evaluate patients and prescribe a visit to a *hydropathic clinic,* where baths were given for therapeutic purposes, or they could use *electrotherapy* for stimulating the nerves and improving the circulation (Bromberg, 1975). Though he studied electrotherapy carefully and exactly followed the instructions of Wilhelm Erb, the leading expert, Freud found it useless (Freud, 1925/1989). Interestingly, it was discovered much later that electrotherapy worked by suggestion when it worked it all. The other treatment technique available to Freud, hypnosis, was the only one believed at the time to operate through psychological, as opposed to physical, mechanisms.

Studies on Hysteria.   Influenced by his observations of Charcot and by news of others who successfully used suggestion, with or without hypnosis, as therapy, Freud began to use hypnosis routinely to treat hysteria. As his patients' memories of past trauma returned through hypnosis, Freud was impressed to witness repeated confirmations of Josef Breuer's discovery: When the emotion accompanying the recall of a significant memory was released, the hysterical symptom disappeared. Though Breuer himself was reluctant, Freud published a paper with him in 1893 describing the successful treatment of various hysterical symptoms and linking hysteria to dissociations of consciousness due to repression (Bromberg, 1975). A series of classic case studies, with Breuer's account of Anna O.'s treatment as the centerpiece, was published as *Studies on Hysteria* two years later (Breuer & Freud, 1895/1974).

Catharsis and Abreaction.   What were Freud's theories about the causes and treatment of hysteria at that time? He believed that we have no idea what is really going on with us when we develop such problems as a phobia of drinking water, going into trances, complete memory loss for significant time periods, or physical problems that make no sense medically. In those cases we have somehow hidden from ourselves vivid memories of highly upsetting events from the past. We also have no direct knowledge of the key emotions that we experienced at the times our symptoms developed, though it's quite likely that we will experience related emotions today without knowing where they came from.

What treatments follow from those ideas? Freud thought it essential for patients to recover the essential memories and emotions and thus gain insight into the real causes of neurotic distress, and the true meaning of the symptom. The processes at work in successful treatment were catharsis and abreaction.

Put simply, *catharsis* refers to (a) establishing the link between an emotion and a repressed memory and (b) eliminating this emotion by abreaction. *Abreaction* means liberating the emotion by expressing it (Freud, 1925/1989). In the case of Anna O. and her reluctance to drink water (see Box 3.1, Chapter 3), catharsis was (a) her recalling—under hypnosis—the memory of the dog drinking from a glass, realizing that she felt disgusted at the time, and recognizing that her disgust over the dog was linked to her difficulty in drinking water, and (b) expressing her disgust by telling Breuer about it, thus relieving her symptom by abreaction.

Transference.   Freud found that catharsis brought excellent practical results, but it was severely limited and did not deal with the most fundamental issues. In any event, he could not hypnotize every patient, and even those that he could did not achieve as deep a state of hypnosis as he desired. He eventually abandoned hypnosis, for two reasons. First, believing that hypnosis only worked with patients with hysteria, he did not wish to restrict his practice to the treatment of that disorder. Second, he had found that even in the most successful of treatments, the excellent results would instantly evaporate if his relationship with the patient became disturbed:

> The personal emotional relation between doctor and patient was . . . stronger than the whole cathartic process, and it was precisely that factor which escaped every effort at control. (Freud, 1925/1989, p. 16)

Freud gave up hypnotism in order to isolate this more important mysterious element lying behind it. In trying to understand why his patients repressed significant memories and emotions, Freud began to focus on underlying sexual themes, but that was enough for Josef Breuer. Parting company with Freud, Breuer abandoned hysteria at that point and followed other professional directions.

Identifying unconscious sexual elements in the all-important rapport between the therapist and the patient, Freud formulated the concept of *transference*—an intense emotional relationship out of proportion to the actual therapy situation (Bromberg, 1975). Transference is now so important that it is theoretically and technically essential to psychoanalysis. Freud explained that transference arises automatically in every analytic treatment, and does not have to be engineered by the analyst. "It can be of a positive or of a negative character and can vary between the extremes of a passionate, completely sensual love and the unbridled expression of an embittered defiance and hatred" (Freud, 1925/1989, p. 26).

Freud identified transference as a universal phenomenon in human relationships, strongly related to what hypnotists call suggestibility, the active ingredient in rapport. The task of the analyst is to make the patient aware of the transference and to show him or her that it is a reexperiencing of emotionally charged interpersonal relationships from the repressed years of childhood.

Repression and Resistance.   The French physician Hippolyte Bernheim had recovered memories from patients after hypnosis by laying his hand on the person's forehead, and insisting that he or she could remember and only had to say it. Freud tried this. Offering assurances and encouragement, and assisted by the touch of his hand, he tried to force forgotten material into the patient's consciousness. He continued the practice, adopted while he was using hypnotism, of having the patient lie upon a sofa while Freud sat behind, seeing the patient but not being seen himself. Initially, he recovered memories by simply asking patients to close their eyes and concentrate. But many people simply could not recover memories, with or without hypnosis. The more alarming, painful, or shameful was the forgotten material, the more difficult it was to recall (Bernheimer, 1990; Freud, 1925/1989; Malcolm, 1982).

To explain the difficulties for physician and patient in gaining access to such material, Freud proposed certain hypothetical mechanisms that operate behind the scenes. He introduced the concept of *cathexis,* the mental energy attached to emotionally charged ideas. This mental energy could be deflected by a competing force, a *counter-cathexis,* that caused the emergence of a symptom. The counter-cathexis operated not only to produce a symptom but also to resist attempts to bring the unacceptable idea into consciousness. This force, *resistance,* had to be overcome before emotionally significant events could be recalled. Freud believed that resistance was the same force that had repressed the feelings in the first place, turning them into symptoms.

Freud's discovery of the forces of resistance and repression was vital in launching psychoanalysis as an innovative form of psychotherapy. According to Freud's emerging theory, attempting to remove specific symptoms in some direct fashion would be doomed to fail, because the symptom is a form of mental defense against the real issue, a hidden, emotionally charged, unacceptable idea bound up with a repressed memory. *Analyzing and interpreting the patient's unconscious resistance to recognizing the real problem* is central to the psychoanalytic treatment that Freud devised (Bromberg, 1975). Following these insights, Freud could no longer accept therapy based simply on catharsis and abreaction of specific emotions. Instead, he had to uncover repressions and subject them to the patient's conscious judgment, so that he or she could maturely accept or reject the formerly unconscious ideas. Because of this change of emphasis, Freud stopped using the term *catharsis* to describe his method of evaluation and treatment. He recognized the "new situation" by calling his method *psychoanalysis* (Freud, 1925/1989).

The Seduction Theory of Hysteria. Freud developed and expanded the idea that mental disorders stem from unconscious conflicts over the wishes, ambitions, and desires aroused during early childhood experiences. Repressed sexual conflicts were especially important. By 1895 Freud was convinced that he had isolated the cause of hysteria. All of his female patients seemed to be telling him, in the material being recovered from the unconscious, that they had been sexually abused—seduced, molested, even raped—by their fathers in childhood. Freud satisfied himself that he had not distorted the material by his own unwitting use of suggestion. He believed his patients, deliberately suspending his criticism so as to maintain a neutral and receptive attitude. In the spring of 1896 Freud published his *seduction theory.* It was widely rejected (Porter, 1987).

Only his friend and colleague Wilhelm Fliess, an ear, nose, and throat specialist who had contributed significantly to the theory of infantile sexuality, was sympathetic (Jaccard, 1995). But the ideas that Fliess was putting forward seemed even more eccentric than Freud's own. For example, Fliess believed in male periods, in the male menopause, and in the physiological equivalence in women of the nose and the vagina, attributing female sexual dysfunctions to a "reflex nasal neurosis" (Porter, 1987, p. 219). In a near-fatal surgical blunder, Fliess operated on the nose of one of Freud's patients, Emma Eckstein, in order to cure her of masturbation, but the patient hemorrhaged and nearly died. Freud later reassured Fliess that he was not to blame for the incident, as Ms. Eckstein had "bled out of *longing*," and "there is no doubt that her hemorrhages were due to wishes" (Porter, 1987, p. 219).

Freud and Fliess remained friends and exchanged letters for many years, but their final parting on the shores of an Austrian lake in 1900 sounds like the dramatic finale of a Sherlock Holmes adventure. Fliess had accused Freud of stealing his ideas and alleged that at their last meeting Freud was so hostile toward him that he actually tried to kill him by pushing him over a precipice (Jaccard, 1995).

In 1897 Freud began to question his seduction theory and eventually came to regard his patients' stories as fantasies. He wrote that it was "hardly credible that perverted acts against children were so general" (Porter, 1987, p. 220). From that point, he interpreted memories of sexual contact between children and parents as unconsciously motivated fantasies. Most psychoanalysts today believe that this was the vital theoretical breakthrough that paved the way for the discovery of the Oedipus complex and the true science of psychoanalysis. However, in recent years Jeffrey Masson has made a case for the opposite view, and indicted Freud for a monumental failure of courage in dropping the seduction theory; he had been right the first time (Masson, 1983, 1986).

Free Association. Realizing that the apparently aimless, wandering thoughts of his patients were actually guided by unconscious mechanisms, Freud began to use the technique of *free association.* Resistance to forbidden ideas, and defenses against revealing them, were evident in patients' avoidance of certain words or thoughts, or in their choice of certain phrases (Bernheimer, 1990).

Elisabeth von R., whose treatment in 1892 provided one of the four case histories Freud contributed to *Studies on Hysteria,* helped teach him the potential value of free association (Gay, 1989). She had pains in her legs and difficulties in walking that defied medical explanation. Freud listened carefully as she let her thoughts and speech wander, uncontrolled by her rational judgment. It emerged that for nearly two years before the death of her ailing father, Ms. von R. had taken the role of his nurse, sacrificing her own social life. She recalled that her first episode of leg pain had been accompanied by a pang of guilt concerning her duties toward her father. She had, rarely for her, attended a social event with an eligible young man and returned home later than planned. On her return she was dismayed to learn that her father had taken a turn for the worse in her absence. She immediately felt faint and clutched the door frame for support. The incident marked the beginning of her pain symptoms, which later developed and spread. Freud's treatment, in which he listened carefully to her apparently random recollections and attended thoroughly to each symptom, was successful.

Encouraged by his good results with Elisabeth and other patients, Freud developed the formal technique of free association. To take the example of a male patient, he would be asked:

> to abandon himself to a process of *free association*—that is, to say whatever came into his head, while ceasing to give any conscious direction to his thoughts. It was essential, however, that he should bind himself to report literally everything that occurred to his self-perception and not to give way to critical objections which sought to put certain associations on one side on the ground that they were not sufficiently important or that they were irrelevant or that they were altogether meaningless. (Freud, 1925/1989, pp. 24–25)

The idea was to contrive a pure method of gaining access to unconscious material without contamination by the analyst's expectations (Porter, 1987). This successful method brought the added benefits of being labor-saving, noncoercive, relevant, comprehensive, and patient-directed. Accordingly, following the procedure of free association became what Freud referred to as "the fundamental rule of psychoanalysis" (Freud, 1912/1989, pp. 357, 359). Uncovering the resistance by free association had to be supplemented by an "art of interpretation" by the analyst, but, Freud argued, this is not difficult to learn.

The Interpretation of Dreams.   The techniques of free association and interpretation soon led Freud to accept the immense importance of dreams. Ego defenses are lowered in sleep, but they are not absent. The repressive resistance of the ego continues as a censor of unconscious impulses, making the forbidden meanings of dreams unrecognizable. Dreams are distorted messages in which coded symbols form the text. In fact, "*a dream is the (disguised) fulfilment of a (repressed) wish*" (Freud, 1925/1989, p. 28).

Asking the patient to free associate to his or her own dream material produced a coherent thought-structure, an understandable, perfectly valid product of the mind's activity. Interpreting dreams psychoanalytically, using their *manifest* or obvious content as the starting point for free association but searching keenly for the all-important *latent* or hidden ideas, removed their apparent absurdity and pointlessness and revealed their meaning.

Freud was struck by the realization that dreams are formed in the same way that neurotic symptoms are formed, but everyone—not just a patient with a neurosis—has dreams.

Therefore, the understanding of dreams by means of psychoanalysis brought the technique out of the clinic and made it applicable to normal psychological phenomena. Freud's significant book on the subject, *The Interpretation of Dreams,* was published in 1900.

The Technique of Freudian Psychoanalysis

The formal procedure of Freudian psychoanalysis, often referred to as *classical psychoanalysis,* was described in six papers on technique that Freud published between 1911 and 1915 (e.g. Freud, 1912/1989, 1913/1989, 1915/1989). Later authorities, such as the U.S. psychiatrists Karl Menninger (1958) and Jacob Arlow (1995), wrote extensively on analytic technique for students and practitioners.

The Psychoanalytic Situation. The participants in psychoanalysis are the analyst and the *analysand,* who is either a patient seeking treatment or a student undergoing a training analysis. As most analysands are patients, we'll use that term from now on. The standard technical procedure of psychoanalysis is *the psychoanalytic situation,* a setting in which the roles of the participants, and the practical conditions of their mutual contract, are clearly and strictly regulated. After two or three initial interviews in which the contract is made, the patient reclines on the couch and produces material for the analysis by free association. The analyst listens attentively, maintaining an attitude of uncritical acceptance and nonjudgmental professional curiosity. Occasionally, the analyst alters the procedure, interrupting the patient's monologue to ask him or her to produce additional associations to an idea, fantasy, or dream already presented.

Freud advised against taking notes during analytic sessions because this taxes the analyst's attention and compels him or her to select the material to be recorded, which runs counter to the principles of psychoanalysis. Arguing that analysts will have little difficulty in remembering important material from the analysis, Freud wrote:

> The technique . . . consists simply in not directing one's notice to anything in particular and in maintaining the same "evenly-suspended attention" . . . in the face of all that one hears. . . . [The doctor] should withhold all conscious influences . . . should simply listen, and not bother about . . . keeping anything in mind. (Freud, 1912/1989, p. 357)

Endogenous Determination of the Material. The setting is arranged so as to minimize the influence on the patient of external factors, such as cues from the analyst as to his or her own opinions, expectations, or preferences as to session content. Analysts do not give advice, talk about themselves, enter discussions about politics, answer questions about their families, or even show like or dislike of the patient; they strive to be as neutral and colorless as possible (Malcolm, 1982). Classical analysts sit out of view of the patient, deliberately remaining aloof and even mysterious. Freud explained that he did not want his own facial expressions to influence the patient's process of free association, but he added, "I cannot put up with being stared at by other people for eight hours a day" (Freud, 1913/1989, p. 371). It is vital to the procedure that any thoughts and associations produced by the patient are *endogenously determined,* coming strictly from within the person, because the analyst does not want the material to be contaminated by conscious defensive processes.

Appointments and Fees.   At the outset, patient and analyst agree upon a schedule of appointments and fees. Proposed deviations from the established contract must be analyzed, because any request by the patient to skip an appointment or delay the payment of a fee—however reasonable the request may sound—could reflect unconscious resistance, requiring analysis, not accommodation. Freud gave several reasons for strictness about fees. Free treatment only serves to strengthen the patient's resistances. Not charging a fee removes the relationship from the real world. And a patient who pays no fee "is deprived of a strong motive for endeavoring to bring the treatment to an end" (Malcolm, 1982, p. 25).

Selection of Patients.   Not everyone is selected for psychoanalytic treatment. A patient with only minor problems would usually be discouraged from embarking upon psycho-analysis for reasons of cost-effectiveness; the typical course of psychoanalytic treatment is long-term and very demanding, financially and intellectually. But a patient with a severe disorder may not be suitable either, if the disorder interferes with the capacity for insight or with the process of producing material in free association. The ideal patient for classical psychoanalysis is an intelligent person with a neurosis—anxiety, dissociation, a sexual dysfunction, or a mild mood disorder—someone who is significantly distressed by symp-toms, yet is not entirely handicapped by them. A patient in analysis needs to be able to make a commitment to change through critical self-scrutiny, and to participate fully in a treatment that may require four or five 50-minute sessions per week for a few years.

Training Analyses.   Other candidates for psychoanalysis may not be patients but psy-chiatrists, psychologists, and others who need to experience a *training analysis* before becoming psychoanalysts themselves. The rationale for a training analysis is partly that future analysts will have thoroughly explored any unresolved personal issues that might otherwise distort their work and partly that "the process to be understood had to be experi-enced" (Menninger, 1958, p. vi). Freud pointed out that the analyst's own unconscious is an important instrument in psychoanalysis, and if the analyst has significant areas of uncon-scious resistance, he or she will have "blind spots" that will lead to an avoidance of deal-ing with certain kinds of material. He initially recommended analysis of one's own dreams as a qualification for becoming an analyst, a procedure he had undertaken himself; but he later endorsed formal training analyses as the appropriate route to psychoanalytic practice. Freud's own unprecedented self-analysis had begun not long before the death of his father in 1896, and the self-analysis was proceeding at the time Freud abandoned his seduction theory of hysteria (Gay, 1989).

The Course of a Therapeutic Psychoanalysis

The Opening Phase.   Psychoanalysis begins with a few face-to-face interviews. The ana-lyst takes note not only of what the patient has to say but also of the manner in which it is delivered, the choice of issues presented or excluded, which matters are brought up first, whether the patient arrives early, on time, or late for appointments, and so on. Psychoanalysts normally avoid standardized history taking, leaving it up to the patient to decide what to mention and when. As with projective tests, with their ambiguous stimulus materials, this allows for the operation of unconscious factors.

The patient takes to the couch and begins the task of free association. The analyst begins to learn the patient's characteristic ways of resisting the expression of troubling material. The analyst may suggest some interpretations at this stage, but will defer interpreting areas of deep conflict until a later stage. This opening stage typically lasts three to six months.

The Regression.   The psychoanalyst deliberately maintains a steady attitude of neutrality as the patient works at cooperating with the procedure. While it is gratifying to the patient to be able to focus in detail upon his or her thoughts in the presence of an attentive professional listener, it is also frustrating. Day after day, the patient spends a full hour in producing material, struggling to obey the fundamental rule, and freely expressing any and all thoughts, ideas, images, memories, and fantasies that come to mind. The analyst listens attentively, but does little else. The patient pays, leaves, and returns the next day. Again, the patient's outpouring of associations is rewarded by the analyst's polite attentiveness. Sooner or later, the patient feels distinctly frustrated at the lack of obvious response from the analyst. A poet compared this frustration to the feeling someone might get if they had to take off all their clothes in front of another person, while the other person does not even remove their overcoat (Menninger, 1958).

From the analyst's point of view, the patient's developing frustration is not only expected—in fact, it is intentionally engineered by the psychoanalytic procedure itself. Psychoanalysis can be seen as a method for putting the patient on the defensive, not for any malicious motive but in order to find out how he or she responds to frustration—what defenses are used, how quickly they are brought out, how successful they are, and so on. The frustration induced by the psychoanalytic situation normally leads to *regression*—a falling back on methods of defense used earlier in life. As the frustration continues, so does the regression, as the patient's ego retreats to more and more primitive ways of dealing with emotional threat. This provides a rich source of material for analysis and aids in the development of transference, as the patient casts about for some means of getting a reaction from the analyst.

The Development of Transference.   In time, the patient becomes ready to relate current issues to unconscious conflicts from childhood. At about that point in the analysis, the analyst begins to take on great emotional significance for the patient; transference has developed. The patient's perception of the analyst becomes inappropriate, and so do the demands he or she places on the analyst. The patient may not be ready at this stage actually to *remember* crucial human interactions from childhood, yet nonetheless *acts* in the analysis as if repeating his or her part in those interactions. Transference could be understood as "a form of memory in which repetition in action replaces recollection of events" (Arlow, 1989, p. 39). Freud described this form of memory as the *repetition compulsion* and gave these examples from male patients:

> For instance, the patient does not say that he remembers that he used to be defiant and critical toward his parents' authority; instead, he behaves in that way to the doctor. . . . He does not remember having been intensely ashamed of certain sexual activities and afraid of their

being found out; but he makes it clear that he is ashamed of the treatment on which he is now embarked, and tries to keep it secret from everybody. (Malcolm, 1982, pp. 28–29)

Analysis of the transference is central to psychoanalysis by definition. Analyzing the transference helps the patient to distinguish reality from fantasy, and the past from the present. It vividly shows the force of persistent unconscious wishes from childhood. Ultimately, the automatic, stereotyped styles of interacting that represented unconscious responses to unconscious fantasies can be replaced. Instead, the patient reaches a position of being able to evaluate more realistically these formerly unconscious fears, self-defeating behaviors, and the like.

There is a parallel between the patient's original neurosis, with its distressing emotions and dysfunctional behaviors, and the stage of the analysis in which transference issues are at their most intense. Thus the events of this stage can be viewed as products of the *transference neurosis,* a form of transitional state between the original neurosis and normal functioning (Bloch, 1982).

Working Through.   We might imagine that a successful transference analysis is accomplished in a dramatic session in which the patient suddenly gains total insight in a momentous, life-changing instant of blinding revelation (and, presumably, follows up by rushing into the street shouting "Eureka!" or "I'm cured!" or something equally suitable). This is not the case (Bloch, 1982). The reality is that analysis of the transference requires much more than even a couple of insightful experiences on the part of the patient. It is a process, a long-continuing effort in which insights arise many times in many different ways. This process of gradually consolidating and deepening the patient's insight is known as *working through.*

Resistance works overtime during the working-through phase of treatment. It is because of resistance that any attempt to hurry the analysis will fail. It would miss the point simply to tell the patient what is in his or her unconscious; Freud derided such an approach as "wild" psychoanalysis:

> The pathological factor is not . . . ignorance in itself, but the root of this ignorance in . . . *inner resistances.* . . . The task of the treatment lies in combating these resistances. . . . If knowledge about the unconscious were as important for the patient as people . . . imagine, listening to lectures or reading books would be enough to cure. . . . Such measures, however, have as much influence on the symptoms of nervous illness as a distribution of menu cards in a time of famine has upon hunger. (Freud, 1910/1989, p. 354)

What is vital is the process of struggling with the patient's unconscious resistance. Working through continues to help overcome the patient's amnesia for significant childhood experiences. In a successful analysis, working through the transference issues is accompanied by the patient's retrieval of forgotten memories of significant past events or fantasies. There is a continual interaction of understanding the transference and recalling past events, so that each facilitates the other.

The analyst also has an unconscious, of course, and although he or she is not undergoing analysis the analyst also experiences frustration to some extent. The effects of the patient on the analyst's unconscious reactions is known as *countertransference.* Menninger gave the example of a laboratory technician who at different times cast his analyst into the roles of a father, a cousin, and an aunt:

> The analyst was a rather warmhearted fellow, and by the accusations of coldness he was only somewhat amused. The accusation that he was like a female seductress, however, he found a trifle disturbing. "Does the patient realize how irrational such accusations are?" he thought. A little later, when he was cast into the role of a stern female judge, he was less annoyed at being made a woman than at being regarded as a moralist. (Actually he *was* somewhat moralistic—more so than he realized.) (Menninger, 1958, p. 87)

The analyst was able to ask himself why that patient was annoying him so much and eventually recognized that, instead of trying to reject his analyst, the patient was indirectly setting up a situation in which *he* would be rejected, thus justifying the anger he felt toward the significant people he had been reminded of in the analysis.

The analyst's responsibility is to face the countertransference issues as squarely, and with as much insight, as possible, aided by his or her training analysis and, if necessary, consultation with colleagues. The development of countertransference is not a therapeutic disaster but a predictable and inevitable part of psychoanalysis. Appropriately handled, it can significantly aid the analyst's understanding of the patient.

Resolution of the Transference and Treatment Termination.   By the time the transference is well understood, and both are satisfied that the major goals of treatment have been met, analyst and patient start to think about ending the treatment. At this point the analyst helps the patient resolve an unconscious attachment to him or her. A firm date for the termination of treatment is established, some weeks in advance, and this agreement is held to as firmly as the provisions of the original contract.

But it's not over yet. Typically, the original symptoms that brought the patient to treatment come back at full force in the weeks before termination. While this might seem a therapeutic calamity, unraveling all the hard work of the previous months or years, the analyst will recognize this as an expected, predictable, well-understood phenomenon that betrays a last-ditch attempt by ego defenses to hold on to the symptoms and resist their replacement by more mature, straightforward, and realistic mental strategies. Treatment ends with the analysis of the patient's fantasies about a future without the symptoms that brought him or her into treatment and without the analyst.

Psychoanalytic Therapy since Freud

Freud did not devise psychoanalysis all at once. His theories and techniques evolved and changed throughout his long career. His close associates also made revisions. Carl Gustav Jung, for example, expanded Freud's concept of libido to include all life-giving forces in human behavior, not just the sex drive, and Freud accepted that theoretical modification. But some of these changes were significant enough that their authors could no longer remain tied to Freud and his views. The famous "dissidents" Jung and Adler may have branched off on their own because of Freud's own intolerance to changes proposed by others (Bloch,

1982). Freud denied being intolerant, but ten years after their departure he characterized Jung and Adler as "heretics" whose "attempts against psycho-analysis have blown over without doing any harm" (Freud, 1925/1989, p. 33).

Carl Jung's Analytical Psychotherapy

Carl Gustav Jung (1875–1961) developed his own system of psychodynamic therapy after his break with Freud and psychoanalysis. The traditional label for Jung's theoretical work is *analytical psychology* (Ryckman, 2000; Walker, 1959), but writers emphasizing Jungian treatment use the phrase *analytical psychotherapy* (Kaufmann, 1989).

In 1906 several psychiatrists in Zurich, Switzerland, had become very interested in psychoanalysis. They included Eugen Bleuler (best known for his later work on schizophrenia) and his assistant Carl Jung (Freud, 1925/1989). With Freud, they held a conference in Salzburg, Austria, in 1908, and founded a psychoanalytic journal with Jung as its first editor. In 1909 Freud and Jung were invited by G. Stanley Hall to present a series of lectures at Clark University in Worcester, Massachusetts, a pivotal event in the history of psychoanalysis in the United States. The *International Psychoanalytic Association* was formed after a conference in Germany in 1910, and Jung was its first president. Bleuler soon left the association because of "misunderstandings with Jung," and then in 1912 Jung led a "secessionist movement" based on rejecting the theories of infantile sexuality and the Oedipus complex (Freud, 1925/1989, p. 32). Jung resigned as editor of the journal in 1913 and as president of the association in 1914 (Walker, 1959).

Jungian Theory.   Jung had a more abstract and universal view of psychodynamics than Freud and was more interested in general unconscious themes that apply to all of us than in focusing on the details of individuals' psychosexual development. Freud's disparaging assessment was that Jung "hoped to escape the need for recognizing the importance of infantile sexuality and of the Oedipus complex as well as the necessity for any analysis of childhood" (Freud, 1925/1989, p. 33).

Libido as the Life Force.   Jung agreed with Freud that a dynamic unconscious was the mechanism behind mental processes, that it is helpful to explore the deeper meaning of dreams, and that transference is one of the most important issues in psychotherapy. But Jung disagreed with Freud's emphasis on sexuality in the neuroses, claiming instead that libido is the life-force itself, encompassing all life-giving energies (Ehrenwald, 1976; Walker, 1959).

Word Association.   Jung had taken an early interest in mythology and the psychology of the occult and, influenced by Freud, decided to learn about hypnotism as a means of studying such phenomena. Accordingly, he traveled to Paris in 1902 to study with Pierre Janet, an international authority on hypnotism. As a result, Jung was attracted to dissociative phenomena such as automatic writing (writing while in a trance), somnambulism (sleepwalking), multiple personality, and related trance states. He was fascinated by states and disorders in which the unconscious part of the personality could sometimes take over the conscious part, though he found that not all disorders could be explained in this way. Seeking a new approach to studying the unconscious, Jung borrowed from the earlier work of Wilhelm Wundt, Sir Francis Galton, and others and examined *word association* (Walker, 1959).

In word association a list of words is presented orally, one word at a time, to the subject, who responds with the first word that comes to mind. People vary widely in the particular words they give in response to stimulus words and in their reaction time, which differs from person to person and from word to word. Jung's experimentation with word association led him to conclude that the results had little to do with a subject's general intelligence, but had much to do with his or her emotional reactions to the thoughts suggested by the words. For example, a hospital staff member who had stolen money took much longer than innocent colleagues to respond to words connected with the theft. Especially significant, patients with neuroses gave unusual responses to standard stimulus words. These responses were connected with emotion-laden experiences of the kind that usually only resurfaced during psychoanalytic treatment. For example, a patient who showed long reaction times or who gave unusual associations to words like "fail," "shame," "self," "hate," and "kill" may have repressed some ideas with a depressive or self-punitive theme. Jung used the term *complex* for an unconscious network of ideas linked to a common theme. Freud accepted and used Jung's term himself, as in the famous example of the *Oedipus complex* (Walker, 1959).

For routine clinical use, Jung constructed a standard word association test, a list of stimulus words that had proved particularly helpful in eliciting material connected with typical neuroses or complexes. In analytical psychotherapy as in psychoanalysis, uncovering hidden, emotionally significant material is a central clinical activity, encompassing both assessment and therapy. Jung's word association test served both purposes: In addition to employing it for gathering essential assessment data, he also used the technique in therapy as a quick way of gaining access to repressed material.

The Collective Unconscious.   As he had expanded Freud's concept of libido, Jung similarly broadened the concept of the unconscious. Not just the material repressed by an individual, it also embraces a *collective unconscious,* containing the entire spectrum of primordial images and archetypes that are common to all humans throughout history. The *archetypes* are inborn predispositions to perceive, think, and behave in certain ways. They are not directly open to awareness but can be observed indirectly in the common themes of art and folklore. Some archetypes take the form of human roles, such as the hero, the Great Mother, and the Wise Old Man. Others are abstractions like rebirth and wholeness. Still others are blueprints for personality development: the persona, the shadow, the animus and the anima, and the self (Kaufmann, 1989).

Jung noticed that the hallucinations and delusions of inpatients with psychoses tend to follow certain themes, such as the belief that one is God, or the mother of the whole of humanity. Many of these themes have parallels in ancient myths. For example, one of the patients at Jung's hospital described to him some strikingly unusual images and visions four years before Jung himself encountered an ancient Greek papyrus dealing with similar material. Because this papyrus had not been deciphered until shortly before Jung read it in 1910, it was clear that the patient could not have read it. Yet the ancient Greek author was describing the same material that Jung's patient reported in 1906 (Walker, 1959). This discovery led Jung to read widely on mysticism—ancient and modern, European and Asian—and to travel to Africa, India, and New Mexico to study original cultures and societies. He developed the idea that creativity, myths, and religion all stem from a universal, collective human unconscious. Normally, the collective unconscious is a mainspring of creativity that inspires productive achievement. But when its material floods into normal consciousness, the result is mental illness, schizophrenia being the prime example. When there is a healthy balance between conscious and unconscious aspects of the personality, all is well (Ehrenwald, 1976).

Introversion and Extraversion.   In addition to the balance of conscious and unconscious elements, the individual's general orientation to the outside world is an important Jungian concept. The two major orientations coincide with the two major personality types, the *introvert* and the *extravert*. Introverts are inner-directed and inward-looking; extraverts are outward-looking and outgoing. In individuals with mental disorders, introversion is associated with schizophrenia, largely marked by withdrawal from social contact and a preoccupation with the inner world of fantasy and imagination; extraversion is associated with hysteria, largely marked by exaggerated emotionality and a lack of interest in symbolism, hidden meanings, and insightful self-exploration.

Jung believed that people without mental disorders could also be described as introverts or extraverts. The introvert prefers being alone, easily withdraws from novelty, and is preoccupied mainly by thoughts. The extravert is sociable, reacts quickly, and willingly seeks out new experiences (Ehrenwald, 1976; Walker, 1959).

Jung postulated four additional personality attributes, each representing a way of relating to the world: sensation, thinking, feeling, and intuition. *Sensing* refers to experiencing stimuli without evaluating or judging them. *Thinking* involves interpreting stimuli through reasoning and logic. *Feeling* means attaching emotional values to stimuli. *Intuiting* describes going beyond the immediate stimuli to envisage what might be made of them (Ryckman, 2000; Walker, 1959). From 1943 to the present the successive revisions of the Myers-Briggs Type Indicator (MBTI), a self-report personality questionnaire based on Jung's personality constructs, have been widely used in educational and counseling settings (Myers & McCaulley, 1985). The MBTI began as a "people-sorting test" devised by Isabel Briggs Myers in a Pennsylvania personnel office. Her interest in Jungian personality typology was inspired by her mother, Katharine Briggs, who had had a lifelong interest in fictional character analysis. She had corresponded with Jung and once met him in New York (Tucker & Duniho, 1994).

Jung's Therapeutic Technique.   It is difficult to give a precise description of Jung's technique of analytical psychotherapy, for three reasons. First, he based his method on Freudian psychoanalysis, and since Freud had perfected his technique after many years' work, few modifications were necessary (remember, Jung disagreed with Freud chiefly on theoretical matters, not on the technique of treatment). Second, the few papers Jung wrote about the practicalities of therapy were quite general and imprecise. Third, Jung believed that "the essence of his method was the avoidance of any set procedures" (Walker, 1959, p. 89).

It's easier to note some of the differences between Freudian analysis and Jungian analytical psychotherapy. Theoretically, Jungians emphasize the importance of social and cultural factors in psychopathology and mental health, but pay little attention to infantile sexual development. In psychotherapy, therefore, while Freud would have persisted in any analysis until the patient talked about his or her sexual development in childhood, a Jungian would only discuss sexual matters if they were pertinent to the particular case. Transference is recognized as important, but it is not given prominence. The analysis of dreams is the major work of psychotherapy, because a central objective of treatment is to open lines of communication between consciousness and the unconscious (Bloch, 1982; Kaufmann, 1989; Walker, 1959). In analytical psychotherapy therapist and patient sit face to face, and the value of their interacting in a collaborative relationship is emphasized (Bloch, 1982). The beneficial influence of the therapist's own personality is openly acknowledged. Analytical psychotherapy is a flexible enterprise in which methods are varied to match the needs of the individual patient (Walker, 1959).

Therapeutic Goals. The highest goal of Jungian treatment is to discover all aspects of oneself and one's creative potential. Fully developing all of one's unconscious capacity is the end result of a key process known as *individuation.* Jung viewed individuation as an innate, creative force that impels us toward achieving wholeness (Bloch, 1982; Kaufmann, 1989).

Typical Problems. Jung cited three main classes of problems requiring treatment: (1) repression of important desires and memories (that need to be recovered and expressed); (2) failure to accept and integrate into one's lifestyle certain types of thinking and behaving derived from the archetypes; and (3) neglect of underdeveloped aspects of the personality (for example, a "thinker" might benefit from developing more openness to sensing, feeling, and intuition; an "extravert" might take a hard look at the possible advantages of an introverted posture). Several *intermediate techniques* could be used to help patients address these issues (Walker, 1959).

Intermediate Techniques. Jung's choice of intermediate techniques reflected some of his theoretical disagreements with psychoanalysis. He viewed neurotic symptoms and dreams not simply as offshoots of repressed conflicts, but as signs of an effort to solve a problem. Once such clues have been identified, *reeducation* can be used to help patients develop neglected aspects of their functioning. *Interpretation,* especially dream interpretation, is essential because it's nearly impossible for patients to understand their behavior fully on their own initiative. Expertise in the symbolism of the archetypes is necessary. Dreams are not simply symbols of repressed desires, but illustrate the creative workings of the unconscious in attempting to make up for a failure to express hidden potentials in waking life. Jung used *free association* through the structured format of the word association test, identifying complexes by finding patterns in words producing slow or unusual responses. *Transference* is important to Jungians, but managing it therapeutically does not require the therapist to be aloof, distant, and impersonal. Jung believed that therapists are most helpful when they react naturally to patients' transference manifestations; therapists' reactions help patients understand their own. This is, nonetheless, a delicate task, and Jung thought it essential for therapists to have been analyzed themselves in order to understand themselves as thoroughly as possible; he claimed to have originated the idea of the training analysis. Finally, Jung devised the technique of *picture making,* in which patients draw or paint themes and images from their dreams. By turning passive recollection into a realistic, creative act, patients can elaborate the themes fully and experience them more vividly (Walker, 1959).

Applications.   Jung did not recommend his technique for everyone, and he often suggested to patients that they seek analysis along the lines of Freud or Adler. He noted that his patients tended to be older than Freud's, about two-thirds being over the age of 40; most had already had some form of psychotherapy. A distinct subgroup were "not suffering from any clinically definable neurosis, but from the senselessness and aimlessness of their lives" (Walker, 1959, p. 87).

A striking feature of Jung's analytical psychotherapy is that, practically alone among the approaches with significant followings in the Western world, it stresses the essential unity of human mythology and spirituality. For that reason it is accessible to anyone, not restricted by cultural boundaries. As a European white male in a respected, mainstream profession, Jung seems an ironic choice for the role of advocate of cross-cultural communication. Nonetheless, he promoted the view that middle-class people from the industrialized Western world could benefit from attending to universal messages from the unconscious. Jung believed that ignoring these messages has deprived people of personal fulfillment and meaningful lives.

Cultures different from Jung's own provide many examples of the merits of close communication between individuals and the dream world of archetypes. The Senoi of Malaysia were remarkable for the value they placed on dreaming, and they perfected techniques of lucid dreaming in which they could control its content for purposes of healthy mental and spiritual development (Marks, 1987). The Naskapi people of present-day Labrador and Quebec have for centuries recognized that they carry within themselves an inner companion, the "big man" or Great Man, an immortal who demands from the individual ethical behavior and an attitude of complete honesty. The big man communicates with the person through dreams and inner voices and confers wisdom, competence, skill, and strength in many areas of life, including the search for food. An overarching goal of life is to deepen and enrich this communication (Honigmann, 1975; Kaufmann, 1989). Central themes of Jungian psychology are that the unconscious archetypes, spiritual and others, are universal and that it is healthy and desirable to be open to communications from the unconscious. Accordingly, everyone, not only the Senoi and the Naskapi, would benefit from attending to such communications as these.

Alfred Adler's Individual Psychology

Alfred Adler (1870–1937) was a Viennese physician who became an associate of Freud after defending the psychoanalytic view of dream interpretation against criticisms published in the popular press. Like Jung, Adler later became a prominent dissenter from Freud and from psychoanalysis; he led the other "secessionist" movement by resigning from the Vienna Psychoanalytic Society in 1911 and forming his own association (Bloch, 1982; Ryckman, 2000).

Adler had been physically weak and prone to illness as a child, and the family doctor had recommended that he counteract this by seeking fresh air and playing outside with other children. Adler developed a lasting social interest from this early contact with playmates.

In addition to overcoming his physical weakness, he also had to cope with some early academic difficulties, but he applied himself vigorously and succeeded. At medical school he was attracted to the egalitarian and humane aspects of socialism and became an advocate of the rights of common people. (Adler's wife, Raissa Epstein, was Russian and a close friend of Trotsky.) This social orientation colored Adler's whole life and work. Initially practicing as an ophthalmologist, he switched to general medical practice, then to neurology. He wrote a book on the health of tailors, a pioneering work in the field of industrial medicine (Mosak, 1995; Ryckman, 2000; Walker, 1957). But Adler is best known, of course, for his contributions to psychodynamic therapy. His theoretical approach is known as *individual psychology.*

Adlerian Psychotherapy.   By contrast with the Freudians, Adlerians do not view unconscious factors as the central elements in personality, psychopathology, and psychotherapy. Adler used the word *unconscious* only as an adjective, not a noun (there are unconscious—not understood—aspects of the person and his or her functioning, but not *an* unconscious as a theoretical construct). Self-defeating or problematic behavior is acquired through the learning of faulty social values. Patients can willingly give up unproductive behavior patterns as a result of insight, and develop alternative lifestyles, preferably ones that are closely tied to positive interactions with people (Bloch, 1982; Mosak, 1995).

Adlerian psychotherapy is seen as a cooperative educational enterprise. The therapist tries to help patients understand and interpret the lifestyles they have adopted and serves as a helping friend, a model, and a source of warm encouragement. Typical patients are regarded as feeling discouraged in their attempts to come to terms with life, rather than as suffering from disorders. Treatment is aimed at clear goals agreed upon by therapist and patient. It is also present-centered; little attention is paid to the influence of the past, except when the patient spontaneously reenacts his or her role in the original family constellation during group therapy. Factors in the therapist-patient relationship are seen as more important in determining therapeutic outcome than the validity of the underlying psychodynamic theory or the use of specified treatment techniques (Bloch, 1982; Mosak, 1995).

Given that neither theory nor technique are essential determinants of outcome, what therapist-patient relationship factors are necessary? Adlerians do not focus specifically upon transference and certainly do not facilitate its development in the psychoanalytic way—having the therapist adopt an aloof, mysterious, impersonal presence. Instead, they emphasize an egalitarian relationship within a warm, permissive, accepting, and nonjudgmental atmosphere. These factors are variations on the traditional virtues of faith, hope, and love (Mosak, 1995).

Development of patients' social interest is the chief goal of therapy, and it is achieved by helping them to reassess their social values. The therapist attends to matters of lifestyle, life tasks, and *basic mistakes* in the patient's general outlook on the world—the *cognitive map.* Common basic mistakes include persistent preoccupation with inferiority feelings or discouragement. People are assumed to be free to continue past patterns or to choose new directions (Mosak, 1995).

Adler's Therapeutic Technique.   The process of Adlerian psychotherapy can be divided into four stages, each defined by a particular aim: to establish a good working relationship;

to understand the patient's lifestyle and goals; to achieve insight through interpretation; and to achieve a reorientation (Mosak, 1995). Adlerians stimulate an equal, collaborative *therapeutic relationship* in which both therapist and patient participate actively. The egalitarian nature of the relationship is reflected in the face-to-face seating arrangement. The therapist avoids being placed in the role of an all-knowing, all-powerful authority, which could encourage dependence on the part of the patient. The therapist equally avoids feeling overpowered by the patient and is careful not to overreact to accusations of being uncaring or insensitive. An alignment of therapist and patient goals is necessary for appropriate cooperation, but misalignment of goals creates what Freudians call resistance and transference.

Patients' lifestyles may lead them unconsciously to place the therapist in a certain role, or to expect certain reactions from him or her. Such stereotyped expectations of the course of a relationship are referred to as *scripts*. Therapists are careful not to accept these specified roles, because psychotherapy—to continue the analogy—involves something similar to proofreading and editing these scripts rather than acting the leading parts.

Adlerians *explore lifestyles and goals*. The patient's sense of his or her place in the family constellation in childhood receives much attention. Adlerians believe that one's later lifestyle is largely influenced by that vital early process of coming to terms with living with parents and older or younger siblings, dealing with the other children in school, and so forth. Early recollections are explored and treated much like projective test responses, because it is assumed that we all construct our own mythology about our lives. The life story and recollections allow the therapist insight into the patient's basic mistakes, errors that arise from confusing personal myths with reality. Basic mistakes include overgeneralizations; rigid rules for conduct; self-criticism; and uncritical acceptance of simplistic platitudes ("You've got to look out for yourself; no one else will" and the like). Adlerians assume that one's lifestyle is consistent and therefore will be expressed in all forms of behavior and communication. It does not matter, then, whether patients talk about everyday issues, dreams, political beliefs, or childhood fantasies—all reflect the lifestyle (Walker, 1957).

Every facet of behavior and communication—descriptions of everyday events, dreams, interpersonal interactions—may provide the therapist and patient with material for *interpretation*. Adlerians prefer interpretation of purposes rather than causes, and they favor an understanding that leads to constructive action rather than the development of an abstract insight (Mosak, 1995; Walker, 1957). Adlerians do not necessarily avoid giving advice. Consistent with the view that patients are discouraged, not sick, therapists offer encouragement, boost self-esteem, and urge patients to abandon negative thoughts and assumptions and replace them by more positive cognitions. The notion that people create their own emotions by choosing what they think is stressed (Mosak, 1995):

> No experience is a cause of success or failure. We do not suffer from the shock of our experiences—the so-called *trauma*—but we make out of them just what suits our purposes. We are *self-determined* by the meaning we give to our experiences; and there is probably something of a mistake always involved when we take particular experiences as the basis for our future life. Meanings are not determined by situations, but we determine ourselves by the meanings we give to situations. (Adler, 1931/1976, p. 293)

Adlerians do not hesitate to persuade patients to change, using *reorientation* to increase personal fulfillment. A current lifestyle may be safe and self-protective without bringing happiness, for example. This idea is reflected in the caption of a popular poster (of the kind that often adorn therapists' offices) depicting a boat at anchor in harbor. The caption, probably written by an Adlerian, reads: "A boat is safe in harbor—but that's not what boats are *for*."

Adler's Influence. Adler developed *family education centers,* forerunners of the community mental health centers that were established in the United States in the 1960s. As was the case with most of his innovations, Adler has received neither recognition nor credit for this pioneering work (Bloch, 1982). Adler's emphasis on the social and cultural context of the individual became central to the work of post-Freudian psychodynamic therapists like Karen Horney, Erich Fromm, and Harry Stack Sullivan (Bloch, 1982). By focusing on the central importance of the meanings people attach to significant life events, Adler's work also influenced the humanistic and existential psychotherapists Rollo May and Carl Rogers and the cognitive therapists Albert Ellis and Donald Meichenbaum.

The Neo-Freudians

Recall that we introduced the *neo-Freudians* Erich Fromm, Karen Horney, and Harry Stack Sullivan in Chapter 3. All three accepted basic Freudian hypotheses about the importance of unconscious motivation and the significance of early childhood development, but they went further than Freud in stressing patients' current social functioning as the chief focus of therapy. To Horney, for example, the goal of therapy was to identify and analyze the patient's unhelpful orientation concerning other people and encourage him or her to move *with* others, rather than toward, against, or away from them. Echoing Adler's view, the essential process in therapy is the development of the therapist-patient relationship, ideally a reciprocal, cooperative accord that can serve as a blueprint for other healthy relationships. The patient achieves greater self-realization as he or she learns to develop more fulfilling ways of relating to others (Bloch, 1982).

Therapeutic Technique. Fromm, Horney, and Sullivan did not specify detailed therapeutic methods and procedures in their writings, but their views can be summarized as follows:

1. The focus in therapy is upon patients' relationship to other people and to themselves, not upon the internal dynamics of id, ego, and superego.
2. Personality types are recognized, but these are labeled in terms of orientation to people, such as "extraverted," rather than in terms of instinctual drives, such as "anal-sadistic."
3. Reviewing current life experiences is more important than retrieving buried memories. Free association is used occasionally, not routinely.
4. Interpretation is used to reveal patients' unconscious attitudes toward other people.
5. While patients benefit from being helped to recognize unconscious material, especially unconscious ideas about relationships with other people, neo-Freudians pay little attention to universally repressed aggression and sexuality.
6. The therapist does not adopt a neutral, mysterious persona but may relate warmly with the patient in a collaborative, participating interaction (Walker, 1957).

In summary, the neo-Freudians Fromm, Horney, and Sullivan largely ignored infantile sexuality and the Oedipus complex and focused, instead, on patients' current relationships with other people. Like Jung and Adler, these psychotherapists fostered warm, egalitarian therapist-patient relationships in which the participants would sit face to face, rather than having the patient in a passive position lying on a couch. Jungians, Adlerians, and neo-Freudians continue to practice their brands of psychotherapy today, of course, but they have also strongly influenced other psychodynamic therapists in addition to many working in humanistic and cognitive therapy traditions.

The Ego Psychologists

In the 1930s Anna Freud (daughter of Sigmund Freud) and Heinz Hartmann attempted to broaden the theoretical scope of psychoanalysis to encompass humans' adaptation to their current social environment. While this approach clearly has much in common with that of the neo-Freudians cited above, the early *ego psychologists* did not reject Freud's drive theory or his concept of libido. Instead, they expanded the psychoanalytic study of ego functions. In time, this led to a significant change in direction for psychoanalysis; attention was turned away from intrapsychic conflict and towards individuals' ego development. This, in turn, encouraged an interest in the *narcissistic neuroses,* especially schizophrenia and depression, because they can be seen as disorders of ego functioning. For example, these disorders can involve poor reality testing and difficulty in sorting out internal representations of significant people in one's life.

Psychotherapy with people with disordered ego functioning requires a more active approach than classical psychoanalysis. Assuming that the therapist has sound judgment, good social skills, and other signs of a healthy ego, the patient may use the therapist as an appropriate model and even identify with him or her. There is no need for the therapist to sit quietly, out of sight, keeping emotionally at a distance so as to deal with unconscious conflict and the analysis of transference. Instead, ego psychologists are more directive and encouraging, and more interested in the events of the patient's daily life. Psychotherapy can thus become a *corrective emotional experience* (Auld & Hyman, 1991).

The Object Relations Theorists

Freud used the term *object* to mean "a person, place, thing, idea, fantasy, or memory invested with emotion" (Hamilton, 1994, p. 322). *Object relations* refers to the psychodynamic theory that focuses on the ways in which people internalize and externalize relationships. Proponents of this theory believe that unconscious internal fantasies are just as important as external social relationships (Hamilton, 1994). Object relations theory is linked with the work of the British analysts Michael Balint, John Bowlby, W. R. D. Fairbairn, Harry Guntrip, Melanie Klein, and D. W. Winnicott, and with the American analyst Otto Kernberg. The related concept of *self-psychology* is especially associated with the work of Heinz Kohut in Chicago.

Karl Abraham.   Karl Abraham (1877–1925), a colleague of Jung, had worked with Bleuler in Zurich. Abraham is known particularly for his development of the psychoanalytic theory of depression. Interested particularly in the oral stage of infantile development, Abraham studied the process through which people act as if they have symbolically taken into themselves objects whom they both love and hate.

Melanie Klein. Abraham conducted a training analysis with Melanie Klein in Berlin; she had previously studied psychoanalysis with Sandor Ferenczi in Budapest. She moved to London in 1926 and became one of the first analysts to treat children under the age of 6. Instead of free association, a technique doubly inappropriate with very young children because they are usually preverbal and very suggestible, Klein developed the technique of play-analysis or *play therapy,* in which themes reflecting unconscious conflict may surface in the child's apparently haphazard use of toys (Walker, 1957).

Object Relations Theory. Object relations theory addresses the type of conflict that arises when people have mixed feelings about, or *ambivalence* toward, a person, thing, or topic. Through the mechanism of *introjection,* a mental representation of an emotionally significant item is incorporated into the ego and thus becomes an object. Klein interpreted children's play behavior as symbolizing difficulties they might be experiencing in current relationships at home; these include relationships with parents, with parts of parents' bodies, and especially with the mother's breast. These can be incorporated as good or bad objects. As Abraham had done, Klein noticed a link between the temporary reactions of a child toward the loss of a loved object and the phenomena and symptoms of clinical depression (Walker, 1957).

Therapeutic Technique. Object relations therapy is guided by theories of how people internalize and externalize their relationships. For example, some patients act so as to get others around them, such as the therapist, to display their unwanted emotions. This way of communicating is known as *projective identification* (Hamilton, 1994). Understanding projective identification allows the therapist to judge whether to be openly warm and caring or to adopt a stance of interested neutrality.

For example, a man dealing with multiple family problems threw himself into his work, minimizing the stress he was under and saying nothing about his own emotions, though he seemed quite tense and anxious. The therapist speculated that this man allowed others to have his emotions for him. With that hypothesis in mind, the therapist warmly expressed the sadness that he felt on listening to the patient's story, a sadness that the patient himself did not seem to be aware of. From that point the patient relaxed. By contrast, a woman who had been sexually abused by a former counselor became anxious when the new therapist showed empathy and concern. The patient seemed to be experiencing the therapist's warmth as dangerous and threatening. The therapist therefore maintained a somewhat more distant attitude of careful professional interest, eventually enabling the patient to stabilize her other relationships (Hamilton, 1994).

Object relations therapy with adults often seems similar to the work of neo-Freudians or ego psychologists, but there is far greater emphasis on oral stage functioning, the stage at which incorporating and introjecting unsatisfying objects first takes place. The therapist will therefore try to recover memories even from as far back as the first 18 months or so of life. To do this, special techniques are necessary. The therapist might use *deep interpretation,* in which a patient may be confronted by a bold and direct statement of possible unconscious issues, without careful preparation to ensure that the patient is ready to accept it. Object relations therapists believe that an incorrect interpretation will do no harm, because there will be no corresponding unconscious element to resonate to it. Because of the prime importance of patients' mental representations of significant other people, transference issues are especially important and receive a great deal of attention (Walker, 1957).

Brief Psychodynamic Therapy

A course of classical psychoanalysis takes a great deal of time. Present-day Freudian analysts still accept Freud's estimate that a typical analysis would take six months to three years, probably even viewing this as an underestimate. But many psychodynamic therapists today question the need for such prolonged treatment and describe briefer versions that preserve the essentials while making therapy more accessible and acceptable to a wider variety of patients (and to the insurance companies that pay a percentage of the cost!). Interestingly enough, Freud and Breuer only took a few weeks to treat hysteria in their first patients. It was only when a broader range of psychopathology was treated, and in more thoroughgoing fashion, that the time required for a typical analysis began to grow so much longer. But some of Freud's earliest associates argued that satisfactory results could be obtained in three or four months (Walker, 1957).

The early analysts who pioneered brief treatment had had short training analyses themselves. Stekel was a Viennese physician who had undergone a short analysis by Freud around 1901 (Walker, 1957), and Ferenczi, a Hungarian general practitioner, was said to have been analyzed by Freud in about six weeks (Brief Psychodynamic Therapy, 1994a). Stekel and Ferenczi explored several variations in psychoanalytic technique, summarized as follows:

1. Early in treatment, the analyst sets a fixed date for the termination of the professional relationship. The rationale for this is to encourage the patient to improve quickly.
2. The analyst threatens to terminate treatment if the patient does not make satisfactory progress.
3. The analyst presents specific themes as material for fantasy (forced fantasy), rather than waiting for the patient to produce them spontaneously in dreams and free association.
4. Forced interpretation, similar to the deep interpretation later used by Melanie Klein, was used to hasten the treatment process.
5. The analyst insists that the patient abstain, while in treatment, from gratifying the needs involved in the disorder. For example, the analyst does not offer reassurance to relieve anxiety and might even ask the patient not to engage in sexual activity for the duration of the analysis if the neurosis has sexual underpinnings. The rationale is to provide motivation for the patient to complete treatment rapidly (Walker, 1957).

What is now known as *brief psychodynamic therapy* developed from this early work, and has been seen as a distinct approach for about thirty years. Factors involved in the growth of brief psychotherapy in the United States in the last few decades include the need for rapid treatment of traumatic stress-related disorders in the aftermath of World War II; the expansion of mental health clinics and hospital-based psychiatry units; the increase in demand for mental health services after the 1963 Community Mental Health Act; limits imposed by health insurance companies and health maintenance organizations on the number of treatment sessions approved for payment; and the challenge posed to traditional psychodynamic therapy by the empirically supported short-term methods of behavior therapy and cognitive therapy (Brief Psychodynamic Therapy, 1994a).

Not simply an abbreviated version of classical psychoanalysis, brief psychodynamic therapy follows similar principles but allows the therapist to address specific present-day concerns and engage in a less neutral professional relationship with the patient. Brevity of treatment is not the central issue; rather, it is the fact of a definite time-limit. For this reason, some therapists call it *time-sensitive* or *time-limited* therapy. Specific goals are established at the outset:

> To get a patient to state concrete and specific goals, one recommendation is to say at the beginning, "If one night while you were sleeping there was a miracle and the problem was solved, how would you know, and how would other people know if you did not tell them?" (Brief Psychodynamic Therapy, 1994a)

Several forms of brief psychodynamic therapy have been described. What follows is a brief sampler of seven of these.

Focal Psychotherapy.   Working in London, David Malan developed *focal psychotherapy* with the aim of rapidly identifying and addressing the theme or focus of patients' conflicts. The therapist explores the patient's early emotional traumas and current social behavior and examines *triangles of conflict* (between hidden wishes, anxiety, and defenses) and *triangles of persons* (involving present relationships, past relationships, and the therapeutic or transference relationship). Resistances are interpreted when they arise as defenses occurring in the treatment situation (Brief Psychodynamic Therapy, 1994b). The most deeply unconscious elements in the two triangles are the hidden wish and wishes concerning past relationships. This material is best reached by identifying the same wishes in current relationships or in the transference.

For example, one of Malan's associates used the "two triangles" method in treating a 28-year-old male advertising executive. The patient had sought treatment because he and his wife had sexual dysfunctions, but they could not be treated as a couple because she refused to participate in psychotherapy. In session 10 (of a course of 26 sessions), the patient told his therapist that he had "defied" his wife by not changing his clothes before going out with her. She had responded by telling him that she had nearly agreed to go to bed with a man she had met casually in the subway. The therapist pointed out that this incident reminded her of the patient's previously reported fantasies of humiliating women (hidden wish; present relationship). He replied that he felt a great deal of anger because of his sense of weakness. The therapist asked about his relationship with his mother (past relationship). He described his unhappy childhood, for which he blamed his mother; he had both wished for and resented being "engulfed" by her. He needed to agree with his mother to avoid losing her (past defense and anxiety). The therapist suggested a connection with herself, in that the patient needed to agree with her to get her to respond warmly to him (past defense, linked with transference defense).

Eventually, the patient expressed anger at his parents, saying that he had "had no adolescence—they were so bloody understanding I couldn't rebel" (Malan & Osimo, 1992, p. 109). He felt relieved when he confided to his therapist that he had had sadistic fantasies about making attacks upon her breasts, anus, and vagina (hidden wish, transference). Finally, he could say of the therapist (in her role as transference object): "I've got mixed feelings— I want [Mommy's] approval, but I also don't care whether you approve or not. I seem to be going through an accelerated adolescence," and of his mother: "I avoid getting to the core of my feeling about her, which is tremendous locked-up anger—a lack of respect, that's what it is—it's terrible to say that. I feel as though a thunderclap has happened" (Malan & Osimo, 1992, p. 109).

Brief and Emergency Psychotherapy.   Used for acute emotional distress as encountered in crisis clinics and hospital emergency rooms, *brief and emergency psychotherapy* was designed by Leopold Bellak as a technique for rapidly identifying continuities between the patient's past and present behavior. The intent is to arrive at a dynamic formulation in which current problems are related to events from the past. The rationale given to the patient is that emotional problems arise when our understanding of present challenges is distorted by the influence of the past. To elicit material, the therapist asks the patient to look at the spontaneous thoughts that arise during everyday activities and may employ a *mediate catharsis* approach by indicating the feelings he or she might have had in a situation described by the patient. This can facilitate the patient's guilt-free examination of thoughts and feelings. Treatment is conducted in a course of five weekly sessions (Brief Psychodynamic Therapy, 1994b).

Short-Term Anxiety-Provoking Therapy.   Peter Sifneos's approach in *short-term anxiety-provoking therapy* is to confront ego defenses directly. The typical patient has a specific problem concerning loss or separation leading to grief. Goals are decided early and put in writing. The therapist repeats the patient's own words at appropriate points to counter resistance (Brief Psychodynamic Therapy, 1994b).

Time-Limited Psychotherapy.   The *time-limited psychotherapy* of James Mann intensifies transference feelings by creating an inflexible time limit of twelve sessions and by assigning central importance, in the last two or three sessions, to the imminent termination. The therapist finds a focus as quickly as possible and identifies persistent themes in the patient's dynamics and symbolic life. The impending end of the therapeutic relationship affords the patient an opportunity to relive earlier separations in a more mature fashion (Brief Psychodynamic Therapy, 1994b).

Intensive Short-Term Dynamic Psychotherapy.   Patients with strong defenses that emphasize intellectualization are seen as good candidates for *intensive short-term dynamic psychotherapy,* described by Habib Davanloo. The therapist confronts resistance directly and stimulates the development of transference by challenging the patient, the aim being to restructure the defenses (Brief Psychodynamic Therapy, 1994b; Prochaska & Norcross, 2003).

Supportive-Expressive Psychoanalytically Oriented Psychotherapy.   The *supportive-expressive psychotherapy* of Lester Luborsky deals with the patient's central conflict by identifying the *core conflictual relationship theme.* Typically, the patient wants something, and would like to get it from some other person, but there are obstacles. In exploring this, the therapist uses the transference but takes an encouraging attitude rather than maintaining neutrality (Brief Psychodynamic Therapy, 1994b; Prochaska & Norcross, 2003).

Time-Limited Dynamic Psychotherapy.   Hans Strupp's *time-limited dynamic psychotherapy* approach involves assessing the roles in which patients unwittingly cast themselves. In a collaborative manner, therapist and patient construct a story outline with the elements: acts of the patient directed at others; the patient's expectations of others; acts of others directed at the patient; and self-directed acts of the patient (Binder, Strupp, & Henry, 1995; Brief Psychodynamic Therapy, 1994b).

Interpersonal Psychotherapy

Myrna Weissman and her colleagues initially developed *interpersonal psychotherapy* as a psychodynamic treatment for depressed women, based on research conducted in the 1970s. Previous research and therapy had focused on depressive symptoms, such as nonrestorative sleep, low energy, and poor concentration. Weissman focused instead on the social relationships of depressed women, assessing how acute depression influenced social, family, and community functioning. Studying 40 depressed women and 40 of their nondepressed neighbors, the researchers were struck by the considerable impairments shown by the depressed women in their daily lives and interpersonal relationships. These impairments affected all significant social roles, but were most obvious in work and family settings. As the women's depressive symptoms improved with medication, their social adjustment improved also, but at a slower rate. By contrast, psychotherapy focused on helping patients cope with personal and social aspects of depression had its greatest positive impact on their social functioning (Weissman & Paykel, 1974).

In the early 1900s the traditional view of the link between psychopathology and social functioning was that mental disorders like schizophrenia are the *cause* of various kinds of impairment. In other words, "impairment of social role performance [is] almost entirely the consequence of the patient's illness" (Klerman, Weissman, Rounsaville, & Chevron, 1984, p. 48). Interpersonal psychotherapists do not deny the disruptive effect of certain disorders on social functioning, but they emphasize the other side of this two-way process, in which disturbance in social roles can both set the scene for the development of disorders and also actively maintain them.

Strategies, Techniques, and Therapeutic Stance.   Interpersonal psychotherapists conceptualize their work at the three levels of strategies, techniques, and therapeutic stance. The *strategies* are seen in three phases of treatment, which is short-term, usually lasting less than one year. The first phase involves diagnosing depression, explaining it to the patient from a medical perspective, and agreeing upon a treatment contract. Interpersonal psychotherapy focuses chiefly on the patient's current social relationships and is directed toward one or two specific, immediate problem areas agreed upon during these initial assessment sessions. The intermediate phase consists of working on the major interpersonal problem areas. Four broad categories of these are of particular interest. *Grief* means depressive symptoms prolonged beyond a normal mourning period after the death of someone very close to the patient. *Role dispute* refers to disagreements with a significant person. *Role transition* includes any major life change, such as marriage or changing jobs. *Interpersonal deficits* describes a pattern of chronic difficulties with social relationships. The termination phase is similar to that of other short-term therapies: Therapist and patient discuss their feelings about the end of the relationship, review the course of treatment, and outline directions for further progress by the patient (Klerman et al., 1984; Markowitz & Swartz, 1997).

Comparing interpersonal psychotherapy with psychoanalytic and cognitive-behavioral approaches illustrates its *techniques* and the *therapeutic stance* of its practitioners. While interpersonal psychotherapists take note of patients' unconscious defensive styles, treatment deals not with internal conflicts but with present-day interpersonal relationships. By contrast with cognitive-behavior therapists, interpersonal psychotherapists avoid such directive methods as giving homework assignments and helping clients practice assertive behaviors or constructive self-statements. Instead, therapists call attention to apparent discrepancies in patients' thoughts, feelings, and behaviors, encouraging them to explore the effects of these on present interpersonal relationships and functioning. Without employing directive techniques, interpersonal psychotherapists ask themselves how they can help patients talk about painful feelings, clarify their wishes, and deal constructively with misinformation (Klerman et al., 1984).

The Place of Psychodynamic Psychotherapy in Contemporary Clinical Psychology

Taken collectively, clinical psychologists' views of psychoanalysis and its offshoots cover the entire range from enthusiastic acceptance to downright rejection. Freud's original work has formed the nucleus of most American psychiatrists' psychotherapy training for almost a century, and this is also true for many clinical psychologists whose doctoral training programs were psychodynamically oriented. These psychologists value the insights that can be derived from a careful and dispassionate study of patients' dreams, fantasies, defensive styles, and ways of relating to the therapist in an intense and prolonged encounter. The various forms of psychodynamic psychotherapy are rooted in a broad theory of mental health and mental disorders that encompasses all aspects of human behavior, cognition, and emotion, from slips of the tongue to arriving late to a therapy session and from specific phobias to acute schizophrenia. Manuals on the techniques of psychodynamic therapy provide guidance on everything from dealing with patients' hostility to setting and collecting fees. Clinical psychologists working in the psychodynamic tradition can call upon a vast literature of helpful references and a worldwide association of like-minded colleagues.

That being the case, what are the criticisms? One of the most telling has been that the psychodynamic approaches are not very *psychological*. Depending on what definition of "psychological" we use, that can seem an extraordinary statement. However, it makes a great deal of sense if we define as psychological the chief elements in the curriculum of a typical college program for a student majoring in psychology. According to what is presented in such programs, what do psychologists do? Above all, they study human experience and behavior by proposing hypotheses and stringently testing them, adopting an experimental paradigm in which the methodology includes operational definition of variables and procedures, random assignment of participants to conditions, using statistical inference to evaluate the results, and so forth. Findings from research programs based on these principles form the basis of courses on cognition, social psychology, perception, and learning.

You have probably caught our drift by now. Sigmund Freud's case histories are fascinating, Melanie Klein's play therapy was an intriguing innovation, and deep interpretation as used by an object relations therapist can make for compelling reading, but what do they have to do with psychology as we understand it today? What statistics have been used to test hypotheses about counter-cathexes or counter-transference? What experiments have tested the effectiveness of classical psychoanalysis? Most of the psychodynamic approaches to therapy are potentially vulnerable to this line of criticism, which has been especially identified with pioneers of behavior therapy like Joseph Wolpe and Stanley Rachman. Their critique of Freud's case of Little Hans (see Box 3.2) was based on the arguments that its method was unscientific and its conclusions illogical (Wolpe & Rachman, 1960).

But there are counterarguments. Supporters of psychoanalysis acknowledge that empirical validation is lacking in some key areas. But experimental science is not the only way to advance knowledge, and not everything is amenable to operational definition and quantification of variables. Psychoanalysis can be viewed as more like deciphering an ancient language or understanding the meaning of a poem than finding out which method of advertising sells more consumer goods. There's nothing wrong with experimental science, properly applied, and there's nothing wrong with classics or literary criticism, either, when they are deployed correctly. In fact, they are highly rational, disciplined enterprises that have increased our understanding in significant areas (Cheshire, 1975, 1979; Conway, 1978). The dispute is over which method for advancing knowledge and understanding natural phenomena is most applicable to mental disorders and their treatment.

Scientifically minded clinicians have recently made a point of identifying forms of psychotherapy that have been validated by experimental research—the *empirically supported therapies* (Kendall, 1998). Those who favor the experimental approach have compared the state of psychotherapy with the state of *pharmacological treatment,* the use of medication. In the United States, the federal Food and Drug Administration regulates the medications that may be used to treat mental health problems, only approving those with scientifically demonstrated safety and effectiveness. But there is no government agency protecting consumers from ineffective or harmful therapy. Instead, it seems that "anything goes" in the field of psychotherapy, where speculation and hunches about treatment effectiveness are favored far more than actual scientific data (Davison, 1998). Concerned about this trend, the Division of Clinical Psychology of the American Psychological Association commissioned a task force to prepare a report on effective psychotherapies (Task Force, 1995).

Promoters of scientific validation point out that research has shown certain treatments to be more effective than others for particular problems and disorders. The most convincing data derive from research using *randomized controlled trials,* in which patients are distributed randomly among different experimental treatments and progress is measured objectively from pre-treatment to post-treatment and follow-up. Table 11.1 lists the empirically supported therapies identified in a recent survey (DeRubeis & Crits-Christoff, 1998).

TABLE 11.1   Forms of Psychotherapy for Adult Mental Health Problems Supported by Empirical Research

	Efficacious and Specific	Efficacious	Possibly Efficacious
Major Depressive Disorder	Cognitive therapy	Behavior therapy Interpersonal therapy	Problem-solving therapy for depression
Generalized Anxiety Disorder	Cognitive therapy	Applied relaxation	
Social Phobia	Exposure therapy Exposure plus cognitive restructuring		
Obsessive-Compulsive Disorder	Exposure and response prevention		Cognitive therapy
Agoraphobia Panic Disorder	Exposure therapy Panic control therapy Cognitive therapy	Exposure therapy Applied relaxation	
Posttraumatic Stress Disorder	Exposure therapy		Stress inoculation training Eye movement desensitization and reprocessing
Schizophrenia			Social skills training
Alcohol Abuse and Dependence			Social skills training Cue exposure Cue exposure plus coping skills training
Substance Dependence	(Opiates)		Supportive-expressive therapy Cognitive therapy Behavior therapy (reinforcement)
	(Cocaine)		Relapse prevention therapy

Source: From DeRubeis, R. J., & Crits-Christoff, P. (1998). Empirically supported individual and group psychological treatments for adult mental disorders. *Journal of Consulting and Clinical Psychology, 66,* 37–52.

Studies establishing treatment effectiveness must be well controlled and meet high scientific standards. Findings that have been replicated by other scientists carry most weight and are most convincing when independent researchers with no particular allegiance to the therapy under study obtain the same results. Treatment is considered *efficacious* if it has brought greater benefit than no treatment in at least two studies by independent research groups. It is considered *efficacious and specific* if it has been shown superior to placebo treatment. The most influential research focuses treatment on specific problems or issues, not clients in general. Improvement due to treatment is evaluated by participants' scores on reliable and valid psychological tests. Finally, it is important that the therapists in the study carefully follow a detailed treatment manual to ensure that they actually use the designated procedures (Chambless & Hollon, 1998).

From the thousands of empirical studies of psychotherapy with adults, several specific therapies have been identified as effective in application to particular, focused client problems (DeRubeis & Crits-Christoph, 1998). Among these therapies, two categories are prominent: cognitive-behavioral interventions and interpersonal psychotherapy. While earlier forms of psychodynamic psychotherapy continue to be vulnerable to the criticism that they have not been supported by controlled research, interpersonal psychotherapy has established its validity as a tried-and-tested approach in application to depression (DeRubeis & Crits-Christoff, 1998; Spanier & Frank, 1998) and bulimia nervosa (Fairburn, 1998).

In support of traditional psychodynamic therapies, it has been pointed out that experimental studies of psychotherapy focus almost entirely on *forms* of treatment, therapeutic procedures, rather than on the skills of therapists and the characteristics of patients (Garfield, 1998). Research on the *process* of therapy, session by session, would be more relevant to psychodynamic therapy. In randomized controlled trials, patients are not matched to treatments or therapists on the basis of which intervention would be prescribed for them. Instead, they are assigned randomly, by contrast with real clinical practice (Persons & Silberschatz, 1998; Seligman, 1995). Furthermore, following a structured treatment manual, as required in research studies, allows clinicians no freedom in adapting therapy to the needs of the particular client (Garfield, 1998).

These interesting points notwithstanding, the data show that, when treatment via an established protocol is compared with treatments tailor-made by clinicians for specific clients, manual-based therapy produces better outcomes (Barlow, 1996b; Wilson, 1996). It would be understandable to assume that the wisdom of experienced clinicians would have the edge over rigid research protocols in providing effective psychotherapy, but evidence for this is lacking—demonstrating that reasonable assumptions can be proved incorrect by controlled experimentation.

Testing treatments objectively would seem to require us to evaluate therapy independent of the personal qualities and theoretical biases of the therapists (Kendall, 1998). Some excellent therapists presumably have personal characteristics that motivate a patient to change successfully even when the techniques used are suboptimal. But if there are therapists who deliver successful treatment regardless of the particular techniques employed, surely we would want to discover their secrets so as to train more professionals to perform like them!

Finally, it can be argued that some forms of psychotherapy are more amenable to traditional psychological experimentation than others. Clinicians working in the psychodynamic traditions are usually more interested in seeking a holistic understanding of patient function-ing than in measuring specific behaviors. They typically seek symbolic connections in the material presented by patients and tend to be more interested in the process of therapy, and in the relationship between the participants, than in objective, statistical data. By contrast, cognitive-behavioral clinicians find the methods and concepts of experimental psychology more congenial and favor focused experimentation. In deciding how to make further progress in evaluating psychotherapies successfully, the conceptual matter of disagreement over goals, treatment targets, and methods is at least as significant as the empirical matter of the need to collect more data on a broader variety of treatments.

B O X   11.1

Focus on Ethics: The "Bait-and-Switch" Tactic in Psychotherapy

Consider the following clinical scenario:

> An overworked businessman with high blood pressure has been sternly admonished by his family physician to do more to deal with his potentially life-threatening hypertension. The patient has com-plied with the regimen of medication prescribed by his doctor, but he has not altered his diet, embarked on an exercise program, or learned to relax. The physician recently found resource materials on the Internet indicating that clinical psychologists can contribute to health care in this area. She learned that health psychology can help hypertensive clients by teaching them relaxation skills, employing cogni-tive restructuring techniques, and using biofeedback. Accordingly, she recommends that her patient consult a clinical psychologist for health psychology input to help deal with his severe hypertension.
>
> The patient consults a psychologist, saying that his doctor suggested that he do so because of his dangerously high blood pressure. The psychologist spends most of this first meeting eyeing him speculatively, saying very little, and leaving it to the patient to break the long silences. Finally, the psy-chologist asks the man about his sex life. He says it's fine, leaves, and never goes back. He tells his family physician that "this psychology baloney is all phooey." *(adapted from Williams, 1985)*

Williams (1985) argued that the psychologist's behavior was highly unprofessional, resem-bling the "bait-and-switch" tactic traditionally employed by unscrupulous retailers—enticing potential customers into the store with the promise of a bargain deal, then, when they arrive, per-suading them to opt for a more costly alternative. The analogy with the psychologist in this example is that the client was expecting some straightforward advice on dealing with his high blood pressure, but instead found that the psychologist had his own agenda—one that probably meant getting him involved in costly, long-term therapy that might not be focused at all upon reducing hypertension. Furthermore, the psychologist's agenda did not include letting the client know the rationale for the therapy being offered.

Because psychodynamic therapy deals with subtle and indirect influences on human behav-ior and attempts to reveal unconscious motives, it is understandably difficult to forecast the course of therapy in detail at the outset. But this could easily mean that clients will not know what to expect unless the psychologist reviews this with them specifically. Clients have a right to be informed at least about the broad parameters of treatment, and there is nothing intrinsically difficult about this

---

BOX **11.1**   **Continued**

for psychodynamic practitioners. Even in the purest classical analysis, the analyst has a few face-to-face sessions with the client at the outset in order to discuss format, expectations, and so on. When a psychologist fails to give clients appropriate advance information about the offered services, he or she risks violating specific ethical standards (Koocher & Keith-Spiegel, 1998).

The APA Ethics Code (American Psychological Association, 2002) includes standards on the subject of informing potential clients about the nature of psychological services so that they can make informed decisions about participating. Standard 3.10, "Informed Consent," reads in part: "When psychologists provide . . . therapy [or] counseling . . . they obtain the informed consent of the individual . . . using language that is reasonably understandable."

Standard 10.01, "Informed Consent to Therapy," includes the following language: "Psychologists inform clients/patients as early as is feasible in the therapeutic relationship about the nature and anticipated course of therapy . . . and provide sufficient opportunity for the client/patient to ask questions and receive answers."

These important standards protect psychologists' clients by ensuring that they are fully informed at the outset about what they can expect from the services offered. When psychologists fail to comply with these standards, their clients can be harmed. Deflecting clients from alternative interventions that may have been more helpful is one example of the kind of harm that could accrue.

---

12 Humanistic, Experiential, and Family Therapies

Humanistic Psychotherapy

In Chapter 3 we noted that the humanistic model of personality, psychopathology, and psychotherapy initially drew most of its concepts from existential philosophy, emphasizing people's innate freedom to choose, take responsibility for their choices, and live very much in the present moment. Healthy living in the here-and-now confronts us with the existential realities of being, freedom, responsibility, and choice, and contemplating existence in turn forces us to face the ever-present possibility of nonexistence. Facing the inevitability of death means coming to terms with *angst* or existential anxiety—a process that is essential to healthy development and a fulfilling life. Each individual's search for meaning in life is his or her ultimate goal and highest aspiration.

Contemporary humanistic approaches to psychotherapy originated in three schools of thought that emerged in the 1950s: existential, Gestalt, and client-centered therapy.

Existential Psychotherapies

> *We rode in an orange-red cart to countries of sadness.*
> *We rode in a red cart of no distinction to no destination.*
> *Do we exist?*
> *—Mary P.**

Existentialists seek the meaning of human existence, and emphasize choice and individuality (as opposed to the idea that our behavior is determined in some mechanistic way). Martin Heidegger (1889–1976) is usually cited as having originated modern existential philosophy. In Heidegger's view, human existence is a continuing, evolving process for each individual. We are not static; we are always becoming something different (Hergenhahn, 1992). These elements of existential philosophy are seen in the forms of psychotherapy developed by Ludwig Binswanger and others, as noted in Chapter 3.

Existential psychotherapists focus on clients' important life themes and issues, but the emphasis is on the quality of the therapeutic relationship itself as the essential agent of change. For example, Irvin Yalom was working with an elderly widow who had recently had her

---

*Source: Mary P., Excerpt from *Black Raspberry Tales*. Reprinted with permission.

purse snatched. The therapist commented that the incident brought home to the client the inescapable fact that her husband was no longer with her. The client wept openly. Yalom wondered what to do next. He was struck by how big the women's purse was and raised the question of whether carrying around so large a bag might have been asking for trouble. The client protested and emptied the bag to prove to Yalom how essential each item was. Therapist and client gazed at the huge pile of belongings overflowing on Yalom's desk and sat in silence, taking it in. Then they both burst out laughing. This was a precious moment that dramatically cleared the air. Afterward, Yalom and the client were much more relaxed and comfortable with each other. This incident had been the catalyst for increasing the intimacy they experienced in what had previously been rather a distant therapeutic relationship (Walsh & McElwain, 2002).

The task of existential psychotherapy is to challenge clients to examine their lives and consider how their freedom is impaired. That helps them to remove obstacles, increase their sense of choice, and exert their will. It is undeniable that there are limitations on our freedom and autonomy as individuals. The term *existential-humanistic* "is often used to denote a therapeutic approach that tempers the humanistic notion of individual freedom with an existential focus on context and responsibility" (Walsh & McElwain, 2002, p. 255). While it is inescapable that we are not free of conditions, we can take a stand and choose what our attitudes toward them will be (Cain, 2002).

Existential psychotherapy seeks to understand the unique meanings of clients' experiences from the subjective point of view of the individual in his or her current phenomenological world. It would contradict the tenets of the model to classify people and their problems by means of a structured, objective diagnostic protocol, or to prescribe fixed intervention techniques established by research using group averages. The collaborative relationship between client and therapist is healing in itself, and does not rely conceptually on a "repair model" (Walsh & McElwain, 2002, p. 272).

The existential approach is not the most widely practiced form of psychotherapy, but its practitioners view it as a refreshing contrast to more mechanistic therapies and are working vigorously to promote it, citing growing experimental support in some areas (Cain & Seeman, 2002). It is also important in having set the scene for more popular humanistic therapies, especially Carl Rogers's client-centered therapy.

Gestalt Therapy

The name most strongly associated with *Gestalt therapy* is Frederick ("Fritz") Perls (1893–1970). Perls was a German physician who initially trained in psychoanalysis, but he became increasingly attracted to phenomenological and existential ideas and eventually developed Gestalt therapy as a blend of psychoanalytic, existential, and other influences (Greenberg & Rice, 1997). Among these other influences was *Gestalt psychology,* a holistic school or system of psychology that was popular in the United States and Europe between the 1930s and 1950s (see Box 12.1).

Gestalt Therapy Concepts.   Perls's studies of Gestalt psychology gave him a holistic view of human physical and psychological functioning, and led him "to view the person as part of an organism/environment field" (Greenberg & Rice, 1997, p. 102). Perls's wife and

B O X **12.1**

Gestalt Psychology

Gestalt psychologists objected to the study of specific elements in perception and learning, arguing that we do not experience the world in isolated fragments but in meaningful configurations (Hergenhahn, 1992). (The German word *Gestalt* refers to "whole," "pattern," or "configuration.") Believing that the whole is more than the sum of its parts, Gestalt psychologists' studies of perception and problem-solving demonstrated that we tend to perceive patterns, not isolated stimuli, and that people and animals can solve problems in flashes of insight in which we suddenly "see" the solution rather than by tedious trial-and-error learning. Perception is organized; our perceptual processes are geared to recognize figures and to distinguish them from backgrounds. This relationship between *figure* and *ground* is an important concept in Gestalt psychology. We do not see patches of color, angles, and lines, but we see people or trees or houses. We do not hear isolated notes of varying pitch, we hear tunes and melodies. In fact, we seem to be programmed for perceiving and detecting *figural goodness*—as if we have an inbuilt preference for certain figures, such as closed circles. Viewing an incomplete circle creates tension, a pressure to close the figure in the appropriate way. Seeking perceptual *closure* is one way of explaining motivation (Hergenhahn, 1992).

The Gestalt psychologists Kurt Koffka, Wolfgang Kohler, and Max Wertheimer developed their system as a field theory in which structures created by brain chemistry impose order on what we perceive, while at the same time the patterns of what is perceived can gradually mold the layout of the human brain (Hergenhahn, 1992).

---

colleague, Laura Posner Perls, cofounded the Gestalt therapy approach with him. They developed Gestalt therapy after leaving Germany in the 1930s for the Netherlands, then South Africa, and later the United States and Canada (Yontef, 1995). Consistent with field theory, in their approach to psychopathology and psychotherapy Fritz and Laura Perls and their associates focused on *process,* or people's development over time, rather than static personality structures, as implied by traditional psychoanalytic models. Fritz Perls viewed a person as very much an ongoing event—physically, a complex and continuing process of digesting food, building up and breaking down chemicals in nerves and muscles, and so forth, and psychologically, a continuous interaction of the person with the ever-changing flux of internal and external stimuli. Gestalt therapists use the term *mental metabolism* as a metaphor for the processes through which people grow emotionally (Yontef, 1995).

In their clinical work Fritz and Laura Perls emphasized the here-and-now awareness of bodily sensations, active experimentation in the form of exercises designed to help clients get in touch with their immediate experience, and genuine encounters with other people. These elements have all been incorporated into contemporary humanistic and experiential therapies (Greenberg & Rice, 1997; Yontef, 1995).

In Gestalt therapy theory people are defined by their *boundaries.* None of us has an isolated, free-standing sense of "I"; our sense of individuality derives from our *contact* with other people or the physical environment. Healthy living means being in good contact, or "being mindful of current reality" (Yontef, 1995, p. 264). If at a given moment we are preoccupied by past issues or worries about the future, our current awareness and functioning will be diminished. In figure/ground terms, the figure is what stands out in our immediate awareness.

For example, the leader of a Gestalt therapy workshop that one of us attended asked the participants to sit around in a circle and focus on immediate sensations, rather than line up in rows of seats and listen to a structured academic lecture. He began by noting that he was sensing some acute bodily discomfort because the workshop organizer had neglected to provide coffee. One of the graduate students present challenged the leader to provide data on the effectiveness of his therapeutic approach, but the leader commented on the posture, body language, and facial expression of the questioner and expressed his emotional reaction to the person's attitude and demeanor. In each case, the presenter focused his awareness on the "figures" that stood out from the ground at each particular moment.

Insight is a vital concept in Gestalt therapy. Insight is a form of awareness in which everything falls into place in a meaningful pattern. Psychotherapy can help people develop insightful self-awareness when this does not occur naturally. As an experiential intervention, Gestalt therapy focuses on process rather than content and is based on the here-and-now interactions between therapist and client. The therapist tunes in to the figures that emerge from the background during therapeutic interactions and tries to gain insight into them (Yontef, 1995).

Gestalt therapy is often associated with some dramatic techniques that were well publicized in the 1960s and 1970s. These include the *empty chair technique* for dealing with "unfinished business" with another person, and thus obtaining closure. In this technique, "Facing an empty chair, the person contacts the imaginary other to express previously inhibited painful emotion" (Strumpfel & Goldman, 2002, p. 197). Despite the clinical value of such strategies, Gestalt therapists oppose the idea that there is a set of established techniques that define the approach. As in the case of other therapeutic approaches, the therapeutic *principles* are far more important than specific *techniques* that may be employed (Yontef, 1995).

Like existential psychotherapy, Gestalt therapy is not commonly practiced as a "free-standing" approach. However, it has had a strong influence on other humanistic schools, and some of its strategies and principles have been popular among eclectic therapists.

Client-Centered Therapy

As noted in Chapter 3, Carl Rogers's introduction of *client-centered therapy* in 1940 was the key event in launching humanistic therapy as a significant force in American psychotherapy. Rogers's central assumption was that clients direct their own personal growth, aided by their own inner resources. Therapists help this process along by setting up the most facilitative climate, a warm interpersonal relationship that is marked by the therapist's genuineness, unconditional positive regard, and empathy (Raskin & Rogers, 1989).

Emphasizing the therapeutic relationship itself, rather than the counselor's expert use of techniques, makes sense if we accept that humans carry within themselves all the resources they need for optimal personal development. Influenced by Maslow, Rogers believed that the individual's innate drive for *self-actualization* is all that one needs to solve personal and emotional problems and to live a fulfilling life. The therapist's task is to liberate this process when it has become blocked, usually when the individual has lost touch with his or her own sense of what feels right and turns, instead, to accepting the judgments and seeking the approval of other people.

For example, in this excerpt from a therapy session transcript the client comments on experiencing feelings in the present moment as opposed to solving problems in a deliberate, structured way, using the analogy of a jigsaw puzzle:

> CLIENT: For the first time in months I am not thinking about my problems. I'm not actually, I'm not working on them.
>
> ROGERS: I get the impression you don't sort of sit down to work on "my problems." It isn't that feeling at all.
>
> CLIENT: That's right. That's right. I suppose what I, I mean actually is that I'm not sitting down to put this puzzle together as, as something I've got to see the picture. . . . It may be that I am actually enjoying this feeling process. Or I'm certainly learning something.
>
> ROGERS: At least there's a sense of the immediate goal of getting that feel as being the thing, not that you're doing this in order to see a picture, but that it's a, a satisfaction of really getting acquainted with each piece. Is that—
>
> CLIENT: That's it. That's it. And it still becomes that sort of sensuousness, that touching [the pieces of the jigsaw puzzle]. It's quite interesting. Sometimes not entirely pleasant, I'm sure, but—
>
> ROGERS: A rather different sort of experience.
>
> CLIENT: Yes. Quite.

(From Rogers, 1961, p. 78; selection also cited by Patterson, 1980)

Consistent with this theory, Rogers gave counselors and psychotherapists a list of heart-felt recommendations: Don't solve problems, but help clients grow. Rely on individuals' drive toward adjustment and healthy development. Emphasize emotional, rather than intellectual, elements in the counseling process. Focus on the immediate situation, not the past. Stress the therapeutic relationship itself as a growth experience (Cain, 2002; Rogers, 1940, 1942).

Amplifying his theoretical assumptions in a later article, "The Necessary and Sufficient Conditions of Therapeutic Personality Change" (Rogers, 1957), he made the following points. Two people, the client and therapist, are in psychological contact. The client is in a state of incongruence (is vulnerable or anxious). The therapist is congruent or integrated—authentic, consistent—in the relationship. The therapist experiences unconditional positive regard for the client, and experiences an empathic understanding of the client's internal frame of reference. The therapist conveys his or her empathic understanding and unconditional positive regard to the client, and the communication of these experiences is effective (Cain, 2002).

Genuineness.   When therapists are genuine (or congruent) in the therapeutic relationship, they are natural and artless, simply being themselves, rather than putting on a false or phony image—even the image of a professional therapist! The opposite of genuineness in the Rogerian sense would be the "game face" people can display as a calculated gambit designed to gain some advantage—as in playing poker, for example.

Unconditional Positive Regard.   Accepting the client unconditionally means that the client does not have to earn the status of a worthwhile human being; he or she has it automatically, and the therapist accepts the client fully no matter what. People often ask client-centered therapists questions such as: "What if the client is a child molester or an axe murderer? Are they still OK, no matter what?" The reply is usually something like this: "Yes, you can always value, prize, and accept the human being, even if you reject his or her behavior. It's just like the religious concept of rejecting the sin, but not the sinner. In any event, even axe murderers ended up behaving that way only because their natural drive for self-actualization was blocked through untoward experiences and circumstances."

Empathy.   Empathy means "tuning in" to and sensing the client's private world as accurately as possible, as if it were one's own private world. The "as if" is important. Therapists do not lose that "as if" quality, or there would be a very confusing blurring of the participants' personal boundaries. Nonetheless, striving to understand the client's feelings and perceptions as vividly as possible, without trying to "become" the client, is vital to client-centered therapy. As in the familiar phrase "to understand all is to forgive all," fully understanding the client's perspective makes sense of things that have seemed unclear or even absurd. It is important to the therapeutic process that the client perceives the therapist's empathy.

In client-centered therapy the therapist's demonstration of empathy, recognized by the client, has the highest priority (Patterson, 1980). The following excerpt illustrates that empathy is not simply a matter of the therapist echoing what the client says. The therapist goes further than that and attempts to elaborate on the feelings behind the client's statement. Because the client is the expert on his or her experience, the therapist offers this tentatively, always seeking feedback from the client as to its accuracy.

> CLIENT: I suppose from the practical point of view . . . what I ought to be doing is solving some problems, day-to-day problems. And yet . . . what I'm trying to do is solve . . . something else that's . . . a great deal more important than little day-to-day problems. Maybe that sums up the whole thing.
>
> ROGERS: I wonder if this will distort your meaning, that from a hard-headed point of view you ought to be spending time thinking through specific problems. But you wonder if perhaps maybe you aren't on a quest for this whole you and perhaps that's more important than a solution to the day-to-day problems.
>
> CLIENT: I think that's it. I think that's it. That's probably what I mean.

(Rogers, 1961, p. 90)

Research on Client-Centered Therapy.   Rogers's contribution to psychotherapy was innovative in focusing on the client as the agent of self-change and unique among the humanistic schools at that time in pioneering systematic research on psychotherapy process and outcome (Bozarth, Zimring, & Tausch, 2002). The earliest phase of Rogers's research focused on *nondirective therapy,* the original label for the approach. On the therapist's side of the interaction, the key hypotheses were that "if therapists accept, recognize, and clarify the feelings expressed by the clients, then there will be movement from negative to positive feelings, followed by insight and positive actions initiated by the clients" (Bozarth et al., 2002). Accordingly, therapy proceeds best when therapists respond to, accept, and clarify clients' expressed feelings rather than attending to the content of what is communicated. Early studies showed that therapists could be reliably classified by observers as directive or nondirective and that the clients of nondirective therapists showed positive changes as therapy progressed in positive feelings, understanding and insight, and planning activity. When therapists' statements interpreted or structured what was said, clients stopped self-exploring, but when therapists reflected expressed feelings, clients continued the self-exploration process. Positive changes in clients included improved self-concept and, in turn, increased acceptance of others (Bozarth et al., 2002).

In Chapter 3 we briefly noted the 1967 Wisconsin project, in which Rogers and his colleagues studied 28 patients with schizophrenia, 16 of whom were treated by client-centered therapy. Consistent with Rogers' hypotheses, high ratings of empathy were correlated with reductions on Scale 8 (Sc) of the MMPI. By contrast, low levels of rated empathy were associated with release from the hospital, producing a contradictory mixture of findings. Despite these somewhat disappointing results, even Rogers's critics agreed that inpatients with schizophrenia were an extremely challenging target for any psychological intervention available at that time (Rachman & Wilson, 1980).

Early research on the outcome of client-centered therapy produced results that seemed predominantly consistent with Rogers's hypotheses that the three therapist-offered conditions are both necessary and sufficient for therapeutic personality change (Truax & Carkhuff, 1967). Therapists' communication of genuineness, unconditional positive regard, and empathy was seen to facilitate client improvement, but most of the studies lacked adequate control groups (Rachman & Wilson, 1980).

Reviews published in the 1970s concluded that the link between the facilitative conditions and therapeutic improvement were, at best, modest. In the much-cited prospective experimental trial that compared traditional psychotherapy with behavior therapy (Sloane, Staples, Cristol, Yorkston, & Whipple, 1975), the key Rogerian conditions were unrelated to treatment outcome. Possible reasons for these disappointing findings include researchers' choice of challenging client groups, such as college underachievers and delinquent girls. Like improving the adjustment of people with schizophrenia, increasing students' academic achievement and preventing delinquent individuals' offending are difficult assignments for any psychotherapist.

Other difficulties have included assembling psychometrically sound measures of such vital constructs as empathy. Much of the research has used external evaluations of empathy, but correlations between judges' ratings of empathy and those of clients have been "low or nonexistent" (Watson, 2002, p. 448). Part of the problem, of course, is that in Rogers's theory only the client can truly judge the accuracy of the therapist's attempts at empathy. Consistent with this, the strongest evidence for a link between empathy and outcome derives from studies using the Barrett-Lennard Relationship Inventory, which obtains client-perceived ratings (Barrett-Lennard, 1973). Ideally, however, the most dependable measurement of empathy as a construct would require an objective, external validation criterion.

Since the 1980s psychotherapy research in general has largely focused on evaluating specific treatment techniques as applied to particular disorders. Client-centered therapy researchers have objected to this focus on procedures because it appears to neglect the client-therapist relationship (Bozarth et al., 2002). To some extent, this difference in emphasis reflects the different goals and treatment targets of client-centered and, for example, behavior therapists. Client-centered therapists aim at general improvement in clients' personality functioning rather than treating specific mental disorders. Critics of client-centered therapy might argue that personal growth is a more limited goal than seeking recovery from particular debilitating syndromes such as panic disorder, major depressive disorder, and obsessive-compulsive disorder. Whatever the reason for the differences in emphasis, studies of client-centered therapy have not examined specific disorders in the same detail as have cognitive-behavioral investigations.

Eclectic Treatment Combinations

As coherent, distinctive systems of psychotherapy, existential, Gestalt, and client-centered therapies are the leading approaches within the humanistic/experiential spectrum of mental health interventions. Many clinicians incorporate aspects of all three of these approaches in their therapeutic work, and much of the therapy delivered today within this general tradition can be seen as eclectic. Probably most forms of eclecticism are unique to the particular practitioner, but some eclectic treatment "packages" that have been studied in their own right can be identified.

A Three-Stage Model of Helping

Rogers's client-centered therapy is a prominent component of the *three-stage model of helping* introduced by Hill and O'Brien (1999). Drawing from psychodynamic, client-centered, and cognitive-behavioral therapies, the three-stage model views psychotherapists and counselors ("helpers") as collaborators and facilitators who guide clients in exploring their feelings, understanding their problems, making choices, and effecting changes. Rather than claiming expertise on how people should live, helpers in this model bring empathy and special helping skills to the therapeutic relationship.

Exploration, Insight, and Action. The three stages in the model are *exploration, insight,* and *action.* In each stage clients are helped to come to terms with their thoughts, feelings, and behaviors as essential domains of psychological functioning. In the exploration stage, clients explore and examine these three domains. In the insight stage, clients seek understanding of them. In the action stage, clients decide what to do on the basis of their exploration and insight (Hill & O'Brien, 1999).

The exploration stage draws chiefly from Rogers's client-centered therapy, the insight stage from psychodynamic therapies, and the action stage from behavioral and cognitive-behavioral approaches. However, *empathic collaboration,* a concept strongly identified with the humanistic position, is vital to all three stages, and humanistic and experiential ideas are prominent among the assumptions underlying the model. For example, in the model people are viewed as being born with varied potentials for development psychologically, physically, and interpersonally, and they tend toward fulfilling those potentials. However, the environment can help or hinder this innate tendency toward healthy development. Early experience provides the foundation for personality development, and attachment and self-esteem are especially important. Healthy emotional environments include relationships marked by "acceptance, love, support, encouragement, recognition, and appropriate challenges" (Hill & O'Brien, 1999, p. 20). While people cannot change their personalities fundamentally, they can learn to accept who they are and make the most of their potential. Determinism is therefore balanced by free will.

Informed by Rogers's work, the exploration stage in the Hill and O'Brien model involves establishing rapport and developing a therapeutic relationship; creating a climate in which clients can "tell their stories"; gaining access to emotion, encouraging emotional arousal, and helping clients experience their feelings; and, in general, learning about clients—their worldviews, their styles of interaction, their problems, their needs. In this delicate initial stage counselors and psychotherapists can err by talking too much, giving advice, trying to be the client's friend or buddy, and failing to listen attentively. Experienced helpers tend, instead, to ask open-ended questions, to allow silences to develop, to withhold premature self-disclosures, and to accept and encourage clients' expressions of emotion. Many of the problems displayed by novice helpers can be attributed to their attempts to reduce their own anxiety by imposing too much structure on the client and the relationship (Hill & O'Brien, 1999).

In the insight stage, therapist and client collaborate to achieve new understandings. These can include gaining greater awareness of the client's potential role in contributing to his or her problems. Therapists "actively work with clients in the insight stage to construct meanings and reframe experiences" (Hill & O'Brien, 1999, p. 23).

In the action stage, therapists guide clients toward making decisions and effecting behavioral changes based on what has been learned during the insight stage. Therapists draw from cognitive-behavioral formulations to inform their guidance of their clients.

Essential Components.   Clinicians following the three-stage model of helping show similarities with cognitive therapists in emphasizing *empathic collaboration* and changing dysfunctional cognitive *schemas.* They also show similarities with psychoanalytic clinicians in focusing on *covert processes,* operating in both client and therapist, that profoundly influence the therapeutic relationship (Hill & O'Brien, 1999). Aspects of the Hill and O'Brien model that have received consistent empirical support in many studies include the therapeutic value of empathy and experiencing (Cain & Seeman, 2002; Hill, 2001).

Process-Experiential Therapy

Leslie Greenberg, Robert Elliott, and their colleagues have combined client-centered therapy with components of existential, Gestalt, and experiential therapies to form *process-experiential psychotherapy.* The twin foci are on the relationship and on therapeutic tasks, but "the client and the quality of the relationship always take precedence over the therapeutic tasks proposed, methods, or goals" (Cain, 2002, p. 40). The emphasis is on processing emotion and reconstructing *emotion schemes.* Clients are helped to integrate information from their emotional and cognitive systems so as to make a more satisfactory adjustment (Cain, 2002).

Because clients are the experts on their experience, therapists do not interpret or advise. Instead, they encourage clients to identify their inner experience and to engage in processes of discovery and choice. The focus is on "present experience and on the current moment-by-moment process of attending to and symbolizing bodily felt referents" (Elliott & Greenberg, 1995, p. 123). There is a natural tendency toward healthy growth that moves the person forward in an adaptive manner. The therapist helps the client in the process of creating new meanings. An essential element is the authentic, genuine relationship between therapist and client, as opposed to the relationship in traditional psychoanalytic therapy—in which the therapist carefully cultivates him or herself as a bland, neutral, blank screen upon which the client's unconscious issues may be projected.

An eclectic combination of concepts and techniques grounded in contemporary emotion theory, process-experiential psychotherapy fosters "a creative dialectic between the client-centered emphasis on creating a genuinely empathic and prizing therapeutic relationship . . . and the active, task-focused, process-directive style of Gestalt therapy" (Elliott & Greenberg, 2002, p. 279). Process-experiential therapy is viewed by its proponents as a research-informed treatment. Another name for the approach is *emotionally focused therapy* (EFT).

Theory of Psychopathology.   Distress and impairment arise when a person is unable to find words or images to symbolize his or her experiences and when the key emotion schemes through which experiences are interpreted are dysfunctional. *Emotion schemes* are "implicit, idiosyncratic organizational structures that serve as the basis for human experience and self-organization" (Elliott & Greenberg, 2002, p. 280). The chief goal of therapy is to help clients gain access to their dysfunctional emotion schemes under conditions that will facilitate change.

Guiding Principles.   The therapist aims at mutual collaboration and co-exploration, and offers interventions in a nonimposing, nonauthoritative manner. A central issue in treatment is the balance between *relationship responsiveness* and *task directiveness.* Six specific principles can be articulated, three of which guide development of the therapeutic relationship, and three of which facilitate completion of therapeutic tasks.

The *relationship principles* are empathic attunement, therapeutic bond, and task collaboration. *Empathic attunement* means that the therapist continually strives to understand the client's experiential world as fully as possible at a feeling level. The *therapeutic bond* means that the therapist communicates empathy, acceptance, warmth, unconditional prizing, and openness. *Task collaboration* means that the therapist facilitates the client's involvement in the goals and tasks of therapy.

The *task facilitation principles* that encourage work on specific therapeutic tasks are experiential processing, growth and choice, and task completion. *Experiential processing* involves facilitating *modes of engagement,* which can be listed as attending and awareness, experiential search, active expression, interpersonal contact, self-reflection, and carrying forward into action. The *growth and choice* principle reminds therapists to focus on fostering client growth and self-determination. The *task completion* principle encourages therapists to facilitate clients' completion of key therapeutic tasks (Elliott & Greenberg, 1995, 2002).

Experiential Response Modes. In employing the six principles, the therapist makes use of several *experiential response modes*. The essentials here are empathic understanding, empathic exploration, process directing (it is essential, of course, that the therapist direct the *process*, not the content, of sessions), and experiential presence.

Therapeutic Tasks. Therapeutic tasks all have three elements: a *marker* of client readiness, a sequence of actions or *operations*, and a desired resolution or *end state*. Typical interventions and tasks are empathic exploration, empathic affirmation, focusing, evocative unfolding, two-chair work for *conflict splits* and *self-interruption*, empty chair dialogue for *unfinished business* or unresolved emotional reactions, and meaning work. *Empathic exploration* is the most characteristic therapist response. It communicates understanding and helps clients approach unclear aspects of experience (Elliott & Greenberg, 2002).

The following exchange illustrates empathic exploration. The client is a 19-year-old woman who has been victimized by crime.

> CLIENT: I just want enough of who I used to be so that I could live like a human being.
>
> THERAPIST: "I don't feel like a human being right now. I feel like some kind of something else that's not human."

(Elliott & Greenberg, 2002, p. 288)

To illustrate the use of two-chair work for conflict splits, a trainee psychotherapist was invited to confront issues posed by his pride, which he viewed as stubbornly stifling his growth and self-expression. Sitting in the *experiencing chair,* he talked aloud to his pride, which was assigned to the *other chair.* (To the trainee, his pride embodied his expectations and self-criticisms.) Then he occupied the other chair and spoke, as his pride, to the now-empty experiencing chair. The two sides gradually converged, became indistinguishable in their experiencing level, and achieved resolution while moving to a higher level of experiencing.

Practical Applications. Process-experiential psychotherapy is chiefly applied in individual therapy, but it also has applications in group and couples formats. It is most helpful for outpatients with less severe pathology and relatively mild distress. Typically, treatment is delivered in 50-minute sessions once per week. Therapists are trained in a series of modules. A vital component of training is experiential learning, in which the trainee may practice the roles of therapist and client (Elliot & Greenberg, 1995).

Research on Treatment Outcome. Elliott (2002) conducted a meta-analysis of 86 studies of process-experiential and other humanistic therapies. He calculated pre–post effect sizes (i.e., *change effect size data*) so that single-group studies could be included, used *statistical* *equivalence analysis* in "proving the null hypothesis," and applied statistical controls for researcher allegiance. An effect size lower than that normally considered to be clinically meaningful was chosen as a criterion for improvement. As a result of this analysis, Elliott (2002) reached the following conclusions. On average, clients in humanistic therapy show large therapeutic changes over time. Client gains are stable, and persist over follow-up intervals that sometimes exceed twelve months. In randomized trials with untreated controls, clients usually show substantially more change than the comparable untreated clients. In clinical trials in which clients were randomly assigned either to humanistic therapy or to another designated treatment, clients in humanistic therapies "generally show amounts of change equivalent to clients in nonhumanistic therapies, including [cognitive-behavior therapy]" (Elliott, 2002, pp. 71–72). Elliott noted that there was strong evidence of an effect for researcher allegiance, suggesting that in future studies researchers would do better to employ disinterested therapists. In this meta-analysis the outcome measures selected were often confounded with treatment type, making it unclear whether more or less discriminating measures or more or less effective interventions were responsible for the observed differences.

Elliott noted, and responded to, potential criticisms of this study as follows. The analysis relied heavily on uncontrolled studies, but he argues that it is more scientific to use all available data. Few studies used treatment manuals, but manuals do not ensure that therapists follow them or perform competently. Furthermore, specific competence checks were used in some of the studies. In any event, the main interventions have been fully described in the literature on client-centered, Gestalt, and process-experiential psychotherapy, often in great detail. Many studies used clients with unspecified diagnoses or did not use the DSM-IV classification. However, insisting that specific diagnoses be the focus of investigation is unscientific. In everyday clinical practice most clients have multiple diagnoses, problems, and issues. Imprecise labels such as "neurotic" do communicate much meaningful information to clinicians, and are readily understood as referring to typical outpatients with moderate distress.

The most scientifically minded psychologists are likely to find Elliott's points less than compelling. However, the recent careful descriptions of the elements of process-experiential psychotherapy by Greenberg and his colleagues will allow replication of these procedures, thus satisfying one of the requirements for systematic research in this area.

Family Therapy

Family therapy can be placed within the broader theoretical context of *family psychology intervention science* (Liddle, Bray, Levant, & Santisteban, 2002). Family psychology interventions can involve assessing and paying attention to several systems and levels of social influence, including peer, school, occupational, community, and neighborhood domains. The broad array of possible interventions draws strongly, but not entirely, from family therapy and the study of family systems (Liddle et al., 2002), but in this section we will focus on traditional family therapy approaches.

As a system of psychotherapy, family therapy had its origins outside mainstream psychology and developed as much from the fields of anthropology, information theory, and cybernetics (Alexander, Sexton, & Robbins, 2002). The family therapy approach entails a unique way of viewing psychopathology. Its practitioners see problems within the context of the *family system*. For example, an early finding was that positive psychotherapeutic change in someone receiving individual therapy could be subtly, perhaps unwittingly, undermined by other family members (Goldenberg & Goldenberg, 1995).

Systems Perspective

A *system* is "a collection of organisms that are interconnected in mutually influential, interdependent relationships with each other" (Miklowitz, 1994, p. 372). Defining a family as a system means viewing family members as interconnected through their emotional attachments. Key assumptions of the systems model are that the system is superordinate to its components and that the behavior of a component can only be understood in terms of the system. Applied to psychopathology, the systems view implies that the presence of a psychological disorder in an individual family member reflects problems in the family system itself. Consequently, treatment involves modifying the structure of the family and the communication processes that take place within it.

A family system has its own regulatory mechanisms that tend to keep it in balance through homeostatic processes. Family systems theory predicts that psychopathology arises when the family's homeostasis is thrown out of balance by some significant event. A designated family member develops a disorder so as to restore the balance. For example, when a family failed to deal appropriately with grief over the death of a grandparent, a teenage boy had an arrest for drunken driving. By forcing the family to confront an undeniable and immediate problem, the boy helped the family restore a suitable equilibrium. Family members are, of course, unaware that these powerful processes are at work (Miklowitz, 1994).

Family members are viewed as *interdependent* in this model, such that a significant change in one individual causes compensatory changes in another. For example, a husband who had played a key role in supporting his wife while she struggled with panic disorder and agoraphobia was adversely affected when she improved dramatically with behavior therapy. In fact, he felt useless after her recovery and attempted suicide. Another man whose wife was treated successfully for agoraphobia suddenly developed low back pain, which improved when his wife stopped going out so much (Hafner, 1977).

Viewed as a system, a family has no memory—implying that family therapists may intervene in the "here and now" at any point, without having to conduct a careful assessment of the family's history. Subgroups within a family may form *triangles* that lend stability and reduce or increase emotional intensity. Many family therapists view their primary task as analyzing these triangles and intervening to change them, thus changing the system. *Feedback* is an essential process. *Negative feedback* is at work when a domestic central heating system keeps the temperature within a specified range. When the temperature rises enough to reach a certain level, the furnace shuts off. When the temperature declines to a designated lower level, the furnace cuts in again. In a family system, negative feedback maintains equilibrium. *Positive feedback* creates an upward or downward spiral, as in the case of a microphone held too close to a loudspeaker—the mike picks up the signal from the speaker, the amplifier feeds that sound back to the speaker, the mike picks up *that* signal, and so forth, resulting in a squealing sound that gets louder and louder. Positive feedback can disrupt a family system and force it to change, a phenomenon of which family therapists may take advantage (Foley, 1989).

Development of Family Therapy

Family therapy was developed by a varied group of people working in isolation from one another. Freud's psychoanalysis and Rogers's client-centered therapy, the leading schools in the 1950s, saw pathology as the result of unhealthy interactions with others. Traditional psychotherapy required the relationship with the therapist to be private, so as to discourage patients from distorting or denying feelings in order to win the approval of others. But in the early 1950s, the pioneering family therapist Don Jackson documented the dramatic effects individual psychotherapy had upon other members of the patient's family (Nichols & Schwartz, 1991).

The child guidance movement was also important. The theory behind child guidance clinics was that, if emotional disorders begin in childhood (via Freudian psychodynamics), then adult psychopathology could be prevented by interventions with children at risk. Rudolph Dreikurs, a student of Adler, was a leading proponent of child guidance clinics in the United States in the 1920s. Gradually, child guidance workers came to believe that children's problems were the offshoot of family tensions.

Some of the early theories turned out to be misguided. "Maternal overprotectiveness" was blamed for the problems of many children. In 1948 Frieda Fromm-Reichmann introduced the concept of the *schizophrenogenic mother,* a domineering, aggressive, rejecting, and insecure parent whose pathological messages were thought to induce schizophrenia. This hypothesis has since been completely discredited.

John Bowlby at the Tavistock Clinic in the United Kingdom started to see his child patients together with their parents and reported improved therapeutic outcomes. Nathan Ackerman extended this approach in 1938 and advocated viewing the family as a single, whole entity when dealing with the problems of any individual within it (Nichols & Schwartz, 1991).

Social work was influential (Clarkin & Carpenter, 1995). In 1917 Mary Richmond published her classic text *Social Diagnosis,* encouraging treatment of the whole family, suggesting the concept of family cohesion, and taking a systems view. Physicians dealing with patients' sexual difficulties inevitably brought in the patients' spouses, and (arguably) marital therapy began in this way. Research on family dynamics in the etiology of schizophrenia was another precursor, exemplified by Bateson's concept of the double bind. Harry Stack Sullivan had focused on interpersonal relations in his work on schizophrenia, and in 1927 he described the "hospital family" as a benevolent substitute for the patient's real family. In Palo Alto, Gregory Bateson headed the project on schizophrenia and Don Jackson led the Mental Research Institute (devoted to treating families). In 1949 Theodore Lidz took a psychodynamic view of the family interactions that were assumed to produce schizophrenia.

Marriage counseling was another contributing development. In 1931 the first report on the psychoanalysis of a married couple was presented at an American Psychiatric Association convention. The author, Clarence Oberndorf, argued that married couples have interlocking neuroses that are best treated in concert (Nichols & Schwartz, 1991).

Schools of Family Therapy

Perhaps the earliest forms of family therapy were *psychoeducational*. This is not really a distinct school, as "probably all therapies have an instructional element" (Clarkin & Carpenter, 1995, p. 208). Because family interactions were once blamed for the development of severe psychopathology, notoriously schizophrenia, families therefore had to be counseled to communicate more appropriately in order to stop manufacturing mental illness. It has since been accepted that the situation is more complex. Disturbed family interactions are most likely the result of, rather then the cause of, severe mental illness in one member. Nonetheless, whatever its cause, disturbed communication in the family can still exert an adverse influence on the disordered individual's rehabilitation. Serious psychopathology in a family member places significant stress on the family in any event. Accordingly, family therapy based on psychoeducational principles makes sense if it focuses on constructive coping and adaptation (Clarkin & Carpenter, 1995).

Cognitive-behavioral family therapy emphasizes such techniques as communication skills training, problem-solving training, and contingency contracting/social exchange/operant learning methods. Foci for attention are attributional styles and distorted assumptions, communication deviance, and expression of negative affect and "expressed emotion" (Clarkin & Carpenter, 1995). Because the cognitive-behavioral approach does not stem from either psychoanalytic or systems theory concepts, it is not regarded as one of the branches of family therapy proper (Guerin & Chabot, 1997).

Otherwise, the various schools within family therapy are unified in having recognizable common elements and, consistent with a "family tree" analogy, can be viewed as forming four major branches. The *communications* approach began with Gregory Bateson and his work on the double bind theory of schizophrenia in Palo Alto in the 1950s. The *psychoanalytic multigenerational systems* approach began with the work of Murray Bowen. The *experiential systems* approach is humanistic with psychoanalytic underpinnings; it is associated with Carl Whitaker and Virginia Satir. The *structural family therapy* approach began with the child guidance movement and is represented currently by Salvadore Minuchin (Guerin & Chabot, 1997).

Communications.   Gregory Bateson's *Palo Alto Communication Model* developed from the theory of the *double bind,* which was later rejected for lack of experimental support (Miklowitz, 1994). In this model the family was described as a "cybernetic system" that either changes to become more adaptive in response to new information, or returns to a state of homeostasis when new, disruptive information is introduced.

In the double bind, two or more people are involved in an important, continuing relationship. A strong command is given, but at the same time there is another command at an abstract level that contradicts the first. The second command may be nonverbal. There is also a perceived threat. The individual receiving these messages may not escape from the situation, but must respond. When this situation has been repeated often enough, not all of these elements need to be present to create the adverse effects of the double bind—"almost any part is enough to precipitate either panic or rage" (Guerin & Chabot, 1997, p. 185).

In one example of the conflicting messages given in a double-bind situation, a mother visited her son in a psychiatric inpatient unit. Approaching him, she said, "Come here, give me a hug, I love you," but her tone was distant, her manner disapproving, and she visibly winced when her son embraced her. When he withdrew, she asked, "Don't you love me any more?" (Barlow & Durand, 1999).

Another example of a double-bind message is found in the command: "Dominate me!" If the person receiving this message does then dominate the other, that would merely be compliance with the command, the opposite of domination (Guerin & Chabot, 1997).

In the *Strategic Intervention* model of Don Jackson and Jay Haley, therapy is viewed as a power struggle over control. The identified patient is in control, and the therapist must therefore change the power balance. One method for doing so is the *therapeutic double bind,* devised as a paradoxical maneuver by Jackson and Haley. The therapist might say to the family member with schizophrenia, "I think you should go on having hallucinations. By having such symptoms, you are playing a vital role in holding this family together." If the individual continues to have hallucinations, then he or she is complying with the therapist, who is therefore in control. If the individual stops having hallucinations in order to defy the therapist, well and good! (Guerin & Chabot, 1997).

In triangulation, two members of a family form a coalition that excludes a third. For example, a mother with marital problems becomes overly close to the daughter in a relationship that excludes the father. The daughter is caught between the parents and may develop a problem that helps restore the homeostasis of the family. Therapy focuses on the original problem, the marital distress, and on the family's attempts to solve it. Techniques include *reframing,* or describing the apparent problem in more benign terms, and *paradoxical intention,* or recommending the opposite of what might be expected—as in the example of the therapeutic double bind cited above (Clarkin & Carpenter, 1995; Miklowitz, 1994).

The *Milan School* of Mara Selvini Palazzoli developed from the strategic model, but was also influenced by the structural approach. By *circular questioning* the therapist forms hypotheses about family dynamics, such as by asking one member to clarify another's views, or to comment on the relationship between two others. The therapist continually revises his or her hypotheses in response. Often, the family has developed a "game" in which some members try to gain control over others. The chief technique is the *counterparadoxical* intervention—the game is identified, and the therapist encourages the family to continue it or even to exaggerate it. This challenges the family to change (Miklowitz, 1994).

Psychoanalytic Multigenerational Systems.   In the *psychoanalytic model* it is important to understand the unconscious conflicts, drives, wishes, and dynamics of each individual and of the family as a whole. What are the causes of psychopathology? A family member experiences intolerable aspects of the self. These are *projected* onto another member, who *identifies* with these attributes and begins to experience them. This is the process of *projective identification.*

In Bowen's *family systems* model people are destined for certain roles in the complex family system. Fusion (failure of individuals to differentiate themselves from the family) is a common problem. *Differentiation* from one's family of origin is a necessary condition for emotional and physical health. The process of differentiation involves defining one's own boundaries, integrating conflicting parts of the self, and tolerating and empathizing with the emotional conflicts and reactions of other people. In a family, each individual is confronted by the tension between discomfort with autonomy or independence and the desire to differentiate and self-regulate. It is seen as better to *respond* (considering others' wants) than to *react* (acting solely on the basis of feelings). Maintaining one's individual identity while staying in touch with the system is the goal for all family members, not only those with symptoms.

Bowen's approach may involve the analysis of triangles occurring across generations, as in the case of a grandmother, mother, and daughter. Schizophrenia is seen as resulting from a lack of interpersonal differentiation that is transmitted from generation to generation. In this pattern, mothers tend to be overinvolved with their sons, who are not encouraged to perform age-appropriate behaviors. The fathers tend to be weak, ineffectual, and underinvolved (Clarkin & Carpenter, 1995; Miklowitz, 1994).

The *object relations* model of family therapy is associated with the work of Boszormenyi-Nagy. In this view, satisfactory relationships with people form a basic need. Not obtaining satisfactory relationships in the family of origin carries over and contaminates new relationships. The identified patient carries the unacceptable impulses of other family members (Clarkin & Carpenter, 1995).

Experiential Systems. The *Symbolic-Experiential* model of Carl Whitaker and Virginia Satir focuses on the family's symbols. The approach is pragmatic and atheoretical. In Whitaker's view, theories are only for students who want to control their anxiety about managing the clinical situation. The emphasis is on the emotional experience created by therapy itself, not on intellectual understanding or insight.

Satir's goals for family therapy are to make three changes in the family system: to enable each member to state openly, in the presence of the others, exactly what he or she perceives; for each person to be respected for his or her unique contribution, rather than for interactions to be based on a power hierarchy; and for "differentness [to] be openly acknowledged and used for growth" (Satir, quoted in Guerin & Chabot, 1997, p. 205). Whitaker might seize upon an instance of the family's disturbance and try to exaggerate it to absurd proportions. For example, he once told a young man who had made a suicidal gesture to make sure he did it right next time and to go one better by taking his therapist with him! (Guerin & Chabot, 1997; Miklowitz, 1994).

Structural Family Therapy. The *Structural Family Therapy* model of Salvador Minuchin is a theory of family process that views pathology as resulting from one's being either enmeshed in or disengaged from one's family. The theory is that pathology in a family member occurs because of dysfunctional hierarchical family structures. For example, parents do not have appropriate power over their children or a pathological relationship has developed between one parent and a child. Hence, the structural model describes a theory of family process in which being either enmeshed or disengaged can result in pathology. The therapist tries either to loosen or to establish boundaries, often doing so directively within sessions. This might involve literally moving people together or away from each other.

Parent-child relationships (and triangles) are important; the therapist looks for alignments and splits (Clarkin & Carpenter, 1995; Miklowitz, 1994).

Criticisms

As with any other approach to psychotherapy, family therapy approaches rest on certain assumptions that may be questioned. For example, Foley (1989) argued for treating families rather than individuals, citing the rationale that family therapy is more logical, faster, more satisfactory, and more economical that concentrating on an individual who is supposed to be in need of treatment. However, he did not adduce empirical data to support that statement. In the next sentence, Foley wrote that the task is to change relationships in the troubled family (1989, p. 455). But who said anything about a troubled family? It is an assumption of family therapy that any individual who appears to need treatment has a troubled family, but this hypothesis is rarely tested empirically. Some family therapists also assume, for example, that the way the members of the family seat themselves in the first session reveals important alliances and splits, but the reliability and validity of such clinical observations as an assessment method are unclear and, likely enough, unknown.

There are considerable difficulties in conducting controlled research on family therapy interventions. These include selecting appropriate measures and outcome criteria, and deciding upon the units of analysis. If the entire family is viewed as the participant in the experiment, what are the dependent variables, and what statistics should be used? If individuals within families are the participants, how can they be randomly assigned to conditions without their families accompanying them? These difficulties are not insuperable, and controlled research on systems of family therapy have been reported. The recent book by Liddle and colleagues (Liddle et al., 2002) promises to help focus future research in this area.

Group Therapy

Practically all forms of psychotherapy evolved in one way or another from Freudian psychoanalysis. A central assumption of psychoanalytic therapy is that hidden or secret material must be carefully brought, against considerable resistance and with many emotional ups and downs, to the patient's consciousness. This assumption seems to require logically that treatment take place in private, confidential conversations between two people, the therapist and the patient (Walker, 1959). But when prominent psychotherapists began to mount serious challenges to Freud's theories, his techniques and procedures were also opened up for criticism. If a critic started questioning the need for dredging up patients' unconscious sexual fantasies, for example, he or she might also question the need for a veil of utter secrecy to surround the treatment. Why not have other people present during therapy sessions? Why not go further and treat more than one patient at once, in the same interview?

Another stimulus for the introduction of group therapy was logistical. Because traditional psychoanalytic treatment usually meant several meetings per week over a span of a few years, the average psychoanalyst—even an especially busy and hardworking one—could treat only a few people in any given year, and not very many over a whole professional lifetime. For clinics or hospitals with a large clientele, traditional psychoanalysis was therefore entirely impractical as a standard form of service delivery. One solution to this logistical problem of providing therapy for larger numbers of people was to treat several of them at once. Group therapy has been described as a product of modern marketing techniques, a method of making psychotherapy available to the small consumer at a price he or she can afford (Ehrenwald, 1976).

Group therapists observed that their technique was not only more economical, but also more effective than traditional therapy. For example, after the Second World War psychotherapists were faced by significant numbers of returning veterans with war-related neuroses. Group treatment was first used simply as a way of providing treatment to as many people as possible, but several psychotherapists reported that the results were superior to those of individual therapy—progress was made more quickly with group therapy, and the outcomes were less superficial (Foulkes & Anthony, 1965).

Some of the advantages of group therapy have been cited as deriving from a sense of belonging and of being accepted by a peer group, especially in the case of the "lonely, isolated city dweller in the depersonalized and alienated urban society of our age" (Ehrenwald, 1976, p. 515). Other beneficial aspects reflect:

> the dramatic shift of authority, of the role of leadership, from parental figures to peer groups . . . the role once delegated to the parish priest, the religious counselor, or the supposedly all-knowing and infallible psychoanalyst is being transferred to the Group . . . guided or even left to its own resources by a self-effacing "facilitator" or group leader. (Ehrenwald, 1976, p. 515)

Generally, group therapists draw from the theories of their preferred individual therapy techniques. Freudian group therapists, for example, see catharsis, transference, and insight phenomena developing in group treatment and typically assume that patients project upon other group members the attributes of the family members with whom they grew up from infancy. Adlerians believe that disclosures made to a group bring about an especially powerful catharsis because of the healing processes in the development of community feeling. Also, participating in a group as an equal with others who also face and overcome problems counteracts inferiority feelings. But practitioners of Jung's analytical psychology see only a limited role for group therapy, because it focuses only on people's social development; Jung was concerned about the group's tendency to keep its members dependent, insecure, and infantile (Walker, 1957).

Group Analytic Psychotherapy

The technique of group analytic psychotherapy consists of having regular meetings of a particular group of patients under the guidance of the same psychotherapist. At first, patients talk to each other about their specific symptoms, then they move on to discussions of their personal difficulties and emotional conflicts. In the process, group members develop and express emotional feelings about the other participants, and they learn to understand and accept the feelings expressed by the others. The principal technique is interpretation, in which patients help others relate their symptoms to the emotions they seem to be experiencing and expressing (Walker, 1957).

Behavior Therapy in Groups

Some of the treatment targets that have been most closely associated with behavior therapy, such as parent training, assertiveness training, treatment of obesity, and social skills training, have been addressed via group therapy both for convenience and for theoretical reasons, especially the social learning theory concepts of modeling and observational learning. Behavior therapists have been divided on how to view behavioral group therapy. Some view it as behavior therapy *in* the group, a matter of delivering the same intervention to multiple participants for convenience. Others view it as behavior therapy that operates *through* the group process (Franks & Wilson, 1973). Combining these views entails seeing the group as "both the context and the vehicle of individual behavior change" (Rose, 1977, p. x).

Research on behavioral group therapy is not reviewed here as a separate topic, because many of the behavior therapy interventions to be cited in Chapter 13, particularly those applied to anxiety disorders, were implemented and studied in group contexts. Behavioral researchers have tended not to draw a sharp distinction between individual therapy and interventions delivered to groups, chiefly because behavioral group therapy often involves homogenous groups of clients, such as people with panic disorder or assertiveness difficulties, who are treated together for convenience or as part of a research protocol.

Humanistic Group Therapy

Humanistic group therapy, including existential, Gestalt, and client-centered group therapies, is aimed at helping clients make positive behavioral and attitudinal changes. The emphasis is on free will, participants' ability to make growth-producing choices, and self-awareness. Self-actualization is viewed as the essential process:

> To operate effectively in a group, the therapist must trust the abilities of the group members to help one another grow in positive directions. Unless this is the case, the therapist may try to exert more control over the group process than is helpful. (Page et al., 2002, p. 340)

Traditionally, group members determine the direction of the group for themselves. This format is known as *unstructured group therapy.*

Research on Humanistic Group Therapy. Studies with psychiatric inpatients (Charles B. Truax) and counseling center outpatients (several European studies) have shown greater overall self-exploration and improvement with high levels of the Rogerian therapist-offered conditions. Representative findings have indicated 85 to 89 percent post-therapy improvement, maintained at a six-month follow-up assessment, and 72 percent of participants improved at a twelve-month follow-up assessment. Positive outcomes were related to participants' perception of therapists' attitudes, and to process measures such as "expression of feelings" and "confidence in the group." Concerning congruence, a 1968 study showed that client-centered group therapy significantly narrowed the gap between client ratings of self and ideal self. Less research was conducted in the United States in the 1970s as Rogers left academia and focused on encounter groups. However, many studies were reported in Europe in the 1980s (Page, Weiss, & Lietaer, 2002).

There has been relatively little research on Gestalt group therapy. One problem is that there are two models: Perls' traditional, individually oriented "hot seat" workshop approach and a more interactional group process approach. Potential researchers have to determine which model would be the more appropriate target (Page et al., 2002). In any event, Gestalt therapists have typically shown less interest in scientific validation of their treatments than others working in the humanistic tradition.

Irvin D. Yalom is the central figure in existential group therapy. In his studies, a "meaning-related curative factor" was cited as most important by most participants. In the medical arena, one study showed that survival rates for female breast cancer patients were significantly increased by existential group therapy (Spiegel, Bloom, Kraemer, & Gottheil, 1989), and this has been cited as an important empirical validation of the approach (Page et al., 2002). However, critics would note that in that study participants in the experimental condition received "weekly supportive group therapy with self-hypnosis for pain" (Spiegel et al., 1989, p. 888). Clearly, group therapy was confounded with self-hypnosis in this study.

Common Features of Group Therapy

Some characteristics of group therapy seem to operate across theoretical boundaries. These common elements include having a limited number of participants; having designated leaders or therapists, whose procedures are based on a theoretical rationale for group treatment; and having the aim of providing a therapeutic experience, with the expectation of beneficial emotional, cognitive, and behavioral change (Shaffer & Galinsky, 1974).

Ballinger and Yalom (1995) identified ten therapeutic factors that operate in group therapy in general, as follows: instilling hope, universality (showing that the individual is not alone and that problems are universal), imparting information, altruism (group members helping one another), corrective recapitulation of problems from the person's original family, developing social skills, imitating others, emotional processing and cognitive reflection, interpersonal learning, and group cohesiveness.

BOX **12.2**

Psychodrama

Jacob L. Moreno (1898–1974) developed psychodrama in the 1920s in Vienna and New York. The technique involves the use of a small theater with a balcony overhead. The psychotherapist acts as producer and the patient as the central character, who enacts poignant past encounters with parents, emotionally significant interactions with friends or others, or even dialogues with elements of a delusional system. Assistants of the psychotherapist play the supporting roles, and the other patients form an active audience, often participating in the action (Ehrenwald, 1976; Rosenbaum & Patterson, 1995).

Moreno viewed psychodrama as "the *depth* therapy of the group. It starts where group psychotherapy ends, and extends it in order to make it more effective" (Moreno, 1956, quoted by Ehrenwald, 1976, p. 532).

Moreno described the treatment of Karl, an American of German ancestry, in New York in 1939. Karl had the paranoid delusion that he was Adolf Hitler. Karl's wife had told Moreno that she had returned home after a brief vacation to find the walls of their apartment covered with pictures of Hitler. Over the next few days Karl had spent hours in front of a mirror, practicing Hitler's speech and mannerisms. He neglected his business and took a job as doorman at a movie theater, apparently because he liked wearing the uniform.

In the first psychodrama session, Moreno's assistants took the parts of Goering and Goebbels, prominent members of Hitler's government. Karl smiled and greeted them, acting as if he knew them well. He stepped up to a microphone and addressed the audience over a public address system. He told them he was making the following announcement to the people of Germany: He was the real Adolf Hitler. The other one was an impostor. The German people should overthrow the impostor and install him, the real Hitler! The audience applauded wildly.

In later sessions Karl enacted events connected with his preoccupation with conquering the world. In one scene, the patient asked the Gestapo leaders from the audience—Goering, Goebbels, Ribbentrop, Hess, and others—to commit suicide with him. He ordered that music from Wagner's *Gotterdammerung* be played in the background. He pretended to shoot himself in front of the audience. During one session, he earnestly asked Moreno, "What's the matter with me? Will this torture never end? Is it real or is it a dream?"

Three months after the beginning of treatment, "Goering" announced to Moreno that "Hitler" wanted a haircut. A real barber was called in and actually cut Karl's hair on the stage. The barber was about to leave when Karl called him back and asked him to shave off the Hitler-style moustache he had worn for months. The barber shaved it off. There was a dramatic silence, then Karl jumped up, felt his face, and shouted, "It's gone! It's over! Why did I do it?"

In the following sessions, his manner and speech gradually changed. He asked to be called Karl, not Adolf. He kissed his wife on the stage and smiled at her. Karl made a "good social recovery" (Ehrenwald, 1976, pp. 532–538).

BOX **12.3**

Focus on Ethics: Multiple Role Relationships

A multiple relationship occurs whenever a psychologist who has a professional relationship with a client also interacts with the client in other capacities—for example, as a business partner. Multiple relationships of this kind are hazardous because there is the risk that the additional relationship may cause harm to the client or may impair the professional relationship. Imagine the situation in which a psychologist invests money in a client's business enterprise while they continue their therapeutic relationship. Several untoward consequences could follow if anything went wrong with the additional relationship. For example, if the psychologist were to fail to meet obligations for regular investments in the client's business, the client's ability to engage fully in psychotherapy could be compromised. If the psychologist were to feel resentful at the client's lack of business acumen, then the psychologist's professional objectivity could be substantially diminished. If the psychologist were to put pressure on the client to spend more time on the mutual business venture so as to increase profits, this could constitute exploitation of the client and thus cause harm (Peterson, 1996).

Multiple relationships "are by far the most frequent cause for disciplinary action, legal action, or both against psychologists; most of these actions involve dual relationships of a sexual nature" (Peterson, 1996, p. 82). Legal and psychological authorities agree unequivocally that psychotherapist-client sexual contact harms the client (Pope & Vasquez, 1998). This is not based on conjecture, but upon the results of a number of studies, many of which compared clients who had been sexually involved with a psychotherapist with matched groups of clients who had not been victimized in this way. Other studies compared clients who had been sexually exploited by psychotherapists with those exploited by nonpsychiatric physicians. The measures used in such studies included clinical interviews, behavioral observation, and standardized psychological assessment instruments. The results of these studies have been summarized as follows:

> The consequences for clients [include] ambivalence, guilt, emptiness and isolation, sexual confusion, impaired ability to trust, confused roles and boundaries, emotional lability, suppressed rage, increased suicidal risk, and . . . [problems] in the areas of concentration and memory and often involving flashbacks, intrusive thoughts, unbidden images, and nightmares. (Pope & Vasquez, 1998, p. 162)

In many jurisdictions, for a psychologist to have sexual contact with a client is not only unethical, it is also illegal. Multiple relationships were the basis for over 40 percent of ethics complaints made to the American Psychological Association (APA) between 1990 and 1993; in the cases that were adjudicated in 1994, sexual misconduct was the largest category of unethical conduct leading to loss of APA membership. Ninety percent of unethical incidents involving sexual misconduct were perpetrated by male psychologists (Peterson, 1996).

Psychologists who exploit their clients sexually do not always set out to do so. Sexual misconduct sometimes arises when a psychologist fails to deal appropriately with a sexual advance from a client. Several options are available when a psychologist recognizes that he or she may be becoming vulnerable to acting unethically in such a case. The psychologist is expected to maintain an objective, professional demeanor with the client at all times, making the client's feelings toward the therapist a therapeutic issue. The psychologist can seek appropriate opportunities to remind the client of the ethical codes governing the practice of psychology and of psychologists' obligations to avoid exploiting or harming their clients. The psychologist can consult a trusted senior colleague to discuss the matter confidentially and explore his or her own emotional reactions to the client, in addition to discussing appropriate professional responses (Nagy, 2000).

13 Cognitive-Behavioral Interventions

The integrative approach known today as *cognitive-behavior therapy* has two main branches. One of these draws directly from focused research on the treatment of specific areas of psychopathology and is aimed at eliminating particular psychological disorders such as panic disorder with agoraphobia, major depressive disorder, or bulimia nervosa. The other combines a variety of behavioral and cognitive techniques to form a holistic treatment method applicable to the broadest range of client problems and issues, from assertiveness deficits to borderline personality disorder, from poor study skills to substance dependence, and from severe family dysfunction to chronic schizophrenia. This broader form of cognitive-behavior therapy addresses both the issues associated with traditional counseling approaches and those that have been the target of the most intensive forms of psychotherapy.

As reviewed in Chapter 3, the history of cognitive-behavior therapy has been marked by several significant transitions. Before 1950, techniques based on conditioning principles were sometimes applied unsystematically to specific habit problems. In the late 1950s behavior therapy began to emerge as a set of empirically based treatment techniques that were subsequently validated in controlled experiments. In the 1970s behavioral clinicians began to go beyond the principles of conditioning and learning to inform their treatments and to draw from experimental work on expectancies and self-guiding covert speech. The new cognitive-behavioral orientation was also influenced by the cognitive restructuring therapies of Beck, Ellis, and others and by studies of clinical applications of self-control, self-management, and coping skills. Contemporary cognitive-behavioral psychologists are involved in health psychology and behavioral medicine in addition to traditional mental health work. And in inpatient and outpatient mental health settings cognitive-behavior therapists now treat the entire spectrum of disorders.

We begin our outline of cognitive-behavioral interventions by describing some of the experimentally based techniques that were devised by the early behavior therapists. This illustrates the empirical basis of cognitive-behavioral work and also delineates the essential interventions from which the current comprehensive approach developed (Thorpe & Olson, 1997).

Behavior Therapy Techniques

Consistent with the topics emphasized in the early works on behavior therapy (Eysenck & Rachman, 1965; Ullman & Krasner, 1975; Wolpe & Lazarus, 1966), our focus in this section is on anxiety-reduction techniques, operant learning techniques, applied behavior analysis, and social skills and problem-solving training.

Anxiety-Reduction Methods

Systematic Desensitization.   In Chapter 3 we described Joseph Wolpe's *systematic desensitization* (SD) as one of the first behavior therapy techniques. Drawn from experimental research on learning processes, it was applied to the treatment of situation-linked anxiety patterns, notably specific phobias. Using clinical series methodology, in which the same treatment procedures were offered sequentially to many clients, Wolpe (1958) reported highly favorable outcomes for systematic desensitization and related extinction-based methods with 210 clients with various disorders. Using more sophisticated experimentation, Lang and Lazovik (1963) showed that SD could also be implemented effectively in a laboratory setting with snake-fearful college volunteers. SD was more effective than no treatment, as gauged by several measures that included a fear-relevant behavioral avoidance test. A companion study (Lang, Lazovik, & Reynolds, 1965) demonstrated that SD was also more effective than a pseudotherapy comparison condition that controlled for nonspecific therapy events, such as expectation of gain and meeting with a therapist to work on problems.

In a methodologically sophisticated study, Paul (1966) provided convincing evidence of the effectiveness of SD for public speaking anxiety by comparing it with traditional psychotherapy methods as delivered by experienced clinicians. Before and after treatment participants made speeches before a panel of trained raters, who assessed performance decrements due to anxiety using a structured behavioral observation protocol. On a battery of measures, SD produced significantly more improvement than traditional psychotherapy and placebo and no-treatment control conditions. A follow-up study two years later confirmed that the effects of SD were lasting and that there had been no emergence of new symptoms (Paul, 1967).

One early study confirmed that the different procedural elements within SD were necessary to the effectiveness of the procedure (Davison, 1968), but other studies, including some with clinic clients rather than student volunteers, have contradicted this finding. Exposure to relevant, feared stimuli is vital, but the relaxation component appears to be unnecessary, and it is not essential for clients to terminate imagined scenes when anxiety arises (Gillan & Rachman, 1974; Marks, 1981a; McGlynn, 1973; Wilson, 1973). As a result, SD was gradually replaced by methods that encourage clients to confront anxiety-provoking stimuli directly, sometimes even at full intensity.

Graduated Real-Life Practice.   In graduated real-life practice, sometimes referred to as "graded practice" or "successive approximation," the client proceeds step by step along a hierarchy of progressively more challenging stimuli, facing actual situations without relaxation. As in SD, the client may withdraw from a situation to regroup at any point if anxiety arises. In an early report on two phobic clients, Meyer (1957) described the successful treatment of agoraphobic symptoms by this method. Like Wolpe, Meyer reasoned that the important principle was that of *stimulus generalization*—the client's anxiety response will extinguish if he or she confronts a stimulus that resembles the phobic stimulus but is far less intense, evoking minimal anxiety. Next, the client can learn to deal with a graded continuum of similar situations. One of Meyer's clients, a woman in her 40s, avoided crowds, travel, and confined areas. She had five sessions of graduated real-life practice, accompanied by the therapist. They took bus rides, entered crowded stores, traveled on the subway, and used elevators. She responded well to the procedure and had maintained her improvement when followed up four months later.

Imaginal Flooding and Exposure in Vivo.   SD and graduated real-life practice involve dealing with anxiety-evoking stimuli cautiously, one step at a time. Confrontive exposure, sometimes called flooding, involves dealing with imagined or real stimuli at full intensity. The first confrontive exposure technique of this kind was *implosive therapy* (Stampfl & Levis, 1967), using imagined stimuli. The theory was that extinction would be most effective when the client is exposed to the original conditioning situation that elicits the greatest fear. The technique involves confronting the client with relevant fantasy material for prolonged periods. Using an "avoidance serial cue hierarchy" derived from the client's current concerns and presented problems, the therapist describes feared scenes in such an involved and dramatic way as to arouse intense anxiety and continues to present the material, at great length if necessary, until the client's anxiety decreases.

The original implosive therapy of Stampfl and Levis included the use of psychodynamic theme material in an attempt to integrate traditional with learning-based therapies. Behavior therapists have abandoned the psychodynamic material and use the term *imaginal flooding* to describe techniques involving confrontive exposure in fantasy.

Confrontive exposure to feared stimuli in real life is known as *exposure in vivo* (Marks, 1981a), which has been extensively studied in application to agoraphobia, specific phobias, and obsessive-compulsive disorder. Exposure in vivo is viewed as an empirical clinical method that may involve extinction, habituation, or other forms of acclimatization to originally feared stimuli. Not convinced that conditioning explanations of phobias have been scientifically proven, Marks avoids conditioning terms, describing the feared situation as an *evoking stimulus* (ES) and the behavior that it calls forth, such as phobic avoidance or compulsive rituals, as the *evoked response* (ER). The technique involves identifying the ES and presenting it until the ER is reduced.

Exposure to the ES will be therapeutic only if prolonged sufficiently. The more protective exposure methods of SD and graduated real-life practice lead to improvement even with brief stimulus presentations, because they evoke only weak anxiety. The confrontive exposure methods of imaginal flooding and exposure in vivo are also effective, despite their use of stimuli that evoke intense anxiety, because exposure is prolonged (Reiss, 1980).

Operant Learning Techniques

Positive and Negative Reinforcement.   Reinforcement refers to the procedures and processes involved when a specific behavior is strengthened or maintained by an operant learning contingency. For example, positive reinforcement occurs when a laboratory pigeon's rate of pecking at an illuminated disk increases when grain is delivered contingent upon the occurrence of that behavior. Positive reinforcers are usually items that may be delivered repeatedly during a learning process, and research has shown that small, immediate reinforcements are more effective in promoting learning than large, delayed ones (Logue, 1995).

Laboratory experimenters using positive reinforcement can accelerate the acquisition of a new behavior using the method of *shaping* or *successive approximation.* The learning task is divided into a series of small steps. When the first step has been learned successfully, a more difficult task is presented. For example, a first step in a shaping program could be to present food whenever the laboratory pigeon enters the half of the chamber nearer to the disk. Next, food could be delivered only when the pigeon points its beak toward the disk. Eventually, the reinforcement is delivered only when the pigeon pecks at the disk.

Behavior may be reinforced or maintained in other ways than by presenting desirable stimuli, such as food or money. Removing an undesirable stimulus may also reinforce behavior. For example, taking aspirin to relieve a headache will be reinforced if the headache goes away. Reinforcing behavior by the contingent removal of aversive stimuli is known as *negative reinforcement.*

Punishment.   When behavior *decreases* as a result of a behavioral contingency, it is possible that some form of punishment is operating. (Other possibilities are that the behavior is under extinction after positive reinforcement, or a contingency that positively reinforces low response rates is in effect.) The clearest example of punishment is found when response rates decrease after a stimulus has been presented contingent upon the response. Another term for this is *response-contingent aversive stimulation* (RCAS). If a child touches a hot stove and burns a finger, and if the child stops touching the stove as a result, then the contingency operating is RCAS, or punishment.

Another form of punishment occurs when the effect of a response is to remove a stimulus, and that is followed by reduced response rates. This is known as *response cost.* If drivers reduce their rate of committing minor traffic violations when they have to pay monetary fines for doing so, response cost is the contingency operating.

Figure 13.1 provides the definitions of the two types of reinforcement and the two types of punishment in terms of the effect on behavior of the contingent presentation or withdrawal of stimuli.

		Effect on Behavior	
		Behavior Increases	**Behavior Decreases**
Scheduled Consequence of the Response	**Stimulus Is Presented**	Positive Reinforcement	Punishment (Response-Contingent Aversive Stimulation)
	Stimulus Is Withdrawn	Negative Reinforcement	Punishment (Response Cost)

FIGURE 13.1   Four Types of Response Consequence in Operant Learning

Extinction. *Extinction* refers to the procedure of disconnecting a reinforcement contingency, and to the effects of this on behavior. To take an example of extinction following positive reinforcement, imagine that the pigeon's disk-pecking has been reinforced with food for some time, but the experimenter now switches off the food-delivery mechanism. Pecking at the disk no longer has any effect. The pigeon ultimately produces fewer and fewer pecks, until, eventually, no further responses are made. Extinction of an operant response has some elements in common with extinction of a classically conditioned response.

Schedules of Reinforcement. In the example of the laboratory pigeon, *continuous reinforcement* occurs when every response is reinforced. After continuous reinforcement, the effects of extinction are usually quite rapid. Imagine encouraging a mute patient to speak by using continuous social reinforcement—every time the patient speaks appropriately, the therapist smiles and nods in an encouraging fashion. Now imagine that, because this therapy was so successful, the patient leaves the institution and begins to deal with people in the community for the first time. What would happen if the patient's first attempts at conversation were not immediately followed by enthusiastic smiles and nods? Right away, there would be an extinction trial for which the patient had not been prepared. For this reason, it is often unrealistic to rely entirely on continuous reinforcement in therapy programs.

In real life, reinforcement is usually intermittent. Behavior does not always produce certain consequences consistently. Pigeons do not always obtain food every time they peck at an object, and drivers are not fined every time they double-park or speed. Starting with the research of Ferster and Skinner (1957), operant learning researchers made extensive studies of the effects on behavior of a variety of alternatives to continuous reinforcement known as *schedules of reinforcement.* For example, in a *variable ratio* (VR) schedule only a fraction of the responses are reinforced, in an unpredictable pattern. The number of responses required to produce the reinforcer varies randomly around a given average value. In a VR 3 schedule, roughly every third response produces reinforcement (sometimes the second response, sometimes the fourth, and so on). This arrangement is more likely than continuous reinforcement to keep the learner responding, and this is true even after extinction has been put into effect and no responses are reinforced. VR schedules apply to gambling. The payoff for gambling is well known to be intermittent and unpredictable, thus reinforcing a stable rate of responding.

When behavior has been maintained by an intermittent schedule such as VR, it can be more difficult for the behaving organism to detect when extinction is in effect (D'Amato, 1970). After all, in VR most responses go unreinforced anyway, even before extinction sets in. One practical consequence of schedules of intermittent reinforcement is that the effects of extinction are delayed, and more responses are made under extinction (Angermeier, 1994).

Rule-Governed Behavior. An obvious question about operant learning in people is, "Why is it necessary to provide elaborate behavioral contingencies and reinforcement schedules to encourage certain response sequences, when all we have to do is to ask the person to do it?" Skinner (1953, 1966) argued that our behavior is ultimately controlled by the actual contingencies operating, not by words. An advantage of operant learning methodology is that it can deal not only with the behavior of verbal individuals but also with that of animals, preverbal children, and people with communication difficulties.

Operant learning theorists recognize the importance of *rule-governed behavior* when behavior is controlled by stimuli that specify the contingency operating (Pierce & Epling, 1995). Examples of such contingency-specifying stimuli are rules, instructions, advice, and laws, and they can be seen as *discriminative stimuli* that set the occasion for adaptive behavior. Theorists contrast rule-governed behavior with *contingency-shaped behavior,* as in the case of the laboratory pigeon, or the patient in a positive reinforcement program to encourage appropriate speech. One of the differences between the two types of behavior is that rules affect how the behavior is performed, whereas reinforcement contingencies influence response rates and the likelihood of the behavior being enacted (Pierce & Epling, 1995). Ultimately, rule-governed behavior increases or decreases depending on the actual reinforcement contingencies operating (Thorpe & Olson, 1997).

Applied Behavior Analysis

Behavior therapists assume that operant learning principles are at work not just in specialized laboratories, but also in the natural environment in which people go about their daily activities. Similarly, the same learning processes can be seen in normal and abnormal behavior. Understanding abnormal behavior in terms of operant learning principles can lead directly to treatments based on the same principles. This enterprise is known as *applied behavior analysis.*

Applying operant learning to problem behavior involves identifying the behavioral contingencies operating. Conceptually, this is as simple as ABC: Identifying the contingency means identifying A, the *antecedent events;* B, the *behavior;* and C, the *consequences,* or the reinforcer (Kazdin, 1994a). In many cases it turns out that an unwanted behavior is being maintained by positive reinforcement. Take the example of a child who repeatedly acts disruptively in class and whose teacher always responds by telling him or her to behave more appropriately. The antecedent events include being in the classroom with this particular teacher. The behavior is the disruptive activity. The consequences appear to be the teacher's stern admonitions to the child to stop acting badly. This formulation immediately raises the issue that the teacher's attention may be reinforcing the problem behavior. The behavior therapist might advise the teacher to ignore the child the next few times it happens, so as to investigate the possibility that unintentional social reinforcement had been maintaining the problem behavior.

Bijou (1963) has argued that ineffective use of reinforcement by parents may delay behavioral development in children. Not reinforcing behavior often enough or soon enough produces too "thin" a schedule of intermittent reinforcement and leads to extinction. Theories like this have led to numerous applications of reinforcement in successful treatment programs.

Applications with Specific Behavior Problems in Individuals.   Azrin and Foxx (1971) devised a rapid method for toilet training profoundly retarded people in institutions. The method combines shaping, positive reinforcement, and some punishment procedures. Nine patients were successfully trained in approximately four days. Findings like this indicate the tremendous potential for reinforcement methods in treating severely disturbed individuals.

Baltes and Lascomb (1975) consulted with nursing home staff who were concerned about the behavior of one of the residents, an elderly woman who had started screaming loudly at intervals throughout the day. The therapists noticed that the resident's screams were always followed by the swift appearance of nurses and others to see what was wrong. The staff members would urge the resident to stop screaming and eventually go away. The therapists hypothesized that the attention of the staff might be reinforcing the resident's screaming. They began to spend time with the resident when she was not screaming, to make sure that she could gain attention appropriately without having to resort to inappropriate behavior. This was somewhat helpful, but the resident would occasionally scream even when the therapists were already present. The treatment plan the therapists adopted was as follows. When they were with the resident, they would pay attention to her, give her candy, and play her favorite music on a tape recorder. Whenever she screamed, they would switch off the music, remove the candy, become silent, and look away from her. When she stopped screaming, the therapists would pay attention again. This strategy proved quite successful. By systematically alternating periods of treatment and no treatment, the authors of the report were able to show that placing the screaming under conditions of extinction was indeed responsible for the improvement. This example illustrates how positive reinforcement can unintentionally sustain unhelpful behavior in a client. It also shows how reversing the contingency, placing the unwanted behavior under conditions of extinction, can prove valuable as therapy.

Ullmann and Krasner (1975) suggested an explanation of somatoform disorders—complaints of physical problems when medical investigations detect no abnormality—in operant learning terms. First, the person observes somebody else gaining some reward from having a medical symptom. Second, the person's own complaint of symptoms is reinforced. (People with somatoform disorders are not deliberately faking their symptoms. Operant learning mechanisms can influence behavior in this way without the person understanding clearly what is happening.) Kallman, Hersen, and O'Toole (1975) described a man in his early 40s with a fifteen-year history of hospital admissions for back pain. He no longer worked and was officially viewed as disabled. Medical investigations had never adequately explained his symptoms. The therapists noticed that the client received a considerable amount of help from his family. Whenever his problems flared up again, family members would take over the chores and bring him breakfast in bed. Because of their suspicion that reinforcement may have been playing a part in the problem, the therapists tried social reinforcement as therapy. Three times a day, a research assistant would spend 10 minutes talking to him. At the end of a visit, she would ask him to walk if he could. In some phases of the therapy, she praised him specifically for his success at standing; in other phases, she praised him only for walking. Whichever response was selected for reinforcement increased, confirming the specificity of treatment (rather than a general increase in the client's morale). The patient progressed well at home for a month before he was brought back to the hospital with the original problems at full force. It turned out that the family had once again reinforced the problem behavior by attention. The therapists reiterated behavioral principles to the family members and used videotapes of the family's communication to make the point. After that, the patient's improvement was maintained at home for at least three months.

An important focus for the treatment of inpatients with chronic schizophrenia has been speech problems, including mutism (the patient does not speak at all), delusional speech, and disorganized speech. Isaacs, Thomas, and Goldiamond (1960) used positive reinforcement to reinstate speech in two patients who had been mute for fourteen and nineteen years. Taking advantage of a patient's sudden interest in a psychologist's chewing gum, the therapists used the gum as a reinforcer. After careful shaping of speech sounds by reinforcement, the patient was able to answer direct questions in group therapy sessions, but only when the original therapist asked the questions! Ayllon and Haughton (1964) reinforced appropriate speech in three delusional patients by listening, showing interest, and giving candy. Reinforcement was made contingent upon either "neutral" or "psychotic" talk, depending on the phase of the study. As expected, reinforcement increased the rate of whichever behavior was the target at the time. In these and similar studies, the techniques used produced clear control of the behavior, but generalization across situations and over time was very poor.

An early study by Ayllon (1963) demonstrated the successful treatment of three problems in a 47-year-old woman who had been hospitalized for nine years for chronic schizophrenia. She stole food, she hoarded towels in her room, and she wore excessive amounts of clothing at one time (such as six dresses, two dozen pairs of stockings, and several sweaters). To encourage her to stop stealing food from other patients in the dining room, the ward staff removed the patient from the dining room whenever she attempted to steal. Removing her from the dining room meant that she had to forgo her meal. This approach eliminated the stealing entirely within two weeks and allowed the staff to maintain the patient on a needed, medically prescribed diet.

The patient also hoarded towels, keeping from 19 to 29 towels in her room instead of the usual one or two. Nurses had to remove towels from the room periodically to maintain the ward supply. Therapy followed the principle of *stimulus satiation,* a concept drawn from laboratory studies indicating that responses typically weaken when the reinforcing stimulus is made too abundant. Accordingly, instead of removing towels from the patient's room, staff members started giving her more and more towels. When the number of towels in the room exceeded 600, the patient began to carry towels out herself. She gave every sign of being tired of them, because she said, "Take them towels away. I can't sit here all night folding towels" (Ayllon, 1963, p. 57). Eventually, the patient was keeping just one or two towels in her room.

The final problem, wearing enormous amounts of clothing, was treated by making the patient's access to the dining room contingent upon her fully clothed weight falling below a certain limit. At first, she was allowed to wear over 20 pounds of clothes, but this allowance was gradually reduced. The patient gradually discarded more and more clothes until she was typically wearing about 3 pounds of clothes.

The Token Economy.   Positive reinforcement methods have been used effectively to encourage long-term psychiatric hospital residents to take an interest in social and other activities that could be pursued outside the hospital after discharge. In the *token economy* a group of patients, often an entire hospital ward, participate in a remotivational program in which specific, designated behaviors are reinforced immediately. The reinforcers used are tokens, standard units such as poker chips, that may be dispensed readily by ward staff. These tokens are later exchanged for more tangible reinforcers, such as candy, small gifts, or additional recreational privileges.

Token reinforcement is possible because of the phenomenon of *conditioned reinforcement* (also known as "secondary reinforcement"). Conditioned reinforcers such as tokens have acquired their power to reinforce behavior. Reinforcers like food, water, and sexual activity are assumed to be primary reinforcers, because people do not have to go through special educational procedures in order for these stimuli to reinforce behavior. By contrast, other stimuli that can reinforce behavior take on their power to do so through learning—such as a friend's smile, a satisfactory grade in a college course, and money. One consistent research finding in laboratory and clinical settings has been that it does not matter how soon after the response the primary reinforcer is presented, provided that the conditioned reinforcer is presented immediately after the response (Kelleher, 1966; Osborne & Adams, 1970).

Initial studies of inpatients with chronic disorders by Ayllon and Azrin (1965, 1968) demonstrated that token reinforcement could be effective in increasing "healthy" behaviors, such as taking care of personal hygiene (Davison, 1969). A combination of money and off-ward pass privileges successfully reinforced appropriate social and self-directed behavior in inpatients who also participated in patient-led problem-solving groups (Fairweather, 1964). The program lasted about six months, and a follow-up assessment was conducted six months after the termination of the project. Compared with traditional treatment, the problem-solving/reinforcement intervention was associated with more social interaction, less pathological behavior, reduced use of medication, shorter hospital stays, and longer intervals before rehospitalization.

In the treatment of institutionalized people with chronic disorders such as schizophrenia, the token economy and related positive reinforcement methods are helpful in increasing specific behaviors like self-care skills and social participation. However, cognitive and affective symptoms such as delusional speech and emotional incongruities typically remain unchanged (Fraser, McLeod, Begg, Hawthorne, & Davis, 1976; Mumford, Patch, Andrews, & Wyner, 1975).

In a landmark study, Paul and Lentz (1977) sought to improve general psychosocial treatment practices for chronic psychiatric inpatients. Patients assigned to token economy and milieu therapy programs were compared with a matched group of patients in a traditional hospital ward program. Eighty-four inpatients were studied for four and a half years, and there was a follow-up assessment one and a half years later. As patients were discharged from the hospital after treatment, similar patients from other units took their places. During the stage of active treatment, 90 percent of the token economy patients and 50 percent of the milieu patients improved. At a follow-up assessment eighteen months later, Paul and Lentz (1977) observed that over 90 percent of the token economy patients were still living in the community. For the milieu therapy and standard treatment groups, the figures were over 70 percent and under 50 percent, respectively (Hartmann & Barrios, 1980).

Despite the striking results of these major studies, mental health professionals have largely ignored them (Bellack & Mueser, 1994). For various reasons, the notably less effective traditional hospital programs continue to be the norm in most state hospitals (Corrigan & Liberman, 1994; Wilson, 1982; Yoman, 1996).

Social Skills and Problem-Solving Training

Inpatients with chronic disorders often show marked deficits in interpersonal skill, social judgment, and conflict-resolution ability, abilities that are necessary for successful functioning in the community. Since the 1970s behavior therapists have focused on teaching social and problem-solving skills to people with schizophrenia seeking to reenter the community (Curran, Monti, & Corriveau, 1982).

Social Skills Training Techniques.   Deficits in *social competence* are central to many forms of psychopathology (Trower, 1995; Zigler & Phillips, 1960), and from its beginnings behavior therapy has employed social skills training techniques in the treatment of a variety of disorders, from social phobia to schizophrenia. The influential book *Behavior Therapy Techniques* by Wolpe and Lazarus (1966), which explained the principles of assertiveness training and related social skills training concepts, provided an initial impetus for this work. Today, *social skills training* (SST) describes a particular group of techniques, including instruction, modeling, behavior rehearsal, praise, prompts, coaching, feedback, reinforcement, and homework assignments (Curran et al., 1982; Trower, 1995). SST is suitable for some chronic inpatients, but it is more appropriate in general for outpatients or for hospitalized patients who may expect realistically to be discharged to the community. Even in those with the most promising prognoses, a typical course of treatment may last over six months.

Specific aspects of social behavior are targeted, such as starting a conversation, paying a compliment, criticizing someone's behavior, expressing feelings, and listening attentively. The chief component of SST is the combination of modeling with behavior rehearsal (role-playing), techniques aimed at redressing hypothesized skills deficits (Bellack & Morrison, 1982). Clients proceed through a hierarchy of training exercises that include instructions, role-playing, feedback and praise for progress, modeling, and real-life practice. The related technique of *rehearsal desensitization* is useful when social anxiety is also present (Piaget & Lazarus, 1969). This procedure combines skills training with anxiety reduction by incorporating into the role-playing procedure some systematic desensitization elements. Therapist and client proceed carefully through a hierarchy of role-play items, carefully graded for the degree of anxiety elicited.

Goldsmith and McFall (1975) extended laboratory work on assertiveness training to the treatment of psychiatric inpatients. Treatment was structured around a 20-item questionnaire that had been validated with 74 outpatients. The situations presented included dating, making friends, interviewing for jobs, and dealing with "more intelligent and attractive" people. Target behaviors included being assertive, knowing when to begin and end a conversation, deciding how self-disclosing to be, and handling silences. In a treatment study, 36 inpatients were randomly distributed among three experimental treatment groups: (1) interpersonal skills training, (2) a pseudo-therapy control, and (3) assessment only (patients in this group were advised that the practice involved in repeated assessments could be helpful). The skills training patients had three one-hour training sessions with modeling, behavior rehearsal, coaching, and feedback. The pseudo-therapy patients explored their feelings instead. The outcome clearly favored the skills training condition, as measured by patients' self-report, ratings of audiotaped role-plays, and a simulated real-life test.

Goldstein, Sprafkin, and Gershaw (1976) described a *structured learning therapy* that includes not only modeling, role-playing, and social reinforcement elements, but also *transfer training* aimed at promoting generalization of the effects of treatment to the patients' lives in the community after leaving the hospital. The results of preliminary studies were encouraging.

Problem-Solving Therapy.   Citing evidence that hospitalized psychiatric patients have problems with "interpersonal problem-solving cognition," Siegel and Spivack (1976) described a *problem-solving therapy* program for chronic patients. Their program involves a series of training exercises dealing with problem identification, goal definition, solution evaluation, evaluation of alternatives, and selection of the best solution (Kendall, 1987). Patients view a series of color slides depicting people in various situations and answer questions about the slides to demonstrate that they have attended appropriately. In another element of the program therapists show patients a color slide of a group of people, then present a different slide including one person from the first slide among a group of different people. The patient is asked to identify the person common to both slides. Other program elements include learning to assess the emotions displayed by people in magazine pictures and learning to ask intelligent questions in a guessing game. Pilot work indicated that the exercises were relevant, held the patients' interest, and were pitched at an appropriate level of difficulty. A study of seven chronic patients in a post-discharge aftercare program showed that an average of fourteen sessions were needed to complete the training. The guessing game seemed particularly helpful as an antidote to thought disorder. A second pilot study produced some evidence that patients' ability to think of suitable solutions to imagined real-life problems improved. Further research has confirmed the value of problem-solving training for chronic patients in aftercare and community settings in the United States and Australia (Bellack & Mueser, 1994; Hansen, St. Lawrence, & Christoff, 1985; Hayes, Halford, & Varghese, 1995; Payne & Halford, 1990).

Contemporary social skills and problem-solving programs begin with an assessment of the demands of the client's setting, then equip him or her with the skills necessary to function effectively in that setting (Trower, 1995, p. 73). This is especially important when the inpatient with schizophrenia is discharged to a family setting with high rates of *expressed emotion,* or criticism, hostility, and emotional overinvolvement (McNally, 1994).

Cognitive Modification Procedures

The holistic therapeutic approach known as *cognitive-behavior therapy,* reviewed in the final section of this chapter, draws from behavioral and cognitive theoretical models (reviewed in Chapter 3) and applies behavior therapy techniques and cognitive modification procedures in the treatment of psychological disorders. In this section we describe the best-known cognitive modification procedures.

Various terms are in common use to label these procedures. *Cognitive therapy* is associated specifically with the approach of Aaron T. Beck (Beck, 1976, 1995; Beck, Rush, Shaw, & Emery, 1979; Beck & Weishaar, 1995), originally focused on depression but now extended to a broad range of applications, including anxiety disorders, eating disorders, marital problems, personality disorders, and even the acute and chronic symptoms of schizophrenia. *Cognitive restructuring* has been used chiefly by Arnold Lazarus (1995) to describe one of the chief components of his multimodal therapy. *Cognitive-behavior modification* was used by Donald Meichenbaum (1977, 1995) to describe the pioneering interventions that were based on his original experimental studies. We use *cognitive modification procedures* here as a generic term for these and similar forms of therapeutic intervention.

Cognitive-Behavior Modification

Self-Instructional Training.   Meichenbaum's techniques were inspired by some unexpected findings from two of his early research studies. One of these involved teaching inpatients with schizophrenia to talk appropriately in one-on-one conversations. By contrast with some of the early behavior therapy techniques, this intervention produced enduring results that generalized to settings beyond the specific locations in which treatment was delivered. Meichenbaum was struck by the method some of the patients used to help themselves produce the appropriate behavior. They repeated to themselves the instructions that had been given them by the experimenter (e.g., "give healthy talk," "be relevant"). The patients were using helpful *self-instructions* effectively to guide their behavior appropriately (Meichenbaum, 1977). Encouraged by these findings, Meichenbaum began employing a deliberate strategy of teaching patients to use self-guiding speech for therapeutic purposes. He developed and tested this technique of *self-instructional training* and applied it to the treatment of impulsive children and other clinical groups (Meichenbaum & Goodman, 1971).

Another important influence on Meichenbaum's cognitive-behavior modification arose from the results of a study he and his colleagues designed to extend Paul's (1966) research on treatments for speech anxiety. As we noted in Chapter 3, Paul had compared systematic desensitization (SD) with traditional psychodynamic insight therapy. Although he had described SD with enough precision to allow other researchers to replicate the experimental procedures, the insight therapy used in the study had been outlined quite vaguely; the therapists simply indicated which books and authors had most influenced their therapeutic work. To rectify that problem, Meichenbaum, Gilmore, and Fedoravicius (1971) designed a study to provide a more definitive test, comparing SD with a form of insight therapy with procedures that could be defined with sufficient clarity and precision. The form of insight therapy they chose was then known as *rational-emotive therapy* (RET; Ellis, 1962), an approach that was viewed as an insight therapy that belonged within the broad category of traditional psychodynamic interventions.

In the Meichenbaum and colleagues (1971) study, treatment was conducted in groups, not in individual treatment sessions, and the experimental version of RET, labeled *self-instructional training* (SIT) for the purposes of the study, replaced the insight therapy. Participants in the SIT condition were asked to think about the test speech they had given before an audience of raters as part of the pre-treatment assessment, to recall what thoughts they had had in the situation (e.g., "What if I make a mess of this speech?"), and to reflect on how helpful or otherwise those thoughts had been. Eventually, they rehearsed statements reflecting more productive attitudes (e.g., "I'll just concentrate on organizing my thoughts and taking it one step at a time. It'll be over soon, anyway."). In other respects the procedures in the study were very similar to those of Paul and his colleagues, but the results were dramatically different—both treatments were shown to be effective, each producing impressive results. There was an additional indication that SIT might be especially useful for those participants whose social anxiety was generalized, also arising in many situations beyond public speaking. Meichenbaum and his colleagues had discovered a new procedure that was as effective as SD, but which, instead of reducing situational anxiety through desensitization, involved persuading people to identify and alter their unhelpful *views* and self-statements.

Self-instructional training was also applied to impulsivity in children and to inappropriate behavior in patients with schizophrenia (Meichenbaum, 1977). The immediate results of these applications were highly encouraging, and the benefits of therapy often extended beyond the behaviors that were specifically targeted, thus promoting greater generalization than the results of operant learning procedures. Initially, Meichenbaum had emphasized the insight aspect of the procedure, but he later focused on clients' rehearsal of helpful, encouraging self-statements.

Stress Inoculation Training.   Encouraged by the success of treatment based on altering self-instructions, and by the indications that it led to generalized improvement in coping skills, Meichenbaum (1977) next pursued the idea of a preventive treatment. Instead of aiming treatment at a specific problem that had already developed, he sought to devise a procedure to equip clients with the skills needed to forestall future problems. In *stress inoculation training,* the treatment procedure progresses through three phases. In the educational phase, the client is given an explanation of the role of unhelpful thinking patterns in producing and maintaining unpleasant emotions and dysfunctional behavior. In the rehearsal phase, the client practices making coping self-statements designed to help deal with stressful events. In the application phase, the client practices using the coping skills while confronting actual stressors. An example of a real stressor used in the training is the cold pressor test, in which the participant immerses a hand and arm in ice-cold water for as long as possible (that is, until the discomfort becomes unbearable). After rehearsal training, volunteers were able to keep their arms immersed in the water for significantly longer periods than people who had not received the training, indicating that the procedure increases people's resilience in tolerating stressful stimuli.

One application of stress inoculation was in anger control (Novaco, 1975). As in other applications, the rehearsal phase is divided into four elements: preparing for a stressor, confronting and handling a stressor, coping with the sense of being overwhelmed by the stressor, and self-congratulation after having dealt with the stressful experience. Novaco's research participants were angry young men who were easily provoked into aggression. For example, a stressor for one client was another man looking at him in an unfriendly way. All too often, the client would quickly harbor thoughts of being judged, belittled, and criticized by the other man, and the usual result was a fist fight and an arrest for disorderly conduct.

Examples of the new self-statements that the client could practice in therapy were similar to the following: (a) *preparing* (when about to enter a bar, for example): "I can develop a plan to deal with this situation so that I won't lose control"; (b) *confronting* (another man looks at him insolently): "I can handle this without losing my cool. I won't give him the satisfaction of getting upset"; (c) *feeling overwhelmed* (the man picks a fight with him): "Even now, I can still cope. It's a strong provocation, but I can relax and defuse this situation. All I need do is keep a cool head"; and (d) *self-congratulation* (leaving, after having handled the situation): "I handled that really well, considering that I have had such a problem with this. Wait till I tell my therapist!"

Stress inoculation training has been applied and tested successfully with police officers, whose work brings them into frequent contact with stressful and potentially dangerous situations that nonetheless call for a measured, professional response.

Constructive Narrative.   Recently, Meichenbaum (1995) has commented on the metaphorical nature of the theories we use to explain behavior change. For example, he suggests that the first common metaphor in the field was conditioning, in which theorists viewed clients' cognitions as subject to the same laws as overt behaviors. Next came information processing, in which cognitions were seen as operating similarly to computer software programs. The latest metaphor is that of constructive narrative, in which clients came to be viewed as "narrators, storytellers and makers of meaning" (Meichenbaum, 1995, p. 149). Using this metaphor, therapists help their clients to alter their stories, to reframe stressful events in their lives, to "normalize" their experiences, to develop a "healing theory" of what happened, and ultimately to build new "assumptive worlds" and new ways to view themselves. Treatment based on this model has elements in common with contemporary brief psychodynamic therapy, and Meichenbaum is optimistic about the potential for the ultimate integration of psychodynamic and cognitive-behavioral therapy.

Rational-Emotive Behavior Therapy

Albert Ellis (1962) developed his cognitive modification technique in the 1950s under the original name of rational-emotive therapy (RET) (see also Ellis, 1988; Ellis & Harper, 1975; Walen, DiGiuseppe, & Dryden, 1992). Ellis worked entirely independently of behavior therapy at first, and his approach was usually categorized together with psychoanalysis as an insight therapy until Meichenbaum brought RET to the attention of behavior therapists in the early 1970s. Initially trained in psychodynamic therapy, Ellis rejected it after becoming more and more dissatisfied with its poor practical results. His work on RET sprang from his earlier interest in philosophy, particularly the work of the Stoics (early Greek and Roman philosophers, such as Epictetus and Marcus Aurelius, who sought to accept events with a stern and tranquil mind). They had argued that people can more or less tolerate any adversity without undue sorrow. The secret is to acknowledge that people are disturbed not by events, but by their view of those events. Ellis's therapy aims at persuading clients to dispute the unhelpful views that make them anxious, depressed, or angry. Although the approach is most closely identified with the rational disputation of irrational ideas, Ellis (1979) has claimed that his technique not only involves cognitive modification but also embraces most of the techniques of behavior therapy, especially real-life activity assignments, self-management procedures, and homework exercises. For this reason he renamed the approach *rational-emotive behavior therapy* (REBT) in the 1990s (Ellis, 1995).

Ellis describes his philosophy and technique as follows:

> REBT is a cognitive-emotive-behavioristic method of psychotherapy uniquely designed to enable people to observe, understand, and persistently dispute their irrational, grandiose, perfectionistic *shoulds, oughts,* and *musts.* It employs the logico-empirical method of science to encourage people to surrender magic, absolutes, and damnation; to acknowledge that nothing is sacred or all-important (although many things are exceptionally unpleasant and incon-

venient); and to gradually teach themselves and to practice the philosophy of desiring rather than demanding and of working at changing what they can change and gracefully putting up with what they cannot. (Ellis, 1995, p. 194)

Ellis describes a three-step progression designated by the letters A, B, and C. A denotes the *activating event*; B the client's *beliefs* about A; and C the emotional *consequence*. An REBT therapist typically takes as a starting point the client's presented problem, usually a disturbing emotion, at C, the last step in the progression. Clients tend to believe, erroneously, that C is caused by A, the activating event that triggers the sequence. As examples of A and C, imagine that the client was confidently expecting an annual salary raise because of especially hard work in recent months, but the employer not only fails to offer a raise but implies that the client's job is in jeopardy because the work output has not come up to expectation. Suppose the client becomes depressed. The behavior of the employer is A; the client's depressive mood is the C. The client believes that A causes C (e.g., "She made me depressed by telling me my work was no good"). But Ellis would urge the client to reject that idea and accept instead that it is largely B, the client's beliefs about A, that causes C.

The beliefs clients can mobilize are of two kinds, rational (rBs) and irrational (iBs). *Rational beliefs* include the following: "I certainly don't like being in this situation; I don't like it one bit. Well, there's no sense whining about it. I'll do my best to turn things around if I can. But even if I can't, I'll cope with the situation somehow." If the client left it at that, the resulting emotion would probably be concern or sadness rather than profound depression or deep despair. Sadness is fairly easy to cope with, but depression is not. Depression and despair would probably be the result of *irrational beliefs* similar to the following: "I must get what I want. I shouldn't get treated in ways I don't like. But I just *did* get treated that way. Therefore this situation is totally impossible, an unheard-of crisis that I simply cannot stand or tolerate." Ellis suggests that such generalized irrational beliefs usually include the ideas that an inconvenient situation must not or should not happen; that when it does happen, it is awful or terrible; and in the face of such a catastrophe, one cannot possibly stand it.

The therapist moves to D in the progression, *disputing* irrational beliefs, pointing out that these beliefs are unrealistic and unhelpful. To challenge the damaging beliefs, the therapist will ask the client to confront questions like, "Why *must* things go the way you want? (You might *prefer* things to be a certain way, granted; but why *must* they be the way you want?) Why is it *terrible* if things do not go your way? (Inconvenient, yes; a pain in the neck, yes; but hardly terrible!) And why can you not *stand* it? (It's a challenge, certainly; but that doesn't mean you cannot possibly stand it!)"

Ellis has advocated his technique as potentially applicable to any problem, because the client is always displeased or dissatisfied with something. That means that REBT can be applied to the client's negative emotional state, whatever it is, by identifying and disputing the irrational beliefs about the situation. In Ellis's view everyone is prone to think irrationally. In our society, we are raised in such a way that we tend to believe statements like, "I must always be loved and approved of by people," or "Any failure is disastrous." Such beliefs are echoed in nursery rhymes, television commercials, and popular songs, and are listed in various research inventories of irrational beliefs such as the *General Attitude and Belief Scale* (Bernard, 1998).

Many clinical psychologists are sympathetic to Ellis's views and find his techniques pragmatically helpful, but some remain cautious about the scientific standing of REBT. Ellis's (1979) description of REBT as including the whole of behavior therapy certainly makes it a holistic approach, but also makes it extremely hard to test (how can you test an approach that encompasses every technique in behavior therapy?). Some empirical findings have been encouraging. Trexler and Karst (1972) found REBT effective with speech anxious students, for example. In another study, three variants of REBT were compared with relaxation training plus counseling, and with no treatment, in 50 community mental health center outpatients (Lipsky, Kassinove, & Miller, 1980). Measures of rational thinking, neuroticism, depression, and anxiety showed that REBT brought greater benefit than the other conditions. This study is important because it dealt with genuine clients who had sought therapy, not with student volunteers. Finally, REBT has been the subject of a critical appraisal by a team of philosophers and psychologists who have examined its conceptual and empirical standing (Bernard & DiGiuseppe, 1989). Some of the contributors to that volume concluded that Ellis has overstated the level of empirical support and scientific validation enjoyed by his method (Haaga & Davison, 1989; Meichenbaum, 1995), and others found fault with its conceptual bases (Lazarus, 1989), yet the tone of these evaluations of REBT was generally positive.

Cognitive Therapy

The most prominent of the leading cognitive modification procedures is the *cognitive therapy* of Aaron T. Beck, a psychiatrist who is best known for his work on depression. The theory, technique, and empirical standing of cognitive therapy have been detailed in several books and chapters (Beck, 1976, 1995; Beck, Emery, & Greenberg, 1985; Beck, Rush, Shaw, & Emery, 1979; Beck & Weishaar, 1995; Dobson & Shaw, 1995; Freeman & Reinecke, 1995).

Cognitive therapy and rational emotive behavior therapy have some features in common. Both were developed in the 1950s, both involve exploring unhelpful beliefs, and the originators of these methods had both been trained initially in psychodynamic therapy. Beck rejected psychoanalytic theory because he did not agree with the notion that depressed clients displayed retroflected hostility (or "anger turned inward"). His experience with depressed outpatients led him to see the potential of exploring, and changing, unadaptive belief systems. This is achieved not only by a form of rational disputation, as in REBT, but also by encouraging the client to attempt specific "experiments" in real life to help challenge the faulty assumptions. For example, a depressed woman whose boyfriend had left her concluded that no one could like her, let alone love her. At the urging of the therapist, she made a deliberate attempt to meet ten people in one week in order to find out experimentally how many of them would reject her. Predictably enough, she was not rejected by all of these people, and the results of that experiment were used as data with which to challenge the general, negative assumption she had made. Central to Beck's cognitive therapy model are the three fundamental concepts of the cognitive triad, cognitive schemas, and cognitive distortions.

The Cognitive Triad.   When a client is in a depressive episode, he or she typically dwells upon negative or pessimistic thoughts about him- or herself, the world, and the future (e.g.,

"I am no good; the outlook is very poor; and there's no hope of it changing for the better"). Self, world, and future form the *cognitive triad* of pessimistic thoughts that require examination in every case of depression (Beck & Weishaar, 1995; Freeman & Reinecke, 1995).

Cognitive Schemas.   Beck observed that depressive clients tend to interpret their experiences on the basis of global, absolute beliefs, such as "I am unlovable." Such beliefs were labeled by Beck as *cognitive schemas.* Any event potentially relevant to such a belief would immediately be interpreted in terms of the schema (Beck, 1995). For example, if a woman were in a depressive episode, and her dating partner did not call her in the evening as promised, she would conclude that this was irrefutable evidence that she was unlovable. Beck's view is that such schemas are only active during episodes of disturbance, as in a depressive episode, and lie dormant between episodes. A schema could develop early in life in response to a significant event. For example, when your best friend moves out of state when you are 7 years old you could conclude, "Whenever you really get to like someone, they abandon you." According to the theory, if a similar event occurs later in life, it could precipitate a depressive episode.

Cognitive Distortions.   Clients experience specific *cognitive distortions* during depressive episodes. Beck lists several of these, each of which, like *selective abstraction,* refers to an exaggeration of the negative aspects of a situation. For example, a depressive client had been looking forward with dread to her annual performance evaluation at work and told her therapist how it went at their next therapy session. "I knew it would be awful, and it was," she said. The therapist asked for more details. "I have a terrible telephone manner," she replied through her tears. The therapist eventually elicited the following. The work performance evaluation had ten parts, dealing with such matters as punctuality, general professionalism, work output, interpersonal effectiveness, and so forth. Each of the ten parts could be rated out of 10 points. The client had received 10 out of 10 on nine items, but on the last the supervisor had said, "I had to find something for you to work on, but your performance has been so good that it was difficult. Perhaps you could try to terminate phone calls from customers a little quicker; you're too polite with them sometimes!" This was the "awful" event that had so troubled the client—a work performance evaluation that had been 97 percent perfect!

According to Beck's model of depression, the scene is set by the development, early in life, of a negative schema concerning loss, personal worthlessness, or the like. This schema is triggered in later years with the occurrence of a relevant event. The client enters a depressive episode, and the cognitive triad and the various cognitive distortions emerge. Treatment is focused upon gently challenging the negative thoughts and encouraging the client to test the pessimistic assumptions empirically.

Several studies have provided support for Beck's theoretical postulates. The general idea that certain thinking patterns correlate with certain mood states has been substantiated in a series of investigations. LaPointe and Harrell (1978) developed a questionnaire on thoughts and feelings and tested it with a college population. A later version of the questionnaire, the Situational Self-Statement and Affective State Inventory (SSSASI; Harrell, Chambless, & Calhoun, 1981) presented volunteers with vignettes about common situations involving frustrations or disappointments. The students indicated which thoughts and feelings they would be likely to have if they were in the situation in real life. For example, a vignette might read, "Suppose you entered one of your paintings in an art contest. You had high hopes of winning first prize, but you did not even get an honorable mention" (after Harrell et al., 1981). Next, the participants would indicate how likely it would be for them to experience each of a group of feelings and each of a group of thoughts. The feelings were angry, suspicious, anxious, depressed, and concerned. An example of the kind of thought that correlated with a "depressed" feeling was: "I may as well give up on art. I knew, deep down, that I would fail. It's hardly worth trying anything any more."

Tested with clinical (psychiatric outpatients and inpatients) and "normal" (students and hospital staff members) participants, the SSSASI showed the same relationships between thoughts and feelings in all groups, but the clients and patients endorsed the negative thoughts and feelings more strongly than the students and staff members (Thorpe, Barnes, Hunter, & Hines, 1983). The results were consistent with Beck's hypothesis that each feeling has a corresponding thought (Beck, Laude, & Bohnert, 1974).

Questionnaire work of this kind tends to support Beck's hypotheses when the focus is on specific self-statements linked to particular feeling states, and Ellis's hypotheses when the focus is on a few classes of generalized irrational beliefs (Bernard, 1998; Thorpe, Walter, Kingery, & Nay, 2001).

Cognitive Restructuring

Following his *multimodal therapy* model, Arnold Lazarus (1973, 1976, 1995) recommends that clinicians attend to seven modalities of client functioning in assessment and treatment, modalities whose initials spell out the acronym "BASIC I.D.": Behavior, Affect, Sensation, Imagery, Cognition, Interpersonal Relations, and Drugs/Diet. Among these, Lazarus has given some prominence to the cognitive modality. As examples of *cognitive restructuring* Lazarus (1995) cites: "Changes in dichotomous reasoning, self-downing, overgeneralization, categorical imperatives, non sequiturs, and excessive desires for approval" (p. 341). By including cognition in his list of modalities, Lazarus helped establish cognitive modification procedures among clinical psychologists. Cognitive restructuring techniques seem very similar to REBT and to cognitive therapy. For example, Lazarus (1973) helps a client deal with distressing thoughts like "I am inferior, evil, and deserve to suffer" by means of rational disputation and *corrective self-talk* (p. 409). Like Beck, he also addresses errors in the *form* of the thinking as well as in the content. For example, with clients who tend to overgeneralize, Lazarus would help them to examine the illogic involved in detail so that they understand the logical error and how to correct it. Lazarus would also include in the cognitive modality areas of ignorance or misinformation, such as a client's lack of knowledge about sexuality.

Coping and Problem Solving

Cognitive modification procedures also owe a great deal to the work of Marvin Goldfried (1980). Taking a broader perspective than most others, Goldfried suggests that clients need more than specific solutions to particular problems. A client who is afraid of cats could be treated by systematic desensitization, for example, to have the fear "removed." But this would not necessarily give the client the skills needed to handle any other anxieties that might happen to arise in the course of a rich and varied life. Instead of treating specific issues one by one, why not teach the client how to solve problems in general? This would involve teaching the client *coping skills.*

D'Zurilla and Goldfried (1971) described the general use of problem solving as a therapeutic strategy. It has potential applications in many areas of client functioning. It involves encouraging the client to adopt an active attitude toward a life problem so that he or she can step back and think about it, define it, generate alternative solutions, make a decision, and try it out. The approach has some similarities with the self-instructional training technique that Meichenbaum and Cameron (1973) used to improve the attention, thinking, and language use of inpatients with schizophrenia. That approach had involved teaching the clients to stop, think ahead, remind themselves of the task at hand, and so on.

Goldfried's (1980) use of coping skills training encompasses anything from physical health and fitness to dealing with the larger community. He focuses on four areas in particular: problem-solving, relaxation, cognitive restructuring, and communication skills. In his discussion of relaxation, for example, he criticizes systematic desensitization for placing the client in such a passive role. Instead of carefully protecting the client from anxiety, Goldfried argues, the therapist would do better to encourage the client to accept anxiety and learn to cope with it during the treatment session. This would equip him or her far better for the real world. Peter Lewinsohn's psychoeducational group approach to teach coping skills to individuals at risk for depression is consistent with Goldfried's model (Hollon & Carter, 1994).

Cognitive-Behavior Therapy: Specific Applications

To illustrate the focused application of cognitive-behavioral methods to specific disorders, we have selected the broad category of anxiety disorders, concentrating on panic disorder, phobias, generalized anxiety disorder, obsessive-compulsive disorder, and posttraumatic stress disorder.

In organizing this section by specific disorders we do not wish to give the misleading impression that every clinical problem has a matching behavioral treatment technique to be used in all cases. That would run counter to proper behavioral practice, in which each treatment plan is based upon an individual behavioral analysis. For example, we shall see that empirical research strongly supports the use of exposure with response prevention to help clients with compulsive rituals and panic control therapy to treat panic disorder. But that does not necessarily mean that all clients will benefit from the same, generic treatment plan. Behavior therapists use research findings on treatment effectiveness judiciously, bringing empirically validated techniques into play when they match the particular pattern of issues presented by the client. It would be inappropriate and unethical to ignore a research-validated "treatment of choice" in formulating a treatment plan and making recommendations to a client. But unthinkingly choosing a treatment technique from a list approved for the particular disorder would be a technical, not a professional, activity that could do clients a disservice. Behavior therapists implement therapeutic techniques based on professional judgments as to which procedures to employ with particular clients.

Anxiety is usually viewed as a clinical problem if it causes the client intense distress or disability. It can be highly distressing to experience panic attacks or other intense anxiety episodes. It is certainly disabling when anxiety leads to avoidance of routine activities, so that one cannot work or socialize. And it is certainly distressing and disabling when anxiety arises in harmless situations or in any or all situations (Mahoney, 1980; Wilson, Nathan, O'Leary, & Clark, 1996).

In the DSM-IV classification the anxiety disorders are grouped into a dozen categories, including categories for medically related and substance-induced anxiety. We shall focus on a representative sample of these in this section.

Panic Disorder

In *Panic Disorder* the client has recurrent, unpredictable panic attacks, at least one of which has been followed by one month or more of worry about having further attacks (or about their consequences). Panic disorder takes two forms, Panic Disorder Without Agoraphobia and Panic Disorder With Agoraphobia, defined of course by the presence or absence of agoraphobia.

A *panic attack* is a definite period of intense fear or distress with at least four from the following list of thirteen symptoms, each of which develops rapidly and reaches a peak within 10 minutes: racing or pounding heart, or palpitations; sweating; trembling or shaking; feeling of shortness of breath; feeling of choking; chest pain or discomfort; nausea or abdominal distress; feeling faint, dizzy, or light-headed; feelings of unreality or detachment; fear of losing control or going crazy; fear of dying during the attack; unusual bodily sensations; and chills or hot flashes. *Agoraphobia* involves anxiety about being in situations that would not allow easy escape if panic symptoms arose (such as being far from home, being in crowded public places, and using public transportation). The client avoids these situations or, if not, experiences marked distress if a trusted companion is not present (American Psychiatric Association, 1994).

Phobias and Obsessive-Compulsive Disorders

A *Phobia* is a persistent, irrational fear of a specific situation or object, resulting in a strong desire to avoid it. The individual recognizes that the fear is exaggerated or unreasonable, but nevertheless feels unable to control the phobia. One of these is Agoraphobia Without History of Panic Disorder, in which the client fears or avoids crowds, public places, travel away from home, and so forth without actually experiencing panic attacks. In Social Phobia the client is distressed by anxiety about being observed critically by others, coupled with the fear of doing something embarrassing. The person almost always experiences anxiety in such situations and often avoids them, interfering significantly with social or work activities. This category is essentially a grouping of specific phobias that have in common a theme of social-evaluative anxiety. Common examples are fears of public speaking, of interviewing for a job, or of eating in a restaurant. In Specific Phobia the client has a phobia of any particular object or situation other than agoraphobic or social phobia situations. Typical specific phobias are fears of small animals or insects; of heights, darkness, or confinement; and of blood, injury, and illness.

The essential problems in *Obsessive-Compulsive Disorder* are: (a) worrying, intrusive thoughts, ideas, or images that the client resists, or (b) an urge to repeat a ritual or stereotyped behavior of some kind while realizing that this is unreasonable and unnecessary.

Generalized Anxiety Disorder

Generalized Anxiety Disorder refers to a pattern of persistent, exaggerated anxiety and worry about the person's general life circumstances. The client finds it hard to control the worry and shows such symptoms as restlessness, concentration difficulties, muscle tension, and sleep disturbance. The anxiety pattern causes definite distress or clear impairment in social or occupational functioning.

Conditioning Theories of Anxiety

Cognitive-behavioral explanations of anxiety disorders begin with laboratory studies of conditioning in animals, as outlined in Chapter 4. For example, obsessive-compulsive disorder has a parallel in several animal studies (Mineka, 1985). Dogs subjected to high levels of shock during avoidance learning often displayed stereotyped behavior patterns with little apparent anxiety. Rats developed "fixations" in another group of studies. They had to jump from a pedestal toward one of two doors. One door would fall open, and the rat would land safely inside, but the other would be locked, so the rat would bump its nose and fall into a net. If the experimenter placed a particular mark on the open door, such as a plus sign, the rats would readily learn to jump toward it, even if the location of door with the plus sign (the door that would fall open) varied from trial to trial. But when the experimenter placed the sign on the doors randomly, so that sometimes the plus sign was on the open door and sometimes on the locked one, it was impossible for the rats to learn the discrimination. Their behavior became stereotyped; they would adopt a policy of always jumping toward the left-hand door, for example, whatever the sign indicated (Yates, 1962). In her own studies, Mineka (1985) has shown that monkeys under stress also display stereotypic and ritualistic behavior. These laboratory responses are very similar to the behavior of obsessive-compulsive clients. In both the lab and the clinic, this behavior involves a stereotyped pattern that has no bearing on what actually happens next.

Mineka (1985) has also pointed out that *experimental neurosis* is a perfect prototype for generalized anxiety disorder. Discovered by Pavlov and others under certain experimental conditions involving conflict, experimental neurosis consists of a group of symptoms in the animals including agitation, rapid heart beat, hypersensitivity, distractibility, and helplessness (inability to perform previously learned responses). Similar phenomena are seen when monkeys and chimpanzees are separated from their parents. This *separation protest* in human and nonhuman primate infants is very similar to symptoms of panic disorder and generalized anxiety disorder (Hecker & Thorpe, 1992).

Classical conditioning processes provide an explanation of some anxiety phenomena. The assumption is that lasting fear of a nondangerous object or situation could be acquired through accidental association with a stimulus that triggers fear or alarm (Barlow, 1988). In this formulation, anxiety is a conditioned response that will predictably extinguish when the conditioned stimulus, the phobic object, is confronted repeatedly in the absence of an unpleasant unconditioned stimulus. Wolpe's (1958) systematic desensitization procedure allows for the extinction of anxiety when the client confronts the feared situation without distress. The various other exposure treatments also developed from basic research on extinction processes, and they all provide a systematic method for the client to follow in confronting feared stimuli.

The classical conditioning explanation of anxiety could apply when the client fears something in particular, as in phobic and obsessive-compulsive disorders. But it is more difficult for classical conditioning principles to accommodate panic disorder and generalized anxiety disorder, because they appear not to involve specific stimuli. Furthermore, classical conditioning does not explain the persistence of anxiety disorders. After all, whenever the client encounters the feared situation without an aversive event taking place, there is the real-life equivalent of a laboratory extinction trial, and we would expect the anxiety (the conditioned response) to weaken. Why does this not happen in specific phobias, for instance, if the conditioning view is correct?

Mowrer (1947, 1960) proposed a *two-factor* or *two-process theory* to explain why anxiety does not seem to extinguish in the way predicted by classical conditioning principles. He argued that classical conditioning works together with a second process to maintain clinical anxiety. The second process is the operant learning of escape and avoidance behavior. In other words, first, anxiety is acquired by classical conditioning, when a previously harmless stimulus is paired with an accidental aversive event. Second, because the situation elicits a conditioned response of anxiety on future occasions, the client understandably escapes or avoids it, thus reducing the anxiety and providing motivation for continued avoidance. Continued avoidance of the feared situation prevents the exposure necessary for extinction to take place. And rapid escape on encountering the phobic object severely limits the client's exposure to only a brief moment, a duration insufficient to allow extinction (Wilson, 1973).

Rachman (1971, 1976) argued that obsessive-compulsive disorder is similar to phobias, and two-factor theory applies to both. Obsessional thoughts are similar to phobias in being conditioned stimuli that elicit anxiety. The client's ritualistic or compulsive behavior serves as an escape response that protects the obsessions from extinction.

Classical conditioning and two-factor theory provide convenient explanations of some anxiety disorders, and they have even inspired the development of effective treatments. But there are many difficult questions about anxiety disorders that conditioning theories cannot answer, requiring us to go further afield for convincing explanations. Animals can learn to avoid aversive stimuli without having been exposed to classical conditioning (Herrnstein, 1969; Herrnstein & Hineline, 1966; Hineline, 1977). Levels of fear and avoidance behavior are often at odds with one another in phobic clients (Rachman & Hodgson, 1974). The victims of major natural disasters do not necessarily develop anxiety, despite having been subjected to highly fear-provoking experiences (Rachman, 1977). Many clients with phobias cannot recall having had an aversive experience with the situation or object they fear (Marks, 1987). Conditioned fear is very difficult to produce in humans in laboratory experiments, and there are many contradictory findings (Harris, 1979). People do not become phobic of random stimuli but tend to fear some things, like spiders, heights, and darkness, rather than others, like houses, trees, and electrical appliances (Marks, 1969; Seligman, 1971).

Counterarguments include Seligman's (1971) proposal that, even though people fear some things more than others, classical conditioning could still operate when phobias do arise. He put forward the concept of biological *preparedness,* suggesting that the stimuli that are prominent in phobias and obsessions are those that would always have been potentially threatening to humans. Prepared stimulus-response connections are biologically important, are easily conditioned, and are slow to extinguish. Experimental evidence on this notion, however, produced mixed conclusions (Ohman, Erixon, & Lofberg, 1975; Silva, Rachman,

& Seligman, 1977). In any event, while conditioning is one possible pathway to fear, there are several others, including observing other people, watching movies, and reading books (Rachman, 1977). An alternative strategy is to focus less on how anxiety develops through conditioning, and more on how it fails to extinguish in certain individuals (Marks, 1981b).

Marks (1981a) developed successful treatments for agoraphobia and obsessive-compulsive disorder by drawing from Baum's (1970) studies of *blocking,* or *response prevention,* in animals. Rats that had been conditioned to fear environments in which they had been shocked were confined there, without the opportunity to escape, after the aversive stimuli had been removed. This technique was highly successful in promoting the extinction of the conditioned anxiety. By contrast with systematic desensitization procedures, confrontive exposure to conditioned stimuli during extinction is empirically more helpful than the technique of gradual approach to feared stimuli (Wilson, 1973).

The clinical equivalents of the blocking procedure are the exposure methods, *exposure in vivo* (in real life) and *exposure with response prevention*—the client remains in contact with highly feared stimuli without escaping, for prolonged periods if necessary, until the anxiety declines. Clients with agoraphobia, for example, are asked to spend 90 minutes or more in crowded shopping malls without retreating at the onset of anxiety. Obsessive-compulsive clients are asked to confront the stimuli that normally provoke them to ritualize, but this time without performing the ritual. In either case, preventing the escape or avoidance response allows the client to confront the feared situation. In clinical practice, these methods have brought significant benefit to highly anxious clients (Marks, 1981, 1987).

Cognitive Theories of Anxiety

Because they involve external cues that can be viewed as eliciting stimuli, phobias and compulsions initially received more attention than other anxiety disorders from conditioning-oriented behavior therapists (Foa & Kozak, 1986). But the development of cognitive restructuring therapies led to an emphasis on *internal cues,* such as sensations of emotional arousal or thoughts of impending catastrophes. Beck's cognitive theory of the causes and treatment of depression has also been applied to the anxiety disorders, especially to panic disorder (Beck, 1985; Beck, Emery, & Greenberg, 1985; Clark & Beck, 1988).

In panic disorder, the client experiences a sudden, unexplained surge of anxiety that rapidly culminates in a terrifying panic attack. This begins with a bodily sensation that would be perfectly understandable in normal circumstances. The client suddenly gets up from a chair and feels a little faint for a second or two, is momentarily startled by the sound of the doorbell, or runs to catch a bus and then notices the sensations of a pounding heart and flushed face. But instead of making a benign attribution concerning such sensations, the client interprets them as meaning something terribly uncontrollable, like a serious disease. These alarming interpretations arouse further anxiety, producing a vicious circle in which normal sensations ultimately escalate into a panic attack. The development of such *catastrophic misinterpretations* of routine bodily sensations is central to the cognitive theory of panic disorder (Clark, 1986).

Cognitive therapy hypotheses have also been applied to obsessive-compulsive disorder (Salkovskis, 1985; Salkovskis, Richards, & Forrester, 1995). One client had obsessional thoughts about having left things in an untidy or dangerous condition. He could be driving his car, for example, and suddenly have the thought that he might have seen a nail on the side of the road a couple of miles back. "If I don't go back and check, and—if it was indeed a nail—remove it, then someone could get a flat tire, lose control of their car, and die." So he would turn his car around and drive back to look for the possible nail. The obsessional thought was the intrusive idea about the nail; the automatic thoughts were that he would be to blame for an awful catastrophe if he did not at least check the situation. According to Rachman (1978), it is not remarkable that the client has occasional *intrusions* of disturbing thoughts or images, because everyone does to one degree or another. What is unusual is that the client goes on to have automatic thoughts, like "I must check," which are related to exaggerated beliefs about personal responsibility. These beliefs, not the intrusions them-selves, lead clients to check or perform rituals. This implies that cognitive therapy for obsessive-compulsive disorder would not concentrate on the intrusive thoughts but upon the automatic thoughts produced by the intrusions, and the general dysfunctional beliefs— the cognitive schemas—underlying those automatic thoughts.

Cognitive-Behavioral Interventions

Phobias.   Early behavioral treatment interventions for anxiety disorders were focused on phobias. In the 1960s analogue research showed that systematic desensitization (SD) was helpful in treating college students with specific phobias, but a more significant challenge was to apply it to clients with agoraphobia in clinical settings. Compared with snake pho-bia and public speaking anxiety, agoraphobia is far more severe, generalized, disabling, and difficult to treat (Marks, 1981b). An initial case report of behavior therapy for agoraphobia-like symptoms described a favorable outcome, but the chief method used was not SD but graduated real-life practice (Meyer, 1957). The results of SD with clinical series of agora-phobic clients were disappointing. Only minimal therapeutic gains were made, and even those were only achieved after a large number of treatment sessions that sometimes went on for more than a year (Cooper, Gelder, & Marks, 1965; Marks & Gelder, 1965; Meyer & Gelder, 1963). The results of controlled comparisons of SD with traditional psychotherapy were no more impressive (Gelder & Marks, 1966; Gelder, Marks, & Wolff, 1967).

One of the most thorough studies of SD with phobic clients was conducted by Gelder, Bancroft, Gath, Johnston, Mathews, and Shaw (1973). Thirty-six clients with agoraphobia, social phobia, or specific phobias were given fifteen sessions of treatment in as many weeks. Clients were randomly distributed among three treatment conditions: SD, imaginal flooding, and "associative psychotherapy" (a placebo-control condition in which clients made free associations to phobic imagery). The last four sessions of treatment were devoted to real-life practice in phobic situations. Clients were assessed before and after treatment and again six months later. Imaginal flooding and SD were both more helpful than associa-tive psychotherapy on various measures of outcome. Clients with agoraphobia did espe-cially poorly with associative psychotherapy.

Used alone, SD is of limited value in treating commonly presented phobias (Marks, 1981). It remains useful in the treatment of some specific and social phobias, especially when the feared events are difficult to replicate in real life (such as criticism by an employer). Nev-ertheless, SD has been generally supplanted by techniques with an in vivo component, like participant modeling or exposure in vivo, especially for agoraphobic avoidance.

Experiments on *graduated real-life practice* (also called "graded practice") with phobic clients often used single-case research methodology. Several studies of this kind were conducted by a team of researchers in Vermont in the late 1960s (Agras, Leitenberg, Barlow, & Burlington, 1967; Leitenberg, Agras, Thompson, & Wright, 1968). One consistent finding was that it is helpful for clients to enter real phobic situations repeatedly (Leitenberg et al., 1968).

In treating agoraphobia, the Vermont team were able to show that feedback on progress from the therapist and praise for specific accomplishments provided added benefit (Agras et al., 1968). Contingent praise was shown to be effective as reinforcement because clients made progress in either distance walked from the clinic or time spent away from the clinic, depending upon which criterion was used for reinforcement. Essential elements in a successful program for agoraphobic clients are practice in real phobic settings (Leitenberg, Agras, Edwardes, Thompson, & Wincze, 1970) and therapist feedback on progress, especially in the early stages of treatment (Leitenberg, Agras, Allen, & Butz, 1975).

Beginning in the late 1960s clinical researchers explored the rapid treatment of phobias by confrontive, prolonged exposure to feared stimuli in the imagination and in real life. Boulougouris and Marks (1969) treated four phobic clients with imaginal flooding and prolonged real-life practice, obtaining impressive results. In a crossover study comparing imaginal flooding with systematic desensitization, Boulougouris, Marks, and Marset (1971) showed that flooding was generally the more effective in a sample of phobic clients. Flooding was particularly helpful to the agoraphobic clients. In another crossover trial with a sample of phobic and obsessive-compulsive clients, Greist, Marks, Berlin, Gournay, and Noshirvani (1980) asked the participants (a) to confront or (b) to avoid feared situations for one week. In the confronting condition, clients were advised to remain in the feared surroundings for as long as it took for their anxiety to diminish, for hours if need be. In the avoidance condition, clients were recommended to take a break from anxiety and steer well clear of fear-provoking situations. The problems dealt with in the 19 clients were compulsive rituals, agoraphobia, social phobia, and specific phobias of wasps, spiders, ants, enclosed spaces, and incontinence (losing control of one's bladder or bowels). Treatment-related changes consistently favored the confrontation condition.

A study of 36 women with agoraphobia showed no clear differences between imaginal and in vivo exposure (Mathews, Johnston, Lancashire, Munby, Shaw, & Gelder, 1976). Some clients followed imaginal procedures, some had exposure in vivo, and there was a combined treatment group. This was an ambitious study in which clients had sixteen 90-minute treatment sessions. It is likely that, with that amount of exposure, all techniques were able to exert their maximum impact.

Barbara Rothbaum and her colleagues have used computer-generated, virtual reality environments in exposure treatment for people with a specific phobia of heights (acrophobia). The procedure is described as *virtual reality graded exposure* (VRGE). The technology involves real-time computer graphics, body tracking devices, and visual displays. Clients wear a head-mounted display with an electromagnetic sensor, so that the virtual environment changes in a realistic way with head and body motion (Rothbaum, Hodges, Kooper, Opdyke, Williford, & North, 1995). Seventeen acrophobic students received treatment in seven 35- to 45-minute exposure sessions (Hodges, Kooper, Meyer, Rothbaum, Opdyke, de Graaff, Williford, & North, 1995). These clients were exposed to three environments: an elevator, a series of balconies, and a series of bridges. The open elevator was presented as located on the inside of a 49-floor hotel; the participant would actually hold onto a waist-high rail that was depicted as a guard rail. The goals of the study were to find out if (1) the simulated environment was realistic, and (2) anxiety could habituate under these conditions. Both goals were clearly reached. The "sense of presence" was such that clients produced a range of anxiety symptoms that included nausea and actual vomiting in one participant. Treated participants showed significant improvement on measures of avoidance and anxiety, whereas a waiting-list control group showed no change.

Analogue studies with student volunteers showed that cognitive modification procedures are potentially effective treatments for anxiety problems (Emmelkamp, 1979). Researchers working with clinical phobias had also been encouraged by the effects of adding cognitive restructuring techniques to behavior therapy (Mathews & Rezin, 1977; Mathews & Shaw, 1973). Emmelkamp, Kuipers, and Eggeraat (1978) reported a crossover study with 21 agoraphobic clients who received group sessions of exposure in vivo and a combination of various cognitive restructuring procedures. Clients improved significantly more with exposure than with cognitive treatment. Other studies with agoraphobic clients added cognitive restructuring procedures to behavioral techniques, without appreciable effects on outcome (Thorpe & Burns, 1983; Williams & Rappoport, 1983).

Similar results were obtained for specific phobias. Biran and Wilson (1981) treated clients with fears of heights, darkness, or being confined. Graduated real-life practice was compared with a battery of cognitive restructuring methods that included relabeling of emotional feelings, elements of rational emotive behavior therapy, and stress inoculation. Guided practice was clearly more efficient and effective in the study than the cognitive treatment package. The practical implications are clear. If a client has a fear of heights, it is far more helpful for him or her to practice walking on the roof of a high building with the therapist than to dispute unhelpful attitudes in the therapist's office.

In studies of social phobia, cognitive modification procedures have produced more encouraging results. Not only are cognitive interventions as helpful as performance-based behavioral treatment for social phobia, but there is also evidence that results from student volunteers are very similar to those observed in clinic clients with this disorder (Emmelkamp, Mersch, & Vissia, 1985; Emmelkamp, Mersch, Vissia, & van der Helm, 1985). In these studies Emmelkamp and his colleagues noticed that some kinds of cognitive restructuring may be more helpful than others. The impression is that it is more helpful to focus on removing self-defeating or negative self-statements than to try to promote "positive thinking." A review of twelve studies of cognitive-behavioral treatment and nine studies of exposure treatment for social phobia revealed, however, that these techniques are equally effective (Feske & Chambless, 1995).

Obsessive-Compulsive Disorder.   Behavioral treatment of *obsessive-compulsive disorder* (OCD) has paralleled the treatment of phobias in some ways, because in both disorders the client is more anxious in some situations than in others. A client with contamination fears and elaborate cleansing rituals is similar to a client with a specific phobia in that the obsessional thoughts are triggered by an external stimulus event, such as the sight of a doorknob in a public building. The client's prolonged hand-washing rituals can be seen as attempts to escape from the feared situation, which in this case is feeling contaminated. As in a phobia, there is an external feared stimulus that leads the client to attempt to escape or avoid.

However, some obsessions are prompted more by internal than external stimuli, and these obsessions are not as easy to formulate in situational terms. Many clients with OCD fear their own impulses, for example, or worry a great deal about the idea that they might think blasphemous thoughts. Salkovskis (1983) described a 23-year-old man who had obsessional ruminations about people being violent toward him. He attempted to neutralize these disturbing thoughts by repeating the exact thoughts, internally, an even number of times, but as soon as he did this the thought would return, and he had to repeat the process. Each episode of this kind lasted from 15 minutes to three hours. Cases like this are different from phobias in that the important stimuli are internal, so different treatment methods have been necessary.

Early case studies described the application of systematic desensitization (SD) to obsessional thinking. Worsley (1970) outlined the treatment of a 24-year-old woman who was greatly troubled by sharp knives and scissors and by the idea that she might harm someone with them. Treatment consisted of SD, with the relaxation component assisted by the use of short-acting barbiturate medication. After the SD sessions, the client progressed to real-life exposure to knives. Twenty-three treatment sessions were held over five months. The client responded well to treatment and was still free of obsessions at a follow-up visit two years later. Although many case studies like this have been reported, a comprehensive review of OCD treatment, completed after the popularity of SD had declined, revealed no controlled studies of this technique in application to OCD (Beech & Vaughan, 1978).

When external stimuli evoke compulsive rituals, therapists can advise clients to confront these stimuli without ritualizing. This procedure, *exposure with response prevention,* is parallel to exposure treatment with phobic clients in that the situation is confronted without escape or avoidance (Stanley & Wagner, 1994).

Modeling has also proved useful in combination with exposure and response prevention. The therapist demonstrates an appropriate behavior sequence while the client looks on, providing an opportunity for the client to acquire adaptive coping skills. It can be helpful to show the client what a reasonably normal hand-washing procedure looks like, for example. Modeling, exposure, and response-prevention can be a particularly powerful technique combination (Rachman & Hodgson, 1980).

Some obsessions are triggered by internal cues. In cases like this it is difficult to identify a suitable stimulus with which to confront the client in therapy. Salkovskis (1983) described the treatment of an obsessional ruminator who tried to neutralize thoughts of violence by repeating them exactly to himself, covertly. The obsessional thoughts of violence were the stimuli, and the neutralizing thoughts (repeating the obsessions in a ritualistic way) were the responses. Treatment would involve having the client confront the stimuli without making the responses, very difficult to do in this case. Salkovskis succeeded in treating this client by preparing an audiotape of the client voicing his unpleasant thoughts, and then playing the tape back to him repeatedly. This treatment may have worked because the exposure could proceed without the escape response (the neutralizing thoughts) being made. The client did not have time to neutralize each thought as it was expressed on the audiotape, because the stimulus tape was under the control of the therapist during these treatment sessions—and the therapist kept the tape running without pause!

Generalized Anxiety Disorder.   The most common of the anxiety disorders (Weissman, 1985), *generalized anxiety disorder* (GAD) poses a challenge for behavioral treatment because it is not linked to particular situations or characteristic behavior patterns. Together with various somatic symptoms of anxiety, the client experiences a series of worrying thoughts or images. This aspect of the problem invites exploration by cognitive therapists, but the worrying thoughts are not as organized or systematic as in obsessive-compulsive disorder, making them difficult to deal with. Hence, specific treatments that have been successful in other applications—systematic desensitization, exposure in vivo, stress inoculation—cannot be applied meaningfully. Behavior therapists have typically armed the generalized anxiety client with as many coping strategies as possible, chiefly drawn from techniques of relaxation training and rational emotive behavior therapy.

Wolpe (1973) recommended *thought-stopping* to disrupt prolonged worrying, and several case reports have illustrated the use of this technique. The therapist asks the client to begin worrying, and to do so in earnest for a few minutes. The client signals the therapist when the worrying is definitely in progress. A few seconds after the client's signal, the therapist suddenly shouts "*Stop!*"—preferably slapping a hand on a desk or table at the same time. The usual effect is for the client to be surprised and startled and for the worrying thought pattern to be disrupted. When the client tries to resume worrying, it is often difficult to reinstate the original thoughts. Nonetheless, client and therapist proceed with the technique. Eventually, the client, not the therapist, shouts "Stop" when the worrying is in progress, and later still the client practices the technique covertly. The utility of this thought-stopping technique is supported by a variety of illustrative anecdotal reports, but compelling experimental data are lacking (O'Brien, 1979).

Deffenbacher and Suinn (1987) proposed a model of generalized anxiety disorder that suggests four suitable intervention targets: (1) taking control of any stimuli that elicit generalized anxiety or worry, (2) reducing fear in general by employing any or all available techniques, (3) controlling autonomic arousal, and (4) changing negative cognitions. These treatment strategies all have some empirical support.

Applying *stimulus control* methods involves helping the client to limit the situations and occasions for the problem's occurrence. The target of this approach has been the client's tendency to worry most of the time and in practically all situations. Theoretically, we assume that if the client has usually worried in various places, then those places have come to set the occasion for worrying. In operant learning terms, those situations have become discriminative stimuli. Borkovec, Wilkinson, Folensbee, and Lerman (1983) applied this technique by asking clients to set aside a half-hour "worry period" each day; to keep track of worrying thoughts when they arise; each time a worrying thought emerges, to postpone worrying about it until the designated time; and then to worry as thoroughly as possible during the appointed half-hour period. The technique has proved successful, but it is not entirely clear why.

Relaxation training is the chief component of the *anxiety management training* approach developed by Suinn and Richardson (1971). Clients are trained in relaxation in the usual manner. Next, they are taught to notice when they become tense and then to use the feelings of tension as a cue to relax. As the treatment program progresses, the therapist presents anxiety-arousing scenes for clients to imagine, and they apply relaxation to reduce these feelings of anxiety. The therapist gradually makes the presented scenes more challenging, while slowly reducing his or her influence on clients' efforts to relax. In a test of this technique, Jannoun, Oppenheimer, and Gelder (1982) treated 27 GAD clients. Anxiety management training was presented as a self-help program. Significant anxiety reduction was achieved, as measured by clients' and independent clinicians' ratings. Improvements had been maintained at a follow-up assessment three months after treatment.

Relaxation training alone can be of significant benefit to generalized anxiety disorder clients. Lehrer (1978) treated ten GAD clients with four sessions of relaxation training and compared them with ten untreated GAD clients. Additional comparison groups included twenty nonclients, ten of whom had relaxation and ten of whom did not. Results were that the treated GAD clients were similar to the nonclients on important measures after treatment.

In a study with Community Mental Health Center outpatients, rational emotive behavior therapy (REBT) proved more effective than relaxation with a sample of fifty adults who appear to have had general anxieties (Lipsky, Kassinove, & Miller, 1980). Ramm, Marks, Yuksel, and Stern (1981) treated twelve generalized anxiety clients by what they described as "anxiety management training." The techniques used, however, involved self-statement modification. In six one-hour treatment sessions, clients learned to adopt either positive or negative self-statements concerning their problems. Results were not very impressive, but both groups improved at similar rates. One month after treatment, the measures no longer showed a significant improvement from pretreatment levels. Later studies have produced somewhat more encouraging results for cognitive interventions for generalized anxiety (Barlow, Rapee, & Brown, 1992; see below).

The most helpful behavioral treatment approach for generalized anxiety disorder has been the combination of relaxation training with some form of cognitive modification procedure. A prospective between-groups study of GAD clients was reported by Woodward and Jones (1980). Clients were randomly distributed among four treatment conditions: cognitive restructuring (a combination of rational emotive behavior therapy and self-instructional training), systematic desensitization (including the use of coping imagery), the combination of cognitive restructuring and SD, and no treatment. The combined treatment group was clearly the most successful intervention; clients in this condition made clinically significant improvement, while those in the other conditions showed little therapeutic change. The combination of relaxation training and cognitive modification has also been found therapeutic by Barlow and his associates (Barlow, Cohen, Waddell, Vermilyea, Klosko, Blanchard, & Di Nardo, 1984). One component of this study was a comparison of somatic and cognitive treatments for GAD in five clients; another four GAD clients served as an untreated control group. The somatic treatments were progressive relaxation training and electromyograph biofeedback, a technique in which clients could observe monitored changes in muscle tension (in this case, the frontalis muscle of the forehead) and thus learn to reduce the tension. The cognitive treatment procedure was derived from stress inoculation and cognitive therapy methods. Eighteen treatment sessions were given. Treated clients improved significantly, while untreated clients did not, on many measures, including reductions in frontalis muscle tension, heart rate, self-report of state anxiety, and clinicians' ratings of problem severity.

A later study by this group focused on 65 carefully diagnosed generalized anxiety disorder clients who were treated by relaxation, cognitive therapy, or the combination of both techniques (Barlow, Rapee, & Brown, 1992). A waiting-list control group provided a baseline for comparison. The active treatments all produced modest therapeutic gains, but clients in these conditions showed significant improvement as compared with the control group participants; the gains persisted over a two-year follow-up interval. Most clients were left with residual anxiety, and there was a substantial dropout rate during the study, yet treated participants used less prescribed medication during the followup.

Panic Disorder.   *Panic disorder* was traditionally one of the most challenging disorders to formulate and treat via cognitive-behavior therapy, but today panic control therapy is well established as the most effective psychological intervention for the disorder.

Initial studies focused on relaxation training and cognitive restructuring. Waddell, Barlow, and O'Brien (1984) described the treatment of three men with panic disorder by cognitive restructuring and relaxation training, the number of treatment sessions ranging from twelve to seventeen. The research design was a multiple baseline across clients, so each client's treatment began at a different time. As gauged by decreases in the number and duration of panic attacks, the program was successful at least up to a three-month follow-up assessment. However, there was an increase in "background" or generalized anxiety in two of the clients. Eleven clients with panic disorder were treated in the study by Barlow and colleagues (1984), cited in the previous section on generalized anxiety disorder. Five of the panic disorder clients were treated by a combination of relaxation, biofeedback, and cognitive-behavioral therapy; six served as a waiting-list control group. Parallel to the results with the GAD clients, the results for panic disorder clearly favored the treated clients, who improved significantly on all major measures while the waiting list clients did not. On the criterion of self-monitored panic attacks in both panic disorder and GAD groups, all ten of the treated clients improved, while four of the ten untreated clients actually got worse.

Theoretical interpretations of panic disorder have combined the somatic and cognitive aspects of the disorder, justifying treatment by relaxation or biofeedback and cognitive approaches. Theorists assume that panic attacks develop because, first, there is a bodily reaction similar to anxiety (whether it was actually triggered by biological factors such as hyperventilation [Ley, 1987] or by external stimuli), and second, the client interprets this in a catastrophic fashion (Clark, 1986; Clark & Beck, 1988; Hecker & Thorpe, 1992). To take hyperventilation as an example, examining both bodily reactions and catastrophic interpretations leads to two logical treatment approaches. First, the client can be told that his or her symptoms are understandable in terms of overbreathing or hyperventilation. This information allows the client to construe the bodily sensations as a normal reaction to hyperventilation, rather than as an unexplained attack of anxiety. Second, the client can be trained to control his or her respiration so that episodes of hyperventilation are less likely to occur.

In a study of respiration control for panic disorder clients, Clark, Salkovskis, and Chalkley (1985) treated nineteen people who had panic attacks and anticipatory anxiety. The clients had been selected from a larger sample of panic disorder sufferers because their symptoms were consistent with the hyperventilation interpretation. Clients were given a rationale and explanation that encouraged them to interpret the sensations of anxiety as the result of hyperventilation, and they were trained in respiration control. After two weeks of treatment there were significant reductions in panic frequency and in the self-report of anxiety. Further reductions took place within six-month and two-year follow-up intervals, although the results here may have been partly due to extra treatment given in the interim. No exposure treatment was given in the study, but behavioral avoidance tests served as an index of improvement for these clients.

Since 1989, the essential techniques used in the psychological treatment of panic disorder have been cognitive restructuring, exposure to somatic cues, and breathing retraining, collectively referred to as *panic control treatment* (Beck & Zebb, 1994; Rapee & Barlow, 1991; Street & Barlow, 1994). The treatment component receiving most emphasis is *exposure to somatic cues,* or deliberately producing and confronting the bodily sensations that the client associates with panic. The theory is that panic disorder does not reflect anxiety about external situations like public places, crowds, or heights. Instead, it reflects anxiety about certain bodily sensations like dizziness, light-headedness, and muscle tension. If the client is anxious about crowds, the therapist would normally recommend exposure therapy, such as confronting crowds until the anxiety declines. Therefore, if the client is anxious about the sensation of light-headedness, the therapist could recommend exposure therapy—confronting the feeling of light-headedness until the anxiety declines.

The *cognitive restructuring* component of panic control treatment is a form of cognitive therapy, applied to the client's implicit schemas construing panic sensations as signs of catastrophic illness (Clark, 1986). Through this type of intervention, clients are able to recognize that, despite the discomfort and distress associated with breathlessness, there is no evidence that they have to be incapacitated by this symptom—in fact, clients can remind themselves that they have always survived everything that has ever happened to them!

David Barlow and his colleagues conducted a large-scale treatment outcome study to compare four conditions: the panic control treatment package (PCT); relaxation training; PCT plus relaxation training (combined treatment); and a waiting-list control (Barlow, Craske, Cerny, & Klosko, 1989). The three active treatments brought significant benefit as measured by panic frequency reduction and general improvement on a battery of measures. The PCT and combined conditions were most successful overall, and significantly more clients terminated treatment early from the relaxation condition. Two years after the conclusion of treatment, clients in the PCT condition were faring best, 80 percent of them remaining free of panic attacks (Street & Barlow, 1994).

Posttraumatic Stress Disorder. Posttraumatic stress disorder (PTSD) is a syndrome of anxiety elements and other symptoms in some individuals who have been subjected to life-threatening stressors and experience emotional distress following the traumatic event (American Psychiatric Association, 1994). Behavioral treatments for PTSD fall into two groups, exposure methods and anxiety management training (Rothbaum & Foa, 1992a). Imaginal flooding has been successfully applied to the psychological problems of combat veterans (Keane, Fairbank, Caddell, & Zimering, 1989), rape victims (Steketee & Foa, 1987), and survivors of automobile accidents (McCaffrey & Fairbank, 1985). Cognitive restructuring methods have also been found helpful for rape victims (Resick, Jordan, Girelli, Hutter, & Marhoefer-Dvorak, 1988). The controversial new technique of *eye movement desensitization and reprocessing* (Shapiro, 1989, 1991a, 1995) is helpful in reducing subjective distress in the short term, but its benefits in treating the full-scale disorder have yet to be demonstrated (Hassard, 1993; Jensen, 1994). Recurrent and traumatic nightmares may be treated by exposure methods and dream reorganization techniques (Marks, 1987; Palace & Johnston, 1989).

Cognitive-Behavior Therapy: Holistic Approaches

As a comprehensive form of psychotherapy, cognitive-behavior therapy is empirically based, problem-focused, goal-oriented, collaborative, and present-centered, emphasizing active interventions to resolve problems through direct changes in thoughts and behaviors (Persons, 1994). Cognitive-behavior therapists are on familiar ground when clients seek outpatient treatment for such well-formulated problems as specific phobias or panic disorder. As we have seen, well-researched treatment packages are available for many disorders and can be confidently recommended as the "state of the art" treatment. But cognitive-behavior therapists are also in their element when clients present with significant distress that does not always map conveniently onto conventional diagnostic categories, and that does not point clearly to one particular type of resolution.

Take the example of a client whose chief concern was a seemingly impossible conflict between following his dream of a career in the creative arts on the one hand and maintaining harmony in his family on the other. His wife had given him an ultimatum: Give up this life of poverty as a struggling artist and take a conventional job with a dependable salary or say goodbye to the kids and me! This client's clinician had to confront some challenging issues. For one thing, specific guidelines from the clinical research literature on how to proceed with this particular problem were notably absent. In any event, the precise goals of treatment would have to be established with the client before any focused intervention could be pursued. One goal could be for him to learn to cope more smoothly with the marital conflict over his career choice. Another could be for him to give up his dream and learn to be philosophical about adopting a more conventional work and family life. Yet another could be for him to learn to be more assertive with his wife and to insist upon maintaining a healthy degree of personal autonomy within the relationship. Cognitive-behavior therapists prefer an egalitarian relationship in which client and therapist carefully review the options and decide jointly upon goals and procedures. In some cases, like this one, negotiating the goals can constitute a significant part of the therapeutic work.

A potentially helpful framework for this client's therapy could be *rational-emotive behavior therapy.* The rationale would be that, whichever direction the client takes, there is likely to be a particular set of advantages and disadvantages. For example, leaving his wife and children would be decidedly negative in removing his family life, but also positive in leaving him free to pursue his vocation without criticism from others. Giving up his artwork would be negative in removing a significant area of fulfilment in his life, but also positive in reducing marital discord. Going on with the uneasy status quo also has its pluses and minuses. And so on. Using the rational-emotive approach, the therapist could ask the client to consider whether it might be unduly and unhelpfully perfectionistic to seek the one right answer to his problems. It could help him to reflect on the idea that, whatever choice he makes, he could probably learn to live without distressing himself. Arguably, no contemplated outcome would have to be awful or insupportable. Using Ellis's ideas flexibly can be a helpful resource in a case such as this one in which there is no obvious area of psychopathology to be eliminated by the faithful application of focused, empirically supported interventions.

In other cases, the client presents a variety of issues with no obvious focus. For example, another client was a single mother who had had to give up her paraprofessional job because of a physical injury. Her husband was in jail for abusing her physically. Her preschool child had special health-care needs. She and her child were living in subsidized housing in a high-crime area. Assisted by special state-funded programs, she was pursuing an associate's degree at the community college. Her concerns included a high level of objective stress from the varied demands on her as mother, student, and recipient of various state-sponsored services; problems with assertiveness in dealing with exploitive and unreasonable neighbors; and difficulties encountered with her academic work because the only time she could study was when her child eventually went to sleep quite late at night.

Cognitive-behavior therapists intervene in such cases by maintaining their empirical, problem-oriented focus and by implementing specific treatment techniques creatively and inventively. One convenient framework for holistic therapy is *multimodal therapy* (Lazarus, 1976, 1995), in which the therapist can use the BASIC I.D. elements as a checklist of areas in which the client would like to increase or decrease particular aspects of functioning. For example, the single mother's modality profile could look like this:

Behavior: Increase my study time and improve my study skills by setting aside particular times for school work each day while Johnny is in daycare. Decrease biting my fingernails and quit or reduce cigarette smoking.

Affect: Decrease anxiety, worry, occasional depressive mood. Reduce guilt over not visiting husband in jail.

Sensation: Increase time spent in genuine relaxation. Decrease headaches, pain from injured shoulder by seeking and following medical advice.

Imagery: Increase my sense of myself as a survivor, a winner who can overcome obstacles and get my associate's degree despite all these problems. Decrease morbid dreams and fantasies of backsliding into letting my husband and parents run my life for me.

Cognition: Increase positive thoughts and successful coping attitudes. Decrease evaluations of myself as a loser who can never make it because the cards are stacked against me.

Interpersonal: Increase appropriate self-assertion with my needy neighbors who keep asking me for rides to town, to babysit for them, and to buy them alcohol and cigarettes.

Drugs/Diet: Increase compliance with physical therapist's recommendations. Decrease smoking, eating junk food.

Pioneering behavior therapists like Joseph Wolpe viewed the enterprise not as a fixed set of procedures but as a flexible clinical approach, focused on the individual client and based upon a unique behavioral assessment. Recently, many clinical psychologists have stressed the importance of validated, empirically supported interventions for particular disorders, parallel to the endorsement of specific pharmaceutical products for the treatment of given disorders by the Food and Drug Administration in the United States (Crits-Christoff, Frank, Chambless, Brody, & Karp, 1995). There is a potential conflict here between two defensible viewpoints. One is that it is inappropriate and unethical for psychologists to offer clients treatments that have not been endorsed as safe and effective, according to appropriate standards of scientific verification. The other is that it is inappropriate and unethical to pre-scribe a course of treatment to a client purely because he or she has a given disorder, ignor-ing elements of his or her personal uniqueness that may have a valid bearing on treatment selection.

The potential conflict here could be addressed by (1) identifying treatments that have been shown effective for clients sharing certain characteristics (such as the disorder they have), (2) assessing the characteristics of each client so as to determine which of the research-validated interventions shows the greatest promise of success, and (3) carefully monitoring therapeutic progress, abandoning interventions that are not working and intro-ducing others as necessary. The problem is that cognitive-behavior therapists do not yet have all the data they need to make such decisions in every case. When a client presents a set of issues for which research has not yet identified suitable treatments, the clinician can choose either not to work with the client, or to be inventive and use cognitive-behavioral principles to design a suitable intervention. The latter option would be preferred by many psychologists working in this tradition. If behavior therapists like Isaac Marks (exposure in vivo) and Edna Foa (trauma processing) had not experimented with new techniques when confronted by relatively unresearched problems, the cognitive-behavioral orientation would probably not exist (Thorpe & Olson, 1997).

BOX **13.1**

Focus on Ethics: The Return of the "Bait-and-Switch" Tactic in Psychotherapy

Consider the following clinical scenario:

> A client consults a cognitive-behavioral psychologist for treatment of a specific phobia of spiders. Treatment proceeds successfully, with a "textbook case" outcome in which the client's phobia is entirely relieved after 30 sessions. Now the client mentions that she has having marital difficulties that she believes are related to some long-standing issues she has in making long-term commitments. She and the psychologist negotiate a revised treatment plan for further weekly therapy sessions with the goal of improving her marriage and resolving her long-term concerns. They agree to review the new treatment plan in one year's time.

A situation similar to this arises fairly frequently in the practice of cognitive-behavior therapy. Sometimes clients are not ready to raise their most difficult concerns with their therapists at the outset and may only feel comfortable doing so after the therapist has earned their trust over a period of many weeks. Sometimes clients may be so impressed with the progress they have made on the problems they presented initially that, for the first time, they begin to hope that seemingly more intractable concerns could also be addressed successfully. Presumably, there is nothing wrong with a client and therapist partnership renegotiating their treatment contract by mutual consent.

But psychologists do need to be aware of the "bait-and-switch" hazard that we discussed in Box 11.1 and ready to address the possibility that under the circumstances of this scenario a client may feel pressured into a longer-term professional relationship than they had contemplated. When a psychologist doubts his or her objectivity in this regard, it is always possible to refer the client to a colleague for a second opinion as to the desirability of an extended treatment plan or to suggest to the client that it may in any event be helpful to make a fresh start with another therapist. On the other hand, if the client's request for further treatment is indeed based upon his or her satisfaction with the therapist and with the work successfully accomplished to date, it may not serve the client well to give the appearance of abandoning him or her by making a new referral. The point is that psychologists are ethically bound to be aware of such potential problems and to make their professional decisions carefully after due consideration of ethical directives.

PART FOUR

Specializations in Clinical Psychology

CHAPTER

14 Clinical Neuropsychology

Dr. P. was a well-liked teacher at a local school of music who consulted with an ophthalmologist when he experienced some peculiar visual difficulties. Dr. P. complained of frequently being unable to recognize his students. Actually, to be more precise, Dr. P. had difficulty recognizing his students when he first saw them, particularly when they were sitting still. However, he would immediately identify them when they spoke. The ophthalmologist could find nothing wrong with Dr. P.'s eyes or vision, in the conventional sense. Nonetheless, he referred Dr. P. on to a neurologist, Dr. Oliver Sacks. In his initial meeting with Dr. P., Dr. Sacks conducted a routine neurological exam, which was essentially normal. However, much to Dr. Sacks's amazement, when leaving his office, Dr. P. "reached out and took hold of his wife's head, tried to lift it off, to put it on. He had apparently mistaken his wife for a hat!" (Sacks, 1970, p. 11).

Dr. P. suffered from a relatively rare form of a neurological condition called *prosopagnosia,* or the inability to recognize faces. In his description of the case, *The Man Who Mistook His Wife for a Hat* (Sacks, 1970), Oliver Sacks details some of the difficulties Dr. P. had putting visual information together to construct, or perceive, a whole object. For example, when presented with a rose and asked what it is, Dr. P. examined the flower and said, "About six inches in length. . . . A convoluted red form with a linear green attachment" (p. 13). Only after he is encouraged smell the object does Dr. P show recognition, exclaiming, "Beautiful . . . an early rose. What a heavenly smell!" (p. 14). He could see all the pieces, but could not put together the whole.

The complex and fascinating relationship between brain functioning and behavior is the purview of *neuropsychology* (Kolb & Whishaw, 1996). Basic neuropsychology is "the science of human behavior based on the function of the human brain" (Kolb & Whishaw, 1996, p. 3). Clinical neuropsychologists work with clients who have experienced impairment in brain functioning. A wide variety of factors can produce brain dysfunction, including head injury, exposure to toxic chemicals, infectious diseases, genetic abnormalities, systemic diseases (e.g., cancer, vascular diseases), nutritional deprivation, and progressive disorders of the central nervous system such as Alzheimer's disease or multiple sclerosis (Goldstein, 1998). Neuropsychologists study the effects of these brain conditions, help identify types of brain dysfunction based upon their behavioral correlates, assess the consequences of brain injury, and help clients to recover from, and cope with, brain impairment.

Much of the work of clinical neuropsychologists is built upon an understanding of the relationship between specific areas of the brain and specific psychological functions. The discovery of *localization of function* in the brain set the stage for the development of neuropsychology. In the following pages, we present a brief history of the discovery of brain-behavior relationships. The reader interested in a more detailed history should see Chapter 1 of Kolb and Whishaw's (1996) *Fundamentals of Human Neuropsychology* or Hartlage (1987) *Neuropsychology: Definition and History,* upon which the following brief history is based.

Discovering Brain-Behavior Relationships:
A Brief History

Human beings' beliefs about the brain and its relationship to thinking and behavior has an interesting—and with the benefit of hindsight, at times humorous—history. As early as the fifth century B.C., Alcmaeon of Croton hypothesized that the brain was the seat of mental activity and had a controlling influence over human behavior. However, later philosophers, notably Aristotle (384–322 B.C.), suggested that the heart was the source of mental processes (he reasoned that the brain served as a radiator whose function was to cool the blood). The Aristotelian view held sway among intellectuals for a few hundred years until the great Roman physician Galen (A.D. 122–c. 199) vigorously attacked them. Galen had served as surgeon for the gladiators for five years before becoming the leading physician in Rome. Through his observations of head-injured gladiators, and his dissections of human corpses, he concluded that the brain was the central organ of human behavior.

Recognition of the brain's importance in regulating behavior is not, of course, the same as understanding how the brain controls behavior. For example, although Galen saw the brain as central, his view of how the brain regulated behavior was misguided. Galen proposed that the internal open spaces in the brain (the ventricles) housed the psychic spirits that controlled behavior. Galen's ventricular hypothesis was the prevailing view for well over a thousand years before it was discredited by Andreas Vesalius (1514–1564). Vesalius showed that the ventricles of animals and humans were about the same size. He concluded, therefore, that since humans have the largest brains (relative to their size), it must be the brain matter and not the ventricles that are important in mental processes.

The beginning of modern thinking about the relationship between the brain and behavior can be traced back the nineteenth century. Franz Joseph Gall (1758–1828) and Johan Casper Spurzheim (1776–1832) proposed their theory of *phrenology* in the early nineteenth century. According to phrenological theory, bumps and depressions in the skull indicated the size of the underlying brain area. Larger specific brain areas, according to the theory, resulted in bumps in the skull above those areas. Conversely, poorly developed areas of the brain resulted in depressions in the overlying skull. Gall and Spurzheim believed that bumps and depressions in various areas of the skull correlated with different mental functions (e.g., language, time perception, ability to do calculations) and personality traits (e.g., cautiousness, secretiveness, self-esteem). Scores of phrenology maps were produced by Gall and Spurzheim and their followers, each map seemingly more complex than its predecessor

Phrenology, although widely popular for a short period of time, was quickly dismissed by serious scholars. However, it would be unfair to dismiss the contributions Gall and Spurzheim made to neurology and our understanding of brain behavior relationships. They proposed that the brain's cortex is made up of functional cells that connect to the brain stem and spinal cord, showing anatomically how the cortex could control muscles and hence overt behavior through its connections to the spinal cord. They also pointed out how the two brain hemispheres could communicate with one another via the corpus callosum. Finally, and most important for our purposes, Gall and Spurzheim's phrenological theory proposed that specific areas of the brain's cortex serve specific functions.

The question of whether the brain was localized with respect to function or operated uniformly was hotly debated throughout the nineteenth century. One of the most important pieces of clinical evidence supportive of the localization view was produced by Paul Broca (1824–1880). In 1861, Broca received a patient who had lost his ability to speak and had some right-sided paralysis but otherwise appeared to be intelligent and normal. The patient (referred to as "Tan" because that was the only utterance he could make) died on April 17, 1861, and Broca performed the autopsy. He discovered that Tan had a lesion on the left frontal lobe. By 1863, Broca had studied eight additional patients who had lost the ability to speak. In every case, they were found to have a lesion on the third gyrus of the left frontal lobe. Although Broca was not the first to suggest the localization of specific functions to specific areas of the brain, his standing in scientific community (he was a respected physician and founder of the Anthropological Society of Paris) provided considerable clout to the theory of localization of function. The posterior portion of the left frontal lobe is still referred to as *Broca's area* and the inability to speak associated with damage to that area is called *Broca's aphasia.*

Besides Broca, Carl Wernicke (1848–1904) is the name most frequently associated with the localization of function viewpoint. In actuality Wernicke disagreed with the strict localization stance and his findings and writings helped to develop the complexity of localization theory. Wernicke observed patients who suffered with aphasia (impairment in the ability to speak) but who did not have damage to Broca's area. Rather, these patients had lesions in the temporal lobe, posterior to (or behind) Broca's area. Patient's with *Wernicke's aphasia,* as it has come to be called, showed a different form of aphasia. They could speak but what they said was confused and made little or no sense. In contrast, patients with Broca's aphasia could not speak. Wernicke developed a model of how language is produced. Put quite crudely, the brain organizes what speech sounds it wants to make in Wernicke's area, then this information is sent via cortical pathways to Broca's area, where the speech movements are programmed. Wernicke's theorizing represented the first successful attempt to map out the brain areas involved in a complicated human function.

Broca and Wernicke contributed to our understanding of brain behavior relationships by working backward. They examined brain-impaired patients and deduced what functions specific areas of the cortex were responsible for based upon what the patient could not do (e.g., if a patient could not produce speech and it was subsequently discovered that he had a lesion in Broca's area, then Broca's area must be involved in speech production). Another way of looking at the relationship between brain anatomy and brain function would be to stimulate specific areas of the brain and observe what behaviors follow. A landmark paper on brain stimulation was published in 1870 by Gustav Theodor Fritsch (1838–1929) and Eduard Hitzig (1838–1907). By applying electrical stimulation to the cortex of dogs, they showed that specific areas of the cortex were responsible for motor activity and other areas were responsible for sensory experiences. Cortical stimulation studies provided further evidence that specific areas of the brain were involved in specific mental and physical functions.

Before ending our discussion of important nineteenth- and early twentieth-century figures in neuropsychology, one additional figure deserves attention. John Hughlings-Jackson (1835–1911) was a neurologist who proposed that the nervous system was organized hierarchically. Lower areas of the nervous system (e.g., the spinal cord) were influenced by higher levels (e.g., the brain stem), which were influenced by higher levels (e.g., the cortex). Hughling-Jackson's ideas helped to organize our understanding of the role the cortex plays in organizing purposeful behavior. From his hierarchical perspective, it could be understood how a variety of areas of the brain are involved in specific functions. To take language as an example, while language is primarily a left-hemisphere function, a person with right-hemisphere damage would likely have difficulty describing spatial concepts, since spatial organization is a right hemisphere function.

Development of Clinical Neuropsychology

While its roots lie in the nineteenth century, clinical neuropsychology is generally considered to have developed in the second half of the twentieth century. In the first half of the twentieth century, psychologists made their first forays into the area by developing tests that could be used to distinguish patients with brain damage from others, usually psychiatric patients. There was little attention paid to identifying the types of brain damage or the specific areas of the brain affected. Instead the focus was on identifying "brain damage" or "organic brain damage" or "organicity." Single tests such as the Bender-Gestalt and the Benton Visual Retention Test were developed for this purpose.

In the same way that World War II impacted the development of clinical psychology (see Chapter 2), it was a huge spur to the development of clinical neuropsychology. The large number of head-injured soldiers and veterans presented a need for careful assessment and treatment as well as a steady source of subjects to study. With much of the training of clinical psychologists occurring at VA hospitals, it is understandable that many of these enthusiastic young professionals developed a significant interest in neuropsychology.

Perhaps the two most important figures in the early development of U.S. clinical neuropsychology were Ward Halstead (1908–1969) and Ralph Reitan (b. 1922). Halstead published a monograph in 1947 in which he described his observations of several hundred people on a battery of very specific tests. Halstead was able to identify reliable differences between patients who were later identified as having brain lesions and normal controls. Ralph Reitan was a student of Halstead's who took his tests and, over the next two decades, systematically related performance on specific tasks to specific areas and types of cerebral damage, including temporal lobe damage, cerebrovascular lesions, and others. Reitan added to Halstead's original battery with additional tests to obtain greater comprehensiveness. In addition, he related specific patterns of test scores to specific functional deficits such as aphasias, deficits in abstract thinking, and specific motor functions (summarized by Hartlage, 1987).

Ralph Reitan had a tremendous impact upon the developing field of clinical neuropsychology. The approach he took to neuropsychological assessment set the standard for the emerging discipline. In addition, he served as mentor to a series of researchers and clinicians who came to work with him at his Indiana University Medical Center Laboratory who went on to other hospitals and universities and spread the word about Reitan's approach to neuropsychology. The Halstead-Reitan battery was the standard in neuropsychological assessment for nearly two decades.

In the mid-1970s an alternative to the Halstead-Reitan battery was developed based upon neurological examination procedures used by the Russian neurologist A. R. Luria (Luria, 1980). Some of Luria's writings had been translated into English in the 1960s. Her curiosity piqued by what she read, Anne-Lise Christensen traveled to the Soviet Union and studied with Luria. Upon her return, Christensen published *Luria's Neuropsychological Investigation* in 1975 along with a manual and kit containing some of the test materials used by Luria. Charles G. Golden and his collaborators used these materials to develop a scoring system, norms as well as some information regarding the tests reliability and validity. The Luria-Nebraska Neuropsychological Battery was published in 1980 (Golden, Hammeke, & Purisch, 1980).

As neuropsychology developed, many clinicians moved away from the use of standardized batteries of neuropsychological tests. Instead, these clinicians chose from a variety of tests and tailored the assessment to the diagnostic issues or the presenting problems unique to each patient. This approach to neuropsychological assessment is probably best exemplified by Murial Lezak (1995). Later in this chapter we will discuss the different approaches to neuropsychological assessment in more detail.

The 1980s and 1990s saw tremendous growth in neuropsychology. While the original neuropsychologists worked in hospitals and university medical settings, increasingly clinical neuropsychologists have moved into independent practice (Putman & DeLuca, 1990). The types of professional activities clinical neuropsychologists pursue have expanded to include not only research and clinical assessment but also forensic work and cognitive rehabilitation. The growth of the field has spurred development of a definition of clinical neuropsychology as well as the proliferation of voluntary certifications for neuropsychologists (see below).

Before further discussion of contemporary clinical neuropsychology, it is important for the reader to have a rudimentary knowledge of the workings of the human brain as well as some understanding of the various ways in which brain functioning can be impaired. We turn our attention to these topics.

A Map of the Human Brain: Structure and Function

Given the incredible power and sophistication of the human brain, one might expect it to be a more awe-inspiring organ to look at. In reality, the human brain is a pretty pathetic sight. Wrinkled and old-looking, the human brain weighs about 1450 grams and resembles a large prune (Drubach, 2000). Looking at the brain from the outside, one can easily see that it consists of two nearly identical halves or hemispheres. Each hemisphere is made up of four lobes, *frontal, temporal, parietal,* and *occipital* (see Chapter 4, Figure 4.3). The outer covering of the brain is called the *cerebral cortex* or simply the *cortex.* Each lobe of the cortex is associated with different brain functions. (For a more detailed discussion of brain structures and functions, the interested reader should see Drubach, 2000, upon which much of the following discussion is based.)

The frontal lobes have a variety of functions and in a way are the most human of the cortices. They are responsible for initiating activity. When we walk, talk, make a lay-up, or play the piano, the signals that direct our muscles to do these actions originate in the frontal lobes. As we saw when we discussed Broca's area, the left frontal lobe is particularly important in directing human speech. Beyond spoken language, however, the left frontal lobes play an important role in directing any form of communication such as writing but also our so-called body language. Frontal lobes are very important in regulating our behavior. In fact, much of what we recognize as personality is mediated by the frontal lobes. The frontal lobes control how we react to the various stimuli that we are exposed to at any given moment. As you read this book, your frontal lobes are being presented with a variety of externally and internally generated stimuli. While reading this text, you may feel hungry or sleepy (hopefully not). You may hear music coming from down the hall and may have intrusive thoughts about other things you would rather be doing at this moment. Whether you close your book and go see where the music is coming from, slip into a daydream, or steadfastly persevere at mastering the material is controlled by your frontal lobes. Because of the importance of the frontal lobes in regulating human behavior, many of the activities associated with the frontal lobe are called *executive functions.*

When one or both of the frontal lobes are damaged, a variety of deficits can result. First, given the importance of these lobes in controlling movement, a person with damage to one frontal lobe will have difficulty moving his or her arms, legs, or facial muscles on the opposite side. If the damage is to the left side, the person likely will have difficulty speaking. He or she might understand what others say, but might not be able to initiate a response. People with frontal lobe damage often appear to lack drive or energy. They appear to have lost their motivation. Others may view them as lazy. Given this slowing down and lack of energy often seen in people with frontal lobe damage, surgeons have sometimes intentionally damaged patients' frontal lobes as a means of controlling their behavior. This procedure is called a frontal lobotomy. One person who had been extremely aggressive prior to a frontal lobotomy reported that he occasionally still thought about killing people, but he could not motivate the energy to do it any more (Drubach, 2000).

Frontal lobe functioning is extremely complex. While some individuals become placid following frontal lobe damage, others lose their sense of inhibition. Part of the functioning of the frontal lobes is to regulate our behavior. It is probably quite common for any of us to have an off-color thought or to take notice of someone we find sexually attractive. Some people with frontal lobe damage cannot help but express these thoughts or act on their impulses. A formerly quiet, conservative business executive who suffered frontal lobe damage shocked his colleagues by making sexually explicit comments at board meetings (Drubach, 2000).

In addition to problems with initiation and inhibition, people with frontal lobe damage often have difficulty planning or organizing their lives. Planning and problem solving are considered to be an executive function associated with the frontal lobes. Patients with damage to the frontal lobes have a difficult time shifting set. They tend to persist in a solution to a problem that has worked in the past but is no longer appropriate. Clinical neuropsychologists use specific tests to evaluate patients' ability to shift set from one problem solution to another. The Wisconsin Card Sorting Test (Heaton, 1981), for example, is sensitive to deficits in ability to shift set. In this test, patients are presented with a set of cards. One of four shapes appears on each card (triangle, circle, plus sign, star) in one of four colors (red, green, blue, yellow). Each card has one to four of the same shapes printed on it (e.g., two red circles, three blue triangles, one red star; see Figure 14.1). Patients must put the cards down in front of four stimulus cards based upon a rule they must figure out. There are, of course, three possible rules, match by color, match by shape, or match by number of shapes. Each time a card is placed the patient is informed whether it is correct (i.e., whether they followed the right rule). The trick is that the examiner changes the rule periodically throughout the test. Each time the subject must figure out what the new rule is. Patients with frontal lobe damage struggle with this task. They have a hard time shifting from one solution that had worked but no longer does to find the new correct solution. Given the frustration this test generates in some patients, we have heard it referred to as the Wisconsin torture test.

The parietal lobes are important in processing sensory information. The primary sensory cortex is located in the parietal lobes. The parietal lobes also play an important role in processing and understanding the sensory component of language. Working in conjunction with the temporal lobes, the parietal lobes are involved in processing language input. Probably the most noticeable deficit associated with the parietal lobes is loss of one's ability to detect tactile sensory stimuli. People with damage to the right parietal lobe may be unable to feel the left side of their bodies. In addition, patients with parietal damage may lose the capacity to understand spoken or written language.

The functions associated with the temporal lobes include processing auditory information, interpreting the meaning of language, learning, forming new memories, and regulating emotions. *Receptive aphasia* is a problem associated with left temporal lobe damage. Patients with this problem can speak perfectly well but cannot understand spoken language even when the speaker is themselves. Some people with damage to the temporal lobes have

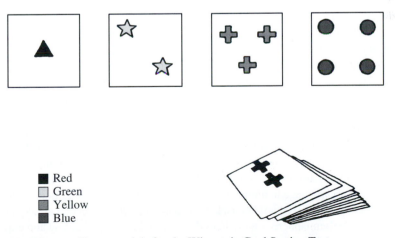

Red
Green
Yellow
Blue

FIGURE 14.1   Test materials for the Wisconsin Card Sorting Test.

Source: From *Neuropsychological Assessment* by Muriel Lezak, copyright © 1976 by Oxford University Press, Inc. Used by permission of Oxford University Press, Inc.

difficulty forming new memories. People who have temporal lobe epilepsy often have emotional disturbances such as severe anxiety, anger or rage attacks, or an uncomfortable déjà vu feeling.

The occipital lobes are responsible for processing visual information. The cells of the occipital lobe are highly specialized for responding to specific shapes, colors, velocities of movement, visual textures, and directions of lines (i.e., horizontal or vertical). All of these specific pieces of information are integrated in the visual cortex to form a meaningful image. Severe damage to the occipital lobes can cause *cortical blindness,* the eyes work perfectly well but the patient cannot see for lack of the brain area needed to interpret the visual stimuli. Less severe damage can result in a failure to recognize common objects. Dr. P., for example, suffered with prosopagnosia. A rare condition that results when a specific area of the occipital lobe is damaged is called *Anton's syndrome.* In this baffling disorder the patient is blind but does not realize it.

Below the cerebral cortex there are a myriad of other brain structures. The *thalamus,* for example, is an important relay station for information. The thalamus helps to select and organize information from the sensory organs before it is transmitted to other areas of the brain. The *basal ganglia* is the name of a group of brain structures including the *putamen* and *caudate nucleus.* Huntington's disease results from damage to the caudate nucleus and is manifested by a deterioration in mental functioning (dementia) and abrupt movements of the limbs. The *cerebellum* is a cauliflower-shaped body that sits at the back of the brain below the cortex. The cerebellum is important in coordinating body movements. People with damage to the cerebellum experience *cerebellar ataxia* (they are unsteady on their feet and have difficulty with coordination).

Before closing our brief discussion of the relationship between brain structure and brain function, let's take a look at some of the functions associated with the brain's two hemispheres. First, some basics: The brain and body have a contralateral relationship. In other words, the right side of the body is controlled by the left side of the brain and visa versa. The two hemispheres of the brain are not separate in most people. A large band of brain fibers called the *corpus callosum* connects the two hemispheres. Some patients with severe epilepsy have had this band of fibers cut, creating in essence two independent brains in the same individuals. Studies of these individuals are fascinating and have helped improve our understand of the characteristics of each hemisphere (see Lepore, Ptito, & Jasper, 1986). In a relatively rare condition called *agenesis of the corpus callosum,* this important structure never develops, resulting in an array of problems for the child (Stickles, Schilmoeller, & Schilmoeller, in press).

Although brain functioning is not so compartmentalized that complex functions such as language can be mapped to specific brain areas, each hemisphere of the brain does appear to be associated with different functions. Speech functioning, for example, is located in the left hemisphere in almost all right-handed people and most left-handers. Given the importance of spoken language to human functioning, the left hemisphere is sometimes called the dominant hemisphere. The left hemisphere also is associated with logical, sequential thinking.

The right hemisphere is more heavily involved in understanding and expressing emotions. People with right hemisphere damage have a harder time recognizing others' emotional expressions and in expressing emotions through facial expressions. Other evidence of the importance of the right hemisphere in emotional expression comes from studies that show that the left side of the face (controlled by the right hemisphere) is better at expressing emotions than is the right. While the left hemisphere controls language, the right is important for interpreting the emotional tone of spoken language. We understand what others say to us by the content of the words but also by the rhythm, pitch, and tempo they use. *Prosody* is the term used to refer to the stress, rhythm, and intonation that provides additional information about a spoken message (Walker, 1997). For example, the sentence "John is really fat" can be understood as a concrete (albeit unflattering) description of John, or it can be interpreted as a sarcastic comment about a very thin John, depending upon where the emphasis is placed. People with damage to the right hemisphere tend to interpret spoken words literally and miss more subtle information conveyed via the speaker's prosody. The right hemisphere is also involved in the processing of most aspects of musical information and is more adept at intuitive thinking.

Causes of Brain Dysfunction

As the discussion above illustrates, much of what we know about the relationship between brain structure and function has been learned by studying individuals who have suffered damage to the their brains. In the next section we review some of the more common causes of brain injury.

Trauma

Trauma to the head is so common in our society that it has been called a "silent epidemic." It has been estimated that someone in the United States suffers a head injury every 15 seconds, with about two million occurring annually (Smith, Barth, Diamond, & Giuliano, 1998). About 25 percent of head injuries are serious enough to require hospitalization. Young adult males are at the greatest risk for head injury (Sorenson & Kraus, 1991). In fact, head injury is the leading cause of death and disability among young Americans (Smith et al., 1998). The most common cause of head injury is motor vehicle accidents, followed by falls, and assaults. Sports and work-related injuries are also fairly common (Sorenson & Krause, 1991). A distinction is usually made between closed head injuries (blunt force to the head without perforation of the skull) and penetrating head injuries (open brain wounds that result from the perforation of the skull). The latter are associated with particularly high rates of mortality.

 Head traumas can damage the brain in a variety of ways. There can be tearing or bruising at the site of impact. However, the brain is not stationary in the skull. A sudden impact can cause the brain to move rapidly or rotate within the skull. It is this moving around of the brain inside the skull that causes diffuse brain damage. Think of how you are pushed backward when a car you are riding in quickly accelerates and then jerked forward if the car suddenly stops. That is what happens to the brain when a blunt object strikes the head with considerable force. This jarring about of the brain can cause lacerations or bruising as the brain strikes against the interior of the skull. In addition, there can be microscopic stretching or tearing of axons. This type of diffuse axonal injury may not be visible through the imaging techniques that have been developed to assess structural damage to the brain (e.g., computerized tomography or CT; Smith et al., 1998).

Cerebrovascular Disease

Cerebrovascular diseases can result in damage to blood vessels that leads to disruption of brain functioning. When someone suffers brain impairment as the result of interruption of cerebral circulation, it is commonly referred to as a stroke. Stroke is one of the most common causes of neurological damage in adults. Stroke is the third leading cause of death in Europe and the United States and the number one killer of adults in Japan and China (Mora & Bornstein, 1998). Stroke causes brain damage by suddenly interrupting blood flow to the affected area of the brain. Consequently, there is a lack of oxygen and nutrients, sometimes accompanied by a buildup of metabolic products that are normally removed in the blood.

Stroke may result from a variety of different forms of pathology. Infarctions result from blocking of blood vessels. Infarctions can develop as a consequence of *atherosclerosis,* a degenerative disease that involves the buildup of fatty deposits or atherosclerotic plaque within the walls of the arteries. Atherosclerosis causes arterial occlusions throughout the body, including those that provide blood to the brain. *Thromboembolic strokes* are caused by a blockage, or occlusion, due to the build up of tissue at a specific site in the blood vessels serving the brain. As the thrombus grows, it gradually cuts off blood flow to the effected area. In contrast, *embolic strokes* are due to arterial occlusion that is caused by an *embolus* (a hunk of atherosclerotic plaque or other debris) from somewhere else in the body that becomes stuck in a cerebral blood vessel. Emboli may be formed in a variety of ways but most commonly develop secondary to heart disease (Mora & Bornstein, 1998).

Besides occlusions of blood vessels serving the cerebral cortex, strokes can also be caused by bursting of blood vessels (Mora & Bornstein, 1998). Cerebral hemorrhage, or cerebrovascular bleeding, can occur anywhere in the brain. Sometimes the hemorrhage occurs when an *aneurysm* bursts. An aneurysm is a dilation (or ballooning) of the blood vessel. In other cases, the hemorrhage is due to a congenital abnormality of the vascular system that may have produced no symptoms throughout a person's life but bursts open in their later years.

Degenerative Diseases

There are a variety of degenerative diseases that affect brain functioning. These diseases are caused by degeneration of neurons in the central nervous system. Alzheimer's disease is probably the best-known example of a degenerative brain disorder. Other examples include Parkinson's disease, Pick's disease, and Huntington's chorea. In Alzheimer's disease there is a progressive degeneration of the cell bodies of neurons. As the disease progresses, overall brain size decreases and there is enlargement of the cerebral ventricles (Allen, Sprenkel, Heyman, Schrame, & Heffron, 1998). Alzheimer's disease is categorized as *cortical dementia* since the cerebral cortex is primarily affected, particularly early on in the disease. Initial symptoms include impairment in memory and intellectual functioning. The most pronounced memory disturbance involves encoding and storing new memories. However, as the disease progresses there is disturbance in memory retrieval. The losses tend to be retrograde— progressing backward in time so that newer memories are lost first while older, well-formed memories are intact. Patients experience significant difficulties in recognizing familiar faces and objects. Eventually, the disease affects speech and the ability to perform voluntary movements (the latter is referred to as *apraxia*).

In addition to the degenerative cortical dementias, such as Alzheimer's disease, there is another class of degenerating brain disorders that are sometimes referred to as *demyelinating disorders* (Allen et al., 1998). Multiple sclerosis is the best known example of a demyelinating disorder. Recall that the myelin sheath is a layer of fat cells that surround the axon of a neuron (see Chapter 4). In multiple sclerosis, lesions or plaques destroy the myelin surrounding groups of nerve cells. As a result, these cells cannot function efficiently. Nerve messages are blocked, distorted, or slowed (Allen et al., 1998). Multiple sclerosis is considered to be an autoimmune disease, since it is believed that the body's own immune system attacks the myelin cells, causing plaques.

Tumors

Tumors may affect brain functioning in one of three ways. Brain tumors develop in the brain tissue itself or the surrounding structures (e.g., meninges, blood vessels, or bone). Metastatic tumors spread to the brain from other parts of the body. Finally, the brain may be damaged indirectly by tumors elsewhere in the body (Berg, 1998). Tumors affect brain functioning by displacing brain tissue in the early stages. Cerebral tissue may be compressed by the growing tumor. The symptoms one experiences with a brain tumor depend upon its size, rate of growth, and location. As the tumor grows, more areas of the brain are affected and impairment in brain functioning increases.

Often brain tumors can be removed surgically. However, the surgery itself can result in damage to the brain. Some tumors cannot be safely removed surgically. Radiation treatment or chemotherapy are typically used to reduce or destroy these tumors.

Chronic Alcohol Abuse and Nutritional Deficits

Consumption of moderate amounts of alcohol is accepted in most societies and may be associated with some health benefits (Burke et al., 2001; Theobald, Bygren, Castensen, & Engfeldt, 2000). However, there is clear evidence that heavy consumption of alcohol over a long period of time is associated with damage to the brain (United States Department of Health and Human Services, 1997). Deficits in memory functioning and emotion regulation observed in chronic alcohol abusers have been linked to damage in specific brain structures. In addition, studies have documented deterioration of the cerebral cortex and damage to the cerebellum in long-term alcohol abusers.

Some very severe and chronic alcohol abusers exhibit a peculiar memory disturbance in which they are unable to form new memories. The first impression one has is that these patients appear to be neurologically intact. They can carry on a reasonable conversation and may tell witty stories. However, as one spends more time with them their problem with recent memory becomes more apparent. They may ask the same question over and over again or repeat the same story. This syndrome was first described by a Russian physician in the 1880s named S. S. Korsakoff and the disorder bears his name. In Korsakoff's syndrome, the patient demonstrates *anterograde amnesia* (the inability to form new memories). In addition, they tend to *confabulate* or make up stories to fill in the gaps in their recent memory. Korsakoff patients typically have no insight into their memory loss (Kolb & Whishaw, 1996). It is now known that Korsakoff's syndrome is due to a severe thiamin (vitamin B_1) deficiency that is the result of chronic intake of large quantities of alcohol and poor nutrition.

Clinical Neuropsychology as a Specialty Area

Clinical neuropsychology is a specialty area within professional psychology. It was formally recognized as a specialty by the American Psychological Association in 1996. The discipline represents an integration of clinical psychology and neuropsychology. Clinical neuropsychologists are professional psychologists trained in the science of brain-behavior relationships. They specialize in the application of assessment and intervention principles based upon the scientific study of human behavior across the life span as it relates to normal and abnormal functioning of the central nervous system (Hannay, 1998). Seven core domains of professional activity of clinical neuropsychologists have been delineated: assessment, intervention, consultation, supervision, research, consumer protection, and professional development (Hannay, 1998).

Division 40—Clinical Neuropsychology of the American Psychological Association defines a clinical neuropsychologist as follows:

> A Clinical Neuropsychologist is a professional psychologist who applies principles of assessment and intervention based upon the scientific study of human behavior as it relates to normal and abnormal functioning of the central nervous system. The Clinical Neuropsychologist is a doctoral-level psychology provider of diagnostic and intervention services who has demonstrated competence in the application of such principles for human welfare following:
> A. Successful completion of systematic didactic and experiential training in neuropsychology and neuroscience at a regionally accredited university.
> B. Two or more years of appropriate supervised training applying neuropsychological services in a clinical setting.
> C. Licensing and certification to provide psychological services to the public by laws or the state or province in which he or she practices.
> D. Review by one's peers as a test of these competencies.

Division 40 encourages clinical neuropsychologists to obtain the ABPP (see Chapter 1) Diploma in Clinical Neuropsychology since this provides the clearest evidence of competence (Division 40 Task Force on Education, Accreditation and Credentiality, 1989)

Clinical neuropsychologists work in general and psychiatric hospitals, private clinics, universities, schools, hospitals, community mental health centers, independent rehabilitation centers, and private practice (Putnam & DeLuca, 1990). In hospitals, they consult to neurology, psychiatry, or other medical services. In addition, they work as part of rehabilitation teams helping people who have suffered brain injuries to improve the quality of their lives. In a hospital setting, clinical neuropsychologists often work closely with neurologists integrating neuroimaging data (e.g., CT, MRI, or PET scans) with neuropsychological assessment findings to better understand patients. Clinical neuropsychologists teach, conduct research, and provide clinical services at universities affiliated with, or housed within, medical centers. For these clinical neuropsychologists, teaching may involve supervision or graduate and post-doctoral students in clinical neuropsychology, as well as medical students and residents. Clinical neuropsychologists in private practice do assessment and psychotherapy and may consult to schools or to courts. Forensic neuropsychologists are often called upon to testify in cases in which questions of whether a person has suffered brain damage or the extent of impairment caused by a brain injury are at issue.

Neuropsychological Assessment

The neuropsychological assessment is the backbone clinical neuropsychology. A neuropsychological assessment typically takes several hours to complete and involves administering, scoring, and interpreting a battery of specific neuropsychological tests. What is a neuropsychological test? Any test that is sensitive to the condition of the brain can be considered a neuropsychological test (Goldstein, 1998). In a good neuropsychological test, changes in brain functioning are reliably correlated with changes in test performance. By examining a client's performance on a variety of specific neuropsychological tests, inferences can be made about brain functioning.

The goal of the prototypical neuropsychological assessment is to specify in exquisite detail the cognitive functioning, including the functional deficits, of the client and to relate their functioning back to known brain systems (Goldstein, 1998). The typical areas of functioning covered in a neuropsychological assessment include general intellectual capacity, language, attention, abstract reasoning, memory, psychomotor speed and accuracy, visual-spatial skills, and visual, auditory, and tactile perception.

Traditionally, neuropsychologists have worked with brain-injured individuals. In the early years, neuropsychological assessment was used as a method of pinpointing what areas of the brain were affected by a brain injury. By examining areas of functional deficit, the neuropsychologist would work backwards to infer what areas of the brain were injured. With the invention of sophisticated imaging technologies for directly observing brain structure (e.g., CT, PET, and MRI scans), this goal for neuropsychological assessment is less important. Nonetheless, neuropsychological assessment of brain-damaged clients continues to be an essential function of the neuropsychologist. Knowing where brain damage is is not the same as knowing how it affects the patient's cognitive capacities. Neuropsychologists describe the functional deficits associated with the injury, document changes in functioning over time, and identify targets and methods for rehabilitative services. In addition, the neuropsychological assessment still has a role to play in identifying brain areas affected by injury since not all forms of brain injury (e.g., axonal stretching) are readily identified with imaging technologies. Neuropsychologists have expanded their work beyond brain-damaged individuals. Neuropsychological assessments have been used in research and clinical work with individuals with learning disabled clients (Rourke & Gates, 1981; Whishaw & Kolb, 1984), individuals with no known pathology (Gold, Berman, Randolph, Goldberg, & Weinberger, 1996), and normal aging (Goldstein & Nussbaum, 1996).

There are a variety of approaches to neuropsychological assessment but these can be organized into two general types: standard comprehensive neuropsychological test batteries and individualized test batteries (Goldstein, 1998). In addition to the neuropsychological tests, a comprehensive neuropsychological assessment also will include one or more measures of personality or psychopathology such as the MMPI-2 (see Chapter 8) and usually tests of academic achievement (see Chapter 7). In the following section we describe standard neuropsychological batteries. Later we discuss some of the individualized tests used to measure specific areas of functioning.

Comprehensive Batteries

The most widely used comprehensive neuropsychological test battery is the Halstead-Reitan (Reitan & Wolfson, 1985). Actually, there are several versions of the Halstead-Reitan battery but the differences among these tend to be minor (Goldstein, 1998). The core battery consists of about a dozen specific tests and takes from six to eight hours to administer. It is not uncommon for a specially trained technician to administer and score the tests, with the neuropsychologist interpreting the results and writing the report. Seven of the core tests are used to calculate an impairment index. There are normative data for brain-damaged respondents for each test. The impairment index is simply the proportion of tests in which the patient's scores is in the range or brain-damaged subjects. An impairment index of .5 or higher is indicative of impaired brain function (Reitan & Wolfson, 1985). See Table 14.1 for a brief description of several of the tests that make up the Halstead-Reitan battery.

The validity of the Halstead-Reitan battery has been examined in a variety of ways. First, early studies by Halstead (1947) and Reitan (1955) showed that the tests were useful in distinguishing brain-damaged from non-brain-damaged patients. As the field of neuropsychology has progressed, it has been important to show that neuropsychological batteries can be used to make more refined distinctions beyond simply identifying the presence or absence of brain damage. Several of the tests in the Halstead-Reitan have been shown to be useful in discriminating patients with left hemisphere damage from those with right hemisphere damage. Beyond this there are few studies that have examined more specific inferences that clinicians might draw from the test battery such as the localization of damage or the type of lesion (Goldstein, 1998).

The Luria-Nebraska Neuropsychological Battery is a more recently developed comprehensive test battery. The Luria-Nebraska consists of 269 items, each of which is scored on a 2- or 3-point scale (0 = normal performance, 1 = borderline performance, 2 = abnormal performance). Thus, the higher the score, the worse the performance. The 269 items are organized into eleven content scales: Motor, Rhythm, Tactile, Visual, Receptive Speech, Expressive Speech, Writing, Reading, Arithmetic, Memory, and Intellectual Processes. Each of the eleven scales can be administered individually and for each, raw scores are converted to T scores.

In addition to the eleven content scales, the developers of the Luria-Nebraska created three derived scales: the Pathognomic, Left Hemisphere, and Right Hemisphere scales. The Pathognomic scale is based upon items taken from throughout the test that are particularly sensitive to brain damage. The Left and Right Hemisphere scales are derived from the Motor and Tactile scales and were designed to detect damage localized to one or the other hemisphere.

When scoring the Luria-Nebraska, procedures have been developed to take into consideration subjects' age and education level. An alternative form of the Luria-Nebraska battery has been published (Golden, Purisch, & Hammeke, 1985) that allows for repeated assessment of the same subject. There is also a children's version of the test battery (Golden, 1981b).

TABLE 14.1   Description of Some Tests from the Halstead-Reitan Neuropsychological Test Battery

Category Test

This is a test of concept identification and abstract reasoning. The subject sits before a screen that presents various series of geometric forms and verbal or numerical stimuli. The subject must figure out the organizing principles that govern the various series and respond by flipping an appropriate switch. The subject is provided with feedback as to whether he or she has identified the correct principle. There are seven different principles to be discerned and the subject is told when one group ends and the next begins.

Tactile Performance Test

For this test, the subject is blindfolded and presented with a series of ten blocks that must be fitted into a formboard with spaces in shapes that match the blocks. The subject does the task first with the preferred hand, then with the nonpreferred hand, and finally with both hands. The blindfold is then removed and the subject is asked to draw the formboard.

The Seashore Rhythm Test

The subject is asked to listen to a series of thirty pairs of rhythmic beats and to judge whether the two sounds in each pair were the same or different. This test requires sustained attention to nonverbal auditory stimuli and the ability to perceive and compare rhythmic sequences.

Speech-Sounds Perception Test

Sixty spoken nonsense words that include the "ee" sound (e.g., *zeeks*) are presented to the subject via audiotape. He or she must identify the correct sound from four choices presented on the answer sheet. This test requires sustained attention, the ability to perceive spoken stimulus sounds, and the ability to relate sounds to visual stimuli.

Finger Tapping

As the name implies, in this test is designed to measure the subject's maximal tapping speed using the index finger of each hand. A specially calibrated apparatus is used so that the subject's response can be compared to normative data. Five 10-second trials are given to each hand. This test assesses fine-motor speed on both sides of the subject's body.

Trail Making Test

In the first part of this test the subject must connect a series of circles that are numbered 1 through 25 and are randomly scattered on a page. In part B, the circles contain both numbers (1 through 13) and letters (letters A through L) and the subject is to connect the circles alternating between numbers and letters (e.g., 1 to A, A to 2, 2 to B, and so on). Subjects are timed on both tasks. The task requires the ability to scan the page continuously to find the next number or letter in the sequence, the ability to shift sets from numbers only to alternating between numbers and letter, and the ability to work under the pressure of time. This test is very sensitive to brain impairment (Reitan & Wolfson, 1985).

Validity studies of the Luria-Nebraska show that the test can discriminate between brain-damaged and normal subjects as well as brain-damaged subjects and those with schizophrenia. There have been several studies of specific neurological disorders such as chronic alcoholism, Huntington's disease, and learning disabilities that tend to support the discriminative validity of the test (reviewed by Goldstein, 1998).

Individualized Neuropsychological Assessment

While some neuropsychologists prefer to use standard comprehensive batteries, others opt for a more individualized approach to assessment in which the clinician chooses a set of specific tests based upon the purpose of the evaluation, the patient's history, and other available information (e.g., records of prior evaluations, imaging studies). This method is sometimes referred to as the hypothesis-testing, or process, approach since the neuropsychologist develops a set of hypotheses about the patient and then chooses a set of tests to examine the hypotheses.

Even when neuropsychologists use the individualized approach, there are certain areas of functioning that are typically covered in a comprehensive neuropsychological assessment. In the following section we discuss the basic areas covered in neuropsychological assessment and some of the tests that are used for assessment of these areas of cognitive and behavioral functioning.

General Intellectual Functioning.   General measures of intellectual functioning or IQ tests, such as the WAIS-III (see Chapter 7), are often included in neuropsychological test batteries. The inclusion of a measure of general intellectual functioning may seem antithetical to neuropsychological assessment since the goal of such an assessment is to identify strengths and deficits in specific types of cognitive functions. In fact, as our knowledge of neuropsychological functioning has increased, the validity of the concept of global intelligence has been called into question. The eminent neuropsychologist Muriel Lezak put it this way "neuropsychological studies have demonstrated that there is no general cognitive or intellectual function, but rather many discrete ones that work together so smoothly when the brain is intact that cognition is experienced as a single, seamless, attribute" (1995, p. 23).

Nonetheless, the assessment of general intellectual ability may serve one or more purposes in neuropsychological assessment. First, if the overall IQ is seen as a composite measure of the individual's abilities in a variety of domains, it can provide an anchoring point against which to measure areas of deficit. The summary IQ is considered a benchmark against which scores on more narrowly focused neuropsychological tests are compared (Moses, Pritchard, & Adams, 1997). The assumption is that an individual who obtains a high average IQ, for example, will score in the above average range on tests designed to measure specific cognitive abilities. There appears to be good evidence for the validity of this assumption (Horton, 1999; Tremont, Hoffman, Scott, & Adams, 1998). A second function of the overall IQ in a neuropsychological assessment is that it can provide information about the patient's functioning prior to the brain damage. Overall IQ scores are clearly impacted by brain injury. However, when using the Wechsler scale, for example, certain subtests have been identified that tend to remain stable in the face of brain injury. So-called "hold" subtests can be used to estimate premorbid (i.e., before the brain damage) levels of intellectual functioning.

Standardized tests of intelligence such as the Wechsler scales or the Stanford-Binet are typically used to assess global intellectual functioning. The Wechsler scales may be particularly useful for this purpose since these scales have been studied extensively with a variety of populations and a great deal is known about the sensitivity of these scales to various forms of disease and intervention (see, for example, McCaffrey, Duff, & Westervelt, 2000). In some cases it is not possible to administer the entire Wechsler intelligence scale in order to obtain an estimate of general intelligence. Some neuropsychologists will use certain sub-tests of the WAIS-III, for example, to estimate IQ. The Information, Comprehension, and Vocabulary subtests are often used since these tests appear to be relatively resistant to brain injury. An abbreviated version of the Wechsler scale for adults, the Wechsler Abbreviated Scale of Intelligence (WASI), was published in 1999 and may be used for estimating full-scale IQ (Psychological Corporation, 1999).

Memory Functioning.   Memory, like intelligence, is not a unitary construct. There are, in fact, many components to memory functioning or many memory systems. Memory involves acquiring information, organizing it, storing it, maintaining it in storage over some length of time and retrieving it. Memory functioning is sensitive to brain impairment. However, some forms of brain injury leave certain memory functions intact but devastate others. In earlier stages of Alzheimer's disease, for example, patients may have difficulty remembering the name of someone whom they met an hour earlier but can provide vividly detailed descriptions of people they knew when they were young adults.

There are a multitude of neuropsychological tests of memory functioning including many tests that were developed for measuring one or more specific aspects of memory and others that are designed to tap into many different components of memory. We will describe a small sample of memory tests. The interested reader should see Lezak (1995), particularly Chapters 11 and 12, for a comprehensive review of tests of memory.

The Auditory-Verbal Learning Test (Rey, 1959) is a test of immediate memory span and provides information about the patient's "learning curve" over repeated trials. Examiners read a list of fifteen words to subjects, who are to remember as many as possible. After the list is read, the subjects say as many words as they can recall. The list is read again and subjects are asked to say back as many words as they can, including the ones they recalled the first time. This procedure is repeated for a total of five trials. The subjects are then presented with a second list of fifteen words and asked to recall as many as possible. Subjects are then asked to recall as many words as they can from the first list. After a 30-minute delay, subjects are asked again to recall as many words as they can from the first list. The introduction of the second list provides for an opportunity to see how prone the subject is to proactive and retroactive interference. The delayed recall provides information about subjects' ability to retrieve information from long-term memory.

The Auditory-Verbal Learning Test provides information about how subjects handle verbal information. Memory for nonverbal information involves some different neural pathways and should be looked at in its own right. Several tests of memory for visual information have been developed. In the Graham-Kendall Memory-for-Designs Test (Graham & Kendall, 1960) the subject is shown a series of fifteen geometric designs, one at a time, for 5 seconds each. Subjects draw what they can recall immediately after each exposure. Figure 14.2 shows the Memory-for-Designs reproductions produced by a 39-year-old minister who sustained a severe concussion in a car accident after which he was in a coma for 16 days about a year before the assessment. The quality of the lines, the placement of the drawings, and the handling of erasures are all types of errors commonly seen in individuals who have sustained brain injury.

David Wechsler developed a comprehensive battery of tests to assess memory functioning in the 1940s (Wechsler, 1945). The Wechsler Memory Scale (WMS) has been

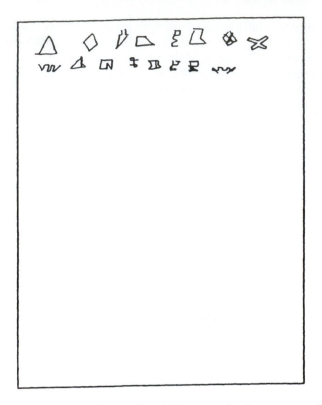

FIGURE 14.2   Graham-Kendall Memory-for-Designs reproduction produced by a 39-year-old minister one year after suffering a severe concussion in a car accident.

Source: From *Neuropsychological Assessment* by Muriel Lezak, copyright © 1976 by Oxford University Press, Inc. Used by permission of Oxford University Press, Inc.

through a series of revisions with the most recent version—the WMS-III—appearing in 1997. The WMS-III consists of 17 subtests, 10 primary and 7 optional, that cover most aspects of memory functioning by evaluating knowledge of personal and current information, immediate and delayed recall of verbal and visual information, learning pairs of words, recalling information from pictures, learning word lists, and recalling information from a brief story. The WMS-III yields composite scores for Immediate Memory, General (or Delayed) Memory, and Working Memory. The test is normed for use with people ages 16 to 89. The technical manual includes extensive information about the scale's reliability and validity.

Abstract Reasoning.   Individuals with some forms of brain damage have difficulty thinking abstractly. They tend to approach problems in an extremely concrete fashion. The Wisconsin Card Sorting Test described earlier is used to assess abstract or conceptual thinking. The subject must discern the rule governing card placement. Subjects' performance on some of the subtests of the WAIS-III can be used to examine abstract thinking as well. Concrete thinking can be seen in subjects' responses on Similarities (e.g., Q: "How are a dog and a cow alike?" A: "They both have four legs.") or on Picture Completion (e.g., when shown a picture of a rowboat without one oarlock and asked what is missing, a concrete response would be "A person in the boat") (Lezak, 1995).

Visual-Perceptual Functioning. Human beings are constantly processing visual information. We must orient ourselves in space, recognize and classify objects, judge distances between ourselves and objects in our visual field, and many others tasks. Many of these visual-perceptual processes occur automatically and outside of our awareness. There have been a variety of neuropsychological tests developed to examine visual-perceptual functioning. Some of the tasks involve little or no physical manipulation of the test material so that problems with motor functioning do not interfere with test performance. Others tasks involve drawing or manipulating objects in space. In the Hooper Visual Organization Test (Hooper, 1983), participants are presented with line drawings of familiar objects (e.g., fish, table, saw). In the drawing, the objects have been dissembled into pieces much like a puzzle. The subject is asked what object is represented in the picture. To perform well, the subjects must mentally rotate the pieces of the drawing to reassemble and recognize the object. A well-known test of visual-perceptual and motor functioning is the Bender Visual Motor Gestalt Test (Bender, 1938). In this test the participant is presented with nine geometric figures one at a time and asked to reproduce each figure while looking at it. This test is a very popular screening measure for problems in visual-perceptual functioning.

Verbal Language Functioning. There are a variety of disorders of verbal functioning that can appear in individuals with brain impairment. The three most prominent types are the *aphasias* (difficulties in verbal comprehension and production), the *dysarthrias* (difficulties with articulation), and *apraxias* of speech (difficulties in the execution of speech tasks). The production and comprehension of spoken language can be disrupted in a variety of ways. Once again a whole host of neuropsychological tests of language functioning have been developed (see Lezak, 1995; Chapter 13 for a review). In these tests subjects are asked to repeat words, phrases, or sentences, to name familiar objects, to follow simple instructions, or to tell stories. In tests of receptive language, subjects point to pictures that correspond with words presented by the examiner.

Other Areas. In addition to those described above, neuropsychologist may choose to assess other areas of cognitive or psychological functioning. Lezak (1995) includes all of the areas already mentioned as well as tests of *attention* (e.g., Digit Symbol, or Trails-Making Test), *academic skills* (e.g., sections from standard achievement batteries; see Chapter 7), *construction* (e.g., Block Design or drawing tests), *motor ability* (e.g., Finger Tapping) and one or more tests of *emotional status* (e.g., Symptom Check List-90-R) in her standard neuropsychological battery.

Putting It All Together

If the previous discussion leaves you with the impression that neuropsychological assessment involves administering and scoring tests, then simply looking at the scores to determine what areas of the brain are damaged, we have given you the wrong impression. A wide array of factors besides brain impairment can influence subjects' performance on neuropsychological tests. The neuropsychologist must evaluate the evidence as a whole, in the context of the patient's personal history and current circumstances, before inferences about specific areas of brain impairment can be made with any validity.

One factor that needs to be considered in evaluating subjects' performance is their level of motivation. Is the patient putting forth his or her best effort? Is he or she interested? Does the person care about how he or she is doing? Simply not trying one's hardest can distort the picture painted by one's performance on neuropsychological tests. How to interpret a lack of motivation on the patient's part can be tricky. Loss of motivation is a characteristic of patients with damage to the limbic system or prefrontal areas of the brain (Lezak, 1995). A lack of effort may be a confounding factor when interpreting test results or it may be evidence of brain damage in and of itself.

Neuropsychological assessments typically take several hours to complete. Fatigue, therefore, is a factor that can affect test performance. As with a loss of motivation, fatigue also can be a symptom of brain injury. Patients who have suffered brain damage relatively recently are particularly vulnerable to fatigue (Lezak, 1995). Examiners need to consider other causes of fatigue as well, however. Patients' physical health status and medications they may take can cause fatigue and influence test results in other ways. Neuropsychologists need to be aware of their patients' health conditions and medications and understand how these may be impacting the patients' performance.

Patients' emotional state, including the presence of mental health conditions, can influence test scores. Anxiety and depression can impair patients' ability to maintain concentration. Depressed mood can also undercut subjects' motivation to perform on tests. More severe conditions such as schizophrenia and bipolar disorder also affect test performance. We are reminded of an experience one of us had during his pre-doctoral internship. A patient was referred for neuropsychological assessment by an opthamologist because of very unusual responses the patient had during an eye examination. After several hours of neuropsychological testing had produced strikingly uneven test performance, the intern asked his supervisor to observe further testing. After about one-half hour of observing, the supervisor interrupted testing to ask the patient if he had ever felt that other people were stealing his thoughts. "Yes!" the patient replied and explained how he had written a popular song but that the lyrics had be stolen out his head. The patient was experiencing a first psychotic break and was later diagnosed with schizophrenia. In order to correctly understand this patient, the supervisor had to shift from thinking about the localized brain functions that specific tests were supposedly examining and look at the whole picture of the patient. A great deal, in fact, is known about how patients with schizophrenia perform on neuropsychological tests (Goldstein, 1998).

Neuropsychological test results need to be interpreted in the context of the patient's life experience. In a perfect world, any patient who suffers a brain injury would have had a comprehensive neuropsychological assessment prior to the accident so that deficits in cognitive functioning could easily be identified by comparing pre-injury and post-injury performance on the same tests. Unfortunately, this rarely occurs. Clinical neuropsychologists must estimate their patients' level of premorbid functioning based upon case history and the pattern of performance across tests. Educational level and occupational achievement are two factors that are considered when estimating pre-injury abilities.

One other factor that can influence neuropsychological test performance deserves mentioning—*malingering,* that is, subjects who purposely perform poorly on tests in order to appear as if they have suffered a brain injury. Hundreds of thousands, or even millions, of dollars are sometimes at stake for patients who claim to have suffered brain damage as the result of an accident. They may be motivated to perform poorly on testing. Other individuals appear to be motivated to appear impaired simply so that they can adopt the societal role of patient. Methods of assessing whether subjects have "faked bad" are built into some psychological tests (e.g., MMPI-2). Often neuropsychologists must rely upon their knowledge of brain-behavior relationships to discern a pattern of faking bad across a series of neuropsychological test scores.

Box 14.1 contains an example report of a neuropsychological evaluation. The report is based upon a real case which has be de-identified. The report was written by a board-certified clinical neuropsychologist (ABBP-CN) whose commentary about the case follows the report.

BOX 14.1

Neuropsychological Evaluation

PATIENT:	**FIRST NAME, LAST NAME,** male
DATE OF BIRTH:	mm-dd-yyyy (age 32)
DATE OF EVALUATION:	mm-dd-yyyy
DEMOGRAPHICS:	
Hand dominance:	Right
Education:	Years/grade level
Marital status:	Married
Occupation:	Insurance salesman
REFERRED BY:	**Dr. Practitioner**
Purpose:	Assess cognitive deficits, assist return to work

Background of referral: This patient was outside his motor vehicle, apparently checking some aspect of it, when he was struck by another vehicle. He sustained injuries to his pelvis, lung, and head. CT scan indicated contusions of both temporal lobes but worse on the left; because of cerebral edema, part of his left temporal lobe was excised. He was in a coma for about three weeks (partly drug-induced), a period of posttraumatic amnesia encompassing six to seven weeks, and in the hospital for two months. He received aggressive medical and rehabilitation services, and was discharged home. After discharge, he continued to receive outpatient rehabilitation in occupational therapy, physical therapy, and still attends speech therapy session twice a week. He has not resumed driving a motor vehicle.

The patient was alert and attentive, well-oriented and cooperative. He understood the nature and purpose of the evaluation. He understood questions, but had difficulty answering them because of significant expressive language deficits. His speech was logical and appropriate to the question, but was halting and somewhat telegraphic in nature. He used circumlocutory strategies, not always selecting the correct word, but the content appeared to be coherent and sensible. He could give only limited history or description of current functioning as a result and often looked to his wife for assistance. His mood appeared to be mildly depressed, but he demonstrated no unusual frustration or impatience with himself. He could appreciate humor. He appeared to be intense, but not anxious or fearful.

(continued)

BOX **14.1** **Continued**

History
Medical history: The patient was health during childhood, with no major illnesses. When he was 8 or 9 years old, he broke his arm and knocked himself out in a bicycle accident. In puberty, he had surgery to remove some breast tissue. On high school graduation day, he was in an ATV accident and injured his foot. In 1987, he was in a motorcycle accident but sustained no serious injuries. He denied history of alcohol or substance abuse. Family medical history is noncontributory.

Family history: The patient is the youngest of two children, born in Small City, and he grew up in this general area. He presently lives in **Small Town in Small State** with his wife and their two children. He was active socially and with hobbies that included hunting, golf, and building his own house. There was no indication of marital or family strain other than in response to his injury.

Education/work history: The patient completed high school with a B average. He attended two years of college, studying construction, and worked for six years with a large construction company. In that position he did drafting and compiled job estimates, and spent time in the field as a supervisor. That position ended when the company folded. He then joined his present employer, **a large insurance company,** as a sales representative after extensive studying. He was rapidly promoted from sales to management and supervised six agents. He has not worked since his injury.

CURRENT FUNCTIONING AND PROBLEMS: **The patient** and his wife reported that he has made a lot of progress since his injury, and he feels lucky to be alive and able to talk at all. He has great difficulty thinking of specific words in conversation, which he partly ascribes to memory problems. He has residual weakness on his left side. He reports very little dreaming, sleeps a lot at night, and naps during the day. He has reduced stamina, gets tired quickly, and staggers and loses his balance. He has no problems with his hearing, but does not always understand what is being said. His vision is good; he believes it is better than before his accident. His appetite is satisfactory, but he gets full more quickly when he eats a meal. He has experienced no change in his sense of taste or smell. Although he can read and write better than immediately after his injury, he has trouble figuring out how to spell a word or what it means when reading. Reading is very slow and frustrating, so he reads very little. His wife has observed that everyday activities are much slower now, that life has just slowed down for him. He has great difficulty when in unfamiliar places—such as a recent family trip to Florida—and relied heavily on his wife to make simple decisions such as which bus to take. His temperament has not changed; he is still the easygoing, "cool" man he was before. He takes frustration well and copes well with stress. He has little difficulty with ADLs, except for slowness and fatigue, and is able to manage clothing fasteners in spite of problems with his right hand. His wife believes that **the patient** has been more realistic about his deficits since their Florida trip and no longer expects to return to work this month.

OBSERVATIONS: **The patient** is a man of average height and weight, dressed very neatly and cleanly in casual clothing. He was socially pleasant, eager to converse, but obviously struggled to express his thoughts. There were frequent occasions in which he lost his train of thought irretrievably and was unable to complete it even with a thoughtful pause. At times he had difficulty with directions or a question, could indicate that he was confused, and accept clarification. His responses to questions or tasks were quite slow, for which he repeatedly apologized. His motivation and cooperation were consistently high. His attention was excellent, and he was rarely distracted. His general activity level was subdued. He verbalized some insight into his areas of weakness, and on some occasions he expressed his frustration at not being able to perform as well as he wished. He responded well to reinforcement and encouragement.

BOX **14.1**   **Continued**

PROCEDURES: Reviews of records, history questionnaire, clinical interview; digit span, spatial span, Trails A & B, IVA Continuous Performance Test; PASAT, grip strength, finger tapping, grooved pegboard, tasks of motor regulation and praxes; sensory examination (tactile, auditory, olfactory, and visual screenings); Judgment of Line Orientation, Facial Recognition, Rey-Osterrieth complex figure, drawing samples; Controlled Oral Word Association, Visual Naming, Sentence Repetition, writing sample; logical memory section of Wechsler Memory Scale, 3rd edition; California Verbal Learning Test; reading comprehension section of PIAT-III, Wide Range Achievement Test, 3rd edition; Wisconsin Card Sorting Test, Verbal Concept Attainment Test; Wechsler Adult intelligence Scale, 3rd edition (WAIS-III); MMPI-2.

TEST RESULTS

Attention/concentration: The patient was able to focus his attention on brief tasks, and perform mental manipulations of information at average levels. He could alternate and sustain attention. He had difficulty with rapidly paced complex operations, which were probably reduced by his language problems. There was no difference between visual or auditory information processing.

Motor functions: The patient had average grip strength on his left and low average on the right. Simple motor speed was low average on his left, borderline on the right. Fine motor dexterity was borderline on the right, impaired on the left. Reaction times were borderline. These scores indicate a pattern of mostly right-sided deficits, but generalized slowing and reductions of basic motor functions. His higher-level motor regulation (sequencing, programming, inhibition) were intact. Praxes were intact.

Sensory processing: The patient had basically intact sensory processing, but he had difficulty verbalizing or naming objects and familiar occurs. There was no suppression to bilateral simultaneous stimulation, upper limb position sense was intact, and auditory detection (finger rubbing) was intact. Visual acuity without glasses was 20/20 OD, 20/30 OS, and 20/20 OU.

Visual-related functions: The patient had excellent visual-spatial orientation and superior visual construction. His discrimination of facial features was borderline.

Speech/language: Except for borderline ability to repeat verbal information, all aspects of expressive language were impaired. He could write only a short paragraph, and it contained several spelling and grammatical errors.

Learning/memory: His recall of visual information was excellent. He could not absorb, process, organize, or retrieve new verbal information even with repetition. Because of the language problems, this may be due largely to language; however, his inability to recognize the information indicated that there may also be some true memory problems.

Academic: The patient's oral reading and math functions were average; his reading comprehension was borderline, and spelling impaired, both below what would be predicted from his education and occupational backgrounds.

Reasoning/intellect: He had intact reasoning and problem-solving abilities when it involved visual material only; verbal reasoning, conceptualization, and problem solving were almost uniformly impaired. His math reasoning was intact. Active mental processing and his ability to apply reasoning powers to a complex visual task were average. He could figure out concepts, response rules, generate and test hypotheses, adjust his behavior to feedback, and shift readily from one rule to another.

(continued)

B O X **14.1**   **Continued**

Emotional/personality: The patient's reading comprehension was not sufficient to cope with the MMPI-2 by himself, so it was read to him. His responses indicated moderately high levels of concern about his physical health and somatic symptoms, perhaps more than is warranted even with his medical history. Although some of his recent functioning suggests depression (sleep difficulties, low energy, sleeping excessively), the test score was in the normal range. He has difficulty admitting problems or personal weakness, so he may underreport symptoms of a more "psychological" nature and direct his stress toward his body. He is a man who is comfortable with others and who prides himself on being strong and self-sufficient; he does not like being so dependent on others.

SUMMARY AND DIAGNOSTIC IMPRESSION

This young man with the history of brain injury from a motor vehicle accident has cognitive deficits consistent with left frontotemporal and temporoparietal foci. There are a few scores that indicate scattered mild disruptions of function in other areas of the brain, a pattern typically seen in closed head injuries.

His attention is adequate for ordinary simple tasks, but not for rapid processing of complex operations such as might be required in his work. His expressive language is undoubtedly not sufficient for his usual work, since insurance sales requires rapid thought and excellent verbal skills. His reading, spelling, and comprehension are lower than he will need on the job. Most sensory-motor and visual processing functions are intact, but he is weaker and slower than he should be. His memory is excellent for visual information, but probably compromised for verbal, although it is difficult to assess verbal memory in the face of his expressive language problems. His reaction times are slowed, but other cognitive functions do not preclude his driving; he will need to be especially careful not to drive when he is tired.

RECOMMENDATIONS

The patient clearly needs to continue his speech therapy. Because of his fatigue and poor stamina, he may need to continue physical rehabilitation, even on his own, to build his endurance.

The patient cannot return to his former job at this time. Whether his language skills develop sufficiently or rapidly enough to enable his eventual return cannot be determined by this examiner or at present. To facilitate his ultimate return to work, he should contact his insurance company to set up consultation with a vocational rehabilitation specialist. If unable to return to his job in the foreseeable future, this consultant could assist him in finding more suitable work.

When **the patient** is ready to return to work, it is important that he do it gradually, especially if it is in the near future and his stamina is still reduced. His tolerance to stress, confusion, noisy environments, and so on is less than he is accustomed to, and he should make arrangements to control those factors in the workplace.

Dr. Smart, Ph.D., ABPP-CN

COMMENTARY ON CASE

This gentleman sustained an injury that resulted in brain injury that was somewhat atypical, in that there was a much clearer focus than usual. In addition to the original blow, edema was sufficient to risk herniation so surgery was performed to save his life. The resulting damage was much more severe but more localized. The bilateral nature of the injury (both temporal lobes affected, as seen as CT scan) would typically show up as scattered, multifocal deficits in his cognitive functions.

BOX **14.1** **Continued**

The severity of the injury can be gauged by the length of coma (3 weeks), and length of post-traumatic amnesia (the gap in memory from the time of the accident until memories are once again stored). In his case, both are associated with moderate to severe brain injury. Numerous studies have shown that unconsciousness of only 30 minutes and PTA of 24 hours will result in at least mild permanent residuals of brain injury. There is a strong correlation between length of these two indices and the severity of injury, and with the long-term outcome.

The case demonstrates the difficulties that are sometimes encountered with neuropsychological examination—confounding of variables. **The patient** had significant expressive language deficits, which interfered substantially with his ability to organize and express his thoughts, to absorb and process verbal information, and to use verbal mediation for reasoning and problem solving. Factoring out such confounding variables can be tricky and relies on the expertise and competence of the examiner.

This case illustrates a somewhat typical pattern for left hemisphere injury, such as is frequently seen following left-hemisphere stroke. In **the patient's** case, it was the result of surgery. The consistency of the right-sided motor weaknesses and verbally mediated cognitive functions all point to the left hemisphere. The lack of right-hemisphere signs (e.g., visual perception, visual memory, performance IQ, and fluid reasoning) is reassuring and indicates that injury to the other sites may have been mild.

This case also illustrates the non-unique character of test findings. There is no single test that is associated with a single, unique diagnosis. It is the *pattern* that reveals possible diagnoses, and the knowledge of the neuropsychologist that can differentiate between the alternatives. In this case, a pattern that is typically observed with CVA certainly cannot be interpreted as attributable to that etiology. It does reveal a pattern of deficits associated with locations within the brain, but not necessarily that single cause. The etiology of any brain dysfunction is usually determined by history, not specific test scores alone.

The test scores also showed that, in spite of significant problems, this man was likely to make an excellent recovery. He was seen in follow-up about six months later and had recovered to the point that return to work was feasible, although not at the high administrative level he had held before the injury. Potential emotional barriers to full recovery could have been activated at this point. When told he would be unlikely to return to his same job, he could have become discouraged, frustrated, or angry. Patients who have been injured as a result of actions of others may sometimes also be held back by factors of secondary gain, in that it is more profitable for them to remain disabled than to recover.

Several important factors were operating to facilitate his good recovery: good premorbid health, high IQ, high occupational level (achievement oriented), good mental health (including self-driven, hard worker), and strong family support system. These are factors that are similar to those important to a strong positive response to psychotherapy.

Rehabilitation

The fact that the bulk of this chapter has focused upon neuropsychological assessment is no accident. The careful assessment and description of cognitive and behavioral functions and deficits in brain-injured patients is the *sine qua non* of clinical neuropsychology. A legitimate question to ask of clinical neuropsychology then is "so what?" In other words, what next? What happens once the assessment is over? For most patients the answer is *rehabilitation.* Loosely speaking, rehabilitation is the process of getting on with one's life after a brain injury.

Assessment and rehabilitation are, in fact, interwoven in clinical practice. Clinical neuropsychologists use their knowledge of the brain and types of brain impairment along with the findings from the neuropsychological assessment to help patients understand what they can expect after the brain injury. Generally speaking, there are three pathways that patients follow after a brain injury. They may deteriorate, as is seen in patients suffering with dementia or most patients with multiple sclerosis. They may recover some or all functioning. Many patients who suffer a stroke recover much of the cognitive and behavioral functions lost in the weeks immediately following the incident. Finally, the deficits a patient has experienced may be stable. Understanding the likely course of a brain impairment is important for designing the appropriate rehabilitation plan.

The role that clinical neuropsychologists play in the rehabilitation of brain-injured patients has increased over the past twenty-five years (Golden, 1981a; Golden, Zillmer, & Spiers, 1992). They serve an important function in the rehabilitation process, but they do not work alone. Typically, clinical neuropsychologists work as part of a multidisciplinary rehabilitation team (Sohlberg & Mateer, 1989). Much of the hands-on work with brain-injured patients is performed by occupational therapists, physical therapists, and speech-language pathologists. Neurologists also participate on the multidisciplinary team, providing consultation and managing patients' medications. Clinical neuropsychologists consult to the team and provide direct services to patients.

As we have seen, the neuropsychological assessment identifies areas of cognitive and behavioral deficit, but also the areas that are still intact. Interventions with brain-injured patients generally have one of two goals. They are designed either to help the person to relearn the lost function or to learn to compensate for areas of deficit. Compensation involves using behavioral or cognitive functions that are still intact to offset deficits. It may also involve helping patients or their families to make adjustments to the patients' physical environment.

Golden and colleagues (1992) suggest five guidelines for developing rehabilitation tasks. First, they should include only one skill area that is impaired. All other skills involved in the task should be functioning well. Second, the task should be one that can be graded from the very simple to a level close to or at normal performance. Third, rehabilitation tasks should be quantifiable so that the patient and therapist can mark progress. Fourth, the patient should be able to receive immediate feedback from the task. Patients need to know how they did. Finally, the task should not be too difficult, so that the number of errors the patient makes can be controlled.

A competent clinical neuropsychologist is first, and perhaps most importantly, a well-trained clinical psychologist. In our opinion, clinical neuropsychologists who have focused their training narrowly on neuropsychology without first developing proficiency at the general skills associated with clinical psychology are likely to be less effective than the well-rounded clinical neuropsychologist. The latter professional will bring to bear the general skills of clinical psychology to his or her professional work as a neuropsychologist. In the area of rehabilitation, for example, there are several important clinical skills that neuropsychologists need. For example, they must to have good interviewing skills so that they can build a strong rapport with their clients (see Chapter 6). They must have a thorough knowledge of psychometric theory (see Chapter 5). Knowledge of functional analysis is important to help brain-injured patients understand and modify their behavior (see Chapter 9). Single-subject experimental designs can help the rehabilitation team to evaluate and modify their treatment plans (see Chapter 10). Finally, clinical neuropsychologists need to be skilled psychotherapists helping their clients to grieve their losses, renegotiate their relationships, manage their emotions, and struggle through countless other challenges they face (see Chapters 11 through 13).

Training and Certification

As the reader can see from the brief history of clinical neuropsychology provided earlier in this chapter, the specialty discipline developed informally. Psychologists working with brain-injured patients applied their skills and knowledge as psychologists to develop tests and strategies for understanding their patients. New psychologists interested in the emerging field sought opportunities to work with Ralph Reitan, Muriel Lezak, and other pioneers. These neuropsychologists took their knowledge with them to the universities and medical centers where they worked and in turn trained the next generation of neuropsychologists. Psychologists with varied training backgrounds trod many different paths to clinical neuropsychology. As the field grew, clinical neuropsychologists formed professional groups to share information and to guide the development of their profession. Division 40 (Clinical Neuropsychology) of the American Psychological Association was formed in 1979 and the American Board of Clinical Neuropsychology was incorporated in 1981 (Bieliauskas & Matthews, 1997). However, it was not until 1997 that representatives of the field got together and developed a set of guidelines for training in clinical neuropsychology (Hannay, 1998). At this conference, held in Houston, Texas, the participants produced a set of aspirational guidelines for training. The following discussion of training is based upon those guidelines.

To be a competent clinical neuropsychologist, the professional must have a solid foundation in the core areas of general psychology (e.g., learning, cognition, social, and personality) as well as knowledge of the core clinical areas (e.g., psychopathology, psychotherapy). However, the clinical neuropsychologist must also possess a strong understanding of neuroanatomy and brain-behavior relationships. Finally, training and experience with the specialized techniques of neuropsychology is necessary. Table 14.2 details the areas of knowledge foundation for clinical neuropsychologists.

Clinical neuropsychology is a post-doctoral specialization. However, the training begins in the graduate program. The majority of clinical neuropsychologists will have doctoral training in clinical psychology, although some come to neuropsychology from backgrounds in counseling or educational psychology. A minority of clinical neuropsychologists

TABLE 14.2   Knowledge Base for Clinical Neuropsychologists

A. Generic psychology core
    1. Statistics and methodology
    2. Learning, cognition, and personality
    3. Social psychology and personality
    4. Biological bases of behavior
    5. Life span development
    6. History
    7. Cultural and individual differences and diversity
B. Generic clinical core
    1. Psychopathology
    2. Psychometric theory
    3. Interview and assessment techniques
    4. Intervention techniques
    5. Professional ethics
C. Foundations for the study of brain-behavior relationships
    1. Functional neuroanatomy
    2. Neurological and related disorders including etiology, pathology, course, and treatment
    3. Non-neurologic conditions affecting CNS functioning
    4. Neuroimaging and other neurodiagnostic techniques
    5. Neurochemistry of behavior (e.g., psychopharmacology)
    6. Neuropsychology of behavior
D. Foundations of the practice of clinical neuropsychology
    1. Specialized neuropsychological assessment techniques
    2. Specialized neuropsychological intervention techniques
    3. Research design and analysis in neuropsychology
    4. Professional issues and ethics in neuropsychology
    5. Practical implications of neuropsychology

Source: From *Proceedings of the Houston Conference on Specialty Education and Training in Clinical Neuropsychology,* September 3–7, 1997, University of Houston Hilton and Conference Center. *Archives of Clinical Neuropsychology, 13,* 157–250.

receive their doctoral training in basic neuropsychology and acquire clinical training, including specialized training in clinical neuropsychology, post-doctorally. Many graduate training programs in clinical psychology offer training in clinical neuropsychology. Some even offer a special neuropsychology track within their clinical psychology training program. Division 40 maintains a list of doctoral training programs that offer training in clinical neuropsychology and can be viewed at their website (www.Div40.org).

Clinical neuropsychologists complete a pre-doctoral internship in professional psychology. The internship need not focus exclusively upon clinical neuropsychology, since one of the goals of the internship year is to complete the training for general practice of professional psychology. However, the internship should offer concentrated training in the science and practice of clinical neuropsychology (Hannay, 1998). The mix of general training to specialized training is determined by the needs of the specific intern.

The Houston Conference participants recommended two years of post-doctoral education and training in clinical neuropsychology for those interested in independent practice. The clinical neuropsychology residency would take place in an organized program under the supervision of a faculty of board-certified clinical neuropsychologists. By the conclusion of training, the resident will have met the following criteria (Hannay, 1998, p. 164):

1. Advanced skill in the neuropsychological evaluation, treatment, and consultation to patients and professionals sufficient to practice on an independent basis
2. Advanced understanding of brain-behavior relationships
3. Scholarly activity, e.g., submission of a study or literature review for publication, presentation, submission of a grant proposal or outcome assessment
4. A formal evaluation of competency in the exit criteria 1 through 3 in the residency program
5. Eligibility for state or provincial licensure or certification for the independent practice of psychology
6. Eligibility for board certification in clinical neuropsychology by the American Board of Professional Psychology

The reader will note that in criterion 6, the Houston participants are explicitly promoting the ABPP as the benchmark measure for independent practice. While they stopped short of requiring the ABPP in clinical neuropsychology, the document makes clear that all clinical neuropsychologists should be ready for ABPP designation. Not surprisingly, this statement about ABPP certification is consistent with the model promoted by Division 40. In this way the discipline of clinical neuropsychology is modeling its training after standard practice in most medical specialization. In medicine it is anticipated that any physician claiming specialization will obtain certification for the appropriate professional board.

While the road to specialization in clinical neuropsychology may be long, the rewards can be substantial. There are many employment opportunities for neuropsychologists, and the profession can be financially rewarding. A survey of APA Division 40 members, carried out in the late 1980s, found that their mean annual income was almost $20,000 higher than the mean annual income for the APA membership as a whole (Putnam, 1989).

BOX **14.2**

Focus on Ethics: Ethical Issues in Advertising

Private practice has been an increasingly popular work setting for many clinical neuropsychologists. In fact, as we saw in Chapter 2, private practice business in clinical psychology, whether in neuropsychology, psychotherapy, or other areas, grew dramatically in the period between 1970 and 1990. And while the rate of growth has slowed, private practice continues to be a very popular option for clinical psychologists. For their practices to succeed, psychologists need clients. In order to attract clients, psychologists need to get the word out about themselves and their businesses. In short, psychologists need to advertise.

(continued)

BOX **14.2**   **Continued**

Following the lead of other professions, most notably medicine, psychologists have traditionally taken a rather staid approach to advertising their businesses. Typically, psychologists might publish a notice in their local newspaper announcing the opening of their practice. Such announcements included the psychologist's name, highest degree earned, area of practice (e.g., clinical psychology), address, phone number, and appointment hours (Koocher & Keith-Spiegel, 1998). In addition to the announcement, psychologists might send letters to professionals in their community who could potentially refer clients to them. Such letters would usually include a bit more information about the psychologist's training and areas of expertise (e.g., "practice limited to psychological assessment and psychotherapy with adult clients").

This reserved approach to advertising was officially endorsed and encouraged by the American Psychological Association. The APA published guidelines for telephone directory listings in 1969 that encouraged psychologists to limit their statements to their name, highest degree, and phone number. If they chose to list area of specialization, this was to be limited to a brief statement (e.g., "practice limited to children"). Listing multiple areas of specialization was considered "a form of self-aggrandizement and . . . unwarranted" (quoted in Koocher & Keith-Spiegel, 1998, p. 260). Psychologists were advised against use of large print, boldface font, and box ads.

The APA Ethical Principles in place at that time similarly enjoined psychologists to show restraint in public statements about themselves or their practices. For example, the 1981 version of the APA Ethical Principles included the following statement about advertisements:

> They do not contain . . . (iii) a testimonial from a patient regarding the psychologist's services or products; (iv) a statement intended or likely to create false or unjustified expectations of favorable results; (v) a statement implying unusual, unique, or one-of-a-kind abilities; (vi) a statement intended or likely to appeal to a client's fears, anxieties, or emotions concerning the possible results or failure to obtain the offered services; (vii) a statement concerning the comparative desirability of offered services; (viii) a statement of direct solicitation of individual clients.

Psychologists whose advertisements included this type of information were subject to sanction by the APA ethics committee.

In addition to the prohibitions on advertising, psychologists were also prohibited from some other methods of attracting clients. Specifically, they could not offer their services to someone who was already receiving similar services from another professional. So, if a psychologist knew that someone was in psychotherapy with another mental health professional, it was considered unethical for that psychologist to suggest that the client switch to him or her. It was also considered unethical for psychologists to receive payment for referring people to other professionals or to pay for referrals made to them.

The circumspect approach to advertising promoted by the APA was probably motivated by a desire to protect the image of professional psychology as well as a legitimate wish to protect consumers against unscrupulous psychologists. However, the restrictions on advertising limited the amount and type of information consumers had access to when choosing among psychological service providers. The American free-enterprise system is based upon the assumption that competition is a good thing. When professional organizations limit competition among their members, consumers are hurt. What may be good for the profession is not necessarily good for the consumer.

BOX **14.2**   **Continued**

The Federal Trade Commission is the government agency charged with ensuring competition in the marketplace and protecting consumers. In the 1980s, the FTC began an investigation of the American Psychological Association. Under pressure from the agency, the APA Board of Directors amended the Ethical Principles of Psychologists in 1989, publishing the revision in 1990. Seven changes to the 1981 version were made. Five of the six advertising prohibitions listed above (numbers iii, v, vi, vii, and viii) were removed. In addition, the prohibition against psychologists' giving or receiving remuneration for referring clients to other professionals and the ban on directly offering one's services to someone who is already receiving similar services from another professional were removed. The current Ethics Code reflects the more liberal approach to advertising demanded by the FTC.

So what has happened since the FTC stepped in? Have professional psychologists gone hog-wild promoting their services? We are pleased to report that, while there are exceptions, it appears that few psychologists have abused the more open advertising guidelines. While we are aware of instances in which psychologists have taken out radio and television advertisements, this practice continues to be fairly rare and what has appeared so far has tended to be tasteful. We are not aware of cases in which psychologists have had former clients give testimonials and few psychologists hawk their one-of-a-kind, unique abilities.

From the preceding discussion, one might form the impression that the FTC promotes an "anything goes" approach to advertising. This simply is not true. The agency holds the view that providing consumers with information is good, as long as that information is truthful. In this way, the FTC and the APA are clearly on the same page. Ethical Standard 5 of the Ethics Code deals with *Advertising and other Public Statements*. Standard 5.01 (a) includes this statement "Psychologists do not knowingly make public statements that are false, deceptive, misleading, or fraudulent concerning their research, practice, or other work activities or those of persons or organizations with which they are affiliated" (American Psychological Association, 2002). Clearly this guiding principle for psychologists is wholeheartedly endorsed by the Federal Trade Commission.

CHAPTER

15

Clinical Health Psychology

Tom, a 48-year-old African American pharmaceutical sales representative, discovers during his biannual physical that he has hypertension (sustained periods of high blood pressure). Tom is particularly troubled by the news because his father, who also had high blood pressure, died of a massive stroke about ten years earlier. Tom knows that he should be more careful about his health. He used to pride himself on being physically fit. In his 20s, Tom played basketball several evenings a week with friends and participated in a men's league at the local YMCA. However, as the years passed, attendance at pickup games gradually dropped off and Tom became aware that the other players in the men's league were getting younger and younger (compared to him). Tom was discouraged by how sore he felt one, two, or even three days after playing ball. He felt increasing pressure from his wife to spend more time with their children. Eventually, Tom quit playing basketball altogether. Tom's job has him on the road a great deal of the time. He often eats in fast-food restaurants and snacks on chips in his hotel room at night. Over the years Tom's weight has steadily increased. He is about 40 pounds heavier than when he graduated from college.

Over the same time period that Tom's exercise decreased and his weight increased, Tom was aware of a gradual increase in his level of stress. After the birth of their third child, Tom and his wife agreed that she would quit her job and devote herself full time to the care of their children. Tom felt pressure to make up for the lost income by working harder. The quarterly bonus checks Tom receives if he reaches his sales quota used to be used to buy extras or to pay for vacations. Tom now depends upon the quarterly bonus checks to pay down the balance on his credit cards. Tom feels it is getting harder and harder to compete with the younger sales representatives. He is also acutely aware that most of the salespeople he started with have either moved on to other companies or moved up to managerial positions. Tom wonders whether he has been looked over for promotions because of his race. Feeling greater stress, Tom has become more irritable, quicker to snap at his wife and children. He feels that his wife is not as supportive of him as she once was and that his marriage is deteriorating.

Why does Tom have high blood pressure? Is it an inevitable product of his genetic makeup? If one parent has hypertension, the chance of his or her offspring having high blood pressure is about 45 percent (Smith et al., 1987). Is it Tom's gender and race? The prevalence rates for hypertension are higher for men than women and African Americans develop hypertension at much higher rates than whites (Herd & Weiss, 1984). Is it due to Tom's diet (high in sodium and fat), his inactivity, and consequent weight gain? Obesity is a risk factor for hypertension, particularly at Tom's age (Alexander, 1984). What about the stress in Tom's life? Could that be the cause of his hypertension? Irritability and a quick anger response are risk factors for high blood pressure (Johnson, Schork, & Spielberger, 1987), as is chronic striving against excessive odds (James, Hartnett, & Kalsbeek, 1983). What about living in a society where discrimination against African Americans, although less overt than in our country's past, is still present? Could racism have caused or exacerbated Tom's hypertension? African Americans with high blood pressure show aggravation of their symptoms when exposed to racism (Armstead, Lawler, Gordon, Cross, & Gibbons, 1989). Or are Tom's health problems related to his failing marriage? Marital satisfaction is correlated with a variety of health indicators (Gove, Style, & Hughes, 1990).

Understanding a disease, like hypertension, with respect to its physical manifestations (elevated blood pressure) as well as the behavioral (lack of exercise, unhealthy diet), personal (anger proneness), environmental (stress), cultural (racism), and genetic factors that may contribute to the etiology and severity of symptoms is characteristic of *health psychology*. Applying this broad model to understand and intervene with specific clients to help them manage or overcome their illness is the an important part of the work of *clinical health psychologists.*

Definitions

Once again, let's start with some definitions. Before we can discuss health psychology, we need a working definition of health. It has long been recognized that health is not simply the absence of disease. In 1948, the World Health Organization defined *health* as "a complete state of physical, mental, and social well-being and not merely the absence of disease or infirmity" (World Health Organization, 1948). By the WHO definition of health, very few people would be considered healthy. The definition appears to be aspirational. Rather than viewing health as an either/or phenomenon (i.e., healthy versus unhealthy), it is probably better to view health as falling along a continuum with severe disability at one end and optimal functioning at the other (Sarafino, 1994).

Health psychology is a subdiscipline within psychology that focuses upon understanding how people stay healthy, the factors that contribute to the onset and maintenance of illness, and how people cope when they are ill (Taylor, 1999). Health psychology has been defined as follows:

> *Health psychology* is the aggregate of the specific educational, scientific, and professional contributions of the discipline of psychology to the promotion and maintenance of health, the prevention and treatment of illness, the identification of etiologic and diagnostic correlates of health, illness, and related dysfunction, and to the analysis and improvement of health care system and health policy formation. (Matarazzo, 1982, p. 4).

As you can tell by the definition, health psychology is a rather broad field within psychology. It has been suggested that the field can be organized into five broad content areas (Johnston & Weinman, 1995):

1. *Health risk behaviors.* This area is focused upon understanding the nature, causes, and health consequences of behaviors that have a detrimental impact upon health.

Examples of such behaviors include smoking, unsafe sexual behavior, and unhealthy eating habits.

2. *Health protective or enhancing behaviors.* The study and promotion of factors associated with developing and maintaining behaviors that prevent illness and enhance health are the primary focus of this area of health psychology. What leads people to exercise, maintain a healthy diet, practice safe sex, floss their teeth, do self-examinations, or participate in preventive medical screenings?

3. *Health-related cognitions.* The theme of this area of health psychology is the cognitive processes that underlie health promoting and health risk behaviors. Health psychologists study the influence of certain kinds of beliefs and attitudes on health behavior. They examine ways of modifying health-related beliefs in order to promote healthy behavior.

4. *Processes influencing health-care delivery.* The aim of this area of health psychology is to understand the psychological factors that impact the effectiveness of health-care delivery systems. What is the quality of communication between health-care providers and patients? How satisfied are patients with services? What aspects of the delivery system promote adherence to medical advice? What are the psychological factors that predict a positive adjustment to surgical procedures? How can health-care providers best prepare patients for medical procedures?

5. *Psychological aspects of illness.* This area of health psychology is interested in questions such as: What is the psychological impact of chronic illnesses? How do patients cope with terminal illness? What factors are associated with quality of life in people with severe disabilities? What predicts adherence with rehabilitation?

Clinical health psychology can be considered a subdiscipline of both health psychology and clinical psychology. Traditionally, clinical psychology has been associated with mental health. Clinical health psychology approaches issues of general health and illness with the methods, models, and assumptions of clinical psychology. As scientist-practitioners, clinical health psychologists aim "to translate research into practical applications that can help people lead healthier lives" (Michie, 1998, p. 155). Clinical health psychology applies knowledge drawn from the larger field of health psychology to the health service setting:

> A clinical health psychologist applies, in professional practice, the specific educational, scientific, and professional contributions of the discipline of psychology to the promotion and maintenance of health; the prevention, treatment, and rehabilitation of illness, injury, and disability; the identification of etiologic and diagnostic correlates of health, illness, and related dysfunction; and the analysis and improvement of the health care system and health policy formation. (Belar, 1997, p. 411)

Models of Illness and Health

Humans' understanding of the causes of illness and health have, of course, changed dramatically over recorded history. As we saw in Chapter 2, Hippocrates proposed a humoral theory of health and illness. When the four basic humors are balanced, humans are in a healthy state. Conversely, illness was thought to result from imbalance among the body's humors. Hippocrates recommended avoiding excesses and eating a balanced diet to maintain one's health. The Middle Ages witnessed the decline of enlightened thought and the ascendance of religion and mysticism in Europe. Like mental illness, physical health was thought to be determined by one's spiritual purity. Sickness was God's punishment for one's sins. Following from this view, priests became the primary ministers of healing and religion and medicine became all but indistinguishable (Kaplan, 1975).

The reemergence of culture and philosophy in the fourteenth and fifteenth centuries in Europe is referred to as the *Renaissance*. Starting in this period and continuing to the present day, remarkable advances have been made in medical technology and theories of medicine. The seventeenth-century thinker René Descartes (1596–1650) made significant philosophical contributions that opened the door for scientific advancement. Descartes argued that the body and the mind (or soul) are separate. The body is a machine and humans can learn to understand the workings of the machine. The body is matter that is subject to natural law. The mind is a separate entity. While it can be studied, it is not subject to the same laws that govern matter. The mind and the body, although separate, do communicate. Descartes even pointed out where mind-body communication takes place—the pineal gland (a small gland at the base of the brain). The soul, according to Descartes, leaves the body at death. Descartes's viewpoint was eventually accepted by the Church, which was important because it led to the Church lifting its sanction against dissection (Engel, 1977). Descartes's view of the mind and body as separate entities is very much a part of Western thought. In fact, this view, which is sometimes called *mind-body dualism* or simply *dualism,* is probably the implicit model most of us have of the relationship between our psychology and our physiology.

In the eighteenth and nineteenth centuries, knowledge of the workings of the human body and the scientific approach to medicine grew dramatically. Several important scientific discoveries and technological advances were made during this time period. The discovery that certain microorganisms cause diseases led to the development of antiseptic techniques that, along with the development of anesthesias, resulted in remarkable advances in surgical procedures (Stone, 1979). The nineteenth century witnessed an increase in the public's faith in physicians and the ascendance of the scientific approach to medicine.

The viewpoint that became dominant in the nineteenth century and remained so throughout the twentieth century is called the *biomedical model*. The basic assumption of the biomedical model is that all physical problems and disorders can be explained by disturbances in physiological processes such as bacterial or viral infection, injury, or biochemical imbalances (Sarafino, 1994). From the biomedical point of view, psychological or social processes are separate from physical processes, and diseases can be understood entirely as a function of the latter.

The successes of the biomedical model have been impressive. Infectious diseases that were once considered life-threatening are now routinely treated with antibiotics. Viral illnesses, such as smallpox, have been all but eradicated thanks to aggressive vaccination programs. Examination of the leading causes of death at the outset of the twentieth century and at its close illustrates the successes of the biomedical model (see Table 15.1). The most common killers in the year 1900, influenza and pneumonia, were responsible for approximately 202 out of every 100,000 deaths (Sexton, 1979). By the end of the twentieth century, these illness accounted for only about 31 deaths per 100,000 (U.S. Department of Commerce, 1997, cited in Taylor, 1999). Several of the leading causes of death at the turn of the twentieth century (e.g., diseases of infancy, tuberculosis, diphtheria), no longer made the top 10 list in the 1990s. Medicine's ability to treat acute viral and bacterial diseases has had a dramatic impact upon the quality and longevity of life for people living in industrialized countries. The average life expectancy for an American born in 1900 was 47.3 years (U.S. Bureau of the Census, 1975). For babies born in the United States in the year 2000 the average life expectancy is 77.1 years (U.S. Census Bureau, 2000).

Examination of Table 15.1 illustrates not only the success of the biomedical approach to understanding diseases and their treatment but also the model's limitations. The leading causes of death in the United States are no longer acute illness. Rather, today the most common causes of death among Americans are chronic illnesses and illnesses that can be directly linked to lifestyle. The biomedical model, while still useful, does not offer a comprehensive account of these illnesses. To more fully explain illnesses such as heart disease, chronic obstructive pulmonary disease, diabetes, and cancer it is necessary to look beyond the physical processes that describe these pathologies. As these illnesses have emerged as the leading causes of death in the twentieth century, various *risk factors* have been identified. Risk factors are "characteristics or conditions that are associated with the development of a disease or injury" (Sarafino, 1994, p. 10). Several of the risk factors for these chronic diseases have to do with the way people behave. Table 15.2 lists five of the leading causes of death and the behavioral risk factors for each. The recognition that behavior plays a significant role in the etiology of disease illustrates one of the limitations of the purely biomedical model. Clearly, there is a need for a more complete model of health and illness. In the fall of the twentieth century, the *biopsychosocial model* emerged (Engel, 1977; Schwartz, 1982). This model views illness as a product of biological, psychological, and social factors.

TABLE 15.1   Ten Leading Causes of Death for People in the United States, 1900 and 1994

1900	1994
1. Influenza and pneumonia	1. Diseases of the heart
2. Tuberculosis	2. Cancer
3. Gastroenteritis	3. Cerebrovascular diseases (stroke)
4. Diseases of the heart	4. Chronic obstructive pulmonary disease
5. Vascular lesions of the CNS	5. Accidents
6. Chronic nephritis	6. Influenza and pneumonia
7. Accidents	7. Diabetes mellitus
8. Cancer	8. Suicide
9. Diseases of early infancy	9. HIV infection
10. Diphtheria	10. Homicide

Source: From S. E. Taylor (1999).

TABLE 15.2   Leading Causes of Death and Their Behavioral Risk Factors

Disease	Behavior Risk Factors
Heart disease	Smoking, lack of exercise, diet, ineffective stress management
Cancer	Smoking, heavy alcohol use, diet
Stroke	Smoking, diet, ineffective stress management
Accidents	Alcohol use, drug use, not using seat belts
Influenza and pneumonia	Smoking, failure to get immunization

Source: From Matarazzo (1984).

Biopsychosocial Model

The biopsychosocial model of health and illness was proposed as an alternative to the biomedical model. Before considering the alternative, let's look at the limitations of the biomedical perspective. The model reduces all illnesses to the biological level. Diseases are understood to be the products of disordered cells, chemical imbalances, or malfunctioning organs. This *reductionistic* model does not acknowledge how broader psychological and social factors impact the biological processes. Instead it focuses upon a single-factor (biological dysfunction) in illness. The biomedical model accepts mind-body dualism. By focusing exclusively upon biological processes, the biomedical model assumes that the mind and the body are best understood as separate entities. Finally, the biomedical model is focused on illness rather than on health. It examines physical aberrations associated with illness and how to rectify these aberrations. (Taylor, 1999). The model's strength is in understanding and modifying disease processes after they have started. It has had some impact upon preventing disease (e.g., viral inoculations, improved hygiene, improved diet) but limited impact upon promoting health.

In contrast, the biopsychosocial model views both illness and health as being the products of biological, psychological, and social factors. The model rejects mind-body dualism, viewing physiology and psychology as inseparably intertwined when it comes to matters of health and illness. Finally, the biopsychosocial model emphasizes both health and illness. Health is not seen as simply the absence of illness but rather as something that is strived for and maintained through attention to biological, psychological, and social needs (Taylor, 1999). We will examine the roles of biological, psychological, and social factors in health and illness in turn.

Biological factors clearly play a central role in health and illness. Biological factors include genetic predispositions, structural soundness or deficits (e.g., malformed aorta), the immune system, the endocrine system, and the body's biochemistry. The human body consists of a complex assortment of interacting physical systems. Damage or dysfunction in one system usually impacts several others. Healthy functioning requires that each system works well and that the various systems interact efficiently.

What are the psychological factors that impact health and illness? There are, of course, many, but they can be broken down into three interacting types: cognitive, emotional, and behavioral (Sarafino, 1994). Beliefs, perceptions, memory functioning, and other cognitive processes can influence health and illness. Take Mary, for example, who is advised by her health-care provider to engage in some form of physical exercise regularly to reduce weight and lower cholesterol. Mary may believe that this is sound advice but does not believe that she can stick to an exercise program. Because Mary has low *self-efficacy* (Bandura, 1977, 1986) when it comes to exercising, she is unlikely to initiate or maintain an exercise program. Emotional functioning is also related to health and illness. It has been suggested, for example, that chronic low levels of depression may be associated with increased risk for cancer (Spiegel, 1996). Anxiety may prevent people from seeking preventive and restorative medical procedures. Finally, as we have already seen, behavior plays an important role in health. All seven of the top health risk factors in the United States, identified by the U.S. Department of Health and Human Services, are behavioral—tobacco use, diet, alcohol use, accidents, suicide, violence, and unsafe sex (cited in VandenBos, DeLeon, & Belar, 1991).

Social influences upon health take place at many levels. Our social environment includes our families, our friends, our community, as well as the larger society within which we live. Within the immediate social environment the behavior and beliefs of one's family and friends impact one's own behavior and beliefs. To take a simple example, if one's family and friends all smoke, one is more likely to pick up the habit as well. In addition to its influence upon health behaviors, one's immediate social environment influences one's health in other ways. "A growing body of literature suggests that people with supportive family and friends remain in better health and recover better from physical and emotional distress than those who are less socially integrated" (Rhodes, 1998, p. 481). At the broadest level, the society within which we live impacts our health. A society that values health promotes exercise, healthy eating, preventive care, and other behaviors consistent with these values. In the United States, for example, health has been explicitly promoted through funding for public service announcement encouraging the use of seat belts, school programs that encourage children to stay away from drugs, and laws requiring warning labels on packages of cigarettes.

The biopsychosocial model is more than the simple recognition that biological, psychological, and social factors impact health. It views the biological, psychological, and social as three large interactive systems. *Systems theory* (Bertalanffy, 1968) sees systems as dynamic entities that consist of many components that are continuously interrelating. Health status is a function of many systems that are linked to one another hierarchically. Cells, the central nervous system, and the immune system are all systems organized within a large system—the human body. Humans, in turn, are part of larger systems—families, groups of friends, communities, and societies. Changes within systems higher in the hierarchy (e.g., society) impact lower levels (e.g., the family), and even lower levels (e.g., the immune system of specific individuals). Changes within the smallest systems (e.g., individual cells), however, also can lead to changes in the body (e.g., illness), which impact larger systems, (e.g., families), which can impact even larger systems (e.g., societies). One need only think of how the changes in a relatively small system, the human immune system, caused by the HIV virus has impacted individuals, families, communities, and societies to understand the interrelatedness among systems.

Adopting a biopsychosocial perspective on health and illness is more than an academic exercise. The clinical implications of the model are significant. First, in the assessment of health problems, one must look at biological, psychological, and social factors. Multidisciplinary teams are often necessary to adequately understand patients' complaints (Schwartz, 1982). Similarly, health intervention often needs to take place at all three levels. For example, a patient with high cholesterol may need medication (biological factor), but also education about diet and exercise (psychological factors). In addition, the patient's recovery may be facilitated by intervening with family members so that they will support the patient's lifestyle changes and referral to a support group for people struggling to manage their cholesterol levels (social factors).

Clinical Health Psychology: A Brief History

Hippocrates might be considered the first clinical health psychologist. His advice to live one's life in moderation and maintain a balanced diet is as sound today as it was in ancient Greece. But we would be stretching a point to suggest that a direct line can be drawn from the ancient Greeks to modern clinical health psychologists. The dawn of clinical health psychology is probably more appropriately placed in the early twentieth century with the work of Sigmund Freud. Freud's description of *conversion hysteria* had a profound influence upon psychiatric thinking about physical illnesses. Recall that *hysteria* was the term used to describe conditions in which no organic basis for patients' physical symptoms could be found (see Chapter 2). Freud argued that these physical symptoms were due to unconscious emotional conflicts (Davison & Neale, 1990). Freud termed the disorder conversion hysteria.

Freud's speculations about the role internal conflicts play in mental and physical conditions gave rise to a broader interest in the relationship between specific illnesses and personality dynamics. In the 1930s researchers and clinicians interested in the relationship between personality and illness formed an association and began to publish the journal *Psychosomatic Medicine*. The field of psychosomatic medicine focused upon the relationship between certain personality patterns and specific forms of illness. Franz Alexander, an early leader in the field, for example, argued that individuals who had an excessive need for dependency and love were prone to develop ulcers (Taylor, 1999). As this example suggests, psychosomatic medicine was strongly influenced by psychodynamic thinking about personality. As the field matured, however, it has incorporated other approaches and theories. Contemporary psychosomatic medicine is interested in the interrelationships among psychological, social, and biological processes (Christie & Mellett, 1986).

The field of psychosomatic medicine was an important forerunner of clinical health psychology. It showed that psychological processes can be useful in understanding biological processes, including disease, heretofore considered outside the realm of psychology. The psychosomatic medicine approach has been criticized, however, on a number of grounds, including the methodological rigor of its research methods, the overemphasis upon personality to the exclusion of other psychological factors, and its identification of certain illnesses as psychosomatic (Engel, 1977).

In the 1960s and 1970s an alternative approach to examining the role of psychological factors in illness emerged. Behaviorally oriented psychologists began to explore the role that learning processes might play in the development, maintenance, and treatment of physical illnesses. *Behavioral medicine* involves the application of principles drawn from classical and operant conditioning to help people modify risk behaviors and manage negative emotions thought to contribute to illness.

Perhaps one of the more interesting contributions of behavioral medicine was the application of learning principles to teach people to modify physiological processes not traditionally thought to be under voluntary control (Blanchard & Epstein, 1978). *Biofeedback* refers to a set of techniques in which patients learn to influence psychophysiological processes by receiving feedback about these processes. For example, a hypertensive patient may learn to relax physically in order to reduce blood pressure. The patient's blood pressure is monitored while the patient relaxes. The patient is rewarded by feedback in the form of a tone or light display when he or she succeeds in lowering blood pressure (Thorpe & Olson, 1997). Behavioral medicine is an interdisciplinary field that applies learning principles to address a variety of health-related issues, including prevention, treatment, and rehabilitation (Sarafino, 1994).

Health psychology emerged as its own field in the 1970s. One marker of the birth of a new field is the creation of an organization of people interested in that area of discovery. The Division of Health Psychology (Division 38 of the American Psychological Association) was formed in 1978. Volume 1 of *Health Psychology,* the division's journal, was published in 1982. There is considerable overlap among health psychology, psychosomatic medicine, and behavioral medicine. The fields have similar goals. What distinguishes them are their traditions and disciplinary affiliations. Psychosomatic medicine grew out of psychodynamic psychiatry. Behavioral medicine developed out of behavior therapy and is interdisciplinary. Health psychology developed as a field within psychology. It applies information and methodologies from many other subdisciplines of psychology including developmental, clinical, physiological, social, and experimental psychology (Sarafino, 1994). While psychosomatic medicine, behavioral medicine, and health psychology have much in common, the latter is clearly a subdiscipline of psychology, utilizes many theoretical perspectives within psychology, and is interested in all aspects of health and health-care delivery. In its short life, health psychology has experienced spectacular growth. By 1990, more research was being done in health psychology than any other area of clinical research in APA-accredited doctoral training programs in clinical psychology (Sayette & Mayne, 1990).

Clinical health psychology emerged as a subdiscipline of psychology at the end of the twentieth century. It is interested in the application of knowledge drawn from health psychology to improve health. "Clinical health psychology aims to translate research into practical applications that can help people live healthier lives" (Michie, 1998). Some of the features of clinical health psychology are a grounding in the biopsychosocial model, knowledge about the relationship between behavior and health, and the ability to work in a variety of health-care settings (Belar, 1997). The American Psychological Association officially recognized clinical health psychology as a specialty in 1997 (Belar, 1997).

Clinical health psychology is one of the fastest-growing areas of specialization within psychology and has been called "a specialty for the twenty-first century" (Belar, 1997). There are many factors that have created the need for an applied health psychology. First, as we have already seen, the major threats to health in the twenty-first century all have significant behavioral risk factors. There is a need for professionals who can work with patients to change risk behaviors, to study the efficacy of their intervention methods, and to consult with other professionals about behavioral risk. Second, the dramatic changes that have taken place in the health-care delivery system in the United States over the past twenty years have created a recognition of the importance of promoting and maintaining health instead of only responding to illness. Third, there is overwhelming scientific evidence demonstrating the role of psychosocial factors in the etiology and maintenance of disease states (Steptoe, 1998). Finally, the emphasis upon "evidence-based practice" in medicine has created a need for professionals who have the skills to scientifically study health-care practices and delivery systems and to apply that knowledge. Thus, there is a growing market for the scientist-practitioner-clinical-health-psychologist.

In the remainder of this chapter we focus upon the role psychological factors play in health and illness and how clinical health psychologists intervene to promote health and treat illness. Let's first look at health promotion and illness prevention.

Prevention and Health Promotion

Stress and Illness

Stress is a term that is used in a variety of ways. We use stress as a noun when we talk about the challenging events we face (e.g., "She has been dealing with a lot of stress lately"). We use stress as a verb (e.g., "He was stressed out."). And we use stress as an adjective (e.g., "Boy, I've had a stressful day"). The definition of stress has produced a significant amount of discussion and disagreement among scholars and researchers over the years (see Steptoe, 1998, for discussion). To reduce the confusion, stress researchers tend to refer to environmental events that are viewed as sources or causes of emotional turmoil as *stressors*. Various terms have been used to describe the emotional response (i.e., feelings of tension) people feel when faced with stressors. *Distress* and *strain* have been used to describe these reaction, but *stress* is still used by many to refer to the negative emotional response to stressful events. Finally, stress is also sometimes defined as a *process* between person and environment. This latter definition includes the stressors and distress. In this tradition, one group of researchers have defined stress as a process in which "environmental demands tax or exceed the adaptive capacity of an organism, resulting in psychological and biological changes that may place a person at risk for disease" (Cohen, Kessler, & Gordon, 1995, p. 3).

As the definition of stress included in the previous paragraph indicates, it is generally recognized that there is a relationship between stress and illness. There is considerable evidence linking exposure to stressors and physical illness (Cohen, Tyrell, & Smith, 1991; Steptoe, 1998). In an early attempt to explore the link between stressors and health, Holmes and Rahe (1967) created a survey of recently experienced life events or life changes (e.g., death of a spouse, jail term, pregnancy, son or daughter leaving home). They found a link between the number of recently experienced life events and their subjects' subsequent health status. Although the Holmes and Rahe measure has been criticized on a variety of grounds (see Ogden, 1996), the link between negative life events and illness has been demonstrated in a variety of ways. For example, natural disasters such as earthquakes or volcano eruptions are followed by increases in health problems and mortality (Adams & Adams, 1984; Tevisan et al., 1992). Individuals who face chronic stressors such as continuously discordant interpersonal relationships or chronic unemployment tend to have poorer health and higher death rates as well (Kiecolt-Glaser et al., 1994; Morris, Cook, & Shaper, 1994).

Stress impacts human physiology in a variety of ways. Sudden, intense stressors initiate a strong sympathetic nervous system response—the "fight-or-flight response" first described by Walter Cannon (1932). Physiologically, the fight-or-flight response involves increased heart and respiration rates, elevations in blood pressure, increased sweat gland activity, and constriction of peripheral blood vessels. These changes prepare the person to escape from the stressor (flight) or face it (fight). The activation of the sympathetic nervous system stimulates the adrenal glands, which releases epinephrine and norepinephrine. These catecholamines produce the keyed-up feeling we experience when we are stressed.

Stress also results in activation of the hypothalamic-pituitary-adrenal (HPA) system (Taylor, 1999). In response to stressors, the hypothalamus releases a peptide called corticotropic releasing factor (CRF), which in turn stimulates the adrenal cortex to release adrenocorticotropin (ACTH). ACTH travels through the body's circulatory system to the adrenal glands, where it stimulates the release of a variety of corticosteroids including cortisol. Cortisol helps the body to cope with stressors by conserving carbohydrates and reducing inflammation caused by an injury.

The human physiological stress response briefly described in the preceding two paragraphs is an adaptive response to immediately experienced stressors that can be effectively coped with through escape or physical confrontation. From an evolutionary perspective, it makes sense for humans to develop this type of stress response when the stressors one needed to cope with were predatory animals or enemies with clubs. However, these responses are not as adaptive when the stressors are those that cannot be escaped by running or coped with by physical aggression. Job pressures, marital discord, and excessive debt produce the same stress response that being chased by a saber-tooth tiger produced in our ancestors.

Excessive or chronic activation of the human stress response can have a negative impact upon one's health. Overproduction of epinephrine and norepinephrine can impair the immune system, produce elevated blood pressure, and sometimes provoke variations in normal heart rhythm. The catecholamines (epinephrine and norepinephrine) impact cholesterol levels. Cortisol also has immunosuppressive effects (Taylor, 1999).

The route from stress to illness likely has multiple intersecting paths (Baum, 1994). There are the direct physiological paths briefly outlined above, but there are also indirect paths between stress and illness. One way that stress may lead to illness is by increasing health risk behaviors. People who react to stress by increasing their alcohol consumption, smoking more cigarettes, pigging out on junk food, or using illicit drugs are at increased risk for the various health problems associated with these behaviors. Conversely, the link between stress and illness may be via behaviors that people don't engage in. High levels of stress may be the reason some people skip preventive health appointments, fail to seek health care when they are sick, are noncompliant with medical advice, quit exercising, and do not take time to foster healthy relationships.

Managing Stress.   The job of applying our knowledge about the link between stress and illness often falls to the clinical health psychologist. From a biopsychosocial perspective, it makes sense that if people can learn to reduce and manage the stress in their lives their risk of developing illnesses would decrease. Prevention of illness is a high priority for many businesses. The annual cost of lost productivity due to stress-related illnesses has been estimated to be in the billions of dollars (Taylor, 1999). *Primary prevention* refers to the task of preventing the development of illness in people who are currently healthy. Learning to effectively manage life stress is a form of primary prevention. Stress management can also be an important for *secondary prevention* (i.e., preventing illness in individuals who are at increased risk or have recovered). For example, stress management is considered an important part of secondary prevention for people who have already suffered a heart attack (Chesney & Rosenman, 1985) or who have high blood pressure (Shapiro, Schwartz, Ferguson, Redmon, & Weiss, 1977).

Comprehensive stress management, whether for primary or secondary prevention, is a fine example of the ways in which clinical health psychologists translate research findings into practice. In addition to elucidating the various links between stress and illness, health psychologists have identified several factors that mediate and moderate the impact of stressors. Clinical health psychologists apply this knowledge when helping clients to manage their own life stressors. Stress management may take place within a psychotherapeutic relationship, a workshop, or as a part of a comprehensive employee assistance program. In the following paragraphs we describe possible components that might be included in a comprehensive stress management program.

Part of a thorough stress management program includes reducing or eliminating dysfunctional coping behaviors. Alcohol use is a good example of a dysfunctional stress management strategy. Drinking small amounts of alcohol can reduce one's stress in the short run. Drinking larger amounts of alcohol, however, can exacerbate stress by leading to ill feelings (hangover), disruption in interpersonal relationships, and impaired job or school performance. Drinking itself is associated with a wide range of health hazards. In the short term, drinking alcohol increases the risk that people will accidentally harm themselves or someone else (Smith & Kraus, 1988). In the long run, chronic excessive alcohol use is linked to a variety of health conditions, including liver damage, hypertension, some forms of cancer, heart disease, and brain damage (USDHHS, 1990). Finally, excessive use of alcohol is likely to impair the acquisition of new, healthier stress management strategies.

Besides alcohol misuse, other maladaptive coping behaviors such as excessive eating, drug abuse, or gambling need to be evaluated. Like alcohol use, these behaviors can exacerbate stress. If identified, these behaviors would be addressed in a comprehensive stress management program.

Stress management should include a component that targets stress at a physiological level. This can be accomplished in a number of ways. Regular physical exercise has been shown to reduce stress (Brown, 1991). In addition, regular exercise has a variety of other health benefits, including lowering blood pressure, increasing metabolism of carbohydrates and fats, improving self-esteem, and reducing anxiety (Conner & Norman, 1998). Regular practice of progressive muscle relaxation is associated with a reduction in stress (Lichstein, 1988). In the typical muscle relaxation procedure, clients learn to focus their attention on specific muscle groups by alternatively tensing and relaxing these muscles (Bernstein & Borkovec, 1973). Nontraditional approaches to relaxation such as *transcendental meditation* are also used by some clinicians to reduce stress (Benson, 1987).

Cognitive behavior therapy (see Chapter 13) is used by many practitioners to help clients learn to manage life stress. Ellis's REBT (Ellis, 1995), Beck's cognitive therapy (Beck & Weishaar, 1995) and Meichenbaum's stress inoculation training (Meichenbaum & Turk, 1982) have all been used in stress management. Cognitive therapy may be a particularly important component of stress management. Irrational self-talk can perpetuate stress in a variety of ways. For example, negative expectations about the likelihood that one can cope with life stressors (e.g., "It doesn't matter what I do, I'll never get a job") can lead to a lack of effort and may perpetuate the problem (e.g., unemployment). To take another example, one's self-efficacy (see Chapter 3) about exercise will impact the likelihood that one will maintain an exercise program (Wilcox & Storandt, 1996). As a third example, cognitive strategies can be used to help clients realistically appraise just how bad are the life stressors they experience. REBT might be particularly helpful here. By objectively examining their interpretation of the stressor (e.g., "In the big picture, how important is it that you get an A on this test?"), clients can learn to manage their emotional reactions.

Cognitive therapy's emphasis upon clients' interpretation of stressors is consistent with contemporary psychological theory about stress and coping (Lazarus & Folkman, 1984a, 1984b). Richard Lazarus and his colleagues have proposed that our appraisal of stressors impacts the degree to which we experience stress when confronted by them. When faced with a stressor, people make a *primary appraisal* of the stressor. If an event is perceived as harmful, threatening for the future, and/or potentially challenging, it is likely to produce stress. However, the level of stress one experiences in reaction to the event is also determined by a secondary appraisal process. In addition to evaluating the harm caused by a negative event, its potential for future threat, and how challenging it is, people also appraise their ability to cope and the resources they can utilize to manage the harm, threat, and challenge. The subjective feeling of stress is determined by the relationship between the primary and secondary appraisal. If a task is evaluated as high in harm, threat, and challenge and the person appraises his or her ability to cope as low, stress will be significant. However, if an event is perceived as moderately threatening, for example, and the client evaluates his or her coping ability positively, stress will be low.

Training in time management and problem solving also may be included in stress management. For many clients, stress is produced by the feeling that there are simply too many things to do. Basic time-management skills include setting specific work goals, prioritizing one's goals, eliminating activities that consume time with little payoff, and setting aside specific blocks of time for specific activities. In problem-solving training, clients learn to define problems in solvable terms, generate and evaluate solutions, and implement and reevaluate the chosen solution.

In addition to the specific therapeutic strategies clinical psychologists use for stress management, they also apply what is known about moderators of stress to help clients learn to manage stress effectively. Two stress moderators identified through research are perception of control and social support. People who have a strong sense of personal control experience less stress in response to stressors than those with a poorer sense of self-control (Sarafino, 1994). Therapists can help clients recognize what aspects of their lives they control and to exercise that control. Similarly, clinicians can apply the knowledge that social support buffers the impact of psychosocial stressors by helping clients to develop and maintain supportive relationships.

Behavior and Health

How people behave has a strong impact upon their health. Engaging in certain behaviors increases the risk of illness, while regularly engaging in other types of behaviors decreases risk. In the following pages we explore ways in which clinical health psychologists help people to engage in health-promoting behaviors and help them stop engaging in health-risk behaviors.

Promoting Healthy Behavior.   There is no shortage of information available to the public about the benefits of various forms of health-enhancing and illness-preventing behaviors. Popular magazines, newspaper articles, TV news magazines, self-help books, and public information announcements provide information about the benefits of regular exercise, eating a balanced diet, and preventive health care (e.g., breast self-examination). With so much information available, one might wonder why everyone does not exercise regularly, eat five or more helpings of fruits and vegetables a day, floss their teeth, see a health-care provider regularly, practice safe sex, and do preventive self-examinations. Health psychology has, in fact, devoted much attention to understanding what motivates people to engage in health-enhancing behaviors and how these behaviors are maintained. For illustrative purposes, we will focus upon exercise as the prototypical healthy behavior.

The health benefits of regular exercise are well documented. People who exercise regularly have greater cardiovascular endurance and lower risk for heart disease (Conner & Norman, 1998). Consistent exercise is associated with increased metabolism of carbohydrates and fats and therefore plays an important role in weight loss and weight management. Regular vigorous exercise appears to be associated with decreased risk for certain forms of cancer (Brownson, Chang, Davis, & Smith, 1991). Other direct physical benefits of regular exercise include improved muscle tone and strength, increased flexibility, lowered cholesterol levels, and improved stress tolerance (Taylor, 1999). There are also psychological benefits to regular exercise such as improved mood, increased self-esteem, and reduced anxiety and depression (Conner & Norman, 1998). With so much to gain by physical exercise, one would think that exercise would be a top priority in most people's lives. Survey studies, however, suggest that this is not the case (e.g., General Household Survey, 1989).

A variety of factors that are correlated with maintenance of regular exercise have been identified. Boys and men are more likely to exercise regularly than girls and women, and younger adults are more likely to exercise than older adults (Sallis et al., 1993; Health Promotion Authority for Wales, 1990). Overweight people are less likely to participate in exercise programs than people who are normal weight (Dishman, 1982). People who are well educated, upper middle class, and who have a history of exercising tend to exercise more than less well-educated, poorer people who did not exercise in their youth (Dishman, 1982, 1991).

With respect to psychological variables, self-efficacy has emerged as an important factor in understanding whether people will initiate or maintain an exercise program (McAuley, 1993; Wurtele & Maddux, 1987). Self-efficacy refers to a person's beliefs about his or her ability to perform the behaviors necessary to cope with the situation and produce positive outcomes (Bandura, 1977). Social learning theory predicts that people with strong self-efficacy beliefs will develop stronger intentions to act, exert more effort to achieve their goals, and persist longer in the face of adversity (Bandura, 1991). As applied to exercise, people with high self-efficacy are more likely to initiate an exercise program, put more effort into the program, and persevere. Self-efficacy has proven to be a useful construct in predicting health behaviors in general (Wallston, 1994) and exercise in particular (McAuley, 1993; McAuley & Courneya, 1992; Wilcox & Storandt, 1996).

When working with individual clients, clinical health psychologists may apply self-efficacy theory and other psychological constructs to help them develop and stick with exercise programs. Many cognitive behavioral treatment strategies are particularly helpful in working toward these goals. For example, therapists might help clients to use *contingency contracting* to set reasonable exercise goals and to reinforce compliance. Self-monitoring would be used to observe compliance. Cognitive restructuring procedures can help clients identify and challenge beliefs about exercise that would interfere with compliance (e.g., "It doesn't matter what I do, I'll never lose weight," "Everyone will laugh at me," "I'm a dork"). Exercise programs that include training in developing plans to respond to thoughts and situations that place people at risk for quitting (e.g., increased stress, schedule changes) have higher rates of exercise maintenance than those that do not include instruction in relapse prevention (Belisle, Roskies, & Levesque, 1987; Simkin & Gross, 1994).

Decreasing Negative Health Behaviors.   Just as behavior can enhance health, behavior can also impair health. As we have already seen, the top health risk factors in the United States are behavioral. Changing health-risk behaviors is an important part of the work of clinical health psychologists.

The quintessential negative health behavior is cigarette smoking. Smoking tobacco is the number one cause of preventable death in the United Stated. Each year about 175,000 cancer deaths and another 350,000 deaths from heart disease can be directly linked to smoking (American Heart Association, 1997; American Heart Association, 1995). In addition to cancer and heart disease, smoking is a factor in a variety of other health problems including emphysema, chronic obstructive pulmonary disease, bronchitis, injuries and deaths due to fires, and low-birth-weight infants (Taylor, 1999). In addition to the negative health effects that can be directly related to smoking, smoking also impacts health through its interaction with other health risk factors. For example, high cholesterol is a risk factor for heart disease. The risk of heart disease is much higher for people who smoke and have high cholesterol compared to people who have only one of these risk factors. In fact, risk of death due to heart disease is greater than would be expected by simply adding the mortality risks of smoking and high cholesterol (Taylor, 1999). Cigarette smoking and alcohol abuse have similarly synergistic effects. The combined use of cigarettes and alcohol is associated with markedly increased risk for illness and death (Hurt et al., 1996). A history of alcohol abuse is a risk factor for nicotine dependence and is associated with poorer smoking cessation treatment outcome (Centers for Disease Control and Prevention, 1997a).

If smoking is so bad for our health, then why would anyone smoke? The behaviors of buying cigarettes, opening the package, putting a cigarette to one's lips, lighting it, sucking the smoke into one's lungs, and blowing it out appear to be influenced by a wide variety of physiological and psychological factors. Smoking one's first cigarettes appears to be influenced by social and cognitive factors. Most cigarettes smoked by adolescents are smoked in the presence of peers (Biglan, McConnel, Severson, Bavry, & Ary, 1984). Preadolescents in the United States have already developed the image of the person who smokes cigarettes as defiant, tough, mature, and unconventional (Dinh, Sarason, Peterson, & Onstad, 1995). Adolescents who view themselves as similar to the prototypical smoker are more likely to smoke (Barton, Chassin, Presson, & Sherman, 1982). A variety of other factors determine whether an adolescent begins to smoke, including whether their parents smoke, exposure to prosmoking information in the media, and social support for smoking (Taylor, 1999).

Once people start smoking, other factors are important in maintaining smoking behavior. Chief among these factors is the physical addiction to nicotine. Once addicted, smokers feel bad when they do not smoke. People who smoke regularly report that they experience increased anxiety, irritability, and moodiness along with decreased ability to concentrate when they stop smoking. In behavioral terms, cigarette smoking is negatively reinforced (i.e., the act of smoking is associated with the cessation of unpleasant feelings).

The reality is, most adult smokers in the United States want to quit (Centers for Disease Control and Prevention, 1997b). Unfortunately, quitting smoking is extremely difficult. People with multiple addiction report that it is harder to quit smoking than it is to quit abusing drugs or to stop drinking (Kozlowski, Coambs, Ferrence, & Adlaf, 1989). Research confirms the impression that it is very hard to quit smoking. A recent review found that only about 7.5 percent of smokers who quit on their own remain abstinent for more than five months (Wetter et al., 1998). Many people turn to health-care providers, including clinical psychologists, for help with smoking cessation.

Clinical psychologists might use a variety of approaches to help clients quit smoking. Some early approaches to smoking cessation focused upon pairing aversive sensations with cigarette smoking. For example, in a procedure called *rapid smoking* (Lichstein, Harris, Birchler, Wahl, & Schmahl, 1973) clients would rapidly smoke cigarette after cigarette focusing their attention on to the unpleasant feelings they experienced. While initial reports for rapid smoking were very optimistic (Lichtenstein et al., 1973), further research has shown that while aversive techniques may help people to quit smoking, by themselves they are not successful at helping people to maintain abstinence (Leventhal, Baker, Brandon, & Fleming, 1989).

Contemporary approaches to smoking cessation tend to focus greater effort on helping people to maintain abstinence. For example, Hall, Munoz, and Reus (1994) tested a brief group cognitive-behavioral intervention. The treatment included an educational component that emphasized the role negative emotions play in cigarette smoking and smoking cessation. Participants monitored their thoughts, interpersonal contacts, daily activities, and mood. They learned strategies for coping with cravings. Cognitive-behavioral strategies for managing depressed mood and anger were also taught. The smokers were encouraged to increase the number of pleasant activities they engaged in and to increase social contact with nonsmokers. Finally, clients learned about dysfunctional thinking patterns that place them at risk for relapse into smoking. Hall and colleagues found their intervention to be helpful especially for smokers who had a history of problems with depression.

Besides cognitive-behavior therapy, a variety of forms of nicotine replacement therapies have been shown to be helpful for people interested in quitting smoking. Nicotine replacement can take a variety of forms but the most common are the nicotine patch and nicotine gum. Contemporary approaches to smoking cessation usually rely upon a combination of psychological and pharmacological approaches. Nicotine withdrawal is carried out gradually while clients learn skills for coping with cravings, managing negative mood states that often set the stage for smoking, and developing strategies for preventing relapse (see Smith et al., 2001, for an example). Unfortunately, even the best smoking cessation methods available are still not particularly successful at helping smokers to remain smoke-free over the long run. A recent meta-analysis found that even intensive smoking cessation therapy and nicotine replacement therapies are only successful in achieving long-term abstinence in about 18 percent of smokers (Wetter et al., 1998). A recent study that combined nicotine replacement with the cognitive behavior therapy approach developed by Hall and colleagues (1994) found that only 25 percent of smokers were abstinent at one year post-treatment (Smith et al., 2001).

Illness

While a significant focus of health psychology is on prevention of illness, clinical health psychologists are also involved with people after they have developed diseases. Clinical health psychologists have participated in the treatment of patients with a variety of forms of illness, including gastrointestinal problems (Turner, 1998), kidney disease (Christensen & Moran, 1998), epilepsy (Baker, 1998), obstetrics and gynecological problems (Alder, 1998; Hunter, 1998), chronic pain (Pearce & McDonald, 1998), and arthritis (Barlow, 1998), among others. Some clinical health psychologists have even specialized in dental health (see Box 15.1). In the next section, we will focus upon three illnesses: diabetes mellitus, headache, and cancer. In each section we will briefly review the role of psychological factors in the disorder and describe ways in which clinical health psychologists work with patients suffering with these problems.

B O X **15.1**

From Mental to Dental Health

Clinical psychology is traditionally associated with the mental health field. Psychological assessment and treatment procedures were originally developed for children and adults with intellectual, psychiatric, and emotional problems. Over its hundred-plus years of existence, however, the field has expanded into areas that were traditionally associated with other disciplines. As we have seen in this chapter, clinical health psychologists research and practice in areas once considered the sole purview of medical doctors. But physicians are not the only ones who are learning to regard psychologists as their colleagues. Dentistry has benefitted from the clinical and research expertise of clinical psychology. From the psychoanalyst's couch to the dentist's chair, what a long strange trip it's been!

As with other areas of health psychology, psychologists contribution to dental health can be broken down into two broad areas: prevention and treatment. Preventive dental care has two goals: prevention of tooth decay (cavities) and prevention of gingivitis (inflammation of the gums caused by plaque). There are basically three components of preventive dental care—brushing, flossing, and professional cleaning. Ideal dental care involves brushing after meals and snacks, daily flossing to remove food particles caught between the teeth, and twice-yearly professional cleaning to remove plaque buildup.

BOX **15.1** Continued

Health psychologists have devised a variety of approaches to help people practice preventive dental care. These can be organized into three types (Kent, 2001). *Educational approaches* are based on the assumption that providing people with information about the importance of proper dental care and how to prevent dental problems will lead them to practice better dental care. Unfortunately, research on educational approaches suggests that information alone is not enough to sustain behavior change (Kent, 2001). *Behavioral approaches* teach people the skills of brushing and flossing but also how to use self-monitoring and reinforcement to maintain preventative behavior. These approaches are often used with children, who place a sticker on a chart each time they brush their teeth. Adults can be taught contingency management strategies in which they reward themselves for longer periods of compliance with their preventive dental plan (e.g., take themselves to dinner on Saturday if they flossed all week). Finally, *social-cognitive approaches* to prevention expand upon educational and behavioral efforts recognizing the importance of people's beliefs in predicting their behavior. Programs that promote the idea that oral health is under the person's control and build people's self-efficacy for preventive care tend to produce lasting changes in dental health care (e.g., Tedesco, Keffer, Davis, & Christersson, 1994).

The most common way in which psychologists get involved with the care of dental patients is helping them overcome anxiety about dental procedures. Some anxiety about visiting the dentist is fairly common, but about 5 percent of people have such a debilitating fear of visiting the dentist that they avoid professional dental care altogether (Kent, 2001). Other people experience extremely high levels of dental fear but force themselves to suffer through cleanings and procedures. People who avoid professional dental care may experience pain and social embarrassment because of their problem. Over half of the people referred to a specialty dental anxiety clinic reported that their dental problems interfered with social activities (Berggren, 1993).

Clinical health psychologists may use a variety of strategies to help patients overcome their anxiety about undergoing dental procedures. Most therapies involve some form of graded exposure, either in real life or imagination, to the dental setting. Patients may be taught muscle relaxation or breathing techniques, as well as cognitive strategies for distracting themselves (Kent, 1998). In consultation with the treating dental professionals, anxious patients may be taught strategies for exerting some control during dental procedures. Simple strategies like the use of a "stop signal" (Wardle, 1983) can increase a patient's sense of personal control during dental procedures.

Patients with dental fear are not the only types of referrals clinical health psychologists might receive from dentists. People who are coping with the effects of oral-facial surgery or temporomandibular joint pain might also be referred, as might patients with special needs. Dental care, whether preventive or restorative, is influenced by people's behavior, emotions, and beliefs. As such, there are many ways in which clinical health psychology can help dentistry.

Diabetes Mellitus

Glucose is the fuel upon which the body runs. But the fuel is of no use if it cannot get to the cells that need it. *Insulin* causes cell walls to become more permeable, allowing glucose to pass into most of the body's cells, where it can be metabolized. In the absence of insulin, most of the body's cells will metabolize substances other than glucose. When fat is metabolized in the absence of glucose metabolism, *ketones* are created and build up in the blood.

These ketones are poisonous and their buildup in the bloodstream can led to coma and death. High level of ketones in the blood stream is called ketoacidosis.

Diabetes mellitus refers to a set of conditions in which insulin production or insulin action is ineffective. The two most common types of diabetes are insulin-dependent diabetes mellitus (IDDM) and non-insulin-dependent diabetes mellitus (NIDDM). IDDM is sometimes called juvenile-onset or Type I diabetes. The onset of IDDM is usually under the age of 30 and occurs rapidly with the sudden onset of symptoms, including severe thirst, excessive urination, and dramatic weight loss. In IDDM, the pancreas essentially produces no insulin. NIDDM is sometimes called maturity-onset, adult-onset, or Type II diabetes. This is by far the most common form of diabetes, accounting for about 85 percent of the cases in developed countries (Bradley, Riazi, Barendse, Pierce, & Hendriecks, 1998). Unlike IDDM, the onset of NIDDM tends to be insidious. Undiagnosed NIDDM may be present for years. In NIDDM, there is insufficient insulin production to meet the body's requirements.

Diabetes effects about 3 percent of the United States population (Aikens & Wagner, 1998). Over 90 percent of people with diabetes suffer with NIDDM and about 6 percent have IDDM (American Diabetes Association, 1996). *Gestational diabetes* occurs in between 2 and 5 percent of pregnancies and tends to remit after delivery (American Diabetes Association, 1996). The risk for NIDDM increases with age. NIDDM is more common in African Americans, Native Americans, and Hispanic Americans (Aikens & Wagner, 1998).

Diabetes mellitus is associated with a variety of health complications. Problems of acute fluctuations in blood sugar levels include coma and infections. Chronic failure to effectively manage one's blood sugar levels is associated with an assortment of health problems. Kidney failure, liver damage, loss of sensations in one's extremities (usually the feet) due to peripheral neuropathy, erectile dysfunction in men, and blindness are all potential complications of chronic diabetes.

Diabetes is a chronic health condition that individuals must manage throughout their lives. Diabetes management is multifaceted and often complicated. A diabetes management plan specifying that patients take the same amount of insulin at the same time every day, eat the same amount and type of food at the same time, and keep their energy expenditures consistent is completely unrealistic (Bradley et al., 1998). Diabetes management involves monitoring blood glucose levels, coordinating insulin and food intake, and monitoring one's activity level. At the minimum, people with diabetes need to assess their blood glucose three or more times a day. They must monitor and limit their calorie intake. NIDDM patients can usually get by with an oral insulin-enhancing agent. However, people with IDDM and people with poorly controlled NIDDM need to give themselves two or more injections of insulin daily. Some patients can be fitted with subcutaneous insulin pumps (Aikens & Wagner, 1998).

Psychological Factors in Diabetes Mellitus.   As the brief description of diabetes management suggests, the regimen is complex, intrusive, and unpleasant. Unsuccessful management is a significant problem. Noncompliance with dietary recommendations and insulin administration is very common in patients with diabetes (Sarafino, 1994). A variety of psychological factors are important in determining the success of diabetes management. Patients must understand what is involved in diabetes management and why it is important. They need to problem solve in order to deal with things that arise but cannot be predicted (e.g., missing an insulin dosage; unplanned physical exertion). They must be motivated to comply with the management plan. They must deal with social pressures that make compliance difficult (e.g., testing one's blood in a social situation; requesting certain kinds of food when needed).

There are a variety of emotional and behavioral problems frequently associated with diabetes. Rates of depressive and anxiety disorders are much higher in people with IDDM or NIDDM than in the general population (Aikens & Wagner, 1998). Stress is also a significant problem for people with diabetes. Diabetes management itself can be stressful. However, there is also evidence to suggest that stress impacts blood glucose levels (Aikens & Wagner, 1998; Bradley et al., 1998). One way that stress may affect blood glucose is indirectly by interfering with diabetes management. Alternatively, stress may more directly impact blood glucose levels through the sympathetic nervous system and pituitary activity (Bradley et al., 1998). Finally, there is an increased prevalence of anorexia and bulimia in women with IDDM, and obesity is a risk and complicating factor for NIDDM (Aikens & Wagner, 1998).

Psychological Intervention. Patients with diabetes may be referred to clinical health psychologists for a variety of reasons. Aikens and Wagner (1998) classified 65 consecutive referrals to the Behavioral Endrocrinology Service at the University of Chicago. Ninety percent of these patients were diabetic. The most common type of referral they received was patients suffering with a depressive disorder (25 percent). The second most common problem was stress affecting diabetes mellitus (21 percent), and some form of anxiety disorder was the third (16 percent). About 13 percent of the patients were referred for failure to adhere to their diabetes management regimen.

There have been several controlled studies of psychological interventions for improving diabetes management. An interesting program developed at the University of Virginia called Blood Glucose Awareness Training helps people with diabetes learn to recognize their blood glucose levels (Cox et al., 1992). In the program, individuals with diabetes learn to monitor their physical symptoms, mood, and the environmental cues associated with different blood glucose readings. They learn to identify the cues that predict high and low blood glucose levels for them. The training has been found to lead to improved accuracy in recognizing blood glucose levels and in diabetes control (Cox et al., 1991; Cox, Conder-Frederick, Julian, & Clarke, 1994; Cox et al., 1995). More general diabetes management programs involve nutrition and education counseling, self-monitoring, weight management, and motivation enhancement strategies (Aikens & Wagner, 1998).

Given how common anxiety and depression are in patients with diabetes mellitus, there have been surprisingly few controlled studies of psychological treatment of these problems in diabetic patients. Clinically, health psychologists frequently use cognitive-behavioral therapies that have been shown to be helpful with nondiabetic samples to treat diabetics with these problems (Aikens & Wagner, 1998). One controlled study found that a combination of cognitive-behavior therapy and intensive behavioral management was more effective at reducing depression in diabetic patients than was the behavioral management program alone (Lustman, 1997, cited in Aikens & Wagner, 1998).

There has been considerably more research on stress management training for patients with diabetes mellitus. Studies of progressive muscle relaxation with or without biofeedback have yielded inconsistent results (see Aikens & Wagner, 1998; Bradley et al., 1998, for review). Taken together the findings suggest that relaxation training may be a valuable adjunct to a more general diabetes management program for some people but not others. Relaxation training appears to be most helpful for patients whose blood-glucose control is particularly sensitive to stress and those diabetics who are generally anxious (Bradley et al., 1998).

Headache

The experience of a headache is near-universal. A recent study found that 91 percent of Danish men and 99 percent of Danish women experience headaches during their lifetime (Rasmussen, Jensen, Schroll, & Olesen, 1991). Descriptions of headaches can be found in writing from the earliest Mesopotamian civilization through the ancient Greeks and, of course, in modern times (Martin, 1998). There have been various attempts to classify headaches. The most recent comprehensive effort was published by the Headache Classification Committee of the International Headache Society (1988). The classification system organizes headaches into thirteen different types, the two most common types being migraine and tension-type headache.

The classic migraine headache is experienced as intense pulsating pain that often starts behind or around the eyes and radiates through the forehead and temporal region. Migraine headaches are often unilateral (one side of the head). Migraine pain is aggravated by routine physical activities such as walking up the stairs. During migraines people are often unable to carry out their daily routines. Migraines are frequently accompanied by other symptoms in addition to head pain. During migraines, people often feel nauseous and may vomit. They report heightened sensitivity to light and sound. Their ability to concentrate may be impaired, and they may be irritable and lose their appetite. A minority of migraine sufferers experience a visual aura (e.g., bright spots or stars) immediately preceding or before a migraine. Migraine frequency varies markedly in people who experience migraines from one a year or less to several migraine episodes a week (Holroyd & Lipchik, 1997).

Tension headache is usually experienced as steady pain on both sides of the head. Sufferers often describe the pain as a pressing or tightening feeling or as a dull ache. Unlike migraines, tension headaches are not accompanied by nausea, vomiting, or visual aura, nor are they as incapacitating. Most people can carry out their usual daily activities while suffering with a tension headache. Tension-headache sufferers report headache pain less than 50 percent of the time. However, some people suffer with tension headaches daily (Holroyd & Lipchik, 1997).

Headaches are much more common in women than men. The lifetime prevalence rates for migraine is about 25 percent for women and about 8 percent for men (Martin, 1998). Similarly, many more women than men report experiencing tension-type headache (Rasmussen et al., 1991; Martin, 1998). Women are also more likely to be disabled by migraine (about 18 percent of women and 6 percent of men) and tension-type headaches (about 5 percent of women and 2 percent of men; Holroyd & Lipchik, 1997). Hormonal changes associated with the menstrual cycle are a likely factor in migraine headache. For example, migraine prevalence is about equal in boys and girls prior to puberty. Prevalence rates for girls increases rapidly in adolescence (Martin, 1998). About 60 percent of women with migraine report that some of their headaches are associated with the menstrual cycle and many women no longer have migraine after menopause (Holroyd & Lipchik, 1997). The degree to which reproductive hormones play a role in tension headaches is not clear.

In the United States, migraine headache is associated with race and income. African Americans and Hispanic Americans have higher rates of migraine than do whites (Stang, Sternfield, & Sidney, 1996). The relationship between race and migraine headache is most likely mediated by societal factors. A study of Ethiopian citizens found very low prevalence rates for migraine in both men and women (Haimanot, Seraw, Forsgren, Ekbom, & Ekstedt, 1995). It has been suggested that prevalence rates of migraine and tension-type headache are higher in developed, Westernized countries compared to developing countries; however, the data are not clear at this point (Martin, 1998).

Psychological Factors in Headache. There appears to be an association between stress and headache. However, the relationship is not a simple one. Typically, no differences in major life events have been found when headache sufferers are compared to control subjects (Martin, 1998). However, when the focus is shifted from major life events to minor daily hassles, differences have often been found. For example, Spierings, Sorbi, Haimowitz, and Tellegen (1996) found that migraine suffers report more daily hassles in the two days preceding a migraine episode.

More important than the number of stressors experienced by headache sufferers may be the way in which they cope with stress. Headache sufferers tend to evaluate the stressful events they experienced more negatively and experience themselves as having less control over these events (Martin, 1998). In addition to reacting strongly to stress, it may be that individuals who suffer headaches frequently do not have social resources to help them cope with stress. Having the support of close friends or family members can help buffer the impact of stress. Headache sufferers perceive that they have less social support and are less satisfied with the support they do have, compared to nonheadache suffers (Martin & Soon, 1993; Martin & Theunissen, 1993).

Negative mood states serve as precipitants to headache episodes in some patients and exacerbate headache pain in most headache sufferers (Martin, 1998). Not surprisingly, prevalence rates for anxiety and mood disorders are higher in headache sufferers than in the general population (Featherstone, 1985; Morrison & Price, 1989).

Personality may be another factor that influences whether, and how severely, one experiences headache but the data here are not so clear. The difficulty in identifying a headache-prone personality is not due to a lack of trying. A review published nearly twenty years ago found over 100 studies of possible relationships between personality and headache (Blanchard, Andrasik, & Arena, 1984). Some avenues of investigation have been more fruitful than others. For example, the so-called "Type A" behavior pattern appears to be a risk factor for headache (Martin, Nathan, & Milich, 1987). The Type A pattern was proposed by two physicians interested in identifying risk factors for cardiovascular disease (Friedman & Rosenman, 1974). The Type A personality is marked by hostility, competitive striving, and a constant state of time urgency.

Psychological Intervention. Contemporary psychological treatment for headache pain started in the 1970s with the development of biofeedback technologies. With the discovery of methods for controlling autonomic functioning, clinicians and researchers began to experiment with the idea of training headache sufferers to control the physiological mechanisms believed to underlie their pain. Tension-type headache was thought to be due to sustained constriction of the muscles around the head. Migraine, on the other hand, was considered to be due to dilation of the cranial arteries (Martin, 1998). *EMG biofeedback* was used to help tension-headache patients reduce tension in the muscles around the head (e.g., frontalis). Migraine sufferers were taught to increase the blood flow to their fingers in order to relieve vascular pressure in the head. *Thermal biofeedback* was used to help patients raise the temperature of their fingertips. In order to raise temperature, blood flow to the fingers must increase.

Since its inception, there have been hundreds of studies of biofeedback for headache pain. EMG biofeedback has been shown to be superior to no treatment and also to various attention control interventions (see Martin, 1998, for review). While EMG biofeedback tends to be helpful, the mechanism by which it works is not at all clear. Reductions in EMG have not been found to correlate with reduction in headaches (Martin, 1998). See Box 15.2 for discussion of an interesting study of the mechanisms of change in EMG biofeedback. Studies of thermal biofeedback tend to find it to be superior to no-treatment comparisons. However, comparisons to credible attention-placebo conditions have tended to find no differences in headache reduction (Martin, 1998).

Relaxation training, without the assistance of any biofeedback equipment, has also been used in the treatment of migraine headache. Learning to relax may increase headache suffers' control over physiological responses and their general level of arousal. In addition, taking time to relax each day may give patients a respite from the stress of the day. Regardless of the mechanism of action, relaxation procedures tend to help reduce the frequency and severity of headache pain in tension-type and migraine headache sufferers (Martin, 1998).

While biofeedback and relaxation training target physiological systems thought to cause or exacerbate headache pain, another set of psychological approaches to treatment targets stress and patients' coping mechanisms. In stress management training, patients learn to identify stressors that either trigger or aggravate headaches and to develop strategies for coping with these stressors. In addition, they learn to identify the ways in which they think about pain and to modify their thinking in order to cope more effectively with the pain. Finally, emotional states associated with headaches (e.g., depression, anxiety) are identified, and cognitive-behavioral strategies are used to manage these emotions (Holroyd & Lipchick, 1997). Stress management that focuses upon cognitive coping training has been shown to be helpful with good long-term results in both tension-type and migraine headache sufferers (Martin, 1998).

Cancer

Few words cause more anxiety among people receiving health-care services than does *cancer*. Even apparently healthy people undergoing medical screening for cancer tend to become distressed (Wardle & Pope, 1992). The fear of cancer in developed countries is easily understood. Cancer is the second leading cause of death in the United States and the third leading killer worldwide (Knight, 1998). Every day in the United States over 3,500 people are diagnosed with cancer and another 1,500 die cancer-related deaths (Parker, Tong, Bolden, &

BOX **15.2**

Change Mechanisms in Biofeedback

Treatments may work for the reasons we think they work. On the other hand, the mechanisms by which a treatment helps clients may be completely different from the ones originally considered. EMG biofeedback is a good case in point. If tension-type headaches are caused by excessive and sustained tension of the cranial muscles, then it follows that reducing tension in these muscles should relieve headache pain. From this logical premise, EMG biofeedback was born. Electrodes connected to a patient's forehead and attached to the right kind of equipment can measure the activity level of the frontalis muscles. Feeding this information into a computer, the patient can see the level of muscle activity. The information on the computer screen provides the patient with feedback about his or her muscle activity. By watching the feedback, the patient can learn to lower the tension levels in his or her frontalis muscles. As we saw in the text, several studies have shown that this relatively simple procedure can help patients with tension headaches reduce the frequency and intensity of headache pain.

Why do EMG biofeedback patients experience less pain after treatment? Because they have learned to reduce the tension in their frontalis muscles, of course. Well, maybe not. Kenneth Holroyd and his colleagues suspected that it was not the reduction in muscle tension itself that led to less headache pain. Rather, it was the belief that one could do something about one's headaches that caused the reduction in pain. Holroyd and colleagues set out to test their hypothesis (Holroyd et al., 1984).

They treated fifty-three college students who suffered with recurrent tension headaches with one of four forms of EMG biofeedback. Half of the patients were treated with traditional biofeedback. That is, when muscle tension decreased, they received feedback that the muscles were more relaxed. The other half of the patients, however, received false feedback. For these patients, whenever they *increased* the tension in the forehead muscles, they were given feedback indicating that they had successfully reduced tension. In addition to manipulating whether patients learned to raise or lower their muscle tension, the researchers also manipulated the type of performance feedback participants received. Half of the participants were led to believe that they were highly successful at reducing muscle tension within and across therapy sessions. The other half of the participants were led to believe that they were only moderately successful. This feedback was bogus (i.e., not related to their actual performance).

The research design used by Holroyd and colleagues (1984) is a 2 by 2 factorial design. What this means is that there were two factors studied (whether patients learned to raise or lower muscle tension and whether they received "high success" or "moderate success" performance feedback) and that each factor had two levels.

What do you think they found? Well, if you guessed that the patients who learned to lower their forehead muscle tension had fewer headaches you would be wrong. In fact, their results suggest that it did not matter whether the patients raised or lowered their muscle tension. What mattered was whether they *believed* that they were successful at controlling their muscle tension. The subjects who received high success feedback showed a significantly greater reduction in headache activity. It appears that it was the *perception of control* that was crucial in reducing headache frequency rather than physiological changes.

Holroyd and his colleagues suggested that two cognitive mechanisms accounted for treatment success. Specifically, they suggested that changes in *self-efficacy* and *locus of control* caused improvement. When headache sufferers believed that their headache pain could be managed by controlling muscle tension (internal locus of control), and they believed that they could successfully control their muscle tension (high self-efficacy), they experienced fewer headaches.

Wingo, 1997). For women, breast, colon/rectum, lung, uterus, and ovarian are the five most common forms of cancer. For men the top five are prostate, lung, colon/rectum, bladder, and lymphoma (American Cancer Society, 1997). For both sexes, however, lung cancer is the leading cause of cancer-related death (American Cancer Society, 1997). Clearly, cancer is a major health concern that impacts millions of people's lives every year.

Technically, cancer is a term that is used to refer to over 200 different diseases (Knight, 1998). What these diseases have in common is abnormal cell growth and cell reproduction. The basic pathology in cancer is a failure of control responses in cellular development. All cells develop, reproduce, and die. This cycle of growth and reproduction is controlled by the cell's genes. In cancer, there is a mutation of the genes that control the cell's growth and reproduction. Usually, cancer develops in one site (e.g., lung, skin, breast) and spreads to other cells at that site. However, cancer can spread to organs adjoining the original site, a process called *metastasis*. In some cases, cancer cells can metastasize to distant regions of the body.

Many forms of cancer treatment are in use today. Surgery is sometimes used to remove cancer cells and surrounding tissue. Surgical procedures have been refined over the years to reduce the amount of tissue removed and to preserve, where possible, the functioning of the affected organ. For example, a procedure called breast-conserving surgery is sometimes used instead of mastectomy for women with breast cancer (Moyer, 1997). *Chemotherapy* involves administration of toxic drugs that kill cancer cells. Chemotherapy is curative for some forms of cancer (e.g., Hodgkin's disease) and is used to slow the progress of more advanced cancers (Knight, 1998). Unfortunately, most chemotherapy drugs affect the body in ways other than by killing cancer cells. Chemotherapy produces physical side effects that can vary from mild to life threatening. Nausea, diarrhea, hair loss, fatigue, and suppression of the body's immune system are some of the more common side effects of chemotherapy. *Radiation therapy* involves the application of radioactive particles to cancer sites and the surrounding tissue. The goal is to kill the cancer cells and adjoining tissue that may have been affected. Depending upon the site and dosage of radiation exposure, treatment can produce nausea, loss of appetite, hair loss, dry mouth, or immunosuppression. Delayed side effects can include sterility or new malignancies (Holland, 1989). *Bone marrow transplantation* is a powerful procedure that was originally used for patients who had diseases that involved failure of the bone marrow (e.g., leukemia, non-Hodgkin's lymphoma; Andersen & Golden-Kreutz, 1998). However, it is being used more frequently with other forms of cancer such as breast cancer (e.g., Winer & Sutton, 1994). In bone marrow transplantation, the patient is treated with very high doses of chemotherapy or radiation therapy or both. Consequently, the patient's immune system is nearly wiped out. Recovery of the immune system is initiated by infusion of bone marrow that was either taken from the patient before treatment *(autologous transplant)* or donated by someone else *(allogenic transplant;* Knight, 1998).

Psychological Factors and Interventions. As the preceding overview of cancer rates, mortality, and treatment suggests, most people have strong psychological responses to the diagnosis and treatment of cancer. Clinical health psychologists have adapted, and in some cases developed, psychological assessment and treatment methods to address the needs of cancer patients and their families. In the following pages we discuss some of the psychological issues cancer patients face and how clinical health psychologists work with them.

Being told that one has cancer evokes a wide variety of strong emotional responses. While difficult for the patient to hear, there is clear consensus among health-care providers that it is morally, ethically, and legally correct to inform cancer sufferers of their diagnosis (Woodard & Pamies, 1992). Empirically, several studies have found a positive correlation between the amount and accuracy of information given to cancer patients about their diagnosis and long-term adjustment in adults and children (Andersen & Golden-Kreutz, 1998). Not surprisingly, recently diagnosed cancer patients report high rates of major depression and depressed mood (Montgomery, Pocock, & Titley, 2003). Anxiety is also common (Schag & Heinrich, 1989). Rates and severity of mood disturbance and psychiatric disorders increase with the severity of the cancer (Andersen & Golden-Kreutz, 1998; Knight, 1998).

Clinical health psychologists use many of the same strategies for managing anxiety and depression in cancer patients as they use with nonmedical patients. Fortunately, it appears that these methods are helpful with cancer patients as well (Andersen, 1993). An illustrative study of melanoma patients demonstrates the value of psychological intervention for recently diagnosed cancer patients (Fawzy, Cousins, et al., 1990; Fawzy, Kemeny, et al., 1990). Eighty people who were newly diagnosed with melanoma were assigned to an experimental support group or a control condition. Patients in the experimental condition were provided with health information, instruction in solving problems related to their illness, and relaxation training in a supportive group setting. Six months after the completion of the treatment, support group subjects reported less depression and fatigue and more vigor. Interestingly, the patients who participated in the support group were also found to have better immunologic functioning than control patients.

Clinical health psychologists can play an important role in helping patients cope with the rigors of cancer treatment. There is, in fact, a large body of research showing that presurgical psychological preparation is associated with positive postsurgical adjustment (see, for example, meta-analysis by Johnston & Vogele, 1993). Typically, clinical health psychologists help patients prepare by surgery by providing them with information about what the patients will experience, both procedurally and physically, pre- and postoperatively. They learn cognitive and relaxation strategies for coping with some of the unpleasant things they will experience. Hypnosis is also sometimes used in surgery preparation. These types of intervention are associated with lower rates of negative affect, less pain, lower usage of pain medication, and shorter length of hospital stay (Johnston & Vogele, 1993).

Chemotherapy and radiation therapy patients commonly experience nausea and vomiting while undergoing treatment (Morrow & Hickok, 1993). For some patients, anxiety, nausea, and vomiting become classically conditioned responses to the cues associated with treatment. A patient treated by one of us, for example, reported that she felt nauseous when she saw the sign for the exit she took to get to the hospital for her outpatient chemotherapy sessions. Clinical health psychologists can help patients cope with the side effects of chemotherapy, including classically conditioned responses, in a variety of ways, including progressive muscle relaxation with guided imagery, hypnosis, cognitive distracting techniques, and biofeedback (Andersen & Golden-Kreutz, 1998).

In addition to nausea and vomiting, psychologists sometimes work with cancer patients to help them cope with other side effects of cancer treatment such as hair loss, fatigue, disfigurement, and sexual dysfunction (Knight, 1998). Clinical health psychologists might also work with the family members of cancer patients to help them cope with their own feelings about their loved one's disease and struggle to provide support and care (Knight, 1998).

Patients with advanced forms of cancer may be referred to psychologists for help in coping with end-of-life issues. As these patients struggle with grief and anxiety about dying, they may be faced with a variety of other concerns. For some terminal patients, issues around communicating with family members are crucial. Others may face difficult decisions about life support and palliative care. For dying parents, concerns about their children may be paramount (Koocher, 1986; Lentz & Ramsey, 1988). These difficult issues are faced by patients who are often in terrible pain, physically weak, and may have impaired cognitive abilities. Not surprisingly, terminal care for cancer patients is extremely stressful for care providers and family members alike (Knight, 1998).

Training and Certification in Health Psychology

Training in clinical health psychology takes place at the doctoral level. Typically, graduate training occurs within a doctoral program in clinical psychology. A recent survey of doctoral programs identified thirty-one clinical training programs that offered specialty tracks in health psychology (APA Division 38 Education and Training Committee, 2000). A small number of programs offer specific training in health psychology with a focus upon direct clinical service to patients (APA Division 38, 2001).

The experiences students obtain in training programs in health psychology are quite diverse. In some programs students spend many hours delivering clinical services in health-care settings, whereas other programs offer course work in health psychology with relatively little emphasis upon clinical work. At this point, there are no mandated standards for doctoral training in health psychology.

Many doctoral students in clinical psychology do not obtain experience in health psychology until their pre-doctoral internship. There are over seventy pre-doctoral internships in the United Stated that offer clinical health psychology as a major component of the training experience. Many more offer some clinical health psychology experience (APA Division 38, 2001).

For the psychologist interested in specializing in clinical health psychology, an increasing number of post-doctoral training programs are available. As with other areas of specialization in clinical psychology, greater emphasis is being placed upon specialized post-doctoral training for people wishing to claim specialization in clinical health psychology.

The American Board of Professional Psychology (ABPP) recognizes clinical health psychology as a specialty area (Belar & Jeffrey, 1990). The American Board of Clinical Health Psychology is the specialty board that is responsible for examining and certifying psychologists interested in board certification. As with all the ABPP-recognized boards, the clinical health psychology board requires licensure for independent practice and at least two years of supervised practice to be considered for specialization. The candidate must submit work samples and sit for a lengthy exam (four to five hours) with a group of board-certified psychologists. As with other specialty boards, the ABPP in Clinical Health Psychology is a completely voluntary credential.

Career Opportunities in Clinical Psychology

As of this writing, the opportunities for psychologists interested in clinical health psychology are quite good. Medical facilities, particularly medical centers that have teaching and research as well as patient-care missions, have expanded the opportunities for employment for clinical psychologists. Because of their varied skills, clinical health psychologists are sought by other types of health-care agencies such as health maintenance organizations, rehabilitation centers, pain management centers, and public health agencies. Some clinical health psychologists work in private practice and those with more academic interests work at colleges, universities, medical or dental schools (APA Division 38, 2001).

In the clinical setting, clinical health psychologists bring to the table a variety of skills. They may utilize cognitive, psychophysiological, personality, or behavioral assessment methods to evaluate the role psychological factors play in patient's medical conditions. The most common interventions used by clinical health psychologists are relaxation training, cognitive-behavior therapy, stress-management, biofeedback, and psychoeducation. However, the full range of psychotherapeutic techniques may be utilized to address individual patients' needs.

Some clinical health psychologists focus their careers on research. In general, clinical health psychology research deals with understanding, and intervening with, health problems from a biopsychosocial perspective. The range of topics a clinical health psychologist might study are as diverse as the fields of psychology and medicine combined. For more in-depth coverage of the many areas of inquiry pursued by clinical health psychologists, interested readers should see Volume 8, *Health Psychology,* in *Comprehensive Clinical Psychology* (Johnston & Johnston, 1998).

As with clinical psychology generally, training in clinical health psychology does not direct psychologists toward either clinical or research careers. As a scientist-practitioners, clinical health psychologists have an array of skills to utilize in their professional careers. As such, the opportunities for research, direct patient care, writing, teaching, and consultation are many.

BOX **15.3**

Focus on Ethics: Expanding One's Practice

Over the past twenty-five years there has been an explosion of scientific knowledge relevant to the practice of clinical health psychology. Consequently, the opportunities for clinical practice have grown and the expansion of clinical practice possibilities in health psychology will likely continue to grow in the decades ahead. It has been suggested, in fact, that "mental health psychology" may lose its place as the dominant area of clinical practice. Psychological practice focused upon the assessment and treatment of mental disorders may be seen as just one domain of health-care psychology (Belar, Brown, et al., 2001).

Psychologists whose training and practice have focused on mental health may be interested in taking advantage of new practice opportunities in health psychology. Is the traditionally trained clinical psychologist competent to work with medical patients? Practitioners can find guidance for defining the scope of their practice expertise in the Ethics Code. Ethical Standard 2, *Competence,* includes the following statements: "Psychologists provide services . . . with populations and in areas only within the boundaries of their competence, based on their education, training, supervised experience, consultation, study, or professional experience," and "Psychologists planning to provide services . . . involving populations, areas, techniques, or technologies new to them undertake relevant education, training, supervised experience, consultation, or study" (American Psychological Association, 2002).

(continued)

B O X **15.3**   **Continued**

Clearly, the onus of responsibility is on psychologists to determine whether they have the education, training, and experience to expand their practices into clinical health psychology. A distinguished group of clinical health psychologists has proposed a self-assessment template to help psychologists determine whether they are prepared to deliver services to patients with medical problems. Cynthia Belar and her colleagues suggest that psychologists answer the following thirteen questions when considering expanding their practice:

1. Do I have knowledge of biological bases of health and disease as related to this problem?
2. Do I have knowledge of the cognitive-affective bases of health and disease as related to this problem?
3. Do I have knowledge of the social bases of health and disease as related to this problem?
4. Do I have knowledge of the development and individual bases of health and disease as it relates to this problem?
5. Do I have knowledge of the interactions among biological, affective, cognitive, social, and developmental components (e.g., psychophysiological aspects)?
6. Do I have knowledge of the empirically supported clinical assessment methods for this problem and how assessment might be affected by information described by questions 1–5?
7. Do I have knowledge of, and skill in implementing, the empirically supported interventions relevant to this problem?
8. Do I have knowledge of the roles and functions of other health-care professionals relevant to this patient's problem?
9. Do I understand the sociopolitical features of the health-care delivery system that can impact this problem?
10. Do I understand the health policy issues relevant to practice with this problem?
11. Am I aware of the distinctive ethical issues related to practice with this problem?
12. Am I aware of the distinctive legal issues related to practice with this problem?
13. Am I aware of the special professional issues associated with practice with this problem?

As the wording of these questions implies, psychologists need not be competent in all areas of clinical health psychology (one wonders whether anyone could) in order to work with patients with medical illnesses. But rather psychologists should focus on specific problem area (e.g., breast cancer, HIV/AIDS, hypertension) when conducting their self-assessment.

There are a variety of methods by which psychologists can expand their domain of competence. These include systematic readings of relevant texts and journals, attending continuing professional education workshops, apprenticing oneself to a competent practitioner, hiring an experienced colleague to supervise one's work, creating a peer network of other psychologists interested in expanding their practices, attending medical grand rounds, and taking advantage of online resources such as listservs relevant to the problem area. When done properly, the expansion of practice is carried out systematically and gradually over a period of months or years.

16   Forensic Psychology

Dr. McDonald appears in court to testify about the emotional state of a psychotherapy client before the client was injured in an auto accident. Dr. Higgombotham discusses the risk a convicted child molester poses to the community and factors that moderate the risk of future sexual offenses. Dr. Walters is asked to evaluate a retired school teacher with Alzheimer's disease and to give an opinion about the teacher's capacity to make a will. Dr. Maxwell is hired by the defense attorney in a murder trial in which the 14-year-old defendant confessed to the crime, and Dr. Maxwell is asked to evaluate the defendant's capacity to understand the Miranda warnings. Dr. Walker evaluates the competence to stand trial of a defendant with schizophrenia facing an assault charge.

Psychologists are frequently called into the legal arena to provide opinions in cases such as the ones described above. Whether clinical psychologists like it or not, the chances of being called into court at some point in their careers are quite high. And it is not only clinical psychologists who attorneys and judges look to for expert advise. A cognitive psychologist may be asked to testify about the validity of "repressed memories" (Loftus, 1993). A defense attorney might call upon an expert on perception to testify about factors that may have influenced the reliability of an eye witness's testimony (see Box 16.1). Psychologists have special knowledge and expertise that the courts value.

Some psychologists specialize in legal work and identify themselves as forensic specialists or *forensic psychologists*. In the criminal justice system, common questions faced by forensic psychologists include: Is the defendant competent to stand trial? And what was the mental state of the defendant at the time of the crime? Forensic psychologists are also involved in noncriminal legal proceedings. In custody hearings, for example, a forensic psychologist might testify about the guardianship or visitation arrangements that would best serve the interest of a child. In civil litigation, the forensic psychologist could be asked to evaluate an individual for mental injury. A forensic psychologist might testify at a hearing about whether an individual should be committed to a psychiatric hospital against his or her will.

Definitions

If any psychologist can end up in court, what does it mean to be a forensic psychologist? Thomas Grisso, a well-known forensic psychologist, offered the following definition: A "forensic psychologist refers to any psychologist, experimental or clinical, who specializes in producing or communicating psychological research or assessment information intended for

BOX **16.1**

Eyewitness Testimony

The research literature on the reliability of eyewitness testimony is vast. Eyewitness reports have been found to be surprisingly unreliable and subject to manipulation (Goodman & Hahn, 1987; Loftus, 1979; McCloskey & Egeth, 1983; Wells & Loftus, 1984; Wells, 1993). To provide a flavor of the types of research that have illustrated the problems with eyewitness testimony, we describe three example studies.

In an oft-cited study, Buckhout, Figueroa, and Hoff (1975) arranged for a simulated crime to be aired on a television news show. Pictures of suspects were then aired and viewers were encouraged to phone in their choice of suspects. Of the 2,145 viewers who phoned in, only 315 correctly identified the perpetrator. This hit rate, 14.7 percent, was no better than would have been expected by chance guesses.

Elizabeth Loftus has studied the effects questioning has on subjects after they witness an event. In one study (cited in Loftus, 1979), college-student subjects were shown a film of a traffic accident. Half of the subjects were asked, "About how fast were the cars going when they hit each other?" The other half were asked the same question only the words "smashed into" replaced "hit." Subjects in the "hit" condition estimated the cars' speed to be 34 miles per hour. The average estimate of subjects in the "smashed into" condition was over 40 miles per hour. In addition, when all subjects were asked questions about the incident one week later, twice as many subjects who were originally asked the "smashed into" question reported having seen broken glass in the film, when in fact there had been none.

What about the confidence with which eyewitnesses report their observations? Intuitively, it would seem that when a witness is certain of his or her observation, the report is more likely to be accurate. Research studies have consistently shown that there is a strong correlation between the certainty with which eyewitnesses report their observation and their credibility as witnesses. Confident eyewitnesses are perceived as more credible witnesses (see Wells, 1993, for review). But studies have also shown that witness certainty is highly malleable. In an innovative study, Luus and Wells (1991) staged a theft. Witnesses believed that they had seen an actual theft. They were asked to identify the thief in a line-up and then to make a statement to a police officer. Between the time they made their identification and when they were interviewed by the officer, they were provided with information that another witness had (a) identified the same person, (b) identified a different person, or (c) decided the thief was not in the line-up. The certainty with which the witnesses made their statements to the police officer varied markedly depending upon the information they were given about the other witness. They were most certain they had identified the right suspect when they believed another witness had identified the same one. The implications of these findings are obvious. When witnesses who tentatively identify suspects later learn of other evidence against the suspects, the witnesses' certainty in their identification goes up. Surely, however, this is not because their memories have improved.

Forensic psychologists familiar with the literature on eyewitness testimony can be valuable assets to the legal system. They are most likely to be called upon by defense attorneys interested in casting doubt on the reliability of eyewitness testimony against the attorneys' clients. Forensic psychologists in such cases would examine the available data and identify factors that might have affected the witness's recall of the event. They might read transcripts of police interviews of the witness to identify factors in the interrogation that could have affected the way the witness recalled the event. They might also try to find out what type of information about the crime the witness was exposed to prior to giving a statement to the police and point out things that may have distorted the witness's recall. The psychologist would then defend his or her findings on the stand by citing the relevant research.

BOX **16.1** **Continued**

Are the research findings that point to the fallibility of eyewitness testimony strong enough to support the expert testimony of forensic psychologists? Some reviewers have concluded that the answer to this question is no. They point out several weaknesses in the literature, such as the fact that most of the research is analogue. That is, very little of it has been done with actual witnesses to real crimes (Yuille, 1993). Others have pointed out inconsistencies in the literature and findings that, while statistically significant, may be of little practical import (Egeth, 1993; McCloskey & Egeth, 1983). Despite these skeptics, there appears to be a consensus among experts on eyewitness testimony that certain psychological findings have been sufficiently established as to be of value to judges and juries (Kassin, Ellsworth, & Smith, 1989).

application to legal issues" (Grisso, 1987, p. 831). Dr. Grisso's definition emphasizes the importance of scientific research for forensic psychologists. They may conduct research on psychological factors relevant to legal issues or consume psychological research findings and share these with the courts in order to assist legal decision making. Competent forensic psychologists base their opinions on scientifically derived psychological knowledge.

As the examples at the beginning of this chapter illustrate, the number and types of issues about which courts look to mental health professionals for information and guidance has grown over the past few decades. Consequently, the number of psychologists who identify themselves as forensic specialists has also increased. In 1991, Division 41 of the American Psychological Association, the American Psychology-Law Society, endorsed a set of Specialty Guidelines for Forensic Psychologists (Committee on the Ethical Guidelines for Forensic Psychologists, 1991). Within the guidelines, the following definition of forensic psychology was offered: "all forms of professional psychological conduct when acting, with definable foreknowledge, as a psychological expert on explicitly psycholegal issues, in direct assistance to courts, parties to legal proceedings, correctional and forensic mental health facilities, and administrative, judicial, and legislative agencies acting in an adjudicative capacity." In other words, forensic psychology is the field of applied psychology in which expertise on psychological issues relevant to legal matters is used to assist courts and other legal bodies.

Psychology and Law: A Wary Alliance

While the courts have often turned to mental health professionals for guidance in complex legal matters, the relationship between psychology and the law has not always been harmonious. Judge David Bazelon described himself as a "disappointed lover" in a paper critical of professional psychology's performance in the legal arena. Judge Bazelon criticized psychologists for offering opinions that ventured far beyond their scientific foundations and for making moral judgments guised as psychological recommendations (Bazelon, 1982). Periodically, psychological testimony has played an important role in high-profile criminal cases such as the trials of John Hinckley, who attempted to assassinate President Reagan, and

Jeffrey Dalmer, who admitted to killing and dismembering fifteen young men over a ten-year period. Mental health experts frequently offer strikingly inconsistent testimony in these cases, and the public may be left with the impression that expert testimony is based upon who is paying the expert rather than any scientific foundation. The value of psychological research findings in the legal system generally has been called into question by some (e.g., Loh, 1981).

Some of the conflict between the psychological and legal professions can be traced back to the basic assumptions that underlie each discipline. Perhaps the most important philosophical difference between the law and psychology is the assumption about the determinants of human behavior (Melton, Petrila, Poythress, & Slobogin, 1987). Psychology holds a deterministic view of behavior. Psychological research is generally directed at identifying the factors, whether intrapsychic, environmental, social, or biological, that influence human behavior. As we saw in Chapters 3 and 4, each of the theoretical models important to clinical psychology has hypothesized various determinants of behavior. The law, on the other hand, emphasizes the importance of free will. Each individual is responsible for his or her conduct. When psychologists describe psychological factors influencing defendants' behavior, it can appear as if the professional is arguing that the defendants are not responsible for their actions.

The philosophical assumptions of psychology and law appear to be mutually exclusive. How then can a psychologist function within the legal setting? Melton and colleagues (1987) offer a partial solution to the dilemma. If the psychologist can resist the temptation, or in some cases the pressure from the examining attorney, to pronounce upon the ultimate legal issue (e.g., was the defendant responsible for his actions?), he or she can still be of assistance to the courts by identifying factors that may have influenced the defendant's behavior. The legal decision about the defendant's behavior is then left to the judge or the jury. The psychologist's findings are interpreted within the legal framework of the case.

A second important difference between the psychological and legal disciplines is in their tolerance for indecision (Anderten, Staulcup, & Grisso, 1980; Melton et al., 1987). The law requires a decision be made about "truth" based upon the evidence available. The defendant is either guilty or not guilty of a crime. In the law, the conclusion of fact is an all-or-none decision. In behavioral science, on the other hand, there is a high tolerance for ambiguity. One of the most common phrases used in the discussion sections of psychological research papers is "more research needs to be done." In fact, science can be seen as an endless search for ultimate truth. Much of the scientific data upon which psychologists rely is based upon comparisons between groups that differ on a particular dimension. The psychologist is faced with the problem of how to apply group data to the individual case. An example will illustrate the dilemma. A convicted violent offender is denied parole because his psychological profile fits that of a group of parolees categorized as "high risk." Research studies have shown that 40 percent of parolees with the same profile have committed violent crimes while on parole. The offender protests that he is "reformed" and that he should be considered among the 60 percent of parolees with this profile who do not commit offenses while on parole (Melton et al., 1987). The legal decision is absolute—parole denied—while the research findings are probabilistic.

The distinction between legal philosophy and the philosophy underlying the behavioral sciences that causes the greatest discomfort for some psychologists is the assumption about the best method of arriving at the truth. The law assumes that the truth is most likely to be derived through an adversarial process. "The logic of jurisprudence is based on the assumption that truth may best be discovered when two persons who support differing conclusions confront each other with passionate, bipartisan debate regarding the merits of their conclusions" (Anderten et al., 1980, p. 764). Attorneys "argue" their cases before a judge or jury who has the responsibility to determine who won the argument. In contrast, science is based upon the assumption that the truth will be discovered through dispassionate employment of the scientific method. In science, all observations should be shared, whether or not they are consistent with one's theoretical position. Many psychologists are surprised when they find themselves on the witness stand facing a hostile attorney who passionately challenges them to defend their views. Most psychologists who testify with any frequency can share at least one humiliating experience in which they were made to feel incredibly inept under intense cross-examination (see Brodsky, 1991).

Expert Witnesses

When psychologists appear in court in their professional role, they are usually appearing as *expert witnesses.* An expert witness is distinguished from a *fact witness.* The latter is usually only able to testify to information obtained through direct observation. That is, fact witnesses can testify about what they saw, heard, read, tasted, felt, and the like. The only types of opinions the fact witness can offer are those based upon their direct perception and that clarify their testimony (Stromberg et al., 1988). Expert witnesses, on the other hand, are allowed, and in fact expected, to offer opinions to the court. The role of the expert witness is to use specialized knowledge to assist the judge or jury in understanding the evidence presented in the case. Psychologists have been recognized as capable of providing expert testimony in cases involving issues of mental disorders since 1962 (Blau, 1984).

When psychologists are on the witness stand, the first questions usually asked are about their education, training, experience, license, and certifications. The attorney doing the questioning is trying to establish that the psychologist is an expert. It is the judge who determines whether the psychologist qualifies as an expert on the matter at hand. The attorney's job is to elicit the information necessary to establish the psychologist as an expert witness. The questioning might go something like this:

ATTORNEY: Please state your name and occupation.

PSYCHOLOGIST: Dr. Lewis Wisnewski. I am a clinical psychologist in private practice.

ATTORNEY: Please tell us about your training and professional experience.

PSYCHOLOGIST: I received my Ph.D. in clinical psychology from the University of Florida in 1986. I did a two-year post-doctoral fellowship in pediatric psychology at Duke University Medical Center. I obtained my state license to practice psychology in Maine in 1989. I worked at the Behavioral and Developmental Pediatrics unit at Eastern Maine Medical Center for four years and have been in private practice for the past three.

ATTORNEY: Tell us, Dr. Wisnewski, do you have an area of specialization?

PSYCHOLOGIST: Yes. I specialize in working with children and families. Specifically, I specialize in working with children with chronic health problems such as asthma or diabetes.

ATTORNEY: Have you done any research in this area?

PSYCHOLOGIST: Yes. I've published several papers on the emotional and social consequences of growing up with a chronic health problem.

ATTORNEY: Beside your research work in this area, do you have any clinical experience working with children with diabetes?

PSYCHOLOGIST: Yes. While at Duke, I worked in a children's diabetes unit. I also consulted with the diabetes clinic at EMMC. At any one time in my private practice, I might be working with six to ten families who have one or more children with diabetes.

In this case, the attorney is establishing the fact that Dr. Wisnewski is an expert in psychological factors in childhood diabetes. Later the attorney will ask Dr. Wisnewski to offer an opinion about the emotional functioning of a specific child he evaluated. Having established Dr. Wisnewski as an expert, the courts will allow him to testify as to his opinions. If this were a child custody case, Dr. Wisnewski might be allowed to offer his opinion as to the custody arrangement that would best meet the child's emotional needs.

Being established as an expert witness does not give the psychologist free rein to offer opinions on anything and everything (Stromberg et al., 1988). It would be inappropriate for Dr. Wisnewski to offer his opinion about whether the father of the child he evaluated is an alcoholic or the likelihood that the father would benefit from treatment unless it has been established that Dr. Wisnewski is also an expert in substance abuse and has evaluated the father. If the opposing attorney is on the ball, he or she will object if a psychologist is asked to offer expert opinion about matters that are beyond his or her expertise.

Being recognized as an expert by the courts can be an ego-boosting experience. Psychologists need to be cautious that they do not abuse the privilege of offering expert opinions. For example, psychologists might be asked for opinions that require inference far beyond the knowledge base of scientific psychology. A question such as "Doctor, what is your opinion as to whether little 5-year-old Johnny is more likely to become a professional hockey player when he grows up if he is placed with his mother or his father?" is best not answered directly. There are no data upon which to base the opinion. To testify that little Johnny would be more likely to make it to the NHL if he is placed with his father (an ex-NHL player himself) than if he goes with the mother (she is sick of hockey) because it seems logical is not offering an expert opinion. Anyone might draw the same conclusion—it takes no special training in psychology. Similarly, psychologists need to be careful about confusing personal and professional opinion. It would be inappropriate, for example, for a psychologist to recommend that a child be placed with her mother rather than her father if the opinion is based upon the fact that the mother shared the same religious beliefs as the psychologist.

In the area of criminal law, psychologists should avoid offering opinion on legal issues (American Psychological Association, 1978), although in practice many psychologists do not follow this advice. Issues such as whether a person is criminally responsible for his or her actions, whether a person should be hospitalized against his or her will, or what is the appropriate sentence for a person convicted of a crime are legal in nature. While mental health professionals have information that can be useful to the courts, it is the judges' role to make these determinations.

Psychology and Criminal Law

Competence to Stand Trial

In the United States, a defendant is required to make a plea in response to a legal charge prior to trial (Winick, 1983). This requirement can be traced back to English common law. Some historians believe that the concept of "competency to stand trial" has its roots in this requirement (see Melton, Petril, Poythress, & Slobogin, 1997). It seems that in English courts some defendants would stand mute rather than respond to the charges. The court in such cases wished to determine whether the defendant was "mute of malice" (i.e., the defendant was being obstinate) or "mute by visitation of God" (i.e., the defendant was unable to respond to the charge because he or she was deaf, must, or "lunatic" (Melton et al., 1997). If the individual was thought to be mute of malice, the courts sought to force a plea by placing increasingly heavy weights upon the defendant's chest, apparently in an effort to squeeze a plea out of the defendant. Those found to be mute by visitation of God were spared this procedure.

Although our legal systems no longer use the weight method to extract pleas, the issue of competence to stand trial continues to be a problem and is raised quite frequently (Melton et al., 1997; Roesch & Golding, 1987), although in most cases defendants are found competent to stand trial. The modern legal definition of competence was established in a landmark case, *Dusky v. United States* (1960). In this case the Supreme Court ruled:

> It is not enough for the district judge to find "that the defendant is oriented to time and place and has some recollection of events," but that the test must be whether he has sufficient present ability to consult with his lawyer with a reasonable degree of rational understanding— and whether he has a rational as well as factual understanding of the proceedings against him. (quoted in Roesch & Golding, 1987, p. 379)

Although specific laws defining competency vary from state to state (Roesch & Golding, 1987; Roesch, Ogloff, & Golding, 1993), in most cases the forensic psychologist is interested in assessing three areas of competency (Maloney, 1985): Can the person appreciate the charges against him or her? Can the person cooperate with counsel? Can the person understand the proceedings in the court? In conducting such an evaluation, the clinician needs to keep several points in mind (Melton et al., 1987; Roesch et al., 1993). First, the focus is on the defendant's competence in the present, not at some point in the past such as the time of the crime. Second, the assessment should focus upon the defendant's capacity to work with the attorney and understand the court proceedings, not the defendant's willingness to do so (mute of malice still doesn't cut it). Third, the assessment is of *reasonable* degree of understanding, not perfect understanding. Fourth, the presence of a mental illness, while often relevant to competence, does not guarantee incompetence. It is quite possible to be schizophrenic, for example, and still be able to understand the charges one is facing, to work with one's attorney, and to understand court proceedings.

Most commentators on the topic of competence to stand trial agree that the threshold for finding a defendant competent is quite low (Melton et al., 1987; Roesch & Golding, 1987; Roesch et al., 1993). The emphasis is upon defendants' cognitive understanding of the judicial procedure, not their feelings about the procedures. Given the fact that legal cases vary in their complexity, it is possible that a defendant may be competent for one type of proceeding, but not another (Roesch & Golding, 1987). For example, in some legal proceedings, the defendant may be required to testify. A defendant who is likely to withdraw into a catatonic state under pressure may be incompetent to stand trial in such a case. However, the same defendant may be competent to cooperate with his or her attorney if the plan is to plea bargain (Roesch & Golding, 1987).

Several instruments have been developed to assist clinicians in assessing competence, including the MacArthur Competency Assessment Tool-Criminal Adjudication (Otto, Poythress, et al., 1998), the Fitness Interview Test (McDonald, Nussbaum, & Bagby, 1991), the Mosley Forensic Competency Scale (Mosley, Thyer, & Larrison, 2001), and the MET-FORS Fitness Questionnaire (Nussbaum, Mamak, Tremblay, Wright, & Callaghan, 1998).

Most defendants who are assessed for competence to stand trial are, in fact, found to be competent (Melton et al., 1987; Roesch & Golding, 1987). However, the defendant who is found to be incompetent presents the state with a difficult moral problem: What is to be done with someone who has been charged with a crime but is not competent to face trial? When the charges are not serious, they are sometimes dropped in an agreement between the state and the defendant and his or her lawyer that the defendant will seek treatment. When the charges are more serious—for example, murder—few would be satisfied with this informal solution. Typically, charges are suspended until such time as the defendant is found competent to face them. The defendant is usually remanded to a psychiatric hospital to receive treatment. Prior to 1972, most states allowed indefinite commitments for incompetent defendants. In a landmark case, *Jackson v. Indiana* (1972), the Supreme Court was faced with the case of a mentally ill deaf-mute who was not likely to be restored to competence with treatment. In *Jackson,* the Supreme Court ruled that a defendant cannot be held for longer than it should reasonably take to determine that he or she is likely to obtain the capacity to stand trial in the foreseeable future.

The *Jackson* ruling, therefore, called to a halt the relatively common practice of involuntarily hospitalizing defendants found incompetent for indefinite periods. Once found incompetent and hospitalized, defendants have limited rights to refuse treatment (Winick, 1983), thus avoiding the situation in which the defendant avoids prosecution by refusing treatment (usually medication) that would likely restore competence.

Other Competencies in the Criminal Process

Competence to stand trial is the most common, but not the only, competence-related issue raised in criminal cases. In the United States, the individual has the right to self-determination. There are situations, however, in which that right is abrogated by the state, presumably acting in the best interest of the individual who is judged to be incompetent to make important decisions, or perform specific acts, for himself or herself. In such cases the state invokes *parens patriae* ("state acting as the parent") power to decide or act on behalf of the individual (Melton et al., 1997).

"You have the right to remain silent. Anything you say can and will be used against you in a court of law." Most people who have watched enough cop shows on television can recite the famous Miranda warnings. This warning, given to prisoners at the time of their arrest, came out of a 1966 United States Supreme Court decision in which the court ruled that statements made by a prisoner were inadmissible as evidence when the prisoner had not been warned of his or her rights (*Miranda v. Arizona*, 1966). In cases in which the defendant has confessed to a crime, the defense attorney may try to make the confession inadmissible by arguing that the defendant was not competent to confess. A forensic psychologist might be consulted in such cases to determine whether a defendant could have understood his or her rights and freely chosen to waive them when the confession was made. It could be argued, for example, that due to mental retardation, the defendant was incapable of understanding his or her right not to make self-incriminating statements (Fifth Amendment) or his or her right to consult with an attorney (Sixth Amendment). Grisso (1981) has found that juveniles very frequently misunderstand their rights as described in the Miranda warning. The mere fact that a mental disorder is present, even a severe disorder such as schizophrenia, does not by itself mean that a defendant's confession is inadmissible. There must be some evidence that the police took advantage of the defendant's condition (Melton et al., 1997). When testifying in a case in which competence to give a confession is the issue, the forensic psychologist might describe a defendant's mental state, level of intellectual functioning, and conditions under which he or she would be particularly vulnerable to influence by the police. The judge will consider this evidence in determining whether to allow the prosecution to use the defendant's confession.

The Sixth Amendment to the Constitution of the United States gives all defendants the right to legal counsel. The Supreme Court has ruled, however, that the Sixth Amendment also gives the defendants the right to refuse counsel and defend themselves, even though the court recognized that this is rarely in the defendant's best interest (Melton et al., 1997). One of the more famous, and bizarre, cases in which a defendant chose to defend himself was the case of Colin Fergusson. On December 7, 1993, Mr. Fergusson was a passenger on New York's Long Island Rail Road. As the train headed for the suburbs, Fergusson opened fire with a 9 mm semiautomatic handgun into a carload of commuters. Six passengers were killed and 19 were wounded by Fergusson. Although two high-powered criminal defense attorneys had agreed to take his case, Fergusson waived his right to counsel and served as his own attorney. His defense, despite the fact that there were scores of eyewitnesses, was that a Caucasian man (Fergusson is black) took the gun from him while he was sleeping and perpetrated the crime. Defending himself, Fergusson was allowed to cross-examine witnesses on the stand, some of whom were individuals he had shot. The following strange interchange took place between Fergusson and Maryanne Phillips, whom he had shot in the chest and who played as if she were dead to avoid being shot again.

> **FERGUSSON:** "It was your statement that you played dead and that you were closing your eyes."
>
> **PHILLIPS:** "I didn't want you to shoot me again."

Prior to Fergusson's murder trial a separate hearing on his competence to stand trial had taken place. The judge determined that he was competent. Although it occured rarely, defendants such as Fergusson were sometimes evaluated for their competence to refuse counsel. Perhaps unfortunately for Fergusson, the Supreme Court has ruled that if a defendant is competent to stand trial, he or she is competent to decide to refuse counsel and defend himself or herself (Melton et al., 1997).

A third competency issue that may arise in a criminal case has to do with the competence of witnesses to the alleged crime, rather than the defendant's competence. Questions are sometimes raised about the competence of witnesses to testify. Competence to testify is most often raised when the witness is a child, is mentally retarded, or suffers with a severe mental disorder. Of these three groups of potential witnesses, children as witnesses have received the most attention (see Box 16.2). The primary issues for the courts are the child's ability to distinguish truth from falsehood and to understand the need to tell the truth (Melton et al., 1987). Even when the child clearly understands the difference between the truth and a lie, questions are often raised about whether the child's memory for events relevant to the alleged crime is true or the product of suggestion. It is not uncommon for a child to be expected to testify months or years after the event in question, having repeated his or description of the event numerous times, and having discussed the event with parents, the police, caseworkers, and a therapist. Legitimate questions about the veracity of the child's testimony can be raised in such cases.

Several other issues of competency arise from time to time in criminal cases. A defense attorney may question his or her client's competence to plead guilty or to refuse an insanity defense. In other cases, the court itself may raise questions about a defendant's competence to be sentenced (see Melton et al., 1997 for discussion). In states that have the death penalty, questions about a defendant's competence to be executed can be raised. No state allows for the execution of an incompetent person. In a famous case involving capital punishment, Gary Gilmore waived his right to appeal his death sentence. The Supreme Court ruled that Gilmore had the right to waive appeal as long as the waiver was "knowing and intelligent" (quoted in Melton et al., 1987, p. 108). As a result, Gilmore was executed by firing squad. The standard for competence to be executed is that the individual understands what it means to be executed and why the execution was ordered. This standard has resulted in some disturbing questions for the courts. In *Perry v. Louisiana* (1989), the court was asked to determine whether a death row inmate could be forced to take psychotropic medication so that he would be restored to competence for his own execution.

The Insanity Defense

The issue involving law and mental health that is probably most familiar to the general public is the insanity defense. If the amount of coverage this issue has received in newspapers, popular magazines, novels, and made-for-TV movies were an accurate indicator, the insanity defense would be among the most frequently used legal strategies in the criminal justice system. When the insanity defense is used successfully in a high-profile trial, such as John Hinckley's, there is usually a public outcry for the abolition of not guilty by reason of insanity (NGRI) laws, accompanied by debates among legal scholars, mental health professionals, and talk-show guests.

BOX **16.2**

Children's Testimony

Kelly Michaels was a young woman in her mid-20s who worked at the Wee Care Nursery School in Maplewood, New Jersey. On August 2, 1988, Ms. Michaels was convicted of 115 counts of sexual abuse against 20 children between the ages of 3 and 5 who had been students at the Wee Care school. The primary evidence against Kelly Michaels was the testimony of 19 children. During the time that Ms. Michaels worked at Wee Care, no other staff members noted any problem with her work performance. Children did not complain about her and parents did not detect anything unusual about their children when they picked them up at the end of the day. In fact, no suspicions had been raised about Ms. Michaels until four days after she had left the nursery school to take a better-paying position. At that time, a 4-year-old student at Wee Care was at his pediatrician's office having his temperature taken rectally when he said to a nurse, "That's what my teacher does to me at school." That afternoon the child's mother notified the New Jersey child protective agency. Over the next two months the students of Wee Care Nursery School were interviewed repeatedly. Based upon these interviews, a bizarre picture emerged of the goings on at the Wee Care Nursery. Kelly Michaels allegedly sexually assaulted the children with knives, forks, spoons, and Lego blocks. She played the piano in the nude, licked peanut butter off the children's genitals, made the children eat her feces and drink her urine, and made them play a game in which they all disrobed and licked one another (the Cat game). Ms. Michaels was sentenced to 47 years in prison (description based upon Ceci & Bruck, 1995).

Given that there were no adult witnesses to the sexual abuse that was alleged to have occurred at the Wee Care Nursery School, prosecutors relied upon the testimony of the child victims to convict Kelly Michaels. But are children reliable witnesses? Are they more vulnerable to suggestive questioning than adults? Is the testimony of children, particularly in cases of child sexual abuse, tainted by overzealous investigators and therapists? Stephan Ceci and Maggie Bruck (1995) examine these and related questions in their book, *Jeopardy in the Courtroom: A Scientific Analysis of Children's Testimony.* Summarizing nearly 100 years of research on children's suggestibility, Ceci and Bruck identify several factors that can contaminate the reports of child witnesses, including interview bias (when an interviewer has strong expectations about what he or she is likely to find, children will often provide corroborating evidence); repeated questioning (when children are provided misleading information over the course of several interviews, they come to believe that the misinformation is true and develop other beliefs consistent with the misinformation), stereotype induction (when the interviewer conveys negative information about someone, such as "She does bad things," the child may form a negative stereotype of that person and provide information consistent with the stereotype), and the use of anatomically detailed dolls (in some investigations of child sexual abuse, the child is provided with one or more dolls that have sexual organs). Reviewing the evidence, Ceci and Bruck suggest that the dangers associated with anatomically correct dolls outweigh the potential benefits. For example, research studies have not consistently shown that sexually abused children play with the dolls in a manner that is distinguishable from nonabused children.

In the following excerpt from an interview with one of the child witnesses in the Kelly Michaels case, note how the interviewer pursues information consistent with the belief that the child was abused by Ms. Michaels:

INTERVIEWER: Do you think that Kelly was not good when she was hurting you all?
CHILD A: Wasn't hurting me. I like her.

(continued)

BOX **16.2** **Continued**

INTERVIEWER: I can't hear you, you got to look at me when you talk to me. Now when Kelly was bothering kids in the music room . . .

CHILD A: I got socks off . . .

INTERVIEWER: Did she make anybody else take their clothes off in the music room?

CHILD A: No.

INTERVIEWER: Yes?

CHILD A: No . . .

INTERVIEWER: Did Kelly ever make you kiss her on the butt?

CHILD A: No.

INTERVIEWER: Did Kelly ever say—I'll tell you what. When did Kelly say these words? Piss, shit, sugar?

CHILD A: Piss, shit, sugar?

INTERVIEWER: Yeah, when did she say that, what did you have to do in order for her to say that?

CHILD A: I didn't say that.

INTERVIEWER: I know, she said it, but what did you have to do? (quoted in Ceci & Bruck, 1995, p. 100)

In the following interview and commentary, one can see the effects of repeated and suggestive questioning. This interview was conducted by Eileen Treacy, the state's expert, approximately two years after the events were alleged to have occurred:

TREACY: I see, and did the kids want Kelly to do that peanut butter stuff?

CHILD A: I didn't even think that there was a peanut butter . . .

TREACY: Well, what about licking the peanut butter?

CHILD A: There wasn't anything about peanut butter . . .

TREACY: Some of the kids told me that things happened with knives. Do you remember anything like that?

CHILD A: No.

(Although the child professes no knowledge of utensil abuse, at trial this child testified to numerous abuse allegations.)

TREACY: . . . Well what about that Cat game?

CHILD A: Cat game?

TREACY: Where everybody went like this, "Meow, Meow."

CHILD A: I don't think that I was there that day.

(Although the child professes no knowledge of the Cat game, at trial she described a cat game in which all the children were naked and licking each other.) (From Ceci & Bruck, 1995, p. 117)

Psychological research such as that reviewed by Ceci and Bruck (1995) has had an impact in the courts. For Kelly Michaels, the impact was significant. Expert psychological testimony played a role in her appeals trial. After five years of incarceration, she was freed on bail when the Appeals Court of New Jersey reversed her conviction (*State v. Michaels,* 1993). In December 1994 the prosecution dropped all charged against Ms. Michaels.

The public fascination with the insanity defense has resulted in, or may be a product of, some widely held myths about the defense. Many people believe that the insanity defense is used very commonly, usually by wealthy defendants, who escape punishment for some heinous crime such as murder. One study, for example, found that the "average" community resident in Wyoming believed that the insanity defense was used 43 percent of the time in criminal cases; students thought it was used 37 percent of the time; and legislators thought it was used in 21 percent of cases (Pasewark, Seidenzahl, & Pantle, 1981). In Wyoming, during the time period in question, the insanity defense was used in about half of 1 percent of criminal cases. Other studies have found it was used even less frequently in other jurisdictions (e.g., Cooke & Sikoski, 1974; Petrila, 1982). Not only is the insanity defense used infrequently, it is usually not successful. The best estimate is that the insanity defense succeeds about one-fourth of the time (Steadman, Keitner, Braff, & Arvanites, 1983). In over 70 percent of these cases of acquittal by use of the insanity defense, the plea was arrived at through a plea-bargain so that the cases never went to trial (Melton et al., 1987). As for the idea that the NGRI defense has helped a disproportionately large number of wealthy individuals escape punishment for violent crimes, the data don't support this myth either. "Historically, in fact, most people who were found not guilty by reason of insanity . . . were poor persons, charged with non-violent or marginally violent crimes, who then were incarcerated for long periods of time in institutions for the criminally insane" (Stromberg et al., 1988, p. 630).

The insanity defense, therefore, appears to have generated interest and debate in scholarly publications out of proportion to its practical impact. That is not to say, however, that it is a trivial issue, for the insanity defense strikes at the heart of the assumption of moral responsibility underlying our judicial system. It is the issue that most strongly pits the determinism assumed by psychological theories of human behavior against the concept of free will upon which our criminal justice system rests (see Golding & Roesch, 1987; Stromberg et al., 1988, for discussion).

NGRI Standards. The U.S. and British systems of justice require that two elements be present for a criminal act: *actus reus,* the voluntary performance of the act, and *mens rea,* the choice or intention to commit the act (Smith & Meyer, 1987). In the insanity defense, the defendant argues for the absence of *mens rea.* The concept of *mens rea* can be traced back to ancient Babylonian Talmud, was present in Greek and Roman laws, and can be identified in British law as far back as King Henry I of England (1100–1135; see Golding & Roesch, 1987). The first documented case of acquittal by reason of insanity occurred in 1505 (Stromberg et al., 1988). In 1724, Lord Tracy argued that the defense was appropriate only if the defendant "doth not know what he is doing, no more than an infant, than a brute, or a wild beast" (quoted in Golding & Roesch, 1987, p. 386). The so-called "wild beast" test was standard until the nineteenth century, when the first, and perhaps most influential, of the modern standards for NGRI was established.

On January 20, 1843, Daniel M'Naghten attempted to assassinate Robert Peel, the prime minister of England. He fired at the wrong man, hitting Peel's private secretary, Edward Drummond, who later died of the injuries. M'Naghten was probably suffering from paranoid schizophrenia and the jury found him not guilty by reason of insanity (Golding &

Roesch, 1987; Smith & Meyer, 1987; Stromberg et al., 1988). M'Naghten's acquittal resulted in such a public uproar that the House of Lords appointed a group of judges to develop a standard for use in insanity defense cases in the future. The M'Naghten standard, as it known, reads as follows:

> Every man is to be presumed to be sane, and . . . to establish a defense on the ground of insanity, it must be clearly proved that, at the time of committing the act, the party accused was labouring under such a defect of reason, from disease of the mind, as not to know the nature and quality of the act he was doing; or if he did know it, that he did not know he was doing what was wrong (M'Naghten's Case, 1843, p. 722)

M'Naghten was adopted in the United States and continues to be the standard in about one-third of the states (Stromberg, et al., 1988). The M'Naghten standard is a tough one to meet. If taken literally, it requires that the defendant demonstrate that he or she did not know that the criminal act was wrong at the time it was committed. It has been criticized for emphasizing cognitive understanding and ignoring perceptual, emotional, and other influences upon behavior.

In 1962, the American Law Institute (ALI) produced its Model Penal Code, which included a standard for the insanity defense (see Golding & Roesch, 1987; Melton et al., 1997; Smith & Meyer, 1987; Stromberg et al., 1988). The ALI standard is:

> A person is not responsible for criminal conduct if at the time of such conduct, as a result of mental disease or defect, he lacks substantial capacity either to appreciate the criminality (wrongfulness) of his conduct or to conform his conduct to the requirements of law. (quoted in Smith & Meyer, 1987, p. 388)

The ALI standard is more liberal than M'Naghten in several ways. First, it allows for the influence of noncognitive factors upon the defendant's ability to "appreciate" that his or her actions are wrong. Second, while M'Naghten is usually seen as an either/or standard (i.e., the person understands that the act was wrong or does not), the ALI standard allows for a not guilty finding if the person lacks "substantial capacity." By the ALI standard, then, *some* capacity to appreciate the wrongfulness is not enough. Third, it adds a volitional component to the standard ("lacks substantial capacity . . . to conform his conduct") to M'Naghten's purely cognitive understanding (Stromberg et al., 1988). In addition, the ALI standard includes the caveat "The terms 'mental disease or defect' do not include abnormality manifested only by repeated criminal or otherwise anti-social conduct" (quoted in Smith & Meyer, 1987, p. 388). This sentence effectively excludes the individual diagnosed as psychopathic, or antisocial personality disorder, from using the defense. The ALI standard has been adopted by many states.

Another approach applied in some states, usually in combination with M'Naghten, is the "irresistible impulse" standard. As the name implies, the standard allows for an insanity acquittal in cases where, while the accused may have understood that his or her actions were wrong, he or she were unable to refrain from acting because of mental illness. The idea is that the behavioral impulse is so strong that it cannot be resisted by force of will (Smith & Meyer, 1987). The difficulty with the irresistible impulse standard is that it is often very difficult to distinguish an uncontrollable act from one that is simply difficult to control. For example, was the alcoholic unable to resist the impulse to rob the liquor store or was the urge simply very hard to control?

In the insanity defense, the judge or jury must make a binary decision: guilty or innocent. Some states have moved beyond this either/or standard to consider the "diminished capacity" defense. The concept of diminished capacity has been applied in two ways. In one, the defendant argues that he or she could not have engaged in an essential element of the charge due to some mental or physical defect. For example, a chronic alcoholic charged with tax fraud might claim that he was so drunk most of the time he couldn't have planned to deceive the IRS (Stromberg et al., 1988). The second way in which diminished capacity has been used is to reduce the seriousness of the charge. For example, a schizophrenic woman might acknowledge that she murdered her husband but argue that she lacked the capacity to plan the murder, thus arguing for the charge to be reduced from premeditated murder to manslaughter. California is one of the states that acknowledges diminished capacity. Perhaps the most infamous case in which the diminished capacity defense was used was that of Dan White, the San Francisco supervisor who intentionally and apparently with premeditation killed two city officials. White was convicted only of manslaughter, however, because he alleged that his mental problems were exacerbated by a diet of sugary junk food. The so-called "Twinkie Defense," while successful in this case, is considered absurd by most legal scholars (Stromberg et al., 1988).

There have been a variety of efforts to reform the insanity defense over the years. The "Guilty But Mentally Ill" verdict has been proposed as a compromise that would allow juries to convict in difficult cases, but treatment, rather than incarceration, would be the consequence. Twelve states have passed statutes allowing a finding of Guilty But Mentally Ill since 1976 (Melton et al., 1987). In these states, a defendant who pleads NGRI can be found not guilty, guilty, insane, or Guilty But Mentally Ill. The latter verdict is given when the defendant is found guilty beyond a reasonable doubt, not insane (i.e., not meeting the standard for NGRI), but mentally ill. Proponents of the Guilty But Mentally Ill statute argue that it offers juries a compromise verdict. The public is defended against dangerous offenders while at the same time providing treatment for the sick (Melton et al., 1997). Critics of these statutes have called the idea that a defendant can be "Guilty But Mentally Ill" an oxymoron and note that the verdict simply side-steps the issue of moral responsibility (Stromberg et al., 1988).

The NGRI Evaluation.   Evaluating a defendant in an NGRI case is a particularly challenging endeavor. The forensic psychologist is presented with the problem of assessing the accused's state of mind when the offense occurred. Depending upon the case this can be weeks, months, or even years prior to the evaluation. Malingering is an important consideration. Having made the NGRI plea, the defendant may be highly motivated to convince the clinician just how crazy he or she really was when the crime was committed. It has been suggested, therefore, that the NGRI mental health evaluation include multiple interviews with the defendant; a review of any clinical records on the defendant; a review of crime investigation records, including witness interviews, confessions, and autopsy reports; a review of criminal history including probation reports; and interviews with mental health or corrections staff who have had contact with the defendant (Melton et al., 1997; Smith & Meyer, 1987).

The Rogers Criminal Responsibility Assessment Scales (R-CRAS) were developed in an effort to improve the scientific rigor of insanity evaluations (Rogers, Dolmetsch, & Cavanaugh, 1983). The instrument guides the clinician through an evaluation of six "psycholegal" criteria relevant to the insanity plea: (1) the client's reliability (i.e., the presence of malingering), (2) evidence of organic brain disturbances, (3) evidence of major psychiatric disorder, (4) cognitive control (i.e., the ability to comprehend the criminality of his or her behavior), (5) behavioral control (i.e., the ability to control criminal behavior), and (6) whether the loss of control (items 3 and 4) were the result of organic (item 2) or psychiatric (item 3) defect. When forensic specialists are provided with identical information, the interrater reliability of the R-CRAS is good. Although not generally accepted as the preferred method of assessing criminal responsibility (see Goldstein, 1992), and not without its critics (see Melton et al., 1997), there is more evidence for the reliability and validity of the R-CRAS method than any alternative methods of assessing defendants who claim the insanity defense (Rogers & Ewing, 1992).

What Happens after an NGRI Acquittal.   Francine Hughs poured gasoline in the bedroom of her ex-husband and set the room on fire. She then drove herself to the police station, where she reported what she had done. Her ex-husband was killed in the fire. Ms. Hughs had suffered physical abuse at the hands of her ex-husband for years, including on the day of his death. In a case involving conflicting psychiatric and psychological testimony, Ms. Hughs was acquitted NGRI. After she was acquitted, Ms. Hughs was reexamined and it was determined that she did not meet the state's requirements for involuntary hospitalization—she was not found to be mentally ill and a danger to herself or others (see *Civil Commitment* below). She was released back into the community (case summary taken from Melton et al., 1987).

The case of Ms. Hughs and others like it draw a great deal of public attention and sometimes understandable outrage. They lead to questions about the guidelines used for dealing with individuals found NGRI. In most states, NGRI acquittals are routinely evaluated to determine whether they meet criteria for civil commitment. If they do, they are involuntarily hospitalized, usually in a facility for the criminally mentally ill until such time as they can demonstrate that they are no longer mentally ill or no longer a danger to themselves or others (Stromberg et al., 1988). In Michigan, for example, defendants acquitted NGRI are committed to a forensic psychiatric facility for 60 days for the purpose of determining whether they are mentally ill and dangerous to themselves or others (Melton et al., 1987). Criss and Racine (1981) found that between 43 and 72 percent of the 60-day NGRI acquittals committed to the Center for Forensic Psychiatry were released after the diagnostic period. Findings such as these lend fuel to the belief that the NGRI defense allows clever criminals to escape punishment. While there are undoubtedly cases in which this is true, other findings indicate that most NGRI acquittals are psychotic and have prior histories of psychiatric hospitalization (see Melton et al., 1987).

Sentencing

"Don't do the crime if you can't do the time." The rates of imprisonment of United States citizens have steadily increased over the past three decades. In 1990, the rate at which this country incarcerated criminals was double the rate of incarceration in 1980 and triple the rate in 1970 (Wrightsman, Nietzel, & Fortune, 1994). There are over a million people behind bars in state and federal prisons and local jails in the United States (Wrightsman et al., 1994). Many see stricter prison sentences as the solution to our country's crime problem, while others see overreliance upon incarceration as contributing to the problem. Incarceration is, of course, not the only form of punishment for convicted criminals. Fines, probation, community service, and other "innovative" sentences are also used.

Whatever the form, punishment of criminals is thought to serve several functions (see Greenberg & Ruback, 1984):

1. *General deterrence.* Punishment of an individual offender is assumed to discourage other potential lawbreakers from committing crimes.
2. *Individual deterrence.* Having been punished for the crime, the criminal is assumed to be less likely to commit future crimes.
3. *Incapacitation.* The community is protected from the offender while he or she is incarcerated.
4. *Retribution.* The goal here is to give the criminal his or her "just deserts." The criminal should not benefit, and should in fact suffer, for having committed the crime.
5. *Moral outrage.* Punishment can help a society vent the frustration and anger that results from being victimized. Thus punishment is thought to serve as a means of societal catharsis, relieving the emotional pain suffered as a consequence of the crime.
6. *Rehabilitation.* Another goal of punishment is to provide the offender with an opportunity to mend his or her ways. The hope is that the criminal will learn new skills or develop different attitudes that will allow him or her to become a productive citizen when the sentence is complete.
7. *Restitution.* Punishment can take the form of financial or other compensation provided to the victim for damages or losses suffered.

Judges are allowed some discretion in meting out criminal sentences. They consider such factors as the circumstances of the crime and characteristics of the criminal (e.g., prior convictions) when deciding upon the appropriate sentence. Some judges have used their discretionary powers in interesting ways. For example, an avid golfer who was convicted of diverting materials and labor (about $300,000 worth) from a California building project to build his private residence near the Pebble Beach golf course was sentenced to 9 months of labor at a public golf course. He was not allowed to play golf himself and was incarcerated when he was not working (Neff, 1987).

The courts sometimes look to mental health professionals for help in providing information they can use to facilitate sentencing decisions. Since a large percentage of criminal cases are resolved without a trial, judges use pre-sentence investigations (often conducted by probation officers) and pre-sentence psychological evaluations to develop a better understanding of the crime and the criminal. The job of the forensic psychologist in these cases is to help the judge to understand the offender as a unique individual different from the stereotype the judge might hold about those convicted of the particular offense (Melton et al., 1987).

One or more of the following three issues are emphasized in the pre-sentence psychological evaluation: (1) the need and potential value of treatment, (2) the offender's personal responsibility for the crime (culpability), and (3) the dangerousness of the convicted offender (Melton et al., 1987). Regarding the need for treatment, forensic psychologists may identify a mental health disorder (e.g., pedophilia, alcoholism) that was a factor in the commission of the crime. They can educate the courts about the amenability of such a problem to treatment and whether the offender is a good candidate for such treatment. Psychologists can also provide the courts with information about the availability of treatment and the likelihood that the offender will comply. A forensic evaluation can shed some light upon the offender's culpability by identifying situational factors that may have contributed to the occurrence of the crime. In some cases this can result in an easier sentence, since the judge may come to see the crime as less of a product of the offender's free choice. The third issue forensic psychologists are often asked to address in pre-sentence evaluations is the degree of risk the offender presents for committing violent acts in the future. Recall that one of the goals of incarceration is to protect the community. Judges want to know: How likely is it that this offender will hurt someone? Can he be safely freed into the community? Will he commit similar crimes again in the near future? Whether mental health professionals have anything to say about the risk for future violence is a controversial issue. Although it is extremely difficult to predict whether a specific individual will or will not commit a violent act (see Box 16.3), forensic psychologists may provide some useful information about factors associated with increased and decreased risk for violence that the courts may find helpful in determining the appropriate sentence (Melton et al., 1987).

As indicated in other areas of criminal law, the ultimate decision in sentencing is up to the judge. It would be inappropriate for the clinical psychologist to make direct recommendations about sentencing (e.g., "This defendant should serve at least two years in the penitentiary and have an extensive probation following his release"). Sentencing should be based upon legal and community standards. While psychologists, trained as clinicians, may tend to emphasize the rehabilitative function the sentence could potentially serve (e.g., recommending probation with mandatory sex-offender treatment), the judge needs to be mindful of the other functions punishment serves in the criminal system.

Civil Commitment

Few professional duties are as stressful to psychologists as those involved in involuntarily committing someone to a hospital against his or her will. This process, known as *civil commitment,* often involves the police, distraught family members, and angry or confused prospective patients. Psychologists might be roused from their bed in the middle of the night in order to evaluate the person in question. They rarely have the time to consult colleagues or resource materials and the evaluation itself may take place in a less than ideal physical location (e.g., the back of a police cruiser; Knapp & Vande Creeke, 1987).

Civil commitment refers to the hospitalization of a mentally ill individual when that individual does not consent to voluntary admission. Civil commitment is another example of the state acting upon its *parens patriae* authority. In this case, the state is acting on behalf of the individual to protect him or her, but also to protect the community. Psychologists have the authority to participate in the involuntary hospitalization process in some but not all states.

Should Psychologists Predict Dangerousness?

Civil commitment laws require mental health professionals to evaluate dangerousness when assessing someone for involuntary hospitalization. Is this person likely to behave violently? Does he or she pose a serious threat of harm to self or others? Involuntary admissions is not the only situation in which forensic psychologists and other mental health professionals are asked to evaluate dangerousness. The decision to discharge a patient from the hospital involves risk assessment. When requesting pre-sentence evaluations, judges often want to know the degree of risk the convicted offender presents to the community. In some states with the death penalty, it must be shown that the offender would continue to behave violently unless subjected to capital punishment before a capital sentence can be given. Mandated reporting laws require psychologists to inform authorities if they learn of children or others who are at risk for abuse. These laws implicitly demand that psychologists evaluate risk and act based upon their findings. Even psychologists who do not routinely interact with the courts or mental hospitals cannot escape the demand to assess risk for violence. Society expects mental health professionals to be able to evaluate risk and act to protect those who are threatened (Monahan, 1993). Shah (1978) noted that there were at least fifteen legal and clinical situations that call upon mental health professionals to assess risk for violence. Failure to do so could leave the clinician open to liability litigation.

But can mental health professionals accurately predict whether a given individual will behave violently? Historically, those who have reviewed the research literature on the prediction of dangerousness have answered with a resounding no! (e.g., Megargee, 1981; Monahan, 1981). In the 1970s both the American Psychological Association (1978) and the American Psychiatric Association (1974) issued statements indicating that their members had no special ability to predict who is going to behave violently. One reviewer at the time drew the following conclusion: "the identification of potentially violent individuals with sufficient accuracy to warrant preventative detention is . . . an impossible quest" (Megargee, 1981, p. 181).

Several factors conspire to make it difficult to predict violence. First, although we are increasingly aware of violence in our society, the fact remains that violent crime is still a relatively rare phenomenon. Overprediction is unavoidable when predicting low base rate phenomena. The following classic example illustrates the low base rate problem as it applies to predicting who will murder:

> Assume that one person out of a thousand will kill. Assume also that an exceptionally accurate test is created which differentiates with 95 percent effectiveness those who will kill from those who will not. If 100,000 people were tested, out of the 100 who would kill, 95 would be isolated. Unfortunately, out of the 99,900 who would not kill, 4,995 people would also be isolated as potential killers. (Livermore, Malmquist, & Meehl, 1968, p. 84)

A second factor that likely contributes to the tendency to overpredict violence is the consequences making a mistake has for the predictor (Melton et al., 1987; Smith & Meyer, 1987). If a clinician declares a patient who would not actually behave violently to be violent and the individual is hospitalized, there are likely to be no negative repercussions for the clinician. On the other hand, should the clinician inaccurately state that a prospective patient is not violent and that individual subsequently assaults, rapes, or murders someone, the mental health professional is likely to be subject to negative publicity and a lawsuit, not to mention having to cope with the guilt of knowing he or she could have prevented another human being from harm. These types of considerations may understandably influence a clinician's judgment.

(continued)

B O X   **16.3**   **Continued**

Clinicians tend to be trained to think in terms of diagnoses, personality factors, cognitive distortions, and emotional influences upon behavior. Violence, on the other hand may be more strongly influenced by environmental factors or the interaction between situational variables and personal predilection. The prediction of dangerousness is a particularly difficult task because clinicians can only guess at the situations in which the examinee will find himself or herself. To take an extreme example, most men and women soldiers who partake in horrific acts of violence in combat never commit another violent act once they are discharged from the service.

In the past two decades, the science of violence prediction has improved. First, several lines of research have identified groups of individuals who engage in violent behavior at relatively high rates. For example, Klassan and O'Connor (1988) identified a group of mental health care recipients for whom the base rate of violent behavior in the community was over 50 percent. There is growing evidence that a subset of individuals with certain mental health conditions present an increased risk for violence (Monahan, 1992). Link, Cullen, and Andrews (1993, as cited in Monahan, 1992) found that patients who endorsed current psychotic symptoms were more likely to engage in violent behavior. Individuals who are diagnosed as psychopaths based upon a particular measure of psychopathy (Hare, 1991) have been shown to be at increased risk for violence (see Salekin, Rogers, & Sewell, 1996, for review).

How to use these new research findings in clinical practice is an issue still open to debate. In a thoughtful commentary on the ethics of violence prediction, Grisso and Appelbaum (1992) note that dichotomous predictions (i.e., the person either is or is not dangerous) cannot be defended based upon current research findings. However, conveying the degree of risk for future violence by describing the probability of violence for an individual given what we know about comparable groups can be defended. For example, reporting that there is a 40 percent rate of violent recidivism among people with similar arrest histories and the same mental disorder would be ethically defensible. Testifying at a commitment hearing that an individual meets diagnostic criteria for a mental disorder and that individuals with that disorder are at increased risk for violent behavior is ethically appropriate (Grisso & Appelbaum, 1992).

Monahan and Steadman (1996) have suggested that mental health professionals use a system for communicating risk that is analogous to the approach used by meteorologists. Weather forecasters routinely used probabilistic statements to describe expected weather patterns (e.g., 70 percent chance of rain). However, when describing rare but dangerous events, they use a categorical warning system (e.g., no warning, hurricane watch, hurricane warning). In mental health, a combination of probabilistic and categorical statements might be used effectively in reporting risk assessment findings.

Although we still can't predict dangerousness as accurately as the courts would like, nor as well as the general public seems to believe we should, forensic psychologists and other mental health professionals do have valuable information to share. The Supreme Court recognized in *Barefoot v. Estelle* (1983) that there is a need to assess potential for future violence and that this need is so great that courts should be allowed to accept clinicians' violence predictions, no matter how flawed they might be. After all, the court concluded, mental health professionals' predictions about dangerousness were "not always wrong . . . only most of the time" (p. 91).

Tracing the history of civil commitment through Western civilization reveals considerable variety in the ways in which the mentally ill have been treated. Ancient Greek writings reveal a benevolent attitude toward the mentally ill. It was recommended that they be cared for in clean, comfortable, and well-lit confines. The Romans appointed a guardian to look after the mentally ill individual's property (Melton et al., 1997). By the Middle Ages, however, there was considerable intolerance for the those suffering with mental disorders. They were often driven out of communities and at times imprisoned (Smith & Meyer, 1987). In Colonial America, the mentally ill were frequently subject to ridicule, harassment, and in some cases public whippings, since the society generally viewed a failure to work as a sign of immorality (Melton et al., 1997). The first hospital specifically created for the care of the mentally disordered in this country was established in 1773 in Williamsburg, Virginia (Smith & Meyer, 1987). This marked a shift from a moralistic to a medical view of the mentally ill in the United States.

In the nineteenth century, most states had statutes that allowed for involuntary hospitalization. Unfortunately, these tended to be vaguely worded, creating the potential for abuse. Husbands, for example, could have their wives committed if they were able to persuade a single physician to sign commitment papers (Smith & Meyer, 1987). A reform movement began in the latter part of the nineteenth century that succeeded in creating some modifications of the commitment laws (Melton et al., 1997). Nonetheless, prior to the middle part of the twentieth century, most state laws required only that the person was "mentally ill and in need of treatment" for involuntary hospitalization to occur:

> Due process was largely dispensed with on the ground that the goal of commitment was therapy, not punishment. Mental institutions during this time period were a backwater of social policy, basically ignored by legislators, policymakers, and lawyers. Police officers, public hospitals, and families demanded that some place be found for disruptive mentally ill persons. As a result, states committed many people for long periods, often to large "mega-institutions" with inadequate medical staff, minimal treatment, and disgraceful living conditions, (Stromberg et al., 1988, p. 552)

Significant reform of the commitment laws did not really begin until the 1960s. People began to view the mentally ill as another group of citizens who had been denied their basic civil rights. Improvements in psychotropic medications made it possible for people with severe forms of mental illness to function in the community. The courts eventually struck down laws allowing for involuntary hospitalizations simply based upon a need for treatment. New laws were developed that placed more safeguards in the civil commitment process. It had to be shown not only that the prospective patients were mentally ill, but also that they posed danger to themselves or to others. In addition, the courts required that the state prove that there was no less restrictive alternative to hospitalization and that the patient would be provided treatment, and not simply be housed, during the course of the hospital stay.

Civil Commitment Laws

Although there is some variability among states in the laws governing civil commitment, most require that the following criteria be met: The person is (1) mentally ill; (2) either dangerous to himself or herself, dangerous to others, or gravely disabled; (3) unwilling to consent to voluntary hospitalization; (4) treatable; and (5) the hospital must be the least restrictive alternative (Stromberg et al., 1988).

The definition of mental illness in most state laws matches the *Diagnostic and Statistical Manual of Mental Disorders* (American Psychiatric Association, 1994) fairly closely. Some states explicitly exclude some disorders such as mental retardation or alcoholism. Mental health professionals are usually most comfortable indicating whether a prospective patient meets this criterion.

The criterion that is most troublesome for mental health professionals is determining whether the person is, in fact, dangerous to themselves or to others. As discussed in Box 16.3, examination of the research on mental health professionals' ability to predict violence is a humbling experience for most psychologists. In fact, the American Psychological Association and the American Psychiatric Association have issued statements indicating that their members are not able to make reasonable predictions about the likelihood of dangerous behavior (see Stromberg et al., 1988). Nonetheless, the courts have not let mental health professionals off the hook. They have proclaimed dangerousness to be a legal, rather than medical or psychological, concept. The court will determine whether a person is dangerous, but mental health professionals need to be involved in the process since, even if they can't predict dangerousness, they have information the courts can use in making a determination (Stromberg et al., 1988).

The issue of dangerousness presents the courts with difficult questions. How serious must the danger be—for example, is exposing one's genitals to strangers dangerous enough to warrant commitment? Does the danger have to be to another person or can it also include property—should a person who threatens to burn down his neighbor's garage because he believes that it is a temple for devil worshipers be hospitalized? How soon in the future must the danger be? Most states require that the danger be "imminent," but the exact definition of this term is open to interpretation. Does there need to be evidence of prior dangerous acts in order to justify hospitalization? Some states require there has been a recent overtly dangerous act, attempted act, or specific threat to meet the criterion for dangerous (see Stromberg et al., 1988, for discussion).

Some case examples illustrate the inconsistencies that result from the difficulty in determining dangerousness. A 27-year-old man was picked up by police because he was blocking the door to the office of a clothing manufacturer. The man claimed that he was owed one million dollars for having designed the manufacturer's line of clothes. The man stated, "Everybody is God. Everybody got sense. God has sense. Be productive . . . I'm productive, making the book of designs for clothes for everybody in the world, in the universe." An examining psychiatrist concluded that the man was suffering with paranoid schizophrenia. The courts ordered him hospitalized on the grounds that if he returned to the manufacturer he might harm someone or be harmed by an irritated employee (Stromberg et al., 1988, p. 559).

A man named Barker was convinced that his common-law wife was having an affair with a neighbor. He was taken into police custody when he called to complain that his neighbor and his wife were engaged in sodomy. Two psychiatrists examined Mr. Barker and both concluded that he suffered with paranoid delusions. Four events that had occurred in the months prior to the civil commitment hearing were presented as evidence of Mr. Barker's dangerousness. First, he tried to punch the neighbor. He missed. Second, while intoxicated, Mr. Barker argued with his wife, fired shots with a revolver through an open door, then faked a suicide attempt by firing a blank shell at his own head. Third, he had shown up at his sister's house one night brandishing a gun and stating that he was looking for his wife. Fourth, he had broken a beer bottle and waved the jagged edges at his wife. After considering this evidence, the courts still concluded that Mr. Barker did not present an immediate risk and ordered his release (Stromberg et al., 1988, p. 559–560).

Most states include a provision for the commitment of mentally ill individuals who do not threaten others or threaten to harm themselves, but are unable to care for themselves. The term "gravely disabled" is used to describe such individuals (Stromberg et al., 1988). Gravely disabled is usually taken to mean that the individual cannot care for his or her basic needs for food, clothing, or shelter.

A person cannot be committed to a hospital unless evidence is presented showing that the individual can benefit from treatment. In the landmark case *Jackson v. Indiana* (1972), the Supreme Court ruled that a deaf, mentally retarded man who had committed a crime could not be held in a hospital until he was competent to stand trial. Since he was essentially untreatable, this would have been a life sentence. Patients have the right to treatment. Today, courts require that the state present evidence that there is a proposed treatment plan for the involuntary patient and that the patient can benefit from the treatment.

The final criterion for civil commitment in most states is that hospitalization is the least restrictive means of providing treatment and protecting the patient and community. With the advent of powerful psychotropic medications, extended periods of hospitalization have become increasingly difficult to justify. Many states have developed short-term crisis stabilization programs, day treatments, and other programs to meet the needs of the mentally ill. Although it is an option that is used infrequently (Miller, 1985), most states permit commitment to outpatient treatment. If the patient fails to comply with outpatient treatment and medication regimes, then involuntary hospitalization can be considered.

Civil Commitment Procedures

Most state laws designate certain people who can initiate civil commitment proceedings. These usually include police officers, mental health professionals, and family members (Stromberg et al., 1988). For the psychologist, this can sometimes mean initiating a petition for the evaluation of a psychotherapy client for commitment to a hospital. By initiating a petition for involuntary hospitalization, the mental health professional is raising the question of civil commitment. When he or she is the petitioner, it is not the mental health professional's role to decide that this is the case.

Involuntary confinement requires an independent assessment of the prospective patient. This emergency evaluation usually takes place at the treatment facility, but some communities, especially in rural areas, use emergency response teams who travel to the prospective patient to conduct the evaluation. For example, a concerned family member may take a suicidal person to the emergency room of a general hospital, where the crisis response team from a psychiatric institution comes to evaluate the person.

Confinement to a treatment facility as the result of an emergency evaluation is only for a limited time (e.g., seven days). In *O'Connor v. Donaldson* (1975), the Supreme Court ruled that a hearing must take place within five to seven days after admission. The preliminary hearing is held before a judge. Usually, two mental health professionals who have conducted independent evaluations of the patient will testify. The treatment facility presents its treatment plan. The judge then decides whether the patient meets criteria for continued involuntary hospitalization. As a result of this hearing, the patient may be confined to the mental health facility for a longer term (e.g., up to 30 days). If additional hospitalization is deemed necessary by the hospital staff, another hearing must take place. Periodic formal hearings to determine whether the patient continues to meet criteria for civil commitment are conducted. It is rare for a patient to be committed to a mental institution for longer than 90 days without another hearing. Unfortunately, hearings can be cursory affairs in some jurisdictions (see Smith & Meyer, 1987; Stromberg et al., 1988). Patients often have a very short notice prior to the hearing; very few are represented by attorneys of their choosing; and the hearing itself may involve little more than the professionals' reports that the patient is mentally ill and dangerous.

Reforms in the civil commitment laws, along with the advent of powerful antipsychotic medications, have dramatically reduced the number of people committed to state and county mental hospitals. On an average day in 1955, 560,000 United States citizens were committed to institutions due to mental illness. By 1972 it was 276,000; in 1975, that number was below 200,000; and in 1981 it was about 138,000 (Melton et al., 1987; Stromberg et al., 1988). While reformation of the civil commitment laws has undoubtedly prevented some people from being hospitalized who in fact did not need to be, the systems currently in place for dealing with the mentally ill in our country are far from perfect. It is widely recognized that many individuals who in decades past would have been chronic residents of mental hospitals now can be found living in the jails, prisons, homeless shelters, and streets of most American cities.

On January 17, 1996, Mark Bechard entered the Servants of the Blessed Sacrament Chapel and convent in Waterville, Maine, and bludgeoned and stomped to death Sister Edna Mary Cardozo and Sister Mary Julien Fortin. He stabbed a third nun and bludgeoned a fourth, neither of whom died. Bechard was known to have a long history of mental illness. He was diagnosed with schizoaffective disorder and had been hospitalized more than two dozen times since 1977. When on his medication, Mark Bechard was lucid. He was an accomplished jazz musician. However, Bechard also had a history of violence, having assaulted his mother, a band member, a girlfriend, and two strangers in the ten years prior to the murders. Mark attended Mass at the Blessed Sacrament chapel frequently and was well known to the sisters. In the days prior to the murders, he apparently had stopped taking his medication. His appearance and demeanor deteriorated. On the night of the murders, Mark threw his trumpet into the garbage. He attended Mass, where he was observed to be talking to himself. Did the mental health system fail Mark Bechard and the sisters of the Servants of the Blessed Sacrament convent? How should his rights to the least restrictive alternative to hospitalization be weighed against citizens' rights to be protected?

Child Abuse and Neglect

Children are victimized more often than adults in our society (Finkelhor & Dziuba-Leatherman, 1994). The best estimates are that somewhere between 5 and 25 children out of every 1,000 are the victims of physical abuse. Children are raped, robbed, and assaulted at rates two to three times higher than that of the adult population as a whole, (see Finkelhor & Dziuba-Leatherman, 1994, for discussion). Children are sometimes the victims of crimes such as neglect or family abduction, for which there is no adult equivalent.

The problems of child abuse and neglect were "discovered" in our country in the 1960s. An important article by Henry Kempe and colleagues published in the *Journal of the American Medical Association* in 1962 is sometimes credited with alerting the nation to the problem of child abuse. The authors identified what they called the "battered-child syndrome." In a four-year period in the mid-1960s, all fifty states enacted mandated child abuse reporting laws. These laws resulted in a dramatic increase in the number of reported cases of child abuse (Melton et al., 1987). The country underwent a similar awakening to the problem of sexual abuse of children in the 1980s.

The problems of child abuse and neglect are particularly challenging ones for the courts to deal with since the perpetrators are often family members. It has been estimated, for example, that about half of the incidents of sexual abuse are perpetrated by a parent (Finkelhor & Dziuba-Leatherman, 1994). The courts must balance the state's interest in protecting the child against the individual's right to family privacy (Melton et al., 1997).

Psychologists and other mental health professionals become involved in the legal issues that stem from child abuse and neglect at three phases. First, mandated reporting laws require psychologists to report physical or sexual abuse of a child, as well as neglect, when they suspect that it has occurred or is likely to occur. If the abuse allegations are substantiated and the perpetrator is a parent or guardian, the courts may remove the child from the home or require the perpetrator to reside elsewhere. The mandate of child protection agencies, however, is to preserve families, or when disruption has occurred, to work toward reunification (Azar, Benjet, Fuhrman, & Cavallero, 1995). Therefore, the second phase at which psychologists often become involved is helping the courts determine what conditions the family must meet for reunification to occur. For example, parents may be required to complete parent education classes or demonstrate that they have maintained sobriety in order to regain custody of their children. The third phase at which mental health professionals often get involved is the most severe. In this phase, the state will move to have the rights of the child's parents permanently terminated.

Termination of parental rights is one of the most serious actions the civil courts can take. To many people this punishment would be more painful than imprisonment. As such, the criteria for termination of parental rights are quite demanding. First, it must be demonstrated that the parent is *unfit* and that his or her unfitness is *not amenable* to intervention. Second, it must be demonstrated that the state has provided the services necessary to remediate the parent's deficits and that either the parent has failed to take advantage of these services or failed to make adequate progress. Third, it must be demonstrated that a better alternative is available for the child (e.g., foster care or adoptive parents; Azar et al., 1995; Melton et al., 1997). The courts frequently look to mental health professionals for information to assist them in determining whether these criteria have been met. As in other areas in which the law and psychology interact, the level of certainty demanded by the law often exceeds that which psychologist can provide (see Azar et al., 1995).

To take the first criterion, the definition of unfit is not clear within the law, nor do we have sound scientific bases for determining what is minimally adequate parenting (Azar et al., 1995). The clinical training of psychologists often leads them to think it terms of what is optimal parenting instead of what is adequate. For example, while most parent-effectiveness trainers would agree that time-out is preferable to repeatedly shouting "stop it" when managing the behavior of a preschooler, it is not clear that engaging in the latter behavior makes a parent unfit. Azar and colleagues (1995) have pointed out that we don't have an empirically based definition of adequate parenting, nor of the goodness of fit between parental style and children's needs.

Mental health professionals often come from cultural and socioeconomic backgrounds that are very different from the families who most often appear at termination hearings (American Humane Society, 1985). These cultural differences may result in misunderstandings that negatively bias the clinician's evaluation. Azar and colleagues (1995) offer the following example to illustrate this point. A Hispanic child who lowers his eyes in front of his parents may be seen as frightened of the parents by an evaluator who does not understand that this gesture is an appropriate sign of respect in the child's culture.

Evaluating the adequacy of services provided to a family is another area in which the clinical psychologist might assist the courts in making termination of parental rights decisions. Behavioral approaches to parent training have been shown to be effective with parents who have mistreated their children (e.g., Azar & Twentyman, 1986). However, high-quality interventions of this sort are often not available to families. Families who are involved with child protective services may receive minimal or no intervention. In fact, the child protective system in this country appears to be in a state of disarray (Azar et al., 1995). Even if families are receiving services for which there is some research support, the question of whether service is adequate for that specific family is often open to question. Culturally diverse or special populations (e.g., drug-addicted parents) may never have been studied. The mental health professional may not have an empirical basis upon which to judge whether the services provided to the family in a parental rights case were adequate. Without some normative data about the efficacy of the specific interventions with this type of family under these circumstances (i.e., intervention ordered by child protective services), the foundation of a psychologist's "expert testimony" can be questioned. Nonetheless, what psychologists can do is educate the courts about relevant theory and research, which may help the courts to make more informed decisions.

Evaluating the appropriateness of the alternative placement for the child who has been taken away from his or her family is another difficult task for the mental health professional. The stress of living in foster care, attending court hearings, and knowing that one may be permanently separated from one's parents may make it very difficult to interpret the child's behavior and evaluate the appropriateness of alternative placements. In addition, while a preferable alternative placement may be available at the time the mental health professional conducts his or her evaluation, the stability of that placement may be unknowable. Foster parents sometimes quit, and the quality of a foster home can change as other foster children move in and out of the residence.

Given the issues discussed above, one may wonder whether it is appropriate for psychologists to testify in termination of parental rights cases. In a thoughtful paper on the subject, Sandra Azar and her colleagues answered this question with a cautious yes (Azar et al., 1995). The psychologist can bring to the court information that might not be otherwise available and can help the court to interpret information presented by others. Azar and colleagues (1995) describe a case in which a mentally retarded mother's repeated failure to come to counseling sessions on time was interpreted as resistance, when in fact it was discovered that she could not tell time. Idiographic evaluation of the primary players in termination of parental rights cases gives the courts a better understanding of the individuals and their behavior. Psychologists can help dispel widely held myths that may prejudice the courts. For example, mentally retarded parents are often assumed to be unfit (Hayman, 1990). However, research studies of mentally retarded parents have raised doubt about the automatic assumption that they cannot adequately care for their children (see Azar et al., 1995; Melton, et al., 1997). With psychosocial support and adequate financial resources, they are often able to provide adequate parenting. The clinical psychologist brings a sophisticated knowledge of the technology and methodology of evaluating treatment outcome that can assist the courts in determining the adequacy of the services provided to the family. The psychologist, therefore, can help the courts determine whether the second criteria for termination of parental rights has been met. It seems then that forensic psychologists can be of assistance to the courts in child protective matters. As in other areas in which psychologists serve the courts, however, caution must be exercised by psychologists so that they do not stray beyond the confines of the current, scientifically derived knowledge base.

Child Custody in Divorce

Marriages frequently end in divorce in our culture. The divorce rate in the United States has risen sharply over the past four decades. Starting in the late 1950s the divorce rate began to climb until it reached a level more than twice as high as in the first half of this century (Guttmann, 1993). It is estimated that about half of all new marriages will end in divorce. When a marriage dissolves, parents are faced with difficult decisions about who will have responsibility for the children and what role the noncustodial parent will play in their lives. The courts may become involved in child custody decisions when divorcing parents cannot agree on where the children should live or how custody should be shared

Not until the late nineteenth century was there much debate over the fate of the children when a marriage ended in divorce. They went with the father. English and U.S. law viewed children as fathers' possessions, or chattel (Melton et al., 1987; Wyer, Gaylord, & Grove, 1987; Wrightsman et al., 1994). In the late nineteenth and early twentieth centuries, the courts began to recognize children as human beings. Consequently, a gradual shift in the standard upon which custody was decided took place. As early as 1881, Justice Brewer argued that the "best interest of the child" should be emphasized in disputed custody decisions (*Chapsky v. Wood*, cited in Wyer et al., 1987). By 1900, fourteen states had statutes emphasizing the best interest of the child (Wyer et al., 1987). Best interest of the child is currently the standard in almost all fifty states.

For the first two-thirds of the twentieth century, best interest of the child translated into maternal custody for all practical purposes. Mothers were routinely given custody based upon the so-called "tender years doctrine," which saw mothers as the natural caregivers for children of tender years. Young children and minor girls of any age were routinely awarded to the mother, while teenaged boys were most often awarded to the father (Wyer et al., 1987). Mother-preference in custody decisions began to erode in the 1970s (Melton et al., 1987; Wrightsman et al., 1994). Ironically, it may have been one unforeseen consequence of the women's liberation movement that, with larger numbers of women working and an increased concern for equality of the sexes, the courts no longer automatically assumed mothers would provide for the best interest of the child.

In the 1980s joint custody plans were adopted by most states (Wrightsman et al., 1994). Joint custody seemed to promise something for everyone—fathers could continue to have influence in the lives of their children, and mothers were relieved of the responsibility of being the sole custodial parent. Research studies comparing joint custody to arrangements in which one parent had custody and the other was allowed visitation tend to show that family members are generally more satisfied in joint custody arrangements (see Wrightsman et al., 1994). Some studies, however, have found that a subset of children have a difficult time switching from one household to another (e.g., Steinman, 1981). Joint custody usually works best when both parents live in the same school district and when animosity between the parents is not so great as to make effective communication about the child impossible.

The fact is, in most cases, custody and visitation decisions are worked out by divorcing parents. Perhaps as few as 10 percent of custody disputes are resolved in court (see Melton et al., 1997). For the cases that do come to trial, however, the disagreement between parents is often intense and there is little interest in compromise. It is in these cases that psychologists often find themselves involved.

A high-quality custody evaluation can be of great value to the judge faced with determining the best interest of a child or children in a contested custody case. In a typical evaluation of this type, the clinician will assess all the principal players in the custody dispute including both parents, the children in question, and the parents' new spouses or live-in partners. In addition, home visits and observations of parent-child interactions are frequently conducted (Ackerman, 1994). Parents and children are interviewed about their custody preferences and the reasons behind their choices. Skilled forensic psychologists bring knowledge of child development, family dynamics, psychopathology, personality functioning, and the effects of divorce on children to bear in their evaluations. When done well, the custody evaluation provides the court with a rich supply of objective and impartial information to use in determining the custody arrangement that best meets the needs of the child or children. Experts disagree on whether psychologists should make specific recommendations about the ultimate issue (i.e., who should be awarded custody). Some evaluators do not usually make a specific recommendation to the court on the ultimate issue. They see their role as providing the court with data it can use in determining the custody arrangement. Other evaluators (e.g., Ackerman, 1994) see it as appropriate to offer recommendations about custody arrangements.

Unfortunately for the courts, and for professional psychology, not all psychologists who have consulted to the courts in custody cases do so with appropriate professional expertise, care, and caution (Keith-Spiegel & Koocher, 1985; Melton et al., 1997; Weithorn, 1987). A long list of problems and abuses has been cited:

> inadequate familiarity with applicable legal standards and procedures; use of inappropriate psychological assessment techniques; presentation of opinions based on partial or irrelevant data; overreaching by exceeding the limitations of psychological knowledge in expert testimony and offering opinions on matters of law; loss of objectivity through inappropriate

engagement in the adversary process; and failure to recognize the boundaries and parameters of confidentiality in the custody context. (Weithorn, 1987, p. vii)

Concerns such as these led the American Psychological Association to develop Guidelines for Child Custody Evaluations in Divorce Proceedings (see Table 16.1; American Psychological Association, 1994). The APA guidelines are aspirational, not mandatory. That is, the association encourages its members to strive to meet the guidelines, but will not penalize them for failure to do so. In this way, the guidelines are akin to the General Principles and not the Ethical Standards in the Ethical Principles of Psychologists and Code of Conduct.

Gerald Koocher commented that conducting custody evaluations ranks second only to having sex with one's clients in activities likely to result in a malpractice suit (Koocher, personal communication, January 27, 1995). Emotions run high in contested custody cases. Frequently, one or both parents are dissatisfied with the outcome. In addition, psychologists need to be knowledgeable in a wide variety of areas to do the job competently. Psychologists who undertake custody assessments must be able to perform psychological evaluations of

---

TABLE 16.1   Guidelines for Child Custody Evaluations in Divorce Proceedings

I.   Orienting Guidelines: Purpose of a Child Custody Evaluation
1. The primary purpose of the evaluation is to assess the best psychological interests of the child.
2. The child's interests and well-being are paramount.
3. The focus of the evaluation is on parenting capacity, the psychological and developmental needs of the child, and the resulting fit.

II. General Guidelines: Preparing for a Child Custody Evaluation
4. The role of the psychologist is that of a professional expert who strives to maintain an objective, impartial stance.
5. The psychologist gains specialized competence.
6. The psychologist is aware of personal and societal biases and engages in nondiscriminatory practice.
7. The psychologist avoids multiple relationships.

III. Procedural Guidelines: Conducting a Child Custody Evaluation
8. The scope of the evaluation is determined by the evaluator, based on the nature of the referral question.
9. The psychologist obtains informed consent from all adult participants and, as appropriate, informs child participants.
10. The psychologist informs the participants about the limits of confidentiality and the disclosure of information.
11. The psychologist uses multiple methods of data gathering.
12. The psychologist neither overinterprets nor inappropriately interprets clinical assessment data.
13. The psychologist does not give any opinion regarding the psychological functioning of any individual who has not been personally evaluated.
14. Recommendations, if any, are based on what is in the best psychological interest of the child.
15. The psychologist clarifies financial arrangements.
16. The psychologist maintains written records.

Source: Adapted from American Psychological Association (1994).

children, adults, and families. In addition, they must have experience and training in child and family development, psychopathology, and family dynamics. Psychologists must have a firm handle on the burgeoning research literature on the effects of divorce on children. In addition, they must understand the divorce and custody laws in their state or jurisdiction (American Psychological Association, 1994).

The Power and Perils of Testifying in Court

It is a rare psychologist who can approach testifying in court with casual aplomb. The experience can be professionally gratifying. As in the fictitious example of Dr. Wisnewski, when providing expert testimony, psychologists are frequently presented with an opportunity to list their professional accomplishments in a public forum. Psychologists then share their knowledge with the court and confidently defend the opinions offered. The experience can also be professionally deflating. On cross-examination, opposing attorneys attempt to cast doubt on psychologists' testimony by making them look ill-prepared or incompetent. Minor weaknesses in the psychologists' professional training or assessment procedures can be made to look like major flaws (Brodsky, 1991). The entire field of professional psychology is also fair game. Cross-examining attorneys have been known to portray clinical psychology as no more reputable than palm reading.

To be effective expert witnesses, psychologists need to understand the legal system, develop good working relationships with the attorneys, prepare carefully, and anticipate the criticisms likely to be leveled at them or their testimony (Brodsky, 1991; Singer & Nievod, 1987; Stromberg et al., 1988).

In the direct examination, the attorney who has brought the psychologist in as an expert witness leads him or her through a preplanned series of questions. Direct examination has four themes: (1) establishing the qualifications of the psychologist (see the Dr. Wisnewski example above); (2) "laying a foundation" for the psychologist's testimony; questions such as "Dr. Smith, did you conduct a psychological evaluation of Mr. Manson?" and "What procedures did you use in your examination?" provide the foundation upon which the psychologist's testimony rests; (3) drawing from the psychologist the factual findings, conclusions, and opinions; and (4) walking the psychologist through a series of hypothetical questions (Stromberg et al., 1988). In each type of questioning, but especially in the fourth, in addition to painting a picture for the judge or jury, the attorney is also anticipating arguments likely to be raised by the opposing side and allowing the psychologist to dispute them under friendly conditions.

In cross-examination, the opposing attorney tries to distort the picture painted by the psychologist during direct examination so that it is no longer clear or looks very different (Stromberg et al., 1988). It is the opposing attorney's job to highlight inconsistencies and weaknesses in the psychologist's testimony. If this fails, the psychologist himself or herself is fair game for attack. Unfortunately for many psychologists, there are now volumes available to help attorneys attack psychological testimony (Ziskin, 1981; Ziskin & Faust, 1988). These books describe strategies and trial techniques designed to nullify the impact of psychological testimony. One common strategy is to draw psychologists into offering opinions about matters that are beyond their expertise. By doing so the attorney can then discredit the psychologist and shake the jury's confidence in the opinions offered in areas about which the psychologist is truly expert (Singer & Nievod, 1988). The following examples provide a flavor of the types of cross-examination questions that, if not answered carefully, can cause the psychologist to appear inept.

> "Isn't there considerable controversy about the usefulness of psychological evidence in regard to legal matters?"
>
> "Can you offer any evidence that the psychiatric theories upon which you base your conclusions have some basis in fact?"
>
> "Has there ever been a scientific study of the accuracy of your professional judgment?"
>
> "So you haven't any idea if the diagnostic opinions you have been offering year after year are really correct?" (Singer & Nievod, 1988, pp. 544–545).

Coping with hostile cross-examination is more art than science. Several authors have offered their advice on this topic (e.g., Brodsky, 1991; Poythress, 1980; Stromberg et al., 1988). Some suggestions frequently offered include:

1. Only answer clear questions. When an attorney's questions include phrases like "isn't it conceivable" or "is it possible" or "never occurs," the psychologist is probably wise to ask for clarification before answering.
2. Do not overstate the certainty of your conclusion. Very little about human behavior is true 100 percent of the time.
3. Review current literature. Few things are more anxiety provoking for a psychologist than to discover on the witness stand that the examining attorney has read the recent research articles or books that the psychologist has been meaning to get around to but has not quite found the time.
4. Conduct a careful examination. This may be the most important advice. The witness stand is no place for a psychologists to discover their errors.

Training and Certification in Forensic Psychology

Forensic psychology has been one of the fastest growing areas of professional psychology over the past two decades. Many clinical psychologists choose to specialize in forensic work and many more spend a portion of their time on forensic cases. As we saw in Chapter 2, while the license to practice psychology in most states is generic, the professional psychologist is legally and ethically bound to practice only within his or her areas of competence. There is no license in forensic psychology. Certification in forensic psychology is voluntary, although in some states only state-certified forensic psychologists can do court-ordered evaluations (Grisso, 1988).

A psychologist may take a variety of paths in developing competence for forensic work (Grisso, 1988; Melton, 1987). Students who know very early on that they want to specialize in forensic work might choose a graduate training program offering joint training in psychology and law. Currently, there are a handful of a joint psychology-law (J.D. and Ph.D.

or Psy.D.) training programs. Students from these programs conduct doctoral dissertations on topics that involve the interaction between psychology and law.

Specialized doctoral training is not the only way of obtaining competence in forensic psychology. Many students who attend clinical training programs offering more general training may begin to specialize in the pre-doctoral internship year by choosing an internship that offers opportunities for forensic training. Completion of a post-doctoral fellowship in forensic psychology may then cap off the specialized training.

Licensed psychologists who are years beyond their graduate training sometimes also develop interest in expanding their practices to include some forensic work. For this professional, Grisso (1988) suggests the following plan for developing competence in an area of forensic work. First, Grisso advises that the psychologist choose one area of forensic work, such as custody evaluations or competence to stand trial, in which he or she would like to gain competence. Second, the psychologist should develop a plan for intensive self-study in this area. For example, one might plan to focus one's professional reading upon the area for a period of three months or more. It can be helpful to connect with an experienced psychologist who would serve as a mentor during the period of self-study. The mentor might suggest readings and meet with the psychologist to discuss specific issues or applications. Third, the psychologist can attend continuing education workshops on the topic. Fourth, the psychologist would take on a few evaluations that he or she would conduct under the supervision of the mentor. Finally, as the psychologist's competence and confidence builds, supervision would be phased out. Grisso emphasizes that developing competence in a single area of forensic work does not make one a forensic psychologist. To be competent in a specific area requires an understanding of the legal and psychological issues of central importance to that area and the specialized methods employed.

Voluntary certification in forensic psychology is offered by the American Board of Forensic Psychology. The ABFP requires a specified number of hours of clinical experience in forensic work and a certain amount of continuing education in forensic psychology, work samples, and an oral examination before a panel of three board-certified forensic psychologists. In the oral examination, forensic psychologists must answer questions not only about their work samples, but also about federal and state case law relevant to mental health, professional ethics specific to forensic work, and other broad areas.

B O X   **16.4**

Focus on Ethics: What's My Role?

Mr. Clemens had been seeing Dr. Mandel for psychotherapy for problems with social anxiety and depression over a period of a few months. During the course of therapy, Mr. Clemens was injured in an accident at work. Dr. Mandel continued to see Mr. Clemens as he recovered from his injuries. Mr. Clemens decided to sue his employer for compensation for injuries, both physical and emotional, he suffered as a result of the accident. On the advice of his attorney, Mr. Clemens asked Dr. Mandel to evaluate him and testify in court about the emotional consequences of his injuries. He explained that he had great trust in Dr. Mandel and that he did not think he would feel comfortable being evaluated by another psychologist.

BOX **16.4** **Continued**

What are the ethical issues facing Dr. Mandel? First, she needs to consider whether conducting the evaluation will have a negative impact upon her other work with Mr. Clemens. If Dr. Mandel's findings do not support Mr. Clemens's case, would this sour the therapy relationship? Second, she should consider whether she can be truly objective in her evaluation. Given the therapeutic alliance with Mr. Clemens, will she be able to evaluate him impartially?

What should Dr. Mandel do? The proper action would be to refuse to conduct the evaluation. Dr. Mandel could explain the conflict. As a therapist, her paramount concern is Mr. Clemens's welfare, whereas as a forensic assessor and potential witness, objectivity and accuracy would be her primary concerns (Canter, Bennett, Jones, & Nagy, 1994). It would be appropriate for Dr. Mandel to offer to refer Mr. Clemens to another professional who could conduct the evaluation. She might offer to assist the client in coping with his anxiety about seeing the other psychologist.

It is possible that Dr. Mandel may end up in court anyway, even if she refuses to do the forensic evaluation. She may be forced to testify if served with a valid subpoena from either side. Dr. Mandel might be asked to testify about her observations of Mr. Clemens over time. However, she also might be pressed to offer an opinion about the impact the accident had upon Mr. Clemens or whether his injuries interfered with treatment. If forced to testify, it is imperative that Dr. Mandel be truthful and frank on the stand and not allow loyalty to her client to distort her testimony.

The fictitious case of Dr. Mandel and Mr. Clemens provides an example of the way in which a psychologist might be drawn into dual professional roles with the same client in a case involving civil litigation. The issue of role clarification can also arise in criminal proceedings, as the case of *Estelle v. Smith* (1981; as cited in Bersoff, 1995) illustrates. Smith had been indicted on murder charges and the state had announced its intention to seek the death penalty. The judge ordered Mr. Smith to be evaluated by a psychiatrist, Dr. Grigson, for the purposes of determining whether he was competent to stand trial. Dr. Grigson concluded that Mr. Smith was competent. Smith was tried and found guilty. After the criminal trial, a separate sentencing hearing was held to decide whether Mr. Smith should be executed. One of the things the jury needed to determine in the sentencing trial was whether Mr. Smith would likely commit violent criminal acts in the future. Dr. Grigson testified that Mr. Smith was a danger to society, basing his testimony on the pretrial competency evaluation. Mr. Smith was sentenced to death.

Had Dr. Grigson been a psychologist, would his behavior have been in violation of the Ethics Code? The primary ethical issue seems to be whether Mr. Smith was deceived into revealing information about himself in the competency evaluation that was used against him in the sentencing hearing. Ethical Standard 9.03, *Informed Consent in Assessments,* directs psychologists to obtain informed consent for evaluations and explains that clients must be given information about the "nature and purpose of the assessment." In practice, psychologists need to inform individuals of the purpose of the evaluation and how the findings are likely to be used. It is not clear what Dr. Grigson told Mr. Smith when he did the competency evaluation. However, if he did not inform him of the possibility that he might testify at his sentencing hearing, then he did not obtain informed consent.

Mr. Smith appealed his death sentence all the way to the Supreme Court. His attorneys argued that his Fifth (the protection against self-incriminating statements) and Sixth (right to counsel) Amendment rights were violated. The Supreme Court sided with Mr. Smith and his sentence was overturned.

The fictitious case of Mr. Clemens and the real experience of Mr. Smith illustrate how important it is for forensic psychologists to clarify their professional roles for all parties in legal cases.

Conclusions and Future Directions

Our intention in writing this book was to give students a broad overview of the multifaceted and diverse field of clinical psychology. We tried to achieve this goal by describing where clinical psychology came from, what it looks like now, and our thoughts are about where the field is going. If we have achieved our goal, then the reader can appreciate the challenge of briefly drawing some general conclusions about clinical psychology. To help organize our thoughts, we return to an idea we introduced in Chapter 1 when we discussed characteristics of the field. We stated that clinical psychology is characterized by four emphases: science, maladjustment, individual, and helping. As we draw the book to a close, let's revisit these four emphases.

Emphases in Clinical Psychology: A Review

Emphasis on Science

As we saw in Chapter 2, the proposal to train a cadre of psychologists to be both scientists and practitioners was considered a bold experiment. In our view, the experiment has succeeded. The greatest contributions clinical psychology has made toward understanding and alleviating human suffering have been through the application of the values and methods of science. While the scientist-practitioner model is no longer the only accepted model for training clinical psychologists, the alternative models still emphasize training in scientific thinking and the importance of the scientific foundation for clinical practice.

Science provides the yardsticks against which we measure the value of the theoretical models (Chapters 3 and 4), assessment methods (Part II), and intervention strategies (Part III) of clinical psychology. For example, scientific constructs such as reliability and validity are the basis upon which psychological assessment techniques are judged. Psychotherapy may be the area in which clinical psychology has most strongly distinguished itself as the discipline most concerned about scientific issues. While many disciplines practice psychotherapy, far and away the lion's share of psychotherapy research has been conducted by clinical psychologists. Clinical psychology has led the way in developing and modifying research strategies for evaluating psychotherapy (Chapter 10). And clinical psychology was the first discipline to organize and promulgate a list of treatments for which there is a level of empirical support.

While there is much to celebrate about clinical psychology's commitment to science, there is also much room for improvement. Many clinical psychologists continue to use assessment techniques for which there is minimal or no research support (see Lilienfeld, Wood,

& Garb, 2000). Similarly, there is a considerable gap between the science of psychotherapy research and psychotherapy practice (Persons, 1995).

Emphasis on Maladjustment

Clearly, the subject matters of clinical psychology are maladjustment, disability, and distress. The discipline developed in guidance clinics, veterans' hospitals, mental health centers, and medical centers. The emphasis of the theoretical models have been upon understanding pathology. Similarly, assessment methods were designed to detect problems or to understand how individuals differ from the norm. Clinical research focuses upon understanding and alleviating psychological problems.

Even as clinical psychology has expanded into non–mental health areas, the emphasis has continued to be upon pathology. For example, clinical health psychology distinguishes itself from the broader field of health psychology by its focus upon disease (Chapter 15). Similarly, in the forensic arena, clinical psychologists are most frequently called in when questions arise about conditions of the mind that may interfere with the judicial process (e.g., criminal responsibility, competence, and the like; see Chapter 16).

Emphasis on the Individual

The theory and practice of clinical psychology has been dominated by a focus on the individual. Theories of psychopathology and psychotherapy have emphasized intra-individual phenomena. Clinical assessment is focused almost exclusively upon the individual client or patient. Data on groups of individuals are used to understand characteristics of the individual. Similarly, in psychotherapy most models are designed to help the individual change characteristics of his or her personality or behavior.

The emphasis upon the individual is not, of course, absolute. Some models of pathology emphasize the role of societal factors. In behavioral assessment, the aim of the functional analysis is to understand how the individual and his or her environment (including other people) influence each other. And, of course, there are psychotherapies that are designed to intervene with multiple people at one time (Chapter 13).

Emphasis on Helping

Clinical psychology is a helping profession. Traditionally, clinical psychologists have studied and worked with individuals with mental health problems. As we saw in Chapter 15, however, the field has expanded into most other areas of health and illness. Clinical research is carried out not only to better understand the various ways in which human beings suffer, but also with the goal of using that knowledge to avoid or alleviate suffering. Similarly, the understanding of an individual that is developed through an individualized psychological assessment is most often used to help that individual directly or to help larger systems (e.g., courts, school systems) to work more productively with the individual. Finally, psychotherapy, the activity most frequently engaged in by clinical psychologists (see Chapter 1), and the activity with which the profession is most closely identified, has as its goal the alleviation of human suffering.

Future Directions

What lies ahead for clinical psychology? Predicting the future of an entire discipline is probably as risky as predicting how a given individual will behave in the future (see Chapter 5, and Chapter 16, Box 16.3). When predicting what a person will do in the future, the best information one can use is how that person has behaved in the past. We assume the same to be true about predicting what will happen in clinical psychology. We look at current trends and hypothesize that they will continue into the future. We discuss four trends we anticipate will mark the future of clinical psychology.

Increased Specialization

In Chapter 2 we noted that the recent history of clinical psychology has seen an increase in specialization. Evidence of increase in specialization can be seen in the proliferation of professional groups for psychologists with specific clinical interests (e.g., 20 of the 53 divisions of the American Psychological Association are related to clinical psychology and there are now 6 sections of Division 12—the Society of Clinical Psychology). ABPP certification (see Chapter 1) is now offered in twelve different specialty areas. The days of the generalist-clinical-psychologist are over.

The trend toward increased specialization undoubtedly will continue. This is probably a natural and healthy development in the life span of the field. As the knowledge base in clinical psychology grows, specialization becomes necessary in order to maintain competence and stay on top of new developments. Increasingly, clinical psychologists will have to define their areas of competence explicitly. As we saw in our sampling of areas of specialization (Chapters 14, 15, and 16), the more established specialty areas have already taken steps to define standards for training and practice in their areas and have developed mechanisms for certifying psychologists in their specialties.

Decrease in Adherence to Theoretical Models

Theory will always have an important role to play in scientific clinical psychology. However, it is our view that adherence to the major theoretical models in clinical psychology (see Chapter 3) is less important in practice and research than it once was. Although radical behaviorists and classic psychoanalysts still exist, they play a more peripheral role in the field than they once did. A few examples may illustrate the point. Take behavior therapy (Thorpe & Olson, 1997; see also Chapter 13). The behavior therapy movement was initiated by a group of pioneers who applied learning theory to help their patients. But learning theory is no longer a central feature of behavior therapy. Cognitive constructs and cognitive intervention, anathema to radical behaviorists, are now generally accepted by most behavior therapists. One need only look at the table of contents of any recent issue of *Behavior Therapy* to see evidence of the ascendance of cognition in behavior therapy.

Contemporary models of psychopathology provide another example of the decreased significance of traditional psychological theories. Current theories of psychopathology are integrative. Anxiety and anxiety disorders, for example, are understood as the products of genetic factors, learning history, cultural influences, cognitive (both conscious and unconscious) processes, and social stressors (see Barlow, 2002, for example).

In the clinical practice arena, the increased emphasis upon accountability and evidence-based practice will likely further erode the loyalty of practitioners to their favorite theories. The managed care revolution in health care (see Chapter 2) has dramatically increased the oversight of psychological practice. Insurance carriers are interested in reimbursing for treatments that work (i.e., that have been shown to be helpful in controlled clinical trials), not for treatments that should work according to the practitioner's preferred theory.

Splitting of Science and Practice

Tension between academic psychologists and practicing psychologists is as old as the field itself. Nonetheless, we see that the gap between scientifically minded clinical psychologists and practice-oriented clinical psychologists is growing. An illustration of the gap between the two groups can be seen in the makeup of professional organizations. Throughout the first half of its lifetime, the American Psychological Association was identified with academic psychology. However, over the past fifty years the makeup and activities of the organization have been increasingly dominated by practice-oriented psychologists. Many scientifically oriented psychologists fled APA for the American Psychological Society. Clinical psychologists who identify strongly with the fields of scientific foundation have formed their own interest groups, such as the Society for a Scientific Clinical Psychology.

The different reactions of clinical psychologists to recent movements in the field illustrate the scientist-practitioner rift. Many clinical psychologists would like to see changes in practice laws that would allow psychologists to prescribe medications. Practitioners tend to be the strongest supporters of the pursuit of prescription privileges, whereas academic clinical psychologists tend to be against it. Similarly, scientifically minded clinical psychologists tended to support Division 12's effort to identify psychological treatments that have empirical support (see Chapter 10), whereas many practitioners were critical of the effort.

Shrinking Psychotherapy Market

On the practice front, a trend that is likely to have a significant impact upon clinical psychology is the shrinking opportunities for psychotherapy practitioners. It is not that there are fewer consumers of psychotherapy. Rather, the share of the psychotherapy market available for clinical psychologists is shrinking. Increasingly, clinical social workers and mental health counselors are obtaining licenses that allow them to practice psychotherapy. These practitioners tend to have less training than clinical psychologists, but they are also willing to provide psychotherapy at a lower rate. In the dollar-conscious health-care market, these providers are very attractive to managed health-care companies and insurance providers.

In addition to the shrinking market share, clinical psychologists are seeing the reimbursement rates for psychotherapy services dropping. In the managed care system, psychologists need to join provider networks in order to see patients covered by certain insurance providers. If a psychologist is not in the network, the insurer either will not pay or will cover a smaller percentage of the fee than for in-network providers. Patients are motivated to see in-network providers because their share of the cost is lower. In order to join a provider network, psychologists typically have to agree to a reimbursement rate set by the insurance company—a rate that, with rare exception, is lower than the psychologist's ordinary fee.

With the shrinking profitability of psychotherapy, many clinical psychologists are diversifying their practices. Some are doing more assessment and consultation work, while others are specializing in neuropsychology or forensic work, where reimbursement rates tend to be higher. Psychotherapy likely will occupy a less central place in the practice pattern of clinical psychologists in years to come.

Concluding Comment: A Focus on Ethics

Most students reading this book are at a point in their lives at which they will soon choose their career paths. Some will choose clinical psychology. Of those who do, some will focus their careers on clinical research, while others will devote most of their professional time to clinical practice, and still others will teach. Many will have careers that combine the various activities engaged in by clinical psychologists (see Chapter 1). Most readers will not become clinical psychologists. Their careers will take them down a wide variety of roads. Regardless of their career path, issues causing them to pause and consider what is right and what is wrong undoubtedly will arise. Struggling with these issues is challenging. To be an ethical professional involves anticipating and recognizing ethical dilemmas and being mindful of personal morals, community standards, cultural considerations, and professional guidelines when choosing courses of action. It is our hope that the discussion of ethical issues throughout this book fostered in the reader a personal commitment to a lifelong effort to act ethically and to encourage ethical behavior in those with whom they work.

APPENDIX A

American Psychological Association's Ethical Principles and Code of Conduct

CONTENTS

Source: "Ethical Principles of Psychologists and Code of Conduct," from *American Psychologist,* 2002, *57,* 1060–1073. Copyright © 2002 by the American Psychological Association. Reprinted by permission.

Introduction and Applicability

The American Psychological Association's (APA's) Ethical Principles of Psychologists and Code of Conduct (hereinafter referred to as the Ethics Code) consists of an Introduction, a Preamble, five General Principles (A–E), and specific Ethical Standards. The Introduction discusses the intent, organization, procedural considerations, and scope of application of the Ethics Code. The Preamble and General Principles are aspirational goals to guide psychologists toward the highest ideals of psychology. Although the Preamble and General Principles are not themselves enforceable rules, they should be considered by psychologists in arriving at an ethical course of action. The Ethical Standards set forth enforceable rules for conduct as psychologists. Most of the Ethical Standards are written broadly, in order to apply to psychologists in varied roles, although the application of an Ethical Standard may vary depending on the context. The Ethical Standards are not exhaustive. The fact that a given conduct is not specifically addressed by an Ethical Standard does not mean that it is necessarily either ethical or unethical.

This Ethics Code applies only to psychologists' activities that are part of their scientific, educational, or professional roles as psychologists. Areas covered include but are not limited to the clinical, counseling, and school practice of psychology; research; teaching; supervision of trainees; public service; policy development; social intervention; development of assessment instructions; conducting assessments; educational counseling; organizational con-

This version of the APA Ethics Code was adopted by the American Psychological Association's Council of Representatives during its meeting, August 21, 2002, and is effective beginning June 1, 2003. Inquiries concerning the substance of interpretation of the APA Ethics Code should be addressed to the Director, Office of Ethics, American Psychological Association, 750 First Street, NE, Washington, DC 20002-4242. The Ethics Code and information regarding the Code can be found on the APA Web site, http://www.apa.org/ethics. The standards in the Ethics Code will be used to adjudicate complaints brought concerning alleged conduct occurring on or after the effective date. Complaints regarding conduct occurring prior to the effective date will be adjudicated on the basis of the version of the Ethics Code that was in effect at the time the conduct occurred.

The APA has previously published its Ethics Code as follows:

American Psychological Association. (1953). *Ethical standards of psychologists*. Washington, DC: Author.
American Psychological Association. (1959). Ethical standards of psychologists. *American Psychologist, 14*, 279–282.
American Psychological Association. (1963). Ethical standards of psychologists. *American Psychologist, 18*, 56–60.
American Psychological Association. (1968). Ethical standards of psychologists. *American Psychologist, 23*, 357–361.
American Psychological Association. (1977, March). Ethical standards of psychologists. *APA Monitor*, 22–23.
American Psychological Association. (1979). *Ethical standards of psychologists*. Washington, DC: Author.
American Psychological Association. (1981). Ethical standards of psychologists. *American Psychologist, 36*, 633–638.
American Psychological Association. (1990). Ethical standards of psychologists (Amended June 2, 1989), *American Psychologist, 45*, 390–395.
American Psychological Association. (1992). Ethical standards of psychologists and code of conduct. *American Psychologist, 47*, 1597–1611.

Request copies of the APA's Ethical Principles of Psychologists and Code of Conduct from the APA Order Department, 750 First Street, NE, Washington, DC 20002-4242, or phone (202) 336-5510.

sulting; forensic activities; program design and evaluation; and administration. This Ethics Code applies to these activities across a variety of contexts, such as in person, postal, telephone, Internet, and other electronic transmissions. These activities shall be distinguished from the purely private conduct of psychologists, which is not within the purview of the Ethics Code.

Membership in the APA commits members and student affiliates to comply with the standards of the APA Ethics Code and to the rules and procedures used to enforce them. Lack of awareness or misunderstanding of an Ethical Standard is not itself a defense to a charge of unethical conduct.

The procedures for filing, investigating, and resolving complaints of unethical conduct are described in the current Rules and Procedures of the APA Ethics Committee. APA may impose sanctions on its members for violations of the standards of the Ethics Code, including termination of APA membership, and may notify other bodies and individuals of its actions. Actions that violate the standards of the Ethics Code may also lead to the imposition of sanctions on psychologists or students whether or not they are APA members by bodies other than APA, including state psychological boards, other state or federal agencies, and payors for health services. In addition, APA may take action against a member after his or her conviction of a felony, expulsion or suspension from an affiliated state psychological association, or suspension or loss of licensure. When the sanction to be imposed by APA is less than expulsion, the 2001 Rules and Procedures do not guarantee an opportunity for an in-person hearing, but generally provide that complaints will be resolved only on the basis of a submitted record.

The Ethics Code is intended to provide guidance for psychologists and standards of professional conduct that can be applied by the APA and by other bodies that choose to adopt them. The Ethics Code is not intended to be a basis of civil liability. Whether a psychologist has violated the Ethics Code standards does not by itself determine whether the psychologist is legally liable in a court action, whether a contract is enforceable, or whether other legal consequences occur.

The modifiers used in some of the standards of this Ethics Code (e.g., *reasonably, appropriate, potentially*) are included in the standards when they would (1) allow professional judgment on the part of psychologists, (2) eliminate injustice or inequality that would occur without the modifier, (3) ensure applicability across the broad range of activities conducted by psychologists, or (4) guard against a set of rigid rules that might be quickly outdated. As used in this Ethics Code, the term *reasonable* means the prevailing professional judgment of psychologists engaged in similar activities in similar circumstances, given the knowledge the psychologist had or should have had at the time.

In the process of making decisions regarding their professional behavior, psychologists must consider this Ethics Code in addition to applicable laws and psychology board regulations. In applying the Ethics Code to their professional work, psychologists may consider other materials and guidelines that have been adopted or endorsed by scientific and professional psychological organizations and the dictates of their own conscience, as well as consult with others within the field. If this Ethics Code establishes a higher standard of conduct than is required by law, psychologists must meet the higher ethical standard. If psychologists' ethical responsibilities conflict with law, regulations, or other governing legal authority, psychologists make known their commitment to this Ethics Code and take steps to resolve the conflict in a responsible manner. If the conflict is unresolvable via such means, psychologists may adhere to the requirements of the law, regulations, or other governing authority in keeping with basic principles of human rights.

Preamble

Psychologists are committed to increasing scientific and professional knowledge of behavior and people's understanding of themselves and others and to the use of such knowledge to improve the condition of individuals, organizations, and society. Psychologists respect and protect civil and human rights and the central importance of freedom of inquiry and expression in research, teaching, and publication. They strive to help the public in developing informed judgments and choices concerning human behavior. In doing so, they perform many roles, such as researcher, educator, diagnostician, therapist, supervisor, consultant, administrator, social interventionist, and expert witness. This Ethics Code provides a common set of principles and standards upon which psychologists build their professional and scientific work.

This Ethics Code is intended to provide specific standards to cover most situations encountered by psychologists. It has as its goals the welfare and protection of the individuals and groups with whom psychologists work and the education of members, students, and the public regarding ethical standards of the discipline.

The development of a dynamic set of ethical standards for psychologists' work-related conduct requires a personal commitment and lifelong effort to act ethically; to encourage ethical behavior by students, supervisees, employees, and colleagues; and to consult with others concerning ethical problems.

General Principles

This section consists of General Principles. General Principles, as opposed to Ethical Standards, are aspirational in nature. Their intent is to guide and inspire psychologists toward the very highest ethical ideals of the profession. General Principles, in contrast to Ethical Standards, do not represent obligations and should not form the basis for imposing sanctions. Relying upon General Principles for either of these reasons distorts both their meaning and purpose.

Principle A: Beneficence and Nonmaleficence

Psychologists strive to benefit those with whom they work and take care to do no harm. In their professional actions, psychologists seek to safeguard the welfare and rights of those with whom they interact professionally and other affected persons, and the welfare of animal subjects of research. When conflicts occur among psychologists' obligations or concerns, they attempt to resolve these conflicts in a responsible fashion that avoids or minimizes harm. Because psychologists' scientific and professional judgments and actions may affect the lives of others, they are alert to and guard against personal, financial, social, organizational, or political factors that might lead to misuse of their influence. Psychologists strive to be aware of the possible effect of their own physical and mental health on their ability to help those with whom they work.

Principle B: Fidelity and Responsibility

Psychologists establish relationships of trust with those with whom they work. They are aware of their professional and scientific responsibilities to society and to the specific communities in which they work. Psychologists uphold professional standards of conduct, clarify their professional roles and obligations, accept appropriate responsibility for their behavior, and seek to manage conflicts of interest that could lead to exploitation or harm. Psychologists consult with, refer to, or cooperate with other professionals and institutions to the extent needed to serve the best interests of those with whom they work. They are concerned about the ethical compliance of their colleagues' scientific and professional conduct. Psychologists strive to contribute a portion of their professional time for little or no compensation or personal advantage.

Principle C: Integrity

Psychologists seek to promote accuracy, honesty, and truthfulness in the science, teaching, and practice of psychology. In these activities psychologists do not steal, cheat, or engage in fraud, subterfuge, or intentional misrepresentation of fact. Psychologists strive to keep their promises and to avoid unwise or unclear commitments. In situations in which deception may be ethically justifiable to maximize benefits and minimize harm, psychologists have a serious obligation to consider the need for, the possible consequences of, and their responsibility to correct any resulting mistrust or other harmful effects that arise from the use of such techniques.

Principle D: Justice

Psychologists recognize that fairness and justice entitle all persons to access to and benefit from the contributions of psychology and to equal quality in the processes, procedures, and services being conducted by psychologists. Psychologists exercise reasonable judgment and take precautions to ensure that their potential biases, the boundaries of their competence, and the limitations of their expertise do not lead to or condone unjust practices.

Principle E: Respect for People's Rights and Dignity

Psychologists respect the dignity and worth of all people, and the rights of individuals to privacy, confidentiality, and self-determination. Psychologists are aware that special safeguards may be necessary to protect the rights and welfare of persons or communities whose vulnerabilities impair autonomous decision making. Psychologists are aware of and respect cultural, individual, and role differences, including those based on age, gender, gender identity, race, ethnicity, culture, national origin, religion, sexual orientation, disability, language, and socioeconomic status, and consider these factor when working with members of such groups. Psychologists try to eliminate the effect on their work of biases based on those factors, and they do not knowingly participate in or condone activities of others based upon such prejudices.

Ethical Standards

1.   Resolving Ethical Issues

1.01 Misuse of Psychologists' Work

If psychologists learn to misuse or misrepresentation of their work, they take reasonable steps to correct or minimize the misuse or misrepresentation.

1.02 Conflicts Between Ethics and Law, Regulations, or Other Governing Legal Authority

If psychologists' ethical responsibilities conflict with law, regulations, or other governing legal authority, psychologists make known their commitment to the Ethics Code and take steps to resolve the conflict. If the conflict is unresolvable via such means, psychologists may adhere to the requirements of the law, regulations, or other governing legal authority.

1.03 Conflicts Between Ethics and Organizational Demands

If the demands of an organization with which psychologists are affiliated or for whom they are working conflict with this Ethics Code, psychologists clarity the nature of the conflict, make known their commitment to the Ethics Code, and to the extent feasible, resolve the conflict in a way that permits adherence to the Ethics Code.

1.04 Informal Resolution of Ethical Violations

When psychologists believe that there may have been an ethical violation by another psychologist, they attempt to resolve the issue by bringing it to the attention of that individual, if an informal resolution appears appropriate and the intervention does not violate any confidentiality rights that may be involved. (See also Standards 1.02, Conflicts Between Ethics and Law, Regulations, or Other Governing Legal Authority, and 1.03, Conflicts Between Ethics and Organizational Demands.)

1.05 Reporting Ethical Violations

If an apparent ethical violation has substantially harmed or is likely to substantially harm a person or organization and is not appropriate for informal resolution under Standard 1.04, Informal Resolution of Ethical Violations, or is not resolved properly in that fashion, psychologists take further action appropriate to the situation. Such action might include referral to state or national committees on professional ethics, to state licensing boards, or to the appropriate institutional authorities. This standard does not apply when an intervention would violate confidentiality rights or when psychologists have been retained to review the work of another psychologist whose professional conduct is in question. (See also Standard 1.02, Conflicts Between Ethics and Law, Regulations, or Other Governing Legal Authority.)

1.06 Cooperating With Ethics Committees

Psychologists cooperate in ethics investigations, proceedings, and resulting requirements of the APA or any affiliated state psychological association to which they belong. In doing so, they address any confidentiality issues. Failure to cooperate is itself an ethics violation. However, making a request for deferment of adjudication of an ethics complaint pending the outcome of litigation does not alone constitute noncooperation.

1.07 Improper Complaints

Psychologists do not file or encourage the filing of ethics complaints that are made with reckless disregard for or willful ignorance of facts that would disprove the allegation.

1.08 Unfair Discrimination Against Complainants and Respondents

Psychologists do not deny persons employment, advancement, admissions to academic or other programs, tenure, or promotion, based solely upon their having made or their being the subject of an ethics complaint. This does not preclude taking action based upon the outcome of such proceedings or considering other appropriate information.

2.   Competence

2.01 Boundaries of Competence

(a) Psychologists provide services, teach, and conduct research with populations and in areas only within the boundaries of their competence, based on their education, training, supervised experience, consultation, study, or professional experience.

(b) Where scientific or professional knowledge in the discipline of psychology establishes that an understanding of factors associated with age, gender, gender identity, race, ethnicity, culture, national origin, religion, sexual orientation, disability, language, or socioeconomic status is essential for effective implementation of their services or research, psychologists have or obtain the training, experience, consultation, or supervision necessary to ensure the competence of their services, or they make appropriate referrals, except as provided in Standard 2.02, Providing Services in Emergencies.

(c) Psychologists planning to provide services, teach, or conduct research involving populations, areas, techniques, or technologies new to them undertake relevant education, training, supervised experience, consultation, or study.

(d) When psychologists are asked to provide services to individuals for whom appropriate mental health services are not available and for which psychologists have not obtained the competence necessary, psychologists with closely related prior training or experience may provide such services in order to ensure that services are not denied if they make a reasonable effort to obtain the competence required by using relevant research, training, consultation, or study.

(e) In those emerging areas in which generally recognized standards for preparatory training do not yet exist, psychologists nevertheless take reasonable steps to ensure the competence of their work and to protect clients/patients, students, supervisees, research participants, organizational clients, and others from harm.

(f) When assuming forensic roles, psychologists are or become reasonably familiar with the judicial or administrative rules governing their roles.

2.02 Providing Services in Emergencies

In emergencies, when psychologists provide services to individuals for whom other mental health services are not available and for which psychologists have not obtained the necessary training, psychologists may provide such services in order to ensure that services are not denied. The services are discontinued as soon as the emergency has ended or appropriate services are available.

2.03 Maintaining Competence

Psychologists undertake ongoing efforts to develop and maintain their competence.

2.04 Bases for Scientific and Professional Judgments

Psychologists' work is based upon established scientific and professional knowledge of the discipline. (See also Standards 2.01e, Boundaries of Competence, and 10.01b, Informed Consent to Therapy.)

2.05 Delegation of Work to Others

Psychologists who delegate work to employees, supervisees, or research or teaching assistants or who use the services of others, such as interpreters, take reasonable steps to (1) avoid delegating such work to persons who have a multiple relationship with those being served that would likely lead to exploitation or loss of objectivity; (2) authorize only those responsibilities that such persons can be expected to perform competently on the basis of their education, training, or experience, either independently or with the level of supervision being provided; and (3) see that such persons perform these services competently. (See also Standards 2.02, Providing Services in Emergencies; 3.05, Multiple Relationships; 4.01, Maintaining Confidentiality; 9.01, Bases for Assessments; 9.02, Use of Assessments; 9.03, Informed Consent in Assessments; and 9.07, Assessment by Unqualified Persons.)

2.06 Personal Problems and Conflicts

(a) Psychologists refrain from initiating an activity when they know or should know that there is a substantial likelihood that their personal problems will prevent them from performing their work-related activities in a competent manner.

(b) When psychologists become aware of personal problems that may interfere with their performing work-related duties adequately, they take appropriate measures, such as obtaining professional consultation or assistance, and determine whether they should limit, suspend, or terminate their work-related duties. (See also Standard 10.10, Terminating Therapy.)

3.   Human Relations

3.01 Unfair Discrimination

In their work-related activities, psychologists do not engage in unfair discrimination based on age, gender, gender identity, race, ethnicity, culture, national origin, religion, sexual orientation, disability, socioeconomic status, or any basis proscribed by law.

3.02 Sexual Harassment

Psychologists do not engage in sexual harassment. Sexual harassment is sexual solicitation, physical advances, or verbal or nonverbal conduct that is sexual in nature, that occurs in connection with the psychologist's activities or roles as a psychologist, and that either (1) is unwelcome, is offensive, or creates a hostile workplace or educational environment, and the psychologist knows or is told this or (2) is sufficiently severe or intense to be abusive to a reasonable person in the context. Sexual harassment can consist of a single intense or severe act or of multiple persistent or pervasive acts. (See also Standard 1.08, Unfair Discrimination Against Complainants and Respondents.)

3.03 Other Harassment

Psychologists do not knowingly engage in behavior that is harassing or demeaning to persons with whom they interact in their work based on factors such as those persons' age, gender, gender identity, race, ethnicity, culture, national origin, religion, sexual orientation, disability, language, or socioeconomic status.

3.04 Avoiding Harm

Psychologists take reasonable steps to avoid harming their clients/patients, students, supervisees, research participants, organizational clients, and others with whom they work, and to minimize harm where it is foreseeable and unavoidable.

3.05 Multiple Relationships

(a) A multiple relationship occurs when a psychologists is in a professional role with a person and (1) at the same time is in another role with the same person, (2) at the same time is in a relationship with a person closely associated with or related to the person with whom the psychologist has the professional relationship, or (3) promises to enter into another relationship in the future with the person or a person closely associated with or related to the person.

A psychologist refrains from entering into a multiple relationship if the multiple relationship could reasonably be expected to impair the psychologist's objectivity, competence, or effectiveness in performing his or her functions as a psychologist, or otherwise risks exploitation or harm to the person with whom the professional relationship.

Multiple relationships that would not reasonably be expected to cause impairment or risk exploitation or harm are not unethical.

(b) If a psychologist finds that, due to unforeseen factors, a potentially harmful multiple relationship has arisen, the psychologist takes reasonable steps to resolve it with due regard for the best interests of the affected person and maximal compliance with the Ethics Code.

(d) When psychologists are required by law, institutional policy, or extraordinary circumstances to serve in more than one role in judicial or administrative proceedings, at the outset they clarify role expectations and the extent of confidentiality and thereafter as changes occur. (See also Standards 3.04, Avoiding Harm, and 3.07, Third-Party Requests for Services.)

3.06 Conflict of Interest

Psychologists refrain from taking on a professional role when personal, scientific, professional, legal, financial, or other interests or relationships could reasonably be expected to (1) impair their objectivity, competence, or effectiveness in performing their functions as psychologists or (2) expose the person or organization with whom the professional relationship exists to harm or exploitation.

3.07 Third-Party Requests for Services

When psychologists agree to provide services to a person or entity at the request of a third party, psychologists attempt to clarify at the outset of the service the nature of the relationship with all individuals or organizations involved. This clarification includes the role of the psychologist (e.g., therapist, consultant, diagnostician, or expert witness), an identification of who is the client, the probable uses of the services provided or the information obtained, and the fact that there may be limits to confidentiality. (See also Standards 3.05, Multiple Relationships, and 4.02, Discussing the Limits of Confidentiality.)

3.08 Exploitative Relationships

Psychologists do not exploit persons over whom they have supervisory, evaluative, or other authority such as clients/patients, students, supervisees, research participants, and employees. (See also Standards 3.05, Multiple Relationships; 6.04, Fees and Financial Arrangements; 6.05, Barter With Clients/Patients; 7.07, Sexual Relationships With Students and Supervisees; 10.05, Sexual Intimacies With Current Therapy Clients/Patients; 10.06, Sexual Intimacies With Relatives or Significant Others of Current Therapy Clients/Patients; 10.07, Therapy With Former Sexual Partners; and 10.08, Sexual Intimacies With Former Therapy Clients/Patients.)

3.09 Cooperation With Other Professionals

When indicated and professionally appropriate, psychologists cooperate with other professionals in order to serve their clients/patients effectively and appropriately. (See also Standard 4.05, Disclosures.)

3.10 Informed Consent

(a) When psychologists conduct research or provide assessment, therapy, counseling, or consulting services in person or via electronic transmission or other forms of communication, they obtain the informed consent of the individual or individuals using language that is reasonably understandable to that person or persons except when conducting such activities without consent is mandated by law or governmental regulation or as otherwise provided in this Ethics Code. (See also Standards 8.02, Informed Consent to Research; 9.03, Informed Consent in Assessments; and 10.01, Informed Consent to Therapy.)

(b) For persons who are legally incapable of giving informed consent, psychologists nevertheless (1) provide an appropriate explanation, (2) seek the individual's assent, (3) consider such persons' preferences and best interests, and (4) obtain appropriate permission from a legally authorized person, if such substitute consent is permitted or required by law. When consent by a legally authorized person is not permitted or required by law, psychologists take reasonable steps to protect the individual's rights and welfare.

(c) When psychological services are court ordered or otherwise mandated, psychologists inform the individual of the nature of the anticipated services, including whether the services are court ordered or mandated and any limits of confidentiality, before proceeding.

(d) Psychologists appropriately document written or oral consent, permission, and assent. (See also Standards 8.02, Informed Consent to Research; 9.03, Informed Consent in Assessments; and 10.01, Informed Consent to Therapy.)

3.11 Psychological Services Delivered to or Through Organizations

(a) Psychologists delivering services to or through organizations provide information beforehand to clients and when appropriate those directly affected by the services about (1) the nature and objectives of the services, (2) the intended recipients, (3) which of the individuals are clients, (4) the relationship the psychologist will have with each person and the organization, (5) the probable uses of services provided and information obtained, (6) who will have access to the information, and (7) limits of confidentiality. As soon as feasible, they provide information about the results and conclusions of such services to appropriate persons.

(b) If psychologists will be precluded by law or by organizational roles from providing such information to particular individuals or groups, they so inform those individuals or groups at the outset of the service.

3.12 Interruption of Psychological Services

Unless otherwise covered by contract, psychologists make reasonable efforts to plan for facilitating services in the event that psychological services are interrupted by factors such as the psychologist's illness, death, unavailability, relocation, or retirement or by the client/patient's relocation or financial limitations (See also Standard 6.02c, Maintenance, Dissemination, and Disposal of Confidential Records of Professional and Scientific Work.)

4.   <u>Privacy and Confidentiality</u>

4.01 Maintaining Confidentiality

Psychologists have a primary obligation and take reasonable precautions to protect confidential information obtained through or stored in any medium, recognizing that the extent and limits of confidentiality may be regulated by law or established by institutional rules or professional or scientific relationship. (See also Standard 2.05, Delegation of Work to Others.)

4.02 Discussing the Limits of Confidentiality

(a) Psychologists discuss with persons (including, to the extent feasible, persons who are legally incapable of giving informed consent and their legal representatives) and organizations with whom they establish a scientific or professional relationship (1) the relevant limits of confidentiality and (2) the foreseeable uses of the information generated through their psychological activities. (See also Standard 3.10, Informed Consent.)

(b) Unless it is not feasible or is contraindicated, the discussion of confidentiality occurs at the outset of the relationship and thereafter as new circumstances may warrant.

(c) Psychologists who offer services, products, or information via electronic transmission inform clients/patients of the risks to privacy and limits of confidentiality.

4.03 Recording

Before recording the voices or images of individuals to whom they provide services, psychologists obtain permission from all such persons or their legal representatives. (See also Standards 8.03, Informed Consent for Recording Voices and Images in Research; 8.05, Dispensing With Informed Consent for Research; and 8.07, Deception in Research.)

4.04 Minimizing Intrusions on Privacy

(a) Psychologists include in written and oral reports and consultations, only information germane to the purpose for which the communication is made.

(b) Psychologists discuss confidential information obtained in their work only for appropriate scientific or professional purposes and only with persons clearly concerned with such matters.

4.05 Disclosures

(a) Psychologists may disclose confidential information with the appropriate consent of the organizational client, the individual client/patient, or another legally authorized person on behalf of the client/patient unless prohibited by law.

(b) Psychologists disclose confidential information without the consent of the individual only as mandated by law, or where permitted by law for a valid purpose such as to (1) provide needed professional services; (2) obtain appropriate professional consultations; (3) protect the client/patient, psychologist, or others from harm; or (4) obtain payment for services from a client/patient, in which instance disclosure is limited to the minimum that is necessary to achieve the purpose. (See also Standard 6.04e, Fees and Financial Arrangements.)

4.06 Consultations

When consulting with colleagues, (1) psychologists do not disclose confidential information that reasonably could lead to the identification of a client/patient, research participant, or other person or organization with whom they have a confidential relationship unless they have obtained the prior consent of the person or organization or the disclosure cannot be avoided, and (2) they disclose information only to the extent necessary to achieve the purposes of the consultation. (See also Standard 4.01, Maintaining Confidentiality.)

4.07 Use of Confidential Information for Didactic or Other Purposes

Psychologists do not disclose in their writings, lectures, or other public media, confidential, personally identifiable information concerning their clients/patients, students, research participants, organizational clients, or other recipients of their services that they obtained during the course of their work, unless (1) they take reasonable steps to disguise the person or organization, (2) the person or organization has consented in writing, or (3) there is legal authorization for doing so.

5. Advertising and Other Public Statements

5.01 Avoidance of False or Deceptive Statements

(a) Public statements include but are not limited to paid or unpaid advertising, product endorsements, grant applications, licensing applications, other credentialing applications, brochures, printed matter, directory listings, personal resumes or curricula vitae, or comments for use in media such as print or electronic transmission, statements in legal proceedings, lectures and public oral presentations, and published materials. Psychologists do not knowingly make public statements that are false, deceptive, or fraudulent concerning their research, practice, or other work activities or those of persons who organizations with which they are affiliated.

(b) Psychologists do not make false, deceptive, or fraudulent statements concerning (1) their training, experience, or competence; (2) their academic degrees; (3) their credentials; (4) their institutional or association affiliations; (5) their services; (6) the scientific or clinical basis for, or results or degree of success of, their services; (7) their fees; or (8) their publications or research findings.

(c) Psychologists claim degrees as credentials for their health services only if those degrees (1) were earned from a regionally accredited educational institution or (2) were the basis for psychology licensure by the state in which they practice.

5.02 Statement by Others

(a) Psychologists who engage others to create or place public statements that promote their professional practice, products, or activities retain professional responsibility for such statements.

(b) Psychologists do not compensate employees of press, radio, television, or other communication media in return for publicity in a news item. (See also Standard 1.01, Misuse of Psychologists' Work.)

(c) A paid advertisement relating to psychologists' activities must be identified or clearly recognizable as such.

5.03 Descriptions of Workshops and Non-Degree-Granting Educational Programs

To the degree to which they exercise control, psychologists responsible for announcements, catalogs, brochures, or advertisements describing workshops, seminars, or other non-degree-granting educational programs ensure that they accurately describe the audience for which the program is intended, the educational objectives, the presenters, and the fees involved.

5.04 Media Presentations

When psychologists provide public advice or comment via print, Internet, or other electronic transmission, they take precautions to ensure that statements (1) are based on their professional knowledge, training, or experience in accord with appropriate psychological literature and practice; (2) are otherwise consistent with this Ethics Code; and (3) do not indicate that a professional relationship has been established with the recipient. (See also Standard 2.04, Bases for Scientific and Professional Judgments.)

5.05 Testimonials

Psychologists do not solicit testimonials from current therapy clients/patients or other persons who because of their particular circumstances are vulnerable to undue influence.

5.06 In-Person Solicitation

Psychologists do not engage, directly or through agents, in uninvited in-person solicitation of business from actual or potential therapy clients/patients or other persons who because of their particular circumstances are vulnerable to undue influence. However, this prohibition does not preclude (1) attempting to implement appropriate collateral contacts for the purpose of benefiting an already engaged therapy client/patient or (2) providing disaster or community outreach services.

6.   Record Keeping and Fees

6.01 Documentation of Professional and Scientific Work and Maintenance of Records

Psychologists create, and do the extent the records are under their control, maintain, disseminate, store, retain, and dispose of records and data relating to their professional and scientific work in order to (1) facilitate provision of services later by them or by other professionals, (2) allow for replication of research design and analyses, (3) meet institutional requirements, (4) ensure accuracy of billing and payments, and (5) ensure compliance and law. (See also Standard 4.01, Maintaining Confidentiality.)

6.02 Maintenance, Dissemination, and Disposal of Confidential Records of Professional and Scientific Work

(a) Psychologists maintain confidentiality in creating, storing, accessing, transferring, and disposing of records under their control, whether these are written, automated, or in any other medium. (See also Standards 4.01, Maintaining Confidentiality, and 6.01, Documentation of Professional and Scientific Work and Maintenance of Records.)

(b) If confidential information concerning recipients of psychological services is entered into databases or systems of records available to persons whose access has not been consented to by the recipient, psychologists use coding or other techniques to avoid the inclusion of personal indentifiers.

(c) Psychologists make plans in advance in facilitate the appropriate transfer and to protect the confidentiality of records and data in the event of psychologists' withdrawal from positions or practice. (See also Standards 3.12, Interruption of Psychological Services, and 10.09, Interruption of Therapy.)

6.03 Withholding Records for Nonpayment

Psychologists may not withhold records under their control that are requested and needed for a client's/patient's emergency treatment solely because payment has not been received.

6.04 Fees and Financial Arrangements

(a) As early as is feasible in a professional or scientific relationship, psychologists and recipients of psychological services reach an agreement specifying compensation and billing arrangements.

(b) Psychologists' fee practices are consistent with law.

(c) Psychologists do not misrepresent their fees.

(d) If limitations to services can be anticipated because of limitations in financing, this is discussed with the recipient of services as early as is feasible. (See also Standards 10.09, Interruption of Therapy, and 10.10, Terminating Therapy.)

(e) If the recipient of services does not pay for services as agreed, and if psychologists intend to use collection agencies or legal measures to collect the fees, psychologists first inform the person that such measures will be taken and provide that person an opportunity to make prompt payment. (See also Standards 4.05, Disclosure; 6.03, Withholding Records for Nonpayment; and 10.01, Informed Consent to Therapy.)

6.05 Barter With Clients/Patients

Barter is the acceptance of goods, services, or other nonmonetary remuneration from clients/patients in return for psychologists services. Psychologists may barter only if (1) it is not clinically contraindicated, and (2) the resulting arrangement is not exploitative. (See also Standards 3.05, Multiple Relationships, and 6.04, Fees and Financial Arrangements.)

6.06 Accuracy in Reports to Payors and Funding Sources

In their reports to payors for services for sources of research funding, psychologists take reasonable steps to ensure the accurate reporting of the nature of the service provided or research conducted, the fees, charges, or payments, and where applicable, the identity of the provider, the findings, and the diagnosis. (See also Standards 4.01, Maintaining Confidentiality; 4.04, Minimizing Intrusions on Privacy; and 4.05, Disclosures.)

6.07 Referrals and Fees

When psychologists pay, receive payment from, or divide fees with another professional, other than in an employer–employee relationship, the payment to each is based on the services provided (clinical, consultative, administrative, or other) and is not based on the referral itself. (See also Standard 3.09, Cooperation With Other Professionals.)

7.   Education and Training

7.01 Design of Education and Training Programs

Psychologists responsible for education and training programs take reasonable steps to ensure that the programs are designed to provide the appropriate knowledge and proper experiences, and to meet the requirements for licensure, certification, or other goals for which claims are made by the program. (See also Standard 5.03, Descriptions of Workshops and Non-Degree-Granting Educational Programs.)

7.02 Descriptions of Education and Training Programs

Psychologists responsible for education and training programs take reasonable steps to ensure that there is a current and accurate description of the program content (including participation in required course- or program-related counseling, psychotherapy, experiential groups, consulting projects, or community service), training goals and objectives, stipends and benefits, and requirements that must be met for satisfactory completion of the program. This information must be made readily available to all interested parties.

7.03 Accuracy in Training

(a) Psychologists take reasonable steps to ensure that course syllabi are accurate regarding the subject matter to be covered, bases for evaluating progress, and the nature of course experiences. This standard does not preclude an instructor from modifying course content or requirements when the instructor considers it pedagogically necessary or desirable, so long as students are made aware of these modifications in a manner that enables them to fulfill course requirements. (See also Standard 5.01, Avoidance of False or Deceptive Statements.)

(b) When engaged in teaching or training, psychologists present psychological information accurately. (See also Standard 2.03, Maintaining Competence.)

7.04 Student Disclosure of Personal Information

Psychologists do not require students or supervisees to disclose personal information in course- or program-related activities, either orally or in writing, regarding sexual history, history of abuse and neglect, psychological treatment, and relationships with parents, peers, and spouses or significant others except if (1) the program or training facility has clearly identified this requirement in its admissions and program materials or (2) the information is necessary to evaluate or obtain assistance for students whose personal problems could reasonably be judged to be preventing them from performing their training- or professionally related activities in a competent manner or posing a threat to the students or others.

7.05 Mandatory Individual or Group Therapy

(a) When individual or group therapy is a program or course requirement, psychologists responsible for that program allow students in undergraduate and graduate programs the option of selecting such therapy from practitioners unaffiliated with the program. (See also Standard 7.02, Descriptions of Education and Training Programs.)

(b) Faculty who are or are likely to be responsible for evaluating students' academic performance do not themselves provide that therapy. (See also Standard 3.05, Multiple Relationships.)

7.06 Assessing Student and Supervisee Performance

(a) In academic and supervisory relationships, psychologists establish a timely and specific process for providing feedback to students and supervisees. Information regarding the process is provided to the student at the beginning of supervision.

(b) Psychologists evaluate students and supervisees on the basis of their actual performance on relevant and established program requirements.

7.07 Sexual Relationships With Students and Supervisees

Psychologists do not engage in sexual relationships with students or supervisees who are in their department, agency, or training center or over whom psychologists have or are likely to have evaluative authority. (See also Standard 3.05, Multiple Relationships.)

8.   Research and Publication

8.01 Institutional Approval

When institutional approval is required, psychologists provide accurate information about their research proposals and obtain approval prior to conducting the research. They conduct the research in accordance with the approved research protocol.

8.02 Informed Consent to Research

(a) When obtaining informed consent as required in Standard 3.10, Informed Consent, psychologists inform participants about (1) the purpose of the research, expected duration, and procedures; (2) their right to decline to participate and to withdraw from the research once participation has begun; (3) the foreseeable consequences of declining or withdrawing; (4) reasonably foreseeable factors that may be expected to influence their willingness to participate such as potential risks, discomfort, or adverse effects; (5) any prospective research benefits; (6) limits of confidentiality; (7) incentives for participation; and (8) whom to contact for questions about the research and research participants' rights. They provide opportunity for the prospective participants to ask questions and receive answers. (See also Standards 8.03, Informed Consent for Recording Voices and Images in Research; 8.05, Dispensing With Informed Consent for Research; and 8.07, Deception in Research.)

(b) Psychologists conducting intervention research involving the use of experimental treatments clarity to participants at the outset of the research (1) the experimental nature of the treatment; (2) the services that will or will not be available to the control group(s) if appropriate; (3) the means by which assignment to treatment and control groups will be made; (4) available treatment alternatives if an individual does not wish to participate in the research or wishes to withdraw once a study has begun; and (5) compensation for or monetary costs of participating including, if appropriate, whether reimbursement from the participant or a third-party payor will be sought. (See also Standard 8.02a, Informed Consent to Research.)

8.03 Informed Consent for Recording Voices and Images in Research

Psychologists obtain informed consent from research participants prior to recording their voices or images for data collection unless (1) the research consists solely of naturalistic observations in public places, and it is not anticipated that the recording will be used in a manner that could cause personal identification or harm, or (2) the research design includes deception, and consent for the use of the recording is obtained during debriefing. (See also Standard 8.07, Deception in Research.)

8.04 Client/Patient, Student, and Subordinate Research Participants

(a) When psychologists conduct research with clients/patients, students, or subordinates as participants, psychologists take steps to protect the prospective participants from adverse consequences of declining or withdrawing from participation.

(b) When research participation is a course requirement or an opportunity for extra credit, the prospective participant is given the choice of equitable alternative activities.

8.05 Dispensing With Informed Consent for Research

Psychologists may dispense with informed consent only (1) where research would not reasonably be assumed to create distress or harm and involves (a) the study of normal educational practices, curricula, or classroom management methods conducted in educational settings; (b) only anonymous questionnaires, naturalistic observations, or archival research for which disclosure of responses would not place participants at risk of criminal or civil liability or damage their financial standing, employability, or reputation, and confidentiality is protected; or (c) the study of factors related to job or organization effectiveness conducted in organizational settings for which there is not risk to participations' employability, and confidentiality is protected or (c) where otherwise permitted by law or federal or institutional regulations.

8.06 Offering Inducements for Research Participation

(a) Psychologists make reasonable efforts to avoid offering excessive or inappropriate financial or other inducements for research participation when such inducements are likely to coerce participation.

(b) When offering professional services as an inducement for research participation, psychologists clarity the nature of the services, as well as the risks, obligations, and limitations. (See also Standard 6.05, Barter With Clients/Patients.)

8.07 Deception in Research

(a) Psychologists do not conduct a study involving deception unless they have determined that the use of deceptive techniques is justified by the study's significant prospective scientific, educational, or applied value and that effective nondeceptive alternative procedures are not feasible.

(b) Psychologists do not deceive prospective participants about research that is reasonably expected to cause physical pain or severe emotional distress.

(c) Psychologists explain any deception that is an integral feature of the design and conduct of an experiment to participants as early as is feasible, preferably at the conclusion of their participation, but no later than at the conclusion of the data collection, and permit participants to withdraw their data. (See also Standard 8.08, Debriefing.)

8.08 Debriefing

(a) Psychologists provide a prompt opportunity for participants to obtain appropriate information about the nature, results, and conclusions of the research, and they take reasonable steps to correct any misconceptions that participants may have of which the psychologists are aware.

(b) If scientific or humane values justify delaying or withholding this information, psychologists take reasonable measures to reduce the risk of harm.

(c) When psychologists become aware that research procedures have harmed a participant, they take reasonable steps to minimize the harm.

8.09 Humane Care and Use of Animals in Research

(a) Psychologists acquire, care for, use, and dispose of animals in compliance with current federal, state, and local laws and regulations, and with professional standards.

(b) Psychologists trained in research methods and experienced in the care of laboratory animals supervise all procedures involving animals and are responsible for ensuring appropriate consideration of their comfort, health, and humane treatment.

(c) Psychologists ensure that all individuals under their supervision who are using animals have received instruction in research methods and in the care, maintenance, and handling of the species being used, to the extent appropriate to their role. (See also Standard 2.05, Delegation of Work to Others.)

(d) Psychologists make reasonable efforts to minimize the discomfort, infection, illness, and pain of animal subjects.

(e) Psychologists use a procedure subjecting animals to pain, stress, or privation only when an alternative procedure is unavailable and the goal is justified by its prospective scientific, educational, or applied value.

(f) Psychologists perform surgical procedures under appropriate anesthesia and follow techniques to avoid infection and minimize pain during and after surgery.

(g) When it is appropriate that an animal's life be terminated, psychologists proceed rapidly, with an effort to minimize pain and in accordance with accepted procedures.

8.10 Reporting Research Results

(a) Psychologists do not fabricate data. (See also Standard 5.01a, Avoidance of False or Deceptive Statements.)

(b) If psychologists discover significant errors in their published data, they take reasonable steps to correct such errors in a correction, retraction, erratum, or other appropriate publication means.

8.11 Plagiarism

Psychologists do not present portions of another's work or data as their own, even if the other work or data source is cited occasionally.

8.12 Publication Credit

(a) Psychologists take responsibility and credit, including authorship credit, only for work they have actually performed or to which they have substantially contributed. (See also Standard 8.12b, Publication Credit.)

(b) Principal authorship and other publication credits accurately reflect the relative scientific or professional contributions of the individuals involved, regardless of their relative status. Mere possession of an institutional position, such as department chair, does not justify authorship credit. Minor contributions to the research or to the writing for publications are acknowledged appropriately, such as in footnotes or in an introductory statement.

(c) Except under exceptional circumstances, a student is listed as principal author on any multiple-authored article that is substantially based on the student's doctoral dissertation. Faculty advisors discuss publication credit with students as early as feasible and throughout the research and publication process as appropriate. (See also Standard 8.12b, Publication Credit.)

8.13 Duplicate Publication of Data

Psychologists do not publish, as original data, data that have been previously published. This does not preclude republishing data when they are accompanied by proper acknowledgment.

8.14 Sharing Research Data for Verification

(a) After research results are published, psychologists do not withhold the data on which their conclusions are based from other competent professionals who seek to verify the substantive claims through reanalysis and who intend to use such data only for that purpose, provided that the confidentiality of the participants can be protected and unless legal rights concerning proprietary data preclude their release. This does not preclude psychologists from requiring that such individuals or groups be responsible for costs associated with the provision of such information.

(b) Psychologists who request data from other psychologists to verify the substantive claims through reanalysis may use shared data only for the declared purpose. Requesting psychologists obtain prior written agreement for all other uses of the data.

8.15 Reviewers

Psychologists who review material submitted for presentation, publication, grant, or research proposal review respect the confidentiality of and the proprietary rights in such information of those who submitted it.

9.   Assessment

9.01 Bases for Assessments

(a) Psychologists base the opinions contained in their recommendations, reports, and diagnostic or evaluative statements, including forensic testimony, on information and techniques sufficient to substantiate their findings. (See also Standard 2.04, Bases for Scientific and Professional Judgments.)

(b) Except as noted in 9.01c, psychologists provide opinions of the psychological characteristics of individuals only after they have conducted an examination of the individuals adequate to support their statements or conclusions. When, despite reasonable efforts, such an examination is not practical, psychologists document the efforts they made and the result of those efforts, clarify the probable impact of their limited information on the reliability and validity of their opinions, and appropriately limit the nature and extent of their conclusions or recommendations. (See also Standards 2.01, Boundaries of Competence, and 9.06, Interpreting Assessment Results.)

(c) When psychologists conduct a record review or provide consultation or supervision and an individual examination is not warranted or necessary for the opinion, psychologists explain this and the sources of information on which they based their conclusions and recommendations.

9.02 Use of Assessments

(a) Psychologists administer, adapt, score, interpret, or use assessment techniques, interviews, tests, or instruments in a manner and for purposes that are appropriate in light of the research on or evidence of the usefulness and proper application of the techniques.

(b) Psychologists use assessment instruments whose validity and reliability have been established for use with members of the population tested. When such validity or reliability has not been established, psychologists describe the strengths and limitations of test results and interpretation.

(c) Psychologists use assessment methods that are appropriate to an individual's language preference and competence, unless the use of an alternative language is relevant to the assessment issues.

9.03 Informed Consent in Assessments

(a) Psychologists obtain informed consent for assessments, evaluations, or diagnostic services, as described in Standard 3.10, Informed Consent, except when (1) testing is mandated by law or governmental regulations; (2) informed consent is implied because testing is conducted as a routine educational, institutional, or organizational activity (e.g., when participants voluntarily agree to assessment when applying for a job); or (3) one purpose of the testing is to evaluate decisional capacity. Informed consent includes an explanation of the nature and purpose of the assessment, fees, involvement of third parties, and limits of confidentiality and sufficient opportunity for the client/patient to ask questions and receive answers.

(b) Psychologists inform persons with questionable capacity to consent or for whom testing is mandated by law or governmental regulations about the nature and purpose of the proposed assessment services, using language that is reasonably understandable to the person being assessed.

(c) Psychologists using the services of an interpreter obtain informed consent from the client/patient to use that interpreter, ensure that confidentiality of test results and test security are maintained, and include in their recommendations, reports, and diagnostic or evaluative statements, including forensic testimony, discussion of any limitations on the data obtained. (See also Standards 2.05, Delegation of Work to Others; 4.01, Maintaining Confidentiality; 9.01, Bases for Assessments; 9.06, Interpreting Assessment Results; and 9.07, Assessment by Unqualified Persons.)

9.04 Release of Test Data

(a) The term *test data* refers to raw and scaled scores, client/patient responses to test questions or stimuli, and psychologists' notes and recordings concerning client/patient statements and behavior during an examination. Those portions of test materials that include client/patient responses are included in the definition of *test data*. Pursuant to a client/patient release, psychologists provide test data to the client/patient or other persons identified in the release. Psychologists may refrain from releasing test data to protect a client/patient or others from substantial harm or misuse of misrepresentation of the data or the test, recognizing that in many instances release of confidential information under these circumstances is regulated by law. (See also Standard 9.11, Maintaining Test Security.)

(b) In the absence of a client/patient release, psychologists provide test data only as required by law or court order.

9.05 Test Construction

Psychologists who develop tests and other assessment techniques use appropriate psychometric procedures and current scientific or professional knowledge for test design, standardization, validation, reduction or elimination of bias, and recommendations for use.

9.06 Interpreting Assessment Results

When interpreting assessment results, including automated interpretations, psychologists take into account the purpose of the assessment as well as the various test factors, test-taking abilities, and other characteristics of the person being assessed, such as situational, personal, linguistic, and cultural differences, that might affect psychologists' judgments or reduce the accuracy of their interpretations. They indicate any significant limitations of their interpretations. (See also Standards 2.01b and c, Boundaries of Competence, and 3.01, Unfair Discrimination.)

9.07 Assessment by Unqualified Persons

Psychologists do not promote the use of psychological assessment techniques by unqualified persons, except when such use is conducted for training purposes with appropriate supervision. (See also Standard 2.05, Delegation of Work to Others.)

9.08 Obsolete Tests and Outdated Test Results

(a) Psychologists do not base their assessment or intervention decisions or recommendations on data or test results that are outdated for the current purpose.

(b) Psychologists do not base such decisions or recommendations on tests and measures that are obsolete and not useful for the current purpose.

9.09 Test Scoring and Interpretation Services

(a) Psychologists who offer assessment or scoring services to other professionals accurately describe the purpose, norms, validity, reliability, and applications of the procedures and any special qualifications applicable to their use.

(b) Psychologists select scoring and interpretation services (including automated services) on the basis of evidence of the validity of the program and procedures as well as on other appropriate considerations. (See also Standard 2.01b and c, Boundaries of Competence.)

(c) Psychologists retain responsibility for the appropriate application, interpretation, and use of assessment instruments, whether they score and interpret such tests themselves or use automated or other services.

9.10 Explaining Assessment Results

Regardless of whether the scoring and interpretation are done by psychologists, by employees or assistants, or by automated or other outside services, psychologists take reasonable steps to ensure that explanations of results are given to the individual or designated representative unless the nature of the relationship precludes provision of an explanation of results (such as in some organizational consulting, preemployment or security screenings, and forensic evaluations), and this fact has been clearly explained to the person being assessed in advance.

9.11 Maintaining Test Security

The term *test materials* refers to manuals, instruments, protocols, and test questions or stimuli and does not include *test data* as defined in Standard 9.04, Release of Test Data. Psychologists make reasonable efforts to maintain the integrity and security of test materials and other assessment techniques consistent with law and contractual obligations, and in a manner that permits adherence to this Ethics Code.

10.   <u>Therapy</u>

10.01 Informed Consent to Therapy

(a) When obtaining informed consent to therapy as required in Standard 3.10, Informed Consent, psychologists inform clients/patients as early as is feasible in the therapeutic relationship about the nature and anticipated course of therapy, fees, involvement of third parties, and limits of confidentiality and provide sufficient opportunity for the client/patient to ask questions and receive answers. (See also Standards 4.02, Discussing the Limits of Confidentiality, and 6.04, Fees and Financial Arrangements.)

(b) When obtaining informed consent for treatment for which generally recognized techniques and procedures have not been established, psychologists inform their clients/ patients of the developing nature of the treatment, the potential risks involved, alternative treatments that may be available, and the voluntary nature of their participation. (See also Standards 2.01e, Boundaries of Competence, and 3.10, Informed Consent.)

(c) When the therapist is a trainee and the legal responsibility for the treatment provided resides with the supervisor, the client/patient, as part of the informed consent procedure, is informed that the therapist is in training and is supervised and is given the name of the supervisor.

10.02 Therapy Involving Couples or Families

(a) When psychologists agree to provide services to several persons who have a relationship (such as spouses, significant others, or parents and children), they take reasonable steps to clarify at the outset (1) which of the individuals are clients/patients and (2) the relationship the psychologist will have with each person. This clarification includes the psychologist's role and the probable uses of the services provided or the information obtained. (See also Standard 4.02, Discussing the Limits of Confidentiality.)

(b) If it becomes apparent that psychologists may be called on to perform potentially conflicting roles (such as family therapist and then witness for one party in divorce proceedings), psychologists take reasonable steps to clarify and modify, or withdraw from, roles appropriately. (See also Standard 3.05c, Multiple Relationships.)

10.03 Group Therapy

When psychologists provide services to several persons in a group setting, they describe at the outset the roles and responsibilities of all parties and the limits of confidentiality.

10.04 Providing Therapy to Those Served by Others

In deciding whether to offer or provide services to those already receiving mental health services elsewhere, psychologists carefully consider the treatment issues and the potential client's/patient's welfare. Psychologists discuss these issues with the client/patient or another legally authorized person on behalf of the client/patient in order to minimize the risk of confusion and conflict, consult with the other service providers when appropriate, and proceed with caution and sensitivity to the therapeutic issues.

10.05 Sexual Intimacies With Current Therapy Clients/Patients

Psychologists do not engage in sexual intimacies with current therapy clients/patients.

10.06 Sexual Intimacies With Relatives or Significant Others of Current Therapy Clients/Patients

Psychologists do not engage in sexual intimacies with individuals they know to be close relatives, guardians, or significant others of current clients/patients. Psychologists do not terminate therapy to circumvent this standard.

10.07 Therapy With Former Sexual Partner

Psychologists do not accept as therapy clients/patients persons with whom they have engaged in sexual intimacies.

10.08 Sexual Intimacies With Former Therapy Clients/Patients

(a) Psychologists do not engage in sexual intimacies with former clients/patients for at least two years after cessation or termination of therapy.

(b) Psychologists do not engage in sexual intimacies with former clients/patients even after a two-year interval except in the most unusual circumstances. Psychologists who engage in such activity after the two years following cessation or termination of therapy and of having no sexual contact with the former client/patient bear the burden of demonstrating that there has been no exploitation, in light of all relevant factors, including (1) the amount of time that has passed since therapy terminated; (2) the nature, duration, and intensity of the therapy; (3) the circumstances of termination; (4) the client's/patient's personal history; (5) the client's/patient's current mental status; (6) the likelihood of adverse impact on the client/patient; and (7) any statements or actions made by the therapist during the course of therapy suggesting or inviting the possibility of a posttermination sexual or romantic relationship with the client/patient. (See also Standard 3.05, Multiple Relationships.)

10.09 Interruption of Therapy

When entering into employment or contractual relationships, psychologists make reasonable efforts to provide for orderly and appropriate resolution of responsibility for client/patient care in the event that the employment or contractual relationship ends, with paramount consideration given to the welfare of the client/patient. (See also Standard 3.12, Interruption of Psychological Services.)

10.10 Terminating Therapy

(a) Psychologists terminate therapy when it becomes reasonably clear that the client/patient no longer needs the service, is not likely to benefit, or is being harmed by continued services.

(b) Psychologists may terminate therapy when threatened or otherwise endangered by the client/patient or another person with whom the client/patient has a relationship.

(c) Except when precluded by the actions of clients/patients or third-party payors, prior to termination psychologists provide pretermination counseling and suggest alternative service providers as appropriate.

APPENDIX B

A Review of Statistical and Psychometric Concepts

Clinical psychologists must understand some basic statistical and psychometric concepts in order to be competent evaluators, therapists, and researchers. A thorough understanding of these concepts is particularly important for psychologists who use psychological tests. What follows is a brief overview of some of the more important statistical and psychometric concepts in psychological assessment. For more detailed coverage, readers should see Anastasi and Urbina (1997), Sattler (1988), or Walsh and Betz (1995).

Basic Statistical Concepts

When a psychological test has been constructed and the administration and scoring procedures standardized, the next step in test development is to establish a set of *norms*. Norms refer to the distribution of scores for a sample of individuals from the population of interest. This sample is referred to as the *normative sample, norm group, reference group,* or *standardization sample* (Cohen, Swerdlik, & Smith, 1992). Who should be included in the normative sample depends upon the purpose for which one wishes to use the test. To take an extreme example, if a psychologist is developing a test of attention and concentration which she hopes to use in identifying first graders with attention deficit hyperactivity disorder, she should not use a sample of college students as the norm group. The *Standards for Educational and Psychological Testing* (American Educational and Research Association, 1985), states, "Norms that are presented should refer to clearly defined groups. These groups should be the ones with whom users of the test will ordinarily wish to compare people who are tested" (p. 33).

Many psychological tests, such as tests of intelligence, use age-matched standardization samples. Tests of academic achievement might use samples of children at different grade levels to establish the norm for each grade. In the clinical area, test developers will often administer a test to a sample of individuals with a specific disorder and another sample with no mental disorder. For example, Steketee, Frost, and Bogart (1996) collected normative data on the Yale-Brown Obsessive Compulsive Scale with a set of individuals with obsessive-compulsive disorder (OCD) and a sample of college students. With these data, a clinician can compare his or her client's score to a sample of OCD sufferers and a non-OCD group.

Having a set of scores of individuals from a certain age or grade level, or with a certain mental disorder, does not mean that it is necessarily appropriate to interpret the score of any individual of the same age or grade level or with the same disorder by comparing his or her score to the sample distribution. The population of 6-year-olds, for example, is made up of children who are male, female, African American, Caucasian, Hispanic, Asian, Catholic, and Jewish, as well as children from urban, suburban, and rural settings, wealthy, poor, single-parent, and two-parent families. Test developers will usually attempt to include in a standardization sample individuals representing different subgroups. Ideally, the percentage of individuals from each subgroup in the sample will match the percentage in the population. So if 12 percent of the population of 6-year-olds in the country are African American, then the standardization sample should be made up of 12 percent African American children. When a test developer makes sure that each subgroup of interest is represented in the normative sample at a frequency equal to its population frequency, the sample is referred to as a *stratified sample*. If the individuals within each subgroup are randomly chosen (i.e., everyone in the population has the same chances of being chosen), then the procedure is referred to as *stratified-random sampling*.

In order to use the data from the normative sample to interpret the meaning of an individual's score, the clinical psychologist needs to know some statistical properties of the distribution of scores. At the very least, he or she needs to know the average score and how variable is the distribution. There are three ways of measuring the average score in a distribution. These are referred to as *measures of central tendency*. The *mean* is the most commonly used measure of central tendency and is in most cases the most useful. The mean is calculated by summing the scores of all the individuals who were administered the test and dividing by the number of scores. So if there are 100 people in the standardization sample, the mean score would be the sum of all of 100 scores divided by 100. Other measures of central tendency include the *median,* the number in the middle of the distribution of numbers (i.e., half the scores are higher and half are lower) and the *mode,* the most frequently occurring score.

Three statistics are commonly used to describe the variability in a set of scores: the *range,* the *variance,* and the *standard deviation*. The range simply refers to the difference between the lowest and highest score. The range is of limited valued in describing the distribution. The variance and standard deviation are much more helpful. The variance and standard deviation both describe the average distance of the scores in the distribution from the mean score. The standard deviation, which is equal to the square root of the variance, is particularly useful because its value is in numerical units that are the same as the scores in the distribution. The standard deviation is also important because it is used in a number of statistical formulas. S, s, and SD have all been used as symbols for the standard deviation of a sample of scores.

The *normal curve* refers to a bell-shaped distribution of scores in which the mean, median, and mode are exactly the same. Many psychological tests will yield an approximately normal distribution of scores if administered to enough people, although few will yield a precise normal curve (Cohen et al., 1992). As a general rule, the larger the number of scores in the sample, the more closely the distribution of scores will approximate a normal curve, although there are many exceptions to this rule. A normal distribution of scores has the following properties:

- 50 percent of the scores fall above the mean and 50 percent fall below.
- Approximately 34 percent of the scores fall between the mean and one standard deviation above the mean.

- Approximately 34 percent of the scores fall between the mean and one standard deviation below the mean.
- Approximately 68 percent of all scores fall within one standard deviation of the mean (i.e., between the mean and ± one standard deviation).
- Approximately 95 percent of all scores fall within two standard deviations of the mean (i.e., between the mean and ± two standard deviations).

Knowing the mean and standard deviation of a normally distributed set of scores tells one a great deal about that set of scores and is very useful in interpreting the score of any one individual. Raw test scores are often converted into *standard scores* to facilitate interpretation of individual scores and to compare scores from different tests. A standard score is a raw score that has been transformed from one scale to another scale, the latter having some properties that ease interpretation. The two most commonly used standardized scores are probably *z scores* and *T scores*. The distribution of z scores has a mean of 0 and a standard deviation of 1. The formula for converting raw scores to z scores is rather simple:

$$z = \frac{X - \overline{X}}{SD}$$

where X is equal to a specific score, $\overline{X}$ is the mean of the sample, and SD is the standard deviation of the sample. Using this formula any set of raw scores can be converted into z scores. With z scores, it is easily understood where an individual score falls relative to the mean score for the distribution. A z score of 1 means the person's score is one standard deviation above the mean of the sample, or better than about 84 percent of the scores in the sample. By converting raw scores to z scores, one can compare scores on tests that have very different distributions. For example, if we know that little Billy received a raw score of 24 on his spelling test and a raw score of 42 on his arithmetic test, we know very little about his performance. However, if by converting the raw scores to z scores, we see that Billy's z score in spelling was .78 and his z score in arithmetic was −1.75, we have a better idea of Billy's relative strengths and weaknesses and might suggest he invest in a calculator.

T scores have a mean set at 50 and a standard deviation of 10. The T score was devised by W. A. McCall (1922, 1939, cited in Cohen et al., 1992) and was named for McCall's mentor, E. L. Thorndike. The distribution of T scores ranges from 0, five standard deviations below the mean, to 100, five standard deviations above the mean. The Minnesota Multiphasic Personality Inventory is a well-known measure that uses T scores to describe where an individual's scores fall on the inventory's scales (see Chapter 8). The deviation IQ (see Chapter 7) is another type of standard score. For most IQ tests, raw scores are converted to IQ scores which have a mean set at 100 and a standard deviation of 15.

Another way in which test scores are sometimes presented is *percentile scores* or *percentile equivalents*. The percentile score refers to the percentage of scores above which the individual's score lies. For example, a percentile score of 75 means that the individual's score was higher than 75 percent of the scores in the sample. While the percentile equivalent is a pretty straightforward way to communicate test results, it can be misinterpreted. It is not uncommon, for example, for percentile scores to be misinterpreted to mean the percentage of items an individual got right. Percentiles are derived scores expressed in terms of the percentage of scores an individual's score supercedes. Percentage scores refers to the percentage of items answered correctly (Anastasi & Urbina, 1997). Figure B.1 presents a normal curve with the percentiles and some standard scores.

Before moving on to a discussion of the basics of psychometrics, it is important to take a moment to review one more statistical concept. The *correlation coefficient* is used to describe the degree of relationship between two sets of scores. For example, imagine the case where a set of students is administered two tests: Test A and Test B. If the person who scores highest on Test A also scores highest on Test B and the person who scores second highest on Test A also receives the second highest score on test B and so on down to the person with the worst score on A also getting the worse score on B, then the two sets of tests

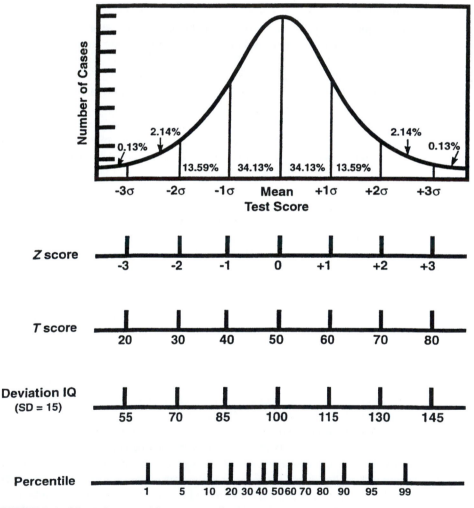

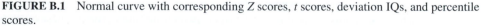

FIGURE B.1   Normal curve with corresponding *Z* scores, *t* scores, deviation IQs, and percentile scores.

scores would be perfectly correlated. The correlation coefficient describing the relationship between the two scores would be +1.00, sometimes referred to as a perfect positive correlation. In this case, knowing a person's relative standing on Test A (e.g., Maryanne received the fifth highest score on Test A), we would be able to predict exactly her relative standing on Test B (e.g., Maryanne's score on Test B was also the fifth highest).

In a perfect negative correlation (correlation coefficient is equal to –1.00), one can also predict a person's relative standing on one set of scores from the other. However, the direction of the relationship between the two scores would be the opposite. In this case, the person who received the top score on Test A would have received the lowest score on Test B.

When there is no relationship between two sets of test scores the correlation coefficient is equal to 0. In this case, knowing where a person scores on one variable tells you nothing about where he or she scores on the other. One's ability to predict a person's relative standing on Test A based upon his or her score on Test B is no better than chance.

The perfect negative correlation, zero correlation, and perfect positive correlation are the extreme examples. In actual practice, correlations coefficients describing the relationship between two sets of scores usually falls somewhere between 0 and plus or minus 1. That is, there is usually some degree of relationship found between two sets of variables. One question that is often of interest is whether the degree of relationship between two sets of variables, expressed as the correlation coefficient, is likely to have occurred by chance. Fortunately, there are statistical procedures that allow us to estimate the probability that the observed correlation between two sets of variables could have occurred by chance. These procedures take into account the size of the sample, as well as the means and standard deviations of the two distributions, and the size of the correlation between two samples. It is possible, for example, for a correlation of .78 to be nonsignificant (i.e., no higher than might be expected by chance) if the sample size is relatively small, while a correlation of .32 may be significant (i.e., unlikely to have occurred by chance) if derived from a large enough sample.

There are a variety of ways of computing the correlation coefficient. The appropriate statistic depends upon the type of data. The most common coefficient is the *Pearson Product-Moment Correlation Coefficient,* or *Pearson r.* The Pearson r takes into account a score's relative position in a group, but also the amount the score deviates above or below the group mean.

Basic Psychometric Concepts

Reliability

The concept of reliability is important in psychological testing but also in diagnostics, behavioral observation, interviewer ratings, and every other form of psychological assessment. Reliability refers to consistency of observations or scores. In the case of psychological testing, it refers to the consistency of scores obtained by the same person when a test is administered at different times, or by different people, or with different sets of equivalent items (Anastasi & Urbina, 1997). Reliability has been used to describe several aspects of assessment consistency. Various reliability coefficients are statistical expressions that describe the degree to which individual differences in test scores, observations, or diagnoses are due to "true" differences in the individual under consideration and how much these differences can be attributed to measurement errors. For example, the reliability of an IQ tests allows one to estimate the degree to which the difference between Bianca's IQ score of 105 and Jerry's IQ score of 88 represents true differences in ability and how much is due to inconsistencies in the test. To put it more technically, "measures of test reliability make it possible to estimate what proportion of the total variance of test scores is *error variance*" (Anastasi & Urbina, 1997, p. 84; italics in original).

There are a variety of ways of assessing the reliability of a psychological test. The most appropriate method depends upon the nature of the test and the nature of the phenomenon of interest. *Test-retest* reliability is the most straightforward means of assessing reliability. The consistency of the test is assessed by administering the test on two occasions. The correlation between the two sets of scores is the reliability coefficient in this case. Test-retest reliability shows the degree of consistency of test scores over time. A low correlation between scores obtained at time one and those obtained at time two suggests that fluctuations in the conditions of the test taker or changes in the test environment have a strong influence on an individual's score.

Several factors can affect test-retest reliability, some of which don't necessarily reflect problems in the test. If a test has a strong practice effects, test-retest reliability might be poor. For example, a test that includes items requiring the examinee to solve novel problems may be vulnerable to practice effects. Once the person figures out the strategy, the problem is no longer novel. The range of scores in the second administration of the test may be restricted by a ceiling effect (that is, everyone scores at or near the top). Test-retest reliability can also be affected by the stability of the phenomena of interest. For example, it would probably be inappropriate to expect a high correlation between two sets of scores on a measure of depression administered six months apart since we would not expect individuals' levels of depression to be consistent over this length of time. On the other hand, six-month test-retest might be appropriate for a measure of general intelligence since intelligence is assumed to be a relatively stable characteristic. Too short an interval between tests can also be a problem. A test taker may recall his or her responses from the first administration during the second, leading to a spuriously high estimate of reliability (Anastasi & Urbina, 1997).

An approach to reliability estimation that avoids some of the difficulties with test-retest reliability is the use of *parallel* or *alternate forms* of the same test. In this approach to reliability, the same set of people is administered two forms of the test. The correlation between the two sets of scores is the reliability coefficient. To use this approach, one must have two truly parallel forms of the test. Items should cover the same content areas, be expressed in the same form (e.g., multiple choice, open response, and so on), have the same number of items, and the same range of difficulty. Instructions, time limits, and testing format must be equivalent (Anastasi & Urbina, 1997).

Parallel form reliability has several strengths. Anastasi and Urbina (1997) point out that this type of reliability coefficient is a measure of both stability of responses over time but also stability of responses to different samples of items. Using alternative forms of the same test reduces, but does not eliminate, the problem of practice effects. Practice at solving certain types of problems (e.g., math word problems) can improve the speed and accuracy of responses to similar types of problems, whereas for other types of problems (e.g., vocabulary words), practice is less of an issue. The biggest drawback of using alternative forms to assess the reliability of a psychological test is the difficulty of independently constructing two forms of the same test that are truly equivalent. For most psychological tests, equivalent forms simply are not available.

It is possible to measure the reliability of a test from a single administration. In fact, there are several ways of deriving a reliability coefficient from a single set of test scores. The most straightforward approach is the *split-half reliability*. As the name implies, this method involves splitting the test items in half and examining the correlation between the sets of scores obtained from each half. The logic here is the same as for the parallel forms reliability. If the test items assess the same construct, then scores derived from one half of the items ought to correlate highly with scores from the other half. The first question to address when doing split-half reliability is how to form two tests out of one. Forming two version by doing a simple odd-even split is one convention for doing split-half reliability: Odd items form one test and even items form the other. The appropriateness of a odd-even split is dependent upon the format of the test. For tests where some items refer back to earlier ones, or where several questions in a row deal with the same reading passage or diagram, an odd-even split does not make sense. In cases such as these, whole groups of items need to be assigned to one-half of the test or the other.

The correlation between two halves of the same test actually yields a reliability coefficient that underestimates the true reliability of the whole test. The reason is that, as a general rule, the more items used to make up a test, the more reliable the test will be. This general rule can be proved mathematically, but it is probably easiest to understand why this is true conceptually. If we are trying to measure a construct accurately and consistently, we are more likely to succeed if we take a large number of samples of behavior than if we take only a few samples. With the split-half method of assessing reliability, we are limited by the fact that we are estimating reliability based upon a sample of behavior that is only half the size of the sample used in the actual test. The Spearman-Brown formula (see Anastasi & Urbina, 1997) is used to estimate the true reliability of a test based upon a split-half reliability coefficient.

Split-half reliability with the Spearman-Brown correction is a method of measuring the *internal consistency* of a test. This approach assesses the consistency of responses to one-half of the test compared to the other. Other methods of measuring internal consistency assess the relationships among all the items of the test. When a test has high internal consistency, the items of the test are assumed to be measuring the same construct. Put differently, internal consistency measures the degree to which the sample of items used in a particular test measure the same domain of behavior. A simple example will illustrate. A test made up of 40 vocabulary words is likely to be more internally consistent than a test made up of 10 vocabulary words, 10 spatial reasoning problems, 10 arithmetic problems, and 10 items measuring perceptual speed (Anastasi & Urbina, 1997).

There are several methods of measuring the internal consistency of a test. The best-known formula was first presented by Kuder and Richardson in a 1937 paper. Several formulas are described in the paper, but the most widely applicable one is formula 20. Thus, the formula has come to be called Kuder-Richardson Formula 20, or KR-20 by some. The Kuder-Richardson formula yields a reliability coefficient that is a measure of internal consistency. Cronbach (1951) showed mathematically that the Kuder-Richardson reliability coefficient is equal to the split-half coefficients that would result from every possible splitting of the test. One limitation of the Kuder-Richardson formula is that it can only be used on tests with a dichotomous response format (e.g., true-false, right-wrong). A more general formula has been derived for use with tests that have alternative response formats (e.g., "always," "sometimes," "rarely," "never"). This formula is known as *coefficient alpha* (Anastasi & Urbina, 1997).

The types of reliability discussed so far are most applicable to psychological testing. As we indicated earlier, however, reliability issues are important in every method of psychological assessment. Certain forms of reliability are particularly important for certain assessment activities. *Interrater reliability* refers to the level of agreement between two observers rating the same behavior or characteristic. The reliability of ratings of psychotherapy clients' level of improvement might be assessed by looking at the correlation between sets of ratings obtained from two independent raters who have observed the same sample of behavior (e.g., videotape of a post-treatment clinical interview). For behavioral observation systems that rely upon a frequency count of specific behaviors, the degree to which different observers agree that the behavior did or did not occur is referred to as *interobserver reliability*. *Diagnostic reliability* refers to the level of agreement between two or more diagnosticians about whether individuals meet criteria for psychiatric (or other) diagnoses and which diagnosis is primary.

For a psychological test to be useful, it must be reliable. When a clinical psychologist administers a test of intelligence, for example, and derives an IQ score, how much stock he or she places in that particular score is dependent upon the reliability of the test. If the test is highly reliable (e.g., reliability coefficient > .90), the psychologist can have confidence that the obtained IQ score is a close approximation of the person's true score (i.e., the hypothetical score the person would obtain if all measurement error was eliminated). A perfectly reliable test would have a reliability coefficient of 1.0. Few, if any, methods of psychological assessment are perfectly reliable. For psychological tests, it is desirable that the reliability coefficient be above .80 (Anastasi & Urbina, 1997). The reliability of a psychological test is one factor a psychologist might consider in deciding whether to use that test as part of a psychological assessment.

Validity

Put simply, validity refers to the degree to which a measure actually assesses what it is purported to assess. In psychological assessment, validity is the degree to which the assessment methods accurately measure the psychological characteristics they are believed to measure. The validity of a psychological assessment method cannot be separated from the purpose of the assessment. A psychological test is not valid or invalid. Rather, the test may be valid for certain purposes with certain groups of people but invalid for other purposes or when used with a different population. The revised Beck Depression Inventory (BDI; Beck & Steer, 1993) is a popular self-report measure of severity of depression. There is an extensive literature supporting the validity of the BDI for this purpose (for review, see Kramer & Conoley, 1992). The BDI is not valid, however, for use with children and is not valid for diagnosing depressive disorders (e.g., dysthymia versus major depressive episode versus bipolar disorder). The proper answer to the question "Is this test valid?" therefore, is another question: "Valid for what?"

Three types of validity generally are recognized: *content-related validity, criterion-related validity,* and *construct-related validity* (American Educational and Research Association, 1985). It is probably more accurate to think of these types of validity as ways of gathering evidence about whether a test measures what we think it measures.

Content-related validity refers to the extent to which a test or other assessment method covers the domain of behavior of interest. Take as an example a test of intelligence. Memory is thought to play a role in intellectual functioning. Therefore, a test of intelligence should include items assessing memory functioning, such as items that require the test taker to recall a string of numbers. However, an intelligence test that includes only these items would have poor content validity since intelligence is more than one's ability to recall number strings. Intelligence tests should include items that assess abstract reasoning, nonverbal problem solving, judgment, and general knowledge, as well as items that assess memory.

Content-related validity is usually emphasized in academic testing. For example, if we assessing what grade level of arithmetic class a 10-year-old transfer student should be placed in, our test should include items assessing number recognition, counting, addition, subtraction, multiplication, and division. The difficulty of the items should match the difficulty expected at the possible grade levels under consideration. In this case, the test might include items that have a difficulty range representative of third through seventh grade.

While content-related validity is emphasized in academic testing, it plays a role in other types of assessment as well. For example, a measure of anxiety—whether a questionnaire, observation method, or interview—should include items that assess physiological aspects of anxiety (e.g., sweating), anxious thoughts (e.g., "I feel nervous") and anxious behavior (e.g., fidgeting; Lang, 1978).

The term *face valid* is sometimes used to describe a psychological test. Face validity refers to how apparent it is to the test taker that the test is measuring a specific construct or quality. For example, a true-false test of depression that consists of the following items:

1. I feel sad.
2. I am blue.
3. I feel down in the dumps.
4. My friends tell me that I am depressed.
5. I sometimes think about killing myself.

would be considered face valid. It should be obvious to anyone taking the test that it is measuring depression. Face validity is not true validity in the technical sense (Anastasi & Urbina, 1997). The term simply refers to whether the test looks valid to the person taking it. Face validity is generally considered a positive feature of a test. If the test content appears irrelevant, foolish, childish, or inappropriate to the test taker, it may result in poor cooperation, which can negatively affect the validity of the test. A test that is highly face valid, however, can be problematic in some circumstances. For example, a psychotherapy client completing the fictitious depression measure described above would find it obvious how to respond if she wants to appear more or less depressed to her therapist. How she scores on this measure may have more to do with the impression she wishes to give her therapist than her true level of depression.

An important way to evaluate the validity of a psychological measure is to assess how closely it relates to some criterion measure. If the criterion is measured at the same time as the assessment method, the term *concurrent validity* is used to describe the relationship.

When the criterion is measured at a later point in time, the correlation between the test and the criterion is a measure of *predictive validity*. Concurrent and predictive validity are types of *criterion-related validity*. Criterion-related validity "refers to the extent to which a measure of an attribute demonstrates an association with some independent or external indicator of the same attribute" (Walsh & Betz, 1995).

The correlation between a newly developed measure of intelligence and an established measure of intelligence is evidence of the concurrent validity of the new measure. A psychiatrist's determination of which individuals meet diagnostic criteria for panic disorder might be the criterion against which a paper-and-pencil screening measure of panic disorder would be tested. High agreement between the individuals diagnosed with panic disorder by the psychiatrist and those identified by the screening measure would be taken as evidence of the concurrent validity of the screening measure. The correlation between the college aptitude test scores of a group of high school seniors and the cumulative GPAs of the same group of students after their junior year in college would be used to evaluate the predictive validity of the college aptitude test.

All forms of validity provide evidence related to *construct-related validity* (Messick, 1995). Most psychological assessment strategies attempt to measure the degree to which individuals possess some theoretical construct. Intelligence, assertiveness, paranoia, verbal reasoning, and schizophrenia are all constructs. They are theoretical postulates that have been put forth to explain or account for a set of observations. Construct validation is the process of gathering data to test the idea that the assessment method actually reflects the construct it is designed to reflect.

Establishing construct validity involves the cumulation of data showing that the measure is related to other things that are believed to represent the construct it is supposed to be measuring and not related to things it should be independent of (Campbell & Fiske, 1959). For example, a group of socially phobic individuals should show higher scores on a measure of state of anxiety administered at a crowded restaurant than when assessed in the security of their homes. If their scores in the two situations are the same, it would call into question the construct validity of the measure. The construct validity of the state anxiety measure would be further supported if it could be shown that scores on this measure are not strongly correlated with scores on a measure of depression. *Convergent validity* is the term used to describe evidence that a test correlates highly with other variables it should theoretically be related to, and *divergent validity* refers to evidence that the measure is not correlated with something with which it should be unrelated.

Reliability and validity are two of the most important factors to consider when evaluating a psychological assessment method. The two concepts are related, but distinct. Reliability refers to consistency and validity to accuracy of measurement. Unless an assessment is reliable, there is no point in considering its validity. An assessment technique cannot be valid if it is not reliable. However, the reverse is not true—an assessment can be highly reliable but completely invalid. On Halloween night 1938, Orson Welles and a group of Mercury Theatre actors broadcast a radio dramatization of H. G. Wells's *War of the Worlds*. The broadcast was so realistic that thousands of people listening believed the earth had in fact been invaded by Martians. The reliability of their assessment of the situation was quite high (most people listening agreed that the earth was under alien invasion); fortunately, the validity of the listeners' assessment was quite low.

REFERENCES

Abramowitz, C. V., & Dokecki, P. R. (1977). The politics of clinical judgment: Early empirical returns. *Psychological Bulletin, 84,* 460–476.

Abramowitz, C. V., & Murray, J. (1983). Race effects in psychotherapy. In J. Murray & P. R. Abramson (Eds.), *Bias in psychotherapy* (pp. 215–255). New York: Academic Press.

Abramowitz, J. S. (1996). Variants of exposure and response prevention in the treatment of obsessive-compulsive disorder: A meta-analysis. *Behavior Therapy, 27,* 583–600.

Abramowitz, J. S. (1997). Effectiveness of psychological and pharmacological treatments for obsessive-compulsive disorder: A quantitative review. *Journal of Consulting and Clinical Psychology, 65,* 44–52.

Academy of Psychological Clinical Science. (2003). www.w3.arizona/edu~psych/apcs/apcs.html

Academy of Psychological Clinical Science (2003, August). *Mission and specific goals.* Retrieved August 18, 2003 from www.psych.Arizona.edu/apcs/purpose.html

Acierno, R., Hersen, M., & Van Hasselt, V. B. (1998). Prescriptive assessment and treatment. In A. S. Bellack & M. Hersen (Eds.), *Behavioral assessment: A practical handbook* (4th ed., pp. 47–62). Boston: Allyn and Bacon.

Ackerman, M. J. (1994). *Clinician's guide to child custody evaluations.* New York: Wiley.

Adams, P. R., & Adams, G. R. (1984). Mount Saint Helen's ashfall: Evidence for a disaster stress reaction. *American Psychologist, 39,* 262–260.

Adler, A. (1976). What life should mean to you (excerpt). In J. Ehrenwald (Ed.), *The history of psychotherapy: From healing magic to encounter.* New York: Jason Aronson (pp. 292–298). (Original work published in 1931.)

Afnan, S. M. (1958). *Avicenna: His life and works.* London: George Allen and Unwin.

Agras, W. S., Leitenberg, H., Barlow, D. H., & Burlington, M. A. (1967). Social reinforcement in the modification of agoraphobia. *Archives of General Psychiatry, 19,* 423–427.

Aikens, J. E., & Wagner, L. I. (1998). Diabetes mellitus and other endocrine disorders. In P. M. Camic & S. J. Knight (Eds.), *Clinical handbook of health psychology: A practical guide to effective interventions* (pp. 191–225). Seattle, WA: Hogrefe & Huber Publishers.

Albee, G. W. (1970). Notes on a position paper opposing psychodiagnosis. In A. R. Mahrer (Ed.), *New approaches to personality classification* (pp. 385–395). New York: Columbia University Press

Albee, G. W. (1990). The futility of psychotherapy. In D. Cohen (Ed.), Special issue: Challenging the therapeutic state: Critical perspectives on psychiatry and the mental health system. *Journal of Mind and Behavior, 11,* (3 and 4), 369–384 (123–138).

Alder, B. (1998). Reproductive and obstetric issues. In A. S. Bellack & M. Hersen (Eds.), *Comprehensive clinical psychology, Volume 8, Health psychology* (pp. 409–427). New York: Elsevier.

Alexander, J. A. (1984). Blood pressure and obesity. In J. D. Matarazzo, S. M. Weiss, J. A. Herd, N. E. Miller, & S. M. Weiss (Eds.), *Behavioral health: A handbook of health enhancement and disease prevention.* New York: Wiley.

Alexander, J. F., Sexton, T. L., & Robbins, M. S. (2002). The developmental status of family therapy in family psychology intervention science. In H. A. Liddle, D. A. Santisteban, R. F. Levant, & J. H. Bray (Eds.), *Family psychology: Science-based interventions* (Chapter 2; pp. 17–40). Washington, DC: American Psychological Association.

Al-Kubaisy, T., Marks, I. M., Logsdail, S., Marks, M. P., Lovell, K., Sungur, M., & Araya, R. (1992). Role of exposure homework in phobia reduction: A controlled study. *Behavior Therapy, 23,* 599–621.

Allen, D. N., Sprenkel, D. G., Heyman, R. A., Schramke, C. J., & Heffron, N. E. (1998). Evaluation of demyelinating and degenerative disorders. In G. Goldstein, P. D. Nussbaum, & S. R. Beers (Eds.), *Neuropsychology* (pp. 187–208). New York: Plenum.

Allport, G. W. (1937). *Personality: A psychological interpretation.* New York: Holt.

American Association on Mental Retardation (1992). *Mental retardation: Definition, classification, and systems of supports (9th ed.).* Washington, DC: Author.

American Cancer Society (1997). Cancer facts and figures, 1997. New York: American Cancer Society.

American Diabetes Association (1996). *Vital statistics.* Alexandria: Author.

American Educational Research Association, American Psychological Association, & National Council on Measurement in Education. (1985). *Standards for educational and psychological testing.* Washington, DC: American Psychological Association.

American Heart Association. (1995). *Heart and stroke facts.* Dallas, TX: Author.

American Heart Association. (1997). *Heart and stroke facts.* Dallas, TX: Author.

American Humane Association (1985). *National analysis of child abuse and neglect reports.* Denver, CO: Author.

American Indians and diabetes. (1997). *American Indian Community Mental Health, 3,* 3–4.

American Psychiatric Association. (1952). *Diagnostic and statistical manual of mental disorders.* Washington, DC: Author.

American Psychiatric Association. (1968). *Diagnostic and statistical manual of mental disorders* (2nd ed.). Washington, DC: Author.

American Psychiatric Association. (1974). *Clinical aspects of the violent individual.* Washington, DC: Author.

American Psychiatric Association. (1980). *Diagnostic and statistical manual of mental disorders* (3rd ed.). Washington, DC: Author.

American Psychiatric Association. (1987). *Diagnostic and statistical manual of mental disorders* (3rd ed., Revised). Washington, DC: Author.

American Psychiatric Association. (1993). Practice guidelines for major depressive disorder in adults. *American Journal of Psychiatry, 150* (Suppl. 4).

American Psychiatric Association, Task Force on DSM-IV. (1993). *DSM-IV draft criteria.* Washington, DC: Author.

American Psychiatric Association. (1994). *Diagnostic and statistical manual of mental disorders* (4th ed.). Washington, DC: Author.

American Psychiatric Association. (2000). *Diagnostic and statistical manual of mental disorders* (4th ed., Text Revision). Washington, DC: Author.

American Psychological Association. (1947). Committee on training in clinical psychology. Recommended graduate training programs in clinical psychology. *American Psychologist, 2,* 539–558.

American Psychological Association. (1953). *Ethical standards of psychologists: A summary of ethical principles.* Oxford, England: Author.

American Psychological Association. (1978). Report of the Task Force on the Role of Psychology in the Criminal Justice System. *American Psychologist, 33,* 1099–1113.

American Psychological Association. (1982). *Ethical principles in the conduct of research with human subjects.* Washington, DC: Arthur.

American Psychological Association. (1985). *Standards for educational and psychological testing.* Washington, DC: Arthur.

American Psychological Association. (1986). *Guidelines for ethical conduct in the care and use of animals.* Washington, DC: Arthur.

American Psychological Association. (1987a). *General guidelines for providers of psychological services.* Washington, DC: Arthur.

American Psychological Association. (1987b). *Guidelines for computer based tests and interpretations.* Washington, DC: Arthur.

American Psychological Association. (1990). *Guidelines for providers of psychological services to ethnic, linguistic, and culturally diverse populations.* Washington, DC: Arthur.

American Psychological Association. (1992a). *Ethical principles of psychologists and code of conduct.* Washington, DC: Author.

American Psychological Association. (1992b). Guidelines for child custody evaluations in divorce proceedings. *American Psychologist, 49,* 677–680.

American Psychological Association. (1993). *Directory of the American Psychological Association, 1993 edition.* Washington, DC: Author.

American Psychological Association. (1994a). *Publication manual of the American Psychological Association* (4th ed.). Washington, DC: Author.

American Psychological Association. (1994b). *Guidelines for child custody evaluations in divorce.* Washington, DC: Arthur.

American Psychological Association. (1996, December). Task Force Report: *On-line psychotherapy and counseling.* Washington, DC: Author.

American Psychological Association. (1997). *1997 Doctoral Employment Survey.* Washington, CD: Author.

American Psychological Association. (1998). *Guidelines for psychological evaluations in child protective matters.* Washington, DC: Arthur.

American Psychological Association. (1999). Accredited internships and postdoctoral programs for training in psychology: 1999. *American Psychologist, 54,* 1079–1098.

American Psychological Association. (2001). *Guidelines for psychotherapy with lesbian, gay and bisexual clients.* Washington, DC: Arthur.

American Psychological Association. (2002). Ethical principles of psychologists and code of conduct. *American Psychologist, 57,* 1060–1073.

American Psychological Association Committee on Training in Clinical Psychology. (1947). Recommended graduate training program in clinical psychology, *American Psychologist, 2,* 539–558.

American Psychological Association Committee of Women in Psychology. (1985). *Statement on proposed diagnostic categories for DSM-III-R.* Washington, DC: American Psychological Association.

American Psychological Association Division 38 Education and Training Committee. (2000). *A directory of program offering health psychology training.* Washington, DC: American Psychological Association.

American Psychological Association Division 38. (2001). *Health psychology web site.* Retrieved December 13, 2001, from http://www.health-psych.org.

Ames, L. (1981). Sylvia Plath: A biographical note. In S. Plath, *The bell jar* (pp. 201–216). New York: Bantam Books.

Anastasi, A. (1982). *Psychological testing* (5th ed.). New York: Macmillan.

Anastasi, A., & Urbina, S. (1997). *Psychological testing* (7th ed.). Upper Saddle River, NJ: Prentice Hall.

Andersen, B. L. (1993). Cancer. In C. A. Niven & C. Douglas (Eds.), *The health psychology of women* (pp. 75–89). Langhorne, PA: Harwood Academic Publishers.

Andersen, B. L., & Golden-Kreutz, D. M. (1998). Cancer. In A. S. Bellack & M. Hersen (Eds.), *Comprehensive clinical psychology, Volume 8, Health psychology* (pp. 217–236). New York: Elsevier.

Anderten, P., Staulcup, V., & Grisso, T. (1980). On being ethical in legal places. *American Psychologist, 11,* 764–773.

Andrews, J. A., Foster, S. L., Capaldi, D., & Hops, H. (2000). Adolescent and family predictors of physical aggression, communication, and satisfaction in young adults couples: A prospective analysis. *Journal of Consulting and Clinical Psychology, 68,* 195–208.

Angermeier, W. F. (1994). Operant learning. In V. S. Ramachandran (Ed.), *Encyclopedia of human behavior* (Vol. 3, pp. 351–366). San Diego, CA: Academic Press.

Anglicus, B. (1991). De proprietatibus rerum. In R. Porter (Ed.), *The Faber book of madness* (pp. 63–64). London: Faber and Faber. (Original work published in 1535.)

Angoff, W. J. (1988). The nature nurture debate, aptitudes, and group differences. *American Psychologist, 43,* 713–720.

Aponte, J. F., Rivers, R. Y., & Wohl, J. (1995). *Psychological interventions and cultural diversity.* Boston: Allyn and Bacon.

Applebaum, P. S., Mirkin, S. A., & Bateman, A. (1981). Empirical assessment of competency to consent to psychiatric hospitalization. *American Journal of Psychiatry, 138,* 1170–1176.

ARACOR. (1998). http://www.aracor.com

Archer, R. P., & Krishnamurthy, R. (1996). The Minnesota Multiphasic Personality Inventory—Adolescent (MMPI-A). In C. S. Newmark (Ed.), *Major psychological assessment instruments* (2nd ed.). Boston: Allyn and Bacon.

Arkes, H. R. (1981). Impediments to accurate clinical judgment and possible ways to minimize their impact. *Journal of Consulting and Clinical Psychology, 49,* 323–330.

Arkes, H. R., Faust, D., Guilmette, T. J., & Hart, K. (1988). Eliminating the hindsight bias. *Journal of Applied Psychology, 73,* 305–307.

Arkes, H. R., Wortman, R. L., Saville, P., & Harkness, A. R. (1981). The hindsight bias among physicians weighing the likelihood of diagnosis. *Journal of Applied Psychology, 66,* 252–-254.

Arkowitz, H. (1992). Integrative theories of therapy. In D. K. Freedheim (Ed.), *History of psychotherapy: A century of change* (p. 261–303). Washington, DC: American Psychological Association.

Arlow, J. (1989). Psychoanalysis. In R. J. Corsini & D. Wedding (Eds.), *Current psychotherapies* (4th ed., pp. 19–62). Itsca, IL: F. E. Peacock.

Arlow, J. (1995). Psychoanalysis. In R. J. Corsini & D. Wedding (Eds.), *Current psychotherapies* (5th ed., pp. 15–50). Itasca, IL: F. E. Peacock.

Armstead, C. A., Lawler, K. A., Gordon, G., Cross, J., & Givvons, J. (1989). Relationship of racial stressors to blood pressure responses and anger expression in black college students. *Health Psychology, 8,* 541–557.

Arnow, B. A., Taylor, C. B., Agras, W. S., & Telch, M. J. (1985). Enhancing agoraphobia treatment outcome by changing couples communication patterns. *Behavior Therapy, 16,* 452–467.

Aronow, E., Reznikoff, M., & Moreland, K. (1994). *The Rorschach technique: Perceptual basics, content interpretation, and applications.* Boston: Allyn and Bacon.

Aronow, E., Reznikoff, M., & Moreland, K. (1995). The Rorschach: Projective technique or psychometric test? *Journal of Personality Assessment, 64,* 213–228.

Asimov, I. (1994). *The human brain: Its capacities and functions* (rev. ed.). New York: Penguin.

Auld, F., & Hyman, M. (1991). *Resolution of inner conflict: An introduction to psychoanalytic therapy.* Washington, DC: American Psychological Association.

Austad, C. S., Hunter, R. D. A., & Morgan, T. C. (1998). Managed health care, ethics and psychotherapy. *Clinical Psychology: Science and Practice, 5,* 67–76.

Ax, R. K., Forbes, M. R., & Thompson, D. D. (1997). Prescription privileges for psychologists: A survey of predoctoral interns and directors of training. *Professional Psychology: Research and Practice, 28,* 509–514.

Ayllon, T. (1963). Intensive treatment of psychotic behavior by stimulus satiation and food reinforcement. *Behaviour Research and Therapy, 1,* 53–61.

Ayllon, T., & Azrin, N. H. (1965). The measurement and reinforcement of behavior of psychotics. *Journal of the Experimental Analysis of Behavior, 8,* 357–383.

Ayllon, T., & Azrin, N. H. (1968). *The token economy: A motivational system for therapy and rehabilitation.* New York: Appleton-Century-Crofts.

Ayllon, T., & Haughton, E. (1964). Modification of symptomatic verbal behavior of mental patients. *Behavior Research and Therapy, 2,* 87–97.

Azar, S. T., Benjet, C. L., Fuhrman, G. S., Cavallero, L. (1995). Child maltreatment and termination of parental rights: Can behavioral research help Solomon? *Behavior Therapy, 26,* 599–624.

Azar, S. T., & Twentyman, C. T. (1986). Cognitive behavioral perspectives on the assessment and treatment of child abuse. In P. C. Kendall (Ed.), *Advances in cognitive behavior research and therapy* (Vol. 5. pp. 237–267). New York: Academic Press.

Azmitia, E. C. (1994). Brain chemicals. In V. S. Ramachandran (Ed.), *Encyclopedia of human behavior* (Vol. 1, pp. 435–441). San Diego, CA: Academic Press.

Azrin, N. H., & Foxx, R. M. (1971). A rapid method of toilet training the institutionalized retarded. *Journal of Applied Behavior Analysis, 4,* 89–99.

Baekland, F., & Lundwall, L. (1975). Dropping out of treatment: A critical review. *Psychological Bulletin, 82,* 738–783.

Baker, D. D., & Benjamin, L. T. (2000). The affirmation of the scientist-practitioner: A look back at Boulder. *American Psychologist, 55,* 241–247.

Baker, G. A. (1998). Epilepsy. In A. S. Bellack, & M. Hersen (Eds.), *Comprehensive clinical psychology, Volume 8, Health psychology* (pp. 487–504). New York: Elsevier.

Ballinger, B., & Yalom, I. (1995). Group therapy in practice. In B. Bongar & L. E. Beutler (Eds.), *Comprehensive textbook of psychotherapy: Theory and practice* (Chapter 11; pp. 189–204). New York: Oxford University Press.

Ballinger, J. R. (1996). URL: http://www.mritutor.com

Baltes, M. M., & Lascomb, S. L. (1975). Creating a healthy institutional environment for the elderly via behavior management: The nurse as a change agent. *International Journal of Nursing Studies, 12,* 5–12.

Bandura, A. (1969). *Principles of behavior modification.* New York: Holt, Rinehart and Winston.

Bandura, A. (1971a). Psychotherapy based upon modeling principles. In A. E. Bergin & S. L. Garfield (Eds.), *Handbook of psychotherapy and behavior change* (pp. 653–708). New York: Wiley.

Bandura, A. (1971b). *Social learning theory.* New York: General Learning Press.

Bandura, A. (1977). Self-efficacy: Toward a unifying theory of behavior change. *Psychological Review, 84,* 191–215.

Bandura, A. (1986). *Social foundations of thought and action: A social cognitive theory.* Englewood Cliffs, NJ: Prentice Hall.

Bandura, A. (1991). Self-efficacy mechanism in physiological activation and health-promoting behavior. In J. Madden (Ed.), *Neurobiology of learning, emotion and affect* (pp. 229–270). New York: Raven Press.

Bandura, A. (1994). Self-efficacy. In V. S. Ramachandran (Ed.), *Encyclopedia of human behavior* (Vol. 4, pp. 71–81). San Diego, CA: Academic Press.

Bandura, A. (1995). Exercise of personal and collective efficacy in changing societies. In A. Bandura (Ed.), *Self-efficacy in changing societies* (pp. 1–45). Cambridge: Cambridge University Press.

Barefoot v. Estelle, 463 U.S. 880 (1983).

Barlow, D. H. (1988). *Anxiety and its disorders.* Guilford Press, New York.

Barlow, D. H. (1991). On the relation of clinical research to clinical practice: Current issues, new directions. *Journal of Consulting and Clinical Psychology, 49,* 147–155.

Barlow, D. H. (1996a). Health care policy, psychotherapy research, and the future of psychotherapy. *American Psychologist, 51,* 1050–1058.

Barlow, D. H. (1996b). The effectiveness of psychotherapy: Science and policy. *Clinical Psychology: Science and Practice, 3,* 236–240.

Barlow, D. H. (Ed.). (2002). *Anxiety and its disorders: The nature and treatment of anxiety and panic* (2nd ed.). New York: Guilford.

Barlow, D. H., Cohen, A. S., Waddell, M. T., Vermilyea, B. B., Klosko, J. S., Blanchard, E. B., & DiNardo, P. A. (1984). Panic and generalized anxiety disorders: Nature and treatment. *Behavior Therapy, 15,* 431–449.

Barlow, D. H., Craske, M. G., Cerny, J. A., & Klosko, J. S. (1989). Behavioral treatment of panic disorder. *Behavior Therapy, 20,* 261–282.

Barlow, D. H., DiNardo, P. A., Vermilyea, B. B., Vermilyea, J. A., & Blanchard, E. B. (1986). Co-morbidity and depression among the anxiety disorders: Issues in diagnosis and classification. *Journal of Nervous and Mental Disease, 174,* 63–72.

Barlow, D. H., & Durand, V. M. (1999). *Abnormal psychology: An integrative approach* (2nd ed.). Pacific Grove, CA: Brooks/Cole.

Barlow, D. H., & Durand, V. M. (2002). *Abnormal psychology: An integrative approach* (3rd ed.). Belmont, CA: Wadsworth.

Barlow, D. H., Esler, J. L., & Vitali, A. E. (1998). Psychosocial treatments for panic disorders, phobias, and generalized anxiety disorder. In P. E. Nathan & J. M. Gorman (Eds.), *A guide to treatments that work* (pp. 288–318). New York: Oxford University Press.

Barlow, D. H., Hayes, S. C., & Nelson, R. O. (1984). *The scientist-practitioner: Research and accountability in clinical and educational settings.* Elmsford, NY: Pergamon Press.

Barlow, D. H., & Hersen, M. (1984). *Single-case experimental designs: Strategies for studying behavior change* (2nd ed.). Elsmford, NY: Pergamon.

Barlow, D. H., Rapee, R. M., & Brown, T. A. (1992). Behavioral treatment of generalized anxiety disorder. *Behavior Therapy, 23,* 551–570.

Barlow, J. H. (1998). Arthritis. In A. S. Bellack, & M. Hersen (Eds.), *Comprehensive clinical psychology, Volume 8, Health psychology* (pp. 427–444). New York: Elsevier.

Barrett-Lennard, G. T. (1973). The intensive group experience: Experiential learning groups in practice: General process description and guidelines. *Canada's Mental Health, 73,* 12.

Barrios, B. (1988). On the changing nature of behavioral assessment. In A. S. Bellack & M. Hersen (Eds.), *Behavioral assessment* (3rd ed.). New York: Pergamon Press.

Barton, J., Chassin, L., Presson, C. C. & Sherman, S. J. (1982). Social image factors as motivators of smoking initiation in early and middle adolescence. *Child Development, 53,* 1499–1511.

Baucom, D. H., Shoham, V., Mueser, K. T., Daiuto, A. D., & Stickle, T. R. (1998). Empirically supported couple and family interventions for marital distress and adult mental health problems. *Journal of Consulting and Clinical Psychology, 66,* 53–88.

Baum, A. (1994). Behavioral, biological, and environmental interactions in disease processes. In S. Blumenthal, K. Matthews, & S. Weiss (Eds.), *New research frontiers in behavioral medicine: Proceedings of the national conference* (pp. 61–70).

Baum, M. (1970). Extinction of avoidance responding through response prevention (flooding). *Psychological Bulletin, 74,* 276–284.

Bazelon, D. (1982). Veils, values, and social responsibility. *American Psychologist, 37,* 115–121.

Beck, A. T. (1976). *Cognitive therapy and the emotional disorders.* New York: International Universities Press.

Beck, A. T. (1985). Generalized anxiety disorder and panic disorder. In A. T. Beck, G. Emery, & R. L. Greenberg, *Anxiety disorders and phobias: A cognitive perspective* (pp. 82–114). New York: Basic Books.

Beck, A. T. (1995). Cognitive therapy: A 30-year retrospective. In S. O. Lilienfeld (Ed.), *Seeing both sides: Classic controversies in abnormal psychology* (pp. 303–311). Pacific Grove, CA: Brooks/Cole. (Original work published in 1991.)

Beck, A. T., Emery, G., & Greenberg, R. L. (1985). *Anxiety disorders and phobias: A cognitive perspective.* New York: Basic Books.

Beck, A. T., Laude, R., & Bohnert, M. (1974). Ideational components of anxiety neuroses. *Archives of General Psychiatry, 31,* 319–325.

Beck, A. T., Rush, A. J., Shaw, B. F., & Emery, G. (1979). *Cognitive therapy of depression.* New York: Guilford.

Beck, A. T., & Steer, R. A. (1993). *Beck Depression Inventory: Manual.* San Antonio, TX: Psychological Corporation.

Beck, A. T., Ward, C. H., Mendelson, M., Mock, J., & Erbaugh, J. (1961). An inventory for measuring depression. *Archives of General Psychiatry, 4,* 53–63.

Beck, A. T., & Weishaar, M. E. (1995). Cognitive therapy. In R. J. Corsini & D. Wedding (Eds.), *Current psychotherapies* (5th ed., pp. 229–261). Itasca, IL: F. E. Peacock.

Beck, J. G., & Zebb, B. J. (1994). Behavioral assessment and treatment of panic disorder: Current status, future directions. *Behavior Therapy, 25,* 581–611.

Beck, J. S. (1994). *Cognitive therapy: Basics and beyond.* New York: Guilford.

Becker, D., & Lamb, S. (1994). Sex bias in the diagnosis of borderline personality disorder and posttraumatic stress disorder. *Professional Psychology, 25,* 55–61.

Beech, H. R., & Vaughan, M. (1978). *Behavioral treatment of obsessional states.* New York: Wiley.

Belar, C. D. (1997). Clinical health psychology: A specialty for the 21st century. *Health Psychology, 16,* 411–416.

Belar, C. D. (2000). Scientist-practitioner ≠ Science + Practice: Boulder is bolder. *American Psychologist, 55,* 249–250.

Belar, C. D., Bieliauskas, L. A., Klepac, R. K., Larsen, K. G., Stigall, T. T., & Zimet, C. N. (1993). National conference on postdoctoral training in professional psychology. *American Psychologist, 48,* 1284–1289.

Belar, C. D., Brown, R. A., Hersch, L. E., Hornyak, L. M., Rozensky, R. H., Sheridan, E. P., Brown, R. T., & Reed, G. W. (2001). Self-assessment in clinical health psychology: A model for ethical expansion of practice. *Professional Psychology: Research and Practice, 32,* 135–141.

Belar, C. D., & Jeffrey, T. (1990). Board certification in health psychology. *Journal of Clinical Psychology in Medical Settings, 2,* 129–132.

Belar, C. D., & Perry, N. W. (Eds.) (1991). *Proceedings of the National Conference on Scientist-Practitioner Education and Training for the Professional Practice of Psychology.* Sarasota, FL: Professional Resource Press.

Belisle, M., Roskies, E., & Levesque, J-M. (1987). Improving adherence to physical activity. *Health Psychology, 6,* 159–172.

Bell, L. V. (1980). *Treating the mentally ill: From colonial times to the present.* New York: Praeger.

Bellack, A. S., & Hersen, M. (Eds.) (1998). *Behavioral assessment: A practical handbook* (4th ed.). Boston: Allyn and Bacon.

Bellack, A. S., & Morrison, R. L. (1982). Interpersonal dysfunction. In A. S. Bellack, M. Hersen, & A. E. Kazdin (Eds.), *International handbook of behavior modification and therapy* (pp. 717–747). New York: Plenum Press.

Bellack, A. S., & Mueser, K. T. (1994). Schizophrenia. In L. W. Craighead, W. E. Craighead, A. E. Kazdin, & M. J. Mahoney (Eds.), *Cognitive and behavioral interventions: An empirical approach to mental health problems* (pp. 105–122.) Boston: Allyn and Bacon.

Bellack, L. (1993). *The T.A.T., C.A.T., and S.A.T. in clinical use* (5th ed.). Boston: Allyn and Bacon.

Bender, L. (1938). A visual motor Gestalt test and its clinical use. *American Orthopsychiatric Association, Research Monographs,* No. 3.

Benjamin, L. T. (1996). Introduction: Lightner Witmer's legacy to American psychology. *American Psychologist, 51,* 235–236.

Ben-Porath, Y. S., & Tellegen, A. (1995). How (not) to evaluate the comparability of the MMPI and MMPI-2 profile configurations: A reply to Humphrey and Dahlstrom. *Journal of Personality Assessment, 65,* 62–58.

Benson, H. (1987). *Your maximum mind.* New York: Times Book.

Berg, R. A. (1998). Evaluation of neoplastic processes. In G. Goldstein, P. D. Nussbaum, & S. R. Beers (Eds.), *Neuropsychology* (pp. 248–269). New York: Plenum.

Berggren, U. (1993). Psychosocial effects associated with dental fear in adult dental patients with avoidance behaviours. *Psychology and Health, 8,* 185–196.

Bergin, A. E. (1971). The evaluation of therapeutic outcomes. In A. E. Bergin & S. L. Garfield (Eds.), *Handbook of psychotherapy and behavior change: An empirical analysis* (pp. ix–xii). New York: Wiley.

Berkerian, D. A. (1993). In search of the typical eyewitness. *American Psychologist, 48,* 574–576.

Berman, J. S., & Norton, N. L. (1985). Does professional training make a therapist more effective? *Psychological Bulletin, 98,* 401–407.

Bernard, M. E. (1998). Validation of the General Attitude and Belief Scale. *Journal of Rational-Emotive and Cognitive-Behavior Therapy, 16,* 183–196.

Bernard, M. E., & DiGiuseppe, R. (Eds.). (1989). *Inside rational-emotive therapy: A critical appraisal of the theory and therapy of Albert Ellis.* San Diego, CA: Academic Press.

Bernheimer, C. (1990). Introduction, part one. In C. Bernheimer & C. Kahane (Eds.), *In Dora's case: Freud, hysteria, feminism* (2nd ed., pp. 1–18.) New York: Columbia University Press.

Bernheimer, C., & Kahane, C. (Eds.). (1990). *In Dora's case: Freud, hysteria, feminism* (2nd ed.). New York: Columbia University Press.

Bernstein, D. A., & Borkovec, T. (1973). *Progressive relaxation training: A manual for the helping professions.* Champaign, IL: Research Press.

Berry, J. W., Poortinga, Y. H., Segall, M. H., & Dasen, P. R. (1992). *Cross-cultural psychology: Research and applications.* Cambridge: Cambridge University Press.

Bersoff, D. N. (1995). *Ethical conflicts in psychology.* Washington, DC: American Psychological Association.

Bersoff, D. N., & Hofer, P. J. (1995). Legal issues in computerized psychological testing. In D. N. Bersoff (Ed.), *Ethical conflicts in psychology* (pp. 291–294). Washington, DC: American Psychological Association.

Bertalanffy, L. von (1986). *General systems theory.* New York: Braziller.

Bessai, J. L. (1976). Self-rating scales of rationality: An update. *Rational Living, 11*(1), 28–30.

Bessai, J. L. (1977, June). *A factored measure of irrational beliefs.* Paper presented at the Second National Conference on Rational-Emotive Therapy, Chicago.

Beutler, L. E. (1979). Toward specific psychological therapies for specific conditions. *Journal of Consulting and Clinical Psychology, 47,* 882–897.

Beutler, L. E., & Fisher, D. (1994). Combined specialty training in counseling, clinical, and school psychology: An idea whose time has returned. *Professional Psychology: Research and Practice, 25,* 62–69.

Beutler, L. E., Machado, P. P., & Neufeldt, S. A. (1994). In A. E. Bergin & S. L. Garfield (Eds.), *Handbook of psychotherapy and behavior change* (4th ed.; pp. 229–269). Oxford, England: John Wiley & Sons.

Bickman, L. (1987). Graduate education in psychology. *American Psychologist, 42,* 1041–1047.

Bieliauskas, L. A., & Matthews, C. G. (1997). American Board of Clinical Neuropsychology, 1996 update: Facts, data, and information for potential candidates. *Clinical Neuropsychologist, 11,* 222–226.

Bierman, K. L. (1983). Cognitive development and clinical interviews with children. In B. B. Lahey & A. E. Kazdin (Eds.), *Advances in clinical child psychology* (Vol. 6., pp. 217–250). New York: Plenum.

Biglan, A., McConnell, S., Severson, H. H., Bavry, J., & Ary, D. (1984). Social and behavioral factors associated with high-risk sexual behavior among adolescents. Journal of *Behavioral Medicine, 13,* 245–262.

Bijou, S. W. (1963). Theory and research in mental (developmental) retardation. *Psychological Record, 13,* 95–110.

Bijou, S. W., & Baier, D. M. (1966). Operant methods in child behavior and development. In W. K. Honig (Ed.), *Operant behavior: Areas of research and application* (pp. 718–789). New York: Appleton-Century-Crofts.

Binder, J. L., Strupp, H. H., & Henry, W. P. (1995). Psychodynamic therapies in practice: Time-limited dynamic psychotherapy. In B. Bongar & L. E. Beutler (Eds.), *Comprehensive textbook of psychotherapy: Theory and practice* (Chapter 3, pp. 48–63.) New York: Oxford University Press.

Binswanger, L. (1956). Existential analysis and psychotherapy. In F. Fromm-Reichman & J. L. Moreno (Eds.), *Progress in psychotherapy* (Vol. 1). New York: Grune and Stratton.

Binswanger, L. (1976). Existential analysis and psychotherapy (excerpt). In J. Ehrenwald (Ed.), *The history of psychotherapy: From healing magic to encounter* (pp. 375–379.) New York: Jason Aronson. (Original work published in 1956.)

Biran, M., & Wilson, G. T. (1981). Treatment of phobic disorders using cognitive and exposure methods: A self-efficacy analysis. *Journal of Consulting and Clinical Psychology, 49,* 886–899.

Blanchard, E. B., Andrasik, F., & Arena, J. G., (1984). Personality and chronic headache. *Progress in Experimental Personality Research, 13,* 303–360.

Blanchard, E. B., & Epstein, L. H. (1978). *A biofeedback primer.* Reading, MA: Addison-Wesley.

Blanchard, E. B., Kolb, L. C., Gerardi, R. J., Ryan, P., & Pallmeyer, T. P. (1986). Cardiac response to relevant stimuli as an adjunctive tool for diagnosing post-traumatic stress disorder in Vietnam veterans. *Behavior Therapy, 17,* 592–606.

Blau, T. (1984). *The psychologist as expert witness.* New York: Wiley-Interscience.

Bleuler, E. (1950). *Dementia praecox or the group of schizophrenias* (J. Zinkin, Trans.). New York: International Universities Press. (Original work published in 1911.)

Bloch, S. (1982). *What is psychotherapy?* Oxford: Oxford University Press.

Blount, R. L., Frank, N. C., & Smith, A. J. (1993). Training the next generation of researchers in clinical psychology. *Clinical Psychologist, 46,* 100–105.

Bobbitt, B. L., Marques, C. C., & Trout, D. L. (1998). Managed behavioral health care: Current status, recent trends and the role of psychology. *Clinical Psychology: Science and Practice, 5,* 53–66.

Bockoven, J. S. (1963). *Moral treatment in American psychiatry.* New York: Springer.

Bongar, B. (1992). The ethical issue of competence in working with suicidal patients. *Ethics and Behavior, 2,* 75–89.

Bongar, B., & Beutler, L. E. (Eds.). (1995). *Comprehensive textbook of psychotherapy: Theory and practice.* New York: Oxford University Press.

Boring, E. G. (1923, June 6). Intelligence as the tests test it. *New Republic,* 35–37.

Borkovec, T. D., & Castonguay, G. (1998). What is the scientific meaning of empirically supported therapy? *Journal of Consulting and Clinical Psychology, 66,* 136–142.

Borkovec, T., Wilkinson, L., Folensbee, R., & Lerman, C. (1983). Stimulus control applications to the treatment of worry. *Behavior Research and Therapy, 21,* 247–251.

Borum, R. (1996). Improving the clinical practice of violence risk assessment. *American Psychologist, 51,* 945–956.

Boulougouris, J. C., & Marks, I. M. (1969). Implosion (flooding): A new treatment for phobias. *British Medical Journal, 2,* 721.

Boulougouris, J. C., & Marks, I. M., & Marset, P. (1971). Superiority of flooding (implosion) to desensitization for reducing pathological fear. *Behavior Research and Therapy, 9,* 7–16.

Boykin, A. W. (1986). The triple quandary and the schooling of Afro-American children. In U. Neisser (Ed.), *The school achievement of minority children* (pp. 57–92). Hillsdale, NJ: Erlbaum.

Boykin, A. W. (1994). Harvesting talent and culture: African-American children and educational reform. In R. Rossi (Ed.), *Schools and students at risk* (pp. 116–138). New York: Teachers College Press.

Bozarth, J. D., Zimring, F. M., & Tausch, R. (2002). Client-centered therapy: The evolution of a revolution. In D. J. Cain & J. Seeman (Eds.), *Humanistic psychotherapies: Handbook of research and practice* (Chapter 5; pp. 177–188). Washington, DC: American Psychological Association.

Bradley, C., Riazi, A., Barendse, S., Pierce, M. B., &

Hendriecks, C. (1998). Diabetes mellitus. In A. S. Bellack, & M. Hersen (Eds.), *Comprehensive clinical psychology, Volume 8, Health psychology* (pp. 277–304). New York: Elsevier.

Brems, C., Thevenin, D. M., & Routh, D. K. (1991). The history of clinical psychology. In *Clinical psychology: Historical and research foundations* (pp. 3–36). New York: Plenum.

Brenner, D. (1982). *The effective psychotherapist: Conclusions from practice and research.* New York: Pergamon Press.

Breuer, J. (1989). Anna O. In P. Gay (Ed.), *The Freud reader* (pp. 61–78). New York: W.W. Norton. (Original work published in 1895.)

Breuer, J., & Freud, S. (1974). Studies on hysteria. In J. & A. Strachey (Eds. & Trans.), *The Pelican Freud library* (Vol. 3). Harmondsworth, UK: Penguin. (Original work published 1895.)

Brief psychodynamic therapy: Part I. (1994a). *Harvard Mental Health Letter, 10*(9), 1–3.

Brief psychodynamic therapy: Part II. (1994b). *Harvard Mental Health Letter, 10*(10), 1–4.

Brill, A. A. (Ed. & Trans.) (1924). *Bleuler's textbook of psychiatry* (4th German ed.). New York: Macmillan.

Brock, A. J. (1916). (Trans.) *Galen on the natural faculties.* London: William Heinemann.

Brock, G. W., & Barnard, C. P. (1992). *Procedures in marriage and family therapy* (2nd ed.). Boston: Allyn and Bacon.

Brodsky, S. L. (1991). *Testifying in court: Guidelines and maxims for the expert witness.* Washington, DC: American Psychological Association.

Brody, N. (1985). The validity of tests of intelligence. In B. B. Woman (Ed.), *Handbook of intelligence* (pp. 353–389). New York: Wiley.

Brodzinsky, D. M. (1993). On the use and misuse of psychological testing in child custody evaluations. *Professional Psychology: Research and Practice, 24,* 213–219.

Bromberg, W. (1975). *From shaman to psychotherapist: A history of the treatment of mental illness.* Chicago: Henry Regnery Company.

Brown, J. D. (1991). Staying fit and staying well: Physical fitness as a moderator of life stress. *Journal of Personality and Social Psychology, 60,* 555–561.

Brown, P. (1990). The name game: Toward a sociology of diagnosis. In D. Cohen (Ed.), Special issue: Challenging the therapeutic state: Critical perspectives on psychiatry and the mental health system. *Journal of Mind and Behavior, 11,* (3 and 4), 139–160; 385–406.

Brown, R. T., & Morris, M. K. (1994). Central nervous system (Vol. 1, pp. 537–547). In V. S. Ramachandran (Ed.), *Encyclopedia of human behavior.* San Diego, CA: Academic Press.

Brown, T. A., DiNardo, P. A., & Barlow, D. H. (1994). *Anxiety disorders interview schedule for the DSM-IV.* Albany, NY: Graywind Publications.

Brownson, R. C., Chang, J. C., Davis, J. R., & Smith, C. A. (1991). Physical activity on the job and cancer in Missouri. *Public Health Briefs, 81,* 639–640.

Bruner, J. S., & Tagiuri, R. (1954). The perception of people. In G. Lindzey (Ed.), *Handbook of social psychology.* Reading, MA: Addison-Wesley.

Buck, J. N. (1948). The H-T-P technique, a qualitative and quantitative scoring manual. *Journal of Clinical Psychology, 4,* 317–396.

Buckhout, R. (1975). Nearly 2,000 witnesses can be wrong. *Social Action and the Law, 2,* 7.

Buckhout, R., Figueroa, D., & Hoff, E. (1975). Eyewitness identification: Effects of suggestion and bias in identification from photographs. *Bulletin of the Psychonomic Society, 6,* 71–74.

Bugental, J. F. T. (1978). *Psychotherapy and process: The fundamentals of an existential-humanistic approach.* New York: Random House.

Bugental, J. F. T. (1987). *The art of psychotherapy.* New York: Norton.

Bugental, J. F. T., & McBeath, B. (1995). Depth existential therapy: Evolution since World War II. In B. Bongar & L. E. Beutler (Eds.), *Comprehensive textbook of psychotherapy: Theory and practice* (pp. 111–122). New York: Oxford.

Burke, G. L., Arnold, A. M., Bild, D. E., Cushman, M., Fried, L. P., Newman, A., Nunn, C., & Robbins, J. (2001). Factors associated with healthy aging: The cardiovascular health study. *Journal of the American Geriatrics Society, 49,* 254–262.

Burns, D. D., & Nolen-Hoeksema, S. (1991). Coping styles, homework compliance, and the effectiveness of cognitive-behavioral therapy. *Journal of Consulting and Clinical Psychology, 59,* 305–311.

Burns, D. D., & Nolen-Hoeksema, S. (1992). Therapeutic empathy and recovery from depression in cognitive-behavioral therapy: A structural equation model. *Journal of Consulting and Clinical Psychology, 60*(3), 441–449.

Burns, R. C. (1970). *Kinetic Family Drawings (KFD): An introduction to understanding children through kinetic drawings.* New York: Brunner/Mazel.

Burns, R. C. (1987). *Action, styles, and symbols in Kinetic Family Drawings (KFD).* New York: Brunner/Mazel.

Burton, R. (1898). *Burton's anatomy of melancholy.* London: Chatto & Windus. (Original title: *The anatomy of melancholy; What it is, with all the kinds, causes, symptoms, prognostics, and several cures of it; in three partitions, with their several sections, members, and subsections, philosophically, medicinally, his-*

torically opened and cut up. Original work published 1651–1652.)

Butcher, J. N. (1987). The use of computers in psychological assessment: An overview of practices and issues. In J. N. Butcher (Ed.), *Computerized psychological assessment: A practitioner's guide.* New York: Basic Books.

Butcher, J. N. (1990). *MMPI-2 in psychological treatment.* New York: Oxford University Press.

Butcher, J. N., Dahlstrom, W. G., Graham, J. R., Tellegen, A., & Kaemmer, B. (1992). Minnesota Multiphasic Personality Inventory—2 (MMPI-2): Manual for administration and scoring. Minneapolis: University of Minnesota Press.

Cahill, S. P., Carrigan, M. H., & Evans, I. M. (1998). The relationship between behavior theory and behavior therapy: Challenges and promises. In J. J. Plaud & G. H. Eifert (Eds.), *From behavior theory to behavior therapy* (Chapter 14, pp. 294–319). Boston: Allyn and Bacon.

Cain, D. J. (2002). Defining characteristics, history, and evolution of humanistic psychotherapies. In D. J. Cain & J. Seeman (Eds.), *Humanistic psychotherapies: Handbook of research and practice* (Chapter 1; pp. 3–54). Washington, DC: American Psychological Association.

Cain, D. J., & Seeman, J. (Eds.). (2002). *Humanistic psychotherapies: Handbook of research and practice.* Washington, DC: American Psychological Association.

Calof, D. (1995). Suppressed memory therapy is legitimate. In W. Barbour (Ed.), *Mental illness: Opposing viewpoints* (pp. 118–126). San Diego, CA: Greenhaven Press.

Campbell, D. T., & Fiske, D. W. (1959). Convergent and discriminant validation by the multitrait-multimethod matrix. *Psychological Bulletin, 56,* 81–105.

Canino, I. A., & Spurlock, J. (1994). *Culturally diverse children and adolescents: Assessment, diagnosis, and treatment.* New York: Guilford Press.

Cannon, W. B. (1932). *The wisdom of the body.* New York: Norton.

Canter, M. B., Bennett, B. E., Jones, S. E. & Nagy, T. F. (1994). *Ethics for psychologists: A commentary on the APA ethics code.* Washington, DC: American Psychological Association.

Carlin, A. S., Hoffman, H. G., & Weghorst, S. (1997). Virtual reality and tactile augmentation in the treatment of spider phobia: A case report. *Behaviour Research and Therapy, 35,* 153–158.

Carroll, K. M., Nich, C., & Rounsaville, B. J. (1997). Contributions of the therapeutic alliance to outcome in active versus control psychotherapies. *Journal of Consulting and Clinical Psychology, 65,* 510–514.

Carson, H. L. (1975). Genetics, human. *Encyclopaedia Britannica* (15th ed.). Chicago: Encyclopaedia Britannica.

Carson, R. C. (1994). Dilemmas in the pathway of the DSM-IV. *Journal of Abnormal Psychology, 100,* 302–307.

Carson, R. C. (1996). Aristotle, Galileo, and the DSM taxonomy: The case of schizophrenia. *Journal of Consulting and Clinical Psychology, 64,* 113–1139.

Carson, R. C., Butcher, J. N., & Coleman, J. C. (1988). *Abnormal psychology and modern life* (8th ed.). Glenview, IL: Scott, Foresman and Company.

Casas, J. M. (1995). Counseling and psychotherapy with racial/ethnic minority groups in theory and practice. In B. Bongar & L. E. Beutler (Eds.), *Comprehensive textbook of psychotherapy: Theory and practice* (Chapter 17; pp. 311–335). New York: Oxford University Press.

Caruso, K. R. (1988). *Manual for the Projective Storytelling Cards.* Sarasota, FL: Professional Resource Exchange.

Cattell, R. B. (1946). *Description and measurement of personality.* New York: World Book Co.

Cattell, R. B. (1950). *Personality: A systematic, theoretical, and factual study.* New York: McGraw-Hill.

Cattell, R. B. (1957). *Personality and motivation structure and measurement.* New York: Harcourt, Brace, Jovanovich.

Cattell, R. B. (1963). Theory of fluid and crystallized intelligence: A critical experiment. *Journal of Educational Psychology, 54,* 1–22.

Cattell, R. B., Cattell, A. K., & Cattell, H. E. (1993). *Sixteen Factor Questionnaire, Fifth Edition.* Champaign, IL: Institute for Personality and Ability Testing.

Cattell, R. B., Saunders, D. R., & Stice, G. F. (1950). *The 16 Personality Factor Questionnaire.* Champaign, IL: Institute for Personality and Ability Testing.

Ceci, S. J. (1991). How much does schooling influence general intelligence and its cognitive components? A reassessment of the evidence. Developmental Psychology, 27, 703–722.

Ceci, S. J., & Bruck, M. (1993). Suggestibility of the child witness: A historical review and synthesis. *Psychological Bulletin, 113,* 403–439.

Ceci, S. J., & Bruck, M. (1995). *Jeopardy in the courtroom: A scientific analysis of children's testimony.* Washington, DC: American Psychological Association.

Centers for Disease Control and Prevention. (1997a). Efforts to quit smoking among persons with a history of alcohol problems-Iowa, Kansas, and Nebraska, 1996–1996. *Morbidity and mortality weekly report, 46,* 1144.

Centers for Disease Control and Prevention. (1997b). Cigarette smoking among adults—United States,

1995. *Morbidity and mortality weekly, 46,* 1217–1220.

Chambless, D. L., Baker, M. J., Baucom, D. H., Beutler, L. E., Calhoun, K. S., Crits-Christoph, P., Daiuto, A., DeRubeis, R., Detweiler, J., Haaga, D. A. F., Bennett Johnson, S., McCurry, S., Mueser, K. T., Pope, K. S., Sanderson, W. C., Shoham, V., Stickle, T., Williams, D. A., & Woody, S. R. (1998). Update on empirically validated treatments, II. *Clinical Psychologist, 51,* 3–16.

Chambless, D. L., & Goldstein, A. J. (Eds.). (1982). *Agoraphobia: Multiple perspectives on theory and treatment.* John Wiley & Sons, New York.

Chambless, D. L., & Hollon, S. D. (1998). Defining empirically supported therapies. *Journal of Consulting and Clinical Psychology, 66,* 7–18.

Chambless, D. L., Sanderson, W. C., Shoham, V., Johnson, S. B., Pope, K. S., Crits-Christoph, P., Baker, M., Bennett Johnson, S, Woody, S. R., Sue, S., Beutler, L., & Williams, D. A. (1996). An update on empirically validated therapies. *Clinical Psychologist, 49,* 5–18.

Chapman, L. J. (1967). Illusory correlation in observational report. *Journal of Verbal Learning and Verbal Behavior, 6,* 151–155.

Chapman, L. J., & Chapman, J. P. (1967). Genesis of popular but erroneous psychodiagnostic observations. *Journal of Abnormal Psychology, 72,* 193–204.

Chapman, L. J., & Chapman, J. P. (1969). Illusory correlations as an obstacle to the use of valid psychodiagnostic signs. *Journal of Abnormal Psychology, 74,* 271–280.

Chemtob, C. M., Bauer, G. B., Hamada, R. S., Pelowski, S. R., & Muraoka, M. Y. (1989). *Professional Psychology: Research and Practice, 20,* 294–300.

Chemtob, C. M., Hamada, R. S., Bauer, G. B., Torigoe, R. Y., & Kinney, B. (1988). Patient suicide: Frequency and impact on psychologists. *Professional Psychology: Research and Practice, 19,* 421–425.

Cheshire, N. M. (1975). *The nature of psychodynamic interpretation.* London: John Wiley & Sons.

Cheshire, N. M. (1979). A big hand for Little Hans. *Bulletin of the British Psychological Society, 32,* 320–323.

Chesney, M. A., Eagleston, J. R., & Rosenman, R. H. (1981). Type A behavior: Assessment and intervention. In C. K. Prokop & L. A. Bradley (Eds.), *Medical psychology: Contributions to behavioral medicine* (pp. 485–497). New York: Academic Press.

Chesney, M. A., & Rosenman, R. H. (1985). *Anger and hostility in cardiovascular and behavioral disorders.* New York: Hemisphere.

Chiras, D. D. (1991). *Human biology: Health, homeostasis, and the environment.* St. Paul, MN: West Publishing Co.

Chorney, M. J., Chorney, K., Seese, N., Owen, M. J., Daniels, J., McGuffin, P., Thompson, L. A., Detterman, D. K., Benbow, C., Lubinski, D., Eley, T., & Plomin, R. (1998). A quantitative trait locus associated with cognitive ability in children. *Psychological Science, 9,* 159–166.

Christensen, A. J., & Moran, P. J. (1998). End-stage renal disease. In A. S. Bellack & M. Hersen (Eds.), *Comprehensive clinical psychology, Volume 8, Health psychology* (pp. 321–338). New York: Elsevier.

Christie, M. J., & Mellett, P. G. (Eds.). (1986). *The psychosomatic approach: Contemporary practice and wholeperson care.* New York: Wiley.

Cicchetti, D. V. (1994). Guidelines, criteria, and rules of thumb for evaluating normed and standardized assessment instruments in psychology. *Psychological Assessment, 6,* 284–290.

Ciminero, A. R. (1986). Behavioral assessment: An Overview. In A. R. Ciminero, K. S. Calhoun, & H. E. Adams (Eds.), *Handbook of behavioral assessment* (2nd ed., pp. 3–11). New York: John Wiley & Sons.

Ciminero, A. R., Calhoun, K. S., & Adams, H. E. (Eds.). (1986). *Handbook of behavioral assessment* (2nd ed.). New York: John Wiley & Sons.

Clark, D. M. (1986). A cognitive approach to panic. *Behaviour Research and Therapy, 24,* 461–470.

Clark, D. M., & Beck, A. T. (1988). Cognitive approaches. In C. Last & M. Hersen (Eds.), *Handbook of anxiety disorders.* New York: Pergamon.

Clark, D. M., Salkovskis, P. M., & Chalkley, A. J. (1985). Respiratory control as a treatment for panic attacks. *Journal of Behavior Therapy and Experimental Psychiatry, 16,* 23–30.

Clark, L. A., Watson, D., & Reynolds, S. (1995). Diagnosis and classification of psychopathology: Challenges to the current system. *Annual Review of Psychology, 46,* 121–153.

Clarkin, J. F., & Carpenter, D. (1995). Family therapy in historical perspective. In B. Bongar & L. E. Beutler (Eds.), *Comprehensive textbook of psychotherapy: Theory and practice* (Chapter 12; pp. 205–227). New York: Oxford University Press.

Cleary, T. A., Humphreys, L. G., Kendrick, S. A., & Wesman, A. (1975). Educational uses of tests with disadvantaged students. *American Psychologist, 30,* 15–41.

Cohen, D. (Ed.) (1990). Special issue: Challenging the therapeutic state: Critical perspectives on psychiatry and the mental health system. *Journal of Mind and Behavior, 11,* (3 and 4), 247–573 (1–328).

Cohen, L. H., Sargent, M. M., & Sechrest, L. B. (1986). Use of psychotherapy research by professional psychologists. *American Psychologist, 41,* 198–206.

Cohen, R. J., Swerdlik, M. E., & Smith, D. K. (1992). *Psychological testing and assessment: An introduc-

tion to tests and measurement (2nd ed.). Mountain View, CA: Mayfield Publishing Co.

Cohen, S., Kessler, R. C., & Gordon, L. U. (1995). Strategies for measuring stress in studies of psychiatric and physical disorders. In S. Cohen, R. C. Kessler, & L. U. Gordon (Eds.), *Measuring stress: A guide for health and social scientists* (pp. 3–26). New York: Oxford University Press.

Cohen, S., Tyrrell, D. A. J., & Smith, A. P. (1991). Psychosocial stress and susceptibility to the common cold. *New England Journal of Medicine, 325,* 606–612.

Comas-Diaz, L. (1993). Diversifying clinical psychology. In L. Comas-Diaz & G. Stricker (Eds.), Special issue: Diversity in clinical psychology: Theory, research, and practice (pp. 45–49). *Clinical Psychologist, 46,* 43–89.

Comas-Diaz, L., & Stricker, G. (1993). Special issue: Diversity in clinical psychology: Theory, research, and practice. *Clinical Psychologist, 46, 43–89.*

Committee on Ethical Guidelines for Forensic Psychologists. (1991). Specialty guidelines for forensic psychologists. *Law and Human Behavior, 15,* 655–665.

Compas, B. E., Haaga, D. A. F., Keefe, F. J., Leitenberg, H., & Williams, D. A. (1998). Sampling of empirically supported psychological treatments from health psychology: Smoking, chronic pain, cancer, and bulimia nervosa. *Journal of Consulting and Clinical Psychology, 66,* 89–112.

Cone, J. D. (1987). Behavioral assessment: Some things old, some things new, some things borrowed? *Behavioral Assessment, 9,* 1–4.

Cone, J. D. (1998). Psychometric considerations: Concepts, contents, and methods. In A. S. Bellack & M. Hersen (Eds.), *Behavioral assessment: A practical handbook* (4th ed.; pp. 22–46). Boston: Allyn and Bacon.

Conner, M., & Norman, P. (1998). Health behavior. In A. S. Bellack, & M. Hersen (Eds.), *Comprehensive clinical psychology, Volume 8, Health psychology* (pp. 1–37). New York: Elsevier.

Connors, G. J., Carroll, K. M., DiClemente, C. C., Longabaugh, R., Donovan, D. M. (1997). The therapeutic alliance and its relationship to alcoholism treatment participation and outcome. *Journal of Consulting and Clinical Psychology, 65,* 588–598.

Constantino, G., Malgady, R. G., & Rogler, L. H. (1988). *Tell-Me-A Story (TEMAS) manual.* Los Angeles, CA: Western Psychological Services.

Conway, A. V. (1978). Little Hans: Misrepresentation of the evidence? *Bulletin of the British Psychological Society, 31,* 285–287.

Cook, T. D., & Campbell, D. T. (Eds.). (1979). *Quasi-*

experimentation: Design and analysis issues for field settings. Chicago: Rand McNally.

Cooke, G. & Sikorski, C. R. (1974). Factors affecting length of hospitalization of persons adjudicated not guilty by reasons of insanity. *Bulletin of the American Academy of Psychiatry, 2,* 251–261.

Cooper, J. E., Gelder, M. G., & Marks, I. M. (1965). The results of behavior therapy in 77 psychiatric patients. *British Medical Journal, 1,* 1222–1225.

Cormier, W. H., & Cormier, L. S. (1991). *Interviewing strategies for helpers: Fundamental skills and cognitive behavioral interventions.* (3rd ed.). Pacific Grove, CA: Brooks/Cole.

Corrigan, P. W., & Liberman, R. P. (1994). *Behavior therapy in psychiatric hospitals.* New York: Springer.

Corsini, R. J., & Wedding, D. (Eds.). (1989). *Current psychotherapies* (4th ed.). Itasca, IL: F. E. Peacock.

Corsini, R. J., & Wedding, D. (Eds.). (1995). *Current psychotherapies* (5th ed.) Itasca, IL: F. E. Peacock.

Costa, P. T., Jr., & McCrae, R. R. (1985). *The NEO Personality Inventory manual.* Odessa, FL: Psychological Assessment Resources.

Costa, P. T., Jr., & McCrae, R. R. (1992). *NEO-PI-R professional manual.* Odessa, FL: Psychological Assessment Resources.

Costa, P. T., Jr., & McCrae, R. R. (1994). *Bibliography for the Revised NEO Personality Inventory and NEO Five-Factor Inventory (NEO-FFI).* Odessa, FL: Psychological Assessment Resources.

Costa, P. T., Jr., & Widiger, T. A. (Eds.). (1994). *Personality disorders and the five-factor model of personality.* Washington, DC: American Psychological Association.

Council for the National Register of Health Service Providers in Psychology. (1989). *National register of health service providers in psychology.* Washington, DC: Author.

Cox, D. J., Gonder-Frederick, L. A., Julian, D. M., & Clarke, W. L. (1992). *Blood glucose awareness training manual.* Charlottesville, VA: University of Virginia.

Cox, D. J., Gonder-Frederick, L. A., Julian, D. M., & Clarke, W. L. (1994). Long-term follow-up of blood glucose awareness training. *Diabetes Care, 17,* 1–5.

Cox, D. J., Gonder-Frederick, L. A., Julian, D. M., Cryer, P., Lee, J. A., Richards, F. E., & Clarke, W. L. (1991). Intensive versus standard blood glucose awareness training (BGAT) with insulin-dependent diabetes: Mechanisms and ancilliary effects. *Psychosomatic Medicine, 53,* 453–462.

Cox, D. J., Gonder-Frederick, L. A., Kovatchev, B., Polonksy, W., Schlundt, D., Julian, D. M., & Clarke, W. L. (1995). A multi-center evaluation of blood glucose awareness training-II. *Diabetes Care, 18,* 523–528.

Craighead, L. W., Craighead, W. E., Kazdin, A. E., & Mahoney, M. J. (1994). *Cognitive and behavioral interventions: An empirical approach to mental health problems.* Boston: Allyn and Bacon.

Craighead, W. E., Craighead, L. W., & Ilardi, S. S. (1998). Psychosocial treatment for major depressive disorder. In P. E. Nathan & J. M. Gorman (Eds.), *A guide to treatments that work* (pp. 226–239). New York: Oxford University Press.

Cramer, P. (1994). Defense mechanisms (Vol. 2, pp. 91–96). In V. S. Ramachandran (Ed.), *Encyclopedia of human behavior.* San Diego, CA: Academic Press.

Criss, M. L. & Racine, R. D. (1981). Impact of change in legal standard for those adjudicated not guilty by reason of insanity 1975–1979 in Michigan. *Bulletin of the American Academy of Psychiatry, 8,* 261–271.

Critchley, D. L. (1985). Evolution of the role. In D. L. Critchley & J. T. Maurin (Eds.), *The clinical specialist in psychiatric mental health nursing: Theory, research, and practice.* (pp. 5–22). New York: John Wiley & Sons.

Critchley, D. L., & Maurin, J. T. (Eds.). (1985). *The clinical specialist in psychiatric mental health nursing: Theory, research, and practice.* New York: John Wiley & Sons.

Critelli, J. W., & Neumann, K. F. (1984). The placebo: Conceptual analysis of a construct in transition. *American Psychologist, 39,* 32–39.

Crits-Christoff, P., Frank, E., Chambless, D. L., Brody, C., & Karp, J. F. (1995). Training in empirically validated treatments: What are clinical psychology students learning? *Professional Psychology: Research and Practice, 26,* 514–522.

Cronbach, L. J. (1949). Statistical methods applied to Rorschach scores: A review. *Psychological Bulletin, 46,* 393–429.

Cronbach, L. J. (1951). Coefficient alpha and the internal structure of tests. *Psychometrika, 16,* 297–334.

Cummings, N. (1995). Impact of managed care on employment and training: A primer for survival. *Professional Psychology: Research and Practice, 26,* 10–15.

Curran, J. P., Monti, P. M., & Corriveau, D. P. (1982). Treatment of schizophrenia. In A. S. Bellack, M. Hersen, & A. E. Kazdin (Eds.), *International handbook of behavior modification and therapy.* (pp. 433–466). New York: Plenum.

Dahlstrom, W. G., Welch, G. S., & Dahlstrom, L. E. (1972). *An MMPI handbook (Vol. 1), Clinical interpretation.* Minneapolis: University of Minnesota Press.

Dain, N. (1964). *Concepts of insanity in the United States, 1989–1865.* New Brunswick, NJ: Rutgers University Press.

D'Amato, M. R. (1970). *Experimental psychology.* New York: McGraw-Hill.

Dana, R. H. (1966). Eisegesis and assessment. *Journal of Projective Techniques and Personality Assessment, 32,* 215–222.

Dana, R. H. (1993). *Multicultural assessment perspectives for professional psychology.* Boston: Allyn and Bacon.

Dana, R. H. (1996). The Thematic Apperception Test (TAT). In C. S. Newmark (Ed.), *Major psychological assessment instruments* (2nd ed.). Boston: Allyn and Bacon.

Darou, W. G., Hum, A., & Kurtness, J. (1993). An investigation of the impact of psychosocial research on a Native population. *Professional Psychology, 24,* 325–329.

Das, J. P., Kirby, J., & Jarman, R. F. (1975). Simultaneous and successive synthesis: An alternative model of cognitive abilities. *Psychological Bulletin, 82,* 87–103.

Dattilio, F. M., & Padesky, C. M. (1990). *Cognitive therapy with couples.* Sarasota, FL: Professional Resource Exchange.

David, H. P. (1975). Mental health and hygiene. *Encyclopaedia Britannica* (15th ed.). Chicago: Encyclopaedia Britannica, Inc.

Davidson, C. V., & Abramowitz, S. I. (1980). Sex bias in clinical judgment: Later empirical returns. *Psychology of Women Quarterly, 4,* 377–395.

Davison, G. C. (1968). Systematic desensitization as a counter-conditioning process. *Journal of Abnormal Psychology, 73,* 91–99.

Davison, G. C. (1969). Appraisal of behavior modification techniques with adults in institutional settings. In C. M. Franks (Ed.), *Behavior therapy: Appraisal and status* (pp. 220–278). New York: McGraw-Hill.

Davison, G. C. (1998). Being bolder with the Boulder Model: The challenge of education and training in empirically supported treatments. *Journal of Consulting and Clinical Psychology, 66,* 163–167.

Davison, G. C., & Neale, J. M. (1990). *Abnormal psychology* (5th ed). New York: Wiley

Dawes, R. (1994). *House of cards: Psychology and psychotherapy built on myth.* New York: Free Press.

Dawes, R. N., Faust, D., & Meehl, P. E. (1989). Clinical versus actuarial judgment. *Science, 243,* 1668–1674.

DeBell, C., & Jones, R. D. (1997). Privileged communication at last? An overview of *Jaffee v. Redmond. Professional Psychology: Research and Practice, 28,* 559–566.

Deffenbacher, J. L., & Suinn, R. M. (1987). Generalized anxiety syndrome. In L. Michelson & L. M. Ascher

(Eds.), *Anxiety and stress disorders: Cognitive-behavioral assessment and treatment* (pp. 332–360). New York: Guilford.

DeLeon, P. H., Bennett, B. E., & Bricklin, P. M. (1997). Ethics and public policy formulation: A case example related to prescription privileges. *Professional Psychology: Research and Practice, 28,* 518–525.

DeLeon, P. H., & Wiggins, J. G. (1996). Prescription privileges for psychologists. *American Psychologist, 51,* 225–229.

Denker, R. (1946). Results of treatment of psychoneuroses by the general practitioner. A follow-up study of 500 cases. *New York State Journal of Medicine, 46,* 2164–2166.

DeRubeis, R. J., & Crits-Christoff, P. (1998). Empirically supported individual and group psychological treatments for adult mental disorders. *Journal of Consulting and Clinical Psychology, 66,* 37–52.

Deutsch, C. J. (1984). Self-report sources of stress among psychotherapists. *Professional Psychology: Research and Practice, 15,* 833–845.

Dickson, D. H., & Kelly, I. W. (1985). The "Barnum Effect" in personality assessment: A review of the literature. *Psychological Reports, 57,* 367–382.

DiNardo, P. A., Barlow, D. H., Cerny, J., Vermilyea, B. B., Vermilyea, J. A., Himaldi, W., & Waddell, M. (1985). *Anxiety Disorders Interview Schedule—Revised (ADIS-R).* Albany: Phobia and Anxiety Disorders Clinic, State University of New York at Albany.

DiNardo, P. A., O'Brien, G. T., Barlow, D. H., Waddell, M. T., & Blanchard, E. B. (1985). *Anxiety Disorders Interview Schedule—Revised* (ADIS-R). Albany, NY: Phobia and Anxiety Disorders Clinic, State University of New York at Albany.

DiNardo, P. A., O'Brien, B. T., Waddell, M. T., & Blanchard, E. B. (1982). *Anxiety Disorders Interview Schedule.* Albany, NY: Phobia and Anxiety Disorders Clinic, State University of New York at Albany.

Dinh, K. T., Sarason, I. G., Peterson, A. V., & Onstad, L. E. (1995). Children's perceptions of smokers and nonsmokers: A longitudinal study. *Health Psychology, 14,* 32–40.

Dishman, R. K. (1982). Compliance/adherence in health-related exercise. *Health Psychology, 1,* 237–267.

Dishman, R. K. (1991). Increasing and maintaining exercise and physical activity. *Behavior Therapy, 22,* 345–378.

Division 40 Task Force on Education, Accreditation and Credentialing. (1989). *Clinical Neuropsychologist, 3.*

Dobson, K. S. (1989). A meta-analysis of the efficacy of cognitive therapy for depression. *Journal of Consulting and Clinical Psychology, 57,* 414–419.

Dobson, K. S., & Shaw, B. F. (1986). Cognitive assessment with major depressive disorders. *Cognitive Therapy and Research, 10,* 13–29.

Dobson, K. S., & Shaw, B. F. (1995). Cognitive therapies in practice. In B. Bongar & L. E. Beutler (Eds.), *Comprehensive textbook of psychotherapy: Theory and practice* (pp. 159–172). New York: Oxford University Press.

Doris, J. (Ed.). (1991). *The suggestibility of children's recollections: Implications for eyewitness testimony.* Washington, DC: American Psychological Association.

Drodz, J. F., & Goldfried, M. R., (1996). A critical evaluation of the state-of-the-art in psychotherapy outcome research. *Psychotherapy, 33,* 171–180.

Drubach, D. (2000). *The brain explained.* Upper Saddle River, NJ: Prentice Hall Health.

Dube, E. F. (1982). Literacy, cultural familiarity and "intelligence" as determinants of story recall. In U. Neisser (Ed.), *Memory observed: Remembering in natural contexts* (pp. 274–292). New York: Freeman.

Dubin, S. S. (1972). Obsolescence or lifelong education: A choice for the professional. *American Psychologist, 27,* 486–496.

Durand, V. M., & Barlow, D. H. (2000). *Abnormal psychology: An introduction* (2nd ed.). Belmont, CA: Wadsworth.

Durand, V. M., & Barlow, D. H. (2003). *Essentials of abnormal psychology* (3rd ed.). Pacific Grove, CA: Wadsworth.

Durham, J. D., & Hardin, S. B. (Eds.) (1986). *The nurse psychotherapist in private practice.* New York: Springer.

Durham v. United States, 214 F.2d 862 (D.C. Cir., 1954).

Dusky v. United States, 362 U.S. 402 (1960).

D'Zurilla, T. J., & Goldfried, M. R. (1971). Problem-solving and behavior modification. *Journal of Abnormal Psychology, 78,* 107–026.

Echeburua, E., Corral, P., Garcia Bajos, E., & Borda, M. (1993). Interactions between self-exposure and alprazolam in the treatment of agoraphobia without current panic: An exploratory study. *Behavioural and Cognitive Psychotherapy, 21,* 219–238.

Edelson, M. (1994). Can psychotherapy research answer this psychotherapist's questions? In P. R. Tally, H. H. Strupp, & S. F. Butler (Eds.), *Psychotherapy research and practice: Bridging the gap* (pp. 124–142). New York: Basic Books.

Edmonds, M., & Clark, E. E. (1989). *Voices of the winds: Native American legends.* New York: Facts on File.

Eells, T. D. (Ed.). (1997). *Handbook of psychotherapy case formulation.* New York: Guilford.

Egan, G. (1986). *The skilled helper.* Monterey, CA: Brooks/Cole.

Egeth, H. E. (1993). What do we *not* know about eyewitness identification? *American Psychologist, 48,* 577–580.

Ehrenwald, J. (Ed.). (1976). *The history of psychotherapy: From healing magic to encounter.* New York: Jason Aronson.

Elkin, I. (1994). The NIMH treatment of depression collaborative research program: Where we began and where we are. In A. E. Bergin & S. L. Garfield (Eds.), *Handbook of psychotherapy and behavior change* (4th ed., pp. 114–139). New York: Wiley.

Elkin, I., Gibbons, R. D., Shea, M. T., Sotsky, S. M., Watkins, J. T., Pilkonis, P. A., & Hedeker, D. (1995). Initial severity and differential treatment outcome in the National Institute of Mental Health treatment of depression collaborative research program. *Journal of Consulting and Clinical Psychology, 63,* 841–847.

Elkin, I., Shea, M. T., Watkins, J. T., Imber, S. D., Sotsky, S. M., Collins, J. F., Glass, D. R., Pikonis, P. A., Weber, W. R., Docherty, J. P., Fiester, S. J., & Parloff, M. B. (1989). NIMH Treatment of Depression Collaborative Research Program: General effectiveness of treatments. *Archives of General Psychiatry, 46,* 971–983.

Elkind, D. (1974). *Children and adolescence: Interpretive essays on Jean Piaget* (2nd ed.). New York: Oxford University Press.

Elliott, R. (2002). The effectiveness of humanistic therapies: A meta-analysis. In D. J. Cain & J. Seeman (Eds.), *Humanistic psychotherapies: Handbook of research and practice* (Chapter 2; pp. 57–81). Washington, DC: American Psychological Association.

Elliott, R., & Greenberg, L. S. (1995). Experiential therapy in practice: The process-experiential approach. In B. Bongar & L. E. Beutler (Eds.), *Comprehensive textbook of psychotherapy: Theory and practice* (Chapter 7; pp. 123–139). New York: Oxford University Press.

Elliott, R, & Greenberg, L. S. (2002). Process-experiential psychotherapy. In D. J. Cain & J. Seeman (Eds.), *Humanistic psychotherapies: Handbook of research and practice* (Chapter 9; pp. 279–306). Washington, DC: American Psychological Association.

Ellis, A. (1962). *Reason and emotion in psychotherapy.* New York: Lyle Stuart.

Ellis, A. (1979). A note on the treatment of agoraphobics with cognitive modification versus prolonged exposure in vivo. *Behavior Research and Therapy, 17,* 162–164.

Ellis, A. (1988). *How to stubbornly refuse to make yourself miserable about anything—yes, anything!* Secaucus, NJ: Lyle Stuart.

Ellis, A. (1995). Rational emotive behavior therapy. In R. J. Corsini & D. Wedding (Eds.), *Current psychotherapies* (5th ed., pp. 162–196). Itasca, IL: F. E. Peacock.

Ellis, A. (1997). Using Rational Emotive Behavior Therapy techniques to cope with disability. *Professional Psychology: Research and Practice, 28,* 17–22.

Ellis, A., & Harper, R. A. (1975). *A new guide to rational living.* North Hollywood, CA: Wilshire.

Ellis, H. C. (1992). Graduate education in psychology: Past, present, and future. *American Psychologist, 47,* 570–576.

Ehrenwald, J. (Ed.). (1976). *The history of psychotherapy: From healing magic to encounter.* New York: Jason Aronson.

Emmelkamp, P. M. G. (1979). The behavioral study of clinical phobias. In M. Hersen, R. Eisler, & P. M. Miller (Eds.), *Progress in behavior modification* (Vol. 8, pp. 55–125). New York: Academic Press.

Emmelkamp, P. M. G., Kuipers, A. C., & Eggeraat, J. B. (1978). Cognitive modification versus prolonged exposure in vivo: A comparison with agoraphobics as subjects. *Behavior Research and Therapy, 16,* 33–41.

Emmelkamp, P. M. G., Mersch, P. P., & Vissia, E. (1985). The external validity of analogue outcome research: Evaluation of cognitive and behavioral interventions. *Behavior Research and Therapy, 23,* 83–86.

Emmelkamp, P. M. G., Mersch, P. P., Vissia, E., & van der Helm, M. (1985). Social phobia: A comparative evaluation of cognitive and behavioral interventions. *Behavior Research and Therapy, 23,* 365–369.

Emmelkamp, P. M. G., van der Helm, R., van Zanten, B. L., & Ploch, I. (1980). Treatment of obsessive-compulsive patients: The contribution of self-instructional training to the effectiveness of exposure. *Behaviour Research and Therapy, 18,* 61–66.

Endicott, J., & Spitzer, R. L. (1978). A diagnostic interview—The schedule for affective disorders and schizophrenia. *Archives of General Psychiatry, 35,* 837–844.

Engel, G. L. (1977). The need for a new medical model: A challenge for biomedicine. *Science, 196,* 129–136.

Entwisle, D. R. (1972). To dispel fantasies about fantasy-based measures of achievement motivation. *Psychological Bulletin, 77,* 377–391.

Epstein, J. (1988). Introduction: What's the usage? In S. Greenbaum & J. Whitcut (Eds.), *The complete plain words by Sir Ernest Gowers.* Boston: David R. Godine.

Erdberg, P., & Exner, J. E. (1984). Rorschach assessment. In G. Goldstein & M. Hersen (Eds.), *Handbook of psychological assessment.* New York: Pergamon.

Erdelyi, M. H., & Goldberg, B. (1979). Let's not sweep repression under the rug: Toward a cognitive psychology of repression. In J. F. Kihlstrom & F. J. Evans (Eds.), *Functional disorders of memory* (pp. 355–402). Hillsdale, NJ: Erlbaum.

Estelle v. Smith, 451 U.S. 459 (1981).

Exner, J. E. (1974). *The Rorschach: A comprehensive system. Vol. 1.* New York: Wiley.

Exner, J. E. (1986). *The Rorschach: A comprehensive system. Vol. 1: Basic foundations* (2nd ed.). New York: Wiley.

Exner, J. E. (1991). *The Rorschach: A comprehensive system. Vol. 2: Interpretation.* New York: Wiley.

Exner, J. E. (1993). *The Rorschach: A comprehensive system. Vol. 1: Basic foundations* (3rd ed.). New York: Wiley.

Exner, J. E., Jr., & Exner, D. E. (1972). How clinicians use the Rorschach. *Journal of Personality Assessment, 36,* 402–408.

Exner, J. E., & Weiner, I. B. (1994). *The Rorschach: A comprehensive system. Vol. 3: Assessment of children and adolescents* (2nd ed.). New York: Wiley.

Eysenck, H. J. (1952a). The effects of psychotherapy: An evaluation. *Journal of Consulting Psychology, 16,* 319–324.

Eysenck, H. J. (1952b). *The scientific study of personality.* London: Routledge and Kegan Paul.

Eysenck, H. J. (1958). Personality tests: 1950–1955. In G. W. T. H. Fleming & A. Walk (Eds.), *Recent progress in psychiatry* (Vol. 3, pp. 118–159). New York: Grove Press.

Eysenck, H. J. (1960). The effects of psychotherapy. In H. J. Eysenck (Ed.), *Handbook of abnormal psychology: An experimental approach* (pp. 697–725). New York: Basic Books.

Eysenck, H. J. (1966a). Personality and experimental psychology. *Bulletin of the British Psychological Society, 19,* 62(1–28).

Eysenck, H. J. (1966b). *The effects of psychotherapy.* New York: International Science Press.

Eysenck, H. J. (1970). A dimensional system of psychodiagnostics. In A. R. Maher (Ed.), *New approaches to personality classification* (pp. 169–207). New York: Columbia University Press.

Eysenck, H. J. (1978). An exercise in mega-silliness. *American Psychologist, 33,* 517.

Eysenck, H. J. (1983). Special Review: M. L. Smith, G. V., Glass, & T. I. Miller. The benefits of psychotherapy. *Behaviour Research and Therapy, 21,* 315–320.

Eysenck, H. J. (1984). Is behavior therapy on course? *Behavioural Psychotherapy, 12,* 2–6.

Eysenck, H. J., & Rachman, S. (1965). *The causes and cures of neurosis.* London: Routledge and Kegan Paul.

Fagan, T. K. (1996). Witmer's contributions to school psychological services. *American Psychologist, 51,* 241–243.

Fairburn, C. G. (1998). Bulimia nervosa. In J. C. Markowitz (Ed.), *Interpersonal psychotherapy.* Washington, DC: American Psychiatric Press.

Fairweather, G. W. (1964). *Social psychology in treating mental illness: Experimental approach.* New York: Wiley.

Fairweather, G. W., & Fergus, E. O. (1993). *Empowering the mentally ill.* Austin, TX: Fairweather.

Farrell, A. D. (1993). Behavioral assessment with adults. In R. T. Ammerman & M. Hersen (Eds.), *Handbook of behavior therapy with children and adults.* Boston: Allyn and Bacon.

Farrell, B. A. (1981). *The standing of psychoanalysis.* Oxford: Oxford University Press.

Faust, D., & Ziskin, J. (1988). The expert witness in psychology and psychiatry. *Science, 241,* 31–35.

Fawzy, F. I., Cousins, N., Fawzy, N. W., Kemeny, M. E., Elashoff, R., & Morton, D. (1990). A structured psychiatric intervention for cancer patients: I. Changes over time in methods of coping and affective disturbance. *Archives of General Psychiatry, 47,* 720–725.

Fawzy, F. I., Kemeny, M. E., Fawzy, N. W., Elashoff, R., Morton, D. Cousins, N., & Fahey, J. L. (1990). A structured psychiatric intervention for cancer patients: II. Changes over time in immunological measures. *Archives of General Psychiatry, 47,* 729–735.

Featherstone, H. J., (1985). Medical diagnosis and problems in individuals with recurrent idiopathic headaches. *Headache, 25,* 136–140.

Federal Register. (1977). *Handicapped Children Rule, 42*(250). Washington, DC: U.S. Government Printing Office.

Feighner, J. P. (1997). Are the new antidepressants Venlafaxine and Nefazodone really different? *The Harvard Mental Health Letter, 13,* (8), 8.

Feinstein, H., & Raw, S. D. (1996). Psychotherapy research is not psychotherapy practice. *Clinical Psychology: Science and Practice, 3,* 168–171.

Feldman, M. D., Ford, C. V., & Reinhold, T. (1994). *Patient or pretender: Inside the strange world of factitious disorders.* New York: John Wiley & Sons.

Ferster, C. B., & Skinner, B. F. (1957). *Schedules of reinforcement.* New York: Appleton-Century-Crofts.

Feske, U., & Chambless, D. L. (1995). Cognitive behavioral versus exposure only treatment for social phobia: A meta-analysis. *Behavior Therapy, 26,* 695–720.

Feyerbend, P. (1982). *Against method.* London: Verso Edition.

Fink, M. (1997). What is the role of ECT in the treatment of mania? *Harvard Mental Health Letter, 13* (12), 8.

Finkelhor, D. & Dziuba-Leatherman, J. (1994). Victimization of children. *American Psychologist, 49,* 173–183.

Fiore, J. (1991). Getting into graduate school in clinical psychology. In Nietzel, M. T., Bernstein, D. A., & Milich, R. (Eds.), *Introduction to clinical psychology* (3rd ed.). Englewood Cliffs, NJ: Prentice Hall.

Firestar, M. (1993). Co-optation is beside the point. *Resources: Workforce Issues in Mental Health Systems, 5,* 15.

First, M. B., Frances, A., & Widiger, T. A. (1992). DSM-IV and behavioral assessment. *Behavioral Assessment, 14,* 297–306.

First, M. B., Spitzer, R. L., Gibbon, M., & Williams, J. B. W. (1995). *The Structure Clinical Interview for DSM-IV Axis I Disorders—Patient Edition (SCID-I/P, Version 2.0).* New York: Biometrics Research Department, New York Psychiatric Institute.

Fleck, S. (1995). Dehumanizing developments in American psychiatry in recent decades. *Journal of Nervous and Mental Disease, 1983,* 195–203.

Flynn, J. R. (1984). The mean IQ of Americans: Massive gains 1932 to 1978. *Psychological Bulletin, 95,* 29–51.

Flynn, J. R. (1987). Massive IQ gains in 14 nations: What IQ tests really measure. *Psychological Bulletin, 101,* 171–191.

Flynn, J. R. (1991). *Asian-Americans: Achievement beyond IQ.* Hillsdale, NJ: Erlbaum.

Foa, E. B., Grayson, J. B., & Steketee, G. (1982). Depression, habituation and treatment outcome in obsessive-compulsives. In J. C. Boulougouris (Ed.), *Practical applications of learning theories in psychiatry* (pp. 129–142). New York: Wiley.

Foa, E. B., Hearst-Ikeda, D., & Perry, K. J. (1995). Evaluation of a brief cognitive-behavioral program for the prevention of chronic PTSD in recent sexual assault victims. *Journal of Consulting and Clinical Psychology, 63,* 948–955.

Foa, E. B., & Kozak, M. J. (1986). Emotional processing of fear: Exposure to corrective information. *Psychological Bulletin, 99,* 20–35.

Foa, E. B., Kozak, M. J., Steketee, G., & McCarthy, P. R. (1992). Treatment of depressive and obsessive-compulsive symptoms in OCD by imipramine and behavior therapy. *British Journal of Clinical Psychology, 31,* 279–292.

Foa, E. B., & Riggs, D. S. (1995). Posttraumatic stress disorder following assault: Theoretical considerations and empirical findings. *Current Directions in Psychological Science, 4,* 61–65.

Foa, E. B., Rothbaum, B. O., Riggs, D. S., & Murdock, T. B. (1991). Treatment of posttraumatic stress disorder in rape victims: A comparison between cognitive-behavioral procedures and counseling. *Journal of Consulting and Clinical Psychology, 59,* 715–723.

Foa, E. B., Steketee, G., & Azarow, B. (1985). Behavior therapy with obsessive-compulsives: From theory to treatment. In M. Mavissakalian (Ed.), *Obsessive-compulsive disorder: Psychological and pharmacological treatment.* New York: Plenum Press.

Foa, E. B., Steketee, G., Grayson, J. B., Turner, R. M., & Latimer, P. (1984). Deliberate exposure and blocking of obsessive-compulsive rituals: Immediate and long-term effects. *Behavior Therapy, 15,* 450–472.

Foa, E. B., Steketee, G., & Milby, J. B. (1980). Differential effects of exposure and response prevention in obsessive-compulsive washers. *Journal of Consulting and Clinical Psychology, 48,* 71–79.

Fodor, I. G. (1985). Assertiveness training for the eighties: Moving beyond the personal. In L. B. Rosewater & L. E. A. Walker (Eds.), *Handbook of feminist therapy: Women's issues in psychotherapy* (pp. 257–265). New York: Springer Publishing Company.

Foley, V. D. (1989). Family therapy. In R. J. Corsini & D. Wedding (Eds.), *Current psychotherapies* (4th ed., pp. 455–500). Itasca, IL: F. E. Peacock.

Follette, W. C., & Houts, A. C. (1996). Models of scientific progress and the role of theory in taxonomy development: A case study of the DSM. *Journal of Consulting and Clinical Psychology, 64,* 1120–1132

Folstein, M. F., Folstein, S. E., & McHugh, P. R. (1975). "Mini-Mental State": A practical method of grading the cognitive state of patients for the clinician. *Journal of Psychiatric Research, 12,* 189–198.

Foster, S. L., Bell-Dolan, D. J., & Burge, D. A. (1988). Behavioral observation. In A. S. Bellack & M. Hersen (Eds.), *Behavioral assessment: A practical handbook* (pp. 119–160). Elmsford, NY: Pergamon Press.

Foster, S. L., & Mash, E. J. (1999). Assessing social validity in clinical treatment research: Issues and procedures. *Journal of Consulting and Clinical Psychology, 67,* 308–319.

Foulkes, S. H., & Anthony, E. J. (1965). *Group psychotherapy: The psychoanalytic approach* (2nd ed.). Harmondsworth, UK: Penguin.

Fowler, R. D. (1985). Landmarks in computer-assisted psychological assessment. *Journal of Consulting and Clinical Psychology, 41,* 748–759.

Fowler, R. D. (1985). Landmarks in computer-assisted psychological assessment. *Journal of Consulting and Clinical Psychology, 53,* 748–759.

Fowers, B. J., & Richardson, F. C. (1996), Why is multiculturalism good? *American Psychologist, 51,* 609–621.

Fox, R. E. (1995). The rape of psychotherapy. *Professional Psychology: Research and Practice, 26,* 147–155.

Frances, C, M., & Wolfe, E. M. (2000). Issues related to postdoctoral education and training in professional psychology: Results of an opinion survey. *Professional Psychology: Research and Practice, 31,* 429–434.

Frank, J. D. (1961). *Persuasion and healing: A comparative study of psychotherapy.* New York: Schocken.

Frank, L. K. (1939). Projective methods for the study of personality. *Journal of Psychology, 8,* 389–409.

Franklin, M. E., & Foa, E. B. (1998). Cognitive-behavioral treatments for obsessive compulsive disorder. In P. E. Nathan & J. M. Gorman (Eds.), *A guide to treatments that work* (pp. 339–357). New York: Oxford University Press.

Franks, C. M. (1969). Introduction: Behavior therapy and its Pavlovian origins: Review and Perspectives. In C. M. Franks (Ed.), *Behavior therapy: Appraisal and status.* New York: McGraw-Hill.

Franks, C. M., & Wilson, G. T. (Eds.). (1973). *Annual review of behavior therapy theory and practice.* New York: Brunner/Mazel.

Fraser, D., McLeod, W. L., Begg, J. C., Hawthorne, J. H., & Davis, P. (1976). Against the odds: The results of a token economy programme with long-term psychiatric patients. *International Journal of Nursing Studies, 13,* 55–63.

Freedheim, D. K. (Ed.). (1992). *History of psychotherapy: A century of change.* Washington, DC: American Psychological Association.

Freeman, A., & Reinecke, M. A. (1995). Cognitive therapy. In A. S. Gurman & S. B. Messer (Eds.), *Essential psychotherapies: Theory and practice* (pp. 182–225). New York: Guilford.

Freeman, F. S. (1955). *Theory and practice of psychological testing.* New York: Holt.

Fremouw, W. J., de Perczel, M., & Ellis, T. E. (1990). *Suicide risk: Assessment an response guidelines.* New York: Pergamon Press.

Freud, S. (1909/1955). Analysis of a phobia in a five-year-old boy. *Standard edition of the complete psychological works* (Vol. 10, pp. 5–147). London: Hogarth Press. (Original work published in 1909.)

Freud, S. (1910/1989). "Wild" psycho-analysis. In P. Gay (Ed.), *The Freud reader* (pp. 351–356). New York: W.W. Norton. (Original work published in 1910.)

Freud, S. (1912/1989). Recommendations to physicians practicing psycho-analysis. In P. Gay, (Ed.), *The Freud reader* (pp. 356–363). New York: W.W. Norton. (Original work published in 1912.)

Freud, S. (1913/1989). On beginning the treatment. In P. Gay, (Ed.), *The Freud reader* (pp. 363–378). New York: W.W. Norton. (Original work published in 1913.)

Freud, S. (1915/1989). Fragment of an analysis of a case of hysteria ("Dora"). In P. Gay (Ed.), *The Freud reader* (pp. 172–239). New York: W.W. Norton. (Original work published in 1915.)

Freud, S. (1915/1989). Observations on transference-love. In P. Gay (Ed.), *The Freud reader* (pp. 378–387). New York: W.W. Norton. (Original work published in 1915.)

Freud, S. (1923/1989). The ego and the id. In P. Gay (Ed.), *The Freud reader* (pp. 629–658). New York: W.W. Norton. (Original work published in 1923.)

Freud, S. (1924/1989). The dissolution of the Oedipus complex. In P. Gay (Ed.), *The Freud reader* (pp. 661–666). New York: W.W. Norton. (Original work published in 1924.)

Freud, S. (1925/1989). An autobiographical study. In P. Gay (Ed.), *The Freud reader* (pp. 3–41). New York: W. W. Norton. (Original work published in 1925.)

Friedman, M., & Rosenman, R. H. (1974). *Type A behavior and your heart.* New York: Knopf.

Fritzler, B. K., Hecker, J. E., & Losee, M. C. (1997). Self-directed treatment with minimal therapist contact: Preliminary findings for obsessive-compulsive disorder. *Behaviour Research and Therapy, 35,* 627–631.

Garb, H. N. (1989). Clinical judgment, clinical training, and professional experience. *Psychological Bulletin, 105,* 387–396.

Garb, H. N. (1997). Race bias, social class bias, and gender bias in clinical judgment. *Clinical Psychology: Science and Practice, 4,* 99–120.

Garb, H. N., Florio, C. M., & Grove, W. M. (1998). The validity of the Rorschach and the Minnesota Multiphasic Personality Inventory: Results from meta-analyses. *Psychological Science, 9,* 402–404.

Garcon, M., & Vinchon, J. (1930). *The devil, an historical, critical and medical study.* New York: Dutton.

Gardner, H. (1983). *Frames of mind: The theory of multiple intelligences.* New York: Basic Books.

Gardner, M. (1995). Suppressed memory therapy is not legitimate. In W. Barbour (Ed.), *Mental illness: Opposing viewpoints* (pp. 110–117). San Diego, CA: Greenhaven Press.

Gardner, R. D. (1975). Opening remarks. In G. Kriegman, R. D. Gardner, R. D., & D. W. Abse (Eds.), *American psychiatry: Past, present, and future* (pp. 1–2). Charlottesville: University Press of Virginia.

Garfield, S. L. (1994). Research on client variables in psychotherapy. In A. E. Bergin & S. L. Garfield (Eds.), *Handbook of psychotherapy and behavior change* (4th ed.; pp. 190–228). Oxford, England: John Wiley & Sons.

Garfield, S. L., (1996). Some problems associated with

"validated" forms of psychotherapy. *Clinical Psychology: Science and Practice, 3,* 218–229.

Garfield, S. L. (1998). Some comments on empirically supported treatments. *Journal of Consulting and Clinical Psychology, 66,* 121–125.

Garfield, S. L., & Kurtz, R. (1974). A survey of clinical psychologists: Characteristics, activities, and orientations. *Clinical Psychologist, 28,* 6–9.

Gaston, L. (1990). The concept of alliance and its role in psychotherapy: Theoretical and empirical considerations. *Psychotherapy: Theory, Research, Practice, Training, 27,* 143–153.

Gay, J., & Cole, M. (1967). *The new mathematics and an old culture: A study of learning among the Kpelle of Liberia.* New York: Holt, Rinehart, and Winston.

Gay, P. (Ed.). (1989). *The Freud reader.* New York: W.W. Norton.

Gelder, M. G., Bancroft, J. H. J., Gath, D. H., Johnston, D. W., Mathews, A. M., & Shaw, P. M. (1973). Specific and nonspecific factors in behavior therapy. *British Journal of Psychiatry, 123,* 445–462.

Gelder, M. G., & Marks, I. M. (1966). Severe agoraphobia: A controlled prospective trial of behavior therapy. *British Journal of Psychiatry, 112,* 309–319.

Gelder, M. G., Marks, I. M., & Wolff, H. (1967). Desensitization and psychotherapy in the treatment of phobic states. *British Journal of Psychiatry, 113,* 53–73.

General Household Survey (1980). London: OPCS.

Gerty, F. J., Holloway, J. W., Jr., & MacKay, R. P. (1952). Licensure or certification for clinical psychologists. *Journal of the American Medical Association, 148,* 272–273.

Giles, T. R. (1983a). Probable superiority of behavioral interventions—I: Traditional comparative outcome. *Journal of Behavior Therapy and Experimental Psychiatry, 14,* 29–32.

Giles, T. R. (1983b). Probable superiority of behavioral interventions—II: Empirical status of the equivalence of therapies hypothesis. *Journal of Behavior Therapy and Experimental Psychiatry, 14,* 189–196.

Gillan, P., & Rachman, S. (1974). An experimental investigation of desensitization in phobic patients. *British Journal of Psychiatry, 124,* 392–401.

Giordano, P. J. (1997). Establishing rapport and developing interviewing skills. In Jr. Matthews & C. E. Walker (Eds.), *Basic skills and professional issues in clinical psychology* (pp. 59–82). Boston: Allyn and Bacon.

Gladis, M. M., Gosch, E. A., Dishnuk, N. M., & Crits-Christoph (1999). Quality of life: Expanding the scope of clinical significance. *Journal of Consulting and Clinical Psychology, 67,* 320–331.

Glaser, R. D., & Thorpe, J. S. (1986). Unethical intimacy: A survey of sexual contact and advances between psychology educators and female graduate students. *American Psychologist, 41,* 43–51.

Goffman, E. (1963). *Stigma: Notes on the management of spoiled identity.* Englewood Cliffs, NJ: Prentice-Hall.

Gold, J. M., Berman, K. F., Goldberg, T. E., & Weinberger, D. R. (1996). PET validation of a novel prefrontal task: Delayed response alternation. *Neuropsychology, 10,* 3–10.

Golden, C. J. (1981a). *Diagnosis and rehabilitation in clinical neuropsychology* (2nd ed.). Springfield, IL: Charles C. Thomas.

Golden, C. J. (1981b). A standardized version of Luria's neuropsychological tests: A quantitative and qualitative approach to neuropsychological evaluation. *International Journal of Neuroscience, 10,* 51–56.

Golden, C. J., Hammeke, T., & Purisch, A. (1980). *A manual for the Luria-Nebraska Neuropsychological Battery* (rev. ed.). Los Angeles: Western Psychological Services.

Golden, C. J., Purisch, A., & Hammeke, T. (1985). *Luria-Nebraska Neuropsychological Battery Manual—Forms I and II.* Los Angeles: Western Psychological Services.

Golden, C. J., Zillmer, E., & Spiers, M. (1992). *Neuropsychological assessment and intervention.* Springfield, IL: Charles C. Thomas.

Goldenberg, I., & Goldenberg, H. (1995). Family therapy. In R. J. Corsini & D. Wedding (Eds.), *Current psychotherapies* (5th ed., pp. 356–385). Itasca, IL: F. E. Peacock.

Goldfried, M. R. (Ed.). (1980). Special issue: Psychotherapy process. *Cognitive Therapy and Research, 4,* 271–306.

Goldfried, M. R. (Ed.). (1992). *Converging themes in psychotherapy.* New York: Springer.

Goldfried, M. R., & Kent, R. N. (1972). Traditional versus behavioral assessment: A comparison of methodological and theoretical assumptions. *Psychological Bulletin, 77,* 409–420.

Goldfried, M. R., & Linehan, M. M. (1977). Basic issues in behavioral assessment. In A. R. Ciminero, K. S. Calhoun, & H. E. Adams (Eds.), *Handbook of behavioral assessment* (pp. 15–46). New York: Wiley.

Goldfried, M. R., & Wolfe, B. E. (1998). Toward a more clinically valid approach to therapy research. *Journal of Consulting and Clinical Psychology, 66,* 143–150.

Goldman, R., & Greenberg, L. S. (1997). Case formulation in process-experiential therapy. In T. D. Eells (Ed.), *Handbook of psychotherapy case formulation* (pp. 402–429). New York: Guilford.

Goldsmith, J. B., & McFall, R. M. (1975). Development and evaluation of an interpersonal skill-training program for psychiatric inpatients. *Journal of Abnormal Psychology, 84,* 51–58.

Goldstein, A. P., Sprafkin, R. P., & Gershaw, N. J. (1976). Structured learning therapy: Training for community living. *Psychotherapy: Theory, Research, and Practice, 13,* 374–377.

Goldstein, G. (1998). Introduction to neuropsychological assessment. In G. Goldstein, P. D. Nussbaum, & S. R. Beers (Eds.), *Neuropsychology* (pp. 63–81). New York: Plenum.

Goldstein, G., & Nussbaum, P. D. (1996). The neuropsychology of aging. In J. G. Beaumont & J. Segent (Eds.), *The Blackwell dictionary of neuropsychology.* London: Wiley.

Goldstein, R. L. (1992). Dr. Rogers' "insanity detector" and the admissibility of novel scientific evidence. *Medicine and Law, 11,* 441–447.

Goncalves, A. S., Woodward, M. J., & Millon, T. (1994). Millon Clinical Multiaxial Inventory-II. In M. E. Maaruish (Ed.), *The use of psychological testing for treatment planning and outcome assessment* (pp. 161–184). Hillsdale, NJ: Erlbaum.

Goode, E. E. (1995). Broad definitions of mental illness may be harmful. In W. Barbour (Ed.), *Mental illness: Opposing viewpoints* (pp. 24–28). San Diego, CA: Greenhaven Press.

Goodenough, F. (1926). *Measurement of intelligence by drawings.* New York: World Book.

Goodman, G. S., & Hahn, A. (1987). Evaluating eyewitness testimony. In I. B. Weiner & A. K. Hess (Eds.), *Handbook of forensic psychology* (pp. 258–192). New York: John Wiley & Sons.

Gottesman, I. I. (1991). *Schizophrenia genesis: The origins of madness.* New York: W. H. Freeman.

Gottesman, I. I., & Shields, J. (1982). *Schizophrenia: The epigenetic puzzle.* Cambridge: Cambridge University Press.

Gould, R. A., Otto, M. W., Pollack, M. H., & Yap, L. (1997). Cognitive behavioral and pharmacological treatment of generalized anxiety disorder: A preliminary meta-analysis. *Behavior Therapy, 28,* 285–305.

Gould, S. J. (1981). *The mismeasure of man.* New York: Norton.

Gournay, K. (Ed.). (1989). *Agoraphobia: Current perspectives on theory and treatment.* London: Routledge.

Gove, W. R., Style, C. B., & Hughes, M. (1990). The effect of marriage on the well-being of adults: A theoretical analysis. *Journal of Family Issues, 11,* 4–35.

Graham, F. K, & Kendall, B. S. (1960). Memory-for-Designs Revised general manual. *Perceptual and Motor Skills, 11* (Monograph Suppl. No. 2-VII), 147–188.

Graham, J. R. (1990). *MMPI-2: Assessing personality and psychopathology* (2nd ed). New York: Oxford.

Graham, J. R., & Lilly, R. S. (1984). *Psychological testing.* Englewood Cliffs, NJ: Prentice Hall.

Green, A. I., & Patel, J. K. (1996). The new pharmacology of schizophrenia. *The Harvard Mental Health Letter, 13,* (6), 5–7.

Green, B. F., Jr. (1981). A primer of testing. *American Psychologist, 36,* 1001–1011.

Green, S. B., & Kelley, C. K. (1988). Racial bias in prediction with the MMPI for a juvenile delinquent population. *Journal of Personality Assessment, 52,* 263–275.

Greenberg, L. S., & Rice, L. N. (1997). Humanistic approaches to psychotherapy. In P. L. Wachtel & S. B. Messer (Eds.), *Theories of psychotherapy: Origins and evolution* (Chapter 3, pp. 97–129). Washington, DC: American Psychological Association.

Greenberg, M. S., & Ruback, R. B. (1984). *Social psychology of the criminal justice system.* Pacific Grove, CA: Brooks/Cole Publishing.

Greene, R. L. (1987). Ethnicity and MMPI performance: A review. *Journal of Consulting and Clinical Psychology, 55,* 487–512.

Gregg, N., Hoy, C., & Gay, A. F. (Eds.). (1996). *Adults with learning disabilities: Theoretical and practical perspectives.* New York: Guilford Press.

Greisinger, W. (1867). *Mental pathology and therapeutics* (2nd ed.; C. L. Robertson & J. Rutherford, Trans.). London: New Sydenham Society

Greist, J. H., Marks, I. M., Berlin, F., Gournay, K., & Noshirvani, H. (1980). Avoidance versus confrontation of fear. *Behavior Therapy, 11,* 1–14.

Grisso, T. (1981). *Juveniles' waiver of rights: Legal and psychological competence.* New York: Plenum.

Grisso, T. (1986). *Evaluating competencies: Forensic assessment and instruments.* New York: Plenum Press.

Grisso, T. (1987). The economic and scientific future of forensic psychological assessment. *American Psychologist, 42,* 831–839.

Grisso, T. (1988). *Preparing for a forensic mental health practice* (cassette recording). Sarasota, FL: Professional Resource Exchange.

Grisso, T. & Appelbaum, P. S. (1992). Is it unethical to offer predictions of future violence? *Law and Human Behavior, 16,* 621–633.

Groden, G., & Lantz, S. (2001). The reliability of the Detailed Behavior Report (DBR) in documenting functional assessment observations. *Behavioral Interventions, 16,* 15–25.

Groth-Marnat, G. (1990). *Handbook of psychological assessment* (2nd ed.). New York: Wiley.

Guerin, P. J, & Chabot, D. R. (1997). Development of family systems theory. In P. L. Wachtel & S. B. Messer (Eds.), *Theories of psychotherapy: Origins and evolution* (Chapter 5, pp. 181–225). Washington, DC: American Psychological Association.

Guevremont, D. C., & Spiegler, M. D. (1990, November). *What do behavior therapists really do? A survey of the clinical practice of AABT members.* Paper presented at the 24th annual convention of the Association for Advancement of Behavior Therapy, San Francisco.

Gurman, A. S., & Messer, S. B. (Eds.) (1995). *Essential psychotherapies: Theory and practice.* New York: Guilford.

Guthrie, D. J. (1975). Medicine, history of. *Encyclopaedia Britannica* (15th ed.) Chicago: Encyclopaedia Britannica.

Guttman, J. (1993). *Divorce in psychosocial perspective: Theory and research.* Hillsdale, NJ: Lawrence Erlbaum Associates.

Haaga, D. A. F., & Davison, G. C. (1989). Outcome studies of rational-emotive therapy. In M. E. Bernard & R. DiGiuseppe (Eds.), *Inside rational-emotive therapy: A critical appraisal of the theory and therapy of Albert Ellis* (pp. 155–197). San Diego, CA: Academic Press.

Has, L. J., & Malouf, J. L. (1995). *Keeping up the good work: A practitioner's guide to mental health ethics* (2nd ed.). Sarasota, FL: Professional Resource Press.

Hafner, R. J. (1977). The husbands of agoraphobic women and their influence on treatment outcome. *British Journal of Psychiatry, 131,* 289–294.

Haggard, H. W. (1929/1946). *Devils, drugs and doctors: The story of the science of healing from medicineman to doctor.* New York: Pocket Books. (Original work published in 1929.)

Hahlweg, K., & Markman, H. J. (1988). Effectiveness of behavioral marital therapy: Empirical status of behavioral techniques in preventing and alleviating marital distress. *Journal of Consulting and Clinical Psychology, 56,* 440–447.

Haimanot, R. T., Seraw, B., Forsggren, L., Ekbom, K., & Ekstedt, J. (1995). Migraine, chronic tension-type headache and cluster headache in Ethiopian rural community. *Cephalalgia, 15,* 482–488.

Hall, C. S., & Lindzey, G. (1970). *Theories of personality* (2nd ed.). New York: Wiley.

Hall, C. S., & Lindzey, G. (1978). *Theories of personality* (3rd ed.). New York: Wiley.

Hall, S. H., Munoz, R. F., & Reus, V. I. (1994). Cognitive-behavioral intervention increases abstinence rates for depressive-history smokers. *Journal of Consulting and Clinical Psychology, 62,* 141–146.

Halstead, W. C. (1947). *Brain and intelligence: A quantitative study of frontal lobes.* Chicago: University of Chicago Press.

Hamilton, N. G. (1994). Object relations theory. In V. S. Ramachandran (Ed.), *Encyclopedia of human behav-* *ior* (Vol. 3, pp. 321–332). San Diego, CA: Academic Press.

Hammen, C., Gitlin, M. & Altshuler (2000). Predictors of work adjustment in bipolar I patients: A naturalistic longitudinal follow-up. *Journal of Consulting and Clinical Psychology, 68,* 220–225.

Hammer, E. F. (1958). *The clinical application of projective drawings.* Springfield, IL: Charles C. Thomas.

Hammill, D. D. (1998). *Detroit Tests of Learning Aptitude* (DTLA-4). Austin, TX: PRO-ED.

Handelsman, M. M., & Galvin, M. D. (1988). Facilitating informed consent for outpatient psychotherapy: A suggested written format. *Professional Psychology: Research and Practice, 19,* 223–225.

Handler, L. (1996). The clinical use of drawings: Draw-A-Person, House-Tree-Person and Kinetic Family drawings. In C. S. Newark (Ed.), *Major psychological assessment instruments* (2nd ed.; pp. 206–293). Boston: Allyn and Bacon.

Haney, W. M., Madaus, G. F., & Lyons, R. (1993). *The fractured marketplace for standardized testing.* Norwell, MA: Kluwer Academic Publishers.

Hannay, H. J. (1998). Proceedings of the Houston conference on specialty education and training in clinical neuropsychology, September 3–7, 1997, University of Houston Hilton and Conference Center. *Archives of Clinical Neuropsychology, 13,* 157–250.

Hansen, D. J., St. Lawrence, J. S., & Christoff, K. A. (1985). Effects of interpersonal problem-solving training with chronic aftercare patients on problem-solving component skills and effectiveness of solutions. *Journal of Consulting and Clinical Psychology, 53,* 167–174.

Hare, R. D. (1991). *Manual for the Hare Psychopathy Checklist-Revised.* Toronto: Multi Health Systems.

Hare-Mustin, R. T., Marecek, J., Kaplan, A. G., & Liss-Levinson, N. (1988). Rights of clients, responsibilities of therapist. *American Psychologist, 34,* 3–16.

Harkness, A. R. (1992). Fundamental topics in personality disorders: Candidate trait dimensions from lower regions of the hierarchy. *Psychological Assessment, 4,* 251–259.

Harrell, T. H., Chambless, D. L., & Calhoun, J. F. (1981). Correlational relationships between self-statements and affective states. *Cognitive Therapy and Research, 5,* 159–173.

Harris, B. (1979). Whatever happened to Little Albert? *American Psychologist, 34,* 151–160.

Harris, D. B. (1963). *Children's drawings as measures of intellectual maturity.* New York: Harcourt, Brace, and World.

Harris, D. B. (1972). Review of the DAP. In O. K. Buros (Ed.), *The seventh mental measurement yearbook* (pp. 562–620). New York: McGraw-Hill.

Harrison, P. L., Kaufman, A. S., Hickman, J. A., & Kaufman, N. L. (1988). A survey of test use for adult assessment. *Journal of Psychoeducational Assessment, 6,* 188–198.

Hartlage, L. C. (1987). Neuropsychology: Definition and history. In L. C. Hartlage, M. J. Asken, & J. L. Hornsby (Eds.), *Essentials of neuropsychological assessment.* New York: Springer.

Hartmann, D. P., & Barrios, B. (1980). Book review (Paul & Lentz, 1977). *Behavior Therapy, 11,* 607–610.

Hassard, A. (1993). Eye movement desensitization of body image. *Behavioural Psychotherapy, 21,* 157–160.

Hatcher, C., Mohande, K., Turner, J., & Gelles, M. G. (1999). The role of the psychologist in crisis/hostage negotiations. *Behavioral Sciences and the Law, 16,* 455–472.

Hathaway, S. R., & McKinley, J. C. (1940). A Multiphasic Personality Schedule (Minnesota): I. Construction of the schedule. *Journal of Psychology, 10,* 249–254.

Hathaway, S. R., & Monaches, E. D. (1963). Adolescent personality and behavior: MMPI patterns of normal, delinquent, dropout, and other outcomes. Minneapolis: University of Minnesota Press.

Hatsukami, D. K., Grillo, M., Boyle, R., Allen, S., Jensen, J, Bliss, R., & Brown, S. (2000). Treatment of spit tobacco users with transdermal nicotine system and mint snuff. *Journal of Consulting and Clinical Psychology, 68,* 241–249.

Havens, L. (1994). Some suggestions for making research more applicable to clinical practice. In P. R. Tally, H. H. Strupp, & S. F. Butler (Eds.), *Psychotherapy research and practice: Bridging the gap* (pp. 88–98). New York: Basic Books.

Hawkins, R. P. (1979). The functions of assessment: Implications for selection and development of devices for assessing repertoires in clinical, educational, and other settings. *Journal of Applied Behavior Analysis, 12,* 501–516.

Hayes, R. L., Halford, W. K., & Varghese, F. T. (1995). Social skills training with chronic schizophrenic patients: Effects on negative symptoms and community functioning. *Behavior Therapy, 26,* 433–449.

Hayes, S. C. (1981). Single case experimental design and empirical clinical practice. *Journal of Consulting and Clinical Psychology, 49,* 193–211.

Hayes, S. C. (1996). Creating the empirical clinician. *Clinical Psychology: Science and Practice, 3,* 179–181.

Hayes, S. C. (1998). Resisting biologism. *Behavior Therapist, 21,* 95–97.

Hayes, S. C., Follette, W. C., & Follette, V. M. (1995). Behavior therapy: A contextual approach. In A. S. Gurman & S. B. Messer (Eds.), *Essential psychotherapies: Theory and practice* (pp. 128–181). New York: Guilford.

Hayes, S. C., Strosahl, K. D., & Wilson, K. G. (1999). *Acceptance and commitment therapy: An experiential approach to behavior change.* New York: Guilford.

Hayes, S. C., Wilson, K. G., Gifford, E. V., Follette, V. M. & Strosahl, K. (1996). Experiential avoidance and behavioral disorders: A functional dimensional approach to diagnosis and treatment. *Journal of Consulting and Clinical Psychology, 64,* 1152–1169.

Hayman, R. L. (1990). Presumptions of justice: Law, politics, and the mentally retarded parent. *Harvard Law Review, 103,* 1201–1271.

Haynes, S. N. (1991). *Models of causality in psychopathology: Toward dynamic, synthetic, and nonlinear models of behavior disorders.* New York: Pergamon Press.

Haynes, S. N. (1998). The changing nature of behavioral assessment. In A. S. Bellack & M. Hersen (Eds.), *Behavioral assessment: A practical handbook* (4th ed., pp. 1–21). Boston: Allyn and Bacon.

Haynes, S. N., & O'Brien, W. H. (1990). Functional analysis in behavior therapy. *Clinical Psychology Review, 10,* 649–668.

Headache Classification Committee of the International Headache Society. (1988). Classification and diagnostic criteria for headache disorders, cranial neuralgias and facial pain. *Cephalalgia, 8* (Suppl. 7), 91–96.

Health Promotion Authority of Wales. (1990). *Health in Wales.* Cardiff, UK: Author.

Heaton, R. K. (1981). *A manual for the card sorting test.* Odessa, FL: Psychological Assessment Resources.

Hecker, J. E. (1990). Emotional processing in the treatment of simple phobia: A comparison of imaginal and *in vivo* flooding. *Behavioural Psychotherapy, 18,* 21–34.

Hecker, J. E., Fink, C. M., Levasseur, J. B., & Parker, J. D. (1995). Perspectives on practicum: A survey of directors of accredited PhD programs and internships (or, What is a practicum hour and how many do I need?). *Professional Psychology: Research and Practice, 26,* 205–210.

Hecker, J. E., Losee, M. C., Fritzler, B. K., & Fink, C. M. (1996). Self-directed versus therapist-directed cognitive behavioral treatment for panic disorder. *Journal of Anxiety Disorders, 10,* 253–265.

Hecker, J. E., Norvell, N. K., & Hills, H. (1989). Psychologic assessment of candidates for heart transplantation: Toward a normative data base. *The Journal of Heart Transplantation, 8,* 171–176.

Hecker, J. E., & Thorpe, G. L. (1987). Fear reduction processes in imaginal and in vivo flooding: A comment on James' review. *Behavioural Psychotherapy, 15,* 215–223.

Hecker, J. E., & Thorpe, G. L. (1992). *Agoraphobia and panic: A guide to psychological treatment.* Boston: Allyn and Bacon.

Hegde, M. N. (1991). *A singular manual of textbook preparation.* San Diego, CA: Singular Publishing Group.

Helms, J. E., & Cook, D. A. (1999). *Using race and culture in counseling and psychotherapy: Theory and process.* Boston: Allyn and Bacon.

Hendrix, J. (1968). Letter to the room full of mirrors. On the dust jacket of the Jimi Hendrix Experience, *Electric ladyland.* Burbank, CA: Reprise Records.

Henry, W. P. (1997). Interpersonal case formulation: Describing and explaining interpersonal patterns using the structural analysis of social behavior (pp. 223–259). In Eells, T. D. (Ed.), *Handbook of psychotherapy case formulation.* New York: Guilford.

Herd, J. A., & Weiss, S. M. (1984). Overview of hypertension: Its treatment and prevention. In J. D. Matarazzo, S. M. Weiss, J. A. Herd, N. E. Miller, & S. M. Weiss (Eds.), *Behavioral health: A handbook of health enhancement and disease prevention.* New York: Wiley.

Hergenhahn, B. R. (1992). *An introduction to the history of psychology* (2nd ed.). Pacific Grove, CA: Brooks/Cole.

Herman, J. L. (1992). *Trauma and recovery.* New York: Basic Books.

Herrnstein, R. J. (1969). Method and theory in the study of avoidance. *Psychological Review, 76,* 49–69.

Herrnstein, R. J., & Hineline, P. N. (1966). Negative reinforcement as shock-frequency reduction. *Journal of the Experimental Analysis of Behavior, 9,* 421–430.

Herrnstein, R. J., & Murray, C. (1994). *The bell curve: Intelligence and class structure in American life.* New York: Free Press.

Hersen, M., & Turner, S. M. (1985). *Diagnostic interviewing.* New York: Plenum.

Heston, L. L. (1966). Psychiatric disorders in foster home reared children of schizophrenic mothers. *British Journal of Psychiatry, 112,* 819–825.

Heyman, R. E., & Neidig, P. H. (1997). Physical aggression couples treatment. In W. K. Halford & M. J. Markman (Eds.), *Clinical handbook of marriage and couples intervention* (pp. 589–617). New York: Wiley.

Hill, C. E. (Ed.). (2001). *Helping skills: The empirical foundation.* Washington, DC: American Psychological Association.

Hill, C. E., & O'Brien, K. M. (1999). *Helping skills: Facilitating exploration, insight, and action.* Washington, DC: American Psychological Association.

Hineline, P. (1977). Negative reinforcement and avoidance. In W. K. Honig & J. E. R. Staddon (Eds.), *Handbook of operant behavior.* Englewood Cliffs, NJ: Prentice-Hall.

Hoberman, H. M., Lewinsohn, P. M., & Tilson, M. (1988). Group treatment of depression: Individual predictors of outcome. *Journal of Consulting and Clinical Psychology, 56,* 393–398.

Hodges, L. F., Kooper, R., Meyer, T. C., Rothbaum, B. O., Opdyke, D., de Graaff, J. J., Williford, J. S., & North, M. M. (1995). Virtual environments for treating the fear of heights. *Computer: Innovative Technology for Computer Professionals,* July, 27–34.

Holland, J. C. (1989). Ratiotherapy. In J. C. Holland & J. H. Rowland (Eds.), *Handbook of psychooncology: Psychological care of the patient with cancer.* New York: Oxford University Press.

Hollon, S. D., & Carter, M. M. (1994). Depression in adults. In L. W. Craighead, W. E. Craighead, A. E. Kazdin, & M. J. Mahoney (Eds.), *Cognitive and behavioral interventions: An empirical approach to mental health problems* (pp. 89–104). Boston: Allyn and Bacon.

Holmes, T. H., & Rahe, R. H. (1967). The social readjustment rating scale. *Journal of Psychosomatic Research, 11,* 213–218.

Holroyd, K. A., & Lipchik, G. L. (1997). Recurrent headache disorders. In S. J. Gallant, G. P. Keita, and R. Royak-Schaler (Eds.), *Health care for women: Psychological, social, and behavioral influences.* Washington, DC: American Psychological Association.

Holroyd, K. A., Penzien, D. B., Hursey, K. G., Tobin, D. L., Rogers, L., Holm, J. E., Marcille, P. J., Hall, J. R., & Chila, A. G. (1984). Change mechanisms in EMG biofeedback training: Cognitive change underlying improvements in tension headache. *Journal of Consulting and Clinical Psychology, 52,* 1039–1053.

Holt, R. R. (1970). Yet another look and clinical and statistical prediction: Or, is clinical psychology worthwhile? *American Psychologist, 25,* 337–349.

Holt, R. R. (1986). Clinical and statistical prediction: A retrospective and would-be integrative perspective. *Journal of Personality Assessment, 50,* 376–386.

Holzberg, J. D. (1960). Reliability re-examined. In M. A. Rickers-Ovsiankina (Ed.), *Rorschach psychology* (pp. 361–379). New York: Wiley.

Homma-True, R., Greene, B., Lopez, S. R., & Trimble, J. E. (1993). Ethnocultural diversity in clinical psychology. In L. Comas-Diaz & G. Stricker (Eds.), Special issue: Diversity in clinical psychology: Theory, research, and practice. *Clinical Psychologist, 46,* 43–89.

Honigmann, J. J. (1975). American sub-arctic cultures. *Encyclopaedia Britannica* (15th ed.). Chicago: Encyclopaedia Britannica.

Hooper, H. E. (1983). *Hooper Visual Organization Test (VOT).* Los Angeles: Western Psychological Services.

Hope, D. A., & Heimberg, R. G. (1993). Social phobia and social anxiety. In D. H. Barlow (Ed.), *Clinical handbook of psychological disorders* (2nd ed., pp. 99–136). New York: Guilford.

Horgan, J. (1996). Why Freud isn't dead. *Scientific American,* December, 106–111.

Horn, J. L., & Cattell, R. B. (1966). Refinement and test of the theory of fluid and crystallized general intelligences. *Journal of Educational Psychology, 57,* 253–270.

Horton, A. M. (1999). Above-average intelligence and neuropsychological test score performance. *International Journal of Neuroscience, 99,* 221–231.

Horvath A. O., & Luborsky, L. (1993). The role of therapeutic alliance in psychotherapy. *Journal of Consulting and Clinical Psychology, 61,* 561–573.

Horvath, P. (1988). Placebos and common factors in two decades of psychotherapy research. *Psychological Bulletin, 104,* 214–225.

Howe, G. (1990). *Schizophrenia: A fresh approach* (2nd ed.). Newton Abbot, UK: David & Charles.

Hoyt, M. F. (1995). Brief psychotherapies. In A. S. Gurman & S. B. Messer (Eds.), *Essential psychotherapies: Theory and practice* (pp. 441–487). New York: Guilford.

Hsu, L. M. (1989). Random sampling, randomization, and equivalence of contrasted groups in psychotherapy outcome research. *Journal of Consulting and Clinical Psychology, 57,* 131–137.

Hull, C. L. (1952). *A behavior system: An introduction to behavior theory concerning the individual organism.* New Haven: Yale University Press.

Hulse, W. C. (1971). The emotionally disturbed child draws his family. *Quarterly Journal of Child Behavior, 3,* 152–174.

Humphrey, D. H., & Dahlstrom, W. G. (1995). The impact of changing from the MMPI to the MMPI-2 on profile configurations. *Journal of Personality Assessment, 64,* 429–439.

Humphreys, L. G. (1979). The construct of general intelligence. *Intelligence, 3,* 105–120.

Hunter, J. E. (1983). A causal analysis of cognitive ability, job knowledge, job performance, and supervisor ratings. In F. Landy, S. Zedeck, & J. Cleveland (Eds.), *Performance measurement and theory* (pp. 257–266). Hillsdale, NJ: Erlbaum.

Hunter, M. (1998). Gynecological problems. In A. S. Bellack, & M. Hersen (Eds.), *Comprehensive clinical psychology, Volume 8, Health psychology* (pp. 361–382). New York: Elsevier.

Hunter, R., & MacAlpine, I. (1963). *Three hundred years of psychiatry, 1535–1860.* London: Oxford University Press.

Hurt, R. D., Offord, K. P., Croghan, I. T., Bomez-Dahl, L., Kottle, T. E., Morse, R. M., & Melton, L. J. (1996). Mortality following inpatient addictions treatment: Role of tobacco use in a community-based cohort. *Journal of American Medical Association, 275,* 1097–1103.

Hurvitz, N. (1973). Psychotherapy as a means of social control. *Journal of Consulting and Clinical Psychology, 40,* 232–239.

INS-Division 40 Task Force on Education, Accreditation, and Credentialing. (1987). Report of the INS-Division 40 Task Force on Education, Accreditation, and Credentialing. *Clinical Neuropsychologist, 1,* 29–34.

Isaacs, W., Thomas, J., & Goldiamond, I. (1960). Application of operant conditioning to reinstate verbal behavior in psychotics. *Journal of Speech and Hearing Disorders, 24,* 8–12.

Jaccard, R. (1995, January 15, 16). Affairs of the mind. *Manchester Guardian Weekly.*

Jackson, D. N. (1985). Computer-based personality testing. *Computers in Human Behavior, 1,* 255–264.

Jackson, D. N. (1986). *Computer-based personality testing.* Washington, DC: Scientific Affairs Office, American Psychological Association.

Jackson v. Indiana, 406 U.S. 715 (1972).

Jacobson, N. S., & Christensen, A. (1996). Studying the effectiveness of psychotherapy: How well can clinical trials do the job? *American Psychologist, 51,* 1031–1039.

Jacobson, N. S., Christensen, A., Prince, S. E., Cordova, J., & Eldridge, K. (2000). Integrative behavioral couple therapy: An acceptance-based, promising new treatment for couple discord. *Journal of Consulting and Clinical Psychology, 68,* 346–350.

Jacobson, N. S., Dobson, K. S., Truax, P. A., Addis, M. E., Koerner, K., Gollan, J. K., Gortner, E., & Prince, S. (1996). A component analysis of cognitive-behavioral treatment for depression. *Journal of Consulting and Clinical Psychology, 64,* 295–304.

Jacobson, N. S., Follette, W. C., & Revenstorf, D. (1984). Psychotherapy outcome research: Methods for reporting variability and evaluating clinical significance. *Behavior Therapy, 52,* 497–504.

Jacobson, N. S., & Hollon, S. D. (1996). Cognitive-behavior therapy versus pharmacotherapy: Now that the jury's returned its verdict, it's time to present the rest of the evidence. *Journal of Consulting and Clinical Psychology, 64,* 74–80.

Jacobson, N. S., Roberts, L. J., Berns, S. B., & McGlinchey, J. B. (1999). Methods for defining and determining the clinical significance of treatment effects: Description, application, and alternatives. *Journal of Consulting and Clinical Psychology, 67,* 300–307.

Jacobson, N. S., & Truax, P. (1991). Clinical significance: A statistical approach to defining meaningful change in psychotherapy research. *Journal of Consulting and Clinical Psychology, 59,* 12–19.

Jacobson, N. S., Wilson, L., & Tupper, C. (1988). The clinical significance of treatment gains resulting from exposure-based interventions for agoraphobia: A reanalysis of outcome data. *Behavior Therapy, 19,* 539–554.

Jahoda, G. (1988). J'accuse. In M. H. Bond (Ed.), *The cross-cultural challenge to social psychology* (pp. 86–95). Newbury Park, CA: Sage.

James, S. A., Hartnett, S. A., & Kalsbeek, W. D. (1983). John Henryism and blood pressure differences among black men. *Journal of Behavioral Medicine, 6,* 259–278.

Jannoun, L., Oppenheimer, C., & Gelder, M. (1982). A self-help treatment program for anxiety state patients. *Behavior Therapy, 13,* 103–111.

Janov, A. (1970). *The primal scream: Primal therapy: The cure for neurosis.* New York: G. P. Putnam & Sons.

Jensen, A. R. (1959). The reliability of projective techniques: Review of the literature. *Acta Pscychologica, 16,* 108–136.

Jensen, A. R. (1969). How much can we boost IQ and scholastic achievement? *Harvard Educational Review, 39,* 1–123.

Jensen, A. R. (1980). *Bias in mental testing.* New York: Free Press.

Jensen, A. R. (1985). The nature of black-white difference on various psychometric tests: Spearman's hypothesis. *Behavioral and Brain Sciences, 8,* 193–263.

Jensen, J. A. (1994). An investigation of eye movement desensitization and reprocessing (EMD/R) as a treatment for posttraumatic stress disorder (PTSD) symptoms of Vietnam combat veterans. *Behavior Therapy, 25,* 311–325.

Jensen, J. A., & Armstrong, R. J. (1985). *Slosson Intelligence Test (SIT) for children and adults: Expanded norms tables applications and developments.* East Aurora, NY: Slosson Educational Publications.

Johnson, E. H., Schork, N. J., & Spielberger, C. D. (1987). Emotional and familial determinants of elevated blood pressure in black and white adolescent females. *Journal of Psychosomatic Research, 31,* 731–741.

Johnson, L. E., & Thorpe, G. L. (1994). Review of psychotherapy and counseling with minorities: A cognitive approach to individual differences, by Manuel Ramirez. *Behavioural and Cognitive Psychotherapy, 22,* 185–187.

Johnston, D. W., & Johnston, M. (1998). Health psychology. In A. S. Bellack, & M. Hersen (Eds.), *Comprehensive clinical psychology, Volume 8, Health psychology* (Vol. 8). New York: Elsevier.

Johnston, M., & Vogele, C. (1993). Benefits of psychological preparation for surgery: A meta-analysis. *Annals of Behavioral Medicine, 15,* 245–256.

Johnston, M., & Weinman, J. (1995). Health psychology. In *Professional psychology handbook* (pp. 61–68). Leicester, UK: BPS Books.

Johnston, M. K., Kelley, C., Harris, S., & Wolf, M. M. (1966). An application of reinforcement principles to development of motor skills of a young child. *Child Development, 37,* 379–387.

Johnstone, T. (Ed. & Trans.). (1914). *Kraepelin's lectures on clinical psychiatry* (2nd German ed.). New York: William Wood and Co.

Jolles, I. A. (1952). *A catalogue for the qualitative interpretation of the H-T-P.* Beverly Hills, CA: Western Psychological Services.

Jolles, I. A. (1971). *A catalogue for the qualitative interpretation of the H-T-P.* Beverly Hills, CA: Western Psychological Services.

Jones, H. G. (1984). Behaviour therapy—An autobiographic view. *Behavioural Psychotherapy, 12,* 7–16.

Jones, M. C. (1924). A laboratory study of fear: The case of Peter. *Pediatric Seminary, 31,* 308–315.

Jones, W. H. S. (1923). (Ed. & Trans.). *Hippocrates,* Vol. 1. London: William Heinemann

Joseph, R. (1994). Limbic system. In V. S. Ramachandran (Ed.), *Encyclopedia of human behavior* (Vol. 3, pp. 67–81). San Diego, CA: Academic Press.

Kadushin, C. (1969). *Why people go to psychiatrists.* Oxford, UK: Atherton Press.

Kafka, M. P. (1991). Successful antidepressant treatment of nonparaphilic sexual addictions and paraphilias in men. *Journal of Clinical Psychiatry, 52,* 60–65.

Kafka, M. P. (1993). Currents Interview: Update on paraphilias and paraphilia-related disorders. *Currents in Affective Illness, 12(6),* 5–13.

Kafka, M. P., & Prentky, R. (1992). Fluoxetine treatment of nonparaphilic sexual addictions and paraphilias in men. *Journal of Clinical Psychiatry, 53,* 351–358.

Kahane, C. (1990). Introduction, part two. In C. Bernheimer & C. Kahane (Eds.), *In Dora's case: Freud, hysteria, feminism* (2nd ed; pp. 19–34). New York: Columbia University Press.

Kahill, S. (1984). Human figure drawings in adults: An update of the empirical evidence, 1967–1982. *Canadian Psychology, 25,* 269–290.

Kallman, W. M., Hersen, M., & O'Toole, D. H. (1975). The use of social reinforcement in a case of conversion reaction. *Behavior Therapy, 6,* 411–413.

Kanfer, F. H., Eyberg, S. M., & Krahn, G. L. (1983). Interviewing strategies in child assessment. In C. E. Walker & M. C. Roberts (Eds.), *Handbook of Clinical child psychology* (pp. 95–108). New York: Wiley.

Kanfer, F. H., & Saslow, G. (1969). Behavioral diagnosis. In C. M. Franks (Ed.), *Behavior therapy: Appraisal and status.* New York: McGraw-Hill.

Kanfer, F. H., & Scheft, B. K. (1988). *Guiding the process of therapeutic change.* Champaign, IL: Research Press.

Kaplan, H. I. (1975). Current psychodynamic concepts in psychosomatic medicine. In R. O. Pasnau (Ed.), *Consultation-liaison psychiatry.* New York: Grune & Stratton.

Kaplan, M. (1983). A woman's view of DSM-III. *American Psychologist, 38,* 786–792.

Kaplan, M. A. (1984). Anna O. and Bertha Pappenheim: An historical perspective. In M. Rosenbaum & M. Muroff (Eds.), *Anna O.: Fourteen contemporary perspectives* (pp. 101–117). New York: Free Press.

Kaplan, R. M., & Saccuzzo, D. P. (1993). *Psychological testing: Principles, applications, and issues* (3rd ed.). Pacific Grove, CA: Brooks/Cole.

Karasu, J. B. (1980). The ethics of psychotherapy. *American Journal of Psychiatry, 137,* 1502–1512.

Karon, B. P., & Widener, A. J. (1995). Psychodynamic therapies in historical perspective: "Nothing human do I consider alien to me." In B. Bongar & L. E. Beutler (Eds.), *Comprehensive textbook of psychotherapy: Theory and practice.* New York: Oxford. (pp. 24–47.)

Kassin, S. M., Ellsworth, P. C., & Smith, V. L. (1989). The "general acceptance" of psychological research on eyewitness testimony: A survey of experts. *American Psychologist, 44,* 1089–1098.

Katz, R. (1994). Post-traumatic stress disorder. In V. S. Ramachandran (Ed.), *Encyclopedia of human behavior* (Vol. 3, pp. 555–562). San Diego, CA: Academic Press.

Kaufman, A. S. (1990). *Assessing adolescent and adult intelligence.* Boston: Allyn and Bacon.

Kaufman, A. S., & Harrison, P. L. (1991). Individual intellectual assessment. In C. E. Walker (Ed.), *Clinical psychology: Historical and research foundations.* New York: Plenum Press.

Kaufman, A. S., & Kaufman, N. L. (1983a). *Kaufman Assessment Battery for Children: Administration and scoring manual.* Circle Pines, MN: American Guidance Service.

Kaufman, A. S., & Kaufman, N. L. (1983b). *Kaufman Assessment Battery for Children: Interpretive manual.* Circle Pines, MN: American Guidance Service.

Kaufman, A. S., & Kaufman, N. L. (1993). *Kaufman Adolescent and Adult Intelligence Test: Manual.* Circle Pines, MN: American Guidance Service.

Kaufman, A. S., Kaufman, N. L., & Goldsmith, B. (1984). *Kaufman Sequential or Simultaneous* (K-SOS). Circle Pines, MN: American Guidance Service.

Kaufman, E., & Kaufmann, P. (1992). *Family therapy of drug and alcohol abuse* (2nd ed.). Boston: Allyn and Bacon.

Kaufmann, Y. (1989). Analytical psychotherapy. In R. J. Corsini & D. Wedding (Eds.), *Current psychotherapies* (4th ed.; pp. 119–152). Itasca, IL: F. E. Peacock.

Kazdin, A. E., (1977). Assessing the clinical or applied importance of behavior change through social validation. *Behavior Modification, 1,* 427–452.

Kazdin, A. E. (1982). *Single-case research designs: Methods for clinical and applied settings.* New York: Oxford University Press.

Kazdin, A. E. (1985). Selection of target behaviors: the relationship of treatment focus to clinical dysfunction. *Behavioral Assessment, 7,* 33–47.

Kazdin, A. E. (1988). Child psychotherapy: Developing and identifying effective treatments. Elmsford, NY: Pergamon.

Kazdin, A. E. (1994a). *Behavior modification in applied settings* (5th ed.). Pacific Grove, CA: Brooks/Cole.

Kazdin, A. E. (1994b). Methodology, design, and evaluation in psychotherapy research. In A. E. Bergin & S. L. Garfield (Eds.), *Handbook of psychotherapy and behavior change* (4th ed.; pp. 143–188). New York: Wiley.

Kazdin, A. E. (1998). *Research design in clinical psychology* (3rd ed.). Boston: Allyn and Bacon.

Kazdin, A. E. (1999). The meanings and measurement of clinical significance. *Journal of Consulting and Clinical Psychology, 67,* 332–339.

Kazdin, A. E. (2001). *Behavior modification in applied settings* (6th ed.). Belmont, CA: Wadsworth.

Kazdin, A. E., & Bass, D. (1989). Power to detect difference between alternative treatments in comparative psychotherapy outcome research. *Journal of Consulting and Clinical Psychology, 57,* 138–147.

Kazdin, A. E., & Weisz, J. R. (1998). Identifying and developing empirically supported child and adolescent treatments. *Journal of Consulting and Clinical Psychology, 66,* 19–36.

Kazdin, A. E., & Wilson, G. T. (1978). *Evaluation of behavior therapy: Issues, evidence and research strategies.* Cambridge, MA: Ballinger.

Keane, T. M., Fairbank, J. A., Caddell, J. M., & Zimering, R. (1989). Implosive (flooding) therapy reduces symptoms of PTSD in Vietnam combat veterans. *Behavior Therapy, 20,* 245–260.

Kehoe, E. J., & Macrae, M. (1998). Classical conditioning. In W. O'Donohue (Ed.), *Learning and behavior therapy* (Chapter 3, pp. 36–58). Boston: Allyn and Bacon.

Keijsers, G. P., Hoogduin, C. A., Schaap, C. P. (1994). Prognostic factors in behavioral treatment of panic disorder with and without agoraphobia. *Behavior Therapy, 25,* 689–708.

Keith-Spiegal, P., & Koocher, G. P. (1985). *Ethics in psychology.* New York: Random House.

Kelleher, R. T. (1966). Chaining and conditioned reinforcement. In W. K. Honig (Ed.), *Operant behavior: Areas of research and application.* New York: Appleton-Century-Crofts.

Kempe, C. H., Silverman, F. N., Steele, B. F., Droegemuller, W., & Silver, H. K. (1962). The battered-child syndrome. *Journal of the American Medical Association, 181,* 17–24.

Kendall, P. C. (1987). Cognitive processes and procedures in behavior therapy. In G. T. Wilson, C. M. Franks, P. C. Kendall, & J. P. Foreyt (Eds.), *Review of behavior therapy: Theory and practice, 11.* New York: Guilford.

Kendall, P. C. (1998). Empirically supported psychological therapies. *Journal of Consulting and Clinical Psychology, 66,* 3–6.

Kendall, P. C. (1999). Clinical significance. *Journal of Consulting and Clinical Psychology, 67,* 283–284.

Kent, G. (2001). Dental health. In D. W. Johnston & M. Johnston (Eds.), *Health psychology, Vol. 8, Comprehensive clinical psychology* (pp. 594–615). Amsterdam, Netherlands: Elsevier Science Publishers.

Kerr, N., Kramer, G. P., Caroll, J. S., & Alfini, J. J. (1991). On the effectiveness of the voir dire in criminal cases with prejudicial pretrial publicity: An empirical study. *American Law Review, 40,* 665–701.

Kety, S. S. (1988). Schizophrenic illness in the families of schizophrenic adoptees: Findings from the Danish national sample. *Schizophrenia Bulletin, 14,* 217–222.

Kety, S. S., Rosenthal, D., Wender, P. H., Schulsinger, F., & Jacobsen, B. (1978). The biological and adoptive families of adopted individuals who become schizophrenic. In L. C. Wynne, R. L. Cromwell & S. Matthysse (Eds.), *The nature of schizophrenia* (pp. 25–37). New York: John Wiley & Sons.

Kiecolt-Glaser, J. K., Malarkey, W. B., Cacioppo, J. T.,& Glaser, R. (1993) Stressful personal relationships: Immune and endocrine function. In R. Glaser & J. K. Kiecolt-Glaser (Eds.), *Handbook of human stress and immunity* (pp. 321–339). San Diego, CA: Academic Press.

Kiesler, C. A., & Morton, T. L. (1988). Psychology and public policy in the "Health Care Revolution." *American Psychologist, 43,* 993–1003.

Kirk, S. A. (1958). *Early education of the mentally retarded.* Urbana, IL: University of Illinois Press.

Kirk, S. A. (1962). Effects of educational treatment. In L. C. Kolb, R. L. Masland, & R. E. Cooke (Eds.), *Mental retardation* (pp. 289–294). Baltimore: Williams & Wilkins.

Klassen, D., & O'Connor, W. (1988). A prospective study of predictors of violence in adult male mental health admissions. *Law and Human Behavior, 12,* 143–158.

Klein, D. F., & Rabkin, J. (Eds.). (1981). *Anxiety: New research and changing concepts.* New York: Raven.

Klein, D. N., & Riso, L. P. (1995). Psychiatric disorders: Problems of boundaries and comorbidity. In C. G. Costello (Ed.), *Basic issues in psychopathology.* New York: Guilford.

Kleinke, C. L. (1994). *Common principles of psychotherapy.* Pacific Grove, CA: Brooks/Cole.

Kleinman, A. (1988). *Rethinking psychiatry: From cultural category to personal experience.* New York: The Free Press.

Klerman, G. L., & Weissman, M. M. (Eds.). (1993). *New applications of interpersonal therapy.* Washington, DC: American Psychiatric Press.

Klerman, G. L., Weissman, M. M., Rounsaville, B. J., & Chevron, E. S. (1984). *Interpersonal psychotherapy of depression.* New York: Basic Books.

Klopfer, W. G., & Taulbee, E. S. (1976). Projective tests. *Annual Review of Psychology, 27,* 543–567.

Knapp, S., & VandeCreek, L. (1987). A review of tort liability in involuntary civil commitment. *Hospital and Community Psychiatry, 38,* 648–651.

Knapp, S., & VandeCreek, L. (1997). *Jaffee v. Redmond:* The Supreme Court recognizes a psychotherapist-patient privilege in federal courts. *Professional Psychology: Research and Practice, 28,* 567–572.

Knapp, T. J. (1988). Introduction. In T. J. Knapp (Ed.) & M. T. Schumacher (Trans.), *Westphal's "Die Agoraphobie"* (pp. 1–57). Lanham, MD: University Press of America.

Knapp, T. J. (Ed.), & Schumacher, M. T. (Trans.). (1988). *Westphal's "Die Agoraphobie"* Lanham, MD: University Press of America.

Knight, B. (1986). *Psychotherapy with older adults.* Newbury Park, CA: Sage Publications.

Knight, S. J. (1998). Oncology and hematology. In P. M. Camic & S. J. Knight (Eds.), *Clinical handbook of health psychology: A practical guide to effective interventions.* Seattle, WA: Hogrefe & Huber Publishers.

Kohn, M. L., & Schooler, C. (1973). Occupational experience and psychological functioning: An assessment of reciprocal effects. *American Sociological Review, 38,* 97–118

Kohn, M. L., & Schooler, C. (1983). *Work and personality: An inquiry into the impact of social stratification.* Norwood, NJ: Ablex.

Kolb, B., & Whishaw, I. Q. (1996). *Fundamentals of human neuropsychology* (4th ed.). New York: Freeman & Co.

Kolb, B., Whishaw, I. Q., & Cioe, J. (1994). Brain. In V. S. Ramachandran (Ed.), *Encyclopedia of human behavior* (Vol. 1, pp. 425–434). San Diego, CA: Academic Press.

Kolb, L. C., Masland, R. L., & Cooke, R. E. (Eds.). (1962). *Mental retardation.* Baltimore: Williams & Wilkins.

Kolko, D. J., & Milan, M. A. (1983). Reframing and paradoxical instruction to overcome "resistance" in the treatment of delinquent youth. *Journal of Consulting and Clinical Psychology.*

Koocher, G. P. (1986). Coping with a death from cancer. *Journal of Consulting and Clinical Psychology, 54,* 623–631.

Koocher, G. P. (1995). Ethics in psychotherapy. In B. Bongar & L. E. Beutler (Eds.), *Comprehensive textbook of psychotherapy: Theory and practice* (pp. 456–473). New York: Oxford University Press.

Koocher, G. P., & Keith-Spiegel, P. (1998). *Ethics in psychology: Professional standards and cases* (2nd ed.). New York: Oxford University Press.

Kopelowicz, A., & Liberman, R. P. (1998). Psychosocial treatments for schizophrenia. In P. E. Nathan & J. M. Gorman (Eds.), *A guide to treatments that work* (pp. 19–211). New York: Oxford University Press.

Koppitz, E. M. (1968). *Psychological evaluation of children's human figure drawings.* Yorktown Heights, NY: The Psychological Corporation.

Koppitz, E. M. (1984). *Psychological evaluation of human figure drawings by middle school pupils.* New York: Grune & Stratton.

Kozlowski, L. T., Coambs, R. B., Ferrence, R. G., & Adlaf, E. M. (1989). Preventing smoking and other drug use: Let the buyers beware and the interventions be apt. *Canadian Journal of Public Health, 80,* 452–456.

Kraepelin, E. (1921). *Manic-depressive insanity and paranoia.* Edinburgh: E. & S. Livingstone. (R. M. Barclay, Trans.; G. M. Robertson, Ed.) (From the Eighth German Edition of the *Text-book of psychiatry,* Vols. 3 and 4.)

Kramer, J. J., & Conoley, J. C. (Eds.). (1992). *The eleventh mental measurements yearbook.* Lincoln, NE: The Buros Institute of Mental Measurement.

Krasner, L. (1992). The concepts of syndrome and functional analysis: Compatible or incompatible? *Behavioral Assessment, 14,* 307–321.

Kravitz, L. S. (1988). *The hidden doctrine of Maimonides' guide for the perplexed: Philosophical and religious God-language in tension.* Lewiston, NY: Edwin Mellen.

Kriegman, G., Gardner, R. D., & Abse, D. W. (Eds.). (1975). *American psychiatry: Past, present, and future.* Charlottesville: University Press of Virginia.

Krupnick, J. L., Sotsky, S. M., Simmens, S., Moyer, J., Elkin, I., Watkins, J., & Pilkonis, P. (1996). The role of therapeutic alliance in psychotherapy and pharmacotherapy outcome: Findings in the National Institute of Mental Health Treatment for Depression Collaborative Research Program. *Journal of Consulting and Clinical Psychology, 65,* 532–539.

Kuder, G. G., & Richardson, M. W. (1937). The theory of estimation of test reliability. *Psychometrika, 2,* 151–160.

Kulynych, J. J., & Stromberg, C. (1998). Legal Update #11: Telecommunication in psychological practice. *Register Report, 24* (1/2), 9–18.

Kutchins, H., & Stuart, K. A. (2000). DSM-IV: Does bigger and newer mean better? In R. Halgin (Ed.). *Taking sides: Clashing views on controversial issues in abnormal psychology* (pp. 8–12) Guilford, CT: Dushkin/McGraw-Hill.

Kutchins, J., & Kirk, S. A. (1997). *Making us crazy: DSM: The psychiatric bible and the creation of mental disorder.* New York: Free Press.

Laidlaw, T. A., & Malmo, C. (1990). Introduction: Feminist therapy and psychological healing. In T. A. Laidlaw, C. Malmo, & Associates (Eds.), *Healing voices: Feminist approaches to therapy with women* (pp. 1–11). San Francisco: Jossey-Bass.

Laidlaw, T. A., Malmo, C., & Associates. (1990). *Healing voices: Feminist approaches to therapy with women.* San Francisco: Jossey-Bass.

Lambert, M. J. & Bergin, A. E. (1994). The effectiveness of psychotherapy. In A. E. Bergin & S. L. Garfield (Eds.), *Handbook of psychotherapy and behavior change* (4th ed., pp. 143–188). New York: Wiley.

Lambert, M. J., DeJulio, S. S., & Stein, D. (1978). Therapist interpersonal skills. *Psychological Bulletin, 83,* 467–489.

Landis, C. (1938). A statistical evaluation of psychotherapeutic methods. In S. E. Hinsie (Ed.), *Concepts and problems in psychotherapy* (pp. 155–169). London: Heinemann.

Landman, J. T., & Dawes, R. M. (1982). Psychotherapy outcome: Smith and Glass' conclusions stand up under scrutiny. *American Psychologist, 37,* 504–516.

Lang, P. J. (1978). Anxiety: Towards a psychophysiological definition. In H. S. Akiskal & W. L. Webb (Eds.), *Psychiatric diagnosis: Exploration of biological predictors* (pp. 365–389). New York: Spectrum.

Lang, P. J. (1979). A bio-informational theory of emotional imagery. *Psychophysiology, 16,* 495–512.

Lang, P. J. (1985). The cognitive psychophysiology of emotion: Fear and anxiety. In A. H. Tuma & J. D. Maser (Eds.), *Anxiety and the anxiety disorders* (pp. 131–170). Hillsdale, NJ: Lawrence Erlbaum.

Lang, P. J., & Lazovik, A. D. (1963). Experimental desensitization of a phobia. *Journal of Abnormal and Social Psychology, 66,* 519–525.

Lang, P. J., Lazovik, A. D., & Reynolds, D. J. (1965). Desensitization, suggestibility, and pseudotherapy. *Journal of Abnormal Psychology, 70,* 395–402.

LaPointe, K., & Harrell, T. (1978). Thoughts and feelings: Correlational relationships and cross-situational consistency. *Cognitive Therapy and Research, 2,* 311–322.

Lapsley, D. K. (1994). Id, ego, and superego. In V. S. Ramachandran (Ed.), *Encyclopedia of human behavior* (Vol. 2, pp. 579–588). San Diego, CA: Academic Press.

Laurent, J., Swerdlik, M., & Ryburn, M. (1992). Review of validity research on the Stanford-Binet Intelligence Scale: Fourth Edition. *Psychological Assessment: A Journal of Consulting and Clinical Psychology, 4,* 102–112.

Lazarus, A. A. (1971). *Behavior therapy and beyond.* New York: McGraw-Hill.

Lazarus, A. A. (1973). Multimodal behavior therapy: Treating the "Basic Id." *Journal of Nervous and Mental Disease, 156,* 404–411.

Lazarus, A. A. (1976). *Multimodal behavior therapy.* New York: Springer.

Lazarus, A. A. (1989). The practice of rational-emotive therapy. In M. E. Bernard & R. DiGiuseppe (Eds.), *Inside rational-emotive therapy: A critical appraisal of the theory and therapy of Albert Ellis* (pp. 95–112). San Diego, CA: Academic Press.

Lazarus, A. A. (1995). Multimodal therapy. In R. J. Corsini & D. Wedding (Eds.), *Current psychotherapies* (5th ed.; pp. 322–355). Itasca, IL: F. E. Peacock.

Lazarus, R. S., & Folkman, S. (1984a). Coping and adaptation. In W. D. Gentry (Ed.), *Handbook of behavioral medicine* (pp. 282–325). New York: Guilford.

Lazarus, R. S., & Folkman, S. (1984b). *Stress, appraisal, and coping.* New York: Springer.

Leary, T. (1957). *Interpersonal diagnosis of personality. A functional theory and methodology for personality evaluation.* New York: Ronald Press.

Leavitt, R. M. (1989, Spring). Suffering in Passamaquoddy. *The Maine Mosaic,* 20–21.

Lebensohn, Z. (1978). Defensive psychiatry or how to treat the mentally ill without being a lawyer. In W. Barton & C. Sanborn (Eds.), *Law and the mental health professionals.* New York: International Universities Press.

Lego, S. (1986). Foreword. In J. D. Durham & S. B. Hardin (Eds.), *The nurse psychotherapist in private practice* (pp. xv-xvi). New York: Springer.

Lehrer, P. (1978). Psychophysiological effects of progressive relaxation in anxiety neurotic patients and of progressive relaxation and alpha feedback in nonpatients. *Journal of Consulting and Clinical Psychology, 46,* 389–404.

Leifer, R. (1990). Introduction: The medical model as the ideology of the therapeutic state. In D. Cohen (Ed.), Special issue: Challenging the therapeutic state: Critical perspectives on psychiatry and the mental health system. *The Journal of Mind and Behavior, 11* (3 and 4), 247–258 (1–12).

Leitenberg, H., Agras, W. S., Allen, R., & Butz, R. A. (1975). Feedback and therapist praise during treatment of phobia. *Journal of Consulting and Clinical Psychology, 43,* 396–404.

Leitenberg, H., Agras, W. S., Edwardes, J. A., Thompson, L. E., & Wincze, J. P. (1970). Practice as a psychotherapeutic variable: An experimental analysis within single cases. *Journal of Psychiatric Research, 7,* 215–225.

Leitenberg, H., Agras, W. S., Thompson, L. E., & Wright, E. E. (1968). Feedback in behavior modification: An experimental analysis in two phobic cases. *Journal of Applied Behavior Analysis, 1,* 131–137.

Leitenberg, H., Rosen, J. C., Gross, J., Nudelman, S., & Vara, L. S. (1988). Exposure plus response-prevention treatment of bulimia nervosa. *Journal of Consulting and Clinical Psychology, 56,* 535–541.

Lentz, R. J., & Ramsey, L. J. (1988). The psychologist consultant on the hospice team: One example of the model. *Hospice Journal, 4,* 55–66.

Leonard, K. E. (1992). Alcohol and violence in context [Review of K. Pernanen, "Alcohol in human violence"]. *Contemporary Psychology, 37,* 1084–1085.

Lepore, F., Ptito, M., & Jasper, H. H. (Eds.). (1986). *Two hemispheres—One brain.* New York: Alan R. Liss.

Lerner, P. M. (1991). *Psychoanalytic theory and the Rorschach.* New York: Analytic Press.

Levenson, H., & Strupp, H. H. (1997). Cyclical maladaptive patterns: Case formulation in time-limited dynamic psychotherapy (pp. 84–115). In T. D. Eells (Ed.), *Handbook of psychotherapy case formulation.* New York: Guilford.

Leventhal, H., Baker, T. B., Brandon, T., & Fleming, R. (1989). Intervening and preventing cigarette smoking. In T. Ney & A. Gale (Eds.), *Smoking and human behavior* (pp. 313–336). New York: Wiley.

Levine, M. (1981). *The history and politics of community mental health.* New York: Oxford University Press.

Ley, R. (1987). Panic disorder: A hyperventilation interpretation. In L. Michelson & L. M. Ascher (Eds.), *Anxiety and stress disorders: Cognitive-behavioral assessment and treatment* (pp. 191–212). New York: Guilford.

Lezak, M. D. (1995). *Neuropsychological assessment* (3rd ed.). New York: Oxford University Press.

Lichstein, K. L. (1988). *Clinical relaxation strategies.* New York: Wiley.

Lichtenstein, E., Harris, D. E., Birchler, G. R., Wahl, J. M., & Schmahl, D. P. (1973). Comparison of rapid smoking, warm, smoky air, and attention placebo in the modification of smoking behavior. *Journal of Consulting and Clinical Psychology, 40,* 92–98.

Liddle, H. A., Bray, J. H., Levant, R. F., & Santisteban, D. A. (2002). Family psychology intervention science: An emerging area of science and practice. In H. A. Liddle, D. A. Santisteban, R. F. Levant, & J. H. Bray (Eds.), *Family psychology: Science-based interventions* (Chapter 1; pp. 3–15). Washington, DC: American Psychological Association.

Liddle, H. A., Santisteban, D. A., Levant, R. F, & Bray, J. H. (Eds.). (2002). *Family psychology: Science-based interventions.* Washington, DC: American Psychological Association.

Lilienfeld, S. O., Waldman, I. D., & Israel, A. C. (1994). A critical examination of the use of the term and concept of comorbidity in psychopathology research. *Clinical Psychology: Science & Practice, 1,* 71–83.

Lilienfeld, S. O., Wood, J. M., & Garb, H. N. (2000). The scientific status of projective techniques. *Psychological Science in the Public Interest, 1,* 27–66.

Linehan, M. M., & Kehrer, C. A. (1993). Borderline personality disorder. In D. H. Barlow (Ed.), *Clinical handbook of psychological disorders* (2nd ed.; pp. 396–441). New York: Guilford.

Lipsky, M. M., Kassinove, H., & Miller, N. J. (1980). Effects of rational-emotive therapy, rational role-reversal, and rational-emotive imagery on the emotional adjustment of Community Mental Health Center patients. *Journal of Consulting and Clinical Psychology, 48,* 366–374.

Litwack, T. R. (1994). Assessment of dangerousness: Legal, research, and clinical developments. *Administration and Policy in Mental Health, 21,* 361–378.

Livermore, J., Malmquist, C., & Meehl, P. (1968). On the justification for civil commitment. *University of Pennsylvania Law Review, 117,* 75–96.

Locke, E. A. (1971). Is "behavior therapy" behavioristic? (An analysis of Wolpe's psychotherapeutic methods). *Psychological Bulletin, 70,* 318–327.

Loehlin, J. C., Lindzey, G., & Spuhler, J. N. (1975). *Race differences in intelligence.* New York: Freeman.

Loftus, E. F. (1979). *Eyewitness testimony.* Cambridge, MA: Harvard University Press.

Loftus, E. F. (1993). The reality of repressed memories. *American Psychologist, 48,* 518–537.

Logue, A. W. (1995). *Self-control: Waiting until tomorrow for what you want today.* Englewood Cliffs, NJ: Prentice Hall.

Loh, W. D. (1981). Perspectives on psychology and the law. *Journal of Applied Social Psychology, 11,* 314–355.

London, P. (1986). Major issues in psychotherapy integration. *Journal of Integrative and Eclectic Psychotherapy, 5,* 211–216.

Loomis, C. C., & Thorpe, G. L. (1992). Review of cognitive therapy with couples, by F. M. Dattilio & C. A. Padesky. *The Journal of Mind and Behavior, 13,* 413–415.

Lopez, S. R. (1989). Patient variable biases in clinical judgment: Conceptual overview and methodological considerations. *Psychological Bulletin, 106,* 184–203.

Lowing, P. A., Mirsky, A. F., & Pereira, R. (1983). The inheritance of schizophrenic spectrum disorders: A reanalysis of the Danish adoptee study data. *American Journal of Psychiatry, 140,* 1167–1171.

Lubin, B., Larsen, R. M., & Matarazzo, J. D. (1984). Patterns of psychological test usage in the United States: 1935–1982. *American Psychologist, 39,* 451–454.

Lubin, B., Larsen, R. M., Matarazzo, J. D., & Seever, M. (1985). Psychological test usage patterns in five professional settings. *American Psychologist, 40,* 857–861.

Luborsky, L. (1954). A note on Eysenck's article "The effects of psychotherapy: An evaluation." *British Journal of Psychology, 45,* 129–131.

Luborsky, L. (1984). *Principles of psychoanalytic psychotherapy: A manual for supportive-expressive treatment.* New York: Basic Books.

Luborsky, L. (1997). The core conflictual relationship theme: A basic case formulation method. In T. D. Eells (Ed.), *Handbook of psychotherapy case formulation* (pp. 58–83). New York: Guilford.

Luborsky, L., Chandler, D. R., Auerbach, A. H., Cohen, D. & Bachrach, H. (1971). Factors influencing the outcome of psychotherapy: A review of quantitative research. *Psychological Bulletin, 75,* 145–185.

Luborsky, L., Crits-Christoph, P., McLellan, A. T., Woody, G., Piper, W., Liberman, B., Imber, S., & Pilkonis, P. (1988). Do therapists vary much in their success? Findings from four outcome studies. *American Journal of Orthopsychiatry, 56,* 501–512.

Luborsky, L., Singer, B., & Luborsky, L. (1975). Comparative studies of psychotherapies: Is it true that "Everyone has one and all must have prizes"? *Archives of General Psychology, 32,* 995–1008.

Lundy, A. (1988). Instructional set and the Thematic Apperception Test. *Journal of Personality Assessment, 49,* 141–145.

Luria, A. R. (1966). *Human brain and psychological processes.* New York: Harper & Row.

Luria, A. R. (1980). *Higher cortical functioning in man* (2nd ed.). New York: Basic Books.

Luus, C. E., & Wells, G. L. (1991). Eyewitness identification and the selection of distracters for lineups. *Law and Human Behavior, 15,* 43–57.

Lynn, R. (1990). The role of nutrition in secular increases in intelligence. *Personality and Individual Differences, 11,* 273–285.

Lynn, R. (1993). Further evidence for the existence of race and sex-differences in criminal capacity. *Social Behavior and Personality, 21,* 89–92.

Machover, K. (1949). *Personality projection in the drawings of the human figure.* Springfield, IL: Charles C. Thomas.

MacKinnon, C. A. (1986). Preface. In J. M. Masson, *A dark science: Women, sexuality, and psychiatry in the nineteenth century.* New York: Farrar, Straus and Giroux.

MacLeod, C. M. (1991). Half a century of research on the Stroop effect: An integrative review. *Psychological Bulletin, 109,* 163–203.

Maher, B. A. (1966). *Principles of psychopathology: An experimental approach.* New York: McGraw-Hill.

Maher, B. A. (1999). Changing trends in doctoral programs in psychology: A comparative analysis of research-oriented versus professional-applied programs. *Psychological Science, 10,* 475–481.

Mahoney, M. J. (1980). *Abnormal psychology: Perspectives on human variance.* San Francisco: Harper and Row.

Maimonides, M. (1904). *The guide for the perplexed* (2nd ed.). Dover Publications. (M. Friedlander, Trans.) (Original work published before 1194.)

Malan, D., & Osimo, F. (1992). *Psychodynamics, training, and outcome in brief psychotherapy.* Oxford, UK: Butterworth-Heinemann Ltd.

Malcolm, J. (1982). *Psychoanalysis: The impossible profession.* New York: Vintage Books.

Malcolm, J. (1990). Reflections: J'appelle un chat un chat (pp. 305–325). In C. Bernheimer & C. Kahane (Eds.), *In Dora's case: Freud, hysteria, feminism* (2nd ed.). New York: Columbia University Press.

Maloney, M. P. (1985). *A clinician's guide to forensic assessment.* New York: Free Press.

Markowitz, J. C. (Ed.). (1998). *Interpersonal psychotherapy.* Washington, DC: American Psychiatric Press.

Markowitz, J. C., & Swartz, H. A. (1997). Case formulation in interpersonal psychotherapy of depression (pp. 192–222). In T. D. Eells (Ed.), *Handbook of psychotherapy case formulation.* New York: Guilford.

Marks, I. M. (1969). *Fears and phobias.* London: Heinemann Medical.

Marks, I. M. (1972). Perspective on flooding. *Seminars in Psychiatry, 4*(2), 129–138.

Marks, I. M. (1981a). Behavioural concepts and treatments of neuroses. *Behavioural Psychotherapy, 9,* 137–154.

Marks, I. M. (1981b). *Cure and care of neuroses: Theory and practice of behavioral psychotherapy.* New York: Wiley.

Marks, I. M. (1987). *Fears, phobias, and rituals: Panic, anxiety, and their disorders.* Oxford University Press, New York.

Marks, I. M., & Gelder, M. G. (1965). A controlled retrospective study of behavior therapy in phobic patients. *British Journal of Psychiatry, 111,* 571–573.

Marks, I. M., Stern, R. S., Mawson, D., Cobb, J., & McDonald, R. (1980). Clomipramine and exposure for obsessive-compulsive rituals: I. *British Journal of Psychiatry, 136,* 1–25.

Marks, I. M., Swinson, R. P., Basoglu, M., Kuch, K., Noshirvani, H., O'Sullivan, G., Lelliott, P. T., Kirby, M., McNamee, G., Sengun, S. & Wickwire, K. (1993). Alprazolam and exposure alone and combined in panic disorder with agoraphobia: A controlled trial in London and Toronto. *British Journal of Psychiatry, 162,* 776–787.

Marks, P. A., Seeman, W., & Haller, D. L. (1974). *The actuarial use of the MMPI with adolescents and adults.* Baltimore: Williams and Wilkins.

Martin, A. (1994 October 16, 28). Avoiding "e" issue. *Manchester Guardian Weekly.*

Martin, P. R. (1998). Headache. In A. S. Bellack & M. Hersen (Eds.), *Comprehensive clinical psychology, Volume 8, Health psychology* (pp. 530–556). New York: Elsevier.

Martin, P. R., Nathan, P. R., & Milech, D. (1987). The Type A behaviour pattern and chronic headaches. *Behaviour Change, 4,* 33–39.

Martin, P. R., & Soon, K. (1993). The relationship between perceived stress, social support and chronic headaches. *Headache, 33,* 307–314.

Martin, P. R., & Theunissen, C. (1993). The role of life event stress, coping and social support in chronic headaches. *Headache, 22,* 301–306.

Mash, E. J., & Hunsley, J. (1990). Behavioral assessment: A contemporary approach. In A. S. Bellack, M. Hersen, & A. E. Kazdin (Eds.), *International handbook of behavior modification and therapy* (2nd ed.; pp. 87–106). New York: Plenum Press.

Masling, J. M. (1997). On the nature and utility of projective tests and objective tests. *Journal of Personality Assessment, 69,* 257–270.

Masserman, J. H. (1943). *Behavior and neurosis.* Chicago: University of Chicago Press.

Masson, J. M. (1983). *The assault on truth: Freud's suppression of the seduction theory.* New York: Farrar, Straus & Giroux.

Masson, J. M. (1986). *A dark science: Women, sexuality, and psychiatry in the nineteenth century.* New York: Farrar, Straus & Giroux.

Masson, J. M. (1992). *The assault on truth: Freud's suppression of the seduction theory.* New York: Harper Perennial. (Original work published in 1985.)

Matarazzo, J. D. (1965). The interview. In B. B. Wolman (Ed.), *Handbook of clinical psychology* (pp. 403–450). New York: McGraw Hill.

Matarazzo, J. D. (1972). *Wechsler's measurement and appraisal of adult intelligence* (5th ed.). New York: Oxford University Press.

Matarazzo, J. D. (1982). Behavioral health's challenge to academic, scientific, and professional psychology. *American Psychologist, 35,* 1–14.

Matarazzo, J. D. (1983). The reliability of psychiatric and psychological diagnosis. *Clinical Psychology Review, 3,* 103–145.

Matarazzo, J. D. (1984). Behavioral health: A 1990 challenge for the health services professions. In J. D. Matarazzo, S. M. Weiss, J. A. Herd, & N. E. Miller (Eds.), *Topics in health psychology* (pp. 3–18). New York: John Wiley & Sons.

Matarazzo, J. D. (1986). Computerized psychological test interpretation: Unvalidated plus all mean and no sigma. *American Psychologist, 41,* 14–24.

Matarazzo, J. D. (1990). Psychological assessment versus psychological testing. *American Psychologist, 45,* 999–1017.

Mathews, A. M., Gelder, M. G., and Johnston, D. W. (1981). *Agoraphobia: Nature and treatment.* Guilford, New York.

Mathews, A. M., Johnson, D. W., Lancashire, M., Munby, M., Shaw, P. M., & Gelder, M. G. (1976). Imaginal flooding and exposure to real phobic situations: Treatment outcome with agoraphobic patients. *British Journal of Psychiatry, 129,* 362–371.

Mathews, A. M., & Rezin, V. (1977). Treatment of dental fears by imaginal flooding and rehearsal of coping behavior. *Behavior Research and Therapy, 15,* 321–328.

Mathews, A. M., & Shaw, P. (1973). Emotional arousal and persuasion effects in flooding. *Behavior Research and Therapy, 11,* 587–598.

Matthews, J. R., & Walker, C. E. (1997). *Basic skills and professional issues in clinical psychology.* Boston: Allyn and Bacon.

Matthews, L. J. (1997). Psychological screening. In J. R. Matthews & C. E. Walker (Eds.), *Basic skills and professional issues in clinical psychology* (pp. 115–134). Boston: Allyn and Bacon.

May, R., & Yalom, I. (1989). Existential psychotherapy. In R. J. Corsini, & D. Wedding (Eds.), *Current psychotherapies* (4th ed.; pp. 363–402). Itasca, IL: F. E. Peacock.

Maziade, M., Roy, M. A., Fournier, J. P., & Cliché, D. (1992). Reliability of best-estimate diagnosis in genetic linkage studies of major psychoses: Results from the Quebec pedigree studies. *American Journal of Psychiatry, 149,* 1674–1686.

McArthur, C. C. (1956). Clinical versus actuarial prediction. In *Proceedings, 1955 invitational conference on testing problems* (pp. 99–106). Princeton, NJ: Educational Testing Service.

McAuley, E. (1993). Self-efficacy and the maintenance of exercise participation in older adults. *Journal of Behavioral Medicine, 16,* 103–113.

McAuley, E., & Courneya, K. S. (1992). Self-efficacy relationships with affective and attitudinal responses to exercise. *Journal of Applied Social Psychology, 2,* 312–326.

McCaffrey R. J., Duff, K., & Westervelt, H. J. (2000). *Practitioner's guide to evaluating change with intellectual assessment instruments.* New York: Kluwer Academic/Plenum.

McCaffrey, R. J., & Fairbank, J. A. (1985). Behavioral assessment and treatment of accident-related post-traumatic stress disorder: Two case studies. *Behavior Therapy, 16,* 406–416.

McCann, J. T., & Dyer, F. J. (1996). *Forensic assessment with the Millon Inventories.* New York: Guilford.

McCarthy, K. (1993, July). Kids' eyewitness recall is focus for conference. *The APA Monitor, 24 (7),* 1, 28–29.

McCloskey, M., & Egeth, H. (1983). Eyewitness identification: What can a psychologist tell a jury? *American Psychologist, 38,* 550–563.

McCrae, R. R., & John, O. P. (1992). An introduction to the five-factor model and its applications. *Journal of Personality, 60,* 175–215.

McDonald, D. A., Nussbaum, D. S., & Bagby, R. (1991). Reliability, validity and utility of the Fitness Interview Test. *Canadian Journal of Psychiatry, 36,* 480–484.

McFall, R. M. (1991). Manifesto for a science of clinical psychology. *The Clinical Psychologist, 44,* 75–88.

McGovern, C. M. (1985). *Masters of madness: Social origins of the American psychiatric profession.* Hanover, NH: University Press of New England.

McGlynn, F. D. (1973). Graded imagination and relaxation as components of experimental desensitization. *The Journal of Nervous and Mental Disease, 156,* 377–385.

McGlynn, F. D, & Rose, M. P. (1998). Assessment of anxiety and fear. In A. S. Bellack & M. Hersen (Eds.), *Behavioral assessment: A practical handbook* (4th ed.; pp. 179–209). Boston: Allyn and Bacon.

McGrew, J. H., Glueckauf, R. L., Bond, G. R., & Frank, R. G. (1996). Health care reform and professional psychology: Overview of key issues and background of book. In R. L. Glueckauf, R. G. Frank, G. R. Bond, & J. H. McGrew (Eds.), *Psychological practice in a changing health care system.* New York: Springer.

McKellar, P. (1957). *Imagination and thinking: A psychological analysis.* London: Cohen & West.

McKown, R. (1961). *Pioneers in mental health.* New York: Dodd, Mead Co.

McNally, R. J. (1994). *Panic disorder: A critical analysis.* New York: Guilford.

McNally, R. J. (1995). Automaticity and the anxiety disorders. *Behaviour Research & Therapy, 33,* 747–754.

McReynolds, P. (1996). Lightner Witmer: A centennial tribute. *American Psychologist, 51,* 237–240.

Meehl, P. (1945). An investigation of a general normality or control factor in personality testing. *Psychological Monographs, 59* (4, Whole No. 274).

Meehl, P. E. (1954). *Clinical versus statistical prediction.* Minneapolis: University of Minnesota Press.

Meehl, P. E. (1957). When shall we use our heads instead of the formula? *Journal of Counseling Psychology, 4,* 268–273.

Meehl, P. E. (1960). The cognitive activity of the clinician. *American Psychologist, 15,* 19–27.

Meehl, P. E. (1965). Seer over sign: The first good example. *Journal of Experimental Research in Personality, 1,* 27–32.

Meehl, P. E. (1973). *Psychodiagnosis: Selected papers.* Minneapolis: University of Minnesota Press.

Meehl, P. E. (1986). Causes and effects of my disturbing little book. *Journal of Personality Assessment, 50,* 370–375.

Megargee, E. (1981). Methodological problems in the prediction of violence. In J. Hays, T. Roberts, & K. Solway (Eds.), *Violence and the violent individual* (pp. 179–191). New York: Spectrum.

Meichenbaum, D. H. (1977). *Cognitive-behavior modification: An integrative approach.* New York: Plenum.

Meichenbaum, D. H. (1995). Cognitive-behavioral therapy in historical perspective. In B. Bongar & L. E. Beutler (Eds.), *Comprehensive textbook of psychotherapy: Theory and practice* (pp. 140–158). New York: Oxford University Press.

Meichenbaum, D. H., & Cameron, R. (1973). Training schizophrenics to talk to themselves: A means of developing attentional controls. *Behavior Therapy, 4,* 515–534.

Meichenbaum, D. H., Gilmore, J. B., & Fedoravicius, A. (1971). Group insight versus group desensitization in treating speech anxiety. *Journal of Consulting and Clinical Psychology, 36,* 410–421.

Meichenbaum, D. H., & Goodman, J. (1971). Training impulsive children to talk to themselves: A means of developing self-control. *Journal of Abnormal Psychology, 77,* 115–126.

Meichenbaum, D., & Turk, D. (1982). Stress, coping, and disease: A cognitive-behavioral perspective. In R. W. J. Neufield (Ed.), *Psychological stress and psychopathology.* New York: McGraw-Hill.

Melton, G. B. (1987). Training in psychology and law. In I. B. Weiner & A. K. Hess (Eds.), *Handbook of forensic psychology.* New York: Wiley.

Melton, G. B., Petrila, J., Poythress, N. G., Slobogin, C. (1987). *Psychological evaluations for the courts: A handbook for mental health professionals and lawyers.* New York: Guilford.

Melton, G. B., Petrila, J., Poythress, N. G., Slobogin, C. (1997). *Psychological evaluations for the courts: A handbook for mental health professionals and lawyers* (2nd ed.). New York: Guilford.

Memoir of the author (unattributed). (1898). *Burton's anatomy of melancholy.* (pp. ix–xiv.) London: Chatto & Windus. (Original work published 1651–1652.)

Menninger, K. (1958). *Theory of psychoanalytic technique.* New York: Basic Books.

Messer, S. B., & Wolitzky, D. L. (1997). The traditional psychoanalytic approach to case formulation (pp. 26–57). In T. D. Eells (Ed.), *Handbook of psychotherapy case formulation.* New York: Guilford.

Messick, S. (1995). Validity of psychological assessment: Validation of inferences from person's responses and performances as scientific inquiry into score meaning. *American Psychologist, 50,* 741–749.

Meyer, R. G., & Salmon, P. (1988). *Abnormal psychology* (2nd ed.). Boston: Allyn and Bacon.

Meyer, V. (1957). The treatment of two phobic patients on the basis of learning principles. *Journal of Abnormal and Social Psychology, 55,* 261–266.

Meyer, V. (1966) Modification of expectations in cases with obsessional rituals. *Behaviour Research and Therapy, 4,* 273–280.

Meyer, V., & Gelder, M. G. (1963). Behavior therapy and phobic disorders. *British Journal of Psychiatry, 109,* 19–28.

Meyer, V., & Levy, R. (1973). Modification of behavior in obsessive-compulsive disorders. In H. E. Adams & P. Unikel (Eds.), *Issues and trends in behavior therapy.* Springfield, Il: C. C. Thomas.

Meyer, V., Levy, R., & Schnurer, A. (1974). A behavioral treatment of obsessive-compulsive disorders. In H. R. Beech (Ed.), *Obsessional states.* London: Methuen.

Michie, S. (1998). Consultancy. In A. S. Bellack, & M. Hersen (Eds.), *Comprehensive clinical psychology, Volume 8, Health psychology* (pp. 153–169). New York: Elsevier.

Miklowitz, D. (1994). Family systems. In V. S. Ramachandran (Ed.), *Encyclopedia of human behavior* (Vol. 2; pp. 371–379). San Diego, CA: Academic Press.

Miller, R. D. (1985). Commitment to outpatient treatment: A national survey. *Hospital and Community Psychiatry, 36,* 265–267.

Miller, W. R. (1983). Motivational interviewing with problem drinkers. *Behavioural Psychotherapy, 1,* 147–172.

Miller, W. R. (1985). Motivation for treatment: A review with special emphasis on alcoholism. *Psychological Bulletin, 98,* 84–107.

Miller, W. R., & Marlatt, G. A. (1984). *Manual for Comprehensive Drinker Profile.* Odessa, FL: Psychological Assessment Resources.

Miller, W. R., & Rollnick, S. (1991). *Motivational interviewing: Preparing people to change addictive behavior.* New York: Guilford.

Millet, P. E., & Schwebel, A. I. (1994). Assessment of training received by psychology graduate students in the area of chronic mental illness. *Professional Psychology: Research and Practice, 25,* 76–79.

Millon, T. (1969). *Modern psychological pathology: A biosocial approach to maladaptive learning and functioning.* Philadelphia: Saunders.

Millon, T. (1981). *Disorders of personality, DSM-III: Axis II.* New York: Wiley.

Millon, T. (1983). *Millon Clinical Multiaxial Inventory manual* (3rd ed.). Minneapolis MN: National Computer Systems.

Millon, T. (1991). Classification in psychopathology: Rationale, alternatives, and standards. *Journal of Abnormal Psychology, 100,* 245–261.

Millon, T. (1996). *Personality and psychopathology: Building a clinical science.* New York: Wiley.

Millon, T., & Davis, R. D. (1996). The Millon Clinical Multiaxial Inventory-III (MCMI-III). In C. S. Newmark (Ed.), *Major psychological assessment instruments* (2nd ed.). Boston: Allyn and Bacon.

Millon, T., Davis, R. D., & Millon, C. (1997). *MCMI-III manual* (second edition). Minneapolis MN: National Computer Systems.

Millon, T., Green, C. J., & Meagher, R. B., Jr. (1982). *Millon Behavioral Health Inventory manual* (3rd ed.). Minneapolis MN: National Computer Systems.

Millon, T., Millon C., & Davis, R. D. (1993). *Millon Adolescent Clinical Inventory (MACI) manual.* Minneapolis MN: National Computer Systems.

Millon, T., Weiss, L., Millon, C., & Davis, R. D. (1994). *Millon Index of Personality Styles manual.* San Antonio, TX: Psychological Corporation.

Milner, J. S., & Campbell, J. C. (1995). Prediction issues for practitioners. In J. C. Campbell (Ed.), *Assessing dangerousness: Violence by sexual offenders, batterers, and child abusers* (pp. 20–40). Thousand Oaks, CA: Sage Publications.

Mineka, S. (1985). Animal models of anxiety-based disorders: Their usefulness and limitations. In A. H. Tuma & J. D. Maser (Eds.), *Anxiety and the anxiety disorders* (pp. 199–244). Hillsdale, NJ: Lawrence Erlbaum.

Mineka, S., & Sutton, S. K. (1992). Cognitive biases and the emotional disorders. *Psychological Science, 3,* 65–69.

Miranda v. Arizona, U.S. (1966).

Mischel, W. (1968). *Personality and assessment.* New York: Wiley.

M'Naghten's Case, 8 Eng. Rep. 718 (1843).

Mohr, D. C., Likosky, W., Bertagnolli, A., Goodkin, D. E.,

Van Der Wende, J., Dwyer, P., & Dick, L. P. (2000). Telephone-administered cognitive-behavioral therapy for the treatment of depressive symptoms in multiple sclerosis. *Journal of Consulting and Clinical Psychology, 68,* 356–361.

Monahan, J. (1981). *The clinical prediction of violent behavior.* Washington, DC: Government Printing House.

Monahan, J. (1992). Mental disorders and violent behavior: Perceptions and evidence. *American Psychologist, 47,* 511–521.

Monahan, J. (1993). Limiting therapist exposure to Tarasoff liability: Guidelines for risk containment. *American Psychologist, 48,* 242–250.

Monahan, J., & Steadman, H. J. (1996). Violent storms and violent people: How meteorology can inform risk communication in mental health law. *American Psychologist, 51,* 931–938.

Monsanto Company. (1990). Genetic engineering is beneficial. In W. Dudley (Ed.), *Genetic engineering: Opposing viewpoints* (pp. 17–24). San Diego, CA: Greenhaven Press.

Montgomery, C., Pocock, M., & Titley, K. (2003). Predicting psychological distress in patients with leukemia and lymphoma. *Journal of Psychosomatic Research, 54,* 289–292.

Mood disorders: An overview—Part II. (1998a). *The Harvard Mental Health Letter, 14* (7), 1–5.

Mood disorders: An overview—Part III. (1998b). *The Harvard Mental Health Letter, 14* (8), 1–5.

Moore, R. (1978). Ethics in the practice of psychiatry—Origins, functions, models of enforcement. *American Journal of Psychiatry, 135,* 157–163.

Mora, C. D., & Bornstein, R. A. (1998). Evaluation of cerebrovascular disease. In G. Goldstein, P. D. Nussbaum, & S. R. Beers (Eds.), *Neuropsychology* (pp. 171–186). New York: Plenum.

Moreno, J. L. (1956). The philosophy of the third psychiatric revolution with special emphasis on group psychotherapy and psychodrama. In F. Fromm-Reichman & J. L. Moreno (Eds.), *Progress in psychotherapy* (Vol. 1). New York: Grune and Stratton.

Morgan, C. D., & Murray, H. A. (1935). A method for investigating fantasies. *AMA Archives of Neurology and Psychiatry, 34,* 389–406.

Morris, J. K., Cook, D. G., & Shaper, A. G. (1994). Loss of employment and mortality. *British Medical Journal, 308,* 1135–1139.

Morrison, D. P., & Price, W. H. (1989). The prevalence of psychiatric disorder among female new referrals to a migraine clinic. *Psychological Medicine, 19,* 919–925.

Morrison, J. A. (1993). *The first interview.* New York: Plenum.

Morrison, R. L. (1988). Structured interviews and rating scales. In A. S. Bellack & M. Hersen (Eds.), *Behavioral assessment: A practical handbook* (3rd ed.; pp. 252–277). New York: Pergamon Press.

Morrow-Bradley, G. & Elliott, R. (1986). Utilization of psychotherapy research by practicing psychotherapists. *American Psychologist, 41,* 188–197.

Morrow, G. R., & Hickok, J. T. (1993). Behavioral treatment of chemotherapy-induced nausea and vomiting. *Oncology, 7*(Suppl.), 83–89.

Mosak, H. H. (1995). Adlerian psychotherapy. In R. J. Corsini & D. Wedding (Eds.), *Current psychotherapies* (5th ed.; pp. 51–94). Itasca, IL: F. E. Peacock.

Moses, J. A., Jr., Pritchard, D. A., & Adams, R. L. (1997). Neuropsychological information in the Wechsler Adult Intelligence Scale-Revised. *Archives of Clinical Neuropsychology, 12,* 97–109.

Mosley, D., Thyer, B. A., & Larrison, C. (2001). Development and preliminary validation of the Mosley Forensic Competency Scale. *Journal of Human Behavior in the Social Environment, 4,* 2001.

Mowrer, O. H. (1947). On the dual nature of learning as a reinterpretation of "conditioning" and "problem-solving." *Harvard Educational Review,* 102–148.

Mowrer, O. H. (1960). *Learning theory and behavior.* New York: Wiley.

Mowrer, O. H., & Mowrer W. M. (1938). Enuresis: A method for its study and treatment. *American Journal of Orthopsychiatry, 8,* 436–459.

Moyer, A., (1997). Psychosocial outcomes of breast-conserving surgery versus mastectomy: A meta-analytic review. *Health Psychology, 16,* 284–298.

Mumford, S. J., Patch, I. C. L., Andrew, N., & Wyner, L. (1975). A token economy ward programme with chronic schizophrenic patients. *British Journal of Psychiatry, 126,* 60–72.

Murray, H. (1938). *Explorations in personality.* Fair Lawn, NJ: Oxford University Press.

Murray, H. A. (1943). *Thematic Apperception Test manual.* Cambridge, MA: Harvard University Press.

Myers, I. B., & McCaulley, M. H. (1985). *Manual: A guide to the development and use of the Myers-Briggs Type Indicator.* Palo Alto, CA: Consulting Psychologists' Press.

Naglieri, J. A., & Bardos, A. N. (1997). *GAMA: General Ability Measure for Adults.* Minnetonka, MN: NCS Assessments.

Nagoshi, C. T. (1994). Behavioral genetics. In V. S. Ramachandran (Ed.), *Encyclopedia of human behavior* (Vol. 1; pp. 345–357). San Diego, CA: Academic Press.

Nagy, T. F. (2000). *Ethics in plain English: An illustrative casebook for psychologists.* Washington, DC: American Psychological Association.

Nasr, S. H. (1975). Avicenna. *Encyclopaedia Britannica* (15th ed.) Chicago: Encyclopaedia Britannica.

Nathan, P. E. & Gorman, J. M. (1998a). *A guide to treatments that work.* New York: Oxford University Press.

Nathan, P. E. & Gorman, J. M. (1998b). Preface. In P. E. Nathan & J. M. Gorman (Eds.), *A guide to treatments that work.* New York: Oxford University Press.

National Commission on Testing and Public Policy. (1990). *From gatekeeper to gateway: Transforming testing in America.* Chestnut Hill, MA: Boston College and Author.

National Institute of Mental Health. (1991). *Caring for people with severe mental disorders: A national plan of research to improve services.* DHHS Pub. No. (ADM)91–1762. Washington, DC: Government Printing Office.

National Institute of Mental Health. (1993). *1994 budget estimate.* Washington, DC: Government Printing Office.

National Institute of Mental Health. (1994). *1995 budget estimate.* Washington, DC: Government Printing Office.

National Institute of Mental Health. (1997). www.nimh.nih.gov/hotsci/petscan.htm

National Institute of Mental Health. (1998). *Mental illness in America: The National Institute of Mental Health agenda.* www.nimh.nih.gov (updated 03/18/98).

Nay, W. R. (1977). Analogue measures. In A. R. Ciminero, K. S. Calhoun, & H. E. Adams (Eds.), *Handbook of behavioral assessment.* New York: Wiley.

Neale, J. M., & Oltmanns, T. F. (1980). *Schizophrenia.* New York: John Wiley & Sons.

Neff, C. (1987, April 8). Scorecard. *Sports Illustrated, 28,* 25–26.

Neisser, U., Boodoo, G, Bouchard, T. J., Boykin, W. A. Brody, N. Ceci, S. J., Halpern, D. F., Loehlin, J. C., Perloff, R., Sternberg, R. J., & Urbina, S. (1996). Intelligence: Knowns and unknowns. *American Psychologist, 51,* 77–101.

Nelson, G., & Walsh-Bowers, R. (1994). Psychology and psychiatric survivors. *American Psychologist, 49,* 895–896.

Nelson, R. O. (1983). Behavioral assessment: Past, present, and future. *Behavioral Assessment, 5,* 195–206.

Nelson, R. O., & Barlow, D. H. (1981). Behavioral assessment: Basic strategies and initial procedures. In D. H. Barlow (Ed.), *Behavioral assessment of adult disorders.* New York: Guilford.

Nelson, R. O., & Hayes, S. C. (1979). Some current dimensions of behavioral assessment. *Behavioral Assessment, 1,* 1–16.

Newmark, C. S. (1996). *Major psychological assessment instruments.* Boston: Allyn and Bacon.

Nichols, M. P., & Schwartz, R. C. (1991). *Family therapy: Concepts and methods* (2nd ed.). Boston: Allyn and Bacon.

Nicholson, R. A., Robertson, H. C., Johnson, W. G., & Jensen, G. (1988). A comparison of instruments for assessing competency to stand trial. *Law and Human Behavior, 12,* 313–321.

Norcross, J. (1990). An eclectic definition of psychotherapy. In J. K. Zeig & W. M. Munion (Eds.), *What is psychotherapy?* San Francisco: Jossey-Bass.

Norcross, J. C., Karg, R. S., & Prochaska, J. O. (1997a). Clinical psychologists in the 1990s: Part I. *The Clinical Psychologist, 50*(2), 4–9.

Norcross, J. C., Karg, R. S., & Prochaska, J. O. (1997b). Clinical psychologists in the 1990s: Part II. *The Clinical Psychologist, 50*(3), 41.

Norcross, J. C., & Prochaska, J. O. (1982). A national survey of clinical psychologists: Characteristics and activities. *The Clinical Psychologist 35*(2), 1–8.

Norcross, J. C., Sayette, M. A., & Mayne, T. J. (1998). Selecting a doctoral program in professional psychology: Some comparisons among PhD counseling, PhD clinical, and PsyD clinical psychology programs. *Professional Psychology: Research & Practice, 29,* 609–614.

Novaco, R. W. (1975). *Anger control: The development and evaluation of an experimental treatment.* Lexington, MA: Heath and Co.

Noyes, L. C. (1977). *Modern clinical psychiatry.* Philadelphia: Saunders.

Nussbaum, D., Mamak, M., Tremblay, H., Wright, & Callaghan, J. (1998). The METFORS Fitness Questionnaire (MFQ): A self-report measure for screening competency to stand trial. *American Journal of Forensic Psychology, 16,* 41–66.

Oakland, T. (1985). Review of Slosson Intelligence Test. In J. V. Mitchell (Ed.), *The ninth mental measurement yearbook* (pp. 1401–1403). Lincoln, NE: Buros Institute of Mental Measurements, University of Nebraska.

O'Brien, J. S. (1979). A modified thought stopping procedure for the treatment of agoraphobia. *Journal of Behavior Therapy and Experimental Psychiatry, 10,* 121–124.

O'Brien, W. H., & Haynes, S. N. (1993). Behavioral assessment in the psychiatric setting. In A. S. Bellack & M. Hersen (Eds.), *Handbook of behavior therapy in the psychiatric setting* (pp. 39–71). New York: Plenum.

O'Connor v. Donaldson, 422 U.S. 563 (1975).

O'Farrell, T. J. (1995). Marital and family therapy. In R. K. Hester & W. R. Miller (Eds.), *Handbook of alcoholism treatment approaches* (2nd ed.; pp. 195–220). Boston: Allyn and Bacon.

Ogbu, J. U. (1978). *Minority education and caste: The American system in cross-cultural perspective.* New York: Academic Press.

Ogden, J. (1996). *Health psychology: A textbook.* Philadelphia: Open University Press.

Ogles, B. M., Lunnen, K. M., Bonesteel, K. (2001). Clinical significance: History, application, and current practice. *Clinical Psychology Review, 21,* 421–446.

Ohman, A., Erixon, G., & Lofberg, I. (1975). Phobias and preparedness: Phobic versus neutral pictures as conditioned stimuli for human autonomic responses. *Journal of Abnormal Psychology, 84,* 41–45.

O'Leary, K. D., Heyman, R. E., & Neidig, P. H. (1999). Treatment of wife abuse: A comparison of gender specific and conjoint approaches. *Behavior Therapy, 30,* 475–506.

Olivier, G. (1980). The increase of stature in France. *Journal of Human Evolution, 9,* 645–649.

Orlinsky, D. E., & Howard, K. I., (1986). Process and outcome in psychotherapy. In S. L. Garfield & A. E. Bergin (Eds.), *Handbook of psychotherapy and behavior change* (3rd ed.; pp. 344–347). New York: Wiley.

Osborne, J. G., & Adams, D. L. (1970, April). *Delays in token exchange and presentation in a token economy.* Paper presented at the Western Psychological Association Convention, Los Angeles, CA.

Othmer, E., & Othmer, S. C. (1994). *The clinical interview using DSM-IV.* Washington, DC: American Psychiatric Association.

Otto, R. K., Poythress, N. G., Nicholson, R. A., Edens, J. F., Monahan, J., Bonnie, R. J., Hoge, S. K., & Eisenberg, M. (1998). Psychometric properties of the MacArthur Competence Assessment Tool-Criminal Assessment. *Psychological Assessment, 10,* 435–443.

Ownby, R. L. (1992). *Psychological reports: A guide to report writing in professional psychology* (2nd ed.). Brandon, VT: Clinical Psychology Publishing Co.

Page, R. C., Weiss, J. F., & Lietaer, G. (2002). Humanistic group psychotherapy. In D. J. Cain & J. Seeman (Eds.), *Humanistic psychotherapies: Handbook of research and practice* (pp. 339–368). Washington, DC: American Psychological Association.

Palace, E. M., & Johnston, C. (1989). Treatment of recurrent nightmares by the dream reorganization approach. *Journal of Behavior Therapy and Experimental Psychiatry, 20,* 219–226.

Pankratz, L. (1981). A review of the Munchausen syndrome. *Clinical Psychology Review, 1,* 65–78.

Parker, S. L., Tong, T., Bolden, S., & Wingo, P. P. (1997). Cancer statistics, 1997. *CA-A Cancer Journal for Clinicians, 47,* 5–27.

Parks, C. W., & Hollon, S. D. (1988). Cognitive assessment. In A. S. Bellack & M. Hersen (Eds.), *Behav-*

ioral assessment: A practical handbook (3rd ed.; pp. 161–212). New York: Pergamon.

Parloff, M. B. (1986). Placebo controls in psychotherapy research: A sine qua non or a placebo for research problems? *Journal of Consulting and Clinical Psychology, 54,* 79–87.

Pasewark, R. A., Seidenzahl, D., & Pantle, M. A. (1981). Opinions about the insanity plea. *Journal of Forensic Psychiatry, 8,* 63–72.

Patterson, C. H. (1980). *Theories of counseling and psychotherapy* (3rd ed.). New York: Harper & Row.

Paul, G. L. (1966). *Insight versus desensitization in psychotherapy: An experiment in anxiety reduction.* Stanford: Stanford University Press.

Paul, G. L. (1967a). Insight versus desensitization in psychotherapy two years after termination. *Journal of Consulting Psychology, 31,* 333–348.

Paul, G. L. (1967b). Outcome research in psychotherapy. *Journal of Consulting Psychology, 31,* 109–118.

Paul, G. L., & Lentz, R. J. (1977). *Psychosocial treatment of chronic mental patients: Milieu versus social learning programs.* Cambridge, MA: Harvard University Press.

Paul, G. L., Stuve, P., & Cross, J. V. (1997). Real-world inpatient programs: Shedding some light—A critique. *Applied & Preventive Psychology, 6,* 193–204.

Pavlov, I. P. (1927). *Conditioned reflexes: An investigation of the physiological activity of the cerebral cortex* (G. V. Anrep, Trans.). London: Oxford University Press.

Payne, P. V., & Halford, W. K. (1990). Social skills training with chronic schizophrenic patients living in community settings. *Behavioural Psychotherapy, 18,* 49–64.

Pearce, S., & McDonald, A. L. (1998). Chronic pain. In A. S. Bellack, & M. Hersen (Eds.), *Comprehensive clinical psychology, Volume 8, Health psychology* (pp. 557–574). New York: Elsevier.

Pedersen, P. B., & Ivey, A. (1993). *Culture-centered counseling and interviewing skills: A practical guide.* Westport, CT: Praeger.

Perry v. Louisiana, 111 S.Ct. 449 (1990).

Persons, J. B. (1991). Psychotherapy outcome studies do not accurately represent current models of psychotherapy: A proposed remedy. *American Psychologist, 46,* 99–106.

Persons, J. B. (1994). Cognitive behavior therapy. In V. S. Ramachandran (Ed.), *Encyclopedia of human behavior* (Vol. 1; pp. 617–626). San Diego, CA: Academic Press.

Persons, J. B. (1995). Why practicing psychologists are slow to adopt empirically validated treatments. In S. C. Hayes, V. M. Follette, R. M. Dawes, & K. E. Grady (Eds.), *Scientific standards of psychological*

practice: Issues and recommendations. Reno, NV: Context Press.

Persons, J. B., & Silberschatz, G. (1998). Are results of randomized controlled trials useful to psychotherapists? *Journal of Consulting and Clinical Psychology, 66,* 126–135.

Peterson, C. (1994). Book review: *The eleventh mental measurements yearbook. Journal of Personality Assessment, 63,* 394–397.

Peterson, C. (1994). Learned helplessness. In V. S. Ramachandran (Ed.), *Encyclopedia of human behavior* (Vol. 3; pp. 57–66). San Diego, CA: Academic Press.

Peterson, C. (1995). Explanatory style and health. In G. M. Buchanan & M. E. P. Seligman (Eds.), *Explanatory style* (pp. 233–252). Hillsdale, NJ: Erlbaum.

Peterson, C. (1996). Common problem areas and their causes resulting in disciplinary actions. In L. Bass & Associates (Eds.), *Professional conduct and discipline in psychology* (Chapter 5; pp. 71–89). Washington, DC: American Psychological Association & Montgomery, AL: Association of State and Provincial Psychology Boards.

Peterson, D. R. (1968). The Doctor of Psychology program at the University of Illinois. *American Psychologist, 23,* 511–516.

Peterson, R. L., Peterson, D. R., Abrams, J. C., & Stricker, G. (1997). The National Council of Schools and Programs of Professional Psychology educational model. *Professional Psychology: Research and Practice, 28,* 373–386.

Petrila, J. (1982). The insanity defense and other mental health dispositions in Missouri. *International Journal of Psychiatry, 5,* 81–101.

Phares, E. J. (1988). *Clinical psychology: Concepts, methods, and profession* (3rd ed.). Chicago: Dorsey.

Phelps, R. (1996). Preliminary practitioner survey results enhance APA's understanding of the health care environment. *Practitioner Focus, 9,* 5.

Phillips, L. (1953). Case history data and prognosis in schizophrenia. *Journal of Nervous and Mental Disease, 6,* 515–525.

Piaget, G. W., & Lazarus, A. A. (1969). The use of rehearsal-desensitization. *Psychotherapy: Theory, Research, and Practice, 6,* 264–266.

Piaget, J. (1980). The psychogenesis of knowledge and its epistemological significance. In M. Piattelli-Palmarini (Ed.), *Language and learning: The debate between Jean Piaget and Noam Chomsky.* Cambridge, MA: Harvard University Press.

Pierce, W. D., & Epling, W. F. (1995). *Behavior analysis and learning.* Englewood Cliffs, NJ: Prentice Hall.

Pilkonis, P. A., Imber, S. D., & Rubinky, P. (1984). Influence of life events on outcome in psychotherapy.

Journal of Nervous and Mental Diseases, 172, 468–474.

Pinel, P. (1806/1962). *A treatise on insanity.* New York: Hanfer Publishing Co.

Piotrowski, C., & Keller, J. W. (1989). Psychological testing in outpatient mental health facilities: A national study. *Professional Psychology: Research and Practice, 20,* 423–425.

Piotrowski, C., & Keller, J. W. (1996). Research on clinical experience: What doctoral students need to know. *Journal of Instructional Psychology, 23,* 126–127.

Piotrowski, C., & Lubin, B. (1990). Assessment practices of health psychologists: Survey of APA Division 38 clinicians. *Professional Psychology: Research and Practice, 21,* 99–106.

Piotrowski, C., Sherry, D., & Keller, J. W. (1985). Psychodiagnostic test usage: A survey of the Society for Personality Assessment. *Journal of Personality Assessment, 44,* 115–119.

Piotrowski, C., & Zalewski, C. (1993). Training in psychodiagnostic testing in APA-approved Psy.D. and Ph.D. clinical psychology programs. *Journal of Personality Assessment, 49,* 394–405.

Pipal, J. E. (1995). Managed care: Is it the corpse in the living room? An expose. *Psychotherapy, 32,* 323–332.

Pipes, R. B., & Davenport, D. S. (1999). *Introduction to psychotherapy: Common clinical wisdom.* Boston: Allyn and Bacon.

Plath, S. (1981). *The bell jar.* New York: Bantam Books. (Original work published in 1963.)

Plomin, R. (1997). Identifying genes for cognitive abilities and disabilities. In R. J. Sternberg & E. L. Grigorenko (Eds.), *Intelligence, heredity, and environment.* New York: Cambridge University Press.

Pope, K. S., & Vasquez, M. J. T. (1998). *Ethics in psychotherapy and counseling: A practical guide* (2nd ed.). San Francisco: Jossey-Bass.

Pope, K. S., & Vetter, V. A. (1992). Ethical dilemmas encountered by members of the American Psychological Association. *American Psychologist, 47,* 397–411.

Popp, C. A., Diguer, L., Luborsky, L., Faude, J., Johnson, S., Morris, M., Schaffer, N., Schaffler, P., & Schmidt, K. (1996). Repetitive relationship themes in waking narratives and dreams. *Journal of Consulting and Clinical Psychology, 64,* 1073–1078.

Porter, R. (1987). *A social history of madness: The world through the eyes of the insane.* New York: E. P. Dutton.

Porter, R. (Ed.). (1991). *The Faber book of madness.* London: Faber and Faber.

Poythress, N. G. (1980). Coping on the witness stand: Learned responses to "learned treatises." *Professional Psychology, 11,* 139–149.

Preskorn, S. H. (1995). Mental disorders are medical diseases. In W. Barbour (Ed.), *Mental illness: Opposing viewpoints* (pp. 29–36). San Diego, CA: Greenhaven Press.

Prochaska, J. O., & Norcross, J. C. (1999). *Systems of psychotherapy: A transtheoretical analysis* (4th ed.). Pacific Grove, CA: Brooks/Cole.

Prochaska, J. O., & Norcross, J. C. (2003). *Systems of psychotherapy: A transtheoretical analysis* (5th ed.). Pacific Grove, CA: Wadworth.

Prout, H. (1983). School psychologists and social-emotional assessment techniques: Patterns in training and use. *School Psychology Review, 12,* 35–38.

Psychological Corporation. (1999). *Wechsler Abbreviated Scale of Intelligence manual.* San Antonio, TX: Harcourt-Brace.

Putnam, S. H. (1989). The TCN salary survey: A salary survey of neuropsychologists. *The Clinical Neuropsychologist, 3,* 97–115.

Putnam, S. H., & DeLuca, J. W. (1990). The TCN professional practice survey: Part I: General practices of neuropsychologists in primary employment and private practice settings. *The Clinical Neuropsychologist, 4,* 199–243.

Quay, H. C. (1986). Classification. In H. C. Quay & J. S. Werry (Eds.), *Psychopathological disorders of childhood* (3rd ed.; pp. 1–34). New York: Wiley.

Rabin, A. I., & Hurley, J. R. (1964). Projective techniques. *Progress in Clinical Psychology, 6.*

Rachman, S. (1971). Obsessional ruminations. *Behavior Research and Therapy, 9,* 229–235.

Rachman, S. (1976). The modification of obsessions: A new formulation. *Behavior Research and Therapy, 14,* 437–443.

Rachman, S. J. (1977). The conditioning theory of fear-acquisition: A critical examination. *Behavior Research and Therapy, 15,* 375–387.

Rachman, S. J. (1978). An anatomy of obsessions. *Behavioural Analysis and Modification, 2,* 253–278.

Rachman, S. J., & Hodgson, R. I. (1974). Synchrony and desynchrony in fear and avoidance. *Behavior Research and Therapy, 12,* 311–318.

Rachman, S. J., & Hodgson, R. J. (1980). *Obsessions and compulsions.* Englewood Cliffs, NJ: Prentice-Hall.

Rachman, S. J., & Wilson, G. T. (1980). *The effects of psychological therapy* (2nd ed.). Oxford: Pergamon.

Rahman, F. (1952). *Avicenna's psychology: An English translation of Kitab al-Najat, Book II, Chapter VI with historico-philosophical notes and textual improvements on the Cairo edition.* London: Oxford University Press.

Raimy, V. C. (Ed.). (1950). *Training in clinical psychology.* New York: Prentice Hall.

Ramirez, M. (1991). *Psychotherapy and counseling with*

minorities: A cognitive approach to individual and cultural differences. New York: Pergamon Press.

Ramirez, S. Z., Wassef, A., Paniagua, F. A., & Linskey, A. O. (1996). Mental health providers' perceptions of cultural variables in evaluating ethnically diverse clients. *Professional Psychology: Research and Practice, 27,* 284–288.

Ramm, E., Marks, I. M., Yuksel, S., & Stern, R. S. (1981). Anxiety management training for anxiety states: Positive compared with negative self-statements. *British Journal of Psychiatry, 140,* 367–373.

Ramsay, M. C., Reynolds, C. R., & Kamphaus, R. W. (2002). *Essentials of behavioral assessment.* New York: Wiley.

Randolph, J. J., Hicks, T., & Masoi, D. (1981). The competency screening test: A replication and extension. *Criminal Justice and Behavior, 8,* 471–482.

Range, L. M., Menyhert, A., Walsh, M., Hardin, K. N., Ellis, J. B., & Craddick, R. (1991). Letters of recommendation: Perspectives, recommendations, and ethics. *Professional Psychology: Research and Practice, 22,* 389–392.

Rapaport, D., Gill, M. M., & Schafer, R. (1945). *Diagnostic psychological testing* (Vol. 1). Chicago: Yearbook.

Rapaport, D., Gill, M. M., & Schafer, R. (1946). *Diagnostic psychological testing* (Vol. 2). Chicago: Yearbook.

Rapee, R. M., & Barlow, D. H. (1991). The cognitive-behavioral treatment of panic attacks and agoraphobic avoidance. In J. R. Walker, G. R. Norton, & C. A. Ross (Eds.), *Panic disorder and agoraphobia: A comprehensive guide for the practitioner* (pp. 252–305). Pacific Grove, CA: Brooks/Cole.

Raskin, N. J. (1994). *Client-centered therapy* (videotape). Washington, DC: American Psychological Association.

Raskin, N. J., & Rogers, C. R. (1989). Person-centered therapy. In Corsini, R. J., & Wedding, D. (Eds.), *Current psychotherapies* (4th ed.; pp. 155–194). Itasca, IL: F. E. Peacock.

Raskin, N. J., & Rogers, C. R. (1995). Person-centered therapy. In J. J. Corsini & D. Wedding (Eds.), *Current psychotherapies* (5th ed.; Chapter 5; pp. 128–161). Itasca, IL: F. E. Peacock.

Rasmussen, B. K., Jensen, R., Schroll, M, & Olesen, J. (1991). Epidemiology of headache in a general population: A prevalence study. *Journal of Clinical Epidemiology, 44,* 1147–1157.

Raue, P. J., Goldfried, M. R., & Barkham, M. (1997). The therapeutic alliance in psychodynamic-interpersonal and cognitive-behavioral therapy. *Journal of Consulting and Clinical Psychology, 65,* 582–587.

Reamer, F. G. (1993). *The philosophical foundations of social work.* New York: Columbia University Press.

Rehm, L. P. (1997). Continuing education for empirically supported treatments. *Clinical Psychologist, 50,* 2–3.

Reisman, J. M., (1991). *A history of clinical psychology* (2nd ed.). New York: Hemisphere Publishing Corporation.

Reiss, S. (1980). Pavlovian conditioning and human fear: An expectancy model. *Behavior Therapy, 11,* 380–396.

Reitan, R. M. (1955). Certain differential effects of left and right cerebral lesions in human adults. *Journal of Comparative and Physiological Psychology, 48,* 474–477.

Reitan, R. M., & Wolfson, D. (1985). *The Halstead-Reitan Neuropsychological Test Battery: Theory and clinical interpretation.* Tucson, AZ: Neuropsychology Press.

Report of Committee on Clinical Section of American Psychological Association. (1935). *Psychological Clinic, 23,* 1–140.

Repp, A. C., & Horner, R. H. (1999). *Functional analysis of problem behavior: From effective assessment to effective support.* Belmont, CA: Wadsworth.

Rescorla, R. A. (1988). Pavlovian conditioning: It's not what you think it is. *American Psychologist, 43,* 151–160.

Rescorla, R. A., & Solomon, R. L. (1967). Two-process learning theory: Relationships between Pavlovian conditioning and instrumental learning. *Psychological Review, 74,* 151–182.

Resick, P. A., Jordan, C. G., Girelli, S. A., Hutter, C. K., & Marhoefer-Dvorak, S. (1988). A comparative outcome study of behavioral group therapy for sexual assault victims. *Behavior Therapy, 19,* 385–401.

Resnick, J. H. (1991). Finally, a definition of clinical psychology: A message from the president, Division 12. *Clinical Psychologist, 44,* 3–11.

Resnick, R. J. (1997). A brief history of practice—expanded. *American Psychologist, 52,* 463–468.

Restak, R. M. (1984). *The brain.* Toronto: Bantam Books.

Retzlaff, P. (1992). *Tactical psychotherapy of the personality disorders: An MCMI-III-based approach.* Boston: Allyn and Bacon.

Retzlaff, P. D. (1996). *Tactical psychotherapy of the personality disorders: An MCMI-III-based approach.* Boston: Allyn and Bacon.

Rey, A. (1959). Sollicitation de la mémoire de fixation par des mots et des objets presentes simultanement. *Archives de Psychologie, 37,* 126–139.

Reynolds, C. R., & Brown, R. T. (1984) Bias in mental testing: An introduction to the issue. In C. R. Reynolds & R. T. Brown (Eds.), *Perspectives on bias in mental testing* (pp. 1–39). New York: Plenum Press.

Reynolds, W. M. (1985). Review of Slosson Intelligence Test. In J. V. Mitchell (Ed.), *The ninth mental measurement yearbook* (pp. 1403–1404). Lincoln, NE: Buros Institute of Mental Measurements, University of Nebraska.

Rhodes, J. E. (1998). Family, friends, and community: The role of social support in promoting health. In P. M. Camic & S. J. Knight (Eds.), *Clinical handbook of health psychology: A practical guide to effective interventions*. Kirkland, WA: Hogrefe & Hogrefe.

Rice, C. E. (1997). Scenarios: The scientist-practitioner split and the future of psychology. *American Psychologist, 52,* 1173–1181.

Richie, N. D. (1992). *Innovation and change in the human services*. Springfield, IL: Thomas.

Robiner, W. N. (1991). How many psychologists are needed? A call for national psychology human resource agenda. *Professional Psychology: Research and Practice, 22,* 427–440.

Robins, L. N., Heltzer, J. E., Croughan, J., & Ratcliff, K. S. (1981). National Institute of Mental Health diagnostic interview schedule: Its history, characteristics, and validity. *Archives of General Psychiatry, 38,* 381–389.

Robinson, L. A., Berman, J. S., & Neimeyer, R. A. (1990). Psychotherapy for the treatment of depression: A comprehensive review of controlled outcome research. *Psychological Bulletin, 108,* 30–49.

Roesch, R. & Golding, S. L. (1987). Defining and assessing competency to stand trial. In I. B. Weiner & A. K. Hess (Eds.), *Handbook of forensic psychology* (pp. 378–394). New York: John Wiley & Sons.

Roesch, R., Ogloff, J. R. P., & Golding, S. L. (1993). Competency to stand trial: Legal and clinical issues. *Applied & Preventative Psychology, 2,* 43–51.

Rogers, C. R. (1940, December). *Some newer concepts in psychotherapy*. Presentation to Psi Chi, University of Minnesota.

Rogers, C. R. (1942). *Counseling and psychotherapy: Newer concepts in practice*. Boston: Houghton-Mifflin.

Rogers, C. R. (1957). The necessary and sufficient conditions of therapeutic personality change. *Journal of consulting Psychology, 21,* 95–103.

Rogers, C. (1959). A theory of therapy, personality, and interpersonal relationships, as developed in a client-centered framework. In S. Koch (Ed.), *Psychology: A study of a science, Vol. III, Formulations of the person and the social context* (pp. 184–256). New York: McGraw-Hill.

Rogers, C. R. (1961). *On becoming a person: A therapist's view of psychotherapy*. Boston: Houghton-Mifflin.

Rogers, C. R. (1976). Carl Rogers on encounter groups (excerpt). In J. Ehrenwald (Ed.), *The history of psychotherapy: From healing magic to encounter* (pp. 542–554). New York: Jason Aronson. (Original work published in 1970.)

Rogers, R. (1995). *Diagnostic and structure interviewing: A handbook for psychologists*. Odessa, FL: Psychological Assessment Resources.

Rogers, R., Dolmetsch, R., & Cavanaugh, J. L. (1981). An empirical approach to insanity evaluations. *Journal of Clinical Psychology, 37,* 683–687.

Rogers, R., & Ewing, C. P. (1992). The measurement of insanity: Debating the merits of the R-CRAS and its alternatives. *International Journal of Law and Psychiatry, 15,* 113–123.

Rollnick, S., & Bell, A. (1991). Brief motivational interviewing for use by the nonspecialist. In W. R. Miller & S. Rollnick (Eds.), *Motivational interviewing: Preparing people to change addictive behavior* (pp. 203–213). New York: Guilford.

Romanczyk, R. G., Kent, R. N., Diament, C., & O'Leary, K. D. (1973). Measuring the reliability of observational data: A reactive process. *Journal of Applied Behavior Analysis, 6,* 175–184.

Rose, S. D. (1977). *Group therapy: A behavioral approach*. Englewood Cliffs, NJ: Prentice-Hall.

Rosenbaum, M., & Muroff, M. (Eds.). (1984). *Anna O.: Fourteen contemporary perspectives*. New York: The Free Press.

Rosenbaum, M., & Patterson, K. M. (1995). Group therapy in historical perspective. In B. Bongar & L. E. Beutler (Eds.), *Comprehensive textbook of psychotherapy: Theory and practice* (Chapter 10; pp. 173–188). New York: Oxford University Press.

Rosenhan, D. (1973). On being sane in insane places. *Science, 179,* 250–258.

Rosenthal, D. (1975). Discussion: The concept of schizophrenic disorders. In R. R. Fieve, D. Rosenthal & H. Brill (Eds.), *Genetic research in psychiatry* (pp. 199–208). Baltimore: Johns Hopkins University Press.

Rosenthal, D., Wender, P. H., Kety, S. S., Schulsinger, F., Welner, J., & Ostergaard, L. (1968). Schizophrenics' offspring reared in adoptive homes. In D. Rosenthal & S. S. Kety (Eds.), *The transmission of schizophrenia* (pp. 377–391). Oxford: Pergamon.

Rosenzweig, S. (1936). Some implicit common factors in diverse methods of psychotherapy. *American Journal of Orthopsychiatry, 6,* 412–415.

Rosewater, L. B., & Walker, L. E. A. (Eds.) (1985). *Handbook of feminist therapy: Women's issues in psychotherapy*. New York: Springer Publishing Company.

Roston, R. A., & Sherrer, S. W. (1973). Malpractice: What's new? *Professional Psychology: Research and Practice, 4,* 270–276.

Rothbaum, B. O., & Foa, E. B. (1992a). Cognitive-behavioral treatment of posttraumatic stress disorder. In P. A. Saigh (Ed.), *Posttraumatic stress disorder: A behavioral approach to assessment and treatment* (pp. 85–110). New York: Macmillan.

Rothbaum, B. O., & Foa, E. B. (1992b). Exposure therapy for rape victims with post-traumatic stress disorder. *Behavior Therapist, 9,* 219–222.

Rothbaum, B. O., Hodges, L. F., Kooper, R., Opdyke, D., Williford, J. S., & North, M. (1995). Virtual reality graded exposure in the treatment of acrophobia: A case report. *Behavior Therapy, 26,* 547–554.

Rourke, B. P., & Gates, R. D. (1981). Neuropsychological research and school psychology. In G. W. Hynd & J. E. Obrzut (Eds.), *Neuropsychological assessment and the school-age child.* New York: Grune & Stratton.

Routh, D. K. (1994). *Clinical psychology since 1917: Science, practice and organization.* New York: Plenum.

Routh, D. K. (1998). Hippocrates meets Democritus: A history of psychiatry and clinical psychology. In A. S. Bellack & M. Hersen (Eds.), *Comprehensive clinical psychology* (pp. 1–48). New York: Elsevier.

Rowntree, L. G. (1943). Causes of rejection and the incidence of defects among 18 and 19 year old selective service registrants. *Journal of the American Medical Association, 123,* 181–185.

Rush, A. J., Beck, A. T., Kovacs, M., & Hollon, S. (1977). Comparative efficacy of cognitive therapy and pharmacotherapy in the treatment of depressed outpatients. *Cognitive Therapy and Research, 1,* 17–37.

Rushton, J. P. (1995). *Race, evolution, and behavior.* New Brunswick, NJ: Transaction.

Rushton, J. P. (1997). Race, IQ, and the APA report on *The bell curve. American Psychologist, 52,* 69–70.

Ruth-Roemer, S., Kurpins, S. R., & Carmin, C. (Eds.). (1998). *The emerging role of counseling psychology in health care.* New York: Norton.

Ryckman, R. M. (1989). *Theories of personality* (4th ed.). Pacific Grove, CA: Brooks/Cole.

Ryckman, R. M. (2000). *Theories of personality* (7th ed.). Belmont, CA: Wadsworth.

Sacks, O. (1970). *The man who mistook his wife for a hat and other clinical tales.* New York: Harper & Row.

Sage, N. (1973, January). Psychology and the Angela Davis jury. *Human Behavior,* 58–61.

Salekin, R. T., Rogers, R., & Sewell, K. W. (1996). A review and meta-analysis of the Psychopathy Checklist and Psychopathy Checklist-Revised: Predictive validity of dangerousness. *Clinical Psychology: Science and Practice, 3,* 203–215.

Salkovskis, P. M. (1983). Treatment of an obsessional patient using habituation to audiotaped ruminations. *British Journal of Clinical Psychology, 22,* 311–313.

Salkovskis, P. M. (1985). Obsessional-compulsive problems: A cognitive-behavioural analysis. *Behavior Research and Therapy, 23,* 571–583.

Salkovskis, P. M., Richards, H. C., & Forrester, E. (1995). The relationship between obsessional problems and intrusive thoughts. *Behavioural and Cognitive Psychotherapy, 23,* 281–299.

Sallis, J. F., Nader, P. R., Broyles, S. L., Berry, C. C., Elder, J. P., McKenzie, R. L., & Nelson, J. A. (1993). Correlates of physical activity at home in Mexican-American and Anglo-American preschool children. *Health Psychology, 12,* 390–398.

Samuel, S. E., & Gorton, G. E. (1998). National survey of psychology internship directors regarding education for prevention of psychologist-patient sexual exploitation. *Professional Psychology: Research and Practice, 29,* 86–90.

Sanders, M. R., & Dadds, M. R. (1993). *Behavioral family intervention.* Boston: Allyn and Bacon.

Sanderson, W. C., DiNardo, P. A., Rapee, R. M., & Barlow, D. H. (1990). Syndrome comorbidity in patients with DSM-III-R anxiety disorders. *Journal of Abnormal Psychology, 99,* 308–312.

Sanford, N. (1953). Clinical method: Psychotherapy. *Annual Review of Psychology, 4,* 316–242.

Sapolsky, R. (1995). Broad definitions of mental illness are beneficial. In W. Barbour (Ed.), *Mental illness: Opposing viewpoints* (pp. 17–23). San Diego, CA: Greenhaven Press.

Sarafino, E. P. (1994). *Health psychology: Biopsychosocial interactions* (2nd ed.). New York: Wiley.

Sarbin, T. R. (1986). Prediction and clinical inference: Forty years later. *Journal of Personality Assessment, 50,* 362–369.

Sarbin, T. R. (1990). Toward the obsolescence of the schizophrenia hypothesis. In D. Cohen (Ed.), Special issue: Challenging the therapeutic state: Critical perspectives on psychiatry and the mental health system. *The Journal of Mind and Behavior, 11,* (3 and 4), 259–284 (13–38).

Sarbin, T. R. (1997). On the futility of psychiatric diagnostic manuals (DSMs) and the return of personal agency. *Applied & Preventative Psychology, 6,* 233–243.

Sarbin, T. R., & Mancuso, J. C. (1980). *Schizophrenia: Medical diagnosis or moral verdict?* New York: Pergamon.

Sarwer, D. B., & Sayers, S. L. (1998). Behavioral interviewing. In A. S. Bellack & M. Hersen (Eds.), *Behavioral assessment: A practical handbook* (4th ed.; pp. 63–78). Boston: Allyn and Bacon.

Sattler, J. M. (1988). *Assessment of children* (3rd ed.). San Diego, CA: Author.

Sawyer, J. (1966). Measurement and prediction, clinical and statistical. *Psychological Bulletin, 66,* 178–200.

Sayette, M. A., & Mayne, T. J. (1990). Survey of clinical and research trends in clinical psychology. *American Psychologist, 45,* 1263–1266.

Scarr, S., & Weinberg, R. A. (1976). IQ test performance of Black children adopted by White families. *American Psychologist, 31,* 726–739.

Scarr, S., & Weinberg, R. A. (1978a). Attitudes, interests, and IQ. *Human Nature, 1,* 29–36.

Scarr, S., & Weinberg, R. A. (1978b) The influence of "family background" on intellectual attainment. *American Sociological Review, 43,* 674–692.

Schaefer, H. H., & Martin, P. L. (1969). *Behavioral therapy.* New York: McGraw-Hill.

Schizophrenia update—Part II. (1995). *The Harvard Mental Health Letter, 11* (12), 1–5.

Schag, C. A., & Heinrich, R. L. (1989). Anxiety in medical situations: Adult cancer patients. *Journal of Clinical Psychology, 45,* 20–27.

Schaie, K. W. (1994). The course of adult intellectual development. *American Psychologist, 49,* 304–313.

Schmidt, B. G. (1946). Changes in personal, social, and intellectual behavior in children originally classified as feebleminded. *Psychological Monographs, 60*(5).

Schnurr, P. P., Ford, J. D., Friedman, M. J., Green, B. L., Dain, B. J., & Sengupta, A. (2000). Predictors and outcomes of posttraumatic stress disorder in world war II veterans exposed to mustard gas. *Journal of Consulting and Clinical Psychology, 68,* 258–268.

Schofield, W. (1964). *Psychotherapy: The purchase of friendship.* Englewood Cliffs, NJ: Prentice Hall.

Schwartz, G. E. (1982). Testing the biopsychosocial model: The ultimate challenge facing behavioral medicine? *Journal of Consulting and Clinical Psychology, 5,* 1040–1053.

Schwartz, J. D. (1978). Review of the TAT. In O. K. Buros (Ed.), *The eighth mental measurements handbook* (pp. 1127–1130). Highland Park, NJ: Gryphon Press.

Scott, A. (1993). Consumers/survivors reform the system, bringing a "human face" to research. *Resources: Workforce Issues in Mental Health Systems, 5,* 3–6.

Sechrest, L., Stickle, T. R., & Stewart, M. (1998). The role of assessment in clinical psychology. In C. R. Reynolds (Ed.), Assessment. Vol. 4 in A. S. Bellack & M. Hersen (Eds.), *Comprehensive clinical psychology.* New York: Elsevier.

Searles, J. S. (1985). A methodological and empirical critique of psychotherapy outcome metaanlysis. *Behaviour Research and Therapy, 23,* 453–463.

Seidler-Feller, D. (1985). A feminist critique of sex therapy. In L. B. Rosewater & L. E. A. Walker (Eds.), *Handbook of feminist therapy: Women's issues in psychotherapy* (pp. 119–129). New York: Springer Publishing Company.

Seligman, M. E. P. (1971). Phobias and preparedness. *Behavior Therapy, 2,* 307–320.

Seligman, M. E. P. (1994). *What you can change and what you can't: The complete guide to successful self-improvement.* New York: Knopf.

Seligman, M. E. P. (1995). The effectiveness of psychotherapy: The *Consumer Reports* study. *American Psychologist, 50,* 965–974.

Seligman, M. E. P. (1996). Good news for psychotherapy: The *Consumer Reports* study. *The Independent Practitioner, 16,* 17–20.

Seligman, M. E. P. (1996). Science as an ally of practice. *American Psychologist, 51,* 1072–1079.

Seligman, M. E. P. (1998). President's column: Is depression biochemical? *American Psychological Association Monitor, 29* (9), 2.

Senger, H. L. (1987). The "placebo" effect of psychotherapy: A moose in the rabbit stew. *American Journal of Psychotherapy, 41,* 68–81.

Sexton, M. M. (1979). Behavioral epidemiology. In O. F. Pomerleau & J. P. Brady (Eds.), *Behavioral medicine: Theory and practice* (pp. 3–22). Baltimore, MD: Williams & Winkins.

Shaffer, J. B. P., & Galinsky, M. D. (1974). *Models of group therapy and sensitivity training.* Englewood Cliffs, NJ: Prentice-Hall.

Shah, S. (1978). Dangerousness: A paradigm for exploring some issues in law and psychology. *American Psychologist, 33,* 224–238.

Shakow, D., & Rapaport, D. (1964). *The influence of Freud on American psychology.* New York: International University Press.

Shapiro, A. E., & Wiggins, J. G. (1994). A PsyD degree for every practitioner: Truth in labeling. *American Psychologist, 49,* 207–210.

Shapiro, A. P., Schwartz, G. E., Ferguson, D. C. E., Redmond, D. P., & Weiss, S. M. (1977). Behavioral methods in the treatment of hypertension: A review of clinical status. *Annals of Internal Medicine, 86,* 626–636.

Shapiro, D. E., & Schulman, C. E. (1996). Ethical and legal issues in e-mail therapy. *Ethics and Behavior, 6,* 107–124.

Shapiro, D. L. (1991). Informed consent in forensic evaluations. *Psychotherapy in Private Practice, 9,* 145–154.

Shapiro, F. (1989). Eye movement desensitization: A new treatment for post-traumatic stress disorder. *Journal of Behavior Therapy and Experimental Psychiatry, 20,* 211–217.

Shapiro, F. (1991a). Eye movement desensitization and reprocessing procedure: From EMD to EMD/R—A new treatment model for anxiety and related traumata. *The Behavior Therapist, 14,* 133–135, & 128.

Shapiro, F. (1991b). Eye movement desensitization and reprocessing: A cautionary note. *The Behavior Therapist, 14,* 188.

Shapiro, F. (1995). *Eye movement desensitization and reprocessing: Basic principles, protocols, and procedures.* New York: Guilford.

Shapiro, M. B. (1966). The single case in clinical-psychological research. *Journal of General Psychology, 74,* 3–22.

Shaw, S. R., Swerdlik, M. E., & Laurent, J. (1993). Review of the WISC-III. *Journal of Psychoeducational Assessment* (Monograph Series: Advances in Psychoeducational Assessment). Germantown, TN: Psychoeducational Corporation.

Shea, S. C. (1988). *Psychiatric interviewing: The art of understanding.* Philadelphia: W. B. Saunders.

Shedler, J., Mayman, M., & Manis, M. (1993). The *illusion* of mental health. *American Psychologist, 48,* 1117–1131.

Sherry, P. (1991). Ethical issues in the conduct of supervision. *Counseling Psychologist, 19,* 566–584.

Shipley, W. C. (1940). A self-administering scale for measuring intellectual impairment and deterioration. *Journal of Psychology, 9,* 371–377.

Shlien, J. M. (1992). Theory as autobiography: The man and the movement [Review of H. Kirschenbaum & V. Henderson (Eds.). (1989), *The Carl Rogers reader*]. *Contemporary Psychology, 37,* 1082–1084.

Shontz, F., & Green, P. (1992). Trends in research on the Rorschach: Review and recommendations. *Applied and Preventative Psychology, 1,* 149–156.

Siassi, I. (1984). Psychiatric interview and mental status examination. In G. Goldstein & M. Hersen (Eds.), *Handbook of psychological assessment* (pp. 259–275). New York: Pergamon.

Siegel, J. M., & Spivack, G. (1976). Problem-solving therapy: The description of a new program for chronic psychiatric patients. *Psychotherapy: Theory, Research, and Practice, 13,*

Sigmon, S. T. (1995). Ethical practices and beliefs of psychopathology researchers. *Ethics & Behavior, 5,* 295–309.

Silva, P. de, Rachman, S., & Seligman, M. (1977). Prepared phobias and obsessions: Therapeutic outcome. *Behavior Research and Therapy, 15,* 65–78.

Silverman-Dresner, T. R. (1989). *Updating the core psychology course: Integrating gender into the curriculum.* New York: Peter Lang.

Silverstein, A. B. (1985). Two- and four-subtest short forms of the WAIS-R: A closer look at validity and reliability. *Journal of Consulting and Clinical Psychology, 52,* 95–97.

Simkin, L. R., & Gross, A. M. (1994). Assessment of coping with high-risk situations for exercise relapse among healthy women. *Health Psychology, 13,* 274–277.

Singer, M. T., & Nievod, A. (1987). Consulting and testifying in court. In I. B. Weiner & A. K. Hess (Eds.), *Handbook of forensic psychology* (pp. 529–554). New York: John Wiley & Sons.

Sinnott, J. D. (1994). Sex roles. In V. S. Ramachandran (Ed.), *Encyclopedia of human behavior* (Vol. 4, pp. 151–158). San Diego, CA: Academic Press.

Skeels, H. M., & Dye, H. N. (1939). A study of the effects of differential stimulation on mentally retarded children. *Proceedings and Addresses of the American Association on Mental Deficiency, 44,* 114–136.

Skinner, B. F. (1953). *Science and human behavior* (pp. 227–241). New York: Free Press.

Skinner, B. F. (1961). *Cumulative record* (enlarged edition). New York: Appleton-Century-Crofts.

Skinner, B. F. (1966). Operant behavior. In W. K. Honig (Ed.), *Operant behavior: Areas of research and application.* New York: Appleton-Century-Crofts.

Sleek, S. (1996, April). Ensuring accuracy in clinical decisions. *The APA Monitor, 26,* 30.

Sloane, B., Staples, F. R., Cristol, A. H., Yorkston, N. J., & Whipple, K. (1975). Short-term analytically oriented psychotherapy versus behavior therapy. *American Journal of Psychiatry, 132,* 373–377.

Slosson, R. L. (1982). *Slosson Intelligence Test* (2nd ed.). East Aurora, NY: Slosson Educational Publications.

Smith, C. P., & Graham, J. R. (1981). Behavioral correlates for the MMPI standard F scale and the modified F scale for black and white psychiatric patients. *Journal of Consulting and Clinical Psychology, 49,* 55–459.

Smith, G. B., Schwebel, A. I., Dunn, R. L., & McIver, S. D. (1993). The role of psychologists in the treatment, management, and prevention of chronic mental illness. *American Psychologist, 48,* 966–971.

Smith, G. S., & Kraus, J. F. (1988). Alcohol and residential, recreational, and occupational injuries: A review of the epidemiologic evidence. In L. Breslow, J. E. Fielding, & L. B. Lave (Eds.), *Annual review of public health* (Vol. 9). Palo Alto, CA: Annual Reviews.

Smith, M. L., & Glass, G. V. (1977). Meta-analysis of psychotherapy outcome studies. *American Psychologist, 32,* 752–760.

Smith, M. L., Glass, G. V., & Miller, T. I. (1980). *The benefits of psychotherapy.* Baltimore: Johns Hopkins University Press.

Smith, R. J., Barth, J. T., Diamond, R., & Giuliano, A. J. (1998). Evaluation of head injury. In G. Goldstein, P. D. Nussbaum, & S. R. Beers (Eds.), *Neuropsychology* (pp. 136–170). New York: Plenum.

Smith, S. R., & Meyer, R. G. (1987). *Law, behavior, and mental health: Policy and practice.* New York: University Press.

Smith, S. S., Jorenby, D. E., Fiore, M. C., Anderson, J. E., Mielke, M. M., Beach, K. E., Piasecki, T. M., & Baker, T. B. (2001). Strike while the iron is hot: Can stepped-care treatments resurrect relapsing smokers? *Journal of Consulting and Clinical Psychology, 69,* 429–439.

Smith, T. W. (1989). Assessment in rational-emotive therapy: Empirical access to the ABCD model. In M. E. Bernard & R. DiGiuseppe (Eds.), *Inside rational-emotive therapy: A critical appraisal of the theory and therapy of Albert Ellis* (pp. 135–153). San Diego, CA: Academic Press.

Smith, T. W., Turner, C. W., Ford, M. H., Hunt, S. C., Barlow, G. K., Stults, B. M. & Williams, R. R. (1987). Blood pressure reactivity in adult male twins. *Health Psychology, 6,* 209–220.

Snider, M. (1992). *Process family therapy: An eclectic approach to family therapy.* Boston: Allyn and Bacon.

Snyderman, M., & Rothman, S. (1987). Survey of expert opinion on intelligence and aptitude testing. *American Psychologist, 42,* 137–144.

Society of Clinical Psychology. (2002). www.apa.org/divisions/div12/

Sohlberg, M. M., & Mateer, C. A. (1989). *Introduction to cognitive rehabilitation: Theory and practice.* New York: Guilford.

Sontag, L. W., Baker, C. T., & Nelson, V. L. (1958). Mental growth and personality development: A longitudinal study. *Monographs of the Society for Research in Child Development, 23* (2, Serial No. 68).

Sorenson, S. B., & Kraus, J. F. (1991). Occurrence, severity, and outcomes of brain injury. *Journal of Head Trauma Rehabilitation, 6,* 1–10.

Spanier, C., & Frank, E. (1998). Maintenance interpersonal therapy: A preventive treatment for depression (pp. 67–97). In J. C. Markowitz (Ed.), *Interpersonal psychotherapy.* Washington, DC: American Psychiatric Press.

Spearman, C. (1927). *The abilities of man.* New York: Macmillan.

Spiegel, D. (1996). Cancer and depression. *British Journal of Psychiatry, 168,* 109–116.

Spiegel, D., Bloom, J. R., Kraemer, H. C., & Gottheil, E. (1989). Effect of psychosocial treatment on survival of patients with metastatic breast cancer. *Lancet, 335,* 888–891.

Spierings, E. L. H., Sorbi, M., Haimowitz, B. R., & Tellegen, B. (1996). Changes in daily hassles, mood and sleep in the 2 days before a migraine headache. *The Clinical Journal of Pain, 12,* 38–42.

Spitzer, R. L. (1975). On pseudoscience in science, logic in remission, and psychiatric diagnosis: A critique of Rosenhan's "On being sane in insane places." *Journal of Abnormal Psychology, 84,* 442–452.

Spitzer, R. L., Endicott, J., & Robins, E. (1978). Research diagnostic criteria. *Archives of General Psychiatry, 35,* 773–782.

Spitzer, R. L., & Williams, J. B. (1985). *Instruction manual for the structured clinical interview for DSM-III.* New York: Biometrics Research Department, New York State Psychiatric Institute.

Spring, B. J., Weinstein, L., Lemon, M., & Haskell, A. (1991). Schizophrenia from Hippocrates to Kraepelin: Intellectual foundations of contemporary research. In C. E. Walker (Ed.), *Clinical psychology: Historical and research foundations* (pp. 259–278). New York: Plenum.

Stampfl, T. G., & Levis, D. J. (1967). Essentials of implosive therapy: A learning-theory-based psychodynamic behavioral therapy. *Journal of Abnormal Psychology, 72,* 496–503.

Stanek, L. J. (1993). Manipulative language, discriminatory practices. *Resources: Workforce issues in mental health systems, 5,* 9–10.

Stang, P. E., Sternfield, B., & Sidney, S. (1996). Migraine headache in a prepaid health plan: Ascertainment, demographics, physiological, and behavioral factors. *Headache, 36,* 69–76.

Stanley, M. A., & Wagner, A. L. (1994). Obsessive-compulsive behavior. In V. S. Ramachandran (Ed.), *Encyclopedia of human behavior* (Vol. 3, pp. 333–344). San Diego, CA: Academic Press.

Stapp, J., Tucker, A. M., & VandenBos, G. R. (1985). Census of psychological personnel: 1983. *American Psychologist, 40,* 1317–1351.

Starr, B. J., & Katkin, E. S. (1969). The clinician as an aberrant actuary: Illusory correlation and the incomplete sentences blank. *Journal of Abnormal Psychology, 74,* 670–675.

State v. Michaels, 264 N. J. Super 579, 625 A. D. 2d 489 (N.J. Super Ad, 1993).

Steadman, H. J., Keitner, L., Braff, J., & Arvanites, T. M. (1983). Factors associated with successful insanity defense. *American Journal of Psychiatry, 140,* 401–405.

Stein, H. F., & Grant, W. D. (1988). *Behavioral science in family medicine: A program for second and third year family medicine residents.* Kansas City, MO: The Society of Teachers of Family Medicine.

Steinman, S. (1981). The experience of children in a joint-custody arrangement: A report of a study. *American Journal of Orthopsychiatry, 51,* 403–414.

Steinmann, A. (1984). Anna O.: Female, 1880–1882; Bertha Pappenheim: Female, 1980–1982. In M. Rosenbaum & M. Muroff (Eds.), *Anna O.: Fourteen contemporary perspectives* (pp. 118–131). New York: Free Press.

Steketee, G. (1993). *Treatment of obsessive compulsive disorder.* New York: Guilford.

Steketee, G., & Foa, E. B. (1987). Rape victims: Post-traumatic stress responses and their treatment: A review of the literature. *Journal of Anxiety Disorders, 1,* 69–86.

Steketee, G. S., Foa, E. B., & Grayson, J. B. (1982). Recent advances in the treatment of obsessive-compulsives. *Archives of General Psychiatry, 38,* 1365–1371.

Steketee, G., & White, K. (1993). *When once is not enough.* New York: New Harbinger.

Steptoe, A. (1998). Psychophysiological bases of disease. In A. S. Bellack, & M. Hersen (Eds.), *Comprehensive clinical psychology, Volume 8, Health psychology* (pp. 39–78). New York: Elsevier.

Stere, L. K. (1985). Feminist assertiveness training: Self-esteem groups as skill training for women. In L. B. Rosewater & L. E. A. Walker (Eds.), *Handbook of feminist therapy: Women's issues in psychotherapy* (pp. 51–61). New York: Springer Publishing Company.

Sternberg, R. J. (1985). *Beyond IQ: A triarchic theory of human intelligence.* New York: Cambridge University Press.

Sternberg, R. J. (1993a). *Sternberg Triarchic Abilities Test.* Unpublished test.

Sternberg, R. J. (1993b). Rocky's back again: A review of the WAIS-III. *Journal of Psychoeducational Assessment* (Monograph Series: Advances in Psychoeducational Assessment). Germantown, TN: Psychoeducational Corporation.

Sternberg, R. J. (1997). The concept of intelligence and its role in lifelong learning and success. *American Psychologists, 52,* 1030–1037.

Sternberg, R. J., & Detterman, D. K. (Eds.). (1986). *What is intelligence? Contemporary views on its nature and definition.* Norwood, NJ: Ablex.

Stewart, A. E., & Stewart, E. A., (1998). Trends in post-doctoral education: Requirements for licensure and training opportunities. *Professional Psychology: Research and Practice, 29,* 273–283.

Stickles, J. L., Schilmoeller, G., & Schilmoeller, C. (in press). A twenty-three year longitudinal review of communication development in an individual with agenesis of the corpus callosum. *International Journal of Disability, Development and Education.*

Stiles, W. B., Shapiro, D. A., & Elliott, R. K., (1986). Are all psychotherapies equivalent? *American Psychologist, 41,* 165–180.

Stone, G. (Ed.). (1983). *National Working Conference on Education and Training in Health Psychology, 2* (5, Suppl.), 1–53.

Stone, G. C. (1979). Health and the health system: A historical overview and conceptual framework. In G. C. Stone, F. Cohen, & N. E. Adler (Eds.), *Health psychology—A handbook.* San Francisco: Jossey-Bass.

Stoolmiller, M., Eddy, M., & Reid, J. B. (2000). Detecting and describing preventive intervention effects in a universal school-based randomized trial targeting delinquent and violent behavior. *Journal of Consulting and Clinical Psychology, 68,* 296–306.

Street, L. L., & Barlow, D. H. (1994). Anxiety disorders. In L. W. Craighead, W. E. Craighead, A. E. Kazdin, & M. J. Mahoney (Eds.), *Cognitive and behavioral interventions: An empirical approach to mental health problems* (pp. 71–87). Boston: Allyn and Bacon.

Stricker, G. (2000). The scientist-practitioner model: Gandhi was right again. *American Psychologist, 55,* 253–254.

Strom, K. (1993). Reimbursement demands and treatment decisions: A growing dilemma for social workers. *Social Work, 37,* 398–403.

Stromberg, C. D., Haggarty, D. J., Leibenluft, R. F., McMillian, M. H., Mishkin, B., Rubin, B. L., & Trilling, H. R. (1988). *The psychologist's legal handbook.* Washington, DC: The Council for the National Register of Health Service Providers in Psychology.

Stromberg, C., Lindberg, D., Mishkin, B., & Baker, M. (1993). Privacy, confidentiality, and privilege. *Psychologist's Legal Update, No. 1 (April),* 3–16.

Stromberg, C., Schneider, J., & Joondeph, B. (1993). Dealing with potentially dangerous patients. *The Psychologist's Legal Update, No. 2 (August),* 3–12.

Strosahl, K. (1994). Entering the new frontier of managed mental health care: Gold mines and land mines. *Cognitive and Behavioral Practice, 1,* 5–23.

Strumpfel, U., & Goldman, R. (2002). Contacting gestalt therapy. In D. J. Cain & J. Seeman (Eds.), *Humanistic psychotherapies: Handbook of research and practice* (Chapter 6; pp. 189–219). Washington, DC: American Psychological Association.

Strupp, H. H. (1963a). The outcome problem in psychotherapy revisited. *Psychotherapy: Theory, Research and Practice, 1,* 1–13.

Strupp, H. H. (1963b). The outcome problem in psychotherapy: A rejoinder. *Psychotherapy: Theory, Research and Practice, 1,* 101.

Strupp, H. H., & Hadley, S. W. (1979). Specific versus non-specific factors in psychotherapy. *Archives of General Psychiatry, 36,* 1125–1136.

Sturdivant, S. (1980). *Therapy with woman: A feminist philosophy of treatment.* New York: Springer.

Sturgis, E. T., & Gramling, S. E. (1988). Psychophysiological assessment. In A. S. Bellack & M. Hersen

(Eds.), *Behavioral assessment: A practical handbook* (3rd ed.; pp. 213–251). Elmsford, NY: Pergamon Press.

Sturgis, E. T., & Gramling, S. E. (1998). Psychophysiological assessment. In A. S. Bellack & M. Hersen (Eds.), *Behavioral assessment: A practical handbook* (4th ed.; pp. 126–157). Boston: Allyn and Bacon.

Sue, D. (1981). *Counseling the culturally different.* New York: John Wiley and Sons.

Sue, D. W., & Sue, D. (1990). *Counseling the culturally different: Theory and practice.* New York: Wiley.

Sue, D., Sue, D., & Sue, S. (1986). *Understanding abnormal behavior* (2nd ed.). Boston: Houghton Mifflin.

Sue, S., Fujino, D. C., Hu, L., Takeuchi, D. T., & Zane, S. (1991). Community mental health services for ethnic minority groups: A test of the cultural responsiveness hypothesis. *Journal of Consulting and Clinical Psychology, 59,* 533–540.

Suinn, R. M., & Oskamp, S. (1969). *The predictive validity of projective measures: A fifteen year evaluative review of the research.* Springfield, IL: Charles C. Thomas.

Suinn, R. M., & Richardson, F. (1971). Anxiety management training: A nonspecific behavior therapy program for anxiety control. *Behavior Therapy, 2,* 498–510.

Sullivan, K. T., & Bradbury, T. N. (1996). Preventing marital dysfunction: The primacy of secondary strategies. *the Behavior Therapist, 19,* 33–36.

Sullivan, T., Martin, W. L., Handelsman, M. (1993). Practical benefits of an informed-consent procedure: An empirical investigation. *Professional Psychology: Research and Practice, 24,* 160–163.

Sundberg, M. D. (1961). The practice of psychological testing in clinical services in the United States. *American Psychologist, 16,* 78–93.

Suzuki, L. A., & Valencia, R. R. (1997). Race-ethnicity and measured intelligence. *American Psychologist, 52,* 1103–1114.

Swan, G. E., & MacDonald, M. L. (1978). Behavior therapy in practice: A national survey of behavior therapists. *Behavior Therapy, 9,* 799–807.

Swartz, J. D. (1978). Review of the T.A.T. In O. K. Buros (Ed.), *The eighth mental measurement handbook* (pp. 1127–1130). Highland Park, NJ: Gryphon Press.

Swendsen, J. D., & Mazure, C. M. (2000). Life stress as a risk factor for postpartum depression: Current Research and methodological issues. *Clinical Psychology: Science and Practice, 7,* 17–31.

Swensen, C. H. (1957). Empirical evaluations of human figure drawings. *Psychological Bulletin, 54,* 431–466.

Swensen, C. H. (1968). Empirical evaluations of human figure drawings: 1957–1966. *Psychological Bulletin, 70,* 20–44.

Sym, J. (1963). Life's preservative against self-killing. In R. Hunter & I. MacAlpine, *Three hundred years of psychiatry, 1535–1860* (pp. 113–115). London: Oxford University Press. (Original work published in 1637.)

Szasz, T. (1961). *The myth of mental illness: Foundations of a theory of personal conduct.* New York: Harper & Row.

Szasz, T. (1990). Law and psychiatry: The problems that will not go away. In D. Cohen (Ed.), Special issue: Challenging the therapeutic state: Critical perspectives on psychiatry and the mental health system. *The Journal of Mind and Behavior, 11* (3 and 4), 557–564 (311–318).

Szasz, T. (1995). Mental disorders are not medical diseases. In W. Barbour (Ed.), *Mental illness: Opposing viewpoints* (pp. 37–42). San Diego, CA: Greenhaven Press.

Taplin, P. S., & Reid, J. B. (1973). Effects of instructional set and experimenter influence on observer reliability. *Child Development, 44,* 547–554.

Task Force on Promotion and Dissemination of Psychological Procedures. (1995). Training in and dissemination of empirically-validated psychological treatments: Report and recommendations. *The Clinical Psychologist, 48,* 3–23.

Tatman, S. M., Peters, D. B., Greene, A. L., & Bongar, B. (1997). Graduate students' attitudes toward prescription privileges training. *Professional Psychology: Research and Practice, 28,* 515–517.

Taylor, S. (1996). Meta-analysis of cognitive-behavioral treatments for social phobia. *Journal of Behavior Therapy and Experimental Psychiatry, 27,* 1–9.

Taylor, S. E. (1999). *Health psychology* (4th ed.). New York: McGraw Hill.

Tedesco, L. A., Keffer, M. A., Davis, E. L., & Christersson, L. A. (1994). Self-efficacy and reasoned action: Predicting oral health status and behaviour at one, three, and six month intervals. *Psychology and Health, 8,* 105–121.

Temerlin, M. K. (1968). Suggestion effects in psychiatric diagnosis. *Journal of Nervous and Mental Disease, 47,* 349–353.

Terman, L. M. (1916). *The measurement of intelligence.* Boston: Houghton Mifflin.

Terman, L. M., & Merrill, M. A. (1937). *Measuring intelligence.* Boston: Houghton Mifflin.

Terman, L. M., & Merrill, M. A. (1960). *Stanford-Binet Intelligence Scale: Manual for the third edition.* Boston: Houghton Mifflin.

Terman, L. M., & Merrill, M. A. (1973). *Stanford-Binet Intelligence Scale: 1972 norms edition.* Boston: Houghton Mifflin.

Teyber, E. (1988). *Interpersonal process in psychotherapy: A guide for clinical training.* Chicago, IL: Dorsey.

Teyber, E. (2000). *Interpersonal process in psychotherapy: A guide to clinical training.* Chicago, IL: Dorsey.

Theobald, H., Bygren, L. O., Carstensen, J., & Engfeldt, P. (2000). A moderate intake of wine is associated with total mortality and reduced mortality from cardiovascular disease. *Journal of Studies on Alcohol, 61,* 652–656.

Thompson, L. W., Gallagher, D., & Breckenridge, J. S. (1987). *Journal of Consulting and Clinical Psychology, 55,* 385–390.

Thorndike, R. L., Hagen, E. P., & Sattler, J. M. (1986). *Stanford-Binet intelligence scale: Fourth edition (Technical Manual).* Chicago: Riverside.

Thorpe, G. L. (1994). Agoraphobia. In V. S. Ramachandran (Ed.), *Encyclopedia of human behavior* (Vol. 1). San Diego, CA: Academic Press. (pp. 57–69.)

Thorpe, G. L. (1998). Agoraphobia (Vol. 1, pp. 39–51.) In H. S. Friedman (Ed.), *Encyclopedia of mental health.* San Diego, CA: Academic Press.

Thorpe, G. L., Barnes, G. S., Hunter, J. E., & Hines, D. (1983). Thoughts and feelings: Correlations in two clinical and two non-clinical samples. *Cognitive Therapy and Research, 7,* 565–574.

Thorpe, G. L., & Burns, L. E. (1983). *The agoraphobic syndrome: Behavioural approaches to evaluation and treatment.* John Wiley & Sons, Chichester, U.K.

Thorpe, G. L., & Olson, S. L. (1990). *Behavior therapy: Concepts, procedures, and applications.* Boston: Allyn and Bacon.

Thorpe, G. L. & Olson, S. L. (1997). *Behavior therapy: concepts, procedures, and applications* (2nd ed.). Boston: Allyn and Bacon.

Thorpe, G. L., Parker, J. D., & Barnes, G. S. (1992). The Common Beliefs Survey III and its subscales: Discriminant validity in clinical and nonclinical subjects. *Journal of Rational-Emotive and Cognitive-Behavior Therapy, 10,* 95–104.

Thorpe, G. L., Walter, M. I., Kingery, L. R, & Nay, W. T. (2001). The Common Beliefs Survey—III and the Situational Self-Statement and Affective State Inventory: Test-retest reliability, internal consistency, and further psychometric considerations. *Journal of Rational-Emotive and Cognitive-Behavior Therapy, 19,* 89–103.

Thurstone, L. L. (1938). *Primary mental abilities.* Chicago, IL: The University of Chicago Press.

Tosi, D. J., Forman, M. A., Rudy, D. R., & Murphy, M. A. (1986). Factor analysis of the Common Beliefs Survey III: A replication study. *Journal of Consulting and Clinical Psychology, 54,* 404–405.

Tranel, D. (1994). The release of psychological data to non-experts: Ethical and legal considerations. *Professional Psychology: Research and Practice, 25,* 33–38.

Tremont, G., Hoffman, R. G., Scott, J. G., & Adams, R. L. (1998). Effect of intellectual level on neuropsy-chological test performance: A response to Dodrill (1997). *The Clinical Neuropsychologist, 12,* 560–567.

Trevisan, M., Jossa, F., Farinaro, E., Krogh, V. Panico, S., Giumetti, D., & Mancini, M. (1992). Earthquake and coronary heart disease risk factors: A longitudinal study. American *Journal of Epidemiology, 135,* 632–637.

Trexler, L. D., & Karst, T. O. (1972). Rational-Emotive Therapy, placebo, and no-treatment effects on public-speaking anxiety. *Journal of Abnormal Psychology, 79,* 60–67.

Trower, P. (1995). Adult social skills: State of the art and future directions. In W. O'Donohue & L. Krasner (Eds.), *Handbook of psychological skills training: Clinical techniques and applications* (pp. 54–80). Boston: Allyn and Bacon.

Truax, C. B., & Carkhuff, R. R. (1967). *Toward effective counseling and psychotherapy: Training and practice.* Chicago: Aldine.

Tryon, W. W. (1998). Behavioral observation. In A. S. Bellack & M. Hersen (Eds.), *Behavioral assessment: A practical handbook* (4th ed.; pp. 79–103). Boston: Allyn and Bacon.

Tucker, I. F., & Duniho, T. (1994). Jungian personality types. (Vol. 3; pp. 13–28). In V. S. Ramachandran (Ed.), *Encyclopedia of human behavior.* San Diego, CA: Academic Press.

Tucker, L., & Lubin, W. (1994). *National survey of psychologists. Report from Division 39, American Psychological Association.* Washington, DC: American Psychological Association.

Tuma, J. M. (Ed.). (1985). *Proceedings of the Conference on Training Clinical Child Psychologists.* Washington, DC: American Psychological Association, Division of Clinical Psychology, Section on Clinical Child Psychology.

Turner, S. M. (1998). Functional bowel disorders. In A. S. Bellack & M. Hersen (Eds.), *Comprehensive clinical psychology, Volume 8, Health psychology* (pp. 305–320). New York: Elsevier.

Ullman, L., & Krasner, L. (1975). *A psychological approach to abnormal behavior* (2nd ed.). Englewood Cliffs, NJ: Prentice-Hall.

Ungar, S. J. (1972, November). The Pentagon papers trial. *Atlantic Monthly,* 22–23, 26–28, 30, 32, 34.

Update on mood disorders—Part II. (1995). *The Harvard Mental Health Letter, 11* (7), 1–4.

Upton, C. J. (1975). Melanesian cultures. *Encyclopaedia Britannica* (15th ed.). Chicago: Benton.

U.S. Bureau of the Census. (1975). *Historical statistics of the United States: Colonial times to 1970, bicentennial edition, Part 2.* Washington, DC: U.S. Government Printing Office.

U.S. Census Bureau. (2000). *Statistical abstract of the*

United States: 2000 (120th ed.). Washington, DC: U.S. Government Printing Office.

U.S. Department of Health and Human Services. (1990). *Alcohol and health* (Publication No. ADM 90–1656). Rockville, MD: National Institute on Alcohol Abuse and Alcoholism. Encyclopaedia Britannica, Inc.

U.S. Department of Health and Human Services. (1997). *Ninth special report to the U.S. Congress on alcohol and health.* Rockville, MD: U.S. Public Health Service.

Vandenberg, S. G., & Vogler, G. P. (1985). Genetic determinants of intelligence. In B. B. Woman (Ed.), *Handbook of intelligence* (pp. 3–57). New York: Wiley.

VandenBos, G. R., DeLeon, P. H., & Belar, C. D. (1991). How many psychologists are needed? It's too early to know! *Professional Psychology: Research and Practice, 22,* 441–448.

Vane, J. R. (1981). Thematic Apperception Test: A review. *Social Psychology Review, 1,* 319–336.

Vincent, K. R. (1991). Black/white IQ differences: Does age make the difference? *Journal of Clinical Psychology, 47,* 266–279.

Vogeltanz, N. D., Sigmon, S. T., & Vickers, K. S. (1998). Feminism and behavior analysis: A framework for women's health research and practice. In J. J. Plaud & G. H. Eifert (Eds.), *From behavior theory to behavior therapy* (Chapter 13; pp. 269–293). Boston: Allyn and Bacon.

Vraniak, D. (1994). Native Americans. In R. J. Sternberg (Ed.), *Encyclopedia of human intelligence* (pp. 747–754). New York: Macmillan.

Vredenburgh, L. D., Carlozzi, A. F., & Stein, L. B. (1999). Burnout in counseling psychologists: Type of practice setting and pertinent demographics. *Counseling Psychologist Quarterly, 12,* 293–302.

Waddell, M. T., Barlow, D. H., & O'Brien, G. T. (1984). A preliminary investigation of cognitive and relaxation treatment of panic disorder: Effects of intense anxiety versus "background" anxiety. *Behavior Research and Therapy, 22,* 393–402.

Wade, T. C., Baker,. T. B., Morton, T. L., & Baker, L. J. (1978). The status of psychological testing in clinical psychology: Relationships between test use and professional activities and orientations. *Journal of Personality Assessment, 42,* 3–11.

Walen, S. R., DiGiuseppe, R., & Dryden, W. (1992). *A practitioner's guide to rational-emotive therapy* (2nd ed.). New York: Oxford University Press.

Walker, J. P. (1997). Adult cognitive, linguistic, and speech disorders. In C. M. Seymour & E. H. Nober (Eds.), *Introduction to communication disorders: A cultural/social approach.* Newton, MA: Butterworth-Heinemann.

Walker, J. R., Norton, G. R., and Ross, C. A. (Eds.). (1991). *Panic disorder and agoraphobia: A comprehensive guide for the practitioner.* Pacific Grove, CA: Brooks/Cole.

Walker, L. (1995). *The abused woman: A survivor therapy approach.* Princeton, NJ: Films for the Humanities and Sciences.

Walker, N. (1959). *A short history of psychotherapy: In theory and practice.* New York: Noonday Press.

Wallston, K. A. (1994). Cautious optimism vs. cockeyed optimism. *Psychology and Health, 9,* 201–203.

Walsh, R. A., & McElwain, B. (2002). Existential psychotherapies. In D. J. Cain & J. Seeman (Eds.), *Humanistic psychotherapies: Handbook of research and practice* (Chapter 8; pp. 253–278). Washington, DC: American Psychological Association.

Walsh, W. B., & Betz, N. E. (1995). *Tests and assessment* (3rd ed.). Englewood Cliffs, NJ: Prentice Hall.

Walter, M. I., Thorpe, G. L., & Kingery, L. R. (2001). The Common Beliefs Survey III, the Situational Self-Statement and Affective State Inventory and their relationship to authoritarianism and social dominance orientation. *Journal of Rational-Emotive and Cognitive-Behavior Therapy, 19,* 105–118.

Ward, C. H., Beck, A. T., Mendelson, M., Mock, J. E., & Erbaugh, J. K. (1962). The psychiatric nomenclature: Reasons for diagnostic disagreement. *Archives of General Psychiatry, 7,* 198–205.

Wardle, J. (1983). Psychological management of anxiety and pain during dental treatment. *Journal of Psychosomatic Research, 27,* 399–402.

Wardle, J., & Pope, R. (1992). The psychological costs of screening for cancer. *Journal of Psychosomatic Research, 36,* 609–624.

Watkins, C. E. (1991). What have surveys taught us about the teaching and practice of psychological assessment? *Journal of Personality Assessment, 56,* 426–437.

Watkins, C. E., Campbell, V. L., Nieberding, R., & Hallmark, R. (1995). Contemporary practice of psychological assessment by clinical psychologists. *Professional Psychology: Research and Practice, 26,* 54–60.

Watson, J. B. (1928). What the nursery has to say about instincts. Experimental studies on the growth of the emotions. Recent experiments on how we lose and change our emotional equipment. In C. Murchison (Ed.), *Psychologies of 1925.* Worcester, MA: Clark University Press.

Watson, J. B., & Raynor, R. (1920). Conditioned emotional reactions. *Journal of Experimental Psychology, 3,* 1–14.

Watson, J. C. (2002). Re-visioning empathy. In D. J. Cain & J. Seeman (Eds.), *Humanistic psychotherapies: Handbook of research and practice.* Washington, DC: American Psychological Association.

Watson, R. I. (1978). *The great psychologists* (4th ed.). Philadelphia: J. B. Lippincott Co.

Webster, C., Harris, G., Rice, M., Cormier, C., & Quinsey, V. (1994). *The violence prediction scheme.* Toronto: Centre of Criminology, University of Toronto.

Wechsler, D. (1939). *Measurement of adult intelligence.* Baltimore, MD: Williams & Winkin.

Wechsler, D. (1945). A standardized memory scale for clinical use. *Journal of Psychology, 19,* 87–95.

Wechsler, D. (1958). The measurement and appraisal of adult intelligence (4th ed.). Baltimore, MD: Williams & Wilkin.

Wechsler, D. (1991). *WISC-III: Manual.* San Antonio, TX: Psychological Corporation.

Wechsler, D. (1997). WAIS-III administration and scoring manual. San Antonio, TX: Psychological Corporation.

Wedding, D., & Faust, D. (1989). Clinical judgment and decision making in neuropsychology. *Archives of Clinical Neuropsychology, 4,* 233–265.

Weinberg, R. A., Scarr, S., & Waldman, I. D. (1992). The Minnesota Transracial Adoption Study: A follow-up of IQ test performance at adolescence. *Intelligence, 16,* 117–135.

Weinberger, J. (1993). Common factors in psychotherapy. In J. Gold & G. Stricker (Eds.), *Handbook of psychotherapy integration* (pp. 43–56). New York: Plenum.

Weinberger, J. (1995). Common factors aren't so common: The common factors dilemma. *Clinical Psychology: Science and Practice, 2,* 45–69.

Weiner, I. B. (1977). Approaches to Rorschach validation. In M. A. Rickers-Ovsiankira (Ed.), *Rorschach psychology.* Huntington, NY: Robert E. Krieger Publishing Co.

Weiner, I. B. (1996). Some observations on the validity of the Rorschach Inkblot Method. *Journal of Personality Assessment, 8,* 206–213.

Weiner, I. B. (1997). Current status of the Rorschach Inkblot Method. *Journal of Personality Assessment, 68,* 5–19.

Weis, H. M. (1993, August). Stigma vs. services (Letters). *APA Monitor, 24,* (8), 68.

Weissman, M. M. (1985). The epidemiology of anxiety disorders: Rates, risks, and familiar patterns. In A. H. Tuma & J. D. Maser (Eds.), *Anxiety and the anxiety disorders* (pp. 275–296). Hillsdale, NJ: Lawrence Erlbaum.

Weissman, M. M., & Markowitz, J. C. (1998). An overview of interpersonal psychotherapy (pp. 1–33). In J. C. Markowitz (Ed.), *Interpersonal psychotherapy.* Washington, DC: American Psychiatric Press.

Weissman, M. M., & Paykel, E. S. (1974). *The depressed woman: A study of social relationships.* Chicago: University of Chicago Press.

Weisz, J. R., Weiss, B., Alicke, M. D., & Klotz, M. L. (1987). Effectiveness of psychotherapy with children and adolescents. A meta-analysis for clinicians. *Journal of Consulting and Clinical Psychology, 55,* 542–549.

Weithorn, L. A. (Ed.). (1987). *Psychology and child custody determinations.* Lincoln: University of Nebraska Press.

Wells, G. L. (1993). What do we know about eyewitness identification? *American Psychologist, 48,* 553–571.

Wells, G. L., & Loftus, E. F. (Eds.). (1984). *Eyewitness testimony: Psychological perspectives.* New York: Cambridge University Press.

West, A., Martindale, C. Hines, D., & Rother, W. T. (1983). Marijuana-induced primary process content in the TAT. *Journal of Personality Assessment, 47,* 466–467.

Wetter, D. W., Fiore, M. C., Gritz, E. R., Lando, H. A., Stitzer, M. L., Hassleblad, V., & Baker, T. B. (1998). The AHCPR smoking cessation clinical practice guideline: Findings and implications for psychologists. *American Psychologist, 60,* 943–952.

Whishaw, I. Q., & Kolb, B. (1984). Neuropsychological assessment of children and adults with development dyslexia. In R. N. Malatesha & H. A. Whitaker (Eds.), *Dyslexia: A global issue.* The Hague: Martinus Nijhoff.

Whitley, B. E. (1979). Sex roles and psychotherapy: A current appraisal. *Psychological Bulletin, 86,* 1309–1321.

Widiger, T. A., & Rorer, L. G. (1984). The responsible psychotherapist. *American Psychologist, 39,* 503–515.

Widiger, T. A., Trull, T. J., Hurt, S. W., Clarkin, J., & Frances, A. (1987). A multidimensional scaling of DSM-III personality disorders. *Archives of General Psychiatry, 44,* 557–563.

Wiens, A. N. (1993). Postdoctoral education—Training for speciality practice: Long anticipated, finally realized. *American Psychologist, 48,* 415–422.

Wiens, A. N., & Matarazzo, J. D. (1983). Diagnostic interviewing. In M. Hersen, A. E. Kazdin, & A. S., Bellack (Eds.), *The clinical psychology handbook.* New York: Pergamon.

Wierzbicki, M. (1993). *Issues in clinical psychology: Subjective versus objective approaches.* Boston: Allyn and Bacon.

Wiggins, J. S. (1973). *Personality and prediction: Principles of personality assessment.* Reading, MA: Addison-Wesley.

Wiggins, J. S., & Pincus, A. L. (1992). Personality: Structure and assessment. *Annual Review of Psychology, 43,* 493–504.

Wilcox, S., & Storandt, M. (1996). Relations among age, exercise, and psychological variables in a community sample of women. *Health Psychology, 15,* 110–113.

Wilkins, W. (1986). Placebo problems in psychotherapy research: Social-psychological alternatives to chemotherapy concepts. *American Psychologist, 41,* 551–556.

Wilkinson, G. S. (1993). *Wide Range Achievement Test: Administration manual.* Wilmington, DE: Wide Range.

Williams, J. B., Spitzer, R. L., & Gibbon, M. (1992). International reliability of a diagnostic intake procedure for panic disorder. *American Journal of Psychiatry, 149,* 560–562.

Williams, J. B. W., & Spitzer, R. L. (1995). The issue of sex bias in DSM-III: A critique of "A woman's view of DSM-III" by Marcie Kaplan. In S. O. Lilienfeld (Ed.), *Seeing both sides: Classic controversies in abnormal psychology* (pp. 71–76). Pacific Grove, CA: Brooks/Cole. (Original work published in 1983.)

Williams, J. M. G., Mathews, A., & MacLeod, C. (1996). The emotional Stroop task and psychopathology. *Psychological Bulletin, 120,* 3–24.

Williams, J. M. G., Watts, F. N., MacLeod, C., & Mathews, A. (1988). *Cognitive psychology and emotional disorders.* Chichester: Wiley.

Williams, J. M. G., Watts, F. N., MacLeod, C., & Mathews, A. (1997). *Cognitive psychology and emotional disorders* (2nd ed.). Chichester: Wiley.

Williams, M. H. (1985). The bait-and-switch tactic in psychotherapy. *Psychotherapy: Theory, Research, and Practice, 22,* 110–113.

Williams, S. L., & Rappoport, A. (1983). Cognitive treatment in the natural environment for agoraphobics. *Behavior Therapy, 14,* 299–313.

Williams, W. M., & Ceci, S. J. (1997). Are Americans becoming more or less alike? Trends in race, class, and ability differences in intelligence. *American Psychologist, 52,* 1226–1235.

Wilson, E. O. (1975). *Sociobiology: the new synthesis.* Cambridge, MA: Harvard University.

Wilson, E. O. (1978). *On human nature.* Cambridge, MA: Harvard University Press.

Wilson, G. T. (1973). Counterconditioning versus forced exposure in extinction of avoidance responding and conditioned fear in rats. *Journal of Comparative and Physiological Psychology, 82,* 105–114.

Wilson, G. T. (1982). Psychotherapy process and procedure. The behavioral mandate. *Behavior Therapy, 13,* 291–312.

Wilson, G. T. (1984). Clinical issues and strategies in the practice of behavior therapy. In C. M. Franks, G. T. Wilson, P. C. Kendall, & K. D. Brownell (Eds.), *Annual review of behavior therapy: Theory and practice* (Vol. 10; pp. 291–320). New York: Guilford.

Wilson, G. T. (1995). Behavior therapy. In R. J. Corsini, & D. Wedding (Eds.), *Current psychotherapies* (5th ed.; pp. 197–228). Itasca, IL: F. E. Peacock.

Wilson, G. T. (1996). Empirically validated treatments: Reality and resistance. *Clinical Psychology: Science and Practice, 3,* 241–244.

Wilson, G. T. (1997). Dissemination of cognitive behavioral treatments: Commentary. *Behavior Therapy, 28,* 473–475.

Wilson, G. T., & Evans, I. M. (1977). The therapist-client relationship in behavior therapy. In A. Gurman & A. Razin (Eds.), *Effective psychotherapy: A handbook of research* (pp. 544–565). New York: Pergamon.

Wilson, G. T., & Fairburn, C. G. (1998). Treatments for eating disorders. In P. E. Nathan & J. M. Gorman (Eds.), *A guide to treatments that work* (pp. 501–530). New York: Oxford University Press.

Wilson, G. T., Nathan, P. E., O'Leary, K. D., & Clark, L. A. (1996). *Abnormal psychology: Integrating perspectives.* Boston: Allyn and Bacon.

Wilson, G. T., & O'Leary, K. D. (1980). Principles of behavior therapy. Englewood Cliffs, NJ: Prentice Hall.

Wilson, P. H., Spence, S. H., & Kavanagh, D. J. (1989). *Cognitive-behavioral interviewing for adult disorders: A practical handbook.* Baltimore, MD: Johns Hopkins University Press.

Wilson, S. R., Thompson, T. A., & Wylie, G. (1982). Automated psychological testing for the severely physically handicapped. *International Journal of Man-Machine Studies, 17,* 291–296.

Wincze, J. P., Richards, J., Parsons, J., & Bailey, S. (1996). A comparative survey of therapist sexual misconduct between an American state and an Australian state. *Professional Psychology: Research and Practice, 27,* 289–294.

Windle, C. (1952). Psychological tests in psychopathological prognosis. *Psychological Bulletin, 49,* 451–482.

Winer, E. O., & Sutton, L. M. (1994). Quality of life after bone marrow transplantation. *Oncology, 8,* 19–27.

Winick, B. J. (1983). Incompetency to stand trial: Developments in the law. In J. Monahan & H. J. Steadman (Eds.), *Mentally disordered offenders.* New York: Plenum.

Wohl, J. (1995). Traditional individual psychotherapy and ethnic minorities (Chapter 5; pp. 74–91). In J. F. Aponte, R. Y. Rivers, & J. Wohl (Eds.), *Psychological interventions and cultural diversity.* Boston: Allyn and Bacon.

Wolf, M. M. (1978). Social validity: The case of subjective measurement or how applied behavior analysis is finding its heart. *Journal of Applied Behavior Analysis, 11,* 203–214.

Wolpe, J. (1958). *Psychotherapy by reciprocal inhibition.* Stanford, CA: Stanford University Press.

Wolpe, J. (1973). *The practice of behavior therapy* (2nd ed.). New York: Pergamon.

Wolpe, J. (1982). Behavioristic psychotherapy: Its character and origin. In J. Wolpe, *The practice of behavior therapy* (3rd ed.; pp. 1–12). New York: Pergamon.

Wolpe, J. (1990). *The practice of behavior therapy* (4th ed.). New York: Pergamon.

Wolpe, J., & Lang, P. J. (1969). *Fear survey schedule.* San Diego, CA: Educational and Industrial Testing Service.

Wolpe, J., & Lazarus, A. A. (1966). *Behavior therapy techniques.* New York: Pergamon.

Wolpe, J., & Rachman, S. (1960). Psychoanalytic "evidence": A critique based on Freud's case of Little Hans. *The Journal of Nervous and Mental Disease, 131,* 135–148.

Wood, J. M., Nezworski, T., & Stejskal, W. J. (1996a). The Comprehensive System for the Rorschach: A critical examination. *Psychological Science, 7,* 3–10.

Wood, J. M., Nezworski, M. T., & Stejskal, W. J. (1996b). Thinking critically about the Comprehensive System for the Rorschach: A Reply to Exner. *Psychological Science, 7,* 14–17.

Woodard, L. J., & Pamies, R. J. (1992). The disclosure of the diagnosis of cancer. *Primary Care, 19,* 657–663.

Woodcock, R. W., & Johnson, M. B. (1989). *Woodcock-Johnson Psycho-Educational Battery—Revised.* Allen, TX: DLM Teaching Resources.

Woodward, R., & Jones, R. (1980). Cognitive restructuring treatment: A controlled trial with anxious patients. *Behavior Research and Therapy, 18,* 401–407.

World Health Organization. (1948). *Constitution of the World Health Organization.* Geneva, Switzerland: World Health Organization Basic Documents.

Worsley, J. L. (1970). The causation and treatment of obsessionality. In L. E. Burns & J. L. Worsley (Eds.), *Behavior therapy in the 1970's.* Bristol, UK: John Wright.

Wrightsman, L. S., Nietzel, M. T., & Fortune, W. H. (1994). *Psychology and the legal system* (3rd ed.). Pacific Groves, CA: Brooks/Cole.

Wulfert, E., Greenway, D. E., & Dougher, M. J. (1996). A logical functional analysis of reinforcement-based disorders: Alcoholism and pedophilia. *Journal of Consulting and Clinical Psychology, 64,* 1140–1151.

Wurtele, S. K., & Maddux, J. E. (1987). Relative contributions of protection motivation components in predicting exercise intentions and behavior. *Health Psychology, 6,* 453–466.

Wyer, M. M., Gaylord, S. J., Grove, E. T. (1987). The legal context of child custody evaluations. In L. A. Weithorn (Ed.), *Psychology and child custody determinations.* Lincoln: University of Nebraska Press.

Yarrow, L. J. (1960). Interviewing children. In P. H. Mussen (Ed.), *Handbook of research methods in child development* (pp. 561–602). New York: Wiley.

Yates, A. J. (1962). *Frustration and conflict.* London: Methuen.

Yates, A. J. (1970). *Behavior therapy.* New York: Wiley.

Yoman, J. (1996). The good news for behavior therapy's converted [Review of P. W. Corrigan & R. P. Liberman, *Behavior therapy in psychiatric hospitals*]. *Contemporary Psychology, 41,* 64–65.

Yontef, G. M. (1995). Gestalt therapy. In A. S. Gurman & S. B. Messer (Eds.), *Essential psychotherapies: Theory and practice* (Chapter 8; pp. 261–303). New York: Guilford.

Yu, L. M., Rinaldi, S. A., Templer, D. I., Colbert, L. A., Siscoe, K., & Van Patten, K. (1997). Score on the Examination for Professional Practice in Psychology as a function of attributes of clinical psychology graduate programs. *Psychological Science, 8,* 347–350.

Yuille, J. C. (1993). We must study forensic eyewitnesses to know about them. *American Psychologist, 48,* 572–573.

Zigler, E., & Phillips, L. (1960). Social effectiveness and symptomatic behaviors. *Journal of Abnormal and Social Psychology, 61,* 231–238.

Zigler, E., & Phillips, L. (1961). Psychiatric diagnosis: A critique. *Journal of Abnormal and Social Psychology, 3,* 607–618.

Zigler, E., & Phillips, L. (1968). Psychiatric diagnosis: A critique. In D. S. Holmes (Ed.), *Reviews of research in behavior pathology* (pp. 27–47). New York: John Wiley & Sons.

Zilboorg, G., & Henry, G. W. (1941). *A history of medical psychology.* New York: Norton.

Ziskin, J. (1981). *Coping with psychiatric and psychological testimony* (Vol. 2; 3rd ed.). Venice, CA: Law and Psychology Press.

Ziskin, J., & Faust, D. (1988). *Coping with psychiatric and psychological testimony* (Vols. 1–3, 4th ed.). Marina Del Rey, CA: Law and Psychology Press.

Zook, A., & Walton, J. M. (1989). Theoretical orientation and work settings of clinical and counseling psychologists: A current perspective. *Professional Psychology: Research and Practice, 20,* 23–31.

Zubin, J. (1954). Failures of the Rorschach technique. *Journal of Projective Techniques, 18,* 303–315.

Zubin, J., Eron, L. D., & Schumer, F. (1965). *An experimental approach to projective techniques.* New York: Wiley.

Zuercher-White, E. (1997). *Treating panic disorder and agoraphobia: A step-by-step clinical guide.* Oakland, CA: New Harbinger.

INDEX